HOME REPAIR WISDOM & KNOW-HOW

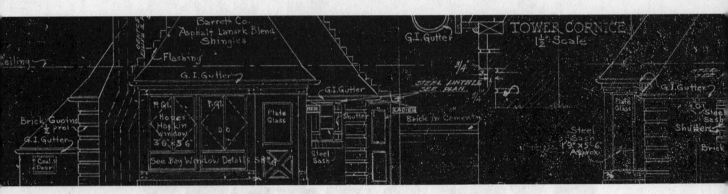

Barrett Co.
Asphalt Lanark Blend
Shingles

Flashing

G.I. Gutter

G.I. Gutter

TOWER CORNICE
1½ Scale

Ceiling

Brick Quoins
4 proj

G.I. Gutter

Coal
Door

F.Gl.
Hopes
Hopkin
Window
3'0" x 5'6"

F.Gl.

D.D.

Plate
Glass

See Bay Window Details Sheet 4

MEN

Shutter

Steel
Sash

STEEL LINTELS
SEE PLAN.

Brick in Cement

Steel
Sash
1'9" x 5'6"
Approx.

Plate
Glass

G.I. Gutter

F.Gl.
Steel
Sash

Shutters

Brick

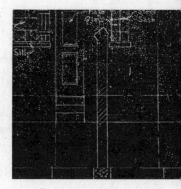

HOME REPAIR WISDOM & KNOW-HOW

Timeless Techniques to Fix, Maintain, and Improve Your Home

From the editors of _Fine Homebuilding_

BLACK DOG
& LEVENTHAL
PUBLISHERS
NEW YORK

Copyright © 2017 by The Taunton Press

Cover design by Carlos Esparza
Cover illustration © Steven Noble
Cover copyright © 2017 by Hachette Book Group, Inc.

Black Dog & Leventhal Publishers
Hachette Book Group
1290 Avenue of the Americas
New York, NY 10104
www.hachettebookgroup.com
www.blackdogandleventhal.com

First Edition: May 2017

Black Dog & Leventhal Publishers is an imprint of Hachette Books, a division of Hachette Book Group. The Black Dog & Leventhal Publishers name and logo are trademarks of Hachette Book Group, Inc.

The publisher is not responsible for websites (or their content) that are not owned by the publisher.

The Hachette Speakers Bureau provides a wide range of authors for speaking events. To find out more, go to www.HachetteSpeakersBureau.com or call (866) 376-6591.

Print book interior design by Ohioboy Design

Compiled by Waterbury Publications, Inc

Library of Congress Control Number: 2016957958

ISBNs: 978-0-316-36290-0 (trade paperback); 978-0-316-36288-7 (ebook)

Printed in the United States of America

LSC-W

10 9 8 7 6 5 4 3 2

Contents

Continued ➜

Contents

Tools & Materials

Outfitting a Tool Belt

By Patrick McCombe

I was recently asked what I thought were the essential tools for greenhorn carpenters and what it would cost to buy them. It's a good question. I have my opinions, but so does everybody else who's been in the trenches. I asked several coworkers who are former carpenters, and we developed a list of core carpentry tools—specifically, the tools that a carpenter needs often enough to keep in a tool belt, itself the first item on the list. I then headed to the nearest home center and bought everything on the list, with the goal of keeping the total within reason.

I got my start in carpentry more than 20 years ago, so although some of my choices are decidedly old school, my emphasis was on high-quality, affordable tools. You should feel free to choose tools based on your budget and on what feels right.

When you go tool shopping, buy good stuff, because there's nothing more frustrating than struggling with bad tools. Assuming you don't lose them, you might still be using some of them 20 years from now.

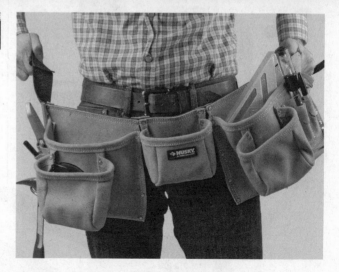

Whether you're a college student buying gear for a summer job, a foreman outfitting a new crew member, or an interested veteran, go to finehomebuilding.com/extras to let us know what you think belongs in a beginner's tool belt.

Continued →

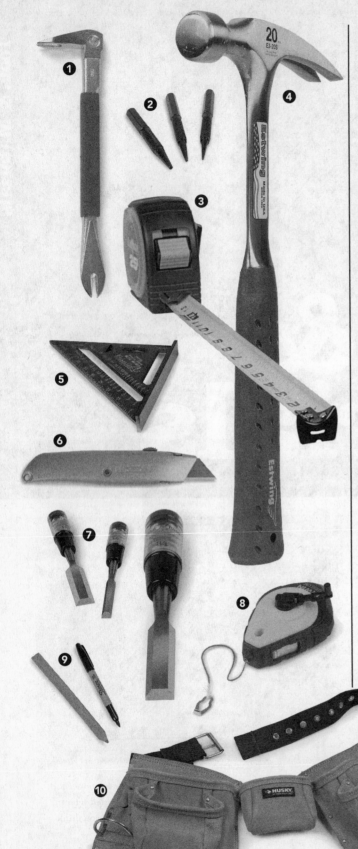

1. CAT'S PAW Modern Japanese-style cat's paws for pulling nails are a vast improvement over traditional styles. I prefer the style with cat's paws on both ends of the tool, but those with both a cat's paw and a pry or molding bar are equally useful.

2. NAIL SETS You'll want all three common sizes of nail sets for driving nails below the surface in preparation for filling. More expensive versions have color-coded rubber grips, which is nice but not necessary.

3. 25- OR 30-FT. TAPE MEASURE On the job site, being able to measure things that are out of reach is key, so pick a tape with a 1-in.-wide blade for longer standout. The 30-ft. (or longer) tapes are nice, but many are a frustratingly tight fit in a standard tool-bag tape holder.

4. HAMMER To me, it matters little whether the handle is wood, steel, or fiberglass, but choose a rip over a curved claw. A 20-oz. model with a smooth face is a good general-purpose choice.

5. RAFTER SQUARE Often called a Speed Square, a rafter square is made for marking straight and angled cuts on everything from rafters and joists to trim and siding. Choose one made from thick plastic or aluminum, as thin aluminum versions bend too easily. For another few dollars, you can get a square with a little book filled with rafter tables—probably a good investment.

6. UTILITY KNIFE Retractable utility knives are good for cutting everything from felt paper and housewrap to insulation and drywall. I like this old-school Stanley because it fits in my belt's holder, but models with a quick-change blade are a worthy upgrade.

7. 3-PIECE CHISEL SET More important than the chisel brand is learning how to keep your chisels sharp (look online at FineHomebuilding.com/extras). You'll need only one in your belt for cutting, scraping, and occasional prying, but having a set of ½-, ¾-, and 1-in. widths should mean that at least one is always sharp.

8. CHALKLINE Chalklines are used for quickly marking long cuts and reference lines. Quick-return chalklines are worth the additional expense when you're snapping long lines like those for wall plates and roof shingles. Use blue chalk when the finished product requires a blemish-free surface; red chalk stains.

9. PENCIL Carpenter's pencils are square so that they won't roll away. Carry two in your belt for when the lead breaks or if you drop one while on a ladder or at another inopportune time. Carry a permanent marker, too.

10. A TWO-POUCH TOOL BELT A carpenter's apron is the uniform of the trade and the best way to keep your gear organized and within easy reach. Choose a rig with an easily adjustable belt because you'll have to fine-tune the fit as you add or remove clothing during the day.

Don't Forget Safety Gear

While browsing the hand-tool aisle at a home center, I noticed that relatively little has changed since I outfitted myself more than 20 years ago. One important thing has changed, though: Safety glasses and ear protection are much better than they used to be. I wish I would have listened when people told me to wear hearing protection; my hearing is permanently compromised from noisy equipment and power tools.

Dust Masks

Skip the cheapest dust masks, which offer little protection, and upgrade to a two-strap model with an N95 rating instead. Wear one whenever you're sanding, scraping, cutting pressure-treated lumber, or doing demo.

Safety Glasses

Get a pair of both clear and tinted glasses so that you'll be protected in all conditions. If you wear corrective lenses, consider prescription safety glasses. You'll find it's money well spent when—not if—something happens.

Hearing Protection

Band-style ear plugs, which store around your neck, are always ready—although the plastic band breaks far too easily. Disposable foam plugs work well, but handling turns them gross quickly. Washable plugs are another option, but their 25-db. noise reduction offers less protection.

Hammers

By Aaron Fagan

The first nail I ever drove was with my father's hammer—a True Temper A16 Rocket, which he had won in a nailing contest at an annual picnic for the hardware dealers of Rochester, N.Y., in 1963. His instruction to me that day sounded quite simple. He said, "It's all about letting the hammer do the work." I am certain that, like anyone wielding a hammer for the first time, I must have made a rather sad scene: There I am, holding the hammer too tightly, my hand and arm singing with vibration; choked too high on the handle; missing, repeatedly; the bent nail mirroring my defeat with its head slumped down; and, ultimately, that ancient rite, the Dance of the Purple Thumb.

That was 30 years ago, and the art of letting the hammer do the work is one I will not master. Still, my story illustrates that hammers, and our history with them, are personal to us. The carpenters I know think that their hammer is the best hammer, and they are happy to tell you why. But hammers, too, have a story to tell. Their designs have evolved over the millennia, always moving us closer to that goal: letting them do the work.

Still Building Rome

We humans have had some time to think about hammers. Even in the Stone Age, there was great sophistication in choosing the right stone for the job, and much later, the right stick, bone, or antler to tie the stone to with sinew or other materials. But it was not until the Roman Empire that a nailing hammer emerged.

Dating from the first century, it had a wood handle attached to a metal head with a striking surface on one side, and a split, curved claw for pulling nails on the other. The Romans made extensive use of nails for construction, and it's a legacy that persists in our nail-sizing system: The "d" stands for the Roman coin denarius, which was presumably worth ten donkeys. Nails were priced per hundred, so one hundred 8d nails was equal to 80 donkeys. At that cost, the ability to extract and reuse those nails seems self-evident.

For centuries afterward, the head and the handle underwent countless interpretations from blacksmith to blacksmith, but these were slight modifications from that Roman design. While the use of steel for hammerheads is thought to date back to the Romans, the widespread use of hickory for handles did not occur until the mid-19th century in America. (Hickory is unique for its strength, density, and excellent shock resistance.) From the beginning of the tool's history, the single greatest design challenge was keeping the head securely affixed to the handle.

Revolutionaries

Around 1840, a carpenter in a small crew hired to build a church in Norwich, N.Y., realized he had left his hammer back home. The local blacksmith was David Maydole, who had been experimenting with hammer designs. (Even though the Industrial Revolution was newly underway in the United States, hammers still came from blacksmiths.) Maydole was frustrated by the tendency for hammerheads to fly off, and he tried to do something about it. Inspired by the extended eye of an adz—a tool similar to an ax—he added a tapered neck to wedge the handle

Continued →

Don't Fly Off the Handle

While David Maydole's adz-eye hammer better secured the head to the hickory handle, handles still broke, requiring a tedious replacement. Todd Coonrad's Douglas design offers both overstrike protection and the ability to more readily change the handle.

a modified patent by Arthur Taylor and Scott Hinman of Elyria, Ohio, and was disingenuously marketed as the "world's standard since 1836." This would have meant that Cheney started making this hammer when he was 15 years old. In addition, Cheney's patented design was for cut nails, whereas the Cheney Nailer's nail starter required wire nails, which didn't come into standard use until 1910.

Cheney's conception of a "hammer that holds the nail"—however indirectly—is at work today in the many modern hammers with a magnetic nail-starting feature. And just as the essence of the Roman claw hammer has endured, so too has Maydole's adz-eye hammer.

The head/handle problem was revisited in 1926 by Ernest Estwing, who introduced a virtually indestructible, forged hammer made from a single piece of solid carbon steel with a lacquered grip made of stacked leather rings. Estwing's design was one of many as a new age of invention dawned. Countless inventors flooded the U.S. Patent and Trademark Office with ingenious modifications and interpretations of the tool.

Postwar Promise and the Age of Science

Hammers are a time capsule containing a compression of history. For example, four-clawed hammers, designed to reduce damage in extracting costly nails for reuse, became popular during the Great Depression. After World War II, a booming economy and new fascination with science meant that hammers would be designed in a completely different way.

During the 1950s, a growing middle class was realizing the promise of the American Dream for the first time, leading to an unprecedented demand for housing. This ushered in a period of reimagining the hammer to meet those demands. Rather than a single crew building one house from start to finish, there emerged framing crews, whose sole charge was to get a house framed quickly and accurately for finish crews to complete. The common hammer—with its short handle, smooth face, and curved claw—had exhausted its potential in this setting and came to be classed as a finish hammer, to be used for tasks less intensive than rough carpentry. Framing became a task for what is now known as the California framing hammer.

Framing hammers began as rigging hatchets, which were the primary tools workers in California used to make wood oil derricks before World War II. A rigging-hatchet head has an ax blade on one side and a short-necked milled hammer face on the other. It is balanced, grabs nails well, and has a heavy head weight for lots of striking power. It has a long hickory handle that is either straight or curved with an adz eye or a teardrop-shape (single-bit) eye. For many carpenters, the downside of using a rigging hatchet for home building was the dangerous blade (unions banned them) and the tool's inability to extract nails efficiently. Crews began replacing the blade with the claws from old hammers. The late Larry Haun, after he had seen a modified hatchet on the job, had his first one made in 1954. The legendary

inside the head, resulting in the adz-eye hammer. As the story goes, the carpenter was so happy with Maydole's hammer that the rest of his crew decided to order them. Word spread, the local store ordered some, and a New York City tool merchant placed a standing order with Maydole for as many hammers as he could make. Though Maydole never patented his adz-eye hammer, in 1845 he founded the David Maydole Hammer Co., which grew to be one of the largest hammer manufacturers in the United States.

In Fly Creek, N.Y., a mere 40 miles away from Maydole's operation, another inventor, Henry Cheney, introduced a nail-starting system near the claw, which he patented in 1871. That, however, is not the design that made his name famous. The popular Cheney Nailer was introduced in 1927, a full 50 years after Henry Cheney's death. That hammer was based on

The Hammer That Holds the Nail

Henry Cheney was the first to conceive a hammer with a nail starter in the head, a feature that is nearly standard on modern tools such as this DeWalt, a lightweight steel hammer that gives titanium tools a run for their money.

Where job-site ingenuity created the California framing hammer, 20th-century science sought to remedy the shortcomings of the solid-steel hammer. Although these hammers were an incredibly strong alternative to wood hammers and were better for pulling nails, they were heavy and provided very little shock absorption. Until this time, little, if any, consideration had been given to the end user. Most previous innovations did not go much beyond getting a hammer to drive a nail without breaking. Arm fatigue, the amount of force expended, and comfort were only of peripheral concern.

In 1955, Plumb introduced the first hammers with fiberglass handles as an alternative to wood or steel. The same year, True Temper introduced the Rocket my father would win in 1963, which boasted a steel-tube handle with a rubberized grip. Hammers such as these signaled the dawn of products marketed as utilizing "space-age technology." Their handles were designed to be shock resistant, ergonomic, stronger than wood, and lighter than solid steel. They were still on the heavy side, however, and did not provide the clarity of sensation that nailing with a wood handle offers. Hammerheads were now being offered with either curved or straight (rip) claws and smooth or milled faces. This period saw the rise of many new hammer designs and materials and also introduced new avenues for refining and building on that progress.

Clash of the Titans

As the study of ergonomics matured, researchers could measure how hammers actually work and then develop ways to change them. For example, they were now able to determine the force required to grip a hammer and to understand the way a hammer distributes force when it strikes; this in turn helped them find ways to curb vibration, increase striking velocity, and optimize the sweet spot on the hammer's face. This continuing quest for a better tool shows how far we have come in our story from rocks tied to sticks, but also how little has changed. A hammer's primary function is still about driving nails and extracting them, but there are other functions a hammer needs to do just as well. A hammer needs to pry boards apart and knock elements into alignment. It's also one of the principal tools for demolition work. Each role calls for specifications no single hammer contains. In an attempt to address as many of these roles as possible, manufacturers in the late 1990s introduced materials such as titanium, graphite, and carbon fiber, and features such as side nail pulls, magnetic nail starters, and interchangeable (milled or smooth) faces.

Because you can swing it faster, a hammer with a titanium head can work just as well as one with a steel head. A titanium hammer transfers 98% of the energy from swinging the hammer to the nail, and does so with dramatically less shock than a steel hammer, which transfers only 70% of that energy to the nail. The two principal complaints are that titanium is five times as expensive as steel, and that titanium hammers are cast as opposed to forged. Stiletto Hammers does offer a removable steel face,

carpenter wrote about this in 2006 ("One Carpenter's Life," *Fine Homebuilding* #177): "I took my Plumb rigging hatchet home and cut off the blade with a hacksaw. I had an old Estwing hammer that supplied the claws. I took the pieces to a friend who had an electric arc welder in his garage, and he put the parts together. Although my hammer was a rough-looking tool, it was now safer to use, and I could drive framing nails easily with one lick. The straight-claw, long-handle California framer was born."

Bob Hart, a Los Angeles framing contractor, was one of the first to manufacture these hammers. He began his business by selling his hammers to lumberyards out of the trunk of his car. The popularity of California framing hammers grew through exemplary designs by such makers as Vaughan and Dalluge, and now virtually every manufacturer offers some version of the tool.

Continued →

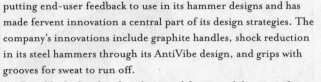

Do Me a Solid

In 1926, Ernest Estwing introduced a virtually indestructible, forged hammer made from a single piece of solid carbon steel with a lacquered grip made of stacked leather rings. In 2001, Mark Martinez began selling the TiBone, the first solid-titanium, lightweight framing hammer.

putting end-user feedback to use in its hammer designs and has made fervent innovation a central part of its design strategies. The company's innovations include graphite handles, shock reduction in its steel hammers through its AntiVibe design, and grips with grooves for sweat to run off.

Possibly the height of aesthetic and functional design in the hammer so far comes from Todd Coonrad. He has a background in industrial design, but it was through his work as a contractor that he began to question and reimagine the hammer. Like many carpenters, Coonrad preferred hickory handles but grew tired of replacing broken ones. In 1995, he developed a unique head-to-handle assembly that not only allows handles to be changed more readily, but, by creating a channel in the handle for the head to slide into, offers overstrike protection, increasing the

Good Vibrations

The True Temper Rocket was one of the first hammer designs that attempted to dampen the vibration of the steel handle. Stanley's AntiVibe technology exploits all of the benefits of steel.

which serves several purposes. Steel makes a more durable face than titanium, but the face can also be switched from milled to smooth or replaced when it wears down.

A nearly standard feature on modern hammers is a magnetic nail starter at the front of the hammer, which was first introduced in 1995 on a production-made framing hammer designed by Mark Martinez. In 1999, after acquiring the Stiletto trademark and production rights, he began selling the first titanium-head framing hammer. In 2001, he produced the first solid-titanium hammer, called the TiBone.

DeWalt, owned by Stanley Black & Decker, makes a 14-oz. hammer designed to deliver the striking power of a 28-oz. hammer. To add strength, the hammer is made by MIG-welding two forged pieces of steel together. Stanley has a long history of

longevity of the handle. The steel head features both a magnetic nail starter and a side nail pull. Coonrad has had licensing agreements with several manufacturers over the years including Hart, Vaughan, and Dalluge, but now he also produces his impeccably crafted hammers through his own company, Douglas. Despite all of this innovation—from the prehistoric discovery of a better striking rock, to Maydole's more secure hammerhead, to today's ergonomic wonders—one truth of hammer design has remained constant: The form of a claw hammer expresses a powerful metaphor of our human ability to revise and create. There is forgiveness of the past in the claw, and hope for the future in its face.

Nails

By Debra Judge Silber

Considering how critical nails are to holding wood-frame houses together, it's surprising that we don't pay more attention to them. The fact is, nails and the connections they make are critical to managing building loads and ensuring a safe, durable structure. Although there are many types of nailed connections used in home building, the three basic wood-to-wood connections here illustrate how nails perform.

In service, nails must resist withdrawal forces and shear (lateral) forces; they must also be resistant to pull-through and to combined (off-axis) forces. How well they perform is dependent on the characteristics of the nail, the wood, and the angle in which the nail is driven. Altering these factors—such as using a ring-shank nail or driving the nail at an angle—has a much greater effect on withdrawal resistance than on shear resistance, which is more dependent on the bending strength of the nail and the bearing capacity of the wood surrounding it. Penetration is also important. The rule of thumb is that at least two-thirds of the nail should extend into the base material. So a 1×3 should be fastened to a 4×4 with a 2½-in. (8d) nail, with ¾ in. of the nail going through the 1×3 and 1¾ in. going into the 4×4.

So the next time you swing a hammer, consider this: There's a lot riding on that nail. Here's how it works.

Anatomy of a Nail

Head

Head size and structure vary with a nail's type and purpose: to avoid overpenetration of the nailed material (such as the broad thin head of a roofing nail) or to embed the head in it (such as the barrel-shaped head of a finishing nail). Embossed nail heads enhance paint adhesion. Head shape has little bearing on withdrawal, but a small head can result in pull-through under force.

Finishing   Roofing

Gauge/Diameter

Gauge is a measure of nail-shank diameter most commonly associated with collated nails. The larger the diameter, the lower the gauge. In general, nails with a large diameter have greater resistance to withdrawal and lateral loads.

Shank

Smooth-shank nails drive into and pull out of most woods more easily than deformed-shank nails, but those deformations—for example, annular rings or helical threads—can improve holding in certain materials such as hardwoods or plywoods. Ring-shank nails can have up to twice the withdrawal capacity of smooth-shank nails.

Annular   Helical

Coating

Sacrificial galvanized (zinc) coatings delay corrosion of steel nails. Hot-dipped galvanized nails are immersed in molten zinc to produce a durable coating; other processes include mechanical galvanization and electrogalvanization. Polymer coatings increase initial withdrawal resistance by increasing friction between the nail and the wood. Driving into hardwoods can remove this coating, however.

Size

The size of nails for wood-to-wood applications is commonly referred to by pennyweight. The term is attributed to the original price per hundred nails and is designated with a "d" (for the Roman coin denarius). Pennyweight identifies nails by size on an established but somewhat arbitrary scale (below) and is not considered the best method of specification. Both shank length and diameter can vary slightly among different nails of the same pennyweight: For example, an 8d common nail measures 2½ in. with a 0.131-in. dia., an 8d box nail measures 2½ in. with a 0.113-in. dia., and an 8d sinker nail measures 2⅜ in. with an 0.113-in. dia.

Penny-Inch Nail Equivalents(common)

2d = 1 in.	9d = 2¾ in.
3d = 1¼ in.	10d = 3 in.
4d = 1½ in.	12d = 3¼ in.
5d = 1¾ in.	16d = 3½ in.
6d = 2 in.	20d = 4 in.
7d = 2¼ in.	30d = 4½ in.
8d = 2½ in.	40d = 5 in.

Material

Typically made from carbon-steel wire, nails also can be made from aluminum, brass, nickel, bronze, copper, and stainless steel. These materials have different friction values and bending strengths, influencing withdrawal and shear capacity.

Point

Most nails have a four-sided diamond point to make driving easier. Sharp points enhance withdrawal resistance, but they can cause wood to split. Blunt points prevent splitting but lessen withdrawal resistance.

Continued ➡

Three Basic Connections

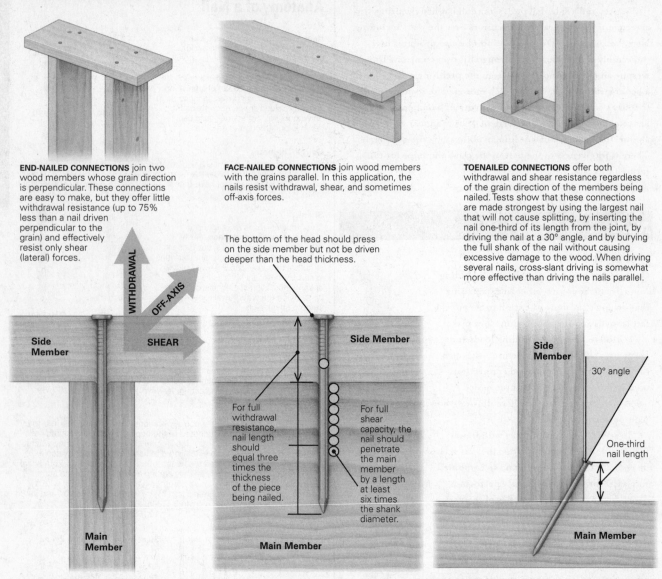

END-NAILED CONNECTIONS join two wood members whose grain direction is perpendicular. These connections are easy to make, but they offer little withdrawal resistance (up to 75% less than a nail driven perpendicular to the grain) and effectively resist only shear (lateral) forces.

FACE-NAILED CONNECTIONS join wood members with the grains parallel. In this application, the nails resist withdrawal, shear, and sometimes off-axis forces.

The bottom of the head should press on the side member but not be driven deeper than the head thickness.

TOENAILED CONNECTIONS offer both withdrawal and shear resistance regardless of the grain direction of the members being nailed. Tests show that these connections are made strongest by using the largest nail that will not cause splitting, by inserting the nail one-third of its length from the joint, by driving the nail at a 30° angle, and by burying the full shank of the nail without causing excessive damage to the wood. When driving several nails, cross-slant driving is somewhat more effective than driving the nails parallel.

WITHDRAWAL

OFF-AXIS

SHEAR

Side Member

Main Member

For full withdrawal resistance, nail length should equal three times the thickness of the piece being nailed.

Side Member

For full shear capacity, the nail should penetrate the main member by a length at least six times the shank diameter.

Main Member

Side Member

30° angle

One-third nail length

Main Member

Other Common Connections

Dovetail Nailing
Nails are driven at an angle through the face of a board to clamp the boards together and to provide better withdrawal resistance than perpendicular face-nailing.

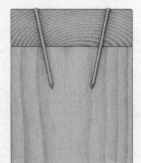

Blind Nailing
This connection is used with tongue-and-groove boards. Nails are driven at a 45° angle, enabling the groove of the adjacent board to fit over the nail.

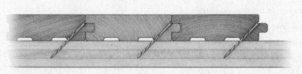

Clinch Nailing
An extralong nail is driven through the wood members being joined, and the tip is then bent and nailed flush for extra withdrawal resistance.

Choosing the Right Framing Nailer

By Michael Springer

Builders often ask for tool tests of framing nailers, but all the variations on the market make that a tall order to fill. There are stick nailers with 20°-, 28°-, and 30°-magazine angles, not to mention coil nailers. Some tools max out at 3¼-in. nails, some at 3½-in. nails, and some at 4-in. nails or longer. Some tools shoot full round-head nails, clipped-head nails, or both. With the variety of models available from the major pneumatic brands, power-tool companies, and lower-cost clone and private-label manufacturers, the framing-nailer category must represent 100 or more tools.

Here, my goal is to condense all the relevant information about these nailers into a brief guide, highlighting the latest technologies and features these tools have to offer.

It All Starts with the Nails

Picking a framing nailer starts with knowing the nails you'll be shooting. You want a tool that you can keep supplied with nails easily and affordably. Regional preferences and sometimes even building codes dictate which fasteners—and therefore which tools—are common in your area.

California and other Western states have adopted full round-head nailers, while most of the rest of the country relies on clipped-head models. Specific code requirements have driven some of the divide, but these geographic tool preferences can be traced back to where the big nailer companies started, or at least to the regional markets where their distribution was originally focused. Think Bostitch in New England, Hitachi in the West, and Paslode and Senco in between. As the major players staked their claims, whatever type of nail their early tools required became the default favorite in the territory.

Regardless of nail type, follow the nailing schedule for each material, component, and assembly you construct as specified by the building code covering your area. Model building codes were written for hand-driven nails, so they specify only the size, spacing, and number of nails used for specific connections and applications, not the type of head. The International Code Council's ESR-1539 report—which is free and widely available online—is written with an awareness of pneumatic nailers and is a good place to find the details of nailed connections (and equivalent connections) required to meet all the model building codes.

Continued →

Know Your Nails

Nail Collation

Framing nailers come in two styles: coil or stick. Coil nailers have an adjustable canister that accepts a coil of nails strung together by two rows of thin wire welded to the shanks of the nails. These nails have a full round head. Stick nailers fit two angled sticks of 25 to 40 nails collated with wire, paper, or plastic, with the head of each nail nested just above the head of the nail in front of it. The style of nail head is usually based on the collation angle.

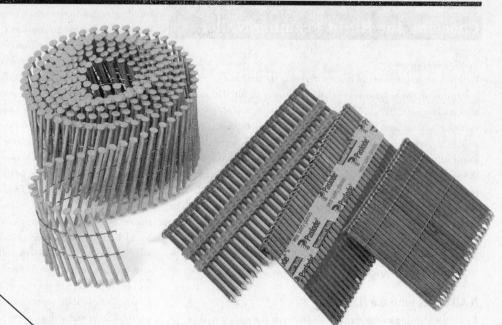

Nail Heads

Full round-head nails are acceptable everywhere in the United States and for every type of framing connection. They are also typically available in thicker shank diameters. The downside is that nail heads take up space in a magazine, so you get fewer nails per stick.

Maximum Nail Diameter

Nailers also have limitations to the maximum diameter of compatible fasteners they can accept. The minimum nail thickness for wall sheathing isn't typically the same as the minimum nail thickness for rafters. This varies by region, though, and also can change based on what the architect or engineer has specified in the building plans. I know a framer in the Southwest who is allowed to use 3-in. by 0.131-in. (10d) nails for everything—an easy task for any framing nailer.

Maximum Nail Length

Some brands have created a new compact-framer category, designed to be lighter and to fit more easily between 16-in.-on-center framing layouts. The dividing line for this category is typically maximum nail length—3¼ in. for compact models, 3½ in. for full size—but the maximum shank thickness also may differ by collation angle and brand.
The max size is often referenced in a nailer's model number. For instance, a domestic model number may express maximum nail lengths of 3¼ in. and 3½ in. as 325 and 350. Foreign models may use 83 and 90, which are the lengths in millimeters. It's worth noting that some compact nailers don't have the guts to shoot into dense engineered lumber well. Even if the longest nails you shoot are 3¼ in., you may be better off with a full-size nailer because of its superior power.

Two Head-Style Options for Paper-Collated Stick Nails

Depending on your region and applicable codes, the type of head on your nails is a big deal, and the head style is usually tied to the collation angle. There are a few variations.

Clipped Head

At steeper collation angles (28° and 30°), manufacturers can pack nails closer together by clipping off one side of the head. The resulting D-shape has less surface area than round heads of the same diameter and causes these nails to be disallowed for some applications. Some of the nails are called notched instead of clipped because the chunk removed from their heads is rounded instead of straight.

Offset Round Head

Available in both 28° and 30° angles, these nails provide the code compliance of a full round-head nail with the tight spacing common to a stick of clipped-head nails.

Must-Have Features for a Quality Framing Nailer

Even an occasional user needs a competent tool. Here are some important features to consider when choosing a nailer.

BALANCE AND FEEL are important to your overall comfort and the control of the tool. Before you plunk down cash, be sure to fill the tool with nails and to hang a hose off the back to evaluate how it really feels. Otherwise, you're just kicking the tires.

THE BODY OF THE NAILER will be either aluminum or magnesium, and the choice is a bit of a toss-up. Magnesium is lighter but more brittle, and it costs more than standard aluminum, which is heavier and more durable. It's best just to go with how the tool feels overall, though. I don't know that anyone buys a nailer based on the material it's cast from.

A SELECTIVE-FIRE SETTING lets you switch the tool from sequential-fire (single-shot) mode to bump-fire mode. The best designs are tool free, but because most users never switch back to sequential fire, replacing or adjusting the trigger assembly once is not a big deal. If you plan to switch back and forth, opt for a nailer that has a toggle switch.

TOP-LOAD VERSUS REAR-LOAD MAGAZINES is a decision you will have to make. For myself and the guys I know, the answer is unanimously in favor of rear load. Hanging the tool down with one hand lets you load in a more comfortable position; the spring-loaded follower can't accidentally slam into the nails and damage the collation strip; the remaining nails can't fall out as soon as you release the follower; and having the follower engaged when loading new nails keeps the last few remaining nails tightly in place so that they won't cause a jam.

DEPTH-OF-DRIVE ADJUSTMENT is important for meeting building codes, and the best setups work without the need for tools. Without this feature, you have to adjust the regulator on the air compressor when you switch from LVL headers to nailing off sheathing. It's not worth compromising on this feature.

Handy Upgrades

Whether you're framing on a regular basis or just looking for some extra perks, try these features.

A few manufacturers are using **NOSE MAGNETS** to hold the last few nails in a stick firmly in place when reloading the magazine. This is a simple, useful addition to help make the reloading process goofproof.

BUILT-IN AIR FILTERS are a welcome addition to keep unwanted gunk out of a nailer's innards. Pads of filter media are useful enough, but the best filters are self-cleaning cartridges that cough out any trapped particles every time you unplug the air hose.

A NONMARRING NOSE CAP allows your framing nailer to become a siding, trim, or deck nailer. Without a cap, the teeth on the nose turn cedar or redwood into hamburger.

Coil Nailers

Coil Nailers

Coil nailers have an adjustable canister that accepts a coil of nails—up to 200 framing nails or 300 sheathing nails at a time—angled at 15° and strung together by two rows of thin wire welded to the shanks of the nails. In most areas of the United States, these nailers are far less popular than stick nailers, but they are common in areas of the Northeast and in a few pockets of Louisiana, Missouri, and Texas. Interestingly, this is what the rest of the world considers a framing nailer.

PROS

- These tools shoot a lot of nails between reloading, potentially saving time.
- The tools' compact size provides some accessibility advantages.
- If a model fits shorter nails and has a protective nosepiece, it can double as a high-volume siding or trim nailer.

CONS

- When fully loaded with hundreds of nails, these tools can be heavy and unwieldy.
- Dropping or bending a coil of nails often renders it unusable and creates expensive waste.

Features for Production Framers

- **A RAFTER HOOK** for keeping your nailer close at hand is a must if you don't want your tool to slow you down. The lack of a hook is not a deal breaker, however. Aftermarket hooks that connect at the air fitting are available and may be preferable to a factory-installed hook that is clumsy or too small.
- **TOENAILING SPIKES** that really grab are the key to fast, accurate toenailing. Look for a nose with especially sharp spikes protruding well out from the sides.

Continued ➜

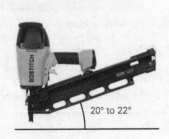

Stick Nailer

Stick Nailers

PLASTIC-COLLATED NAILERS fit round-head nails collated between 20° and 22°. A stiff collating strip—typically plastic but also available in rigid paper—allows enough space for full-size heads with the nails situated side-by-side. Two

20° to 22°

sticks of nails fit in the magazine for a load of about 60 nails. Full round-head nails have been a necessity in some parts of California for a while, so these tools are particularly big on the West Coast and in much of the West in general.

PROS

• Round-head nails are allowed for every connection type, so these tools can be used anywhere in the United States with their standard fasteners. (Some codes require the use of round-head nails only.)

• Round-head nails are typically available in larger shank sizes than other types.

• The easier manufacturing of plastic-collated nail sticks makes them significantly less expensive than the paper- or wire-collated nails used in other nailers.

CONS

• Nails of the standard plastic-collated variety spew out bits of plastic shrapnel, which is a nuisance when they ricochet off the wall into your face or leave the floor dotted with scattered shards.

• The long, low magazine keeps the nose of the tool from fitting into tight spots as easily as higher-angle stick nailers.

WIRE-WELD-COLLATED NAILERS have their own specific collation angle and their own specific homegrown market. These tools started strong in the Northeast and have stayed strong, with 80% of their sales in New England. Overall, the 28° tools are similar to the 30° type (they

28°

share the same pros and cons), but 28° clipped-head nails are typically collated with thin wires tack-welded to the side of the nails. Plastic-collated and paper-tape versions of 28° nails can be found, even some with round heads, but before you bring one out to build shear walls in California, make sure you can get fasteners for it. These tools are largely unknown in much of the country, and their diet of special fasteners may not be on the menu far from home.

PAPER-COLLATED NAILERS have magazine angles anywhere from 30° to 35°, but the fasteners they fit are usually referred to as 30° nails. These tools are known generically as clipped-head nailers or paper-tape nailers. Standard clipped-head nails for these tools are collated with paper tape glued along the sides of nails that are packed shank to shank. Magazines typically fit two sticks of these densely packed nails, providing about 80 nails.

30° to 35°

PROS

• The steep magazine angle of the tool affords its nose the deepest reach into corners.

• Tighter packed sticks of nails hold significantly more fasteners per load than the sticks in full round-head nailers.

CONS

• Clipped-head nails are not approved for structural connections in some areas, so more specialized offset round-head nails may be needed.

• These tools require more expensive fasteners than full round-head nailers.

Hammer Drills and Impact Drivers

By Jeremy Hess

Cordless drills and impact drivers are as common on the job site as tape measures and hammers. Manufacturers are continually improving their tools and batteries in an attempt to build the cordless package that weighs the least, runs the longest, and stands up best to the rigors of job-site use. The latest improvement in this progression is brushless motors. I recently took a look at six brushless hammer-drill and impact-driver combo kits to evaluate their features and their performance in real-world tasks.

All of the kits come with two batteries and a charger and can be purchased as the base for a cordless-tool arsenal. One of the kits offered only two other compatible tools: an oscillating saw and an impact wrench. The other kits offer a larger selection of additional tools, ranging from circular saws and reciprocating saws to specialty metalworking tools and nailers. Manufacturers try to entice purchasers with low prices on these two-tool kits, hoping they'll buy additional tools and batteries later. This hope is justified, since most users want to stick with one battery platform.

Brushed vs. Brushless Motors

Whether corded or cordless, the typical tool motor is constructed of an armature, a commutator, and brushes. This type of motor is inexpensive to build and free of complex electronics. There are downsides, however. For example, the carbon brushes that ride against the commutator slowly wear away until they need replacement. Even worse, the drag created takes away from the useful power of the motor.

Instead of brushes, brushless motors have electronic circuitry that alternates the current to the motor's magnets to make the motor rotate. The absence of brushes eliminates the efficiency-robbing friction and allows for a more compact design for the motor and the tool.

Batteries Vary

While all kits in this test contained lithium-ion (Li-ion) batteries, not all batteries had the same amp-hour rating. The higher the amp-hour rating, the more fuel the battery can hold. A higher amp-hour rating doesn't make the motor more powerful or increase performance; it simply means the battery has a longer run time. The tested kits have batteries ranging from 2 to 5 amp-hours (Ah).

Because of this variation, comparing the number of holes drilled or fasteners driven without some interpretation is not that meaningful. For each kit, then, I compared the number of holes drilled and fasteners driven to its batteries' amp-hour rating. This allowed me to evaluate performance on a more-level playing field. I also included the gross numbers because they matter, too, especially since batteries are a large part of a cordless platform's overall cost.

Shared Features

The tools in all six kits in this test shared many features. They come with some configuration of LED worklights, although the positioning and the number of lights vary, and some work better than others. All tools have a metal belt clip that can be mounted on either side of the tool.

Impact drivers are great for installing large screws and bolts and for tightening nuts. At full power, though, they're not well suited for smaller screws and tightening up delicate hardware, so all of the drivers except two had controls that slow the motors for greater precision when needed. This feature allows the same impact driver to go from installing ledger bolts for a deck to tightening canopy screws for a ceiling fan. Changing this setting is as easy as pushing a button.

All of the hammer drills had two speeds and multiposition clutches.

Continued ➜

Hammer Drills vs. Rotary Hammers

By Matt Higgins

There are times when a conventional drill just won't get the job done. For example, when you're installing a deck ledger against a concrete foundation and need to drill lots of holes, you need a more specialized tool. That's when you might pick up a hammer drill or a rotary hammer. While the names are often used interchangeably, they are not the same tools.

Hammer Drill

As the name implies, this tool delivers a hammering action as it drills. This action is created by two internal metal disks with ridges. As the disks spin against each other, the ridges ride up and down and cause the chuck to move in and out. Hammer drills can have the hammering action turned off; with the flip of a switch and the swap of a bit, you can go from drilling in concrete block to boring into wood framing. Typically, these tools can use up to a ¼-in.-dia. bit when working on poured concrete. A ⅜-in.-dia. or smaller bit can be used in block and masonry.

Because of the mechanics needed to create the hammering action, a hammer drill is typically more bulky than a traditional drill. That said, many of today's hammer drills aren't shaped and sized all that differently from traditional drills. A standoff handle to keep the tool steady is one telltale feature of a hammer drill.

Rotary Hammer

For larger holes, a rotary hammer is the go-to tool. A rotary hammer uses a piston to compress air that moves a striker to create the hammering action. The rate of the blows is slower than with a hammer drill, but those impacts are far more powerful.

Think of the hammer drill as delivering numerous jabs and the rotary hammer as hauling off with haymakers. The power of the rotary hammer means less work for the user, but it also means that the rotary hammer is not suitable for use on wood or metal.

While hammer drills typically are outfitted with a standard adjustable chuck, rotary hammers have a spring-loaded chuck that corresponds directly to the size of the bits being used. This means that you must use only bits that fit that specific chuck. SDS-plus are the most popular bits and are designed for drilling holes with diameters from ⁵⁄₃₂ in. to ¾ in. SDS-max bits step the capability up to a range of ⅜ in. to 2 in.

Since the hammering force isn't created by a spinning mechanism, as it is with hammer drills, rotary hammers can be switched to hammer-only mode. This is useful for light demolition work such as tile removal. Rotary hammers are generally bigger, weigh more, take on bigger tasks, and require less work from the user. They do, however, cost more, so if the job doesn't call for it, purchasing a rotary hammer might be overkill and wasted dollars.

Screw Bits

By Matt Higgins

There's a wide variety of drive systems in the hardware world, and most of us have a healthy collection of bits, ranging from star-drive to square-drive to hex. It's easy to spot the differences between most of the styles, but two that are commonly mixed up—even by the more experienced—are the Phillips and Pozidriv bits. Despite their similar appearance, these two systems are not interchangeable. Here's how to tell the difference between them.

PHILLIPS It makes no difference when you're tightening a cup hinge on a cabinet door, but the Phillips design wasn't actually invented by someone named Phillips. Rather, John Thompson sold his design to Henry Phillips, who then formed a new company, improved the design, and worked to get the drive system to become the standard in numerous industries, especially automotive. The key improvements of the Phillips system over the slotted system are that its bits self-center and will cam out (slip out) when a fastener is sufficiently seated. On a production line, these features are huge time savers. The most common Phillips sizes are 1, 2, and 3 (from smallest to largest), and the bits typically have "ph" indicated on them. The patent on the Phillips design expired in 1966, but the Phillips Screw Company has continued to improve on the cruciform-shaped drive, which has led to other drive systems from the same company, such as the Pozidriv.

POZIDRIV When trying to tighten up that previously mentioned cup hinge with a Phillips bit, you probably should be using a Pozidriv. The Pozidriv also has a self-centering design, but the shape is modified for improved engagement. The sure sign that a screw is Pozidriv is the four tick marks or indentations around the cross. Viewed from the side, the difference between Phillips and Pozidriv bits is unmistakable. A Pozidriv has ribs between each of the four arms of the cross. This adds the increased grip. A Phillips bit fits in a Pozidriv screw head, but it will most likely cam out before the fastener is fully tight. This can damage the fastener and is why that cup hinge loosens up so quickly when a Phillips bit is used. A Pozidriv bit does not fit in a Phillips screw. Pozidriv bits are available in driver sizes from 0 to 5 (from smallest to largest) and have "pz" marked on them.

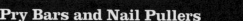

Pry Bars and Nail Pullers

By Don Burgard

Pulling nails isn't nearly as fun as driving them, and separating two pieces of wood nailed together can be a chore, but whether you're a building professional or a DIYer, you've undoubtedly had to do both plenty of times. For situations where nail heads are above the wood's surface, using your hammer's claw to pull the nails may work just fine. Likewise, the hammer claw may be all you need to pry apart two boards. Sometimes, though, you need to dig below the wood's surface to grab onto a nail or slide a tool delicately between a piece of molding and the wall. In these situations, you need a specialty tool.

Although pulling nails and prying apart boards are different tasks, the tool used for both is often the same: some variation of

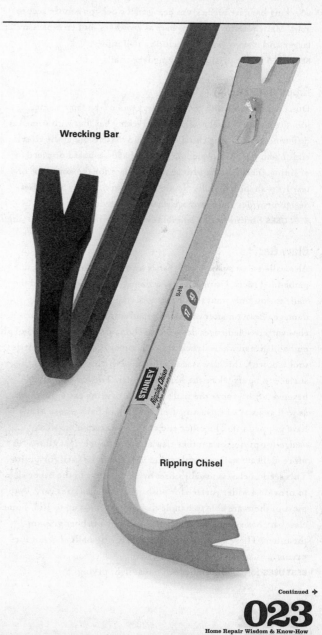

Wrecking Bar

Ripping Chisel

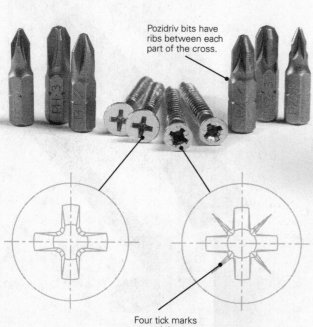

Pozidriv bits have ribs between each part of the cross.

Four tick marks around the cross indicate Pozidriv.

Continued ➜

a bar with one end designed for pulling nails and the other end designed for prying (and perhaps also for pulling nails).

The vocabulary for this category of tools isn't precise, and manufacturers mix and match certain features on their nail-pulling and prying tools, but there are enough common characteristics that it's possible to put these tools into the groups described here. If you do demolition work of all sorts, you likely can put tools in all five groups to good use. If you only occasionally need to pry and pull, you may get all the power and finesse you need from just a couple of these tools.

Wrecking Bar

With a name like "wrecking bar," this tool is clearly not for delicate work. It's got a nail puller on one end and a prying wedge on the other. Big enough to handle extracting nails larger than 16d, it can also pry apart nailed pieces of framing lumber. Most wrecking bars are made from hexagonal stock for a more secure grip. Many refer to wrecking bars as crowbars, but crowbars are larger and may or may not include a nail puller.

BEST USES Heavy prying, removing large nails

Ripping Chisel

Don't confuse this with the upholstery tool of the same name. A job-site ripping chisel resembles a wrecking bar, but with some key differences. A ripping chisel widens and flattens out at the chisel end, making it able to slide easily under a loose board or piece of siding. This flat area also provides a place for the same type of teardrop-shape nail puller found on flat bars. Finally, the offset design provides more leverage when twist-prying.

BEST USES Sliding under and removing loose boards, twist-prying

Claw Bar

Also called a cat's paw, a claw bar is a great tool for digging out embedded nails. Using a claw bar damages the wood around the nail, so you only want to use this tool in places where surface damage doesn't matter or can be repaired. One end has a curved claw with beveled edges designed to slide just under the head of an embedded nail when struck with a hammer. On a Japanese-style tool (shown), this claw is at a right angle to the handle, and the surface to be struck by the hammer is flat. The claw's sharp, beveled edges groove the nail's shank, providing extra purchase as well as a way of extracting finish nails and nails whose heads have popped off. The other end can have a simple beveled wedge for prying or another claw at a lower angle that allows for more-delicate nail removal; either way, it can be used for prying. This second claw is usually offset by 90° relative to the other claw to provide a wider surface for pushing. Claw-bar sizes vary, but most of them are able to handle digging out nails up to 16d. Some claw bars have a nail puller on one end and a rubber grip on the other. These are meant only for removing nails and not for prying.

BEST USES Removing embedded nails, light prying

Flat Bar

A flat bar is perhaps the most useful demolition tool. It can't dig out embedded nails like a claw bar, but it's meant for prying and for pulling all types of nails. In addition to being able to remove nails whose heads are at least slightly above the wood's surface, it's a great tool for removing plywood and clapboard siding. The design of the flat bar provides space for a nail puller of a different sort: a teardrop-shape opening near one end of the bar that grabs a nail and allows it to be removed by pulling up rather than pushing down.

BEST USES Removing small to medium nails, light to medium prying, removing plywood and siding

Molding Bar

When a flat bar is still too fat to get behind a piece of trim without damaging it, you need a molding bar. The molding bar's prying end is especially thin and wide. The thin edge allows the tool to get behind a piece of trim without damaging it, and the wide surface spreads out the prying force, making it less likely that the piece will snap. There is often a slot at the end, which can be used to pull nails from the surface of the molding. The claw at the other end is usually similar to the distinctive claw on a Japanese-style cat's paw. Its flat edge provides a suitable striking surface.

BEST USES Separating trim from walls and siding, removing embedded nails

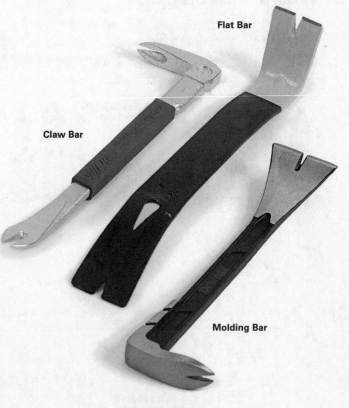

Flat Bar

Claw Bar

Molding Bar

Sawblade Tooth Angles

By Don Burgard

Tooth count is an important feature in how a sawblade performs—for example, cutting crown molding with a 14-tooth blade will create a mess, and cutting plywood with an 80-tooth blade will take a long time and possibly burn the wood. If you're about to buy a new sawblade, though, you'll also want to consider tooth angles.

Top-Bevel Angle

Blades with flat-top teeth, known as flat-top-grind (FTG) blades, are fine for ripping, but when you're cutting across the grain, you need a blade whose teeth are beveled. Beveling the teeth on a sawblade allows them to score the wood, which results in a more precise cut. Common angles are 10°, 15°, and 20°. The greater the angle, the more precise the cut. On an alternate top-bevel angle blade, or ATB, these angles alternate left to right from tooth to tooth; on a combination blade, top-bevel teeth alternate with flat-top teeth. ATB blades generally cut very well, but they tend to dull more quickly than FTG blades. Also, the greater the bevel angle—some high alternate top-bevel (HiATB) blades have angles as high as 38°—the higher the likelihood they will dull quickly. Blades with triple-chip-grind (TCG) tooth configurations alternate flat-top teeth with slightly taller teeth that are beveled on both sides at a 45° angle.

Hook Angle

The angle created by the face of a tooth and an imaginary line from the tip of the tooth to the center of the blade is known as the hook angle. The sharper this angle, the more aggressive the cut. Rip blades can have hook angles as high as 22°, which allows them to plow through long lengths of wood quickly and without excessive heat buildup. On the other hand, blades designed for cutting melamine and similar materials often have negative angles—up to negative 6°. Cutting with low-hook-angle blades is slower than doing so with high-hook-angle blades, and it requires more power. These cuts are cleaner, however, and produce less tearout. On a sliding miter saw or a radial-arm saw, a blade with a negative hook angle reduces the chance of the blade grabbing the stock and feeding too quickly.

Relief Angles

A metal sawblade spinning at a high rate and engaged in constant contact with wood is going to get hot. To reduce the friction that can leave burn marks along the cutline, manufacturers angle the teeth of some sawblades to minimize the surface area that comes into contact with the wood and to provide space for dust and chips (and the heat they contain) to escape. The top-relief angle is generally 12° for softwood and 15° for hardwood. Slight radial-relief and tangential-relief angles help to prevent burning along the sides of the kerf, although they can produce scratch marks.

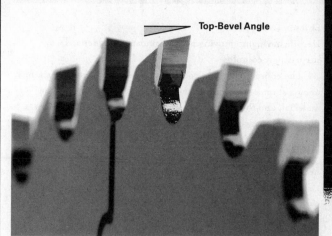

Top-Bevel Angle

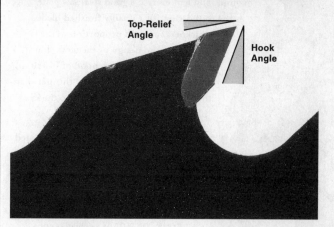

Top-Relief Angle

Hook Angle

Radial-Relief Angle

Tangential-Relief Angle

Continued →

Circular Sawblades

By Justin Fink

Despite having no moving parts, circular sawblades are surprisingly complex.

The common carbide-tooth sawblade has to make three kinds of cuts at once: the cut into the material, the cut through the material, and the cut on the way out of the material. Through the engineering of the saw plate and teeth, the blade is able to perform each of these three cuts.

The wrong blade may still make the cut, but it won't necessarily make it well or make it repeatedly without failing. Here's how circular sawblades work.

A. SAW PLATE Laser-cut to shape and then heat-treated, ground, and hammered, a good steel saw plate is the foundation for a quality finished blade. Plate thickness varies in proportion to the size, number, and design of the teeth, but it typically is in the neighborhood of 0.020 in. to 0.025 in. (less than 1/32 in.) thinner than the width of the teeth attached to the saw plate's outer edge.

B. CHIP LIMITER These small horns—located behind each tooth or after several—are added to certain blades to limit the amount of bite that each tooth takes, which reduces the chances of kickback.

C. EXPANSION SLOT As sawblades cut a kerf through wood, they create enough heat to cause the saw plate to expand. Slots cut into the saw plate dissipate the heat and provide room for expansion so that the blade won't warp. The slots are usually terminated with a rounded end to eliminate the chance of stress cracks, and they often are filled with plastic or a soft metal such as copper to reduce noise as the blade spins.

D. COATING More than window dressing, the Teflon-like coatings used on many sawblades are designed to reduce friction, to prevent wood resin from sticking to the saw plate, and to help make the blade easier to clean.

E. TOOTH COUNT The number of teeth on a sawblade contributes to the speed and smoothness of the cut. Fewer teeth provide faster cuts with rougher results, while more teeth cause blades to cut more slowly but with finer results.

F. VIBRATION DAMPENERS Vibration, which can come from the saw itself and from contact with the material being cut, causes the blade to wobble from side to side, which contributes to tooth wear, creates additional heat, and leads to inferior cuts. To dampen this vibration, manufacturers laser-cut various patterns through the middle of the saw plate. The presence of a good antivibration design is revealed by knocking the saw plate with a hammer; if it rings, it will vibrate.

G. GULLET Acting as a sort of storage compartment, the gullet is where the wood that's removed from the kerf is held until the blade rotates out of the cut and releases the waste. The gullets are curved to retain strength, and sized based on the type of cut and amount of material that each tooth has to handle. For example, a blade with relatively few teeth means that each tooth is cutting more material, so the gullets are large.

Tooth Grind

The shape of the sawblade's teeth, particularly along its top cutting edge, determines how it cuts material. The grind on each tooth of a given blade may be identical, or it may be a mixture of different grinds, designed to work in concert. There are numerous variations to the type, shape, size, and angle of the teeth, but the most common grinds are flat, beveled, and chamfered.

FLAT This squared-off shape makes teeth extremely durable and resistant to fracturing, but it's designed to chip away at the wood, so it's not known for clean cuts. Flat-ground teeth are typically found on blades designed to cut along the grain (rip cut), where cutting speed is the top priority. But flat-ground teeth also play a supporting role on blades that include other, more specialized teeth.

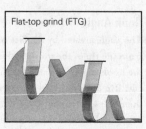
Flat-top grind (FTG)

BEVELED If a flat-ground tooth is a spoon, a beveled tooth is a knife. Rather than grabbing and pulling its way through the material with a digging action, it cuts with a slicing action. Beveled teeth are usually set at opposing angles so that one tooth shaves through the right side of the kerf and the other shaves through the left side. Sometimes this beveled sequence is followed by a single flat-ground tooth (called a raker) to clear away the V-shape waste left by

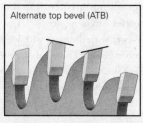
Alternate top bevel (ATB)

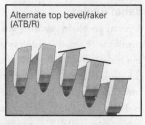
Alternate top bevel/raker (ATB/R)

the beveled teeth. This ATB/R configuration, found on what are often called combination blades, leaves clean results along both cut edges. The steeper the angle of the bevel, the cleaner the edges and faces of the cut, but also the faster the teeth will dull.

CHAMFERED These teeth are designed to survive in dense materials—tropical hardwoods, laminate counters, nonferrous metals, and so on—that would dull other grinds quickly. Chamfered teeth are usually combined with flat-ground teeth. The high, flat center of the chamfered tooth creates the first chip, leaving the sides for the flat-ground tooth that follows behind it.

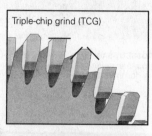
Triple-chip grind (TCG)

Handsaw Revival

By Brian Pontolilo

If you're trimming an entire house and you don't have a power miter saw, you're crazy. But if you think handsaws are old fashioned, you're wrong, although you're probably not alone. Even in an age of laser-guided power tools, saw manufacturers continue to improve and reinvent the handsaw.

Purists might argue that their 100-year-old Disston handsaw will outperform any new saw. They'll laugh at the quality of modern saws and complain that new saws are throw-away tools because many of them can't be resharpened. In many ways, they're right. A well-maintained Disston crosscut saw makes easy work of cutting through most wood. And when the blade dulls, it can be filed and set to cut as if it were new. Of course, you have to know how to file and set the teeth, and if you're cutting particleboard or other man-made products, the glue may dull the blade faster than you can sharpen it.

Modern handsaw design is a response to the evolution of home building. Handsaws are used less, and sharpening is a lost art. Today's handsaws are designed to cut modern materials easily and without dulling.

Beyond Basic Crosscut Saws and Ripsaws

Once there were two standard saws used by carpenters, one for crosscutting and one for ripping. Because most ripping now is done with a circular saw or on a tablesaw, ripsaws are a dying breed. Many new handsaws are capable of both crosscutting and ripping. Marketed as general-purpose saws, they are designed to cut solid lumber, engineered wood, and other man-made materials. There are also some innovative handsaws designed to cut specific materials such as drywall, composite decking, and synthetic trim.

Traditional Japanese handsaws also have influenced the evolution of modern handsaws. The most notable difference between a Western-style saw and a Japanese handsaw is that the Western saw cuts on the push stroke and the Japanese saw cuts on the pull stroke. Japanese saws have inspired manufacturers to rethink both the blade and handle design of their saws.

Different Strokes for Different Folks

Traditional Western crosscut saws cut on the push stroke. The tips of the teeth score the wood, and the edges of the teeth sever the wood fibers. Western-ripsaw teeth also cut on the push stroke, but the teeth work more like a series of chisels. The teeth on both types of saw are set alternately so that the kerf—the groove created by the saw—is wider than the blade, reducing friction as the saw moves deeper into the cut. Cutting with a Western-style saw requires sharp, properly set teeth and good technique because the blade has a tendency to bend during cutting.

Many carpenters have been won over by Japanese-style saws that cut on the pull stroke. The appeal of these saws is easy to understand. When you pull the saw across the material, tension keeps the blade straight, allowing pull saws to have thinner blades. A thinner blade requires less strength to move through the wood and produces a more refined cut. The blade design—with three cutting edges on the crosscut saws and two on the ripsaws—cleans sawdust from the kerf as you cut. Unfortunately, sawdust tends to land on the stock and can make the cutline difficult to see.

Some new handsaws are designed to cut on both the push and the pull stroke. The tooth design is similar to a crosscutting pull saw, but the teeth are filed to cut in both directions. These aggressive saws are more difficult to use, but they cut faster (some manufacturers claim 50% faster) than saws that cut only on one stroke.

As Tooth Design Evolves, Saws Can't Be Resharpened

Most Japanese pull-saw blades are too complex to be sharpened. Instead, the blades are designed to be removed from their handles and replaced. Removable blades can be an advantage. You can withdraw the blades from their handles to fit the saws into a toolbox, and you may need to buy only one handle for many different types of blade.

Likewise, many new Western-style saws cannot be resharpened. In an effort to make saws that can stand up to the glues and synthetics found in modern building materials, manufacturers have developed methods to harden the steel so that blades stay sharper longer. Electronically heat-tempered steel teeth, recognized by their blue and black color, are designed for performance and longevity, but they can't be filed.

Fortunately, most new handsaws are priced fairly. Machine-made general-use carpenter's saws and replacement blades for pull saws are often about the same price. Sawblades that are not hardened and can be refiled and reset likely were hand-sharpened and set by the manufacturer. If you want to buy a saw that can be resharpened, plan to spend more money and more time looking for a saw.

One Rule Applies to All Saws

All sawblades have a number of points, or teeth per inch. Most manufacturers specify points per inch, or the number of cutting

Continued ➡

The Original Cordless Saw

From a quick cut through a single piece of framing lumber to a precise cut to remove a piece of rotting trim, handsaws often get the job done more quickly, more safely, and more accurately than their powered counterparts. Before you buy a handsaw, it is a good idea to understand how different saws work, and why some cost more than others.

Western-Style Carpenter's Saws

Traditional Western-style saws cut on the push stroke with teeth that are hand-filed and set by the manufacturer. The saws can be filed and set when the blade dulls or the set is thrown off. Crosscut-saw and ripsaw blades differ in tooth design and the number of points per inch (ppi) or teeth per inch (tpi). The blades on traditional Western saws range from 20 in. to 26 in. long, and the handles are wooden and bolted to the blades.

Japanese Pull Saws

Traditional Japanese pull saws cut on the pull stroke, allowing for thinner, finer-cutting blades. Due to the complexity of the tooth design and their inexpensive nature, blades usually are replaced instead of resharpened. The blade can be removed easily from the handle, and one handle often can be used for more than one type of blade. The straight bamboo handle makes it easy to control the saw and line up a cut, and it can be used with two hands.

Modern Hybrids

Many modern handsaws are designed with new users and new uses in mind. Because handsaws are used less often, especially for ripping, many new saws are not designated for crosscutting or ripping but for general use. The average blades are shorter, and the teeth cannot be filed because they are hardened to stay sharp even when cutting man-made building materials. Some saws are made for specific materials. The plastic handles are designed for ergonomic comfort and control.

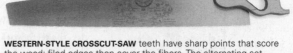
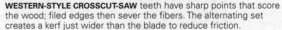

WESTERN-STYLE CROSSCUT-SAW teeth have sharp points that score the wood; filed edges then sever the fibers. The alternating set creates a kerf just wider than the blade to reduce friction.

WESTERN-STYLE RIPSAW teeth are larger and usually have fewer points per inch than crosscut saws. Ripsaw teeth also are set alternately, but instead of cutting with the tips and the edges, the front of the teeth cut like a series of chisels.

JAPANESE CROSSCUT-SAW teeth work similarly to the crosscut teeth on a Western-style saw with two slight differences: They are reversed to cut on the pull stroke, and they have an extra bevel near the top of the blade.

JAPANESE RIPSAW teeth also cut with chiseling action. The teeth are small at the heel of the blade where you start the cut and larger toward the toe. This makes it easy to begin a stroke.

AGGRESSIVE-CUTTING HANDSAW teeth use a design similar to Japanese saws, but each tooth is sharpened on both sides to cut on push and pull strokes. With only 8 ppi, this 15-in. blade is designed to cut faster than most traditional saws.

HARDENED PULL-SAW teeth use traditional Japanese sawtooth design on induction-hardened steel to cut easily through wood as well as modern materials like plywood and particleboard. These larger teeth don't cut as fine as some traditional Japanese saws, but they cut faster.

tips in 1 in. of blade. Coarse blades with fewer points per inch cut fast but leave a rough edge. Blades with more points per inch make smoother cuts, but cut more slowly.

This rule applies to all saws and is important to consider whether you're buying a Western-style saw or a Japanese pull saw. If you are going to cut only framing lumber, where smooth edges are unnecessary, a saw with 9 points per inch will do the job quickly and with little effort. If your task is to cut veneered plywood, a saw with 12 or more points per inch will avoid splintering the veneer and will leave a smooth edge. Although the saw will cut more slowly, the control is an advantage when you are trying to cut accurately.

Saw Handles Are Designed for Control and Comfort

The D-shaped handles on Western-style saws offer the best grip for pushing a saw though a cut. The handles are usually wood, though some manufacturers have switched to lighter, more comfortable plastic handles. Most handles attach to the blade with bolts that can be loosened to adjust the handle's position or tightened if the handle works loose. Some handles are molded to the blade without bolts. These handles still can loosen from the blade but can't be tightened.

Traditional Japanese saws have straight, easy-to-pull handles that can be used with one or two hands. With a long handle that extends straight out from the blade, it is easy to cut a precise line across the stock.

Many of today's general-carpentry saws that cut on the pull stroke have pistol-grip handles. They don't offer the same amount of control as the straight handles on Japanese saws, but the pistol-grip handles are more comfortable for making quick cuts. Just as you should choose a blade based on the material you are cutting and the level of finish your work requires, you should choose a handle based on comfort and the amount of finesse you need to get the job done.

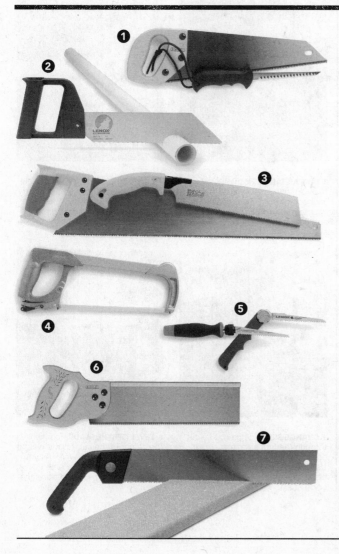

How Many Handsaws Do You Need?

The truth is that you can cut PVC with a string, and if you have a general-carpentry saw, you can handle most occasional jobs. But if you cut a lot of one type of material, or if you just like tools, there are a bunch of useful saws you should know about.

1. Just for Drywall
There are two saws that are handy to have when you're hanging drywall—one with a wide blade for straight cuts and a smaller, more nimble one for curves and circles.

2. PVC Saw
With fine teeth and a wide blade, this type of saw is used to make smooth cuts through all sizes of PVC pipe, leaving a clean, ready-to-glue edge.

3. Crosscut Or General-Purpose Carpentry Saw
This is the saw you reach for to finish the cuts for a stair stringer or a roof rafter, or for other general uses. You can choose a Western-style saw or a pull saw, depending on how you are most comfortable cutting.

4. High-Tension Hacksaw
This tool is often the remedy for a stripped screw or a rusty bolt. And if you don't own pipe cutters, a hacksaw makes easy work of cutting copper pipe. This high-tension frame offers three blade positions for regular cuts, flush cuts, and cutting in tight spaces.

5. Recip-Saw Blade Handles
You can't carry a reciprocating saw in your tool belt, but you can carry the most important part. These two handles allow you to hand-saw with any recip-saw blade.

6. Backsaw Or Detail Saw
If you need to cut miters for casings or crown molding, or if you need to cut a piece of trim in place, this saw is your best bet for a precision cut. The ridge along the top of a backsaw stiffens the blade for straight, fine cutting.

7. A Modern Saw for Modern Material
It's hard to cut through synthetic materials without the sawblade bogging down in the kerf. This saw is designed to stay sharp when cutting man-made material, and the raker teeth clean out the kerf as you cut.

Continued →

Using a Pull Saw

By Will Beemer

You probably won't need a pull saw every day, but it's a great tool to have when the need arises. Unlike Western-style saws, which cut on the push stroke, Japanese-style saws cut on the pull. Pulling on the blade takes advantage of steel's higher tensile strength compared to its compressive strength. As a result, the extrathin blade on a Japanese saw cuts straighter and with greater accuracy than the blade on a Western saw.

You'll find pull saws useful for cutting casing and base trim in place and for cutting small moldings. In short, they are great tools for using any time you need to make a precise, easily guided cut.

Japanese saws are available in a number of different styles. Perhaps the most useful for carpenters is the Ryoba. This type of saw has two sets of teeth: one set for crosscuts and one for rips. You can tell the difference between the two sets by looking at how light reflects along the teeth. If the light reflects the same on every tooth, it's a rip blade. The teeth are usually bigger, too, but not always. If you see a bright reflection on every other tooth, it's a crosscut blade. It used to be that Japanese-style saws were rare (and expensive), but now you can find them in just about every hardware store and home center.

Shark 10-2440 Fine Cut Saw

9½-in. blade with 9-point (rip) and 17-point (crosscut) diamond-shaped teeth and ABS handle

1. START THE CUT. Once you've marked the top and sides of the stock, gently push the saw against your thumb as you pull back on the handle. Your thumb should guide the blade so that the teeth are in the center of the line. Keep your thumb above the teeth to prevent getting cut.

2. MOVE YOUR THUMB AWAY. Once the kerf is established, you can move both hands to the handle. Both thumbs should be lined up on top of the handle.

3. TAKE A STANCE. Position your body so that your dominant hand is directly behind the cutline and your feet are spread shoulder width apart. Hold the blade at a 45° angle, and cut with a steady, even rhythm.

4. DON'T CUT A LINE YOU CAN'T SEE. Position your body so that you can see the cut progressing. You may need to crouch down to keep the blade from blocking your line of sight.

5. CHANGE SIDES. Once you've cut through the first side, move your body to the other side of the stock. Use the existing kerf to line up the blade. Once again, cut with the blade at a 45° angle.

6. LEVEL OFF THE BLADE. To finish the center of the cut, let the weight of the saw do all the work. As you near the end of the cut, grab the offcut to prevent splitting along the grain.

Bench Planes and Block Planes

By Don Burgard

Any decent woodshop is going to have a variety of hand planes, but these tools are far less common on a job site. Still, a hand plane may be just the right tool for those places in a house where wooden parts need to fit precisely, such as cabinets, doors, and trim. In these places, planes can smooth surfaces, remove minuscule amounts of material at a time, and clean up areas cut by other, less precise tools. In many places, planes can reduce or even eliminate the need for sanding. Moreover, because planes are much quieter than power tools, if you whistle while you work, you'll be able to hear yourself.

Bench Planes

Bench planes are so called because they are most often used at a woodworking bench. They are held with two hands, with the front hand holding a knob and the back hand gripping a handle (called a tote). The blades on bench planes are angled at 45°, and they are positioned with the bevel side down. A chip breaker lies on top of the blade in a bench plane; it directs wood shavings up and away and helps to reduce the stuttering or skipping movement known as chatter.

To distinguish bench planes of different sizes, most manufacturers use a numbering system established in the 19th century. For an entry door that needs to be trimmed, or even a large cabinet door, the most useful bench plane is likely a no. 7 or no. 8 plane. These planes, known as jointers, have a long sole

that allows them to create a flat surface over a long area. Jointer planes can get the job done quickly and evenly, although their size and cost may have you looking for an alternative. A no. 8 plane is 24 in. long, and a Lie-Nielsen model can cost several hundred dollars.

If you frequently need to surface smaller areas, a smoothing plane (no. 4 and no. 4½) or a jack plane (no. 5 and 5¼) may also come in handy. Senior editor Andy Engel has found that a no. 5 is generally an adequate job-site substitute for a jointer plane, and its length (14 in.) and cost make it easier to justify adding to your toolbox.

Block Planes

At only 6 in. to 7 in. long, a block plane is designed to be used with one hand, and it can fit easily inside a tool pouch. For projects such as cabinets, these small planes have a variety of uses: chamfering, cutting end grain, leveling corner joints, trimming miters, cleaning up saw cuts, and smoothing straight and curved edges. Block planes are available in standard and low-angle versions. The blade on a standard-angle block plane is set at 20°; the blade on a low-angle block plane is set at 12°, which is better for cutting end grain and adjusting miters. Because the blade angle on both of these models is much lower than that on a bench plane, chatter is naturally reduced; at the same time, the risk of tearout is greater. The reduction in chatter means that a chip breaker is unnecessary. As a result, the blade is positioned bevel side up, effectively increasing the blade angle and allowing the blade itself to direct shavings away.

If a carpenter has only one plane on a job site, it's likely to be a standard-angle block plane. These handy little tools are useful for back-beveling miters, chamfering edges, scribe-fitting panels, and angling cedar shingles for woven corners. (No plane is worth using if it's dull. Be sure you understand how to tune up a block plane—there are resources online.)

Continued →

Laser Levels

By Gary M. Katz

When my editor asked me to do a head-to-head test of laser levels, I was confused. I explained that there are three general types—dot, line, and rotary—with dozens of models to choose from.

"Let's test the levels most of our readers are likely to use," he replied, pushing to narrow the focus. "Doesn't one type of laser level do it all?"

No. There's no such thing as a laser level that does it all. But each type of laser performs a variety of leveling and layout tasks, and of course, there are ranges of function within each type. Matching a level's features with the type of work you do and the amount you're willing to spend is the big challenge. You might end up with one laser or several. But if you make smart choices, these high-tech devices will save you huge amounts of time and trouble.

For Greater Accuracy, Expect to Pay More and See Less

In laser levels, accuracy typically is measured in the amount of error over a certain distance. Several variables affect accuracy.

The light-emitting diode is one. Although a bigger dot or broader laser line is easier to see, it's also less accurate because level can be anywhere within the width of the projected light. Better-quality diodes emit tighter dots or lines. Most lasers emit red light, but some manufacturers are offering green lasers, claiming that green is more visible. While this might be true, the technology required to project green light requires significantly more power than red light, so batteries don't last as long.

The self-leveling mechanism built into more-expensive laser levels also has a bearing on accuracy. The mechanism contains a tiny internal pendulum as well as magnets that dampen the pendulum's movement, keeping the diode stationary when someone walks across the floor. Too much dampening can have an adverse effect on accuracy.

Although it's true that more-accurate laser levels usually cost more than less-accurate models, the degree of accuracy required really depends on the work you do. Not everyone requires 1/8-in. accuracy over 100 ft. Foundation and grading contractors may require that degree of precision, but many carpenters would be thrilled with reliable accuracy of 1/4 in. over 50 ft. When buying any laser level, check the accuracy rating given by the manufacturer, and make sure it meets the tolerances for the work you do.

Detectors Make Laser Levels More Versatile

In the past, many laser levels could be used only indoors, in rooms that weren't too bright. Today, improvements in laser technology have overcome both brightness and distance limitations. All three laser-level categories—dot, line, and rotary—feature models that can be used with a detector. This device can be positioned some distance away from the laser's diode and moved up or down until the detector picks up the level projection, blinking or beeping in response.

Teaming a laser level with a detector broadens the scope of the work you can do. When you can't see the line, the detector can. Used outdoors, the laser and detector work like a transit and rod. If handling a broad range of exterior layout tasks is important, make sure to look for a laser level that works with a detector.

Lasers Find Level in Different Ways

Lasers run the gamut when it comes to leveling systems. Manual-leveling models rely on knobs and vials, just like old-fashioned builder's levels. The least-expensive rotary levels have this feature. Self-leveling lasers come in two varieties. Some models must be placed on a surface close to level, within 3° to 5°. Others are equipped with a bubble vial that enables you to get the unit close to level (within 3° to 5°) before the laser's self-leveling mechanism can work. Dot and line lasers require a dampening system to help steady the line, preventing wild fluctuations caused by someone walking on a floor.

If you want a rotary laser level that does all the work of getting level, look for an automatic self-leveling model. For a significant

Three Different Approaches Can Get a Unit Level

MANUAL-LEVELING Much like earlier laser levels, manual-leveling rotary levels require a bit of adjustment. Most are simple to operate; they have one or two bubble vials and adjustment knobs built into the unit. Whether you're shooting level or plumb, set up the device close to level, fine-tune the knobs until the bubble vials are level, and you're ready to go.

SELF-LEVELING The best dot and line lasers are self-leveling. The pendulum-and-magnet leveling mechanism is simple and reliable, with few moving parts and a compact size. For the self-leveling feature to work properly, you set the unit roughly level (within 3° to 6°, depending on the model), and the pendulum and magnets take over, leveling the unit.

AUTO SELF-LEVELING These lasers are equipped with sensors and a servomotor that level the instrument perfectly as soon as it is switched on. One important point to note about automatic self-leveling lasers: They need an automatic shutoff, just in case the tool or tripod is kicked and knocked out of level. Without this shutoff, the instrument could relevel automatically—without the operator's knowledge—at a new elevation.

jump in price, you'll get a tool equipped with sensors and motors for true automatic self-leveling.

Dot Lasers Get You Level, Square, and Plumb

Dot lasers project a simple point. The least-expensive models shoot one dot off the end of a torpedo-type level and are for interior use only. The most-expensive units are self-leveling, shoot five dots, and can be used outside.

Dot Laser

A dot laser won't eliminate the need for a spirit level, but it can replace a water level, a transit, a builder's level, and a plumb bob. Dot lasers are the brightest among the laser-level types; more-expensive units cast dots that are strong enough to see in a brightly lit room and outside.

The most useful models shoot plumb dots (one up and one down) as well as square dots (two horizontal dots that are level and square to one another).

WHY YOU NEED ONE: Plumb dots are faster and more accurate than a plumb bob, and they're not affected by wind or extreme height. Also, transferring lines from a floor to a ceiling, or from a top plate to a bottom plate, becomes a one-person, one-step process.

Square dots are useful for framing walls or squaring foundations. They make the method of measuring a 3-4-5 triangle nearly obsolete. Set up a square-dot laser on one corner, align the first beam with the edge of one wall, and the other beam casts a dot down the length of the adjacent wall. When a dot laser is used with a calculator to find precise diagonal length, laying out even the most complex wall system becomes a fast, easy, one-person job. Many carpenters avoid setting up batterboards, or at least reduce layout time dramatically, by using a dot laser.

Until recently, dot lasers were the smallest instruments available, so it's no wonder they're popular among framers and finish carpenters. Many fit easily in a tool belt, bucket, or box.

Line Lasers Give You Level and Plumb Lines at the Press of a Button

Line lasers cast a line of colored light. Like inexpensive dot lasers, the simplest line lasers project from a torpedo or similar type of level. More-expensive models cast up to four lines 90° from one another.

Line lasers are not as bright as dot lasers, and they generally are limited to indoor use unless they are equipped to work with detectors. Also, the farther the line is cast, the more the beam degrades. In fact, some line lasers are difficult to detect in a large, bright room.

WHY YOU NEED ONE: Line lasers can replace spirit levels, stringlines, plumb bobs, and sometimes water levels, but only newer incarnations of this laser type replace builder's levels.

Models equipped with level and plumb lines create a crosshair, which is helpful for centering layouts on projects like tilework, cabinet installations, flooring, and more.

Lines cast by lasers generally are limited to less than 180°. If you're working on multiple walls

Line Laser

in a room or home, you often have to turn the laser manually to cover the entire area. Some units cast a 360° horizontal line but don't project a vertical line. Units equipped with a dot enable extended working range outside.

Some pricier line-laser models offer the ability to lock the line at any angle, which is helpful when casting a parallel line to an out-of-level ceiling or installing handrails and skirtboards parallel to stairs.

Rotary Lasers Project Lines the Farthest

Rotary lasers shoot a single bright dot that spins to create a 360° line. When it comes to job-site productivity, including new con-struction, remodeling, and even foundation excavation, rotary lasers can't be beat. Less-expensive models are manual-leveling and less

Rotary Laser

accurate (¼ in. over 100 ft.) than high-end models. The more-expensive units project a highly visible beam, automatically level themselves, and are more accurate (⅛ in. over 100 ft.).

WHY YOU NEED ONE: Most rotary lasers have several speeds or variable speeds. At slow speeds, the dot is more visible, but the line might not be continuous. At higher speeds, the spinning dot creates a solid line, but the line won't be visible in bright light. In fact, rotary lasers are never visible outdoors, and only the most expensive units are powerful enough to cast a visible line in a large, bright room. But that's not a problem because rotary lasers are used almost exclusively with detectors.

Using a detector might sound like a hassle, but actually, it's a joy. Set up a rotary laser near the center of a new job site, and one person working with a detector can set batterboards or formboards for footings, flatwork, or grading—alone.

Continued ➡

Set Them Where They Need to Be

Figuring out where to set up a unit sometimes can be a big hurdle in deciding how best to use it. This explains why most lasers come with accessories that offer a variety of mounting options. These options cover most job-site conditions and accommodate different trades. Other accessories, such as the Laserjamb (www.laserjamb.com), also are available. On the Laserjamb, the laser mounts to a telescoping pole via a tripod attachment and can be placed anywhere in a room with ceilings lower than 12 ft.

TRIPOD. Just about all lasers come ready to fasten to a tripod. Many rotary kits include the tripod and surveyor's rod.

NYLON STRAP. Several dot and line lasers come with a strap for suspending units from pipes, braces, and scaffolding.

VACUUM. Some small units come with a built-in vacuum-powered suction device that sticks to the wall and doesn't leave marks.

WALL BRACKETS. Most rotary and many line lasers come with brackets that can be nailed to a wall or hung on a suspended ceiling track.

MINI-TRIPODS. Many models come with folding stands that have multiple adjustments for setting up on uneven surfaces.

MAGNETS. Most often part of a separate mounting bracket, which comes with the tool, this method is useful for mounting to metal studs, ductwork, and garage doors.

Several rotary lasers also are engineered to cast vertical lines: Tilt the head of the instrument, and the tool can shoot plumb lines over long distances for framing tall walls or door openings, aligning special architectural features, or laying out a perfectly plumb elevator chase.

The rotary function can be halted so that the laser projects a simple dot. Many also have line settings, which enable you to cast a nonrotating line. Although some rotary lasers can take the place of a dot laser, rotaries don't project a crosshair like line lasers.

Durability and Portability Are About More Than the Case

Lasers come in all sizes and shapes. To be useful, dot and line lasers must be small so that they're always available, on your tool belt or in your toolbox or bucket, right near where you're working. Dot lasers generally are the smallest and the most portable, though several companies manufacture smaller line lasers. Many larger line lasers come with built-in adjustable bases and some with built-in degree scales for turning accurate angles.

Most small dot and line lasers are encased in rubber and can survive a short fall, which is important because these instruments take a beating on the job site. I've dropped several of my line and dot lasers and never had a problem. Although not all manufacturers agree, I can't help but believe that a built-in locking mechanism—a lever that secures the pendulum when the tool is switched off—provides additional protection.

Rotary lasers are another story. With their expensive sensors and servomotors, auto self-leveling lasers always should be stored in protective cases and locked safely in a truck or van because these tools are susceptible to damage and theft.

A Tripod Isn't the Only Setup Option

Perhaps the best thing about laser levels is that they don't require a whole lot of user interaction. When focused on performing a specific layout task, you simply place the laser somewhere, turn it on, and get to work. Lasers sometimes have to be set up in peculiar places, so manufacturers have produced creative mounting devices for a variety of setup scenarios.

All laser levels come ready to attach to a tripod. Although tripods are great for rotary lasers because they frequently are used outside, dot and line lasers require a little more flexibility.

As a carpenter, I've learned to appreciate the concept of utility. To be prized, like a set of scribes or a circular saw, a tool must perform several tasks, it must be portable, and it must be easy to set up and store in a toolbox or bucket. This is also true for laser levels. I've stopped looking for the perfect all-in-one laser level. I'd rather have a tool I can depend on, one that's there when I need it. And I've also learned as a contractor that it's good to have several lasers because the guys on my crew always need to borrow one.

Specialty Levels

By Don Burgard

Needing to find level and plumb is basic to just about every aspect of building and remodeling. While the market for laser levels continues to grow, you can still find a variety of spirit levels on most job sites. Not all spirit levels are long and straight, however. Inventive minds have discovered that a small container filled with colored liquid and a bubble can be incorporated into a variety of designs, each of which can offer an easier and sometimes more accurate way to get a reading.

Bull's-Eye Level and Cross-Check Level

The bubble in a bull's-eye level floats inside a convex disk instead of a cylindrical vial. Level is achieved when the bubble finds the bull's-eye in the center of the disk. A bull's-eye level is useful when placing items such as large appliances that need to be level in two directions. The cross-check level provides the same information, but it does so with two cylindrical vials at a right angle to each other. When the bubbles in both vials are centered, the object the device is resting on is level.

Post Level

Made of plastic and either hinged or molded into a 90° angle, a post level is attached with a rubber band or elastic strap. It registers plumb with a center vial and level with a vial on each side of the angle. While its design makes it ideal for fitting around posts, a post level can also be attached to a large-diameter pipe.

Torpedo Level

Designed to fit into tight spaces, torpedo levels pack a lot of features into a small package. Usually about 8 in. to 10 in. long, most of these levels have at least three vials: one each for level, plumb, and 45°-angle measurements. Some include a fourth vial for measuring 22.5° or 30° angles. Rare-earth magnets along one edge of many torpedo levels keep the level from moving when it's against ferrous metal. Some manufacturers groove this edge so that it fits better around pipes. If you carry a torpedo level with magnets in your tool belt, however, you may find it annoying to have to scrape away bits of steel from fasteners and drill shavings.

Manufacturers have customized torpedo levels to a remarkable extent. Johnson, for example, has 17 different torpedo levels listed on its website. One of them is designed for welders, two have luminescent vials, and one has a thumbscrew for attaching to a pipe before bending an angle.

Line Level

This tiny level attaches to a taut stringline and is used to find level for two points on a span. Its degree of accuracy is not precise, and it can't be used for finding level across the entire span (even the tightest stringline will sag a little), but it's good enough to use for projects such as setting fence posts, checking the pitch of a driveway, or ensuring a level retaining wall. The trick is to position the level in the center of the string. The farther the tool is from the center, the less accurate your reading will be.

Virtual Bubbles

If there's a smartphone in your pocket, you already have a multipurpose leveling tool; you just need to download any one of many apps offered in both the Google Play and Apple iTunes stores. These apps display a virtual vial and bubble, but they also calculate angles to one or two decimal points. Many apps display both cylindrical and circular vials and automatically toggle between the two depending on whether the phone is on edge or lying flat. Don't trust a smartphone app to give you a reading that's as accurate as what you can get from a tool designed specifically for that purpose, however.

Continued ➜

Pressure-Treated Lumber

By Don Burgard

Until 2004, pressure-treated wood for residential use was preserved with chromate copper arsenate (CCA), and the level of treatment was generally the same for all lumber. Because of concerns over arsenic's toxicity, CCA has since been replaced for residential use by a host of preservatives, some of which have themselves been replaced by even newer formulations. Compared to CCA, these preservatives contain higher amounts of copper, which is expensive, so manufacturers produce pressure-treated lumber with different retention levels.

Retention level measures how much of the preservative is retained in the wood after the pressure treatment ends. It's expressed in pounds per cubic foot (lb. per cu. ft.) of wood fiber. The higher the retention level, the better equipped the wood is to ward off decay from insects and moisture. Wood with a lower retention level has a lower amount of copper and, therefore, a lower cost.

In order to get to the required retention level, some species of lumber (such as Douglas fir, hem-fir, and spruce-pine-fir) have to be incised, which allows the preservative to penetrate the wood more deeply and uniformly. Tests conducted by Forest Product Laboratory have found that this practice results in a reduction in bending strength and stiffness. For this reason, incising is more common with timbers and more substantial boards.

Use the Right Fasteners and Hardware

It's important to know retention levels not only because you don't want to pay for lumber rated for ground contact if you're installing a mudsill or framing a raised deck, but also because the copper content of these preservatives should guide your choice of fasteners and hardware. Copper is corrosive, so this choice is crucial. Generally, fasteners and hardware made from stainless steel and hot-dipped-galvanized (HDG) steel are recommended for pressure-treated lumber. However, lumber with the highest retention levels—such as that used in coastal and below-grade applications—should be used with stainless steel only, which is more resistant to corrosion than HDG steel. And of course, if you're using fasteners made of stainless steel, you must use stainless-steel hardware; combining stainless-steel fasteners with HDG hardware (and vice versa) will result in faster corrosion of the galvanized parts.

AWPA minimum retention levels (in lb. per cu. ft.)			
Preservative	Above ground	Ground contact	Ground contact, heavy duty
ACQ	0.15	0.40	0.60
CA-B	0.10	0.21	0.31
CA-C	0.06	0.15	0.31

ACQ and CA

Most of the preservatives used for treating wood intended for residential applications fall into two categories. In the first category are alkaline copper quaternary (ACQ) and two formulations of copper azole (CA-B and CA-C). The American Wood Protection Association (AWPA) has established minimum retention levels for wood treated with these preservatives (see chart). The label of a board treated with ACQ or CA lists the retention level.

MCQ and MCA

The second category of preservatives includes wood treated with two variations of ACQ and CA: micronized copper quaternary (MCQ) and micronized copper azole (MCA). Unlike with ACQ and CA, in which the copper is dissolved chemically in an organic solvent, the copper in MCQ and MCA is present in microscopic particles suspended in water. Significantly, this makes the copper less corrosive to fasteners and hardware than the copper in wood treated with ACQ and CA; moreover, it can be placed in contact with aluminum. Another advantage is that wood treated with MCQ and MCA keeps more of its natural color.

MCA- and MCQ-treated wood has not been tested by the AWPA. Instead, manufacturers have sent their products to the International Code Council Evaluation Service (ICC-ES), which provides research reports on innovative building products that it deems equivalent to standardized products. For each product, the ICC-ES report provides a minimum retention level. The labels for these products, however, usually just state "above ground," "ground contact," or "ground contact / freshwater use," which correspond to progressively higher retention levels.

Is It Green, or Isn't It?

In 2002, Chemical Specialties received a Presidential Green Chemistry Challenge Award from the EPA for its development of ACQ. A summary on the EPA's website says, "Replacing CCA with ACQ is one of the most dramatic pollution prevention advancements in recent history."

Pressure-treated wood has sometimes had a difficult time being considered an environmentally friendly product, however. This perception persists despite the fact that by extending the life of the wood, the same chemicals that are cause for concern mean that fewer trees have to be cut down.

Wood treated with MCQ and MCA has added a new element of confusion. Some of these products have received recognition from third-party environmental certifiers. For example, Australia-based EcoSpecifier has identified Wolmanized lumber as a Verified Product, and the MicroPro treatment has been certified as an Environmentally Preferable Product by Scientific Certification Systems. At the same time, there are concerns about the presence of nanoparticles of copper—that is, particles that are 1 to 100 nanometers in at least one dimension—in these formulations. (A nanometer is a billionth of a meter.) Materials that small have different properties, and the potential toxicity of nanoparticles of copper has not been established. The EPA's website includes this statement: "EPA is working with the Consumer Product Safety Commission to evaluate if there are any potential human and environmental effects from exposure to micronized copper."

The greenest preservatives used in residential construction may well be two newer formulations that include no copper or any other metal: EL2 (sold in Ecolife-branded lumber) and PTI (sold in lumber branded as Wolmanized EraWood and Wolmanized L3 Outdoor Wood). Because these preservatives are nonmetallic, there is no danger of any metal leaching out over time, and corrosion of fasteners and hardware is less likely. The AWPA has established minimum retention levels for EL2 and PTI, but only for above-ground use, so wood treated with these chemicals is limited to places where it won't be in prolonged contact with water.

Fasteners for Pressure-Treated Lumber

By Don Burgard

The high level of copper in lumber treated with ACQ or CA speeds up the corrosion of most fasteners, so for decks or other outdoor projects made from pressure-treated lumber, code requires the use of fasteners that offer good corrosion resistance. Many manufacturers have developed proprietary fastener coatings that they claim offer sufficient protection against corrosion when used with pressure-treated lumber. In addition, most codes permit the use of silicon-bronze or copper fasteners in these situations. However, stainless-steel and hot-dipped-galvanized (HDG) fasteners are typically recommended and are the most common. Before using either, it's essential to understand the differences between them.

Stainless Steel

Stainless steel has a higher chromium content than other types of steel. In contact with oxygen, chromium forms an invisible protective layer that prevents steel from corroding. If the surface is damaged, the layer will self-heal as long as oxygen remains present. Fasteners made of stainless steel offer the highest level of protection against corrosion; however, they are a good bit more expensive than HDG fasteners. In applications with sheet-metal hardware such as joist connectors, stainless steel's cost disadvantage multiplies because the hardware must be secured with fasteners of the same type. You can't use stainless-steel nails with an HDG connector, for example; the stainless steel will speed up the corrosion of the connector's zinc coating.

Stainless-steel fasteners are available in different levels of corrosion resistance. Grades 304 and 305 offer sufficient protection in most regions, but grade 316 is best for coastal areas. Grade 410 is designed more for hardness than for resistance to corrosion. Although it's great for masonry screws, fasteners made from it aren't sufficiently corrosion resistant and so shouldn't be used with pressure-treated lumber.

Continued ➜

Hot-Dipped Galvanized

Galvanization adds a layer of zinc to the exterior of steel to enhance its corrosion resistance. Although several methods of galvanization exist, hot-dipping creates a metallurgical bond between the zinc and the steel substrate and so offers the best protection against corrosion. Fasteners are lowered into a vat of molten zinc at a temperature of about 850°F. The American

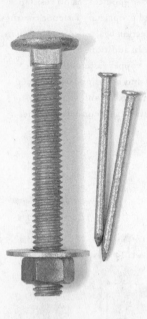

Galvanizers Association claims that a damaged area of the coating up to ¼ in. will continue to receive protection from the surrounding zinc. Because the zinc coating is sacrificial, however, it eventually will corrode. Still, the cost of HDG fasteners (and any connectors used with them) is so much lower than that of stainless-steel fasteners that they are the common choice for noncoastal areas. Be sure that the HDG nails and connectors you use meet the ASTM A153 standard, which ensures that the zinc coating is of a sufficient quality and thickness.

The distinctive rough appearance of HDG nails is not found on HDG bolts and screws, which are spun in a centrifuge to clear the threads of excess zinc. Still, there's enough coating remaining on the threads that nuts have to be tapped oversize to fit the bolts. Nongalvanized nuts won't fit, but they shouldn't be used anyway. HDG bolts and screws are subject to an additional ASTM standard, F2329, which regulates HDG threaded fasteners.

Wall Scanners

By Rob Yagid

They used to be called stud finders, the pocket-size gadgets that could detect the location of framing behind drywall and plaster. That term, however, is now a bit misleading because better-quality tools detect much more than studs. Wall scanners, as some companies refer to them, can detect studs, live electrical wires, and metal pipe. Some can even detect the difference between ferrous and nonferrous metal, and do so with remarkable accuracy. Not all wall scanners operate exactly the same.

The best wall scanner costs $100 or more. You can drop that kind of cash and just trust that the unit will work as it should. Before purchasing a wall scanner, though, it's helpful, and certainly reassuring, to understand precisely how it works.

Wood- and Metal-Stud Detection

Capacitive sensors in the middle of the scanner detect the location of wood and metal framing components. The wall scanner generates an electric field that can penetrate a wall cavity up to 1½ in. Materials influence this electric field differently based on their dielectric constant. Wood and metal studs have a much higher dielectric constant than the voids of air filling the stud bays and have a greater influence on the electric field. The capacitive sensors analyze this influence in the electric field to determine the presence of a stud in the wall. Simultaneously, an inductive sensor distinguishes wood members from metal components.

Live-Wire Detection

Circuitry in the top of the unit houses 50/60 Hz. sensors to detect the presence and position of live wires. The sensors act as a receiver, and if they detect a 50/60-Hz. signal—the frequency in which AC current is transmitted from power plants to residences—within the wall cavity, the unit flashes and beeps. On this unit, a bar graph on the display screen helps to determine the precise location of the live wire. The number of segments displayed in the bar graph indicates the strength of the AC signal. These sensors are suitable for detecting only 110v to 230v wires, and will not detect nonlive wires or telephone cables. These sensors can detect live wires at a depth up to 2 in. inside a wall cavity.

An illumination ring indicates the detection status of building materials within the wall cavity. This illumination ring glows green when no object is found in the wall, orange when an object is near, and red when the scanner has found an object.

The display screen on this unit indicates the type of building material and its location. Here, the unit is indicating the centerpoint of a nonferrous (nonmagnetic) piece of metal, such as copper.

Wood- and Metal-Stud Detection

Live-Wire Detection

Ferrous- and Nonferrous-Metal Distinction

An inductive sensor in the middle of the wall scanner locates and distinguishes nonferrous metal, such as copper supply lines, from ferrous metal, such as older, cast-iron waste lines. The sensor generates a magnetic field, which is boosted in the presence of a ferrous (magnetic) object, or deformed in the presence of a nonferrous (nonmagnetic) metal. The two types of metal are determined by analyzing the degree of deformation between the magnetic fields in what is called the phase shift. Nonferrous metal creates a 90° phase shift, while ferrous metal creates a 0° phase shift. An inductive sensor can detect metal up to a depth of 4¾ in. inside a wall cavity.

Metal-Cutting Snips

By Don Burgard

The home-building industry uses sheet metal sparingly, but the places where it is used—gutters, ducts, flashing—are often essential in helping a house to be energy efficient and watertight. If you enter your local home center expecting to find a set of all-purpose snips for those moments when you need to replace a piece of duct or to cut a piece of flashing, however, you're liable to be taken aback when you encounter a wall of tools with names such as duckbill tinners and long-cut offset aviation snips. Unless you do a lot of HVAC work, you probably don't need an array of tools for cutting sheet metal. In order to choose the specific tools that will make the cuts you most often need to make, though, you need to know the differences between them.

Also, be sure to check the maximum metal thickness a pair of snips is capable of cutting. Trying to cut heavy-gauge metal with light-gauge snips is a recipe for sore hands and a damaged tool. Metal-cutting snips fall into two basic categories: tin snips and aviation snips.

Tinners

Tin snips, or tinners, resemble a pair of scissors, and this simple design means few problems with malfunctioning or breaking. Compared to scissors, though, they have longer handles and shorter blades. The handles have large openings to accommodate hands with gloves, which are essential when dealing with sheet metal, whose corners and cut ends can be razor sharp. Regular tin snips work best on long, straight cuts, although they also can be used to cut gentle curves. Duckbill tin snips get their name from the shape of the blades, which are tapered and allow for cutting sharper curves than regular tin snips. This design difference comes at a sacrifice, though: Duckbill tin snips can't handle metal of the same thickness as regular tin snips. The simple design and solid construction of most tin snips means that you will likely never need to replace them, although you may need to resharpen the blades from time to time.

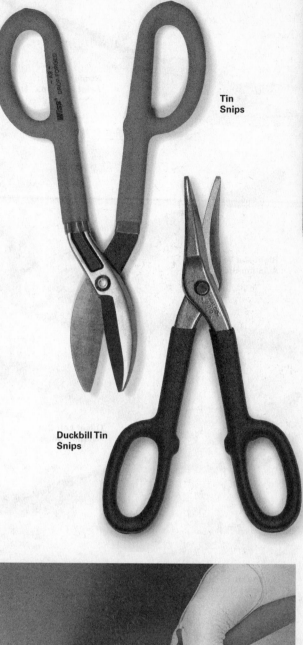

Tin Snips

Duckbill Tin Snips

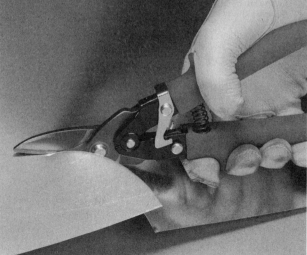

Continued ➔

Straight-Cut Aviation Snips

Right-Cut Vertical Aviation Snips

Offset Left-Cut Aviation Snips

Long-Cut Aviation Snips

Bulldog Aviation Snips

Aviation Snips

Aviation snips are so-named because they were developed to cut sheet metal in the airplane-manufacturing industry. Aviation snips are also known as compound snips because they have two pivot points instead of one. This reduces the amount of force necessary to make cuts and, therefore, reduces user fatigue. Aviation snips are also spring-loaded, further lessening fatigue, and have a hook lock to keep them closed when not in use.

Standard aviation snips come in three basic styles that are sold separately or as a set. These variations are necessary because sheet metal is stiff, is often in large pieces, and sometimes must be cut after it is in place. Most manufacturers color-code the handles.

Aviation snips are not designed to make long cuts in the middle of a sheet. For that, you're better off with a pair of tinners. If you have only aviation snips, however, you can make such a cut by using the left-cutting and right-cutting snips together. With one in each hand, walk the tools across the sheet, alternating cuts between left and right. You'll end up with a waste strip in the middle.

Manufacturers have developed variations on the standard aviation-snip design to meet specific needs. Vertical snips, available in left- and right-cutting styles, have blades positioned at a 90° angle to the handles. These snips make overhead cuts much easier, and they can reach tight locations that regular aviation snips can't. The drawback is in cutting strength; because of the angle and the different grasp that must be used, these snips can't cut through the 18-ga. galvanized steel or 20-ga. stainless steel that regular aviation snips can handle.

Offset aviation snips also have angled blades, but the angle is not as severe as on vertical snips. Offset snips are helpful for making cuts in locations where the user's hands might get in the way or where the user doesn't have a free hand to move the cut metal out of the way. With offset snips, you also can cut diamond lath without shredding your gloves.

Other variations include long-cut aviation snips, which have extralong blades for making long cuts quickly, and bulldog aviation snips, which have short blades that increase the leverage needed for cutting through seams and thicker metals. Bulldog snips are also good for cutting notches.

Color-Coded Handles

The handles on standard aviation snips are color-coded:
RED SNIPS are best for cutting to the left, YELLOW SNIPS are best for making straight cuts, and GREEN SNIPS are best for cutting to the right.

Sump Pumps

By Don Burgard

Basements provide space for storage, recreation, and mechanicals, but because they are at least partly below grade, they are prone to leaking from a high water table or from excessive rainfall. Leaks not only can damage the stuff we store in our basements, but they also can create the conditions for mold and mildew to grow.

Many houses have a sump pump to move water from the basement to the outside, where it is directed away from the house. This device gets its name from the pit, or sump, that is created in the concrete slab to collect excess water. In a proper installation, a drain system directs water from the foundation to the sump, where it is discharged by the pump. The pump, therefore, needs to be powerful enough to lift the water from the sump to the discharge location. In a typical basement, this is often through the rim joist.

When purchasing a sump pump, don't be fooled by the gallons-per-hour (GPH) or gallons-per-minute (GPM) number that some manufacturers highlight on the packaging. This number usually reflects the amount of water the pump will discharge at a static head of 0 ft. Static head is the vertical distance water must be pumped. In a basement with a 10-ft.-tall ceiling and a pump discharging water through the rim joist from an 18-in.-deep sump, the static head is closer to 12 ft. If a particular sump pump's capacity is 4800 GPH at a static head of 0 ft., its capacity at a static head of 12 ft. will be significantly lower. (And the figure you really need to know is the total dynamic head. See "Sizing a Sump Pump" on p. 42 for instructions on how to determine it.)

It's also important to establish how much filtration you need. If your sump was built correctly, it should allow water to enter but not rocks and other debris. If you're confident that solids won't be a problem, you can buy a sump pump with minimal filtration. If you think the occasional small rock may enter the sump, you'll be better off with a pump that can handle solids. The impeller design that accommodates solids also reduces the pump's capacity, though, so you'll need a more powerful (and more expensive) pump.

When shopping for a sump pump, you will have two basic options: submersible and pedestal.

Submersible Sump Pump

A submersible pump is compact and designed to be placed on the bottom of the sump. It can be made of cast iron, stainless steel, plastic, or a combination of steel and plastic. Cast iron is generally considered the most durable, and because it's the heaviest of the materials, a cast-iron pump is the least likely to move around inside the sump. The advantage of having a pump that's constantly submerged in water is that it stays cool even when it's working at maximum capacity. The downside is that pumps with housings of lesser quality are maore likely to develop leaks prematurely.

A submersible pump can have one of three switch

Submersible
Sump Pump

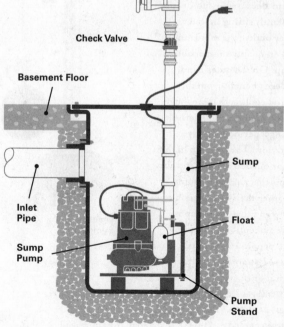

Check Valve

Basement Floor

Inlet
Pipe

Sump
Pump

Sump

Float

Pump
Stand

Continued →

mechanisms. The first two use a float that rises and falls with the water level. When the float reaches a certain height, it trips the switch and turns on the pump. With a vertical-float switch, the float rides up and down on a rod. With a tethered-float switch, the float swings in an arc with changes in the water level. If your sump is narrow, you probably don't want a pump with a tethered float, which can get caught on the edge of the sump. The third switch mechanism uses a diaphragm, which responds to water pressure rather than water level.

MATERIAL: cast iron
SOLIDS CAPACITY: ½ in.
PUMPING CAPACITY: 1500 GPH at a total dynamic head of 20 ft.

Pedestal Sump Pump

With a pedestal pump, the motor and the impeller are separate, with the impeller sitting atop a pedestal that rests on the bottom of the sump, and the motor at the opposite end of a column long enough to raise the motor above the basement floor. The advantage of this design is that the motor doesn't need to be in a waterproof housing; therefore, the cost of a pedestal pump is less than that of a submersible pump. Because the motor isn't constantly sitting in water, it may outlive the motor in a lower-quality submersible pump. On the other hand, it doesn't benefit from the natural cooling that the water provides and so may overheat during a period of heavy operation. The location of the motor outside of the sump also means that a pedestal pump is noisier than a submersible pump and that the pump is more susceptible to damage from people and objects. Pedestal pumps use only vertical-float switches.

MATERIAL: cast iron (base), stainless steel (column)
SOLIDS CAPACITY: ½ in.
PUMPING CAPACITY: 1200 GPM at a total dynamic head of 20 ft.

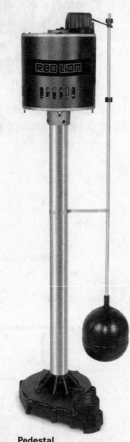

Pedestal Sump Pump

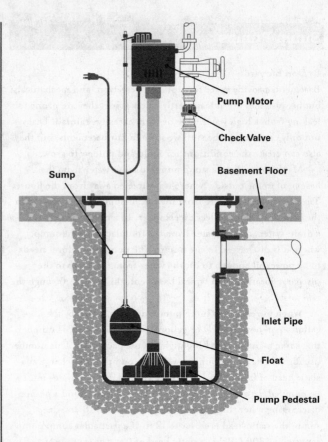

Pump Motor
Check Valve
Basement Floor
Sump
Inlet Pipe
Float
Pump Pedestal

Sizing a Sump Pump

If you're replacing a pump that could always handle the volume of water it needed to handle, your decision is simple: Buy a new pump with the same capacity. If you're replacing a pump that wasn't up to the task or that failed prematurely because it was oversize (and therefore cycled on and off too frequently), or if you're installing a sump pump for the first time, it's important to get the sizing right.

First, you need to know how much water must be pumped out every minute. This figure is known as the system capacity. If you're proactively replacing an old pump that still works, or if you have a backup pump (both good ideas), you can find out the system capacity by measuring how much water accumulates in one minute after the pump has run. It's best to do this during a heavy rain. For an 18-in.-dia. sump, an inch of water is approximately equal to 1 gal.

Second, you need to know the total dynamic head. This is the sum of the static head (the vertical distance a pump must direct the water) and the

Chart A	Equivalent length of pipe due to fittings		
Pipe size	90° elbow	45° elbow	Check valve
1¼ in.	3.5 ft.	1.8 ft.	11.5 ft.
1½ in.	4.0 ft.	2.2 ft.	13.4 ft.
2 in.	5.2 ft.	2.8 ft.	17.2 ft.

Source: "Sizing Up a Sump Pump," Land and Water Series, University of Illinois Extension, 2005

friction head (the effect on water flow of friction from pipes, valves, and fittings). To find the static head, use a tape measure. To find the friction head and the total dynamic head, follow these steps:

Chart B	Friction loss per 100 Ft. of schedule-40 PVC		
Gallons per minute	1¼ in. pipe	1½ in. pipe	2 in. pipe
10	1.78	0.83	NA
12	2.48	1.16	0.34
14	3.29	1.54	0.45
16	4.21	1.97	0.58
18	5.25	2.41	0.72
20	6.42	2.96	0.88
25	10.39	4.8	1.38
30	13.6	6.27	1.81

1. USING CHART A, determine the equivalent length of pipe for your fittings and valves. Add this figure to the total length of horizontal pipe.

2. USING THE SYSTEM CAPACITY AND PIPE DIAMETER, find your friction loss in chart B.

3. MULTIPLY THE FRICTION-LOSS FIGURE by the sum of the equivalent length of pipe and the total length of horizontal pipe, then divide by 100. This is the friction head.

4. ADD THE FRICTION HEAD to the static head to get the total dynamic head.

Take the example of an installation with a static head of 12 ft. If you're using 1½-in. schedule-40 PVC pipe and you have two 45° elbows, one 90° elbow, and a check valve, the equivalent length of pipe is 21.8 ft. (2.2 ft. + 2.2 ft. + 4 ft. + 13.4 ft.). Let's say that the total length of horizontal pipe is 75 ft.

If your system capacity is 20 GPM, the friction loss per 100 ft. is 2.96. Do the calculations to get the friction head: 2.96 × (21.8 ft. + 75 ft.) ÷ 100 = 2.87 ft.

To get the total dynamic head, add the static head and the friction head: 12 ft. + 2.87 ft. = 14.87 ft. Round this up to 15 ft. Now you have the information you need to find a pump that's sized right.

Paintable Caulks and Sealants

By Aaron Fagan

Nearly every discussion about caulks and sealants begins by acknowledging that there is a bewildering array of these products on the market, each of which is formulated out of a wide balance of compounds for either specific or general applications. The very terms caulk and sealant can be confusing, as there is no industry standard to distinguish the two. Generally, the distinction is qualitative: Caulk is a lower grade of sealant. Pure silicone is a superior sealant for most substrates. It's waterproof and holds up to UV exposure and weather extremes; however, it cannot be painted. The great race with manufacturers has been to develop a product that exploits the UV resistance, flexibility, and waterproofing of silicone, combined with the ease of application, paintability, and enhanced substrate adhesion of other compounds. An advanced degree in chemistry isn't required to make sense of these products, but you do need to know the gap you're going to fill.

Water-Based Works Best Inside

For certain interior applications—such as baseboards, windows, doors, and trim—water-based caulks are the ideal choice. While these products are often marketed for interior or exterior use, they perform best indoors—that is, as long as the area won't face major temperature changes, heavy UV exposure, or high moisture levels. A variety of terms is associated with this affordable class of products, including vinyl, acrylic, latex, latex-acrylic, and acrylic-latex. Better-quality versions are referred to as siliconized latex, siliconized acrylic, or latex plus silicone. They usually contain a small amount (less than 2%) of silane, a form of silicone, to promote better flexibility and adhesion. Special paintable, siliconized-latex formulations that include an antimicrobial or biocide additive for wet-prone areas are available and are often labeled "kitchen and bath" or "tub and tile." These products are easy to smooth into joints with a finishing tool or wet finger, and any excess can be cleaned up with water. You can also find a wide palette of color choices if you don't want to paint.

Hybrids Own the Outdoors

For exterior applications— such as windows, siding, and doors—there is a large class of hybrid sealants on the market. First developed in Japan over 30 years ago, these have been slow to gain widespread use in the United States and remain three times more expensive than simple water-based caulks. Labeled as "hybrid" or "paintable silicone," modified-silicone polymers or silane-modified polymers (SMPs) have become increasingly exotic as manufacturers have tried to create a single product that

Continued →

features ease of application, paintability, superior adhesion, flexibility, and durability in all manner of weather. Despite their complex chemistry, hybrid sealants have low concentrations of volatile organic compounds (VOCs). All of them require mineral spirits for cleanup.

These products are labeled as being paintable. Still, a product may not adhere well or last long if it's not the right product in the right place under the right conditions. Knowing where you need to apply the product, and weighing that against the label, will help. Checking the label includes checking the expiration date.

All About Foam

By Justin Fink

The first time I saw a professional spray-foam gun was when my friend Andy pulled his Pageris gun from a green protective case to air-seal and insulate around a window he'd just installed. The gun had a larger can than those that dispense foam through a straw, and it offered far better control over the size of the bead. In addition, Andy didn't have to come up with a use for the other 90% of the can's foam that he didn't need on this job. I decided right then that I was done blowing foam through a straw. It took me much longer to learn how to maintain one of these guns, though.

Andy's gun and carrying case were fairly high-end, but I opted for an entry-level gun from EFI (efi.org) —essentially the other end of the price spectrum in this category. That first gun lasted about a month before it became too clogged to function. I replaced it with a different model, then killed that one by snapping off the trigger while forcing it too hard. The next one met its end when I bent the barrel. This buy-break-replace pattern continued until I spoke with Peter Conlon from Todol Products—a company that specializes in polyurethane foam and that imports the Pageris gun Andy owned. I was surprised that Peter didn't laugh at my stories of repeated gun failure, but that's because he hears this from contractors every day.

Conlon taught me that although it doesn't take much to ruin one of these spray-foam guns, maintaining it and making it last isn't difficult either. You just have to understand the tool and the foam that it dispenses.

A Delicate Tool

The first lesson to learn is that the internal workings of a foam gun are fully sealed and always under pressure. Once the first can of foam is screwed into the adapter, the tool fills with foam, and a can must always be attached to maintain the sealed system. That means that 24 hours a day the foam inside the gun is trying to get out, and moisture in the air is trying to get in to react with the uncured polyurethane resin. This makes for a pretty delicate

Gun vs. Straw

What Does Foam Cost?

Cans of straw-dispensed foam are typically smaller than their gun-dispensed cousins, making it tricky to make a direct comparison. Taken on a cost-per-ounce basis, the straw foam is usually slightly cheaper, but that doesn't factor in realistic yield from the two different cans.

How Much Foam Is in the Can?

The listed yield for a can of spray foam—either straw- or gun-dispensed—is based on measurements from ideal laboratory conditions. In the real world, results vary based on the age of the can, how it was stored, how it's applied, and whether the propellant in the can escapes, which may be a problem when a can of straw foam isn't held in the correct position. In order to compare yield between straw-dispensed and gun-dispensed foam, I used 10-in.-dia. footing tubes as a form of graduated cylinder. To eliminate variables, I used Dow's Great Stuff Gaps & Cracks foam for all of the tests. Once each can was spent and the foam was cured, I peeled away the cardboard to look at core samples and to compare the yield.

Disappointing Yield?

Although I did the test at room temperature, laid the foam

balance, and life in the trades is anything but delicate.

When the field of battle is the back of my bouncing pickup truck, I can guarantee that any encounter between a spray-foam gun and just about any other tool is going to end badly for the gun.

The problem is that if the barrel of the gun takes a hit, the rod will bend, and the seal at the tip will no longer be airtight. The same goes for the long can of foam that is secured to the adapter on the gun by just a few coarse threads. In either case, once foam has a chance to leak out or moisture has a chance to leak in, the foam inside the gun will cure and the tool will be inoperable.

The same risks of leakage apply when using the tool to foam around abrasive surfaces such as brick or concrete. In these cases, the delicate needle on the business end of the gun should always be protected by a sacrifical tip.

The Keys to Getting Light and Fluffy Foam

I haven't found a particular polyurethane foam that I like more than others, but I have learned some tricks for getting the best and most foam out of each can.

The first step is to shake the can heartily. The propellant and the resin need to be thoroughly mixed to get the best cell structure on a chemical level. This should be done before using a can for the first time and occasionally during use.

Polyurethane cures by reacting with the moisture in the air. If very little or no moisture is available, the light and fluffy foam will collapse into itself as it cures. A light spray of water applied to surfaces before filling voids with foam will go a long way toward getting foam to cure properly. This is especially important when working in areas of low humidity, but it's also best practice when filling deep voids. In the case of deep voids, apply the foam in layers, misting lightly between them. It only takes an ounce of water to cure an entire can of polyurethane foam, so think in terms of a spray bottle, not a garden hose.

Finally, it's crucial to have the can itself at room temperature (between 60°F and 80°F). Even if it's cold outside, a warm can of foam will yield satisfactory results. The propellant in the can boils at –10°F, so if the can is 60°F when you pull the trigger, the foam boils dynamically— like splashing water on a hot frying pan—and you get the best foam and the highest yield. If a can has sat in the truck during a cold night, the propellant will have contracted and the polyurethane thickened. Now you're asking the gun to push a thicker product with a less-than-optimal amount of pressure. You can end up with diminished yield, and certainly a much, much slower application speed.

Cleaner Helps, But It Isn't a Cure-All

Just about every company that sells spray foam and foam guns also sells foam-gun cleaner. Essentially a can of acetone, the cleaner is screwed on and sprayed through the gun to clear out uncured foam. The key is to remember that acetone has no effect on polyurethane resin, but only on the propellant. So as the cleaner is run through the gun, the propellant is dissolved, but the polyurethane resins are

---

in fluffy beads, and let each ring set up before adding more on top, both the gun foam and the straw foam skinned over on top but didn't cure as well throughout. Each layer of foam from the straw can took so long to harden that I was sure the can was defective, a theory that was supported by the large, uncured cavern in the middle of the cylinder (which later collapsed and hardened). Surprisingly, though, a second test yielded the same results. The pockets were also present in the gun-dispensed foam, although they were much smaller, and none appeared to be uncured.

Just Add Water

Manufacturers of some cans of foam, both straw-dispensed and gun-dispensed, recommend misting water either into the cavity to be foamed or onto the uncured foam itself. Polyurethane is a moisture-curing resin, and the water is said to help speed up the curing process. I was interested to see if a light mist of water sprayed into the footing tubes before applying each layer of foam would help the foam to cure more fully and thereby eliminate the uncured pockets from the first experiment. Indeed, just two spritzes from a spray bottle before each layer of foam yielded foam that was firmer, that cured in minutes rather than hours, that expanded to roughly twice the yield of the cans in the first test, and that left hardly any voids.

Gun Yield
83 cu. in.
per oz. of foam

The foam spritzed with water set up firmer, cured faster, and yielded almost twice the volume with fewer voids.

Gun Yield
48 cu. in.
per oz. of foam

Straw Yield
69 cu. in.
per oz. of foam

Straw Yield
36 cu. in.
per oz.
of foam

Test 1

Test 2

Continued ➜

left behind. Building up like plaque on the walls of an artery, this resin will eventually either gum up the internal components of the gun or prevent openings in the tool from fully sealing.

The only regular maintenance you have to worry about with these tools is pulling the trigger once a month to purge the barrel. Uncured foam sitting in the barrel of the gun starts to separate a bit over time, and may cure. Pulling the trigger until regular foam is flowing again will clear out any separated resin.

That's not to say that you should never clean the tool, though. Best practice is to run cleaner through the gun for every eight to 10 cans of foam you consume. Screw on a can of cleaner, aim the gun at a piece of white paper, and pull the trigger. The cleaner will dissolve the propellant in the barrel of the gun and will physically push any uncured resins out. The spray will start as dark yellow, then lighten up, and eventually turn clear, which is when you should stop. If any specks of cured foam blast out during cleaning, it's usually an indication that moisture is leaking into the gun from somewhere, probably through the ball valve. After releasing the trigger, unscrew the can of cleaner from the gun, poke the ball valve with a Q-tip, and listen carefully. A hissing sound indicates that the ball isn't sealing completely, possibly because debris is clogging the ball-valve opening. If there's no hissing, you're set.

Is There More Than One Flavor of Foam?

A common misconception is that spray-foam guns are limited to small air-sealing and insulation jobs. It's true that the bread and butter of this category are expanding foams (for general-purpose sealing of gaps) and low-expansion foams (for sealing around windows and doors), but the number of other options for these tools is growing.

ADHESIVE With various ASTM, building-code, and APA standards to back their reliability, adhesive foams are an attractive substitute for conventional tubes of construction adhesive. One can is equivalent to between 10 and 20 quart-size tubes.

FIREBLOCK Less expensive than the intumescent caulk used to seal penetrations, many plumbers and electricians are now using fire-rated foam, usually orange, to meet code requirements.

EXTERIOR Although conventional polyurethane spray foam degrades if left unpainted and exposed to UV light, several companies make UV-resistant foams, usually black in color, specifically for exterior applications.

PEST RESISTANT Popular for their ability to turn away insects and rodents with their bitter taste or added scents, pest-resistant foams are a no-pesticide approach to blocking everything from bees to squirrels.

Why You Should Upgrade to a Foam Gun

There's a reason most pros use foam guns rather than throwaway straws: The guns offer better control over bead size, can be held at a broader range of angles during use, and are reusable.

Bead Control

Bead control on a can of straw foam is virtually nonexistant. Foam guns, however, allow you to dial in the maximum bead size—typically between ⅛ in. and 1¼ in.—using the threaded knob on the back of the tool. Plus, the triggers usually have decent sensitivity.

Sacrificial and Extension Tips

Reducers, available in plastic and metal depending on the gun, are great for foaming into tight crevices. Because the seal at the tip of foam guns is crucial to maintain, they're also a good idea when applying foam along an abrasive surface such as masonry.

Reuse

When you pull the trigger on a can of straw-dispensed foam, you have just started a race against the clock to use up the entire can before the foam hardens in the straw and the nozzle. With a gun, the foam can be doled out at whatever speed or quantity you desire. You then can leave the can on a shelf for a month.

Cleaner Compatible

Although they sometimes get a bad rap in terms of maintenance, foam guns are easy to maintain once you understand how they work. Always keep a can of foam on the gun, pull the trigger once a month to purge stagnant foam from the barrel, and run cleaner through the tool from a screw-on can after every case or so of foam you use, as shown here.

Concrete Hand Floats

By Justin Fink

Once a concrete slab has been poured, screeded, and bull-floated, it's time for hand floats.

A bull float, which is used to smooth 95% of a slab, has a tendency either to pull a small amount of concrete away from the edges of the slab or to push concrete toward the edges. A hand float is used to level and smooth these areas so that they match the rest of the slab. Floats also can be used around obsta-cles, such as pipes and drains, where more precision is needed.

These tools are made in several shapes and sizes, and from four materials. According to Marshalltown Company product manager Jim Bowie, it's a common misconception that price is the deciding factor; each material's effect on the concrete should be considered.

A steel trowel should never be placed on the concrete until all bleed water has evaporated. This tool compresses the top layer of the slab, which adds strength to the surface and gives the slab a durable finish. If used too soon, though, a steel trowel closes the pores of the concrete and traps water below the surface, which would more than likely cause the top layer to delaminate.

WOOD A wood float is the least expensive option, but it isn't durable over the long haul. Because a wood float constantly soaks up bleed water, is dragged over a rough concrete surface, and is hosed down after use, it loses its edge over time. This creates a rough, fuzzed-up surface that pulls and drags at the surface of the concrete rather than smoothing it. This effect sometimes can be useful, though, especially when working with really stiff concrete or concrete that is setting up too hard. Wood also is preferred when applying shake-on color hardeners, which need to be worked into the top surface of the slab. Although redwood is a common material choice in this category, some companies also sell floats made from hard species, such as Marshalltown Company's Xtra-Hard, which is made from jarrah, a wood denser than teak. They cost a few dollars more than redwood.

RESIN Laminated-canvas resin floats have an extremely dense "waffle" surface that gives the concrete the same slightly rough texture as a wood float. The advantage to paying twice the cost of a wood float is that you get a much more durable tool. Canvas resin doesn't soak up water, so it won't fuzz up after repeated use on wet concrete and after being hosed off at the end of a job.

ALUMINUM Aluminum floats have many of the same characteristics as magnesium floats, but they are roughly 30% heavier and 30% stronger. Like magnesium, aluminum opens the pores of fresh concrete, allowing bleed water to evaporate. Although many contractors prefer a certain float for each type of concrete, aluminum has no real specialty or added benefits in any common situation.

MAGNESIUM Although they are slightly weaker than their aluminum counterparts, magnesium floats are lighter and are the most popular choice among professionals. Magnesium smooths the surface of fresh concrete and opens the pores for proper evaporation, all without pulling the surface like a wood or resin tool. Most magnesium floats are extruded or cast. Extruded floats are made by pushing molten magnesium through a die (think Play-Doh), so the floats are the same profile from end to end. Molten magnesium can be cast into any shape desired. Some contractors like a float with more knuckle room, and a cast float can be made with small pedestals that raise the handle for more room.

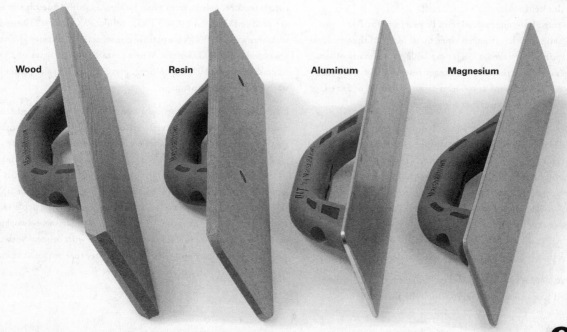

Wood   **Resin**   **Aluminum**   **Magnesium**

Continued →

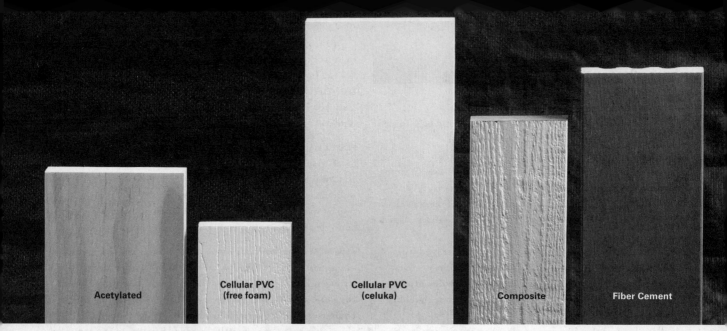

Acetylated | Cellular PVC (free foam) | Cellular PVC (celuka) | Composite | Fiber Cement

Today's Best Exterior Trim

By Gary M. Katz

Not too long ago, the only material used for exterior trim was old-growth lumber—Douglas fir and redwood on the West Coast; yellow pine, white pine, and cedar on the East Coast; southern yellow pine and cypress in the South. Because of changes in forestry and the introduction of innovative materials, home builders and homeowners today have a host of trim products to choose from. All of these engineered-trim options promise to be decay resistant and easy to work with and to perform better than the new-growth lumber stocked at the lumberyard. However, each has its own unique properties that you need to understand before using it in the field.

I first wrote about engineered trim 10 years ago for *Fine Homebuilding*, and a lot has changed since then. Many of the products I reviewed in that story are no longer available, while many others have changed so much that they no longer resemble the originals. It's time to take a fresh look at modern exterior trim in order to help you choose the right product for your next project.

ACETYLATED A process using acetic acid (concentrated vinegar) changes the wood fibers in the various species that are used so that their cells can no longer absorb moisture. This makes the wood dimensionally stable and indigestible, so it holds paint better and is more resistant to rot and insects. Unfortunately, acetylated wood is expensive, and availability is limited. Although the manufacturer says the smell dissipates, you may have to endure a strong odor if you have a lot of trim to install. The biggest benefit of Accoya is that it looks and handles like regular lumber.

CELLULAR PVC (FREE FOAM) Most cellular-PVC trim is made using the so-called free-foam process, in which the material cools slowly as it leaves the injection die. Free-foam PVC is consistent throughout its thickness, and the inner core is smooth and has the same density as the outer skin. To minimize expansion caused by solar heating, PVC trim should be painted either with a light-colored conventional paint with a light-reflectance value (LRV) of 55 or greater, or with a light-reflecting paint with an LRV of 40 or greater. Free-foam PVC should be securely fastened with screws and PVC-compatible construction adhesive. Joints should be glued with PVC cement.

CELLULAR PVC (CELUKA) As celuka PVC leaves the injection die, water cools the expanding foam, creating a PVC trimboard with a dense outer skin and a more granulated core. The manufacturer claims that this makes celuka PVC more dimensionally stable and more impact resistant than free-foam PVC. But because the core has a rough texture, celuka trim must be thoroughly sanded if the edges are profiled. Like free-foam PVC, celuka PVC is best fastened with screws and PVC-compatible construction adhesive. Joints are glued with PVC cement. When installing both types of PVC in cold weather (40°F or colder), leave 3/16-in. gaps at joints for warm-weather expansion.

COMPOSITE Made from northern hardwood fibers collected from milling operations and mixed with adhesive resins, the company that manufacturers this type of composite adds a zinc-borate treatment for rot and insect resistance, and then the material is compressed under ultrahigh pressure, much like how OSB is made. But compared to OSB, the wood fibers that make up this composite are far smaller, so you can create edge profiles and route patterns into the boards using standard woodworking machinery with carbide blades and bits. As with other wood-based products, miters are not recommended because seasonal changes in humidity cause them to open up over time.

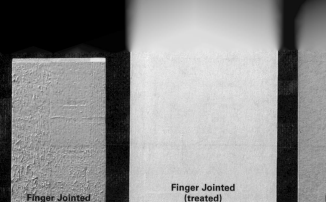

Finger Jointed   Finger Jointed (treated)   Fly Ash   OSB   Polyurethane

FIBER CEMENT Fiber-cement trimboards are made from a lower-density formulation of the same materials that make up fiber-cement siding (sand, cement, and cellulose fibers). Over the last 10 years, fiber-cement products have changed radically. New additives have reduced moisture absorption, and the addition of fiberglass has improved strength and durability. Fiber-cement boards cannot be routed or shaped, and they must be cut with carbide-tipped blades. Personal protective equipment and dust collection are a must because of the risks associated with breathing silica dust. Fiber-cement trim provides a durable finish and eliminates on-site painting.

FINGER JOINTED Finger-jointed boards are straight and free of knots as well as the coffee-colored stains caused by them. To get wider boards, some finger-jointed stock is also edge-glued. Finger-jointed exterior trim is made from eastern white pine, cedar, and imported radiata pine. For appearance, convenience, and dimensional stability, finger-jointed exterior trim is almost always coated with primer. The quality of the priming varies greatly from manufacturer to manufacturer. Look for boards manufactured with a thick coat of primer that sufficiently masks the finger joints. One example undergoes a multistep priming process.

FINGER JOINTED (TREATED) Some finger-jointed trim includes organic-based treatments to protect the wood from insects and rot. These treatments also reduce the amount of moisture the wood can absorb, though not as effectively as acetylation. However, treated finger-jointed boards are much less expensive than acetylated stock. Like untreated finger-jointed stock, treated finger-jointed boards are easily shaped and routed on the job site with ordinary woodworking tools. As with other wood-based trim products, you should avoid exterior miters because seasonal wood movement causes them to open.

FLY ASH The most recent engineered-trim option is made from resin and fly ash, a waste product of coal-generated electricity. Trimboard made from fly-ash doesn't absorb moisture and has no thermal expansion. Fly-ash trim is also impervious to insects and rot. TruExterior is cut and edge-profiled with standard woodworking tools and can be painted with any exterior-rated coating. The manufacturer claims that sawdust generated from cutting or milling fly-ash trim is no more carcinogenic than wood sawdust, and the fly ash used for making the boards is tested thoroughly for harmful contaminants.

OSB OSB trimboards are made from compressed wood fibers and resin and are wrapped with a textured overlay that gives the boards the appearance of solid lumber, provides protection from the elements, and improves paint adhesion. The manufacturer further protects the boards with zinc borate, which improves its resistance to moisture, insects, and rot. OSB is one of the most affordable types of exterior trim, but it can't be routed or shaped like wood. In addition, OSB can't be mitered or laminated, and it is susceptible to swelling caused by moisture.

POLYURETHANE Decorative architectural elements such as pediments, gable louvers, brackets, finials, and medallions made from polyurethane are common in residential construction. However, polyurethane boards aren't nearly as common because the material is more expensive than other options and is easily damaged by impact. Polyurethane expands and contracts less than other plastic-based options, and it has a smooth surface and crisp edges that make it a convincing stand-in for wood trim. Polyurethane trim is first bedded in polyurethane adhesive and then fastened with corrosion-resistant fasteners.

Continued →

How Modern Exterior Trim Stacks Up

Trim type	Description	Warranty	Cutting and milling	Best uses
Acetylated	Natural wood treated with acetic acid	50-year limited (above ground); 25-year limited (ground contact)	Machines and routs well with a little fuzzing using standard carbide tools. Dust collection is beneficial.	High-visibility projects where unpainted natural wood is part of the design and is on display
Cellular PVC (free foam)	Free-foam cellular PVC	Azek, 25-year limited; Kleer, lifetime limited on product, two years on labor; Versatex, 30-year limited	Machines and routs very well with standard carbide tools. Dust collection is beneficial.	Ideal for close-to-grade applications. Good for trim that requires custom edge treatment or milling.
Cellular PVC (celuka)	Water-cooled cellular PVC	25-year limited	Cuts with standard carbide tools, but machined edges are rough. Dust collection is beneficial.	Ideal for close-to-grade applications but not edge profiling. More impact resistant than free-foam PVC.
Composite	Compressed hardwood fibers protected with borate-based preservative	50-year limited	Machines and routs well using standard carbide tools. Dust collection is beneficial.	Avoid close-to-grade locations and areas subject to regular wetting.
Fiber cement	Primed fiber cement with additives for reducing moisture absorption and improving strength	15-year limited	Cuts with specialty carbide tools. Must use dust collection.	Impervious to insect damage. Unaffected by heat and direct sun.
Finger jointed	Finger-jointed primed western red cedar	15-year limited with one factory coat of primer; 25-year limited with two factory coats	Machines and routs well with a little fuzzing using standard carbide tools. Dust collection is beneficial.	Minimal exposure to rain or splashback. Good for custom dimensions and profiles.
Finger jointed (treated)	Edge-glued and finger-jointed radiata pine protected with borate-based preservative	30-year limited	Machines and routs well with a little fuzzing using standard carbide tools. Dust collection is beneficial.	Greater exposure to water and insects than untreated. Good for custom dimensions and profiles.
Fly ash	Fly ash and adhesive with fiberglass reinforcement	20-year limited	Machines and routs very well using standard carbide tools. Must use dust collection.	Ideal for close-to-grade applications
OSB	Compressed wood strands protected with zinc-borate preservative	Five-year 100% on material and labor; 50-year prorated	Cuts with standard carbide tools but does not rout or machine. Rips must be sealed. Dust collection is beneficial.	Projects with tight budgets. Cut edges should be hidden, as they look unfinished.
Polyurethane	Polyurethane foam with primer	Lifetime limited	Cuts with standard tools but does not rout or machine. End cuts and exposed interior turn yellow if left unprimed.	Avoid locations where it will be damaged by string trimmers or impact.

Movement	Prohibitions and warnings	Fastening requirements	Finishing requirements	Job-site storage
Moves 80% less than nonacetylated wood of the same species	Use with stainless-steel flashing. Keep 6 in. above grade and 2 in. above roofing materials.	Stainless-steel nails or screws only. Use the same nailing pattern as with untreated wood.	Seal end cuts with exterior primer or clear sealer.	Elevate and protect from weather.
Expands in length with temperature. Securely fasten to restrict movement and prevent buckling.	Leave a ³⁄₁₆-in. gap at butt joints with temperatures up to 40°F and a ¹⁄₁₆-in. gap at temperatures from 80°F to 100°F.	8d stainless ring-shank nails or screws. Use PVC cement for gluing joints. Use PVC-compatible adhesive to bond PVC to wood.	100% acrylic paint with a urethane additive and medium to high LRV (over 55%)	Store out of direct sun, and keep at ambient temperature during installation.
Expands in length with temperature. Securely fasten to restrict movement and prevent buckling.	Leave a ³⁄₁₆-in. gap at butt joints with temperatures up to 40°F and a ¹⁄₁₆-in. gap at temperatures from 80°F to 100°F.	8d stainless ring-shank nails or screws. Use PVC cement for gluing joints. Use PVC-compatible adhesive to bond PVC to wood.	100% acrylic paint with a urethane additive and medium to high LRV (over 55%)	Store out of direct sun, and keep at ambient temperature during installation.
Minimal expansion	Keep 6 in. above grade, 1 in. above roofing materials, ½ in. above concrete, and ¼ in. above flashings.	6d or 8d 16-ga. corrosion-resistant finish nails or headed nails. Nails must penetrate 1¼ in. into framing. Bond with waterproof wood glue.	Prime end cuts, then coat with high-quality oil or acrylic-latex primer. Paint with acrylic latex.	Elevate and protect from weather.
Minimal expansion	Maintain ¼-in. space between wall flashing and siding materials and 2-in. space above decks, paths, steps, driveways, and roofs.	Stainless-steel finish nails (except for fascia installations without subfascia, which should be nailed directly to rafter ends with 6d siding nails)	Don't use stain or oil- or alkyd-based paint. 100% acrylic topcoats are recommended.	Elevate and protect from weather.
1% increase across the grain for every 4% increase in moisture content	Keep 8 in. above grade and 2 in. above decks and roofs.	Don't use finish nails. Use ring-shank or splitless stainless-steel or HDG siding nails or screws. Countersunk nails must be sealed and filled.	Prime all field cuts. Apply two coats of 100% acrylic solid-color stain or paint.	Elevate and protect from weather.
1% increase across the grain for every 4% increase in moisture content	Do not use for railings or trellises. Moisture content must be below 18%. Keep 8 in. above grade and 2 in. above decks and roofs.	Don't use finish nails. Use ring-shank or splitless stainless-steel or HDG siding nails or screws. Countersunk nails must be sealed and filled.	Prime all field cuts. Apply two coats of 100% acrylic-latex exterior paint.	Elevate and protect from weather.
Minimal expansion	Approved for ground contact	Stainless-steel or galvanized finish nails 24 in. on center	Oil or latex paint	Keep level and protected from weather.
Minimal expansion	Leave a ³⁄₁₆-in. gap between other materials and at joints for sealing. Leave a similar gap between siding, windows, and doors.	8d HDG siding nails 24 in. on center. Maintain 1-in. penetration into framing. Countersinking requires sealant and possible additional nailing.	Use high-quality acrylic-latex paint. Semigloss or satin oil or alkyd paints are also acceptable.	Elevate and protect from weather.
Allow ³⁄₁₆ in. per 18 ft. for expansion and contraction.	Avoid high heat, and allow material to acclimate to ambient temperature before installation.	Bed material in a bead of polyurethane adhesive, and use corrosion-resistant nails and screws. Use polyurethane adhesive on all joints.	Fill large holes with auto-body filler. Fill small holes with exterior spackle. Paint with acrylic-latex.	Store on a flat, level surface in a cool area out of extreme heat.

Continued →

Guide to Gas Fireplaces

By James Cleland

Gas fireplaces and stoves are easily the most popular segment of the home-hearth industry, outselling wood-burning models nearly three to one. Convenience is the driving force behind the popularity of gas. There's no cordwood to haul, store, and stack. There's no ash to clean up, and no smoke smell filling the house. Instead, there's a steady supply of fuel piped directly to the unit. When you want a fire, you can have one up and running with the push of a button, often without getting up from your seat. When it's time for bed, you can shut down the fire just as easily.

Although it's simple to use a gas fireplace, it's not so simple to install one. Further complicating matters, there are three basic types, and the design options are nearly limitless. To keep up with Houston's booming housing market, the company I work for installs dozens of fireplaces every week.

Here, I share what I've learned about choosing among the three basic gas-fireplace types. I also explain what it takes to install and maintain a gas fireplace and identify the features and accessories you should consider when planning a purchase.

Gas Is a Different Experience

Although gas fireplaces are convenient, wood purists often counter that splitting and storing firewood is great exercise and that having a good supply of wood means a reliable source of heat in all conditions without the risk of a disrupted fuel supply. In addition, those who like building and tending fires likely will be disappointed by the experience of a gas fire. The flames are less varied, the color is uniform compared to a wood fire, and there's no opportunity to move logs around with a poker.

But even though they don't crackle or produce that sweet smell of smoke, gas fireplaces continue to look more realistic every year. Manufacturers use real firewood to make the molds for casting the log sets, and then they often hand paint them, further adding to their realistic look. My favorite recent innovation is LED lighting in the bottom of the firebox that simulates the look of glowing coals.

Sizing and Installation

Excluding custom commercial models, gas fireplaces are sized from about 10,000 to about 50,000 Btu of heat per hour. The size of the unit should be based on the size of the space where it's located, not the whole house. Unfortunately, many buyers have a "bigger is better" mentality, which can lead to an oversize fireplace that drives folks out of the room. Besides heat output, the physical dimensions of the fireplace should be considered, as a fireplace that's too big or too small looks out of place even to casual observers. Manufacturers have sizing charts and online calculators that take into account the size of the room and the size of the wall.

Installing a gas fireplace is often more complicated than installing a wood fireplace. A manufactured wood fireplace is typically installed by the fireplace dealer without additional subcontractors, but a gas fireplace requires an electrician to run the cable that powers lights and the ignition system, as well as a plumber to run the gas or propane line to the unit. Coordinating the subtrades is the builder's responsibility for new-home installations. In retrofits, this subcontracted work can be handled by the fireplace dealer, the homeowner, or a general contractor.

Venting

Perhaps one of gas's best attributes is that venting options are greater than with wood. With a wood-burning fireplace, you pretty much have to go straight up through the roof or straight up the outside of an exterior wall with insulated flue pipe, which can be expensive and, depending on the floor plan, may not be possible at all. Masonry chimneys are even more costly and inflexible when it comes to venting.

The first option for venting a gas fireplace is to choose one that doesn't require venting in the first place. While this may seem like an easy installation, my company advises clients to steer clear of unvented fireplaces for a number of reasons (see "Is 'Vent Free' a Good Idea?" on p. 55). Next, there are models that use standard B-vent flue pipe and are vented atmospherically through the roof like a gas furnace or water heater. Generally speaking, you can use two elbows for snaking around obstacles, and you need to maintain manufacturer-specified rise-to-run ratios so that the appliance drafts correctly. Finally, there are direct-vent fireplaces, which have the most-flexible venting options. Direct-vent models send their combustion by-products directly through a wall or roof using two-chamber pipe that also acts as a combustion-air intake. Even though the flue pipe used with a direct-vent gas fireplace costs more than B-vent flue pipe, the total installed cost is often less, because a more direct route to the exterior of the building often means using less pipe. Direct-vent flue pipe also can be run horizontally in joist cavities, and some direct-vent models can accommodate up to four 90° elbows in their flues. For especially long and complicated runs, a power vent fan can be added to the vent system to improve draft. This fan can be placed either at the vent termination or at an accessible spot along the vent pipe. With any gas fireplace, it's critical to follow the manufacturer's installation instructions exactly.

How It Works

The gas supply comes into the bottom of the fireplace housing, where it connects to the main gas valve. Older models had a fuel-wasting standing pilot, but modern fireplaces have an electronic ignitor that lights the pilot, which in turn lights the burner. Once the pilot is lit, the gas valve opens and the burner ignites. Many units have a remote control to change flame height and Btu output by opening or closing the gas valve. Near the gas valve is a battery compartment and a manual ignition system, which makes it possible to use the fireplace in power outages.

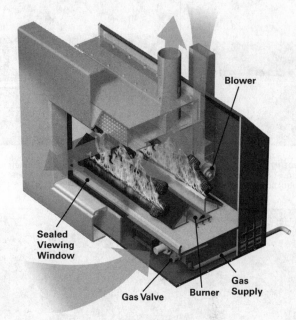

Blower

Sealed Viewing Window

Gas Valve   **Burner**   **Gas Supply**

Two Ways to Vent

ROOF CAP A roof-vent termination looks a lot like a chimney cap for a wood-burning fireplace, but it has two pipes inside: one for combustion by-products and a second for combustion air.

WALL CAP A wall-vent termination typically makes installation easier, but it gets hot when the stove is operating, which can create a risk of burns when the termination is close to outdoor walkways or seating areas.

Continued →

MODERN Gas fireplaces used to look just like their wood-burning counterparts, but new designs take many forms. This model, for example, has a long narrow firebox fit for modern spaces. There are also sophisticated remote controls that enable you to change the flame height and output, set a timer, and control built-in lighting.

OUTDOOR Gas fireplaces are becoming more common in outdoor rooms and entertainment areas, where they provide a natural gathering spot and can take the chill off during a cool evening. This model is made from stainless steel for corrosion resistance.

TRADITIONAL Freestanding gas stoves provide a traditional look with modern convenience. Available in several finishes, this cast-iron stove vents through the top for a classic woodstove look. Stoves and fireplaces also can be vented through the rear, which is often an easier installation method.

The instructions explain proximity to combustible materials and how close vent terminations can be to windows and doors, overhangs, porches, and walkways.

Is "Vent Free" a Good Idea?

At first glance, there's something very appealing about a vent-free gas fireplace. Not having a flue saves money on installation and allows you to put the fireplace anywhere. Unfortunately, the fireplace's combustion by-products aren't magically treated. Instead, the gases, which include carbon monoxide (CO), are released into the room. CO in sufficient concentration can cause fatigue, dizziness, and even death. To make these fireplaces safer, manufacturers include a sensor that shuts off the appliance if oxygen level drops to an unsafe level. Running a gas appliance without a flue also puts a lot of water vapor into the air. This vapor can lead to condensation on windows and doors that obscures the view and can rot or discolor sashes and sills. Excess indoor humidity can also aggravate allergies because it causes dust mites and mold to flourish. With today's tighter houses, I believe there's no place for unvented gas appliances, fireplaces included.

Useful Features

The heat from a gas fireplace is mostly radiant, so it works best when you're directly in front of it. If you're hoping to heat a larger space more efficiently, consider a model with an electric blower, which is an option on many models. I think it's also a good idea to opt for a gas fireplace with adjustable flames so that you can control the amount of heat being produced. This is especially important in my area, where it's seldom cold enough for a raging fire.

The biggest innovations in gas fireplaces in recent years have come in the form of increasingly sophisticated remote controls. Multifunction remotes can control flame height, built-in lighting, and circulation blowers. They also can be programmed to a specific thermostat setting—automatically adjusting the burner as needed—and can be set to shut off the fire after a predetermined amount of time, much like the sleep timer on your television. A new batch of electronic controls are expected to work with smartphones and tablets.

Maintenance

Modern gas fireplaces are durable and long lasting, and we see few problems related to product failure. When we do get a service call, the problem is usually a result of improper maintenance.

Unlike the superefficient blue flame of a cookstove, fireplaces have a fuel-rich yellow flame (meant to replicate a wood fire) that produces more soot than a blue flame. As a result, every year the burners and ignition system should be cleaned by a manufacturer-certified technician.

Continued ➜

Drinking-Water Filtration Systems

By Don Burgard

Two atoms of hydrogen and one atom of oxygen—this simple formula makes possible the presence of life on our planet. Not only do we humans owe our existence to H2O, but we must consume it every day for optimal health. The water that comes into our homes from wells and municipal distribution systems contains more than just hydrogen and oxygen, however.

The EPA regulates 86 different water contaminants. The Contaminant Candidate List from 2009 included 116 additional contaminants known to exist in drinking water in the United States that the agency considered regulating from that point on.

To determine if you need to filter your water, start by obtaining your utility's consumer confidence report (CCR). Water utilities are required by law to provide this annual report, which documents the contaminants present in that utility's water system. This will give you an idea of which contaminants you need to focus on. Because a CCR applies to the system as a whole and not to your home's water supply, a more accurate picture of the contaminants you are ingesting can come only through a test of your household water. (For households whose water is supplied by a well, of course, a test is the only way to find out about contaminants.) To find an approved laboratory, go to epa.gov/safewater/labs.

Carafe Systems

The easiest way of accessing filtered water is by using a carafe with a built-in carbon filter, which traps contaminants in the porous surface of its tiny granules of carbon. Many people choose these systems primarily for the way they improve the taste of tap water, mostly through reducing chlorine, which is added to public water supplies as a disinfectant. Depending on the particular system, they can reduce the presence of a number of contaminants as well. With this type of system, as with all water-filtration systems, read the manufacturer's list of contaminants the system has been tested to filter out to make sure that it includes those present in your water.

Large families may find carafe systems inadequate. The amount of water that a carafe holds may not be enough, and the short life of the filters, which last for about 40 gal. each, may require frequent changing.

Faucet-Mounted Systems

The base in these systems attaches directly to the faucet after the aerator has been removed, then a replaceable carbon-filter cartridge is inserted into the base. Though much more convenient than the carafe systems, even the slimmest faucet-mounted system can look like an ugly appendage, especially if it doesn't match the finish of the faucet. (Some manufacturers offer systems in a variety of finishes.) Depending on the model, filters in faucet-mounted systems last for between 100 gal. and 200 gal. These systems are meant to be used with cold water only; hot water can damage the filter.

Faucet-mounted systems can reduce the water flow, sometimes significantly. This optimizes the work of the filter, but it may be a nuisance if you need lots of filtered water at a given time. A switch allows you to bypass the filter when washing dishes or hands. On this setting, the flow rate is normal.

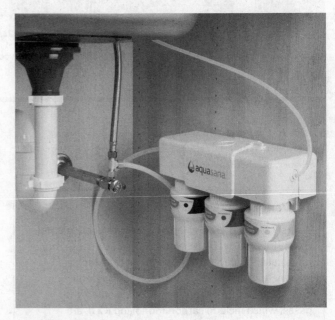

Undersink Systems

Installed (where else?) under the sink, these systems are connected to the cold-water line. Aside from the dedicated faucet they require—which allows you to run unfiltered water from the main faucet, thereby extending the life of the filter(s)—their presence is invisible. Undersink systems are available with one, two, or three filters. One-stage systems include a carbon filter. Two-stage systems may include two carbon filters, or they may include one carbon filter and one sediment filter. (If your tap water contains a lot of sediment, a sediment filter can keep the carbon filter from clogging.) Three-stage systems usually include two carbon filters and one sediment filter. The more filters you have, the longer you can go between changes. For example, Aquasana's three-stage system filters 600 gal., while its two-stage system filters 500 gal. and its one-stage system filters just 200 gal.

Reverse-Osmosis Systems

Reverse osmosis (RO) is a technique used by some municipalities and military units to transform seawater or water that's otherwise unfit for human consumption into potable water. On a much smaller scale, RO systems can filter household water as well. Typically installed under the sink, an RO system begins with either two carbon filters or a sediment filter and a carbon filter. From there, water moves through a filter with a semipermeable membrane that allows water to pass but not contaminants that are larger than a water molecule. The water then proceeds to a storage tank. When the dedicated faucet is turned on, water flows directly to it or through one more carbon filter first. The filters in an RO system usually need to be replaced annually.

RO systems get high marks for thorough filtering, but they come with at least three drawbacks. First, the large space they require limits the storage capability of the undersink area. Second, they filter out the minerals that give water its taste and that are necessary for optimal health. People who eat a well-balanced diet get most of these minerals from their food, but a study reported by the World Health Organization found that when food was cooked in demineralized water, it lost much of its mineral content. Third, the contaminants that the membrane filter traps need to be flushed out by water flowing in the opposite direction of the purified water. This water simply goes into the drainpipe. As a result, an RO system consumes far more water than it produces for drinking. In fact, a three-to-one ratio is not uncommon.

The Facts About Ceiling Fans

By Patrick McCombe

There are 16.7 million ceiling fans sold every year in the United States. They are so popular that most homes have three or more. Most people say that they use their fans to stay comfortable and to save on air-conditioning and heating costs. People also routinely say that the fans keep their homes cooler. These widely held beliefs about ceiling fans are far less straightforward than most people realize.

When used incorrectly, ceiling fans actually can add to your utility costs instead of reducing them. The good news is that if you understand how ceiling fans work and know how to pick the proper fan for a space, these devices can indeed make you more comfortable and save you money on your utilities.

The first thing to know about ceiling fans is that they cool people, not rooms. Like all fans, ceiling fans make you feel more comfortable on a hot day because the breeze they produce speeds the evaporation of sweat from your skin. This evaporative cooling doesn't work on inanimate objects or air, so leaving a ceiling fan running in an unattended room won't help cool the space. You should always turn off ceiling fans when nobody is in the room.

When you're in the room, ceiling fans can save you money on your air-conditioning costs in two ways. For starters, they can keep you comfortable on days with less intense heat, allowing you to resist turning on the air conditioner. Since a typical ceiling fan uses about 100w on high speed, compared to a central air conditioner's 2000w to 5000w, the energy savings are easy to calculate. By setting your air-conditioning thermostat a few degrees higher on the hottest days, you can use the fan to stay comfortable. These savings are harder to document.

A 1996 research project conducted by the Florida Solar Research Center found that Florida homes using ceiling fans had the same thermostat settings as Florida homes without ceiling fans. If we assume that the homeowners with fans accurately reported their fan use and their thermostat settings, we have to assume that they were using the fans without adjusting the thermostat. As a result, their ceiling fans weren't helping to save energy. Moreover, the rooms where the fans were located actually were warmer, since the motor in a ceiling fan can be as hot as 100°F at full speed.

Saving on cooling costs with a ceiling fan simply comes down to occupant behavior. If you can be comfortable with a higher thermostat setting while running the fan, you will save money because the fan uses less electricity than air-conditioning. Just be sure to turn the fan off when you leave the room.

Winter Savings Remain Unproven

Fan manufacturers and some who offer advice on saving energy recommend running ceiling fans in the winter, too. The theory is that by running in reverse, the fan mixes the warm air that's close to the ceiling with the cooler air close to the floor but doesn't

Continued →

High Style
It used to be that all ceiling fans looked like they came from the set of Casablanca, but times have changed. Now you can get fans in virtually any finish and blade configuration. Some models are meant to go unnoticed, while others are meant to be showpieces. There are even fans with hidden and asymmetrical blades.

the fan's breeze may make you feel colder than you would without it." Once again, he suggests experimenting in order to know how running the fan affects comfort.

Match the Fan to the Room

Ceiling fans range in size from 3½ ft. to 7 ft. or more. Recommendations vary from manufacturer to manufacturer, but there are general guidelines on how big a fan should be for a given space. Rooms that are 90 sq. ft. or less should have a 42-in. fan. Rooms from about 90 sq. ft. to 100 sq. ft. require a 44-in. to 46-in. fan. Rooms that are 100 sq. ft. to 150 sq. ft. need a 52-in. to 54-in. fan. For large rooms with multiple seating areas, Alex Reed, marketing director for Big Ass Fans, suggests installing more than one fan or going with a larger model so that everybody can feel the cooling breeze.

To get the maximum cooling effect, a ceiling fan should be 8 ft. to 9 ft. above the floor and directly over the seating area. If the room has a higher ceiling, use an extension rod to lower the fan.

Increase Size to Boost Efficiency

Having some guidance on how to match a fan to the size of the room makes sense, but if you want a more energy-efficient fan, you should probably go with a larger model than what manufacturers and even Energy Star recommend. This is because larger fans move more air per watt than smaller fans. The amount of air moved in cubic feet per minute (cfm) per watt of electricity used is known as a fan's efficacy. This measurement is found on the fan packaging in a 4-in.-wide by 3-in.-tall energy-information label, making it easy to compare models. The amount of air movement per watt is given at the highest speed. Energy Star fans give the efficacy at three speeds.

produce a breeze felt by the room's occupants. Theoretically, this allows you to keep the thermostat at a lower setting. Unfortunately, energy saving from wintertime fan use hasn't been researched.

Jonathan Coulter, an efficiency expert at Advanced Energy in Raleigh, N.C., recommends doing your own testing over a few days to see if running the fan in the winter can save on heating costs in your home. He suggests lowering the thermostat about 5°F and running the fan on low speed, then trying the same thermostat setting with the fan off. If the fan helps you stay comfortable with a lower thermostat setting, you should use the fan because it uses less energy than running your heating system.

If using the fan doesn't help you stay comfortable with a thermostat setting that's 5°F lower, try a thermostat setting that's lower by only 2°F, and repeat the test with and without the fan. If the fan still doesn't help you stay comfortable, return the thermostat to its original position and leave the fan off.

Keep in mind that there are some conceivable drawbacks to running a fan during colder weather. According to Coulter, the first problem is that the fan creates a breeze that makes occupants feel cold, so they turn up their thermostat in response, increasing their energy consumption. In addition, homes with a lot of warm air at ceiling level generally have other problems, such as poorly designed heating systems or large air leaks that contribute to air stratification. Solving those problems first will save more energy and provide greater comfort than running a ceiling fan.

Coulter does point out that homeowners who use wood-burning and pellet stoves for heating can sometimes be more comfortable running ceiling fans as a way to distribute the hot air that collects close to the stove. But he adds, "The air around the stove is often about the same temperature as body temperature, so

Outdoor Options

Outdoor fans, which are built with rust-resistant housings and hardware, create a welcome breeze to keep you cool and keep the bugs away. Damp-location models are made for protected areas such as covered porches and patios. Wet-location models have sealed housings and weather-resistant blades that make them safe in unprotected locations such as pergolas.

Knowing the performance at all three speeds is helpful because it sometimes makes sense to choose a larger fan and then run it on low or medium speed. When building scientist Allison Bailes went looking for a ceiling fan recently, he could have chosen the recommended 44-in. fan that delivers about 60 cfm per watt at high speed, but instead he chose a 52-in. model that produces 117 cfm per watt on medium speed. A downloadable chart at the Energy Star website (energystar.gov) shows that the most efficient fan sold today is a 60-in. model that delivers 1124 cfm per watt on low speed and 711 cfm per watt on high.

Prices Vary

Ultra-energy-efficient fans cost more than less efficient fans. To achieve their unsurpassed efficiency, many of these fans have DC motors, which are more expensive than AC motors but use about 70% less energy. Also, speed control with DC motors is more precise: Six or seven speeds are common, compared to three for AC motors. There are multiple manufacturers on the market that use DC.

Blades are another reason for significant price differences between fans. Less expensive models have blades made from flat pieces of plastic or pressed fiberboard. The blades are mounted on the motor at an angle so that they move air. Flat blades are less efficient and move less air than the airfoil-shape blades found on ultra-energy-efficient fans, but they cost less to manufacture. Ceiling fans with LED lighting also cost more than fans using conventional compact-flourescent and Edison-style light kits, which are commonly found on less expensive fans.

From Pull Chain to Remote Control

Making fans easy to turn on and off should be a priority. At a minimum, fans should be turned on and off with a wall switch rather than a pull chain.

Some wall-mounted fan switches allow you to change fan speed and lighting level in addition to turning the fan on and off. Depending on the model and your home's wiring, these controls often don't need a fan-mounted receiver for operation. As a result, installing one of these controls can be as easy as swapping a light

Cool Controls

Some wireless controls allow you to change the fan speed and the light level from your smartphone or tablet. They feature sophisticated electronics that turn the fan on and off when you enter or leave the room. It also monitors temperature and humidity and learns your comfort and lighting preferences based on your past adjustments.

Continued →

Period Details

Nothing kills the look of period-appropriate decor faster than the wrong fan slapped in the center of a ceiling. Fortunately, there are ceiling fans available to match most architectural periods. Manufacturer websites and lighting showrooms are the best places to get help in matching a fan to an architectural style.

switch. You also can find fans that include a handheld remote control. Remote controls are especially helpful in bedrooms, where you can turn off the lights or adjust the speed without getting out of bed.

In addition to traditional remote controls, there are smartphone apps that allow you to adjust fan speed and lighting level from almost anywhere. Fanimation's FanSync is one example. This system works with most models from most manufacturers.

And then there are those that work with your smartphone system. They allow you to control the fans' speeds, to adjust lighting, and even to set a gradual wakeup alarm with increasing light levels and fan speed. Some models of these high-tech fans also features an occupancy sensor that starts the fan and/or turns on the lights when you enter the room and then shuts everything off when you leave.

When you're considering a new fan, Jeff Dross of Kichler Lighting recommends that you consider how you want to control the fan early in the selection process, as it's often less expensive to buy one with remote- or app-based controls than to add the capability later. "It's much like buying a car," he says. "Options are less expensive when you have them installed on the car when you order it. If you try to install them after you've bought the car, they're very expensive."

Safe and Sturdy Mounting

Subject to the constant stress of a spinning motor, and with a 40-lb. fan attached, the electrical box that holds up your fan has an important job. Required by the National Electric Code (NEC), heavy-duty "fan-rated" boxes are usually connected to the home's framing with robust mounting screws that come with the box. They also include screws for mounting the fan's hanging hardware that are larger than what's included with standard electrical boxes. There are many styles of fan-rated boxes available, in both plastic and metal versions, for new construction and remodels. Choosing plastic or metal is often based on personal preference, as both types work fine.

FOR OLD WORK. Retrofit boxes like this model install through the hole that's cut for the box itself. The telescopic mounting bar expands when turned with a wrench until the teeth on the ends sufficiently grab the joist. The electrical box is then attached to the bar with a pair of bolts.

FOR NEW WORK AND MORE. Available in many styles, fan boxes for new work are attached directly to the framing. They're used primarily for new construction and whenever the framing is open, but they also can be used for retrofit installations in ceilings with attic access.

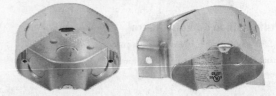

Contents

Carpentry

Three-Legged Sawhorses

By Brian Campbell

Sawhorses support most everything carpenters work with or on. In the not-too-distant past, most carpenters built, rather than bought, their horses. I still do, because having custom sawhorses that can handle multiple functions means you can haul around less stuff and can use smaller work vehicles and tight workspaces efficiently.

I recently set about to improve my sawhorses without making them cumbersome or complicated. To handle the irregular ground of job sites, I made them three-legged. To make them sturdy but not too heavy, I glued two layers of ¾-in. CDX plywood together. (Lighter versions can be built with one layer of ¾-in. or 1⅛-in. plywood.) One end of the rail serves as a leg. The other leg section meets the rail at 15°, interlocking via half-lapped notches. I've now made rails in lengths ranging from 4 ft. to 8 ft.

I bored and slotted the pieces to reduce weight without an appreciable loss of strength. The holes also allow the sawhorses to carry worktables, a tablesaw, or a miter saw, and to accommodate applications such as infeed/outfeed support. U-shaped sacrificial plywood caps protect the rails when I'm cutting on them. The hardware for the adjustable-height components is easily sourced through suppliers such as Rockler or Woodcraft.

Accessorize Your Own

A box slotted to fit around the rail supports a miter saw. Stock is supported by adjustable-height outfeed supports. A tablesaw rests on pipe clamps secured in the holes in the horses. Additional accessories are limited only by your imagination.

STORE WORKPIECES EFFICIENTLY. Great for storing trim or for use as drying racks, mini-shelves attach to the horses with T-bolts.

CAMS SUPPORT A MITER-SAW STAND. Dowels from the cams ride in holes in the sawhorse. Rotating the cam changes its height.

Continued →

Handy hold-down. Commonly available at woodworking suppliers, a bench dog used sideways clamps a workpiece solidly.

Job-site workbench. T-bolts and knobs allow the slotted supports to hold the benchtop at a variety of heights.

Glued-up ¾-in. plywood

4-in. holes for clamping and hanging tools

Keyhole slots for T-bolts to secure adjustable-height accessories

15°

¾-in. holes for various accessories

Horse Sense

With one 8-ft. sawhorse coming out of a single piece of ¾-in. plywood, these work platforms are cheap. They're also sturdy and versatile. Lay out and cut the components, then glue them together before cutting the 15° slots for the half-laps. You'll probably also want to sand the edges of the joined pieces so that they're smooth and flush.

15°

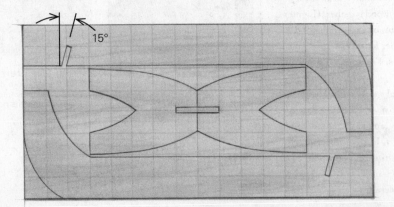

Cutting with a Handsaw

Handsaws offer some distinct advantages over power saws. A handsaw is small and lightweight, so it's easy to pack and carry. A handsaw also is a lot quieter than a circular saw and makes less of a mess. When you have only a few boards to cut, reaching for a handsaw is often faster than taking the time to run an extension cord and set up a power saw. And where a power tool might be cumbersome and dangerous—cutting overhead or on a ladder, for example—a handsaw offers a safe alternative.

Choosing the best handsaw for the job is the first step in making clean, accurate cuts (see "Handsaw Revival," p. 27). But learning to use the saw properly is equally important. Because handsaws are not very good for cutting less than ⅛ in. off the end of a board, measuring and cutting accurately on your first attempt is essential.

5. DON'T LET THE BOARD BREAK. Unsupported, the cutoff can cause the stock to tear toward the end of the cut. For a clean finish, clamp the stock to a sawhorse and support the cutoff with your free hand. Finish the cut with smooth, gentle strokes.

Cut Lumber with a Long Saw and a Low Horse

1. MARK THE CUT. On thick material, mark the cutline on two adjacent faces. Some saw handles allow you to lay out 45° and 90° lines without reaching for a square.

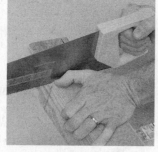

2. USE YOUR THUMB TO START THE CUT. With the sawblade on the waste side of the cutline, use your thumb to align and steady the blade. Hold the saw at a low angle and pull to get started.

3. PUT YOUR WEIGHT BEHIND THE BLADE. A good stance is important when you're using a handsaw to cut thick material like this 4×4. Low sawhorses or other supports will enable you to get your hand, elbow, and shoulder in line with the blade.

4. USE FULL STROKES AT 45°. Long strokes save energy and produce smoother cuts. Keep the blade at 45° when crosscutting.

Tips for Making Common Cuts Accurate

1. RIP WITH THE RIGHT SAW. Ripping a board (cutting with the grain) is usually more difficult than crosscutting. Use the right saw: a traditional Western-style ripsaw, a Japanese ripsaw, or a modern hybrid saw. Cutting action is best with the blade at a 60° angle. If the kerf starts to close and pinch the blade, use a wedge to keep it open.

2. GO VERTICAL FOR NOTCHES. When notching the end of a board or finishing the cuts for a stair stringer, cut with the saw perpendicular to the stock. This way you won't cut any deeper on one side of the board than on the other.

3. CUT MOLDINGS IN PLACE WITH A GUIDE BLOCK. When a power saw isn't an option for making a clean, accurate cut in an installed molding, use a backsaw with a square block of wood as a guide.

4. DON'T SCRIBE THE FLOORING. Instead, trim door casing in place when installing new flooring. Use a straight-handled, fine-toothed pull saw guided by a scrap of the new flooring.

Continued →

Fast and Accurate Wall Framing

By Mike Norton

If there's a glamorous job in carpentry, it's not framing. It might be finish work; everything looks so good after that final piece of molding is nailed in place and the job is complete. Framing, on the other hand, is called "rough," and it requires an experienced imagination to see the finished product in its earliest stage. But framing embodies the physics of the structure, and if you don't get it right, the house will fail. You'll also have a hard time nailing your fancy trim where there is no blocking.

Whether the plans call for traditional stick framing or optimum-value engineering, the skills are relatively simple: straight and square cuts, a good hammer technique, economy of motion, and a strong back. There are a few tricks, however, that make the job easier and the results more professional. Here, I'll explain some of the methods I've picked up, using a simple exterior wall as an example.

Layout is Critical

Even though you're probably the one who laid the sill plates and framed the deck, it's still a good idea to make sure that the deck is square before framing the walls. The simplest method to use is to check the corners by measuring a 3/4/5 triangle and then extending the angle with a reference chalkline. I've found it faster, however, to use a laser that shoots two lines at 90°. Two people can square up a deck in about 10 minutes, and there's less chance for error. If the deck isn't square, it's usually within a ¼-in. tolerance that we can correct by moving the plate location marks out beyond the deck edge or inward toward the center of the deck.

After squaring up the deck, we snap lines for the plates. While we're at it, we also snap a reference centerline across the deck so that we can check that walls are parallel or, when it's snapped to represent the ridgeline, use it to lay out a gable wall.

We frame the walls flat on the deck by first toenailing the bottom plates down on edge along the chalklines. After double-checking the window and door schedule, we mark these locations on the plates. I also figure out where the partitions intersect the wall and mark the location of the backers. If there's a conflict between the partition's placement and the eventual locations of interior trim, I usually call the architect before making the necessary adjustments.

Framing layout is a critical part of the process, so I always double-check my measurements. I cut the bottom plate to length first, then the top plates. I usually wait to install the second top plate until adjoining walls are raised so that the plate ties the walls together.

With the bottom and top plates placed together temporarily, I start marking the layout from the left and go right. After I mark the first stud on the bottom plate, I drive a nail at the line and pull 16 in. from there, marking the X beyond the line that indicates the stud location. At the same time, I transfer the layout to the top plate.

If I have a straight wall and a simple floor frame above, I mark the floor-joist layout onto the second top plate's face so that we don't have to do it after we lift the wall.

Cutting Duplicate Components All at Once is Faster

I've found that it's more efficient to have one of the crew designated as the cut man at a chopsaw. (Mounted on a stand with adjustable stops, the saw makes production work simple and accurate.) Wall studs, headers, window and door parts, and other

---

Lay Out the Plates Once

It's usually easiest to build walls on the deck and then lift them into place. The first step is to mark out stud, window, and door openings on the plates.

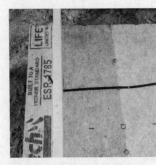

AN OUNCE OF PREVENTION. A length of metal packing strap nailed to the plate and deck is good insurance against a wall dropping off the deck's edge as it's raised.

TOE THE PLATE. Lay the bottom plate on edge, and align it with the chalkline. Toenail it to the deck, nailing every 2 ft. or so. Once the wall is built, the completed structure is anchored to the deck and is less likely to move as it's raised.

NO MATH, JUST MARK. When laying out a plate, it's faster to mark the edge of the first stud, drive a nail into the first mark, and then pull 16-in. intervals from there.

EFFICIENT LAYOUT. For a quick layout, place the top plate behind the bottom plate, and mark both at the same time. This temporary placement also keeps deck clutter to a minimum.

Get Square and Parallel Walls with a Laser

A key step in laying out walls is to establish square corners and parallel walls, a task streamlined with the use of a laser. Once square corners have been set, the plate layout lines can be snapped.

A GOOD LASER MAKES LAYOUT FASTER AND MORE ACCURATE. The author uses a laser that fires a constant beam in five directions that is visible in daylight. The first step is to mark the plate width in all corners, set the laser, and aim it toward the first target.

HIT THE BULL'S-EYE. Placed on the next corner over the plate mark, the target indicates when the laser is lined up.

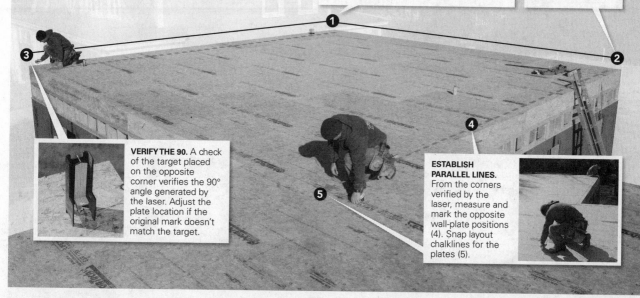

VERIFY THE 90. A check of the target placed on the opposite corner verifies the 90° angle generated by the laser. Adjust the plate location if the original mark doesn't match the target.

ESTABLISH PARALLEL LINES. From the corners verified by the laser, measure and mark the opposite wall-plate positions (4). Snap layout chalklines for the plates (5).

Production-Style Assembly

Assigning one carpenter the task of cutting parts at the chopsaw station means that the rest of the crew can keep nailing.

MULTIPLE WINDOWS. If there are a number of identical windows, it's faster for the cut man to make parts and assemble the windows as units.

AN ORGANIZED LIST. After assigning each window a letter designation and listing the parts' measurements, cut and stack the parts in discrete piles.

ALWAYS CHECK FOR SQUARE. After the wall has been nailed together, measure both diagonals to make sure the wall is square before starting to sheathe.

EASIER ON THE GROUND. It's safer, faster, and neater to cut out the window openings with a circular saw as the sheathing is installed.

Continued →

Raise and Straighten the Walls

As walls are completed, lift them into a standing position, lean them outward an inch or so, and brace them temporarily. Before setting rafters or floor joists, straighten the top plates with springboards, and check them with a taut stringline that's stretched along the top plate.

LIFT IN STAGES. It's sometimes easier and safer to pull up the wall to just above the crew's knees, rest it on sawhorses, then shift hand positions to push up the wall the rest of the way.

SET THE SPRINGBOARDS. With the wall braced, start the straightening process by nailing one end of a pine 1×8 to the underside of the top plate or to a header.

TACK THE BOTTOM. While one carpenter pushes down on the board, the other checks the string with a 2x gauge. The trick is to increase the tension by overbending the board so that it pulls the wall into the string. The first carpenter then tacks the springboard end to the deck and releases the tension on the board.

PULL THE WALL. One carpenter pushes a shorter leg into the underside of the springboard, bringing the top plate back toward the string. When the gauge indicates that the top plate is straight, the other carpenter nails the leg to the springboard, locking it and the wall into place.

duplicates all get cut there.

If the house has many of the same windows, I put together a cut list so that we can cut the legs below the window and the cripples above at the same time as the headers and sills. On the list, I group the windows with the same header length so that the cut man can cut everything without having to adjust his jig.

It's usually easier for the cut man to cut and assemble the headers, jacks, sills, legs, and other pieces into door and window units that we then can incorporate into the frame. If they're all various sizes, we assemble the doors or the windows as part of the wall. When the houses are fairly complicated and have different wall heights and large windows of different sizes, I have someone ready on the deck to cut all the legs and cripples as we frame the wall. Because the width of the header stock can vary by ¼ in. from one 2×10 to another, most times we cut the cripples to

Trick of the Trade

Pull the string tight, make a loop around your finger, and twist it.

Anchor the loop on the lower nail, and pull up on the string.

While keeping tension on the string, pull down hard to compress the wraps on the loop. Loosen the tension on the string, and the knot comes undone.

length, install them, and then cut the jacks to the corresponding length. The rough opening's height may decrease by a fraction of an inch, but as long as the window fits in the rough opening, it's OK.

Sheathing Layout is Important

Once we've assembled a wall on the deck and measured its diagonals to make sure it's square, we begin sheathing. We pay careful attention to the engineer's plans, including the nailing pattern on the sheathing and the location of vertical sheets of plywood to hold down the corners of the house. If a wall is over a certain height or the engineer requires longer sheets for a hold-down, we install blocking across the wall at the point where the seams meet.

We often use 4×8 plywood sheets to span from the mudsill to about a foot under the top plate of the wall. We then can use 4×10 sheets to span from that point to the second top plate of the second-floor wall. We also cut out windows and doors as we sheathe the walls, rather than doing so after we stand them up. It's safer, faster, and more precise.

Bracing and Straightening

After we've raised a wall, we nail the plates to the deck and temporarily brace the wall with 2×6s so that it's pushed outward slightly. This makes it easier to raise an adjacent wall; it's also easier to pull the wall straight than to push it.

To straighten the walls, we nail a 2x block to each end of a wall at the top plate, then run a taut line between the two. Next, we install roughsawn 1×8 springboards at 8-ft. intervals. We cut them to length so they can span a 45° angle from the top plate to the deck, then we nail one end to the underside of the top plate. While one person checks the string with a 2x block, another flexes the board downward and tacks the lower end to the deck.

We jam a short length of board between the deck and the middle of the springboard and push it away from the wall until the gauge block shows that the wall is straight. Then we tack the short board to the springboard and the deck, locking the wall in.

Continued →

Framing for Efficiency

By Steve Baczek

The frame of a Passive House may not be as exciting as the thick layers of insulation, the high-tech mechanical systems, or the triple-glazed windows, but it plays a very important supporting role—pun intended—in achieving success.

I chose every component of the framing package in this house with care, and for a specific reason. The exterior sheathing provides airtightness, the double-stud walls and raised-heel roof trusses are a cost-effective means of supporting or containing above-average levels of insulation, and the floor trusses easily span the open floor plan and provide plenty of room for the many ducts necessary for the ventilation system and supporting mechanicals.

Two Walls, Two Air Barriers

The chief function of the double-stud walls is to hold insulation. Measuring 14 in. from the interior face of the 2×4 inner wall to the exterior face of the 2×6 outer wall, the wall assembly provides a 5-in. thermal break between halves.

In addition to the taped sheathing seams and the picture-frame-style application of Tremco acoustical sealant, the wall is redundantly air-sealed with a 4-in.-thick coat of closed-cell foam sprayed against the inside face of the sheathing. The remainder of the cavity is filled with 10 in. of dry, dense-packed cellulose, bringing the wall assembly to an overall thermal resistance of about R-52.

Some energy-conscious builders and architects might wonder why anybody would design a building that represents the height of energy efficiency, and specify walls with 2×6 studs spaced 16 in. on center and structural headers over every window—details that fly in

The Construction Sequence Is Guided by Blower-Door Tests

The airtightness requirement for Passive House certification is less than or equal to 0.6 air changes per hour at –50 Pa (ACH50). This number can also be expressed as 177 cubic feet per minute at –50 Pa (cfm50). I prefer to use the cfm figures because the larger number makes any changes in performance easier to track.

Phase 1 Primary Air Barrier

TEST RESULT

The primary air barrier in this house is formed by the slab, the exterior sheathing, and the plastered ceilings below each roofline. Backed up with a thick, continuous bead of Tremco acoustical sealant at all seam edges, the 7⁄16-in.-thick Zip System OSB was chosen because of its butyl-based seam-sealing tape, which partners with the water- and air-resistive barrier that's bonded to the exterior side of each sheet. The rough openings at windows and doors are left uncut so that the builders can test the airtightness of the shell before moving to the next step of the process.

Phase 2 Secondary Air Barrier

TEST RESULT

A 4-in.-thick coat of closed-cell polyurethane-foam insulation is sprayed on the inner face of the wall sheathing. Running continuously from the subslab insulation to the top plates, the foam performs a couple of functions. First, it acts as a secondary air barrier should there be any air leakage through the sheathing seams or the acoustical sealant. Second, with an insulation value of roughly R-27, it ensures that the inner surface of the sheathing remains above the dewpoint, eliminating the risk of condensation in the extrathick wall assembly.

the face of advanced-framing techniques.

Given that these walls are thermally broken by the cavity between the inner and outer stud walls, the only advantage to framing with studs set on 24-in. centers would be a small cost savings in lumber. But on this house, which is located in a coastal high-wind zone, that small savings would have been offset by the additional structural measures required of a wall 24 in. on center.

For the headers, all of which are thermally broken with a piece of 2-in.-thick rigid foam, I have found that consistency pays even if it results in a minor energy penalty. I try to minimize decisions for the builder to increase the likelihood that the things I need to be done right will be done right. Also, for what it's worth, the high-performance triple-glazed windows necessary in a Passive House are two to three times the weight of a typical double-glazed window, so a robust window frame is a good thing.

At the top of each wall, bridging the gap between the interior and exterior stud walls, is a rip of ¾-in. plywood, which has a couple of duties. First, it caps and isolates the cavity space of the double-stud wall. Second, it overhangs the interior wall plate, providing a means to connect the interior ceiling to the wall assembly, maintaining the continuity of the air barrier. A third function is one I hadn't planned for but that the builders found very useful: a walking surface. By attaching bracing below the plywood flange, the builders were able to walk the walls easily while installing the floor and roof trusses.

Strong, Wide-Open Floor Framing

One of my goals in designing a successful Passive House is to get as much of the structural load from the floors and roof as possible to the outside of the house. This allows me to keep an open floor plan, which is helpful in moving conditioned air around the

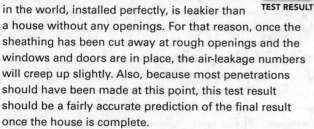

Phase 3 Windows and Doors

106 cfm50
TEST RESULT

Even a house with the best windows and doors in the world, installed perfectly, is leakier than a house without any openings. For that reason, once the sheathing has been cut away at rough openings and the windows and doors are in place, the air-leakage numbers will creep up slightly. Also, because most penetrations should have been made at this point, this test result should be a fairly accurate prediction of the final result once the house is complete.

Phase 4 Insulation and Mechanicals

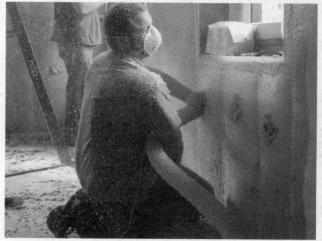

110 cfm50
TEST RESULT

With the more-delicate control functions handled as close to the outside face of the building as possible, the space between the outer and inner stud walls and the space in the attic offer an opportunity for more-cost-effective insulation to provide the bulk of the thermal resistance. Cellulose insulation is packed into the walls to a density of 3.6 lb. per sq. ft., adding R-37 to the overall thermal resistance of the wall assembly. In the attic, loose-fill cellulose is piled to a depth of 24 in., providing an R-92 insulated lid above the ceiling air barrier of the house. At this stage, minor leakage typically stems from final work on mechanical rough-ins and other last-minute tweaks.

Continued ➔

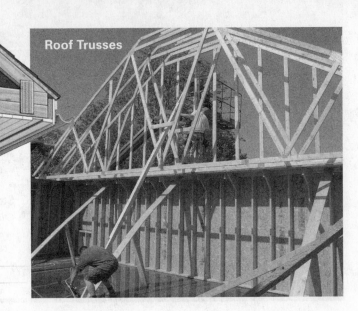

Roof Trusses

house. To achieve this open floor plan, I needed engineered floor joists, which can span longer distances than dimensional lumber.

Although it's largely heated by the sun in the winter, a Passive House still relies on mechanical systems. In addition to the standard plumbing and electrical, this house has lots of ductwork for ventilation. Without a basement or conditioned attic, just about everything has to run through the floor joists that support the second level.

This combined need for a long span and room for lots of mechanicals made open-web floor trusses an easy choice. They are cost-effective and sturdy, and they eliminate concerns about the placement of penetrations or the need for mechanical chases.

This Attic Is for Insulation

Because the attic will hold 24 in. of loose-fill cellulose, I didn't even attempt to provide storage or living space up there. Forfeiting any claim to the attic made roof trusses an easy choice compared to a traditional stick-built roof, and allowed me to get the house dried in and prepped for the uppermost portion of the primary air barrier: the ceilings.

To ensure that this ceiling air barrier—a layer of veneer-plastered blueboard—would be continuous, the plaster installers hung and finished the ceiling before any interior partition walls were framed. That approach not only eliminated the hundreds of linear feet of joints between top plates and ceiling joists—all of which are weak points in an air barrier—but it made the hanger's job easier because full sheets of blueboard could be used.

Multipurpose Components

Because the attic won't be used for anything but insulation, raised-heel roof trusses were a quick and cost-efficient means of putting a lid on this house and of providing a way to hang and finish the ceiling air barrier before partition walls went in. The interior frame provided the typical mounting surface for fixtures

Floor Trusses

Outside Frame

Removing Interior Walls

By Chris Ermides

I busted open my first wall sometime in high school. It wasn't an act of vandalism; I was helping my dad to remove the wall between our kitchen and dining room, and not without trepidation. Walls are built for a reason, I thought, if not to hold up the house, then to have a place for outlets and light switches. Besides, I knew there was stuff in walls that I couldn't see. Lucky for me, my dad believed in doing everything slowly and methodically. We didn't tear down the wall. We assessed it first to see if it was bearing any weight, and then we tried to sniff out what might be hidden behind the plaster. When all that work was done, we dismantled the wall.

Since that first experience, I've removed a lot more walls. To learn more about the process, I interviewed a bunch of remodeling contractors who do this work daily. This article is a collection of what I've learned, but the truth is that the basic process is much the same as what my dad taught me almost two decades ago.

Unbuild the Walls

Walls are built in an organized way, and that's how they should be taken down. Studs go up first, and they come down last. Trim goes in last, and it comes off first. That might sound trivial, but there are plenty of people who take a different tack. Cutting

and finishes, but it also served as a barrier to contain the cavity insulation before the final wallboard was installed.

Open-web floor trusses offer long spans and the ability to run mechanicals between the first and second floors—a saving grace in a house where the attic is off-limits and there is no basement.

The outside frame supports most of the floor load and all of the roof load. It also holds part of the primary air barrier, and with the help of diagonal bracing, provides the necessary wind-shear resistance for this coastal site.

Continued →

BEFORE

AFTER

through a wall with a reciprocating saw and then attempting to remove full sections might seem like the most efficient approach, but it's dangerous. Attacking an enclosed wall haphazardly with a power tool or sledgehammer is like peeling away the shingles on a roof with a backhoe bucket.

With the basic precautions shown here, you can begin to dismantle a wall safely at any time. However, it's important to know if a wall is bearing weight before messing with the framing. Spotting a load-bearing wall isn't always easy, but there are some telltale signs). If you're unsure, hire an engineer. An engineer is also the person to consult when sizing a beam to replace a bearing wall. That beam can be mounted within the finished ceiling in line with the joists above, where you won't be able to see it, or below the joists, where it can be trimmed as an architectural detail (find more information on FineHomebuilding.com). I'm not going to cover how to do that here, though; this story is about taking down walls efficiently. After you have determined whether the wall is bearing weight, the next step is to figure out what's in it.

Pretend the Wall Could Shock You

Chances are good that electrical wires are running in and through the wall you want to remove. Light switches, fixtures, and outlets are obvious indicators, but don't think that they tell the whole story. Look in the basement and attic for cables that enter or exit the wall.

Turn off the power to the circuits you discover before even starting to remove the plaster and lath or the drywall. It's possible that old wiring in the wall could be in bad shape. Even if it's not, though, accidentally loosening or damaging wires during demolition can cause immediate and latent danger, including shock, electrocution, and fire.

Even after you've done your electrical investigative work, be ready for weird stuff. Cliff Popejoy, an electrical contractor in Sacramento, Calif., was called to a house after the home-owner got a shock from touching the washing machine and the wall at the same time. Two of the walls were plaster on metal lath, and both were energized to 120v because a piece of lath was touching the hot terminal of a non-GFI receptacle.

Once you are inside the wall, dealing with electrical wiring means rerouting or dead-ending circuits. An electrician is the best person

Spot and Support Load-Bearing Walls

Bearing walls carry roof, ceiling, and floor loads. They often run perpendicular to floor and ceiling joists, but that isn't the rule. Sometimes walls that run parallel to floor joists are also load-bearing. Look in the basement for girder beams, and trace their path to the roof; some homes have more than one. While these drawings illustrate some common signs of bearing walls, they don't represent a definitive list. The smartest, safest approach is to consult an engineer, and assume that the wall you're going to remove is bearing weight until you prove otherwise. Properly sized beams must replace bearing walls.

This post supports the structural ridge, which is common in vaulted ceilings.

The wall beneath this post is carrying the ridge/hip point load.

A stiff knee or kneewall is possibly carrying some roof load. In older homes, this approach might take the form of posts, which aren't necessarily running plumb to the bearing point below.

This first-floor wall is bearing weight from the floor joists above, as well as the roof load. Bearing walls often run inline with a beam in the basement. They can be offset from their bearing points, however.

This wall is carrying the ceiling joists and possibly some roof load.

Temporary support. Before cutting into the framing of a load-bearing wall, build a temporary wall to pick up the load. Use a 2×8 or 2×10 for the top plate to minimize potential damage to the finished ceiling. Cut the studs ¼ in. long to take some weight off the wall, and screw or nail them in place every 16 in. You also can support the load with a header and posts in lieu of studs to make walking through the temporary wall easier. Be sure that the load path has adequate support below. And remember, the wall might need support on both sides.

This wall is carrying floor joists and an offset load from the wall above.

Continued →

Investigate What's in the Wall

SIGNS OF EXTRA WORK AHEAD. Note the number of utilities passing through the bottom of the wall, but don't assume they tell the whole story. Turn off the power and water to any fixtures and plumbing in the wall and in the walls above and below the wall to be removed; wire and pipe might pass through them as well.

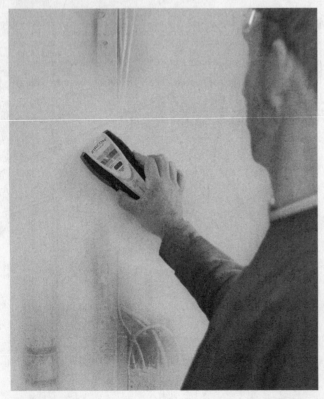

USE A SENSOR. Even if you know that wire and pipe enter the wall from below, it's possible that more is hidden inside. To eliminate as many surprises as possible, use a tester that finds live wires and metal as well as studs.

Protect Floors and Manage Dust

MASONITE TAKES A BEATING. If the floors are to remain, take time to protect them from screws, nails, and other debris. A layer of ⅛-in. Masonite over plastic offers great protection. Sheets of Masonite are reusable and easy to come by.

CONTAIN DUST. Clear plastic isolates the area without blocking light. Furring strips or telescoping poles hold it tight to the floor and ceiling. Protect your lungs with a respirator, and beware of lead paint.

THICK PROTECTION IN A ROLL. Ram Board offers good protection and comes in rolls. It's durable, easy to install, and reusable. It won't take a beating like Masonite, but it comes close.

Inexpensive, but thin. Red (or brown) rosin paper is readily available and cheap, but it won't take much of a beating. Save it for tiled or carpeted floors.

REMOVE DUST. Mount a fan in the window to pull dust out of the house. Cover floor registers and return-air grilles. Furnace filters work well for this purpose if the heating system will be running during the job; otherwise, tape them shut with cardboard.

to do the job. If you're tackling it yourself, though, keep these things in mind.

The best way to reroute cable is to remove it back to the last undisturbed box (at a receptacle, switch, or fixture) and to run new cable. This is easy with modern (grounding) nonmetallic (NM) cable. If the wiring is old armored cable, flexible metal conduit (EMT), or knob-and-tube, it's time to check with the code official to see what materials must be used.

If the part of the wiring that you're removing doesn't feed anything and you can't follow the wiring back to an existing box, you need to dead-end the wiring in its own electrical box. Code requires that the box be accessible. If you can't put it in a basement,

Dismantle the Wall, Don't Demolish It: Tips for Careful Deconstruction

START WITH A KNIFE, NOT A HAMMER Run a sharp utility knife along the edge of each piece of trim to break the painted or caulked seam. Use a taping knife and a hammer to pry trim from the wall one piece at a time so that it can be reused later.

SEVER THE CEILING-TO-WALL JOINT For plaster-and-lath walls, run a reciprocating saw along the joint between the wall and the ceiling. Take care not to cut any deeper than the plaster's depth (usually about ⅝ in.). Use a sharp utility knife where drywalled ceilings and walls meet.

PULL THE PLASTER, THEN THE LATH Using a sledgehammer or a framing hammer, tap the plaster between studs. Start from the bottom, and work up to the ceiling. This breaks the keys off the plaster, releasing it from the lath. Pulling it off is as simple as scraping it with a utility knife.

PULL DRYWALL IN BIG PIECES, NOT LITTLE CHUNKS Cut the drywall into large sections about 2 ft. wide by 6 ft. long. Starting from the top, fold down each section. The leverage and weight of the drywall will make popping it from the screws or nails easy.

FREE THE CABLE, DON'T PULL IT When you have no choice but to work around wire or pipe, cut a sawkerf just above and just below the wire. Then tap the section with a hammer to free the wire from the stud.

TWIST THE STUD, THEN PULL IT Knocking studs loose with a hammer works, but it often splits the stud, rendering that part useless. You can cut the nails by running a metal blade in a reciprocating saw between the stud and the plate, but if the wall is bearing weight, you'll reciprocate more than the blade. Stanley's FuBar has a cleverly designed jaw that makes twisting the stud free easy.

SPLIT THE PLATE AROUND PIPES AND WIRE Once the studs are removed, pull the nails from the plate, then cut it on both sides of the pipe or wire. Finally, split the remaining piece with a chisel. This method also works for top plates.

---

a crawlspace, or an attic, you'll have to put it in a wall or cabinet and cover it with a blank plate.

Although low-voltage wiring (doorbell, thermostat, intercom, telephone, cable, etc.) can be spliced outside a box, it's bad practice to seal a splice inside a wall. Follow the wire back to the attic, the crawlspace, or the basement, and splice the cable there. Or use a low-voltage ring and a blank coverplate in the wall so that the splices are accessible.

See Pipes? Think Flood Insurance

If you're lucky, electrical cable will be the only thing you have to deal with, but don't proceed under that assumption. Unlike electrical cable, pipe generally runs in a straight path, so it is fairly easy to sleuth out. Check in the basement for plumbing lines and in the attic for vent pipes.

There aren't as many indicators of hidden pipe as there are of electrical work. The proximity of kitchen faucets and bathroom fixtures can offer some clues. If you suspect there is plumbing in the wall, turn off the water at the closest shutoff before beginning any demolition.

There are lots of good reasons to hire a licensed plumber to reroute supply, drain, or vent pipes. Most states allow nonlicensed plumbers to remove only fixtures that are attached to a shutoff valve; anything beyond the shutoff valve, as well as drain and vent piping, must be removed and rerouted by a licensed plumber.

But the best reason could be that licensed plumbers have insurance to cover damage caused during remodeling work. While

Continued ➡

modern copper and PEX plumbing can be resilient, jostling old galvanized and copper pipe can weaken joints elsewhere. And given the fact that 4-in. cast-iron pipe weighs about 2 lb. a foot, removing 8 ft. from a stack can be dangerous.

Black iron and flexible gas lines are another concern. These lines should be rerouted only by a licensed gas contractor.

All this investigative work will pay off by giving you a good idea of what's lurking behind the finished surfaces. When the trim and wallboard are gone and the studs and plates are down, you might have to reroute some wires or pipes, but you won't be scrambling to make emergency repairs.

A Tool Set for Every Demo Task

Pry as he might, toolmaker Joe Skach couldn't find the best tool to remove the siding on his house, so he developed his own. He didn't come up with a new bar that does a few different things. Skach came up with a system: a collection of handles, blades, and fulcrums that can be arranged for any demo-specific task. The Artillery Pry Bar System can be configured and assembled to fit whatever task you need. Pop drywall with ease, scrape plaster from lath, and pry that stubborn bottom plate loose without losing your breath.

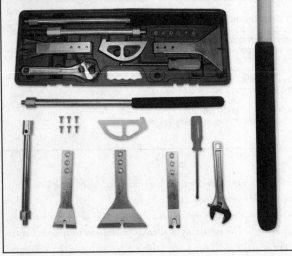

Build a Temporary Brace Wall

By Scott Grice

When I talk to my clients about improving sight-lines and traffic patterns in their homes, the conversation often leads to somebody saying, "Well, let's just tear out that wall," followed by, "Can we do that?" As a remodeling contractor, I've learned that a simple "yes" is the best answer. When I get around to figuring out how to tear out that wall, things can get more complicated. The first step is to determine if the wall is load-bearing. If it is, I need to support the structure temporarily while the demolition and rebuilding work are done. There are different ways to provide support, but if the joists above are perpendicular to the wall, the easiest option is to build a temporary brace wall.

I use a 2×10 for the top plate to spread the weight over a large-enough area to avoid cracking the ceiling finish. For the bottom plate and studs, 2×4s are sufficient. If the brace wall needs to span a long distance, I break it up into 8-ft. or shorter sections to make it manageable for one person to build. I build the wall 3 ft. to 4 ft. from the opening—in this case, to enlarge the doorway beyond the cabinets. This distance is close enough to support the load adequately, yet it gives me enough room to work comfortably.

If I'm dealing with a multistory structure or if I think there is a significant load, I consult an archi-tect or an engineer. Also, when I'm working over a crawlspace or a basement, I build a secondary brace wall below if I need to continue the load path down.

Place and Plumb the Middle Stud First

4. SNUG IS A GOOD FIT. I like to be able to tap studs in place. If I have to pound on a stud with my hammer to get it in place, then it should be trimmed. After the center stud is snug, I start on the outside and work back to the center.

5. NO NAILS NEEDED. There's no benefit to nailing the studs to the plates. If they are fit properly, they will remain in place. Nailing the wall together would only make it harder to take apart.

1. MEASURE FOR THE STUDS. I set both the top and bottom plates on the floor and stand on them while measuring for the studs. When reading a bent tape, I err on the long side. After cutting a stud or two, I get a feel for guesstimating the measurement.

2. DON'T SAY NO TO A HELPING HAND. With the first stud within close reach, I lift the 2×10 top plank flat to the ceiling (with the help of a *Fine Homebuilding* photographer holding the other end of the board). I then wedge the center stud in place; the center stud holds the top plate until I add more studs.

3. PLUMB THE CENTER STUD. After I mark the locations of the ceiling joists on the top plate, I measure from the plumbed stud to match the lay-out marks on the bottom plate.

TIP If you've cut one stud too short, you can wedge it by using a nail as a shim. If the stud is too short by more than the thickness of a nail shank, then you'll need to shim it or replace it.

A Tool Set for Every Demo Task

Using a typical stud finder to locate ceiling joists can be frustratingly inconclusive. However, a rare-earth magnet is a surprisingly accurate alternative. It's strong enough to stick to fasteners even if they're buried in old plaster. A quarter-size magnet works great and can be purchased online (www.woodcraft.com). Use two-part epoxy to affix a small block of wood to the magnet as a handle. To use the homemade stud finder, run the magnet over the surface of the ceiling until it sticks. Chances are that you've located a drywall screw in the center of a joist.

Continued →

Installing a Big Beam

By Andy Engel

Remodeling carpenters routinely set large beams in cases such as the one shown here, where the beam replaces a bearing wall. Whether a beam is made from engineered lumber or regular old 2×12s, the challenge is weight. Here, a new beam was made from three 16-ft.-long 1¾-in. by 11⅞-in. LVLs. It would have been difficult to raise the assembled beam, but the trick is to raise one piece at a time and then fasten the three together in place.

Replacing a wall with a beam requires carrying the loads while the old wall is being removed and the new beam is being installed. I built a temporary wall about 1 ft. beyond the old wall before removing it. I was lucky in that the joists above overlapped by several feet and so the temporary wall could be held back that far, which provided more room to work. In most cases, a temporary wall has to be built much closer to the existing wall, or even in contact with it, to catch the joist overlap and to support the floor.

This beam was engineered for its loads. (Lumberyards often provide this service for free.) Each end of the beam imposes a substantial load that requires a direct path through the framing to the foundation. Here, one end of the beam landed above the foundation wall, while the other was directly over a column in the basement. To complete the load path, all I had to do was place squash blocks (double or triple studs cut to the depth of the floor joists) between the bottom of the subfloor and the main beam below. In other cases, I might have had to add new columns and footings to carry the newly concentrated loads.

3. USE THE BEAM DEPTH TO SIZE THE JACKS. Measure the depth of the beam stock, and mark that on the king studs. Measure up to the mark from the bottom plate to determine the height of the jacks.

4. INSTALL JACK STUDS AND STOP BLOCKS. Two jacks were required at each end, but only one was installed at first to ease setting the beam. Temporary blocks on the jacks guide the beam placement.

5. MEASURE THE BEAM LENGTH. Pull a tape between the king studs to determine the beam length. Deduct ¼ in. from that number so the beam members don't bind while being installed.

1. INSTALL KINGS AND PLATES. King studs tie the beam ends to the existing framing. Cut a new bottom plate long so that fasteners don't split it, screwing it to the framing below where the king and jack studs will go. Cut the plate flush to the jack studs later.

2. MARK THE BEAM LOCATION. To keep the beam straight, snap a chalkline on the joists between the edges of the king studs for a guide.

6. SLIP THE PLIES INTO PLACE. With the top leaning in, place both ends of the first ply at once onto the jack studs. A few sledgehammer taps along the bottom face stand the ply up.

7. INSTALL THE REMAINING PLIES LIKE THE FIRST. Nails can be used to join the plies, but structural screws set with an impact driver are better at drawing them into full contact with one another. Follow the designer's fastening schedule.

8. FASTEN TO THE JOISTS. Join each joist to the beam with a 3½-in. #10 multi-purpose screw driven at an angle. In some circumstances, framing hardware is required to resist seismic or uplift loads.

Use the Right Hardware

In combination with an impact driver, structural screws by manufacturers such as FastenMaster, GRK, Screw Products, and Simpson Strong-Tie are increasingly used in place of nails and lag bolts. Although they're more expensive than those options, structural screws have some advantages. The GRK RSS screws used here require no pilot holes to minimize wood splitting, and they are configured to draw layers together as they are driven. Although multipurpose screws are not as strong as structural screws, they are useful for toe-screwed connections and temporary assemblies. In areas where seismic and wind-uplift forces are big concerns, specific hardware such as hurricane ties are required to connect the beam to the rest of the framing.

Multipurpose screw   Structural screw

9. A WIDE OPENING. With the second jack studs placed, the bottom plates trimmed, the squash blocks placed below, and the temporary wall removed, the new beam is ready for drywall.

Hurricane tie

Continued →

A Hammer Has More Than One Lever Point

Pulling Stubborn Nails

By John Ross

My second job in construction—after I got through scraping a big stack of foundation formboards—was to remove the nails from a pile of salvaged 2×4s. It didn't take long for me to discover how easy it is to break a wooden-handled hammer while pulling nails. At the time, I didn't own two hammers, but my boss did. Before he would let me borrow one of his hammers, he taught me a few tricks.

In its nail-pulling function, a hammer works like a lever. I learned that reducing the distance from the nail head to the fulcrum, or pivot point, reduces stress on the hammer. You can do this in a couple of ways just by changing the hammer's position. Also, a couple of common tools, such as a cat's paw and a pair of end-cutting nippers, make nail-pulling easier.

For pulling finish or siding nails, I like to have a flat bar handy. I can put it under the hammer or nippers and avoid denting the wood.

If you spend any time pulling nails, you'll quickly realize that the rough-textured surface on galvanized nails makes them much harder to pull out. They're also more likely to bend or break. For these reasons, I use galvanized nails only when I am absolutely sure I won't have to remove them.

PULLING STRAIGHT BACK IS THE HARDEST WAY. With a straight-clawed framing hammer, the fulcrum quickly moves to the front of the hammer, the point farthest from the nail. This is the least-preferred method for removing tough nails. It requires the most effort and puts the most stress on the hammer handle. Placing a block under the head of the hammer will help. It reduces the fulcrum's distance to the nail and makes it easier to pull out the nail.

LEVERING TO THE SIDE IS EASIER. Using the side of the hammer's claw as the fulcrum provides the most leverage. Unfortunately, the nail will be removed a correspondingly short distance. By re-engaging the nail and levering the hammer back and forth, you can pull out the nail in increments.

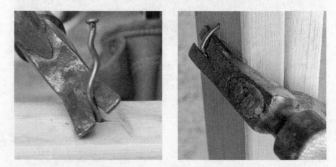

ONE TURN WILL WORK. Instead of rocking back and forth, the hammer can be levered in one direction. If the hammer handle can pass by the edge of the wood, as shown at left, the nail can be twisted out with one motion.

Other Tools Make Pulling Nails Easier

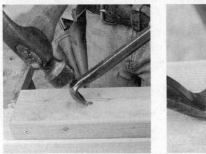

A CAT'S PAW GRABS AN EMBEDDED NAIL. The hook of a cat's paw is designed to be driven under the head of a nail flush with the surface. The tight curve on a cat's paw provides plenty of pulling force as you push the handle.

A HAMMER PROVIDES MORE TRAVEL. One pull with a cat's paw typically won't free a nail. By slipping a hammer under the cat's paw, the travel will be enough to clear the nail.

Lighter Puller

A hammer and a cat's paw make up a significant chunk of my tool bag's heft. Luckily, Stiletto Tools (www.stiletto.com) has found a way for me to shed some weight without shedding tools.

Besides their famously light hammers, Stiletto has introduced a claw bar (model TICLW12) that tips the scale at just over 8 oz., about half the weight of the one I usually carry. This lighter titanium tool is pound for pound much stronger than steel. It has an engineered webbed handle and sharp pry tongs.

The cool feature on this claw bar is its Dimpler, located on the side of the head. When positioned over a nail head and struck with a hammer, it crushes the wood fibers and allows the pry tongs to grab the nail easily. The Dimpler lets me remove an embedded nail without digging into the wood. The only drawback is that the lighter weight and convenience of this claw bar don't come cheap.

Nippers Take Care of Finish Nails

PULLING NAILS THROUGH THE BACK SAVES THE SURFACE. The smaller head of a finish nail allows it to be pulled through the back of a board with a pair of end-cutting nippers. This prevents the "show" side of the molding from being damaged.

A FLAT BAR PROTECTS THE TRIM. If the nail has to be removed from the front, put a flat bar under the nippers or hammer. The pressure from the nippers then is spread over a larger area, minimizing the chances of denting the wood.

Continued →

Baseboard Done Better

By Gary M. Katz

Carpenters new to finish work often cut their teeth on baseboard, and for good reason. Baseboard has many of the basic joints that form the foundation for trim carpentry. Over the years, I've shown a lot of carpenters better ways to run baseboard. Whether you're a veteran or new to the task, I'll share some tips that will improve both the speed and the quality of your trim work.

Measure Once, Measure Precisely

The first key to installing any trim, especially baseboard, is recording accurate measurements on a cutlist (sidebar, right). After years of practice, I've learned how to read a measurement when the tape is bent into a corner. But there are several other ways to measure precisely (sidebar opposite). One method is with a measuring block. For the block, cut a piece of baseboard to an exact length that's easy to remember and add (4 in. is the length I normally use). Stick the block at one end of a run, measure to it, and add the length of the block.

For measuring to the eased edge of casing, simply lay the block

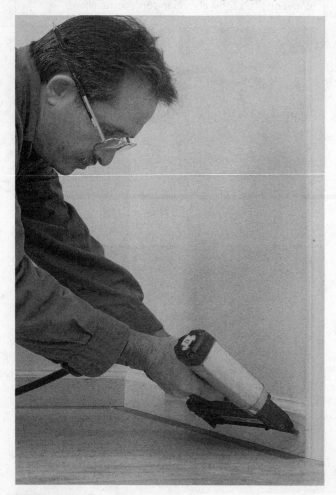

flat and take a precise measurement to the crisp edge of the block. The same strategy works for an outside corner, but make sure to check the angle with a protractor to ensure that the cuts will leave you with a tight joint.

My rules for measuring change slightly depending on the length of the piece. For pieces longer than 6 ft., add about ⅛ in. so that you can spring the piece into place for a tight fit. For pieces shorter than 6 in., subtract a little so that the piece slips in easily between the casing and the corner. For everything else, measure precisely to the nearest ¹⁄₃₂ in.

Cutting Corners Made Easy

Once you've recorded all your measurements on a cutlist, it's

The Cutlist Shorthand Shortcut

Whether it's printed on paper or on a scrap piece of wood, an accurate cutlist is the work order you take to your chopsaw. Start at a door and work around the room counterclockwise, recording the measurement for each piece and the type of joint for each end. If possible, keep most of the copes on your right side for easier right-handed cutting.

B = butt joint
C = cope
OC = outside corner

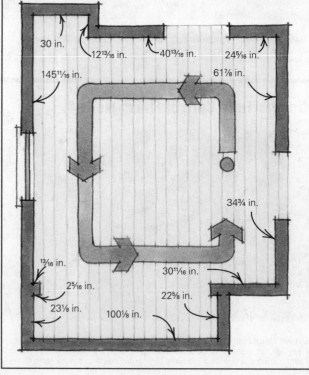

30 in.
12¹³⁄₁₆ in.
40¹³⁄₁₆ in.
24⁵⁄₁₆ in.
145¹¹⁄₁₆ in.
61⅞ in.
34¾ in.
¹³⁄₁₆ in.
2⁵⁄₁₆ in.
23⅛ in.
100⅛ in.
30¹¹⁄₁₆ in.
22⅝ in.

Measure Each Length Precisely

Accurate measurements translate to tightly fitting trim. If you're not comfortable reading a tape measure bent into a corner, the techniques shown here yield exact dimensions.

A Block Eliminates Guesswork

A measuring block makes it easy to get exact inside-corner measurements. Measure to the mark left by the block, then add 4 in.

 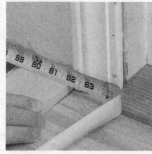

Eased edges of casing can be tough to measure to, so lay a block flat and measure to the edge.

Accurate Angles and Edges

The rounded edge of drywall corner bead can make measuring an outside corner difficult, so a block works well.

Outside corners aren't always 90°, so be sure to check the angle of the corner with a protractor.

High-Tech Measuring Option

Whenever I measure long lengths, I grab my laser measuring tool instead of a tape. Despite being bulky and heavy, this highly accurate tool is perfect for measuring into tight corners, and it works great for other trim details as well.

Laser Distance Measuring Tool

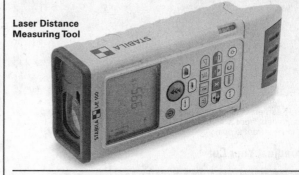

time to head for the miter saw, which, by the way, should never be on the floor. Working on a stand with support for the work on each side of the saw is more efficient and more accurate. Many commercial stands have built-in wings, or you can go for a homemade version (*Fine Homebuilding* #114). Either way, the wings should support the work so that it stays flat on the saw.

I also attach a straight, flat auxiliary fence to the saw. This added fence supports the trim as it's being cut and serves as a measuring aid, too. Make the auxiliary fence the maximum height your saw will cut, or at least as tall as the trim you're cutting and slightly longer than the fence on the saw.

You made the cutlist so that you don't have to visualize the joints as you cut them. Now it's important to teach your-self which way to swing the head of the saw to make a cut for a corner.

Continued ➔

Measure and Cut the Stock

The next step in precise trim installation is transferring the numbers from the cutlist to the stock. An auxiliary fence on the chopsaw comes in handy at this stage.

Measure for Outside Corners

For outside corners, the short point of the miter is always against the fence (photo above left). After making the miter cut, align the short point with the end of the saw fence, then hook your tape on the fence to take the measurement. Spring-clamp longer boards to the saw fence before measuring (photo above right).

Measure for Inside Corners

For inside corners, the long point is always against the fence. When pulling a measurement from a square cut or an inside corner, lay the piece flat to keep the tape from slipping off the end.

Microadjust Your Cut

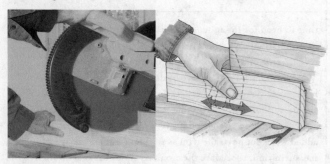

Guide the cuts accurately by placing your fingers against the fence and your thumb on the face of the board. Creep up on the exact cut by making incremental adjustments with your thumb.

Instead of visualizing the joint or the location of the baseboard, you can memorize two simple rules: For inside corners, the long point is always against the wall and the fence; and for outside corners, the short point is always against the wall and the fence. Armed with these two rules and the cutlist, you're ready to start cutting.

The Fence Helps with Measuring

Measuring from the butt end of a board is easy. After making a square cut, lay the board flat on the saw table, and hook the tape on the end. Laying the board flat minimizes the chance that the end of the tape will slip off.

Measuring for an inside-corner cut is also simple. Make the 45° mitered cut for the coped end first. Again lay the board flat and face down, and this time, hook your tape measure on the long point of the cut.

For measuring outside-corner cuts, I put the auxiliary fence to use. Instead of "burning an inch" (measuring from the 1-in. mark), align the short point of the cut with the end of the saw fence, and pull the measurement from the edge of the fence. I spring-clamp longer pieces to the fence before measuring, or I flush the short point with the end of the extension wing, then hook my tape on the extension wing to pull the measurement.

I always use a sharp $2^5/10$ pencil to mark measurements. The harder lead keeps the pencil sharper longer, and crisp, clean lines are essential for accurate cutting.

Controlled Cuts

You're finally ready to cut. Just align the blade on the line and cut away, right? Wrong! It's imperative that the blade cut exactly at the line, and absolute control of the material and saw is the only way to ensure an accurate cut.

To control the material, keep your free hand locked behind the auxiliary saw fence, with your thumb over the material. Begin the cut with the measurement mark 1/8 in. or so away from the blade. Now raise the blade, and using your thumb as a micro-adjuster, slide the material over slightly and let the blade enter the material again. Repeat the process until the blade is exactly at the line, and only then cut through the piece.

A Jigsaw Makes the Best Copes

Here's where I generate all those nasty letters to the editor: Coped corners are faster and more accurate than miters (45° angle cuts on both pieces). For a crisp joint line, miters have to line up exactly in a corner. If the coped piece is off plumb slightly or not quite square to its neighbor, it's harder to detect. The extra couple of minutes needed to cope more than makes up for the fussing that most miters require for a good-looking fit.

I still use a coping saw if I'm installing only a piece or two. The key thing you have to remember when using a coping saw is to keep the sawblade moving. Don't try to cut quickly, and don't push too hard on the blade. Instead, move the saw at a comfortable

Install the Pieces in Order

Spread the cut pieces around the room close to where they will be going. Then work around the room in roughly the same order that you took the measurements. For inside corners, always install the square-cut or butt-end corner pieces first.

Distribute the Cut Pieces

Place the lengths of baseboard around the room near where they are going to be installed.

Fitting Small Corner Pieces

Small pieces go in first and are held in place by adjacent pieces.

Glue Up an Outside Corner

For outside corners, spread glue evenly along both mating faces. Assemble the joint with 23-ga. pin nails.

Fitting an Inside Corner

To fit a coped corner, line up a utility knife along the edge of the miter cut (photo above left), and notch the butt end slightly for the top of the miter (photo above right). For tight-fitting pieces, tap the coped piece with a hammer and a block until it slips into place.

---

machinelike rate that you can maintain throughout the entire cut.

I've recently switched to using a jigsaw for copes, but it's equipped with a Collins Coping Foot (www.collinstool.com). The coping foot replaces the base, or table, of a jigsaw, and its shape allows you to follow the profile of a molding from the back side of the material while keeping the saw base in contact with the material.

Be sure to use the right blade with the jigsaw. Collins recommends a Bosch 244D blade (www.boschtools.com). With only 6 teeth per inch and deep gullets, the blade cuts aggressively and clears the kerf of waste quickly. The teeth also have a wide set, so the blade cuts a wide kerf, which allows you to scroll-cut almost any profile. The wide set of the teeth means you also can remove material with the side of the blade to tune the cope.

The step-by-step process of coping with a jigsaw is much better illustrated visually (sidebar p. 87). In simplest terms,

Continued →

Tips for Problem Spots

Keeping baseboard straight will improve the look of a crooked wall or an out-of-square corner. When drywall is damaged or missing, keeping the board plumb can be tough.

Shim Long Boards

Longer boards spring into place for tight joints (photo above left). Check them with a string, and shim them straight, if necessary (photo above right).

Shim Corner Returns

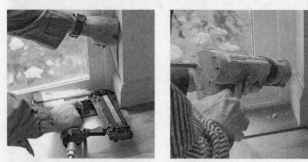

Shim corner returns square (photo left), and caulk the gap along the top (photo above).

Missing Drywall in Corners

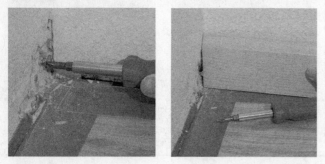

Where the drywall is missing, insert a drywall screw to keep the base plumb in the corner (photo left). Adjust the screw until it's even with the wall (photo right).

secure the board, and begin the cope with a series of relief cuts at critical points on the profile. For the colonial baseboard pictured here, I made two cuts. I first cut the sliver that forms the miter at the top of the intersecting pieces—the one that always breaks off before you can get the board nailed in. (I don't make those little slivers wafer thin anymore. Instead, I leave them at least ⅛ in. thick, and then I mortise the intersecting piece of baseboard to accept the overlapping sliver, as you'll see in the next section).

The second cut is to the point where the plinth, or the flat section of the baseboard, meets the curved profile. After making the relief cuts, it's just a matter of following the profile with the saw held at a slight angle to create a back bevel.

Installation Is the Easy Part

After you've run through your list, and cut and coped every piece, spread the pieces around the room close to where they're going. I generally install baseboard in the same order that I measured and cut it, except that I insert any small pieces (up to about 2 in. wide) first, such as between casing and a corner. Don't try to nail these small pieces, or they'll split. Instead, let the intersecting board hold them in place.

For this type of baseboard, which is only 3½ in. tall, don't bother trying to locate the studs. The wall plate is usually high enough for me to hit with 2½-in. finish nails. For those areas where I need to nail higher, I simply find a stud with a magnet.

In a coped corner, always install the butt end piece first. Then slip in the coped piece. Pressing the coped piece tightly to the wall, plunge the blade of a utility knife into the top of the butt end using the edge of the miter cut as a guide. Remove the coped piece, and cut a notch deep enough to accept the overlapping sliver on the coped end.

Now the coped piece can go in permanently. If your copes are accurate, the fit will be tight. Tap the butt end of the coped piece with a block and hammer until the two pieces marry tightly in the corner and the butt end of the coped piece slips into position.

For outside corners, always test-fit the pieces before nailing them in. When you're satisfied with the joint, apply glue to the mating surfaces of both pieces. Wipe off the excess glue, taking care not to get glue on the baseboard's finished face. The glue joins the two pieces and also seals the ends of the boards. For stain-grade installations, sealing keeps the ends from absorbing more stain and becoming darker than the rest of the board. I preassemble outside-corner joints using a 23-ga. pin nailer that leaves almost invisible nail holes. Then I nail the whole assembly into place.

Keep Baseboard Straight When the Walls Aren't

As you can see from my cutlist, I sometimes like to cope both ends of longer pieces. With the little bit of extra length I give them, they spring into place with tight pressure-fit joints at both ends.

Most carpenters I know just nail the board tight to the wall. If there are any bows or bellies in the wall, though, making a piece of trim conform to them only accents the flaws. It's a good idea to

Coping with a Jigsaw

An odd-looking jigsaw base called the Collins Coping Foot ❶ allows you to cope quickly and accurately. Be sure to use an aggressive blade (6 tpi) with a wide set. Pull the saw toward you to make a relief cut at the top of the miter, ❷ leaving the sliver big enough so that it doesn't break off easily. The next relief cut ❸ is where the profile begins. Keeping the saw at an angle, follow the top profile ❹. Switching to a push stroke, cut the flat part of the profile, ❺ or the plinth.

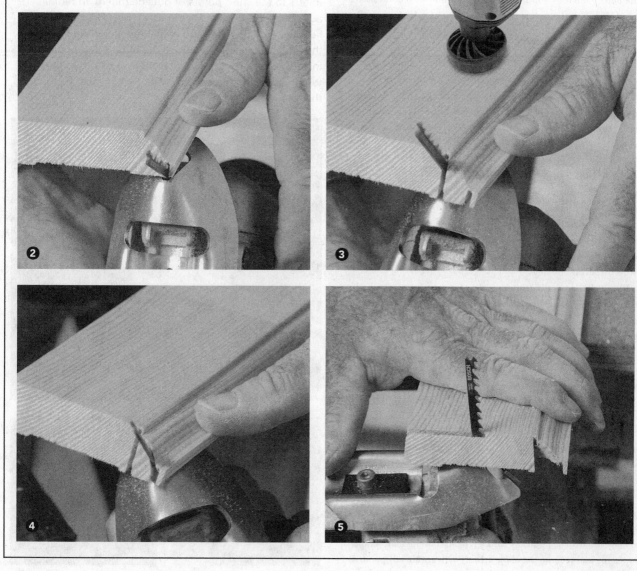

check long pieces with a string before nailing them in. Shim the baseboard so that it looks straight to the eye, then caulk any gaps between the top and the wall. The straight baseboard will make a crooked wall look straighter.

Preassemble all short sections, such as around a column, around an end wall, or for a drywall return at a door opening. Again, if the two sides aren't square to each other, installing an out-of-square joint just makes the return look worse. Instead, make the joint square, shim the short piece, and caulk the top edge.

Finally, in areas where drywall is broken or missing, insert a drywall screw to keep the baseboard straight and plumb. Simply adjust the screw until the head is flush with the surrounding drywall. The screw head backs up the base to keep the joint looking good while the baseboard hides the drywall defect.

Flawless Two-Piece Baseboard

By Nick Schiffer

In the world of building, finish carpentry is the second-to-last step before the homeowners move in—or in the case of a remodel like this one, before they reoccupy the room. My job is to make sure that the framers, drywall installers, and flooring guys who came before me look good, and that the painter who comes after me isn't left with the task of hiding sloppy joints, excessive nail holes, and oversize gaps.

Although many houses are trimmed with a one-piece, shaped baseboard that mimics the look of a traditional two-piece installation—a product known as speedbase—I still prefer the real deal: flat stock topped with a separate cap molding. This two-piece installation takes a bit longer, but it provides more leeway for finesse when it comes to hiding waves in walls and keeping joints tight at corners, even if they aren't square.

Clear the Room and Prep the Area

My process for installing baseboard on remodel jobs is essentially the same as it is in new construction. The only notable exceptions are that remodels typically include a bit more job-site protection, may require that I set up my saw outside or in a garage if the house is occupied, and likely involve removing the existing baseboard before installing the new.

Ideally, I remove all furniture and set up my miter saw and other tools right in the room that I'm working in. At the least, I move all the furniture to the center of the room and cover it with a drop cloth, then I find a nearby spot to set up shop for cutting.

I protect the floor of the room with kraft paper—holding it off the wall by a few inches so that it won't interfere with the baseboard—and seal doorways with plastic sheeting. With the room prepped, I remove any existing baseboard with a thin flat bar and a hammer.

Unless the baseboard is being saved, my priority is to keep the drywall intact. If the baseboard splits or breaks in half, I'm not concerned, but holes made in the wall that won't be covered by the new trim mean extra work. If the baseboard comes off in long lengths, I cut it into shorter sections on the miter saw so it can be loaded into a barrel alongside broken pieces and shorter remnants for carrying to the Dumpster.

To eliminate the chance of the new baseboard being hung up by old nails and debris, I pull any nails left behind in the wall, scrape away caulk, and vacuum the whole area. If walls are already painted, I mark stud locations with pieces of painter's tape or with pencil marks on the paper that covers the flooring. If the walls will be painted after my installation, I mark the studs just above where the new baseboard will go.

First Comes the Flat Stock

For paint-grade jobs like this one, I use primed finger-jointed pine for the flat stock. Once I've cut pieces and positioned them

Two-Piece Baseboard Flat Stock

Cuts Must Be Accurate

If you want to make efficient use of your accurate measurements, then your cuts have to be accurate, too. My measurements are of the actual walls, which means the lengths on my cutlist are from the long points of inside miters to the short points of outside miters. To remain accurate, I mark my stock the same way. On this piece, I cut the outside miter and measured along the face of the stock to mark the inside of the miter's short point. For inside corners, I typically miter the two pieces of flat stock together, setting the saw to make a 44.5° miter to ensure that the visible seam is tight.

Keep Flat-Stock Joints Tight, Flush, and Tidy

My priorities when installing flat stock are making tight joints and getting a good fit between trim and flooring. This means scribing where necessary and sometimes adjusting the angle of a miter or marking a piece in place for a recut. Doing so yields tight joints that come together with no space or need for filler. I cut long pieces just a hair beyond the mark and then spring them into place. For outside corners, I focus first on the miter, holding nails back from the nearest studs until the miter has been glued and clamped. (I use Collins miter clamps.) Once the glue sets, I tack the corner to the studs and remove the clamps.

Scribing for a Tailored Fit

In minor cases, a pencil and a shim are all you need to trace the contours of the floor onto the piece of stock. From there, you can follow the scribed line, removing most of the waste on a tablesaw and fine-tuning the scribe with a jigsaw, a block plane, and/or a sander. Severe waves in the floor may require using wider flat stock so that the top edge of the baseboard remains at a constant height while the bottom edge follows the humps and dips in the floor.

Scribing Dips

For dips in the floor, set the extrawide stock in position so that it spans the entire depression in the floor. Set your scribes to the desired finished height at the highest point of the floor, and then mark the entire piece.

Scribing Humps

If there is a hump in the floor, shim up both ends of the baseboard to get it level, again setting scribes to the desired finished height.

Continued ➔

Reinforced Splices

The traditional approach to making splices is to create a scarf joint (cutting the end of each piece on an angle), which ensures the largest glue surface possible. I prefer to handle splices with butt joints, though, which allows me to cut the trim pieces slightly long and spring them into place without worrying about one piece slipping past the other and creating an open joint. Normally a butt joint wouldn't be as strong as a scarf joint, because the end grain of wood doesn't glue together as strongly as the face grain, but I reinforce butt joints with a pair of tenons set into slots cut with a Festool Domino tool.

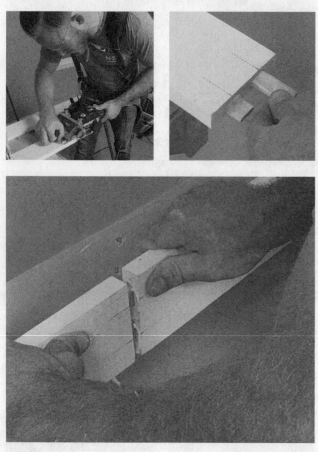

Two-Piece Baseboard Cap Stock

The Cap Hides the Flaws

The more flexible cap molding can conform to wavy walls and hide gaps behind the less flexible flat stock. But if the walls are severely wavy or have out-of-square corners, I switch to an 18-ga. brad nailer to fasten the cap molding to the flat stock below rather than into the wall. In these cases, caulk hides the gap between cap and wall.

on the floor where they will be installed, I look for places that will require excessive scribing along the bottom edge of the baseboard where it meets the floor. If the installation will be finished off with shoe molding, then scribing isn't usually necessary, but shoe molding isn't used much in my region.

All the flat stock is fastened with a pair of 2½-in.-long 15-ga. finish nails into each stud, and the mating mitered pieces of both inside and outside corners are coated with wood glue before being fitted together. I assemble most corners right in place, and I like to leave the first piece loose at least one stud back from the corner until the second piece has been fitted and clamped and the glue has dried.

Small jogs and runs of trim with outside corners are often easier to fasten together on the workbench with glue and miter clamps and then to drop into place as one piece.

For long walls, it's necessary to splice together two pieces of stock with either a traditional scarf joint or a reinforced butt joint.

Cap Molding Follows Suit

The key to a quick cap-molding installation is to keep updating the cutlist as the flat stock is installed. If a piece of flat stock is cut to the measured length and ends up being a bit too long or an angle needs to be adjusted, I erase the original measurement on

Clean Copes by Hand

Because the cap is more visible than the flat stock it covers, inside corners are best handled by coping one piece of cap molding to fit against the other. This technique allows for slight deviations from square without tweaking the angle of the miter, and the seam will stay tight throughout the year, even if the cap expands or contracts with changes in seasonal humidity. There are many ways to cope a joint, but I learned to do it by hand. After cutting the piece to a 45° angle, I remove the waste with a coping saw held at a slight negative angle. I work my way from both sides of the end grain toward the center, then do a final cleanup with 180-grit sandpaper to leave a cleanly contoured profile.

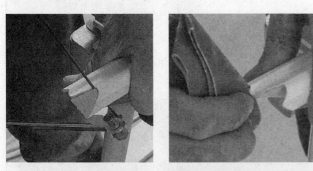

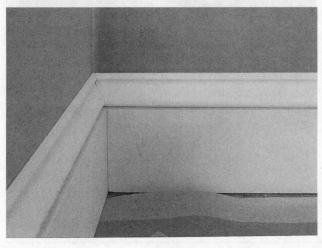

the cutlist and write in the updated measurement so that the cap molding can be cut right on the first try.

Unlike the miter joints on the inside corners of the flat stock, I prefer coped joints at inside corners of the cap stock, which ensures that the joints will fit tight through seasons of expansion and contraction. At this point, I map out which pieces will require a cope and on which end, adding that information to the cutlist as well.

In most cases, I fasten the cap tight to the wall using 2½-in. 15-ga. trim nails, always placing the nails in an area of the cap profile that will minimize hassle when the painter fills and sands the holes. The cap molding can follow the contours of the wall to a certain extent, concealing slight waves and gaps that the thicker, flat stock can't conform to, but I don't blindly follow contours of badly waved walls. If inside or outside corners are clearly out of whack or a long run has a big dip, floating the cap away from the wall is often less noticeable than trying to follow it snugly. In these cases, I switch to an 18-ga. brad nailer to fasten the cap molding to the flat stock below rather than into the wall studs, and then I fill the gap between cap and wall with caulk.

Most cap moldings are too small to be bored out easily with a Festool Domino tool, so rather than relying on butt joints and tenons for splices, I go with the traditional scarf joint. I cut the joint as steep as my miter saw allows to provide as much face grain as possible for the glue joint, but I avoid cutting these pieces overly long, as springing them into place often leads to a misaligned joint.

Clean Returns

Miter returns are a clean way to terminate the cap molding in situations where the end of the run of trim will be visible. These tiny returns are prone to splitting when nailed, so I assemble the pieces with fast-setting CA glue, such as 2P-10 (fastcap.com), and then install them as one unit.

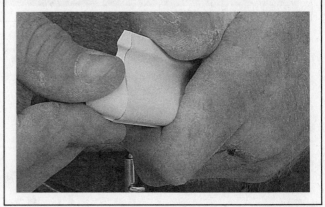

Continued →

Measure and Make a Cutlist

The installation starts with careful measurements and a detailed cutlist, which improves accuracy and reduces trips back and forth to the saw. For consistency, I always start at a doorway and work clockwise.

I make my cutlists with three columns. The first column is for length measurements, which I take along each wall at floor level. The next two columns are to indicate the type of cut needed on each end of every piece of stock.

I check all inside and outside corners with an angle-finder—an indispensible finish-carpentry tool—to determine if off-angle joints are necessary. I mark conventional inside and outside miters (90° angle) with the length and type of miter necessary on each end. OR indicates an outside miter on the right end of the piece of stock, OL indicates an outside miter on the left end, and IR and IL are for inside-right and inside-left miters. If I encounter an out-of-square corner (greater or less than 90°), then I write the adjusted angle that will be needed.

Inside Crown Corners

By Tucker Windover

I can still remember my first day on a finish-carpentry crew. I spent most of my time keeping one eye on the lead carpenter, trying to pick up as many new tricks as I could. I watched him cope and fit a couple of pieces of crown molding. His movements were fluid. His process looked easy. But I didn't quite understand why we had to complicate a joint that could be made with two simple miters. I asked if it would be OK to miter the corners instead of coping them, and the lead said, "Go for it—if you can make it look right and convince me that it will stay that way." So I attempted to do it the easy way, or what I thought would be the easy way. In truth, I didn't make it through a single room before turning to a coping saw.

I've learned a lot since then, and in my opinion, a coped joint is preferable to a miter in several ways. Due to wood movement, miters tend to open at the short point or the long point. A coped corner stays tight as each piece of trim expands and contracts in sync. A coped joint also fits well when installed in a room with minor imperfections, such as one with corners that are out of square or ceilings and walls that are less than straight, level, and plumb. The smallest bump of joint compound can throw a mitered corner out of proper alignment.

A coped joint is also more adjustable. If there is a gap in the joint, you often need only to pry the other end of the trim to

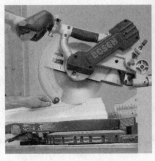

STEP 2 Create a stop that replicates the ceiling position. The distance between the stop and the miter saw's fence should match the ceiling projection. Check the stop location with the marking jig. This setup guarantees that the molding is cut in the same position as it will be installed.

STEP 3 Cut a 45° miter, and measure for length. Place the top edge of the molding down against the stop, and the bottom edge of the crown against the saw's fence. If coping to the left, the long point of the miter will be at the bottom edge of the crown (photo above). Make the miter. Then, using a measurement taken between the corners of the wall, measure from the long point of the miter to mark the trim's length.

Miter the Stock

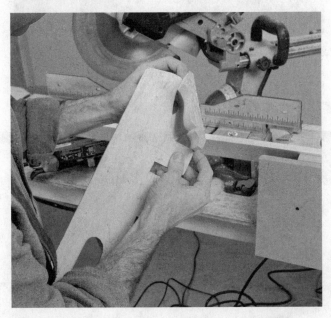

STEP 1 To start, make a marking jig. Label the top of a rectangular scrap of ½-in. plywood as ceiling and its right side as wall. Measure the molding's ceiling projection and its drop down the wall by nesting it in a framing square. Transfer these measurements to the piece of plywood, and cut between the points, removing the jig's corner. This jig will be used to ensure proper crown positioning throughout the cope and the installation.

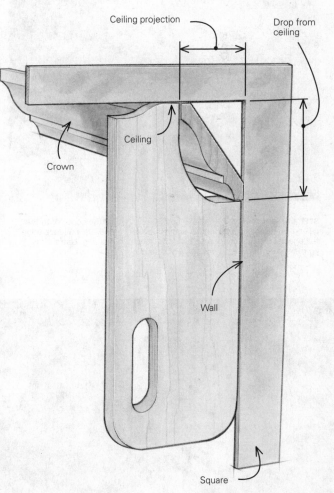

Ceiling projection

Drop from ceiling

Crown

Ceiling

Wall

Square

Continued →

squeeze the joint tight. Finally, the coped joint is much more forgiving. This makes it a faster joint to make because there is less fussing over the fit. If a piece of trim is cut slightly short, say by ⅛ in., the gap is covered by the subsequent piece of coped trim. When you're mitering a corner, any error in length will be revealed.

Still, the coped joint has limitations. Certain crown profiles can't be coped. In these instances, I create a hybrid joint by coping what's copable and mitering what's not. When working with medium-density fiberboard (MDF) trim, I miter the inside corners instead of coping them. MDF trim is more stable than wood, but when coped, its edges become too fragile. I miter crown when installing it on kitchen cabinets that I know to be straight, level, and square. Also, I find that when preassembling crown for a column or a fireplace mantel, mitering works best.

Some people believe that coping is difficult or time-consuming. I can assure you that with a little practice, coping becomes as easy and as fast as tying your shoes.

Cope the Cut

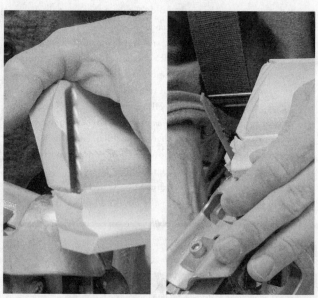

STEP 4 An auxiliary fence helps to secure the trim for the cope. With the ceiling-side edge of the trim flat against the fence and the wall-side edge flat against the stand, snug up a stop to keep it in position. Use the marking jig to be sure that the trim is seated correctly.

STEP 5 A jigsaw fitted with a coping foot (www.collinstool.com) and a Bosch T244D blade increases the speed of the cut. When used correctly, this setup provides a very precise, controlled cope. If the jigsaw doesn't suit you, there is nothing wrong with using a traditional coping saw. With either tool, make several relief cuts before following the profile of the molding. Hold the saw somewhat less than vertical to give the cope a slight back cut.

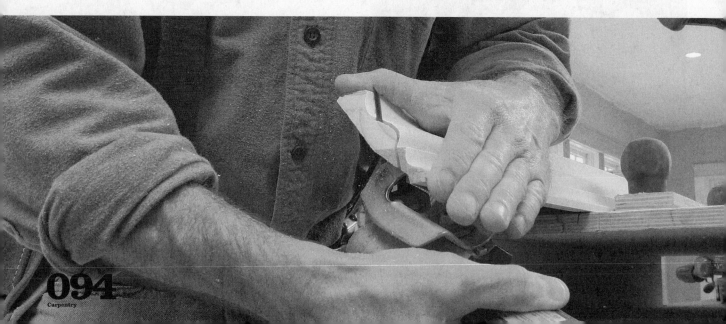

Test the Fit

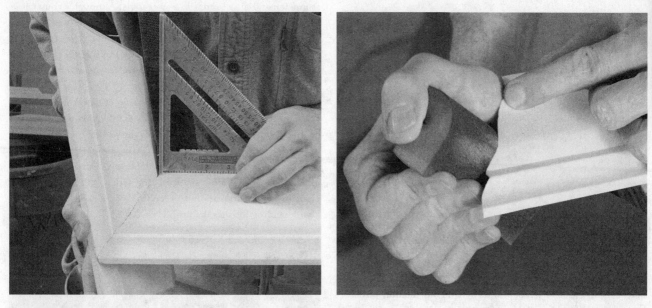

STEP 6 Use a scrap of the molding to test the accuracy of the cope. Whether the corner is less than or greater than 90°, the coped joint stays tight. If the joint isn't as tight as you'd like, fine-tune the cope with a rasp or a sanding sponge.

Install the Crown

STEP 7 Cut the trim to length with a 90° cut. This butt end is covered by the adjacent coped piece of trim. Cut pieces of trim more than 8 ft. ⅛ in. long. The compression helps to keep the corners tight over time. When installing the trim, don't nail within 2 ft. of each end until the joint fits the way you want it.

Going Against the Grain: I Miter

As a student of two old-school carpenters, I was taught to cope the inside corners of crown molding. I installed my crown that way for 15 years because it was the only way the old guys would allow it to be done. However, 20 years ago, fellow finish carpenter Craig Lawrence suggested to me that it was a lot easier and faster to miter inside corners. I was skeptical, but tried the approach and found that he was correct. Since then, I have mitered all my crown-molding corners with nary a complaint.

With the miter approach, you simply set up some stops, pull the trigger, and slice through the stock for a perfect cut every time. I even back-cut each piece a degree or so to accommodate out-of-square corners. If this is not done, the joint will open in front. I leave the ends of the first piece of crown loose until I have the second one up and in position. This allows the corner to be tweaked until it fits. I then glue the pieces together, which I have found helps to form a tight-fitting joint. Finally, I wipe the joint with caulk to blend the pieces together, using colored caulks for stained wood. My advice? Develop a system that works for you, but give miters a try.

Continued ➔

Reproducing Traditional Moldings

By Bill Rainford

Before the American Civil War, most, if not all, architectural moldings were made in a wide variety of profiles by hand with molding planes. In the postwar period, mills became mechanized but often maintained their own sets of profiles. Although there were long periods of overlap and regional variations, it wasn't until the early 20th century that standardization of molding profiles became the norm. Standard profiles are great, unless you do a fair amount of work on old houses.

When reproducing a molding profile for a historic property, you often have to make a choice between having molding knives made, removing that detail, or replacing the profile with what is available in your area. For short runs of molding, though, there is a way to get the best of both worlds.

Recently, I was asked to re-create some of the original moldings from the Alvah Kittredge House in Boston. Built in 1836, the house had fallen into disrepair, but it now is being restored by the nonprofit Historic Boston Inc. Using a few traditional molding planes, a rabbet plane, and a tablesaw, I'll use the example of reproducing one antique molding profile to show how many other trim profiles can be created from scratch.

Break Down the Profile

The first step in the reproduction process is analyzing the molding profile. You can take a cross-section diagram from the architect's plans, a historic plan book, or a catalog. A more immediate method, however, is to trace the profile onto a piece of heavy card stock or even thin sheet metal. (The profile is easier to handle and measure when it's two dimensional.) If I can't pull a piece of molding, I use a profile gauge.

Once I have the profile, I can figure the dimensions of the stock and mill as much as I need. In this case, I bought 5/4 clear white pine to match the original and milled it to a full inch thick and 8 in. wide. When choosing stock, I select the straightest grain, which makes planning easier.

Remove Stock in Stages

Once I've rendered the profile, I start to strategize how to remove as much material as I can with power tools. Although a router is handy for some profiles, a dado stack on the tablesaw was the most efficient stock remover for this particular profile.

With power equipment, it's always safest to stay a bit back from the lines and to finish with the rabbet or plow plane, rather than risk tearing out the stock.

The sequence of planes is a progression of defining areas. You establish guidelines, then use them to steer the next part of the profile. Before I make any cuts, I draw the profile on both ends of the stock. Next, I score a line with a cutting or marking gauge to identify major transitions. After the tablesaw, I use a succession of hand planes to remove stock, ending with a rabbet or block plane to ease the transition between the hollow and the round. Hand-sanding finishes the profile.

The Craftsman
Bill Rainford started out helping his father and grandfather with carpentry projects around the house. His childhood exposure to the trade grew into a lifetime love of woodworking. Bill went on to graduate from the North Bennet Street School's preservation-carpentry program. He has returned there to lead workshops in preservation and also teaches traditional building at Boston Architectural College. When not teaching or building, he can be found exploring historical sites with his wife.

Copy the Profile

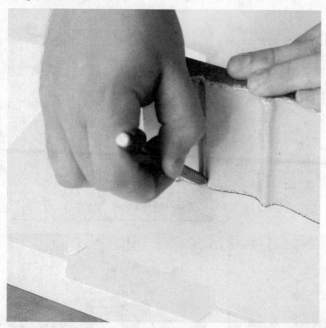

TAKE A SAMPLE. The most accurate method of copying a molding profile is to trace the profile's contour onto a piece of heavy paper. To minimize the hazards of working with materials that could be covered with lead paint, wear a respirator and gloves.

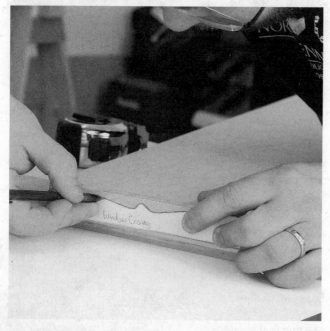

PLAN STOCK REMOVAL. Once the profile has been traced onto card stock, cut out the silhouette, and trace it onto the trim stock. It's an easy way to see where the most stock can be removed with power tools and where hand planes are most valuable.

Profile Gauge

Also known as a molding comb or contour gauge, this tool is a flat arrangement of thin teeth or pins pushed over a molding to capture its profile and transfer it to stock or paper. The first models available were made of steel, which tended to rust. Still available from manufacturers such as Johnson or General, the better models are made from stainless steel or plastic. I use plastic models available in 5½-in., 12-in., and 18-in. lengths.

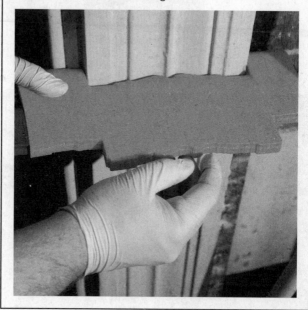

Continued ➜

Shape the Profile in Stages

Establish the Field

Define the Cuts with One Pass.
To reduce tearout and to delineate the work area clearly, use a marking gauge to incise a line on both sides of the profile.

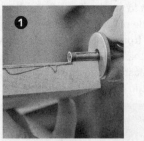

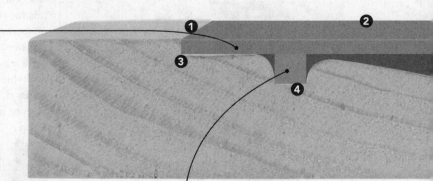

Plow the Grooves

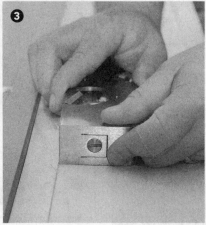

Remove the Waste Fast.
After setting up a ¾-in.-wide dado stack, raise the blades to the correct height, and remove the excess stock in several passes, resetting the fence position at each pass.

Clean Up the Bearing Surface.
Use the shoulder plane to smooth the dadoed area. Then turn it on its side, and square up the perimeter edges.

Define the Outer Edge.
With the blade set to the required depth and the fence to the correct width, run a narrow plow plane along both edges.

In a Perfect World, One Machine Would Do It All

For 20 ft. of trim, I've found that using molding planes is nearly as fast as a machine. The router bits of their day, molding planes were created to cut one profile, and like router bits, there's a fair number to choose from. For anyone who wants to start working with these traditional planes, I recommend the following four.

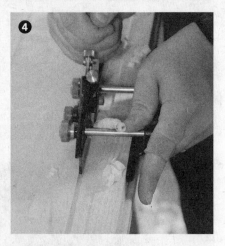

Shoulder Plane This type of metal rabbet plane is used to square up dadoes and tenons.

Narrow Plow Plane A narrow cutter and adjustable fence make this tool ideal for dadoes and grooves.

Snipe's Bill Plane This tool is used to cut in a narrow quirk or to start a fillet that could be followed up with a wider rabbet plane.

Hollows and Rounds These planes are made to be used in matched pairs. It's best to get pairs that were made by the same maker, as the radii vary a bit from maker to maker.

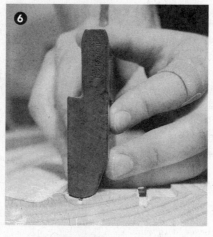

Shape the Curves

Define the Inner Lines.
Set a fence on the stock, and make passes with a snipe's bill plane to the depth of the profile.

Rounds Cut Hollows.
With the inner groove as a guide, use the round plane to cut the dip on each side of the center rib.

Hollows Cut Rounds.
Working from the outer groove, create the rounded portion of the profile with the hollow plane.

Sticking Board

Before I start to plane stock for moldings, I set up a sticking board, which is a length of ¾-in. plywood a little wider and longer than the stock I'll be planing. I screw a full-length MDF fence to one side and locate four brass threaded inserts in one end of the board. Machine screws threaded into the inserts serve as stops and can be raised or lowered, depending on the thickness of the stock.

Continued →

Tame Tricky Transitions

By Tucker Windover

Often, a builder or a homeowner hires an architect or designer to provide plans that include only enough detail to obtain a permit, which means that a lot of the design is left to work out in the field. Framers tend to focus on the bones and the structure, and it's not until the trim carpenter is on the job that the final details are resolved.

There might be a window installed close to the ceiling, and no one notices that the casing almost touches the ceiling until the trim guy tries to install the crown molding. Or the walk-in shower is framed, and no one has considered how the tile, the baseboard, and the curb to the shower will tie together. Another tricky spot is where a window is set close to an entry door—so close that they cannot be trimmed separately, meaning the trim carpenter has to make sense out of trimming them as a single unit.

Trim carpentry is the icing on the cake, and everything shows. Every house has some funky corner or door opening where I just stop and ask, "How are we going to trim this out?" It's the trim carpenter's job to resolve those challenges. What I mostly want to accomplish in these situations is a resolution that draws the least amount of attention to the problem. I usually can accomplish this either by showing a clear termination point or by maintaining a clean, continuous line. These kinds of problems show up at the staircase in almost every house.

Maintain Continuous Lines

Running trim refers to those elements such as baseboard, chair rail, or crown that travel around a room. Whenever I run trim, I try to maintain a continuous flow of lines and to avoid choppy alignments that seem arbitrary or illogical.

For example, in most situations, a chair rail should be aligned with the window stools. Unless there's a major separation between the two (as in the high paneling of the Arts and Crafts style), a slight discrepancy looks like the designer or installer didn't care.

One example I commonly face is when the crown molding intersects with a roofline or the underside of a stairwell. To get around this, I build a soffit onto the angled ceiling that allows the crown to run around the room without changing its relation to the wall.

The soffit is a piece of 1x stock beveled on one edge to match the angle of the ceiling. Its width is determined by the angles of the ceiling and the crown. It has to be wide enough so that the crown can turn the corner and still maintain its spring angle. I use a plywood gauge that mimics the specific crown angle to set the soffit's location. That location also should include a ¼-in. reveal at the bottom of the crown. After snapping a reference chalkline, I nail the soffit to the ceiling, then continue the crown installation across the soffit.

Continuous Crown

A line of crown molding can pass across a change in angle (such as at the top of the stairs) via a soffit. Built onto the angled wall, the soffit's width should be roughly equal to the widest part of the angle of the crown.

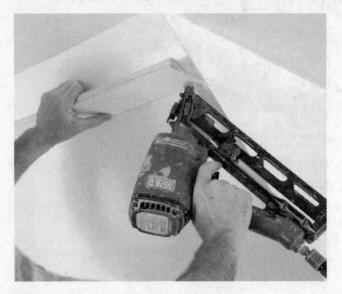

Snap lines, and install the soffit.
Chalklines determine the lower position of the crown. The plywood soffit, beveled to the wall's angle, must be wide enough to create a surface perpendicular to the ceiling.

Mark the ¼-in. reveal on the plywood soffit

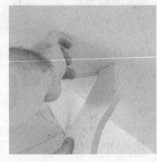

Mark the top of the crown from the wall

Tool of the Trade.
Take a 2-in.-long slice from the intended crown molding, and use it to trace the desired spring angle onto a 12-in. by 6-in. piece of MDF or plywood. Cut out the basic angle of the crown, then remove enough of the rest of the blank so that it's easy to hold with one hand. Place this spring gauge against the ceiling to mark the crown's position and to check the ¼-in. reveal on the plywood soffit.

Mark the ¼-in. reveal on the plywood soffit

Continuous Cap Ties the Stringer to the Baseboard

Rather than terminate the two pieces of base cap at the intersection of the stringer and base, bisect the angle and miter them together to create a continuous line.

Mark lines on the wall.
Use a scrap piece to establish the point where the two caps intersect. Hold the first piece in place, transfer the intersection and end points onto the stock, and cut the miter.

Check the cut with scrap.
Position the mitered upper cap, and check to see that the miter's short point intersects the lower line. Repeat the process with the lower cap.

Fine-tune the fit.
With both scrap miters in place, note any adjustments that are needed, cut the cap stock to length, and miter the ends.

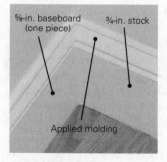

⅝-in. baseboard (one piece)

¾-in. stock

Applied molding

Don't make the transition obvious.
When ⅝-in.-thick baseboard is used throughout a house, it isn't compatible with the heavier stringer stock used for stairs. The easiest solution is to use a run of thicker baseboard stock from the stairs to the next inner corner, where the transition from ¾ in. to ⅝ in. won't be noticed.

Resolve Conflicts at the Baseboard

The trim packages that we typically use feature a base cap as a detail on the underside of the outside stair stringer. You can address the intersection of the base and the stringer in two conventional ways. One of them is to use a triangular piece of stock below the stringer that creates a 90° angle into which the base then butts. I like to use this method when the stair and base cap profiles don't match and can't be mitered.

I think it looks better to maintain the continuous lines of the molding when possible, rather than to have them stop and then start again. I prefer the second option, which is to fit the base to the angle of the stringer. I miter both pieces of cap into this obtuse angle, using a 90° jig on the miter saw.

There's also a potential problem with the compatibility of the baseboard and the stair-stringer stock. Typically, the stringer is made from ¾-in. stock, but the base that's commonly installed (known as speed base) is ⅝ in. To avoid a glaring discrepancy at the intersection of the stringer and the base, I use a piece of ¾-in. stock as a transition piece from the stringer to the nearest inside corner, and cope it and the cap into the thinner stock. The transition is less noticeable and in a less prominent place.

Use a Miter-Saw Jig for Cutting Obtuse Angles

To make the respective base caps of the stringer and the baseboard intersect equally, you have to split the angle formed at the inside intersection in half. The tricky part comes when you try to cut the angle, which is somewhere in the vicinity of 109°. I clamp a 90° jig onto the miter-saw fence, hold the stock against the jig, eyeball the marks on the stock, and cut the correct angle, which ends up at about 19°.

Continued →

In a Perfect World, Walls Are Straight

Along a continuous line of trim, the points from corner to corner need to be straight. In many of the houses that I trim, I sometimes have to fix a mistake in the wall at the chair rail. The reason is that the chair rail becomes the demarcation line between the two paint colors of the drywall above and the paneling below. The different paints accentuate that line, so any deviation from a flat plane, such as a dip in the wall, becomes obvious. If the dip is especially bad, I fix it before the painters arrive.

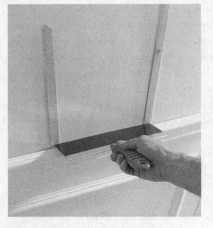  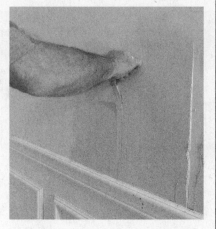

PREPARE THE GROUNDS. With a flat bar, pop out the chair rail so that it's straight. Rip a few shims into ¾-in.-wide strips. Measure the gap between the rail and the wall, then cut the fat end of the shims to match the gap. Insert the shims vertically, spaced at the width of the broad knife that you use. (The author's is 10 in. wide.) Tack them in place with a small nail.

APPLY THE FIRST COAT. Mix up some setting-type drywall compound, and trowel it onto the wall, using shims as grounds for the knife.

REPLACE THE GROUNDS WITH MUD. When the compound is dry, remove the shims and fill the voids with more compound.

10 Tips for Fast Trim

By Joe Milicia

Perhaps nowhere does the old saying that time is money ring truer than in carpentry. To stay in business, I need to work quickly, and I need to do so while maintaining a high standard of quality. For instance, if I only have a couple of days to complete a crown-molding installation and I end up spending 40% of my time making extra trips up and down ladders or hunting for materials, I'm not only cutting into my earnings, but I'm spending far less time cutting and fitting joints precisely.

That's why any professional who installs trim will benefit from a production approach that eliminates wasted time while bolstering accuracy. While whole books have been published about the production approach, I've boiled down my method to 10 essential tips that every trim-installation job can benefit from. Even if you don't make your living as a carpenter, these select strategies will help you to create a better-looking job that allows you to move on to other projects faster.

Admittedly, no two trim jobs are the same, and no two carpenters are either. What saves time for one person may make another person develop a sore back, and different materials sometimes demand an adjusted workflow. The tips here are an organizational starting point and should be optimized to suit the way you work and to fit the work at hand.

Job Preparation

The key to efficiency is creating good cutlists, a process that begins with a series of site assessments. At my company, we typically create a rough-cut list and a final list. Before the job starts, we take an inventory of the types and sizes of the windows and doors we have. We order trim specifically for each window and door size. This minimizes wasted time and ensures that we don't have splices on trim around windows and doors. Also to cut down on splices, we order the longest lengths of crown, baseboard, and shoe molding available.

If by a stroke of luck we are awarded a job at the framing stage, we stop by after the rough mechanicals are installed and take a few photos. These photos help to identify the location of nailing hazards such as wiring and pipes before they are hidden behind the insulation and drywall. We organize the photos by floor and eventually attach them to the cutlist as a reminder of potential trouble areas. When the drywall is installed, we can quickly make reference marks for these obstacles to prevent complications or delays in our trim installation.

For similar reasons, we check all the rooms for discrepancies, such as drywall that sticks proud of the window-jamb extensions, or low spots in the ceiling that will interfere with splices in the crown.

We make our assessments in the order in which we work, from the top of the house down and from the crown down in each room. This lets us begin the work without any finished flooring and allows other contractors to come in behind us as we complete each room.

Make Cuts in Two Stages

We begin with a rough-cut phase in which we measure each trim piece, write its dimension on the drywall behind its intended location for future reference, then cut it about 3 in. long. We bundle rough-cut trim packages for each room together.

Rough-cutting adds an extra step to the job, but there are four very good reasons to do this with all of the trim. First, it allows us to prepare the trim in such a way that we can later cut out any knots or imperfections that would lead to callbacks. Second, it helps us to confirm that we ordered the right quantity of trim, as we can reference our cutlist while moving through the stack of material. Third, it gives us greater control over our use of the stock. For example, when we're installing door and window

---

1. Increase Efficiency with a Dedicated Production Area

In a production area such as this, you can mill and assemble window trim while at the same time organizing rough cuts of base moldings that will eventually be coped and cut to final length. Despite its small space, this cut room and assembly setup creates a workflow where neither work areas nor carpenters create a bottleneck.

Continued →

2. Visualize a Plan of Attack

To make your cutlists, always begin with a visual layout of each room. Walk each room and take an accurate count of trim lengths to minimize the splices in crown and base trim and to make sure that the splices are put in the least conspicuous spots and on the flattest surfaces of the room. Move around each room from left to right, numbering each board on the cutlist and marking it if it is a left or right cope. Being consistent in measuring each room is important, as it ensures that you don't miss any sections. Use this cutlist to rough-cut the trim. If some of the boards have knots in the middle, use them for the shorter pieces. This ensures that the best long boards remain intact for the longest runs.

3. Windows Require a Large Assembly Table

Make your worktable large enough to fully support casing during assembly and glue-ups. A table that's too small won't provide enough support or an adequate clamping surface. By keeping a glue-brush jar full of water nearby, cleaning joints during casing assembly becomes second nature instead of a step that can be forgotten.

Avoid coping short lengths of trim, as these are difficult to fit.

Start at the hardest spot—here, the outside miters with the short legs to the wall.

Locate crown splices out of sightlines and away from low spots in the ceiling, which are the most difficult places to get an even splice.

Measure rough cuts for crown and base at once. One carpenter can make short work of developing a rough-cut list by measuring the wall lengths and adding 3 in. for waste.

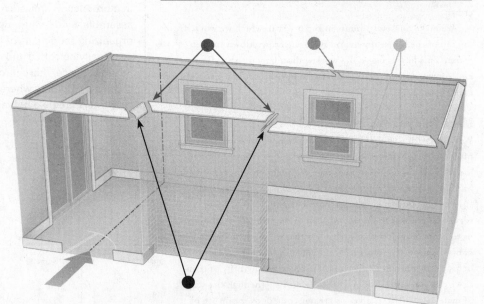

casing, we like to cut the miters at the middle of the trimboards rather than at the ends, which are more prone to snipe marks from milling and to checks. Finally, rough-cutting means that one carpenter can cut copes on one end of the crown, base, and shoe molding while another carpenter continues taking door and window measurements around the house. Cutting copes ahead of time, leaving the opposite end long, saves a lot of time when it comes to final cutting and installation.

Once the rough-cutting is done, we create a final cutlist to guide dimensioning the trim all the way through installation. A cutlist can be developed in many forms. Ours are not so much lists as they are attack plans. You can make a cutlist look like a checklist, a floor plan, or a combination of both.

Whatever its appearance, the final cutlist should include all the information you need for production. For large projects, we like to put the floor number first, followed by a number for each window and door. We start with the room to the left of the stairs and then work left to right. For example, door 301 would be the first door on the left of the third floor.

On most of our jobs, we create a cut room in a large, centrally located space to create some semblance of an assembly line. Ideally, the room can stay intact throughout the project. If large enough, the room also houses our glue-up worktable, where we assemble the door and window casings, and in some instances, even the built-up trim elements if the design calls for them.

With the Cut Room Organized, Begin the Assembly

Whenever we can, we place the stock pile to the left of the cutting station, with the saw situated along one wall, and the opposite wall reserved for pieces that have been cut to length. This allows

4. Don't Be Fussy When You Don't Have to Be

Carefully cutting drywall for an outlet isn't necessary when the drywall will be covered by baseboard trim. Be sure, however, to locate the outlet so that when the shoe molding is added later, the outlet will appear centered on the baseboard.

5. Create Strong Joints Quickly

Biscuit miters for strength. But instead of marking the center of a biscuit to align the tool, register the biscuit joiner's edge to the tip of the miter to speed the process. Have enough miter clamps on hand to reinforce each joint as the glue sets. Enough clamps for three windows keeps the production line moving without having to wait for glue to dry before assembling the next window.

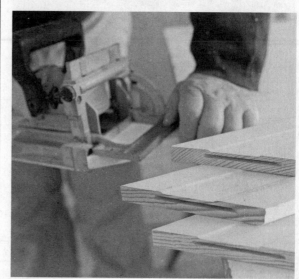

Continued ➜

6. Custom-Fit Stools to Maintain Quality

To maximize efficiency, remove the wallboard where necessary, and fit all the stools at once. Hold a section of casing in place to establish where the stool's mitered return intersects the casing's edge.

7. Reference Marks Help You Stay Organized

When fitting a trim component such as a window stool around the jamb, make a small tick to reference its ideal position. This saves time when fitting the dimensioned pieces later and ensures that the stool doesn't get installed in the wrong opening.

8. Use Screws When Needed

While finish nails satisfy most fastening tasks, certain components need to be pulled into place and demand the increased holding power that screws provide. On paint-grade trim, use trim-head screws, then fill the holes with putty and sand them flush.

9. Clamp When You Can

Look for opportunities to use clamps to hold trim in place. Here, double-hung sashes allow clamp placement where the carpenter would have a difficult time pushing the trim into place. Once the entire assembly is secured, the clamps are removed and the trim stays put, with a consistent reveal.

the cut man simply to turn around rather than being forced to walk around the length of the miter-saw stand. We set up another workstation to do all of our left and right copes. On the job pictured here, space was a little tight, so we used both the table and the wall to stage material.

After installing the crown, we move on to window and door trim before attacking the base and shoe. While we tackle nearly every job with this approach, we're careful never to pigeonhole ourselves into any given process. For example, on this job, we installed the flat casing on the windows and doors first and then went back and completed another cutlist for the backband. Sometimes trying to do everything ahead of time simply isn't as efficient as breaking up the process into more manageable chunks. Our crew has been working together for a while and falls into a natural rhythm, but we like to approach jobs with flexibility and always stay on the lookout for new efficiencies.

10. Don't Cut Corners for Speed

Door casings require two trips to the saw. First, scribe and cut the side leg to the floor (bottom left). Then mark the leg's length to maintain the proper reveal across the head casing (bottom right). Finally, use two fastener sizes to secure the casing. For trim-to-trim connections, 18-ga. fasteners work well; 16-ga. fasteners secure the trim to the framing (below).

Adding Detail with Built-Up Molding

By Rick Arnold

When I'm asked for ideas to upgrade the interior of a house, the first thing I say is "Change the trim." The dramatic difference that built-up trim makes easily justifies the extra cost. As a carpenter, installing an interesting three-piece casing is always more fun than working with boring old clamshell or colonial casing. Because it consists of multiple pieces, built-up trim is actually much more forgiving than single-piece trim. One piece follows the window or door jamb, and a second follows the wall. Then a third piece joins the two, concealing any gaps. As my kids would say, sweet.

A few companies offer architecturally correct built-up trim arrangements (in this article, I used the Greek Revival series from Windsor One; www.windsorone.com). But much the same effect can be achieved with a little imagination and some stock trim from a lumberyard or building-supply store (see "More Casing

Continued →

Options," p. 111). To test trim combinations, make up small sections with all the details.

Window Trim Starts with the Stool

For built-up trim, I prefer a thicker stool with bullnose edges. To find the length of the stool, I assemble a short section of the built-up side casing. Then I set it in place near the bottom of the window, making sure to leave a 3/16-in. reveal on the inside of the window jamb. I make a light pencil mark on the wall along the outside edge of the trim section, then I repeat the process on the other side. I make the marks low enough to use as a reference later when installing the apron.

Next, I measure the distance between the pencil lines and add 3 in. The extra length allows the ends or "ears" of the stool to extend 1½ in. past the edge of the trim, rather than the ¾ in. typically used with conventional molding. The extra length also accommodates the decorative trim that will be applied to the apron.

I make sure the finished stool is deep enough for the built-up trim to land without overhanging. Ideally, the stool should extend ¾ in. to 1 in. beyond the outermost edge of the trim. To maintain the profile of the stool on all three faces, I cut 45° miters on the ends and install small return pieces that fit between the miters and the wall. I glue and nail the return pieces to the stool before nailing the stool into place.

Flat Casing First

The first part of the built-up molding that I install is the flat casing. I measure from the top of the stool to the inside edge of the top jamb of the window, then add 3/16 in. for the reveal. After squaring one end of a piece of stock, I mark the length along the inside edge (in this case, the beaded edge). I cut a 45° angle using the mark as the target for the short point of the angle.

I repeat the same step for the opposite side of the window,

Start with the Stool

After mocking up the trim to double-check the look, scribe the casing width on the wall to determine the length of the stool and apron. Once cut and returned on the ends, the stool is nailed through the top into the windowsill.

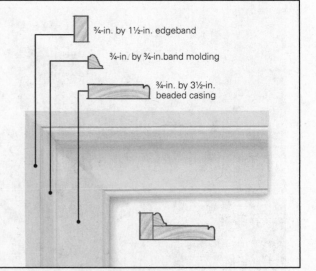

Three-Piece Casing

Combining off-the-shelf moldings creates a complex look without custom milling. The three-piece casing used here is from the Greek Revival series by Windsor One (www.windsorone.com). On the following pages, you'll find designs composed of more common moldings.

¾-in. by 1½-in. edgeband

¾-in. by ¾-in. band molding

¾-in. by 3½-in. beaded casing

Don't Forget the Reveal

To get the length to the short point of the first side piece, measure from the stool to the inside edge of the frame, then add ¾₆ in. for the reveal. Nail the side pieces only to the jamb at this point.

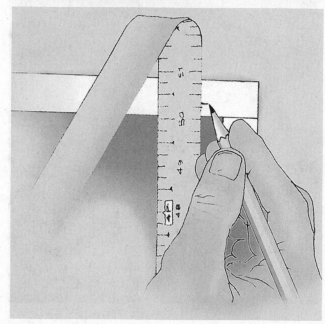

making sure to reverse the direction of the cut. If I'm trimming a lot of windows that are the same height, I check a few to make sure they are exactly the same, then cut all the pieces at once rather than completing one window at a time.

Before nailing in the pieces, I use a biscuit joiner to cut a slot into the mitered ends. Miter joints that are reinforced with biscuits are less likely to come apart over time. Taking care to keep an even reveal, I nail the side pieces into the edge of the window jamb using 1¼-in. nails.

I find the length for the top piece of casing by measuring from long point to long point on the two side pieces. After marking the top piece, I cut it just a bit long, usually by the thickness of my marks. Then I test-fit the piece, shave it if necessary, and cut the biscuit slots. To shave a hair off the miter, I place it tight against the chopsaw blade, raise the blade, turn on the saw, and bring the blade back down. By the way, I start with the wider windows first so that if I cut a top piece too short, it still can be used on a narrower window.

I glue and insert the biscuits into the side pieces with a little more glue on the mitered edges of both top and sides. I wipe the glue with my finger to ensure a thin, even coat. Next, I push the top piece into place and rock the side pieces back and forth until the miters align. If I had nailed the outside edges of the side pieces, I wouldn't be able to adjust the fit so easily. Finally, I nail the top piece into the edge of the jamb and drive a nail through the edge into the side pieces near the long points.

Add Decorative Layers

Trim pieces are added to build up the molding, beginning with the edgeband. I determine the length of the outside edgeband by measuring the outside edge of each flat side piece, from the stool to the long point. After marking that length on a piece of the edgeband, I cut the 45° angle, using the mark as the target of the short point.

The edgeband is flexible enough that it can follow all but the most severe irregularities in the wall. So as I install each piece, I press it hard against the wall. I nail the edgeband into the edge of the flat stock only. Just as with the flat casing, I measure for the top piece of edgeband between the long points, cut it a touch long, fit it, and then glue and nail it into place.

Next, I go back and nail the flat casing into the stud framing. If the framing allows, I nail as close to the outside edge of the casing as possible so that the nail holes will be covered by the final filler trim. It's a good idea to find the edge of the framing beneath the wallboard before running any trim. At this point, I also nail up through the stool into the bottom edge of the flat casing.

To complete the built-up molding, I mark and cut the filler trim that sits just inside the outside edgeband. I use the same measurements that I took for the edgeband, only this time the measurement is to the long point of the 45° miters on the filler trim. Instead of installing the sides first and then the top, I work my way around each window. I make the pieces slightly long so

Continued ➔

that they spring tightly into place. I secure them to both the flat casing and the edgeband using 1¼-in. nails.

Trim the Apron Before It Goes On

For the look I prefer, the length of the apron is the same as the distance between the first pencil marks that I made on the wall. The apron is constructed out of the same flat stock as the window casing. Just as I did with the stool, I bevel both ends of the apron and then cut, glue, and pin the small return pieces in place. Next, I cut and install the decorative trim that runs along the top of the apron. If I have a lot of windows to trim, I can work more efficiently by making all of the aprons at one time.

Finally, I hold the assembled apron hard against the underside of the stool and then fasten the apron to the stud framing. Also, I carefully shoot a few nails down into the apron through the top of the stool.

Sides First, Then Top

Measure between the sides to get the distance between the long points of the top piece. After fitting the top piece, glue the biscuits and miters and fasten the top piece to the jamb edge.

Start Adding Layers

Measure along the outside edge of the flat casing to find the length of the outside edgeband at its short point. Press the edgeband against the wall, and nail it to the edge of the flat stock.

More Casing Options

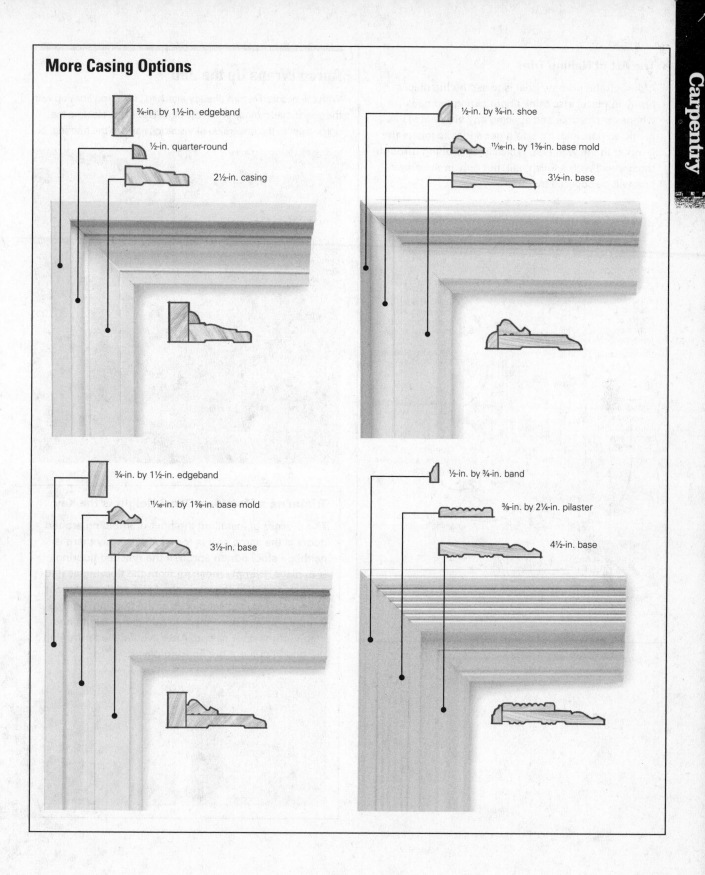

¾-in. by 1½-in. edgeband

½-in. quarter-round

2½-in. casing

½-in. by ¾-in. shoe

¹¹⁄₁₆-in. by 1⅜-in. base mold

3½-in. base

¾-in. by 1½-in. edgeband

¹¹⁄₁₆-in. by 1⅜-in. base mold

3½-in. base

½-in. by ¾-in. band

⅜-in. by 2¼-in. pilaster

4½-in. base

Continued ➜

The Art of Nailing Trim

Although the primary goal is to secure the pieces firmly in place, also think about hiding the nails whenever possible and spacing any visible nails as neatly as possible. It's also a good idea to locate the framing in the wall first, typically by probing through the drywall with a finish nail, but only in the areas that will be covered by trim.

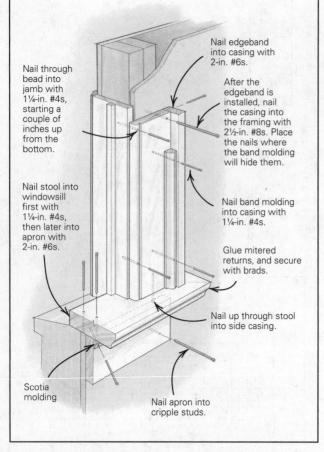

Nail through bead into jamb with 1¼-in. #4s, starting a couple of inches up from the bottom.

Nail stool into windowsill first with 1¼-in. #4s, then later into apron with 2-in. #6s.

Scotia molding

Nail apron into cripple studs.

Nail edgeband into casing with 2-in. #6s.

After the edgeband is installed, nail the casing into the framing with 2½-in. #8s. Place the nails where the band molding will hide them.

Nail band molding into casing with 1¼-in. #4s.

Glue mitered returns, and secure with brads.

Nail up through stool into side casing.

Apron Wraps Up the Job

With the decorative trim already attached, the apron lines up with the pencil marks made when the stool is laid out. Holding the apron tight to the underside of the stool, nail it to the framing.

Trimming a Matching Door? Height is the Key

The process of installing the built-up molding around doors is the same as it is for windows, only there is neither a stool nor an apron. If the finished flooring is in place, I simply measure from the flooring as if it were the stool. In this case, the finished floor had not been installed, so I set pieces of the flooring in place temporarily and used them to gauge the length and height of the door casing. After I've finished trimming the door, I pull out the flooring pieces.

Beadboard Wainscot

By Rick Arnold

I love to transform a room with wainscot. My favorite type and the easiest to install is beadboard. Whether in a Victorian house with stained-beadboard panels or in a cottage with painted beadboard, a room can morph from blah to beautiful quickly. By matching trim details such as the cap (chair rail) and baseboard with the rest of the millwork (casing, crown), wainscot can enhance the whole style.

For this project, I installed paint-grade tongue-and-groove beadboard planks, which are the best type I've worked with (sidebar p. 117). These ½-in.-thick preprimed boards, made from engineered lumber, have a finished width of about 3 in. After the first board is secured, the rest are mostly self-supporting, so whole walls can be dry-fit. And because baseboard hides the bottom ends of the boards in most cases, installation goes quickly, and I have to pay attention only to critical areas.

Beadboard Basics

I like to glue beadboard to a clean substrate, so with existing drywall, I cut an inch or so below the top of the future wainscot cap and remove the drywall from there down. In older houses where removing lath and plaster would be messy and impractical, I clean the area as best as possible and make sure to attach the beadboard to the plaster with polyurethane glue.

Continued ➜

Forgiving Installation

Bullnose and cove molding finish the top of the beadboard.

To complement the colonial trim in this house, the wainscot cap is a simple bullnose, which rests on top of the beadboard and is supported by a ¾-in. cove molding. A standard 3½-in. colonial base covers the bottom edges of the beadboard and returns at the edge of the casing.

Beadboard

Engineered Lumber

For paint-grade beadboard, engineered lumber has all the benefits of both regular wood and medium-density fiberboard (MDF) stock. It has the feel, workability, and look of standard lumber, but it enjoys the stability of MDF. Also, its dimensional measurements stay consistent from one board to the next. On this project, I used WindsorONE SPBC4 beadboard (www.windsorone.com; 707-838-7101).

Baseboard molding covers bottom edge of beadboard.

A Guide Strip Keeps the Top Straight

Start by snapping a level chalkline around the room to indicate the top of the beadboard (usually about 35 in. from the floor). Then tack on a temporary straightedge with small brads. Keeping the top of the beadboard in a straight line provides an even edge for the cap to rest on.

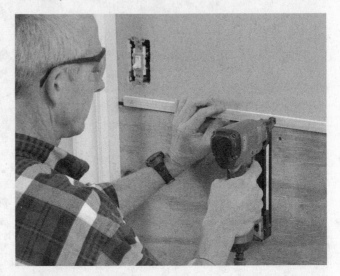

Start Plumb and Stay Plumb

Tack the first board in place, and check it with a level to make sure it's plumb. If need be, plane the board on the casing side until the leading edge is plumb. Then check every couple of feet to make sure that the beadboard is staying plumb. You can correct for plumb in the field by opening a slight gap between two boards at the top or bottom.

Nail Where It Won't Show

In place of nailing along the length of the boards, run horizontal beads of construction adhesive about 16 in. apart on the plywood. Then face-nail the top and bottom of each board where trim will hide the nails.

Approach Side of the Window

Scribe the Vertical Line...

First, dry-fit the last full board before the window casing. Then, placing the scribe guide tight against the casing, trace the cutline on the dry-fit board.

Fit Around Windows

Before running the beadboard, I put in the casing and the stool (without returns) around each window. But I leave the apron off until after the beadboard is installed.

The ability to dry-fit tongue-and-groove beadboard is a real plus when installing it around a window. To get precise cutlines around window casing and other obstacles, I make a scribe guide by ripping the tongue off a length of beadboard. This gives me the exact finished width of a board. Each side of the window receives slightly different treatment depending on the direction I run the beadboard.

Scribe guide

...Then the Horizontal Line
Holding the scribe guide against the bottom of the stool, mark the horizontal cut on the dry-fit board. The actual cut should be made about ⅛ in. Below that line.

Slip In a Sliver
Install the scribed board against the window casing first, then slide the last full board into place from the top down.

Continued ➜

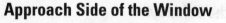

Exit Side of the Window

Scribe the Lines
On the other side of the window, dry-fit an extra board under the window to space a full board properly for the scribe. Then use the scribe guide as before to mark the vertical and horizontal cutlines.

Scribed Board Completes Wrap
After removing the extra dry-fit board, fasten the scribed board into position. Now you're ready to continue down the wall.

Electrical Boxes: Two Ways to Measure

The electrical code prohibits any combustible material, such as wooden beadboard, from being inside the area of an electrical box. When beadboard is installed after the electrical boxes, a box extension must be put in to avoid a code violation.

For Electrical Boxes That Share a Seam Between Boards
Simply dry-fit the first board, then mark and cut it accordingly. Once both sides are cut and checked for fit, fasten them to the wall.

For a Box That Falls Within a Single Board
Mark the top and bottom on the plywood, then transfer the marks to the dry-fit board. Measure from the adjacent board for the vertical cuts.

Folded Finish in a Corner

I don't bother to fit the corner board precisely for the first wall because the edge is covered by the corner board from the other wall. To make sure that I don't end up with a narrow sliver in the corner, I take a quick measurement of the wall. If need be, I start with a half-piece instead of a full board.

A Smart Start

Narrow slivers of beadboard are difficult to install in a corner. To avoid them, a quick overall mea-surement will tell you whether to start at the casing with a full board or to rip the first board in half.

Dry-Fit for Perfect Corners
After dry-fitting the last full-width board, push the scribe guide hard into the corner and draw the cutline. Then cut the scribed board to become the final corner piece.

Accordion Fit
To complete the corner, pull the shared edge of the last full board and the scribed board out from the wall, seating their outside edges in place. Then spring the boards into place..

Other Material Choices for Beadboard

Over the years, I have installed different types of beadboard. Some worked better in certain situations than others, and some I just should have avoided. A general rule of thumb is that the thinner the stock, the shallower the beaded profile. Shallower profiles fill with paint, and their shadowlines don't look nearly as nice as deeper beads milled in thicker stock.

MDF Sheets

Medium-density fiberboard (MDF) sheet-stock beadboard comes pre-primed in 4-ft. widths. Take extra care to seal cut ends when installing it in moisture-prone areas such as bathrooms.

Plywood Sheets

Usually ¼ in. thick, 4-ft.-wide plywood beadboard can be stained or painted. However, I've seen it split along a grain line and across bead lines occasionally, so it should be handled with care.

MDF Planks

Preprimed MDF planks are available in certain areas of the country and usually come either two beads or four beads wide. As with MDF sheet stock, I avoid using these planks in high-moisture areas, and I prime all cuts to keep the boards from absorbing moisture.

Wood Planks

Beadboard planks are available in different wood species. Typical thicknesses are ¼ in., ½ in., or ¾ in., with finished widths of 3 in. or 5 in. Planks come with a primed or natural finish. Solid wood shrinks and swells in response to humidity changes, and unfinished pine beadboard is the worst; it never seems to stop moving. To minimize moisture absorption and wood move-ment, I stain or paint the boards before I install them.

Continued ➜

Installing Iron-On Edging

By Tim Snyder

Iron-on edging (also known as edgebanding) offers a quick, inexpensive way to cover the exposed edges of plywood and other sheet goods. It's a great way to finish off frameless cabinets and shelf edges. Thanks to the heat-activated glue that coats the back of the edging, no clamping is required, and the mess is minimal. You can install the edging with a household iron, an edge-trimming tool (sidebar, p. 119), and a sharp 1-in. chisel. A couple of shopmade jigs make the job even easier.

Start by choosing the type of edgebanding you need. Plastic edging comes in several colors, and wood edging is available in different species. It's all sold by the lineal foot. Wood edging is usually less expensive than plastic edging. For either material, you can expect lower prices when ordering larger quantities.

Edging in a $^{13}/_{16}$-in. width is good for $^3/_4$-in.-thick material; 1-in.-wide edging also is available.

Installing iron-on edging involves a few basic steps. First, you have to make sure that the edges you want to cover are smooth and flush. Then you cut the material slightly longer than necessary and iron it down. Finish by trimming the edges and ends, then sanding all the corners smooth.

Wood and Plastic Options

Plastic edgebanding goes well with laminate or melamine-covered shelves. Black, white, and several other colors are available. Wood edging is made from real wood veneer and is available in different species.

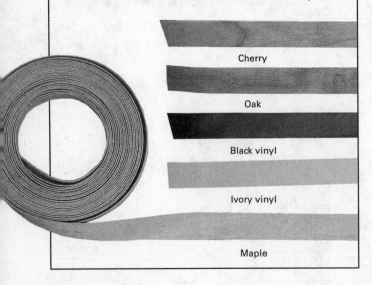

Cherry

Oak

Black vinyl

Ivory vinyl

Maple

Get Edges and Edging Set, Then Iron It On

1. MAKE SURE CORNERS ARE FLUSH. Where two pieces of plywood join, edges need to be flush. If necessary, use a block plane to take down high edges. Then smooth the joint with 120-grit sandpaper wrapped around a block of wood.

2. CUT A LITTLE MORE THAN YOU NEED. Because ends as well as edges will be trimmed, cut each piece an inch or two longer than it needs to be. A sharp chisel makes a quick, clean cut.

3. "TACK" DOWN ONE END, THEN IRON IT OUT. Empty any water from the iron, and set the temperature to high, or "cotton." Hold one end of the edging in place, and press the iron down on it to activate the glue. Sometimes the edging can be centered over the plywood edge. In other situations, it's better to keep the edging flush along one side. Move the iron slowly along the edging to make sure the adhesive melts and bonds. If the edging slips out of alignment, hold the iron over the misaligned area to remelt the glue and realign the edging.

TIP: Avoid using a length of edging that includes a finger joint. This joint doesn't look good in a stain-grade project, and it's a weak spot that could come apart.

Trim and Sand to Get Ready for Finish

4. USE SIMPLE JIGS TO MAKE MITER AND SQUARE CUTS. Screw together a few pieces of wood, and you have easy ways to make precise miter and square cuts in edging before or after it's applied. The jigs guide a 1-in. chisel.

5. THE EDGE TRIMMER CAN DO ONE EDGE OR TWO. Squeezing both sides of the trimmer and pushing it along the edge will trim excess edging along both sides. You also can separate the sides and trim just one edge at a time.

6. TRIM INSIDE EDGES WITH A CHISEL. When the edge-trimming tool can't be used (along an inside edge, for example), use a chisel to pare away excess edging. Work with the bevel facing down for maximum control.

7. SAND TO REMOVE GLUE AND TO EASE THE CORNERS. Wrap 120-grit sandpaper around a block of wood, and do final smoothing with the block held at a 45° angle.

Edge Trimming Made Easy

You can use a block plane to trim away excess edging, but it's easier to get smooth, flush edges with an edge-trimming tool. The one shown here comes with replaceable cutters.

Miter jig

Square-cutting jig

Continued ➜

8 Basic Rules to Master Trim Carpentry

By Tucker Windover

I'm a busy contractor with a half-dozen trim carpenters working on two or three jobs on any given day. Needless to say, I've had a number of employees on my crew of carpenters over the years. To maintain quality and consistency, I've written up a list of work habits and procedures that I've organized in a three-ring binder. On their first day, every new carpenter receives a copy. It's as much a list of results as a list of techniques. Each point sounds minor by itself, but added together, this list creates a foundation for efficient finish carpentry. Even veteran carpenters can let these simple guidelines slip away from them over time, and that can result in careless work. Finish carpentry is more than just tight miter joints. It's a method of work defined by standards that can be easily replicated.

1. Keep the Site Clean

I knew a guy everyone called Yard Sale because he left tools all over the job site. He could never put his hands on the tools he needed. To set up an efficient site, keep tools organized, plan tasks for simple repetition, and lay out job-site materials so that they are easy to access and find.

IT'S BETTER TO HAVE SOME MATERIAL IN EACH ROOM RATHER THAN TO HAVE ONE BIG PILE. Start each project by unpacking the doors and setting them at the openings where they will be installed. This is the time to double-check that the doors swing correctly, that the doors don't swing over a light switch, and that they open cleanly against walls. Stock enough window casing, door trim, and baseboard in each room to complete that room. This way, it's much easier to account for missing material.

CORRAL STAIR PARTS AT THE STAIRS. These smaller pieces are easy to misplace, so put everything within easy reach of the stairs. The risers go in one pile, with treads nearby and newel posts next to the handrail fittings.

2. Be Neat About Nailing

One good work habit to develop is establishing a pattern to your nailing. On standing and running trim, place nails regularly in pairs every 16 in., or until the material is tight. This keeps the work neat and orderly. Avoid nails inside molding profiles; it's hard for a painter to fill and sand these holes. Use 2-in. nails for baseboard because 2½-in. nails will eventually hit a wire in a 2×4 wall. Use 18-ga. nails for wood-to-wood connections and 15-ga. nails for applying molding over drywall and for setting doors.

ALWAYS USE A NAIL SET. In an average 2800-sq.-ft. house, there might be 5000 nails in the trimwork. The painters shouldn't find one unset nail after the finish carpentry is complete.

3. Think and See Straight and Parallel

Installing most trim is the discipline of connecting two points with a straight line. At this stage in the building process, the work sometimes becomes more a game of appearances than of perfection. The trick is to make bows, bends, and out-of-plumb conditions appear straight and true.

SNAP A LINE AS A GUIDE FOR THE BOTTOM EDGE OF CROWN MOLDING. If there are waves in the ceiling, at least the bottom edge will be true. Thin gaps at the ceiling can be caulked, and wider gaps can be reduced by flexing the crown to conform to the ceiling.

AFTER THE CARPENTERS ARE GONE, NO ONE INSPECTS THE HOUSE WITH A LEVEL. Converging lines, however, will stand out to anyone with a good eye. This is especially true where a door is set close to a wall, as in a hallway. If the wall is out of plumb and the door is hung plumb, the casing will show a taper against the wall. However, the aesthetics must be balanced with the door's function, especially if a door is likely to be kept open. Hung out of plumb, a door may swing shut by itself. In that case, the door must be installed so that it operates properly.

Continued ➔

4. Improve the Surfaces Before the Finish Goes On

It may not be noticeable now, but after semigloss paint hits the trim, any sawblade marks, tearout, or imperfections will stand out like a sore thumb. Carry a piece of 150-grit sandpaper in your tool belt. On wood that gets a clear finish, erase or lightly sand out pencil marks. Sand field joints so that they become flush. When you walk away from the work, the stock should be ready for paint or stain.

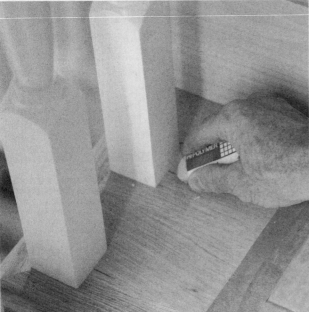

5. Make Miters Flush

After door and window casings are painted, mating surfaces that aren't flush will stand out. A miter should be tight and flush, but a thin gap in the miter can be filled with caulk and will disappear. Uneven surfaces will stand out and should be leveled. A shim placed under one side of the miter can help to line up the joint. Tack it in place, and trim the excess. A little sanding can blend discrepancies between the two sides.

6. Know When to Make Precise Cuts

Not every joint shows, so don't waste valuable time on cuts that don't matter.

Open

USE YOUR TIME WISELY. There are plenty of times when a miter or cope will be covered with a successive layer of trim, so only the visible part of the joint needs to be tight. Corners are almost never square, so miters cut at 45° (photo above) will often show a gap. Instead, use a back-beveled miter that creates a tight outside joint; the gap (photo below) will be hidden by the band molding. Likewise, shoe molding will cover gaps under a run of baseboard. When installing base or crown at an inside corner, the first piece can be cut a little short because the small gap will be covered by the cope of the next piece.

Tight

7. Always Use a Reveal on Standing Trim

Avoid a flush joint on layers of standing trim, such as applied window stool or door casings. Typically, any additional layer of trim on a door or window jamb should have a reveal, or it will leave a distracting seam. The size of the reveal depends on the proportions of the trim, but a 3/16-in. reveal is a good rule of thumb.

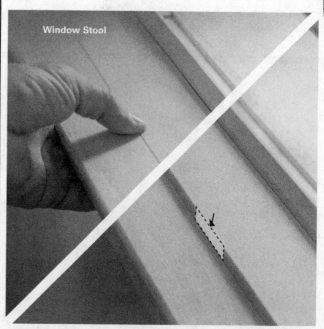

Window Stool

Window Casing

Continued →

8. You Don't Have to Pull Out Your Tape Every Time You Mark and Measure

Most trim measurements can be made faster and more accurately with a more appropriate technique. Choose the most appropriate method for the task at hand.

FOR REPEATED MEASUREMENTS OR A SERIES OF MEASUREMENTS TAKEN FROM THE SAME REFERENCE, USE A STORY POLE. They are typically made from scrap at hand and have the room to display measurements legibly.

MARK A PIECE OF STOCK IN PLACE. After cutting one end to fit, locate the stock, and use a knife or sharp pencil to scribe the cutline.

PINCH STICKS LET YOU TAKE AN EXACT MEASUREMENT between surfaces and transfer it to the stock. The simplest version consists of identical rips of ¾-in. stock that are extended and locked in position with a spring clamp. Bevel the outer stick ends for a more accurate read.

Tip

1. To measure any angle, cut a scrap piece of the stock, hold it in place, and mark the outside and inside lines.

2. Next, place the stock on the opposite side, and mark the lines.

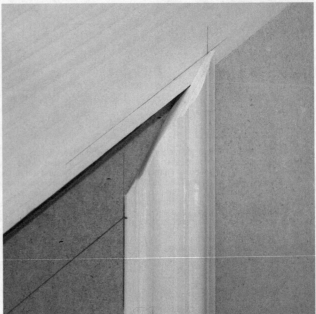

3. Transfer the crossed marks onto the scrap, and use it to determine the angle of the cut.

Router Tricks Trim

By Gary Striegler

My editor recently called me a tool junkie. My wife has called me the same thing, but with a few expletives. In my defense, when you've been building as long as I have, you can appreciate how important it is to have a good collection of tools close at hand wherever you are.

I won't tell you how many routers I actually own, partly because I stopped counting 10 years ago. But despite the grief routers might cause me on occasion, they have gotten me out of a lot of jams on the job. Of the many I own, the trim and midsize D-handle models are the two I reach for most.

Different Routers for Different Jobs

The first trim routers were called laminate trimmers because they made quick, clean work of flush-cutting laminate for countertops. Today, more powerful motors and a variety of accessories make trim routers a staple for most finish carpenters. One of my favorite features is that I can safely use my trim router with one hand, leaving the other hand free to hold the workpiece.

I use a trim router when I need to make short, shallow cuts in doors, cabinets, and trim. Because most have only 1-hp motors and ¼-in. collets, they shouldn't be commissioned for heavy work like cutting detailed profiles into a piece of hardwood. I don't use anything larger than a 1-in.-long by ½-in.-dia. straight bit in my trim routers. Larger-diameter bits put too much strain on the motor.

For bigger tasks that require more power, such as cutting deep mortises or plowing wide dadoes, I use a 1½-hp D-handle router. The D-handle allows me to use one hand or two, and it is easy to control.

If you don't own either of these tools or the bits I mention here, show this article to whoever is likely to give you a hard time about a tool purchase. Together, they'll save you an incredible amount of time, which will let you find reasons to buy more tools.

Patch Blowouts on Trim After It's Installed

Pneumatic nail guns are nice, except when fixing an errant nail adds to my list of things to do. Bondo or wood filler works when the blowout is not large and deep. But nothing does the trick quite like a dutchman, or wooden patch, especially when the blowout happens in the jamb reveal. I used to use a hammer and chisel to make the mortise for a dutchman. Now, I plow a better mortise in half the time with a trim router equipped with a ½-in.-dia. pattern bit. The bit doesn't need to have a large cutting length; I usually use one about ½ in. long to keep the router closer to the cut, which gives me more control.

When working with stain-grade trim, I make the dutchman from the same material and match the grain. If it's paint-grade trim I'm patching, I don't worry about wood type too much.

I often use headless pins to provide extra holding power for the

Trim Router   D-Handle Router

The Bits I Use the Most

Bits equipped with a bearing that matches the cutting diameter follow a template aligned to the cutline, which makes setup quick and easy. Pattern bits have a bearing mounted on top of the cutting area that follows a template mounted to the top of the workpiece. Flush-trim bits have a bearing mounted on the bottom that follows a template mounted below the workpiece. Dado bits aren't equipped with a bearing, so they require the use of a guide for the router. Their deep, nearly hollow center allows waste to exit the dado as you cut. No matter which style you're using, buy carbide-tipped bits that have two flutes. Carbide lasts longer, and two flutes make a cleaner cut than one.

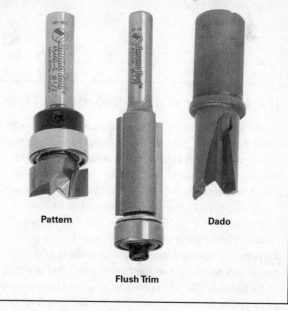

Pattern   Dado

Flush Trim

Continued →

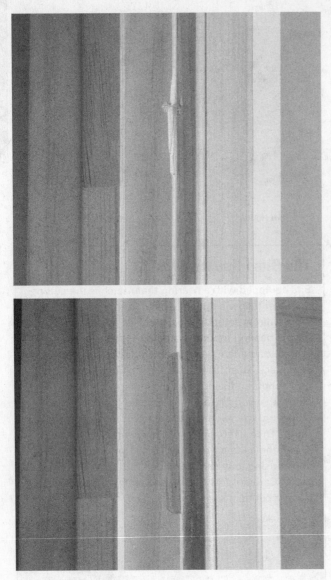

dutchman, but I've seen them clamped in place with masking tape as well. Either way, after the glue dries, a quick pass with 120-grit paper on a random-orbit sander makes the patch practically disappear.

This approach also works for replacing damaged sections of profiled trim, especially if the trim is already installed.

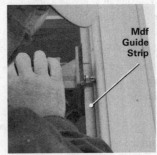

Mdf
Guide
Strip

SET THE DEPTH Nail an MDF guide strip to the jamb using headless pins; then adjust the bit depth to match the jamb's reveal.

PLOW A MORTISE With the router on, push the bit into the jamb until the bearing registers. Then follow the guide until the blowout is gone.

FIT THE DUTCHMAN It's faster to radius the dutchman than to square the corners of the mortise. Make the dutchman a bit thicker than the mortise's depth.

FASTEN AND SAND Glue and nail the dutchman with headless pins. Once the glue dries, sand the patch flush with the jamb.

House Treads in a Skirtboard for a Tight Joint

I build stairs on site by wrapping framed stringers with hardwood treads and plywood risers. One of the most challenging parts of this process is creating a tight fit between stair treads and a skirtboard. You can scribe and butt the tread to the skirtboard, but it takes a lot of time and doesn't account for seasonal movement of the stringers or treads, which can cause the joint to open. For a better joint, I house the treads in the skirtboard. (1) After scribing the skirtboard to the stringers, I plow a dado for each tread using a template and a 1⅛-in. pattern bit. The bit creates a radiused end for the tread's bullnose, so I make sure to stop the bit exactly where the tread needs to end. The guide should be rigid enough that it won't flex and has to be perfectly flat, so I make one by gluing up a couple of pieces of 6-in.-wide ¾-in. MDF. (2) After installing the skirtboard, I test-fit each tread. I shim the tread as needed to push it tight to the top and front of the dado.

USE A SUBBASE AND A GUIDE STRIP. With a square as a guide, start by plowing a starter dado on one end of the board, then make an oversize router base with a 12-in.-sq. piece of ¾-in. MDF. In the center of the MDF, drill a hole larger than the diameter of the bit you're using, and run screws through the router's base to secure it. Then attach a strip of clear stock, such as pine or poplar, that fits the first dado; it should fit snugly but slide freely. To make it easier to register the template in the dado, run the strip just past the subbase so that it's visible. A few headless pins hold it in place.

Get Clean, Evenly Spaced Dadoes to Make Dentil Molding on Site

I hang a lot of custom built-up crown that includes dentil molding, and I often make the dentil molding on site. Some carpenters do this by ripping multiple dadoes on a tablesaw, but I have found that using a router is faster, is more accurate, and produces cleaner cuts.

I plow dadoes across a length of 1×6 poplar; then I rip the board to width. To space the dadoes evenly, I attach a subbase and a guide strip to my D-handle router. The subbase creates a wide, stable surface for cutting, and the guide strip rides in the previously cut dado. Centering the subbase on the router ensures that at least 3 in. of the strip locks into the dado before the bit engages and as it exits the cut.

The size of the bit I use depends on the size of the dentil molding I'm making, but I prefer to use bits with a ½-in.-dia. shank; smaller shanks can flex, which affects the cut. They also break more easily when plowing large dadoes.

Trim a Cabinet Face Frame in Place

When rough openings for appliances are too small, they often need to be widened on site. Modifying cabinet face frames can be nerve-racking, especially when the cabinet is already installed. I've tried plenty of approaches to this task, many of which left me disappointed with the results. The most precise way I found is with a ½-in.-dia. flush-trim bit and a trim router.

I pin a piece of flat stock, typically MDF, to the cabinet behind the stile I'm cutting as a guide for the bearing. Keeping in mind that the bearing is the same size as the bit's cutting diameter, I select stock based on the amount of material I plan to take off (typically ¹⁄₁₆ in. to ⅛ in. at a time).

I like to use a trim router here because I can grip it with both hands for complete control while still having clear sight of the bit as it's removing material. If I need to take more than ⅛ in. off at a time, I switch to a D-handle; the added power produces a cleaner cut.

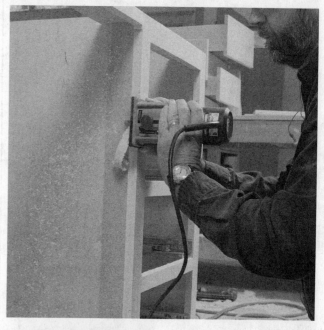

MOVE IN THE RIGHT DIRECTION. When the bit is to the left of the stile, as it is here, move from the top down. When it's to the right of the stile, move from the bottom up. Keep both hands on the router, and move slowly. Straight bits produce a radiused corner. The radius size depends on the bit's diameter and the amount of material you're taking off. Use a ½-in.-dia. bit to keep the radius as small as possible. The smaller it is, the less work you'll have to do with a chisel.

Continued ➜

Mortise Tricky Door Hardware with Simple Jigs

It's easier to mortise a latch plate, ball catch, and slide bolt before hanging the door. When mortising a latch plate, I dismantle the jamb before it's installed and set it up on a workbench. A short pattern bit and a trim router are good for latch-plate and ball-catch mortises. Slide bolts require a deep mortise, so I use a longer pattern bit and a D-handle router.

Latch Plate

MAKE A SELF-CLAMPING JIG. Cut a dado into a piece of ¾-in. MDF to register on the doorstop. Then make a cutout the same size as the latch plate. Hold the template down with one hand, and plow the mortise with the other. Use a corner chisel to square radiused corners with a quick tap of the hammer.

Ball Catch

BALL CATCHES GET A SADDLELIKE THREE-PIECE JIG. Nail and glue two 4-in.-long pieces of ¾-in. MDF, ripped to match the door thickness, in between two pieces of ¾-in. MDF. Space the ripped sections apart the length of the ball latch. Glue shims inside the opening on each side piece so that the opening width matches the ball-catch plate. Center the jig on the hole, and clamp it in place. Place the router onto the jig, locating the bit in the hole. Make a test cut near the hole to double-check the depth.

Slide Bolt

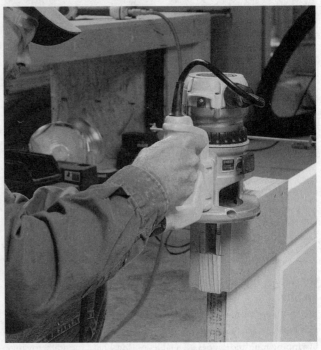

SLIDE BOLTS GET A SIMILAR JIG AND TWO CUTS. Slide bolts like the one shown here sit in a mortise cut into the door's corner. Use a pattern bit with a cutting diameter that matches the width of the slide-bolt plate. Make the first cut with the bit set to the plate depth.

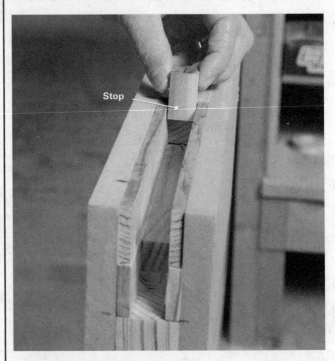

Stop

ADD A STOP FOR THE SECOND CUT. Make a second, deeper cut to the bolt's depth. Before making the cut, drop a stop into the jig to keep the bit from carrying through the end of the shallow cut where the plate will register. Make this cut in two passes.

Crown Molding for Kitchen Cabinets

By Gary Striegler

When I started building, ceilings were 8 ft. tall. In the kitchen, a clunky soffit dropped down a foot above the cabinets, limiting them to 7 ft. in height. When ceiling heights grew to 9 ft., kitchen cabinets grew another foot or so to about 8 ft. Who couldn't use the extra storage? But that was the limit for kitchen cabinets, because close to no one can reach higher than that without a ladder. Still, in my market, ceiling height continued to grow to about 10 ft. What do you do with the space above the cabinets? One solution is to leave it open as display space. Of course, that adds costs for lighting and display items, never mind the extra dusting.

In response, some of my clients asked about taking their upper cabinets all the way to the ceiling, which at least minimizes the dusting. But just growing the upper cabinets by 2 ft. would put the proportions way out of balance. Plus, manufacturers don't want

to warrant a door that tall. One solution was to add a set of short cabinets with glass doors. That cuts way back on the dusting, and the extra row of cabinets looks great. However, it can add several thousand dollars to the cabinet budget. I needed a third option that would be less expensive than adding cabinets and involve less maintenance than open tops. The solution turned out to be adding a decorative frieze above standard wall cabinets.

The whole assembly is relatively inexpensive to build, consisting merely of a flat frieze board that supports crown, panel, and bolection molding. It looks great, ties into the kitchen crown molding, and needs little dusting. It took my lead carpenter and me a bit over a day to build the frieze for the kitchen shown here. Kitchens vary, of course: Ceiling height, cabinet height, style, and finishes will affect your final design. Because this custom kitchen was later painted on site, the frieze ended up blending seamlessly with both the room and the cabinets. If you use prefinished cabinets, you can get from most manufacturers finished plywood and moldings that can be used in the same way.

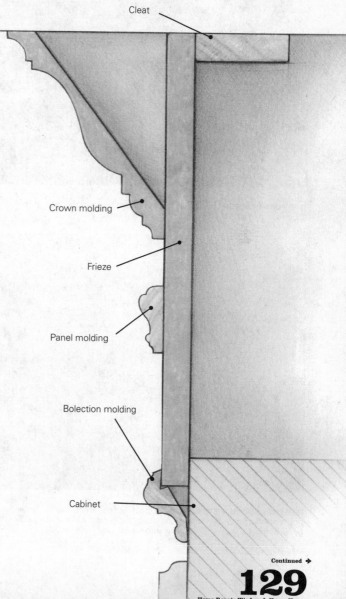

Cleat

Crown molding

Frieze

Panel molding

Bolection molding

Cabinet

Continued ➜

Cleats Outline the Frieze

Fasten the top of the frieze to cleats nailed to the ceiling and plumb with the face of the cabinets. To ensure that the top of long runs of frieze will be straight, I establish two endpoints and snap a chalkline on the ceiling. I make the cleats from scraps of whatever the frieze-board material is—in this case, ¾-in. MDF. The material doesn't matter as much as making sure it's straight so that any irregularities don't telegraph to the face of the frieze.

REINFORCING A CORNER. When there are no joists at a corner, reinforce the cleats by adding a second layer.

TWO POINTS MAKE A LINE. Use a level to plumb up from the face of the cabinet and to establish the endpoints of the cleat.

NAIL THE CLEAT TO THE CEILING. If the cleat crosses joists, nail to them. If not, spread glue on the back of the cleat, and secure it while the glue sets by driving nails at opposing angles into the drywall.

Frieze Board is the Foundation

Because this kitchen was going to be painted, my lead carpenter and I ripped the frieze board from ¾-in. MDF shelf board. MDF is stable and holds paint well, and shelf board is a convenient way to buy it. We mitered the outside corners and butted the insides. The inside and outside corners had to look good, but the fit against the ceiling and the tops of the cabinets didn't matter much since we were adding moldings in both places.

MARK THE CABINET. Because they're so close, any variation in spacing between the frieze board and the tops of the doors would be obvious. Mark the frieze location carefully.

NAIL THE FRIEZE BOARD. Be sure to hit both the tops of the cabinets and the cleats on the ceiling.

CHECK FOR PLUMB. To ensure tight joints, it's crucial that the frieze be plumb. Sometimes a shim or two is required.

NOTCH, AND ADD NAILERS AS NEEDED. Some pieces of frieze board will extend behind others. Notches allow them to clear the cabinets and the cleats. Nailers provide attachment for the abutting frieze board.

Mark the Crown's Location

When installing crown molding for cabinets, the lengths are typically short, so I like to mark the crown for cutting by holding it in place. To ensure I'm holding it at a consistent angle, I mark the location of the crown's top on the ceiling and its bottom on the frieze board. I determine the crown's drop from the ceiling by holding a scrap inside a square and noting the measurement, which I use to make a gauge block.

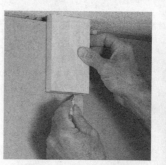

MARK THE CROWN'S BOTTOM. Use a block cut to the length of the crown's drop to mark the location of the crown's bottom on the frieze.

MARK THE CROWN'S TOP. To locate the top, hold a scrap of crown to the bottom line.

Add a Nailer for the Crown

When the joists run perpendicular to the cabinets, they provide nailing every 16 in. When they don't, a piece of 2x stock glued to the drywall offers a solid attachment for crown. Once it dries, carpenter's glue does a surprisingly good job of holding the nailer in place. The trick is securing the piece until the glue dries. For that, drive in long finish nails at opposing angles.

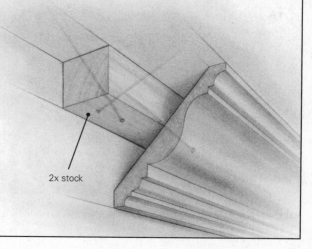

2x stock

Continued ➜

Tackle Tough Pieces First

I start with the most difficult sections, which are typically the short ones, or where there's a piece with two inside corners. Sections with short runs are easier to assemble on a bench; that way, you're sure to get a tight fit. I cut one end of the longer sections, then hold the pieces in place to check the fit before marking the other end for cutting.

FASTEN THE JOINT. Spread some glue inside the joint, and reinforce it with brads.

ASSEMBLE SHORT SECTIONS. Use glue and brad nails to join short sections to longer pieces prior to installation.

Bolection Molding Adds Interest

I had options for the panel molding below the frieze board, but I selected a bolection molding. Most panel moldings (also known as base cap) are ¾ in. thick and would just butt up to the frieze. Bolection molding is milled so that the top edge of the molding lips over the piece above, hiding the joint as well as adding depth and interest. When being cut, bolection molding has to be held at the angle it will be installed.

ADD A SACRIFICIAL SHIM UNDER THE BOLECTION WHEN CUTTING. To get the correct angle, make the shim the same thickness as the piece the molding lips over.

NAIL THE BOLECTION HOME. Hold the lip of the bolection molding tight to the edge of the frieze when nailing.

NAILING IN PLACE. Holding the crown on the lines, fasten it to the frieze and ceiling.

Panel Molding Breaks Up a Wide Board

Adding a panel mold below the crown breaks up the wide frieze and adds interest. I find that placing the band of panel molding about two-thirds of the way between the crown and the bolection is about the right proportion. Unlike the crown and the bolection, panel molding is simply cut flat against the fence.

LOCATE THE BOTTOM OF THE PANEL MOLD. Holding a block against the crown ensures a consistent line.

MARKING IN PLACE MAKES FOR ACCURATE CUTS. Make sure the first end of the piece fits well, then mark the second end with a sharp pencil.

NAIL THE PANEL MOLDING ALONG THE LAYOUT LINES. Particularly with longer pieces, installing along the lines straightens any warped molding.

Cutting Crown Miters on the Flat

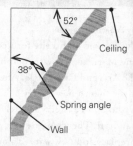

52°
Ceiling
38°
Spring angle
Wall

Wider crown, such as the 7-in. material used here, can't be cut standing up on most miter saws, so it has to be cut lying flat. If the crown is the most common configuration, which springs off the wall at 38° and meets the ceiling at 52°, set the saw at a 33.9° bevel and a 31.6° miter. Most compound-miter saws have marks or detents at these locations. Many newer saws bevel to the left and the right, but older saws as well as some new ones bevel to one side only, usually with the saw tilting to the left, as shown here.

Set the miter angle to the left. To cut the left half of an outside corner or the right half of an inside corner, set the miter 31.6° to the left, and position the bottom of the crown against the fence.

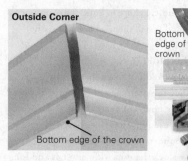

Outside Corner

Bottom edge of the crown

Bottom edge of the crown

33.9° Bevel

31.6° Miter

Set the miter angle to the right . To cut the left half of an inside corner or the right half of an outside corner, set the miter 31.6° to the right, and position the top of the crown against the fence.

Inside Corner

31.6° miter

Top edge of the crown

Continued ➔

Modern Mantel Made Well

By Sebastian Eggert

I've worked at this site for a couple of years now, helping Frank and Marie to renovate their house with a contemporary take on the Arts and Crafts style. After installing trim on the first floor, I made them a new cherry handrail for the stairs. The latest project was to build a cherry mantel that would echo the newel post and handrail. They had carefully chosen the slate that surrounded the fireplace and now wanted a mantel that would frame the slate and tie into the room's scheme of simple trim.

I drew up a plan for a rectilinear mantel that would introduce a pattern of light and shadows around the fireplace. To make sure I maintained a safe distance between the fire and the wood, I checked with the local code (modeled on the 2012 IRC), which states, "No combustible material placed within 12 in. of the fireplace opening (such as mantels or decorative fireplace surrounds) shall project more than ⅛ in. of each 1 in. clearance from the opening."

Since the wall around the fireplace was lumpy and out of plumb, I knew I would have to scribe the parts to fit. Rather than assembling the legs, frieze, and shelf as a unit, I chose to build the components in the shop and then scribe and install them separately on-site.

Prepare the Stock for Scribing

After drawing the design, I picked out stock that was the appropriate size and that had the grain patterns I thought would add to the piece. I had saved a board of curly cherry for a project like this and now planned to use it as the frieze board—the star of the show. As continuity is important in a clear-finished piece like this, I made sure to choose stock that was wide enough and long enough so that I could maintain the grain patterns going around mitered returns.

Working with rough lumber, I had to mill all the parts. Of course, I could have designed a similar surround using factory-surfaced stock found at the lumberyard. At the joiner, I planed one face and one edge of each piece, then ripped and planed the opposite edges to make the stock slightly bigger (about ⅛ in.) than I needed so that I could correct any cup or bow after the initial milling.

When milling the legs, I dadoed their backs to make scribing them to the wall easier. I could have made them from thinner stock and ripped a long miter along the outside edges, but then the grain wouldn't have been continuous. I also dadoed the back of the thick shelf to ease the scribing process.

Assembly on the Bench

The basic plan was to build up the frieze board, attach the shelf to it, and then apply the bands of trim. Once I had milled the legs, I would wait to fit them together with the parting strip and the shelf-and-frieze assembly on-site.

Although it was a gorgeous piece of wood, my prized frieze board wasn't quite wide enough, so I started the assembly by

A Three-Piece Approach

Shelf/frieze
The shelf is connected to the frieze with screws driven through its top. Trimmed with flat stock, the design leans toward Arts and Crafts. Without traditional pegged joinery, cloud lifts, and other embellishments, though, it has a more modern look.

Parting strip
A parting strip eases the transition between the frieze and the legs. The parting strip also reads as the top of the legs, which can be interpreted as columns with a capital supporting the frieze and shelf.

Legs and trim
The surround's legs are milled from solid stock. To help conceal the gap between the legs and the slate, as well as the parting strip and the slate, a small piece of square trim is applied to the inside perimeter of the surround.

Build the Parts in the Shop

Many mantels are built as single units, but because this project required a good deal of scribing, I built up the shelf and frieze as one unit and the legs and parting strip as separate pieces. I then assembled everything on-site

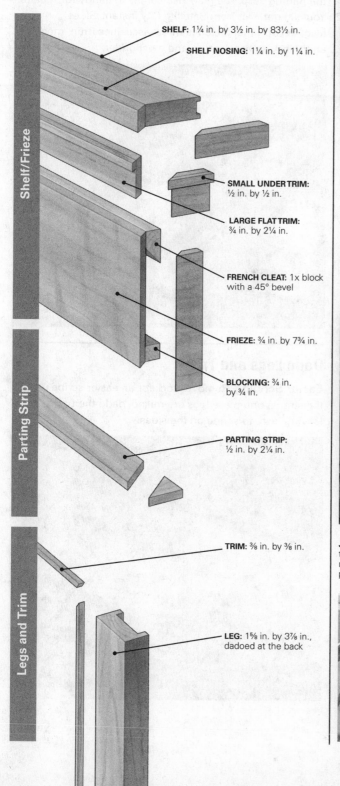

SHELF: 1¼ in. by 3½ in. by 83½ in.

SHELF NOSING: 1¼ in. by 1¼ in.

SMALL UNDER TRIM: ½ in. by ½ in.

LARGE FLAT TRIM: ¾ in. by 2¼ in.

FRENCH CLEAT: 1x block with a 45° bevel

FRIEZE: ¾ in. by 7¾ in.

BLOCKING: ¾ in. by ¾ in.

PARTING STRIP: ½ in. by 2¼ in.

TRIM: ⅜ in. by ⅜ in.

LEG: 1⅝ in. by 3⅞ in., dadoed at the back

Shelf/Frieze

Parting Strip

Legs and Trim

Build the Shelf/Frieze

SHELF: NO FASTENERS. After dry-fitting the miters, glue and clamp the front edge of the band to the shelf. Cauls made from ¼-in. hardboard covered with packing tape (so they won't stick to the glue) register the top of the band to the shelf. Use a long bar clamp to glue the mitered returns.

FRIEZE: WIDE, MITERED RETURNS. Glue the returns to the miters, using tape to hold each piece in alignment, then fasten the joint with a couple of pin nails.

JOIN THE SHELF AND FRIEZE WITH SCREWS. After drilling four pilot holes through the shelf into the frieze, remove the clamps, apply glue, then reclamp the two pieces and secure them with 3-in. #10 screws. Wooden plugs conceal the screws.

ADD SIMPLE LAYERS OF TRIM. With the shelf-and-frieze assembly turned upside down, dry-fit the two smaller layers of trim, then apply glue, clamp in place, and use a few pin nails to secure the miters.

Continued ➜

edge-gluing a piece of cherry to the top of the frieze, where the joint would be covered by trim. Next, I wrapped the shelf with a band of 1¼-in.-thick stock to hide the end grain. The 1¼-in.-thick shelf was well seasoned and less than 4 in. wide, so I wasn't worried about the band popping off at the mitered corners when the humidity changed. I clamped the long front piece to the shelf and marked the miters before cutting them on a chopsaw. I made sure to leave enough material at each end of the piece so the off-cuts could be used as mitered returns with a continuous grain pattern.

To reduce tearout, I cut the stock using a sacrificial fence and bed made from ¼-in. MDF. After gluing and clamping the band along the front edge, I attached the mitered returns and left them to dry.

Returning to the frieze, I sanded and scraped off any dried glue and then cut the mitered returns at both ends. Although I could have used a crosscut sled on a tablesaw or a sliding compound-miter saw to make this wide cut, I used a sliding tablesaw instead. (These big tablesaws have a sliding carriage on the left that pushes past the blade. They're great for cutting sheet goods or straight-lining rough lumber, too. Mine is made by SCMI.) I cut the short returns on a compound-miter saw, then applied glue to both sides of the miter, taped the returns in place, and fastened them with pin nails.

I flipped the frieze onto its face and added the bottom piece of blocking and one-half of the French cleat, a length of 1x stock ripped to a 45° angle. After sanding the mantel shelf, I glued and clamped it to the frieze, then fastened the two pieces together with countersunk #10 screws and plugged the holes.

With the frieze attached to the shelf, I turned the unit upside down on my bench so that I could fit and attach the next two pieces of trim below the shelf. I was very careful to keep the miters clean, especially with these smaller pieces, and I reinforced the glue with a few pin nails.

The last piece to assemble in the shop was the parting strip. Like the other components, it has mitered ends. Because the stock was too thin to nail, I attached the returns with cyanoacrylate (CA) glue. I've found that it's best to apply a layer of thin-viscosity glue to the surface to act as a primer, then apply a second coat of a glue with thicker viscosity, stick the pieces together, and hit the joint with a quick spray of accelerator.

Finish the Parts

When the glue was dry, I sanded all of the mantel components with 180-grit paper, using a random-orbit sander on the larger surfaces and a small foam sanding block for the thinner pieces. I wanted an understated finish for this project, but one that still made the wood grain pop, so I chose a penetrating oil made by BioShield. I applied a liberal coat of the finish with a foam brush and wet-sanded it with 320-grit wet/dry paper. I let it penetrate for about 20 minutes before wiping it off with a clean cloth, then disposing of the combustible wet cloth outside. The next day, I applied a second coat without sanding. Subsequent coats deepen the finish and provide better protection.

A Slick Return

CA Glue I use cyanoacrylate (CA) glue in different viscosities for attaching pieces too small for nails or clamps. Here I used it to glue the thin mitered returns on the parting strip. The glue also comes in handy for repairs. You can get a kit from Satellite City Instant Glues (caglue.com) that includes three viscosities (thin, medium, and thick), an accelerator, and a debonder.

Dado Legs and Trim

Easier Scribing Remove stock for an easier scribe. After the simple one-piece legs are milled, dado the backs, leaving ½ in. to scribe on the sides.

Scribe and Install the Parts On-Site

With all of the mantel components already assembled, installation was a matter of scribing and fastening. I started with the legs, ensuring that they were plumb and level across their tops. With their height established, I scribed and attached the parting strip and then the shelf-and-frieze assembly.

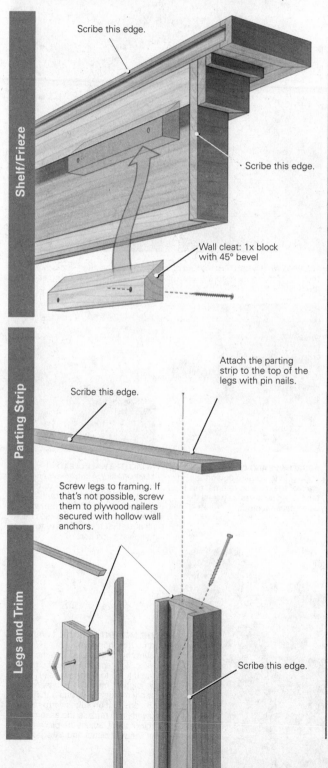

Shelf/Frieze

Scribe this edge.

Scribe this edge.

Wall cleat: 1x block with 45° bevel

Parting Strip

Scribe this edge.

Attach the parting strip to the top of the legs with pin nails.

Screw legs to framing. If that's not possible, screw them to plywood nailers secured with hollow wall anchors.

Legs and Trim

Scribe this edge.

Scribe the Legs and Trim

THE RIGHT SETUP. After positioning the leg plumb side-to-side, shim it plumb to the wall. Set the compass points to the widest gap, then draw scribe lines down both sides of the leg.

SNEAK UP ON THE SCRIBE. After clamping the leg onto a worksurface, use an angle grinder equipped with a chainsaw carving blade. Check the fit, and adjust the scribe as needed.

Fit Parting Strip

ADJUST THE REVEAL. To compensate for the uneven plaster, position the parting strip on the legs and use the compass to mark the amount to be scribed. The result should be an equal reveal over the legs on both sides.

Continued ➔

Installation from the Ground Up

After protecting the floor with mats and setting up my tools, I found the framing in the wall around the fireplace. I began to scribe the legs to the drywall, which was ½ in. out of plumb over 5 ft. I taped a couple of shims together and placed them between the top of each leg and the wall, set my compass to the widest gap, and drew the scribe line down both sides of the leg.

Outside, I used a variety of tools to pare to the scribe line. I have found that a fast way for removing a lot of stock is an angle grinder fitted with a chainsaw blade made by King Arthur (katools.com). I place the back side of the blade flat against the wood, angle it down slightly, and pull back with light strokes. For removing stock on end grain, I use an angle grinder with an abrasive wheel. For touch-ups, I rely on a Makita 9031 narrow-belt sander and a sharp block plane.

After a couple of trial fits, the legs were ready to mount to the wall. On the bottom end of the legs, I drilled a pilot hole ½ in. from the floor. On the top end, I drilled diagonally through the end grain, then drove trim-head screws through both holes and into the framing. (The screw hole at the bottom of each leg gets plugged.) After fitting the parting strip, I attached it to the top of the legs with pin nails. Next, I braced the shelf-and-frieze assembly in position, scribed the back and sides until the shelf was level front to back, then scribed the top so that the shelf conformed to the wall.

With the shelf in place, I marked its height and length on the wall and then removed it to install the 12-in. wall cleats. By nesting the cleats together on the back of the frieze, I could take a measurement from the top of the shelf to the bottom edge of the wall cleat. I then transferred this dimension to the wall. Initially, I attached each cleat with a single screw and hung the shelf and frieze to test the fit. To make minor adjustments, I planed the bevel edge of each cleat until the shelf and frieze were seated against the parting strip correctly. To make significant adjustments, I removed the screw and repositioned the cleat. When everything fit as it should, I locked the cleats in place with additional screws, applied a bead of construction adhesive on each cleat, and reinstalled the shelf-and-frieze assembly. I finished up by pin-nailing a ⅜-in. square band around the inside perimeter of the mantel and installing the baseboard on each side of the legs.

Hang the Shelf/Frieze

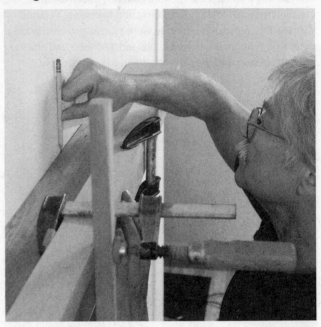

SCRIBING WITH A CRUTCH. Instead of trying to hold the shelf in place while scribing, clamp a block to the shelf, then clamp to the block a long stick that reaches the floor.

AGGRESSIVE AND CAUTIOUS. Use an angle grinder to pare down the end grain of the mitered returns, this time using an abrasive wheel that won't cause tearout.

ATTACH THE WALL CLEATS TEMPORARILY. After measuring from the top of the shelf to the underside of the cleat, transfer the cleat measurements to the wall. Use only one screw to attach each cleat so that it will be easy to adjust the cleat's position.

THE MOMENT OF TRUTH. Carefully drop the shelf-and-frieze assembly onto the cleats, align it to the leg on each side, and check the fit. (It may need a tap to settle properly.) If the fit is good, remove the assembly, apply more screws and a thin bead of construction adhesive to the wall cleats, and replace the assembly. If the fit is off, adjust the placement of the wall cleats and try again.

Laying Out Basic Stair Stringers

By Andy Engel

The essence of laying out stair stringers is straightforward. You use a framing square to draw the stair's notches on the stringer, then you cut them out. If you've done the math (it's grade-school stuff) and the layout right, the tread cuts will be level and the riser cuts plumb.

The International Residential Code (IRC) governs the maximum rise (the height of each step) and the minimum run (the depth of each step), which are 7¾ in. and 10 in., respectively. Many jurisdictions, particularly in the Northeast, allow an 8¼-in. rise and a 9-in. run. Treads on stairs with a run of less than 11 in. must overhang the riser below by a minimum of ¾ in. and a maximum of 1¼ in., so tread depth is actually larger than the run.

Finding Rise and Run

Measure from the finished floor at the bottom of the stairs to the finished floor at the top to find the overall rise. If the finished floor isn't in place, measure from the subfloor, adding the thickness of the upper flooring and subtracting the thickness of the bottom flooring. If the finished floor won't be in place when you install the stringers, add its thickness to the height of the bottom riser, or shim the stringers.

Let's say the overall rise is 46 in. To find the minimum number of risers required for the stair, divide the overall rise by the IRC's maximum rise of 7.75 in. That works out to 5.93, which rounds up to six risers. (Always round up; rounding down results in a taller rise that's not code compliant.) Now divide the overall rise by the number of risers: 46 in. ÷ 6 = 7.66 in., or 7¹¹/₁₆ in. There is always one less tread than there are risers. This stair would have five treads.

Maximum run is governed by materials and building limitations. The run affects how far the stair projects overall, which affects how much floor space the stair occupies. Common nominal 12-in. tread material measures 11¼ in., creating a code-compliant tread overhang on stairs with runs between 10 in. and 10½ in. Using a 10-in. run, this six-riser, five-tread stair would project out 50 in. from the top landing. If you wanted a stair that was not quite as steep, you could add another riser and tread: 46 in. ÷ 7 = 6.57 in., or a riser height of 6⁹/₁₆ in. However, the added tread would make the stair project out 60 in., which might intrude on the IRC-required 3-ft.-deep landing at the bottom. The IRC also requires 80 in. of headroom measured plumb above the line of the tread nosing. Shallower stairs can impinge on this headroom.

You can make a stair shallower by using a bigger run, but this creates another problem. There should be at least 5 in. of stringer stock left at the back after cutting the notches. Using 2×12 stringer stock and a 10-in. run barely leaves 5 in., and a bigger run would leave even less.

After you've decided the rise and run, lay out the stringer with a framing square. Consistent layout is crucial. The IRC allows no more than a ⅜-in. variation in riser height or run depth over a stair. Aim for none. Clamp a strip of wood to the square so that its edge aligns with the stair's rise and run dimensions. This creates a guide that helps make the layout precise.

1. CLAMP A GUIDE TO THE SQUARE. To make it easy to align the framing square on the stringer consistently, clamp a straight wood strip to the square. On the outer edges of the square, align the strip with the run dimension on one leg and the rise dimension on the other.

2. FIND THE CROWN. Sight down the edge of the stringer stock to determine if it crowns. If it does, lay out the stringer so that the crown on the completed stair will face upward.

3. LAY OUT THE FIRST TREAD AND THE SECOND RISER. Hold the square so that the leg with the tread dimension is closest to the end of the stringer stock but far enough from the end to allow for a riser below. Try to lay out the notches so that cutting them gets rid of knots and defects.

Continued ➜

4. LAY OUT THE SECOND TREAD AND THE THIRD RISER. Slide the square up, and carefully align the tread dimension with where the riser line below intersects the edge of the stringer. Continue up the stringer until you've laid out as many treads as are needed.

5. MARK THE BACK OF THE TOP TREAD. You don't have to lay out the upper riser; just make a mark so you know exactly where the tread ends.

9. DON'T OVERCUT THE NOTCHES. Stop the circular saw at the back of the notch, and finish the cuts with a handsaw. Cutting beyond the notch with the circular saw is faster, but it weakens the stringer.

6. MARK THE PLUMB CUT AT THE TOP OF THE STRINGER. Flip the square around to the bottom of the stringer, and mark a cutline from the back of the top tread to the bottom of the stringer.

7. LAY OUT THE BOTTOM RISER. Holding the guide tight to the stringer, align the riser dimension with where the first tread intersects the stringer, and mark the first riser. Extend this line all the way.

8. ADJUST THE FIRST RISER HEIGHT. Deduct one tread thickness from the first riser, or that step will be higher than the rest. Add the thickness of the finished floor to the riser if the flooring isn't installed.

10. USE THE FIRST STRINGER AS A TEMPLATE. To lay out subsequent stringers, align the cut stringer with the edge of the stringer stock, and draw lines. Make the cut, removing the pencil line.

A New Approach to Classic Cabinets

By Mike Maines

The room in the southwest corner of our 1830s Greek revival is by far the fanciest in the house, with its tall baseboards and door casing with flat planes meeting at an angle instead of the more common rounded field. Even the windows are fancy—at least by the standards of rural Maine—with the casings running to the floor and a flat panel under each that is finished to match the walls. The existing fireplace surround, however, was not very attractive.

My wife and I appreciate the history of our house, but we have no desire to live in a museum. So we decided it was time to design and build a fireplace surround, complete with a pair of bookcase cabinets, that would be honest to the spirit of the house but updated with a slightly modern feel.

Over the years, I've refined my approach to building cabinets without the luxury of a fully stocked cabinetry shop, so I knew this was a project I could tackle on site.

Modernizing the Style

The design process involved a lot of sketches and scribbles, but it breaks down simply: The fireplace surround is proportioned to be stocky and proud, just like the house. The flanking bookcases have clean lines and flush surfaces. Meant to evoke classical columns, they look traditional without being fussy. The two pilasters (the legs of the mantel) sit on plinth blocks. The frieze (or lintel) projects beyond the pilasters by ¼ in., just like the plinth blocks. The mantel shelf is 1¼ in. thick, just like most of the other horizontal components, with a flat, angled molding supporting the shelf. After considering many options for the supporting molding, we settled on a simple, angled crown. I realized later that this matches the crown molding on the house's exterior, which gave me confidence that I was on the right track.

Start with the Right Materials

Most of this project makes use of two materials: solid ¾-in. (nominal 4/4) D4S (dressed on four sides) poplar lumber and ¾-in. veneer-core birch plywood. Poplar is my go-to material for paint-grade trim and cabinetry. It is hard, stable, affordable, relatively knot-free, and usually straight-grained. It is also easy to work with both hand tools and power tools, and it's readily available here in the Northeast.

For carcases, I like to use a good grade of veneer-core plywood. When choosing between plywood panels, my first decision involves the quality of the face veneer, which in order from best to worst is graded AA, A, B, C, D, and E. Here, I used plywood with a grade-B face, which is better than shop-grade plywood but not the fully grain-matched product that is typical for stain-grade work. The back side of the plywood can be graded as 1, 2, 3, or 4. I chose a grade-1 back, which is nearly as nice as the grade-B face except that it can have more filled knots. I like birch for the face veneer because it has a discreet but still slightly apparent grain pattern, yet it costs a little less than other veneers. I prefer veneer-core plywood over MDF-core plywood because it's lighter and the dust is

Face Frames Come First

Everybody wants to build the boxes first and then add the face frames. Even if you have the room to work around a bunch of boxes while you try to mill, assemble, and install the face frames, why bother? Maybe you like to build each cabinet separately from start to finish. Good luck making a living with that approach. To make money, you need to be fast. Build the face frames first, then set them aside.

HIDDEN SCREWS. After marking the rail positions on the stiles, fasten each rail with at least two pocket screws. For wider rails, use more screws, and make sure to favor the outer edges of the boards to help prevent cupping. Once fastened, the frame can be sanded smooth on both sides and set aside.

SHELF-PIN HOLES ON THE CHEAP. Instead of buying a jig, mark and drill the desired pin layout into ¼-in. plywood. Clamp the template along the edge of the side pieces, and use a self-centering shelf-pin drill bit to bore the holes.

PAIRS OF POCKETS. The face frame is screwed to the case sides through pocket holes drilled in pairs. Use only one hole out of each pair; if the first screw pushes parts out of alignment, you have a second option right there.

Continued ➜

not as nasty. Finally, I use ¾-in. plywood for carcases because it's thick enough to accept screws and pocket-hole joinery.

The cabinet backs for this project were made from red birch coated with a clear oil finish. Not just any red birch (which in the Northeast, at least, usually refers to the heartwood of a yellow birch or sometimes a paper birch), the boards in this project were cut from logs recovered from the bottom of Maine's Moosehead Lake. The boards I chose have tight grain, rich color, lots of character, and a great story to go with them.

To be true to the house, we decided to use traditional butt hinges for the doors, albeit installed in my slightly nontraditional manner, which allows for some adjustment if the doors warp a bit.

Traditional Work Can Still Use Modern Joinery

Although I considered using my Festool Domino joiner to build the face frames, I ultimately opted for the speed and simplicity of pocket-screw joinery on these parts. I like to add a dab of glue to the joints; end-grain gluing only has one-tenth the strength of edge-grain gluing, but I think it contributes to the joint staying tight and not telegraphing through the paint.

For joining the plywood carcases, I used my no-fuss, adjustable method in which each box is constructed loosely and then tweaked as needed to fit the more-rigid face frame. I have tried every possible way to join face frames to carcases; my go-to method for paint-grade work is to glue the face frames on, tacking them in place with 18-ga. brad nails. The downside to that method is that the filled nail holes sometimes telegraph through the paint. Because our new house has an intermittently wet basement, I expect significant fluctuations in humidity, so I chose my "high-end" system of attaching the face frames with pocket screws.

The backs presented an unusual challenge. I typically use plywood because it's self-squaring and easy to attach with screws or narrow-crown staples. But solid wood needs room for seasonal movement. I bought the red birch planks rough-sawn, then milled them to ¾ in. thick, straightened them with a track saw, and grooved their edges with a router. The groove was sized to accept plywood splines that hold everything in plane but still allow the solid boards to expand and contract. I drilled pilot holes in the perimeter and center of each board, but to allow for expansion, I used the Domino to create elongated slots at each edge of the wider boards. All the boards are attached to the carcase with bugle-headed cabinet screws.

To attach the cabinets to the wall, I used #10 wood screws with finishing washers, placed to lower their visibility once the shelves were installed and loaded with books. I shimmed the cabinets adequately at the floor, so the screws in the wall aren't bearing any weight.

The cabinets and the trim are both finished with Sherwin-Williams' All Purpose Latex Primer and topcoated with two coats of Benjamin Moore's Advance waterborne alkyd paint in a semigloss finish. I had planned to use my Graco airless spray gun for the primer coat only, because I think a brushed finish is more appropriate for an old house like ours, but once I went through the effort to mask everything off, I decided to spray the two topcoats as well. The finish came out great, and I highly recommend the paint, which flows out better and dries harder than regular latex paints. My wife and I love the way the new fireplace surround ties the room together.

Assembly Should Leave Room for Adjustment

If you've cut all the parts correctly, the face frame and the plywood should line up perfectly. Here's how to assemble the carcases when they don't.

START WITH NAILS. Tack the plywood box together with 15-ga. or 16-ga. finish nails. It will be a little floppy, but that's a good thing at this point.

HIDDEN ATTACHMENT. After nailing the box together, align the long sides of the face frame to the cabinet, and fasten them with pocket-hole screws. The screws will be covered by end panels after installation.

TAP IT INTO ALIGNMENT. Use a hammer and block to tap the tops, bottoms, and any fixed shelves into alignment, then fasten them with pocket screws.

SECURE IT WITH SCREWS. After everything is aligned, fasten through the sides of the cabinet with 1⅝-in. screws. Shorter screws won't hold well, and longer screws may lead to splits.

SOLID BACKS MEAN EXTRA STEPS. After slotting the edge of each back board to receive a ¼-in.-thick plywood spline, fasten the boards with screws in a combination of countersunk and slotted holes to allow for seasonal movement.

Scribe for a Tight Fit

I usually leave a stile that will butt against a wall or other finished surface ¼ in. to ¾ in. wider than necessary so that it can be scribed for a perfect fit. After marking the scribe in place, I lay the cabinet flat on its back so that I can cut to the line and then finish the edge with a block plane.

TRIM THE FAT. Use a track saw to remove as much wood as possible without reaching the scribe line. Back-cutting at a 30° bevel makes the hand-planing easier.

FINISH WITH CARE. For a simple scribe, use a block plane to shave up to the line. Complicated scribes may need a jigsaw or an angle grinder with a sanding disk.

Doors That Break All the Rules

A typical cabinet door consists of a framework of rails and stiles—usually assembled with cope-and-stick, mortise-and-tenon, or other joinery—with grooved edges that capture a panel. The frame holds the panel but allows it to expand and contract seasonally. For this project, I tried a new technique.

I used the Festool Domino tool to cut slots on all edges of the ¾-in. plywood panels, rails, and stiles, and on the ends of the rails. After cutting a rabbet around the panel to create a reveal, I glued the panels right in their frames.

MARK TO AVOID MIX-UPS. Arrange the door parts with their finished sides facing up. Draw a triangle in the center of the panel, then mark each stile and rail with the corresponding portion of the triangle that matches its position relative to the panel. Mark the same number in each triangle so that you know the grouping and orientation of each part.

SLOTS, NOT BISCUITS. In terms of layout and use, operating the Domino is very similar to operating a biscuit joiner. Mark both pieces where they will join, dial in the height and depth, and plunge the tool into each piece to create a matching slot.

A RABBETED SHADOWLINE. To disguise the joint between panel and door frame, and to create a nice reveal, rabbet the edges of each panel on the finished side. Hit the rabbets with spackle, primer, and a light sanding before assembly.

Continued ➔

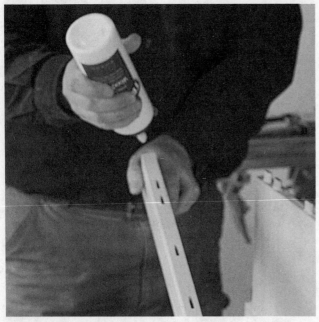

GLUE AND CLAMP. After inserting glue and tenons into the edges of the plywood panel, dab glue into the tenon holes of the stiles, rails, and along their edges. Position the rails first, repeat the process for the stiles, and then clamp everything together. Using a straightedge as a guide, adjust the position of the clamps to ensure that the doors are flat.

The Tricks to Quick Butt Hinges

I chose the BH2A series of butt hinges from Cliffside Industries because I like the adjustment offered by their slotted holes. When working with these butt hinges, I like to follow two tricks I learned from a local cabinetmaker. First, mortise the door only; the other leaf of the hinge will create a nice reveal. Second, don't bother with stopped mortises; cut them right from the front of the door through to the back.

SITE-MADE MORTISE JIG. Plywood scraps are all that's needed to make a custom hinge jig. A router with a flush-bearing bit rides the jig to cut the through mortise.

PLAN FOR ADJUSTABILITY. Place the hinges with the horizontal holes on the door and the vertical holes on the cabinet, and you'll have some room for adjusting.

HANG AND ADJUST IN PLACE. With the hinges in place on the cabinet doors, hold the doors in position while you transfer the hinge locations to the face frame. Attach the door, and tweak as needed for a perfect close.

A Faster Approach to Custom Cabinets

By Mike Maines

When designed and constructed properly, built-in cabinets can bring both style and storage to many parts of a home. Over the years, I've refined my approach to constructing cabinets to decrease the time and tools it takes to build them while ensuring their strength and good looks. I used my technique to build the Douglas-fir kitchen island featured here for my home, but I've followed the same process to make stain- and paint-grade kitchen cabinets, bookcases, linen cabinets, pantries, desks, bathroom vanities, and storage cubbies.

Your Shop is Where You Make It

The beauty of this system is that the setup is simple and doesn't rely on the space or tools found in big cabinet shops. Being able to set up shop in a driveway, a garage, or a small room has always been helpful in keeping my work on schedule.

The tools you need to construct these cabinets are likely sitting in the back of your truck. For cutting components to size, you need a miter saw, a portable tablesaw, a circular saw, an edge guide to cut sheet goods safely, and a portable thickness planer. To fasten the carcase and face frames together, you need a 16-ga. or 18-ga. finish nailer, a screw gun, a pocket-screw jig (www.kregtool.com; www.pennstateind.com), a bunch of screws, and some glue.

A Hybrid Design Makes Face-Frame Cabinets Better

Cabinets are typically designed in one of two ways: frameless or with face frames. Each has its merits. Face-frame cabinets are traditional and strong, and they can be scribed to fit seamlessly against a wall. Frameless cabinets are quicker to put together and can be used in conjunction with adjustable, hidden, and now soft-close hinges.

I've done a lot of historically informed work, and frameless boxes just don't provide the appeal of face-frame cabinets with inset doors. Although frameless cabinets allow a bit more space inside, their end panels tend to look tacked-on, crown molding is hard to detail properly, and filler strips are heavily relied on during installation. I use the benefits of both styles by building a hybrid cabinet. Flushing the inside of the carcase to the inside of the face frame allows me to use hardware designed for frameless cabinets while still providing the traditional look, ease of installation, and strength of face-frame construction.

Screws, Glue, and Quality Hardware Hold It Together

Traditionally, face-frame cabinets are constructed with dadoes, grooves, dowels, or mortise-and-tenon joinery to lock together each component. These techniques create strong assemblies too, but require much more time.

I assemble face frames with fine-thread, 1¼-in. square-drive washer-head pocket screws and yellow glue. I tack the carcases together with finish nails and then drive 1⅝-in. drywall screws for strength. I've used drywall screws for years and have never had a cabinet fail, but it's important to use stronger screws when attaching a cabinet to the wall.

Beyond box strength, cabinets are often measured by the quality of their hardware. The best hinge for this hybrid system is a 32-mm cup hinge made by Blum (www.blum.com) or Mepla (www.mepla-alfit.com). Adjustable, self-closing, and quick to install, they are usually my first choice. In more historically accurate work where a visible hinge is preferred or when I don't want a hinge to intrude on storage space, I like to use Cliffside's 2-in. butt hinges (www.cliffsideind.com). I use a trim router to mortise the door for a single leaf and don't mortise the face frame at all, which helps to provide just the right reveal between the door and the face frame.

I've used all three types of drawer slides (see "What's the Difference," *Fine Homebuilding* #184), but when I have a choice, I opt for the Blum Tandem, an undermount full-extension unit that is forgiving to install and smooth to operate.

For adjustable shelves, I like to drill groups of three to five holes where I think the shelf should be. This allows some adjustability while avoiding the factory-made look of a continuous row of holes. Often, I use paddle-type supports installed in a 5-mm hole. For heavy-duty applications, such as a bookshelf, I like an L-shaped pin in a ¼-in. hole.

Get Doors and Drawer Fronts That Fit the Second Time

I order or build doors and drawer fronts before the built-ins are complete so that I can finish the job quickly. To be sure they fit the way I want them to, with the perfect reveal, I have them built to the exact size of the face-frame opening written on my plans. Once on site, I fit them tight into their openings. I reduce their size on all sides a heavy ¹⁄₁₆ in. by taking measurements from the face frame, not the door or drawer front itself, and rip them on the tablesaw.

Continued →

Good Proportions Are No Accident

Although my built-in cabinets are assembled easily, there's no guarantee they'll look good in a home. A cabinet constructed with wacky proportions won't look or function as well as it should. To start, make a scale drawing on paper of each piece you intend to build. Having this reference on hand will give you a clear idea of what you're building and help you to create a detailed cutlist. I follow a few basic rules when it comes to designing cabinets.

BUILT-IN CABINETS THAT WILL BE USED AS WORKSTATIONS generally have countertops 36 in. above the floor, so boxes should be built to a height of 34½ in. to 35 in., depending on the thickness of the countertop. Cabinets that aren't task-oriented can be any size and are built without toe kicks. I distinguish these units by building the bottom rail taller or shorter than the house's baseboard. When in doubt of any proportions, I use the golden rectangle, a shape 1.6 times as high as it is wide. I also find the widths of components by dividing similar members by 1.6 as done with the end-panel rails.

Drawers can be made as wide as 36 in. when used with quality undermount drawer slides.

End stiles on open shelving should lap the front edge of the shelf by ¼ in.

WHEN MULTIPLE CABINET BOXES ARE LINED UP in a row, they appear more fitted when tied together with a single face frame. I connect the boxes by hiding a screw behind each door hinge. You can make all the face-frame components the same size, but that can make the rails look fat and the end stiles look skinny. Instead, I like to adjust their widths so that the built-in looks more balanced.

Face-frame rails should be 1 in. or 1¼ in. wide.

Divide the width of the bottom rail by 1.6 to determine the width of the panel's top rail. In this case, its width should be either 3⅛ in. or 3⁷⁄₁₆ in.

A 5-in.- or 5¼-in.-wide bottom rail on the end panel matches the dimension of the toe-kick space, plus the width of the face frame's bottom rail.

A toe kick should measure 4 in. off the finished floor and be built into assemblies only where someone will be working directly above them. This gives the unit a more furniturelike appearance.

Stiles in the middle of the face frame should measure 1½ in. across their width.

The standard width for door and drawer rails and stiles is 2¼ in. But widths as large as 3¼ in. still look good.

The stiles on the end of a face frame should be 1¾ in. wide to add mass to the assembly and to cover the edge of the end-panel face frame.

DOORS SHOULD ALWAYS BE TALLER THAN THEY ARE WIDE and should never exceed 20 in. in width; otherwise they project too far into a space when opened. Even an 18-in.-wide door can be too large on certain units. Drawers should be left with a flat face when they're shorter than 4½ in., which is typical, and can be detailed to match frame-and-panel doors when they're taller.

Cut All the Face-Frame Components at Once

When milling 1×6 face-frame material to size, I like to fine-tune its final width with a planer, not a tablesaw. I rip the face-frame stock ⅛ in. wider than I need on a tablesaw. Then I remove the last ⅛ in. with a planer. The planer produces more precise dimensions and smoother cuts.

RIP STOCK TO WIDTH. Use a tablesaw to square all boards with rounded edges. Then cut all face-frame components ⅛ in. wider than their final dimension.

PLANE SIMILAR PARTS TOGETHER. Instead of planing each board individually, plane all the end stiles, then inner stiles, then rails to their exact width.

CHOP TO LENGTH. Armed with a fence and a stop made of scrap material, and a cutlist, chop all the face-frame material to its precise length. Stack all the material to make a complete face frame.

Assemble the Face Frames First

I build all the face frames before I build their corresponding boxes. This not only saves room on the job site, but it also allows me to use the face frames for reference when a dimension comes into question during carcase construction.

LAY OUT THE PARTS, AND MARK POCKET-HOLE LOCATIONS. Dry-fit the face-frame components so that their grain and color look best. Mark the boards to show their orientation in the assembly and where they'll be pocket-screwed.

A POCKET-HOLE JIG MAKES ASSEMBLY EASY. Drill two pocket holes in the end of each rail and each inner stile.

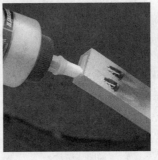

SQUEEZE THE GRAIN TO ELIMINATE SPLITTING. Put a bit of wood glue on the board end before securing a locking C-clamp so that it exerts equal pressure on the grain of each component. The clamp should be placed in line with the pocket hole being screwed.

QUALITY CONTROL. Check to be sure that every component is aligned and secured properly before building subsequent frames. Accuracy here is crucial because the dimensions of the face frame might be used as a reference when building the boxes.

Continued ➜

Build the Boxes

Box assembly is a relatively straightforward process. Before the sides of the boxes are fastened together, though, I drill pocket holes and the holes for shelving pins.

CUT SHEET GOODS safely. Full sheets of plywood should never be cut on a tablesaw. Instead, use a straightedge clamped to the sheet's surface and a circular saw with a fine-toothed alternate top bevel (ATB) sawblade.

DRILL POCKET HOLES IN GROUPS OF TWO. When preparing the sides of the carcase that will be joined with the face frame, drill two holes instead of one for each connection point. This extra step will come in handy when attaching the face frames.

TACK AND SCREW TOGETHER THE BOX PARTS. Nailing the box with 16-ga. finish nails makes it easier to keep pieces in place while they're locked together with 1⅝-in. drywall screws.

SUPPORT THE BOX AND THE DRAWER SLIDES. On top of each box and below each drawer, ¾-in. plywood crosspieces add strength, a place to connect the face frame's top rail, and a surface to attach countertops and undermount drawer slides.

Jig Tip
I make a simple jig out of thin MDF to orient shelf pinholes 1½ in. from the front and back of the box. I usually place the first hole 12 in. off the bottom of the box and drill holes in 1½-in. increments above and below.

Attach the Face Frames to the Boxes

A face frame can be nailed to a box with 16-ga. finish nails. However, the holes still need to be filled, and the gun can scuff the face-frame surface. Another way to attach face frames is with biscuit joinery, a solid solution, but one that demands a lot of time and a massive arsenal of clamps. By attaching the face frame with pocket screws, I get an immediate, permanent connection while leaving the face of the cabinet clear.

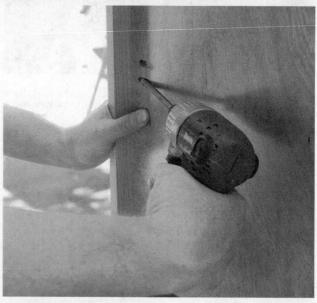

PICK A HOLE, BUT NOT JUST ANY HOLE. Although I drilled groups of two pocket holes in the box, only one hole in each set needs to be screwed. The face frame should flush with the inside of the box perfectly, but if it doesn't, having multiple holes gives you the flexibility to push and pull the face frame into alignment.

Dress Up an Exposed End Panel

Built-in cabinets usually have their sides buried in a wall. Sometimes, however, the sides and even the back are exposed to public view. I detail these areas to hide pocket holes in a couple of ways.

On my kitchen island, I'm using a stock of reclaimed Douglas-fir edge and center bead that has been collecting dust in my garage for years. I simply fill the face-frame opening with the boards, attaching them with an 18-ga. pin nailer. Held tight against the carcase, the ¾-in.-thick face frame would leave a ¼-in. reveal where it meets the end stiles of the front face frame. So I fur out the end panel with ³⁄₁₆-in. plywood strips to reduce the size of the reveal.

If I'm not going to use beadboard on a built-in, I fill the face frame with ½-in. plywood to create a flat recessed panel. Alternatively, I cover the entire side of the carcase with a sheet of ¼-in. plywood that can be stained or painted to match the wood I've used, then glue and nail the face frame to it.

COVER YOUR TRACKS. To hide pocket holes and screws used to assemble the cabinet, wrap exposed faces with a decorative material, such as stain- or paint-grade plywood, beadboard, or edge and center bead.

Bookcases Transform an Unused Wall

By **Brent Benner**

I like books, the kind with paper pages and dust jackets, and I hope they survive the rise in popularity of electronic books. But then, I spend my days building cabinets, not computers. And lucky for me, although e-books might be diminishing the need for bookshelves, there always will be a demand for attractive, efficient storage spaces and quality construction.

This project started when my clients realized that they needed more storage space for books in their Manhattan apartment. The target area was a wall in the bedroom that had two closet doors. The challenge was designing the bookcases around the steel door jambs and between mechanical chases and irregular plaster walls. Because I would build everything in my shop, I had to have accurate site measurements. I figured that making both horizontal and vertical story poles was the best way to avoid mistakes. I marked on the story poles the door locations, plumbing chases, and spaces needed so that I would have room to scribe the bookcases to the walls.

In general, it's a really good idea to measure the walls where a cabinet's face frames will intersect, not back at the corner. (This was especially true here because the walls in this apartment were concrete, out of square, and not parallel.) Back in the shop, I based all my measurements on the pole, which meant there was a lot less chance of a transcription or math error.

Continued →

To visualize the project and solve design issues, after measuring the space I also took a couple of photos of the location and then drafted a design with the help of Google SketchUp.

The idea was to use the available space, so I drew a big cabinet between the doors, and a narrow cabinet on one side. A short cabinet would sit above each of the doors and tie the unit together. All told, the cabinets would create about 35 cu. ft. of book space.

Building a Strong Cabinet is Time Well Spent

Bookcases are simple to build and a great project for woodworkers of all skill levels. I built the cases and shelves with ¾-in. cabinet-grade plywood and the face frames with ¾-in. poplar. To make the boxes stiff and avoid the bother of nailing cleats, I used ½-in. cabinet-grade plywood for the backs. After ripping the box sides to width, I made a story pole to lay out the shelf spacing and then used it to mark the sides. Although I often make adjustable shelves, for this project I used fixed shelves that were fitted into dadoes on the cabinet sides. This arrange-ment gave the cabinet more rigidity. I glued and clamped the box sides and shelves together, and tacked them with a couple of finish nails per joint. Once the basic box was assembled, I cut the plywood to fit the back, then stapled and glued it into place.

Next, I attached the poplar face frame. To give the project a custom look, I milled the stock to size and then added a bead detail that was mitered at the corners. (For more on my technique, see "Master Carpenter," "Dress up cabinet face frames with a mitered integral bead," *Fine Homebuilding* #200). I joined the face-frame sections together with pocket screws and then fastened the entire frame to the case with glue and biscuits. I also primed and finish-painted everything before installation to save time, although the clients eventually settled on another color.

Make the Boxes Fit

To support a bookcase, I usually build a separate base from 3-in.-wide strips of ¾-in. plywood that resembles a shipping pallet. Because each base is separate, it can be leveled and aligned prior to positioning the bookcases. As these tall bookcases extended from the floor to the ceiling, I also could stand them upright and then place them on the base without hitting the ceiling.

Once the bases are in position, I like to start on one side and fit each cabinet, then set it aside. After the scribes are complete, I assemble the cabinets. At this job, I started with the short left-hand cabinet. Next, the large middle cabinet had to be fit between two doorways. The thin right-hand cabinet had to be scribed around a horizontal chase and along an unplumb wall. On complicated scribes like this, it's best to remove stock in stages and test the fit as you go, rather than try to scribe and cut all in one pass. The walls were also a problem. Working with conventionally framed stud walls, I screw the cabinets to the framing, hiding the screws if possible. At this job, the walls were concrete, and I used concrete screws that required pilot holes to secure the bookcase. It was easy enough to fasten the baseboard to the cabinet bases, but I had to glue triangular blocking to the ceiling so that I could nail up the crown molding.

The last component of this job was the trim. I had to match the existing profiles, but instead of having a custom profile made, I found an online molding catalog (www.gardenstatelumber.com) and ordered what I needed. I coped the new stock to the old with a coping foot made for a jigsaw. I also made use of my narrow-profile air-powered sander to adjust the fit of the copes. Finally, a shoe molding obscured any discrepancies between the baseboard and the flooring.

Measure on Site

Use a story pole to determine the exact horizontal and vertical size of a space. It's more accurate than using a measuring tape. Take two long pieces of 1×2 and extend them to each side, then mark where they cross. Chases, door frames, and other obstacles can be marked right on the poles. Although it's tempting to measure only at the plane of the wall, it's best also to measure the walls, top and bottom, where the face frames will inter-sect. Take the poles back to the shop, and use the measurements to build the drawing.

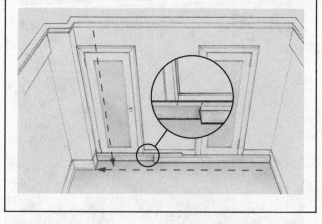

Measure Twice, Cut Once

Accurate on-site measurements prevent mistakes in the shop

Rip, Then Rabbet

Start by ripping the plywood to width and cutting rabbets for the corners and back with a dado stack. After marking the dado positions for the shelves, use a T-square dado jig to guide a router through the dadoes. Use a $^{23}/_{32}$-in. straight plywood bit so that the shelves fit snugly.

Assemble the Box

Glue the rabbeted corners together, and apply bar clamps. To keep the sides from distorting, lay a piece of plywood that's cut to the overall width of the box across the sides to act as a gauge.

Production Shelving

After cutting the shelves and nosing to length, biscuit and glue them together. It's faster to clamp them in pairs, using scrap as cauls to spread out the clamping pressure.

Make the Frame and Attach

Bead the face-frame stock on a router table, and then cut it to length. Miter the beads, then assemble the rails and stiles with pocket screws. After the shelves are glued and tacked into their dadoes, biscuit, glue, and clamp the face frame onto the box.

Continued →

Installation Calls for Order

After the bases are in and cabinets are scribed, fit them all together.

1. Separate bases make installation easier

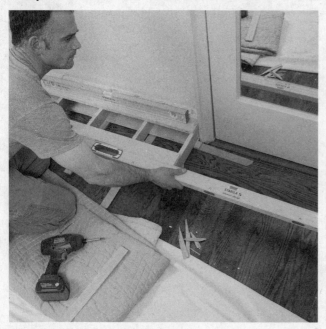

Separate Bases Make Installation Easier

After cutting the existing trim back with a multitool or reciprocating saw, place and level the cabinet bases. Made slightly smaller than the cabinets, the bases can be adjusted so that they're flush to the cabinets' faces while avoiding discrepancies in the corners or intersections of walls and floors. Once shimmed level, they can be screwed to the floor.

2. Scribe to fit, then set aside

2. Scribe to Fit, Then Set Aside

With the cabinet positioned plumb and level, the scribe is set to the amount of overhang on the right. (The author uses FastCap's AccuScribe, but any compass will work.) Follow the contour of the wall, and mark the cabinet's left side. Cut to the line with a jigsaw set to a 15° angle. The back cut makes it easier to make any adjustments to the scribe with a hand plane and/or sandpaper.

3. Fit the cases in order

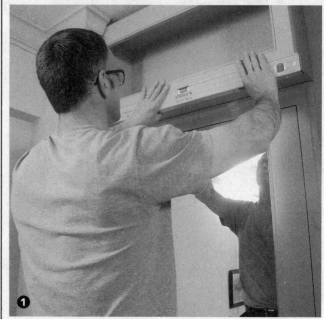

3. Fit the Cases in Order

The left cabinet (1) was scribed first, the middle cabinet (2) was checked for its fit, and the right-hand cabinet (3) was scribed in place. After the left-hand and middle cabinets were screwed into the wall and to each other, the right-hand cabinet was attached to the wall, and the last cabinet (4) was screwed to the adjacent cabinets.

Tricks for Trim

On this job, the concrete walls and ceiling were somewhat uneven, and the crown would need plenty of nailing to make it conform to the ceiling and to match the existing crown. I glued triangular blocks with construction adhesive so that there would be backing on 16-in. centers. The crown was installed left to right, the bottom reveal was kept constant, and the top of the profile was adjusted as needed. After I roughed out the basic cope with a miter saw and a jigsaw, I used an air-powered narrow-profile sander to fine-tune the cut.

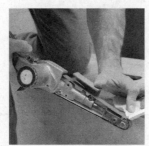

The baseboard was also installed left to right. To make tight miter joints, I cut both halves of the outside miter a little long and pinned them together before scribing them into their final positions. A shoe molding covers any discrepancies between the floor and the baseboard.

Cabinet Door Shoot-Out

No matter who you are or what you do, you can always find a conflict between tradition and innovation. You can't have one without the other, because if it's successful, an innovation becomes the tradition. That's how progress works. Because both old and new have their advantages, sometimes they can coexist. In the world of cabinetmaking, there are lots of traditions and innovations that coexist, sometimes in the same shop.

For this article, Fine Homebuilding brought two cabinetmakers into our shop to see how they would approach the construction of a simple cabinet door. We specified that the door should be made of cherry with a ½-in. cherry-plywood panel that would add strength to the door but not overcomplicate the process. There are lots of issues at play here: the role of craftsmanship in the shop versus production work on the job site, handwork versus machine work, centuries-old joinery versus a relatively new approach, plus the opportunity for some bragging rights among friends. In the end, both approaches proved well suited to their particular applications.

Mortise and Tenon

By Scott Gibson

I have a lot of confidence in a traditional mortise-and-tenon door. The wood-to-wood contact is substantial, meaning there's a large glue area, and the joints are highly resistant to racking. A door with tight-fitting joints is extremely durable.

The process is more time-consuming than making cope-and-stick joints with a router, and it isn't as well suited to making doors on a job site. That said, the work goes surprisingly fast once the machine settings have been dialed in. For tooling, I use a tablesaw and a mortising machine in addition to a few basic hand tools. Mortises could be cut with a drill press or even a portable drill plus a chisel, but the mortising machine is faster and more accurate.

It may be overkill to make doors the way I do, but it wouldn't be the first time I overbuilt something. The advantage I see is that with one setup, mortise-and-tenon joinery can be used to make all the frame-and-panel parts, face frames, and doors for a kitchen's worth of cabinets. It takes some fiddling to get the setup, but once that's done, many pieces can be run off quickly.

Continued ➔

1. Set Up

MAKE A TEST PIECE FIRST FOR SETUP. The one fixed dimension of the mortise and tenon is determined by the size of the mortiser chisel, so the tenon and panel groove are sized to the mortise. A test mortise is cut with a benchtop mortiser fitted with a ¼-in. bit. Measuring the width of the mortise with a set of dial calipers is an accurate way to determine the necessary thickness of the tenon and the panel groove.

2. Groove Stiles and Rails

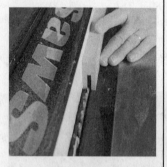

TWO PASSES CUT THE PANEL GROOVE. Although the groove is often cut with a dado stack, it also can be cut with a single tablesaw blade. Because the panel groove measures ¼ in. wide, it can be cut by positioning the fence so that the blade cuts just to one side of the centerline. Registered from either side of the stock, the blade cuts a centered groove in two passes.

3. Mortise Stiles Only

DIALING IN THE MORTISES. After the panel groove is cut, the mortiser is set up to cut on center and to the correct depth. Here, the mortises were cut to 1⅝6 in. deep to make room for glue and a 1¼-in.-long tenon.

4. Tenon the Rails

TENONS ARE CROSSCUT ON THE TABLESAW. Using either a single blade or a dado stack, tenons are cut by first registering the fence at a distance from the blade equal to the length of the tenon. The first pass will cut the cheeks, so it's important that the miter gauge be square to the blade. Moving the stock away from the fence and making repeated passes removes the waste. It's a good idea to check the setup on scrap first.

CHECK THE FIT, AND ADJUST IF NEEDED. Each joint should be tested to ensure a tight fit before assembly. It's best if the tenon needs a few swipes with a plane to fit, rather than having to add a shim.

5. Rabbet the Panel

CUT AND RABBET THE PANEL. Once the frame is ready to be assembled, the panel can be cut. In this case, ½-in. plywood was chosen for a more substantial door. After the panel was cut to size, a rabbet was routed along its back edge.

6. Assemble the Door

THE LAST STEP IS ASSEMBLY. After a thin, even coat of glue is spread on the mating parts, the rails and one stile are joined. Next, the panel is inserted into the groove, the second stile is attached, and the door is clamped. Measure diagonals to make sure the door stays square in the clamps.

Cope and Stick

By Joseph Lanza

I don't know if it qualifies yet as traditional, but millwork factories were producing cope-and-stick joinery a hundred years ago. If you have a table-mounted router, cope-and-stick bits offer a quick, accurate way to make cabinet doors without a big investment.

With a glued-in plywood panel, cope-and-stick doors are extremely strong. Solid-panel doors can be made stronger by adding interior rails or stiles, but for larger doors, cope and stick may not be the best choice, unless the joints are reinforced with slip tenons or dowels. The extra work required might tip me in favor of using mortises and tenons for larger doors.

Although maybe not the best choice for period reproductions, cope-and-stick doors are a good option for jobs that don't require the structural or emotional benefits of mortise-and-tenon joinery. Most of the modern solid-wood cabinet doors in this country are made with a simple cope-and-stick joint, and the vast majority are holding up just fine.

1. Set Up

A TWO-BIT APPROACH. Cope-and-stick router bits are available as single arbors with interchangeable cutters or in sets of dedicated cope and stick bits. The two-bit sets are more accurate and take much less time to set up. (The Amana set used here also can be used to make interior passage doors.) Many sets include thin brass or steel shims that can be inserted between the cutters to match the relative size of the profile to the thickness of the stock.

2. Cope Rail Ends Only

CUT THE COPE FIRST TO REDUCE TEAROUT. After chucking the cope bit into the router, adjust the bit height so that the profile is centered in the stock, and check with a test piece. The opening in the fence should be just large enough to allow the bit to spin without hitting the fence. With a straightedge, check that the bearing is in line with the fence. When cutting, use a backing block to keep the stock square to the bit and to prevent the grain from blowing out at the back of the piece. Cope all rail ends.

3. Stick the Stiles and Rails

SWITCH TO THE STICK BIT. After switching bits, align the middle cutter with the stub tenon on the coped end. Run a test piece to make sure the mating cope and stick align. Run all rails and stiles.

Continued ➜

4. Rabbet the Panel

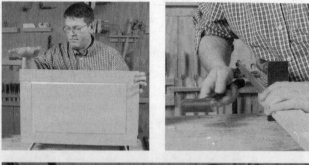

PREP THE PANEL. Dry-fit the rails and stiles, then determine the panel size. Because plywood won't move seasonally, the panel can be cut within 1/16 in. of the actual size. The router table is set up with a straight or dado bit to cut the ¼-in. by ½-in. rabbet on the back.

5. Assemble the Door

ASSEMBLY TIME. It's always a good idea to have a dry run when gluing up a door. If everything fits tightly, apply glue and assemble the rails, stiles, and panel. Clamp at both ends near the rails, and check that the door isn't curling because of too much clamp pressure. Parts that slide out of alignment under pressure can be adjusted back into place with a dead-blow mallet. Finally, check the diagonals to make sure the door is square.

Create a Curved Stair Riser

By Mike Belzowski

As a carpenter, I am always attracted to a finely crafted staircase. Stairs are a place where a carpenter's work really can shine, and they make a statement about the rest of the house. In my house, I wanted to incorporate some curves in the staircase, both to add visual interest and to make the project more challenging.

I designed these stairs with a broad starting step whose curve gradually straightens out over the next two treads. The traditional way to make curved risers is to cut shallow kerfs into the back of the stock so that it will bend more easily. I've never liked that method, which can cause the kerfs to telegraph through to the surface and interrupt the fairness of the curve. Instead, I chose to laminate thin pieces of stock around a form. When this method is complete, the riser's curves are exactly the way I want them. Here, I'll break down my approach to the curved bottom riser and tread.

First, Draw the Plan

Templates are an important part of my stair-building process, especially when I do curved work, and they're based on a full-size drawing. After taking measurements of the existing stair framing and checking to see that everything is level and plumb, I draw the first three risers in plan, full scale on a sheet of ¼-in. plywood.

For accuracy's sake, I draw the risers as equal rectangles, laid out from the centerlines, and then add the radiused ends and curved front. At this point, the lines I've drawn represent the inside of the risers. I add the thickness of the riser stock to all the layout lines and draw in the nosing projection of the treads. I also draw in the wall location and determine newel-post position and centerline on the handrail and balustrade.

The building code says that tread depths cannot vary by more than ½ in. within a staircase, but after talking to the local inspection department, I was able to have a different depth on each of the first three steps.

Build a Form for the Riser

To create an accurate form, I made a ¼-in. plywood pattern based on the full-scale drawing of the inside dimensions of the riser. I made it just over half the size of the plan view so that when I trace it onto the form stock, both sides are identical and the curve is fair across the middle.

Next, I set up a router with a ¼-in. up-spiral bit on a trammel, screwed the trammel to the center of the radius, and routed the radiused end. After cutting out the rest of the shape close to the line with a jigsaw, I faired the curves to the line with a block plane and a spokeshave.

I traced the riser pattern onto a sheet of ¾-in. particleboard, flipping the pattern to get both sides. Again, I used a jigsaw to rough-cut the shape, leaving about 1/16 in. from the line. I screwed the pattern to the particleboard and trimmed half with a router

Use Patterns, Templates, and Forms

The foundation of a curved starting step is the riser. On this job, the riser was laminated from thin layers of poplar and walnut. Making a perfect laminating form starts with a pattern for half of the turn. The pattern can be flipped to make a symmetrical template. The template is repeated, and the layers are glued up into the form.

MAKE THE PATTERN FIRST. To make accurate curves for the pattern, use a router attached to a plywood trammel that's screwed to the center of the curve's radius.

TEMPLATE FOR LAYERS. Use a half-pattern to rout each side of symmetrical layers of particleboard that then are stacked into a clamping form.

THE STURDY FORM. Glued and screwed together, the stack of layers creates a rigid, smooth, and consistent form that won't buckle under clamping pressure.

Mold Thin Layers into a Stair Riser

ONLY AS THIN AS IT NEEDS TO BE. After resawing the laminations and then testing their ability to bend to the target radius, plane all the strips to the thickness that bends without breaking, which in this case is slightly less than 3/32 in.

ASSEMBLY-LINE GLUE-UP. Once the laminations have passed a dry-run clamping test, lay flat each pair of mating pieces, cover them with glue, and fold them together. Repeat the process until the entire 7/8-in.-thick stack is glued together.

Glue Applicator

When I'm gluing up a project, I want to get the glue spread as quickly and evenly as possible. After using various applicators and rollers, I found a hopper glue spreader that works great. Made of aluminum, the hopper holds about a pint of glue that's trigger-released onto the 7-in. roller. It works best with PVA-type glues and cleans up with water.

Continued →

and the pattern bit. Then I flipped the pattern and repeated the procedure on the other half.

This full-size shape became the pattern for the next seven layers of particleboard, using the same process. When they were all cut, I glued and screwed them together, making sure to keep them lined up. A few quick passes with a belt sander took out any minor rough spots on the outside edge.

The Layers Must Be Thin Enough to Bend

Once the form was finished, I milled the solid-wood laminations. I could have used bending plywood, but it's only available in 8-ft. lengths. I wanted the laminations to be continuous, and the riser is more than 13 ft. long. With solid wood, I also could customize the thickness to its ability to bend around a certain radius.

I tried a couple of test cuts to see whether the piece would bend easily around the form. Once I dialed in the thickness, I resawed the layers from a piece of 4/4 stock, always planing one side before cutting the next piece, and sent them through the planer to clean up the bandsaw marks.

Each lamination ended up at a little less than $3/32$ in. thick, and I made eight layers of poplar for the substrate and two layers of walnut for the finish layer.

Plan Carefully for an Easy Glue-Up

I didn't want any surprises with more than 13 ft. of laminates oozing glue and starting to dry, so I first clamped the pieces dry around the form. I checked to see that they conformed evenly to the form and that there were enough clamps. When I was confident that everything would work out, I removed the clamps and cauls, set the laminates aside, and applied a coat of butcher's wax to the form as a glue resist. (Packing tape works, too.) I spread out the laminates in order and began by applying glue to the first two pieces, then put the glued surfaces together and repeated until the entire stack was glued. The glue I used here is Unibond One (vacupress.com), a newer one-part PVA glue that doesn't creep, has an open time of 15 minutes (as opposed to the five to 10 minutes of regular yellow glue), and creates a rigid glueline. After laying the cauls on top, my helper and I wrapped the ends with plastic to keep everything

Maximize Clamp Pressure

You can increase the efficiency of a clamp by using a caul to disperse the pressure over a wider area. After discovering that a clamp's pressure radiates from the clamp at about a 45° angle, I made a caul for projects like this from a 7-in.-wide length of ¼-in. bending plywood to which I glued 1x blocks every 2 in. During glue-up, I attach a clamp at each block. The thickness of the blocks spreads the clamp's pressure over a wider area so that I can use fewer clamps.

READY, SET, CLAMP. When the laminations are glued, lay the clamping caul on top of the stack, wrap each end with plastic, and carry it to the form. Start by applying clamps at the center, then clamp the ends loosely. Work from the center to the ends, applying a clamp at each caul block.

together, then carried the stack to the form.

Clamp Carefully, but Quickly

Now comes the tricky part: We had to clamp the laminated stack onto the form with even pressure before the glue set. Even with the caul, this form required about 65 clamps, which all took time to get into place. We started by putting a couple of clamps in the middle, and then we loosely clamped the ends in place so that they wouldn't ride up as we progressed toward the ends. When I was satisfied that the laminations were clamped evenly, I let the assembly dry for 24 hours.

While the riser dried, I glued up white-oak boards to make the tread, then drew and cut out a full-scale template of the tread on ¼-in. plywood. I used the template as a guide to lay out the tread. After the riser was installed, I used it to check the fit of the tread.

After tracing the template onto the tread, I used a jigsaw to cut nearly to the line and then cleaned up the profile with a pattern bit. I added the bullnose on the edge with a ½-in. roundover bit referenced from both sides.

Use a Template to Locate the Riser

When the riser and tread were finished, I made another template to the inside dimensions of the riser and cut it so that it would fit over the stair framing and sit on the first rough tread. Using a Speed Square, I plumbed down to the floor and marked out where the inside edge of the riser would sit. I also used the template to make eight radiused ends from ¾-in. A/C plywood for blocking.

I located the first layer of blocking at each end by screwing them to the floor. A curved piece filled out the center. After locating the newel supports, I added another layer of blocking, then scribed and cut the riser to fit. I filled in the blocking until it was flush to the riser's top, attaching the riser with pocket screws as I went.

I checked the tread template's fit on the framing and the amount of overhang for the riser. When it was dialed in, I traced it onto the tread, made the necessary cuts, and dropped the tread into place. To avoid any visible nail holes, I fastened the tread in the areas that would be covered by the newel posts and by the shoe molding.

CLEAN UP THE EDGES. When the glue is dry, use a scraper to remove dried glue from the riser's top edge. Even it up with a router and flush-trim bit, using the top of the form as a bearing surface.

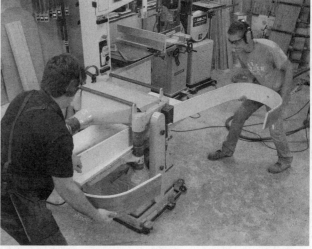

PLANE IT STRAIGHT. Remove the riser from the form, and turn it over so that the clean edge rides on the planer bed. Carefully feed the riser through the planer, taking light passes until the riser measures its correct width.

Continued →

Installation Starts with Blocking

To locate the riser blocking, tack into place a template sized to the riser's inside dimensions, and use a square to position the first layer of plywood blocking. Using the same template, mark and trim the riser to length. With a double layer of plywood blocking screwed to the floor and the steel newel supports bolted in place, attach the riser from the inside with pocket screws.

TACKLE THE BLOCKING ONE LAYER AT A TIME. Start with the blocking attached to the subfloor. Add small pieces of blocking to support the final double layers of plywood that will fill out the riser. Shims below the riser will allow the flooring to slip beneath without scribing.

Make a Perfect Roundover

Unless you use a router table with a fence, the critical aspect of using a roundover bit is the placement of the bearing. There's never any problem with the first cut because there's plenty of surface for the bearing to ride on. The second cut is trickier. The most common mistake is setting the bearing too deep, which makes the bit dive into the surface. To make the second cut properly, register the top edge of the bearing just past the centerline.

PROFILE THE TREAD. After finalizing the tread's shape, add a bullnose profile with a ½-in. roundover bit. To avoid tearout of the grain, climb-cut the ends of the tread by carefully pushing the router in the same direction as the bit's rotation.

FIRST TREAD GOES DOWN ON THE FIRST TRY. After checking and adjusting the fit of the full-size tread template, transfer the template's measurements to the tread, making the necessary cuts and dropping it into place.

How to Make a Stair-Rail Easement

By Charles Bickford

Of all the components of a house, stairs can be one of the most complicated to design and build. Add curves, and the usual rectilinear procession of a stair carriage becomes difficult, especially when it comes to the railing. Building codes specify that the balusters supporting the rail must maintain regular intervals and be at a consistent height. Following that example, the railing must be centered over the balusters and must descend at a rate equal to that of the treads, dropping into a curve known as an easement to meet the top of the newel (the volute). If the stair landing sweeps out over the last few treads, however, the easement has to drop and curve over a short span. This shape is hard to make because it doesn't have a straight stretch long enough to support a router or a shaper.

Builder Richard Walston told me that a five-axis CNC machine can carve almost anything that can be drawn. "But they can't do these easily," he says. "Small parts are harder to cut, and it's not cost-effective to make one or two." The only way to make this part is by hand.

Build a Cradle for the Blank

Here's a basic procedure for making an easement: Glue up a

Slow Down at the Curves

The function of the easement is to unite the railing's 37° rake with a flat, level volute, all in the space of one tread and riser. To do this, it must mate exactly with the railing profile, then start a new falling line while twisting sharply to meet the level face of the volute. The completed railing also must look and feel natural.

Easement must be hand-carved to match the curved rail section's profile.

Easement must twist to accommodate both the curve and drop of the rail.

Easement begins directly above the second-tread nosing.

Volute must be level on top of the newel.

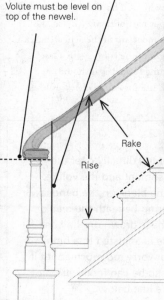

Rake

Rise

Parts and Pieces

1. Straight Rail Section
2. Curved Rail Section
3. Curved Easement
4. Volute
5. Newel Post
6. Starting Step

Continued →

blank, cut a rough shape with a bandsaw, and carve. The trick to cutting the rough shape of the easement is to fix the blank at the final angle of the railing, which Richard explained as he pulled out a squiggle of ¼-in. MDF that had been cut into the plan view of the volute and the easement. He drew the rail's centerline, then used a compass to draw along that line a series of circles whose diameters equal the rail's width. After marking a line to bisect each circle, he hot-glued a 12-in. piece of 1x to each line. The inside edges of the 1xs represented the rail's centerline.

To determine the descent of the easement, Richard clamped a piece of cardboard onto the sticks, then marked the upper end of the easement by lining up the location with a square. After marking the easement's junction with the volute, he removed the cardboard and laid it flat. With a trammel set to a radius that would intersect the end points of the easement, he drew a curved line on the cardboard to represent the upper edge of the easement.

Richard's son Ed had glued up two pieces of 8/4 mahogany to make the easement blank. Next, they drew the volute and easement shape on a piece of MDF. Using a 37° pitch block, they supported the blank so that it covered the pattern on the MDF. With the blank at the correct rake angle, they were ready to cut out the rough shape on the bandsaw by following the lines on the MDF.

Rough Out the Shape on the Bandsaw

A big bandsaw sits by itself in one corner of the shop. Made in Germany by Hema, the saw has a 31-in. vertical capacity; for this job, it was fitted with a ¼-in. blade on high tension. With Ed guiding the piece and associate Ray Becker acting as the spotter, they cut the inner radius and then the outer radius. They turned the blank (which was still attached to the base) on its side, traced the top descent line onto the inner surface, and cut. Ed used a square to draw a line below that was parallel to the first, and then cut that to complete the helical blank.

Before starting to carve the profile, Ed bolted the easement blank onto the volute and the upper part of the rail. Next, he clamped the assembly onto a shop mock-up of the actual staircase and checked the location and height of the volute with a laser.

After making sure that everything looked as it should, he brought the three pieces to the job site for a final check. In this

Trick of the Trade

The glued-up blank is mounted directly over the plan-view outline of the easement and the volute. When Ed starts to cut out the blank on the bandsaw, he's guiding the cut by peering beneath the blank and following the outline that's drawn on the base. Because the bandsaw blade is adjusted to a high tension, he doesn't have to worry too much about it drifting away from the cut, so he can focus attention on keeping the blade on the line below.

Get from Plan View to 3D Pattern

The easement blank must be held and rough-cut at a precise angle so that it will mate with the other railing components. Because of its position, the rake, or falling line, of the easement is slightly different from that of the railing. Using a form, the Walstons can plot out the falling line and transfer it to the blank.

START WITH A PLAN VIEW. After drawing or tracing the outline of the easement and the volute, draw a centerline and then a series of circles that define the width of the railing. Next, draw a line that bisects each circle.

WORKING IN 3D. Hot-glue a 12-in. piece of 1x stock to the intersection of the centerline and each circle's bisecting line. The inside edges of the 1xs now represent the midline of the rail.

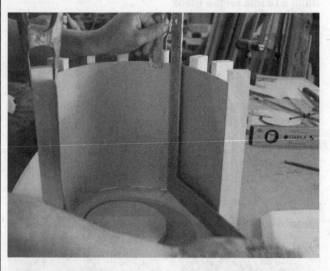

FIND THE BEGINNING AND END. With a piece of cardboard clamped onto the form, use a square to transfer the end points of the easement from the plan view to the cardboard.

CONNECT THE DOTS. Lay the cardboard flat, and with a trammel set to a radius that will intersect both end points of the easement, draw a curved line on the cardboard to represent the upper edge of the easement. Working with a normal rise and run, the Walstons start with a radius of about 24 in. and adjust until the trammel hits both points.

Rough Out the Blank at the Rake Angle

The Walstons stacked and glued together two pieces of 8/4 mahogany to form the blank. The blank is mounted over another plan view of the easement and is supported at the angle of the rake so that the first cuts will be plumb and will match the rest of the railing.

Inside and Outside Cuts

MOUNT THE BLANK. After drawing a plan view of the easement and volute onto a square of ¼-in. MDF, make a rise block equal to the rake of the stairs, and hot-glue it to the square. Also, use hot glue to attach small blocks to support the easement blank.

START THE CUTS. Using the support blocking as a handle, guide the sawblade through the inside radius, followed by the outside radius. Have a glue gun ready to attach more support blocks if necessary.

Top and Bottom Cuts

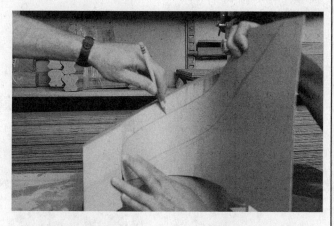

BRING BACK THE CARDBOARD. Although the blank was cut at the rake angle of the railing, it needs to be sawn to the line that was generated by the cardboard pattern. Trim the pattern, and transfer the line onto the blank.

SLICE AWAY THE TOP. While the rough shape is still attached to the base, turn it on its side and cut along the pencil line. It's a good idea to leave a generous margin beyond the line so that you have room to carve.

The Automach

In addition to the grinder and the Proxxon rotary tool, Ed used an Automach electric carving tool. It has a reciprocating head that rapidly indexes one of several profiles of steel blades when it's pushed into the work. The operator controls the depth and angle that the tool cuts. On this project, Ed used the Automach to relieve the edges of the top and the hollow sides of the railing. He was able to excavate a fair amount of stock quickly with a wide-profile gouge, changing direction from time to time to avoid tearout. The Auto-mach Power Carver, sold with five different blades and wrenches, is available online.

assembly, if the volute's height and position are on the money, then the angle and length of the easement are correct. Before disassembling the rail, Ed transferred reference marks from the straight rails to the curved section to make sure they mated cleanly.

Carve Away Everything That's Not the Easement

When the Walstons make straight rail sections, they use a combination of a shaper and handheld routers to make the profile. None of that process works for this little curved section, so the profile must be carved by hand.

Ed brought a portion of straight rail and the easement blank that was still bolted to the volute back to the shop. After wrangling the blank into a comfortable position on the workbench, he used a pencil to transfer the lines of the railing profile onto both ends of the blank.

He lined up his tools: a DeWalt grinder, a Proxxon rotary tool, an electric carving tool, and sandpaper. He used the carving tool to relieve the upper notch that defines both sides of the railing crown. He switched to light passes with the grinder and the rotary tool as he moved down the curve, where the grain starts to change direction.

Using this first cut as a reference, Ed marked the midpoint on the side and used the grinder to take an even ¼ in. away from the lower half up to the midline in an even pass. He continued to rough out the profile, switching between tools as the work required and sanding by hand with 40-grit paper to get the surface close. He also hand-carved the transition between the volute and the easement, using a thin chisel to cut the line that coils into itself at the top of the volute.

Once the major elements were complete, he brought the combined easement and volute back to the site, where it was bolted into place. A final sanding with 120-grit paper smoothed out the transitions and left the railing ready for the finishing crew.

Continued ➔

Stop and Check the Fit

Once the easement blank is roughed out and the ends are trimmed to fit, the blank should be checked for accuracy. Bolted to the next railing section and to the volute, it's usually checked on the staircase at the job site to make sure that it brings the volute level, flat, and directly over the center of the newel.

Curved Rail Section

Curved Easement

Volute

Starting-Step Template

In a Perfect World, the Site and the Shop Are One

To avoid the chaos that is part of working on the job site, Richard and Ed fabricate many of the stair parts in their shop. Because they need to perform periodic checks to make sure everything will fit at the proper angle and position, they build a mock-up wall that replicates the curvature of the stair rail rather than go back and forth to the job site. (They use LVL studs that stay perfectly straight.) They also cut out a replica of the starting tread from ¼-in. MDF that has been marked out with the newel and volute locations. When the lower curve of the rail is roughed out, they can clamp it onto the wall and then check its height and position with a laser plumb bob that is placed on the newel's outline.

Carving Is a Careful Process

Ed starts the carving process by transferring layout lines to the blank and then removing material with an electric carving tool, a rotary tool, coarse sandpaper, and an angle grinder fitted with a sandpaper disk. The various angles of the workpiece require that he frequently change either his position or the position of the workpiece while keeping it from moving around.

Tune Up a Block Plane

By Patrick McCombe

If you want to take your finish carpentry to the next level, you'll need to master the block plane, the secret behind fast, accurate scribes on stain-grade trim and the quickest way to ease edges, adjust inset cabinet doors, and tweak miters.

The first step in becoming proficient with this important tool is learning how to sharpen it. I like diamond stones for sharpening because they're durable. The downside is that they're expensive—but they should be a one-time purchase.

Fine diamond stones can produce an edge sharp enough for most work, but for a plane that's a joy to use, you'll want to hone with something finer. I use a Norton 4000/8000 combination-grit water stone, which produces a supersharp edge with only a little more effort.

Water stones will eventually dish out in the center, so you'll need to flatten them occasionally by running them against the most abrasive diamond stone. When the water stone has a uniform color and appearance, you can stop flattening.

If you can't afford diamond stones, you can use sandpaper glued with 3M Super 77 spray adhesive to pieces of float glass or granite countertop. Compared to the diamond stones, the sandpaper may seem like a bargain, but the finer grits (available online) are still a few dollars per sheet.

Flatten the Sole

One often-overlooked step in preparing a new plane is flattening the sole and the back of the blade (also known as the iron). Fortunately, you have to do this only once. I flatten a plane bottom by running it back and forth over the 60-micron diamond-stone surface. I stop when the bottom has uniform

striations across its length and width. There's no need to polish the flattened sole further, but a little paste wax will prevent rust and help the plane to glide.

Flatten the Blade

With the sole now flat, I flatten the back of the blade. Holding it flat on the stone, I move it sideways over the four diamond-stone surfaces, looking for uniform scratch marks before switching to the next-higher grit. The 9-micron diamond stone is fine for most work, but if you want a really sharp edge, you'll want to use a water stone, too.

I use the 4000-grit side of my water stone first, then the 8000-grit side. Keep the water stone wet to create an abrasive slurry.

Stanley 12-960 Block Plane

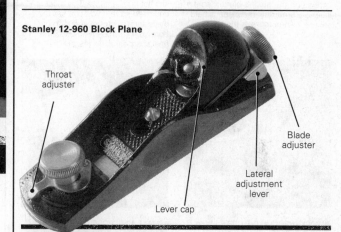

Throat adjuster

Lever cap

Blade adjuster

Lateral adjustment lever

1. FLATTEN THE BOTTOM. After removing the blade, flatten the plane bottom with a 60-micron diamond stone or 220-grit sandpaper. Keep the abrasive wet, and run the plane back and forth until uniform scratch marks are covering the bottom.

2. FLATTEN THE BLADE. With the bevel side up, move the blade back and forth sideways until uniform striations cover at least the bottom quarter of the bevel end. Move to the next-finer grit when the blade gets a uniform polish.

Continued ➡

3. SET UP THE GUIDE. Set the guide's registration jig at 25°, and put it on the honing guide. Tighten the two screws on the guide's blade clamp a little at a time until the blade is held securely. Then remove the jig.

4. CHECK THE ROLLER. With the jig on the stone, rotate the guide's eccentric roller until the bevel sits flat on the stone. The roller is designed so that you can set the blade for a microbevel during final honing. A microbevel makes the final sharpening go faster.

5. WORK THROUGH THE GRITS. Using moderate downward pressure, move the guide back and forth until the bevel gets a uniform striated appearance. Do the same with each grit in turn. Rotate the diamond stones often so that they wear evenly.

6. MAKE A MICROBEVEL. Use plenty of water as you hone, and wipe the blade when you switch grits. Once you've worked through the diamond stones, switch to the water stone. Adjust the guide's roller so that only the leading edge is touching. Start with the 4000-grit side, then move to the 8000-grit side.

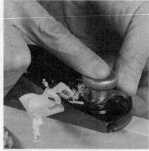

7. REMOVE THE BURR. Place the blade flat on the 8000-grit stone with the back side down. Use a gentle side-to-side motion to remove the burr. Wipe the blade, and then put it back in the plane with the bevel facing up.

8. TAKE A PASS. Adjust the blade for a thin shaving, and make a test pass on a softwood board. Make lateral adjustments until the blade takes an even shaving the full width of the blade. Adjust the throat so that it's as close to the blade as possible without clogging.

Sharpening Tool Kit

While expensive, diamond and water stones should be a one-time purchase. If funds are tight, you can use sandpaper bonded to a piece of float glass.

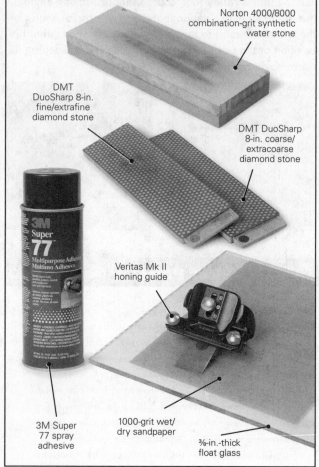

Norton 4000/8000 combination-grit synthetic water stone

DMT DuoSharp 8-in. fine/extrafine diamond stone

DMT DuoSharp 8-in. coarse/extracoarse diamond stone

Veritas Mk II honing guide

3M Super 77 spray adhesive

1000-grit wet/dry sandpaper

⅜-in.-thick float glass

Hone the Bevel

Block-plane blades are sharpened at a 25° angle. I've never been able to master manually guiding the blade at a consistent angle, so I use a honing guide to keep the blade in the proper position. With the blade in the guide, I work through the series of diamond stones and then both sides of the water stone. When honing on the water stones, I adjust the guide's eccentric roller so that the mark on the adjustment knob is in the six-o'clock position to produce a micro-bevel. This makes final honing go faster because you're sharpening less of the blade.

As you work through the grits, you'll feel a burr developing on the back of the blade. Leave it alone until you're done honing. Then remove the burr by holding the blade flat (bevel side up) and gently moving the blade from side to side.

Once all this is done, reassemble the plane, and take a test pass to make sure it is creating an even shavig. If the plane is taking more stock on one side, use the lateral adjustment lever to true the blade.

Contents

Walls & Ceilings

Hanging Drywall on Walls

By Myron R. Ferguson

I love working with drywall. That's not normally the sentiment you hear because, let's face it, hanging drywall is hard, dusty work. But there are ways to make it easier.

A good finished look starts with properly hung panels, which reduces the work of taping, mudding, and sanding. I try to use the biggest sheets possible to limit the number of seams I have to cover. If I'm working by myself, I can use 4-ft. by 12-ft. sheets. When I have a helper, I use 16-ft.-long sheets, if they are available at the supply store.

After I finish hanging the ceiling in a room, I hang the walls. I start where I can hang a full sheet without cutting it. Then I move to abutting walls where smaller pieces are required. This method limits the number of seams, which saves time and reduces waste. If my fastener misses a stud and finds nothing but air while I'm securing a sheet, I remove the fastener right then so there is no chance it will create a blemish on the finished wall.

Even if you are hanging just a few sheets, invest in a heavy-duty T-square to guide your cuts and a stiff-bladed keyhole saw to cut holes for outlet boxes and plumbing penetrations. Also, I use a fixed-blade utility knife called the Rasp-N-Knife that has a useful rasp built into the handle (www.warnertool.com).

Hang from the Top Down

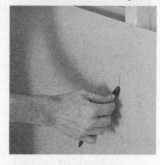

MARK THE STUDS BEFORE YOU LIFT. Position the drywall directly below where it will be installed. With a builder's crayon or pencil, mark each stud's location 7 in. down from the top edge.

RAISE THE TOP SHEET INTO PLACE. I use my left hand to lift and my right hand to stabilize. This way, my free hand can grab the cordless screwdriver when the sheet is in place.

Continued →

THE CRUCIAL MOMENT. When working alone, lifting and fastening a sheet at the same time can be awkward. I hold up the sheet with my left hand and brace it with my shoulder while I drive the first screw.

SECURE FROM THE CENTER OUT. I drive the bottom center screw first and then move out, first along the bottom edge, then up each stud at 16 in. on center. I use 1¼-in. fasteners for drywall thicknesses of ⅝ in. or less.

LIFT THE LOWER PANEL INTO PLACE. I lever the lower panel up against the upper panel's bottom edge with a drywall-lifting tool.

Use a T-Square to Cut a Full Sheet

Hold the T-square in place while you cut. Make the cut in the panel's good side. For safety, keep your top hand well off to the side and out of the path of the cutting blade. I use my foot to keep the bottom of the T-square in place. I start at the bottom and make the score in one motion.

Finish the cut. I snap the board by lifting the center and pulling the board toward me. Then I insert my utility knife in the break and cut the paper on the back.

Cut the Drywall in Place to Save Time

Score the back first. If there is scrap left in door and window openings, score the back of the sheet flush with the opening. Then break the scrap to the inside.

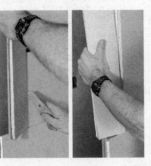

Work from the smooth side to complete the cut. With the scrap pulled toward me to create a crease, I score the paper the full length. To ensure a clean edge, I push the scrap away from me to break the paper.

Driving Solo

I used to hang drywall by lifting the sheet and securing the perimeter with nails. Then, to secure the field, I had two free hands: one to hold the screw and one to hold the driver. Of course, I needed a third hand to manage the cord. That all changed when I bought a cordless driver with collated fasteners. It hangs on my belt within easy reach. It weighs about the same as a corded driver, but it doesn't have a cord to contend with. As on my corded driver, the internal clutch releases before the screw is overdriven and can break the drywall board's surface. The best feature is the collated strip of fasteners that enables me to drive screws with one hand while my other hand holds or braces the drywall. The strip holds enough 1¼-in. screws to secure one sheet.

Cordless driver with collated fasteners

How to Hang Airtight Drywall

By Myron R. Ferguson

Stopping air leaks is the single most important part of making a house more energy efficient. You can stop air on the outside with plywood, housewrap, and tape, but the best air barrier is a system that incorporates the whole wall or roof assembly.

As it turns out, drywall is excellent at stopping air. If you doubt that, try to blow through it. The weak spots are the seams between sheets and the holes that you have to cut for windows, doors, electrical boxes, and can lights. The process for installing drywall as an air barrier is called the airtight-drywall approach (see "Energy-Smart Details" online at finehomebuilding.com), and it relies on caulks, sealants, canned foam, and gaskets to seal the weak spots.

The first step to airtight drywall is to identify what building scientists call the thermal boundary—insulation to us regular folks. The air barrier needs to be continuous along the thermal boundary. This is especially important where interior walls join exterior walls at rim joists or in places where chases are run for plumbing or electrical work.

We decided to hang drywall in the garage shop in Fine Homebuilding's Project House using the airtight approach, partly to show you how to do it and partly so that the editors could make me do their dirty work. The outside of the house eventually will be covered with housewrap and rigid-foam sheathing. The drywall, therefore, is not the primary air barrier but is the interior part of an air-barrier system.

Materials You'll Need

To seal up this garage shop, I used flexible caulk, construction adhesive, and cans of expanding foam. Various types of gaskets are also often used in airtight-drywall jobs. The most basic material, of course, is drywall. To minimize the number of seams I need to fill, I buy the longest sheets I can get my hands on—12-ft. sheets in this case. When hanging big sheets overhead, it's worth considering the new ultralight drywall available from most drywall manufacturers. I wish that the editors had thought to order some of that for this job.

Flexible caulk is used around the perimeter of the walls and ceilings, around window and door openings, and around electrical boxes. It has to be flexible caulk; caulks that dry out over time can leave gaps. Likewise, if structural settling occurs, a caulk that stretches and flexes will help to prevent gaps from forming.

Construction adhesive runs along framing members. Bonding the drywall to the rafters, ceiling joists, and studs isolates each framing cavity, making a single leak much less of a problem down the road. One thing I really like about using a latex drywall adhesive is the amount of open time. You can apply the adhesive to the studs and have up to 30 minutes of open time to fasten sheets of drywall.

Expanding foam is useful for filling larger gaps such as where ceilings meet walls, where sloped ceilings meet flat ceilings, or where walls meet floors.

Another product that I use for airtight-drywall jobs is factory-shaped foam insulation that fits around electrical boxes in walls. For can lights and other ceiling-mounted fixtures, I make my own box with rigid foam or drywall.

Before hanging any sheets, I apply a bead of flexible, stretchable caulk to all gaps in the framing, including the gap between the double top plates, the gap between the jack studs and the king studs, the gap between the bottom plate and the subfloor, and any other gaps where air can leak through. The builder can complete this part of the job well before you show up to hang drywall.

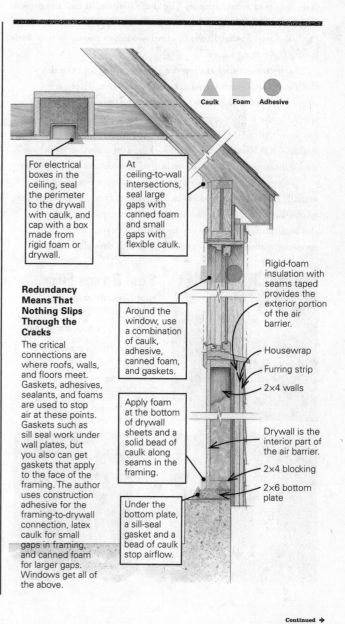

Caulk Foam Adhesive

For electrical boxes in the ceiling, seal the perimeter to the drywall with caulk, and cap with a box made from rigid foam or drywall.

At ceiling-to-wall intersections, seal large gaps with canned foam and small gaps with flexible caulk.

Redundancy Means That Nothing Slips Through the Cracks

The critical connections are where roofs, walls, and floors meet. Gaskets, adhesives, sealants, and foams are used to stop air at these points. Gaskets such as sill seal work under wall plates, but you also can get gaskets that apply to the face of the framing. The author uses construction adhesive for the framing-to-drywall connection, latex caulk for small gaps in framing, and canned foam for larger gaps. Windows get all of the above.

Around the window, use a combination of caulk, adhesive, canned foam, and gaskets.

Apply foam at the bottom of drywall sheets and a solid bead of caulk along seams in the framing.

Under the bottom plate, a sill-seal gasket and a bead of caulk stop airflow.

Rigid-foam insulation with seams taped provides the exterior portion of the air barrier.

Housewrap

Furring strip

2×4 walls

Drywall is the interior part of the air barrier.

2×4 blocking

2×6 bottom plate

Continued →

Plan a Strategy for Tricky Spots

This particular garage has 2×4 studs sitting on a 2×6 bottom plate atop a concrete-block stemwall about 10 in. tall. Before I came in, the editors placed 2×4 blocks in the bottom of each stud cavity. These blocks gave me a surface to glue the bottom of the drywall sheets to; without them, a considerable amount of air could flow through the gap. Another challenge on this job was that one of the walls had a big conduit running from the electrical service panel outside to the breaker panel inside. We removed the conduit's fastening brackets so that we could slide a sheet of drywall behind it. After the drywall was sealed, the conduit itself could be boxed out. It's unwise to box out a chase before drywall because this introduces long cracks to seal.

The garage ceiling is a broken cathedral ceiling, meaning that it slopes up to a flat expanse. The slope is about 51 in.; the drywall sheets are 48 in. Rather than hang a 3-in. strip, I cut a foot off the full sheets so that I could put up two larger pieces, which made taping the ceiling easier.

At the transition between the sloped ceiling and the flat ceiling, there was no solid backing for adhesive. There are a couple of ways to deal with this problem: Apply solid blocking, as we did at the bottom of the wall, or use canned foam to seal the gap after the ceiling has been hung. The best approach is to add backing, but because we added blocking at the bottom of the wall, we used canned foam on the ceiling to illustrate both approaches.

Some tricky spots may not become apparent until you are actually hanging the drywall. In old houses, framing may not be perfectly square, so you can end up with oddly shaped gaps at the butt joints. Fix such a gap by cutting a drywall scrap to fit, screwing it into position, and filling it with drywall compound.

Seal Boxes First

THREE WAYS TO MAKE A BOX AIRTIGHT. The cheapest way to seal an electrical box is to caulk or foam the holes in the back and to seal the perimeter to the drywall. This method is fine for a garage shop. A better way is to use a premade electrical box cover, usually made from EPS foam, that wraps around the box and is caulked and foamed in place. For new construction, airtight electrical boxes, such as the one pictured below are a good choice.

Latex caulk

Foam

Latex caulk

Installation Is Not All That Different

As with typical drywall jobs, I hang the ceilings first, then the walls. When applying caulk and adhesive to the framing, do not skimp—goop it on. This is not the place to save money on a job. Run the bead beyond where the end of the sheet will land. This will keep the seal continuous from one panel to the next.

When placing the sheets, be careful not to smear the caulk and adhesive too much. The framing is only 1½ in. wide, so smearing the sealant can compromise the integrity of the air barrier significantly. On ceilings, align the edge of the sheet you are hanging against the one you are butting it to. Snug the sheet into place, pushing it tight against the framing without sliding it back and forth. Cutting the sheets ¼ in. short is a good way to ensure that they will fit. On walls, prevent smearing the sealant by tilting the panels into place top first, holding the bottom away from the framing. When the top is in place, push the sheet against the framing, bedding it into the adhesive. Seal the perimeter between ceiling and walls with caulk or canned foam after the hanging is complete.

Properly fastening the drywall holds it tight against the framing and sealant, making a tight air seal. The best way to fasten drywall is to begin along one edge, then move toward the center, fastening the other edge last. This ensures that the center of the panel is tight against the framing. For panels that cover electrical boxes, tack the sheet in place, cut out the box with a router, and finish fastening the panel. For large sheets, I screw off the top edge of the sheet before cutting out the boxes. For smaller pieces, I may fasten a top corner and the opposite bottom corner first.

When using a router to cut around electrical boxes, be patient and careful with your cutting. This may take an extra minute, but it will save a lot of repair work later. When cutting out boxes overhead, I turn off the router before removing the bit from the drywall so that the router will not blow drywall dust in my face. Brush out the dust left behind from the router before sealing the box opening with caulk.

Corners, Intersecting Walls, and Other Obstructions

The best corners are floated so that the drywall is not attached to wood that could form a drywall crack. To pull off an airtight-drywall job in this situation, install the first sheet into the corner without fastening the edge to a stud. Only caulk it. Next, apply a bead of caulk to the edge of the first sheet and bed the second sheet into it, fastening the edge into a corner stud. Use drywall clips if there is not a stud within 10 in. of the corner.

For plumbing or conduit runs, such as the large electrical conduit in this shop, slide the drywall behind the pipe, and box it out later. Intersecting walls pose a similar problem: A poorly detailed intersection amounts to a huge hole in the air barrier. It is important to make sure that the drywall air barrier is continuous in these places.

After Hanging the Room, Fill the Gaps

One of the great things about drywall is that the seams don't have to be perfect. Gaps can be filled with foam and mud. After the ceiling and walls are hung, go along the perimeter and fill gaps with foam or caulk. For gaps larger than ¼ in., use expanding foam; for smaller gaps, use caulk. Big globs of caulk will make the taping job a nightmare, so smooth the bead with your finger before it sets up. Likewise, cut off foam after it cures. To complete the air seal, tape the seams and the inside corners as you would for any other drywall job.

Hang the Ceilings Next

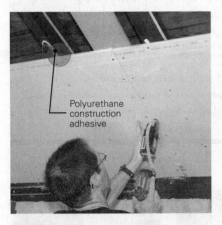

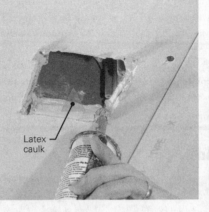

BUTT SEAMS ARE BEST MADE BETWEEN FRAMING MEMBERS. The author likes to use a backerboard that pulls the ends of the panels back, allowing a tapered seam. Adhesive on the face of the framing isolates each framing cavity, so if there is an air leak, it will be contained to one cavity. The adhesive also adds a bit of shear strength and reduces fastener pops.

SEAL THE HOLES. Cut out holes for junction boxes and light fixtures with a router, and then seal them with caulk. It is better to seal holes with caulk after the drywall is attached (as opposed to before hanging the sheet) because the drywall router or saw might damage the caulk joint. When sealing the edges of boxes like this, make sure to brush off the dust so that the caulk can stick to the drywall.

SEAL THE PERIMETER. After completing the ceiling, apply canned foam along the perimeter gap between the framing and the drywall. Let it expand, and cut it off before hanging the walls. Notice here that gaps between framing members were sealed with caulk before hanging any sheets.

Hang the Walls Last

A TIGHT SEAL AT THE BOTTOM. If it was not done on the preconstruction walk-through, seal all the gaps between framing members with flexible caulk. Here, the author seals between the 2×4 blocks and 2×6 bottom plate. The blocks provide a solid surface for adhesive, which will isolate the framing cavities.

WINDOWS GET THE ROYAL TREATMENT. Use both latex caulk and polyurethane construction adhesive to seal around window openings. Rather than just running a bead of adhesive around the window rough opening, the author uses flexible caulk on the jack studs, sill, and header. This serves as insurance against building movement at this potential hole in the envelope.

FOAM THE BIG CRACKS. After the walls and ceiling are hung, spray canned foam along the bottom of the wall and in any large gaps or cracks. Cut off the expanded foam with a drywall saw or utility knife. Seal smaller gaps with caulk. Smooth the bead with your finger to make taping a little easier.

Continued →

Pick and Prepare Joint Compound

By Patrick McCombe

Contrary to what most people think, ready-mix joint compound is not ready to use straight from the bucket. It needs to be mixed for the compound to spread evenly, which leads to a professional-looking finishing job with less sanding.

Ready-mix compounds are available in several versions. At home centers, you'll find regular and lightweight all-purpose compounds. At drywall-supply stores, you may also see taping, topping, and ultralight compounds. I've found that regular-weight all-purpose compound works fine for most drywall-finishing projects. Lightweight all-purpose compound is a good option when you have to carry a lot of compound far from the truck, but it's softer when dry, which makes it susceptible to

damage. Lightweight compound sands more easily than regular compound, however, so if you're new to finishing, it's worth a try.

Powdered setting compound, which is mixed with water before use, hardens chemically, making it a better choice for patching holes, for thick applications, and for the tape coat. It is also stronger and doesn't break down with exposure to water, making it good for bathrooms and other wet areas. Don't, however, dump it down the drain when cleaning up.

Most lumberyards and home centers have setting-type compounds with 45- and 90-minute set times, but drywall suppliers often have compounds available with set times from 5 to 210 minutes. The number on the bag is the average time that it takes for the compound to firm up enough to apply another coat. This time can vary with temperature and humidity.

Preparing both ready-mix and setting-type compound is an important first step in becoming proficient at drywall finishing.

Preparing Ready-Mix Compound

1. POP THE TOP. A new bucket of joint compound may look mixed, it may look dry, or it may have a little water on top. In any case, start mixing the compound with a mud masher or a drywall mixing paddle in a ½-in., low-speed (450-650 rpm) drill. You'll soon notice that the compound has fluffed up and feels softer.

2. ADD A FEW OUNCES OF WATER. You can use joint compound at the packaged consistency for filling corner bead and fastener heads, but you should add a few ounces of cool water and remix to make applying tape and second and third coats easier.

3. THE RIGHT MIX. Thinned compound should be the consistency of soft butter. Don't add too much water, because soupy compound is messy and difficult to work with.

Store for Later Use

Scrape down the sides of the bucket, and level the compound before covering it with a wet rag, a thin layer of water, or the clear plastic wrap that came on the compound to prevent it from drying out. Return the lid to the bucket, and seat it all the way around with a series of hammer blows.

What to Buy

These paddles and compounds will help the job to go smoothly.

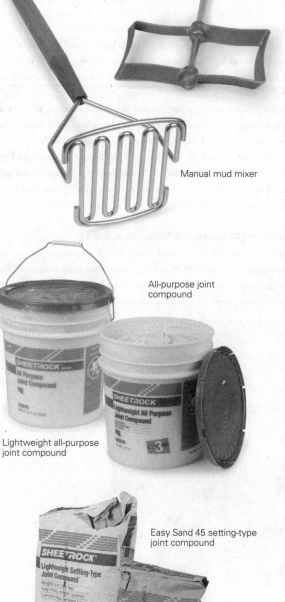

Drill-powered mixing paddle

Manual mud mixer

All-purpose joint compound

Lightweight all-purpose joint compound

Easy Sand 45 setting-type joint compound

Durabond 90 setting-type joint compound

Preparing Setting-Type Joint Compound

1. WEIGH IT OUT. A bathroom or kitchen scale is more accurate than eyeballing when you're mixing a partial bag for a small job or when you can't use a full bag within the working time specified in the directions. Zero the scale with the empty bucket on top, and weigh out the desired amount.

2. ADD POWDER TO WATER. Following the mixing instructions on the bag, pour the proper amount of water in a second bucket. If you're mixing a partial bag, maintain the same ratio of water to powder specified for a full bag in the directions. Shake in the powder, then mix. Go slowly at first to minimize flying powder.

3. MIX, THEN WAIT. Mix the compound thoroughly, and then let it rest for the time specified on the bag, usually 10 minutes. If necessary, add a little water, and remix to get to the proper working consistency. Too much or high-speed mixing will accelerate set times. The compound shown above right is the perfect consistency.

Throw Out Overly Stiff Compound

When the compound starts to get a little hard to spread, switch to corner bead or other areas that use a lot of compound quickly. Don't try to rescue any hardened compound with additional water. Instead, start over with a new batch.

Continued →

Premixed All-Purpose Joint Compound

By Myron R. Ferguson

Most of us who do drywall work prefer premixed, all-purpose, drying-type compound because it's readily available and can be used straight from the bucket.

All-purpose compounds can be used for all phases of drywall finishing, including embedding tape, filling fastener holes, and repairing minor wall damage.

This type of joint compound is available in three weights. They each cost about the same for a 5-gal. pail, but each performs differently on the wall.

Heavyweight Compound Is the Most Durable

Most manufacturers don't label their compound products with the term heavyweight. That's bad marketing. Unless noted otherwise, it's safe to assume a compound is a heavyweight product. If in doubt, pick it up. A 5-gal. pail weighs around 60 lb., roughly 10 lb. heavier than midweight compound and 20 lb. more than lightweight compound.

When I embed tape and corner beads or when I complete plaster repairs, I use heavyweight compound. I also like it for texturing walls or ceilings by hand or for using spray equipment.

Because heavyweight compound has a higher water content than lighter compounds, it shrinks more as it dries. This means fastener holes and drywall damage could require more coats of compound to achieve a perfectly smooth finish.

When it's dry, heavyweight compound provides the hardest finish of the three, which makes it the most-difficult compound to sand; it also is the most resistant to scratches and other damage.

Lightweight Is the Most Forgiving

By adding expanded perlite to their compound formula, manufacturers produce a lightweight compound that weighs about 35% less than heavyweight compound. It's designed to make taping easier because you don't have to break your back lugging around a heavy bucket of mud. It also has a low shrinkage rate, so it requires fewer coats than heavier compound.

I use this compound for fill and finish coats because it smooths and feathers easily. Lightweight compound is drier than other compounds, so it doesn't perform well in automatic taping tools; it is still good for texturing, however. Lightweight compound is so soft when it's dry that it's the easiest to sand, but it's also the least durable. To help avoid dents and scratches that can ruin a finish, I suggest priming as soon as possible.

Be sure to read the compound label before beginning a drywall project. Some manufacturers design their lightweight products to be used only as fill and finish coats over tape embedded in heavyweight compound, not as all-purpose products.

Midweight Combines Benefits of Both

Like heavyweight compound, midweight compound can be used in automatic taping tools. It's also excellent for texturing. Midweight compound shrinks less than heavy compound, dries harder than light compound, and is relatively easy to sand.

These traits give midweight compound some of the performance features of a heavyweight product, with some of the convenience and the ease of use of a lightweight material.

LIGHTWEIGHT COMPOUND IS EASY TO SAND. Because it's not as hard as other compounds when it's dry, it's less durable.

MIDWEIGHT COMPOUND IS VERSATILE. It's not as widely available, but it's easier to work with than heavyweight compound and more durable than lightweight.

HEAVYWEIGHT COMPOUND IS HARD ON THE USER. Not only is this compound extremely heavy to lift, but it also requires more effort to spread and sand.

Cutting Drywall

By Myron R. Ferguson

I recently taped and finished the drywall in two new houses of about the same size. Different contractors had hung the drywall in each house. In the first house, the joints between the sheets were good—not so tight that there was damage from force-fitting, and not so open that the joints needed to be filled with setting compound before I could start taping. Moreover, every electrical box was cut out perfectly, a fairly rare occurrence. In the second house, 62 electrical boxes were miscut, and there were big gaps between some sheets that I had to fill. Plus, I had to fix some areas that had been damaged when sheets that had been cut too long were forced into place. Fixing that long list of mistakes added about 8 hours of labor for me. Don't worry, though; I added enough to the price to cover my time.

Cutting drywall well is not a surgical procedure that requires years of training and practice. It just takes the proper attitude. If you go in thinking, "The taper can fix that," you won't end up with a high-quality job. It's simple: Don't make mistakes the taper will charge you to fix. The following techniques will help you achieve that end.

Cutting Drywall to Length

It's better to cut drywall sheets ¼ in. short. Otherwise, they may get damaged during installation. Drywallers hang ceilings first, so gaps at their edges will be hidden by the wall sheets. Walls are similar. The sheets on succeeding walls will cover gaps on the previous walls. Extra care is called for with the drywall sheets on the final wall in a room, because those ends won't be covered. Leave about a ⅛-in. gap at each end, which you can cover easily with mud and tape.

1. Mark each edge of the sheet. Framing isn't always square and plumb, so if the measurements differ, use the shorter one. There's no need for a pencil; mark the cut with a knife tick.

2. Cut drywall to length using a T-square and a utility knife to score the paper on whichever side is facing you. For the cleanest cut, make one continuous score that goes through the paper face.

3. Once scored, place one hand on each side of the cut, gently lift, and bend the board backward to snap the gypsum core.

4. A knife cut through the paper on the other side of the board separates the two pieces. If the first cut was through the back of the board, make the second cut from the front to avoid visible paper tears.

Cutting Off Just a Smidgeon

Because it's hard to snap drywall unless there's enough on each side of the knife cut to grasp, cutting off a sliver calls for different techniques. And cutting off a couple of inches differs from cutting off just half an inch.

1. To remove very small amounts, start by beveling one edge.

2. Continue by beveling the second edge.

3. Clean up the resulting angled end with a drywall rasp.

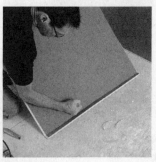

Cutting Off an Inch
To shorten a piece of drywall by an inch or two, score it normally, hold it with the scored end on the floor, and give the piece a sharp blow with your hand.

Continued ➜

Cutting Corners

With outside corners, it's often easier to install the drywall before cutting it to length. This saves time and results in a precise fit, even if one wall is out of plumb and a nonsquare cut is needed.

1. Screw the sheet in place, score the back side, and snap.

2. Holding the piece that's being removed so it doesn't drop and tear the paper, cut the face along the fold.

Cutting Drywall to Width

Because precision isn't usually essential, cuts on the long dimension of drywall sheets can be freehanded. In some cases, the cuts are eyeballed along a chalkline; most of the time, though, only a tape measure and a drywall knife are needed.

1. To cut the long edge of a drywall sheet, pinch a tape measure at the desired measurement, then slide your fingers along the edge of the drywall while holding the knife against the hook at the other end of the tape.

2. Snap the board, then cut the paper on the other side, starting and ending the cut about 1 in. from the ends to keep the cutoff from dropping. Snap the cutoff forward to free it from the remaining paper. Clean up the edges with a drywall rasp.

Angled Cuts

If the edges of the piece you're cutting won't be parallel—for example, an angle to fit below a stair or because a ceiling's width varies—snap a chalkline and cut along it.

Essential Tools

There are a lot of specialty tools for cutting drywall. Some are helpful, while others just take up space in your toolbelt. Here are the basic ones you'll need for every job.

For cutting drywall, a utility knife with a stationary blade provides more stability when making deep cuts or beveling an edge. Commodity blades are fine and are typically changed twice a day.

Drywall saws are made of heavy steel and won't bend when driven into the drywall. They aren't as sharp as wood saws, and they have widely set teeth for aggressive cutting.

A drywall rasp levels cut edges so they'll fit without snagging.

Drywall routers make fast, clean cuts, but they create a lot of dust and are loud. Hearing protection is a must.

Most of the time, a 48-in. T-square is fine. But if you're hanging 9-ft. high walls, you'll also need a 54-in. T-square for the 54-in.-wide drywall. Look for squares made from thicker aluminum for more rigidity.

Cutting Openings

Because doors and windows will be trimmed with casing that extends a couple of inches onto the wall, these openings do not have to be cut precisely. I prefer to cut them with the sheet tacked in place. A word of caution: If the jambs extend beyond the framing, don't place any fasteners adjacent to them. Fasteners that push the drywall tight to the jambs can create pressure that will break the sheet or tear the paper once you start cutting.

1. Measure the distance from the ceiling to the top of the opening, and from the opening's edges to the nearest wall or installed sheet of drywall. Mark these measurements in the face of the board.

2. Use the measurements you took previously to score the back of the sheet where the top of the opening will fall, then tack the sheet in place.

3. Cut out the sides of the opening with a drywall saw or drywall router.

4. After cutting the sides to the top of the opening, snap the board at the back cut made prior to installation, then finish the cut with a knife.

Cutting Out Electrical Penetrations

It's faster and more accurate to cut out for electrical boxes, lights, or fans with the drywall tacked in place. Make sure the wires are pushed toward the back of the box so that they won't be damaged by the saw or the router bit, and don't fasten right next to the penetration until after you cut. You can make the cuts with a drywall saw, but pros use a drywall router. Routers are faster and leave a cleaner edge than a drywall saw. The downside is that they create more dust. Still, if you're going to hang drywall in anything more than a room or two, it's worth the money to buy a router.

1. If the penetration is in the middle of a board, note its distance from adjacent walls or already-hung sheets of drywall. Hang the board, then mark the center of the penetration on the face.

2. Using a ⅛-in. guided bit in a drywall router, plunge into the penetration, then move over until the bit hits the side of the box, fan, duct, or light.

3. Lift the bit out and over the side of the penetration, then reinsert it. Keeping the bit in contact with the outside surface of the penetration, move the router in a counterclockwise direction.

4. With the hole fully cut, a light hammer tap causes the dust to fall out so that it won't interfere during taping.

Cutting With a Drywall Saw

1. To cut with a saw, push it through the drywall into the center of the penetration, and cut over until you find a side. Repeat until you've located each side.

2. Follow the side of the penetration with the saw while putting a slight outward bevel on the cut.

3. Trim around the outside of the cut with a utility knife if needed to allow the board to seat tight to the framing.

Continued →

Using a Drywall Router

By Andy Engel

For years, I avoided using a drywall router to cut holes for electrical boxes, lights, windows, doors, and so forth. To use this small tool, you hang the sheet, make a plunge cut with the ⅛-in. self-guided helical bit, and follow the edge of whatever it is you want to fit the sheet around. I'd tried one on a few occasions, with results such as mangled wires and overcut drywall. I reverted to doing things the carpenter's way: laying out the holes with a square and a tape measure, then cutting them with a knife and a keyhole saw. This was slow, but at least I was on familiar ground.

Still, every drywall pro I knew used routers to make quick, clean, and accurate cuts. There had to be something to these tools. They don't cost a lot either, and the bits are only a few bucks each. Tool use usually comes easily to me, so my failure with drywall routers was both out of character and frustrating. And I wasn't alone; many carpenters I've talked with are buffaloed by these tools.

When faced with a big project of my own, I finally decided to figure it out. After a few missteps, I'm cutting holes in drywall faster and more accurately than ever. Here's what I learned.

1. SET THE BIT DEPTH. The tip of a drywall bit is smooth, so it can bear on the edge of whatever you're cutting and guide the cut. Set the bit depth so that the smooth section will be about ⅛ in. beyond the back of the drywall.

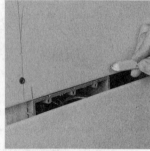

2. MARK A STARTING POINT. For cuts near an edge, mark the abutting sheet. For middle-of-the-board cuts, mark the center of the cutout before hanging the board. This is a starting point and a reminder that something is there to cut around.

3. DON'T MANGLE WIRES. Most of what gets cut out with a drywall router are electrical boxes, and that spinning bit can seriously damage wires. Make sure the power to the box you're cutting around is off, and push wires to the back.

4. HANG THE BOARD. Don't screw near what you're cutting out. Fasten too closely, and the pressure on the sheet can tear the paper face as the cut is finished. Finish fastening after completing all cuts.

5. TAKE THE PLUNGE. Push on the sheet with your hand or knee so that the drywall is tight to the object you're cutting out. Turn on the router, and push the bit through the drywall.

6. MAKE THE LEAP. Move the router outward until the bit hits an edge of what you're cutting out. Pull the bit out, then reinsert it on the far side of the edge.

7. GO COUNTERCLOCKWISE ON OUTSIDE CUTS. Moving in this direction requires only light pressure to follow the box edge, as the bit rotation pulls it inward. If you cut clockwise on the outside, the rotation will push the bit away from the box, causing you to overcut.

8. TAKE YOUR TIME. Slow the cut near corners, pushing the bit lightly against the object so that it turns as it reaches the corner. If the router stops moving easily, you may have hit a nib on an electrical box or a projecting piece of extension jamb. Gently move the bit around the obstacle, then cut on, as shown below.

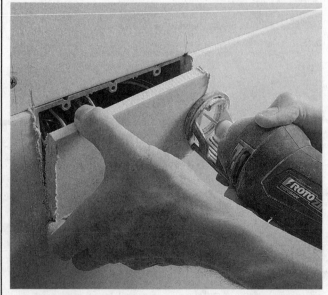

Go Clockwise on Inside Cuts

Unlike recessed lights, electrical boxes, and windows with jambs that extend beyond the stud faces, rough openings are cut from their inside. Set the bit deeper so that the tip clears the eased edges of framing lumber, and cut clockwise.

Makita XOC01

RotoZip SS355

Drywall Routers and Bits

The RotoZip is the granddaddy of drywall routers, so much so that the job-site term for a drywall router is a RotoZip. A number of companies now make drywall routers, however, and there are even cordless versions, such as Makita's XOC01, which I tried out on an earlier job. Both tools have their place. The RotoZip has more power, and because it's corded (the 6-ft. cord could be longer; drywall screwguns come with 16-ft. cords), there isn't a battery to run out of power, which makes it a better choice on a larger project. On the other hand, the Makita has enough power, the batteries have plenty of life, and not having cords to trip over is hard to overrate, particularly on tight remodeling jobs. Both tools use the same ⅛-in. helical bits that guide the cut by riding on whatever you're cutting out.

Self-guiding bit

Taping and Finishing Drywall Corners

By Myron R. Ferguson

When taping and finishing drywall, people seem to struggle most with inside corners. The temptation is to try to work on both sides of a corner at once. If you do that, while you are working one side, the edge of the taping knife or the wet drywall compound (mud) that can build up on its edge will mess up the mud on the other side. It can lead to an even bigger mess at the point where the wall meets the ceiling and three corners come together.

There is a trick to it, but before tackling the corners, tape the flats. Then bed the tape in all three corners (two ceiling and one wall), finish-coat one side of each, let dry, and finish-coat the other sides. You can generally do half of a corner one day, and the other half the next. In humid conditions, it can take longer for the mud to dry.

The drying time can be problematic on small jobs that you could otherwise finish in a day. To speed things up, use setting compound instead of regular drywall mud from a bucket. Setting compound, which comes as a powder that you mix with water, is available in several formulations that harden in times ranging from 20 to 90 minutes. Setting compound might not be worth the time and expense on a larger job that will take multiple days anyway, but it can let you finish a small job in time for supper.

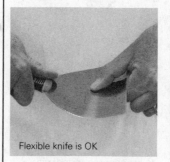
Flexible knife is OK

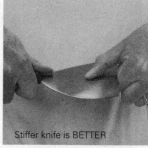
Stiffer knife is BETTER

Choose the Right Taping Knife
Stiffer knives do a better job of removing excess mud and of creating a smooth surface than more flexible knives. Unlike with flat joints, where a variety of taping-knife widths are called for, when taping corners, one 6-in. knife is all that you need.

Continued ➔

Embed the Tape

1. FILL THE CORNERS WITH MUD. First, coat the side whose edge is covered by the abutting sheet so that coating the second edge fills any small gaps. Fill gaps larger than ¼ in. with setting compound.

2. CREASE AND POSITION THE TAPE. Tear the end that goes into the corner to a point to avoid building up layers of tape. Press the tape lightly into place with your fingers.

3. EMBED THE TAPE WITH A TAPING KNIFE. Center the tape with a light pass of the knife, then apply more pressure to smooth the tape and remove excess mud behind it. Tapping the tape with your finger should leave only a slight indentation.

4. CHECK FOR BUBBLES. Squeeze out any bubbles with a taping knife. The tape should be firmly embedded, with its creases straight and with no excess mud on the wall.

Finish-Coat One Side

5. COVER ONE SIDE WITH MUD. First, scrape off any chunks or ridges of dried mud that might interfere, then spread on enough new mud to completely cover the tape.

6. REMOVE THE EXCESS. Letting its inner edge ride against the corner, hold the knife at a steep angle. Feather the mud by applying pressure to the outside edge.

7. SMOOTH IT OUT. Hold the knife at a shallow angle for the final pass, smoothing out imperfections to minimize the need for sanding.

8. ALLOW THE MUD TO DRY. With one side of each corner finish-coated, scrape off any chunks after the mud has dried.

Finish-Coat the Next Side

9. REPEAT THE PROCESS. Finishing the second side involves the same steps as finishing the first side. Use the first side to guide the knife, and smooth the new mud in several passes.

10. ALL CORNERS ARE COATED. There may be a few small chunks of mud standing proud. When the mud dries, scrape or sand it smooth. It's now ready to be primed.

Flawless Drywall Finish

By Myron R. Ferguson

When I visit a job site to estimate a drywall project, the homeowner almost always wants what drywallers call a Level 4 finish: two sanded coats of compound over the embedded tape.

If the drywall is to be wallpapered, textured, or painted with flat paint, a Level 4 finish is perfectly acceptable. But at this level of finish, any joints and imperfections can show when they're under a coat of glossy paint or flooded with bright light.

Another problem with a Level 4 finish occurs when sanding: The compound becomes smooth, but the drywall's paper facing gets rough. If that weren't enough, there are areas of the drywall that don't get sanded, so every sheet ends up with three different textures and porosities. Each reflects light differently, which produces an inconsistent wall surface.

You can solve these problems by moving up to a Level 5 finish, which the Gypsum Association recommends for areas with severe lighting or glossy paint. A Level 5 finish has an additional skim coat of compound spread over the entire wall to give the wall a uniform surface and to make joints disappear.

There are several ways to get to a Level 5 finish, but perhaps the simplest is to skim-coat over a Level 4 finish with watered-down joint compound. The compound can be applied either by trowel or with a ½-in.-nap paint roller. The compound is then immediately removed with a wide knife.

There are also primer surfacers made by several drywall and paint companies. These superthick coatings are applied in a single heavy layer (typically 15 mils to 20 mils wet) over a sanded Level 4 finish.

These primer surfacers offer both a Level 5 finish and a primed, ready-for-paint surface. While a product like USG's Sheetrock Tuff-Hide (www.usg.com) is more expensive than conventional primer, it costs less than a hand-applied Level 5 finish and one coat of primer.

Unfortunately, these new primer surfacers require a huge sprayer to apply them. USG says it takes a sprayer with a minimum output of 1 gal. per minute and a pump pressure of 2700 psi to 3000 psi to spray Tuff-Hide. A machine like this sells for several thousand dollars and weighs 130 lb., which is why I apply a Level 5 finish by hand for all but the biggest jobs.

Gypsum-Board Finishes

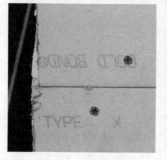

LEVEL 0 No taping, finishing, or accessories are required. This level of finish is useful for temporary construction or when the final level of finish has yet to be determined.

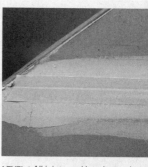

LEVEL 1 All joints and interior angles have tape set in joint compound. The surface is free of excess compound. Tool marks and ridges are acceptable, and tape and fastener heads need not be covered with compound. This level of finish is often described as "fire taping" and is seen typically in garages and other unfinished areas that require a fire separation. Surface appearance doesn't matter.

LEVEL 2 All joints and interior angles have tape set in joint compound and wiped with a joint knife, with a thin coating of compound left on the joints and interior angles. Fastener heads are covered with one coat of compound, and tool marks and ridges are acceptable. This level of finish is often specified for use under tile and in mechanical areas where surface appearance is not a concern.

LEVEL 3 A Level 3 finish has a second coat of compound on taped joints, interior angles, fastener heads, and accessories. The compound is smooth and free of tool marks and ridges. This level of finish is often specified when the finished surface will have a heavy texture.

LEVEL 4 This level has joint tape embedded in compound and two additional coats of compound on top to hide the tape and to smooth the surface. Fasteners are concealed with three coats of compound. Finally, the compound is sanded with fine-grit paper and primed. This level of finish is not recommended under gloss, semigloss, or enamel paints.

LEVEL 5 Level 5 finishing requires all the steps of a Level 4 finish, but with an additional skim coat of compound applied to the entire wall or ceiling. This level of finish is recommended where gloss, semigloss, and enamel paints are specified or where severe lighting conditions occur.

Continued →

6 Steps to Level 5

1. SAND FIRST. Starting with a Level 4 finish, go over all the joints, corners, and fastener heads with 220-grit sandpaper. The author prefers a Radius 360 pole sander because of its large sanding head and its resistance to flipping over.

2. WIPE DOWN THE WALLS. Brush down the walls with a soft push broom, and scrape off any errant blobs of compound that could interfere with skim-coating. A 2-in. paintbrush is great for cleaning out electrical boxes.

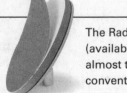

The Radius 360's hook-and-loop disks (available in 150 and 220 grit) are almost twice as big as the paper on a conventional pole sander.

3. THIN OUT THE MUD. Use a heavy-duty drill with a paddle to mix up the compound. Add water a little at a time until the mud's consistency is similar to pancake batter.

4. USE A THICK-NAP ROLLER. Dunk a ½-in. to ¾-in.-nap roller into the joint compound, remove it, and let the compound pour off. Try to keep the floor relatively free of compound, which can be very slippery.

5. GET ROLLING. Start at a corner and work toward the opposite wall. You can coat about 24 sq. ft. to 30 sq. ft. before the compound starts drying. This room will get wainscoting, so the author isn't skimming the bottom 3 ft. of the wall.

6. SCRAPE OFF THE EXCESS. Remove the excess compound with a 10-in. or 12-in. drywall finishing trowel held at a 45° angle. You can put the excess compound back into the bucket, but remix often to keep the mud at the proper consistency.

Drywall Patch

To repair a hole in drywall or plaster, I square up the hole, cut a drywall patch slightly larger than the hole, and use a Surform file to size the patch for a friction fit. Then I apply a bead of polyurethane glue to the edge of the patch before slipping it into place slightly below the surface of the wall. After a few minutes, the glue foams up and fills the gap between the patch and the wall. Polyurethane glue is activated by moisture, so slightly wetting the edges of the drywall makes the glue foam even more and fill the gap more fully. Gloves are essential, as it takes weeks for the glue to wear off.

When the glue has set, I use a paint scraper to knock off the bulk of the hardened glue before sanding the surface flush with an orbital sander. Because polyurethane glue is brittle when cured, it is easy to scrape and sand. I use drywall compound over the patch and mesh drywall tape on the seams. The tape is insurance against joint failure, but on some jobs, I have eliminated the tape and haven't had any problems with cracks at the joints. —Joe Rabbitt

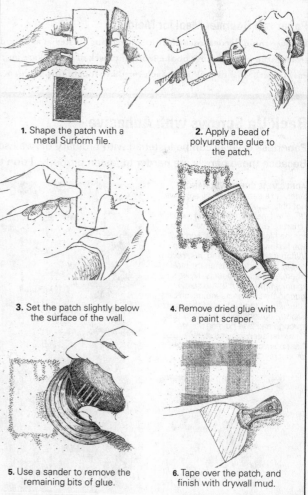

1. Shape the patch with a metal Surform file.

2. Apply a bead of polyurethane glue to the patch.

3. Set the patch slightly below the surface of the wall.

4. Remove dried glue with a paint scraper.

5. Use a sander to remove the remaining bits of glue.

6. Tape over the patch, and finish with drywall mud.

Continued →

Fight Mold with Paperless Drywall

By Myron R. Ferguson

Let's face it—there's been a lot of talk about mold in the past few years. The topic has gotten plenty of attention in the news, has been the focus of lots of building-science research, and has made many homeowners nervous. Here's the thing: Mold spores are everywhere and are nearly impossible to avoid, never mind eliminate. What we can do, though, is help to prevent those mold spores from taking root in our indoor living spaces. That's where products like paperless drywall come into play.

Mold needs four things to grow: oxygen, water, a temperature between 40°F and 100°F, and an organic food source. Considering this group of ingredients, it's not surprising that mold is commonly found on lumber in the basement, on the wall behind the sink in the kitchen, and on the wallpaper adhesive in the bathroom.

The first step in preventing mold growth is to get firm control over the level of moisture in the air (see "Breathing Fresh Air Into Bathroom Ventilation" online at finehomebuilding.com). After that, the focus should be on eliminating the organic food source.

Paper Is a Gourmet Meal for Mold

Because mold decomposes organic (once living) material as a food source, the paper facings on the front and back of drywall are an easy target. Most drywall manufacturers have fought this problem

by offering modern versions of the old wax-coated "greenboard" that has been used in bathrooms for years. Many of these modern paper-faced products even scored a perfect 10 on the ASTM standard for mold resistance. For the ultimate peace of mind, though, a few drywall manufacturers have now created paperless drywall, removing all sources of organic food.

By replacing drywall's paper facing with an inorganic fiberglass mat, products like Dens-Armor Plus (shown in this installation)

Back Up Screws with Adhesive

Paperless drywall can be fastened with ordinary drywall screws. I use 1¼-in. screws for both ½-in. and ⅝-in. panels. Because these panels are harder to fasten properly, I don't rely on screws alone.

ADHESIVE IS CHEAP INSURANCE.
Applying a bead of drywall adhesive not only reduces the number of fasteners necessary on wall panels (chart p. 185), but it also makes up for the high likelihood that some of the fasteners will be set too deep. Without the paper facing, it's much easier to overdrive fasteners into fiberglass-faced products. Make sure to adjust the clutch of the screw gun so that fasteners are driven until they indent the surface of the board slightly, but not so far that they tear through and lose holding power. Consider adhesive and screws to be best practice with fiberglass-faced products.

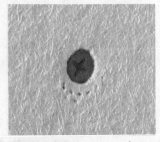

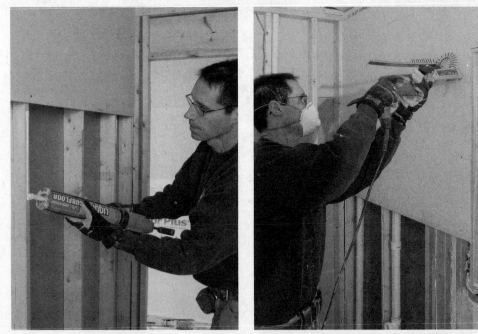

offer excellent mold resistance compared to standard paper-faced wallboard products. But don't get a false sense of security; these products are only as good as the installation.

For example, I once had a truckload of paperless drywall delivered to a job site, and when I started to install the product, I noticed that the back side of one sheet was dirty. I guess the drywall must have been stacked at a convenient height for a lunch or a coffee break because somebody had spilled coffee or soda on it. Then dirt and sawdust from the lumberyard and the job site clung to the sheet. If I hadn't noticed the stain and tossed the sheet, I would have quickly defeated the mold resistance of the paperless drywall. If paperless drywall isn't handled properly or installed correctly, the job may be little more than a pricier route to the same place.

Paperless products behave similarly to standard paper-faced drywall, but they are a bit more fragile to handle and install, require different products to tape, and typically must be finished to a more uniform surface before being painted. Learn these quirks, though, and you're likely to have a successful experience with paperless products.

Put Away Power Tools to Minimize Dust

Because paperless drywall has fiberglass facings on the front and back, it's in your best interest to keep airborne dust to a minimum. I recommend wearing a dust mask when cutting these products. Drywall dust alone warrants a mask. Add fiberglass to the equation, and your throat and lungs can become seriously irritated. Also, gloves and a long-sleeve shirt will help you to avoid getting itchy slivers of fiberglass on your hands and arms.

Window and door bit   Standard ⅛-in.-dia. bit

AVOID THE ROUTER WHERE POSSIBLE. Drywall routers are a fast method for making drywall cutouts. In fact, they leave an even cleaner cut in paperless drywall than in regular paper-faced products. However, they create an enormous amount of fiberglass-laden dust. For cutting around electrical boxes, the small amount of dust is a fair trade-off for the more accurate cutout, but for door and window openings, use a utility knife and a handsaw.

IF YOU USE A ROUTER, USE IT SMART. If you can't bring yourself to part with the drywall router, there are still ways to minimize the dust. Begin by avoiding the larger ¼-in.-dia. "window and door" drywall bits. Bigger bits can be pushed harder and faster and are less likely to break, but they also create much more dust than the standard ⅛-in.-dia. bits.

GLUE MEANS FEWER SCREWS. There are several brands of drywall adhesive on the market, but any construction adhesive that meets ASTM C-557 can be used. If the local building inspector wants to see the proper amount of fasteners and can't verify what's behind the walls, consider the belt-and-suspenders approach: adhesive and standard screw spacing. See the chart at right to compare fastening schedules with and without adhesive.

Framing	Walls	Walls withadhesive	Ceilings	Ceilings withadhesive
16 in. o.c.	Every 16 in.	Every 24 in.	Every 12 in.	Every 16 in.
24 in. o.c.	Every 12 in.	Every 24 in.*	Every 12 in.	Every 16 in.

Continued ➜

Switch to Inorganic Tape

Paper tape set in premixed joint compound is a manufacturer-approved option for finishing joints on paperless drywall, but most encourage the use of setting-type compound and mesh tape, which further reduces the chances of mold growth by removing a food source. Standard mesh tape is widely available and a fine choice, but I prefer fiberglass tape, which has a thinner open-fiber weave. Either way, these tapes come with their own set of rules.

EMBED THE TAPE WITH CARE. Apply the mesh tape in a thinned mixture of compound because it's easy to cut through fiberglass tape accidentally with the edge of a taping knife. Likewise, use a corner knife to avoid tears on inside corners, a relatively new knife for the rest of the seams, and fairly gentle handling all around.

Use a relatively new taping knife for working with mesh tape. The older the knife, the sharper the edges will be.

Sand Where You Can; Skim-Coat Where You Can't

Fiberglass-faced wallboard has a slightly rougher surface than paper-faced drywall, and there's a lot of fuss about how to make this surface blend with the smooth-sanded taped seams. A typical drywall job is taken to what's known as a level-4 finish: two coats of joint compound on all seams. Paperless drywall can be finished to the same level, but only if you plan to roll on a high-solids primer. It's not much extra work either to sand all the walls lightly to knock down the fiberglass texture or to do a level-5 finish (two coats of joint compound on all seams, followed by a skim coat of the entire surface).

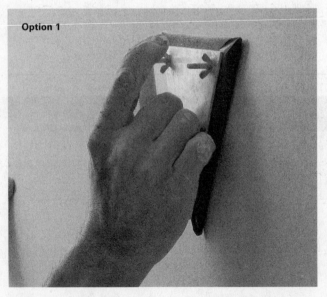

Option 1

Lightly sand the walls and ceilings after applying the third coat of joint compound to the seams. Unlike paper-faced drywall, these products become smoother when sanded. The trade-off to this faster approach is more airborne fiberglass dust, so protect yourself accordingly.

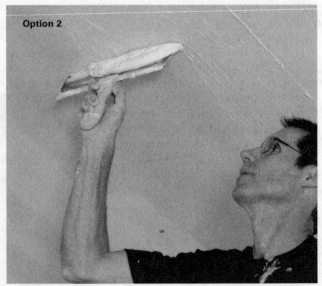

Option 2

Skim-coating the entire surface of the drywall with a thin layer of joint compound is fine if you're comfortable with taping knives. In fact, this is the best option for any type of drywall that will be coated with high-sheen paint or exposed to strong raking light at any point in the day.

Alternatives to Painted Drywall

By Courtney Fadness

Painted drywall is so ubiquitous in home construction that it's easy to overlook other options. Certainly, painted drywall has its virtues. It's inexpensive, easy to install, easy to modify, and it works in any space. An inherent quality of drywall is the smoothness of its finish. However, left on its own, drywall can actually look a bit too perfect, a bit too sterile, and thus lack character and richness—even if painted in the most perfect shade. Visual interest is born from creating visual tension. This is most easily achieved by utilizing contrast. Instead of leaving every room clad in drywall alone, I create interest, depth, and richness in interior spaces by incorporating alternative wall treatments with materials such as wood, tile, and natural stone. Here I discuss these options and highlight the details within projects that successfully put these materials to use.

Wood

Ideal Use: Living rooms, dining rooms, and bedrooms

Consider: Vertical or horizontal planking, board-and-batten treatments, paneling, wainscot, detailed moldings

Wood is an incredibly versatile surface treatment, partly due to the vast array of finish options available. Natural, stained, painted, pickled, whitewashed—all can be used to support a conceptual direction. Wood left in its natural finish feels cozy and warm. Painted wood lends itself to a fresh, clean, and overall subtle effect. Wood treatments can be used to create architectural character as well. For example, a traditional quality can be created by adding a board-and-batten treatment to walls, or by introducing moldings such as an oversize base, cornice, and picture rail. Wood also can be employed to enhance or diminish existing features of a room. Run vertically, wood boards can visually lift the ceiling. Similarly, horizontally oriented boards visually expand the width of the space.

Design example: Planking in a living room

6-in. poplar shiplap planks create clean, crisp, horizontal lines that keep the space from feeling overly tall by countering the vertically oriented fireplace and doors.

The distinctive ¼-in. channel between each board creates texture and adds graphic interest in an otherwise sparse, contemporary space.

The white painted finish on the boards does a better job of reflecting natural light than painted drywall and creates a bright, airy feel.

Simple, square-edge base moldings and window and door casings mimic the crisp detailing of the wall boards and reinforce a clean, unfussy look.

The width of the planks on the wall is similar to the width of the wood flooring, creating harmony among the materials and helping to unify the room.

Continued ➜

Tile

Ideal Use: Kitchens, bathrooms, halls, stairways

Consider: Porcelain, ceramic, glass, mosaic, brick

Tiles in various sizes, textures, colors, patterns, and mosaics are readily available at a variety of prices. An added benefit of using tile for walls is protection against elements such as water, dirt, and stains. Depending upon the tile selected, the effect can be subtle or dramatic. If tile is already present in flooring, backsplashes, fireplaces, and wet areas, try expanding its use to create more impact. Tile the entire bathroom rather than just the shower enclosure. Extend the kitchen backsplash up to the ceiling rather than a few inches above the countertop. Tile can be used to reinforce a particular aesthetic direction or to provide a contrast to it.

Design example: Tile in a kitchen

The walls are treated with a 3×6 white subway tile applied in a running-bond pattern with a dark-gray grout.

The tile and cabinetry are kept similarly hued so as to unify the two walls and enhance the flow between these components.

The subtle texture of the tile softens the transitions between the many features found in the kitchen—window casings, cabinetry, appliances, and lighting—without completely diminishing the contrast.

Natural Stone

Ideal Use: Entryways, halls, stairs, powder rooms, baths, kitchens

Consider: Marble, slate, limestone, bluestone, fieldstone, granite, soapstone

Though a hard material, natural stone has unrivaled depth and richness. Utilizing natural stone for a wall-surface treatment is a fantastic way to bring the warmth of nature indoors. It also provides a great opportunity to borrow exterior materials and details, blurring the indoor/outdoor distinction. This concept is particularly successful when used in entryways, halls, stairs, or any spaces that include a lot of glazing and that have a connection to the outdoors. The veining in natural stone allows it to be treated as the art in a room; natural stone can be used to create feature or accent walls, which instantly add character to a blank space.

Design example: Natural stone in a hall

The walls and columns are covered with Lueders limestone applied in a random pattern of squares and rectangles in various sizes.

Applying exterior surface materials on the interior creates continuity between indoors and outdoors and helps draw the eye toward the view.

The color palette is kept soft and neutral to balance the texture and varied dimension of the stone.

The random layout and rough finish reinforces the organic qualities of the stone, adding depth to the space while softening the visual coldness of full-height glazing.

The dark walnut floor contrasts with the light color of the stone, creating lift and drawing the eye upward.

Make Old Walls Smooth and Sound

By Tim Leahy

The historic mansions that my crew and I work on in Newport, R.I., are sometimes bankrolled by folks who can afford to restore them to their original glory. This means that we strip paint off hundreds of feet of woodwork and repair a lot of plaster walls. Last winter, we were hired to paint the interior of the Eisenhower House at Fort Adams State Park. Because the house is state-owned, the budget was tight. Lucky for us, the woodwork was in great condition, but the walls needed serious attention. Hairline cracks, poorly made patches, and large sections of peeling paint were evident in several rooms that needed to be painted. We made them new again with a technique I've used on many preservation projects.

After scraping loose paint and securing crumbling plaster, my crew and I covered the walls with wide fiberglass mesh, then applied two thin coats of joint compound. At about way less than a dollar per sq. ft. plus minimal labor, the results can't be beat. The walls are clean and smooth, and they won't crack again. Also, any potential lead hazards are now safely contained. While we

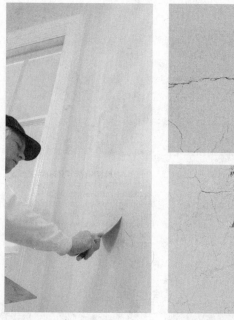

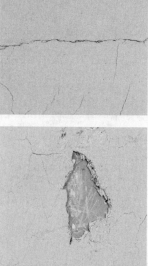

CRACKS, PEELING PAINT, AND BAD PATCHES disappear with a wide roll of adhesive mesh and two thin coats of joint compound

typically use this approach on plaster walls, it works on drywall as well. Before we touched the fiber-glass mesh or opened a bucket of mud, though, we inspected the walls to make sure they were sound.

Get It Clean, Dry, and Dull

As time goes by, plaster succumbs to substrate movement, moisture, alterations, and repairs. On the surface, mildew, chalking, paint failure, and cracks were all easily visible. Before applying the mesh, we scraped and/or sanded any loose or flaking paint and leveled old patches and imperfections.

Deep cracks indicated structural movement, so I brought in one of our carpenters to assess the problem. He determined the cause and that it had been addressed long before we'd gotten there. At that point, my crew and I inspected the plaster more carefully, then stabilized loose areas.

We looked for paint that flaked off easily and for bulges in the surface, which indicate that the plaster keys had broken, releasing plaster from lath. When necessary, we used plaster washers and screws to tighten the wall back to the lath.

Some of the plaster flaked off in chunks. In these instances, we chipped away at the loose plaster until we reached an area where the keys were clearly intact. We then patched holes smaller than 8 in. dia. with setting-type compound, such as Durabond 45. Although we didn't need to patch anything larger than 8 in., I typically patch large areas with drywall. Setting compound can slump when applied over big areas, requiring multiple coats and sanding. It's best to attach the drywall directly to lath; cutting away lath undermines its strength around sound plaster keys.

We scraped away all flaking paint until we reached a place where it still adhered soundly to the wall. Because we were working in a home that predates the 1970s, we did all this with lead safety in mind. I suggest reading "Lead-Paint Safety, at Home and on the Job" (online at finehomebuilding.com) and visiting the EPA's Web site (www.epa.gov/oppt/lead) for guidance.

Once the walls were patched and sound, we vacuumed them to remove dust that would interfere with the adhesive on the mesh. We used trisodium phosphate (TSP) and a damp rag to clean areas that were chalky or had greasy residue.

Self-Adhesive Mesh Adds Strength

The fiberglass mesh we use comes in 3-ft.-wide by 75-ft.- or 150-ft.-long rolls. We apply it in vertical strips, overlapping each seam 1 in. to 2 in. Unrolling the fiberglass is easier if you approach it as a two-person job.

We started in one corner of the room and worked from the ceiling down to the baseboard. I like to run the mesh past inside and around outside corners by about an inch, then overlap the next section. Doing so makes for a stronger joint that is unlikely to crack. As with wallpaper, we let the mesh run long by about an inch at the ceiling and at the baseboard, then trimmed it later.

The key to rolling the mesh is to have about a foot

Continued ➜

well-adhered before trying to unroll large sections. This takes advantage of the adhesive's strength. Using an open palm, we smooth the fiberglass over the wall, working from the middle out to the edges. Every once in a while, it is necessary to peel a bit back and reposition it to keep it smooth and wrinkle-free. I find it easy to trim the mesh with a utility knife and a taping knife or wallpaper edging tool.

All-Purpose Compound Does the Trick

For the skim coat, we used USG's all-purpose joint compound because it is premixed and sands easily. To make the compound easier to apply, I mix it with a paddle mixer.

Although a wide taping knife might seem like the most logical tool for this job, it isn't. Wide taping knives have a bend in the center to help float taped joints. For this application, a perfectly flat knife is key. I've found that a 5-in. knife is a good choice. We applied the mud in a two-stroke fashion using a 5-in. knife. The first coat should be only as thick as the mesh itself, so with the first stroke, we applied the mud to the wall. Then we scraped it

off with the second. We also made sure to work the knife in the proper direction of any overlapped seams so that we didn't lift the mesh.

After allowing the first coat to dry overnight, we inspected the surface. We knocked off small nibs or ridges with a taping knife or with 120-grit sandpaper. We trimmed bubbles or wrinkles flush with a razor knife and filled them with compound.

We then applied another coat in the same fashion, again removing the excess compound to leave a tight, neat surface. Once the second coat was dry, we used a fine sanding sponge to smooth out minor imperfections. I didn't worry about areas where the mesh was slightly visible because the primer and paint would cover them. You also can use joint compound to spot-coat areas where the mesh sits proud of both coats.

Once the walls were well vacuumed, we applied an acrylic primer, then two coats of wall paint. The wall profile and slight irregularities were not changed in this project, but the surface is as it used to be: even and smooth.

Cover the Walls With Mesh

PEEL, STICK AND ROLL. Start each section by peeling several inches away from the roll, then pressing it against the wall. Let an inch or so run onto the ceiling. Keep the roll horizontal to ensure that it stays in a straight line down the wall.

UNROLL A FEW FEET AT A TIME. After a large section is adhered, unroll the mesh with two hands. Pull it tight as you go. Unroll, then smooth a few feet at a time. Make sure every inch is adhered.

KEEP IT SMOOTH AND STRAIGHT. Use your hand to press and smooth the mesh onto the wall. Peel back the fabric, and reposition it as needed to remove wrinkles. Overlap each section by 1 in. to 2 in.

TRIM TO FIT. Use a taping knife and a utility knife to trim the mesh around the casing, the baseboard, and the ceiling. Press the mesh into the joint, then trim it with the knife.

Overlap Inside and Outside Corners

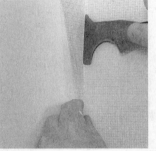

LAP, DON'T BUTT. Butting two pieces into an inside corner will result in cracks over time. Instead, run the mesh about 2 in. past the corner. Smooth it out to remove wrinkles, then go back and tuck it tight into the joint using a 6-in-1 tool or a taping knife.

OVERLAP, BUT GIVE IT ROOM. Overlap the next piece, holding it back from the corner about ½ in. Keeping the overlapping edge away from the corner will ensure that it won't be snagged when joint compound is applied. Wrap outside corners the same way.

Apply Two Thin Coats of Compound

USE A SIDE STROKE. Using a 5-in. taping knife, apply the compound to the wall with a side-to-side stroke. Be sure not to lift the mesh where it overlaps and where it has been trimmed.

SCRAPE IT OFF. Pull the compound off the wall. Keep the knife tight; the first coat should fill only the mesh. Cover the entire wall, keeping this first layer tight to the mesh. Let the first coat dry, then lightly sand and recoat in the same manner.

Work the Room

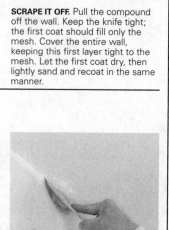

PULL TO CUT IN. Work inside corners horizontally from the inside out. Move in this fashion from the top down. Don't run the knife from top to bottom with one edge tight to the corner.

MOVE DOWN FROM THE CEILING. After the baseboard is cut in and the wall is coated, work along the ceiling.

Sand the Highs, and Fill the Lows

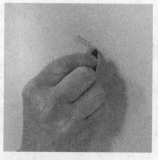

SAND LIGHTLY. Allow the first coat to dry, then sand the entire surface with a fine-grit sanding sponge. Scrape down high edges first with a taping knife. Repeat this process after the second coat has been applied and dries. Spot-coat areas where the mesh sits proud of the second coat.

CUT OUT BUBBLES. Check for bubbles after each coat dries. Cut out the mesh with a razor knife. Then fill with compound, and sand lightly. Some bubbles can be cut and coated as the compound is applied.

Use Wide Mesh and a Narrow Knife

Although covering walls with adhesive mesh and applying two thin coats of drywall compound take a little time, the process requires minimal sanding and costs far less than a dollar per sq. ft.

Plaster Washers and Screws
Reinforce plaster that has pulled away from lath with 1⅝-in. drywall screws and plaster washers.

All-Purpose Joint Compound
Coat the mesh with two thin layers of all-purpose joint compound. Allow each layer to dry 24 hours before recoating and/or priming.

Adhesive Mesh
Apply 36-in.-wide adhesive fiberglass mesh over the entire wall to create a strong, unified substrate for the skim coats.

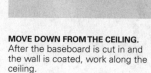

5-In. Taping Knife
Use a knife this size to apply the compound to a wall or ceiling. The work goes quickly. Wider knives curve in the center, so it's difficult to get a smooth, even layer.

Continued ➔

A Simple Approach to Paneled Wainscot

By Gary Striegler

I've done wainscot lots of different ways, and each job has its own balance of cost, complexity, and final appearance. But one of my favorite methods is to build a pocket-screw-joined frame on my workbench or sawhorses, fasten plywood to the back and panel molding to the front, and then install the whole thing in prebuilt sections. I like this system because it's fast but doesn't sacrifice final appearance for that speed. Plus, when installed over wavy walls, these big sections can help create a flat run.

Although this room started with bare walls—which makes it easier to plan the many layers of trim necessary to tie everything together nicely—wainscot can easily be added to an already-trimmed room, too. The important thing is to spend time planning how the various pieces of trim will work together. Do this and you'll be rewarded with work that looks like it was meant to be there.

It All Starts at the Openings

Whether you're working in a new room or doing a trim makeover to an existing space, wainscot always starts at the same place: the windows and doors.

Build Up Casing at Windows and Doors
Casing must be built up with a backband to accommodate the thickness of the layered wainscot trim.

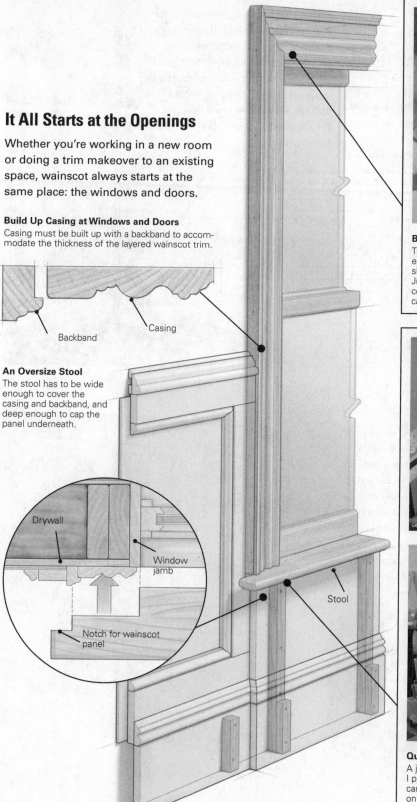

Backband

Casing

An Oversize Stool
The stool has to be wide enough to cover the casing and backband, and deep enough to cap the panel underneath.

Drywall

Window jamb

Notch for wainscot panel

Stool

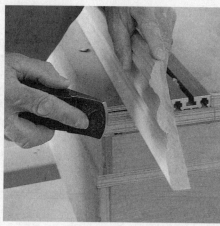

Back-Bevel for Tight Miters
The trick to tight miters is to bevel the back edges of each piece with a sharp block plane. This helps the show face of the trim to come together without gaps. Just be sure to leave enough material at the inside corner of the miter so that when it's assembled you can't see a beveled gap.

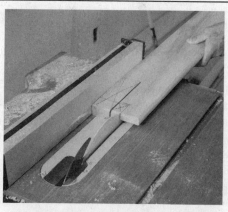

Quick and Clean
A jigsaw is one way to notch a window stool, but I prefer to use a tablesaw and a miter saw. Made carefully, a stopped cut on a tablesaw and a tilted cut on a miter saw are the best combination of speed and accuracy.

Continued →

Plan It on the Wall

The height of the paneling is partially driven by the ceiling height of the room—between 30 in. to 40 in. from the floor is common—and then adjusted to ensure that the rails and stiles will have appropriate reveals on all sides once the baseboard and cap molding have been installed.

Once the vertical positioning has been determined and marked with a chalkline, you can better establish the proportions of the horizontal layout. I find that an odd number of panels is most pleasing to the eye, and I avoid making panels that are taller than they are wide. Here's how to find the panel width.

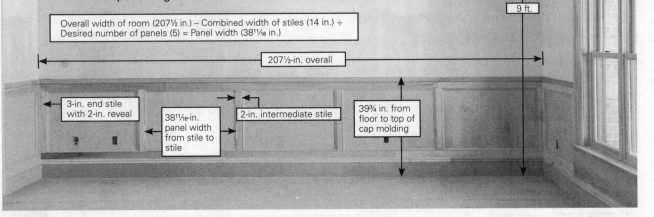

Overall width of room (207½ in.) – Combined width of stiles (14 in.) ÷ Desired number of panels (5) = Panel width (38¹¹⁄₁₆ in.)

207½-in. overall

9 ft.

3-in. end stile with 2-in. reveal

38¹¹⁄₁₆-in. panel width from stile to stile

2-in. intermediate stile

39¾ in. from floor to top of cap molding

Build It on the Bench

I typically see carpenters build the frame of paneled wainscot right on the wall, or build the frame and fasten it to the wall without the panel molding attached. There aren't many benefits to building paneled wainscot piece by piece, right on the wall. It's harder to get good joints in the wainscot frame this way, and you'll spend more time working on your knees as you measure, adjust, fit, and fasten all of the panel molding. I prefer to build as much of the wainscot as possible on a worktable or on sawhorses, where I can work comfortably. Only after I assemble the frame, add a plywood backer, and install the panel molding do I fasten the whole assembly into place on the wall.

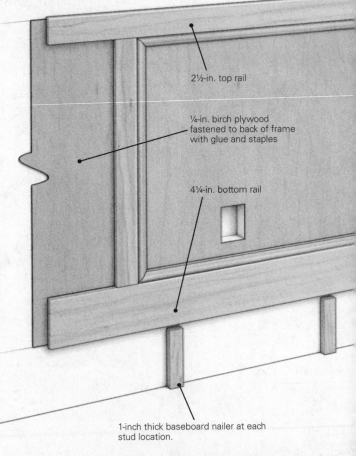

2½-in. top rail

¼-in. birch plywood fastened to back of frame with glue and staples

4¼-in. bottom rail

1-inch thick baseboard nailer at each stud location.

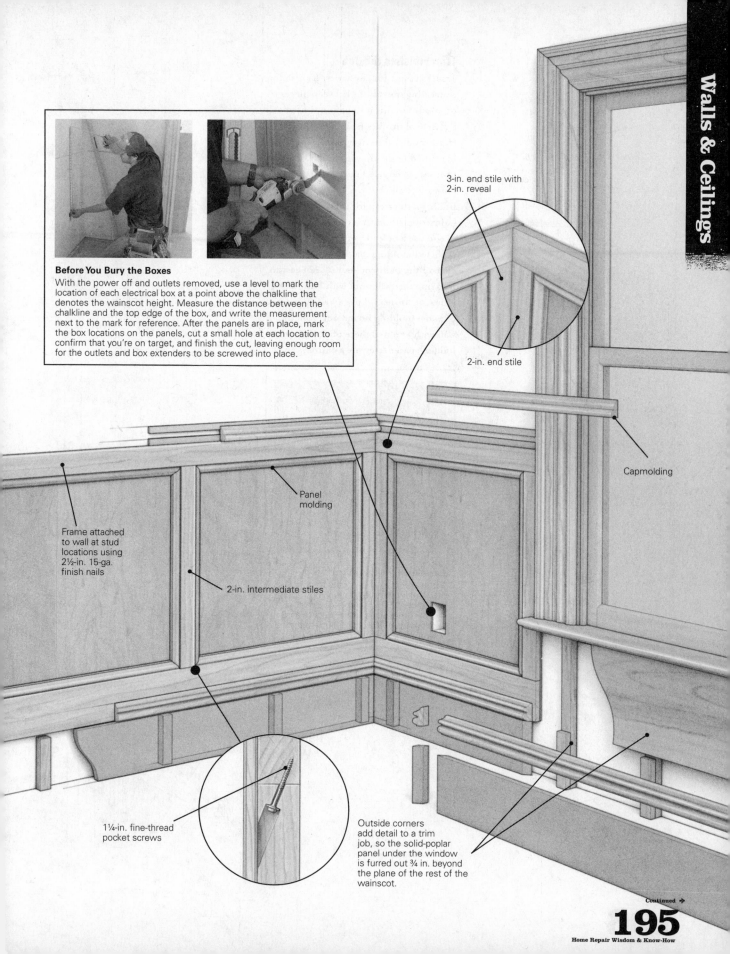

3-in. end stile with 2-in. reveal

2-in. end stile

Capmolding

Before You Bury the Boxes

With the power off and outlets removed, use a level to mark the location of each electrical box at a point above the chalkline that denotes the wainscot height. Measure the distance between the chalkline and the top edge of the box, and write the measurement next to the mark for reference. After the panels are in place, mark the box locations on the panels, cut a small hole at each location to confirm that you're on target, and finish the cut, leaving enough room for the outlets and box extenders to be screwed into place.

Panel molding

Frame attached to wall at stud locations using 2½-in. 15-ga. finish nails

2-in. intermediate stiles

1¼-in. fine-thread pocket screws

Outside corners add detail to a trim job, so the solid-poplar panel under the window is furred out ¾ in. beyond the plane of the rest of the wainscot.

Continued ➡

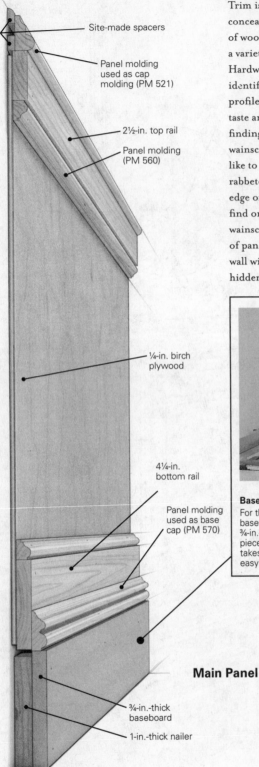

Site-made spacers

Panel molding used as cap molding (PM 521)

2½-in. top rail

Panel molding (PM 560)

¼-in. birch plywood

4¼-in. bottom rail

Panel molding used as base cap (PM 570)

Main Panel

¾-in.-thick baseboard

1-in.-thick nailer

Site-routed stool

Solid ¾-in. poplar

Panel Under Window

¾-in.-thick and 1-in.-thick nailers

Trim Finishes the Job

Trim isn't just for aesthetics; it's also for concealing transitions between pieces of wood. On this installation, I used a variety of profiles from White River Hardwoods (whiteriver.com), which are identified in the drawing at left. Trim profiles are largely a matter of personal taste and scale, but you may have trouble finding a stock cap for this particular wainscot method. A lot of carpenters like to use a bolection molding—a rabbeted molding that laps over the edge of the wainscot—but it's not easy to find one that will work with 1-in.-thick wainscot. Instead, I use a hefty piece of panel molding furred out from the wall with a routed piece of poplar and a hidden spacer to create a custom cap.

Baseboard from Shelving
For the flat portion of the two-piece baseboard, the author likes to rip ¾-in.-thick MDF shelving stock into 5-in. pieces. The material is inexpensive and takes paint well, plus its 12-ft. lengths are easy to handle.

Hanging Drywall Overhead

By Myron R. Ferguson

There is an old saying that I once read on a drywall contractor's business card: "The bitterness of poor quality remains long after the sweetness of low price is forgotten." I keep these words of wisdom in mind whenever I begin a drywall job. Good workmanship is especially important in ceiling-drywall installations because correcting poorly planned, sagging, or sloppy ceilings can be difficult.

In any room that will have drywall on both the walls and the ceiling, the ceiling always comes first. Why? The material easily can be cut to fit, and the wall panels will help to support the outside edges of the ceiling panels to prevent sagging.

I prefer to buy drywall based on the size of the ceiling to be covered. The general rule is to use the largest panels possible to eliminate as many nontapered (butted) seams as possible. Many people don't realize that drywall is available in lengths up to 16 ft., in both 48-in. and 54-in. widths. Although 54-in.-wide drywall

Planning Is Critical

When it comes to installing drywall overhead, a little bit of planning goes a long way toward preventing misaligned panels, sagging ceilings, and butt seams that are difficult to finish.

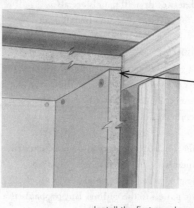

It's smart to install overhead panels first so that the wall panels will help to support the edges of the ceiling.

Install the first panel snug and square against the top plate of the wall to prevent a compounding alignment problem.

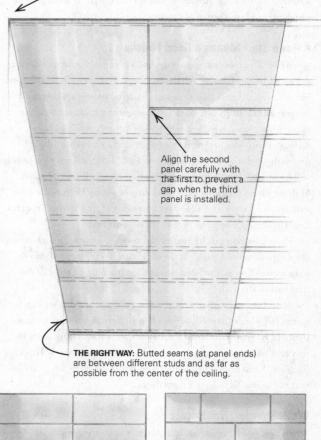

Align the second panel carefully with the first to prevent a gap when the third panel is installed.

THE RIGHT WAY: Butted seams (at panel ends) are between different studs and as far as possible from the center of the ceiling.

POORLY PLACED: Butted seams are lined up and in the center of the ceiling, where they're harder to hide.

TOO MANY: Butted seams are staggered, but there are too many. The one in the center of the ceiling will be highly visible.

Continued ➔

seldom is used on ceilings, it can be handy for eliminating an extra seam.

For example, on a 16-ft.-long ceiling, I will use one 16-ft. panel rather than two standard 8-ft. panels. Using a larger single panel means less work taping and finishing seams.

The strength and thickness of drywall panels are also important considerations for successful ceiling installations.

Perpendicular or Parallel?

For several reasons, hanging drywall perpendicular to the overhead framing members is a good idea. First, it allows the untapered ends of each panel to be butted together over the open space between framing members and back-blocked to give the panel a slight taper.

A perpendicular orientation also allows each sheet of drywall to float over the framing members, making uneven joists or trusses blend in over its length; plus, it's much easier to see the framing when fastening the panels to the ceiling. But probably the most important reason to hang the panels perpendicular to the overhead framing is because drywall is approximately three times stronger in the long direction than it is in the short direction, which means less chance of sagging.

A Good Start Means a Good Finish

When it comes to hanging drywall on ceilings, the question I am asked most often is "Where do I begin?" Every job is different, but my recommendation is to start hanging panels against the longest wall, and put in extra effort to get the first row as straight as possible. As each subsequent row of drywall is hung, keep it tight against the previous row to prevent a compounding problem. If the ceiling is more than 16 ft. long, at least two panels will be in each row, which means butted seams. If one or more of these pieces gets attached out of line—even by ⅛ in.—the gaps will become larger and the edges more out of line as you progress. Starting straight helps to reduce these problems.

Problems also can be caused by bowed top plates, which often are a sign of bowed walls. In these situations, it's a good idea to snap a chalkline as a reference mark for the outside edge of the first run of drywall.

Most times, starting with a 48-in.-wide panel and letting seams fall where they will is fine. But if there is a row of recessed lights 12 ft. from one side of the room, avoiding a long seam in this area will make it easier to tape when the time comes. In a case like this, I just trim a few inches or a few feet off the first run so that the seams fall where I want them.

Work Smarter, Not Harder

When you're lifting panels into place, a helper is invaluable. Don't grip the ends of the panel while the center sags down; hold it in from the ends a little to help support the entire sheet. If you're working alone or if you simply want to make the installation easier, consider using a lifting tool to help carry the load.

Smarter Lifting and Stronger Fastening

1. Drywall Lift
Available from most rental centers, these hand-crank or hydraulic lifts enable a single person to do the job of two or three. The lift adjusts to various heights and holds the drywall against framing members to allow for easier fastening on walls or ceilings.

2. Adjustable Benches
Also known as step-up benches or trestles, these 4-ft. by 9½-in. aluminum benches can be used to reach ceilings up to 10 ft. high. The bench height is adjustable from 18 in. to 32 in.; optional attachments increase the height to 48 in.

3. T-Support
This homemade tool can be assembled from scrap lumber and sized to fit the ceiling height. Make it tall enough to span the distance between the floor and the underside of the drywall being installed, plus an extra ½ in. to get a tight fit. The horizontal arm should match the width of the panel being installed.

4. Stiff Arm
A more modern version of the T-support, this metal tool adjusts to different heights and holds a panel firmly in place against the overhead framing. Unlike a homemade T-support, a stiff arm won't fall down once the panel has been fastened to the framing.

Take Care When Fastening

It's important to set screws to the proper depth. Some self-feeding screw guns have an adjustable depth setting, and special attachments for cordless drills stop the screw right where you want it.

For ceilings framed 16 in. on center (o.c.), I place screws 12 in. apart. If the ceiling joists are 24 in. o.c. or if I'm installing fire-code drywall, I drive screws 8 in. apart.

Too Deep
The paper facing of the drywall will tear and could result in the sheet pulling off the screw.

Not Deep Enough
The head of the fastener will cause problems when you mud and tape the ceiling.

Properly Set
The screw dimples but doesn't break the surface of the drywall. This provides the strongest connection and allows for easier finishing.

Make a Butted Seam into a Tapered Seam

Each of the long sides on a sheet of drywall has a tapered edge so that tape and joint compound can be applied without creating an obvious bump between sheets. It's always a good idea to plan the ceiling with as few butted joints as possible, but sometimes they can't be avoided. In these cases, it's smart to use a backer to pull the butted ends of each sheet together and create a slight bevel. These backers can be purchased from a number of suppliers or made on site from shimmed plywood.

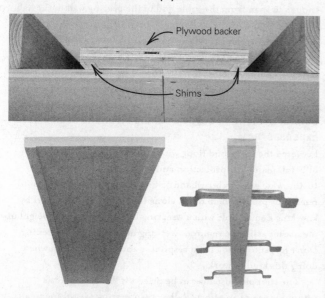

Plywood backer

Shims

A MANUFACTURED BACKER, this 53-in.-long, ½-in.-thick MDF board has a beveled recess down the center. Slim and flexible, it requires only about ½ in. of clearance behind the drywall for installation.

THE BUTTHANGER relies on metal brackets and a 1×3 board to provide tapered backing for butt joints. The pivoting brackets make this a good choice for working around diagonal bracing or pipes, and they can usually be purchased for less than $10 a piece, a good choice for smaller jobs.

When you're fastening each panel, secure the edge that's butting against the top plate or previous run first, making sure that it doesn't overlap or leave any gaps. To help attach the panel tight against the overhead framing, fasten from one long edge across the face to the other edge. If you attach both edges and then attach the center, the panel may not pull tight against the ceiling.

Tacking up panels with drywall nails is fine, but use drywall screws in the face of the panel because they provide a much stronger anchor. Screws typically should be spaced 12 in. apart and need to penetrate the framing only ⅝ in.

When you're hanging drywall on a ceiling taller than 8 ft., it makes sense to finish securing each panel completely before moving to the next because the scaffolding or adjustable benches are already in place. If you're working on a lower ceiling that can be fastened while you're standing on the ground, you can tack each sheet in place, then go back and finish fastening after the whole ceiling is covered. Don't wait until the next day, though, because once the panels start to sag and change shape, it's difficult to snug them up to the framing members again.

Making Accurate Cutouts

If the ceiling will have cutouts for recessed lights, vents, or electrical boxes, take measurements for them before tacking the drywall panels in place. Simply write down the measurements on or next to the surface measured from so that they can be recalled easily later.

Next, tack the panel in place, keeping the fasteners away from the planned cutout to help reduce some of the pressure against the back of the drywall. Transfer the measurements onto the panel to be cut, and use a drywall router or wallboard saw to make the cuts. It's important to take your time making the cutouts; a mistake means a repair.

Finish Up with a Quick Checklist

When all the drywall panels have been installed, do a walk-through, looking for unfastened areas and double-checking that all cutouts have been made. Also, check for poorly set fasteners; too deep is bad, and not deep enough is a huge pain when it's time for mudding and taping.

Continued →

A Few Innovative Tools and Materials

Ceilings commonly are finished with ½-in. regular or ⅝-in. fire-code drywall. Standard 4×8 sheets weigh about 58 lb. and 70 lb. respectively. Both types can be attached perpendicular to 16-in. or 24-in. o.c. framing.

Lightweight ½-in. Drywall

If you're looking for a lightweight option that doesn't sacrifice stiffness, there are ½-in. panels available that are are stronger and less expensive than a ⅝-in. panel and weigh about 10 lb. less than a typical ½-in. panel.

Drywall Adhesive

Drywall adhesive reduces the number of fasteners needed to secure each panel. It also has excellent shear strength and is not affected by changes in temperature or moisture. This means less chance of nail or screw pops. Note: Adhesive should be applied only to the framing, not to overlapping kraft paper or plastic sheeting.

Drywall Screws

Drywall screws rather than drywall nails—especially in the center, or field, of the panel—provide stronger attachment. Screws should be long enough to penetrate ⅝ in. into the framing. Longer screws are more likely to push outward as lumber dries and shrinks, which can lead to screw pops or bumps on the finished surface of the ceiling.

Cordless Self-Feeding Screw Gun

With drywall screws eclipsing drywall nails and batteries replacing power cords, it's no surprise that many drywall installers are switching to cordless self-feeding screw guns to reduce the time and effort needed to fasten each panel.

From Flat Ceiling to Cathedral

By Mike Guertin

Most of the homes in my neighborhood are ranch style, built in the late '50s and early '60s. They all seem to have low ceilings that often measure 88 in. high, which makes them feel cramped and dark. Such a low ceiling is especially out of scale in a 16-ft. by 18-ft. family/living room, as was the case in a ranch I was remodeling. A quick peek in the attic confirmed that the framing was conventional rafters, not trusses. This meant that I could transform the room by adding a structural ridge and reframing the ceiling. The new ceiling would add about 42 in. of height at the center and improve the character of the room. By recycling the existing ceiling joists, I'd need to buy only drywall and a bit of lumber.

Finish the Design Before Starting Work on the Demolition

I had two options for the ceiling design (drawings p. 201): a monoslope vault that ran uninterrupted from the exterior wall to the interior bearing wall; or what I would call a gable vault, which created a false ridge in the middle of the room. This second option seemed in keeping with a ranch house, more so than the monoslope of '80s contemporary-style homes. To gain the greatest height in the new ceiling, I decided to insulate and drywall right to the underside of the existing 2×6 roof rafters.

Before tearing out the plaster ceiling, I moved the rock-wool ceiling insulation to another part of the attic to minimize demolition mess. I also rerouted electrical wiring that crossed the ceiling joists. In the attic, I slipped in a pair of 2×12s long enough to span from the gable end to the bearing wall in the hall that would support the roof once the ceiling joists and strapping were removed. The old ceiling joists act like rafter ties for the roof, resisting the outward thrust of the rafters and preventing the exterior walls from bowing outward. A new structural ridge beam beneath the ridge would accomplish the same goal.

Careful Demolition Saves Both the Floor and Lumberyard Expenses

I covered the hardwood floor with moving blankets, then a layer of 6-mil plastic for protection and for easier cleanup. The old 16-in.-wide gypsum board and ½-in.-thick plaster are easiest to remove by pulling them down along the seams. I usually start by knocking a small hole with a wrecking bar and letting the weight of the plaster assist the removal, working my way across the ceiling. Don't forget to wear a good respirator and eye protection when doing this kind of work.

The strapping usually can be pried off the ceiling joists without much of an effort. Rather than beating everything to a pulp with a wrecking bar after I'd cleared the rafters, I used a reciprocating saw fitted with a bimetal blade to cut the toenails pinning the joists to the plates; this process prevented the joist ends from splitting. Once the nails had been removed, the strapping and the joists would provide much of the lumber needed to frame the new ceiling.

Shims Correct Roof Sag, and New Rafters Extend to a False Ridge

Plans call for two skylights to be installed after the roofing is replaced, so this was the perfect time to frame the roof in preparation. I doubled the rafters on each side, then added the headers above and below the future skylight locations.

The roof rafters had an obvious sag in the middle of the room.

Rather than ignoring it, I ripped tapers on some 2×3s and nailed them to the underside of each rafter to create a uniform ceiling plane. I recut the old ceiling joists and used them to frame the other side of the new ceiling at the same 5-in-12 pitch of the existing roof. I side-nailed the false rafters to the roof rafters at the top and toenailed them to a beam at the bottom. The end wall was framed with 2×4 studs and cleated along the top to carry the ceiling drywall.

After installing new lighting and air-conditioning registers, I hung and finished the drywall, blew in cellulose insulation, then painted. The results were better than I expected.

Framing for New Space

Because I removed the ceiling joists that reinforce the walls against the weight and thrust of the roof, I added a structural ridge. The double 2×12 beam spans from the outer gable wall to an interior bearing wall and is supported at both ends by king and jack studs. I also added new rafters to frame the other half of the gabled ceiling.

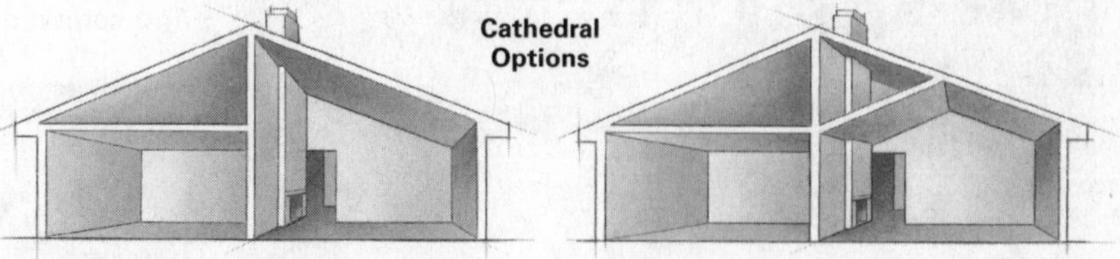

Cathedral Options

A monoslope ceiling extends from the exterior wall's top plate to the roof ridge.

A gabled ceiling creates a false ridge at the room's centerline.

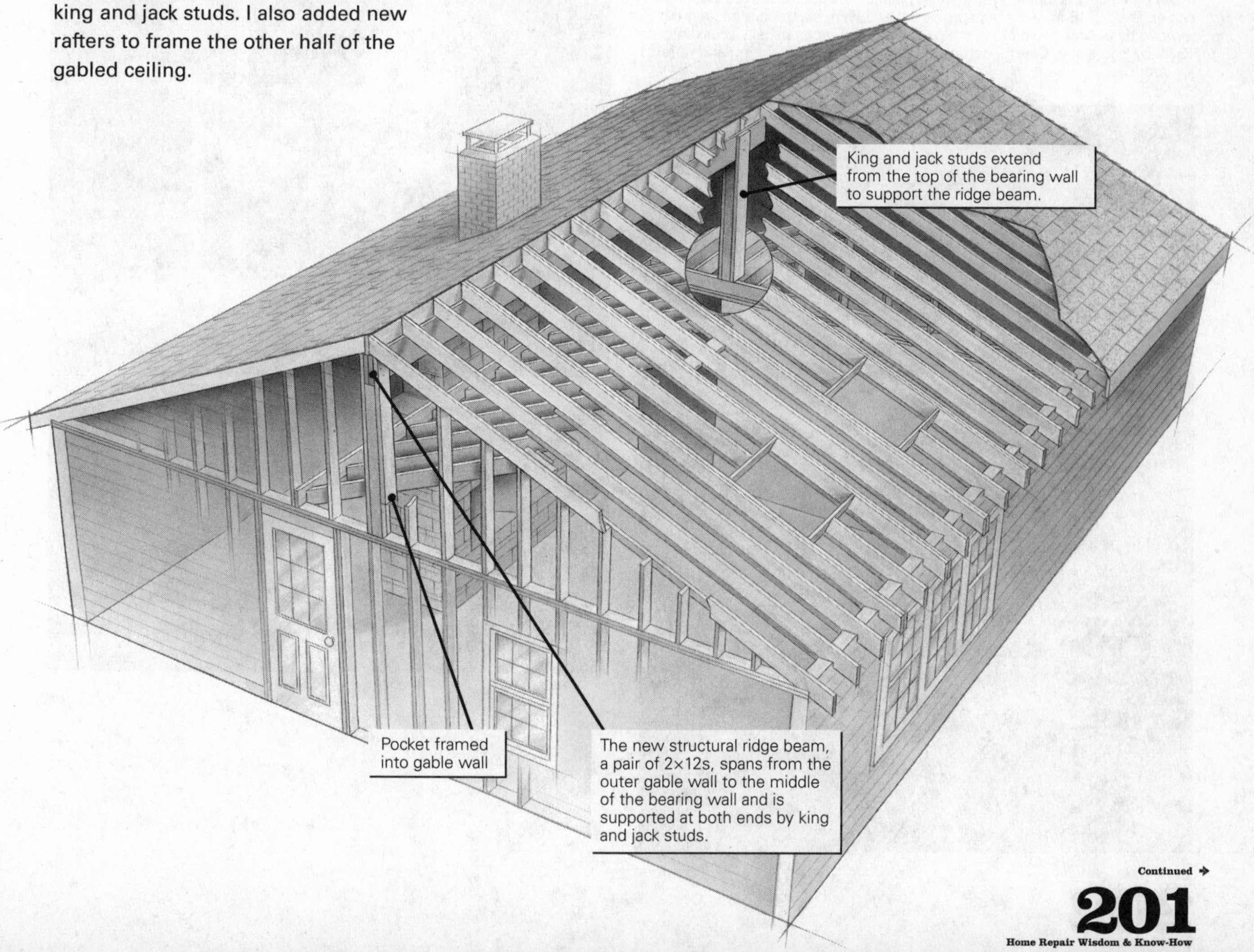

King and jack studs extend from the top of the bearing wall to support the ridge beam.

Pocket framed into gable wall

The new structural ridge beam, a pair of 2×12s, spans from the outer gable wall to the middle of the bearing wall and is supported at both ends by king and jack studs.

Continued ➜

Protect the floor during demolition. Hardwood floors are protected by moving blankets under a layer of 6-mil plastic, which also makes cleanup easier. The old 16-in.-wide gypsum board and ½-in. plaster are easiest to remove by pulling down along the panel edges. Pieces usually break into 16-in. by 8-ft. slabs. Careful demolition also preserves strapping and rafters for later use.

Retrofit a Structural Ridge Beam Before Demolition

Before tearing out the ceiling, I brought a double 2×12 beam to the attic to support the portion of the ridge where I would remove the ceiling. The existing ridge board bears directly on the top edge of the new beam. With the beam's far end set in a pocket at the gable, I raised the inboard end of the beam into place by using a pair of 2×6 king studs as a lifting jig. These uprights had holes drilled every 6 in. for a ½-in.-dia. steel rod I inserted as a safety stop. (1) At each stop, I slid the rod through the holes to support the beam. After an initial manual lift by hand, I used a hydraulic jack to raise the beam level (2). Finally, tight-fitting jack studs were driven under the beam and screwed to the king studs (3).

Straighten a Sagging Roof with Tapered Shims

The roof above the living room sagged to the point where I couldn't ignore it. The ridge was bowed, and the rafters had an obvious sag in the middle of the room. To determine the severity of the problem, I set two stringlines as guides, one just above the top wall plate and one at the centerline of the room. Both lines were blocked out 2½ in. from the face of the rafters and strung from opposite sides of the room. After consecutively lettering the rafters, I clamped a long, straight 2×3 to the side of each one. I lettered each 2×3 with the same letter as the rafter and aligned it with the stringlines at each end. After using the edge of the rafter to scribe the shim, I unclamped the 2×3s, ripped them along the scribe lines, and screwed each one to the underside of its rafter. In addition to straightening the interior plane of the roof, the 2×3s added extra depth to the rafter bays for extra insulation. Alternatively, I could have sistered each 2×6 rafter with a 2×8 or 2×10, but that would have used more lumber and also would have reduced the width of the bays and their insulation.

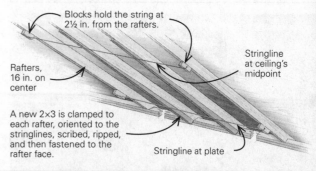

Blocks hold the string at 2½ in. from the rafters.

Rafters, 16 in. on center

Stringline at ceiling's midpoint

A new 2×3 is clamped to each rafter, oriented to the stringlines, scribed, ripped, and then fastened to the rafter face.

Stringline at plate

Frame Now for Skylights Later

Sister rafters without the tails are cut from the old ceiling joists. After the roof nails protruding through the sheathing are bent flat adjacent to the rafters, the top of a sister rafter is aligned alongside the existing one. Oriented this way, the only friction to overcome is at the seat cut and the top cut. Clamps draw the rafter tops together, and I rap the bottoms with a hammer until they're tight (1). Nails are staggered and spaced 12 in. apart to hold each pair together (2).

Combine Insulation and Venting

Custom vent chutes made from 1-in. rigid-foam insulation are fit in each rafter bay; 1-in.-wide strips taped along the edges space the panels off the roof sheathing and form the vent channel. Added later, 6 in. of blown cellulose will create a ceiling insulated to R-25.

Make a Better False Ridge with Straight Lines

I used a plumb bob at both ends of the room to locate the center (1), then snapped a chalkline on the ceiling between them (2). The chalkline indicated where the bottom of the false rafters would cross the existing ones to form the vault. I drove screws into the rafters partially to support the rafter tops, and I toenailed the tails into the double 2×6 that supported the old ceiling along the face of the interior fireplace wall (3). Each rafter top then was spiked to the primary rafters with four 12d nails.

Continued →

Recycled Ceiling Joists Make Good Rafters

Careful demolition saved me a trip to the lumberyard. After finding the centerline, I used the old joists as the new rafters on the gable vault. The open gable end was framed last.

RENT A HELPER. Drywall lifts are usually available at local rental outlets and are worth every penny. They save time and make solo installation of even a 12-ft.-long sheet an easy task. With the addition of skylights, the finished ceiling adds light and space to the living room.

Contents

Roofing & Siding

Perfect Roof Rafters

By Sam Koerber

My process for framing a roof starts the same as anybody else's: laying out and cutting a pattern rafter, which I then use as a template to cut the rest of the rafters to make up the roof frame. Just like everybody else, I choose a flat, straight, and dry piece of stock for the pattern rafter, which I crown so that any natural arch is facing up when installed, and I set the piece atop a pair of sturdy sawhorses that are at a comfortable working height. From there, I get a bit more fussy than most with the layout, which I believe pays off big time in terms of the quality of my frames.

Lessons Learned from Timber Framing

Most of the time, framers use a 6-in. rafter square to lay out the plumb and seat cuts of a rafter. But two practices on recent jobs have convinced me to change up my approach. First, I've begun to incorporate components of timber framing into otherwise stick-framed houses; second, I do exposed rafter tails on most builds. Timber framing has taught me to use chalklines and a framing square for accurate layout on boards that don't have a reliable straight edge for reference. It also has taught me that a knife makes crisper layout lines than a pencil. Those same layout techniques have improved the consistency of the exposed rafter

tails, ensuring that they not only look crisp and uniform but that they line up nicely without trimming and shimming once in place. Now, even on roofs without exposed rafter tails, I use this technique because it works better than the conventional methods.

Lumber, even the dimensioned stock we use for framing, is far from perfect. Referencing the ridge, seat, and other cuts off the edge of a board can throw off the layout more than you might think. Wany edges from the milling process, natural dips and humps in the board, and knots and other grain patterns all affect the trueness of a board edge. The conventional approach means trying to fit a long 2x between walls and roof when the layout of the angles is based only on the 6 in. of wood that is directly in contact with the rafter square. Snapping your reference lines eliminates the inaccuracies.

Trust Your Rafter

Does such a fussy level of accuracy really matter with rough framing? My answer is that it's not about being perfect for the sake of perfection; it's about making the rest of the job go easier. If I'm confident that my rafters are laid out and cut to a high level of accuracy, I can trust them. This way, if they don't fit perfectly, I have a clue that something else in my framing is out of whack and needs to be adjusted. Maybe the top plate is a little crooked, the walls are slightly out of plumb, or the ridge board is cupped, crooked, or set too high or too low. Two wrongs don't make a right, and correcting these other components makes more sense

Continued ➜

Pattern Rafter

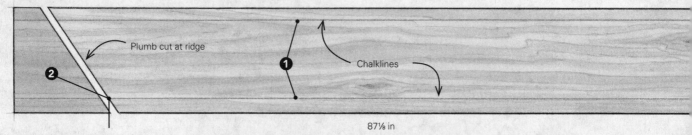

Plumb cut at ridge

❷

❶ Chalklines

87⅛ in

1. START OFF STRAIGHT. Mark 1 in. and 8 in. from the top edge on both ends of a 2×10, then snap a crisp chalkline between each pair of marks (0.5mm string is best) to create dead-straight reference lines.

2. MARK THE RIDGE PLUMB CUT. Align your framing square to the chalkline on the appropriate numbers—the 8-in. and 12-in. marks for this 8-in-12 pitched roof—and scribe a line for the ridge plumb cut. I use a utility knife for all cross-grain marking because the knife line is more accurate than the sharpest pencil line, and it shears off cleaner when cut with a circular saw.

3. FOLLOW THE LINE. Measure from the intersection of the chalkline and plumb cut—starting from the 1-in. mark for accuracy—to mark the rafter length. Adjust this line by half the thickness of the ridge to mark the plumb line that represents the sheathing's outside face.

Accurate Layout Relies on a Reference Line

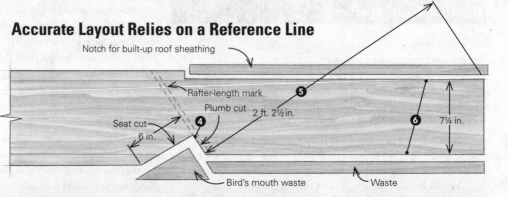

Notch for built-up roof sheathing

Rafter-length mark

Plumb cut

❺

❹ 2 ft. 2½ in.

Seat cut

6 in.

❻ 7¼ in.

Bird's mouth waste

Waste

4. SQUARE UP FOR THE SEAT CUT. The bird's mouth is 6 in. wide—the combined width of the top plate and the wall sheathing—and referenced off the line that marks the rafter length.

5. ADD THE OVERHANG. Reference your framing square off the plumb cut of the bird's mouth to calculate the desired amount of overhang, which is measured perpendicular from the bird's mouth plumb cut.

6. CUT THE TAILS. Use the chalkline as a reference when marking the depth of the notches on the top and bottom of the tail, and connect them with a sharp pencil, which won't wander to follow the grain.

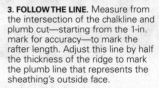

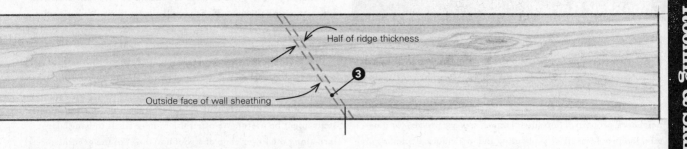

Half of ridge thickness

Outside face of wall sheathing

3

The Pattern Is Set

Add blocks. The rafter template is completed with a reference block screwed near each end of its top edge to ensure that the peaks and tails all line up, regardless of crowns in the middle of the board.

Well-Tailored Rafter Tails

Cutting 2×8 tails out of a 2×10 rafter yields crisp-edged exposed tails that will be aligned well without shimming, and it allows space for the top of the tail to be notched and padded with built-up sheathing to keep roofing nails from poking through below.

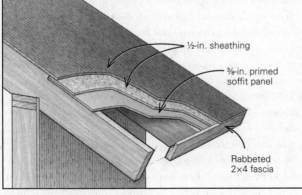

½-in. sheathing

⅜-in. primed soffit panel

Rabbeted 2×4 fascia

to me than altering the ridge or seat cuts of a perfect rafter to fit a problematic frame.

I've found this process to be well worth the extra time spent doing layout. It's satisfying to be able to maintain control over the building throughout the roof framing process.

Finding the Rafter Length Is Easy

All you need to find the length of a rafter is the width of the building, the desired roof pitch, and a basic calculator. The math may look intimidating at first, but go through the steps once and you'll see how easy it is.

Measure between the insides of the plates at the bottom of the wall (the easiest place to get an accurate read), and then add in the plate width and sheathing thickness: 133 in. (plate to plate) + 12 in. (total combined width of plates and sheathing) = 145 in.

A standard gable has two rafters that meet in the middle, so divide this number in half: 145 in. ÷ 2 = a rafter run of 72.5 in.

The roof pitch provides the next two numbers in the calculation. We want an 8-in-12 pitch, so multiply the run by 8, then divide the result by 12 to get the rise: (72.5 × 8) ÷ 12 = a rafter rise of 48.33 in.

The key formula here is $a^2 + b^2 = c^2$. Plugging the run and rise into the formula lets you solve for c, the rafter length: $72.5^2 + 48.33^2$ = 7592.0389 Hit the $\sqrt{}$ to find the square root, which is 87.134 in.

Carpenters don't deal in decimals, but converting the 0.134 remainder into 16ths is simple: 0.134 × 16 = 2, which is ²/₁₆, or ⅛ in. The final calculated rafter length is 87⅛ in.

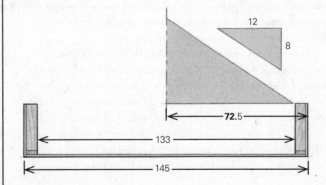

12

8

72.5

133

145

Continued ➜

Low-Risk Reroof

By Stephen Hazlett

I am a roofing contractor by trade and a problem solver by nature. The biggest problem I solve every day is how to tear the roof safely off an occupied home and install a new roof while protecting the interior, the siding, the landscaping, the windows and doors, and the neighbors' property. I don't have a secret, esoteric process for quick, safe, foolproof tearoffs, but planning and meticulous efficiency come as close as possible. I carry a big tarp behind the seat of my truck to cover the house with, but thankfully, I've never had to use it.

On second thought, maybe there is a secret to this type of work: Don't tear off more than you can reroof quickly, and keep a big tarp handy.

The Most Important Tool Is Information

When planning a roof replacement, a lot of information should be gathered in advance: roof pitch, type of decking, number of existing layers of roofing, the history of roof leaks, and the way leaks were resolved.

Writing the proposal is the next step in planning the workflow. I break down the project into a logical progression: what my crew and I can accomplish each day. In doing this, I take into account ladder and scaffolding placements, access for dump and delivery trucks, and electrical-outlet locations. The most-important things I look for are where the old roof debris is going to land and how I can avoid damaging the siding, the landscaping, the awnings, and the lawn.

When I measure roof area, I confirm the thickness of the roof decking so that I'll have patch stock on hand. In my area, many of the homes built in the '20s were sheathed in #2 southern yellow pine. This ¾-in.-thick decking tends to hold up better than the ⅜-in. or ½-in. plywood sheathing used in houses built in the '60s, '70s, and '80s.

Some roofing contractors prefer to have materials delivered to the rooftop after the old roofing has been torn off, but I have materials delivered at least a day before work starts. We enjoy the peace of mind that comes from knowing we have everything we need on site before the first shingle is torn off.

Because every project we do involves an occupied home, weather always is a concern. The morning a reroof is scheduled to begin, I start tracking the weather at 5:30 a.m. I make a "go" or a "no-go" decision by 7 a.m., based on the size and complexity of the roof, the size of the crew, and the rain's estimated time of arrival.

If the job is a go, I notify the crew between 7 a.m. and 7:15 a.m., and we are on site by 8. If I decide the project is a no-go, I notify the homeowner that the project has been postponed.

Protect the House with Plywood and Tarps

Once we arrive on site, we are in constant motion. Everything has been planned, so there is no need to waste time. The first things off the truck each morning are usually an assortment of large ground tarps. The ground tarps are spread out beneath the work area. Anything thrown off the roof lands on them. We have an assortment of sizes from 30 ft. by 40 ft. to narrow runners that fit between garages and fences, and in other tight spots.

Delicate shrubs and flowers often are covered with sawhorses, empty trash barrels, or sheets of oriented strand board (OSB), along with more tarps. Some houses need no more protection than ground tarps and shrub shields, but a couple of additional steps might be useful. We often use bungee cords to hang a large tarp along the lower edge of a roof and down to the ground. This allows the gutters to catch nails and small debris, and the tarp often can be used as a chute to direct larger roof debris to a specific location. We sometimes install roof jacks and planks along the lower roof edge to catch debris and to protect awnings or a swimming pool. This is also a good strategy when houses are extremely close to each other. In that case, all debris is tossed carefully to a specific safe landing area.

Tear Off a Little at a Time

Our main tearoff tool is the Shing-Go shovel, which we call a shingle eater. We can remove 99% of the shingles from the roof with shingle eaters; for the rest, we use an assortment of pry bars, flat bars, and tin snips (for stubborn flashing). Shingle eaters can damage siding easily, so we stay about a foot away from sidewalls. I generally use my Estwing Roofer's Bar to clear out the wall flashing and the adjacent shingles. This bar works better for me than the common flat bars that most roofers use.

We prefer to start from the ridge and work our way down the roof, each worker tearing off a swath (we call it a rack) about 5 ft. wide. A race always is going on to see who can tear off their rack first. A crew of three workers usually tears off an area about 15 ft. wide from the ridge to the gutter in one pass, then moves down the ridge and tears off the next 15-ft.-wide section.

The trick to using a shingle eater is to get it under shingles and not pull it back out. The teeth on the blade of the tool allow you to hook each roofing nail and pull it out with a levering action. I have found that it is less strenuous and more productive to sit on the roof and tear off shingles to my left or below me (I am right-handed). This position is safer because it keeps my center of gravity low. It also allows me to employ my body weight favorably in a rocking motion while pulling down on the handle and levering the shingles and nails off the decking. Inexperienced crew members who bend over and push the shingle eater with their arms and shoulders simply can't keep up with my pace.

Plywood decking allows a much faster tearoff because there are far fewer board edges to catch the teeth of the shingle eater. I find that 1×8 decking is difficult to work with; sometimes I have to tear off sideways along the length of each deck board to avoid catching an edge every few inches. Tearing off along the length of each board also puts less torque on the decking and causes fewer split boards.

With experienced roofers, tear-off can go surprisingly quickly, often within an hour. If I am working solo, I might tear off the old roof until about 10 a.m. before I start reroofing. Remember, there

Sweating the Details Keeps the Job Running Smoothly

Be Prepared at the Start

• Have materials delivered a day early. This ensures an early start if weather permits.

• Know the thickness of the roof sheathing, and have plenty of patch stock on hand for the inevitable repairs.

• Begin tracking the weather early. By 7 a.m., you'll be able to make a fairly safe guess as to whether the reroof is a go or a no-go.

Different Sites Call for Different Strategies

• Each house requires a different level of protection. Simple jobs might need no more than ground tarps. Houses with close neighbors might need plywood and tarps to protect walls.

• Plan for debris removal. A ground-tarp landing zone, a dump truck parked in the driveway, or subcontracted waste removal are common ways to handle this.

• Keep an extralarge tarp in the truck. A roofer's badge of honor is the roof-size tarp that's still in the wrapper behind the seat of his pickup truck. Tip: Don't take the tarp out of the wrapper unless you really need to cover the roof; you'll never get the tarp back into the package.

Manage the Workflow

• Buy doughnuts for the crew. Roofers love doughnuts, and these carbs go a long way if rainclouds start moving in and you need everyone to work through lunch.

• Only unbutton what can be buttoned up in a day. If the weather is unsettled, break the job down into what can be reshingled before and after lunch.

• Keep ahead of the tasks. As one task is completed, another is usually ready to begin. By thinking ahead and shifting personnel strategically, you can optimize workflow with less wasted time. If you're racing the weather, this mode can be a big time-saver.

PROTECT SIDEWALLS. When neighbors are close, tarps and plywood shield walls in the shingle landing zone. Keep panels close to vertical, or they'll damage the house when heavy piles of shingles hit them.

CARRY WASTE TO THE TRUCK. If the driveway can accommodate a dump truck, carry shingles to it rather than pushing them off the roof onto a tarp. A crew member can switch between tearoff and cleanup.

CLEANUP IS THE LAST STEP. A large ground tarp catches most of the debris, but it's a good idea to sweep the lawn with a rolling magnet to pick up errant nails.

Continued ➔

is a finished, occupied home underneath the roof.

Clean, Repair, and Dry in the Roof

Once the old roofing is torn off, we use a plastic lawn rake to clear off loose shingle pieces; then we sweep down the roof deck to remove the loose debris and shingle grit that can make footing hazardous. Next, we cut out rotten wood and replace it with new solid material. Anyone not needed to replace decking pulls out nails left by the shingle eaters. After the wood replacement is finished, we nail off the entire roof deck with 8d nails in a nail gun and then sweep off the roof deck one last time.

With a clean, solid, safe roof deck, the tearoff is complete, and we can begin the new-roof installation. We install drip edge around the perimeter of the roof. Then we install peel-and-stick

Chimney Flashing Matters

This roof was replaced at least a couple of times with no attention paid to the chimney flashing. Obviously, there is a history of leaks—just look at the black tar buildup. Rather than fix the flashing the right way during a reroof, someone took the easy (expensive in the long run) way out. Worse, this chimney was replaced recently, and the mason didn't insert counterflashing into the mortar. The leaks rotted the decking around the chimney and required substantial replacement. The step flashing installed between the shingles and the chimney should be covered by counterflashing set into the mortar as the chimney is built. In retrofit situations, however, this isn't possible. The next-best thing is to grind deeply into the mortar and insert counterflashing.

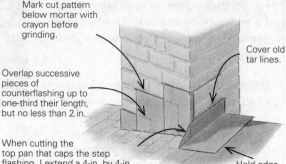

Mark cut pattern below mortar with crayon before grinding.

Cover old tar lines.

Overlap successive pieces of counterflashing up to one-third their length, but no less than 2 in.

When cutting the top pan that caps the step flashing, I extend a 4-in. by 4-in. square past the chimney and bend it over to form a triangular ear that directs water away from the masonry.

Hold edge about 1 in. beyond drip edge.

1. A LITTLE BAD FLASHING CAN CAUSE A LOT OF DAMAGE. This roofer cuts the patch stock in place after nailing one end of the board. His sawblade is set to the depth of the patch stock.

2. START WITH A PLAN. I use a crayon to mark just below the mortar joints before I start grinding them out. I try to insert counterflashing above any old tar lines to give the best possible look.

3. EXTRA PROTECTION. Use roofing membrane along the side, top, and bottom of the chimney. I fold it up the chimney wall as a final line of defense against windblown rain. Cut back the felt about 18 in. so that the membrane can stick to the roof.

4. STEP FLASHING FIRST. After the peel-and-stick membrane is in place, I shingle and step-flash the roof. This front-apron flashing piece extends over the lower shingles and under the first piece of step flashing.

5. COUNTERFLASHING COVERS STEP FLASHING. The front piece covers the chimney's apron flashing, and the bottom corner piece folds around the face of the chimney. Successive pieces overlap each other.

6. READY FOR THE REAR PAN. The counterflashing shown at left covers the last piece of step flashing and folds around the top corner. The pan piece (shown in drawing) comes next.

7. THE FINAL PIECE. The top piece of counterflashing covers the top pan, which has a triangular ear that extends past the chimney. The counterflashing should turn the corner and have its top edges tucked into the masonry.

8. SEAL THE JOINTS. I like Geocel (www.geocelusa .com) sealant because of its excellent longevity. Forced into the horizontal saw kerf, the sealant most likely will outlast the roof shingles. I also daub the exposed nails in the front apron.

membrane along the lower edge of the roof. We install at least one 3-ft.-high course along the bottom edge. If a single course doesn't extend high enough up the roof to correspond with a point at least 12 in. inside the wall, then we might need to install a second course. Check local codes for this detail because unexpectedly doubling the peel-and-stick membrane on a large job can take several hundred dollars out of your pocket. I also put peel-and-stick membrane in valleys and around chimneys.

I use #30 builder's felt to dry in any roof decking not covered with the peel-and-stick membrane. After the whole roof is dried in, we usually snap a chalkline, marking every other shingle course. If three-tab shingles are being used, we snap a couple of vertical lines to maintain a 6-in. shingle offset. We like to rack three-tab shingles straight up the roof on smaller or steep roofs and stairstep larger or easy-to-walk roof areas. No vertical chalklines are necessary for dimensional shingles, only a few horizontal course lines.

Lunchtime is anywhere from 10:30 a.m. to 1 p.m., depending on progress and the weather outlook. I like to have all chalklines snapped before lunch so that when we return, we can begin installing new shingles immediately. I frequently use lunchtime as a chance to grind out the mortar joints in the chimney for reflashing. Doing this work at lunch means that I won't spew dust and grit on my coworkers.

Shingling the Roof Is the Easy Part

We use air guns to install roofs. I usually establish either the vertical "rack" pattern or the stairstep pattern myself, while the next-experienced roofer extends the pattern across the roof. At this point in the job, if we have a third man on the crew, he often is kept busy stocking the roof with bundles of shingles. We try to arrange our work so that once shingles have been laid, we won't need to climb or walk on them again.

After the roof pattern has been stepped in, I jump over to flashing work, and the third man moves to shingling. On this job, there were no valleys to replace, but you can read another one of my articles on roofing, "A Durable Roof-Valley Repair" (see p. 230), for a discussion of that. This roof, however, had a couple of chimneys that needed counterflashing retrofit into them. The chimneys had been rebuilt only a few years ago, but as is common, the mason didn't incorporate counterflashing into the brickwork. If the counterflashing isn't built in to the brickwork, you have to cut it in deeply with a grinder. During a heavy rain, water can be absorbed far into the brick, allowing it to get behind flashing that's not inset deeply.

About a half hour before we are through for the day, the third man on the crew starts folding tarps, packing up tools, loading the truck, and cleaning the yard of errant nails with a rolling magnet.

These details about protecting the outside and inside of a house during reroofing go a long way with my customers as well as my insurance agent. Most of all, though, it's the way I would want to be treated if I were the customer.

Extra Steps Improve Durability

DRY IN WITH HEAVY-DUTY FELT. Use peel-and-stick membrane along the eaves, and #30 builder's felt for the field. The felt paper is held in place with staples if it is to be shingled right away. On new construction, the felt sometimes is nailed with button-cap nails until it can be shingled.

STEP INTO ESTABLISH THE PATTERN. Nail drip edge along the roof perimeter, then begin to shingle. Stepping each shingle back 6 in. allows one roofer to establish the pattern while another fills the field.

Steep Roofs Can Complicate Your Strategy

• Tear off and reroof in gutter-to-ridge swaths before moving sideways. This minimizes scaffold and roof-jack setups.

• Use scaffolding on the roof. We set up slater's jacks and 2×12s along the lower edge of the roof and a second course about midway to the top. If you own as many jacks and planks as we do, you can cover the entire roof area. This method is the safest and fastest for large crews.

• Use a harness and rope. Coupled with a roof ladder and a 2×12 set in roof jacks along the bottom eave, this can be an effective one- or two-person setup.

SLATER'S ROOF JACKS ARE EXTRAWIDE. This allows them to hold up to a 2×12 plank rather than a 2×10 typical of other roof brackets

CATCH THE SHINGLES. Roof jacks with a 2×12 catch the shingles while a scaffold below provides a place to stand and toss shingles into the landing zone.

A SAFE SETUP MAKES THE JOB GO MORE QUICKLY. Tied off to the ridge, this roofer has the extra peace of mind that a misstep won't be fatal. The roof ladder provides safe footing while tearing off from top to bottom.

Continued ➜

Step Flashing

By Gary Herman

Installing step flashing correctly is one of the first things I teach a new member of my crew. The first rule of flashing is that water runs downhill. The second rule of flashing is that sometimes rule No. 1 isn't the whole truth and that water also runs uphill, as when it wicks up inside debris or backs up behind ice. For this reason, I like to lap all flashing by at least 2 in.

It's important to remember that a building always is moving. If you nail step flashing to the wall and to the roof, you're asking for trouble. Most of the time, I like to avoid putting any extra holes in the roof surface, so I nail step flashing to the sidewall only, where both the next piece of flashing and the siding will cover the nail head. The bottom corner, where you start the course of flashing, is made from two pieces of bent step flashing lapped over each other and caulked in place.

BASIC MATERIALS GET THE JOB DONE: Roofing caulk, galvanized roofing nails, tin snips, and step flashing (either flat or prebent).

Corner Flashing Comes First

1. MAKE CORNER FLASHING FROM STEP FLASHING. Once you've shingled up to the sidewall, cut a piece of step flashing at a 45° angle from the outside corner to the bent seam. Bend it down and back to sit flat on the corner. Then sink two nails in the wall near the top, one on each face.

2. LAY A BEAD OF SEALANT. Where the next piece of flashing will overlap, apply a bead of caulk to seal the corner. This spot is prone to leaking because there is not a full 2 in. of overlap. Use a sealant designed for roofing. Not all caulks can withstand the heat and exposure of being on the roof.

The Flashing Alternates with the Shingles

3. BEND THE FIRST PIECE ALONG THE PLUMB LINE. The first piece of step flashing needs one bend so that it laps cleanly over the corner flashing installed in the previous step. Make sure the caulk joint between these two pieces is bedded evenly. Then sink one nail into the sidewall to hold the step flashing in place.

4. BEGIN THE WEAVE. With step flashing, you do a little flashing, then a lot of roofing, then a little more flashing, and so on. Each piece of step flashing laps over the shingle below and under the shingle above. The bottom edge of the flashing should extend just below the nail line. Attach each piece with a single nail high enough to be covered by the next course of flashing, the building wrap, and the siding.

The Top Requires Another Custom Piece

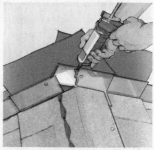

5. THIS ROOF ENDS IN A PEAK. For the first side, cut the step flashing along the fold line, and bend down the lower flap. Drive one nail to hold it in place.

6. CAULK THE TOP. Once you've come up the other side with step flashing and shingles, you're ready to put on the final piece. Apply a vertical bead of caulk as shown.

7. MAKE THE LAST PIECE OF FLASHING. This is the brother to the one you already put on the peak. Cut along the fold line, bend down the flap, and press the pieces together along the caulk joint. Sink one nail into the wall to secure the last piece.

8. ONCE YOU'RE DONE, HALF OF THE FLASHING WILL BE COVERED BY SHINGLES. After the building paper and the siding go on, almost all of it will be covered, which is one of the main reasons flashing has to be installed carefully to begin with.

Synthetic Roofing Underlayments

By Martin Holladay

A milestone in any construction project is drying in, usually defined as the day the roof sheathing is covered with underlayment. Building codes require the installation of asphalt felt for several reasons: Underlayment keeps the sheathing dry until the roofing is installed, it provides some protection against leaks in case wind-driven rain gets past the roofing, and it provides a slight improvement in a roof's fire resistance.

For years, roofers chose between basic #15 or heavier #30 asphalt felt, which are commodity products sold under many brand names. Both types of felt are made from recycled corrugated paper mixed with sawdust; to provide water resistance, the paper is impregnated with asphalt. These days, however, roofers also can choose from a variety of synthetic roofing underlayments: sheet products made of laminated polypropylene or polyethylene plastic.

Synthetic roofing underlayments look and feel similar to housewrap. Unlike housewrap, though, most synthetic roofing underlayments are vapor barriers, so they shouldn't be used on unventilated roofs.

These plastic underlayments also offer higher resistance to UV radiation, better traction for roofers, and more square footage of coverage at a lower weight. They are not, however, intended or approved to replace peel-and-stick membranes in areas prone to ice dams.

Not-So-Slippery Slope
Although Grace's Tri-Flex Xtreme is skid-resistant when dry, its surface is designed to swell slightly so that it becomes even more tacky when wet.

Doesn't Mind Construction Delays
Most synthetic underlayments can be left exposed for six months and some for 12 months. The woolly, tan-colored Opus Roof Blanket, though, is approved for 30 months of UV exposure.

Breathe Easy
Rated at 550 perms, Cosella-Dörken's Delta-Foxx underlayment is by far the most vapor-permeable product in this category, making it ideal for use over unvented assemblies or under slate, clay, or tile roofing.

Traditional Felt Still Competes with Newer Synthetics

Although synthetic roofing underlayments have several advantages over asphalt felt, asphalt felt remains popular as a roofing underlayment for several good reasons.

While the price of asphalt felt fluctuates somewhat, it's still the least expensive option. The cheapest of these options is #15 felt. The #30 felt costs about twice as much per sq. ft. as the #15 felt. Synthetic underlayments cost more than twice as much as the #15 felt. Vapor-permeable synthetic underlayments are the most expensive option, ranging from betweem four to twenty times the price of the #15 felt.

According to Dyami Plotke, a manager at Roof Services in Islip, N.Y., "For a standard roof assembly, where the felt and asphalt shingles are installed on the same day, it doesn't make any difference what underlayment you use, so the lower cost of the standard felt is a big advantage. Where the synthetics outperform felt by a mile is in their tear resistance. Synthetic underlayment allows us to bring a building to a watertight condition just by papering it, without installing the roofing immediately—and it will stay watertight for months. That's why we always use synthetic underlayment under specialty steep-slope products like slate and tile, which are slow to install."

Cap Fasteners Aren't Optional

Although asphalt felt doesn't seal around fasteners as effectively as peel-and-stick membranes, it is less likely to leak at nail and staple penetrations than a synthetic underlayment. Synthetic underlayment punctured by staples or common roofing nails can, with the help of capillary action, lead to leaks. That's why plastic-cap nails or staples, which help to seal penetrations, are a must when installing synthetic underlayments. Cap fasteners can be installed with a compatible pneumatic tool or, in the case of cap nails, manually.

Some roofers also have reported that synthetic underlayments allow more wicking at laps than asphalt felt. For areas that need sealing—including vulnerable laps—use caulk rather than the traditional black roofing cement.

Exposure Limits and Warranties

In their technical-data sheets, manufacturers of synthetic roofing underlayment list maximum time limits, ranging from two months to 30 months, for exposure to the weather. A word of warning, however: There is little evidence that 12-month products actually perform differently from four-month or six-month products, so it doesn't make much sense to rely on these numbers when selecting a product.

Despite the fact that Cosella-Dörken's underlayments have an excellent reputation for durability, the company recommends that roofing be installed "as soon as possible." Product manager Peter Barrett explains, "Plastic begins to degrade as soon as it is exposed to UV light. Once degradation starts, it will go on, even when covered by roofing, since heat and oxidation continue to act on the plastic. Most manufacturers are just giving a guess on the durability of their products. They're gambling that nobody will actually uncover them to see how they're holding up. Warranties are mostly used as marketing tools; these numbers are not an expression of durability."

Continued →

Tailor the Installation to the Roof

Asphalt-felt roofing underlayment has specific installation instructions outlined in the code book. To date, there are no such code guidelines for synthetic underlayments, so the installation for these products is dictated by manufacturers. Below are some of the more generic details, as well as areas that may differ from brand to brand. Not installing synthetic underlayment according to manufacturer requirements is a quick way to void the warranty.

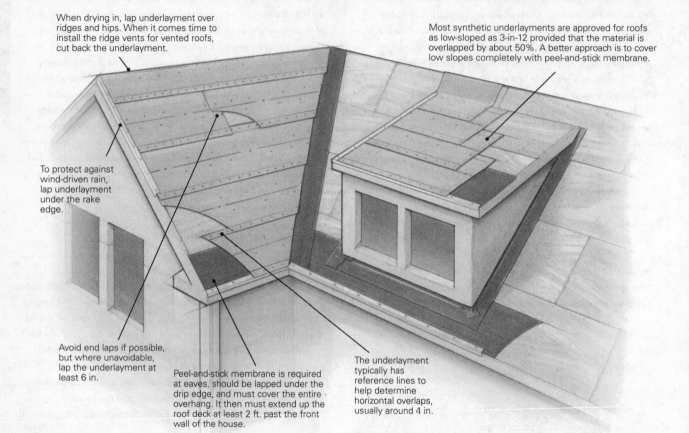

When drying in, lap underlayment over ridges and hips. When it comes time to install the ridge vents for vented roofs, cut back the underlayment.

Most synthetic underlayments are approved for roofs as low-sloped as 3-in-12 provided that the material is overlapped by about 50%. A better approach is to cover low slopes completely with peel-and-stick membrane.

To protect against wind-driven rain, lap underlayment under the rake edge.

Avoid end laps if possible, but where unavoidable, lap the underlayment at least 6 in.

Peel-and-stick membrane is required at eaves, should be lapped under the drip edge, and must cover the entire overhang. It then must extend up the roof deck at least 2 ft. past the front wall of the house.

The underlayment typically has reference lines to help determine horizontal overlaps, usually around 4 in.

Which Brand Should I Choose?

Most roofers aren't too picky about which brand of synthetic underlayment they use, and in many cases, the options will be dictated by your specific region. "In terms of performance, I think that synthetic felt is a commodity product," says Plotke. Because slippery underlayments can be dangerous, the deciding factor for many roofers is traction. According to evaluations made by Fine Homebuilding editorial adviser Mike Guertin, the tested underlayments that showed the greatest slip resistance in both wet and dry conditions were Titanium UDL, RoofLiner, and Tri-Flex Xtreme. Under wet conditions, Sharkskin didn't perform as well as the top-rated underlayments. This segment of the market is growing quickly, however, and there are well over a dozen products that Mike has not had the opportunity to investigate.

To keep track of the product options as they multiply and to weigh in with your own product reviews, visit our online Material Guide at finehomebuilding.com/materialguide.

Features Aside, It Comes Down to Permeance

Most synthetic underlayments have permeance ratings under 1 perm, making them effective vapor barriers. Because these underlayments don't allow roof sheathing to dry upward, manufacturers recommend that they be used only over ventilated spaces (that is, vented cathedral ceilings or vented attics) that allow downward drying.

Of course, just because an attic is currently vented doesn't mean it will stay that way. A few years down the road, a homeowner might decide to install spray polyurethane foam on the underside of the roof sheathing; at that point, the sheathing will no longer be able to dry downward. If this possibility worries you, stick with asphalt-felt underlayment. (Asphalt felt is the original "smart" vapor retarder; it has a permeance of about 5 perms when dry, but a much higher rating of 60 perms when wet.)

Although underlayment manufacturers often don't distinguish between different types of roofing when making ventilation recommendations, some experts do. According to building scientist Joseph Lstiburek, "Having a vapor-permeable underlayment is a big deal if you have a tile roof or a cedar-shingle roof—a roof that is assembled like a vented rain screen. It's very beneficial to be able to dry the roof deck upwards. But the permeance of the underlayment doesn't matter when asphalt shingles are involved." In other words, if you are installing a type of roofing that doesn't allow upward drying, you don't have to worry about the permeance of your underlayment.

Lstiburek tempers his advice with the commonsense observation that underlayment permeance isn't worth obsessing over. "The permeance of the underlayment is irrelevant if everything blows off the roof," he says. "This vapor-permeance is arcane stuff, and none of it matters if you forget to fasten and flash everything properly."

Although most synthetic underlayments are vapor barriers, there are exceptions. Several manufacturers produce products with a vapor permeance that is as high as, or even higher than, asphalt felt. The higher the permeance, the faster water vapor can pass through a material. Any material with a perm rating of 10 or greater is highly permeable.

These products are signifi-cantly more expensive than vapor-impermeable underlayments, so if you want a vapor-permeable product, you may prefer to stick with asphalt felt.

A final note: Although it's perfectly acceptable to use asphalt felt on the roof and as a water-resistive barrier on walls, the same isn't true of vapor-impermeable synthetic roof underlayments. These products are not approved for use on a wall, unless, of course, you're using one of the vapor-permeable options.

5 Roofs That Will Last a Lifetime

By Harrison McCampbell

I'm an architect specializing in moisture problems and solutions. Unfortunately, much of my consulting work involves roofing failures. To me, this is lunacy; we've been building roofs that don't leak for a long time, starting with thatch about 30,000 years ago. Clay-tile roofing appeared around 10,000 B.C., followed by copper (3000 B.C.), slate (2500 B.C.), and wood shakes (12th century A.D.).

Today, these ancient roofing materials are overshadowed easily by asphalt shingles, which are used on about 60% of houses. But asphalt shingles don't satisfy the needs of all homeowners. Historic homes often require traditional materials, and extreme climates can narrow roofing choices. And some people just don't like the look of asphalt.

Consider Regional Style and the House's Scale

If price is your only consideration, then 15-year three-tab asphalt shingles beat any other material hands down. If durability is most important, then a permanent solution such as standing-seam

Premium-Grade Asphalt Shingles
Offer Warranted Longevity

While most folks are familiar with 25-year warranties for asphalt shingles, manufacturers now offer premium architectural or dimensional grades that compete with tile, slate, and wood shingles for longevity. Or at least the warranties do: 50-year warranties are now common, and some manufacturers offer transferable lifetime warranties. These extended warranties beg the question as to what has changed in the asphalt-shingle industry.

"More weight and better design," explains Husnu Kalkanoglu, vice president of research and development at CertainTeed's exterior products division. "A 20-year three-tab shingle may weigh approximately 200 lb. per square, whereas a higher-warranty shingle will be much, much heavier, up to 500 lb. per square. This is because of two things: more asphalt and multiple layers."

Asphalt sheds water and provides a base for embedding granules. Made from different sizes of ceramic-coated crushed rock or ceramic beads, the granules do more than provide color; they also protect the asphalt from UV-degradation. More asphalt allows the granules to bed deeper, which means the asphalt can provide waterproofing protection longer. The other part of the design—multiple fiberglass-mat layers—also boosts life expectancy by adding strength and protection against weathering.

copper might bubble to the top of your list. But thesethings aren't the only considerations.

Think about the style and structural integrity of your house. Clay tiles are common along the southern tier of the United States, but less common in New England. Also, the scale of the roofing material ought to match the scale of the house. Small roofs look goofy with large concrete tiles. The existing roof structure might dictate what you can and cannot do easily. Some old houses have 2×4 roof framing on 2-ft. centers. This framing simply isn't strong enough to support a heavy roof. But a lighter material, such as metal, often can be installed directly over existing shingles.

Climate matters, too. Traditional choices typically evolve in an area because they work well. Tile roofs do well in hurricane-

Continued ➔

prone areas (with proper detailing). A standing-seam terne-coated stainless-steel roof resists the corrosive salt air of a coastal climate. A lifetime roof might not be worth the investment if you're planning to move within a few years. And depending on your roofing choice, you could get a break (or take a hit) on your homeowner's insurance. Finally, think about repairing the roof. If a large branch falls on your roof after a storm, will you need a total reroof? Can you actually walk on it to make the repair? Clay tile and slate are brittle, so repair can be a challenge; metal roofs can be slippery to walk on.

Installation Matters Because Warranties Are Relative

Proper installation is critical with any type of roofing material. Improperly installed roofs can leak. Sloppy installation details can void the warranty. Installation details are specified according to how a material is developed and tested in the manufacturer's lab, and the warranty is written according to this research to provide a consistent product that the manufacturer can stand behind.

But realize how warranties originate: as a sales tool. Asphalt shingles, for example, used to be differentiated by their weight: 200 lb. per square as opposed to 250 lb. per square (a square equals 100 sq. ft.). This means little to a consumer, so marketers translated these numbers into serviceable life: 15-year, 30-year, and—more recently—even lifetime warranties.

Some features in a warranty, however, are aimed more at the sales aspect and less at the "stand behind their product" part. Prorated warranties (those that pay less as time goes on) are a good example. This sliding-scale compensation limits losses while allowing the manufacturer to put a big number on the time scale. Another warranty hook is transferability. Some manufacturers

Wood Roofing
Simple to Install on Complex Roofs

Available in red cedar, white cedar, Alaskan yellow cedar (which is actually cypress), white oak, and southern yellow pine, wood shakes and shingles have a long track record. But for all that's available, red-cedar shakes from British Columbia are the most prevalent.

Canada produces 90% of the world's shakes and shingles.

In spite of the red, white, and yellow in their names, all shakes and shingles weather to gray after a year or so. While it's possible to use kiln-dried (KD) prestained shingles on a roof, it's difficult to maintain the color, especially if you want it to match a house's sidewalls. Prestained shingles also require extra installation attention. "Be very careful of your spacing," advises Lloyd Clefstad, president of www.woodroof.com. "When wet, KD shingles can expand 4%, which, without the proper spacing, will cause buckling, breaking, and eventually roof leaks."

Class A, B, and C fire ratings are available based on factory-applied treatments, but some cities in California don't allow any type of wood roofing regardless of its fire rating.

Standing Seam
The Best Metal Roof

Corrugated-aluminum roofing long has been a favorite due to its long-lasting, low-maintenance qualities and its fire- and wind-resistance capabilities. But aluminum is extremely soft, and corrugated sheets have exposed fasteners, which can leak over time. Steel is considerably stronger but heavier; its longevity depends on a rust-resistant coating. Factory-applied coatings (Enduracote, Galvalume, Kynar, terne) afford the best protection as well as a varied color selection. Light-colored roofs can reduce air-conditioning costs substantially.

"Standing-seam copper roofing is my favorite residential-roof system, for its durability and good looks" says Rick Ragan, owner of Southern Roofing Inc. in Nashville, Tenn. "Because standing-seam panels have concealed fasteners, the roof should never need to be replaced."

Metal roof panels also are manufactured with contours or textures to imitate the look of roof tiles and wood shakes, but these lightweight preformed panels dent under foot traffic or storm-related damage. "Those panels may be OK in places without many trees or high winds, but I've pulled enough trees off of roofs after hurricanes to stay away from them," says builder Michael Chandler in Chapel Hill, N.C.

take advantage of the average homeowners' 10-year stay in a house and void a warranty when the original buyer transfers ownership.

"I don't have any faith in our ability ever to collect on an asphalt-shingle warranty," says roofing contractor Stephen Hazlett of Akron, Ohio. "On almost every roof, I have to deviate from the recommended procedures." Such deviations are often from the specified nailing pattern. A shingle could butt against a chimney or a waste-stack flashing, requiring a nail a couple of inches away from the specified location. If the placement doesn't match the shingle company's specs, the manufacturer might not honor the warranty. While some manufacturers offer more liberal nail-placement specs, most are strict about nail location.

While Hazlett hasn't had a warranty problem, he thinks a warranty's real value is relative: A 50-year shingle might or might not last 50 years, but it will outlast a 15-year shingle substantially.

Bottom line for warranty shoppers: Look for transferable warranties and, if possible, warranties that aren't prorated.

For asphalt roofs, qualified installation contractors are ubiquitous, but for more exotic materials, qualified installers can be scarce. Look to trade organizations for local contacts.

What's on My House?

I always have liked California mission- or Mediterranean-style homes. The mission "pan and barrel" tile, set in mortar, is my favorite residential roof. Copper is my metal roof of choice for its looks and durability. Did I use either when I reroofed my own house last year? No. I used a laminated 30-year asphalt shingle because mission tiles would have looked silly on my brick ranch and asphalt shingles were about one-third the price of copper.

Slate

A Traditional Choice That Lasts Hundreds of Years

One of the most prestigious building materials is experiencing a rebirth. Slate production and use essentially have doubled in the last decade, and many quarries have modernized their facilities to handle slate more efficiently. Most slate quarries are

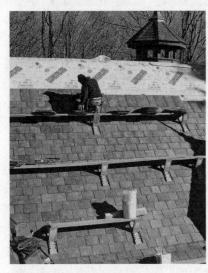

in the Eastern United States and Canada, each producing its own distinct colors.

Slate roofing went through a bottleneck in the 1950s with the increased use of asphalt roofing, and many old-timers who knew trade secrets are gone. That's why it can be challenging today to find truly skilled installers who know the correct details for starter courses, valleys, ridges, and even the staging that allows an installation to be completed without anyone walking on the slate. The advent of power tools hasn't had much effect on how slate roofs are installed. It's still a process done largely by hand. But the reward for this labor-intensive process is a roof with exceptional character and longevity.

Roof Tiles

Made with Clay or Concrete

The earliest clay-roofing tiles were made by bending moist sheets of freshly mixed clay over the thighs of workers, thus forming a tapered half-barrel shape that allowed for a distinctive over-under pattern across the roof. With the mass production of clay tiles, both barrel and flat, features such as lugs and dips were incorporated to help interlock and stabilize the tiles as they were laid one on another. From a limited range of options, colors now are almost limitless, finishes are either dull or glazed, and some tile even is textured to look like wood shakes.

Both clay and concrete are fireproof, with excellent wind resistance when installed properly. But installation can be tricky: You need to install wood battens on the roof and along the hips and ridges as well, tiles need to be cut with a diamond-blade saw, and underlayment

must be exceptional, often #90 rolled roofing. Because roof tiles last a long time, you need to use durable fasteners and flashings. Tests by the Tile Roofing Institute have shown that wind clips and specially placed adhesives let tile roofs sustain 125-mph winds. The biggest disadvantage with concrete and clay is weight, but this problem is solved easily with beefed-up framing.

Continued →

PVC Roof Trim

By John Spier

Framing defines the bones of a building, but a well-executed trim job highlights its design for the world to admire. If done properly, the individual trim components blend together, their arrangement is smooth and harmonious, and the trim looks good for years to come. Trim installation is also a very satisfying part of the job that marks the transition from rough frame to fine finish.

For almost thirty years, I've been building and renovating on Block Island, R.I., a place where houses are routinely blasted by wind-driven salt, sand, debris, and precipitation, occasionally all at once. I've learned to have my clients invest in quality materials to resist these forces of nature, and for the past decade, this has included PVC exterior trim. As with using any new material, installing PVC has a learning curve, but after working with it for a number of years, I feel like I've developed techniques that allow the material to perform at its highest potential.

Recently, I built the house shown here and trimmed it in PVC. The design includes an upper roof marked by almost rounded gables and a pair of A-style dormers. A lower roof shelters a porch encircling the first floor. With their longer lengths and variety of joints, the house's roof soffits and fascias provide good examples of the methods I use to work with the material.

Good Or Bad, PVC Isn't Wood

Although PVC trim is weatherproof, its plasticity makes it harder to work with, especially if you're used to working with wood. First, because of its flexibility and long lengths, it's difficult for one carpenter to move efficiently. It took a couple of jobs for me to find an efficient method for carrying and cutting the floppy material.

Its flexibility also means that PVC will telegraph every bump and ripple in the framing, rather than bridging and hiding them, so the framing needs to be straight before I start to trim. I use shims, saws, a grinder, and an old power plane to smooth things out.

The other tricky aspect of PVC is its finish. PVC crosscuts, rips, and routs smoothly, but the exposed core doesn't have the same smooth surface as the factory faces and edges. When I look back at my earlier PVC-trim jobs, it's usually the ripped edges and cut ends that I notice first. In the early years, the material's porous interior structure tended to capture mold and dirt. Since then, manufacturers have refined the material's composition. Even so, I've learned to plan carefully so that only factory edges are exposed.

When that is not possible, I smooth ends and edges that will be visible with a slow pass of a sharp plane. I also use a block plane to ease sharp corners. Some professionals advocate wiping down cut edges with acetone to seal the material, but that's an additional level of toxicity that I prefer not to have on the job.

Make PVC Joinery Stick

I've used the gamut of fastening systems for PVC trim. In the past, I hand-nailed trim with stainless-steel nails, but the nail heads

How to Handle Floppy Boards

PVC TRIM STOCK ARRIVES ON-SITE IN LONG LENGTHS: 18 ft. for 3/4 stock and 20 ft. for 5/4 stock. It lacks the rigidity of wood unless it's carried on edge, which makes it hard to balance on a miter-saw stand.

SMALLER IS GOOD. Keep a cordless saw near the stock pile, and cut pieces to rough length before carrying them to the miter saw and trimming to exact size.

PLAN FOR SUPPORT. Enlist the help of another carpenter, or use a couple of tall folding sawhorses that you can move around as needed. You can also scab a board across an interior wall to support the stock in line with the saw table.

LASER ASSIST ON A MITER SAW. I've done a lot of trim work over the years with a Hitachi C10FSB sliding compound-miter saw, whose laser is especially useful for fine-tuning trim. It projects a well-defined, sharp line that makes shaving a degree from a cut much easier and faster.

were visible and detracted from a clean appearance. I now use a combination of pneumatic nails and Cortex screws and plugs. I fasten soffits with stainless finish nails because the holes there aren't as noticeable. I hang fascias using just a few nails where they will be hidden by a second fascia layer, and then I finish fastening with screws and plugs.

On jobs that are to be painted, I nail everything pneumatically and fill the nail holes with a shrink-resistant and UV-resistant vinyl or epoxy exterior filler made for PVC. If the dried filler is not painted afterward, its porous texture tends to attract dirt and can look shabby.

I also keep in mind the ambient temperature when I'm installing PVC trim. I don't get scientific about it, but in hot weather, I fit pieces tighter; in cold weather, I leave some expansion room at the unglued butt joints between long soffit pieces. About $1/16$ in. between boards seems to work well. At the corners, I cut miters a bit proud of the framing, especially in hot weather, to allow the framing to move. When the temperature drops, the trim can shrink and still retain the integrity of the joint. I use 23-ga. pin nails to hold miters together

Straight Soffits Simplify Assembly

Fix the Framing

Align soffits with the outside edge of the 2x subfascia. Before installing them, make sure the subfascia is straight. If it's not, adjust the framing. In addition to creating an even substrate for installing the fascia, this makes for faster trim installations with tighter joints.

PUSH IT OUT. Before the soffits are attached, use stringlines to check the straightness of longer runs of subfascia. Here, slightly longer blocking is hammered into place to push out the subfascia.

PULL IT IN. When the subfascia is too far out, cut back the rafter tails with a reciprocating saw.

Find and Bisect an Angle

The simplest way to get accurate miters and bevels without special tools is to hold a couple of scraps in position, mark where they overlap, and cut across the diagonal points using a miter saw. Fine-tune the angle until the scraps fit perfectly, and make note of the saw setting.

Start with the Rake

MARK IT IN PLACE. Measure soffits by holding the first piece in place and marking its length, rather than using a tape to transfer measurements at the saw. Fasten soffits with pneumatic nails in every piece of blocking.

ASSIST THE GLUE BOND. Keep a fresh glue joint tight with 23-ga. pin nails driven through the miter.

STRAIGHTEN AS YOU GO. With the outside edge exposed, it's easy to straighten a wayward soffit with a well-placed shim.

The Right Glue

I've done some comparative and destructive testing of PVC glues, and I've found that generic high-strength glues, typically used for plumbing or conduit work, are more affordable and work very well. On the other hand, purpose-formulated glues, such as Azek's proprietary brand, offer a longer working time. It's a good idea to buy the smallest cans available. Even though the unit cost is higher, I almost never get through an entire can before it gels and becomes useless.

Continued →

Finish at the Eaves

BEGIN AT THE CORNER. Start at one end of the soffit with a miter, keeping the outside edge flush to the subfascia.

SIMPLE IS BEST. In the field, join soffits using butt joints without glue, and leave a space at the sheathing or beam for drainage. Fasten the board at each rafter tail with at least two nails.

Straight Soffits Simplify Assembly

As the most visible part of the roof trim, the fascia needs to run straight and neat. Bumps and uneven joints in the framing can prevent the fascia from making even contact with the soffit, so sand or grind them flat. To minimize seasonal movement, secure the fascia joinery with glue and nails.

Make a Flat Base

Bevel the edge for a better fit. Where the subfascia can't be adjusted, use a right-angle grinder to remove material on the top edge of the soffit so that the fascia will install plumb and tight.

Level the field. The grinder comes in handy where adjoining lengths of subfascia don't align.

Rake meets eave. Miter and glue the rake's plumb cut, then mark and trim the bottom edge flush with the eave.

Secure the Joints

One nail helps. After finding the correct angle, cut and glue the fascia pieces, making sure they stay even with the plane of the roof sheathing. A 16-ga. nail provides insurance.

Miters Start the Eaves

Begin with a guide. To install the fascia at the eaves, use a mitered scrap to set the position of the first full-length piece's miter.

Scarfs stay put. At 45°, scarf joints offer more gluing surface than a butt joint. To keep a scarf from moving during installation, put a fastener at least a foot away from the joint, then glue and fasten the joint.

Almost ready for the roof. Installed with straight lines and tight joints, the finished soffits and fascias define the edges of the upper and lower roofs, as well as the lines of the house.

Cut Fascia Miters Long

Cutting stock about 1/16-in. longer and miters at about 46°, rather than 45°, keeps corners tight, even when the temperature drops and the PVC shrinks. The more acute angle also creates

Gaps behind mitered fascia.

a small space at the back of the miter, so glue won't squeeze out in front. PVC glue doesn't structurally bridge gaps, however, so don't weaken the joint by overcutting more than a couple of degrees.

Good Reasons to Paint PVC

Although it's completely weatherproof, PVC looks better when it's painted. Cut edges have a rough texture if not smoothed with a hand plane or wiped with acetone. Left unpainted, they capture dirt and mold over time. The same is true with filling nail holes. The paint seals the porous texture of the recommended filler and prevents dirt from sticking to the surface.

while the glue sets, a holdover from the way I've always trimmed with wood. On return visits, I've found that those PVC miters stayed tight.

Start with the Soffits

Roof trim consists of two main components: soffits and fascias. It's possible and occasionally better to install fascias first and then fill underneath later, but soffits generally are where you establish your initial straight lines. The outer edge of the soffit provides a straight fastening surface for the fascia, and without the fascia in the way, the soffit is easy to hold and shim straight as needed. Another consideration is that soffits should always ventilate and drain; I use butt joints in the field, and I don't fit the soffits tightly to the sheathing.

One of the secrets to efficient soffit work (or work on any roof trim, for that matter) is to make angled cuts on the smaller pieces that are easier to handle and mark. I never try to fit a joint at both ends of a long length of trim, and I try to do as little measuring as possible. It's much faster and more accurate to scribe a piece than it is to measure once on the house and a second time at the saw. And if I can place joints well above eye level, they are much less likely to be noticeable. Finally, when I'm cutting trim, I have a mental overview of the lengths that I need and how they will best come out of the stock. I keep track of my cutoffs, I know where I will be able to use them, and I allocate lengths so that soffit and fascia joints are staggered by a few rafter bays.

Keep the Fascias Looking Sharp

Fascias are the most obvious and visible trim component on most houses, the element that defines the shape of the roof and makes the visual transition from siding to roofing. They need to be straight and plumb. Because of PVC's flexibility, I have to ensure that the framing beneath the fascias also is straight.

I install the rake fascia first, starting with a plumb cut at the peak. If I know the exact roof pitch, I can transfer the angle to the miter saw and make the plumb cut; alternatively, I can mark the board plumb with a short level and then cut to the line. Holding the board in place, I mark and cut the lower end where it transitions into the eave fascia.

Next, I cut the eave fascia. I use a mitered scrap to establish the

Continued ➔

first corner, and then I use scarf joints in the field. (During the framing stage, I add a 2x subfascia for strength and stability, so when I'm trimming, I don't need to worry about aligning trim joints over rafter tails.) With a helper supporting the other end, I can usually hold the last piece of fascia in place and mark the cut.

Many houses have a second, narrower piece of fascia on the rakes called a double rake; I install this after the eave fascia is done by snapping a line, working from the peak, and cutting it flush at the eave corner. I often switch from the plumb cut I used on the rake peak to a butt joint on the double, which covers most of the plumb cut and helps to keep water from penetrating to the framing.

Chimney Flashing

By Dyami Plotke

By the time my roofing company was called to take a look at the leaking chimney featured here, the sheathing around the chimney was rotten, and the roof rafters beneath were showing signs of water damage.

When the asphalt shingles on this roof were replaced several years ago, the roofer put a new layer of architectural shingles on top of the existing three-tab shingles and reused the house's original aluminum chimney flashing. He patched several small leaks in the flashing corners with roofing cement, but didn't touch the flashing otherwise. Had the roofer done a better job with the chimney flashing, the customer would have been spared the headache and expense of replacing the chimney flashing and patching the roof a few years later.

Copper Flashing Is Worth the Money

We almost always replace aluminum flashing with copper. Of course, copper costs more than aluminum, but it's the superior material for several reasons. For starters, it looks good, it lasts almost forever, and it solders great. More important, though, it's more malleable than aluminum. The flashing pieces can be formed by eye at the metal brake and can be adjusted easily by hand on the roof. When it's time for new shingles, the flashings and counterflashings can be bent out of the way and repositioned without damage.

Flashing and Counterflashing Work Together

Flashing a chimney correctly involves two layers of water-shedding metal: flashing and counterflashing. The front of the chimney has a single piece of flashing, the apron, as the first layer; the back has a similar piece called the pan. The step flashing, which is the first layer on the sides of the chimney, is made from L-shaped pieces of copper lapped so that they shed water running down the roof. The horizontal leg goes under the shingles, and the vertical goes up the sides of the chimney. Ideally, neither leg is fastened; nail or screw holes compromise the watertightness of the flashing.

Because there are no nails or screws to hold the vertical leg tight to the chimney, water running down the masonry can get

past the step flashing and leak into the house. To prevent this, the flashing's vertical legs are covered with counterflashing. The counterflashing directs falling rain and water running down the chimney over the first layer of flashing. This creates a finished assembly that looks good and, more important, is watertight.

As was the case on this job, original counterflashings are often installed in a stepped pattern following the mortar lines of the brick. We generally don't install new flashing in mortar joints. Instead, we cut a 1¾-in.-deep groove about 6 in. above the roof deck all the way around the chimney with an angle grinder. Then we install a single piece of counterflashing into the groove.

Underlayment and Apron

The first piece of metal chimney flashing, the apron, is placed on the down-slope side of the chimney. Here, it laps over one three-tab shingle to match the two layers of existing roofing. This shingle is unnecessary when there is only one shingle layer.

1. MAKE A CUT FOR COUNTER-FLASHING. Cut the groove for the apron and counterflashing with a ¼-in.-thick diamond tuck-point blade on a 4½-in. grinder. Making the groove before reshingling prevents staining the new shingles with brick dust. The dust is slippery, so sweep the sheathing right after cutting.

Peel-and-stick underlayment

½-in. OSB sheathing patch

1¾-in.-deep by ¼-in.-wide groove for counterflashing

Three-tab shingles

2. INSTALL PEEL-AND-STICK. A layer of mineral-surfaced underlayment installed over the OSB sheathing patch and under the shingles provides a second layer of defense against water intrusion. Lap the underlayment onto the chimney sides, then wrap it around the chimney corners.

Copper apron

3 FIT THE APRON. Install the apron on the down-slope side of the chimney. Tuck the vertical leg's top edge into the groove cut around the chimney, then lap the horizontal leg onto the shingles in front of the chimney.

With this method, there are fewer seams, which translates into fewer potential leaks. It's also faster and, therefore, less expensive to do it this way. To hold the counterflashing in the groove, we tuck the V-shaped bend at the top into the groove and use small folded pieces of copper to spread the bend, locking the counterflashing in place. We also rivet the corners with copper pop rivets. These mechanical connections help to hold the counterflashing in place, which in turn helps the sealant at the top of the counterflashing to last up to 20 years.

A Quality Job Is in the Details

We give our counterflashing two bends at the bottom, which makes it look and perform better. The lowest bend is called the strength hem. It stiffens the metal and provides a clean, even edge. The upper bend, which also adds strength, is called the kick. The kick breaks surface tension, preventing water from working its way under the counterflashing. We also make our step flashing from 6-in. by 8-in. pieces instead of the 5-in. by 7-in. pieces commonly found on low-budget roofs. These bigger pieces of step flashing mean fewer leaks from wind-driven rain and heavy snow.

Continued ➜

Step Flashing and Pan

The apron is cut where it transitions from horizontal to vertical. Then it's folded around the chimney to prevent wind-driven rain and snow from getting behind the step flashing and finding their way into the building. The first piece of step flashing is trimmed so that its bottom leg laps onto the apron.

Expansion anchors

Copper pan

The pan is cut and folded around the chimney.

6-in. by 8-in. step flashing

Peel-and-stick underlayment

Sealant at corner

1. TURN THE CORNER. Trim the vertical leg on the first piece of step flashing so that the horizontal leg can lap onto the apron. Tuck the vertical leg behind the apron to keep out wind-driven rain and snow. Fill the small hole where the two parts meet with a dab of solvent-based elastomeric sealant.

2. CONTINUE UP THE SIDES. Install step flashing between the chimney and every course of shingles, ideally without fastening. You can use a single fastener in the uppermost corner of the vertical face to keep the flashing in place if necessary, but fasteners should never be placed in the horizontal leg.

3. INSTALL THE PAN. Once the shingles are even with the up-slope side of the chimney, install a pan made from a single piece of copper to direct water around the chimney. Attach the pan to the masonry using expansion anchors near the top of the vertical leg.

Where's the Cricket?

Chimneys that are built anywhere along the rain-carrying parts of a pitched roof (not at the ridges) create a dam that can stop water from draining and allow it to pool behind the chimney. The dam that is created by the chimney can be especially problematic in cold climates, where the chimney can become a collector for snow and ice.

Behind large chimneys, we install a cricket. Shaped like a tiny hip roof, a cricket diverts water and snow around the chimney for better drainage. We install crickets when the chimney is wider than 24 in. (perpendicular to the slope), which is consistent with the shingle manufacturers' instructions. For smaller chimneys like the one pictured here, a one-piece copper pan is all that's necessary to carry the roof water around the chimney.

Counterflashing

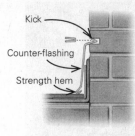

Kick

Counter-flashing

Strength hem

Counterflashing is what makes step flashing work. The counterflashing pan and apron are made in oversize lengths ahead of time and then cut to length on the roof. A bead of water-block mastic is run under the pan, and a bead of M-1 polyether sealant (chemlink.com) is applied to the top edge of the pan for secondary waterproofing.

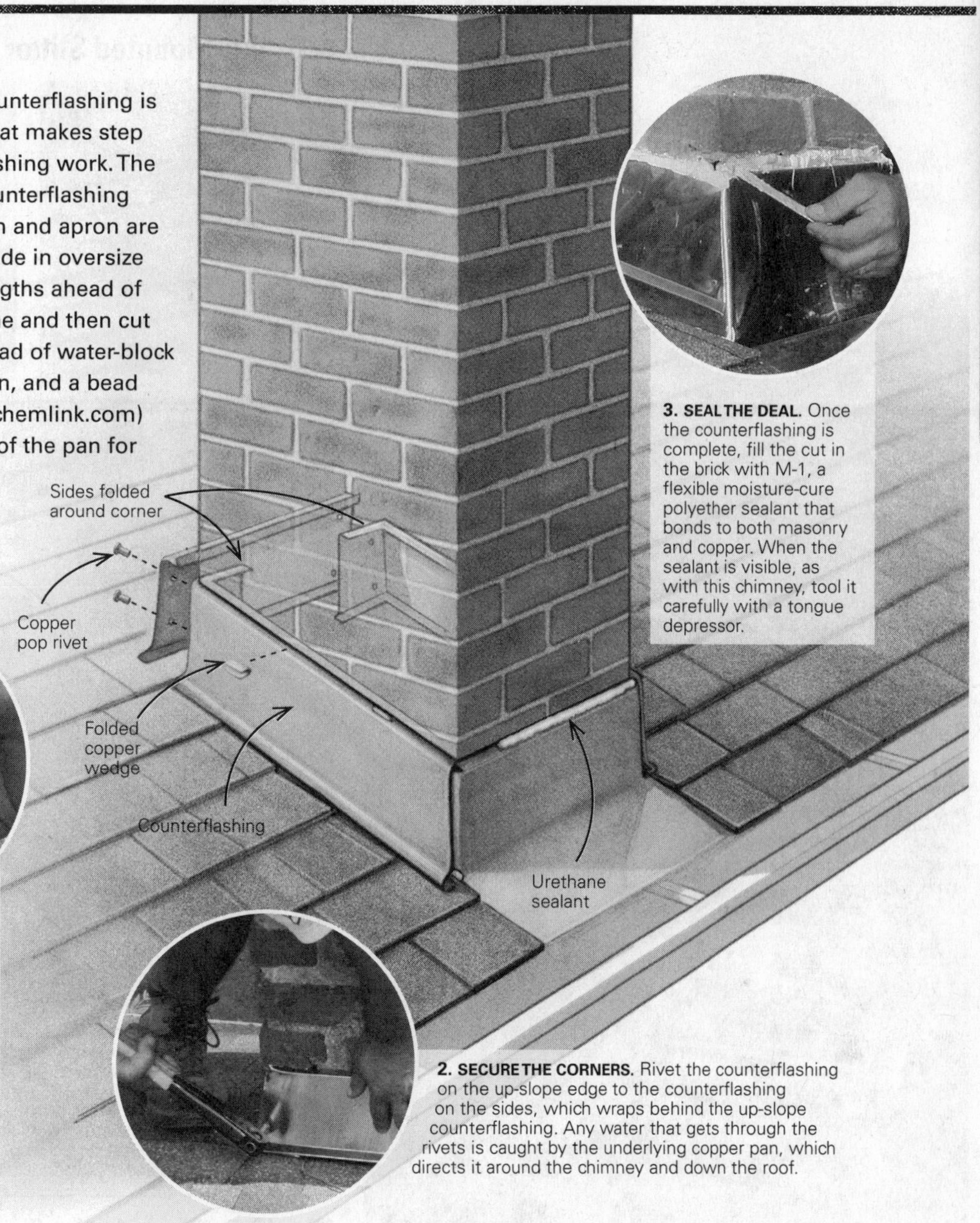

Sides folded around corner

Copper pop rivet

Folded copper wedge

Counterflashing

3. SEAL THE DEAL. Once the counterflashing is complete, fill the cut in the brick with M-1, a flexible moisture-cure polyether sealant that bonds to both masonry and copper. When the sealant is visible, as with this chimney, tool it carefully with a tongue depressor.

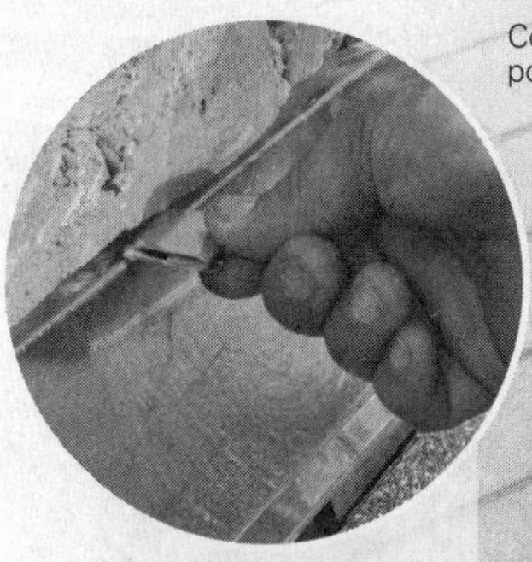

Urethane sealant

1. MAKE A MECHANICAL CONNECTION. Rather than rely solely on caulk or sealant, use wedges of folded copper spaced every 8 in. to 12 in. to hold the counterflashing in its groove. Spread the folds in the wedges with a screwdriver to lock the flashing in place.

2. SECURE THE CORNERS. Rivet the counterflashing on the up-slope edge to the counterflashing on the sides, which wraps behind the up-slope counterflashing. Any water that gets through the rivets is caught by the underlying copper pan, which directs it around the chimney and down the roof.

Using a Sheet-Metal Brake

By John Mahan

As a slate-roofing contractor, I bend most of my own drip-edge flashing. For small jobs or for bending metal on site, I use a portable sheet-metal brake just like those available at tool-rental centers. Sometimes called a siding brake or an aluminum brake, this tool can be used for cutting and bending flashing for windows and doors, and for cladding for exterior soffits and fascias. It also can be used for any number of small projects that require bent light-gauge sheet metal or vinyl. When renting a brake, make sure a slitter is included for cutting sheets to width.

Bending a drip edge is a good project to demonstrate how to use a brake. As shown in the drawing and the photo above, a drip edge requires several different kinds of bends, from a slight kickout to a full fold.

I prefer 16-oz. or 20-oz. sheet-copper flashing rather than aluminum or painted galvanized steel. Copper is expensive, but it lasts longer and looks better than any other flashing choice.

When you're using a brake, it's a good idea to use a piece of scrap for a mock-up to ensure that all the bends can be made

Continued →

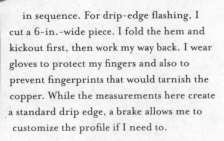

in sequence. For drip-edge flashing, I cut a 6-in.-wide piece. I fold the hem and kickout first, then work my way back. I wear gloves to protect my fingers and also to prevent fingerprints that would tarnish the copper. While the measurements here create a standard drip edge, a brake allows me to customize the profile if I need to.

A Brake-Mounted Slitter Cuts Copper to Width

MOUNT THE SLITTER ON TOP OF THE BRAKE. A slitter is mounted only after a sheet is locked in place. It's removed before any bending is done. A pair of sharp-edged opposing rollers do the actual cutting. To determine the offset distance between the leading edge of the clamp and the cut, clamp a scrap piece in the brake, and nick the edge. The offset here is 1½ in. Add the offset to the desired width of 6 in., and measure back from the clamp's leading edge. Lock the sheet in place, and push the slitter along the rails with a single fluid motion to make the cut.

The Hem Seam Is the First Fold

1. START THE HEM SEAM WITH A FULL FOLD. Insert the 6-in.-wide sheet ½ in. into the brake. Lock the sheet in place by pulling the top handle forward. Then lift the bending plate as far as it can travel.

1. CLAMP UPPER handles control the clamp, which locks in place to hold the sheet metal firmly between two long jaws.

2. LEADING EDGE The sharp front edge of the clamp is where the metal is bent.

3. BENDING PLATE Parallel to the clamp jaws, the hinged bending plate is pulled up by a pair of lower handles to create the bend.

2. COMPRESS THE HEM SEAM, THEN CREATE THE KICKOUT. The top of the clamp's leading edge can be used to complete full folds. Release the piece, then place the folded edge on the brake's hinge. Engage the bending plate fully. To create the kickout, flip the piece; then lock the hem seam in the brake, and lift the bending-plate handle 30°.

Two Folds Complete the Profile

3. INSERT THE PIECE WITH THE KICKOUT UP. Leave 1½ in. between the clamp's leading edge and the kickout. The angle of this middle fold matches the roof's pitch. It doesn't have to be exact, so use the mock-up to get the angle correct through trial and error.

4. BEND THE LAST FOLD IN TWO STEPS. First, place the piece in the brake with the middle fold down. Leave 1 in. between the clamp's leading edge and the middle fold. Lock the piece in place, and lift the bending plate's handle as far as it can travel. Second, flip the piece so that the fold is against the bending hinge. Compress the fold to finish the drip edge.

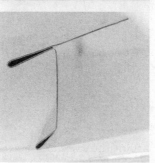

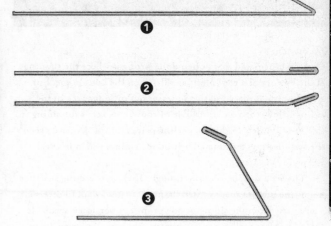

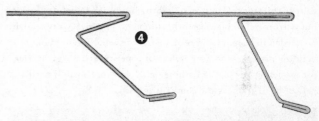

Leave No Trace

If you aren't wearing gloves when you handle copper flashing, the oil on your fingers can tarnish the surface and make the pristine flashing look like a crime scene. Although these marks go away with time, the first impression of a less-than-perfect job might not. To keep himself and his customers feeling good about his work, John Mahan wears special MBT-free gloves. (MBT, or mercaptobenzothiazole, is a chemical that can cause an allergic reaction in some people.) The gloves (www.deltagloves.com) are thin with textured fingertips for a better grip. Yet they are tear- and puncture-resistant—durable enough for a professional roofer.

Continued ➜

Bending Kick-Out Flashing

By Andy Engel

One flashing detail that's often done wrong is where the flashing at the bottom of a roof meets a wall. When the bottom piece of step flashing is placed so that it drains out onto the face of the siding below, the regular dribble of roof water keeps the siding in this location wet, leading to peeling paint and rot. I've even seen the step flashing terminated behind the siding, which is a real recipe for disaster.

There's a simple solution, though: Kick-out flashing installed below the bottom piece of step flashing creates a dam to divert water away from the siding. A polypropylene version is available from DryFlekt and comes in a variety of colors. However, I never seem to have one on hand, or I'm using copper flashing and want the kick out to match, so I usually bend one from aluminum or copper coil stock. Galvanized flashing is too stiff to bend this way, but vinyl coil flashing can work, although a pop rivet or two might be needed to keep it from relaxing out of shape. I figured out the bending pattern by folding a piece of paper, which is a great trick for modeling any sort of flashing detail. For tools, you'll need a pair of hand seamers and some tin snips.

1. START WITH COIL STOCK. Use a knife and a straightedge to cut a 12-in. by 14-in. piece of flashing from the same metal used for the roof's step flashing.

2. MAKE A 90° BEND. Use a straightedge to make a bend that will leave 6 in. of flashing on the roof and 6 in. going up the wall.

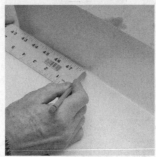

3. MEASURE THE FIRST BEND. Mark the flashing 6 in. from the end to locate the approximate location of the first fold.

4. POSITION SEAMERS FOR THE NEXT BEND. Hold the seamers at an angle slightly beyond 90° in relation to the first bend so the bottom of the flashing will drain. Keep the seamers away from the first bend or the metal might tear at the corner point.

5. BEND THE FLASHING UPWARD. As you push the seamers forward, the metal on the other side of the bend will follow, beginning to form the dam.

6. FOLD THE FLASHING LIKE WRAPPING A PRESENT. Bend the leg that will abut the house at 90° and the roof leg a bit greater than 90° to encourage drainage.

7. FLATTEN THE BENDS. Use a block (and, if needed, a hammer) to make the flashing smooth and crisp.

8. MAKE IT PRETTY. You can leave the end square, but rounding it off with a pair of snips makes it look less obtrusive.

Bending Copper Chimney Flashing

By Dyami Plotke

When my roofing company flashes a chimney, we save time on the roof and make our lives easier by bending the various flashing parts ahead of time on a metal brake. We use a brake rather than bend by hand because it gives the flashing crisp, straight bends that look and perform better than the somewhat wrinkly bends of hand-formed chimney flashing.

When I make flashing parts, I prefer to use our company's spacious metal shop. The room's bright lights and large worktable make it easier to move and lay out the pieces. When you're looking for a space to lay out and cut sheet metal, look for a place large enough to allow you to rotate the longest lengths of flashing that you'll be using. It's also smart to spend some time setting up a good-size worktable, even if it's just a scrap of plywood on sawhorses.

Our metal shop has a large stationary brake, but we also use portable brakes that we carry in the back of our vans. The layout and bending techniques are the same for both tools. The least expensive 8-ft. and 10-ft. portable brakes common on roofing and siding jobs cost hundreds of dollars, but they are available at rental yards and for rent from many home centers as well. If you're bending only smaller pieces, you can buy a smaller brake for a few hundred dollars.

We use 16-oz. copper for most of our residential flashing work. We like copper's malleability, and we like that it's easy to solder. Prepared correctly, copper flashing shouldn't need attention for decades.

When you're bending any type of flashing, the first step is to cut the material to length and width. Our shop has a large shear that I use for cutting the stock to width, but you also can use snips. I like aviation snips for hand-cutting because they require less effort than traditional tin snips. Use care when handling the stock, because cut edges can be extremely sharp. Make the pieces longer than you need, and cut them to exact size on the roof.

Once the piece is cut to size, I lay out the various bends on the flat stock. I mark the bends by measuring from one side of the flashing only so that any slight discrepancy in the width will be hidden by a hemmed edge. Some flashing profiles involve flipping the flashing stock multiple times for bends in opposite directions, so I mark the bends on both ends of the flashing with a hammer and a dull punch. The resulting dimple shows on both sides of the stock, saving time and reducing the number of mistakes.

Once I've marked the stock, I plan the order and the direction of the bends so that I don't crush or distort the flashing piece while I make additional bends.

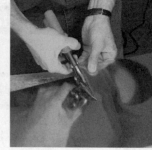

1. CUT THE STOCK. Copper generally comes in 3-ft.-wide by 8-ft.-long sheets. Begin by marking the stock with a nail or a scratch awl so that the mark won't rub off. Then cut the stock to width and length with aviation snips. The length can't exceed the length of the brake. Copper is expensive, so plan cuts for minimal waste.

2. MARK THE BENDS. Use a hammer and a dull punch to mark the various bends on both ends of the stock. The resulting dimple can be seen on both sides of the stock for making bends in either direction. Marking all the bends at once saves time.

3. EYE THE ANGLE. Underbend the flashing pieces so that they hold tight to the roof. Copper flashing can be opened or closed by hand for the perfect fit. Aluminum and steel flashing are less malleable.

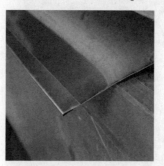

4. HEM THE EDGE. Exposed flashing edges should have a ½-in. hem for a neat appearance and greater strength. Bend the stock as far as the brake allows, and then flatten the bend by closing the brake's jaws.

Continued →

A Durable Roof-Valley Repair

By Stephen Hazlett

When I started my roofing business almost 20 years ago, I quickly found myself specializing in roof repair, mostly reflashing valleys and chimneys on older roofs. Years later, those projects are still my favorites. Repair work has provided me with an excellent opportunity to learn from other peoples' roofing mistakes.

Old Roofs Usually Aren't Worth Fixing

The quality and efficiency of a valley repair are determined largely by how well you can unzip the old valley. Thirty-year dimensional shingles in pretty good shape are a perfect candidate for valley repairs. Old wafer-thin 20-year shingles usually are not worth repairing because they're too delicate. It's better to replace the entire roof than to fool around with patches. Ironically, 50-year shingles are nearly as unsuited to repairs, but for a different reason. The seal-down strip is too good, which makes it almost impossible to separate the shingles without causing extensive damage. Here's one tip: You may be able to cut the seal-down strips on 50-year shingles using a long, thin knife, such as an old bread knife. Warm the blade with a heat gun, and use the back of the blade (not the serrated cutting edge) to slice through the sticky tar.

During warmer months, I usually start a valley repair around 7 a.m., when the shingles are cool and easy to separate. I try to unzip the valley quickly because by 9 a.m., the shingles are often too hot to separate cleanly. During cooler months, I start later (from 8:30 a.m. to 9 a.m.) to give the shingles a chance to warm enough to be pliable.

Roofing Tools Work Better Than Carpentry Tools

A few basic tools are necessary for a valley-flashing replacement project. First, you need a utility knife with a hook blade rather than one with a straight blade. The hook blade allows you to cut an underlying shingle from the top without damage to the membrane below. A standard utility-knife blade, on the other hand, forces you to cut from below the shingle with the blade tip protruding above the shingle being cut. This slow technique is a pain in the neck.

The second item is a roofing hatchet. I prefer an Estwing hatchet (www.estwing.com) for its all-steel construction and its flat, blunt blade, which tapers to a wedge-shaped head. These features make the hatchet ideal for separating shingles from each other. With heavy weight and a short handle, this tool has enough punch even in tight spaces. Typical carpentry hammers are too light and have a long handle that interferes with the short strokes needed for remodel roofing. They also lack a tapered hatchet blade.

The third tool is a roofer's pry bar. It must have just the right length and just the right angle in the shank to reach under a

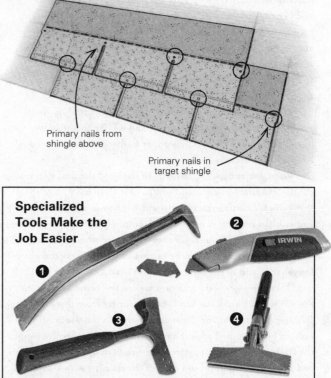

Primary nails from shingle above

Primary nails in target shingle

Specialized Tools Make the Job Easier

1. A roofer's pry bar is the right length and angle for popping shingle nails.
2. A hook blade in a utility knife won't damage the underlying surface.
3. A short, heavy roofing hatchet with a tapered head makes quick work of separating shingles in tight spaces.
4. A metal seamer makes straight, clean bends in metal flashing.

Your Best Defense Is a Good Beginning

1. REMOVE SHINGLES FROM THE TOP DOWN. If reusing the shingles you remove, take care not to rip the shingles, and keep them in order. Four primary nails are driven into each shingle just below the tar line, but the primary nails from the shingles above it also penetrate the target shingle. When removing shingles, pull all eight nails to avoid damage.

2. A CLEAN VALLEY IS A HAPPY VALLEY. Sweep all nails and other debris out of the valley. Loose debris could puncture the peel-and-stick membrane or interfere with its adhesion.

3. BACKUP LAYER. Granulated peel-and-stick membrane provides a safe walking surface and a watertight seal. I sink a button-cap nail in the upper corner of the peel-and-stick membrane, then pull off the backing. After the backing is removed, slip the membrane under the shingle ends.

Continued ➜

shingle and pop out roofing nails. I now use an Estwing Roofers' Bar, which is almost perfect (it has a little too much spring for me). Ordinary carpenters' flat bars don't have the right weight, angle, and length for the job.

Although not pictured, another indispensable item is a 2-ft. by 3-ft. piece of foam rubber about 4 in. thick. This pad provides a nonskid surface to kneel, sit, and place tools and materials on. It saves a lot of wear and tear on roof shingles as well as on my knees.

Unzip Valleys from the Top Down

Begin removing shingles from the top, and work your way down the valley. If the roof you are repairing is a second-layer roof, be careful to remove only the top layer of shingles from the valley.

Roofs have two types of valleys: cut and woven. If you have been cursed with a woven valley, you'll have to dismantle both sides of the valley at the same time. To unzip a cut valley, work one side at a time, starting with the overlying side. Break the seal on the course above the first shingle you want to remove using a roofing hatchet or a pry bar. Next, break the seal under the target shingle. Slide the pry bar under the shingle, and tap it under the head of each roofing nail. Pop out each nail using the pry bar as a lever. Finally, because two sets of nails penetrate each shingle, remove the nails holding the shingle above the target shingle.

At this point, I'm able to move fairly quickly, breaking the seal and pulling out the nails on each shingle, working my way down the roof. After removing the shingles from one side of the valley, I throw down the stack of shingles onto a ground tarp, and I repeat the process on the second side of the valley. Last, I sweep the exposed roof decking clean, and I inspect for damage and missed nails.

Why Use W-Type Valley Flashing?

W-type valley flashing performs better and is easier to work with than V-type valley flashing. The extra rib in the center stops water rushing down one roof slope from pushing its way under the shingles on the opposing slope. The rib stiffens the metal so that it's less likely to bend while being carried. Also, the rib absorbs most of the expansion of the metal on sunny days, so W-flashing is less likely to buckle.

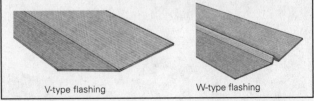

V-type flashing   W-type flashing

The Start of a Durable Valley: Peel-and-Stick Membrane

I begin the new valley installation by putting down a layer of peel-and-stick underlayment membrane. I prefer an underlayment with granulated coating because it's safer to walk on, but for longer life, smooth membranes are less abrasive to the underside of the valley flashing. The backing on this material can be slippery, so when using long pieces, I put a button-cap nail along the top edge to stop the entire piece from sliding off the roof. With the underlayment positioned, remove the split-sheet backing one side at a time. I carefully lift adjacent shingles, then slip the underlayment up under them if necessary.

When installing peel-and-stick membrane, you must work fast because as the temperature grows warmer, the sticky side becomes stickier. Before installing the membrane, keep it in the shade or in the garage and as cool as possible. If working during warm weather or if working alone, it's easiest to install overlapping short pieces (about 8 ft. long) of underlayment. Work from the bottom up to cover the entire valley.

Valley Flashing Has a Track Record

I follow the membrane with W-type valley flashing. In almost 20 years of roofing, I never have been called to repair a W-valley. I can get painted-aluminum W-type valley flashing in black or brown from my supplier. Copper is also available.

The top and sides of the metal tuck under the shingles, but the bottom needs to be bent to fold over the roofline. Because the valley featured here was formed by the junction of two unequally pitched roofs, the angle cuts at the bottom were weird; rather than cutting by eye, I used a framing square to trace the cuts. After trimming with tin snips, I bent the bottom with an ordinary hand seamer to form a neat return, which hooks onto the drip edge. A few small bends on the center notch that fold back on themselves close the gap that would be sure to attract ice dams, wasps, leaf debris, and other undesirables.

When I'm replacing a valley less than 10 ft. long, one piece of

Fit the Flashing to the Valley

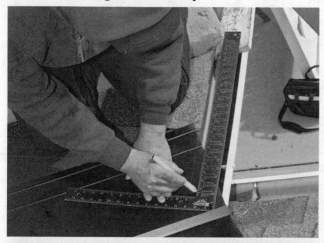

5. KEEP NAILS AT THE EDGE. I nail within the outer inch of the valley flashing about every 10 in. When reinstalling the shingles, I don't let any shingle nails penetrate the metal.

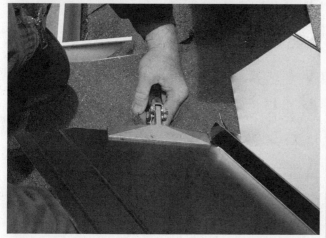

4. FOLD THE METAL OVER THE DRIP EDGE. Lay the first length of metal flashing in place, and cut it about an inch beyond the roof's edge. Then use a metal seamer to bend the flashing over the drip edge. This prevents water from freezing its way up the roof in winter. Also, bend flaps over the raised ridge to keep out insects.

6. USE A STRING TO KEEP THE VALLEY STRAIGHT. I stretch a string from the bottom to the top of the valley and align the first piece of flashing to it. As I add successive pieces of flashing, I restretch the string to keep the alignment perfect.

flashing can run the entire valley, and I can place it accurately by eye. If I need several pieces of flashing to run the length of a valley, I use a chalkline to align the flashing. I align these sections as I work up the valley with the string stretched the length of the valley. Getting the metal as straight as possible is important because any irregularity will be magnified when the valley is shingled. I nail the flashing about 1 in. from the edge, every 10 in. or so.

When Installing Shingles, Cutting Corners Is a Good Thing

With the valley flashing installed, the project is nearing completion quickly. The existing courses of shingles act as layout guides for reinstalling the valley shingles one side at a time. Lay the shingle ends over the valley flashing, but keep nails in the outer inch of the flashing.

After completing one side of the valley, I snap a chalkline and trim that side with a hook blade. Using the fat and skinny profiles of my utility knife as a gauge, I mark a slightly narrower reveal at the top of the valley and expand to a wider reveal at the bottom. Long valleys or those draining a large area should have a larger reveal so that during heavy runoff, water won't work its way under the shingle edges.

After both sides of the valley are reshingled and trimmed, be absolutely certain to clip the top corners of the shingles with a slight back cut. Clipping these shingles prevents leaks caused by a shingle tip diverting water out of the valley stream and back under the shingles. Old shingles with broken seal-down strips can be resealed with roofing caulk. I don't run a bead of tar up the valley along the edges of the shingles because the tar could prevent water from draining out if it got in via windblown rain or through undiscovered imperfections.

Continued ➜

For Roof Repairs, Existing Shingles Set the Layout

  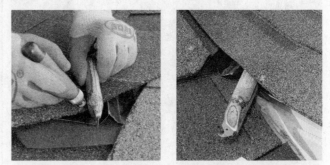

7. KEEP NAILS OUT OF THE VALLEY. Lay shingles over the valley flashing to be cut later. The existing shingles provide a layout guide.

8. MAKE A TAPERED LINE DOWN THE VALLEY. Because the bottom of the valley handles more water than the top, you should taper the shingle cut. It also looks better. I use my utility knife as a guide: the thin side for the valley top and the wide side for the valley bottom.

10. CUTTING SHINGLES IS A TWO-STEP PROCESS. Cut down the valley first, then work your way back up to trim off the underlying shingle corners (see drawing, facing page). By cutting the leading edge of shingles in a valley, you can discourage water from working its way into the interior of the roof.

11. YOU CAN'T START IN THE VALLEY IF YOU HAVE TO MATCH EXISTING SHINGLES. But because I stripped the small roof on the right side of this valley, it was like working on a new roof. Run the shingles through the valley and cut them later after snapping a chalkline. Keep nails out of the valley, although it's OK to nail in the outer inch of the flashing.

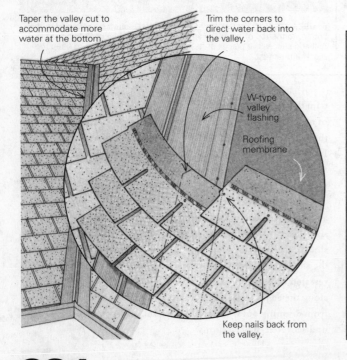

Taper the valley cut to accommodate more water at the bottom.

Trim the corners to direct water back into the valley.

W-type valley flashing

Roofing membrane

Keep nails back from the valley.

Cut Valleys Are Easier to Unzip Than Woven Valleys

There are two types of closed valleys. In woven valleys, shingles are interlaced from adjoining sides; in cut valleys, they are laid one side over the other. Both options work, but an open valley with metal flashing is the most durable choice.

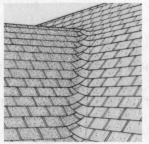 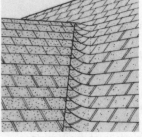

Woven Valley   **Cut Valley**

10 Roof Goofs and How to Fix Them

By Stephen Hazlett

As a roofer, I'm frequently called to solve the mysteries of leaky roofs. Surprisingly, it is not damage from wear and tear that causes most roof leaks but mistakes made during installation or reroofing. Some of these mistakes are impractical to repair after the fact. Others are repairable even years after the original installation.

When customers call about a leaky roof, they often have a good idea of where the leak is coming from. Regardless, I start my investigation with a few questions. How long has the roof been leaking? Has it leaked in that area before? How old is the roof?

If the leak has been appearing on and off for years, the problem is likely poor design or poor material choices. If the roof is 20 years old, it just may be worn out. If it is new (two to three years old), the problem is most likely faulty installation.

I first ask to see the water damage inside the house. I try to determine if the leak is even coming from the roof. What appears to be a leaky roof is sometimes a problem with siding or windows.

After I look inside the house, I go to the rooftop, where I usually can narrow the potentially leaky area to a 12-ft. radius around the damage inside. I examine the shingles. If they are in good shape, I look for punctures from nail pops or tree limbs, then check exposed fasteners. Poorly installed plumbing vent stacks, cable-wire guides, and satellite-dish mounts are always suspects on a leaky roof.

If I still haven't found the source of the leak, I look at the step flashing against sidewalls and chimney flashings. I also inspect all valleys. A valley is susceptible to leaks, and it's one place where I won't do repairs. If I find problems in a valley, I replace the entire valley.

1. Poorly Fastened Sheathing

Sloppy deck installation on new roofs and poorly prepared decks on reroof jobs are among the most common problems I investigate. Poorly fastened sheathing curls along the edges, absorbs water, and swells. This movement causes the nails to pop

out. Loose nails puncture the shingles and cause leaks. Tracking down the offending nail is often harder than the repair itself. Once I find and remove the loose nail, I replace the damaged shingle. Nail pops are to be expected over time. On an older roof, they are not a big concern. On a new roof, however, nail pops are a sign of a sloppy installation and frequently are followed by more problems.

2. Misaligned Starter Courses

It's surprising how often I see leaks because the butt joints between starter-course shingles line up perfectly with the joints between first-course shingles. This layout translates into a leak every 3 ft. along the bottom edge of a roof and will cause the rafter tails, wall sheathing, top plates, and drywall to get wet and rot. If the sheathing is not damaged, the repair is simple: Pull out a few nails, and slip a 5-in. by 7-in. piece of aluminum flashing between the starter course and the first course to cover the exposed joints. You can fasten the flashing with a single nail or with a bead of caulk between the flashing and the starter course and another bead between the flashing and the first course. If the sheathing is damaged, I remove several courses of shingles, replace the damaged wood, and install waterproof membrane with a properly aligned starter course.

WRONG: The butt joints between the starter course and the first-course shingles line up.

FIX: Slide a 5-in. by 7-in. piece of aluminum flashing between the two courses, covering the seams. Fasten the flashing with one roofing nail placed to the side.

Drip edge

RIGHT: The butt joints are offset.

Waterproof shingle underlayment

Rake drip edge

Starter course: shingles with the tabs cut off

First course starts with half of a tab removed from the shingle.

First-course shingles overhang drip edge by ¾ in.

3. Lazy Nailing

If shingles are not fastened properly, the wind can get under them, lift up the edges, and give water an easy path into the roof. Examples of lazy nailing include too few fasteners; fasteners placed too high or too low on the shingle; staples shot in vertically

Continued ➜

instead of horizontally; and not storm-nailing (six nails per shingle in high-wind areas). Always follow the nailing guidelines on the shingle wrappers, and storm-nail shingles on all roofs in high-wind areas or on roofs steeper than 10-in-12 pitch.

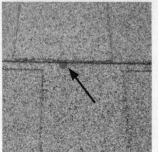

NAIL PLACEMENT IS IMPORTANT. Nails should be driven through the nailing strip, just below the seal-down strip, where they'll be covered by the tabs of the next course of shingles. Exposed nails give water a way into the roof.

TYPICAL NAILING PATTERN: four nails per shingle

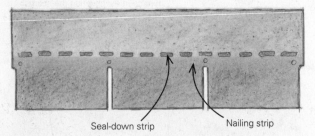

Seal-down strip   Nailing strip

STORM NAILING PATTERN: six nails per shingle

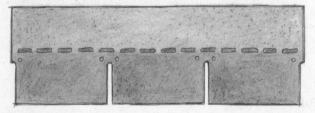

4. Dumb Roof Design

Roof goofs can occur during design and during remodeling. Design mistakes include misdirected gutter spouts, valleys draining against a sidewall, bad dormer locations, chimneys that block water flow, and excessively complicated rooflines. You can't do much about these design flaws once a house is built, but you should pay close attention to areas where roof design promotes problems.

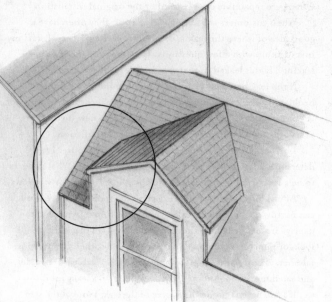

5. Flawed Shingles

Here's one that may surprise you: Shingles with continuous seal-down strips can cause leaks themselves. Water that gets under the side edge of a shingle with a continuous adhesive strip won't be able to escape and will migrate sideways until it finds an exit point, usually a joint between two shingles. This joint is where the leak begins. Valleys, chimneys, waste stacks, and roof vents are the most likely places for water to get under shingles. These leaks are difficult to track down and repair. The solution is to use shingles with breaks in the adhesive strip. And don't use pieces of shingle smaller than the sections between breaks. If you must use continuous-strip shingles, make sure the valley and chimney flashing doesn't dump water where it easily can find its way under the shingles.

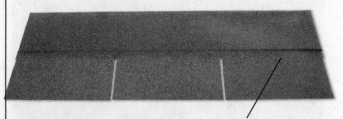

AVOID CONTINUOUS SEAL-DOWN STRIPS. They may seem like a good idea, but water that gets under the shingle can't escape. Shingles with segmented seal-down strips give water an exit every few inches.

6. "Breaking the Bundles"

Some roofers make a big mistake when they load shingles onto the roof by folding the bundles over the ridge. Ironically, delivery crews call this "breaking the bundles," and that's exactly what happens. Breaking the bundles can create stress fractures and separates shingle laminations, reducing the life span of a new roof. Always store shingles flat on the roof. Because cold shingles are more prone to breaking, limit cold-weather roofing to emergency repairs. Don't bend the shingles over the ridge. Folding bundles of shingles over the ridge can damage the shingles and diminish their life span. Lay the bundles flat on the roof, and use a board to prevent them from sliding down the roof.

DON'T BEND THE SHINGLES OVER THE RIDGE. Folding bundles of shingles over the ridge can damage the shingles and diminish their life span. Lay the bundles flat on the roof, and use a board to prevent them from sliding down the roof.

7. Misplaced Step Flashing

Another common problem is improperly sized step flashing. Step flashing should be in line with the top of the shingle course being flashed and should extend down to the top of the shingle tab, about 7 in. on standard shingles or about 8 in. on metric shingles. Even properly sized step flashing can cause a problem if it is out of position. Because correctly placed step flashing covers the adhesive strip on a shingle, it won't let the next shingle seal down in that area. Some people try to solve this minor problem by moving the step flashing up an inch or so, extending the top edge of the flashing above the top of the shingle. When the top of the flashing is nailed, it transforms the top edge of the shingle into a fulcrum, and the flashing lifts up the bottom edge of the next course, causing a gap that water can enter. The installer then tries to fix the problem by nailing at the bottom edge of the flashing. This nail won't be covered by the next piece of step flashing and can cause a leak. Improperly installed step flashing should be stripped and replaced.

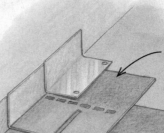

STEP FLASHING NO-NO. Nailing above the top of the shingle will cause the flashing to lift up the bottom of the next course of shingles. An extra nail to hold down the flashing is a potential leak spot.

STEP FLASHING DONE RIGHT. The flashing should be in line with the top of the shingle and nailed only once in the upper corner. The flashing pieces should overlap 2 in.

8. Sloppy Chimney Flashing

A lot of roof leaks are blamed on chimney flashing, and for good reason. Before replacing the chimney flashing, though, spend a little time to rule out other possibilities such as a cracked mortar cap or missing chimney bricks. The most common chimney-flashing error is when roofers don't take the time to insert counterflashing into the mortar. Properly installed counterflashing is bent on a sheet-metal brake, producing sharp, straight, L-shaped bends that seat cleanly in the mortar between brick courses. Chimney flashing bent without a brake is a red flag to me; it signifies sloppy detailing. When I find a roof with poor chimney flashing, I look closely for additional problems.

Continued ➜

10. Careless Valley Shingling

I'm surprised by how many valleys have no flashing. An alarming new practice is using peel-and-stick waterproof membranes as valley flashing. Some less expensive waterproof membranes are warranted for only five years. Fifty-year shingles over a five-year membrane isn't a good investment in a valley where lots of things can go wrong. The only sure way to fix a leaky valley is to reroof the entire valley. I install a waterproof membrane and W-type valley flashing on almost all valley repairs. (For a complete discussion of shingling valleys, go to www.finehomebuilding.com). Fixing a leaky valley usually means reshingling the entire valley. Start at the top, and remove one full shingle width from each side of the valley. Neatness counts a great deal here because the tidy disassembly of the valley determines how well it goes back together.

CHIMNEY FLASHING IS BEST LEFT TO THE EXPERTS. Chimneys have great potential for leaks. If masons don't set counterflashing into the mortar or if the flashing fails, nails and caulk are not a solution. The mortar must be cut with a grinder so that carefully bent new flashing can be inserted between brick courses.

FIXING A LEAKY VALLEY USUALLY MEANS RESHINGLING THE ENTIRE VALLEY. Start at the top, and remove one full shingle width from each side of the valley. Neatness counts a great deal here because the tidy disassembly of the valley determines how well it goes back together.

9. Roof-Mounted Upgrades

Leaks can be caused easily by the many roof penetrations inflicted by homeowners and remodeling contractors. TV-antenna or satellite-dish mounts, skylights, and roof vents never should be installed haphazardly, yet they often are. In the natural realm, overgrown branches can abrade roof shingles, and overly shady roofs can encourage moss growth that will degrade shingles.

Closed-Cut Valleys Are Often Done Wrong

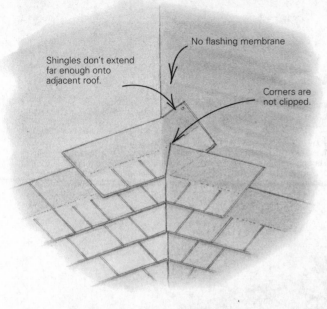

No flashing membrane

Shingles don't extend far enough onto adjacent roof.

Corners are not clipped.

Open Valleys With W-Type Valley Flashing Are Superior

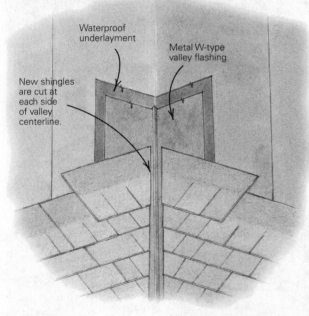

Waterproof underlayment

Metal W-type valley flashing

New shingles are cut at each side of valley centerline.

Removing a Damaged Shingle

Some roof repairs—nail pops, for example—require replacing single shingles. Removing the damaged shingle without damaging the surrounding shingles is the tricky part. This process is best done while shingles are cool enough not to melt underfoot and warm enough not to crack. In the summer, I handle this part of the repair before 8 a.m. In the winter, I do only emergency repairs.

1. The first step is to break the bond created by the seal-down strips below and on the two courses above the shingle you want to remove. Breaking this bond may be difficult with some newer laminated shingles. A 50-year shingle with a 110-mph wind warranty has an aggressive adhesive bond. In these cases, I cut the adhesive strip with a pry bar.

2. With the bonds broken, I can remove the four nails holding the damaged shingle.

3. Before I remove the shingle, though, I have to remove four more nails driven through the course above.

4. Now I can pull out the damaged shingle, slip in a new shingle, and renail all the loosened shingles.

When refastening shingles, don't put new nails in the old nail holes; they'll pop right out. Instead, nail next to the holes and put a dab of sealant over the old holes. While your caulk gun is handy, seal down all the loosened shingle tabs with a dab of sealant.

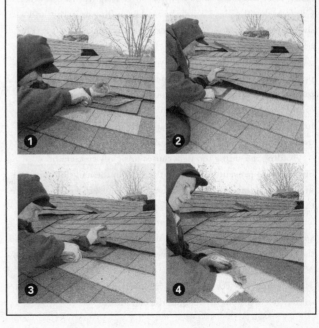

Continued ➜

Removing Vinyl Siding

By Patrick McCombe

Free of visible fasteners, vinyl siding may look impenetrable to the uninitiated, but it's actually the easiest cladding to remove and replace for remodeling or repairs. Because cold weather makes it more difficult to work with vinyl siding and makes cracking the siding more likely, though, it's best to wait for warmer temperatures before attempting removal.

Pulling vinyl apart is safer and easier to do with an inexpensive siding-removal tool. The tool's small hook grabs the bottom of a siding course and pulls it free from the course below it. You can find the tool at home centers and siding dealers for under $10.

Where adjoining pieces overlap, you need to separate the courses. To make sure you're not trying to unhook a molded area that won't separate, look at the siding from below. The connection between courses has a seam. The molded areas in the middle of the course do not.

To remove a piece of siding, unhook the piece above it by inserting the removal tool where the pieces overlap. Use the tool to pull down on the hooked edge, then gently pull the siding from the piece below it. When the pieces separate, slide the tool along the hooked edge while lifting the loose end away from the building.

Once the piece is free, hold it out of the way while you use a cat's paw to pull the siding nails. After you've removed all the nails, push the siding piece straight down to free it from the course below. Continue pulling nails and removing courses until you've removed all that's necessary.

To reinstall vinyl siding, reverse the removal process. Hook the siding onto the course below or the starter strip (for first courses). Confirm that the piece is fully hooked by pulling up gently and sliding it side to side. If it doesn't slide easily, make sure it is fully hooked onto the course below.

Pushing on the overlap with your palm will often reveal any problem spots. Small humps—especially those that yield when pushed on—are spots where the courses are not fully mated. Push on the area while pulling up on the siding until the two pieces are fully joined. You'll often hear a satisfying zipping sound as two uncooperative siding pieces are joined together.

Nailing the siding too tight causes unsightly creases and buckling. To prevent this, center the nails in the nail slot but don't drive them home. There should be the thickness of a dime between the nail head and the siding.

Don't fully insert the siding into J-channel, outside corners, and window flanges. Leave ¼ in. between the end of the siding and the receiving channel to allow for expansion. In temperatures below 40°F, leave ⅜ in.

One final tip: For long runs with overlaps, orient the overlaps so they're consistent throughout the elevation.

1. INSERT THE REMOVAL TOOL. Starting at a receiving channel or overlap, slide the removal tool between two pieces of siding.

2. PULL DOWN AND OUT. Unhook the siding from the previous course by sliding the tool along the seam while gently pulling down and out with the tool and your other hand.

3. PULL THE NAILS. Use a cat's paw to pull the siding nails. Put the cat's paw between the nail and the siding to prevent breaking the slotted nail hole.

4. SLIDE THE PANEL DOWN. Once the nails are removed, unhook the siding piece from the previous course by pulling it straight down. Gently bend the panel to free it from receiving channels.

5. REVERSE THE STEPS. Reinstall panels by pushing in and up until they fully grip the course below. Fully hooked siding panels slide easily for expansion and contraction.

6. DRIVE THE NAILS. Centered in the slot, drive in hot-dipped galvanized or aluminum roofing nails. Leave 1/16 in. to 1/32 in. between the nail head and the siding.

7. RECEIVING CHANNELS FIRST. Before reattaching the bottom edge with the siding tool, insert the piece into J-channel, corners, and trim.

8. REATTACH WITH TWO HANDS. Use the siding tool to pull down on the upper panel while you push inward with your other hand. Work from one end toward the other.

9. TEST THE CONNECTION. Pull up gently on the siding after reinstallation to be sure the two pieces are fully attached.

Vinyl-Siding Tools

Working with vinyl siding requires a pair of specialized tools. To unhook a vinyl-siding panel from a preceding course, you'll need a siding-removal tool. The tool's small hook frees or reattaches it to the course below. The top course and those below windows and other obstructions generally require a snap-lock punch, which makes small tabs that lock panels into utility trim.

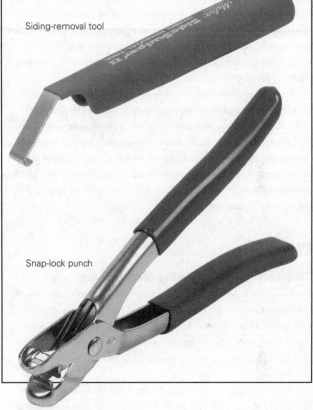

Siding-removal tool

Snap-lock punch

Continued ➜

By Scott Gibson

No siding is more dominant in new residential construction than vinyl. Near-universal availability, low cost, and minimal upkeep all helped to make it the principal siding material in one-third of all new houses built in 2012, according to the U.S. Census Bureau.

But what if—despite its widespread appeal—you're not a fan of plastic siding? If you're aiming for a traditional shingle or clapboard style on your house, your alternatives include a variety of solid-wood species, as well as engineered wood and fiber cement. While the low cost and low-maintenance requirements of vinyl may have overshadowed its competitors in the broader market, a side-by-side comparison still can be worthwhile when you're choosing a cladding for your new house or re-siding project.

Regardless of the type of siding you're considering, it makes sense to look at three criteria: appearance, durability, and cost (including the cost of installation). Here's a look at how the three big siding categories—wood, fiber cement, and vinyl—compare on these points. Although brick and stucco are strong regional players (brick is the single most common choice in the South), they call for specialized installation techniques outside the skill set required for the options considered here.

Wood

Staunchly Traditional, Fading Market Share

Early settlers used mostly wood siding because that's what was available. In terms of market share, however, it's been downhill ever since. In no part of the country does wood siding currently account for even one-tenth of new single-family homes. In the South, it's a faint blip on the screen (3%), according to Census Bureau figures.

Wood siding is made from solid material or short scraps and offcuts glued together with finger joints. Species commonly used for siding run the gamut from cedar and redwood to pine, fir, and other locally available woods. When sourced locally, wood siding can be sustainable in every sense of the word.

Nothing Looks Quite Like Wood

Wood siding is available in many forms: sawn shingles, split shakes, tapered clapboards, and planks that can be applied either horizontally or vertically. It's adaptable to a range of architectural styles, and for certain types of houses, such as New England Capes, it has been the choice for generations of builders. In terms of appearance, wood remains the ideal against which all its lookalike substitutes are measured.

There's No Durability without Maintenance

The best grades of wood (clear heartwood of western red cedar, Alaskan cedar, and redwood, for example) have a long life expectancy if they're installed correctly. Lesser grades, such as pine, won't last as long. All types of wood are more durable with a coat of paint or stain. That means regular maintenance for the life of the product. Depending on climate, weather exposure, and other factors, paint may need attention in seven to 10 years. Leaving wood untreated is an option with some species (cedar shingles, for example, are often left unfinished), but expect the color to fade to gray. Untreated shingles and clapboards may curl or split.

Wood siding can last a long time when properly installed and maintained, but it can rot quickly when installed poorly. Wide eaves, protective porches, and good air circulation may not matter for vinyl or fiber cement, but it can help to extend the life of wood siding.

Top Grades for Top Dollar

Wood siding comes in a broad range of profiles, grades, and wood species, all of which affect its cost. Top grades of clear siding are expensive: In material cost alone, cedar siding is the highest of any siding discussed here. Local species can cost much less. You'll still pay a premium for the best material, however, and availability and quality vary widely depending on the lumber supply where you live.

Wood siding is installed relatively easily, and it has unrivaled workability. It's easily cut and shaped with simple carpentry tools, is light in weight, and is safe to handle. Wood siding probably lasts longer when installed over a vented rain screen, which aids drying and prevents water from being trapped between the back of the siding and the sheathing. While very effective, it's an extra construction step with added costs. The cost of proper installation, as well as the costs involved in periodic maintenance, should be considered when comparing wood to other siding options.

Fiber Cement

Durable and Noncombustible

Patented in Austria more than a century ago as Eternit, fiber-cement siding is made of sand, portland cement, and cellulose fiber. It's sold under at least a half-dozen brand names in the United States. Fiber cement may look like painted wood, but, say manufacturers, it is impervious to wood-boring insects and won't rot. Fiber-cement siding is noncombustible and comes with warranties of up to 50 years. On the downside, it's heavy and brittle, and cutting it produces dangerous silica dust.

Think Hard, Brittle Wood

From a distance, fiber cement and wood are visually indistinguishable. Like vinyl, fiber-cement siding is available in a number of forms that look much like traditional wood siding. Lap siding is typically $5/16$ in. thick and 12 ft. long and available in widths of $5\frac{1}{4}$ in. to 12 in. It's installed with an overlap of $1\frac{1}{4}$ in.

In addition to smooth and textured lap siding, there are individual and panelized shingles as well as panels in sheets up to 4 ft. by 10 ft.—and panels made to look like brick and stone.

Fiber-cement siding can be ordered primed, unprimed, or factory-finished in one of nearly two dozen colors. Fiber cement must be painted; manufacturers recommend 100% acrylic latex paint.

Do Fiber-Cement and Wood Siding Need a Rain Screen?

Instead of nailing siding against housewrap or asphalt felt, many builders now install vertical furring strips or a plastic drainage mat between siding and a water-resistive barrier (WRB). This type of installation (one including an air gap directly behind the siding) is usually called a rain-screen installation. A rain-screen gap offers at least four benefits:

• It limits wicking by providing a capillary break between the back of the siding and the WRB.

• It allows moisture held in the siding and sheathing to be redistributed to adjacent materials by evaporation and diffusion, thereby limiting damage due to water that concentrates at leak points.

• It provides a path for liquid water to drain down to weep holes at the bottom of the wall.

• It provides a path for moving air, which helps to dry the siding and sheathing quickly if they get damp. Wet-wall disasters are so common and so expensive to repair that an increasing number of building experts recommend that all siding installations include a rain-screen gap.

Most wet-wall fiascos are caused by elementary (but all-too-common) flashing errors. A rain-screen installation is a type of insurance policy that can prevent a small workmanship error from leading to disaster.

If you are installing wood or fiber-cement siding, a rain screen provides you with an extra benefit: The paint job will last longer.

Continued →

Tough to the Core

With an inherent resistance to fire, insect damage, and rot, fiber-cement siding comes with lengthy warranties, which are often transferable. CertainTeed and Maxitile, for example, offer a 50-year prorated warranty. James Hardie offers a 30-year nonprorated warranty on its fiber-cement products.

Factory-finished products require minimal maintenance. James Hardie offers two climate-driven paint formulations for its factory-finished siding; both finishes have a 15-year warranty. CertainTeed's ColorMax finish has a 15-year warranty covering peeling, flaking, and cracking.

Installation Boosts Cost

National averages indicate that it costs as much to install a square of fiber cement as it does to buy it. There are a few reasons for this: Fiber-cement siding is relatively heavy (a 4-ft. by 8-ft. panel weighs 73 lb., compared to about 20 lb. for a 12-ft. piece of 8¼-in. lap siding). It's also somewhat brittle. More important, cutting fiber-cement products can create dust that contains crystalline silica, a serious health threat. Special vacuum-equipped saws or shears should be used. Proposed OSHA rules designed to protect workers may tighten job-site regulations in the future.

Vinyl

Low Price, Long Life

Combining durability and low maintenance with a low price, it's no mystery why vinyl (PVC) has become a dominant siding material. Pricier plastic options include polymer (polypropylene) siding, which uses an injection-molding process to give products a highly defined, three-dimensional profile; and cellular PVC, which has a weight and density similar to wood.

Despite its practical advantages, some homeowners and builders just don't like plastic siding. It has been attacked for everything from unsightly trim details to the inherent toxicity of manufacturing polyvinyl chloride. Two common criticisms of PVC involve the release of vinyl chloride and dioxin, both carcinogens, either during the manufacturing process or when PVC is burned. The vinyl-siding industry, however, says that manufacturing was modified years ago to control exposure to vinyl chloride and that vinyl is an "extremely small source of dioxin."

If Wood Can Do It, So Can Plastic

Plastic siding is manufactured in a number of profiles meant to look like traditional wood siding, including shingles, clapboards, shiplap, and board and batten. It's available in hundreds of colors, including dark colors, and can be purchased with an integral EPS backing to increase overall R-values.

According to David Johnston, senior technical director of the Vinyl Siding Institute, insulated siding can add between R-2.5 and R-3 to a wall's R-value. Although it's somewhat more expensive than other grades of vinyl siding, it tends to appear flatter on the wall.

The thickness of vinyl siding ranges from ½₅ in. to ½₀ in. (builder grade). Thicker and more expensive grades of vinyl siding are stronger and more rigid than entry-level products.

Two Words: Plastic Lasts

Low cost is an important advantage of vinyl, but it's not the only one. Vinyl siding requires virtually no maintenance, lasts for decades, and won't trap moisture against the sheathing as other types of siding can. With no wood-fiber content, it won't absorb water and won't rot.

The right vinyl will stand up in a storm. According to the Vinyl Siding Institute, some products meet 150-mph building-code requirements in Miami and Texas, and several can withstand 190-mph winds.

Expensive Is Better Than Cheap

There's no formal grading system for vinyl siding as there is for wood, but three important variables are the thickness of the material, the type of nail hem, and the type of capstock, which is co-extruded with the substrate as a color layer. Economy vinyl is light and easy to install. National data indicates the installation cost of polymer siding is higher than for any other siding.

How Green Is Your Vinyl?

Few questions can touch off an argument faster than this one. Bill Walsh, founder of the Healthy Building Network, points to a variety of concerns, including PVC's reliance on chlorine gas for its manufacture and the toxicity of its chemical components and by-products. In a blog post at GreenBuildingAdvisor.com, Walsh called vinyl "the worst plastic for the environment and the antithesis of a green building material."

Yet the U.S. Green Building Council's LEED program does not prohibit PVC building products, and the vinyl industry has prepared a lengthy report to document its claim that vinyl siding has a much lower environmental impact than brick, fiber cement, or stucco.

Writing in Fine Homebuilding a few years ago, Betsy Pettit, an architect and the president of Building Science Corp., noted that all siding materials have environmental costs. Because of vinyl's long service life, its suitability for recycling, and its track record for trouble-free installations, however, Pettit concluded, "Yes, vinyl siding is green."

The answer? PVC is not a perfect material for siding, but neither are most alternatives.

Factory-Finished Siding

By John Ross

It sounds too good to be true. Choose any color for the cedar or fiber-cement siding you want to install. Eliminate the hassle and expense of a site-applied finish, and get a 25-year warranty against paint failure.

When I first heard this pitch, I thought there had to be a catch; otherwise factory-finishing would be the industry standard. Sure, it's true that western red cedar and fiber cement are both premium siding materials because of their dimensional stability and paint-holding ability. But isn't 10 years about the best you're going to get before you have to repaint?

It turns out that a maintenance-free 25-year warranty for factory-painted siding is something that you can believe in. For the past 30 years, the Forest Products Lab has been assessing paint durability by watching siding weather. According to a study that was published in 1994, the lab found that western red-cedar boards that were not exposed to weather prior to being painted were in almost-perfect condition after 20 years of exposure.

Painted fiber-cement siding hasn't been tested for as long as painted-wood siding, but its excellent dimensional stability suggests a similar longevity for the finish. However, the finish for both

The Factory Is a Better Place to Paint a House

The weather, the chaos, and the plain old dirt of the job site can't compete with the conditions inside a machine-finishing plant. In a plant, siding is never exposed to the elements, paint application is measured to the millimeter, and temperature and humidity are kept at optimal levels. Located throughout the country, machine finishers typically are certified to apply top-quality finishes from major manufacturers like Cabot, Sherwin-Williams, and PPG, and are set up to coat a wide range of materials, including siding and panel products.

ACCLIMATION. Finish isn't applied until the raw material has had time to reach the plant's controlled temperature and humidity.

APPLICATION. High-speed rollers, canted to match the beveled siding's profile, force the paint into crevices to ensure complete coverage.

INSPECTION. The ends and edges are touched up by hand during a visual inspection.

AIR CIRCULATION. Giant racks ensure even, complete drying.

products has to be applied under ideal conditions. Unpainted siding cannot be exposed to the sun prior to finish application. The painting has to be done at the right temperature, in the right humidity, and in a dust-free environment.

A Factory Provides the Perfect Environment for Finishing

Just about all the variables that can affect the quality of a site-applied siding finish are eliminated in a finishing plant. Indoor temperature and humidity are easily controlled. Unfinished siding is kept clean, dry, and out of direct sunlight.

Found across the country, independently owned finishing plants, known as machine finishers, typically gain certification to

Continued ➜

Western Red Cedar and Fiber Cement Become Maintenance-Free Siding Options

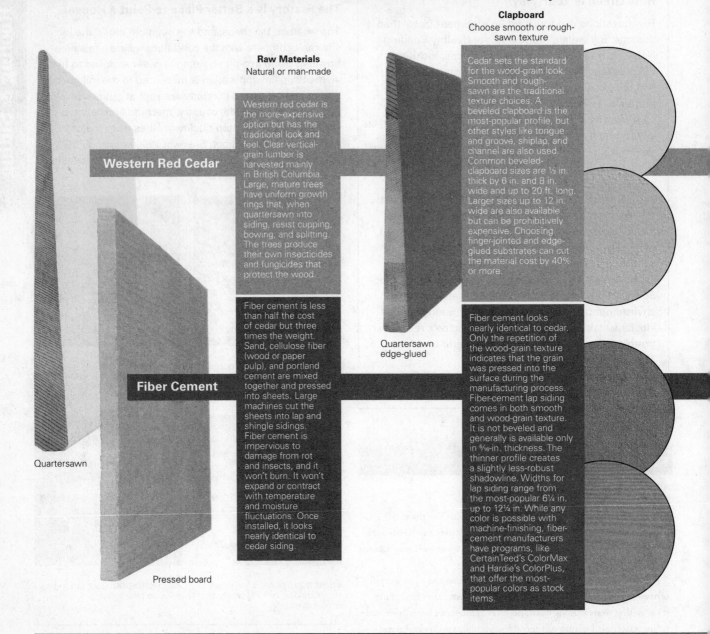

Raw Materials
Natural or man-made

Clapboard
Choose smooth or rough-
sawn texture

Western Red Cedar

Western red cedar is the more-expensive option but has the traditional look and feel. Clear vertical-grain lumber is harvested mainly in British Columbia. Large, mature trees have uniform growth rings that, when quartersawn into siding, resist cupping, bowing, and splitting. The trees produce their own insecticides and fungicides that protect the wood.

Cedar sets the standard for the wood-grain look. Smooth and rough-sawn are the traditional texture choices. A beveled clapboard is the most-popular profile, but other styles like tongue and groove, shiplap, and channel are also used. Common beveled-clapboard sizes are ½ in. thick by 6 in. and 8 in. wide and up to 20 ft. long. Larger sizes up to 12 in. wide are also available but can be prohibitively expensive. Choosing finger-jointed and edge-glued substrates can cut the material cost by 40% or more.

Fiber Cement

Fiber cement is less than half the cost of cedar but three times the weight. Sand, cellulose fiber (wood or paper pulp), and portland cement are mixed together and pressed into sheets. Large machines cut the sheets into lap and shingle sidings. Fiber cement is impervious to damage from rot and insects, and it won't burn. It won't expand or contract with temperature and moisture fluctuations. Once installed, it looks nearly identical to cedar siding.

Fiber cement looks nearly identical to cedar. Only the repetition of the wood-grain texture indicates that the grain was pressed into the surface during the manufacturing process. Fiber-cement lap siding comes in both smooth and wood-grain texture. It is not beveled and generally is available only in ⁵⁄₁₆-in. thickness. The thinner profile creates a slightly less-robust shadowline. Widths for lap siding range from the most-popular 6¼ in. up to 12¼ in. While any color is possible with machine-finishing, fiber-cement manufacturers have programs, like CertainTeed's ColorMax and Hardie's ColorPlus, that offer the most-popular colors as stock items.

Quartersawn
edge-glued

Quartersawn

Pressed board

---

apply finish from one or more siding and/or paint manufacturers. Thanks to their durability, dimensional stability, and favorable painting qualities, western red cedar and fiber cement are the most-popular siding options for factory finishes.

"Honestly, I can't think of a good reason not to prefinish," says Brent Stewart, vice president of purchasing for Russin Lumber Corp., a factory finisher in Montgomery, N.Y. "But most homeowners don't know that this process is available."

Stewart says that factory-finishing, also called machine-finishing, is becoming more popular because quality and availability are improving. "For the customer, better quality control means

there's not a big mystery about what they are going to get," Stewart says. Also, better quality control makes it more likely that the lumber retailer will recommend a factory-finished product. This represents a major change for the industry compared to five years ago. Now you can find factory finishers by contacting paint manufacturers or your local lumber retailer.

To see how the factory-finishing process works, I visited a plant that specializes in finishing western red-cedar and fiber-cement siding. Both materials are shipped to the finisher direct from the manufacturer. Once at the plant, the siding is allowed to acclimate to the plant's temperature and humidity for several days.

Shingles
A variety of shapes and styles

Cedar sidewall shingles can make a house look rustic or refined. Typically quartersawn from premium-grade lumber, they vary in width from 4 in. to 12 in. and can be applied in a nearly endless combination of patterns. Decorative ends such as ovals, octagons, and circles allow skilled installers to weave elaborate patterns. Shingles can be purchased individually or collated on a plywood substrate. More options include smooth, grooved, or rough-sawn textures. At least one company, Stave Lake Cedar (www.stavelake .com), offers an 18-year no-tannin-bleed warranty for its machine-finished coatings.

Stave Lake textured shingles

Fiber-cement shingles come in a wide variety of shapes, widths, and textures. However, fiber-cement shingles are not typically individual pieces but rather larger panels with a shingle pattern cut into them. The panels can be installed faster than individual pieces yet are overlaid to create a traditional shingled look. As fiber-cement manufacturing improves, companies are experimenting with more stylized looks. One example is from the Japanese company Nichiha. Its Sierra Premium Shake is a ½-in.-thick panel product. Deep grooves and repeated channels create the shingle look. During the finishing process, oxidizing stains collect in the grooves for a rich, variegated look.

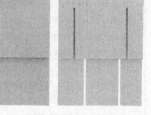

Nichiha Sierra Premium

CertainTeed shingle panels

Before it is primed, cedar is sanded on the back side to improve the primer's adhesion. During priming, cedar gets an alkyd oil primer to help prevent tannins or extractives from bleeding through. Fiber cement gets a special latex primer. Both materials are finished with an acrylic-latex finish coat.

The application methods vary depending on the finisher. But essentially, the siding is fed into a machine that floods the top and bottom surfaces with finish. The machine then uses rollers and high-speed brushes to force the paint into the siding's crevices. Close monitoring ensures that an even 6-mil layer of paint is applied to the siding. After the application of the finish, the siding is placed on racks to dry. To speed up the drying process, some factory finishers bake on the paint in ovens.

Factory-Finished Siding Saves You Money

It's not hard to find out how much factory-finishing costs. In about 10 minutes, my local lumberyard worked up quotes for me on several different finish options for 5760 lin. ft. of beveled cedar clapboards and fiber-cement lap siding: about enough material for a 3000-sq.-ft. house. I was interested in comparing the cost of unfinished cedar clapboards and primed fiber-cement siding with machine-finished versions of the same siding. The lumberyard sales rep told me that a factory finish could be applied for about $1200 per coat on either substrate. For primer and two finish coats, my factory-applied paint job would cost $3500 (figures cited from 2014).

Getting a reliable estimate for site-painting a house is more difficult. The cost of paint is easy enough to figure, but the cost of getting it on the house depends a lot on site conditions, such as whether the house is one story or two, or if it is on a slope. A painter in Fairfield County, Connecticut, figuring for scaffolding, equipment, and paint, roughly estimated such a project as costing up to $10,000 for one primer coat and two finish coats. These bottom-line price comparisons make factory-finished siding look very attractive.

Continued →

Fiber-Cement Siding Can Come with a Transferable Warranty

All three fiber-cement manufacturers mentioned here (Nichiha, CertainTeed, James Hardie) offer warranties that cover the siding itself as well as the factory finish, as long as you use the proprietary finish applied by the manufacturer. Although 25-year warranties are available with a special-order extra finish coat of paint, the typical single-coat warranty is 15 years. The substrate warranty, which can be up to 50 years and which primarily covers delamination, and the proprietary-finish warranty are transferable to a new homeowner, which factors positively in a home's resale value.

If you want to go beyond the limited selection of proprietary finish colors available from fiber-cement manufacturers, your lumberyard can arrange to have an independent machine finisher apply a much-broader selection of color choices. In this case, the fiber-cement manufacturer still warrants the substrate, but the paint warranty comes from the paint manufacturer. Choose this finish option, and you can get up to a 25-year warranty against finish failure.

For cedar siding, the warranty for a factory finish comes from the paint manufacturer and is typically for 15 to 25 years, depending on how many coats are applied. These warranties aren't transferable, and if there's a problem with the siding itself, you'll have to contact the siding manufacturer or installer to address these issues.

Some Site-Painting Required

For cedar siding, factory finishers recommend that a final whole-house coat be applied on site to seal the end grain and the face nails. Even if all the siding is factory-finished, the fresh end cuts need to be painted as the siding is installed.

Hugh Schreiber, a remodeling contractor in Berkeley, Calif., has done his share of painting (see online at Fine Homebuilding. com), but he has also installed Hardie's ColorPlus fiber-cement lap siding.

Schreiber says a more-streamlined installation is the biggest advantage of using factory-finished siding. "Brushing carefully to cut in the trim where it meets the siding is a huge hassle," he says. "The prefinished siding saved me from having to do that. I painted the trim before the siding went up, and nothing had to be cut in."

That said, a factory-finished product has some disadvantages. Schreiber says he had to be more attentive in handling each board to avoid scratches and to get the siding in place with the proper orientation; he prefers the factory-finished end to abut the trim. For Schreiber, the extra care that he had to take while handling the siding was worth the trouble. "As a guy who has painted a lot, I will use prefinished siding again," he says. "The paint job was cleaner and tighter all the way around."

The biggest deterrent to factory-finishing might simply be the schedule. Jim Florian, an estimator at H.P. Broom Housewright Inc. in Hadlyme, Conn., says that it's difficult to get homeowners to think about siding colors early in the design phase of a building project. While they are still trying to choose bathroom fixtures, they might not be ready to think about exterior-color choices.

To take advantage of factory-finishing but avoid painting himself into a corner, Florian says there is a middle road. "Whether it's cedar or fiber cement, we'll spec a primer coat and just one finish coat instead of two. This saves time and money over site-painting everything. To get the best seal against the weather, we apply a final coat on site." This also leaves room for flexibility. If the home-owner wants to make a slight change before the final coat, say from buttercup yellow to sunflower, there is no added cost.

Green Comparison

When comparing the relative greenness of western red-cedar and fiber-cement siding, the key issues are the raw materials going into the products, impacts of manufacturing, durability, and maintenance. At the most-basic level, wood is the greenest building material available because its production absorbs carbon dioxide and produces oxygen, while well-managed forests provide habitats for wildlife, cleanse water, and offer a range of other ecosystem benefits. If western red cedar carried certification based on standards from the Forest Stewardship Council (FSC), we would have third-party verification of well-managed forestry, but to date, British Columbian western red cedar has not been FSC-certified.

By comparison, the raw materials for fiber-cement include portland cement (a highly energy-intensive material) and wood fiber (often sourced from as far away as New Zealand). The energy used to produce fiber cement generates significant air pollution as well as carbon-dioxide emissions.

If we delve more deeply into the life cycle of siding, the picture grows murkier. Some western red cedar, for example, is sawn into large billets in British Columbia, then is shipped to China for milling into siding.

The other significant issue is durability and the need for regular painting. This is where fiber cement often outshines cedar. Conventional wisdom is that fiber cement is more stable than cedar and needs less fre- quent repainting, especially if installed over a rain screen. With factory finishing, though, these differences are minimized. By finishing wood before exposed surfaces have been damaged by UV light, the paint lasts a lot longer, so the environmental impacts (and costs) of frequent painting are reduced, further improving the environmental advantages of cedar over fiber cement.

Note that in fire-prone regions, there's another reason to choose fiber cement over cedar: fire protection.

Proper Installation Techniques Ensure Longevity and Keep Warranties Valid

If water becomes trapped behind siding, it can cause bubbling paint and siding that warps, rots, or delaminates. It's also likely to void siding and paint warranties. To help prevent moisture damage, a space created behind the siding (called a rain screen) allows water to drain down or evaporate. The traditional method of ensuring healthy siding involves installing vertical furring strips over builder's felt (drawing right). Alternatively, a housewrap with a rain screen incorporated into it can be used. Several manufacturers make drainable housewraps, one of which is shown below.

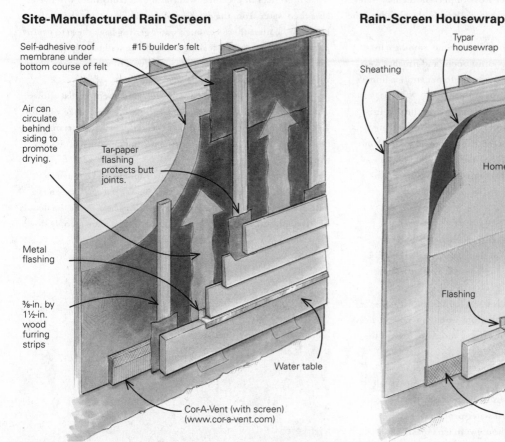

Site-Manufactured Rain Screen

Self-adhesive roof membrane under bottom course of felt

#15 builder's felt

Air can circulate behind siding to promote drying.

Tar-paper flashing protects butt joints.

Metal flashing

⅜-in. by 1½-in. wood furring strips

Water table

Cor-A-Vent (with screen)
(www.cor-a-vent.com)

Rain-Screen Housewrap

Typar housewrap

Sheathing

Home Slicker mesh

Flashing

Clapboard

Water table

Home Slicker screen repels insects.

Hide Your Handiwork

Siding nails can be ordered with any paint color on the head. Maze Nails (www.mazenails. com) keeps stocks of nails to match all CertainTeed and Hardie standard colors. Typically, hand-driven nails with a blunt tip and thin shank are used on cedar, while pneumatic fasteners with a steeply cut tip and thick shank secure fiber cement. When hand-nailing, use a polyurethane cap on the hammer (available from the nail manufacturer) to avoid damaging the finish. An aluminum nose on a pneumatic nailer protects factory-finished fiber-cement siding.

Color-matching paint kits coat cut ends on site. Several bottles should come with your siding order, but if you've chosen a custom color, it's smart to order extra touch-up paint.

Continued ➜

Vented Rain Screens

By Justin Fink

Water is lazy. It will never work hard to find its way into your house. In fact, water always will follow the path of least resistance. That's why the roofing membrane, asphalt shingles, siding, housewrap, and all the flashing details on a house are installed so that they lap over each other. They work to prevent the lazy water from being sidetracked as it follows its path from the clouds to the ground.

But houses are made of wood, and over time, wood shrinks and expands. Nails loosen, siding joints open, and finishes wear away. It eventually becomes easier for water to penetrate a home's outer layers of defense, especially the siding.

Once water has gotten through that outer layer, its potential for causing problems increases, and its potential for escaping or drying is greatly reduced. To prevent this trapped water from causing damage behind the siding, we need to give it an easy way out. It needs a place to go and a way to dry—and a vented rain screen offers both.

Trust Me, Your Siding Leaks

For many people reading this, the biggest challenge will be accepting the fact that the siding on their house leaks. So I'll be clear: It doesn't matter whether your house is clad with shakes, shingles, clapboards, vinyl, or stucco, your siding leaks. How do I know? Because water always finds a way behind siding, whether through gaps or cracks in the installation, wood movement, heavy downpours, or the heat of the sun driving moisture toward the cooler back of the siding.

Don't panic. Leaks are part of the reason that houses are built with weather-resistive barriers such as housewrap or felt paper under the siding. Even when installed correctly, though, housewrap isn't a guarantee against water problems.

Siding installed tight against housewrap isn't ideal for a number of reasons. Yes, housewrap is designed to shed water, but it does have a weakness. Surfactants in soap and power-washing chemicals, and tannins and sugars from wood siding, can reduce the surface tension of the water, allowing it to pass through the microscopic openings in the housewrap. Also, dirt can clog these openings, allowing liquid water to pass. The best way to eliminate this problem is to create a physical gap between the back of the siding and the face of the housewrap.

Less Than an Inch Makes Drainage Possible

Providing a physical gap between the back of the siding and the surface of the housewrap is like eliminating a bridge between two land masses. Remember that liquid water is lazy, so when given an uninterrupted conduit for drainage and all the appeal of gravity, it will follow that path every time. As long as that path runs straight down the back of the siding to daylight, bulk water isn't a threat.

Water drainage is only one part of the assembly, however. For a rain screen to function properly, it must also have a steady flow of air to help promote drying.

Ventilation Is the Second Half of the Equation

Except for vinyl, most types of siding are considered reservoir products. That is, they are like dense sponges: Even when coated with paint on all sides, they still can absorb water.

Differences in pressure (wind) and heat (sunshine) will drive absorbed water from the exterior of the siding toward the cooler back side. Unless there's enough water getting back there to drain physically or enough air leaking through the wall to help the water dry, it just sits. That's where the second part of a rain screen comes into play: the ventilation.

Located at the bottom of a wall, the same opening that allows water to drain in a rain-screen setup also acts as an intake vent for air. With another vent at the top of the wall, air will constantly flow behind the siding, picking up and removing moisture on its way out.

The concept is simple, and it usually doesn't take much to convince builders and homeowners that a vented rain screen is a best practice for long-lasting siding and a dry house. It's the details of a vented rain-screen system that seem to bog many people down.

The Concept Is Simple. The Details Raise Questions.

The theory behind a vented rain screen is straightforward: Water can drain, and air flowing behind the siding can intercept moisture that has penetrated, helping the wall to stay dry. The details can be tricky, though, and there is ongoing discussion (sometimes argument) over the best way to handle crucial details. Here are answers to the most common questions.

❶

How Much of a Gap Should I Leave Behind the Siding?

The size of the gap depends on how much water you expect and, in some cases, how much you want to alter details for trim, windows, and doors. A ⅜-in. gap is a good place to start, but even a ¹⁄₁₆-in. gap is better than none at all. A ¼-in. or ⅜-in. gap will allow many types of siding to be installed without having to fur out trim, though 5/4 stock will be needed. The illustrations shown here use 1×3 furring strips to create a ¾-in. space.

❷

What's the Best Way to Keep Insects Out of the Air Intake/Water Drainage Openings?

The easiest way to keep insects out of the airspace is to use a corrugated vent strip with insect screen or filter fabric. It is attached at the bottom of the wall, over the housewrap, and is hidden by the first course of siding. The site-made approach is to staple up strips of insect screen over the housewrap at the bottom edge of the wall before the battens or open-weave membrane is installed. Then, before the siding is attached, the screen is folded up and stapled over the front face of the battens or membrane.

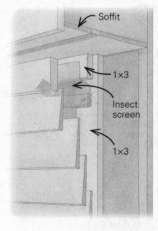

③ Exhaust options
④ Transitions
① Gap size

Water that gets behind siding is allowed to drain.

Airflow behind siding keeps wall dry.

⑤ Windows and doors
⑥ Corners
② Air intake/water drainage

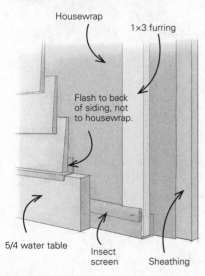

Housewrap

1×3 furring

Flash to back of siding, not to housewrap.

5/4 water table

Insect screen

Sheathing

❸

Is It OK to Tie the Exhaust Into the Attic Vents, or Is a Frieze-Vent Setup Better?

This is one of the more controversial details in a vented rain-screen setup. According to building scientist Joseph Lstiburek, it doesn't matter much either way. Venting into a soffit is fine, as long as the soffit is connected to the attic ventilation. Although building scientist John Straube agrees that venting into a soffit isn't likely to be a huge deal, he prefers to see the rain screen vented at the frieze so that potentially moisture-laden air coming from behind the siding can mix with outdoor air before being drawn into the attic.

Vent into Soffit

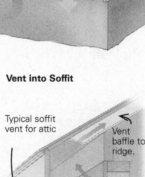

Typical soffit vent for attic

Vent baffle to ridge.

Vent at the Frieze

Soffit

1×3

Insect screen

1×3

Continued ➜

❹

Are Wood Strips the Best Option? If So, Do They Need to Be Pressure-Treated?

Best is a matter of circumstances, but wood is still a fine choice for site-made rain-screen systems. Plywood or OSB of various thicknesses can be ripped into strips and fastened over the housewrap, but most builders opt for the convenience of ¼-in. lath or 1×3 furring strips. The 1x strips are also common when installing siding over 1½-in. or thicker rigid foam. The strips hold the foam in place and provide solid nailing for the siding. Although it takes time, wood strips can even be notched and installed horizontally, an acceptable method behind sidewall shingles or vertical siding. Regardless of the type of wooden strip, pressure-treated stock is not necessary because the strips will be able to dry easily if they get wet.

❺

Is It Necessary to Vent at the Top and Bottom of Each Cavity, or Will One Opening Provide Enough Airflow and Drainage?

Many builders don't bother with exhaust vents in shorter sections of a rain-screen wall, such as below a first-floor window. According to Straube, however, one vent opening does not provide anywhere near the performance of a flow-through setup. That said, don't worry about intake/exhaust vents right at the window; just leave a gap for air to flow around the window.

❻

Should Corner Boards Be Vented So That Air Can Flow Around Corners, Too?

According to Straube, the best approach is to isolate each face. The goal is to prevent rainwater from hitting one face of the house and being dragged around the more vulnerable corners by pressure differences. Straube also notes that a 1×3 nailed over a layer of housewrap is fine; there's no need to seal the corners with caulk or foam. You still can help these corners to stay dry by providing intake vents at the bottom of the corner boards that either tie into the attic ventilation or vent out the frieze.

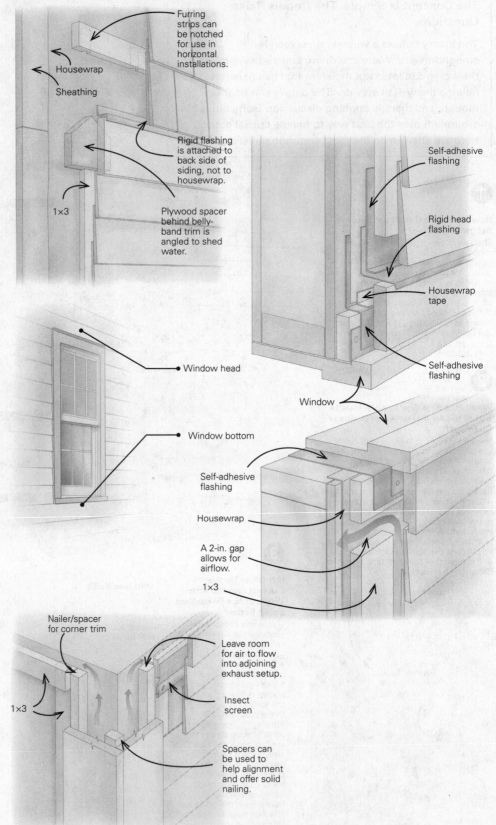

Furring strips can be notched for use in horizontal installations.

Housewrap

Sheathing

Rigid flashing is attached to back side of siding, not to housewrap.

1×3

Plywood spacer behind belly-band trim is angled to shed water.

Self-adhesive flashing

Rigid head flashing

Housewrap tape

Self-adhesive flashing

Window head

Window bottom

Window

Self-adhesive flashing

Housewrap

A 2-in. gap allows for airflow.

1×3

Nailer/spacer for corner trim

Leave room for air to flow into adjoining exhaust setup.

1×3

Insect screen

Spacers can be used to help alignment and offer solid nailing.

Contents

Electrical Systems & Lighting

An Electrical Tool Kit

By Brian Walo

I could easily blow everything I earn as a professional electrician in a single afternoon buying fancy tools that I might use some day for some thing. When I check back into reality, though, I have to admit that it's still the most basic electrical tools that I always reach for. Besides, if I'm going to remain efficient, I have to choose the tools that provide the most bang for my buck and leave my electrical-tool bucket light enough to move around easily.

Also, some tools in my kit (not shown here) are basic items that apply to all sorts of remodeling tasks. I choose these tools based on their use in electrical applications, though. For instance, rather than a heavy 18v drill/driver, I carry an ultracompact model with long-lasting Li-ion batteries to save space without sacrificing run-time. This kit won't get you in and out of complex jobs, but for most of the electrical work found in remodeling, it will be your new best friend.

Drivers

1. PHILLIPS HEAD #2 AND #3: Almost every screw that was once slotted for a flathead screwdriver now accepts a Phillips head, too. The #2 and #3 are the two must-have sizes for electrical work.

2. FLATHEAD ³⁄₁₆ IN. AND ¼ IN.: I hate slotted screws, but they are common. For electrical cover plates, ³⁄₁₆ in. is the standard size; among other things, the ¼-in. size comes in handy as a "beater" for breaking the spot welds on the knockouts of a metal electrical box.

3. NUT DRIVER: Most grounding screws for metal workboxes have a ⁵⁄₁₆-in. hex head. I find a ⁵⁄₁₆-in. nut driver to be the quickest means of tightening them.

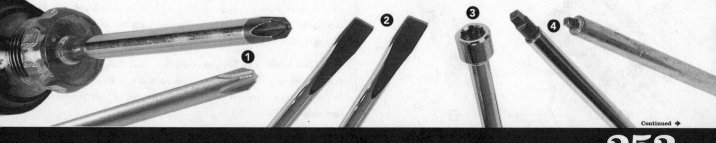

Continued →

4. ROBERTSON #1 AND #2: These square-drive screwdrivers are my favorite tool, and no one else I know uses them. Most new devices (receptacles, switches, etc.) feature screws that can be driven with Phillips, flathead, or Robertson (square) screwdrivers, the latter of which provides the most positive grip.

Testers

1. ANALOG/DIGITAL MULTIMETER: This is my first line of defense against electrical shock and an excellent diagnostic tool. I can double-check that I shut off the right breaker by using the multimeter's AC-voltage function; I also can figure out which cable runs to a light from a particular switch box. I use a clamp-on multi-meter because it limits my exposure to bare conductors when I need to take an amperage reading on live equipment. (For more in-depth information on using a multimeter, see "Make Sure the Power Is Off" on p. 258.)

2. NONCONTACT VOLTAGE DETECTOR: This little tool has a big gee-whiz factor because you can check for voltage without touching bare wires. Because different types of wire insulation and other nearby conductors can interfere with the electrical field, this tool can be less than 100% reliable. Read the safety manual, and understand the tool's limitations. This is not an empty safety reminder, either. I have two pairs of wire strippers with arc holes that resulted from relying on this device before cutting a cable.

3. GFCI-OUTLET TESTER: This little tester is the quickest way to check a GFCI outlet for proper wiring and fault protection. It's also a fast way to figure out which breaker powers a given circuit.

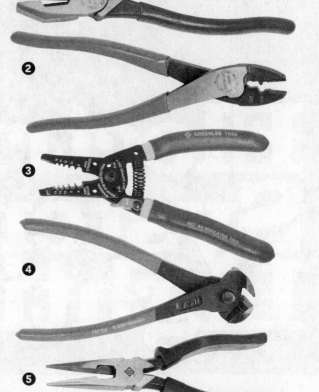

Pliers

1. SIDE-CUTTING (AKA LINEMAN'S): Whether I'm pulling and clipping cable, or twisting wires together, these pliers are the most crucial and frequently used tool I own.

2. CRIMPERS: Find a pair that is long and slender so that you can crimp together ground wires deep inside an electrical box. I also like crimpers with a cutter built in to the nose for slicing through the copper crimping sleeve to separate old ground-wire connections.

3. STRIPPERS: Even the most basic wire strippers are adequate, but I look for a set that has a long nose for reaching into tight spots and serrated jaws to help me pull wire through the back of electrical boxes.

4. END CUT: This tool will be your first choice for pulling out cable staples from a stud or yanking nails from electrical boxes or can lights. A good set has sharp tangs and a solid bite for clipping through nails and staples.

5. NEEDLE NOSE: The fairly precise control of these pliers is great for getting me out of jams—for instance, if I drop a screw in the back of a crowded electrical box or need to pull some cable through a hole in a stud or plate.

Materials

1. ELECTRICAL TAPE: Black tape is the standard, but I also carry rolls of white and green so that I can mark grounded and ungrounded conductors for easy identification.

2. WIRE NUTS: If I had to pick one wire nut to cover the bulk of my day-to-day work, it would be 3M's Performance Plus Tan/Red wire connectors. These nuts handle from #22 to #8 AWG (American wire gauge) wires, depending on the number of conductors.

3. CRIMPING SLEEVES AND BONDING SCREWS: Most, if not all, codes require grounding conductors to be joined together, especially where they enter a metallic workbox. A jar of various sizes of copper crimping sleeves and #10 green ground screws is a must-have.

4. CABLE CLAMPS: These important but often-overlooked clamps secure and protect cable where it enters a light fixture, a workbox, or an electrical panel. I keep both ½-in. and ¾-in. plastic clamps and a few metal clamps in a range of sizes up to 1½ in.

5. STAPLES: Most of the cable I install is #12 and #14 AWG, so I keep lots of insulated staples in these two sizes.

6. SCREWS: When I have to install workbox extensions in a kitchen back-splash or I lose a fastener from a fixture, #6×32 and #8×32 screws save the day. I buy them long and cut them to length with my strippers.

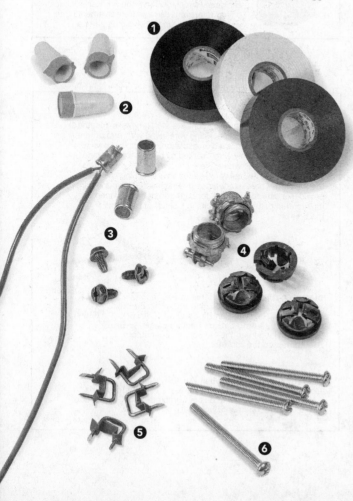

Aren't You Forgetting ...

Diagonal Cutters?

Often called "diags" or "dykes," these cutters are a common electrical tool. I typically use strippers or lineman's pliers for most tasks suited to dykes, so I really can't justify their placement in my essentials kit.

Multibit Screwdriver?

I don't actually own a multibit screwdriver, but I am guilty of borrowing them. If you don't have room for individual drivers of all shapes and sizes, a good combo driver is a fine choice, but only if it's fully equipped. Don't keep carrying it around if half the bits are lost.

Fish Tape?

Running new wires through existing walls is a frequent task for electricians who work on remodeling projects. To be honest, though, I don't own a single fish tape or anything else designed for snaking wires. Instead, I carry 10 ft. of ½-in. PEX tubing.

Household Electricity

By Cliff Popejoy

Electricity is a form of energy we use every day, from opening a garage door, to lighting a desk lamp, to running a clothes washer. If you're not a trained electrician, you likely interact with household electricity at its point of use—an outlet, a light switch, or an appliance. But that's just the end of the line. What's happening upstream?

At its most basic, an electrical current is the movement of electrons from atom to atom. A conductor, such as copper wire, allows easy movement of those electrons from one point to another. An insulator (the plastic coating on a conductor) prohibits this movement, containing the current.

Current is defined as the number of electrons passing a given point during a given time and is measured in amperes, which is often shortened to amps. Voltage is the pressure that drives the flow of electrons. The relationship between voltage and amperage is sometimes compared to the flow of water through a pipe, with voltage being the water pressure and amperage being the amount of water. This analogy illustrates another point regarding amperage and voltage: If one is increased and the other is decreased proportionally, the amount of work performed stays the same—just as a low-volume, high-pressure stream through a hose delivers as much water as a high-volume, low-pressure stream.

Multiply the volts and amps in a circuit, and you get watts, the unit used to measure the power needed to support an electrical demand, or load. As you can see in this illustrated overview, the relationship between voltage, amperage, and watts has practical applications in the wiring of a home for the safe and effective delivery of electricity.

Here's how it works.

1. Power
Utility power enters the house underground or via overhead drop wires that provide both 120v and 240v power (the common notation is 120/240v), typically at 200 amps. A third wire is the neutral and is the path by which electrons, having dropped off most of their energy at a household load, return to the local transformer.

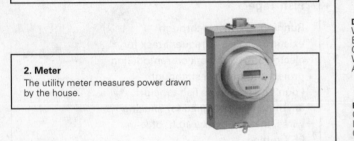

2. Meter
The utility meter measures power drawn by the house.

3. Breaker Panel
Here, incoming power is divided among circuits, which are loops that carry power from the panel to the load and back. Circuits are designed to carry current at specific amperages, from 15 amps to 50 amps in a typical house. The capacity of these circuits may add up to more than the incoming 200 amps because not all circuits draw their maximum amperage at the same time.

4. Breaker
A breaker with a specific amp rating protects each circuit from overload. For safety, the breaker capacity (called ampacity) must be appropriate to the size (gauge) of the wire attached to it. Overload occurs when electric loads draw more amps than the circuit can handle. For example, if two 1600w hair dryers are plugged into a 120v, 20-amp circuit (which can safely supply 2400w), the breaker will cut power to prevent damage from overheating to wires, switches, and other circuit parts.

5. Wiring
Modern branch-circuit wiring consists of nonmetallic-sheathed cable that holds a bare grounding wire along with two or three copper conductors encased in insulation. Electricity flows to the load on the supply wire, marked by black insulation (and red on 240v circuits where there are two supply wires). The white-sheathed neutral wire returns any remaining charge to the panel. The bare (sometimes green-sheathed) ground wire provides a path to the panel for current that has escaped its intended path, which results in a cutoff of power at the breaker.

Supply

Ground

Neutral

12-3   G   TYPE NM-B

DIAMETER/GAUGE the Diameter, or Gauge, of a Wire Determines the Amperage It Can Handle. For Example, 14-Ga. Wire Can Be Used on 15-Amp Circuits, but 20-Amp Circuits Require Larger 12-Ga. Wire. The Gauge and the Number of Conductors Are Printed on the Jacket.

RESPECT THE NEUTRAL! When Correctly Wired, the Neutral Conductor is Energized When Power is Passing Through a Load—That is, When a Circuit is Complete. This Current Can Cause Electrocution or Shock, Despite Its Name.

6. Branch Circuit

These circuits transport electricity to loads and back to the service panel. Here are some common branch circuits.

• **GENERAL-PURPOSE (LIGHTING) CIRCUITS** are 15-amp or 20-amp circuits that carry 120v power to multiple lights and receptacles.

• **DEDICATED BRANCH CIRCUITS** deliver power to a single load, such as a large appliance, or to a group of loads as specified under the National Electric Code to prevent overload. These include 120v, 20-amp kitchen-appliance circuits and bathroom-receptacle circuits. (It's good practice to provide a dedicated 20-amp circuit to each bathroom receptacle to support the amperage drawn by hair dryers.)

• **240V CIRCUITS** are dedicated circuits that provide extra power to air-conditioning compressors, electric water heaters, and other heavy-duty appliances that draw a lot of amps. Doubling the voltage means the amperage can be reduced by half, allowing the use of smaller-gauge wire that is less costly and easier to install.

• **120/240V (MULTIWIRE) CIRCUITS** service loads that require both 120v and 240v, such as electric clothes dryers and ranges. The 120v runs lights, motors, and controls, while the 240v supplies the heating elements. Amperage is typically 30 amps to 50 amps.

Is it 110v or 120v? 220v or 240v?

The nominal voltage for homes in the United States is 120/240v. Before a national power grid was created and voltages were standardized, some local generators delivered electricity at 110/220v. Today, those values are outdated and incorrect.

Continued →

By Clifford A. Popejoy

Household voltage can cause serious shock and even death, so the only way to work safely on wiring is with the power off. The good news is that when used as shown here, a voltage/continuity tester and a noncontact voltage tester will tell you if the power to the wires or fixtures you are working on really is off. They also can provide other valuable information about wiring and fixtures. As far as I'm concerned, these testers are must-have tools whether you're a professional electrician working on a panel, a homeowner replacing a light fixture, or a remodeler about to knock down a wall.

Two Testers Work Together

Every trade has special tools, and the more specialized the work, the more specialized the tools. Most residential electrical projects and basic troubleshooting work can be handled by two tools: a voltage/continuity tester and a noncontact voltage tester. Used together, these two tools can all but eliminate the chance of shock or electrocution. But there's a catch. The most-expensive electrical tester you can find—complete with beeps, flashing lights, and digital readouts—won't do you any good if you don't know how to use it. Take the time to read and follow the manufacturer's instructions. Also, no matter what kind of tester you are using, remember that batteries can die and leads can loosen or break, so always check the tester on a circuit you know to be live before getting started. It's also a good idea to send in the owner's registration card so that you can be contacted if there are any product recalls. Finally, please retire the tester if and when it is worn out or damaged.

Voltage/Continuity Testers Are Your Main Line of Defense

This tester indicates whether there is voltage on a wire or a piece of equipment. Most models indicate the level of voltage as well. You can buy voltage testers and continuity testers separately, but it's smarter to buy a tester with both functions so that when voltage is not detected, the tester will automatically switch to continuity mode (see "What is Continuity?" p. 259). Voltage can be considered the pressure be-hind electrical power, and it is always measured across two points: typically from hot (live) to ground, or from hot to neutral. Ground (also known as earth) potential is defined as 0 volts and is used as a point of reference.

The voltage/continuity tester has a pair of wire leads with insulated probes that terminate in metal tips. The probe tips are placed in contact with the points being tested, and if voltage is present, it will be indicated on the tester with a light, a beep, vibration, or a combination of these. A good tester allows you to slip one of the probes into a slot on the body of the tester; this way, you can read the results and keep your eyes on the receptacle at the same time.

The electrical aisle at the hardware store is likely to have at least a half-dozen voltage testers with a wide range of prices. I recommend that you avoid the very cheapest models because their leads are often short and poorly soldered. A midrange model will likely indicate voltage level and have better leads. A high-end model like the Vol-Con Elite shown below (www.idealindustries.com) will have replaceable leads and more testing functions.

When shopping for a tester, always look for an Underwriters Laboratory (UL) listing and a Category III rating, which ensures that the tester won't melt or blow up if it's accidentally exposed to a surge of high voltage.

Noncontact Testers Are a Great Sidekick, but Only If You Know Their Limitations

I often use a pen-shaped noncontact voltage tester in addition to a voltage/continuity tester. Why? It's

CAUTION: Before You Get Started

It's important to lock or tag out a breaker panel when you're working so that nobody mistakenly turns the power back on. You can purchase locks and warning tags, but at the very least, close the door of the panel and put a piece of tape across it that reads "Danger: Do not touch. Electrician working."

Voltage/
Continuity
Tester

small and fast, and it's able to detect an energized wire where a voltage tester can't. I typically use this tester to double-check the results of a voltage/continuity tester, or to check for voltage in a cable or wire where there's no exposed metal to touch the probes of the voltage tester. But this type of tester has some noteworthy limitations.

A noncontact tester works by detecting the difference in electrostatic charge between its plastic tip and the body of the person holding it. For instance, a wire or other object energized by AC-voltage usually has an electrostatic charge in it. You and your hand holding the tester usually do not. When you're holding the tester and touch it to an energized cable, wire, or other surface, a light goes on (or flashes), and a beep might sound. Some testers are more sensitive than others and could indicate voltage when held near, but not in contact with, an energized object. The VoltAlert tester shown at left (www.fluke.com) detects voltage without metallic contact. The important thing is to make sure the model you choose is rated Category III or higher.

If noncontact testers are so safe and easy to use, why not use them for everything? If you try to use the tool without being relatively well grounded, there might not be sufficient difference between you and the tip of the tester to trigger the voltage indicator. This can be a problem if you're holding the tester in a gloved hand, are standing on a fiberglass ladder, or are working in an area of low relative humidity (an attic, for instance). It's also a problem if you are working in tight quarters and your body is accidentally brushing up against the jacket of a live cable.

Also, unpowered cables or wires might show voltage when tested with a noncontact tester. That's because the tool could detect electrostatic charge that has bled over from an adjacent energized cable or wire, an effect called phantom voltage or ghost voltage.

Finally, a noncontact tester might not show that a cable is live if the cable is in contact with a well-grounded surface (lying on a concrete floor or in contact with a grounded metal surface, for instance). In this case, the electrostatic charge from the AC-voltage is bled off to the concrete floor.

In spite of these limitations, I still consider this tester essential. Double-checking results with a noncontact tester can save your life.

Test a Receptacle for Power

Receptacles are one of the most-common elements of a residential electrical system, especially because building codes require one every 12 ft. in most areas of a house. They also

What Is Continuity?

Continuity is indicated when an electrical circuit is complete. For example, if you touch the probes of a continuity tester to the terminals of a light switch, it should show continuity when the switch is in the "on" position, and no continuity when in the "off" position. I rely on continuity to verify that a ground and neutral are properly connected at the breaker panel, and therefore safe to use as reference points in voltage tests.

are a good demonstration of how the two voltage testers can work together to ensure that power is off and the box is safe to work in.

After I've shut off the breaker that I think is feeding power to the receptacle, I take a few seconds to check for voltage with a voltage/continuity tester while the receptacle cover plate is still in place.

To test for power, put one probe in the receptacle's taller neutral slot, then put the other probe into the hot (shorter) slot (1). If you get a no-voltage result, make sure the probes are in contact with the metal strips in the slot by moving the probes side to side in a slight arcing motion. If I get voltage at the face of the receptacle during any of these tests, I know that I've shut off the wrong breaker. So I go back to the panel, look for the correct breaker, then start again.

To test for correct grounding, I use the continuity function on a voltage tester (2). If the receptacle is wired correctly, the tester should indicate continuity between the neutral slot and the grounding hole because the neutral and the ground should meet at the service panel. If you get continuity between hot and ground (or hot and neutral), it means there might be a load on the circuit, like an incandescent light left in the "on" position.

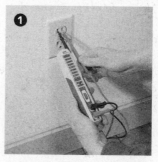
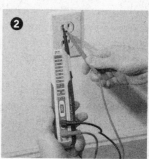

Noncontact Tester

Continued →

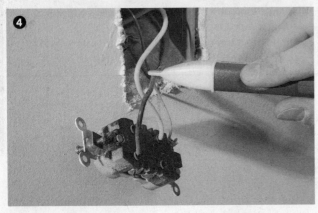

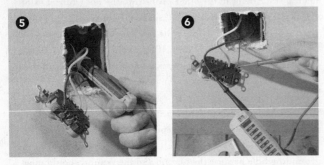

If I've gotten no signs of voltage so far, I can be 90% sure that the circuit is dead. But a noncontact tester has limitations that can lead to false-negative results, and I want to be 100% sure that the power to this receptacle is off before I handle the wiring (6). So I do one last check of each bare wire for voltage to ground, this time with a voltage/continuity tester. The ground reference in a receptacle box is typically either the grounding terminal or the neutral terminal on the side of the receptacle.

Testing Switches Is Different

There's a big difference between checking voltage at a receptacle and checking voltage at a switch: A switch has no neutral. There might not even be a neutral in the switch box, and if the wiring is old, the box might not be grounded. In the case of a switch, I use a noncontact tester to identify the hot wire and team up a voltage/continuity tester with a portable ground to determine whether there is voltage to the switch.

Unlike a receptacle, a light switch can't be checked for voltage with the cover plate still on. So after shutting off power at the appropriate breaker, remove the cover plate, and use a noncontact tester to check for voltage at each switch terminal.

If there's no voltage, unscrew and remove the switch from the box, treating it as if it is live (1). Then use the noncontact tester to check each terminal. Next, trace each wire back into the box to check for breaks in the wire, and rule out the danger of another unknown live circuit running through the box. Note: As shown at left, you might find a neutral (white) wire marked black to indicate that it is being used as a hot.

What if there are no terminals (2)? If the switch is old, the wires might be connected via back-wire holes. A non-contact tester will still indicate voltage through the wire insulation, but a voltage/continuity tester will need a bit of exposed bare wire to

If the voltage/continuity tester shows no voltage at the face, I unscrew the cover plate, remove the receptacle-strap screws, and carefully pull the receptacle away from the box for a closer look. At this point, I still am treating the receptacle as if it is powered. The receptacle face might be dead, but that could be due to an intermittent, poor connection to the receptacle, or a wire in the box could be live and loose.

To test for power inside the box, I use a noncontact tester (testing it first on a known live circuit) to touch each of the wires near the point where they land on a terminal or enter the back of the receptacle (3). Run the tip of the tester along each wire back into the box (4). You never know if a live wire is broken farther back in the box, sometimes inside the wire's insulation. Also, the noncontact tester alerts you to other live circuits that could be just passing through the box on the way to another box (5).

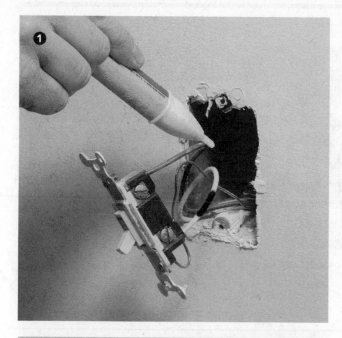

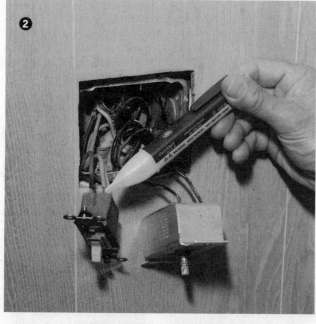

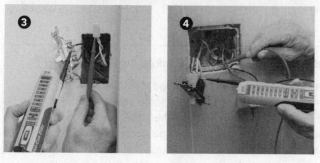

place the probes on. To do this, rotate the wire while pulling it out of the back-wire hole.

You might have noticed that the switch has two, or sometimes three, hot terminals. But you won't find a neutral terminal, and maybe not a ground. A noncontact tester doesn't need a neutral or a ground as a reference point, but the goal is to double-check results with a voltage/continuity tester (3). If the switch is in a metal box, that's a good candidate for a ground reference, but don't assume a metal box is grounded without checking first. If the box is plastic, you can probably still find two or more neutral (white) wires spliced together with a wire nut and tucked in the back of the box. If there are no neutral wires either, you will need to use a portable ground reference.

Metal boxes may not be grounded (4). Check for continuity between the metal box and a neutral (or a portable ground) before using it as a ground reference.

Most of the time, I'm working in an electrical box that has a neutral wire or a bare copper grounding wire, or the box itself is grounded. If installed correctly, any of these things acts as a ground reference when I use a voltage/continuity tester. But there are times when I don't have a nearby ground, as when there's an ungrounded switch box with no neutral in it, which is pretty common in a house 50 years old or older. To get around this, I use a three-prong extension cord plugged into an outlet in some other area that I know is properly wired and grounded. This way, I can insert the probe into the grounding hole in the end of the extension cord and use that as a reference point when testing for voltage.

Using a Voltage Tester

By Cliff A. Popejoy

Doing your own electrical work is satisfying, gets the job done on your schedule, and saves you money. That said, working with household current puts you within reach of a lethal dose of electricity. That's why it's essential to do electrical work with the power off. According to a government report, about one person dies every week in a construction-related electrical accident. To verify that power is off, use a voltage tester. Several different testers are shown here.

For basic wiring tests, I like a simple, rugged tester such as the Ideal Vol-Con Elite with shaker (www.idealindustries.com). This tester vibrates when voltage is present, help-ful even if I can't see the indicator lights. The Vol-Con Elite also has a noncontact tester that identifies live wires through insulation as well as a similar feature in which one probe discerns voltage in a single wire. I run into this frequently with knob-and-tube wiring.

When shopping for a voltage tester, buy quality. Look for an Underwriters Laboratories (UL) listing and a Category III rating, which means the tester won't melt down in the event of unexpected high voltage.

Continued →

Test Loose Wires with Clips and Caps

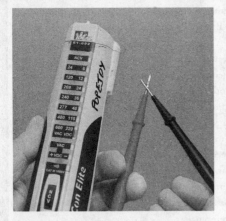

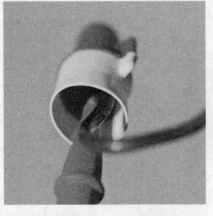

1. CHECK THE TESTER'S BODY, PROBES, AND WIRES FOR SIGNS OF WEAR. Turn on the tester, cross the probe tips, and shake the wires. The continuity light and buzzer should remain on. Last, check the tester on a known live circuit. If the tester isn't reliable, have it repaired or replace it.

2. DON'T HOLD PROBES ON LOOSE WIRES. Put a wire nut on the end of loose wires, and place the probe in the wire nut. Make sure wires are free of oxidation or crud to avoid incorrect readings.

3. USE AN ALLIGATOR CLIP on the neutral if you're checking voltage at several points, such as several hot wires to a neutral wire. This way, you can focus on the probe checking the hot wires.

A Few Simple Tests

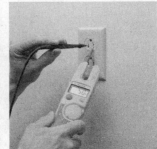

1. CHECK FOR VOLTAGE. Unlike plug-in testers, probe testers verify voltage both within the slots of a receptacle and on side terminals. Place one probe on the neutral (or taller) slot first, then on the hot (shorter) slot. The tester should read 120v. Remove the probes in reverse order. Hold the probes back from the tip to avoid shock if a wire moves or your hand slips.

2. QUICK RECEPTACLE TEST. Check for obvious problems in a grounding (three-hole) outlet by placing the tester's probe in the two vertical slots. The tester should read 120v. A properly grounded receptacle should read 120v with one probe in the shorter, hot slot and one probe in the grounding hole, as shown above. If these tests show no voltage, either power is not present, or the neutral (or ground) wire is interrupted or absent. .

3. QUICK RECEPTACLE TEST. Check for obvious problems in a grounding (three-hole) outlet by placing the tester's probe in the two vertical slots. The tester should read 120v. A properly grounded receptacle should read 120v with one probe in the shorter, hot slot and one probe in the grounding hole, as shown above. If these tests show no voltage, either power is not present, or the neutral (or ground) wire is interrupted or absent.

4. DEALING WITH PHANTOM VOLTAGE. Here's the situation: You think that you've turned off the correct circuit breaker, but a hot-to-neutral receptacle test reads 50v. If the circuit is de-energized, it should read 0v. Or, if the circuit is mislabeled and is still on, the tester should read 120v. You may be getting a false-positive reading, known as phantom voltage. Phantom voltage is caused by a live cable that induces a harmless voltage on a parallel de-energized cable. The simplest way to get a true reading is to use a solenoid-type tester, such as the Ideal Vol-Con Elite.

Two More Dependable Testers: Feature-Packed Or Simple

The Fluke T5-600 (us.fluke.com) is a rugged voltage tester with all the features of a multimeter. It checks for continuity, and it reads voltage, amperage (a built-in fork reads current through the wire's insulation), and ohms. The Greenlee GT-11 Non-Contact Voltage Detector (www.greenlee.com) does quick checks for voltage through insulation. I use it to double-check volt-meter results before touching a bare wire.

Common Wiring Mistakes

By Joseph Fratello

Whether to save time or money, lots of nonelectricians do electrical work. This is espe-cially true during the rough-in phase of new construction: drilling holes, running wire, and nailing up boxes. Remodelers take on tasks as seemingly mundane as installing a new light fixture. As an electrical contractor, I've hired many union and nonunion electricians over the years, and most were horribly misinformed about the electrical trade and the building codes. If professionals have a hard time keeping up with important details, I imagine that carpenters and do-it-yourselfers are going to have a harder time. Before tackling electrical work, you should be aware of a few things.

First, check with your local or state building department to see what licenses or permits are required. The National Electrical Code dictates minimum requirements for safe electrical installation, but local building authorities often impose their own codes. Second, in some areas, homeowners are not allowed to perform electrical work unless they are licensed or certified electricians. It's a good idea to check with your local or state building authorities before doing any work. In many instances, a homeowner can hire a licensed electrician who can pull a permit and supervise any rough wiring that the homeowner might do. Potential liabilities are involved (sidebar p. 265), but various resources clearly explain the correct methods that make electrical work code-compliant and safe. If you're ready to go to work, keep reading. The following is a list of mistakes to avoid during electrical installations.

Romex Needs Its Jacket Whole

On more than one occasion, I have seen wires punctured by a long fastener that missed its mark. When using nonmetallic sheathed cable (often referred to as Romex), you must maintain a 1¼-in. clearance from the edge of a stud to protect the wire from errant drywall screws or long trim nails. It's hard enough to fix the damage properly, but the risk that the damaged wire could remain unnoticed and start a fire inside the wall cavity is worse.

What can you do if you are working on a 2×4 wall and need to bring eight wires into a box? Cable Stackers, a 3M product (www.3m.com), hold up to eight wires and make it easy to position them correctly.

In some circumstances, you have no choice but to bore a hole closer than 1¼ in. from a framing edge. There, you must install a steel nail plate, either ¹⁄₁₆ in. thick or UL-listed for that purpose, to protect the wires from damage.

Keep Low and Line Voltage Apart

I often see two-gang boxes installed with a cable or phone jack in one half and a 120v outlet in the other. If an exposed conductor of a low-voltage wire comes in contact with 120v, the higher voltage can damage whatever is at the end of the low-voltage wire. A solid connection between the exposed low-voltage wire and a 120v wire also can cause the insulation to melt and start a fire. You can't run communication wires (phone, cable, or other low-voltage wires)

---

1. Protect Wiring from Nails and Screws.

PROBLEM There must be a 1¼-in. clearance from the edge of a wood-framing member to any wire to keep drywall screws and long trim nails from puncturing the insulation and causing a short.

SOLUTION Wiring passing through holes closer than 1¼ in. to the framing face must be protected with nail plates. Several runs of wiring can be corralled with inexpensive Cable Stackers, which maintain the distance mandated by code.

2. Don't Mix Line-Voltage and Low-Voltage Wires.

PROBLEM Parallel runs of line- and low-voltage wires cause interference in electronics and/or communication, such as TVs and telephones. Also, any uninsulated contact between low- and line-voltage wires in a box can damage equipment or cause a fire.

SOLUTION Maintain a minimum of 6 in. between parallel runs, and you won't have to shout over the phone. Don't bring low voltage and line voltage together in the same box. Instead, use separate boxes or a box that has an approved divider.

Continued ➜

3. Don't Stuff Too Many Wires into a Switch or Outlet Box.

PROBLEM Overcrowded boxes can overheat, cause insulation to melt, and potentially cause a fire. **SOLUTION** f the box is too small, use a larger box and a plate known as a plaster (or mud) ring.

into a box occupied by 120v or higher unless the communication wire or the box is rated for that use.

A similar situation concerns proximity. Phones, cable boxes, computers, and televisions all are susceptible to interference, a condition made worse when line voltage and low voltage are run parallel through the same hole. The extent of the interference depends on the quality of wire you use and the amount of current passing through the line-voltage wires. When I run low-voltage wires parallel to line-voltage wires, I fasten the low-voltage wires at least 6 in. away from the line voltage.

When you run line- and low-voltage wires in the same hole, you risk having the line voltage cross over into the low voltage, which can also cause a fire. One unfortunate incident I witnessed could have been easily avoided by keeping the wires separated.

A carpenter was adding extra bracing for floor joists in the basement of a house we had wired. As he was nailing, he didn't look to see what was on the other side of the joist. He drove a 16d nail straight through a 120v electrical line and into a thermostat wire that the HVAC contractor had run through the same hole

after the rough wiring was complete. When the 120v crossed into the thermostat wire, it destroyed the entire home-automation system, along with all the control boards for the heating and air conditioning. Although many people blamed the carpenter for the mishap, the HVAC contractor had violated the code and was responsible for the damage. The HVAC mechanic who ran the wire lost his job.

Overcrowded Boxes Can Start a Fire

When too many wires, outlets, or switches are crammed into a box, the heat generated doesn't have enough airspace to dissipate and in turn can melt wire insulation and has the potential to cause a fire.

The problem is made worse when you add dimmers to a crowded switch box. Dimmers generate a substantial amount of heat on their own; combined with the heat potential of the wires, a bad situation can be made worse. I've never seen a box catch fire as a result of being overfilled with wires, but I have seen a few melted dimmers. The next time you try to cram eight wires into a single-gang box, think about who would be responsible if the box caught fire.

The easiest way to learn how to calculate the maximum wire fill of any box is to use the NEC Handbook, which has a section dedicated to this subject; you also can read "More Wires Need Bigger Boxes" (*Fine Homebuilding* #144 or finehomebuilding.com).

Read Labels Before Installing New Light Fixtures to Old Wires

The last time you put up a new light fixture, did you notice the little tag on the fixture that says, "If your house was built prior to 1987 or has 60°C wiring, consult a qualified electrician"? Wire is rated for the safe operating temperature of the conductors. Newer light fixtures are made with 90°C wires, which means the wire inside the fixture is rated to operate safely at temperatures up to 90°C.

Problems occur when you connect the new fixture to old wires in the house. Most homes built before 1987 were wired with 60°C conductors; the new fixture can create heat that can overpower the

4. Use a Splice Box When Installing a New Fixture to Old Wire.

PROBLEM Because of compatibility issues related to safe operating temperatures, new fixtures can overload an older wiring system and cause a fire if improperly installed.

SOLUTION A splice box and a minimum of 3 ft. of new wiring should connect a new light fixture to a circuit wired before 1987. It's the preferable alternative to rewiring the entire circuit. Here's a good way to determine the wiring's age: Insulation jackets made after 1987 are stamped with the date of manufacture (inset photo right); those made prior to 1987 have no date.

older wires' capacity and possibly cause a fire.

A couple of solutions exist. The first option is to replace the old wire from the switch to the light with new wire. Unless you are renovating, however, that's not very attractive. The second option is far more common. If there is access above the light (in an attic or kneewall space), you can remove the wire from the existing fixture box and install it in a junction box. You can then splice on a new piece of wire (make sure it is the same wire gauge) and run the new piece from the junction box back to the fixture box. You should have at least 3 ft. of new wire from the splice box to the fixture box. By installing the new wire in the fixture box, you will be code-compliant and not have to worry that the new light will cause a fire.

Protect and Organize Wire Runs

In countless basements, I have seen tangles that resemble spaghetti hanging from the ceiling. Code says that you may not staple wires to the bottom of a floor joist unless the wire is 6-2, 8-3, or larger. Smaller wires must be run through bored holes or be attached to a running board. One reason you are not allowed to run wires across the bottom of floor joists is to eliminate the temptation to use the 12-2 wire for your kitchen GFI as a place to hang laundry. Current-carrying wires are meant to support only their own weight.

If a lot of wires are already hanging from the bottom of the floor joists, you can run the wires through raceways that fasten to the bottom of the joists. You simply mount a small plastic clip to every other joist; after you've run the wires through the clips, you snap a plastic cover over the entire assembly. The clips allow easy access if you need to run more wires. Some people might think that is expensive, but this product is a tremendous time-saver. Pulling wires through the clips is much easier than pulling wires through drilled holes, and you save time because you no longer need to drill all those holes in the floor joists.

5. Don't Use Wire Runs as a Clothesline.

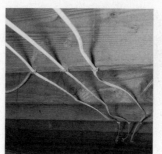

PROBLEM Wires are commonly stapled across the undersides of floor joists, where the wires are often used to support hanging objects.

SOLUTION When running wire through a floor system, drill properly sized holes, or use a running board that's at least a 1×4. Large runs of wire can be organized with raceways, a system of plastic clips (www.speedwayelectricalproducts. com) that support the wires. Removable covers look tidy.

Pull Wires, but Don't Burn Them

Specific rules dictate the number of wires you may run through a single hole. Various calculations are involved, but the NEC Handbook shows you the right way to calculate the permissible amount of wires. This mistake often goes ignored yet can lead to problems, one of which relates directly to a house's structural integrity.

Sometimes people drill four or five 2½-in. holes through the floor joists across the basement to bring all the circuits back to the panel. They then jam 20 or more wires into each of the

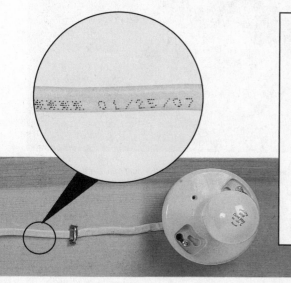

Know Your Liability

The biggest risk anyone takes is that their electrical work can cause a fire. In addition to possible injury and property damage, a fire is usually followed by the question of liability. Unless state or local laws dictate otherwise, when you perform an electrical installation of any kind, you are responsible for that installation for as long as it exists. It's fairly easy for a carpenter or a painter to replace an outlet, but if something goes wrong, the building department or the home-owners' insurance company will investigate to see who performed the work. Electricians carry liability insurance, but in most cases, a carpenter's insurance isn't going to cover your electrical work. If in doubt, have your work checked by a licensed electrician.

Continued →

6. Don't Crowd Holes with Too Many Wires.

PROBLEM Running too many wires through the same drilled hole can cause friction burns on the insulation jacket as the wire is pulled. Damage is often not visible and could cause a fire.

SOLUTION Check the NEC Handbook to determine the correct number of wires for a specific size hole.

7. Make Sure Recessed Lights Don't Become Fire Hazards.

PROBLEM Unless the fixture is rated for insulation contact (IC), there must be 3 in. of space between the fixture and any insulation.

SOLUTION If you retrofit non-IC recessed fixtures, secure the insulation so that it cannot spring back and contact the light after it's installed. .

8. Relocate Smoke Detector with Bad Placement.

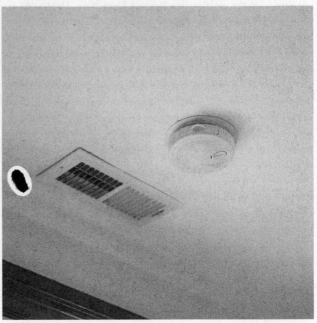

PROBLEM A common mistake is to install a smoke or carbon-monoxide detector too close to an HVAC duct.

SOLUTION The increased circulation around the duct can dilute air quality and fool the detector. Make sure there's at least 36 in. of space between the duct and the detector. .

9. Don't Bury Splice Boxes. It's Dangerous.

PROBLEM Splice boxes installed behind drywall are impossible to find and service. Problems such as short circuits might go undetected and cause a fire inside the wall.

SOLUTION Find a spot where the splice box is accessible and still not obvious. In kitchens, try mounting a box slightly above the upper cabinets. Unless the room is enormous, you will never see it. If the cabinets go to the ceiling, mount a box in the back of the cabinet; the only part you will see is a flat blank plate.

holes. Whoever is drilling the holes often doesn't take the time to read the engineered-lumber literature that outlines the proper locations and maximum sizes of the holes, which in turn can affect the building's structural integrity.

During the rough-wiring stage, I have seen five wires jammed into a ⅞-in. hole. This overcrowding causes burning, a term electricians use to describe the damage that occurs when the insulation of one wire is dragged across the stationary insulation of another wire. This dragging tears the insulation off the stationary wire. Subsequent runs can cover the burned wire, which can go unnoticed and leave exposed conductors inside the wall. I install a maximum of three wires per ⅞-in. hole, which leaves me plenty of room as I pull.

Insulate over Recessed Lights the Right Way

Unless recessed lights are IC-rated (insulation contact), you must keep 3 in. of space between the light and the insulation. When non-IC lights have insulation that is pressed up to them or over them, there are usually two outcomes.

The first is that the light works intermittently. Most recessed lights have a built-in thermal protector. When the thermal protector becomes too hot, it cuts off power to the light, which allows the fixture to cool down. This feature helps to reduce, but doesn't eliminate, the risk of fire. The lights blink intermittently, generating complaints that the light is wired incorrectly. Instead, there is a good chance that insulation is jammed against the fixture, causing the thermal protector to cycle on and off.

The second outcome is more serious. When thermal protectors fail (and they do), lights can become extremely hot, overheat, and cause a fire. For peace of mind, I buy IC-rated lights for an entire house; they cost only a few dollars more. Many code jurisdictions already require the use of IC-rated lights, so check with your local building department to see what type of lights you should use.

Smoke Detectors Require Their Space

Most builders either pay no attention to this code or don't even know it exists. Improper installation of a smoke or carbon-monoxide detector can interfere with the proper opera-tion of the detector. Air ducts can push or pull air away from a detector, which can delay the amount of time it takes for the detector to warn a home's occupants.

When you unpack a smoke or carbon-monoxide detector, it should have a diagram that indicates where you can and cannot locate it. The diagram should indicate the proper distance from the wall, the distance from air ducts, and the proper locations for installation on sloped ceilings.

Make Splice Boxes Accessible

I was once in a house where the previous contractor had buried a junction box. It took me hours to find the box, which cost hundreds of dollars. The customer was extremely lucky that the previous electrician used a metal box instead of a plastic box, because all the wires were melted in the box, and the beam that the box was connected to was charred. This house was close to catching fire.

Burying a splice box is a code violation, and is dangerous and inconsiderate to anyone who has to work on the house in the future. When a connection fails in a buried box, it can be almost impossible for an electrician to find it, unless he is the person who buried it.

If walls are open and you are running new wires, either replace the wire with a longer piece or install an accessible junction box. Most of the time, a single-gang box works. The idea is to be creative and find a place for an accessible junction box. It keeps you code-compliant and headache-free.

Continued ➜

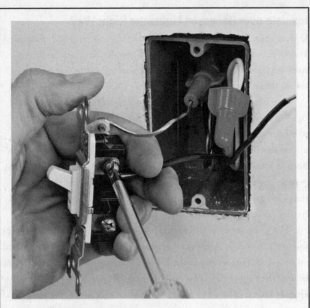

Work Safely with Electricity

Follow these steps, in order, to minimize the risk of shock or electrocution.

1. Identify the problem and the solution.

2. Identify the circuit(s) you need to work on, and determine the means for disconnecting the circuit (breaker or fuse). If the circuits are not identified in the panel, you'll have to do some testing to find out which breaker or fuse controls which circuit. Even if they seem well labeled, it's still prudent to do some testing to verify.

3. De-energize the circuit(s) by turning off the breaker or pulling the fuse.

4. Verify the correct circuit has been shut off by checking the wiring and fixtures on that circuit with an electrical tester. (See "Make Sure the Power Is Off," p. 258.)

5. Lock out the panel to prevent anyone from energizing the circuit while you're working. You can simply tape the panel door shut and mark it with a warning. Visit finehomebuilding.com/extras for a video demonstration.

6. Complete your work on the circuit.

7. Double-check to make sure the wiring is properly secured to the device (switch, socket, or fixture) you're working on, and the ground wires are properly attached.

8. Replace any cover plates removed during the work.

9. Re-energize the circuit and confirm operation.

Worry-Free Wiring Repairs

By Brian Walo

When I tell people that I'm an electrician, they always say the same thing: "I'll do anything but electrical work." It's true that working with electricity can be dangerous, but so can working with power tools or even a kitchen knife. The keys to being safe are following a few basic rules and knowing something about the fundamentals of electricity. Whether you're replacing a broken switch or outlet or

Replace an Outlet

Outlets (aka receptacles or sockets) are easily the most abused portion of a home's electrical system—constantly pushed, pulled, wiggled, and jiggled. If you suspect an outlet is bad, plug in a lamp and wiggle the plug around a little. If the light flickers, you've found the problem. After you've turned off the power and unscrewed the faulty outlet from the box, you're likely to see one of three configurations, depending on whether the outlet is in the middle or at the end of a circuit, and whether it's wired so

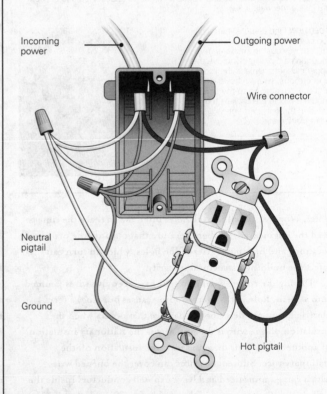

Incoming power

Outgoing power

Wire connector

Neutral pigtail

Ground

Hot pigtail

SPLICING WIRES WITH PIGTAILS (short wires) to the outlet ensures continuous current downstream even if the outlet fails.

updating a fixture, the procedure is basically the same—provided you can follow a few simple rules and pay attention to detail.

It also helps to know a little about electricity itself. The fundamental electrical concept that guides my work is that of the circuit. At its most basic level, electricity flows in a circle. A battery is a good example. Batteries have a positive and a negative terminal—an "in" and an "out" if it's easier to think of it that way. Looping a wire from one terminal through a lightbulb and back to the other terminal completes the circle and lights the bulb. Transfer that idea of a circular path to your home wiring, and you'll have a much easier time making sense of any repairs you need to make.

Home Electricity at a Glance

The conductor (wire) that supplies power to a switch, socket, or lamp is called the "hot" or "in" side of the power supply. It's typically a black or red wire and is a constant power source coming from the electrical panel to outlets, switches, and lights.

A hot conductor must be paired with a neutral conductor (wire) to make a complete circuit. Neutral conductors are generally white or gray and constitute the "out" portion of the circle. If you look at an

that power runs both through and past it (using pigtails; drawing left) or just through it (drawing center).

How-To

1. Plug in a lamp or use a tester to identify the proper circuit. (You might use nearby switches to determine if it's a switched outlet; see below.) Turn off the power, and check to be sure using a testing device.

2. Unscrew the outlet and pull it out of the box. If you haven't already determined whether the outlet is switched, check the side tabs now.

3. Once you've assessed the setup of the outlet, remove the wires from the terminal screws (or backstabs, if they're being used; see p. 271) and attach the new outlet in the same way. In a typical nonswitched receptacle, the green (or bare) ground wire goes to the green grounding screw; the neutral (white) wire(s) goes to the silver terminal(s); and the hot (black) wire(s) goes to the gold terminal(s).

4. Secure the new outlet and replace the cover plate.

5. Re-energize the circuit, and check your work.

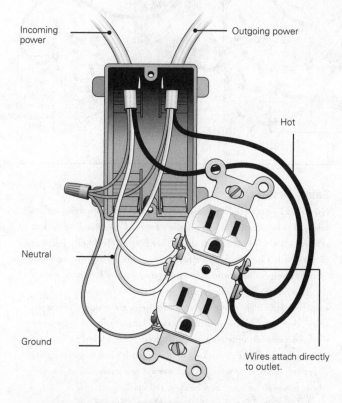

Incoming power — Outgoing power

Hot

Neutral

Ground

Wires attach directly to outlet.

Incoming power

ATTACHING HOT AND NEUTRAL WIRES directly to the outlet's terminals is quicker and results in a less crowded box, but if the outlet fails, it can interrupt power downstream.

AT THE END OF A CIRCUIT, there is only one cable coming into the box, and all wires are connected directly to the outlet (no pigtails).

Continued ➜

Swap Switched Outlets

Switched outlets are just that—outlets controlled by a switch so that you can plug in a lamp and use a switch to turn it on and off. Most homes have at least a few switched outlets for code reasons.

Most switched outlets have a constant power source on one half of the outlet and a switched power source on the other. The easiest way to tell is if you have two different color hot wires attached to the same outlet, and the little metal tab between the hot (gold) screws has been removed, enabling each outlet to operate independently. The drawing below shows one arrangement in which the switch controls only the bottom half of the split-tab outlet. The top half of the split-tab outlet and the next outlet in the circuit have constant power.

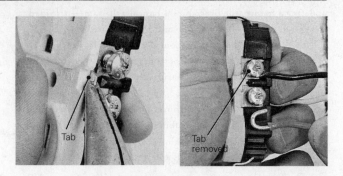

Tab

Tab removed

When replacing a switched out-let, you need to remove the tab between the hot terminals on the new outlet so that they can operate independently. Be sure to attach the hot wires as they were on the old device so that the same half remains switched.

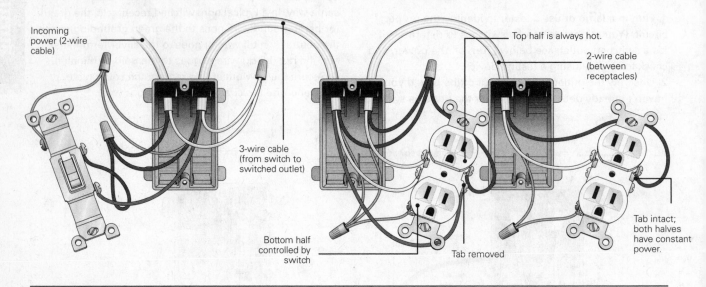

Incoming power (2-wire cable)

3-wire cable (from switch to switched outlet)

Bottom half controlled by switch

Tab removed

Top half is always hot.

2-wire cable (between receptacles)

Tab intact; both halves have constant power.

---

unplugged lamp, you can trace the path of electricity from the small end of the plug (hot/in), through the switch, through the bulb, and back to the large end of the plug (neutral/out). What this means is that every circuit in your house is really just a circle of energy.

Most residential electrical systems installed in the past 50 years also include a grounding conductor or ground wire. This additional wire helps to safeguard against electric shock or fire in the event of an electrical fault (any unintended discharge of energy, as when a loose wire contacts metal) by channeling that excess energy back to the ground and/or panel, where it should trip the breaker or blow the fuse. Grounding wires are generally bare or sheathed in green insulation and are not intended to carry electricity unless there is a malfunction. Never use a grounding wire in your home as a hot or neutral conductor because this incorrect usage presents a serious shock hazard.

Safety First—and Last

Now that I've covered the basics of how the system works, let's talk safety. I joked earlier about people's fears of electrical work, but in reality, a little fear is a great thing. My fear of electricity helps me to maintain a healthy respect for the systems I work on, and your fear will help to keep you safe by alerting you to potential hazards.

The number-one safety rule I stress with my coworkers is something my high-school driving instructor once said: "If you don't know, don't go." Know your limitations. Unless you know that what you're doing is completely safe, don't do it. That means turning off the power when you're working on a circuit. It's not worth the risk of getting shocked or electrocuted, even if you have to shut down the whole house to be sure the wires you're handling are off.

I always shudder when I hear people say, "It's OK—it's only 120 volts" when referring to the possibility of electric shock. Let me be perfectly clear: 120v household current can and will kill you if you don't protect yourself. The sidebar on p. 268 outlines the safe work procedure I use. I advise you to use it, too.

Another crucial safety rule is to follow any and all directions provided with the devices or equipment you're working on. Even the most basic electrical devices come with directions, so take the time to read through them before you start, and again after you're done to make sure you didn't miss anything. When I come across a problem in someone else's wiring, 99% of the time it's because someone didn't follow simple directions.

Common problems with light fixtures

The biggest mistake I find with light fixtures is that they aren't installed in a box: I remove the light, and there's nothing behind it but a hole in the wall with a wire dangling out. All electrical connections within the confines of your home should be inside an electrical box approved for that use. Boxes not only provide a means to mount fixtures and wiring securely, but they also shield framing and other combustible materials in the event of a failed connection.

The second most common problem I uncover is that most light fixtures are not grounded. I can't count the number of light fixtures I've removed, only to have the ground wire come leaping out at me. I can only speculate that a lack of understanding is what makes this such a common problem.

So, to reiterate: Make sure that all fixtures are mounted in a box, and that the fixture's grounding wire, if it has one, is securely fastened to the circuit's ground wire and to the screw on the fixture box, if it is a metal one. If yours is an older, ungrounded system (without a ground wire), use a replacement approved for ungrounded systems, or consult an electrician about installing a ground wire or adding GFCI (ground-fault circuit interrupter) protection to the circuit.

Tips for Trouble-free Wiring

MAKE A TIGHT CONNECTION To ensure strong connections, twist wires together before screwing on the wire nut. This is particularly helpful when wiring fixtures with stranded wire leads; the physical differences between stranded and solid wiring can make these connections tricky. When making a connection between one stranded and one solid wire, I like to make at least one full wrap of the stranded wire around the solid wire, leaving the stranded wire a hair longer than the solid to be sure the strands engage the threads in the wire nut when it's twisted onto the pair. If I'm making a connection between a stranded wire and more than one solid wire, I use pliers to twist the solids together in a group; then I wrap the stranded wire around the group before capping with a wire nut, again leaving the stranded wire just a little long.

MAKE A MAP Before disconnecting wires in an electrical box, draw a quick sketch of what you see (noting wire color and connections) or snap a digital photo. Taping and numbering wires also help to keep things straight.

WRAP IT RIGHT Always wrap wire around screw ter-minals in a clockwise direction (the same direction they will be tightened). This prevents the wire from backing away from the screw as it's secured.

BE CERTAIN ABOUT THE CIRCUIT Tracking down the breaker or fuse that supplies power for a given circuit can be tricky. If you're replacing a switch, leave the light on and flip the breakers until the light goes out (you may need a helper to watch for you). It's a fast, easy way to determine which circuit controls that light. If you're working on an outlet, plugging in a lamp or vacuum cleaner provides you with a visual or audible indicator.

BUY THE RIGHT DEVICE New outlets and switches are required to be marked permanently with amperage and voltage ratings so that you know what you're getting. Household switches

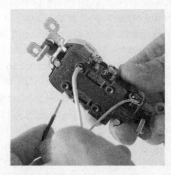

and recep-tacles typically operate on 120v current; most lighting circuits are 15- or 20-amp capacity circuits (you'll see the amps on the breaker or fuse). In most cases, the National Electrical Code allows for 120v/15-amp switches and receptacles on residential circuits rated up to 20 amps, so you really don't need more than basic 15-amp toggle switches and receptacles to be up to code. Some stores sell "heavy-duty" 20-amp devices for more money, but you probably don't need them unless you're replacing a 20-amp rated device or you like spending extra money.

AVOID "BACKSTABS" Push-wire slots or "backstabs" are holes in the back of a switch that allow you to push a wire into an anti-reverse terminal, making a connection similar to a Chinese finger cuff. I'm not a big fan of backstabs. I've repaired numerous problems resulting from them, so if possible, I move the wires from the backstabs to the screw terminals. If you are replacing an electrical device that has more than two conductors wired to it, you might still be able to avoid the backstabs by using pigtails or by purchasing a special screw-type backwire terminal. If you must use the backstabs, be aware that most of them accept only 14-ga. wire, so don't try to force 12-ga. wire into the hole.

Continued ➡

Replace a Three-Way Switch

Whereas a single-pole switch is one switch that controls one fixture, a three-way switch is used when two switches control the same fixture. It may seem counterintuitive to call them "three-way" because they work in pairs. The name refers to their operation, so don't let it confuse you. The wiring will do that.

One reason three-way switches confuse people is because they are wired differently depending on the relative position of the fixture(s) and the switches. But there are some common denominators. Three-way switches have three terminal screws: Two are typically brass-colored, and one is usually black or dark and labeled "common." The coloring and labeling are important because the wiring must be connected in a specific way for the switches to operate properly. The common on one switch is the "in" side of the setup from the power source, and the common on the other switch is the "out" to power the light. Two other wires, called travelers, run between the switches. Power on the travelers alternates depending on whether the switches they're connected to are off or on. If the sequence completes the circuit, the light is on. If not, it's off.

Below are three typical setups you'll find when replacing a three-way switch. All things considered, the key to a simple three-way switch (pun intended) is to distinguish correctly the hot (common) wire from the travelers and to route all three to the correct terminals. The best way to do this is to identify and mark the wires carefully before disconnecting the old switch.

How-To

1. Turn off power to all the boxes containing the switches. Three-way switches can be tougher to replace than single-pole switches because there are at least two boxes involved, and you need to make sure the power is off to all the switches in each box. Verify everything is off by using a testing device.

2. Remove the cover plate, typically with a 3/16-in. flat-blade screwdriver.

3. Unscrew the switch from the box and pull it out to access the terminal screws. Make a note of which wire is attached to the common terminal, and mark it. The common carries power either in to the switch or out to the fixture. The travelers' connections don't really need to be distinguished from one another as long as you know which two wires they are. Taping the two travelers together and leaving the common loose is another way to keep from getting confused.

4. Remove the wires from the screw terminals on the switch, and replace it with the new switch. Reattach the ground wire to the green ground screw; make sure the traveler wires go to the traveler terminals, and the common wire goes to the common terminal. See the drawings at right for additional wiring details that apply to your specific situation.

5. Replace the cover plate, and restore power to the circuit. Test the switch for proper operation.

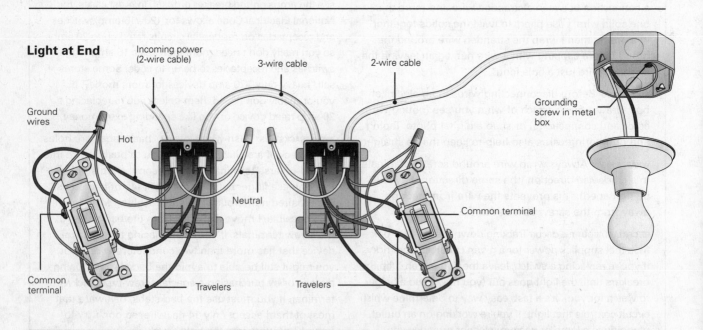

Light at End

Incoming power (2-wire cable)

3-wire cable

2-wire cable

Ground wires

Hot

Neutral

Grounding screw in metal box

Common terminal

Common terminal

Travelers

Travelers

Light First

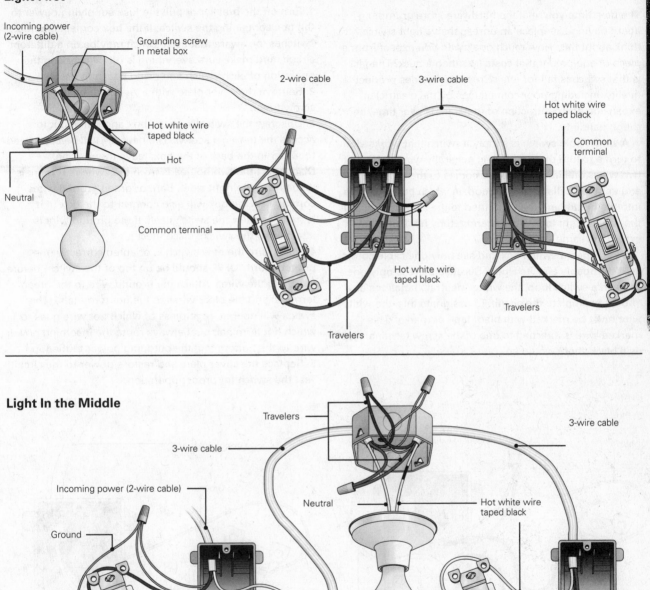

Incoming power
(2-wire cable)

Grounding screw
in metal box

2-wire cable

3-wire cable

Hot white wire
taped black

Common
terminal

Hot white wire
taped black

Hot

Neutral

Common terminal

Hot white wire
taped black

Travelers

Travelers

Light In the Middle

Travelers

3-wire cable

3-wire cable

Incoming power (2-wire cable)

Neutral

Hot white wire
taped black

Ground

Common
terminal

Neutral

Common terminal

Ground screw

Ground screw

Travelers

Travelers

Continued →

Replace a Single-Pole Switch

The next time you're at the hardware store grumbling about having to replace an unresponsive light switch, think about this: How much quality do you expect from a piece of equipment that costs less than a buck? The fact is that switches fail for lots of reasons besides product quality, including poor connections by the electrician, expansion and contraction of metal parts over time, and rough handling.

A single-pole switch is simply a switch that works alone to turn a fixture on and off. It is generally wired in one of two ways: one in which power comes to the switch first; and another, called a switch loop, in which power comes into the fixture and then is routed to the switch. Although the wires might look a bit different, they hook up to the switch the same way.

If you open a switch box and see only one cable coming in, it's probably a switch loop. Because there is only one cable in a switch loop, the white "neutral" functions as a "hot" to complete the circuit. To designate this, the white wire must be marked with black tape or marker. This marked wire is attached to one of the screw terminals just as a black "hot" would be.

How-To

1. Turn off the breaker or pull the fuse supplying power to the box containing the switch. If the box contains multiple switches, be aware that each switch may be on a different circuit, and make sure everything is off by checking the operation of each switch and using a testing device.

2. Remove the cover plate with a ³⁄₁₆-in. flat-blade screwdriver.

3. Unscrew the switch from the box and pull it out to access the terminal screws. The neutrals will be connected together in the back of the box; leave them alone. Disconnect the two hot leads from the switch's terminals (usually on the right side). Bare or green ground wires coming into the box will also connect to the box (if it is metal) and/or the switch itself. If the ground wire is attached to the switch, disconnect it.

4. Make sure the new switch is oriented correctly (the printed word "OFF" should be on top of the switch) before attaching the wires. Attach the ground wire to the green terminal and the black wires to the hot terminals. (The switch will operate regardless of which hot wire goes to which hot terminal, but I always route the incoming power wire to the bottom and the outgoing power to the top.)

5. Replace the cover plate and restore power to the circuit. Test the switch for proper operation.

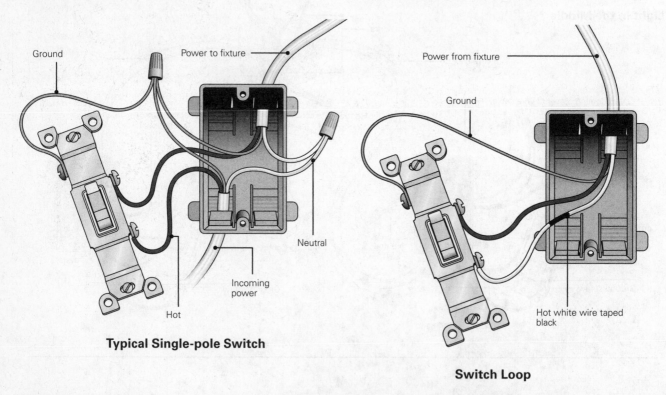

Ground

Power to fixture

Neutral

Incoming power

Hot

Typical Single-pole Switch

Power from fixture

Ground

Hot white wire taped black

Switch Loop

Replace a Light Fixture

Installing a new light fixture is about as straightforward a process as you will encounter when working on your electrical system. Perhaps because it's such a seemingly easy task, even the most electrically gun-shy folks I know will readily change out a light fixture. Perhaps that's also why, in the course of my remodeling work, most of the light fixtures I'm asked to change out are incorrectly installed (see "Common problems," p. 271). Considering that most light fixtures are conductive (metal) and a part of the system that you will have routine contact with (changing bulbs, dusting, etc.), proper installation, including grounding, is a must. If yours is an older, ungrounded system, be sure to use an approved replacement or consult a professional.

How-To

1. Always shut down power to the circuit the light is on instead of relying on the switch to determine that the power is off. With the numerous ways that wiring and switches can be configured, such as a switch loop, it's possible to have the switch in the off position and still have power in the fixture box.

2. Remove the old light, marking which wires attach to which colored leads on the old fixture. Install a fixture box if one does not exist. Your local home center carries a variety of "old work" box options (seemingly counterintuitive because it's a new fixture, but you're installing it into an existing or "old work" application).

3. Install the mounting bracket for the new light fixture on the box, making sure it's securely fastened and the screw studs that support it are level so that it won't hang crookedly. After the bracket is installed, hold the fixture up to it and adjust the depth of the mounting-screw studs so that they allow for a tight fit of the fixture to the wall.

4. Connect the fixture's wire leads to the appropriate leads in the box. The fixture's ground lead (if it has one) should be attached to the grounding wire and/or to the green-colored grounding screw on the box (if it is a metal one). Then connect the neutral (white) fixture lead to the neutral cable wire, and connect the black fixture lead to the hot cable wire.

5. Attach the light securely, re-energize the circuit, and check your work.

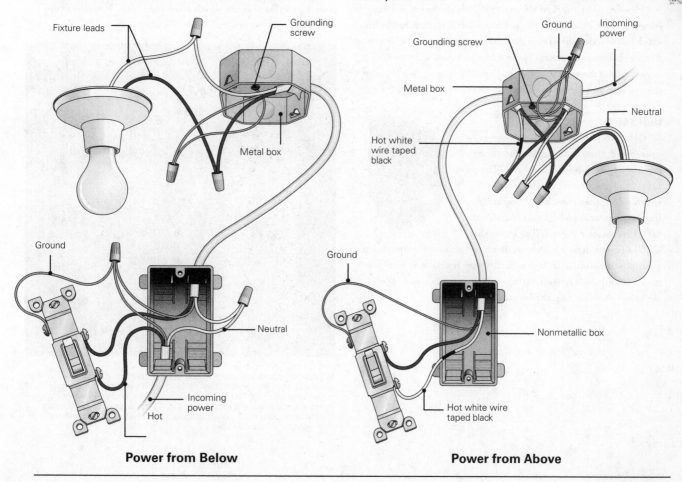

Power from Below

Power from Above

Continued →

Ground-Fault Circuit Interrupters

By Brian Walo

By constantly metering the flow of electricity between the hot and neutral conductors, a GFCI protects you from shocks by assuming that even a minor difference between the two conductors indicates a problem, triggering the device to shut off power. For this reason, GFCI protection is typically a code requirement for potentially wet areas such as bathrooms, kitchens, and outdoor areas, where the chances of electrocution are heightened. The two most common GFCI categories are receptacles and circuit breakers.

Receptacle

Oftentimes, a GFCI receptacle makes much more sense than a breaker. If you need GFCI protection for only one receptacle, say a new outlet on your porch, an inexpensive GFCI receptacle saves you money. And if you do need to protect several outlets, electrical codes allow for a GFCI receptacle to protect every downstream receptacle connected to it.

However, with shock or electrocution, time is the enemy. For instance, when a hair dryer plugged into a GFCI receptacle falls into a sink full of water, the disruption in the line has to travel only a short distance before being sensed by the device and cutting the power. Now consider the same scenario, but with 100 ft. of wiring between the problem and the device. Time may not be on your side.

Breaker

GFCI breakers connect to the circuit at its source and, therefore, protect the entire circuit. This can be good and bad. The good is that you can protect an entire circuit's worth of receptacles with one breaker, so the potential cost savings over individual GFCI receptacles is great. The bad is that GFCI breakers have a higher tendency to "nuisance" trip—due to poor power conditions, lower-quality wire insulation, or other non-ground-fault type situations—which means a trip to the electrical panel to reset the breaker.

Running Electrical Cable

By Andy Engel

When I was a builder, I wired all of my houses with my partner, an electrician. Of course, that doesn't fully qualify me as an electrician, but I know a bit about grunt work, such as pulling cable. Even something seemingly as simple as pulling wire through the framing goes better when you know a few tricks.

There's a difference between cable and wire. Wire refers to the individual conductors the electricity runs through. Cable is a group of wires wrapped in some sort of outer sheathing, usually vinyl. Electrical cable typically is composed of two or three insulated 12-ga. or 14-ga. copper wires, plus a bare ground wire. The name for this configuration is nonmetallic sheathed cable, or NM, or Romex, which is Southwire's brand of NM. A few jurisdictions require NM to be run in conduit, but most residential wiring is done with NM run through holes in the framing or stapled to the sides of framing members.

If not installed correctly, NM cable can kink and twist. Repeated bends at a kink can break the wire. Plus, kinky cable is much harder to pull through the framing. Finally, neatly installed cable looks professional and is easier to trace if you find yourself confused about which cable does what. With the proper technique, anyone can pull cable like a pro.

1. ALIGN THE HOLES. It's easier to pull cable if the holes through the framing are in a straight line. Eyeball the line, and use a consistent body posture to keep the holes aligned. Drill ¾-in. holes. Center holes in the framing members, and never drill closer than 2 in. to the edge of a joist or rafter. Put the holes about 1 ft. away from electrical boxes so that there's room to staple the cable near the box.

2. PREP THE CABLE. Before running cable through the framing, unroll 10 ft. or 20 ft. on the floor. This will prevent the cable from twisting and kinking as it would if you just pulled it off the roll. Although special tools are available for unrolling cable, you can simply unroll the cable using your arms like a football referee indicating illegal formation.

3. WORK CAREFULLY. Thread the cable through the holes, and give it a tug. Keep an eye on the cable roll; you may need to feed more out as you go.

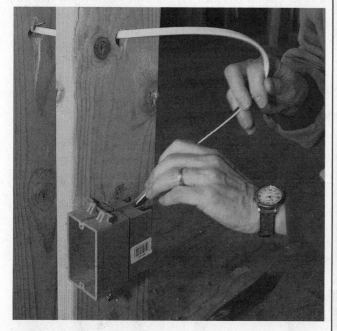

5. STAPLE WIRE FLAT. When cable runs along studs, joists, or rafters, keep it flat and neat, and staple it about every 4 ft. The maximum distance code allows between staples is 4½ ft. Don't damage the sheathing by driving the staples too hard, and keep the cable at least 1¼ in. from the edge of the framing.

6. KEEP YOUR WORK NEAT. You can arrange multiple parallel cables neatly using stackers. Stackers also provide airspace to keep wires from overheating and are especially handy near multiple-switch boxes and breaker panels.

7. USE NAIL PLATES WHEN NECESSARY. When a cable hole is within 1¼ in. of the edge of a stud, code requires nail plates to prevent drywall fasteners or finish nails from damaging the cable.

4. FEED THE BOXES. After running all the cables in an area, strip the sheathing back at least 6 in. (9 in. is better), feed the wire into the boxes, and staple the cable to the framing within 8 in. of plastic boxes and within 12 in. of metal boxes. Make sure there's no unsheathed wire outside the box.

Wiring Toolkit

Although pricey, a heavy-duty ½-in. angle drill is essential for running more than a few feet of cable. It fits between studs on 16-in. centers, and its self-feeding bits pull themselves through the wood, saving operator fatigue. You'll also need a cable stripper and lineman's pliers.

Milwaukee
3107 heavy-duty
right-angle drill

Greenlee
self-feeding
drill bit

Ideal
Lil' Ripper
Stripper

Klein lineman's pliers

Continued ➡

Nonmetallic Sheathed Cable Wire Sizes

By Brian Walo

You may know it as Romex or house wire, but nonmetallic sheathed cable (NM) has become a mainstay of residential wiring since it became available almost a century ago. NM is a quick, easy way to get power where you want it and is relatively cheap compared to other methods of wiring. The construction of NM has evolved from a braided-fabric outer jacket surrounding two conductors (no ground wire) into the color-coded, plastic-jacketed, multiconductor cable assembly we use today. Even with the emergence of color-coded jackets and the widespread availability of home-wiring "how-to" books, there is still some confusion on what size wire is required for a particular application.

Like other multiconductor cable assemblies, NM contains several insulated conductors housed in an outer jacket in a variety of configurations. The most common gauges include 14-, 12-, or 10-AWG solid copper in two- and three-wire configurations. NM is usually labeled by the gauge of the conductors and the number of conductors in the assembly. Regardless of the manufacturer, a label includes the wire gauge separated by a slash from the number of insulated wires in the outer jacket. For instance, 12/2 signals that two insulated 12-AWG conductors are housed in the outer jacket. All NM now has an integrated bare ground wire that usually is excluded from the description on the package. The versions of NM you'll most commonly need are a two-wire version for constructing basic circuits and a three-wire version that comes in handy for wiring three-way and four-way switches, switched receptacles, or a bath or ceiling fan with separate switches for the fan and light.

Because NM is generally used for wiring one- and two-family dwellings, the stock available at your local supplier likely has the most common wire gauges and configurations for residential circuits. Lighting and receptacle circuits in single-family dwellings have a maximum circuit capacity of 15 or 20 amps, which require 14-AWG or 12-AWG conductors, respectively, but most stores are likely to carry 10 AWG and even some larger gauges. The heavier 10-AWG wire is typically used for the loads that most water heaters, AC-unit compressors, and electric clothes dryers draw, and it is generally paired with a 30-amp-maximum fuse or circuit breaker.

Using a variety of wire gauges is crucial to safely managing the heat produced in the wire by the electricity as it flows, and each gauge is paired with an established maximum capacity for a fuse or circuit breaker. This pairing is important, because a circuit attached to a breaker that is sized improperly might serve as a gigantic heating element in your walls and give your fire department something to do for a few hours. You can always use a bigger wire than the code-required minimum, but you'll pay for it. For example, a 50-ft. roll of 10/2 is almost double the cost of a roll of 12/2 and nearly triple that of a roll of 14/2.

Most NM these days has a color-coded outer jacket: white for 14 AWG, yellow for 12 AWG, and orange for 10 AWG. This color-coding makes identification of new wiring easy, but it can lead to some confusion in older homes if you don't pay close attention to the existing wiring. I often find DIY-style wiring that has tapped into 12-AWG/20-amp circuits (which was encased in a white outer jacket for a period of time) with new 14-AWG/15-amp wiring.

Other mistakes made with NM are the result of using it in an application for which it is neither designed nor approved. Some of the more common are installing it outdoors, leaving it exposed to sunlight, and running it underground. For these places, UF-B is usually the best cable to use. Similar in construction and configuration to NM, UF-B is UV-resistant and can be run outdoors as well as directly buried in some applications.

14/2 With Ground
NM in a white sheathing is 14 AWG, suitable for 15-amp circuits.

12/2 With Ground
Yellow-sheathed NM covers 12-AWG cable, which can handle a circuit up to 20 amps.

10/3 With Ground
A 30-amp circuit needs 10-AWG conductors, which are contained in orange-sheathed NM.

Is Your Old Wiring Safe?

By Clifford A. Popejoy

Some materials used in old houses are better than their modern counterparts, like three-coat plaster versus drywall. When it comes to electrical wiring, though, older does not mean better. Electrical material sand safety devices have improved considerably over the past century.

Is old wiring safe? It may be. Or it may present a shock, electrocution, or fire hazard due to deterioration from age, poorly executed modifications, or lack of capacity to meet modern power demands. Older wiring that's in good shape, however, can continue to serve, and selective upgrades can be used to meet today's needs.

A visual inspection of the panel and exposed wiring is the first step in evaluating an electrical system. Although I can't possibly describe everything that could go wrong with old wiring and how to fix it, I can describe some of the signs of an electrical system that needs repair or replacement.

Get to Know Your Old Wiring

When electrical wiring first was installed in new homes, the wires were run on a series of porcelain knobs and tubes. In a knob-and-tube system, the splices were soldered and wrapped in electrical tape. Junction boxes, if there were any, were small.

Armored cable, or BX, also was used in early electrical systems. Originally designed to protect the wires inside, the armor also acted as the grounding conductor in later versions of the cable.

Loomex, a predecessor of the nonmetallic (NM) sheathed cable used today, became available in the late 1920s. Nonmetallic cable first had only two wires with a tar-soaked cotton jacket. Later, a grounding wire and plastic sheathing were added. The insulation on the wires was made more heat resistant in 1984. This cable, used widely today, is labeled NM-B.

When current travels through a wire, the friction creates heat that can damage the wire's insulation. Consequently, all wiring is protected by fuses or circuit breakers. In early electrical systems—5-, 20-, 25-, and 30-amp—Edison fuses provided this protection.

The second generation of over-current protection is the circuit breaker. A circuit breaker is a switch that senses when there's too much current and opens, interrupting the circuit. The advantage of breakers is that they can be reset after the problem has been fixed. If a fuse melts, it has to be replaced. When I inspect old wiring, I begin at the fuse box or breaker panel.

First, Inspect the Panel

As greater demands were made on old electrical systems, fuses would melt due to overloads. People often installed an oversize fuse, or installed a coin or metal slug to bypass the fuse and keep it from melting. When I evaluate a fuse box, I take out each fuse

Red Flags in the Fuse Box and Breaker Panel

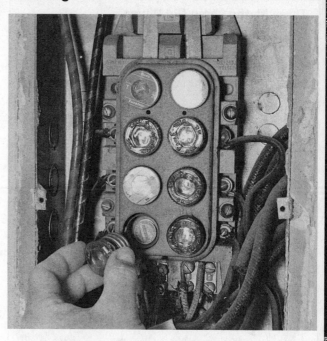

1. COINS OR SLUGS BEHIND THE FUSES. In this case, a penny is not a sign of good luck, but rather a sign that the wiring may have been damaged by the bypassed overcurrent protection.

2. HACKED PANEL COVERS. Circuit b. reakers are designed to work only in specific panels. To save money, mismatched and oversize breakers may have been installed, and the panel cover modified to fit

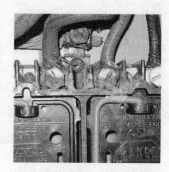

3. RUST. On screws, wire, armored cable, or the box itself, rust is a sign of deterioration. Rust can create poor connections and potential safety hazards.

4. MELTED WIRE. Exposed copper wire is dangerous because it can cause arcing, shock, and electrocution. Melted insulation is a sign of overheating.

Continued ➜

Three Myths About Old Wiring

The design, materials, and installation techniques of older wiring are very different from today's systems. As a result, there are many misconceptions about older wiring. Here are three of the most common myths:

MYTH #1 Knob-and-tube wiring must be replaced. When the opportunity presents itself—during a remodeling project, for instance—I usually recommend replacing old wiring. Some insurance companies won't issue new policies  or will charge higher premiums for houses with knob-and-tube wiring. However, if it is inspected, proves to be in good condition, and meets your needs, there is no reason to rewire your house.

MYTH #2 Old nongrounding circuits are unsafe. Most new appliances, lamps, and tools have two-prong plugs that don't need a grounded outlet. These two-prong plugs are double-insulated, reducing the chance of shock or electrocution 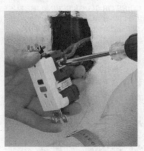 and the need for a grounded circuit. What is unsafe is using an adapter to make a three-prong plug work in a nongrounded outlet. If you need to plug in a surge protector or other grounded device, run a new circuit that has an equipmentgrounding conductor.

MYTH #3 GFCIs won't work with old wiring. A GFCI receptacle will work fine in an old electrical system even if the circuits don't have a grounding conductor. The GFCI self-test button will work, too. Because there's no grounding conductor, though, a plug-in continuity tester won't trip the breaker.

and look for a coin or slug. If I find one, I know the wiring on that circuit probably is damaged and needs to be evaluated further before it can he deemed safe.

Likewise, if I find a bunch of 30-amp fuses in a box, there is a good chance the circuits are overfused. Thirty-amp or larger circuits are used for 240v appliances or for subpanel feeders, so there should be only a pair of 30-amp or larger fuses for each of these circuits. I also check the gauge of the wires on each circuit to determine if the fuse size is appropriate. If the homeowner intends to keep the fuse box as the main panel or as a sub panel, I install type-S inserts before I replace the fuses. The inserts make it impossible to install oversize fuses.

Homeowners with newer electrical panels sometimes install oversize circuit breakers on overloaded circuits. Using the coffeemaker and toaster at the same time no longer trips the breaker, but it's likely that the wiring has been overheated and damaged as well.

I've also found electrical panels missing covers. This makes resetting a breaker unsafe. And I've seen the cover notched to accommodate a breaker not designed for the panel. This is dangerous because breakers and panels work together as a system, and only breakers listed for use in a specific panel are acceptable. If the cover is missing or has been hacked up, I buy a new one or have a new one made, replace the mismatched breaker, and carefully inspect the wiring for that circuit.

Inside all electrical boxes, I look for rusted metal, melted plastic, exposed copper on the hot and neutral wires, and loose connections.

Look for Failing Wires

After I inspect the fuse box or breaker panel, I look at all the accessible wiring, usually in the attic and basement. I check for signs of deterioration or of improper modification. If I find bare wire where the insulation has fallen off, or brittle insulation that will fall off soon, I know there's a risk of shock, electrocution, and fire.

I inspect modifications to knob-and-tube wiring. Original splices should have a neat layer of friction tape and should be supported by knobs on both sides. Nonoriginal splices should be made in electrical boxes. Open splices can fail and arc. The National Electrical Code (NEC) does not allow knob-and-tube wiring to be buried in insulation, although some jurisdictions do, as long as it has been inspected by an electrician and there is a sign warning that the wiring is present. (Go to www.finehomebuilding.com for more on old wiring and code issues.)

I begin my evaluation of armored cable at places where it's exposed to moisture because rust is the most common cause of deterioration. I also make sure the fittings that connect the cable to electrical boxes are not rusted or loose. Rust and bad connections impair the grounding path. If I spot rusted cable, I test the quality of the grounding path with a special tester. (Go to www.finehomebuilding.com for more on these testers.)

With NM cable, I first check to see if the sheathing is

deteriorating or has been chewed by rodents. Then I look in a few boxes to see how the grounding conductor is terminated. During the transition to grounded circuits, some electricians clipped off the ground wire or wrapped it back onto the sheath. If grounding outlets are installed in a system without a grounding wire, I replace the outlet with a nongrounded or GFCI (ground-fault circuit interrupter) receptacle.

Some NM cable installed in the 1960s had aluminum conductors. If I find branch circuits with aluminum wiring, I inspect all connections. Because aluminum expands and contracts, it can work itself loose. I make sure that all the switches and outlets are rated for aluminum wriring. I also look inside junction boxes and behind outlets and switches. Looking in these areas, I can tell if past electrical work was done properly.

Rewire or Upgrade?

After I inspect an electrical system, I have to decide whether to recommend rewiring the house or just doing selective upgrades. If much of the cable sheathing or conductor insulation is in bad shape, if there are no fixture boxes, or if testing shows poor connections, I recommend a rewire. If only one or two areas have deteriorating insulation and it looks as if the original installation and any modifications were well done, and the results of voltage-drop testing are acceptable, then selective replacement or upgrading is an option.

Folks often worry about nongrounded circuits. If wiring is in good shape and grounded outlets aren't needed—for three-prong plugs or surge protectors—these circuits are fine.

Older wiring and the small outlet boxes that often were used with it can be difficult to rework. If you need or want to add GFCI outlets, for example, you may find it difficult to install the GFCI in a small box without damaging the old wires. In this case, I install a junction box at a point where the original wiring is in good shape, and splice and run new cable to the outlet. If the outlet box is still too small, I remove the old electrical box and install an old-work box.

If a house's wiring is in good condition but is overloaded, adding a few new circuits is the best solution. Installing new circuits to serve the kitchen-counter and bathroom outlets, computers, dishwashers, and garbage disposals takes a significant load off existing circuits and costs much less than rewiring the house.

If I'm adding new circuits, I have to decide if the fuse box or breaker panel has enough capacity and breaker spaces to handle new circuits. If the service is an original 120v, 50- or 60-amp fuse box or breaker panel, or if I need to add branch circuits to a fuse box, I recommend upgrading to a modern panel and 200-amp service.

It is also time to upgrade the service when the load calculations show a demand larger than the existing service or when no space is available for new circuits.

Finally, if the panel is rusted or if the hot buses are badly

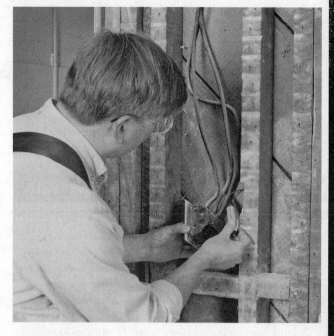

1. POOR ADDITIONS. Other than knob- and-tube, wires should be in a cable or conduit. Loose current-carrying wires are vulnerable to damage.

2. MISSING ELECTRICAL BOX. Switches, outlets, and splices should be installed with electrical boxes.

3. CHEWED CABLE. Rodents can be a problem with nonmetallic cable. Chewed cable should be repaired or replaced.

4. BAD CONNECTIONS. During an inspection, all connections should be checked. Because the armor on this BX cable acts as the grounding conductor, a bad connection means poor or no ground.

5. DETERIORATING SHEATHING. The insulation on old wiring can be brittle. Brittle insulation crumbles, exposing wires and creating a hazard. Small areas of deteriorating cable can be fixed; lots of deteriorating cable should be replaced.

Continued →

pitted, it's time to upgrade. If all you need is one or two additional 20-amp circuits, and the panel has capacity and breaker space, there's no reason to replace a panel just because it is old.

Looking at the condition of wires, and their supports and connections, is a big part of inspecting an old electrical system. If you inspect the wiring in your house and still have concerns, call an electrician who has expertise in old wiring and has the special equipment to test the safety and reliability of the circuits and overcurrent protection.

Running New Wires Through Old Walls

By Charles Bickford

Renovating a house is akin to surgery: calculated mayhem, followed by judicious repair and renewal. Sometimes the job is of the minor, outpatient variety, and sometimes the job is more like a heart transplant. Electrical renovations fall somewhere between the two extremes, not life-threatening to the patient, but tricky work just the same.

Like doctors, most electricians believe in doing no harm, at least as it applies to existing walls. (Why spend more time cleaning up and repairing the damage?) The veteran electricians I talked to all winced at the thought of making big holes in plaster walls, and only as a last resort would they remove baseboard or trim to run a wire. Instead, they'd rather practice noninvasive surgery and drill a series of holes hidden behind interior walls to create a new path for wire. The trick then is to thread a flexible rod, string, or steel tape back down that new path and use it to pull the wire through. Fortunately, the electrical code doesn't require that you staple these wires to the framing.

To learn about the art of snaking wire, I spent time watching different master electricians practice their craft. These guys rely on a number of special tools, many of which are explained here. But what really makes them successful are large measures of creativity, patience, and a thorough understanding of a particular house's structure.

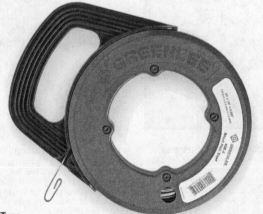

Fish Tape
Available in steel and nonconductive nylon, fish tapes are sold in sizes ranging from 25 ft. to 240 ft.

Start a Tiny Hole to Go from the Basement to the First Floor

1. Determine the position of the outlet or switch in the wall. To locate the corresponding spot in the basement, drill down in a convenient place (between two floorboards, for instance, or next to the baseboard) with an insulation batten. The long thin wire batten is easy to find and leaves a small hole that's easy to patch.

2. Downstairs, find the wall-plate location by measuring over from the protruding wire batten. (You also can find the plate by locating the nail ends that anchor the plate to the floor.)

3. From the basement, use a ¾-in.-dia. bit, and drill an access hole up into the stud bay.

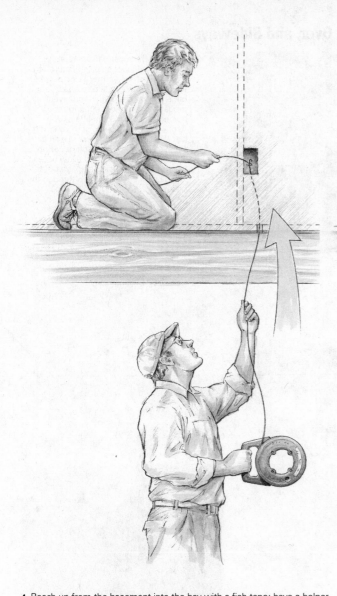

4. Reach up from the basement into the bay with a fish tape; have a helper grab the tape from above and pull up. Fishing longer runs may require repeated attempts to snag the end of the tape. Thin, flexible steel tape is the most common fishing tool. Many electricians cut two lengths from a reel, about 12 ft. and 2 ft. long, and use them for the majority of their work. The grabbing end of the tape is bent back onto itself into a hook. Another common method is to drop a weighted line from above down into the basement and reverse the procedure.

5. Once you've pulled the tape through, you have to secure it to the Romex. First, strip back the jacket about 4 in., cut the paper wrap, and trim back two connectors to the jacket. Now loop the remaining conductor (most contractors use the bare ground) through the bend in the tape, and tightly wrap the connection with electrician's tape. Don't be stingy with the tape (you don't want the fish tape and Romex to separate in the wall), but be sure that the electrical tape is smooth and won't get hung up as it passes through the wall.

"At the end of my Fish Tape, I Make a Half-dozen Loops of Twine and Tape Them Securely to the Tape Hook. Inserted Into the Wall Cavity, the Rat's Nest Increases my Chances of Grabbing It from the Other Direction."

—David Albanese, electrical contractor, Wind Gap, PA.

Continued ➜

Avoid Those Hot Wires!

by Clifford A. Popejoy

When you're blindly drilling holes through framing, you run the risk of drilling into an existing circuit, breaking a wire, causing an arcing fault, or worse, electrocuting yourself. Here are a few preventative measures:

• First, look for nearby outlets, switches, and fixtures, and estimate the wiring paths. For a house wired in cable (i.e., BX or Romex), most switches have cable running to the top plate; a ceiling fixture has a cable running to the switch that controls it. Receptacle outlets may have cable running to them from any and all directions.

•You also can get a stud finder that detects live wires behind drywall. However, I use a touchless AC-voltage detector that has adjustable sensitivity. It beeps at a rate determined by the sensitivity setting, and when you get close to the 60-Hz. electromagnetic field created by line voltage, the beeping rate increases.

• Of course, there's no detector for when a drill bit goes through a wall and into a television set. Mark the long shaft of your drill bit with white tape at 16-in. intervals. If you're not hitting a stud at the right interval or if you're hitting something too soon, stop and find out why.

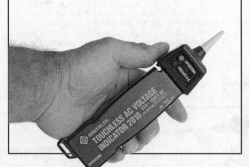

Going Up, Over, and Sideways

1. One of the most difficult snaking jobs is to connect a ceiling fixture to a wall switch when there's no access from above. In addition to a flex bit, extensions, and fish rods, you'll probably need to cut out and repair some drywall. To connect a ceiling fixture and wall switch, start by cutting box locations in both areas. Open an access hole at the junction of ceiling and wall, large enough to allow access to the top plate. Using a spade bit or flex bit, drill a ¾-in. hole up through the plates.

2. Depending on the direction of the joists, you may have an open run to the ceiling-fixture location, or you may have to use a flex bit to drill from the ceiling location across ceiling joists to the wall plate. Made for long-distance drilling, a common flex bit consists of a ¼-in.-dia. shaft that is 48 in. long, ending in a modified auger. Connected to a 48-in. extension, the bit can drill into framing nearly 8 ft. away. Flex bits are a little tricky to use because they can wander and pop out of the drywall sideways instead of drilling through their intended targets.

Flex Bits
These bits are available in bore diameters ranging from ¼ in. to 1 in., and in lengths up to 72 in.

48-in. extension

Fish Rods

When they have to push to find the hole they've drilled, especially in insulated walls, electricians go to the truck for these 4-ft. lengths of ¼-in.-dia. fiberglass rod. The rods can be screwed together for a longer reach. Like fish tape, they are connected directly to the wires with electrical tape. Some electricians prefer the thinner models made by Bergstrom for their flexibility.

3. Thread a fish rod from the ceiling-fixture location to the plate-access hole. Bring the Romex up from the switch location, attach to the tape, and pull it through.

Modified auger

Most flex bits have a small hole where you can attach a wire, then pull the bit and wire back through the holes you've drilled.

"If you want to add more recessed lights to a ceiling, first cut a hole for the new fixture. Then pull down a nearby existing fixture, drill through the joists into the desired bay, and fish the wire."

—Jason Zelek, Zelek Electric, Old Lyme, CN.

"When screwed together end to end, fish rods can loosen as you twist and push them. I duct-tape them together at the ferrules to keep them united."

—Mark Carlson, Roger Electric, Danbury, CN.

Continued ➡

Go Through the Top Plate to Get from the Attic to the Second Floor

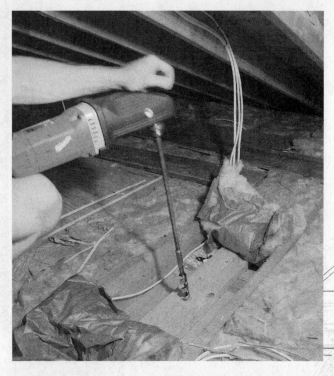

2. Drop a weighted line down through the hole from above, bouncing the weighted end off any obstacles until it reaches the opening below, where a helper can snag it.

1. In many ways, this method is identical to coming from the basement, except that it's upside down. Once you've picked a spot for the second-floor switch, for instance, use an insulation-batten wire to drill up from the ceiling below or to find the top plate upstairs by measuring from a reference point common to both levels. Drill a ¾-in.-dia. hole through the wall's top plate.

Weighted Line

One of the most common low-tech tools is a spool of twine that's weighted at one end, often with ⅜-in. nuts. Electrician David Albanese prefers cotton twine that terminates with 12 in. of sash chain; Karl Linck likes to weight the line with beaded chain. Both like the line weighted with chain because it flows easily over obstacles.

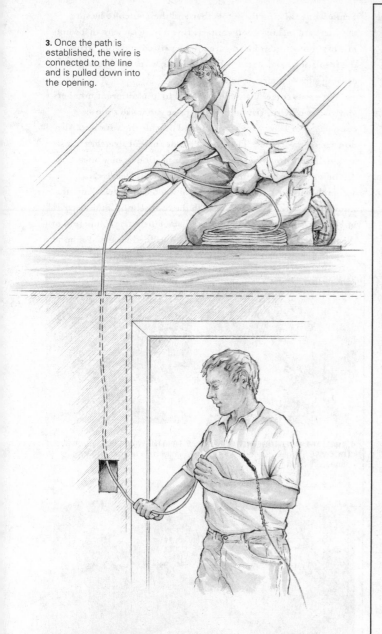

3. Once the path is established, the wire is connected to the line and is pulled down into the opening.

"I don't recommend running wires down beside a chimney in older houses; they sometimes have hot spots that could melt the plastic insulation and create a fire hazard."

—Karl Linck, electrical contractor, Kohler, Wis.

To Feed the Attic, Find the Path of Least Resistance

If you must run wires to the second floor, the easiest method is to pull them up from the basement to the attic and then rout them down. Overall, it's best to bring the wires up in the center of the house. Several options are available.

• In many houses, you can bring the wires up a plumbing chase.

• Building codes allow the use of the space around a chimney, providing it's modern construction.

• Snaking wires down interior walls is a possibility, but usually requires drilling down from the attic and drilling up from the basement to make the connection. Walls adjacent to a staircase offer possible routes as well.

• In older houses that are balloon-framed, the exterior walls often have no blocking and offer the easiest path. Modern platform-framed houses present a more difficult job; their exterior walls are not only insulated but also contain horizontal plates and fire blocking.

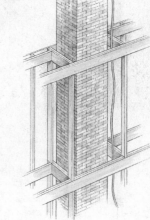

Plumbing chase

Space around a chimney

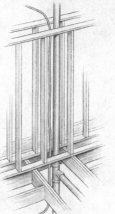

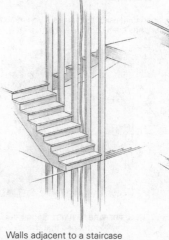

Walls adjacent to a staircase

Balloon-framing

Continued →

Splicing Wires

By Andy Engel

You might think that joining wires together in an electrical box is simple, but people get it wrong far too often. I'm not even talking about figuring out which wires attach to each other; I'm just talking about making the connections. One of the most common errors is when the bare ends of the wires don't make full contact. This often happens when more than two wires are joined, although it also occurs when joining the smaller, stranded wire of a light fixture to the larger-gauge main wiring. What usually happens is that one wire slides down onto the insulation of the other wires rather than their bare ends. This can prevent a plug or light from working. It can also cause arcing, which in turn can start a fire. To avoid this, you have to hold the wires firmly while twisting them together and then watch to be sure the wires are making good contact. If you notice a wire that's not making contact, it's best to snip all the twisted ends off, strip the insulation, and start fresh. Retwisting wires can break them, causing a broken circuit or arcing.

Wire nuts come in a variety of sizes to join different numbers and gauges of wire. Using the wrong size can make a loose connection or leave bare wire exposed outside the wire nut. Also, don't reuse a wire nut. The spring inside the nut stretches in use, and used nuts don't make as good a connection as new ones.

Before using a wire nut, take a look inside it. Debris can accumulate in the opening. A bunch of wood chips packed into the nut with the wires will interfere with the connection. If the electrical box is in a damp environment, put a dab of dielectric compound on the wires before twisting on the nut. This will reduce the likelihood of corrosion, which can also interfere with the connection.

1. EVEN THE ENDS. Hold the unstripped wires side by side as if you're about to twist them together, and trim the ends even using linesman's pliers.

2. STRIP THE WIRES. Remove about 1 in. of the insulation from the wires with strippers.

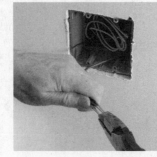

3. PREPARE TO TWIST. Gather the wires together so that the insulation is in alignment, and grab the bare ends with linesman's pliers.

4. TWIST THE WIRES TOGETHER CLOCKWISE. To make a good connection, twist the bare copper tightly, and wrap the insulated sections together two to three turns.

5. TRIM THE WIRE ENDS. Leave about ⅝ in. of bare copper showing.

6. ROUND THE TWIST. Cutting the wire ends leaves the group flattened, making it hard to fit into a wire nut. Lightly squeeze and twist the cut ends of wire to make them round.

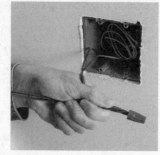

7. TWIST ON A WIRE NUT. Use the right size nut, and twist clockwise until it's firmly seated.

8. CHECK THE CONNECTION. The individual conductors shouldn't move when tugged, and no bare wire should show below the wire nut.

Know your wire nuts

There's a range of wire-nut sizes to fit the range of wire gauges and the number of conductors that might need to be spliced. Using too small or too large a wire nut can result in a poor connection or one where the bare wire is not enclosed within the wire nut, which increases the chance of a short circuit and of arcing. Read the information on the wire-nut packaging to be sure you've got the correct size.

In addition to size, wire nuts differ in other ways. Some, made for outdoor use, contain a glob of nonhardening silicone to keep water out of the connection. Others have wings on them to ease tightening, although the wings can make it harder to fit the wires back into a tight electrical box. If you encounter once-common aluminum wire, special wire nuts that contain an antioxidant compound allow you to splice it with copper safely. This matters, because oxidized aluminum-wire connections can lead to fires. Wire nuts for grounding conductors have a hole in the top for routing a pigtail to a ground screw.

| Winged wire nut | Grounding wire nut | Standard wire nut | Waterproof wire nut |

Problem-Solving Electrical Boxes

By George Socaris

When I started in the electrical business 30 years ago, only a few types of electrical boxes were available, most of them the same shape, just different sizes. Installing new electrical fixtures in older homes and accommodating untimely modifications in new construction demanded a lot of head-scratching and plenty of messy, difficult work with a reciprocating saw and other tools. Cramped spaces, absent framing members, varying wall thicknesses, and indecisive homeowners are just a few of the factors that made me wish for innovative solutions.

Legions of frustrated electricians are probably responsible for the boxes shown here. Today, I'm grateful for the time and trouble I can save if I have the right selection of boxes on hand. Among the many different types of boxes that are currently available, the ones featured here are my favorites, mainly because of how frequently they help me to solve problems quickly and cleanly.

Problem: Installing New Boxes in Old Walls

Snaking wires is tough, but retrofitting electrical boxes runs a close second, especially when space is tight and framing isn't in the right location.

Solution: Old-Work Boxes That Mount with Tabs, Brackets, and Toe Screws

If you can cut an accurately sized hole, these boxes retrofit easily in drywall, plaster, paneling, and cabinets. The ones shown here are single gang (i.e., designed for one switch or receptacle), but most come in multiple-gang form as well.

The rear tab flips up and pulls tight behind the drywall as the screw is turned.

An Old-Work Box Is Secured within an Opening in the Drywall Using Screws and Mounting Tabs

Once the opening is cut, insert the box, and turn the mounting screws with a screwdriver or a drill until the tabs tighten to the back of the drywall.

Front tabs at box corners rest on the finished wall surface.

Continued ➜

Toe Screws Are Built in for Easy Installation

Cut a hole in the wall at the edge of a stud, and this box goes in easily. Because the box is easy to move, it's also a great choice in new construction when homeowners are indecisive about fixture locations.

One side of the box is reinforced and has holes for toe screws.

Bring 14-ga. wire into the box on the shallow side and 12 ga. in on the deeper side where there's more room.

A Shallow-Depth Sconce Box Doesn't Mount to Framing

This box is ideal when mounting lightweight lights on the wall above a sink where you're likely to encounter a vent pipe. Run wire long in the stud bay, and cut a round hole in the wall. Then pull out the wire, and install it in the box. Insert the box in the opening, and turn the screws until the steel mounting bracket pulls tight to the back of the drywall.

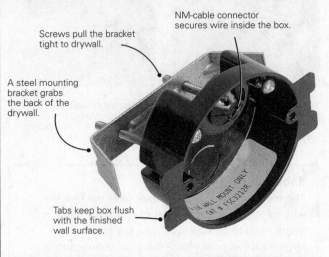

Screws pull the bracket tight to drywall.

NM-cable connector secures wire inside the box.

A steel mounting bracket grabs the back of the drywall.

Tabs keep box flush with the finished wall surface.

A Shallow-Depth Box Gains Space with a Side Compartment

Cut an opening for a single-gang box, and bring wires into the box through the side compartment. Replace the access panel, and tuck the box into the wall opening. Flip-out tabs pull the box tight to the wall.

Corner tabs rest on the finished wall.

Flip-out tab

Insert a narrow screwdriver to move tabs when they get stuck.

Removable panel provides access to wires during installation.

Shallower than a regular box, this box achieves nearly the same volume by being twice as wide.

Wall opening

Problem: Changing Wall Thickness Creates a Code Violation

The International Residential Code (IRC) requires that box openings come within ¼ in. of a finished wall surface, depending on the type of finished surface. A tile backsplash, wainscot paneling, or baseboard adds significant depth to wall thickness.

Solution: Adjustable-Depth Boxes and Box Extensions Bring Box Openings Flush with Finished Wall Surfaces

Using adjustable boxes when framing is exposed is the best approach. But box extensions are the right fix when the boxes already are installed and the drywall is up. These boxes come in multiple-gang versions as well.

Add nails or screws to rear tabs to keep mounting plate from twisting.

Turn the screw to move the box in or out.

An Adjustable-Depth Box Needs to Be Secured to a Stud Before the Drywall Is Installed

It is perfect for roughing in tiled or mirrored backsplashes, or for running outlets in baseboards.

Ears help the mounting plate clip onto steel studs or grab onto 2x framing.

A Box Extension Is Used When Wall Thickness Changes Around an Existing Box

The extension sits on top of the finished wall surface and slides inside the existing box. The outlet or switch is secured directly to the existing box using long screws.

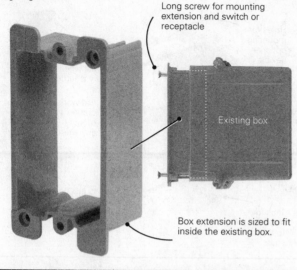

Long screw for mounting extension and switch or receptacle

Existing box

Box extension is sized to fit inside the existing box.

Problem: Fan Location Lands Right on a Ceiling Joist

For layout and design reasons, fans and other ceiling-mounted fixtures often end up in the path of a ceiling joist.

Solution: Boxes Designed to Be Secured Directly to Joists

Modifying the framing or installing shallow-depth boxes used to be the solution, but the boxes shown here offer a less invasive approach.

A Low-Profile Fan Box with Side Wire Compartments Fastens to a Ceiling Joist

The box slips into an accurately cut opening in the ceiling and installs flush with drywall. The side compartments provide added volume for wires.

Saddle design allows wire to enter box from both sides of joist.

Single-leg design

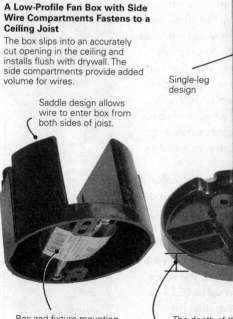

Box and fixture-mounting screws come taped in the box, so they're handy when the fixture is ready to be installed.

The depth of the round section matches the drywall thickness.

Metal-Sheathed Wire Requires a Metal Box

When working in old houses, I often encounter old metal-sheathed wire called BX (armored) cable. BX cable is used exclusively in metal boxes because its sheathing acts as the ground. A special clamp secures the cable to the box and engages the metallic sheathing, grounding the box and the cable. A new version of armored cable, called MC (metal clad) cable, also must be installed in a metal box. MC cable is secured in a box with a special clamp, but the box is grounded by a separate green grounding wire that attaches to a screw inside the box. MC cable is most common in commercial applications, but it is used often in residential retrofits when adding wire in a box that already contains BX cable. Nonmetallic cable can be used in a metal box that contains either BX or MC cable. However, the proper clamps must be used to secure the NM cable in the box, and the uninsulated ground wire must be attached to it with a grounding screw.

The aluminum wire found in older BX cable is wrapped around the metal sheathing. The clamp secures the wire and grounds the metal box.

Like NM cable, newer MC cable includes a separate ground that is secured directly to the metal box with a grounding screw.

Continued →

A Flush-Mounting Plate Fastens Directly to a Ceiling Joist on Top of the Drywall, Eliminating the Need for a Box

The plate becomes a finished part of a fan or chandelier's canopy. It also can work as an extension over existing ceiling boxes. Run wire through a hole in the finished ceiling, and insert it through a knockout in the plate. Secure the wire to the plate using the NM-cable connector provided.

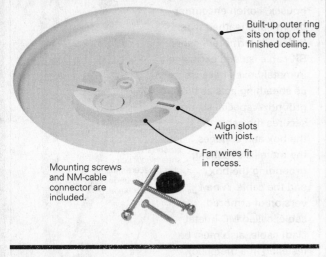

Built-up outer ring sits on top of the finished ceiling.

Align slots with joist.

Fan wires fit in recess.

Mounting screws and NM-cable connector are included.

A Low-Voltage Mounting Bracket Is the Simplest Solution for Securing Low-Voltage Cover Plates to a Wall

The new-work version can be mounted to a stud using nails or mounting tabs, while the old-work version can be installed in any wall surface at any time.

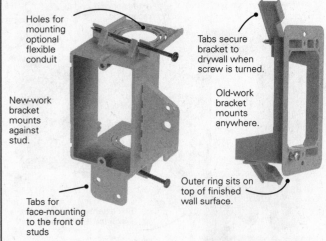

Holes for mounting optional flexible conduit

New-work bracket mounts against stud.

Tabs for face-mounting to the front of studs

Tabs secure bracket to drywall when screw is turned.

Old-work bracket mounts anywhere.

Outer ring sits on top of finished wall surface.

Problem: Adding Telephone, Internet, Cable, and Speaker Wire Near Outlets and Switches

Low-voltage lines usually need to be installed near standard line voltage that feeds switches and receptacles, but the two wiring types must be kept separate.

Solution: Boxes and Brackets That Secure Cover Plates but Keep Wires Separate

Two types of dual-voltage boxes are useful to have on hand, as well as dedicated low-voltage boxes suitable for new construction and retrofits.

Nails for mounting box to stud

Hole for mounting optional flexible conduit

Low-voltage side

Line-voltage side

A Line-Voltage Box with a Low-Voltage Side Bracket

These boxes are used most commonly for outlet/cable and outlet/Internet combinations. Either combination can be housed under the same plate.

In this box, line- and low-voltage wires can be housed in either side, or the box can be used with all line-voltage wire at a later date.

Removable divider plate keeps line and low voltage separate within the same box.

Don't Overstuff the Box

Just because wires fit into a box doesn't mean they're in there safely. Overstuffing a box with too many wires might not seem like a big deal, but it's actually a significant safety concern. Live wires generate heat, and that heat needs airspace to dissipate effectively. When there isn't enough "free air" to allow the wires to cool, they can overheat and cause a fire. To keep this from happening, each box comes with a volume rating stamped inside. That number refers to the maximum amount of space within the box that wires and devices like outlets or switches can occupy.

There is a formula to calculate how much volume wires and devices occupy, but the equation can become tricky quickly. Refer to section E3805.12 in the IRC for specific instructions. In the example to the left, the wires and outlet add up to 15.75 cu. in., which is less than the 20.3-cu.-in. volume rating for this box.

Each 12/2 conductor occupies 2.25 cu. in.

Combined grounds occupy 2.25 cu. in.

The receptacle occupies 4.5 cu. in.

Wire a Switch Box

By Brian Walo

Part of my job as a professional electrician is keeping my work neat and organized. A tidy work box makes it easier to install lights, switches, and outlets, and it helps future electricians to s_ what's going on inside the box. Inspectors look for tidiness, too because neat wiring makes short circuits and arcing less likely.

For me, part of being organized is maintaining some conventions with regard to how I run the cables into a switch bo_ When possible, I run the cable that's feeding power into the box through a bottom knockout. Cables going to lights or receptacle down line go through knockouts in the top. If there's an exterio_ light and an interior light in the same switch box (a common scenario at exterior doors), the cable closer to the door goes to the outside light; a cable farther from the door feeds the interio_ light.

Nothing in the code says you have to run specific cables through specific knockouts, and never assume that somebody else's wiring follows your conventions. Using your own conventions is simply a way to know what wires go where when you're looking at your own work, which is handy when you have make changes or troubleshoot down the road.

Finally, always check with a voltage tester to make sure powe_ is off to each switch (see "Make Sure the Power Is Off," p. 258). Some boxes contain more than one circuit.

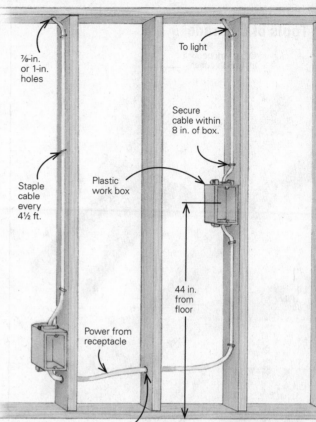

7/8-in. or 1-in. holes

To light

Secure cable within 8 in. of box.

Staple cable every 4½ ft.

Plastic work box

44 in. from floor

Power from receptacle

Holes 1½ in. from stud face

1. RUN THE CABLE. Cables running parallel to framing members should be stapled no less than every 4½ ft. near the center of the board. Although there are no hard-and-fast rules, be consistent with box placement. A distance of 44 in. from the floor works for adults, kids, and people in wheelchairs. Code requires that cables be protected from damage and installed in a neat or "workmanlike" manner. Keep the cable free of loops and twists to make pulling easier

2. LABEL YOUR CABLE. Untwist each cable, and label it so that the writing will be below the box when the cable is in the box and stapled. Although labels may seem like an unnecessary hassle, using them in boxes with multiple switches makes it easier to hook up the switches later.

3. BRING THE CABLES INTO THE BOX. A plastic box has tabs that secure the wires. The tabs are often connected to the box from the molding process. Pull up the tab a little bit with needle-nose pliers or a flat screwdriver, and give the cable a slight bend before pushing it into the box.

Electrical Systems & Lighting

Continued ➔

Tools of the trade

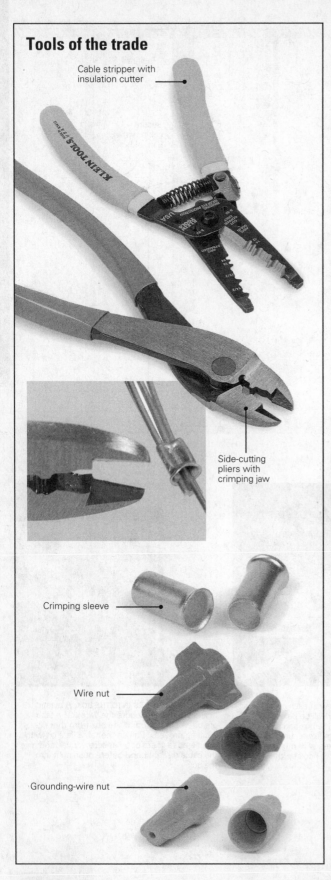

Cable stripper with insulation cutter

Side-cutting pliers with crimping jaw

Crimping sleeve

Wire nut

Grounding-wire nut

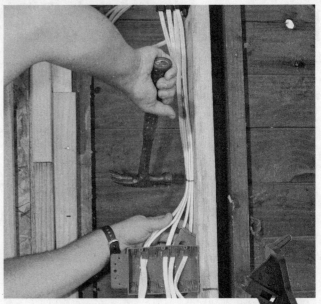

4. SECURE CABLES ALL AT ONCE. Make sure all the cables extend 3 in. or 4 in. beyond the front of the box. It's best to feed in all the cables, making sure they're neat and untwisted, and then to staple them no more than 8 in. from the box. A cable stacker is a great tool for arranging four or more cables.

5. PREPARE THE CONDUCTORS. With the wires in the box and secured with staples, clip off the labels with an insulation cutter, and tuck them into the knockouts where the cables enter the box. Remove the rest of the insulation by cutting it with a utility knife, starting about 2 in. from the end. (Be sure to cut away from yourself.) While holding the conductors, pull down the outer insulation. When you're done, cut off the insulation with side cutters, and slip the label on the cable's hot conductor.

6. Connect neutrals first. White (neutral) wires often are connected together in a switch box. Route them along the back of the box to a central location, cut them to length, and use wire strippers to expose about ¾ in. to 1 in. of copper conductor on each wire. Twist the conductors with pliers, trim the bundle, and cap it with a wire nut. Carefully fold the bundle so that it lies flat in the back of the box. Consult the wire-nut package for guidance on properly sizing wire connectors.

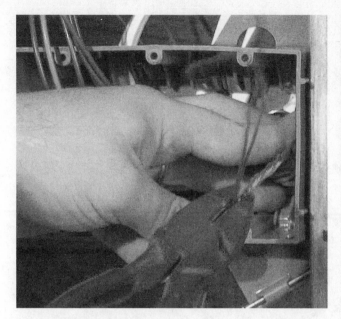

7. CONNECT GROUND WIRES NEXT. Run bare copper ground wires along the back of the box, and route them to a single point. Twist the wires together as a single unit, and cap them with a wire nut or crimping sleeve. Make sure there's a 4-in.-long length of wire (a pigtail) for every grounded switch in the box.

9. FOLD THE WIRES INSIDE. Each single-pole switch will have a pair (line and load) of black wires. Near exterior doors, put the black wire feeding outdoor light fixtures closest to the door. Carefully fold the wires into the box without tangling them. Push the wires to the back of the box so that they're not damaged during drywalling. When it's time to install the switches, pull out the black and ground wires, and connect them to their respective switch terminals.

8. HOT WIRES ARE LAST. On a single-pole switch, the black (hot) wire feeding power to the switch is connected to one of the terminals, and the load wire is connected to the other. You can have a single feed supply power to more than one switch by adding pigtails under a wire nut. The box also contains a cable for a three-way switch. Its red conductor is treated the same as the black conductors.

Electrical Terms

CABLE. A group of individual conductors bundled together for ease of installation. Most residential cable is wrapped in a flexible plastic outer jacket.

CONDUCTOR. Copper or aluminum wire that carries electrical energy. Most residential cable has two or three conductors and an equipment ground wire.

GROUND CONDUCTOR. Provides an alternate path to ground when an electrical component or system has a fault. More accurately described as an equipment ground, this conductor either is bare or has green insulation in a code-compliant installation.

HOT (UNGROUNDED) CONDUCTOR. A current-carrying conductor with electric potential relative to ground or neutral. Hot wires have black or red insulation in the most readily available nonmetallic sheathed cable.

KNOCKOUT. A prepunched hole in a switch box. The hole is connected to the box until it is knocked out for the installation of cable or electrical tubing (conduit).

LINE VS. LOAD. Line voltage refers to power coming into a device, like a switch. Load refers to power going out of the device.

NEUTRAL CONDUCTOR. Called a grounded conductor in the electrical code, a neutral wire is the return path back to the utility transformer and has white or gray insulation.

Continued ➜

Wiring a Single-Pole Switch

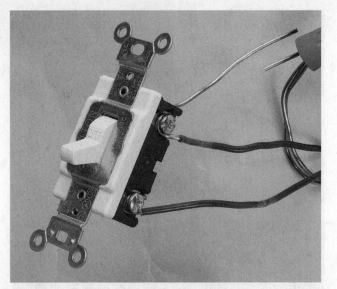

By Dave Balaban

Installing a single-pole switch is just one in a series of tasks that make up an electrician's work, but along with running rough wiring and installing boxes, it's a task that anyone can do and save some money in the process. When wiring a switch, there are two scenarios: You're connecting two feeds (one power, one to the fixture) or one feed (from the fixture to the switch). The tools you need are basic: Phillips-head and slotted-head screwdrivers, a pair of wire strippers, electrician's tape, yellow wire nuts (for two conductors), red wire nuts (for three conductors), lineman's pliers, and a utility knife. If you'd like more information on residential wiring, please consult Fine Homebuilding's online archive (www.taunton.com/store/fharchive) and Rex Cauldwell's book *Safe Home Wiring Projects* (The Taunton Press, 1997).

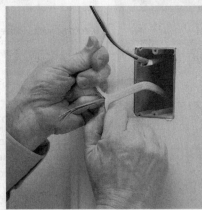

1. LEAVE YOURSELF ENOUGH SLACK. Pull 8 in. to 10 in. of Romex through the box, then trim it back to a 6-in. length, measured from the outside face of the box. The cutters on lineman's pliers cut cleanly and easily through Romex cable.

2. THERE ARE TWO WAYS TO SKIN A PIECE OF ROMEX, but here's the most foolproof. Make a shallow cut about 2 in. long at the end of the Romex. Now grab both black and white conductors, and pull them apart in opposite directions so that the jacket rips, continuing until the tear reaches the inside of the box. Now cut the jacket away, leaving about ½ in. inside the box.

3. STRIPPING THE JACKET WITH A KNIFE IS TRICKIER. Starting where the Romex comes into the box, carefully insert the tip of a sharp utility-knife blade into the jacket's center, and slice the jacket all the way to the end of the Romex. Trim the jacket away close to where the Romex enters the box and carefully inspect both black and white insulations for cuts. Any nicks should be covered completely with two wrappings of electrical tape.

Switch to a Dimmer?

Used instead of a standard switch, a dimmer gives you more flexibility in lighting control. Installation is often easier than a single-pole switch because many dimmers require wire nuts to connect to the power source rather than the screw terminals found on conventional switches.

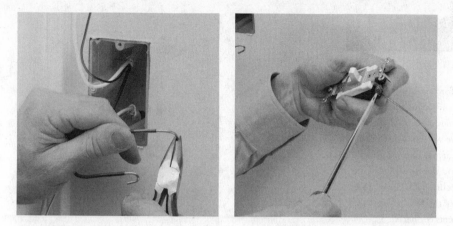

4. STRIP AND BEND THE HOOKS. Strip each wire's insulation back about ¾ in. Make an open-ended loop on the black wires with needle-nose pliers or wire strippers. Next, make a loop in a 6-in. length of bare ground wire, fasten it around the green screw terminal, and tighten the screw snugly.

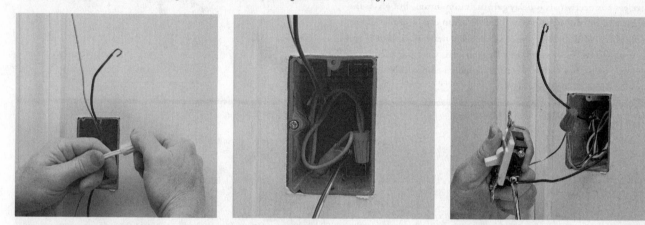

5. CONNECT THE PAIRS. With a yellow wire nut, join the white wires, then use a red wire nut to join the two grounds and a short length of ground that's connected to the switch. Gently push these sets into the back of the box. Now attach the black wire loops to the switch terminals. Always remember to wrap the wire clockwise around the screw so that when the screw tightens, it carries the loop with it.

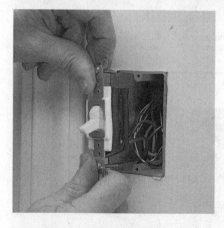

6. FOLD THE WIRES BEHIND THE SWITCH, NOT ON THE SIDES. After wrapping the switch body with a layer of tape, fold the black wires back into the box neatly, then push in the switch on top of the wires. Finish by securing the switch's screws to the box.

Indispensable Tool

If you watch late-night television, you may have seen advertisements that feature a guy yelling about some appliance that performs a host of tasks, all for an unbelievable price. You probably won't see this wire stripper from Klein Tools (www.kleintools.com), but it's worthy of a good yell: It's the tool you want when you're doing electrical work. Its jaws are gauged to strip five different wire sizes. They also can cut wire and bend hooks, and they have a serrated nose for gripping. The plastic-padded handles are curved for a comfortable grip.

Continued →

Multimedia Wiring

By Brian Walo

Because I'm an electrician, the responsibility for installing the wiring for the phone, TV, internet, home-network, and various audio systems often falls on my shoulders. I'm a big fan of technology, so this type of wiring tweaks my inner geek. These systems are radically different from each other, but don't be intimidated. Each relies on low-voltage wiring that is bought in bulk and can be routed through your house following a few basic guidelines. The only major differences are the terminations on each end of the various types of wiring, and subsequently how each of the systems connects.

Voice & Data

Video

Audio

Voice & Data

Wireless connectivity is quickly gaining momentum, but given the speeds and reliability with which information can be transmitted, Cat5 cable is still the workhorse of the data-networking world and has replaced two-wire telephone lines as well. Cat5 has become a generic term, but Cat5e, which is backward compatible, is the more common choice nowadays.

RJ45 Plugs

1. Untwist and arrange the pairs of wires in preparation for the fitting (see chart p. 299).

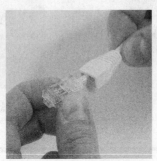

2. Slide all the ordered wires into the fitting at the same time, making sure that they are seated fully.

3. Insert the fitting into the crimper, and squeeze to secure the wires in place.

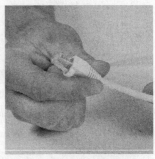

4. Slide the strain-relief boot in place to protect the wires from damage.

RJ45 Wall Plates

5. Use a punch-down tool to set each unstripped wire into the appropriate slot in the jack.

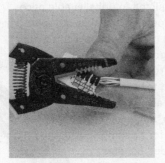

6. Once all the wires are inserted into the appropriate colored slot, snip off the waste.

7. Press down the included cover to protect and secure the wires.

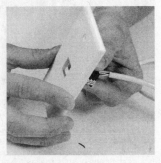

8. Slide the jack into the back side of a wall plate to finish the job.

Toolbox

Invest in a Set of Crimpers

Besides a pair of wire strippers that can handle small gauges (24AWG), Cat5 installations require crimpers to attach the RJ45 and RJ11 fittings.

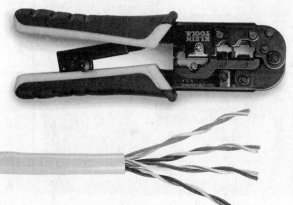

One Cable, Many Options

Each Cat5 cable has four pairs of color-coded copper wires (one solid, one striped). The cable can be used for phone or data; only the fittings and wire configurations change. RJ45 data plugs can be wired in two ways (T568A and T568B). Both configurations are compatible from cable to cable but must be kept consistent within the same cable. RJ11 phone fittings use only three of the four pairs, which is enough for three phone lines.

T568A   T568B   RJ11 plug

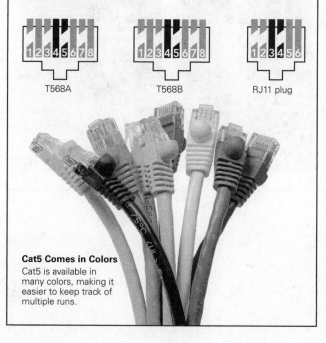

Cat5 Comes in Colors
Cat5 is available in many colors, making it easier to keep track of multiple runs.

Basic Phone Connections

Up to three separate phone lines can be carried by one Cat5 cable. Blue wires are often used for the primary phone line, but it doesn't matter which pair you use as long as it's consistent from one end of the cable to the other.

RJ11 Plugs

1. Untwist three of the four pairs of wires, arrange them using the chart (left), and clip the ends ½ in. from the sheathing.

2. Insert the ordered wires into the fitting; then secure them with the crimpers to complete the termination.

RJ11 Wall

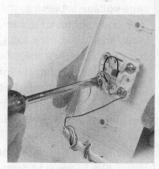

1. Strip about ½ in. off the sheathing on the pair of blue wires so that they can be wrapped on a screw terminal.

2. Attach the solid-blue wire to the red terminal and the striped-blue wire to the green terminal on the back of the jack.

Continued →

Don't Take Shortcuts When Running Low-Voltage Cables; Follow the Code

Although low-voltage wiring doesn't carry enough power to electrocute you, a sloppy installation can create nicks in adjacent low-voltage and line-voltage cables. This can lead to line voltages running unexpectedly through low-voltage cables, posing a serious risk of electrocution or fire.

STRUCTURED WIRING PANELS Structured wiring panels are a dedicated point of convergence for all your home audio, video, and data systems. These boxes are usually one part of a family of components designed to work together. My favorite system is OnQ, made by Legrand.

Traditionally, low-voltage cable is run from one jack to the next in a series, but a structured wiring panel allows for a better method of wiring. The "home run" method, which uses a single length of cable from the panel to each intended location, uses more cable and takes longer to install, but it greatly increases signal quality.

WATCH OUT FOR CROSSTALK Never run low- and line-voltage cables into the same workbox unless there is a code-approved divider. You also never should route low- and line-voltage cables through the same holes or share staples. If the cables became chafed during the installation, the low-voltage wires could present shock and fire hazards. Finally, maintain a gap between parallel cables. If they must cross paths, have them do so at a 90° angle to minimize overlap.

DRILLING HOLES IN WALL FRAMING Holes can't be larger than 40% of the stud depth in load-bearing walls (60% in nonbearing walls), or larger than one-third the height of the framing member. They can be anywhere along the length of a joist, rafter, header, or beam, but they must be a minimum of 2 in. from the top and bottom edges of the wood, and at least 2 in. away from any other holes. Any holes made at floor and ceiling levels must be sealed to create a fire barrier between floors, and any holes within 1¼ in. of the edge of the framing member must be protected with a ¹⁄₁₆-in.-thick metal plate to prevent damage from errant fasteners.

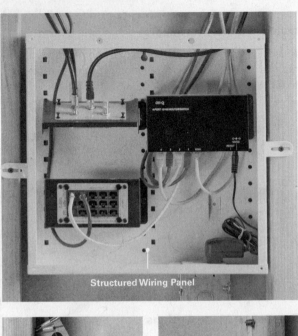

Structured Wiring Panel

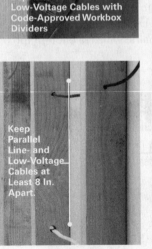

Separate Line- and Low-Voltage Cables with Code-Approved Workbox Dividers

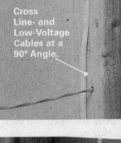

Cross Line- and Low-Voltage Cables at a 90° Angle.

Keep Parallel Line- and Low-Voltage Cables at Least 8 In. Apart.

Holes at Floor and Ceiling Levels Must Be Fire-Sealed.

Video

Coaxial cable has been around for a long time, and it is still the carrier of choice for both cable and satellite television feeds. Most installers have upgraded from the old RG59 coaxial cable to the thicker RG6. There are many variations, such as RG6U and RG6Q, but aside from features such as UV-resistance and slight differences in applying fittings, I treat all the RG6 varieties as equal.

1. Remove ¼ in. of the outer layers to expose the central copper conductor.

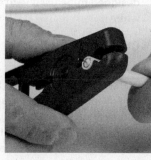

2. Carefully strip away ¼ in. of the outer jacket to expose the braided shielding.

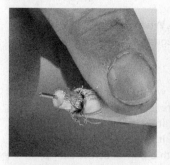

3. Gently fold back the braided shielding to expose the foil-covered white dielectric.

4. Slip the fitting over the stripped cable until it's flush with the receiving end.

5. Open the crimper tool, and insert the cable assembly into the handle.

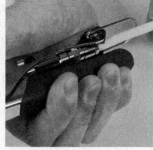

6. Squeeze the crimper firmly to compress the fitting onto the end of the cable.

Toolbox

Coaxial Tools Are a Must

Because coax is a wire within a wire and any connection must keep those two wires separate from one another, you need special tools that remove the layered material in stages. These two get the job done.

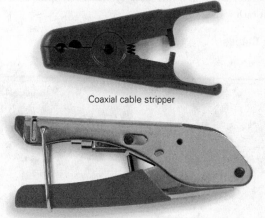

Coaxial cable stripper

Compression crimper

Four Fittings to Choose from

The standard fitting for coaxial cable is called an F-connector, and it is sold in a variety of styles. Whichever style you choose, make sure that it's designed for use with the cable you're installing. For instance, an RG6Q cable needs an RG6Q connector.

Twist and push-on

Both twist and push-on fittings are aimed at the do-it-yourself crowd because they can be installed without any special tools. Both are also difficult to use and are more likely to come loose.

Crimp

These connectors require a hexagonally shaped or similar crimping mechanism that equally distributes the pressure on the cable lines without damaging the cable itself.

Compression

By far the easiest to install, compression fittings are the least likely to damage the cable and are the only type I use. However, they require a special crimper (shown above).

Twist   Push-on   Crimp   Compression

Continued ➜

Audio

Almost every remodeling project these days includes some sort of audio wiring. Common requests are for simple things like running wires for the rear-channel speakers in a surround-sound setup. The tricky part of audio wiring is sorting out and keeping track of the components. Remember, no matter how complicated the installation, you're just connecting the dots between point A (the source) and point B (the speaker). Label everything at both ends of each wire as you go.

Audio Cables

1. Peel back the outer jacket, and strip ½ in. off the red and black wires.

2. Slip the base of the connector over the wire, leaving ¼ in. of copper exposed.

3. Fold the stranded wire over the tip of the base.

4. Screw on your choice of fitting.

Audio Wall Plates

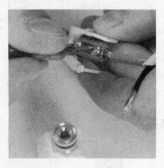

1. Insert ½ in. of bare wire into the back of each binding post, and tighten the set screws.

2. Snap the posts into the back of the wall plate.

Toolbox

Stranded Strippers

All that you really need for working on audio cable is a decent pair of wire strippers, but make sure they are designed to be used with stranded wire.

Choose the Right Wire Gauge

Rather than getting caught up in marketing hype, just check the output ratings for each of the speaker connections for all your equipment. The largest wattage rating for each run determines the wire size. Distance factors into the choice as well. Use 16-ga. wiring for runs up to 80 ft., 14-ga. wiring for runs between 80 ft. and 200 ft., and 12-ga. wiring for anything longer than 200 ft. When in doubt, step up the wire gauge to a larger size.

The Fuss Over Fittings

Leaving the ends of audio wiring bare is the simplest route. The only danger here is the potential for stranded wires to unravel and fray, leading to a poor connection or a short circuit. The other option is to terminate audio cables with a pair of screw-clamp connectors so that installation involves just sliding the stranded wire into the fitting.

Pin Connectors

A step up from bare wires, pin connectors provide a cleaner connection without risking frayed wires. They fit in both spring clips and binding posts.

Spade Connectors

The forked ends of these fittings slide around the sides of a binding post to provide a solid connection. If you choose them, make sure that the size of the spade matches the size of the binding post.

Banana Plugs

These are a popular choice because rather than being connected to a spring clip, they plug directly into the center of a binding post.

Pin   Spade   Banana

The Indispensable Digital Multimeter

By Brian Walo

If I had to carry only one device for electrical work, it would be a digital multimeter. Most of the other electronics I carry are adjuncts that do some of the same things a basic, quality multimeter can do. Available in various shapes and sizes, these fairly small, stout boxes consist usually of a display, wire leads that attach to the item being tested, and switches or knobs to choose between multiple metering functions—hence the tool's name.

The original multimeters were analog, and they used a needle and gauge (like a speedometer in your car) to give readings. Digital multimeters (DMMs) are now more common; they use an LCD screen to display readings with numerical values. Quality and functions differ from one model to another, and prices vary accordingly.

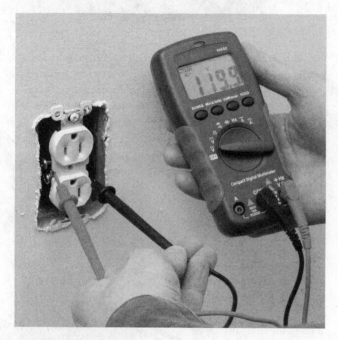

A Sparky's Sidekick

The quality of a digital multimeter (DMM) and the features it offers are going to play a driving role in cost, so you don't want to buy more meter than you're going to need. (The model shown here is an Amprobe AM-60.) I'm a tool junkie, so I understand the desire to buy the best. But even though all the available bells and whistles sound really cool, you probably won't need a DMM capable of measuring 1000 amps for your next remodel. Functions I consider useful but not strictly necessary are temperature and noncontact voltage detection. I wouldn't spend extra on a DMM with these functions because I have tools that do the same things and cost less. That said, there are some basic functions that are must-haves for residential work.

DISPLAY A simple lamplit display will get the job done, but if I had to buy a new meter tomorrow, I'd get one with a bright backlit or other high-contrast display, the bigger the better. Milwaukee's meters have a particularly nice white-on-black display.

MAX AMPS Since 400 amps is typically the absolute max for service to a residence in my area, I like a meter that can read slightly above that range, just to be on the safe side.

RANGING Changing the range of the multimeter allows you to dial in the precision of the readout. If you're measuring a 120v circuit, it's more helpful to have the range of the multimeter set between 0v and 200v than it is to have it set between 0v and 1000v. It's also a matter of safety, as setting the range too low could mean blowing a fuse in the multimeter. I prefer an auto-ranging meter so I don't have to think about setting the dial, but there are meters with both auto-ranging and manual-ranging functions.

CATEGORY RATING Developed to ensure that the right diagnostic tools are used for the wide variety of applications, category ratings appear on all multimeters, ranging from category I (cable, telephone, etc.) to category IV (commercial and industrial power distribution).

Category III is ideal for residential work and is approved for fixed installations such as residential panels, circuit breakers, wiring, receptacles, and fixtures.

DURABILITY Like any electronic device, a multimeter typically doesn't like to be dropped, rained on, or left in the sun. But Klein's MM500 meter is sealed completely against dust and water and is designed to withstand up to a 10-ft. drop.

ACCURACY Digital multimeters commonly have an accuracy of ±0.5%. Unless a multimeter is listed as "true RMS," it can be assumed to be an "average-responding" tool. Electricity travels through wiring in waves, so an average-responding meter essentially takes an educated guess at how much current is flowing based on

Continued →

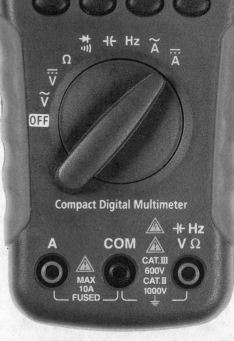

Compact Digital Multimeter

the assumption of a perfect waveform of electricity. True-RMS meters take actual measurements but are more geared for working with computers filled with semiconductors (or building a robot in your basement) than for doing residential electrical work.

LEADS Most, if not all, DMMs come with probe-tipped leads. Some more expensive models include alligator clips, which can be attached to conductors rather than having to be held in place.

STYLE Some meters include a split fork, a hook, or a clamp that allows you to measure the amps running through a wire or cable without having to expose the conductors. All three styles do essentially the same thing, but each has a niche. Fork meters can fit into tighter spaces, which is helpful when cables are run close together. Meters with hooks or clamps make hands-free operation easier.

Fork   Hook   Clamp

Three Key Functions

Even the most basic, dirt-cheap multimeter is designed to measure at least three fundamental components of electrical energy: volts, amps, and ohms. You can't get by without these three basic functions, and aside from the very cheapest of available options, which might not include an a.c.-voltage function, you'd be hard-pressed to find a meter that doesn't do all three.

If you think of electricity like water flowing through a pipe, volts would be like the pressure (electrical "psi"), the amps would be like the number of gallons per minute (electrical "volume"), and ohms would be akin to anything limiting water flow, such as pipe diameter or obstructions inside the plumbing.

ANALOG VS. DIGITAL I've used numerous analog and digital multimeters (DMMs). Each has its pros and cons, but I'll take a stout DMM over an analog model any day of the week. Because analog meters have moving parts that must be calibrated, they're more delicate and susceptible to damage from the rigors of job-site use. Also, unlike DMMs, analogs generally have to be set manually to a specific range for measurements, which can lead to incorrect readings or even damage to the meter if you're not paying careful attention to the settings or where the leads are plugged in. Still, it's worth noting that although DMMs offer more consistent results, they aren't always as true to reality as a comparable analog meter with similar specs. DMMs also can pick up "phantom" voltage— nonexistent voltage induced into a circuit by other nearby sources—that analog meters won't register. I'd still rather have a DMM, since they're easier for me to read and are less sensitive to the beatings I dole out every day. I've also found that you can get a good-quality digital meter with numerous features for less than a good-quality analog these days.

VOLTAGE Our appliances and devices are designed to operate at specific voltages, such as the 120/240-volt services supplied to millions of U.S. homes. Anything above that designed voltage can result in catastrophic damage, which is why surge protectors are so important for computers and other electronic devices. Voltage drop, which is when the voltage reaching a device is less than designated, is also a concern. This can be caused by bad wire splices or junctions, loose connections within the circuit or on the panel, oxidation or corrosion of a connection or conductor, wiring that's too small for the load being carried, and many other variables.

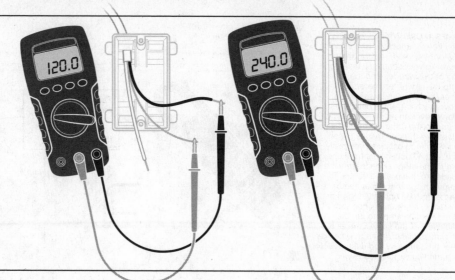

VOLTAGE IN USE: First, set your multimeter to a.c. voltage. Touch one of the leads to the neutral or ground wire*, and touch the other lead to the suspected hot wire. The meter will indicate what voltage is present within the conductors. A 120v circuit should read 120v between hot and neutral or hot and ground, and 0v between neutral and ground. A 240v circuit should read 240v between the two hot conductors, and 120v between each of the hot conductors and the ground. If the 240v circuit has a neutral wire (typical for appliances like ovens and dryers), you should get 120v between black and ground or black and neutral, and 120v between red and ground or red and neutral.

OHMS Measured in ohms, resistance is what slows down the flow of electricity and creates heat. Therefore, it's helpful to know what, if any, resistance is present in your wiring that should not exist.

Resistance can be created by anything that changes the characteristics of the device or wiring connected to it. For example, a staple that's overdriven to the point of damaging the wire, wiring that's too small for the breaker it's attached to, corrosion on conductors and devices, or poor connections can all lead to resistance.

Continuity is the ability of electricity to flow through a component. It's measured by way of the resistance of the wiring and/or device. A multimeter's continuity function can tell you whether there's a fault in a run of wiring, can be used to trace runs of wiring between workboxes, and can allow you to test the function of devices such as toggle switches, which have to be completely disconnected from all wiring.

AMPS While voltage remains more or less constant, amperage varies based on use. For instance, if you have a toaster plugged into the wall, your multimeter will show voltage running through the wire, but if the appliance is off, no amps will be flowing through the wire.

Amps are important because they measure how much electricity you're using when you turn on the oven or when the air conditioner cranks up. Having too many amps running through a circuit creates friction (resistance), which creates heat. If the breaker doesn't trip soon enough, a fire could start.

I use the amp function most often to balance the load in a breaker panel. If you have a lot of equipment on one leg of the service and the other leg isn't carrying anything, your neutral has to carry a more substantial load, which wastes energy and may create an overload. This is more of a problem with heavy 120v

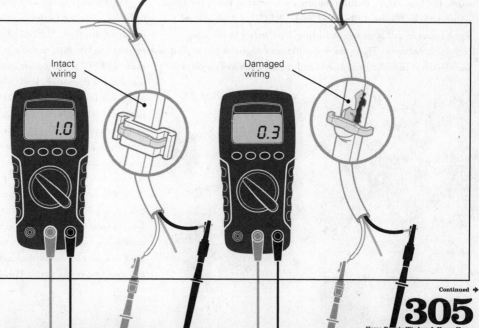

OHMS IN USE: To check a wire for a fault, it must first be completely de-energized and disconnected from all other wiring. Clip one lead to the hot conductor and one to the neutral conductor. As long as the opposite ends of the wiring aren't touching anything, most meters will read 1* (for infinite resistance) in a perfectly intact section of wiring. If you get a reading other than 1, there is something in that run of wiring that's bridging the hot and neutral. This could be an errant drywall screw or an overdriven staple that has damaged the insulation and allowed a fault in the line.

*Verify the reading in your DMM's manual.

Intact wiring

Damaged wiring

Continued →

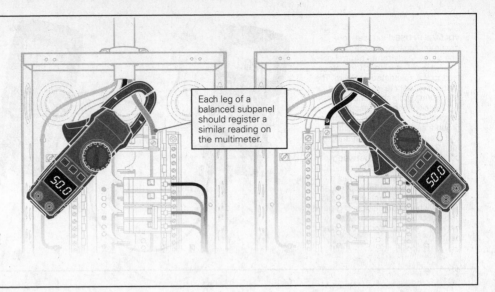

loads (such as those from a tablesaw or a window air conditioner) than for 240v circuits on a double-pole breaker.

If you expect to do this type of work, I recommend using a clamp-on meter because it allows you to check amperage safely without having to touch any exposed conductors.

Electrical Conduits

By Brian Walo

Electrical conduit is needed in certain locations to protect wiring from damage that can occur from drywall screws, abrasion, or UV rays, which degrade insulation when wires are run outside.

With several varieties of conduit available at most home centers and supply houses, it's essential to know the merits of each and what you can and cannot do with it. As with any electrical work, the best source of information about what to use is the latest edition of the National Electrical Code (NEC), and it's always a good idea to call your local building department to see what code(s) it enforces. There are two different categories of conduit for electrical installations: plastic and metal. Each has its place in the residential environment, and some jurisdictions require one type over another for a particular application.

Plastic Conduits

Rigid PVC pipe, electrical nonmetallic tubing (ENT), and liquid-tight flexible nonmetallic conduit (LFNC) are the most likely plastic conduits to be found in a residential setting.

Because it's approved for direct burial and—if it's a schedule-80 pipe—can be used to meet the NEC's requirement for "protection from physical damage," rigid PVC is run in most new underground service entrances to the electrical-meter enclosure. Sizes range from ½ in. dia. to 3 in. dia. for common residential applications. Rigid PVC is inexpensive; can be worked easily without expensive tools; and can be used in walls, outside in the sun, and underground. Connections are made with PVC glue. Rigid PVC can become brittle in cold weather, so check manufacturers' acceptable temperature ranges.

Most homes in my area have at least one 6-ft.-long "whip" of LFNC attached to the exterior air-conditioning unit. The major advantages of LFNC are that it's flexible, waterproof, and resistant to UV rays, making it safe to use outdoors. Because it's made of PVC, it can be cut easily. (I use a PEX-tubing cutter for this.) A few drawbacks limit its use: It tends to cost over twice as much per foot as rigid PVC, the cost of its associated liquid-tight fittings is relatively high, and it cannot be used where it would be subject to physical damage. However, it is easily the best choice for numerous applications for exterior work—such as with equipment near swimming pools and hot tubs—and its flexibility often makes it the only suitable conduit for a particular application.

ENT, or "Smurf tube" (nicknamed because of its light-blue color), is a corrugated, flexible PVC plastic tubing used mostly for dry interior work or in certain places, such as a basement or crawlspace, where moisture exists on the interior of a building. ENT is easier to install than rigid PVC, although it and its fittings are about twice the price. However, not all jurisdictions allow for

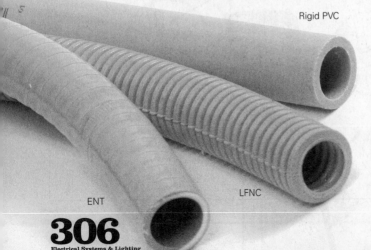

Rigid PVC

ENT

LFNC

residential wiring with ENT, and there are some places in a house where it cannot be installed—for example, it can't be used for exposed work, and with a few exceptions, it needs to be protected from physical damage. However, it can be encased in concrete and within slabs when the appropriate fittings are used, making it a viable choice for roughing in kitchen islands on a slab.

Metal Conduits

Most metal conduits are made of galvanized steel, but some types also can be found in aluminum. The most common steel conduits seen in a residential application, and the ones most commonly available from local home centers, are rigid metal conduit (RMC), electrical metallic tubing (EMT), flexible metal conduit (FMC), and intermediate metal conduit (IMC).

Size Matters

The last and sometimes most important consideration when choosing conduit is the size of pipe needed to run wiring safely. The size of each conductor (that is, each individual wire), the conductor configuration (stranded versus solid wire), and the type and temperature rating of the insulation on the wire itself (for example, THHN or XHW) determine how many conductors you can legally run through each pipe. There are a number of good reasons for playing by the rules here—most important, to avoid starting a fire. Running too many conductors through a length of conduit doesn't leave enough free airspace to allow the wiring to stay within an acceptable temperature range. This can cause overheating and degradation of the insulation. Because of the number of variables involved, you must consult code books to determine the appropriate sizing for your conduit installation.

RMC is the thickest, stiffest, and heaviest of the four and requires special tooling to bend and thread. Most homes in my area have only one run of RMC, if any, and it's used for the service-entrance mast that attaches to the electric-meter base. Given the amount of tension on the mast from the overhead service wiring, and the importance of protecting the service-entrance conductors from damage, RMC is clearly the pipe of choice for this application. However, all other applications within a typical residence can be done with another type of metal or plastic conduit, so RMC's further use is limited more to commercial and industrial settings. Most RMC is made of galvanized steel, but it is also available in aluminum.

FMC is a helically wound, flexible tubing most often made from aluminum. Because it cannot be used outside or in other wet locations, FMC is somewhat limited in its usefulness, but there are a few applications where it is the clear choice. For instance, most new direct-wire cooktops and ovens require a section of FMC for connection to a power source that can remain flexible during the actual installation of the appliance, and many furnaces and heat pumps are coupled to their disconnect with a short whip of FMC. For that reason, many newer ovens and cooktops come wired with FMC attached, and most home centers and supply houses stock at least ½-in.-dia. and ¾-in.-dia. FMC and associated fittings. It can be cut with a hacksaw, but specialized cutting tools are available.

EMT is a thin-walled metal conduit most often found in galvanized steel, but it's also available in aluminum. EMT is relatively inexpensive; can serve as protection from physical damage; and can easily be bent, cut, and installed with a minimal amount of special tools. EMT can be installed outdoors, provided all fittings, supports, and fasteners are made of corrosion-resistant materials. I often see EMT in older homes to protect the ground wire coming out of the meter base, but it can satisfy several other needs in residential construction and renovation. I have used EMT quite a bit as a means for protecting exposed wiring, such as on garage walls for new receptacles or light fixtures.

IMC (not pictured) is thinner than RMC, but thicker and far more rigid than EMT. It's rarely used in my area, but some electricians may choose it over RMC for its lower cost and lighter weight. It's code-approved for the same uses as RMC.

FMC

EMT

RMC

Continued →

Wiring a Master Suite Addition

By Clifford A. Popejoy

It's amazing how electrical-code requirements have evolved for the wiring in bedrooms and bathrooms, the rooms that make a master suite. These safety requirements are intended to protect against electrical fire in the bedroom when we're asleep and vulnerable, and against shock and electrocution in the bathroom where electricity and water can be a dangerous combination.

When I started working on this 350-sq.-ft. master-suite addition, I received an electrical plan that met minimum code requirements in most instances and exceeded them in others. After going over the plan and examining the existing electrical system, I explained to the homeowners how I would integrate the new and old wiring, meet all the code requirements, and add a few upgraded features that would improve the comfort and convenience of their new master suite.

Begin by Examining the Old Wiring

With the electrical plan in hand, the first thing I did on this job was to examine the existing wiring to determine two things: its condition and its existing capacity. (Go to www.finehomebuilding.com to read more about examining old wiring.) In any master-suite addition wired to meet National Electrical Code (NEC) requirements, chances are you'll need to add at least two new circuits. I knew that here, though, I would want to add more.

The main electrical panel was at the far corner of the house, and the existing subpanel was in bad condition. It didn't have a separate equipment-grounding conductor, which meant that there was no place to hook up the grounding wires from the new branch circuits properly; it also wouldn't accept the arc-fault circuit interrupter (AFCI) breaker required for bedroom circuits. These issues and the fact that the subpanel was failing, causing the lights to blink, simplified the decision to replace both the subpanel and the feeder cable that supplied power from the main panel.

If you decide to add circuits to an existing panel (main or sub), the first thing you should do is figure out what power is supplied by the panel (what the highest actual loads are) and compare it to the panel's capacity as marked on the panel label. If the panel is in good condition, has the capacity and the open breaker spaces, and will accept the necessary breakers, you're all set.

The electrical plan for this job included some features that exceed code minimums, including three-way switched outlets in the bedroom and three-way switches for the ceiling-fan light. It also left out a few requirements, including an outlet and a smoke detector in the hallway immediately outside the bedroom and an exterior light fixture near the east-facing entry door.

The homeowners suggested two additional outlets: one outside for outdoor tools and appliances, and one in the master closet for charging cell phones. I suggested two additional exterior light fixtures, one by each entry door; changing the 6-in. can light in the shower to two 4-in. lights; installing an additional recessed light in the bedroom; and putting in a phone line at the cable-TV outlet for TiVo (not shown on plan).

The power for a master-suite addition rarely can be pulled from existing circuits. Bathrooms require at least one dedicated 20-amp circuit that can serve either one bathroom's outlets, lights, and fan, or only the outlets for all the bathrooms in the house. The latter option is a poor choice; a hair dryer alone can max out a 20-amp circuit. Here, I added one circuit for just the two bathroom outlets.

The NEC has no requirement that governs how many circuits are needed for general-use outlets and lights in residential bedrooms. For receptacles in commercial buildings, there is a requirement to assume 180 volt-amps (watts) of demand per standard duplex outlet. This translates to 10 outlets on a 15-amp circuit or 13 on a 20-amp circuit. I like to use it as a rule of thumb in houses as well.

Editing an Electrical Plan

Electrical plans show approximate locations for outlets, lights, fans, and smoke detectors. The plan also shows how fixtures and outlets should be switched. Using the legend, you can decipher more information, including the type of light fixture or outlet to install. Before installing boxes or fixtures, make sure the plan meets local code requirements. Then, walk around and place the boxes and fixtures on the floor near their approximate locations. This will help you to identify problems with the plan. On this project, I made changes to bring the plan up to code, to make the addition more convenient, and to make an art niche more attractive. (Changes described in blue boxes; moved items highlighted in yellow.) What you won't find on an electrical plan is a breakdown of circuits or information on where to run cable.

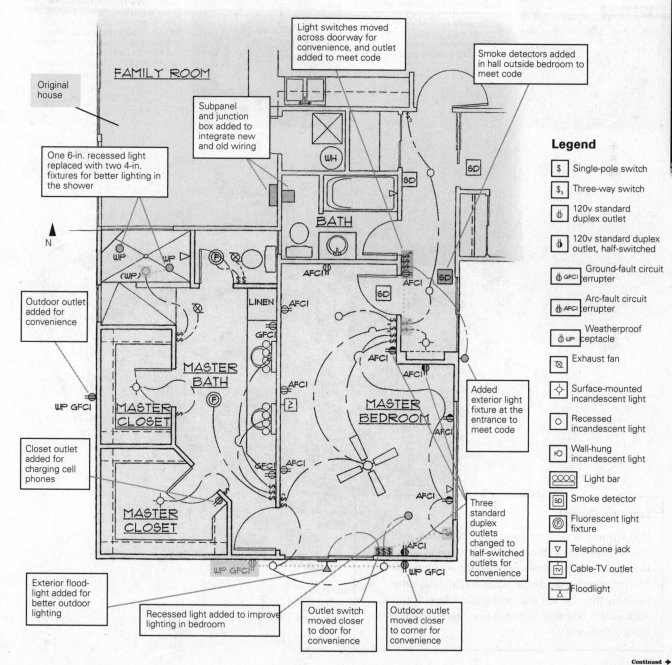

FAMILY ROOM

Original house

Light switches moved across doorway for convenience, and outlet added to meet code

Smoke detectors added in hall outside bedroom to meet code

Subpanel and junction box added to integrate new and old wiring

One 6-in. recessed light replaced with two 4-in. fixtures for better lighting in the shower

BATH

WH

N

WP   (WP)   WP

Outdoor outlet added for convenience

LINEN   AFCI

AFCI

GFCI

AFCI   SD

MASTER BATH

MASTER CLOSET

WP GFCI

Closet outlet added for charging cell phones

AFCI

AFCI

MASTER BEDROOM

Added exterior light fixture at the entrance to meet code

MASTER CLOSET

GFCI   AFCI

AFCI

Three standard duplex outlets changed to half-switched outlets for convenience

AFCI

$$$

WP GFCI   WP GFCI

Exterior floodlight added for better outdoor lighting

Recessed light added to improve lighting in bedroom

Outlet switch moved closer to door for convenience

Outdoor outlet moved closer to corner for convenience

Legend

$	Single-pole switch
$₃	Three-way switch
⊕	120v standard duplex outlet
⊕	120v standard duplex outlet, half-switched
⊕ GFCI	Ground-fault circuit interrupter
⊕ AFCI	Arc-fault circuit interrupter
⊕ WP	Weatherproof receptacle
⊗	Exhaust fan
⋄	Surface-mounted incandescent light
○	Recessed incandescent light
⊦O	Wall-hung incandescent light
〇〇〇〇	Light bar
SD	Smoke detector
Ⓕ	Fluorescent light fixture
▽	Telephone jack
TV	Cable-TV outlet
⊥	Floodlight

Use a Subpanel to Update an Old Electrical System

Adding a subpanel is sometimes the best way to integrate new wiring with an old electrical system. For this addition, a new subpanel was installed to replace an old, failing subpanel in a poor location. Here are some other circumstances where a subpanel can save the day:

• If the main panel doesn't have enough open breaker spaces for the new circuits.

• When AFCI breakers aren't available for an older electrical panel.

• If it's a long way from the new wiring to the main panel. Pulling one feeder cable would be more convenient than pulling several branch-circuit cables.

• If you expect to need more circuits in the same part of the house in the future.

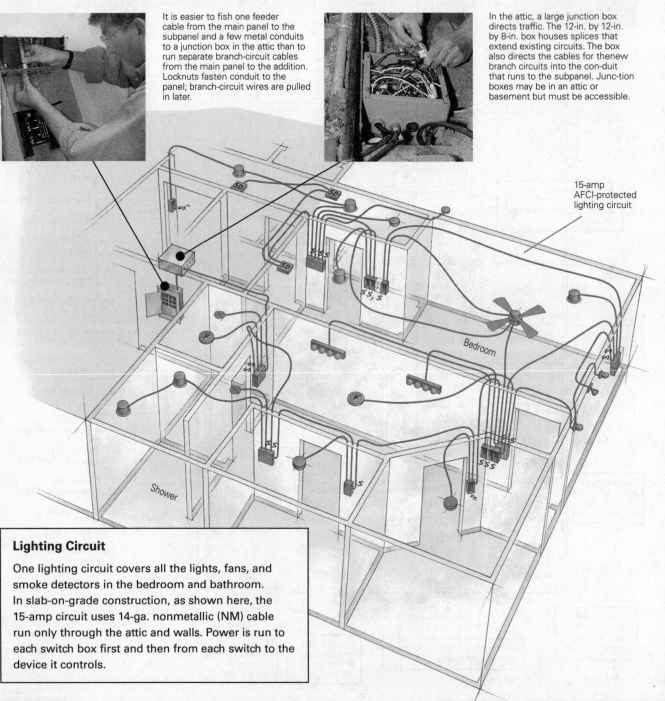

It is easier to fish one feeder cable from the main panel to the subpanel and a few metal conduits to a junction box in the attic than to run separate branch-circuit cables from the main panel to the addition. Locknuts fasten conduit to the panel; branch-circuit wires are pulled in later.

In the attic, a large junction box directs traffic. The 12-in. by 12-in. by 8-in. box houses splices that extend existing circuits. The box also directs the cables for the new branch circuits into the con-duit that runs to the subpanel. Junc-tion boxes may be in an attic or basement but must be accessible.

15-amp AFCI-protected lighting circuit

Bedroom

Shower

Lighting Circuit

One lighting circuit covers all the lights, fans, and smoke detectors in the bedroom and bathroom. In slab-on-grade construction, as shown here, the 15-amp circuit uses 14-ga. nonmetallic (NM) cable run only through the attic and walls. Power is run to each switch box first and then from each switch to the device it controls.

Including the outdoor outlets, the bedroom here has 13 receptacles. One 20-amp circuit might have been OK, but I wanted plenty of power available for large tools and appliances at the two outside outlets, so I separated the outlets into two 20-amp circuits. Finally, one 15-amp circuit supplies power to the bedroom and bathroom lighting (including fans and smoke detectors). Together with a dedicated circuit for a hot-water booster (not shown on plan), I pulled five new circuits. This is more than twice as many circuits as required by the NEC, with plenty of power to supply the additional lights and outlets without causing future overloading problems.

Avoid a Shock in the Bathroom

Outlets in the bathroom must have ground-fault circuit interrupter (GFCI) protection because of their proximity to water sources. GFCIs trip when they detect current leaking out of the circuit, which can cause shock or electrocution. This can be done with a GFCI breaker in the panel or with GFCI outlets in the bathroom.

To me, GFCI outlets make more sense than GFCI breakers because they are more convenient to reset when they trip. And they will trip sooner or later, if not because of dangerous current leakage, then because of humidity and dust allowing current to leak between the prongs of an appliance plug or even across the face of the outlet.

Install Outlet And Switch Boxes First

According to the NEC, no point along an undisturbed wall in a room may be more than 6 ft. from an outlet, and any section of wall more than 2 ft. long must have an outlet. Also, consider convenience when locating outlets and switches. The right height is as important as the right location. A good rule of thumb is to put outlets at 18 in. (from the subfloor to the top of the box) and switches at 48 in. Don't forget telephone jacks and cable-TV outlets during rough-in. Installing the boxes before pulling wire makes it clear where the cables should be run.

Aligning a Box
Face-nailing boxes are quick to install; the depth is set as soon as the box is fastened to the stud. Most boxes that fasten to the side of a stud have nibs that set the depth so that the face of the box is flush with ½-in. drywall.

Blocking for Trim
When hanging a box next to a doorway or window opening, use 2x blocking as a spacer so that the cover plate will not conflict with the casing.

Combo Box
This box has a line-voltage side and a low-voltage side. It's quick to install and lessens the clutter behind the TV where these days, you need power, a cable outlet, and a telephone jack.

Horizontal Outlets
If limited space between a backsplash and a mirror in the bathroom calls for the outlets to lie on their sides, a 4-in. square box and a single-gang plaster ring do the trick.

Sturdy Fan Boxes
If the plan calls for a ceiling fan, install a fan-rated box. This saddle-style box slips over 2x blocking. It is sturdy and offers enough space to splice a three-way switch.

Adjustable Hangers
Use adjustable brackets for ceiling fixtures. A round (4 in. dia.) fixture box on a telescoping hanger bracket makes it easy to position most ceiling fixtures between trusses or joists.

Continued ➔

Drill Holes with Wire Runs and Stapling in Mind

The NEC requires nonmetallic cable (such as Romex) to be secured within 8 in. of a box without clamps or 12 in. of a box that has clamps, and every 4½ ft. A cable running through a horizontal hole is considered secured. Drilling holes may seem like grunt work, but drilling the right number of holes in the right locations makes pulling and stapling the cable easier.

Attic Runs
Drill one ¾-in. hole in the top plate for each switch in every box. Individual holes make pulling the cables a lot easier, and smaller holes let you get away without installing nail plates.

Cable Dispenser & Stapling
Pulling cable through the holes is easy when the cable feeds neatly. Available at electrical-supply houses, wire dispensers pay it out without kinks, snags, or damage to the cable. Leave plenty of extra cable to work with before stapling the run to the framing.

Outlet Runs
Run the outlet cables well above the boxes. You can eyeball the row of holes between receptacle boxes, but make sure they are about 1 ft. above each box. This way, you can staple the cable before it enters the box without bending it sharply, which can damage the insulation.

Cable Clips
One clip can do the job of many staples. When running multiple cables to one box, it can be difficult to staple all the cables to the framing within 8 in. of the box. Cable clips can be nailed to the stud and can alleviate the need for stapling.

The NEC also requires that a bathroom have an outlet within 36 in. of the sink. This bath had two sinks, and although one outlet would have satisfied the NEC, it wouldn't have been convenient for the homeowners. Instead, the plan called for two receptacles above the backsplash; the first in line was a GFCI outlet, and it protected the downstream outlet as well.

In this case, because of a large mirror above the counter, there wasn't enough space for vertically oriented outlets. I used 4-in.-sq. deep junction boxes with plaster rings so that I could install the outlets horizontally. The deep boxes also gave me plenty of room for the bulky GFCI and the 12-ga. wires.

Precautions for Safe Sleeping

Per the NEC, all circuits supplying power inside a bedroom must have AFCI protection for fire safety. This is provided by a special circuit breaker that recognizes certain arcing or sparking, and cuts the power.

To meet this AFCI-protection requirement, the panel where the circuit originates has to have an arc-fault breaker available

Receptacle Circuits

Codes didn't regulate the number of outlets allowed on these circuits. It did demand specific types of breakers or outlets for certain areas. AFCI-protected circuits for the bedroom outlets and GFCI-protected circuits for the bathroom outlets were required. Twelve-ga. cable is run through the attic to the first, or home-run, box and through the walls between outlets. On the east wall (the green circuit), five outlets are half-switched (the top of the outlet is controlled by a switch) for lamps and similar appliances.

20-amp
AFCI-protected
outlet circuit

Bedroom

20-amp
AFCI-protected
outlet circuit

Shower

Master closet

20-amp GFCI-protected
bathroom-outlet circuit

Master closet

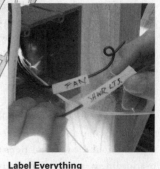

Label Everything
For multigang switch boxes, make sure that each wire is labeled. Remove the paper from scraps of the cable jacket to label the wires for each switch.

for use in it. Older panels may not be compatible with AFCI breakers. I won't use any breaker in a panel unless it is listed by Underwriters Laboratories (UL) for use in that panel. The listing means the breaker has been designed and tested to work in the panel. It's not just a matter of physical fit; the listing is a guarantee that the breaker and panel will work together even under extreme conditions.

Smoke detectors are required by the National Fire Code, not by the NEC. Whatever the source of the requirement, wiring for interlinked hardwired smoke detectors with battery backups is required in all new construction. Although this requirement has several aspects, the most basic mandate is for a smoke detector in each bedroom and one in the area outside bedrooms. I installed one additional smoke detector beyond that shown in the plan, at the far end of the hallway leading to the new master suite. Besides offering better protection, this unit will make it easier to extend the linked-detector circuit to the rest of the house in the future.

It's Up to You to Research Codes

The code requirements I've discussed are from the 2002 National Electrical Code because that's the version used by my local building department. Many jurisdictions adopt the NEC but make amendments. For instance, some cities require AFCI protection only for bedroom-receptacle outlets. Others limit the number of outlets allowed on a branch circuit. It's up to you to find out which version of the NEC is being used in your area and whether any amendments have been adopted. This information should be available in writing.

Continued ➜

Wiring a Bathroom

By Clifford A. Popejoy

If you want to invest some sweat equity in the house or addition you're building, you might consider taking on the job of rough-wiring: installing boxes, running cable, and preparing the boxes before the drywall is hung. If the walls are open, it's a straightforward job, and most building departments allow homeowners to do their own wiring. The task of installing the main service panel is complex and is best left to a professional electrician, but you'll save money by doing the rest of the work yourself. And there's no better place to start than the bathroom, a space that's fairly dense with electrical needs but not overly complicated. Recently, I wired a small bathroom that was part of a new Habitat for Humanity house in Sacramento, Calif. The details of the job demonstrate the necessary steps for attaching boxes, running wire, and making the preliminary connections.

Circuit Design and Code Requirements

As with all good building projects, you have to start with a plan. Usually generated by the architect or designer, a plan lists where the lights, outlets, switches, and other fixtures are to be located. It's also the best place to review the space's code-compliance.

The National Electrical Code (NEC) and the local codes that are based on the NEC allow the lights, fan, and outlets in one bathroom to be supplied by one 20-amp circuit, or for all bathroom outlets in the house to be supplied by a 20-amp circuit. In the latter scenario, the bathroom lights and fans are connected to general-purpose 15-amp circuits. Either option is less than ideal.

A single handheld hair dryer can come close to overloading a 20-amp circuit all by itself, so I always put each duplex outlet on its own 20-amp circuit, and the vent fan and lights on one separate 15-amp circuit. If you're in doubt as to a circuit's capacity, do the load calculations to make sure you're not overloading it (see "How To Figure Circuit Loads," p. 319).

All bathroom outlets must have GFCI (ground-fault circuit interrupter) protection. Most inspectors want to see outlets at or above the level of the counter, although the code does not specify height. Code does require a duplex outlet within 36 in. of the edge of each sink. If there is a double sink, put an outlet between them. Consider installing a pair of duplex outlets near each sink if, for instance, a hair dryer or curling iron are part of the morning routine. I strongly suggest running a separate 20-amp circuit for each outlet box, or even a 20-amp circuit for each duplex outlet. Here I installed two outlets, each on its own 20-amp circuit.

Even if the bathroom has an operable window (which is still code-approved as a venting option), install a vent fan. Vent-fan sizes are based on the amount of air the fans can exhaust, measured in cubic feet per minute (cfm). Fans should be sized according to building code, based on the square footage of the

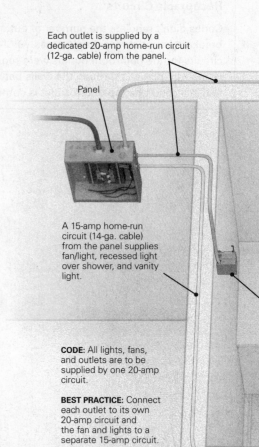

Each outlet is supplied by a dedicated 20-amp home-run circuit (12-ga. cable) from the panel.

Panel

A 15-amp home-run circuit (14-ga. cable) from the panel supplies fan/light, recessed light over shower, and vanity light.

CODE: All lights, fans, and outlets are to be supplied by one 20-amp circuit.

BEST PRACTICE: Connect each outlet to its own 20-amp circuit and the fan and lights to a separate 15-amp circuit.

bathroom. Some fans incorporate a motion sensor and timer, while others have a humidity sensor (humidistat). If a fan doesn't have either one, control the fan with a manual timer that can be set for at least 60 minutes.

A Bathroom Needs Good Lighting

In a bathroom, light sources should use fluorescent or LED lamps to conserve energy. In some areas, they're required in order to meet the energy code. There should be both ambient and task lighting; the latter is especially useful at the vanity mirror and shower. A combined vent fan and light fits the bill for ambient lighting.

Avoid using recessed ceiling lights for vanity task lighting, because the strong downward light casts too many harsh shadows. Best practice is to eliminate shadows by mounting a fixture on each side of the mirror. At the very least, install a single long-bar fixture above the mirror that gives a strong, even light.

It's helpful to have task lighting in the shower area. Recessed lights with wet-location LEDs provide a strong source of illumination. The typical light-colored, reflective shower surfaces

Start with a Code-Compliant Plan

An electrical plan is a map of fixture placement and circuitry that satisfies code requirements. Beyond ensuring a safe electrical rough-in, the plan is also the place where the comfort and convenience of the bathroom can be established through well-placed lights, fans, outlets, and switches.

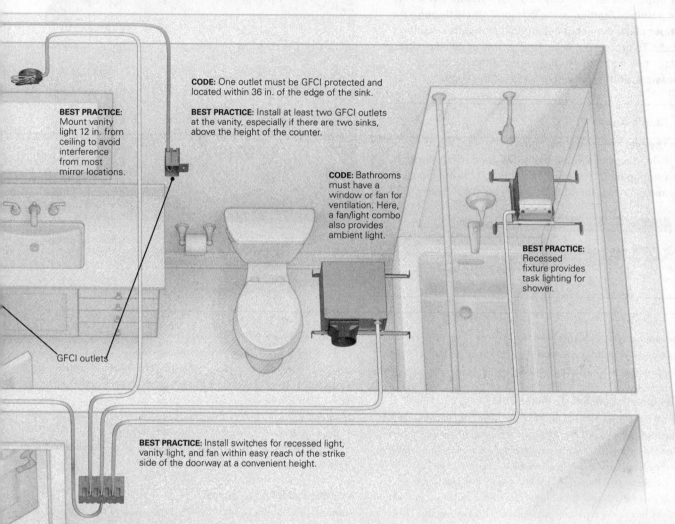

BEST PRACTICE: Mount vanity light 12 in. from ceiling to avoid interference from most mirror locations.

CODE: One outlet must be GFCI protected and located within 36 in. of the edge of the sink.

BEST PRACTICE: Install at least two GFCI outlets at the vanity, especially if there are two sinks, above the height of the counter.

CODE: Bathrooms must have a window or fan for ventilation. Here, a fan/light combo also provides ambient light.

BEST PRACTICE: Recessed fixture provides task lighting for shower.

GFCI outlets

BEST PRACTICE: Install switches for recessed light, vanity light, and fan within easy reach of the strike side of the doorway at a convenient height.

Boxes for Switches, Fixtures, and Outlets

Plastic boxes are strong, inexpensive, and commonly used in residential work. Choose deep boxes with thicker walls; these high-volume boxes make wiring easier and safer because there's more space for heat to dissipate.

Nail-On Boxes

Tabs on the side register these boxes to the face of the stud so they end up flush with the drywall.

Ceiling Light-Fixture Boxes

These light-duty boxes are made with adjustable mounting arms that allow a range of positions between the joists.

Adjustable-Depth Boxes

Once one of these boxes is attached to the framing, it can be made flush to the wall surface by adjusting a depth screw. These are a great option for tiled surfaces.

Metal Boxes

These are usually used only when working with metal conduit or metal-sheathed cable, but because the vanity-light-fixture box location was on a stud, the author used a shallow, 3-in. metal pancake box to provide the necessary support.

Continued ➜

When Running Cable, Drill Holes First

Plan the route between the breaker panel and the switch or outlet box for each cable so that it has as few bends as possible. Starting at the box, drill a hole through the upper plate, then continue drilling along the circuit's route. To protect the cable from screw or nail damage, place holes as close to the center of the framing as possible, and never within 1¼ in. of the edge.

Ship's Auger

The bit I like to use is a heavy-duty ⅝-in.-dia or ¾-in.-dia. ship's auger that's designed to cut through framing nails. Here, a 7½-in.-long bit for drilling studs and a 17½-in.-long bit for plates are from Bosch.

IN CONTROL, AND SAFE. Brace the drill with both hands so that if the bit hits a nail, the drill doesn't suddenly sprain your wrist or knock you off your feet.

---

spread the light, so shadows are not an issue. Smaller 4-in.-dia. fixtures work well for a normal shower, but larger showers might need one or two 6-in.-dia. fixtures.

The Installation: Set Up Boxes First

When it's time to start work, I first check the door swings on the plan to make sure the light switches won't be hidden behind the door when it's open. Next, I place the outlet and switch boxes on the floor just below their intended location.

I like to start by mounting the outlet boxes over the vanity so that there is at least 1 in. or more (I prefer 2 in.) from the bottom of the box to the top of the backsplash. This ensures that there's no chance of conflict with backsplash installation. Here, the plans indicated a 36-in.-tall vanity cabinet with a tile counter and a standard 4-in. backsplash. I mounted the boxes at 45 in. from the floor to the bottom of the box.

When outlets are to be located in the backsplash, I center their boxes in the vertical dimension. If the backsplash is tile, I try to work with the tile installer so that the box works well with the design.

My next step on this project was installing the box for the task lighting over the vanity. I've found that if I locate the box 12 in. below the ceiling, either centered on the cabinet or on the sink, it usually avoids any conflicts with the height of most vanity mirrors. For a vanity that's more than 4 ft. long, a box mounted on each side of the mirror works well.

At the doorway, I mounted a deep four-gang box for holding the lights and the fan switches. For the sake of appearance, I set

this box at the same height as the vanity outlets.

I located the vent-fan box between the ceiling joists, close to the shower and the toilet. I prepped the box by removing the most easily accessed knockout before nailing the arms to the joists, remembering to orient the fan's duct fitting in the direction of the flex-duct run.

The last fixture to install is the recessed light above the shower. Like the fan, the fixture's mounting arms can be adjusted to move the light's position between the joists.

Running Cable to the Boxes

Nonmetallic-sheathed cable (NM-B) is the standard for residential work. The most common types, 12-ga. (yellow sheathing) and 14-ga. (white sheathing), are available with either two or three insulated conductors plus a ground. The lighter 14-ga. is used for 15-amp circuits, and the heavier 12-ga. is used for 20-amp circuits.

Before I start to pull cable, I trace the cable paths, called home runs, from the bath back to the panel. On this job, the bath was powered from a subpanel. These particular home runs are for each 20-amp outlet and for the circuit that powers the lights and fan, which are all switched from one box. After checking for potential obstacles and planning the route with the fewest turns, I started drilling holes and pulling cable.

I use a right-angle drill with a 17½-in.-long ship's-auger bit to drill the holes in the plates above each box or fixture and in subsequent joists or blocking. When drilling through plates, I stay as close as possible to the center. Any hole that's closer than

Pull Cables the Easy Way

To run cable, feed it up into the joists and to the panel. Leave enough to reach the bottom of the panel, and work back, stapling the cable along its path. Back at the box, estimate about a foot of length beyond the box, cut it from the coil, and then feed the cable through the hole on the top plates and down the stud to the box.

NO LOOSE CABLES. The NEC states that cable must be supported horizontally every 4½ ft. Insulated staples, plastic clips, and drilled holes provide the bulk of the support. Cable must also be supported within 9 in. of a box without clamps, or within 12 in. of a box that has clamps.

IT'S EASIEST TO RUN ONE CIRCUIT AT A TIME. Keep track of each circuit by running one cable at a time. Although a tempting short-cut, it's never a good idea to run more than two cables through the same drilled hole.

Continued →

Get the Boxes Ready

The last step in the rough-in process is to get the switch boxes and outlet boxes ready so they can be finished once the drywall is installed. The most complicated box to make up is the gang box of four fan and light switches that's powered by one home-run circuit to the panel.

Strip Jackets for 14/3

At each box, the jacket or sheathing has to be removed from the cable. You could use a utility knife, but the blade can nick the conductor insulation. You could also start a cut with a knife a few inches from the cable's end, then use the heavy thread that's encased in the 14/3-cable sheathing to slit the jacket, or use the bare copper ground wire as a rip cord. I like to use a special pair of stripping pliers (Klein, Ideal, or Crocks) that cuts the jacket but not the conductor insulation.

Label Cables

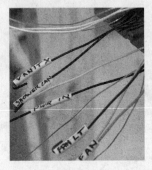

If I'm bringing more than one cable into a box, or bringing cables to the panel, I label the function of the cable on the jacket with a black marker. After stripping off the jacket, I slip it over the hot (black) lead.

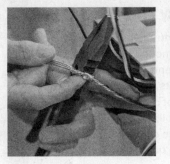

ALL GROUNDED. Twist together the grounds, and secure them with a copper crimp sleeve so there's enough length for each to be connected to its switch.

NEUTRALS NEXT. After trimming back ¾ in. of insulation on each wire, join the neutral conductors with a twist-on connector, and fold them into the box.

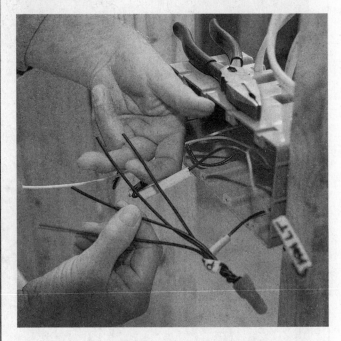

HOT PIGTAILS. Label the hot (black) leads, and then fold them back into the box, except for the powered lead from the panel. Cut 6-in.-long pigtails from scrap black wire, and connect them to the powered lead. Fold the assembly into the box. The pigtails will later be connected to the switches.

1¼ in. to the edge must be protected by a nail plate. I keep the holes in joists toward the middle as well. Modern I-joists have precut knockouts in the OSB web for running wire, which is a real time-saver.

Many people start with running the cable through the hole on the top plate above each box, but that creates a lot of friction and makes pulling the cable difficult. I've found that the easiest way to run cable is to place the roll on the floor at the switch or outlet box and then feed the cable up into the framing and to the destination (fixture, fixture box, or panel). To ease the pulling process, I run no more than two cables through a hole. When the cable is threaded through the drilled holes, I leave enough surplus

at the panel, then retrace the cable's path, stapling as I go. When I get back to the roll, I estimate the length I need to get back to the box, cut the cable, and then thread it through the top plate and staple it to the stud.

Finalize the Process

With the cable cut to rough length and stapled up, the next step is to make up the boxes. Holding the cable next to the box, I cut it so that when it's routed into the box, there's about a foot of cable extending from the box. I strip back the jacket so that when the cable is in place, it will extend ¾ in. into the box. With a screwdriver, I spread open a clamp on the top of the box and pass

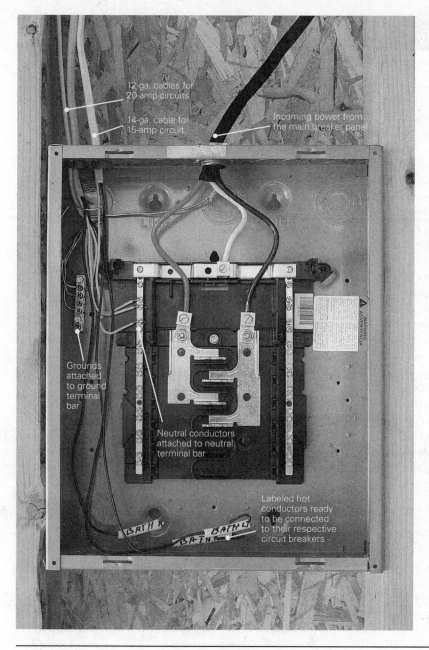

12-ga. cables for
20-amp circuits

14-ga. cable for
15-amp circuit

Incoming power from
the main breaker panel

Grounds
attached
to ground
terminal
bar

Neutral conductors
attached to neutral
terminal bar

Labeled hot
conductors ready
to be connected
to their respective
circuit breakers

BATH R

BATH L   BATH L

Prep the Panel

All circuits terminate at the breaker panel. (In this instance, the bath was powered by a subpanel.) Cut grounds and neutral conductors to length, and secure them to their respective terminal bars. After labeling the hot conductors, don't cut them to length; just fold them into the box.

How to Figure Circuit Loads

Here's an example that illustrates how to calculate a circuit load. A 15-amp bathroom lighting circuit is powering two bathrooms that have the following loads:

- Two wall sconces, each with four bi-pin-base CFLs that draw 0.39 amps each: 8×0.4 amps = 3.2 amps
- Two combo fan/light units, each drawing 1 amp: 2×1 amp = 2 amps
- Eight recessed-light fixtures with 75w halogen incandescent lamps. A 75w lamp draws 0.625 amps (75w/120v):8×0.625 amps = 5 amps
TOTAL AMP LOAD 3.2 + 2 + 5 = 10.2 amps

the cable through, then neatly fold the conductors back into the box. Cables routed into fans and recessed cans are connected to the fixtures' leads.

For multiple gang boxes powered by a home run to the panel, the grounds are connected together, as are the neutral conductors. The hot conductors feeding each fixture are labeled and tucked into the box. Separate pigtails connected to the supply lead and the grounds will ultimately be assigned to their respective switches.

At the other end of the circuit, I route cable into the breaker panel. I connect the grounds and neutrals to their respective terminal bars, then label the hot conductors and tuck them into the box to await their later connection to the breakers.

Continued →

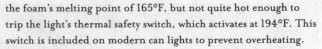

Air-Sealing Can Lights Safely

By Larry Armanda

I've been an electrical contractor and a building-performance professional for more than 35 years. Over the past two decades, I've read countless articles in Fine Homebuilding and other magazines that describe the use of enclosures built from drywall and foam insulation to air-seal can lights in attics. Sealing these notoriously leaky fixtures—which waste energy, allow moisture into the attic, and contribute to ice dams—is a good idea. Unfortunately, the way many builders and weatherization professionals approach the work is potentially dangerous. The problem is that heat generated by the lightbulb and trapped within the enclosure can melt the wiring's plastic insulation, leading to arcing and fire.

Air-sealing can lights safely isn't a new concern of mine. I did my first research in 2001 and published the results in Home Energy, a magazine for the weatherization industry.

I recently completed new research into the subject. This time I built a more comprehensive test rig that mimicked common ceiling construction, and I tested five types of air-sealing enclosures: three homemade versions (2-in. polystyrene insulation, 1-in. foil-faced polyisocyanurate insulation, and ⅝-in. drywall) and two manufactured enclosures (CanCoverIt and Tenmat). In turn, I installed these enclosures over fixtures (with the can light's thermal safety switch bypassed so that I could determine the maximum temperature inside the various enclosures) and taped them to the drywall ceiling with foil tape, similar to how weatherization crews would install them.

Attics Add to the Problem

Summertime attic temperatures prevent heat within the enclosure from dissipating, which adds to the risk of shorted wiring and fire. To simulate the worst-case scenario, I built a large insulated box over my test-light setup and heated it to 135°F with a 300w lightbulb. (Attics in my part of Pennsylvania routinely get this hot on summer days.) I ran a total of 35, 12-hour tests with seven different lightbulbs in each of the five enclosures. I recorded the temperatures inside the enclosures in three locations and inside my "attic" test space with a four-channel HOBO data logger. What I found is alarming.

The highest temperatures recorded approached 250°F with a standard incandescent bulb. Although this isn't the bulb that these fixtures are designed for, weatherization crews routinely find them in can lights. Even with the correct bulb, though, temperatures inside the boxes routinely exceeded 160°F, high enough to degrade the insulation on older versions of nonmetallic-sheathed (NM) cable, which is rated to 140°F. This type of cable was installed from the mid-1960s until 1984.

I also found that foam enclosures could get hot enough to melt when the lights had halogen flood lamps or conventional Edison-base lightbulbs. In some cases, temperatures were above the foam's melting point of 165°F, but not quite hot enough to trip the light's thermal safety switch, which activates at 194°F. This switch is included on modern can lights to prevent overheating.

Older cans don't have a thermal switch, so when they're enclosed, it's conceivable they would keep getting hotter until either the wiring or the enclosure melted. Although I didn't see any melted wires during my comparatively brief periods of testing, I've seen NM cable that's exposed to long-term heat from early fluorescent ballasts: The inner insulation gets brittle and melts, leading to shorts and electrical fire. I did, however, see evidence of localized melting in the extruded-polystyrene enclosure I built. This enclosure was in service only for 12 hours at a time. You can imagine what might happen if the light was left on with the wrong bulb for a few days or more.

Building a Safe Enclosure

Given the problems with conventional methods of air-sealing can lights, I've come up with what I consider the safest way to do it. For starters, I recommend a manufactured Tenmat enclosure (tenmat-us.com), which is made from mineral wool and is fire resistant. You also can use drywall enclosures. They sufficiently resist heat, although they are more susceptible to mold growth in homes with high humidity because the paper facing is a good food source for mold.

Make sure the wiring that supplies the can light is designated NM-B, which is rated to 194°F. If the wiring is not NM-B, install a junction box about 18 in. away from the fixture, and use a short length of modern NM-B to connect the older wire and the fixture. Put the junction box on a mast so that it's not buried in insulation and is easy to find for any future work. Finally, use high-quality UL-181 foil duct tape or a fireblock-type spray foam to seal the enclosure to the drywall ceiling.

Choose the Right Bulbs

I found that you can keep the fixture sufficiently cool and safe by using the correct reflector bulbs. Unfortunately, the right bulb is often replaced with an Edison-style or halogen reflector bulb when the correct bulb burns out. The best way to prevent the installation of the wrong bulb is to install an LED can-light conversion kit. These conversion kits have life spans of about 50,000 hours (almost four years of nonstop use), making it unlikely that someone will swap one out for a potentially dangerous incandescent light.

Many of these retrofit kits claim to be airtight, so you might be tempted to install one and forget the can-light enclosure altogether. Unfortunately, when researchers tested supposedly airtight kits in the past, they found that most were improperly installed, reducing their effectiveness. I don't know of any research that's been done to confirm the airtightness of modern LED retrofit kits. Until we know for sure, I think appropriately constructed can-light enclosures are still the best solution, short of removing the can lights altogether.

An Accident Waiting to Happen

Heat generated by the bulb and trapped within the enclosure can have a dangerous effect on the surrounding materials. There are four potential problems with the way many can lights are air-sealed.

Fixture

Older non-IC can lights don't have a thermal safety switch, so temperatures inside an enclosure can climb until the foam box melts or the insulation on the wires melts or catches fire.

Wiring

Nonmetallic-sheathed cable installed before 1984 is rated for 140°F. Testing reveals that temperatures inside the box can reach 171°F, even with the correct 65w PAR 30 incandescent bulb.

Enclosure

Polystyrene insulation starts to melt at 167°F, yet internal temperatures can exceed 170°F with the correct bulb and approach 250°F when a standard A19 Edison-style bulb is installed.

Bulb

Weatherization crews and electricians routinely find the wrong bulbs installed in ceiling-mounted can lights, but even the correct bulb can make the inside of the enclosure over 170°F—too hot for older wiring.

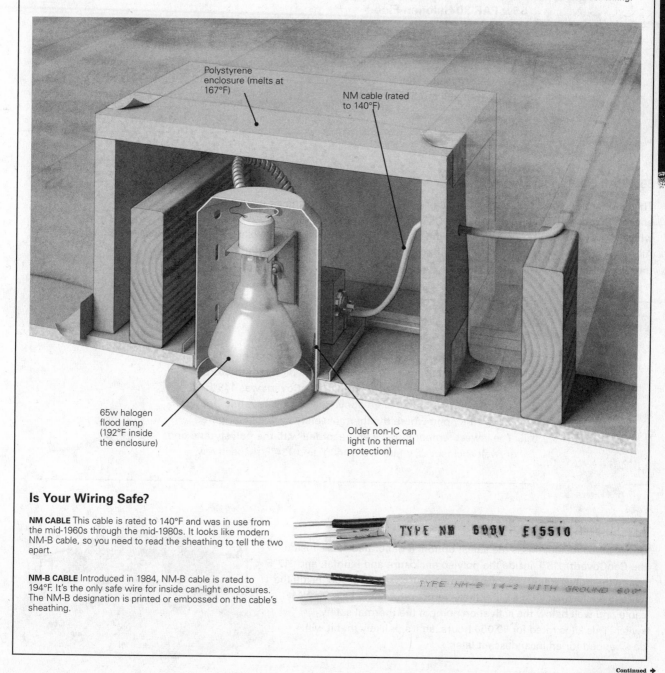

Polystyrene enclosure (melts at 167°F)

NM cable (rated to 140°F)

65w halogen flood lamp (192°F inside the enclosure)

Older non-IC can light (no thermal protection)

Is Your Wiring Safe?

NM CABLE This cable is rated to 140°F and was in use from the mid-1960s through the mid-1980s. It looks like modern NM-B cable, so you need to read the sheathing to tell the two apart.

NM-B CABLE Introduced in 1984, NM-B cable is rated to 194°F. It's the only safe wire for inside can-light enclosures. The NM-B designation is printed or embossed on the cable's sheathing.

Continued ➜

Even the Right Bulb Can Be Dangerous

75w A19 Standard Bulb

This Edison-style incandescent bulb generated the highest temperatures inside all five enclosures. It produced 245°F in the polystyrene cover, well above the material's melting point of 167°F. It raised the temperature to 246°F inside the polyisocyanurate and Tenmat enclosures. The CanCoverIt reached 224°F, and the drywall enclosure reached 216°F. All of these temperatures would have tripped the thermal safety switch and easily exceed the rating of NM cable and even modern NM-B cable.

65w PAR 30 Halogen Flood

This common bulb produced 192°F in the polystyrene, polyisocyanurate, and Tenmat enclosures, which is very close to the point where the fixture's thermal safety switch will activate (194°F), turning off the light. These temperatures also easily exceed the rating of NM cable. The CanCoverIt (183°F) and the drywall enclosure (164°F) were cooler, but still too hot for NM.

65w PAR 30 Standard Flood

This is the traditional bulb for common can-light fixtures. Even so, the air inside the polyisocyanurate enclosure reached 175°F. The Tenmat was 173°F, and the polystyrene and CanCoverIt reached 167°F, which is very close to polystyrene's melting point. At 156°F, the drywall enclosure was the coolest. All of the enclosures reached temperatures that exceed the temperature rating of NM cable but that are below the activation point of the thermal safety switch.

22w LED Lamp

Even though many people think of LEDs as generating little heat, the polyisocyanurate enclosure reached a high temperature of 145°F. The Tenmat was 144°F, and the CanCoverIt was 143°F. All of these temperatures were above the NM-cable rating but well below the point where the thermal safety switch is triggered. The lowest temperatures were recorded with the polystyrene and drywall enclosures, which were 140°F and 134°F, respectively.

13w Utilitec LED Trim Kit

Of the bulbs tested, this is the safest option. It generated 123°F inside the CanCoverIt, 118°F inside the polyiso enclosure and Tenmat, and 117°F inside the polystyrene. The lowest temperature was recorded inside the drywall enclosure (106°F). All of these temperatures are safe for NM cable and well below the activation point of the thermal safety switch. This kit is rated for 50,000 hours, so it's unlikely that it will be swapped for an incandescent later.

Four Factors That Make a Safe Enclosure

Fixture

Modern can lights have a thermal switch that turns off the fixture when the temperature reaches 194°F. It's an important safety device, but it's set too high to protect older wire from the heat trapped within the enclosure. Older can lights often don't have this safety feature, so they should be replaced with modern versions before any air-sealing occurs.

Wiring

Modern nonmetallic-sheathed cable identified as NM-B is rated for 194°F. Testing reveals that temperatures inside the box reach 171°F with the correct 65w PAR 30 incandescent bulb, but modern cable won't be enough if somebody installs the wrong bulb, which can bring temperatures inside the enclosure to 246°F.

Enclosure

Made from mineral wool, the Tenmat enclosure won't melt like polystyrene insulation, and the larger version (model FF135) is big enough to maintain the code-required 3-in. clearance to the fixture even when there's a joist nearby. The Tenmat cuts easily with scissors for fitting it around cables and the mounting hardware.

Bulb

Even if you take all of the other steps described here to protect the wiring from damage and use a heat-resistant drywall or Tenmat enclosure, the wiring is still at risk if somebody installs the wrong bulb. The best way to prevent this is to install an LED can-light conversion kit, which is dimmable, has good color rendition, and should last for 50,000 hours.

Junction box 18 in. from fixture

Mast

NM cable

Tenmat FF135 (fire-resistant mineral wool)

UL-181 foil tape

LED retrofit kit (118°F inside the enclosure)

IC-rated can light (thermal safety switch activates at 194°F)

NM-B cable (rated for 194°F)

Continued ➔

Grid-Tied PV Systems

By Debra Judge Silber

If it seems like more and more roofs in your neighborhood are sprouting shiny black photovoltaic (PV) arrays, you're not alone: In 2013, the number of home PV installations in the United States grew 60%.

While some home PV systems operate independent of the electrical grid, grid-tied systems are far more common. Electricity produced by these systems is used first to satisfy the home's load; any surplus is fed into the utility-maintained grid. When the system is not producing electricity (at night, for example) the house draws power from the grid like any other home.

Distributed generation (DG) is the feeding of electricity into the power grid from multiple locations. DG is a hot topic right now, as the popularity of PV has generated fierce debate between home-power advocates, utilities, and regulators over pricing, regulations, and connection requirements.

The conversion of light to electricity occurs in a solar cell the size of a CD case, but the process doesn't end there. It is the "balance of system" equipment that conditions, monitors, and distributes that power so it can be used to run your TV, computer, and refrigerator (as well as your neighbors'). These components are what make PV power practical.

Here's how it works.

One Meter, Or More?

The number of meters required for a grid-tied system varies. Where net metering is offered, customers often have a single, bidirectional meter that records both electricity drawn from the grid and excess fed into it. Homeowners pay only for the net difference. Two meters are required in areas using "value of solar" tariffs. Under this new (and hotly contested) pricing system, customers sell all the energy they produce to the utility at a specific "solar" rate and then buy back what they need.

1. Photons (light energy) hit photosensitive cells, producing a flow of electrons (an electric current). Cells are combined into modules (sometimes called panels), which are grouped in arrays. An array produces electricity in the form of direct-current (DC) power that flows continuously as long as light hits the modules.

2. DC power travels via cable from the array to the inverter.

3. A DC shutoff, often built into the inverter, allows manual disconnection of the current coming from the array.

4. The inverter converts the DC power to alternating current (AC) and conditions it to match the frequency, sine curve, and voltage of current produced by the grid. A grid-tied inverter will not operate unless it can "read" AC against which to match the DC entering it. That is why grid-tied PV systems typically can't supply power during a grid outage. For power during an outage, a hybrid system incorporating a battery is needed.

5. Safety features, including grounding equipment, surge protection, and disconnection switches, are also part of the system. Grounding equipment provides protection against shocks in the event of a short circuit. Both the array and balance-of-system components should be grounded. The National Electric Code NFPA 70 provides more information on grounding and other safety components.

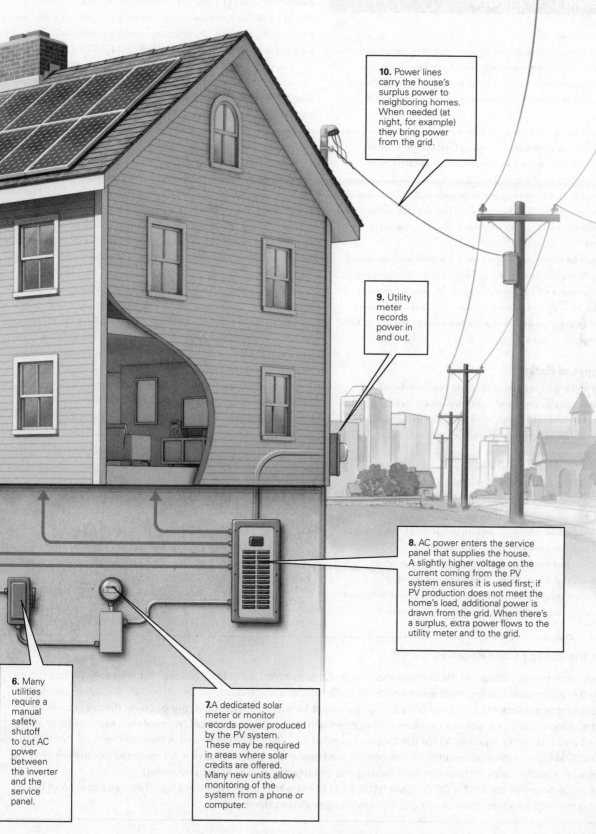

10. Power lines carry the house's surplus power to neighboring homes. When needed (at night, for example) they bring power from the grid.

9. Utility meter records power in and out.

8. AC power enters the service panel that supplies the house. A slightly higher voltage on the current coming from the PV system ensures it is used first; if PV production does not meet the home's load, additional power is drawn from the grid. When there's a surplus, extra power flows to the utility meter and to the grid.

6. Many utilities require a manual safety shutoff to cut AC power between the inverter and the service panel.

7. A dedicated solar meter or monitor records power produced by the PV system. These may be required in areas where solar credits are offered. Many new units allow monitoring of the system from a phone or computer.

Continued →

Recessed Can Lights

By Martin Holladay

The chief virtue of recessed can lights is that they are unobtrusive. If you look at a can light with an infrared camera, though, you'll usually see evidence of air leaks at the perimeter of each fixture. In most cases, these innocent-looking circles are actually holes in your ceiling.

Not only do recessed can lights leak air, but warm lightbulbs also make the situation worse, turning the holes into small chimneys. The heat source accelerates the stack effect, speeding up the flow of air. Still worse: Each fixture is almost as big as a gallon of milk, and it takes up room in your ceiling that should be filled with insulation. The hot spots are located right where your insulation is thinnest. That's why recessed cans are a major cause of ice dams.

You may be thinking, "I don't have that problem, because I installed a fiberglass batt on top of each fixture." Unfortunately, fiberglass batts are no solution. If you check, you'll probably see that the batts on top of your fixtures are black. The stains are caused by the dust that the insulation has filtered out of the escaping stream of hot air.

Three Types of Fixtures

There are at least three types of recessed can fixtures. Older fixtures had holes in them and depended on air leaking through the ceiling to stay cool enough to be safe. The manufacturers of these older fixtures warned installers that the fixtures should never be covered with insulation.

Eventually, manufacturers developed recessed cans that are labeled IC (insulation contact). These improved units are designed to operate safely even if they are covered with insulation. The fixtures include a thermal switch that turns off the fixture if a high-wattage bulb causes the unit to overheat. (Once the unit cools to a safe temperature, the light comes back on.)

However, just because a fixture is rated for insulation contact doesn't mean that it isn't leaky. When a house is tested with a blower door, a smoke pencil held near a recessed can fixture—even one that is IC-rated—often shows significant air leaks.

The best recessed cans are those labeled IC-AT (insulation contact, airtight) or those that are labeled as complying with ASTM E283 (an air-leakage test). Some labels may note that the fixture complies with "Washington state requirements," which simply means that the fixture has passed the ASTM E283 test.

The design of IC-AT fixtures differs from manufacturer to manufacturer. Some units depend on a gasket included with the trim kit to seal the crack between the drywall and the fixture; needless to say, any of the included gaskets must be installed for the fixture to be airtight. If the installer forgets the gasket, the AT label won't mean much.

Start with an Inspection

The first step is to determine the type of fixture you have. You can usually tell from indoors if a recessed can is IC-rated. First, remove the trim and then remove the bulb. Look inside the fixture with a flashlight. If there are holes or slits in the side of the can, it is probably not IC-rated. Look for a label; most IC-rated fixtures include the letters "IC" in the model number.

If you know that the fixture is IC-rated but you're not sure if it is airtight, look for the letters "IC-AT" near the model number. If you can't find a label, climb into the attic (if you have access), and look at the fixture from the attic side. An airtight fixture has a metal shroud over the entire fixture, without any holes or slits, and has a gasketed assembly where the electrical cable enters.

An older fixture without a thermal switch should be removed and discarded. Once the fixture has been removed, the most energy-smart option is to patch the drywall and install a surface-mounted fixture (for example, a pendant light or track lighting). If you insist on replacing the recessed can, install a newer fixture with an IC-AT rating. If the existing fixture is IC-rated but not airtight, it's possible to install an airtight cap on the attic side of the fixture, as long as you have access to the attic (see "Make or Buy a Can-Light Cap," p. 327). If you lack access from above, remove the fixture, and replace it with a surface-mounted fixture.

If the fixture has an IC-AT rating, you can leave it in place. If you have access to the attic, however, it's worth verifying that the fixture is covered by insulation.

Another way to cut down on air leakage through a can—especially one installed in a cathedral ceiling—is with an LED

What the Energy Code Requires

The two most recent versions of the International Energy Conservation Code (IECC) require that any recessed-can fixture installed in an insulated ceiling must meet the ASTM E283 airtightness standard and be labeled for insulation contact.

According to section 402.4.5 of the 2009 IECC, "Recessed luminaires installed in the building thermal envelope shall be sealed to limit air leakage between conditioned and unconditioned spaces. All recessed luminaires shall be IC-rated and labeled as meeting ASTM E283 when tested at 1.57 psf (75 Pa) pressure differential with no more than 2.0 cfm (0.944 L/s) of air movement from the conditioned space to the ceiling cavity. All recessed luminaires shall be sealed with a gasket or caulk between the housing and the interior wall or ceiling covering."

The requirement in the 2012 IECC (in table R402.4.1.1) is more succinct: "Recessed light fixtures installed in the building thermal envelope shall be airtight, IC rated, and sealed to the drywall."

Make or Buy a Can-Light Cap

For years, weatherization contractors have been retrofitting airtight caps on leaky recessed cans, including older fixtures that lack a thermal switch. However, some experts call this practice risky, because fixtures without a thermal safety switch might overheat. The safest approach is to remove these older fixtures and to replace them with new IC-rated fixtures or surface-mounted fixtures.

Working from the attic side, it's safe to install an airtight cap above a leaky IC-rated fixture. You can build your own box or cap from foil-faced rigid foam or gypsum drywall. A homemade box should belarge enough to leave 3 in. of clearance on the sides and top of the fixture. Seal all seams and wiring penetrations with tape or canned spray foam.

Once you've built the cap, make a notch for the electrical cable, then seal the cap to the drywall with canned spray foam. The installed cap should be covered by a generous layer of insulation. Finally, from the interior side, remove the fixture trim, and carefully caulk the seam between the drywall ceiling and the fixture.

At least three manufacturers sell caps for recessed cans. Tenmat makes the sturdiest covers; they are made of fire-resistant mineral wool. Tenmat covers are available from Energy Federation Inc. (efi.org). Other choices include Seal-A-Light covers, which are available from Shamrock Enter-prises (sealalight.com), and Owens Corning SmartCap covers, which are available from The Home Depot.

BUILD A BOX Ou Can Make Your Own Can-Light Covers from Scraps of Foil-Faced Polyisocyanurate Rigid-Foam Insulation, Shown Here, or Drywall.

All seams should be sealed with housewrap tape, foil tape, or canned spray foam.

CAPS ARE INSULATION SAFE Made from Mineral Wool, Tenmat's Can-Light Covers Can Be Used to Create an Airtight Enclosure Around Existing Recessed Lights and Isolate the Fixture from Surrounding Insulation.

Spray foam

conversion kit. These kits include airtight compartments that can be inserted to replace an existing fixture's can and lamp trim. Examples of LED conversion kits include the Cree LR6 LED conversion kit and the Cooper All Pro LED conversion kit.

If you follow the recommendations here, you can reduce air leakage through your recessed cans. Don't forget to install a compact fluorescent (CFL) or LED lamp, not an incandescent.

Better yet, eliminate all your recessed cans. With the range of fixtures now available—surface-mounted ceiling fixtures, pendants, sconces, track lights, cove lights, and floor lamps—it's easy to design an elegant lighting scheme without any recessed cans.

Continued ➤

Retrofitting Recessed Lights

By Clifford A. Popejoy

They're called a lot of things: can lights, downlights, high hats. Whatever you call them, there is no denying that replacing an old fixture with one or more recessed lights can modernize and brighten just about any space. Recessed lights are available for every type of ceiling, and the trim kits that go with them are available in different colors and styles (sidebar p. 329). The lighting effect you create can range from functional to dramatic.

To install recessed lights, you need to make three decisions: getting the right fixtures, determining location and spacing, and figuring out how to get power to and between the lights. Once you work out these details, the installation is light work.

Recessed lights come in a variety of sizes, shapes, and lamp types. Here, I used a 6-in. fixture made to take an energy-efficient fluorescent lamp. Because this is a retrofit, I chose a remodeling fixture that is designed to be installed from below. This type of fixture has retaining clips that lock into place behind the drywall to hold the fixture in the ceiling.

In this room, the recessed lights will be the main light source, so I spaced the fixtures at 4-ft. intervals. Installing a series of recessed lights in only one joist bay is easy. But because these lights are spaced to illuminate the whole kitchen, I had to drill through joists to run wires between the lights. When I drill inside a ceiling or wall, I am careful not to hit anything but the joists. Pipes, wires, and ducts often are close to a joist, so probing inside the ceiling before drilling is a good idea.

As I'm settling on the location of the cans, I'm looking for power. In this room, I replaced an existing light fixture. I identified which circuit the light was on, cut the power, and locked out the breaker. Before using existing wiring, though, make sure the cable is marked NM-B, which signifies that the insulation is rated for modern light fixtures.

If the cable is too short or isn't rated NM-B, install a separate junction box and splice NM-B-rated cable to the existing wiring. This junction box has to be accessible from somewhere inside the house. If the junction box is not accessible from an attic or crawlspace, it must have a removable access panel.

Mark the circular cutouts on the ceiling using the template that comes with the recessed-light fixtures. I could cut the hole with a drywall saw, but to avoid making a mess, I use a specialty

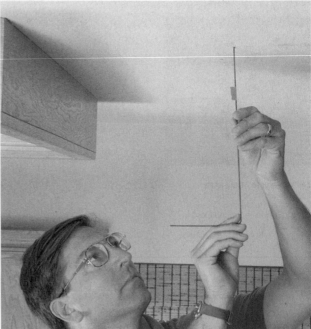

PROBE BEFORE YOU CUT. Bend a coat hanger to the radius of the fixture. Mark the depth cf the fixture with tape. Spin the hanger as you push it into the ceiling to check fcr framing, ductwork, or pipes.

NEW TOOL

OLD SCHOOL

MAKE A CLEAN CUT. You can mark the ceiling with a template and cut the opening with a dry- waff saw. The author uses an adjustable round-hole cutter that captures the dust while drilling the hole (www. nora lighting.com).

RUN CABLE BETWEEN THE HOLES. Use a fishing wand to pull cable between the openings. Cut the cable, leaving enough length to wire the fixture while it rests atop the ladder.

The Right Lights for Your Ceiling and Style

Remodeling fixtures are chosen for the specific ceiling they will be installed in. Trim and baffle kits are chosen for style and light quality.

Light Fixtures

AN ALUMINUM (IC-RATED) CAN won't overheat in an insulated ceiling.

A 4-IN. CAN is perfect for tight spaces, like a soffit over a kitchen sink.

THIS ANGULAR CAN works in a sloped ceiling.

FLUORESCENT LAMP holders maximize energy efficiency and are suitable for any type of ceiling.

Baffle and Trim

A WHITE TRIM RING blends into most ceilings. A reflective baffle produces strong light.

A BLACK EYEBALL-STYLE baffle focuses a mellow light n a particular direction.

Continued ➜

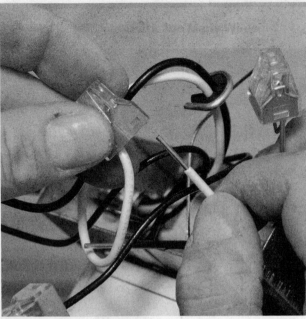

drill bit that cuts circles and has an integral dust and cutoff collector (top photo, p. 329).

The fixtures that I used on this project have push-in wire connectors that make it easy to splice the wires. If the fixture doesn't come with connectors, then I use wire nuts to splice the hot, neutral, and grounding fixture wires to their respective conductors. If the location is difficult to reach, like a tall ceiling, I temporarily wire up and test the fixtures on the ground before I install them.

I have learned that it is worthwhile to take the time to find a faulty fixture before installing it in a 15-ft-high ceiling.

Splicing the stranded fixture wire to the solid 14-ga. or 12-ga. conductors requires a bit of finesse. Be careful not to damage the stranded wires. After putting the cover on the fixture's junction box, I slip the fixture into the hole and snap open and lock the retainer clips to hold it in place. The baffle goes in next, then the bulb, and finally the trim ring. All that's left is to restore power to the circuit and flip the switch.

SPLICE THE WIRES INSIDE THE JTMICTION BOX. With the fixture resting on the ladder, remove the junction-box cover. Pry out the opening for the incoming and outgoing wires. Use the push-in wire connectors that come with the fixture, or splice the wires with wire-nut connectors. Be careful not to damage the stranded fixture wire. Remember to replace the junction-box cover.

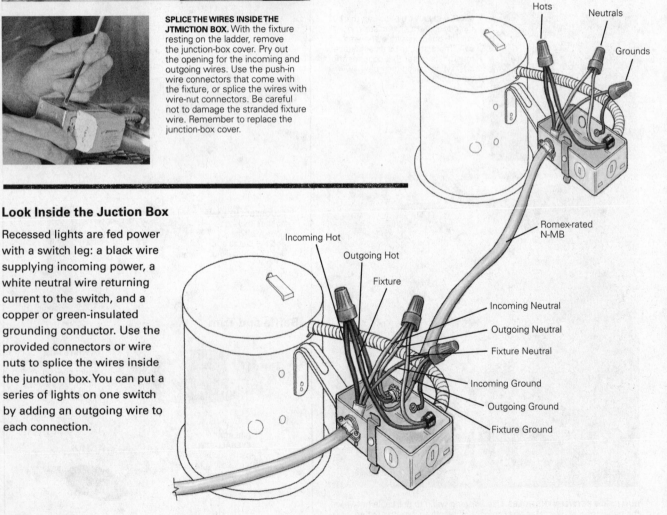

Look Inside the Juction Box

Recessed lights are fed power with a switch leg: a black wire supplying incoming power, a white neutral wire returning current to the switch, and a copper or green-insulated grounding conductor. Use the provided connectors or wire nuts to splice the wires inside the junction box. You can put a series of lights on one switch by adding an outgoing wire to each connection.

Hots
Neutrals
Grounds

Romex-rated N-MB

Incoming Hot
Outgoing Hot
Fixture
Incoming Neutral
Outgoing Neutral
Fixture Neutral
Incoming Ground
Outgoing Ground
Fixture Ground

SLIP THE FIXTURE INTO THE HOLE. Push the cable into the ceiling while you slip the fixture arm with the junction box into the hole. Straighten the housing, and push it into the ceiling. It should fit snugly.

SET THE RETAINING CLIPS TO LOCK THE FIXTURE INTO THE CEILING. Then install the baffle and trim kit. If the trim ring is not integral to the baffle, snap it into place to complete the installation.

Customize Your Room with Recessed Cans

Task Lighting

A Single Recessed Light Can Be Placed Directly Over a Work Area for Task Lighting. Here, a Recessed Light Provides Enough Extra Light Over the Sink That the Whole Kitchen Doesn't Have to Be Lit Up to do the Dishes. This Strategy Also Can Be Used in Dark Hallways, Stairwells, and Corners.

Wall Wash

A painting is easy to highlight with a recessed light. An eyeball-style baffle directs light only to where you want it to shine. This also is called accent lighting.

Downlighting

A series of recessed lights works great as downlighting, or as room's main light source. In general, a 6-in. fixture creates a pool of light equal to its distance from the floor. Here, 4-ft. spacing creates an even level of ambient light.

Continued ➜

Retrofitting a Ceiling Fan

By Clifford A. Popejoy

A ceiling fan is a great way to improve your comfort at home, and one of the most common retrofit projects is one that replaces an existing ceiling light with a fan that includes a light. Ceiling fans are easier than ever to assemble and install; in fact, I recently walked a friend through the process in an afternoon. Easy or not, there are a couple of important safety issues to keep in mind: avoiding electrical shock and getting the fan solidly attached to the ceiling framing.

Before you do anything, find out if the circuit has the capacity to run the new fixture. Most fan/light fixtures use two to three times more power than a standard light fixture. If the circuit was close to capacity before, you don't want to overload it.

Map out the circuit to determine what's on it. The easiest way is to turn off that particular circuit breaker and see what else no longer works. Add up the wattage of the lights and appliances that are fed by the circuit; be sure to include things that may not be used all the time, such as space heaters. If the total wattage is

Choosing the Right-size Fan

In the interest of proportion and efficiency, you have to match the fan size to the room. The chart below provides the basic guidelines; choose the next largest size if the fan is to be installed in a room with a high ceiling.

Room size (sq. ft.)	Overall blade diameter (in.)
100	36
144	42
225	44-48
400	52-54
500	56-60

more than 1800w for a 15-amp circuit or more than 2400w for a 20-amp circuit, the circuit definitely is overloaded. Although not required by code, it's advisable to keep the load below 80% of those figures.

Remove the Old Box, and Check the Existing Wires

Just shutting off the existing light at the wall switch doesn't guarantee that power is off in the ceiling box. The ceiling light's circuit should be turned off at the service panel. Use a voltage tester to confirm that the fixture and all the wires in the box are de-energized, and make sure they'll stay that way while you're working on them. (For more information, see the lockout/tagout video tip at www.finehomebuilding.com).

Now take a close look at the cables coming into the box; take notes on how they're connected. Sometimes it's helpful to label the wires with masking tape and a felt-tip pen. If the old ceiling box is a ½-in.-deep pancake-style box, removing it is usually just a matter of pulling some nails or a couple of screws. For a side-nailed box, I've found that the best removal tool to use is a hacksaw blade in a holder, or a reciprocating saw outfitted with a thin, short blade to cut the nails. Be careful that you don't chew up the wiring as you cut.

After removing the box, check the wires. If the insulation on the wires is old and deteriorated, use electrical tape or heat-shrink tubing (available in most electronics-supply stores) to insulate them. If the insulation is too cracked and you have access from above, cut back the old wires, install a splice (or junction) box, and run new cables to the fan-box location. If the wiring is armored (BX) cable, make sure the metal jacket is in good condition; if it's rusty or corroded, install a junction box and run new cable.

Finish Up with Solid Support and Elementary Wiring

During retrofits, the most common mistake is not to upgrade the outlet box. Use a fan-rated outlet box that's secured to solid

---

Use a Fan-Rated Box

Before installing a ceiling fan, electrical code requires that you use a fan-rated outlet box that will support the extra weight and the motion associated with a fan. A fan-rated box will be labeled as such inside and typically can support up to 70 lb.

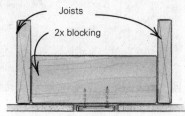

Low Profile
A ½-in.-deep pancake box is meant to be screwed to a joist or block. It's used if only one cable is coming into the box.

Joists
2x blocking

Deeper Profile
A 2¼-in.-deep box can be attached to blocking between joists and is roomy enough to handle more than one cable. It is also available in a saddle-mount configuration.

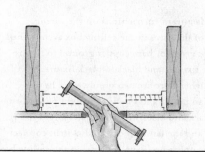

No Blocking, No Problem
Paired with a deep box, this hanger is meant to span between two joists and takes the place of wooden blocking.

Continued →

Installing a Ceiling Fan Is a Straight Forward Job

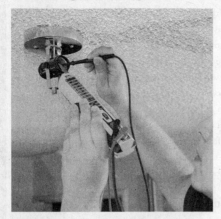

1. MAKE SURE THE OLD FIXTURE IS DEAD. After cutting power at the service panel, use a contact voltage tester to test the wires in the fixture box. Cover all but the end of the probe with electrical tape, which reduces the chance of shorting the probe to the fixture's shell if the power is not off.

2. INSTALL THE HANGER. After removing the old box, install the new. In this case, we used a fan-rated hanger bar and outlet box. The hanger bar is inserted first, squared up to the joists, and centered in the hole. The bar then is twisted clockwise, which pushes the barbed ends into the joists.

3. INSERT THE NEW BOX. Remove a knockout and insert a plastic cable clamp before attaching the box to the hanger bar. Slip the cables into the cable clamps as you slide the box into the hole.

5. SAVE YOURSELF A HEADACHE. Once you've identified all the parts, thread the wires through as you assemble the fan motor, canopy trim ring, canopy, and base. Make sure the parts are assembled in the right order now, rather than later. Don't attach the blades until the fan body is in place.

6. HANG THE MOTOR. After attaching the base or hanging bracket to the fan box with 10/24 or #12 screws, hang the fan body from the hook on the base, and splice the wires together with heavy-duty wire nuts.

7. SECURE THE MOTOR. Insert two screws into the mounting plate, then lift the fan body onto the screws and secure it to the plate. Add a third screw if included by the manufacturer, and then slide the upper canopy in place.

An Extension Keeps the Fan at the Right Height

A fan is most efficient when its blades are 7 ft. to 9 ft. from the floor. For higher or sloped ceilings, fans typically are suspended from extension rods, available in varying lengths from manufacturers.

blocking or framing. Also, when assembling the fan, be sure to use the rubber isolation pads included with it; they're meant to reduce wobbling and to stop fan noise from telegraphing to the ceiling.

Follow the manufacturers' instructions on the wiring. Typically, the colors of the wires in the ceiling box are matched with the fixture wires: green or bare copper ground to fixture green, white to white fixture, and black to black fixture.

For a fan with a light, there are two supply wires in the fixture, one for the fan power and one for the light power (often black and blue, or black and black with a blue stripe). If you're controlling the light and the fan with one wall switch, connect both of them to the supply wire (usually black) in the ceiling box.

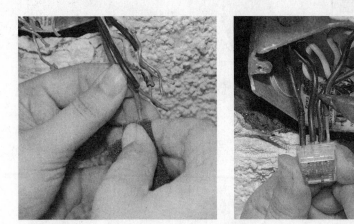

4. CLEAN WIRES FOR A BETTER CONNECTION. Use the manufacturer's locknuts to attach the box, then clean the exposed wire ends with a nylon scrubby and make the splices as needed. Here, we used a UL-listed pressure connector because the wires were short and there was no practical way to splice in longer cables.

8. ATTACH THE LIGHTS. This model included a light fixture, which attached to the underside of the fan body. The wiring connections usually are made with a snapfitting, and then the fixture is screwed to the fan body.

Be Sure the Power Is Off

In older houses, alternative wiring schemes might literally shock an otherwise careful electrician. For instance, there may be power in the ceiling box even after the light is turned off at the wall switch. In one common scenario, power goes to the ceiling box and a switch loop is dropped to the switch. Or the box is used as a junction box, either for the light circuit, or for the light and a different circuit.

A third possibility is that the wiring is just messed up; for instance, the hot and neutral wires may be reversed. Be sure to test the wiring with a good voltage tester (see "Building Skills," *Fine Homebuilding* #172). Also, use a ground reference—the grounded conductor socket of an extension cord that's plugged into a grounded outlet known to be good—with your voltage tester to check the polarity of wires, especially old ones that may not be color-coded.

If there are two wall switches, there will be a three-conductor-with-ground cable (12-3 wg) from the switch box to the ceiling box. I use the black conductor to control the light, and the red to operate the fan. By convention, the switch for the light should be the one located closest to the door.

The light-fixture part of the fan is installed after the fan is hung. Some fan models have a factory-installed modular connector for the light fixture. Remove the cover at the bottom of the fan housing, plug in the light fixture, and fasten the fixture to the fan housing.

On other fan models, the light-fixture wires connect to the corresponding supply wires with twist-on wire connectors. I usually toss those and use the type that have wire springs inside;

they make for a better connection.

Some ceiling-fan models have a remote-control unit that fits into a switch box so that no wires are needed between the wall switch and the fan. There must be power at the fan and at the switch, but sometimes, it's a lot easier to get power at those two locations and not have to run a switching cable between them.

The job isn't complete until you've checked the fan to make sure it's balanced. Run the fan at the highest speed; if it shakes or wobbles, check all the mounting hardware, starting with the ceiling box. Are all the screws, washers, and spacers in place, and tight? Then examine the fan blades and arms, and replace any that are bent or warped.

Continued →

Retrofit Undercabinet Lights

By Rex Alexander

The good thing about European-style cabinets is the crisp lines of the frameless box and full-overlay doors. The bad thing is that this design makes it hard to conceal undercabinet lighting. When I custom-build Euro-style cabinets, I add a 2-in.-deep tray under the upper units to hide wires and transformers. However, one customer rejected that idea because she thought she would need the extra space and wouldn't need lights. A few years later, she called back a little sheepishly and said she had changed her mind. After being in the kitchen, she realized she needed the lighting. To keep down costs, we decided to find an option that wouldn't require the work of an electrician.

I wanted to keep the cabinet lines as clean as I could and didn't want to disturb the glass-tile backsplash, so I chose not to add anything under the cabinet. Instead, I found some xenon puck lights that fit the bill. These models from American Lighting (www.americanlighting.com) are line voltage and don't require bulky transformers. All I had to do was install an outlet inside the cabinet and then somehow conceal the wires. I routed a wire chase in the bottom of the cabinet and covered it with a false bottom panel made of the same melamine. All that's visible is a cabinet edge thickened by ¾ in.

As tempting as it was, running a new outlet from one of the nearby outlets above the counter is not allowed by the electrical code. After cutting a hole in the cabinet back, I pulled a new circuit from the panel and installed the outlet.

In a different scenario, I might have had an electrician hardwire fixtures to remote transformers and/or the panel, eliminating the outlet and the plugs. But I would still conceal the wiring with this method.

PLUNGE TO THE CHASE. A plunge router with an up-spiral straight bit plows a fast mini-chase into the cabinet's lower panel to hide the cord. Finish excavating the chase to the cabinet side with a chisel.

 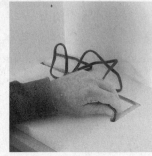

CONNECT THE DOTS. Drill a ½-in. hole through the cabinet side, and repeat the routing and chiseling process on the adjacent cabinet. Next, check that the fixture wires run smoothly in the chase with enough slack to reach the outlet.

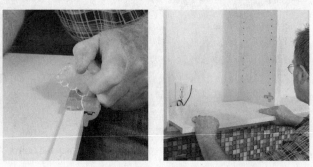

FALSE BOTTOM WITH CLOSE TOLERANCES. Cut a piece of ¼-in. or ½-in. melamine to fit tightly into the bottom of the cabinet. Rip and glue ¼-in. strips onto the sides to make room for the wire. Cover the edges with iron-on melamine tape.

LOCATE THE FIXTURE. These pucks were centered in the middle of each cabinet. Use a hole saw of the appropriate diameter to cut through the lower applied end of the cabinet. Follow with a ½-in.-dia. drill bit to cut through the melamine for the wires.

CABINET SURGERY. Decide where the outlet is best placed, and mark the outline of the cuts. After drilling holes at each of the corners, use a saw to cut both the cabinet back and the drywall behind carefully. Fish the wire up, and install the outlet box.

Compact Cordless Saw

Somewhere along the line, I picked up a small VPX lithium-ion cordless reciprocating saw made by Black & Decker. I used it one day when I didn't have anything else handy, and I found that it was a great tool for some little jobs. It's compact and lightweight, though not particularly strong. I hide it under the rest of the tools in my van.

Contents

Plumbing

Sensible Plumbing

By Dave Yates

"We have very low pressure at the master-bathroom shower, and if any other plumbing is used, we literally have no water coming out of the showerhead." The frustration in my new customer's voice was palpable, and during the drive to his country estate, thoughts about the root causes of his home's water-pressure woes ran through my head. I pulled into the driveway of what had to be a multimillion-dollar home. How could a house that looked this great be suffering so much internally?

I saw the problem almost as soon as I descended the stairs to the basement: a single pair of ½-in. PEX lines—one hot and one cold—running 75 ft. along the ceiling, with T-fittings spliced in at intervals to serve fixtures on the three floors above. The master bath's lines were last along this undersize flow-through system, and as you might guess, the master bath was on the third floor.

What were they thinking? Simply put, they weren't. Good plumbing isn't rocket science; it's applied science. Boil it down and you've got about 25% knowledge and 75% common sense. The problem is that most rough-plumbing jobs are won or lost by a bid process that emphasizes cost-cutting over performance. But doing things right and controlling costs are not mutually exclusive ideas. Both of them need to be engaged in designing and installing a plumbing system that makes sense.

At its most basic, plumbing is simply the practical application of hydraulics and physics to bring clean, healthy water from a municipal water main or a well to the places in the house where it's needed—and when we're finished with it, to remove the waste via the sanitary-sewer system to the municipal sewer or septic tank. Doing this sensibly does that while taking the long view by promoting the conservation of water and energy, ensuring delivery of water at safe temperatures, planning for future maintenance, and most important, guaranteeing satisfactory performance from day one. Here, I'll outline the simplest, most sensible ways to ensure that that happens.

It All Starts with Enough Water

The first step in designing any well-performing plumbing system is calculating how much water will be required for the PDL (peak-demand load). The term is more often associated with energy demands, but I use it to describe the amount of water required to meet the needs of the primary fixtures should they be used simultaneously. Once that's determined, I usually use a percentage—60%—as a basis for the system's capacity unless the owners are available to indicate actual usage habits.

PDLs vary widely but can easily be determined by checking the manufacturers' specification sheets for the fixtures to be installed in the house. At the very least, generalizations can be drawn based

Continued →

on federal regulations, which limit showerheads to 2.5 gal. per minute (gpm) at 80 psi, lavatory faucets to 1 gpm, kitchen sinks to 2.2 gpm, and toilets to 1.6 gal. per flush (gpf). Water-saving fixtures, such as those under the EPA's WaterSense designation, use less. Generalizations can get you into trouble, however, as I found recently when some homeowners called me to find out why the European rain showerhead they had installed was barely drizzling lukewarm water down on them. Never mind that the thing was mounted 10 ft. in the air in a shower big enough for a football team—it had a listed flow rate of 2.5 gpm and was being fed by a 90-ft.-long run of ⅜-in. pipe.

The big culprits that throw PDL calculations off are showerheads and whirlpool-tub fillers; they deserve full attention in terms of number, position, and flow rates. Ask the homeowner, if there is one, what his or her family's bathing habits are, and consider that in your calculations. If it's a spec house and a second-floor bath has a walk-in dual shower, that's a red flag where flow and adequate hot water are concerned. Above all else, pay attention to the master bath, because if the head of the house isn't getting enough water, someone's going to hear about it. If you don't have the time or information available to tally up every fixture's flow rate, there's information on PDL in Appendix E of the International Plumbing Code.

Get the Water There, Fast and Hot

I'm working right now on a 12,000-sq.-ft. house, and it's not unusual in a house like that to see a ⅜-in. water line running 150 ft. from manifold to faucet. I'm sure the guy who installed it was thinking, "Hey, it works at 50 ft., so I guess it'll work at 150 ft."

Getting the sizing and layout of supply lines right isn't terribly complicated, but these days, there's more than one way to deliver water: a flow-through trunk-and-branch system; a home-run system with each fixture having its own water line run to a central manifold; or a hybrid of the two. This is where your diligent PDL homework should pay off. If the home's water is to be distributed

by a flow-through system, each group of bathroom fixtures will be served by a pair of hot/cold water lines that need to meet that branch group's PDL. A home-run system's individual-fixture water line(s) must meet the PDL for that fixture. A hybrid system can provide lower material and labor costs than those of a home-run system by combining fixtures into groups where a drop-off in flow or water-pressure to the neighboring fixture either won't be noticed and/or won't create a potential scalding issue. An example is a dishwasher tied onto the kitchen-sink hot-water line and toilets tied onto bathroom-sink cold-water lines. In all systems, the total PDL must be considered for the main-trunk hot/cold lines or main hot/cold feeds to the manifold(s).

Most flow-through trunk-and-branch systems I see miss the mark by just one pipe size. An optimal distribution system for the average home will use 1-in. trunk lines with a combination of ¾-in. and ½-in. branch lines. (The ¾-in. lines go to baths and showers; everything else gets ½ in.) When I'm using a home-run system, I'll run 1-in. lines at least to the manifold's cold- and hot-water inlets.

Typically, though, I find trunk lines are ¾ in. with ½-in. branches, which leads to consumer complaints regarding temperature and pressure fluctuations. Those narrow trunk lines will save a couple hundred bucks in the course of a job—but it's not always the best way to plumb a house.

Pipe size, along with pipe material and the velocity of water running through it, all figure in the amount of water pressure (in psi) lost along a run of piping (the chart above offers an example). There's also friction loss due to fittings and valves, as well as a standard loss of 1 psi for every 2.31 ft. of rise. So a static pressure of 30 psi in the basement at a well pump will drop off to less than 15 psi on the third floor of a three-story McMansion due to the 35-ft. rise from pump switch to showerhead. A master bathroom with dual shower valves is headed for problems unless the designer or installer properly sizes the supply lines. Charts showing pressure losses for all pipe sizes and types as well as friction losses are easily found in code books.

Sensible Supply

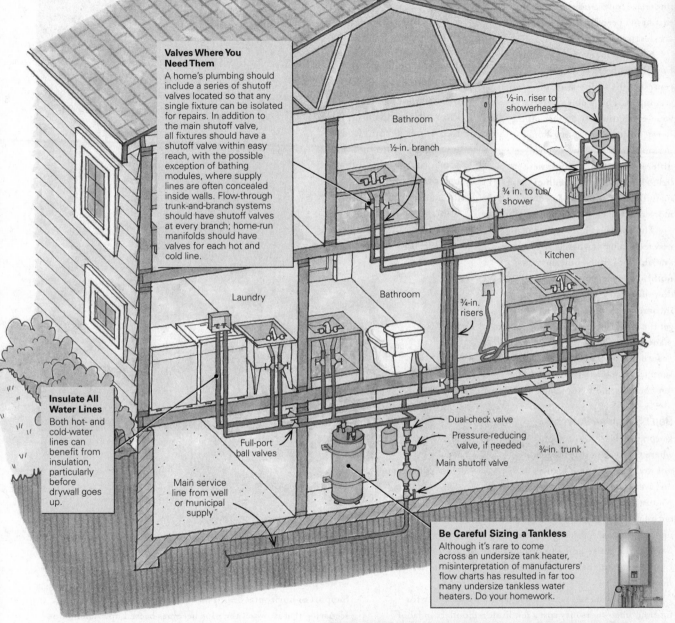

Valves Where You Need Them

A home's plumbing should include a series of shutoff valves located so that any single fixture can be isolated for repairs. In addition to the main shutoff valve, all fixtures should have a shutoff valve within easy reach, with the possible exception of bathing modules, where supply lines are often concealed inside walls. Flow-through trunk-and-branch systems should have shutoff valves at every branch; home-run manifolds should have valves for each hot and cold line.

Insulate All Water Lines

Both hot- and cold-water lines can benefit from insulation, particularly before drywall goes up.

Bathroom

½-in. riser to showerhead

½-in. branch

¾ in. to tub/shower

Kitchen

Laundry

Bathroom

¾-in. risers

Dual-check valve

Pressure-reducing valve, if needed

¾-in. trunk

Main shutoff valve

Full-port ball valves

Main service line from well or municipal supply

Be Careful Sizing a Tankless

Although it's rare to come across an undersize tank heater, misinterpretation of manufacturers' flow charts has resulted in far too many undersize tankless water heaters. Do your homework.

Enough Water, All the Time

You can't plumb a house well without an accurate estimate of supply needs, the peak-demand load. PDL is easily determined by checking manufacturers' specs for the fixtures to be installed in the house, or drawn from federal regulations that govern flow limits. The chart at right illustrates the PDL calculations for the house in this illustration.

Fixture	PDL in gpm	Quantity	Total gpm
Shower/tub filler	2.5	1	2.5
Lavatory sinks	1	2	2
Toilet	1.6	2	3.2
Kitchen sink	2.2	1	2.2
Dishwasher	2	1	2
Ice maker	0.5	1	0.5
Laundry tub	5	1	5
Clothes washer	5	1	5
Hose faucet	5	1	5

Total potential PDL: 27.4

Continued ➜

Size That Water Heater Right

I don't typically see tank-style water heaters that are grossly oversize or undersize for the task at hand. But that hasn't been true in the case of tankless water heaters.

Early on, many manufacturers' flow charts didn't accurately represent the temperature of water coming in. The problem was, if you were getting 40°F water off the street, what came out in gallons per minute at 120°F was much different from what people were led to believe. To the credit of these manufacturers, their charts are now more realistic.

The answer is not to avoid using new technologies when they're available and fit the bill; there's nothing sensible about that. But do your homework. Find out the incoming water temperature, and get the right information from the manufacturer regarding flow rates to ensure that what's getting installed is up to the job based both on water temperature and fixture demand.

Don't Skimp on Valves

In competitive-bid situations where the low bid gets the job, it's not unusual for home-owners to discover during a crisis that they've got just one shutoff valve for their entire plumbing system. This sets up the potential for going without water in the entire house until a plumber arrives for a repair. Even home-run manifolds can be purchased without valves to shave costs.

Adding in the valves that make maintenance easier for future homeowners may cost a few hundred dollars in labor and materials—enough to cost a conscientious plumber the job. Better-quality plumbing systems will incorporate additional shutoff valves in the water-distribution lines, and the best systems will incorporate individual-fixture shutoff valves to isolate any type of problem until it can be repaired without affecting the remainder of the home's plumbing system.

Pressure Loss Over Distance: PEX

Pipe sizing is based on the following factors: gallons per minute (gpm) at peak load, velocity, and pressure drop caused by resistance to flow. Plumbing codes limit flow to 8 ft. per second (fps) to avoid noise and hydraulic erosion. Although tubing can carry flow rates in excess of 8 fps, the following chart illustrates the loss of pressure (in psi per 100 ft.) for PEX tubing at 8 fps.

Tube size	⅜ in.	½ in.	⅝ in.	¾ in.	1 in.
Maximum gpm at 8 fps	2.25	4.5	6.5	9	15
Psi loss per 100 ft. (60°F water)	32.5	25.9	20.3	17.17	12.72

Sources: Watts, Viega, and Uponor

Support Your Local Waste Line

Drainage lines in a home normally rely on gravity to carry away waste. Standard fall tilts at ¼ in. per ft. in the direction of flow. Support of horizontal drains means designing for a worst-case scenario—that is, when the pipe becomes backed up. Water alone weighs 8.34 lb. per gal. Pack in solids and grease, and it doesn't take a rocket scientist to understand why plastic drains require support every 4 ft. I've come across more than my share of plastic hanger strap, which, while lightweight and easy to handle, can stretch, become brittle, and break off, causing drain-line sags that collect solids and water that build into problems.

The advent of low-consumption fixtures is causing some folks to hesitate in their use of high-efficiency toilets that use 1.28 gal. per flush or less. The concerns center on what's called "drain-line carry," the distance a toilet flush will carry simulated

Sensible Drainage, Waste Removal, and Venting

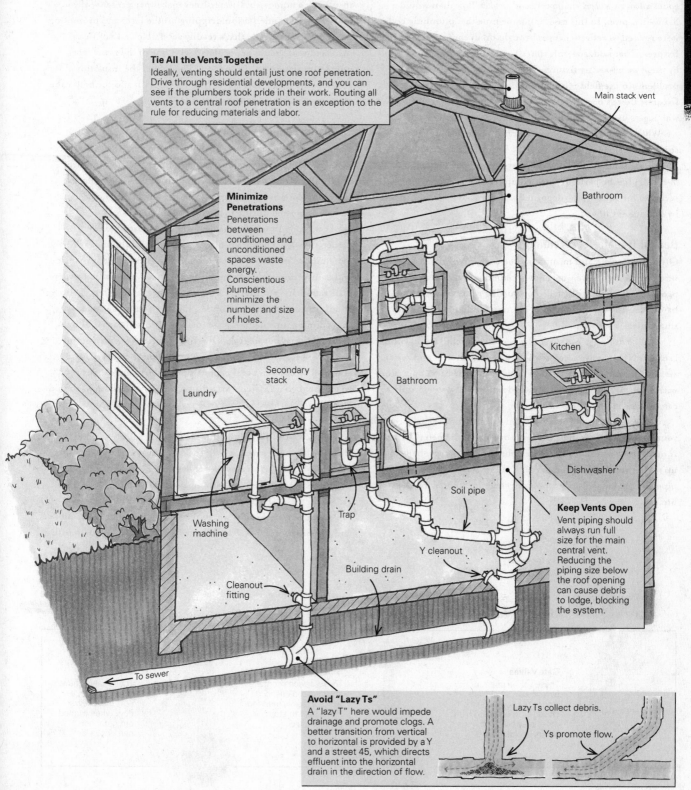

Tie All the Vents Together
Ideally, venting should entail just one roof penetration. Drive through residential developments, and you can see if the plumbers took pride in their work. Routing all vents to a central roof penetration is an exception to the rule for reducing materials and labor.

Main stack vent

Bathroom

Minimize Penetrations
Penetrations between conditioned and unconditioned spaces waste energy. Conscientious plumbers minimize the number and size of holes.

Kitchen

Secondary stack

Laundry

Bathroom

Dishwasher

Keep Vents Open
Vent piping should always run full size for the main central vent. Reducing the piping size below the roof opening can cause debris to lodge, blocking the system.

Soil pipe

Trap

Washing machine

Y cleanout

Building drain

Cleanout fitting

To sewer

Avoid "Lazy Ts"
A "lazy T" here would impede drainage and promote clogs. A better transition from vertical to horizontal is provided by a Y and a street 45, which directs effluent into the horizontal drain in the direction of flow.

Lazy Ts collect debris.

Ys promote flow.

Continued ➤

human waste. The challenge here is that the larger diameter, 4-in.-minimum-size, below-grade pipe required by plumbing codes allows a wider, shallower, and weaker flow than would a 3-in.-dia. pipe. In this case, it may be time that plumbing codes were revised to reflect changes brought on by these water-saving fixtures. That said, the only times I've seen changes brought on by these water-saving fixtures. That said, the only time I've seen problems in the field related to drain-line carry and low-flow fixtures, there's been a belly or sag in the middle of the line, which gets us back to the issue of support.

While on the subject of waste drains, note this: T-fittings should never be laid on their backs. Drainage cascading into this "lazy T" will not be directed downstream, as it would using a Y-fitting, but be partially diverted upstream, setting up a perfect scenario for solids to be deposited that may not be scrubbed away by subsequent flows.

Design Trouble-Free Venting

Often overlooked and misunderstood in terms of their importance, vents are what allow a plumbing system to function properly. Improperly installed or missing vents can wreak havoc, causing drains to siphon out traps and toilets to perform sluggishly.

Unlike drainage lines, vent lines can run uphill or downhill as long as no bellies are created where water will collect and restrict airflow. In vent lines, T-fittings may lie on their backs and, along with Y-fittings, be installed upside down so that water droplets can use gravity to drain away.

Vent piping should always be run full size for the main central vent; side branches can be the same or smaller diameter. Vents should never be reduced because debris (leaves, birds, balls tossed up on the roof) has the potential to fall into the larger diameter pipe and get lodged at the point of reduction, rendering the vent useless.

Insulate Lines When Walls Are Open

While it's more common to find hot-water lines insulated, insulating a home's cold-water lines makes perfect sense if you want to avoid condensation dripping off the lines and promoting mold growth. Any line that's readily accessible and not in an insulated wall should be insulated with one of the many types of pipe insulation on the market. The higher the insulation's R-value, the more resistant to heat loss or gain and the better the transfer of stable water temperatures.

Leave No Penetration Unsealed

The average home leaks air, allowing heated air to exit in winter and hot, humid air to enter during summer, wasting as much as 40% of a household's annual energy budget. Commonsense plumbing designs minimize the number and size of holes, cuts, and voids created during the installation phase.

Long gone should be the days when oversize holes were drilled through a home's timber skeleton for plumbing. While penetrations need to be large enough to accommodate expansion and contraction without generating noise, all penetrations where exfiltration and infiltration will occur—specifically, those between conditioned and nonconditioned spaces—need to be sealed shut. Simply stuffing fiberglass insulation into those voids may look satisfying, but fiberglass doesn't block airflow. Expanding closed-cell foam or fire caulking will prevent the energy loss affecting most homes and is best applied during construction when roughed-in systems are still accessible. Vent systems should be designed with as few roof penetrations as possible.

Maximize Scald Protection

If you've built a new house over the past decade, chances are that plumbing codes (in areas where codes have been adopted and are enforced) required the bathing-module faucets be classified as "scald guard." There are three types: P-only, which react to pressure changes; T-only, which react to temperature fluctuations; and combination P/T valves. What you most likely ended up with,

Rating Valves: Ball Valves Are Best

Gate Valves
These valves interrupt flow by inserting a flat plate across the liquid's path. If closed or opened too hard, gates may break off from stems in older valves.

Globe Valves
These devices contain an internal baffle in which a disk is inserted into a seat to stop the flow of liquid.

Ball Valves
These valves have a sphere with a port that allows flow when aligned but not when perpendicular.

Support Waste Pipes
Horizontal plastic piping must be supported every 4 ft. The support used must be strong enough to support the line when it's completely full (i.e., clogged).

Protect from Punctures
Nail plates protect plumbing lines passing through studs from inadvertent punctures.

Seal Penetrations
Penetrations should be minimized and sealed with foam, not stuffed with fiberglass.

Plumbing As It Ought to Be

A conscientious waste-and-vent job includes drain-pipe support and foam sealant at penetrations, as well as nail plates to protect pipes from punctures.

Watts #1170 thermostatic mixing valve

due to costs, are pressure-balance faucets that work well—as long as the hot- and cold-water temperatures are always the same. In the real world, hot- and cold-water delivery temperatures are constantly changing. Pressure-balance scald-guard faucets are blind to temperature changes. One that is adjusted to deliver a maximum of 120°F during the winter when cold water enters the home at 40°F will deliver much hotter water when cold water enters the home at 80°F. T-only scald-guard faucets are an improvement in safety and cost a little bit more, but the P/T combination scald-guard valves offer premium protection with pricing that's no longer cost prohibitive.

At the same time, tank-style water heaters should be equipped with an ASSE- listed (American Society of Safety Engineers) thermo-static scald-guard device. Codes governing these water heaters allow the storage temperature to exceed the thermostat's setting by up to 30°F. A water heater that's set for 120°F can, therefore, deliver 150°F water and still meet code. Each year in the United States, more than 100,000 people seek medical treatment for hot-water scald burns, with more than a quarter of them children and the elderly, whose skin is thinner and more susceptible to scald burns.

Continued ➡

Better Undersink Plumbing

By Rex Cauldwell

The plumbing system under the average kitchen sink is ill-conceived. Traditional plumbing designs drain slowly and are prone to leaks. This is because the plumbing usually is constructed with small-diameter trap-pipe material, configured with impeding 90° elbows, and connected with numerous compression joints that seal via plastic or rubber gaskets that can leak after only a few years or if pipes are jostled. Making matters worse, water-supply and drain lines occupy much of the central area of the cabinet, limiting storage space.

Frustrated with the downfalls of traditional undersink plumbing systems, I now construct plumbing so that all the drain tubes and water-supply lines fit snugly and securely against cabinet walls. While making this modification, I do simple upgrades in hardware, and as a result, I not only increase storage capacity in the cabinet but also am left with a better-performing plumbing system that drains faster and is less likely to clog, leak, or be damaged by everyday household abuse.

The Downfalls of Traditional Sink Plumbing

1. The 90° turns in small-diameter tubing reduce drainage capabilities. These areas are also susceptible to clogs.

2. Thin-walled PVC with a 1-in. interior diameter slows water flow significantly.

3. A freestanding unit in the center of the cabinet is less durable than one supported by cabinet walls. It also takes up valuable storage space.

4. Unsupported water lines come directly through the middle of the cabinet floor.

5. Compression joints are sealed with rubber or plastic gaskets. These joints are prone to leaks, especially when jostled.

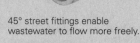

1 Flexible rubber elbows allow the plumbing system to absorb impact and are easy to remove if the system needs cleaning.

2 90° PVC elbows should not be used often, but sometimes are necessary when space is tight.

3 1½-in. schedule-40 PVC increases water flow, reduces clogs, and has greater durability than standard 1-in. plastic pipe.

4 45° street fittings enable wastewater to flow more freely.

5 A double-Y fitting has a large diameter that reduces bottlenecking in the system.

6 The dishwasher connection is made with a ½-in. chrome or galvanized nipple, a ½-in. by ¾-in. reducing bushing, and a 1½-in. slip by ¾-in. thread bushing.

7 A 1½-in. schedule-40 trap prevents sewer gases from escaping the plumbing system. It also captures items that have dropped down the drain.

8 A flexible T-fitting connects the plumbing system to the subfloor drain line. It also allows the rigid section of the plumbing to move when bumped.

9 A 1½-in. PVC cleanout fitting provides a vent tie-in point and access to the subfloor drain.

Well-Designed Parts Improve Plumbing Performance

The 1½-in. schedule-40 PVC used in this setup improves water flow, while the glued joints offer better leakproof connections than standard compression fittings. Also, the thick rubber components are removable, which allows the drainage system to be taken out if valuables need to be removed from the trap.

A 2×6 helps to support water-supply lines.

In new construction, bring supply and drain lines through the floor at the back of the cabinet. In retrofits, try to do the same by rerouting pipes from the basement. In the setup shown here, access in the basement was limited, so I moved the supply lines to the next-best place: the side of the cabinet.

Primed and glued joints offer a far superior connection than twist-on compression joints.

Unlike the setup pictured, opposite, my system contains less-aggressive angles that create faster water flow and reduce the risk of clogging.

A reducing coupling ties the 1½-in. drain line to a 2-in. subfloor drain.

Protective flange

Attaching Pipe When Bowls Are Different Depths

My plumbing system can be adapted for single- and double-bowl sinks. With the latter, you might have problems aligning the plumbing against the back wall if the bowls are of different depths and the strainers below are uneven in height. To compensate for different strainer heights, use a 1½-in. schedule-40 cleanout fitting as a spacer. Apply thread sealant to the female end of the fitting, and screw it to the strainer threads. Attach the flexible 90° elbow to the hub on the cleanout fitting with the provided clamp.

Three Venting Options

- Add an air-admittance valve at point. **9**
- Install a vent that runs into the wall cavity and through the roof.
- Widen the subfloor drain line to 2 in. The increased diameter eliminates siphoning, so no vent is needed. With this system, check with your building inspector for approval.

Air-admittance valve

Continued ➡

Fixing Leaky Copper

By Georg Efird

New construction has dominated my plumbing business in Asheville, N.C., for the past two years. My crew and I spent our days installing PEX tubing. The work was clean and quick. Before housing starts picked up, though, and since they've declined, I spent the majority of my time working with copper. These jobs often involved repairing or tapping into copper water lines in old houses.

Whether you're cutting out a leaky joint or tapping into an existing line, there's a methodical, easy-to-learn process to working with copper. Like any trade-based skill, however, practice is the path to mastery. The steps outlined here and some hard-earned tips that I've acquired over the years can save you some time and money on most repairs involving solder.

Turbulent Flow Weakens Joints

Leaks happen, and they happen for many reasons. More often than not, leaks develop over time, especially in tees, 45° elbows, and 90° elbows, which are subject to significant force as water flows. Water slowly eats and erodes copper in these areas. Improper soldering techniques are also a common source of leaks.

The erosive power of water at these diversion points is why fittings are made of a harder copper than piping. Well water or water that contains sediment or sand can be especially hard on fittings. Sand is particularly bad for copper water systems because of its abrasive quality. Sand can cause pinholes to develop around connections, creating small leaks that can be difficult to spot. Wiping each joint with a dry rag is a good way to test for leaks.

The fittings at the water heater are common trouble spots, too. If the fittings are overheated during the installation process, the Teflon tape around threaded connections can melt, causing the joint to leak. Teflon can break down over time due to heat as well.

To prevent leaks, be sure to protect threaded joints from excessive heat during soldering. I use a tubing cutter and a wet rag to isolate these and any other joints I want to protect.

First, Flush the System

To be soldered, a joint needs to be free of water. Water won't allow the joint to heat properly, impeding the solder's bond to the pipe. The best way to ensure that water doesn't creep into the area I'm working on is to drain the system. I do this by turning off the water heater, turning off the water, then opening all the valves in the house.

I turn off electric water heaters at the breaker. To ensure that no one turns on the breaker before I'm finished, I clip a safety lock-out tag on the switch. (Tape works, too.) If it's a gas water heater, I turn

2 Ways to Remove a Leaky Joint

To solder copper properly, all joints need to be free of water. After locating the leak, turn off the water main, then open all fixtures. Removing a joint allows trapped water to purge from the system. Use a 5-gal. bucket to catch the water.

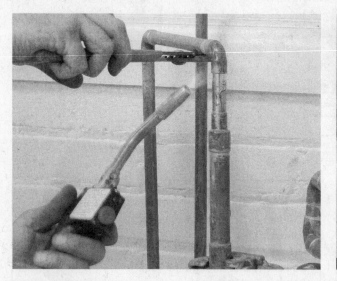

SWEAT IT OFF The least invasive way to remove a leaky fitting is to sweat it off. Heat the pipe and fitting together at the same time, lightly tapping the section with a wrench until the joint can be pulled apart. Wipe away the excess solder while it's hot. Wear eye protection, and watch out for splattering solder. A wet cloth and Channellock pliers are a safe way to handle hot pipe.

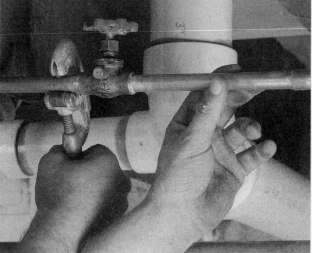

CUT IT OUT If the joint won't sweat off, it needs to be cut out. Place a pipe-cutter wheel far enough back from the joint to clear any hardened solder. Be sure the pipe sits squarely on both wheels. Then spin the cutter around the pipe, tightening the wheel slightly with each full revolution until it breaks free. In tight quarters, use a mini-cutter.

Dam the Drip

A ball of white bread stuffed inside piping will absorb trickling water. Once the water is turned back on, the bread should be purged from the plumbing via an exterior hose bib or a washing-machine-hose line. Plumber's bread works the same way and won't become moldy in your plumbing kit.

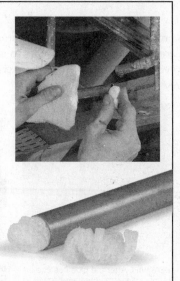

Clean the Pipe and the Fittings

Cleaning the copper removes oxidation, which prevents solder from bonding properly. Fitting brushes fit perfectly around the pipe or in the fitting, so they're easy to use. Don't touch cleaned areas; oil from your hands could impede the solder's bond. Once all pipe and fittings are clean, apply flux, and assemble the pieces.

REAM Use the flare tool attached to the tubing cutter to remove the lip remaining from the cutter wheel. Hold a reamer firmly inside the pipe, and turn it, cutting away the inner lip.

CLEAN Sand the last 1 in. to 2 in. of pipe, then run the sanding cloth over the edge of the pipe as well to remove any burrs left from the reaming tool. Next, scrub the fitting with sanding cloth. Both surfaces should shine like a new penny.

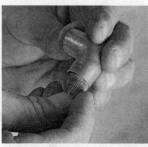

FLUX Apply a thin coat of flux around the pipe and inside the fitting. Don't gob it on. Flux liquefies when heated, so it can bubble and get in the way of solder.

CRIMP THE JOINT Flux acts like a lubricant, so an assembly of pipe and fittings can become unruly. To keep work from falling apart, turn the pipe out of alignment, then crimp the joint slightly with Channellock pliers. This snugs up the fitting, allowing it to hold in any direction. Don't bear down too hard on the pliers, though, which could deform the pipe or the fitting.

it to its lowest setting. Next, I turn off the main water valve and the cold-water valve on top of the water heater. Then I open all faucets in the house, hot and cold, to relieve pressure. This includes hose bibs and toilets, which will drain the rest of the system.

Because I do this work regularly, I have a small supply house in my truck. Piled high in various bins are tees, elbows, and shutoff valves of all sizes, as well as various lengths of pipe from old jobs. I'm able to determine by eye the size of the copper pipe that needs replacing. If you can't size by eye, the most foolproof way to make sure you get the right size is to take a piece of the existing pipe to the hardware store.

Once I've gathered the materials I need, I place a bucket under the section of pipe I plan to remove. Then I sweat or cut out the section and allow any trapped water to drain into a bucket.

If any exterior hose bibs are easily accessible, I like to use my shop vacuum to help blow water through the pipes and out the bib. Opening the relief valve on the water heater helps to break the vacuum if water is still draining. I typically open the relief valve regardless.

Ream, Clean, and Flux

Whether I'm working with piping that's 60 years old or brand new, creating a leak-free joint still requires the same basic steps. The process starts with reaming the ends of the pipe that I just cut. Tubing cutters leave a lip around the inside of the piping. Although it looks insignificant, it decreases the inside diameter enough to affect water flow.

Next, I clean the ends of the pipe and the fittings to remove oxidation, which prevents solder from bonding properly to copper. Although I consider fitting brushes to be well worth the money for this task, I prefer sanding mesh. It's inexpensive and durable, and it works just as well wet as it does dry.

Once I've cleaned the pipe and fittings until they're as shiny as a new copper penny, I apply flux and assemble the pieces. I

Continued ➜

Apply Heat, Then Fill the Joint

Spray nearby combustibles with water for about a minute to protect them from the torch flame. Sheet metal or fire-retardant cloth can also be used to protect plastic piping and framing. If it's necessary to reach past fittings that need to be soldered, solder the farthest ones first to avoid scalding yourself. Wipe down the joint with a damp rag once it has cooled. Don't reheat already-soldered fittings unless absolutely necessary.

HEAT Apply heat from the bottom of the pipe about ½ in. back from where the pipe enters the fitting. Keep the tip of the blue flame no closer than a quarter-inch from the pipe. After 3 to 7 seconds, slowly move the heat closer to the fitting. When soldering shutoff valves, open the valve to prevent damaging the washer.

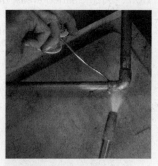

SOLDER After 10 seconds, apply solder from above (the 12 o'clock position) where the pipe meets the fitting. Move the solder back and forth over the joint. Hold the flame between the 4 o'clock and 8 o'clock position to keep flux and solder from dripping into the torch head. A properly heated fitting should draw liquefied solder into the joint. If the solder doesn't melt immediately, remove the torch tip and continue to heat both the pipe and the joint. A properly soldered joint should have a thin, even band around it.

HEAT WIPE After the pipe has cooled but is still warm, use a wet towel to wipe down all pipe to remove flux, which is corrosive. Inspect each fitting connection before turning the water system back on.

DIVERT AND ABSORB THE HEAT Copper is a great heat conductor, so it's important to keep areas like nearby shutoff valves and threaded fittings from overheating. Use a tubing cutter to absorb the heat. The cutter's wheels create an alternate path, but they need only to touch the pipe. Wrapping a vulnerable area with wet cloth provides good protection, too.

like flux that comes with a brush under the lid because it helps the flux to stay clean. If the brush is already in the container, it is less likely to pick up dirt that could end up on a pipe or fitting. On that note, I'm also careful that I don't touch cleaned areas; oil from my hands could interfere with the solder bond.

Before lighting the torch, I make sure to protect plastic piping and framing in the area I'm about to solder. If wood is the only fire hazard around, I spray it with water for about a minute to protect it from the torch flame. More often than not, though, I use sheet metal or fire-retardant cloth to protect plastic piping and framing. In tight areas, I often solder a section before I install it.

Solder Follows Heat

A properly heated fitting should accept solder in a liquid state. The position of the joint—horizontal or vertical—doesn't matter. Liquid solder overcomes gravity to flow toward heat. The amount of solder needed per joint should match the diameter of the fitting. For example, a ½-in.-dia. pipe joint requires only ½ in. of solder. Sometimes I extend only what I plan to use to make sure I don't overfill the joint, which would likely drip. Excess cured solder in the joint could affect water flow. Keep a wet cloth and a bucket handy to catch solder drippings.

With solder and torch in hand, I heat the pipe, then the fitting. Next, I add the solder, working from the lowest fitting up. If it's

necessary to reach past fittings that need to be soldered, I try to solder the farthest ones first to avoid scalding myself. I also make sure to open all shutoffs that will be heated to avoid damaging washers.

If solder starts to melt on a joint, then hardens immediately without flowing into the joint, it means there is still water in the line. I turn off the torch, then remove the fitting after it has cooled. I try to drain the pipe again or dam the water using white bread or plumber's bread.

If soldering isn't an option, it's possible to use a different method. Compression fittings were the solder-free choice for a while, but thanks to new technology, SharkBite fittings (www.sharkbite.com) are a better option. These fittings slip onto copper, PEX, or CPVC tubing, making them incredibly handy for transitioning between different materials. These fittings are pricey, though. A ½-in. elbow can be more than 10 times as expensive as one made of copper. Copper is clearly the most economical choice when multiple joints are involved.

Once I'm done soldering, I wait until every joint is cool to the touch. Then I turn on the water system. I like to keep all faucets open for several minutes to let air and flux drain from the system. Then, one by one, I turn off each fixture beginning with the lowest in the house and working up to the highest. Finally, I look around each joint for leaks. If they exist, I repeat the process. If not, I pack up my things and trust the solder.

Pipe Placement 101

By Brad Casebier

As a plumbing contractor, I am responsible for making sure that the water-supply lines and drainpipes are where they are supposed to be when my crew and I show up to set the fixtures. The best way to ensure a correct rough-in is to follow the instructions for each individual fixture specified in the "cut sheets," or product diagrams. These measured drawings, which show locations for supply and waste lines, are available at manufacturers' websites and from suppliers that sell the product line.

If you're working on a relatively basic kitchen or bath, you can use the typical dimensions shown here, which work with 80% or more of the entry-level to mid-level fixtures we install. There are exceptions to these rules, however, especially with high-end products. I always encourage clients to make selections early; I also remind them that any changes later will result in extra charges and that the extras don't stop with me. A big redo can involve several trades—including carpenters, drywallers, and tilesetters—and can cost hundreds, even thousands, of dollars. It also can mean a delay in the project, which can affect financing and occupancy.

Here are some of the kitchen, bath, and laundry-room plumbing problems we see regularly. Described as gotchas, these items often fall through the cracks and lead to problems down the road.

Kitchen Rough-In

Most folks focus on cabinets, countertops, and appliances when planning a kitchen, but the plumbing is equally important. Get the pipes in the wrong spot, and you'll be tearing into finished work.

Common Kitchen Gotchas

Used for everything from meal prep to family arbitration, the kitchen is the center of a family's life. Avoid these problems, and yours will be the site of domestic bliss.

Changed Cabinet Layout. Plumbing rough-in is often based on the floor plan, but cabinet layout is often changed by cabinetmakers or kitchen designers brought in later. Make sure your layout is based on the most up-to-date information possible.

No Room for the Garbage Disposal. Rough-in kitchen drains so that the trap is about 8 in. Off center (opposite from where the disposal will hang); this will ensure plenty of room for connections. Keep supply lines about 20 in. Above the floor for the same reason.

Noisy Gas Lines. Make sure any corrugated stainless-steel tubing (csst) used for a gas oven and cooktop is sized adequately; otherwise, the pipe can make an annoying whistling sound every time the appliance is used.

Forgetting the Fridge. Add a water-supply box with a valve behind the fridge for the ice maker and water dispenser. Some high-end refrigerators have specific locations, but flipping the box upside down and setting it on top of the bottom plate generally works fine.

Poorly Placed Pot Filler. It's customary to set pot fillers 54 in. High and on the left third of the cooktop, but it's a good idea to ask the family chefs if they have a specific pot they plan to use with the filler.

Air-Starved Islands. It can be tricky to vent sinks in kitchen islands. If you're considering an island sink, check the local plumbing code.

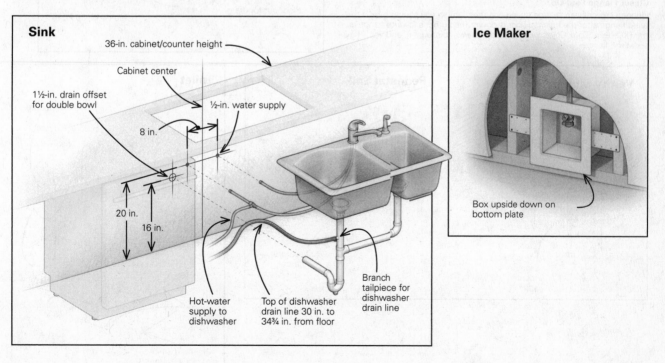

Sink

36-in. cabinet/counter height

Cabinet center

1½-in. drain offset for double bowl

½-in. water supply

8 in.

20 in.

16 in.

Hot-water supply to dishwasher

Top of dishwasher drain line 30 in. to 34¾ in. from floor

Branch tailpiece for dishwasher drain line

Ice Maker

Box upside down on bottom plate

Continued →

Bathroom Rough-In

The safest bet is to select bath fixtures before any plumbing work starts. If you must get the rough-in under way, these dimensions work for most entry- and mid-level fixtures.

Common Bathroom Gotchas

Even though a bathroom is usually the smallest room in a house, a lot can go wrong when you're building it. Use this list to avoid some of the most common bathroom-plumbing missteps.

Too-Tight Toilet.
While code requires only a 30-in. space for a toilet, 15 in. from a cabinet or adjacent wall can make you feel claustrophobic. Try for at least a 34-in. opening, and make sure there's space for the paper holder. Roughing in 13 in. instead of 12 in. from the back wall leaves room for the trim and the drywall.

A Rockin' Throne.
Wobbly toilets ruin wax seals in short order. Add extra blocking around the waste riser, and make sure the toilet is shimmed and caulked at trim-out.

No Room for the Escutcheon.
It's best to know the type of base trim that will be installed. A tall baseboard can interfere with the trim ring around the toilet stub-out. The same thing can happen when supply lines are too close to cabinet backs and sides.

Sacrificed Structural Members.
Plumbed with a 3-in. waste line, toilets are generally placed 12 in. from the wall, but 10-in. and 14-in. rough-in models are available for working around beams and other obstructions.

Too-Low Tub Spout.
Tub fillers, including the curving end, must be at least 1 in. above the tub's flood level; this fix is expensive when tile is involved.

Closet Flange Foul-Up.
Flooring choices can change during construction, so you should mount the toilet flange after the finished floor is down. The author's favorite flange is the TKO from Sioux Chief. Use stainless screws to mount it, and you'll have a lifetime flange.

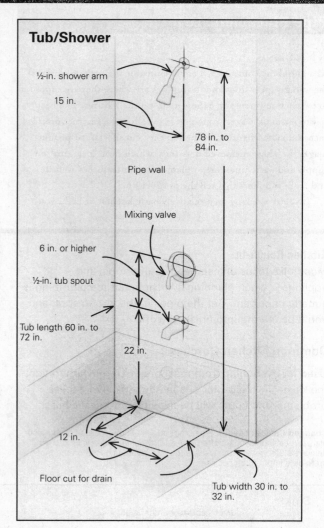

Tub/Shower

½-in. shower arm

15 in.

78 in. to 84 in.

Pipe wall

Mixing valve

6 in. or higher

½-in. tub spout

Tub length 60 in. to 72 in.

22 in.

12 in.

Floor cut for drain

Tub width 30 in. to 32 in.

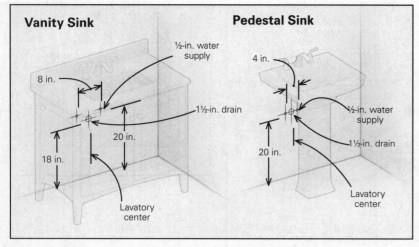

Vanity Sink

½-in. water supply

8 in.

1½-in. drain

20 in.

18 in.

Lavatory center

Pedestal Sink

4 in.

½-in. water supply

1½-in. drain

20 in.

Lavatory center

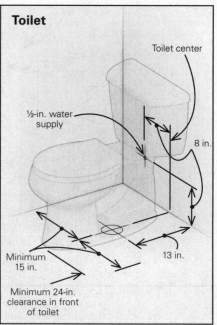

Toilet

Toilet center

½-in. water supply

8 in.

13 in.

Minimum 15 in.

Minimum 24-in. clearance in front of toilet

Which Pipe and Strapping Are Right?

When it comes to drain, waste, and vent applications (DWV), both PVC and ABS have great long-term performance, although we see more PVC in Texas because it seems to handle summertime heat without softening better than ABS. We still use cast iron for some second-floor plumbing and on the drops from second to first floor because cast iron is better at muffling drain sounds. Supply piping continues to be a rodeo. I have had great success with Rehau PEX and Viega PEX, but copper still is used in quite a few of our projects.

When it comes to gas pipe, old-school schedule-40 steel is still my favorite choice. Corrugated stainless-steel tubing (CSST) has its place, but we rarely use it.

It may not be the sexiest product, but "strap iron" is the staple of all residential plumbers for securing DWV and gas systems. There are many fancy products that we use as well, but the main thing is to be sure that pipes are secured every 4 ft. horizontally. This rule of thumb covers most products. See the table at right for specific UPC and IRC requirements.

Laundry Rough-In

A burst washing-machine hose can cause thousands of dollars in damage. Keep shutoffs accessible, and close them whenever the equipment is inactive. Also, include an overflow pan (with a drain) when the laundry area is in finished living space.

Common Laundry Gotchas

Laundry areas have become much more than spaces for washers and dryers, but this added complexity has created a host of potential problems.

Inaccessible Shutoffs.

Washing-machine outlet boxes are typically set at 42 in., but this can be a problem when you want a counter-top over a front loader. You might have to set the box in a remote location to keep it accessible.

The Nonutility Sink.

We like to rough-in utility-sink drains between 10 in. and 12 in., because the depth of the basin is often unknown and because a lower drain gives you greater flexibility.

Noisy Gas Lines.

As in kitchens, make sure any corrugated stainless-steel tubing (CSST) used for a gas dryer is sized adequately. If it isn't, it might produce a whistling noise when the appliance is used.

No Plan for Filtration.

Installing a water softener or filter is expensive if there is no water-softener loop or drain installed. It's cheap enough to stub out a 2-in. drain, 24 in. above the floor. Form a loop outside the drywall with the supply and return lines, and include a ball valve for easier connections later.

The Forgotten Vent.

Remember that dryers need a vent, and the closer the vent is to an exterior wall, the better. Vents under ground-level decks are bad practice, as are uninsulated vents running through unconditioned spaces in cold and mixed climates.

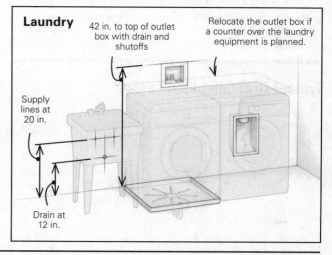

Laundry
42 in. to top of outlet box with drain and shutoffs

Relocate the outlet box if a counter over the laundry equipment is planned.

Supply lines at 20 in.

Drain at 12 in.

Pipe material	Uniform Plumbing Code		International Residential Code	
	Horizontal spacing	Vertical spacing	Horizontal spacing	Vertical spacing
ABS/PVC	4 ft.	10 ft.; provide midstory support if pipe is 2 in. or less	4 ft.; provide for expansion every 30 ft.; provide support at each horizontal branch connection	Base and each story; provide midstory support; provide for expansion every 30 ft.
Threaded-steel water pipe	12 ft.	15 ft.	¾ in. or less: 10 ft. 1 in. or greater: 12 ft.	25 ft. and every other story
Cast iron	5 ft., but 10 ft. is OK when 10-ft. lengths of pipe are used	15 ft.; at the base and each story	Every other joint unless 4 ft. or more; within 18 in. of joints; all horizontal branch connections; no hangers on couplings	15 ft.; at the base and each story
Copper tubing	1¼ in. or less: 6 ft. 1½ in. or greater: 10 ft.	10 ft.	1½ in. or less: 6 ft. 2 in. or greater: 10 ft.	10 ft. and each story
CPVC	¾ in. or less: 3 ft. 1 in. or greater: 4 ft.	10 ft.; provide midstory support if pipe is 2 in. or less	1 in. or less: 3 ft. 1¼ in. or greater: 4 ft.	Each story; provide midstory support
PEX	32 in.	10 ft.; provide midstory support if pipe is 2 in. or less	32 in.	Base and each story; provide midstory support
Threaded-steel or brass gas pipe	½ in. or less: 6 ft. ¾ in. and 1 in.: 8 ft. 1¼ in. or greater: 10 ft.	½ in or less: 6 ft. ¾ in. and 1 in.: 8 ft. 1¼ in. or greater: each story	½ in. or less: 6 ft. ¾ in. and 1 in.: 8 ft. 1¼ in. or greater: 10 ft.	½ in or less: 6 ft. ¾ in. and 1 in.: 8 ft. 1¼ in. or greater: each story

Continued →

Prep and Glue Plastic Fittings

By Mike Lombardi

In my nearly 40 years as a plumber, I've seen just about every possible plumbing mistake, but improperly prepared PVC and ABS connections are what I see most often. Failing to ream or chamfer plastic pipe before it's glued to the fitting is the most common error. Sooner or later, the burr left on the pipe results in a clog, usually during a dinner party or some other inopportune time.

Another problem I see regularly is connections that aren't primed or that have insufficient glue. The solution is easy: Follow the directions on the product container, and hold the connection for 15 seconds while the glue sets.

Dry-fitting (assembling without glue) is the best way to ensure that your work is professional looking and accurate, but keep in mind that it's tough to seat unglued pipes into fitting sockets fully. The resulting difference in length can affect slope and the fit of the pipe, so limit dry-fitting to about four connections before gluing. Finally, wait an hour before running water through any recently glued connections.

1. ESTABLISH A BEGINNING AND AN END. Determine the heights of drains, sewer connections, or other fixed starting and ending points. Work toward connecting them while maintaining a minimum downward slope of ¼ in. per ft.

2. PIPES NEED PROPER SUPPORT. If you're connecting to a length of pipe, make sure it's well supported first. Space hangers every 4 ft. to 6 ft.

7. REMOVE BURRS. After cutting pipes to length, remove any burrs by scraping around the pipe's circumference with a utility knife. Do this on both the inside and outside edges.

8. PRIME FIRST. ABS piping doesn't require primer, but you should prime both male and female sides of any PVC connections. Ensure a neater job by holding the pipe or fitting so that excess primer drips off instead of running down the side.

Typical Drain and Vent Layout

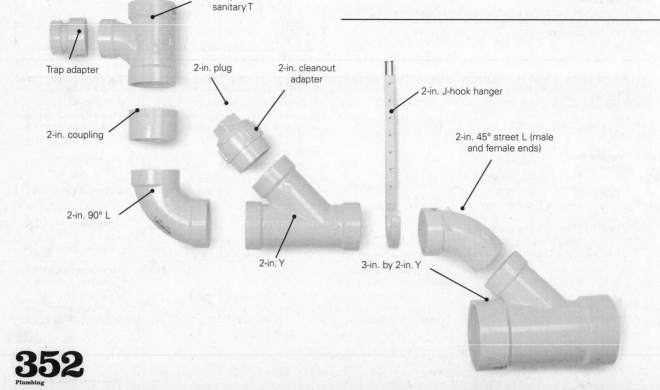

2-in. by 1½-in. reducer coupling

2-in. by 1½-in. sanitary T

Trap adapter

2-in. plug

2-in. cleanout adapter

2-in. coupling

2-in. J-hook hanger

2-in. 45° street L (male and female ends)

2-in. 90° L

2-in. Y

3-in. by 2-in. Y

3. DRY-FIT FIRST. Dry-fitting ensures that pipes are routed and sloped correctly, but limit dry-fitting to about four connections. After marking the pieces, plan the order of reassembly so that you don't work yourself into a corner.

4. CHECK THE SLOPE. A torpedo level is extremely handy for checking that pipes and fittings are sloped for proper drainage. When using the level vertically, make the bubble just touch the line.

5. MEASURE THE PIPE. When it's time to measure for pipe sections, hold a measuring tape between fitting sockets. If necessary, enlist a second set of hands to keep everything in proper position.

6. CUT THE PIPE. There are handsaws for cutting plastic pipe, but most plumbers use a reciprocating saw with a plastic-cutting blade. A miter saw with a combination blade also produces smooth, straight cuts. You also can use a wood-cutting handsaw.

9. GLUE BOTH SIDES. Apply two coats of glue to the male side and a single, light coat to the female side of the connection. Push the parts together with a quarter turn, and hold for 15 seconds while the glue sets.

Making Transitions

Use flexible couplings to connect virtually any type of drain, waste, and vent pipe with any other type of pipe. These couplings are often referred to by the trade name Fernco, which is one of the largest makers. Because the fitting is made from rubber, these connections can sag over time, creating debris-catching low spots, so make sure the pipes on both sides of the joint are well supported.

Plumbing Cement: ABS, PVC, and CPVC

By Justin Fink

Residential water can be routed through a variety of different pipes, and those pipes are joined in different ways. Copper pipes are joined to their fittings with solder, steel pipes rely on threaded connections, and PEX tubing has a wide variety of crimp, expansion, and compression joints. But ABS, PVC, and CPVC pipes rely on solvent-weld cements to create a watertight bond between components. Your choice of cement will be dictated by the type of pipe being joined, your local inspector's preferences, and the environmental conditions during assembly.

Material

They don't appear much different at a quick glance, but ABS, PVC, and CPVC pipes are dissimilar animals, chemically speaking. Because these plumbing connections rely on a solvent-weld joint—where the plastic melts together to form a connection stronger than the pipe itself—those differences are extremely important.

According to Oatey Technical Service, PVC and CPVC cements can be too aggressive on ABS pipe and fittings, especially foam core. PVC solvent cement has a temperature rating of 140°F when cured and cannot be used on CPVC pipe and fittings, which are approved for 180°F continuous operating temperature. These dangers may not be immediately evident, but they can lead to major problems with joints over the long haul. Multipurpose cement would seem an attractive universal choice, but it is not accepted by plumbing code, and therefore, its uses are limited.

Color

The color of the necessary primers and cements allows the building inspector to verify visually that the appropriate product was used for each installation. ABS cement is typically black, but it can be milky white. PVC cement is clear, gray, or blue (for use without a primer in many nonpressure installations). CPVC cement is either

Continued ➜

ABS

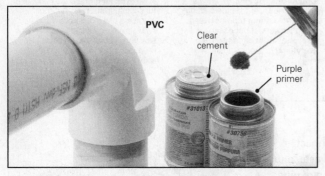

PVC

Clear cement

Purple primer

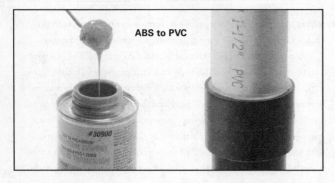

CPVC

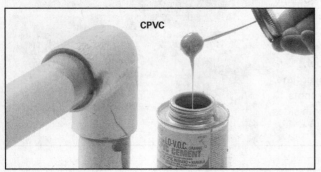

ABS to PVC

1-1/2" PVC

yellow or orange, depending on the brand of pipe.

The inspector also will know to look for purple primer on all PVC and CPVC joints (no primer is necessary for ABS), though clear primer can be used in areas where it is approved by code or on jobs not subject to inspection.

Green-colored transition cement must be used when ABS is being connected to PVC, a common situation when joining household drain, waste, and vent systems to the outgoing city sewer lines at the street.

Consistency

Cements are available in three viscosities, and the choice is directly related to the diameter of the pipe being joined. Regular cement is the thinnest and is intended for pipe up to 2 in. in dia. Medium-duty cement is a bit thicker and is approved for pipes up to 6 in. in dia. Heavy-duty cement is also available for pipes up to 12 in. in dia.

Shutoff Valves

By Don Burgard

Shutoff valves allow plumbing work to be done in a specific room or even at an individual appliance, such as a dishwasher, without having to shut off the water for the entire house. Ball valves are the most common type nowadays, but houses of any age can contain gate valves and globe valves, too. Whether you're installing new valves, replacing old valves, or just wanting to know more about your house's plumbing, it's important to know the differences between ball, gate, and globe valves.

Ball Valves

Ball valves are valued for their longevity and their ability to work perfectly after years of disuse. Inside a ball valve, a sphere usually made of brass, chrome-plated brass, or stainless steel has been drilled through from one end to the other. Attached to the top of the sphere is a lever whose range of movement is just a quarter turn. Move the lever parallel to the pipe, and the opening in the sphere aligns with the water flow. Move it perpendicular to the pipe, and a solid section of the sphere blocks the flow. You can control the flow by moving the lever between 0° and 90°. A partially open ball valve, however, can leave the silicone or PTFE seats on either end of the ball susceptible to deformity from uneven pressure.

One advantage to quarter-turn valves such as ball valves is that they can be shut off quickly. The disadvantage is that this makes water hammer more likely. For that reason, it's best to turn the lever on a ball valve slowly. The levers themselves give ball valves two advantages over wheel-operated valves: First, it's much easier for persons of all abilities to move a lever than to turn a wheel. Second, it's possible at a glance to tell if a ball valve is open. Ball valves have one potential disadvantage over wheel-operated valves: Because shutting off the water flow means turning the lever perpendicular to the pipe, a ball valve may not work in certain tight locations.

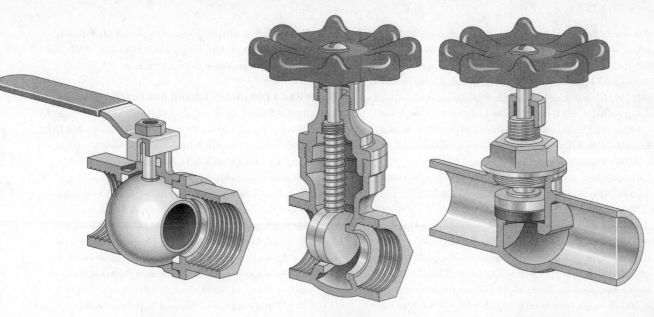

Ball Valves   Gate Valves   Globe Valves

Gate Valves

A gate valve is operated with a wheel that moves a gate up and down. When the gate is in the lowest position, it blocks the flow of water; when it's in the highest position, water can flow freely. Gate valves have either rising stems, which enable you to tell visually if they are open or closed (although not as clearly as the lever on a ball valve), or nonrising stems, which don't. Gate valves are susceptible to corrosion, which can prevent them from opening or closing fully. A heavily corroded stem can even break, rendering the valve useless. Because they open and close slowly, gate valves won't create water hammer. They should be used only in the fully open and fully closed positions. If a valve is left partially open, the gate will vibrate and may become damaged.

Globe Valves

Unlike ball valves and gate valves, globe valves are designed for limiting the flow of water. They are operated with a wheel and a stem like gate valves, but the stem is attached to a stopper that seals shut a baffle—essentially two half-walls that force the water to flow in an Z-pattern. Like gate valves, globe valves close slowly and won't produce water hammer. Because the baffle makes it impossible for water to flow through the valve freely, even in the fully open position, a globe valve reduces water pressure. That reduction, however, makes the stopper and seat less vulnerable to damage than the gate in a gate valve. For water to flow through a globe valve efficiently, the valve must be installed so that the water encounters the top half-wall first. The International Residential Code prohibits globe valves from being used for the main shutoff and the water heater; these locations must have full-open valves, either ball valves or gate valves.

PEX Water Pipe

By Andy Engel

Most of us grew up in homes with copper pipes, and they were reliable enough that we gave them little thought. Joining them takes soldering skills so simple that my father taught me when I was about 10. But a relative newcomer, PEX, is mounting a serious challenge to copper plumbing, despite the latter's long history of reliability.

PEX is a clumsy acronym for cross-linked polyethylene, meaning that it's a strong plastic suitable for potable water. Popularized as the go-to product for radiant-floor heating, PEX has seen its use for potable water grow by about 40% annually. This isn't happening on a lark. The scuttlebutt among plumbers is that PEX is every bit as reliable as copper, yet costs less and is faster to install.

My own experience with PEX involves two underfloor heating systems. The plastic pulls through holes in joists and studs with slightly more difficulty than Romex. Fittings for PEX are expensive, but you don't use many.

What Is PEX Anyway?

Polyethylene is a common plastic whose inert nature makes it valuable for food containers (or in this case, potable-water pipes). You likely poured milk into your morning coffee from a polyethylene jug. PEX differs from your milk jug in that it's cross-linked—its molecules are rearranged to resemble a chain-link fence—which greatly increases the plastic's strength.

Although the polyethylene PEX is made of comes from oil, it is one of the more environmentally friendly plastics. No pipe is without environmental cost. Although much of the copper used

Continued ➜

for pipe is recycled, all of it originally came from mines. And the manufacture of another plastic pipe, CPVC (chlorinated polyvinyl chloride), is said to release dioxin, a potent carcinogen.

Cross-linked polyethylene, although chemically the same as the milk jug, is much tougher and has a "shape memory," allowing it to be stretched or kinked and return to its original shape with time or heat. PEX's shape memory is so strong that at least two manufacturers, Rehau and Uponor, rely on it to create leakproof joints, rather than on crimped metal fittings.

Three different processes are used for cross-linking this plastic, and the resulting products are called PEXa, PEXb, and PEXc. The original, PEXa, dates from the 1950s and has been sold in Europe for radiant-floor heating since 1971. Rehau's Lance MacNevin says PEXa is more forgiving than either PEXb or PEXc, claiming that it can be stretched to about 400% of its manufactured length before failure. But even PEXb and PEXc can stretch substantially. Because of PEXc's cross-linking process (cross-linked with a laser beam while lying flat), it tends to stay flat when rolled out. If you've ever found yourself being followed by a coil of pipe when installing an underground plastic water line, you'll appreciate this seemingly small advantage. PEXb and PEXc are somewhat less expensive than PEXa.

Copper Has a Long Track Record and Few Drawbacks

The American Society of Testing and Materials (ASTM) standard governing copper pipe and fitting sizes was implemented in 1932. That means you can buy a fitting at the hardware store today that will slide right onto a 75-year-old copper pipe.

Studies have shown that copper has anti-microbial properties, perhaps helping to keep your water safe to drink. About the only functional downside to copper is that it is susceptible to developing pinholes in areas with corrosive acidic well water. Andy Kireta Jr. of the Copper Development Association agrees that corrosion can happen, but he notes that "because we have historical data that indicate the areas prone to acidic water, we know to recommend conditioning to neutralize the water's pH in these places." Kireta also points out that "copper tube is one of only a handful of materials that can be recycled and maintain the same level of purity as the original product. That is, you can melt down old copper pipe and use it to make new copper pipe. Most recycled materials, such as steel, paper, and plastics, drop a notch in quality each time they're recycled."

The last plastic pipe to make serious inroads into copper's market dominance was polybutylene, a flexible gray tubing that had problems with leaky fittings. Blame and lawsuits flew like snow in a New England blizzard, and polybutylene disappeared from the market in the mid-1990s. CPVC is approved for domestic potable water, but it doesn't have a huge market share.

If Copper Worked and Plastic Failed, Then Why Risk Using PEX?

With many plumbers gun-shy of plastic pipe after the polybutylene debacle, why take a chance on the PEX generation? First, PEX isn't polybutylene. Polybutylene failed for a number of reasons, one of which was that the fittings were made of a type of plastic that didn't react well with the chlorine used by many municipal water-treatment facilities.

All approved PEX tubing meets ASTM standards. Pipe intended for potable water must meet additional National Sanitation Foundation (NSF) and American National Standards Institute (ANSI) rules. To ensure compliance, samples are tested

No Soldering Required.
Rolls of plastic tubing are far easier to snake through joist and stud bays than are lengths of rigid copper pipe. For this reason, PEX is an excellent choice for remodeling and retrofit situations, allowing you to snake plumbing lines almost as easily as you can snake wire. PEX has a much better resistance to bursting when frozen than copper, and is far less expensive, about 50¢ per ft. vs. 85¢ per ft. for copper, with far fewer fittings to buy.

Tough Tubing, Tougher Connection

These sections of tubing were put to the tests, both tensile and compression. In both cases, the connection held fast.

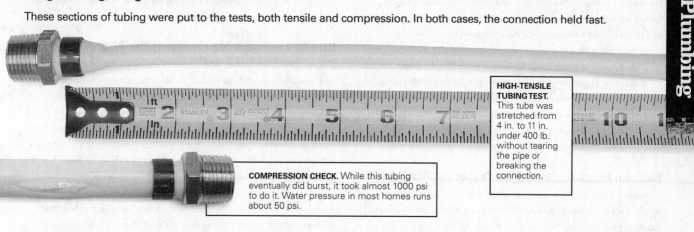

HIGH-TENSILE TUBING TEST. This tube was stretched from 4 in. to 11 in. under 400 lb. without tearing the pipe or breaking the connection.

COMPRESSION CHECK. While this tubing eventually did burst, it took almost 1000 psi to do it. Water pressure in most homes runs about 50 psi.

annually, and unannounced audits of PEX manufacturing plants are made three times a year.

Second, PEX often performs better than copper: It isn't susceptible to pinhole leaks because it's chemically inert; it won't clog with mineral scale because its inner surface is smoother; and it has superior resistance to bursting from frozen water. Jim Bolduck, a Cumberland, Maine, plumber, told me about a PEX-plumbed house he'd seen that had lost its heat in the dead of winter. "That house froze so solid that the boiler split open," said Bolduck. "All the PEX survived, though."

Dana Bres, a research engineer with HUD's Partnership for Advanced Technology in Housing (PATH), points out another asset: "Quality control for all types of plumbing tube (PEX, copper, and CPVC) is excellent, so the pipes themselves rarely leak. Leaks happen at joints, and copper plumbing is loaded with joints. PEX comes in rolls hundreds of feet long, which minimizes the number of joints and the potential for leaks." In 2004, PATH listed PEX plumbing systems using plastic distribution manifolds as one of the top-10 emerging technologies.

PEX and Copper Can Combine for Remodeling

Like CPVC, PEX comes in the same outside diameters as rigid copper pipe (nominal diameter plus ⅛ in.). At least one manufacturer, Watts Radiant, makes compression fittings that work with all three types of pipe. In fact, in my own house, I needed an emergency repair fitting after drilling a hole through a PEX heating line. The old-time plumbing store I went to didn't carry PEX fittings, but they did sell me a

compression coupling for copper pipe. That was five years ago, and although it's not a code- or manufacturer- approved joint, it doesn't leak, either.

For blended systems, PEX manufacturers have fittings that join to PEX at one end and either solder to copper or glue to CPVC on the other. Additional fittings allow PEX to terminate and stub out of the wall or floor.

PEX Can Be Run Like Copper, But That Won't Maximize Its Potential

You can configure PEX plumbing systems several ways, and it's possible to do so in ways that save water. PEX can be configured

PEX Doesn't Have to Be Messy.
Although some plumbers complain that PEX installations are messy, others enjoy the drama of the final hookup to the manifolds. Red (hot) and blue (cold) tubing can make a confusing mass of pipe understandable.

Continued ➤

like a traditional copper system, with larger-diameter trunk lines teeing off to smaller branch lines that feed individual fixtures. Doing so will eliminate some elbows and their potential leaks, but it doesn't take best advantage of PEX's properties.

The PEX industry pushes several other configurations, all of which start out at a plastic or copper manifold, where the hot and cold mains split off to various parts of the house. With manifold systems, each branch has its own shutoff valve, analogous to an electrical system's circuit-breaker panel. Using PEX with manifolds can save water and energy because hot water reaches remote sinks more quickly.

National Plumbing Codes Treat Copper and PEX Equally

Because PEX and copper are the same outside diameter, one might wonder how the inside diameters compare. After all, inside diameter determines flow rate. The walls of PEX pipe are thicker, so the inside diameter is smaller. For several reasons, however, all U.S. plumbing codes treat copper and PEX interchangeably when considering adequate water flow. The inside of PEX is smoother than copper, and PEX offers fewer flow restrictions because it is bent into sweeping curves instead of turning with sharp elbows the way copper and CPVC do.

Although PEX has been part of national plumbing codes since the early 1990s, not every jurisdiction has adopted those codes. Before using PEX for potable water, check with your local building inspector.

Normal PEX Isn't UV-Tolerant

One major shortcoming is that left unprotected, PEX deteriorates when exposed to the sun's UV-rays. Copper doesn't have this problem. Most PEX is warranted for only 30 days of direct sun exposure, but some premium lines coated with a UV-inhibitor are good outside for a year. Even the best PEX can't be left exposed outside, so copper must be used for pipe that's to be exposed to the elements. If you're using PEX under a slab, either cover the pipe where it stubs out of the concrete, or spend more for PEX with a UV-inhibitor.

PEX also is susceptible to damage from certain oil- or solvent-based compounds, and can allow these compounds to pass through the pipe and into the water. Never bury PEX (even if coated with a UV-inhibitor) in contaminated soil, and avoid oils and greases when working with PEX.

How Do I Persuade My Plumber to Use PEX?

I've spoken to a number of plumbers about PEX and didn't find one who flat out refused to use it. Most plumbers who've used it were enthusiastic. Those who were reluctant fell into two camps. A common concern was voiced by Dave Trone, a plumber in Columbia, N.J.: "Plastic and brass expand at different rates, and I think that leaks where PEX pipe joins to brass fittings are simply a matter of time." The other concern I heard surprised me. "It just doesn't look as neat as copper," said one Nebraska plumber.

Although it's true that joints between PEX and brass don't have copper's 75-year track record and that leaking polybutylene fittings are still a sore spot with some plumbers, a representative from Zurn Industries addressed Trone's concerns: "PEX is the most engineered and tested plumbing material out there. Its shape memory allows it to expand and return to size repeatedly, so we're confident of the long-term viability of the joints." Then he showed me a PEX-brass connection that had been subjected to 990 lb. per sq. in. (psi) pressure. The joint had held tight, but the PEX tube burst. Residential water systems generally run at less than 50 psi.

When I brought up the Nebraska plumber's complaint about neatness with Rehau's MacNevin, he replied, "We hear that occasionally. That's why we also make PEX in 20-ft. rigid lengths that can be used in visible locations like a basement."

Manufacturers seem concerned that leaks caused by poor workmanship could undermine the acceptance of PEX, so many offer on-site training and certification to licensed plumbers. In fact, many of the biggest players, such as Rehau and Uponor, won't sell their product to uncertified installers. But because PEX and its fittings are sold through plumbing-supply houses, enforcement of this mandate is spotty. Other manufacturers, however, believe their systems are so simple to use that they're sold at Lowe's and The Home Depot. PEX and its fittings are also readily available online.

If your plumber still isn't buying into PEX, bring up labor savings. Says Bres: "In a recent PATH field evaluation of otherwise identical

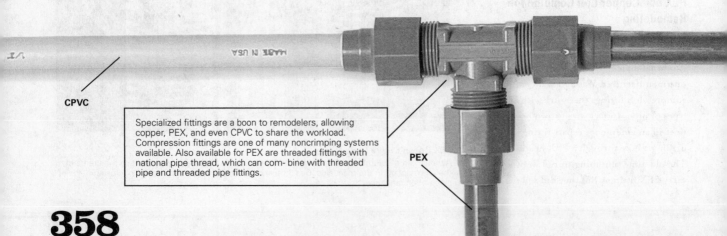

CPVC

PEX

Specialized fittings are a boon to remodelers, allowing copper, PEX, and even CPVC to share the workload. Compression fittings are one of many noncrimping systems available. Also available for PEX are threaded fittings with national pipe thread, which can com- bine with threaded pipe and threaded pipe fittings.

A Leakproof Joint Made Faster Than Soldering

There are many systems for crimping PEX joints. Some are available only to licensed plumbers, but online stores will sell to anyone. The Zurn system is fast and easy.

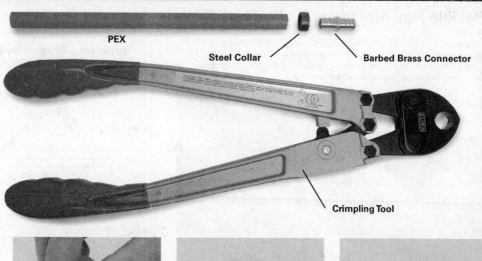

PEX

Steel Collar

Barbed Brass Connector

Crimpling Tool

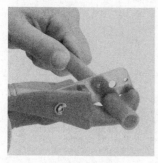

Cut the tubing squarely with a sharp blade in a special PEX-cutting tool.

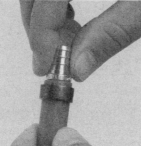

Slip a steel collar over the tube, then insert a barbed brass connector into the tube.

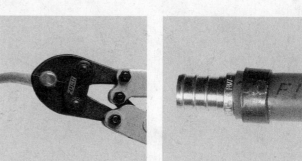

Squeeze the collar with the proprietary crimping tool, and you're done.

homes, it appears that using PEX shaves a day off the plumbing installation, reducing the install time from three days to two."

When I plumbed my new house in 1999, I ran PEX for the radiant-floor heat. For the potable-water system, though, I reflexively used copper because conventionally, that's how you plumb a house. I had a good time soldering the joints and figuring out the system. Being a competent but slow do-it-yourself plumber, I needed about a month's worth of weekends to do the job.

If I had my house to plumb over again, I'd configure PEX in a submanifold system. I think that approach offers the best bang for the buck, and it makes good use of PEX's advantages. Because I'd want to do the work myself, several of the best systems on the market that require pro installation immediately would be out of contention. So my choices would be limited to materials I could buy online or locally. Given that, I wouldn't shop for a particular brand. All the PEX manufacturers I spoke with left me feeling comfortable with their products. I'd look for a supplier of a system; that is, I'd want the fittings and the pipe to come from one manufacturer. I'd look for a supplier happy to provide advice and support. And I'd expect the job to take about half the time.

Copper

Collet

A reusable slip-in fitting uses stainless-steel teeth inside the collet to lock the tubing in place. An internal O-ring makes the seal. To remove, push in the collet while pulling out the tube.

Special fittings allow you to connect copper and PEX in various ways, depending on your needs.

Continued ➜

Flexible Pipe Also Offers Design Flexibility

Incorporating manifolds into the layout can save water and energy because you eliminate most of the pipe between the water heater and the faucet. Although blue (cold water) lines are shown in these layout examples, hot-water layout would be similar.

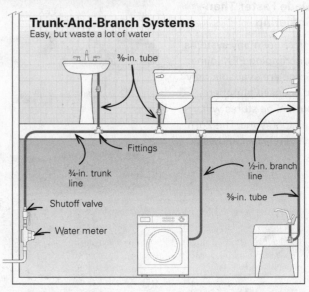

Trunk-And-Branch Systems
Easy, but waste a lot of water

⅜-in. tube

Fittings

¾-in. trunk line

½-in. branch line

⅜-in. tube

Shutoff valve

Water meter

Traditional systems consist of large-diameter (usually ¾ in.) trunk lines to distribute water throughout a house. Smaller branch lines (½ in. and ⅜ in.) tee off to feed individual fixtures. Trunk-and-branch systems have several disadvantages, notably a large number of fittings, which are costlier, slower to install, and more likely to leak than a single run of pipe. Also, a lot of water goes down the drain before hot water reaches the faucet.

Home-Run Manifold Systems
Use the least hot water and the most pipe

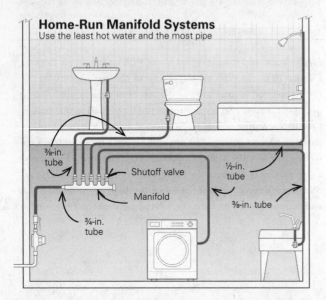

⅜-in. tube

Shutoff valve

Manifold

¾-in. tube

½-in. tube

⅜-in. tube

A large-diameter (¾ in.) main water line feeds the manifold; smaller lines run from the manifold to each fixture. Any fixture in the house can be shut off at the manifold. And because home-run systems don't rely on a large pipe for distribution, you save both water and energy. Simply put, you don't have to leave the faucet running as long before hot water reaches the sink. This design flexibility has a cost, however. Because a dedicated line is going to each fixture, you use a lot of PEX and drill a lot of holes.

Submanifold Systems
Can Be Designed to Save Hot Watermost Pipe

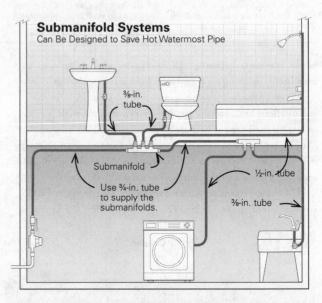

⅜-in. tube

Submanifold

Use ¾-in. tube to supply the submanifolds.

½-in. tube

⅜-in. tube

There are many ways to design submanifold systems, which require far less pipe and drilling than a home-run system. Rather than one main manifold, each bathroom, laundry, and kitchen gets its own submanifold. The simplest system, pictured here, won't save any water over a trunk-and-branch system, but other submanifold systems can be configured as water and energy savers by incorporating a main manifold and a recirculating pump.

Making Basic PEX Connections

By Bruce Norman

MPEX has made plumbing easier. The components are user-friendly for plumbers and leave water systems immediately ready for inspection. The material doesn't require glue joints to set up, and there is no flux to flush out of the system.

Because PEX's flexibility means fewer joints to connect, jobs are completed faster and with less chance of leaky joints. PEX resists the heat loss and scale buildup common to metal pipe.

PEX also has an advantage over alternative materials in cold weather because of its ability to expand rather than crack and break in freezing conditions. This flexibility also greatly reduces water hammer, the sound of metal pipe banging against a house's framing. New adaptive fittings and brackets make PEX even easier to install.

There are two methods to connect PEX that don't require a plumber's license. (Expansion fittings require a plumber's license in many parts of the country.) The push-fit method is great for quick repairs and requires no special tools other than a pipe cutter. For clamp-ring connections, I use a generic crimper, available at most plumbing-supply stores, and stainless-steel band clamps. When planning a PEX plumbing project, remember that only brass fittings (as opposed to plastic fittings, which are sometimes sold in home centers) are approved for underground or underslab use.

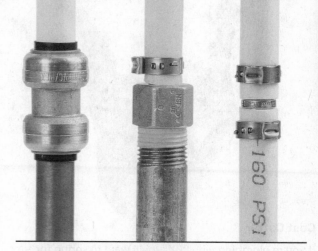

A Fitting for Every Situation

Push-Fit Fitting
Uses metal tines to hold the tubing, in this case PEX and copper, against an O-ring seal. The fittings are sized by the tubing's outside diameter.

Clamp-Ring Connection
Connects PEX to existing metal pipe. PEX tubing is crimped onto the male end, and the female end is either soldered or threaded onto existing pipe.

In-Line Fittings
Used to connect separate lengths of PEX tubing, to create a branch line, or to add a valve.

A Push-Fit Connection

INSERT THE SUPPORT SLEEVE. This piece prevents the PEX tubing from collapsing and breaking the seal. Some manufacturers integrate the support sleeve into the fitting.

INSERT PEX TUBING. For a watertight seal, ensure that the PEX end you want to connect has a straight cut, that the tubing is clean, and that there are no scratches on the outside of the tubing.

INSERT THE COPPER PIPE. The copper-pipe end does not require a support sleeve, but like the PEX, the exterior must be clean and smooth. Finally, to ensure a tight seal, give a final push to both pieces entering the connection. This type of fitting can also connect PEX to PEX.

A Clamp-Ring Connection

FIT THE ADAPTER TO THE EXISTING PIPE FIRST. Whether the adapter fitting is threaded on galvanized pipe or soldered to copper, make the connection to the existing pipe first. Then slip the ring on the PEX tubing, and fit the PEX over the male end of the adapter.

CLAMP THE RING WITH A CRIMPER. Position the ring over the middle of the adapter's male end and tighten with a stainless-steel clamp-ring crimping tool. Proper placement ensures that the ring compresses the PEX tubing over the ribs for a watertight connection.

Continued ➤

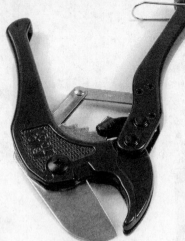

Cost Cutter

If you're plumbing with PEX, you'll want to spring for a tubing cutter rather than rely on a utility knife. However, when it comes to cutting PEX, almost any PVC cutter will do the job. The BrassCraft PVC cutter has a ratcheting cutter action that can cut plastic, vinyl, or rubber tubing up to 1⅝ in. in dia. I thought it was a little clumsy to use but still left a reasonably clean cut. If you look hard, you might be able to find a cutter for less online; you'll definitely find some that cost more.

In-Line Support
Runs of PEX tubing with typical in-line PEX-to-PEX connections should be supported every 3 ft. How-ever, at valve or branch joints, where extra weight could put stress on the line, it is a good idea to add a support clip next to the connection.

Making Hot-Water Recirculation Pay

By Dave Yates

I love potable hot-water recirculation systems, and not just because I sell and install them. By far, the most common reason why customers ask for my company to install recirculation pumps on their domestic hot-water systems is the long wait they have to endure before even a trickle of warm water arrives at their shower or sink. Recirculation eliminates this irritating wait and can save between 8000 and 20,000 gal. of clean drinking and bathing water per household per year. It also avoids sending your money down the drain by lessening water and sewage charges incurred if you are billed based on the gallons used in your home or business. This waste occurs despite mandated limits on showerhead flow—2 gal. per minute (gpm) for WaterSense heads; 2.5 gpm generally—that save on water once you're in the shower. The lower the flow, in fact, the longer the wait for hot water.

The traditional way to eliminate both the wait and the waste has been a mechanical recirculation system, but the pumps these systems rely on—even the more sophisticated pumps that limit recirculation to a few hours a day—incur electrical costs and contribute to heat loss through pipes. In the past year, however, a real drop in the cost of recirculation has become possible with the introduction of pumps powered by electronically commutated motors (ECMs) that reduce electrical-power consumption dramatically.

A Recirculation Primer

In both new construction and retrofits, the installation of hot-water recirculation systems is relatively simple. These systems may include a dedicated return line, or they may be cross-connected so that water that has cooled while sitting in the hot-water pipes bypasses the faucet and returns to the heater through the existing cold-water line. With a dedicated return line, water is typically circulated by a pump that either runs constantly, or is controlled by a timer or an aquastat. A cross-connected system has a hybrid T with an internal thermal valve that allows water from the hot-water pipes that has cooled to bypass fixtures and return to the heater when recirculation is activated.

There is a catch, however: The average induction-motor recirculation pump uses 87w, and that electrical draw can add up. A few of the constant or timed versions typically used in these systems are available in low-wattage and low-flow versions—as low as 33w/0.2 gpm in residential applications. How much these low-wattage versions save depends on the run time and cost of electricity. ECM pumps, however, can run on as little as 5w. They can be positioned in the system in the same way as traditional induction-motor pumps and are no more difficult to install.

Recirculation: Two Scenarios

with a Dedicated Return Line

There are several variations on how a hot-water recirculation system might be installed and activated. This illustration presents a simplified view of a system with a dedicated hot-water return line. It eliminates warm water in cold-water lines.

Using Cold-Water Lines as the Return

When a dedicated return is not possible (in some retrofits, for example), hot and cold lines are cross-linked via a thermostatic bypass valve so that the cold line can return too-cool water from the hot-water supply back to the heater.

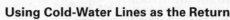

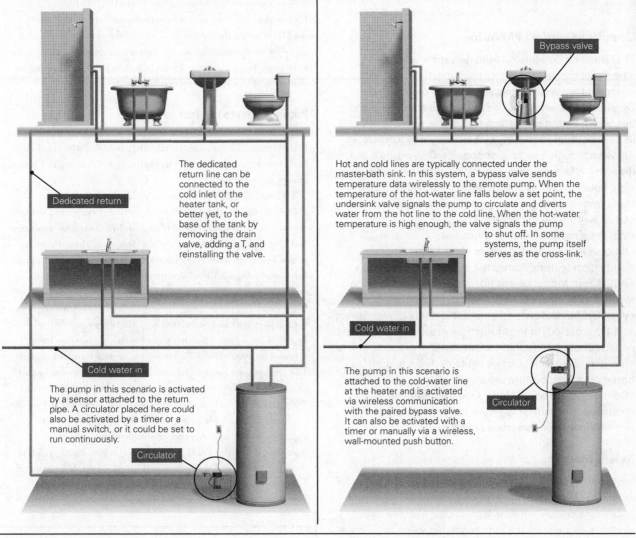

The dedicated return line can be connected to the cold inlet of the heater tank, or better yet, to the base of the tank by removing the drain valve, adding a T, and reinstalling the valve.

Dedicated return

Cold water in

The pump in this scenario is activated by a sensor attached to the return pipe. A circulator placed here could also be activated by a timer or a manual switch, or it could be set to run continuously.

Circulator

Bypass valve

Hot and cold lines are typically connected under the master-bath sink. In this system, a bypass valve sends temperature data wirelessly to the remote pump. When the temperature of the hot-water line falls below a set point, the undersink valve signals the pump to circulate and diverts water from the hot line to the cold line. When the hot-water temperature is high enough, the valve signals the pump to shut off. In some systems, the pump itself serves as the cross-link.

Cold water in

The pump in this scenario is attached to the cold-water line at the heater and is activated via wireless communication with the paired bypass valve. It can also be activated with a timer or manually via a wireless, wall-mounted push button.

Circulator

Explaining Ecm Technology

Traditional AC (alternating current) induction motors run at one speed using full power. Their operation generates heat, which wastes energy and results in wear on the components. In addition, most induction-motor circulators used in residential applications are substantially oversize, adding to their power consumption.

ECMs are brushless DC (direct current) motors and use a permanent-magnet rotor that runs at variable speeds and requires much less energy. ECMs also run much cooler, increasing circulator efficiency and dramatically reducing power consumption. Among the more sophisticated pumps introduced in the U.S.

market in recent months is the Grundfos Comfort PM Auto, a "smart" ECM pump that, according to its manufacturer, can reduce energy use by 95% over a traditional induction-motor pump. Although the upfront cost of an ECM pump is roughly twice that of an induction-motor pump, the additional cost is more than offset by the energy savings year after year.

Less Energy, Less Cost

ECM technology for both hydronic heat and potable water has been used for more than a decade in Europe, where significantly higher electrical costs drove the shift away from induction motors.

Continued ➜

The New Kids on the Block:

ECM Circulators for Domestic Hot Water

Both Grundfos and Xylem have introduced ECM circulators for domestic hot-water recirculation in the United States. Here's a quick review of how each one operates.

Grundfos Comfort PM Auto

The Grundfos Comfort PM Auto features a unique auto-adapt mode that enables the pump to "learn" household hot-water habits and respond proactively. Despite its sophistication, this pump is easy to set up and use, with a button on the back that makes scrolling through its various programs (auto, 24/7, temperature) a breeze. In my view, though, one of its strongest selling points is the disinfection feature that automatically circulates water every eight hours to protect against bacterial growth that can result from leaving warm, stagnant water sitting in pipes.

• Uses 5w to 8.5w of power.
• Varies its motor speed for efficiency.
• If no usage is detected within eight hours, the disinfection feature flushes the system for 15 minutes.
• AutoAdapt Mode: Learns hot-water-usage patterns to automatically turn on slightly in advance of demand.
• Vacation Mode: Turns on if no hot water is drawn during a 24-hour period, then automatically resumes its learned pattern upon the first hot-water usage.
• Temperature Mode: Can be set to cycle on and off based on a temperature sensor.
• Constant-Circulation Mode: Operates 24/7/365.
• Installed in a dedicated return line or in existing water-heater lines in a cross-linked system.

Xylem Models

Xylem makes ECM pumps under several brands, including Bell & Gossett. A key feature of Xylem's ECM circulators is their wireless technology. In cross-linked systems, this allows the remote mixing valve to activate the pump—located out of sight and hearing at the water heater—without a physical connection. The same goes for the optional wireless push-button activator, which plugs into any wall socket. The pump can also be set on a timer.

• Units use from 10w to 20w of power.
• Wireless models with on-demand sensors or push buttons are available.
• Installed in a dedicated return, under a sink, or in existing water-heater lines in a cross-linked system.

About five years ago, ECMs began appearing in the United States, first in air-based blower motors for heating-and-cooling systems and then in circulators for hydronic heating-and-cooling systems. I have been using both in my own home for the past four years and have reduced my electrical-energy consumption for moving both air and water by more than 90%. I was particularly intrigued when the same technology was introduced in the United States in pumps designed for domestic hot-water (DHW) recirculation. Unlike those used in heating applications, pumps designed for DHW recirculation are built to withstand the higher water pressure within potable-water systems and are made using either a low-lead bronze alloy or a stainless-steel impeller housing to comply with restrictions against lead in drinking water.

Putting Them to the Test

I first encountered ECM circulators in 2003 while attending the International Symposium on Heating trade show in Frankfurt. I was immediately impressed by their über-efficiency and low energy consumption.

When ECM pumps became available here for hydronic heating systems, I decided to do an electrical evaluation using my own home as a test case. My custom hydronic heating system had 11 induction-motor circulators (five more than the average zoned hydronic system). I monitored its electrical consumption for a year using a Kill-A-Watt meter and then replaced the older circulators with 10 low-watt zone valves and two Grundfos Alpha ECM circulators. After monitoring the electrical consumption for another year and correcting for differences in heating degree-days, I found that my power consumption had been reduced by more than 90%, saving me several hundred dollars. The savings on a more common six-zone system would be just under half of the initial investment (the difference between an ECM circulator and six zone valves, and six standard circulators).

Since then, ECMs have gained wide acceptance in air- and water-based heating-and-cooling systems, and most manufacturers offer ECM models for hydronic water systems. With the promise of similar reductions in power consumption, I suspect the same acceptance of ECM technology for DHW recirculation is just around the corner.

How Hot-Water Recirculation and ECMs Can Save You Money

It's hard to predict how much a hot-water recirculation system will save because the data varies widely based on household water use; water-heater type, efficiency, and fuel; wastewater-disposal costs; pipe runs; and whether or not the pipes are insulated. But for comparison's sake, in a household that typically lets 14,000 gal. of water run down the drain annually while waiting for the desired temperature (a typical manufacturer's estimate), the cost of waste—including the water, the sewage disposal and the electricity—is estimated to be more than $500.

Cheaper Hot Water

By Dave Yates

As a mechanical contractor, I've been responding to homeowners' concerns about high energy bills for a long time. And now, with fuel costs escalating at an alarming rate, these calls are becoming more frequent, and more urgent.

Heating water for domestic purposes—showers, laundry, dishes, and the rest—accounts for 12% to 26% of a home's energy use. But you can put your hot-water system on an energy diet without sacrificing comfort. The six strategies that follow range widely in cost and complexity, but all will reduce your energy bills and your carbon footprint.

Insulate Your Water Heater

THE FACTS: If your tank-style water heater pre-dates the 2004 federally mandated increase in tank insulation, it's costing you money every day in standby heat losses.

THE FIX: Adding an insulating jacket is inexpensive and takes less than an hour. If you have a gas- or oil-fired water heater, follow the jacket's instructions carefully to avoid cutting off combustion air or interfering with exhaust. All appliances using fossil fuels produce deadly carbon monoxide (CO) during combustion. The combustion-air intake and exhaust draft are two components that keep CO in check. If either is compromised, dangerous levels of CO can leak into the home.

When insulating electric water heaters, be sure to allow access to the elements and the wiring inlet for future service. The inlet/outlet should be accessible for routine inspection (leaks), and the temperature and pressure (T&P) relief valve should remain exposed with its drip leg extended within 6 in. of the floor for annual testing and for observation of any water discharge.

THE SAVINGS: Wrapping an older water heater with an insulation kit can cut standby heat losses by 25% to 45%, saving you 5% to 10% on your water-heating costs.

This insulation jacket from Energy Efficient Solutions (www.energyefficientsolutions.com) has an R-6 value and fits most tanks up to 80 gal.

Insulate Your Home's Hot-Water Pipes

THE FACTS: Every foot of bare ½-in. copper tubing carrying 120°F water around a 70°F home loses 14.1 BTU an hour; ¾-in. tubing loses 19.1 BTU per hour (1 BTU is the amount of energy needed to raise the temperature of 1 lb. of water by 1°F). You can substantially reduce this loss by insulating the hot-water supply lines.

THE FIX: Pipe insulation comes in 6-ft. strips and is typically fiberglass or foam-based material. Choose the best you can afford; fiberglass or elastomeric foam will save you more than cheaper foam tubing.

Insulation should fit snugly over the tubing to prevent condensation, and all joints and slits should be firmly sealed. Foam pipe insulation is often available with a preglued slit; you can use contact cement to seal butt ends or mitered joints. Some cements require adequate ventilation, so read and follow all instructions. Fiberglass insulation should be handled according to manufacturers' instructions. (Always wear safety glasses when working with fiberglass.) Costs range from the low end for R-2 insulation to the high end for R-8 UV-resistant Armaflex, used to insulate exterior piping in solar systems.

In a retrofit, the amount of piping accessible for insulating depends on the home's style. The main distribution lines in most houses are accessible through the basement; only the risers in the walls can't be accessed. In one-story homes, then, this means you can insulate all but a few final feet of piping.

Fiberglass

Foam

Elastomeric foam

THE SAVINGS: If three family members shower for 20 minutes a day each, with hot water traveling 50 ft. through uninsulated ¾-in. pipe from the heater to the shower, the daily energy loss adds up to 975 BTU. Insulate that same run of piping with 1-in. fiberglass, and the energy loss is reduced to just 233 BTU. (That's like not having to heat almost 542 gal. of water a year.) By insulating the pipes, the family above saves enough in a year to buy a large pizza if their water heater is gas-fired and twice that if it burns oil.

Find and Repair Leaks and Drips

THE FACTS: Leaky plumbing that's not causing damage—such as a faucet dripping into a sink—is often ignored. But a single hot-water faucet that drips once a second (60 drips per minute) costs

Continued ➔

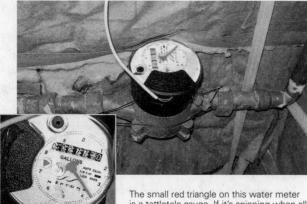

The small red triangle on this water meter is a tattletale gauge. If it's spinning when all faucets are shut off, you have a leak.

a homeowner with a gas-fired water heater $22 a year in wasted BTU alone. Depending on where you live, you might also pay for water and its disposal; at my house, that adds about $24. Not bad? If that leak is actually a dribble that fills one 8-oz. cup a minute, it'll cost $348 annually—plus $230 for the water and its disposal. If your water heater runs on electricity or oil, these numbers will be even higher.

THE FIX: Most leak repairs are manageable for any handy homeowner and can be done with little expense. Leaks in more remote areas can easily go undetected, but many can be found with a little investigation.

If you have municipal water, the meter probably has a tattletale spinner; if the faucets are all shut off and it's spinning, you've got a leak. If the meter doesn't have a tattletale gauge, record the reading in the evening after your last use and again in the morning before using any water. If there's a difference, then you have a leak.

Well-water systems present a different challenge for detecting leaks. In this case, a pressure gauge like the Watts IWTG can be screwed onto any available hose-thread faucet. Open the faucet, return to the well tank, and close the outlet valve. This isolates the home's piping from the well tank. Water is essentially noncompressible, so even a minute leak—like a slow drip—will show up on the gauge as a decrease in pressure.

Other areas to check visually for leaking hot water include the water heater's inlet, outlet, boiler drain, and relief-valve ports, where leaks can be

A Watts gauge helps to detect leaks in well systems. For testing, screw it onto a laundry spigot or any hose-thread faucet.

wicked into surrounding insulation and evaporated quickly by the heated storage tank. Other common leakage sites include pinholes in piping; joints that weep where solder has cracked or where threads are not adequately tightened; and joints between different types of piping.

Once you've found the leak, the first step—whether you tackle the repairs yourself or call in a pro—is shutting off the water (something everyone in your household should know in case of a plumbing emergency). Next, you have to determine what you need to repair the leak. Pipe and joint leaks can be sealed with do-it-yourself kits sold at home centers; the kits contain a wide variety of push-on self-sealing fittings or compression fittings that adapt to virtually any type of piping. You might want to call in a pro if soldering or special tools (PEX crimp ring or expander tools) are required.

If a faucet or toilet is leaking and you're tackling the repairs yourself, I suggest you first search the Internet for your toilet or faucet model. You're likely to find an exploded parts view along with details about repairs or parts to order. Armed with this information, a trip to your local big-box retailer won't be half as frustrating as it would be if you were to stare blindly at a wall lined with thousands of parts. Once you have the parts, complete the replacement according to the manufacturer's directions.

THE SAVINGS: Let's say you've discovered several drippy faucets. You check the water-meter reading over an eight-hour period and find you've lost 4 gal. (that's 126 drips per minute). Is it worth your time and effort to fix the faucets? Repair parts might cost $5 to $50 and a few hours of your time. If the leaks are on the hot side and you heat with oil, those drips cost about $185 a year. Chances are the repairs will last for 10 years (or longer), saving you $1845 over the long run.

Add a Thermal-Expansion Tank

THE FACTS: When water is heated, it expands. Heating 40 gal. of 40°F water to 140°F generates ¾ gal. of thermal expansion. Without an expansion tank, this water leaks out of the tank's temperature and pressure (T&P) valve, ruins the water heater, or causes a leak in the piping—the weakest link in the chain. T&P relief valves discharge under three conditions: pressure that is 150 psi (pounds per square inch) or above; temperatures above 210°F; or when the valve is worn out or fouled with debris. A badly leaking relief valve can double or triple your water-heating bill.

THE FIX: A properly sized thermal-expansion tank (TXT) should be installed to accommodate the increase in volume as water is heated. You'll find TXTs in home centers next to the water heaters. Installation instructions come with each tank.

Grip fittings available today have virtually eliminated the need to solder piping, so the trickiest part of installing a TXT is providing proper support. Because water weighs 8.34 lb. per gal., good support is essential to prevent stressing newly installed joints. Provide that support with metal hanger strapping; don't

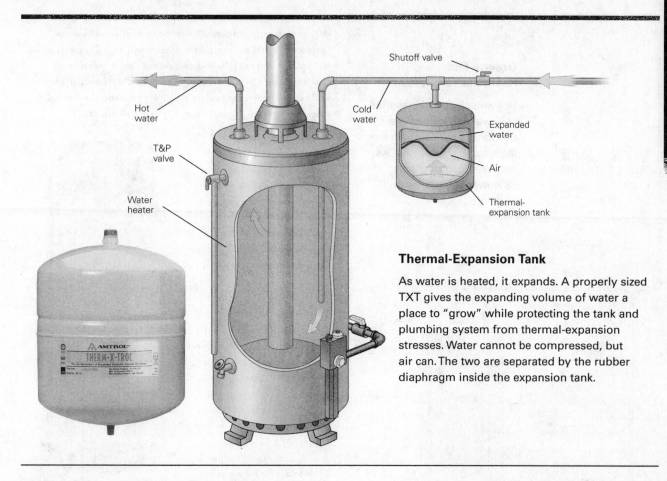

Hot water

T&P valve

Water heater

Shutoff valve

Cold water

Expanded water

Air

Thermal-expansion tank

Thermal-Expansion Tank

As water is heated, it expands. A properly sized TXT gives the expanding volume of water a place to "grow" while protecting the tank and plumbing system from thermal-expansion stresses. Water cannot be compressed, but air can. The two are separated by the rubber diaphragm inside the expansion tank.

---

use the cheap plastic stuff. Most thermal-expansion tanks for residential use come in two sizes: 2-gal. and 4.5-gal. For an extra $15, your system will be better protected by the larger one.

THE SAVINGS: Adding a properly sized TXT can save money by reducing wear and tear on your home's plumbing. The water heater will last longer; the faucets won't wear out as quickly; and piping and fittings won't break, split, or develop leaks caused by high pressure. It's a wise investment.

Add a Gravity-Fed Recirculation System

THE FACTS: A family of four wastes as much as 12,000 gal. of water every year waiting for hot water to travel from the heater to the tap. That wait wastes water and energy, and puts an unnecessary burden on sewage-treatment systems.

THE FIX: Recirculating systems eliminate the wait by delivering instant hot water to all the fixtures in your house. Most systems use an electric pump, but even energy-efficient pumps cost money to run. You can put the pump on a switch, timer, or motion sensor for efficiency, but you sacrifice the convenience of hot water on demand.

If you really want to save energy dollars and always have hot water at the tap, ask your plumber about a gravity-fed

recirculation system. If you want to reduce your water-heating bill to $0, consider combining gravity-fed recirculation with a solar water heater, as I did in my home.

This is how gravity-fed recirculation works: When water is heated, its molecules expand and become less dense. Gravity causes the denser, and therefore heavier, cold-water molecules to sink to the lowest point in the system. All that's needed to set up circulation between the hotter water at the top and the colder water at the bottom is a loop that returns from wherever the desire for instant hot water is located to the lower connection of the water heater. This generates a thermal circulation flow that gently moves hot water out to the end of the loop and back through the return. The entire loop must be well insulated to prevent wasting energy and short-cycling. With no moving parts to wear out, this system supplies instant hot water throughout the house 24 hours a day.

THE SAVINGS: At between $600 and $1400, the initial cost of a recirculation system might seem like a deal breaker, but if you consider the return on investment (rather than payback), you'll see the real value a recirculation system can offer. Let's say you're wasting 12,000 gal. a year waiting for hot water to come through. Eliminating that waste with a gravity-fed recirculation system saves you $265 in water, sewage, and water-heating costs (in my case, roughly half that expense was for heating the water). Now, if you're

Continued ➔

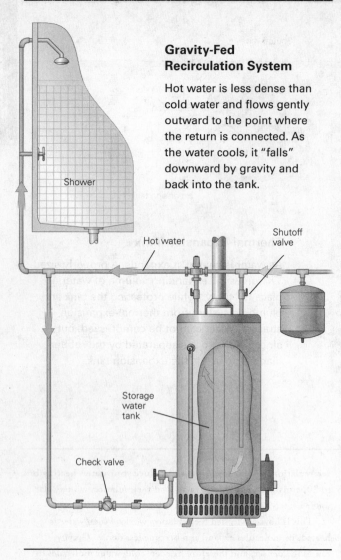

Gravity-Fed Recirculation System

Hot water is less dense than cold water and flows gently outward to the point where the return is connected. As the water cools, it "falls" downward by gravity and back into the tank.

Shower

Hot water

Shutoff valve

Storage water tank

Check valve

---

efficient based on the energy factor (EF), a measure of overall efficiency. Energy efficiency is not the same as cost efficiency, however. Electric storage-tank heaters have a high EF, yet typically cost more to operate; the wiser economic choice would be an appliance with a lower fuel cost, even if it's a bit less efficient. Also, while all indirect water heaters are highly efficient, their actual efficiency depends on the boiler they're connected to.

THE FIX: TRY A NEW TANK.

Replacing a tank-style water heater is a relatively straightforward task. Due to federally mandated changes, today's models are safer and more efficient than those from just a few years ago. One change is beefier insulation (making them slightly bigger, so measure the space first). The feds have also lowered the BTU input, which, while boosting efficiency, also lowers the water heater's gallon-per-hour recovery rate. As a result, you might need to increase storage volume by installing, for example, a 50-gal. model in place of a 40-gal. one.

You can expect to spend $500 to $1900 for a good-quality water heater. The range is due to the variety of gas and oil tank-style water heaters available today: atmospheric chimney-vented, where exhaust exits unassisted through a chimney (the least expensive to purchase, but the most expensive to operate); indirect-vented, where an electric blower exhausts combustion gases through horizontal piping (moderately more expensive to purchase and more demanding to install correctly); and high-efficiency sealed-combustion models with direct vents, in which both exhaust and combustion air are hard-piped to and from the home's exterior (the most expensive, but the least costly to operate). Sealed combustion also eliminates combustion-related outdoor-air infiltration, which adds to a home's heating load.

THE SAVINGS: Switching out an old tank style with 63% efficiency for another with 67% efficiency won't save you much, but upgrading to a 90% efficient, sealed-combustion model is a step in the right direction.

THE FIX: GO TANKLESS. Although tankless and tank-style water heaters both operate at roughly 82% thermal efficiency when their burners are on, tank-style water heaters lose so much heat during standby mode that their actual efficiency averages 63%. If you install a tankless model and use the same number of gallons

---

saving a total of $265 annually and the system costs $1200, the annual ROI is an attractive 22%. A hefty tax-free return and no waiting for hot water—it doesn't get better than that. A recirculation system powered by a pump will save you somewhat less.

Least

Efficiency

Most

- Oil storage tank
- Propane-gas storage tank; natural-gas storage tank
- Propane-gas tankless; natural-gas tankless
- Electric storage tank
- Electric tankless
- Indirect water heaters attached to electric, oil, or gas boilers
- Solar

Toss Your Old Tank and Try Some New Technology

THE FACTS: Efficiencies for water-heating systems range from 63% to 99%, and savings rise markedly with these efficiencies. Because upgrading your water heater can save significantly on energy costs, start by evaluating its efficiency. This chart lists household water-heating systems from least to most

of hot water, you could save that 19% difference. But here's the catch: Because there's no threat of running out of hot water with a tankless heater, some people who've installed them start using more hot water, wiping out any savings. Used with restraint, however, tankless models can be more efficient than tank-style water heaters and save money.

THE SAVINGS: Many of my customers switch from tank to tankless for the endless supply of hot water, rather than the cost savings. The cost of replacing a tank-style water heater with a tankless model ranges from $1500 to $2900. If you control your hot-water use and get the maximum 19% savings, you'll save about $76 on a typical annual water-heating bill of $400.

THE FIX: USE YOUR BOILER. If you have a boiler for hydronic (water-based) heating, you can add an indirect water heater, essentially a tank that stores potable water heated through the boiler. Installed properly, an indirect water heater's operating efficiency will closely match the boiler's; when used with a high-efficiency modulating condensing boiler, the overall efficiency can range well above 90%. Because the boiler's full BTU output is

devoted to making domestic hot water, these models can meet the output of tankless water heaters. With no need for fuel lines or flues, highly insulated indirect water tanks can be located remotely from their energy source (the boiler) and closer to the points of use, reducing the wait for hot water. Adding an indirect water heater to a hydronic-heating system costs $1600 to $2800. These units last up to 30 years, and in life-cycle cost comparisons offer one of the lowest-overall costs for domestic hot water.

THE SAVINGS: An indirect water heater is as efficient as the boiler to which it's connected, from 78% to 98%. The range of savings is just as broad: Depending on water usage, fuel type, and other factors, you could save from about $50 to $400 a year.

THE FIX: GET STOKED BY THE SUN. Solar hot-water systems provide free hot water, but at an up-front cost that might seem too steep: $6000 to $12,000, on average. Maybe that's why the minute solar is mentioned, everyone asks about the payback. Federal and local incentives can help offset the cost. Currently, the federal residential tax incentive for solar installations equals 30% of the system's cost or $2000. Solar hot-water systems fall into two

LIQUID SUNSHINE. The author assembles the Viessmann vacuum-tube solar array that produces 80% of the hot water for his home.

categories: flat panel and vacuum tube. Both systems work well when properly installed and can last 30 years or longer.

THE SAVINGS: My home's Viessmann 30-vacuum-tube system produces about 80% of our hot-water needs (typical savings are 70% to 80%). My payback is expected to be 12 years, but my ROI at today's energy costs is 5%—better than current CD rates. As fuel costs increase, so does my ROI, which also shortens the payback time. Showering in liquid sunshine feels better, too.

NOTE: Prices cited in this article are from 2008.

Indirect Water Heater

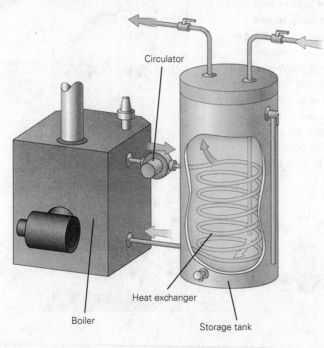

Circulator

Boiler

Heat exchanger

Storage tank

Continued ➜

Hot-Water Recirculation Systems

Rob Yagid

The integration of a recirculation system is a more advanced plumbing technique than standard whole-house plumbing design.

A recirculation system is designed to provide hot water to each of the home's hot-water taps instantly. Beyond providing convenience and increased comfort, a recirculation system saves thousands of gallons of fresh water annually that would otherwise go down the drain as a home-owner waited for hot water to travel from the water heater to the faucet or showerhead. (For more on the significance of this water savings, see "Bringing the Water Shortage Home," online at finehomebuilding. com.)

There are two basic systems: those that rely on an electrically operated pump, and those that are gravity fed and rely on thermosiphoning. Here's how a recirculation system works.

½-in. insulated branch line

¾-in. insulated hot-water trunk line

¾-in. insulated return line

Shutoff valve

Demand-Controlled System

Gary Klein, managing director at Affiliated International Management and a former energy specialist at the California Energy Commission, has studied recirculation systems and has found that a demand-controlled circulation system— one that operates on a pump activated by a switch or motion sensor—uses the least amount of energy and saves the most water. It also costs the least to operate. However, while this system provides hot water quickly, it doesn't do so as quickly as other setups.

1. A switch or motion sensor located near each fixture activates an energy-efficient circulation pump.

Exhaust flue

2. The circulation pump houses a temperature sensor and a check valve that prevents water from entering the return line. The pump moves ambient-temperature water sitting in the line back to the water heater. The sensor lets the pump know when hot water has arrived at the farthest tap and shuts off the pump. Alternatively, a sensor can be placed on the return line immediately after the last tap in the system and hardwired to the pump. This will yield even lower pump run-times.

The return line is connected to the water heater through the existing drain valve.

Gravity-Fed System

Master plumber Dave Yates likes the simplicity of a gravity-fed system when it's applicable. A gravity-fed system relies on thermosiphoning, in which hot water rises to the top of the system and denser cold water falls to the bottom. For such a system to work, the water heater needs to be located below the hot-water taps it will serve. While pipe insulation and short plumbing runs help to reduce standby heat loss and energy consumption, this system uses more energy than others because it is operating 24 hours a day. However, because there are no pumps to install or maintain, this system is arguably the most user-friendly.

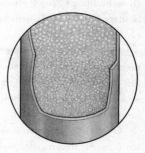

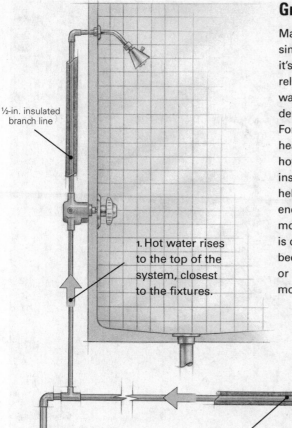

½-in. insulated branch line

1. Hot water rises to the top of the system, closest to the fixtures.

Exhaust flue

¾-in. insulated hot-water trunk line

2. Water that cools in the system is heavier and denser than the hot water being supplied and falls through a return line to the lowest point in the system, the water heater.

¾-in. insulated return line

The return line is connected to the water heater through the existing drain valve.

3. A check valve keeps water in the water heater from flowing back into the return line.

4. Cool water is heated and circulated through the hot-water supply lines, starting the thermosiphoning process over again.

Shutoff valve

Continued →

14 Tips for Bath Plumbing

By Mike Lombardi

I've been a plumber for almost 40 years. I learned the trade from some really good plumbers, but I've also learned from making mistakes and seeing the mistakes of other pros and amateurs. This experience has made me a better plumber and has helped me to build a loyal clientele. A recent job, a full bath remodel at Fine Homebuilding's Project House, offered the perfect opportunity to share some of my favorite hard-earned lessons for better and easier bath plumbing.

The job included moving the sink and the toilet to make room for a new barrier-free tile shower, so we tackled all the typical full-bath rough-in tasks. We used as many cost-saving strategies as we could think of—provided they didn't sacrifice the quality or the longevity of the job.

One thing that always makes jobs like this go easier is to have locations for fixtures, tile, and plumbing decided well before rough-in starts. Changes and rework can quickly blow any budget. Plumbers and tilesetters don't like redoing their own work, and they will charge accordingly to fix problems resulting from poor planning.

2. USE THE RIGHT NUMBER OF WRAPS. Start threaded connections by covering the male side of the fitting with three wraps of Teflon tape. Larger pipes will take up to six wraps. Wrap the tape in a direction that follows the pipe or fitting as it's tightened.

1. ASSEMBLE WHAT YOU CAN. It's often easier to dry-fit and assemble fittings before tucking them into a stud or joist cavity. For example, attaching the supply lines and shower arm before putting the mixing valve into the wall provides more room for turning wrenches and pliers.

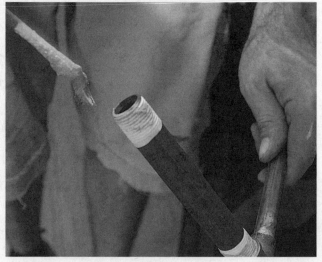

3. USE PIPE DOPE, TOO. Thread-sealing compound lubricates the tape so that it doesn't shred, and it also provides extra insurance against leaks. The author prefers Hercules Megaloc (herchem.com) nonhardening thread sealer.

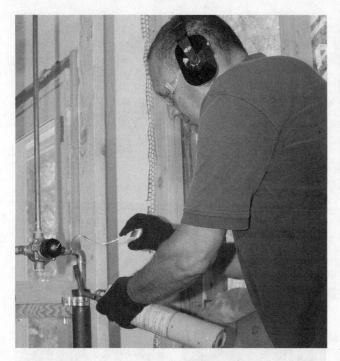

4. WEAR YOUR SAFETY GEAR. Spattering solder, dripping PVC primer and glue, and general overhead work contribute to the high incidence of on-the-job eye injuries among plumbers, so it's important to wear eye protection. Pro-quality plumbing torches are loud, so wear hearing protection when soldering.

5. WIPE SOLDERED JOINTS. Best practice is to wipe soldered joints after you sweat them, but it's not just about looking neat and clean. Soldered copper connections depend on a layer of flux, but flux is corrosive and should be removed while it's still hot. Always use a dry rag to remove flux. A wet rag cools the joint too suddenly, resulting in a weaker connection.

6. KNOW THE WALL FINISH. The difference in thickness between one type of tile and another can determine if a shower valve's handle and trim ring will fit. You often can order different trim kits to compensate for thick wall tile, but it's easier to set the valve in the right spot.

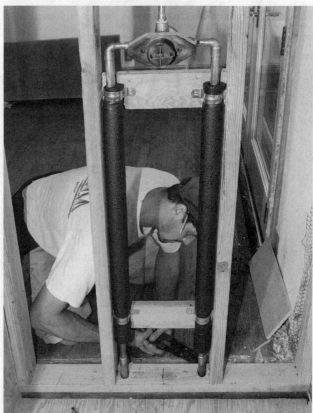

7. MIX AND MATCH. PEX tubing saves labor and works great, but the author prefers the added rigidity of copper for supplying shower valves, shower arms, and valve stub outs. Insulating the copper reduces noise, saves energy, and prevents condensation, which can lead to mold growth.

Continued ➜

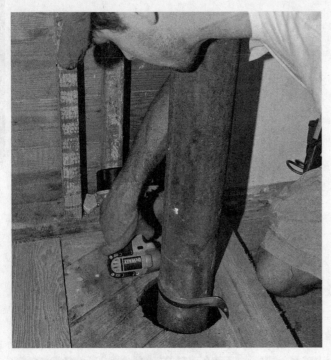

8. SECURE VENTS AND STACKS BEFORE CUTTING. Existing waste lines and vents are often perfectly serviceable, but you often need to add, move, or eliminate pipes during remodeling work. Secure existing pipes with two-hole straps before cutting into them, or risk bringing down all the pipe above you.

9. REAM PIPE CUTS. The little burrs left when you cut plastic drain pipe tend to snag whatever nastiness is passing through the pipe. Eventually, the rough edge creates a clog big enough to require professional drain clearing. Deburring also makes dry-fitting easier. Copper supply lines also should be reamed.

ABS cement   PVC primer and cement

10. USE THE RIGHT GLUE. PVC and ABS use different cements for joining pipe and fittings. ABS piping doesn't require primer, but you should prime both male and female sides of any PVC connections. Ensure a neater job by holding the pipe or fitting so that excess primer drips off instead of running down the side of the pipe. Apply two coats of glue to the male side and a single, light coat to the female side of the connection.

11. INCLUDE CLEANOUTS. Code requires cleanouts where pipes transition from vertical to horizontal.

12. USE THE RIGHT SLOPE. Sloping waste lines from ⅛ in. To ¼ in. Per ft. Allows proper drainage and keeps solid waste moving along.

13. USE DISH SOAP FOR FLEXIBLE COUPLINGS. Plumbers often depend on flexible couplings for making repairs and connecting the different kinds of pipe used in waste lines and vents. Make it easier to slide the tight-fitting couplings onto the pipes they're joining by first adding a few drops of dish soap.

14. AAVS ARE YOUR FRIEND. Air-admittance valves allow air into drain lines while preventing sewer gas from escaping. They're great for remodeling work, as they can replace many feet of vent piping. Just make sure they're accessible. Covering them with HVAC return registers in inaccessible locations allows them to breathe and provides future access.

A New Plumber's Tool Kit

You may already have a reciprocating saw or a handsaw that you can use for cutting plastic waste lines and vents, but you'll need some new tools for working with copper and PEX supply lines. Nonpro plumbers might balk at spending the money for an aluminum pipe wrench when steel versions cost half as much, but aluminum wrenches are easier to carry and do less damage when you drop them. You can get cheaper torches, too, but self-lighting versions free a hand for wiping joints and other tasks.

Tubing cutter

Compact tubing cutter

Solder and flux kit

Self-lighting torch

Ridgid 23468 ½-in. and ¾-in. PEX crimp tool

4-in-1 fitting brush

14-in. aluminum pipe wrench

12-in. tongue-and-groove flat-jaw pliers

Continued ➜

Plumbing a Basement Bathroom

By Mike Guertin

Adding a bathroom in a basement might sound like a complicated project, but the plumbing part of the job isn't much different than any above-grade bath. It's simple and straightforward to bring in the small-diameter supply lines for hot and cold water. Cutting the slab and digging the trench for the waste lines are the tasks that set this project apart. I work with my plumber, Paul Murray, to map out the best fixture layout, and we then divide the tasks required to complete the project. I tackle the slab work, and he lays the drain and supply piping. Of course, the sewer-outlet pipe on most of my projects is above the basement-floor elevation, so we have to install a tank to collect the sewage and a pump to send it up to the level of the sewer outlet. The rough-in process takes several days for us to complete; then we can schedule the inspections.

Plan the Drain Layout First

Rather than completely breaking out the concrete slab in the prospective bathroom, I cut trenches where the drains will run. This saves me from having to move lots of broken concrete and then repour the slab. I chalk a proposed fixture layout on the concrete slab, then meet with Paul. We review options, and he recommends layout changes that minimize my work and simplify his drain- and vent-pipe arrangement. He also identifies suitable locations for the sewage-ejector tank and draws the final trench layout.

The bathroom in this project is typical and includes a toilet, a pedestal sink, and a one-piece shower stall. Other plumbed fixtures, such as a washing machine, a utility sink, a kitchen sink, and a dishwasher, can be tied in to the same drain system.

A Saw and a Sledgehammer Open the Floor

Before I start breaking up the concrete slab, I make cardboard templates of the drain-riser positions for the shower and the toilet. The templates register to the adjacent wall plates or wall layout lines, so after the slab is removed and the trench is dug, Paul has a guide for installing the drains.

The largest drainpipe will be 3 in. dia., but the trenches need to be wide enough to be shoveled out. I usually make them 10 in. to 12 in. wide to leave extra working room for fittings. To cut the slab, I use an old worm-drive saw fitted with a dry-cut diamond blade; it must be plugged into a GFCI-protected outlet. The blade cuts only 2½ in. into the slab, which typically is 3 in. to 5 in. thick, but that's deep enough to give me a good, clean fracture line. A gas-powered concrete saw would cut all the way through the slab, but the exhaust inside a poorly ventilated basement would be overwhelming and would migrate into the living space above.

As the saw cuts, I flood the blade with water to cool it, as well as to speed the cut and to minimize dust. I pour a puddle of water on the floor and use a brush to sweep it to the rear of the blade.

The blade draws the water forward into the cutting action. The water can be pushed back into the blade until it becomes thick slurry. After every few feet of cutting, I collect the slurry in a bucket or a shop vacuum and start a fresh puddle.

A few whacks with a 10-lb. sledgehammer crack the concrete between the sawcuts; I use a pry bar to pop out pieces of the slab. Once a hole is started, the pieces come out easily. A word of caution: Some slabs are placed over plastic vapor retarders. When I encounter them, I try to be careful not to damage the plastic. I slice it down the middle of the trench and fold back the sides so that I can reuse it when backfilling.

Everything Flows Downhill, so Pitch the Trench Accordingly

I use a 3×3 (3-in.-dia. by 3-in.-dia.) elbow fitting to establish the starting depth at the farthest point in the drain run from the ejector tank—in this case, the toilet. To accommodate the 3-in.-dia. elbow, I start the bottom of the trench about 4 in. below the bottom of the slab. This leaves enough space above the drainpipe for the slab to be repoured to its full thickness. The trench needs to be pitched at ¼ in. per ft. I use a 6-ft. level with a pitch vial to gauge the slope as I'm digging. Any tangent trenches from incoming fixture drains need to be sloped at the same pitch, starting where they meet the main trench level. The area directly beneath the shower drain needs to be dug several inches deeper than the trench level to accommodate the trap.

The drain line terminates at the sewage-collection tank. These tanks are usually made of thick plastic and have an inlet hole drilled in the side. The pit for the tank needs to be excavated deep enough so that the bottom of the inlet hole matches the bottom of the trench. This level might cause the top of the tank to be beneath the slab level if the drain runs are long. It's important to let the trench level establish the level of the tank and not just position the tank flush with the top of the slab, or there might not be enough pitch in the drainpipes for the sewage to flow properly. On this project, the tank top needed to be 2½ in. below slab level.

Don't Forget the Vent Lines

It takes me half a day to break out the slab and to dig the trenches. Then Paul returns to in- stall the drains. Using the cardboard templates, he dry-fits, then glues together the pipes and fittings, running them into the sewage tank. A rubber bushing seals the pipe to the tank.

Once all the pipes have been laid, we backfill about three-quarters of the way around them to keep the pipes from shifting. The top of the trench is left exposed for the rough-plumbing inspection. If I'm working in an area that has a high water table, I fill the tank to the inlet, or I weight it with rocks to prevent it from floating if the groundwater level rises.

While the drain lines are exposed, Paul installs the plumbing vents. Proper venting is required by code and is necessary for the drains to work. The vents equalize air pressure inside drains and

Everything Flows Downhill to a Tank

The key to a basement plumbing system is a tank with a pump that raises gray water and sewage to the main waste line, where gravity can take over. To keep everything flowing properly to the sewage tank, the drain lines from the fixtures should be pitched ¼ in. over a 12-in. run. Here, the fixture farthest from the tank, the toilet, determines the tank's vertical position.

AN ECONOMICAL (AND FRIENDLIER) WAY TO CUT CONCRETE. I outfit an old worm-drive saw with a dry-cut diamond blade. To cool the blade and to reduce dust, I puddle a little water near the line and sweep it behind the blade as it cuts. The saw must always be plugged into a GFCI-protected outlet.

TAKE OUT ONLY AS MUCH AS YOU NEED. Scored by the sawcuts, the slab is easily broken out with a sledgehammer, then carted away in chunks.

KEEPING IN PITCH. As the plumber lays out the drains, he continually checks his work with a torpedo level equipped with a pitch vial.

Sewage Ejector: The Guts of the System

The sewage-ejector pump sits inside a plastic tank. It has a float-controlled switch that activates the pump when the sewage level reaches the discharge height. The sewage is pumped up and out through a 2-in.-dia. pipe to the main waste line, where the sewage flows naturally (due to gravity) rather than under pressure. A check valve mounted on the discharge pipe prevents the sewage in the discharge pipe from flowing back into the tank. In the event of a pump failure or a maintenance check, the pipe can be disconnected beneath the check valve, and the sewage inside the pipe above the valve will not leak out.

Many pumps, including the one I installed, can be serviced only by removing the tank cover and disconnecting the drain. My plumber recommends a pump by Liberty (www.liberty pumps.com) with a cover-mounted panel that allows easier access to the switch. All ejector pumps are powered by regular household current; the power cord plugs into any nearby GFCI- protected outlet.

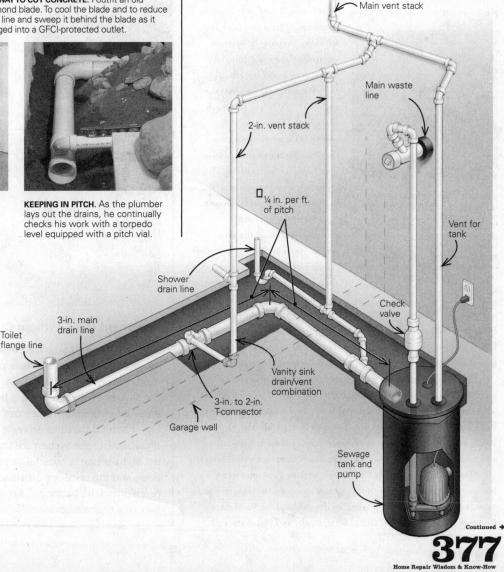

Main vent stack

2-in. vent stack

¼ in. per ft. of pitch

Main waste line

Vent for tank

Check valve

Shower drain line

3-in. main drain line

Toilet flange line

3-in. to 2-in. T-connector

Vanity sink drain/vent combination

Garage wall

Sewage tank and pump

Continued ➔

prevent traps from being sucked dry. Ideally, we run a vent pipe to the exterior of the building or tap into an existing vent pipe in the floor above. A vent pipe can be run through a wall above, can be concealed in a closet, or can be run on an exterior wall. On this project, we tapped in to a vent pipe on the first floor as part of a more-extensive remodeling project. Although air-admittance valves are an alternative for venting difficult locations and can be used to vent fixtures in a basement bathroom, don't use them to vent the sewage tank itself. We have run into problems with both odors and poor pump flow when we've used air valves in the past. Pumps perform much better when they are vented atmospherically.

Leave Yourself Options After Patching the Slab

After the inspector's approval, I backfill around the pipes. The cardboard templates are used to position the shower, sink, and toilet risers precisely. While the backfill is still loose, the pipes are easy to shift a little to match the templates.

I then wrap the risers with strips of corrugated cardboard or surround them with a piece of larger-diameter pipe. The toilet stub, for instance, is left unglued to the fitting below so that it can

Isolate the tank lid, but not the tank. I use a ring of cardboard as a form around the sewage tank's lid so that the repoured patch sits on top of the tank rim but doesn't interfere with the removal of the lid. In some regions, seasonally high water tables can lift the tank right out of its hole if it's not secured.

be trimmed later to match the finished-flooring level when the toilet flange is mounted. The spacer keeps the concrete away from the pipe so that the stub later can be cut to length and glued. The spacers also leave a little wiggle room for fine-tuning the drain risers to match the fixture outlets. This is especially important when you're installing a one-piece shower.

Once the pipes are positioned, I flood the area several times with water to ensure that the backfill is packed tightly around them. The water helps to consolidate the soil and to fill in any gaps. The soil often settles when it's flooded, so I add more dirt flush with the bottom of the old slab and then flood the area again. Finally, I cover the trench with 6-mil plastic as a vapor retarder and tape it to the existing plastic vapor retarder when it is present.

The slab patch usually doesn't require enough concrete to warrant bringing in a ready-mix truck, so I either mix concrete in a wheelbarrow by hand or in a portable mixer. I mix the concrete stiff and then pack it into the trench. I run an Arkie Wall Banger (www. loyola.com/icf) or a concrete vibrator over a plastic cutting board and finish off the surface with a magnesium float and a steel trowel.

After the concrete cures for a couple of days, Paul returns for a few hours to install the supply tubing and to mount the shower mixing valve. I install the subfloor panels, the drywall, and the finished flooring before Paul's final visit to set the toilet and install the sink.

Patching the Slab Is a Small but Intensive Job

Once the drains are in place and I've backfilled, I like to compact the fill with water; any resulting low spots are filled and compacted again.

Before I pour concrete, I isolate the drain risers with a wrap of cardboard, which gives me room to adjust the drain after the concrete is set.

After mixing a small, stiff batch of concrete and packing it into the trench with a wooden float.

I finish by running a vibrator (an Arkie Wall Banger) on a nylon cutting board and, finally, by using a magnesium float and a steel trowel.

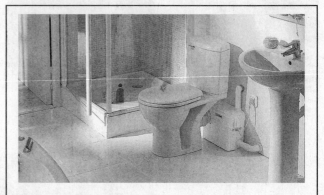

Basement Bath without Cutting the Floor

Saniflo bathroom systems (www.saniflo.com) eliminate the need to break up the basement slab. Rather than running beneath the floor, 2-in.-dia. drainpipes connect the sink, shower, or toilet to a floor-mounted tank with an ejector pump; the pipes can run above floor level, either behind the finished walls or on the surface. The drawbacks to the system are that the pump is visible, the shower pan is raised 6 in. to 7 in. off the finished floor, and the price is a bit steep. With headroom at a premium in the bathroom, I could afford to lose only 2 in. of a typical shower-stall floor.

Replace a Shower Mixing Valve

By Ed Cunha

I do most of my plumbing work on Cape Cod, where there's no shortage of older homes, so it's pretty common for me to replace the old two-handle controls on a tub or shower with a new mixing valve.

In addition to offering the convenience of a single-lever control, a modern mixing valve uses a pressure-balancing mechanism to protect bathers from sudden temperature changes. If someone turns on the dishwasher or flushes a toilet while you're in the shower, a pressure-balanced valve instantly detects the change in water pressure and maintains the hot-to-cold mix you selected.

Here are two ways to complete the job. The first technique is to open the wall behind the plumbing and switch out the valves. The second method is to remove the tile, replace the valves, and retile. Obviously, I'd rather go with the former instead of the latter.

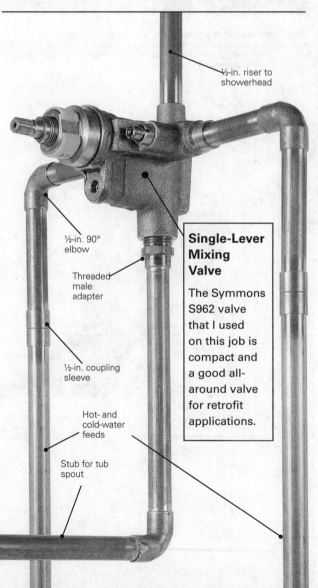

½-in. riser to showerhead

½-in. 90° elbow

Threaded male adapter

½-in. coupling sleeve

Hot- and cold-water feeds

Stub for tub spout

Single-Lever Mixing Valve

The Symmons S962 valve that I used on this job is compact and a good all-around valve for retrofit applications.

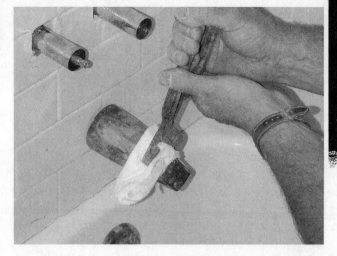

1. THE CHROME HAS TO COME OFF. Pry off the cover plates that hide each handle's installation screws, then remove the screws, handles, and backing plates. In case the spout will be reused, I protect its finish with a rag as I unscrew it with channel-lock pliers.

2. CUT AN ACCESS PANEL. If there's not an access panel behind the tub's plumbing wall, you'll have to cut through the wallboard. I transfer measurements from the tiled side of the wall to the back and cut out a rectangular panel. A panel that extends from stud to stud is easier to patch.

3. A TINY CUTTER FOR TIGHT SPACES. A standard tubing cutter is too large to use in the wall space, so I use a mini-cutter to cut the hot and cold lines that feed the old valve. I make these cuts at the same level so that I'll have an easier time fitting the new valve.

Continued ➜

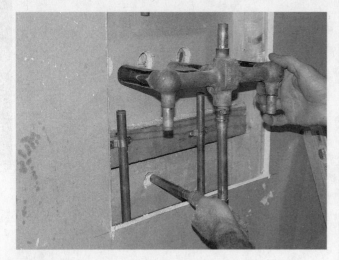

4. LIFT OUT THE OLD VALVES … After cutting the riser line that feeds the showerhead, I can pull the old valve free. I'm careful not to damage drywall edges.

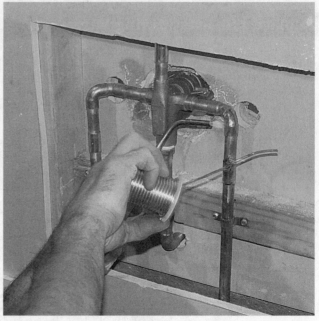

7. FLUX, ASSEMBLE, AND SOLDER. Make sure the elbows, couplings, and short tubing sections join the new valve securely to the old lines. Clean and flux the joints, then solder with the entire assembly in place. To protect the valve's washers, I open the valve before soldering.

5. …AND MAKE ROOM FOR THE NEW. I'll reuse the central hole for the tub spout, but I need to enlarge the hole so that it will accept the body of the new valve. I use a pair of tile nippers to clip away the tile and backerboard. The unused hot and cold holes will be covered by the goof plate.

8. FINISHING UP. To install the finish trim, I first slip the dome cover over the valve. To cover the holes on each side of the valve, I use what's known as a goof plate. After inserting the diverter control, I screw the goof plate onto the valve and attach the selector handle.

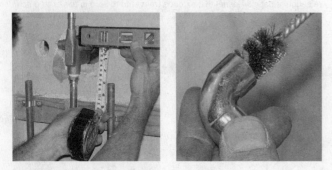

6. DRY-FIT AND MEASURE. The valve's showerhead and tub-spout pipes are in place; now I can measure for the new tubing to connect the hot and cold supply lines. I prep all mating joints with 120-grit emery cloth and a cleaning brush.

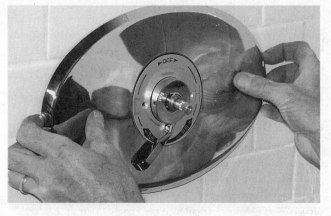

9. NOT ALL GOOF PLATES ARE CREATED EQUAL. The large faceplates used to conceal holes in the shower wall are made to fit around specific valves. To avoid multiple trips to the plumbing supplier, check the fit of the valve cover plate and goof plate.

10. PREPARE FOR THE SPOUT. After measuring the interior length of the tub spout and factoring in the dimension of the male adapter, I mark the proper tubing length.

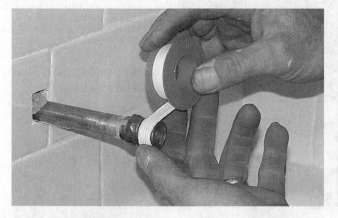

11. DON'T FORGET THE TAPE. I cut, clean, flux, and solder the male adapter onto the tubing. When it has cooled down, I wrap the threads with Teflon tape.

12. A GOOD FIT IS SNUG AGAINST THE WALL. If I've measured correctly, the spout will thread onto the adapter and fit tightly against the tile.

Valve Replacement from the Front: How to Make the Best of a Tricky Tile Job

If I don't have access behind the shower and have to go through the tiled side of the wall, I call my favorite tile man, Tom Meehan. He has to remove and reinstall a small section of tile around the old valves so that I can install the new valve. (1) Tom uses an angle grinder fitted with a diamond blade to cut a rectangle into the wall around the valves. A helper with a vacuum catches the dust. (2) He pulls out the section, removes a few more tiles, and (3) screws in a wood cleat at the top to catch the backerboard later. (4) Now I can remove the old plumbing and install the new valve. When space is too cramped to use a heat shield, I spray combustible surfaces with a thermal shield gel. (5)

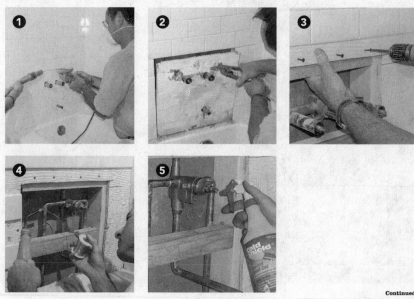

Continued →

Replace a Sink Trap

By Bruce Norman

Sink traps may need replacement for a few different reasons. Because the undersink area is regularly used as storage, the exposed trap assembly is bumped and jostled, and can become damaged. Also, the trap assembly might not have been installed correctly, and its horizontal runs could be insufficiently pitched and not drain well. Finally, the trap could be an outdated configuration, such as an S-trap, which has been eliminated under most code jurisdictions. While some traps can be taken apart and cleaned to restore proper flow, I recommend rebuilding the entire trap assembly.

The two materials most often used for sink plumbing are PVC and ABS (acrylonitrile butadiene styrene). For the repair featured here, I used ABS because the joints are bonded with one-part glue as opposed to the two-part glue needed for PVC. I use glued joints wherever possible but incorporate threaded unions at the trap and tailpieces for serviceability. For this sink, I added a cleanout below the trap assembly, which is required by code. Then I added the sanitary tee to allow for venting.

Originally, there was no vent to this old S-trap system, which is common for old plumbing. Most codes require the vent to be restored to allow liquid to drain quickly. In this case, I installed an air-admittance valve (AAV). Check with your local building department for any restrictions if you choose to use an AAV.

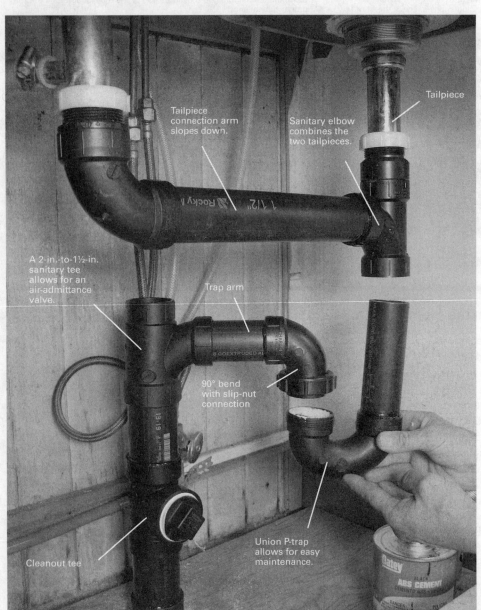

Tailpiece connection arm slopes down.

Sanitary elbow combines the two tailpieces.

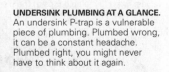
Tailpiece

A 2-in.-to-1½-in. sanitary tee allows for an air-admittance valve.

Trap arm

90° bend with slip-nut connection

Cleanout tee

Union P-trap allows for easy maintenance.

UNDERSINK PLUMBING AT A GLANCE. An undersink P-trap is a vulnerable piece of plumbing. Plumbed wrong, it can be a constant headache. Plumbed right, you might never have to think about it again.

Combine the Tailpieces, Then Build from the Bottom Up

1. CONNECT THE TAILPIECES. Use a 90° bend and a sanitary tee with slip-nut connections to draw the drain water into one tailpiece. The connection arm should slope down by ¼ in. per ft. If needed, provide a stub for the dishwasher drain in the tailpiece.

2. MEASURE TO CONNECT THE CLEANOUT. Hold the clean-out close to the floor but high enough to allow easy access to it. Measure between the hubs, and add ¾ in. for each flange. In this case, a 3¼-in. clear distance plus 1½ in. for the two flanges demands a 4-in. connector pipe.

Dry-Fit the Connections Before Gluing

3. WORK YOUR WAY UP. Hold the 2-in.-to-1½-in. sanitary tee and the union P-trap in place. Measure the distance from the cleanout tee to the sanitary tee. Remember to add ¾ in. for each hub flange.

4. AIM THE T TOWARD THE TAILPIECE. Sight from behind the tailpiece to align the sanitary tee. There is some room for error, but try to get it as close as possible.

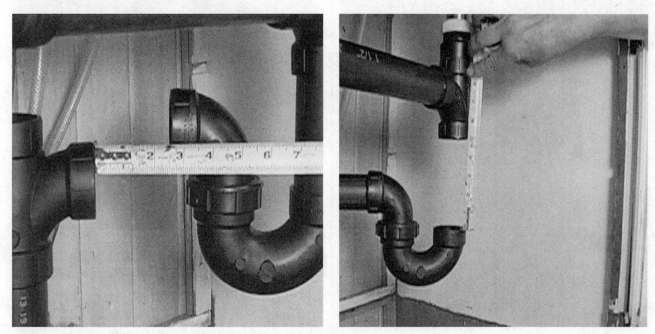

5. MEASURE FOR THE TRAP ARM. Dry-fit the P-trap with a scrap piece of pipe. Measure between the hub flanges, and add 1½ in. (¾ in. for each). Once the trap arm is cut, repeat the process to measure for the vertical tailpiece connection.

Glue Everything but the Threaded Connections

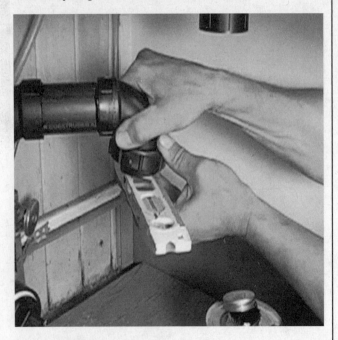

6. LEVEL THE THREADED P-TRAP CONNECTION. Before the glue dries, level the threaded end of the union P-trap in both directions. This allows the rest of the connections to fit together squarely.

7. USE PIPE DOPE ON THE P-TRAP THREADS. When gluing the P-trap into place, use pipe dope on the threaded portion that connects to the union elbow. Dope ensures that this vulnerable spot won't leak over time.

Quiet the Monsters in the Pipes

Stories of monsters in drain lines originated with unvented plumbing. The simple act of dumping a big pot of spaghetti water down the drain can awaken the beast. As water drains, the pressure buildup causes a grumbled protest accompanied by an occasional clank in the pipes below. Once the flow gets going, though, suction takes hold, and the hot water is ingested through a plumbing system that probably has more turns in it than a giant-size Silly Straw. If you bend over and peer down the drain just as the slurping sound gets loudest, it will suddenly stop, and you'll be welcomed by a belch of raw sewer gas that has come through the now-empty P-trap.

Quelling the monster is an easy fix—and economical too. You can buy an air-admittance valve (AAV) at your local plumbing-supply store. For more on venting with an AAV, look online at finehomebuilding.com.

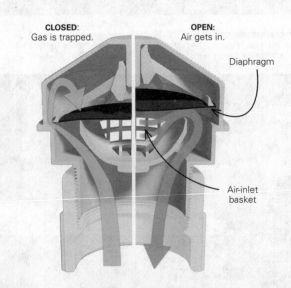

CLOSED: Gas is trapped.

OPEN: Air gets in.

Diaphragm

Air-inlet basket

Replacing a Garbage Disposal

By Ed Cunha

As a plumber, I get a lot of calls about garbage-disposal problems. I've seen an amazing variety of items take a disposal out of commission—everything from knickknacks to twist ties, bottle caps, and beef bones. But a disposal also can stop working for other reasons. The motor can overheat and seize, or an internal part can simply wear out or break.

When I arrive on the job, I have a strategy that tells me in a matter of minutes if the existing disposal can be fixed. If the troubleshooting tips don't work, there is a good chance your disposal is beyond repair. New disposals are relatively inexpensive and easy to install, so even if the old disposal is shot, it's not the end of the world.

Because a disposal can mash fingers just as easily as it mashes food waste, I never work on this appliance without making sure the power is off. You might simply be able to unplug the disposal from a receptacle inside the cabinet. Otherwise, you'll need to flip a switch or a circuit breaker.

Troubleshoot First

RESET THE MOTOR. When the disposal's motor is overloaded, an internal circuit breaker can trip and shut down the unit. Pressing the red reset button on the underside of the disposal restores power, and the motor might be able to free itself.

SPIN THE GRINDING CHAMBER TO CLEAR THE JAM. With the power off, wedge a broom handle against the side of the grinding chamber, and use your hand as a pivot point. Alternatively, some units might accept a Jam-Buster Allen wrench that could free the jam.

Remove the Old Disposal

1. DISCONNECT THE DRAIN LINE. The drain outlet is near the middle of the disposal. On this unit, I could loosen the drain and disconnect the disposal by hand. Near the top, disconnect the dishwasher inlet as well.

2. REMOVE THE DISPOSAL WITH A TWIST. I like to sit on the floor and support the disposal with my foot. You don't have to be as flexible as you might think to do this. With both hands, rotate the disposal counterclockwise until the mounting assembly disconnects.

3. REMOVE THE MOUNTING ASSEMBLY. With a screwdriver, loosen the mounting screws and pry off the snap ring on the lower part of the assembly. Once that's removed, gently break the putty bond of the sink strainer, and remove the assembly from above.

4. INSTALL THE STRAINER AND MOUNTING ASSEMBLY. Remove old putty from the lip of the drain. Apply new putty to the strainer, and press it in place. From below, slip on the paper gasket, the backup flange, and the mounting ring, in that order. Without pushing up on the assembly, install the snap ring and tighten the screws against the backup flange.

5. WIRE THE DISPOSAL FOR POWER. Whether direct-wiring the power source or installing an outlet plug, the operation is the same. On the bottom of the disposal, firmly secure the ground wire. Then connect like-color wires: white to white, black to black. Push the wires back into the housing and attach the cover plate.

6. HANG THE DISPOSAL ON THE MOUNTING ASSEMBLY. I use my foot to support the disposal the same way I did when I took it off. Align the mounting tabs with the mounting ring, and twist the mounting ring clockwise until it clicks into place. After the drain line is reconnected, fill the sink with water, and look at all the joints for possible leaks.

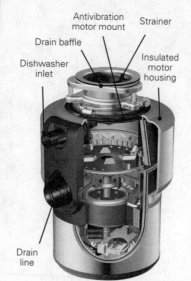

Antivibration motor mount
Strainer
Drain baffle
Dishwasher inlet
Insulated motor housing
Drain line

A Quieter Grind

Garbage disposals can pulverize the scraps of food from a four-course meal, but they also can grind after-dinner conversation to a halt. The folks at InSinkErator (www.insinkerator.com) have tuned their ears to this problem and are trying to improve the around-the-sink ambience. Their ¾-hp Premier model has more-than-adequate power, but also incorporates sound-dampening features like a specially designed drain baffle, an insulated motor housing, and an antivibration motor mount. Available at home centers, it won't chew up the home-repair fund.

Continued →

Installing a Frostproof Outdoor Faucet

By Carl Vonnoh III

Whether you're an avid gardener or you'd just like to have an extra outdoor faucet instead of an extra 100 ft. of garden hose, the simplicity of this installation will make you think twice about paying a doctor's wages to a plumber who doesn't dress nearly as well.

Find a Reference Point

A new outdoor faucet can go just about anywhere; the location depends on your needs. Once the location is chosen, take careful note of any distinct reference points that can be seen from both inside and outside the house, such as a foundation vent, a gas pipe, a dryer vent, or the edge of a basement window. These reference points simplify the transfer of measurements between interior and exterior walls. For this project, my reference point was an HVAC exhaust pipe.

When I'm planning the layout of new plumbing, I always try to use a single length of pipe to reach the house's existing waterline. One length of pipe means less labor and less chance of future leaks. I also leave myself about 6 in. of extra pipe to be on the safe side; the excess can be cut off when I'm ready to solder the joint.

With all my measurements in hand and with my reference point chosen, I transfer the interior measurements to the exterior wall of the house to locate the exact point where I should drill. The siding on this house was vinyl, so I used a 1-in.-dia. wood bit to drill through both the siding and the rim joist behind it. If the siding were brick, I would use a 1-in.-dia. masonry bit, then switch to a wood bit.

Anatomy of a Frostproof-Faucet Installation

If installed properly, an outdoor faucet should not require seasonal repair or replacement. Although there are a few subtleties to the job, the fundamentals of a properly functioning and long-lasting outdoor faucet are twofold: Keep the plumbing installation clean and simple, and learn how to operate the faucet properly.

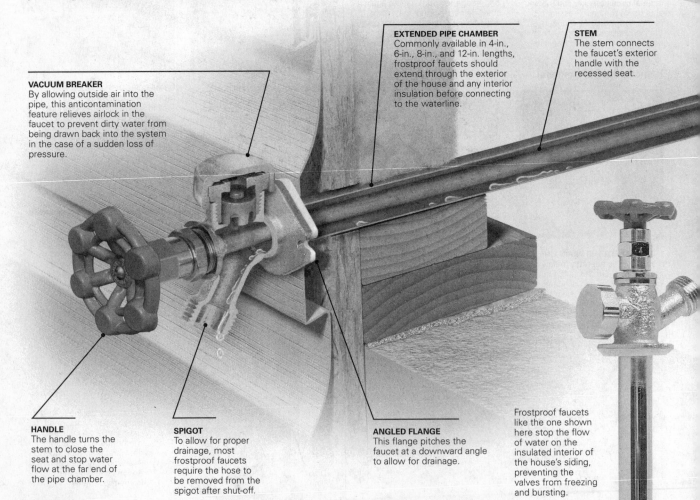

EXTENDED PIPE CHAMBER
Commonly available in 4-in., 6-in., 8-in., and 12-in. lengths, frostproof faucets should extend through the exterior of the house and any interior insulation before connecting to the waterline.

STEM
The stem connects the faucet's exterior handle with the recessed seat.

VACUUM BREAKER
By allowing outside air into the pipe, this anticontamination feature relieves airlock in the faucet to prevent dirty water from being drawn back into the system in the case of a sudden loss of pressure.

HANDLE
The handle turns the stem to close the seat and stop water flow at the far end of the pipe chamber.

SPIGOT
To allow for proper drainage, most frostproof faucets require the hose to be removed from the spigot after shut-off.

ANGLED FLANGE
This flange pitches the faucet at a downward angle to allow for drainage.

Frostproof faucets like the one shown here stop the flow of water on the insulated interior of the house's siding, preventing the valves from freezing and bursting.

Start Outside

TRANSFER MEASUREMENTS TO THE OUTSIDE WALL. The indoor measurements are transferred to the outside wall to locate the exact drilling point. For drilling through vinyl or wood siding, use a wood bit, but a masonry bit would be appropriate for drilling through concrete or brick.

OPEN THE HANDLE, AND SOLDER THE JOINT. Before soldering the faucet to the new copper pipe, turn the handle to prevent the seat from melting.

KEEPING IT CLEAN. Use a ½-in. cap to keep dirt and debris out of the pipe as it slides through the wall.

SEAT
The seat helps to prevent frozen valves by stopping the flow of water on the warm interior side of the house's siding and insulation.

FAUCET CONNECTION
Most frostproof faucets accept soldered or threaded connections.

PIPE BRACING
Securing the new pipe to the floor joists prevents rattling caused by water flow.

T-FITTING
Connect the new pipes with the existing plumbing by replacing the 90° elbow with a T-fitting.

Finish Inside

CUT THE EXISTING WATERLINE. Use a small pipe cutter to open the old pipe to prepare for the new joint. After opening the downstream faucet, pull the existing pipes down slightly to drain the remaining water.

TIE INTO THE EXISTING WATERLINE. A soldered T-fitting connects the new pipes with the old. Be careful when using a torch near flammable materials.

Continued →

Assemble the Faucet First

Once the hole is drilled, I'm ready to prepare the faucet. I suggest installing a frostproof, antisiphon faucet long enough to penetrate the siding, the sheathing, and the insulation before it connects to the water supply (see p. 386).

I solder the faucet to the proper length of pipe (photo p. 387) before I slide it through the hole I made in the house. (For more on soldering, see "Building Skills," *Fine Homebuilding* #162.) On this project, I matched the new pipe to the existing ½-in.-dia. copper plumbing.

After installing the angled flange, I mark the faucet's screw holes with a sharp pencil, then remove the faucet for easier access when drilling.

Shut Off the Water, and Head Inside

Once the new faucet has been slid into place, turn off the water at the nearest valve upstream from where the new faucet connector is going to be installed.

If I've shut off the main water supply to the house, I open any existing outside faucets as well as an interior faucet to drain the water out of the pipe. Without that drainage, soldering would be impossible.

Longer Pipes, Fewer Joints

Because I used a single long length of copper attached to the faucet, the pipe already should be close to the existing waterline. If the new pipe falls short of the existing waterline, I need to bring it as close as possible by soldering any necessary extensions and connections before cutting the existing pipe.

Any time that you're soldering near flammable materials like floor joists, it's a good idea to keep handy a flame-resistant fabric panel or a spray bottle filled with water to protect the flammable materials from the intense heat of the torch.

When the new pipe is braced against the joists and is close enough to the existing cold-water line to accept a ½-in. T-fitting, cut the existing waterline with a pipe cutter. The pipes should have drained by this time; if they have not, pull them down slightly to allow them to finish draining.

The most common way to tie a new length of pipe to the existing plumbing is to use a ½-in. T-fitting, but for this project, I had to extend the existing water pipe to meet the new faucet pipe. Whether you extend the old pipe or not, the best way to find the exact location that the new pipe should connect with the old is simply to overlap them and make a mark.

Check for Leaks

After soldering the new piece of pipe to the existing waterline, wait a few moments for the solder to appear dull, which means that it has finished cooling. Once the connection between the pipes has solidified, turn on the water and inspect your work. Next, make sure to shut off any faucets that had been opened prior to soldering, including the new faucet. When the water has refilled the pipes, check to make sure that no joints have leaks. If I find leaks in any of the joints, I shut off the water, drain the system, and then replace the leaky section rather than resolder the joints.

Contents

Doors & Windows

Install a Prehung Exterior Door

By Andy Engel

Installing a prehung exterior door is straightforward. Assuming the wall is plumb and that the rough sill and opening are flashed, the first step is to check the rough sill for level. If it isn't level, set the door unit in place, and shim the low side until it is level. Add shims about every 6 in. for solid support. Remove the door unit without disturbing the shims, then bed the shims in window and door sealant.

Before placing the door in the opening permanently, squeeze several thick beads of sealant across the top of the sill flashing to keep out wind and rain.

Place the Door from the Outside

Most prehung doors are held closed for handling with some sort of bracket that fastens from the inside. If there's another way into the house, I leave this bracket in place for convenience. If this is the only easy way into the house, then I remove the bracket before proceeding so that I can get in the house through the new door.

Working from the outside, guide the unit into the opening, leading with the sill. When you feel the bottom of the door trim hit the side of the house, let the unit slide down until its sill rests on the rough sill. Push the top in until the trim is tight to the house.

Drive one 2½-in. deck screw through the door trim near the top hinge. This holds the door and allows adjustments while you continue working from the inside.

Shim the Door Plumb

You already shimmed the door sill level, so you can pretty much put away your level. Now it's a matter of shimming and fastening the unit so that the gaps between the door and the frame are uniform. Assuming the door is square, the unit will automatically be plumb when it's properly shimmed. Look first at the top of the door on the latch side. If the gap here is narrow, shimming the near bottom of the door frame at the latch side should open it up. If the gap is wide, shimming behind the lower hinge should close it.

Once you're happy with the gaps, shim behind each hinge, and replace the two innermost screws at each hinge with a 2½-in. screw driven into the stud. Moving to the latch side, shim behind the latch and about 12 in. above and below the latch to even out the gaps. Each set of shims should get two screws, one through the inner side and one through the outer side of the jamb.

After you've shimmed and screwed the frame, check the door's function. It should open and close without hitting the frame. If it hits the frame, back out the screws, adjust the shims, and rescrew. Once the door functions well, score the shims with a knife, and snap them off. Finally, go outside and use 2½-in. deck screws spaced about every 12 in. to screw the door trim to the house.

Continued →

Step-by-Step

1. CHECK FOR LEVEL. With the wall plumb and the opening flashed, check the sill for level. Use wood shims spaced every 6 in. as needed. Bed the shims in window and door sealant.

2. SET THE DOOR. After placing three continuous beads of sealant across the length of the rough sill, insert the door in the opening.

3. DRIVE ONE SCREW. Install one screw through the door trim near the top hinge. This keeps the unit from toppling while still allowing it to be shimmed plumb.

4. MIND THE GAP. Check the space between the top of the door and the head jamb on the latch side so that you know where to shim first.

5. SHIM THE HINGES. To open the gap above the latch side, add shims behind the bottom hinge. To close the gap, reduce the shim thickness or shim the other side.

6. FASTEN THE HINGES. With each hinge shimmed so that the top gap is even, replace the two short inner screws with 2½-in. screws driven into the framing.

7. ADJUST THE LATCH JAMB. Once the hinge-side jamb is fastened, shim behind the latch-side jamb to even the gap.

8. FASTEN THE JAMBS. Double-check the gap around the door, then drive two screws through each set of shims and into the framing.

9. SCORE AND SNAP. After screwing through the shims, score them deeply with a sharp utility knife, then snap them off flush with the jamb.

10. SCREW THE DOOR TRIM. After you've secured the jamb, screw the exterior trim to the framing. Use 2½-in. deck screws spaced about every 12 in.

Shimming

Start with two shims made from cedar shingles. Insert one thick end first, then insert the second so that the tapers oppose each other. Sometimes there's room for only one shim. At other times, the studs will have warped, and you'll need to insert shims with their tapers running in the same direction. Cut the shims as needed so that the fat end is the right thickness.

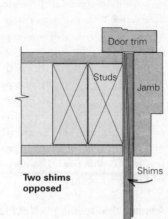

Two shims opposed

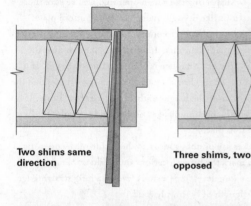

Two shims same direction

Three shims, two opposed

Plumb Perfect Prehung Doors

By Andy Engel

Several years ago, I walked onto a job site to find one proud employee. On his own initiative, he'd hung all the doors in the house alone—in less than three hours. Initially, I was impressed, but the 20 years that I'd been building houses tempered my excitement with skepticism. A little voice in my head said that I would regret not having given him a to-do list before I left—one so easy and so short that when I got back, I might find him in the pasture behind the house, practicing his Frisbee throw with a dry cow patty.

The first door I checked was sufficiently nailed, opened freely, and didn't swing on its own when I let it free from my hands. But the rest of the doors had plenty of problems. Besides the fact that my proud employee didn't once use a level, he also failed to put shims in all the key places. What got me most, though, was that more than a few of the doors were swinging the wrong way. I'm all for getting things done fast, but accuracy is key when it comes to hanging doors. To minimize such mistakes in the future, I developed a door-hanging process that I could easily teach to my crew. It starts with making sure the right door ends up in the right opening.

Mark the Rough Openings

Ordering doors doesn't take much effort on my part because my salesman does it. But it does warrant a couple of hours of my time and attention to ensure that the doors show up without incident. That's why my salesman and I walk through the house room by room with the floor plans in hand before the electrician starts his rough-in. I like to get door orders out of the way before the drywall is installed to allow enough lead time for the order. At this stage, the walk-through is a good opportunity for me to catch any errors in rough-opening sizes or locations that my framers might have made. It also lets me visualize potential errors in door swing on the plans and to correct them as needed.

During this walk-through, I measure the rough openings to make sure they're 2 in. wider than the door size; this leaves ¾ in. for each jamb leg and ¼ in. of shim space on each side of the door. The door sizes usually already account for a ⅛-in. reveal around the door (for example, a 36-in. door will measure closer to 35¾ in.).

I write the size and swing of each door in permanent marker on the trimmer stud of its corresponding rough opening. This becomes the final size. I mark the plans if the size or swing has changed, and I make sure that my salesman makes the final list so that if a door shows up that doesn't match what's written on the trimmer, it's his problem

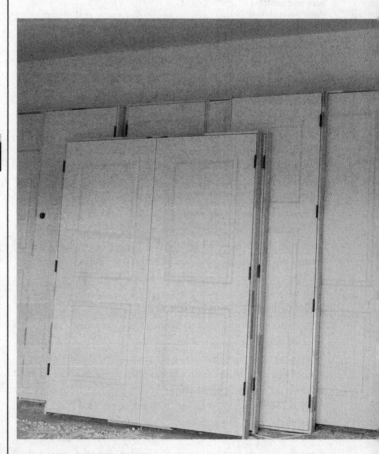

Hinges face away from the wall.
On concrete floors, a vapor barrier protects doors from moisture. Here, the barrier is not in place yet.

Continued ➡

Size and swing.
Write the door size and swing on the hinge-side trimmer stud of each rough opening before the drywall is installed.

---

to fix, not mine.

Marking the door swing on the trimmer stud also informs subcontractors who need to make decisions based on this information. Electricians need to know the door swing to locate light switches. HVAC contractors position return-air vents and feed registers according to door swing as well.

Finally, my hardwood-flooring contractor needs this information for certain rooms if he shows up before we hang the doors. Flooring transitions between wood and tile, for example, should happen under a closed door. If he knows the swing, then he can make the transition in the right place even if the door isn't installed yet. This process isn't ideal, though. I do my best to get the doors in before any flooring is in place. Then I can set the jamb legs directly on the subfloor and let the flooring contractor work around them as he goes.

Have a Place to Store the Doors

There's nothing worse than not having a place to store all the interior doors for a house when they are delivered to a job site. That many doors—often 30 or so for the houses I build—take up a lot of space. So before the truck shows up, I make sure to have a safe, secure place to store them.

It is always a good idea to store millwork of any kind in a controlled climate. Doors can scratch walls, though, so if I'm storing them inside, I put them in rooms like the kitchen, where drywall damage will be covered by cabinets. No matter where the doors end up, they're stacked with the hinges facing away from the wall.

If I have to put the doors in the garage, I lay down heavy plastic or tar paper to keep moisture from wicking into the jamb legs and the door bottoms. On that note, though, I rarely store solid-wood doors in the garage because they're most prone to movement in humid conditions.

As they're coming off the truck, I inspect each door for damage. The damage I discover usually happens on the jambs. I look for splits in the jambs, edges that have been nicked, and evidence that the door frame came apart in shipping or from rough handling. Solid doors are hard to damage, but I have seen holes in hollow-core doors. All wood doors can be scratched pretty easily. Anything that isn't repairable (within reason) on site goes back with the truck, and my sales rep gets a phone call.

Assume the Opening Is Not Plumb

Before I hang even one door, I move all the doors to their respective rough openings. Once the doors are spread out, I start the hanging process by inspecting the rough opening. I make sure there aren't any obstructions like drywall, nails, or a long bottom plate.

The only time I use a level is to plumb the rough opening. I check the edge of the hinge-side trimmer stud first to make sure that the wall is plumb (i.e., the bottom plate is plumb to the top plate). If it isn't, the door will open or close on its own. If my level shows that the wall is within 3/16 in. over the height of the door, I leave it alone. If it's out of plumb, I tap the bottom plate as needed and toenail it to the subfloor to keep it in place.

Once the plates are plumb, I move to the inside of the opening. I use black tape to mark the hinge locations on my door-hanging level. If you don't have a long level, tape a short level to a long straightedge like a 3-in.-wide length of 3/4-in. plywood.

Clear all potential obstructions.
Trim back the drywall on both edges of each trimmer stud using a rough-cutting handsaw.

Shim the hinge side plumb

Plumb the opening with one shim at each hinge location indicated by the black tape on a door-hanging level. Nail the bottom shim first, then the top, then the middle. Use long cedar shims, which are easier to handle and offer more adjustability because of their size.

1. Starting at the bottom-hinge location, nail the shim in place so that the thick end will face the hinge knuckle. Orient all three shims this way. As the drawing shows, when the jamb is installed, the nail to the right holds the jamb tight to the thick end of the shim. The nail to the left will push the jamb slightly, as indicated by the blue arrow. This will splay the jamb a bit, minimizing the possibility that the door will bind. The movement is so slight that the eye will never pick it up.

2. With the bottom shim nailed in place, slide the top shim between the level and the jamb until the level reads plumb.

3. Slide the third shim in until it just touches the level. If you push it in too far, you're likely to nudge the level slightly out of plumb. Trim each shim once it's nailed in place. If you're installing doors directly on the subfloor, place a shim on the floor at the hinge side to raise the jamb slightly.

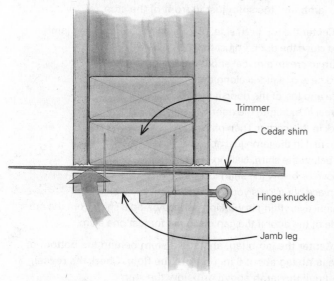

Trimmer

Cedar shim

Hinge knuckle

Jamb leg

If the flooring Is already installed

If the flooring is already installed, the jamb legs need to be cut. Using a level and a shim, determine the difference in height (if any) across the width of the opening. If the floor is level, trim both jamb legs so that the door will clear the finished floor by about ½ in. If the floor is out of level, trim that much more off the jamb leg on the high side.

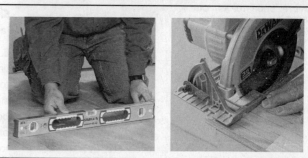

Continued →

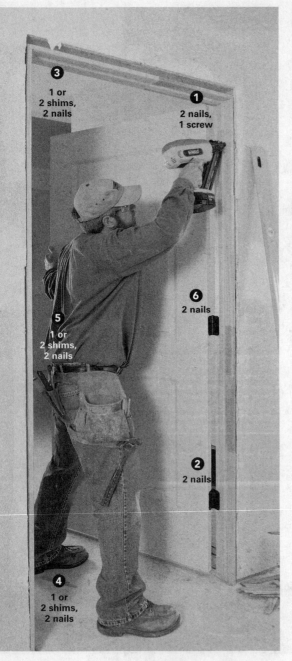

3
1 or
2 shims,
2 nails

1
2 nails,
1 screw

6
2 nails

5
1 or
2 shims,
2 nails

2
2 nails

4
1 or
2 shims,
2 nails

MOVE THE DOORSTOP AS A LAST RESORT. If the door is slightly warped or if the jamb is slightly bowed, the only option might be to move the doorstop. Use a block of scrap 2x and knock the stop where a nail or staple attaches it to the jamb, not between them. Tapping the stop between nails or staples won't move the stop sufficiently and could split it.

Shim and nail, then repeat

Start by nailing the hinge side in place. Then shim and nail the latch side to create an even reveal (or space) between the door and the jamb, about the thickness of a nickel. Follow the sequence described below, adjust the door as needed, then finish the installation with one more nail through each shim. Don't shim or nail the head jamb; the casing will keep it in place.

1. Align the jamb so that it is centered between the drywall on both sides. Next, place one nail through the jamb and the shim just in front of the stop. Then replace the middle screw of the top hinge with one that's 2½ in. long. The top hinge bears much of the door's weight; this screw solidly anchors the door to the framing. Be aware that overtightening this screw can compress the shim and kick out the bottom of the door, causing it to catch on the latch-side jamb leg.

If the door needs adjusting, this corner of the jamb is the last thing to be adjusted.

2. Center the hinge-side jamb at the bottom; then nail through the jamb and the shim just in front of the stop.

3. Center the top latch side, place a shim near the head jamb, and close the door. Adjust the shim to create a reveal about the thickness of a nickel along the side and top of the door. If the reveal is too tight, the door will stick in this corner. Then place one nail in the jamb just above or below the shim. Nailing above or below the shim locks it in place but allows you to adjust

it until everything is working perfectly. Add a shim from the other side of the door if the gap is too big for just one shim.

4. Center the jamb leg, and add a shim behind the bottom of the jamb leg about 6 in. up from the floor. Check the reveal, and nail the jamb above or below the shim.

5. Shim behind the latch to even the reveal, then tack the jamb in place above or below the shim.

6. Add one nail, then close the door and check the reveal one last time. Adjust the shims as needed to tune the reveal. Then move to the other side of the door and close it to make sure it meets the stop. If adjustments are needed here, make them in this order: at the bottom of the latch side, at the bottom of the hinge side, at the top of the latch side, and finally at the top of the hinge side. Remember to remove the long screw if making any adjustments there.

Centered the easy way

If a door is centered between two walls, as at the end of a hallway, there should be an even space between the casing and the drywall on both sides. It's possible to hang the door as previously described by placing it in the opening and shimming it until it is perfectly centered, but that takes a lot of time. To save time and to ease installation, you can hang the door with the casing attached. This approach makes centering a tall door, like the one shown here, more convenient as well.

ATTACH THE CASING LEGS. After removing any nails that were holding the door in place for shipping, nail the casing to both jamb legs using 18-ga. brads. Make sure the casing is perfectly straight, and create an even reveal along the jamb. Leave the head casing off; it will be cut to fit once the door is hung.

CENTER THE TOPS FIRST. Tip the door in place; then center it by measuring the space between the drywall and the casing. Next, place one 15-ga. finish nail through the casing and into the trimmer stud to the left of the top hinge.

PLUMB THE HINGES. With a long level tight to the hinges, adjust the bottom of the jamb until it's plumb. Nail through the casing and into the trimmer stud. Adjust the latch side until the reveal is even, and nail it in place through the casing as well. Finally, install shims from the other side of the door, replace the top hinge screw, and nail the jamb as you go. Once the installation is complete, add the head casing.

I plumb the hinge-side trimmer stud with one shim at each hinge location. I tack the bottom shim in first, then move to the top, then the middle. Finish nails can work here, but sometimes, the impact from the nail gun splits the shim or blows the nail right through it. Drywall nails are a good alternative.

Some people think it's necessary to double-shim here to counter the effect of the shim's taper, but I disagree. Unless the stud is twisted, I put the thick edge of the shim on the hinge-knuckle side. I use one shim to cock the jamb just enough to keep the hinges from binding. Besides, using one shim is quicker. Once the shims are in place, I use a utility knife to trim them flush with the drywall.

Tip the Door into Place

Although the hinge-side trimmer stud is ready, the opening is not done yet. Installing the doors before any flooring is in place is ideal because I don't have to cut any jamb legs. It saves me time at this stage, but the best part is that it ensures a tighter transition once the flooring is in place. But I don't count on a level subfloor.

Before I place the door in the opening, I put a shim on the floor with the thick part toward the hinge knuckle to raise the hinge side of the jamb slightly. Raising this jamb leg a bit ensures that I'll get the right reveal across the top of the door. Otherwise, if I set the door on

the floor and this side is lower than the latch side, I have to cut the latch side once it's hung.

I tip the door into the opening and start by securing the hinge-side jamb leg to the trimmer stud. I often slip a wedge under the door to hold it open and in place while I'm working. I tack the top corner in place and replace the middle screw on the top hinge with a 2½-in.-long screw that fastens into the trimmer stud. Then I tack the bottom corner and move to the top of the latch-side jamb leg. I use one or two shims as needed in each location of the latch side, making sure that the jamb remains aligned with the wall plane.

Once the door is hung, I double-check the reveal around the door. If the reveal is even and if the door is working properly, I make sure it is closing fully against the doorstop. If it doesn't meet the stop, I adjust the jamb legs as needed. Occasionally, the stop might have to be moved with a wood block and a hammer.

When the door is operating to my liking, I finish by adding one or two more nails at each shim location along both jambs. Then I trim the latch-side shims. Although this is the end of the hanging process, it's also my least favorite thing to do. I've found that a sharp utility knife is ideal for the thin end of the shim and that a dovetail saw works best on the thick end.

Continued ➜

Cutting a Prehung Exterior Door

By Andy Engel

Most times when you need a prehung exterior door that's shorter than normal, it's easiest to order it from the lumberyard. It's possible, however, to shorten the unit yourself.

Manufacturers typically allow wood doors to be trimmed by ½ in. at the top and 1½ in. at the bottom. You can cut more away from the bottom without hitting one of the dowels that hold the door together. If possible, I like to cut the top of a prehung exterior door because then I don't need to remove and reinstall the door-bottom weatherstripping. Here, though, enough had to come off that I cut the bottom.

Disassemble the Unit

Take the door out of its frame, and place it on a surface that won't scratch the door, with the protruding hinges facing down. That keeps the hinges out of the saw's way when the cut is made.

Remove the door-bottom weatherstripping carefully so that it can be reinstalled. Mark the cut on each edge of the door, and clamp a shooting board to the door, with the edge of the board indexed on the marks. Position the clamps with their long ends down so that they won't interfere with the saw, and place a block under each clamp to protect the other side of the door.

To prevent tearout, score the door with a sharp knife before cutting it with a circular saw. With the saw's baseplate against the fence of the shooting board, cut slowly but without stopping.

Reattach the door-bottom weatherstripping with spray adhesive and staples, or with caulk and low-profile screws or roofing nails.

Cutting the Frame

Cut the same amount from the bottom of the frame as you cut from the door. Because exterior-door frames are rabbeted, in addition to shortening the jamb legs, you need to recut the rabbets for the sill.

Cut the fasteners holding the jambs to the sill with an oscillating multitool. You also can use a hacksaw. Don't worry about caulk residue or minor splitting on the jamb legs; they'll be cut off later.

Before cutting the jamb legs, mark the new location of the sill rabbet, measuring the cut and the angle from the original rabbet. If you shorten the jambs before marking the new rabbet cut, you lose the reference point. Pull out the weatherstripping, and keep it out of the way with a spring clamp. Later, shorten it with a knife, then stuff it back into its kerf. Mark the height cut on the outside of the jambs, and cut a sill rabbet with a circular saw and chisel.

On a wood jamb, seal cuts with primer. The bottom of the jamb shown here is plastic, so no primer was needed. Apply a bead of paintable exterior sealant such as urethane caulk to the end of the sill, and reassemble the frame. I used stainless-steel decking screws.

That's it. You're done—except for installing the door, but that's another story.

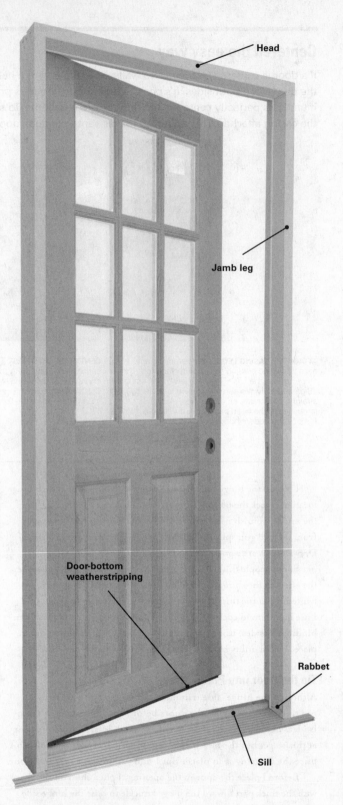

Head

Jamb leg

Door-bottom weatherstripping

Rabbet

Sill

1. REMOVE THE BOTTOM WEATHERSTRIPPING. Use a putty knife or 5-in-1 tool to break the sealant bond between the weatherstripping and the door and to pry out any fasteners. Work carefully so that the weatherstripping can be reused.

2. SCORE THE VENEER. After laying out the cut and clamping the shooting board to the door, score the door's veneer with a knife to minimize tearout.

3. CUT THE DOOR. Use a sharp, new 40-tooth blade in a circular saw. Let the shooting board guide the cut.

4. REATTACH THE DOOR BOTTOM. Spray adhesive on both surfaces creates an instant bond. Staples reinforce the connection.

5. LAY OUT THE RABBET CUT. After carefully removing the sill from the door frame, mark the edge of the new rabbet. Duplicate the existing rabbet's angle.

6. CUT DOWN THE DOOR FRAME. Before recutting the rabbet, mark the jamb legs to length, and cut them down. A cleat between the legs keeps them from flopping.

7. SET THE SAW TO CUT THE RABBET. With the wide part of the saw's baseplate on the thick part of the jamb, set the depth of the blade so that it barely touches the rabbet on the jamb.

8. CLEAN UP THE RABBET. After making a series of cuts with the saw, clean out the waste with a sharp chisel. A spring clamp holds the weatherstripping out of the way.

9. REASSEMBLE THE FRAME. Use corrosion-resistant screws to fasten the sill back in place.

Make a shooting board

Shooting boards are jigs that keep the saw's baseplate from damaging the workpiece, serve as a fence, ease layout, and minimize chipping. They can be made in any length and are custom to each saw. Start with a base made of ¼-in. plywood or hardboard that's about 12 in. wide. Glue to one edge of the base a piece of ¼-in. plywood that's about 5 in. wide. This will serve as a fence, so be sure it has straight edges. The amount of base to the side of the fence must be wider than the base of your circular saw. Once the glue has set, cut off the excess stock by running the circular saw along the fence. The edge of the shooting board is now indexed exactly to the sawblade, so there's no guesswork about where to place the shooting board.

Continued ➡

Trim the Bottom of a Door

By John Ross

The necessity of trimming a door goes along with remodeling projects where the floor rises because of added carpeting, new tile, or extra layers of subflooring (or in my case, whenever my penchant for area rugs gets the best of me). As someone who has remodeled other people's homes as well as my own, I have tackled this project over and over. To trim a door problem-free, I call on the same skills I use for other finish-carpentry projects, such as built-ins, wainscoting, and countertops.

Although you can use straightedge guides, special saws, and zero-clearance throat plates to cut finished work, I use a 4-ft. level clamped to the door and a thin-kerf blade in my circular saw for a task like this. I also use a utility knife to score the door and some masking tape to protect the surface of the door. Finally, I need a gauge block, which I usually make from a piece of thin plywood.

Mark and Score Where You'll Cut

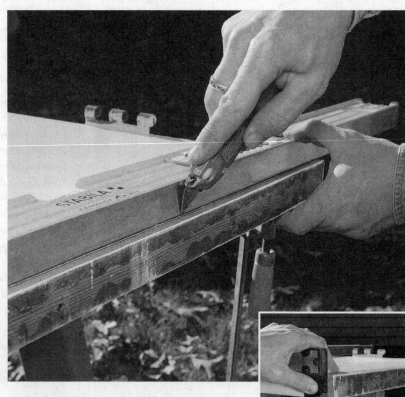

1. MARK THE DOOR FOR THE CUT. At the bottom of the door, I put tape on both the hinge side and the strike side (the side with no hinges). I place the rug against the closed door and mark both pieces of tape ¼ in. above the rug. Because this is an area rug and not wall-to-wall carpeting, I want the door just to clear the rug after it is trimmed.

2. DRAW THE CUTLINE. With the door set on sawhorses, I connect the two marks with tape, then use the level to draw a straight line between them.

3. SCORE THE CUT TO PREVENT TEAROUT. Clamped to the door, the level works well as a guide while I make several shallow passes with a utility knife to score the cutline. As an extra precaution, I tape and score the end of the door where the circular-saw blade will exit.

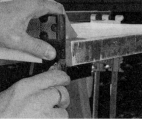

Use a Gauge Block to Line Up the Cut

4. MAKE A GAUGE BLOCK. This scrap of wood is cut at the exact distance from the edge of the blade to the edge of the saw's baseplate.

5. USE THE GAUGE BLOCK TO SET THE LEVEL BACK FROM THE CUTLINE. The block should just cover the scored line. The level is secured to the door with two clamps.

8. EASE THE EDGE. To prevent the bottom of the door from splintering over time, I ease the edge using a small block plane. Some 80-grit sandpaper wrapped around a sanding block works just as well.

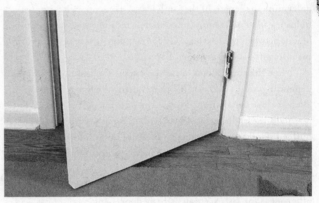

9. THE PAYOFF. The trimmed door clears the rug easily and doesn't look awkward.

6. TAPE THE DOOR, NOT THE SAW. To avoid marring the door, I put down two layers of tape next to the level. I tape the work because it's faster than taping the bottom of the saw and because it's easier to clean up.

The Right Blade for a Clean Cut

For general finish work, I use a sharp thin-kerf blade in my circular saw. It removes less material, so it's easier on the saw. I've had good results with Freud's Diablo 24-tooth framing blade (D0724X) (www. freudtools.com). Although you can buy pricier finish-cutting blades with more carbide-tipped teeth, this framing blade delivers smooth cuts and doesn't overwork the saw.

7. MAKE THE CUT. I set the cutting depth so that the blade just cuts through the door and focus on the baseplate when making the cut. The baseplate edge stays in contact with the level while the bottom runs flat on the door. To prevent the blade guard from dragging on the door, I hold it retracted during the cut.

Continued ➔

Jigs for Jambs

By Jim Chestnut

There seem to be as many ways to hang a door as there are carpenters to hang them, so after many years of running a trim crew, I came up with a few of my own ways to make the work easier and the results better.

When it comes to hanging doors, I believe that the jamb legs should bear fully on the subfloor. Nails alone (especially the light-gauge nails used these days) won't support the weight of the jamb and door over time. Trimming the jamb legs to closer tolerances requires accurate measuring and cutting techniques. Instead of marking a level line and then measuring each side to determine the length of the jamb legs, I came up with a jig that holds my level and almost immediately tells me the difference in length between the two legs. Of course, this jig works well if I'm installing doors on a finished floor, too.

When the time comes to cut the jambs, I adjust my technique depending on the project. If I'm removing the doors from the jambs before installation, I tack a spreader across the legs to maintain the opening, and I cut with a chopsaw paired with an outfeed stand to support the jamb. More often, I keep the doors and jambs intact, mark the jamb lengths, and cut them with a circular saw and a crosscut jig.

Here's a look at my jamb-measuring and cutting jigs and some other ideas for fast, accurate, sturdy door-hanging.

A Convenient Way to Measure Jamb Legs

I make a jig from 5/4×6 stock that I rip to about 4⅝ in. I nail a crossbar 48 in. from the bottom, which is a comfortable height. Then I take apart a broken folding rule, paint over the numbers to avoid confusing myself, and tack a 6-in. length to each side of the stick so that the rule's center (marked with a zero) is equal to the top of a level sitting on the crossbar. Having rules on both sides lets me use the jig for both left- and right-hand doors.

I begin measuring with a reference jamb length— let's say 80⅝ in. (80 in. for the door, ½ in. for the clearance to the floor, and ⅛ in. for the gap at the head). I register the jig against the hinge side, level across, and mark the strike side (1). Then I fit the jig onto the strike side, where I can see any difference in height between the hinge and the strike side of the jamb (2). I write the measurement in 16ths as shown on the rule—minus 2, for instance—and subtract it from the reference length. The strike-side length becomes 80½ in. After the legs are cut, I know the jamb head will be square when the door is installed.

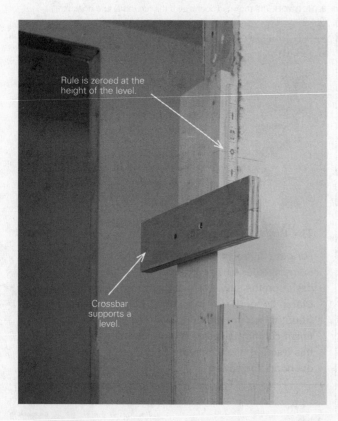

Rule is zeroed at the height of the level.

Crossbar supports a level.

Gauge the Gap, Gauge the Cut

On most jobs, I send my apprentice Hearty around with a jamb jig and graduated shims to check thresholds for level. (A large part of an apprentice's life should involve crawling around on the floor.) If the floor slopes, the jamb needs to be cut slightly off-square to match. Hearty shoves a graduated shim (1) into any gaps beneath the jig and measures the gap created by the angle. He then marks the measurement on the drywall next to the rough opening. The carpenter responsible for cutting the jambs adds or subtracts that amount from the target length. (2) By inserting his own graduated shim to the mark indicated for that door between the jamb edge and the plywood crosscut jig's stop, the carpenter reproduces the angle of the threshold, and his cut matches the floor.

GUESSTIMATE NO MORE. To determine the width of a small gap quickly, I grab some shims, then graduate their tapers in 1/16-in. increments. I use a set of dial calipers; all I have to do is lock the jaws at the desired thickness, shove in the shim until it is snug, and mark it. You can buy accurate calipers for less than $25. The best thing is that as long as the marks are measured with the same calipers, the marks are identical from one shim to the next, regardless of the length or the taper of the shim. An apprentice can use one to measure, a carpenter can use a different one to cut, and the jamb will bear equally on the floor.

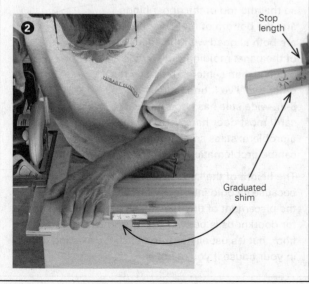

Slick Techniques for Fastening Doors

Upper Jamb First

For stronger door assemblies, I prefer 3-in. screws instead of nails. (Nails are great to locate the door, but screws hold better.) I remove the side stop and drive a screw through the shims. When reapplied, the stops hide the screw heads. Alternatively, I drive a long screw into the hinge, as long as I can match that screw to the existing screw heads.

Lower Jamb Adjustments

When shimming the jamb plumb, I find it easier to adjust the shims if I nail above and below the shims. Once the jamb is where I want it, I drive a screw through the shim. Small blocks tacked to the drywall register the jamb's hinge side to the drywall's face.

Stop length

Graduated shim

Door-Jamb Crosscutting Jig

Fence must be equal to the jamb width.

Continued ➜

Build Your Own Interior Doors

By Paul Levine

As a cabinetmaker, I build doors all the time. But when it came time to make doors for my house, I cringed. Full-size doors have little in common with their cabinet-size counterparts. They are thicker and heavier, requiring beefy joinery to stand up to the strain of their own weight, not to mention daily use. So after making the first of the 11 doors I needed, I realized that the joinery and assembly methods I was using were not going to fly. I agonized for a few weeks but finally came up with a good plan that didn't require special tools or processes.

A typical interior door is assembled with dowels, which provide lots of surface area for a strong glue bond, but the two-part setup of dowel jigs makes them fussy to work with. My design provides for just as much glue area as a doweled door, but it requires only one cutting operation instead of two. With one dado-blade setup, I can cut grooves to accept the loose tenons as well as the ½-in. plywood or medium-density fiberboard (MDF) used for the panels. The frames, panels, and tenons are then glued together. To eliminate fussy alignment work during glue-up, I let the stiles and tenons run long, then trim the door to size with a circular saw and edge guide once the glue has set up.

For under $100 in materials (not including hardware), I can build thicker-than-average, paint-grade frame-and-panel doors, and I can customize them with my choice of molding. But one of the best things about this setup is the freedom to do what you want. By substituting mahogany, for instance, for the frame and mahogany crotch veneer on the panels, you get a dramatically different door without really changing the process.

One Method, Countless Variations

I built traditional paint-grade four-panel doors for my house, but the beauty of this method is that the same techniques can be applied to any design, using any type of wood, to achieve a custom look. Here are a few options.

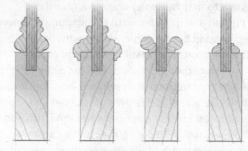

Molding options

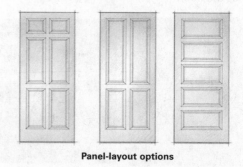

Panel-layout options

Plan for the Hardware

As shown in the drawing below, I size and locate the components of the door with the hinges and knob in mind. I like to set hinges so that the top of the upper hinge and the bottom of the lower hinge are both aligned with the edges of the panel molding. The middle hinge is then centered between the other two. I've found that a 4-in.- to 5-in.-wide stile has enough meat to carry most door hardware without a problem; stiles smaller than that can be problematic.

The height of the knob also needs to be considered because it could interfere with the panel molding or the placement of the middle rail. A comfortable height for doorknobs is between 36 in. and 39 in. from the floor, but it's usually best to match the existing doors in your house if you're not sure.

Rail

Stile

1. The grooves that hold the panels and tenons all can be cut on a tablesaw with a stacked dado set to ⅜-in. width. By running both sides of each stile and rail against the rip fence, I can cut a perfectly centered groove ½ in. wide and 1 in. deep. I like to cut the grooves just a hair wider than the thickness of the panel, then cut the floating tenons to fit snugly.

2. I use a straightedge to make sure the door stays flat as clamps are tightened. I size stiles, rails, and tenons to let the door run long when it's assembled.

3. After sanding both sides of the door flat with a belt sander (you can also pay a local millwork shop to run the doors through a wide belt sander), I trim the top and bottom of the door, then rip a 3° bevel on the strike-side stile.

4. Rabbeted panel moldings are available, but stock molding from the local lumberyard or home center can be rabbeted on the tablesaw to fit the frame-and-panel door. Install the panel molding after you've finished routing the mortises for the lockset and hinges, and after you've cut the bevel for the strike side; these doors are too heavy to be riding across the tablesaw on their moldings.

Panels for moist areas
If the doors will be in a moist area, such as a bathroom, I use Titebond III glue (www. titebond.com), which is waterproof, and Medex (www.sierrapine.com) rather than standard MDF or plywood. Medex is more expensive, but it is almost impervious to moisture.

I use stock planed from 8/4 to a finished thickness of 1¾ in., a nice step up from typical 1⅜-in.-thick interior doors.

Grooves are 1 in. deep and just a hair wider than the panel stock to make assembly easier.

Floating tenons are made of the same stock as the stiles. Size them for a snug fit.

By Ben Graham and Mike Lamp

We recently completed a deep-energy retrofit to an 80-year-old Vermont farmhouse. The many improvements we made included new windows, new mechanical systems, and the addition of 4 in. of exterior mineral-wool insulation. Not surprisingly, the project also called for new energy-efficient exterior doors to complement the home's high-performance building envelope.

For an ultra-efficient house like this one, entry doors are often sourced from Europe, where high-performance doors are more mainstream than in the United States. Unfortunately, most European offerings have a sleek, modern appearance, and our clients wanted something that would fit the style of their farmhouse. With limited options, we set out to build a pair of attractive entry doors that would rival the efficiency of the best-performing units on the market. In addition, we wanted to do so by using common building materials that are readily available.

The 3½-in.-thick R-10 doors that we built are made from site-harvested cherry. They are filled with 2-in. rigid-mineral-wool insulation and include triple-pane low-e glass. We installed the doors in custom-built jambs with a crucial double-weatherstripping detail to help make the entry airtight. Finally, we outfitted each door with the best-built hardware we could find.

High-Performance Components

An ultra-efficient entry door depends on durable, high-quality components. Weatherstripping, glass, and insulation all contribute to a door that looks good, saves energy, and operates easily.

Insulated Glass
Triple-pane low-e glass with 0.24 U-factor

Insulation
Roxul ComfortBoard IS mineral wool

Weatherstripping

WS64 brush sweep

WS15 silicone weatherstripping

GG05 foam weatherseal

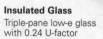

An Insulation Sandwich

Once all of the door's parts were milled, the exterior-side components were assembled by capturing the tongue-and-groove planks that make up the door's lower half in a glued-up frame. It was critical for all of the parts to be in perfect alignment so the cleats that attach the front of the door to the back would fit without struggle. The rest of the assembly was driven largely by an anticipation of wood movement and attention to airtightness.

DRIVE IN THE CLEATS. Once the glue is dry on the exterior panel, the three cleats are driven into the sliding dovetails. The cleats are made from two layers of quartersawn white oak with a 1-in. XPS-foam thermal break in between. They are held together with countersunk ¼-in. bolts.

ADD AN AIR BARRIER. The tongue-and-groove boards that make up the front and back panels are gasketed for weathertightness, but a breathable weather barrier on the exterior side of the door provides a second line of defense. It's sealed to the door skin with weathersealing tape.

ASSEMBLE THE BACK. With the door's center already insulated with 2-in. rigid mineral wool, the boards that make the door's interior panel are slid on the dovetails one at a time. Paste wax makes the process easier. The center board has tongues on both edges to receive boards on both sides.

GLUE UP THE PANEL. The stub-tenon joints where the door's rails and stiles meet are secured with waterproof glue and then clamped with pipe clamps. Temporary spacers (card stock about ³⁄₃₂ in. thick) ensure even gaps between the tongue-and-groove boards during assembly.

CUT THE ARCHED TOP. The door has an arched top that's cut in three passes with a router on a trammel arm. With the door's curved top as a starting point, curved laminations of ³⁄₁₆-in.-thick stock will be made later for the door's top edge, head jamb, and curved stops.

Continued ➜

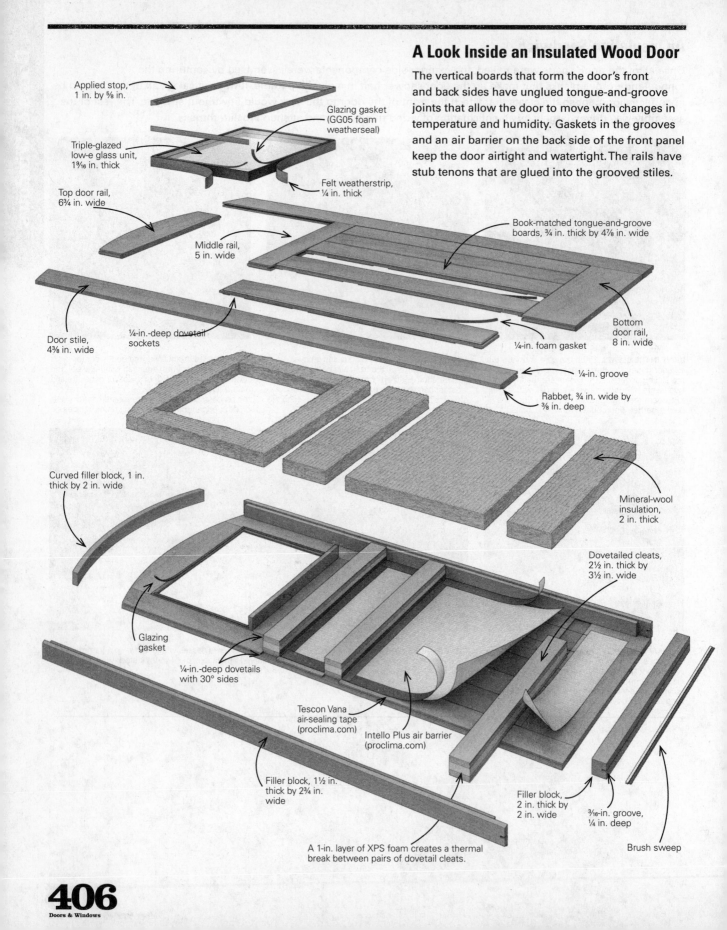

A Look Inside an Insulated Wood Door

The vertical boards that form the door's front and back sides have unglued tongue-and-groove joints that allow the door to move with changes in temperature and humidity. Gaskets in the grooves and an air barrier on the back side of the front panel keep the door airtight and watertight. The rails have stub tenons that are glued into the grooved stiles.

Applied stop, 1 in. by ⅝ in.

Glazing gasket (GG05 foam weatherseal)

Triple-glazed low-e glass unit, 1⅛ in. thick

Felt weatherstrip, ¼ in. thick

Top door rail, 6¾ in. wide

Middle rail, 5 in. wide

Book-matched tongue-and-groove boards, ¾ in. thick by 4⅞ in. wide

Door stile, 4⅜ in. wide

¼-in.-deep dovetail sockets

¼-in. foam gasket

Bottom door rail, 8 in. wide

¼-in. groove

Rabbet, ¾ in. wide by ⅜ in. deep

Curved filler block, 1 in. thick by 2 in. wide

Mineral-wool insulation, 2 in. thick

Dovetailed cleats, 2½ in. thick by 3½ in. wide

Glazing gasket

¼-in.-deep dovetails with 30° sides

Tescon Vana air-sealing tape (proclima.com)

Intello Plus air barrier (proclima.com)

Filler block, 1½ in. thick by 2¾ in. wide

Filler block, 2 in. thick by 2 in. wide

³⁄₁₆-in. groove, ¼ in. deep

Brush sweep

A 1-in. layer of XPS foam creates a thermal break between pairs of dovetail cleats.

A Heavy Door in a Thick Wall

The home's 4 in. of exterior insulation meant that the door jambs had to be 11 in. wide, so they were built in two parts with the joint hidden by the applied stop. The stop has two layers of soft silicone weatherstripping, ensuring that the door is airtight but closes easily. To stop air infiltration further, the home's water-resistive barrier was carefully taped to the jambs with air-sealing tape.

FASTEN THE JAMBS AND INSTALL THE STOP. Once the side jambs are plumb and securely fastened with structural screws, the first layer of the two-layer stop is fastened to the head jamb with 1-in. screws. Then the side stops are coped around the head stop and screwed in place. The screw heads will be hidden by the second stop.

HANG THE DOOR. Once the first-layer stops are in place, the door is hung from its hinges and closed. The second stop is then held tight to the door and fastened through counterbored holes that will be filled with grain-matched cherry plugs later.

SLIP IN THE JAMB EXTENSION. Once both stop layers are in place, the assembled, three-sided jamb extension is fit to the main jamb with a rabbeted half-lap joint. A ¼-in. gap in the joint between the main jamb and the jamb extension allows for seasonal expansion. The gap is hidden by the stop.

INSTALL THE CASING. The jambs are taped to the house's water-resistive barrier with air-sealing tape, and then the casing is installed with screws. The screw holes are counterbored so they can be plugged later.

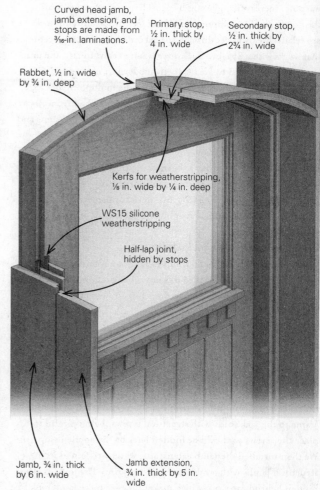

Curved head jamb, jamb extension, and stops are made from ³⁄₁₆-in. laminations.

Primary stop, ½ in. thick by 4 in. wide

Secondary stop, ½ in. thick by 2¾ in. wide

Rabbet, ½ in. wide by ¾ in. deep

Kerfs for weatherstripping, ⅛ in. wide by ¼ in. deep

WS15 silicone weatherstripping

Half-lap joint, hidden by stops

Jamb, ¾ in. thick by 6 in. wide

Jamb extension, ¾ in. thick by 5 in. wide

Aesthetics and Performance Drive Design

One of the first decisions we had to make was whether to build inset or overlay doors. In the United States, virtually all residential entry doors are inset. The door swings into the frame and lands on a stop. High-performance European doors, which are described as overlay, close onto their frame. Proponents of overlay doors say they seal tighter and are therefore more efficient. However, overlay doors require rabbeted or post-style hinges, which are costly and hard to find in the United States.

Rather than order hinges from Europe for several hundred dollars, we decided to build inset doors and add a second layer of weatherstripping to boost their airtightness.

For weatherstripping, we opted to use silicone flipper seals from Research Conservation Technology (conservationtechnology.com) along the head and side jambs. These soft silicone weatherstrips easily compress to accommodate a wood door's seasonal movement, and they make the door easy to close. The strips are installed in one sawkerf that aligns with

Continued →

the door's rabbeted edge and in a second kerf cut into the applied stop. On the bottom of the door, we installed a brushed sweep to seal the door to its bluestone threshold.

Perhaps the most challenging aspect of the doors' design was finding suitable hardware. For high-performance homes, we encourage all of our clients to select multipoint locks for their doors. The bolts at the top and bottom can help prevent a wood door from warping, increase airtightness by providing even pressure against the door's weatherstripping, and boost security. Multipoint locks are relatively easy to get through special order, but finding a setup that works with a 3½-in.-thick door is not as easy. In fact, the units we found that would fit are distinctly modern in appearance. Given the options, our clients decided to forego the multipoint lock and instead install a high-quality traditional mortise lockset from Rocky Mountain Hardware, which accommodates the door's thickness and is in tune with the farmhouse style.

Another essential component was the glazing, as each door's design included a window, a thermal weakpoint in any entry door. To retain efficiency, we selected triple-pane low-e glass panels from Cardinal Glass. The 1⁹/₁₆-in.-thick insulated windows have a U-factor of 0.24, which is roughly the equivalent of R-4.

Performance Hinges on Installation

We assembled the doors and jambs in the shop to make installation easier. The doors are installed like any other prehung unit, with some extra complications due to their 140-lb. weight and their two-part jambs that accommodate the home's extrathick walls.

We devoted the same amount of attention to insulating and air-sealing during the installation that we put into the construction of the doors so that air leaks would not compromise the doors' efficiency. We started by pulling the hinge pins and removing the door from the jamb. We then shimmed the hinge-side jack stud plumb with flat shims and screwed the door frame to the jack studs with structural screws, being careful to place the screws so they'd be hidden later by the applied stop. We then installed the jamb extensions, which are joined to the structural jambs with a rabbeted half-lap joint. The joint is also hidden behind the stop, which makes the two-piece jamb look like a single piece of wood. We carefully taped the door frame to the home's housewrap with air-sealing tape and then filled around the frame with canned spray foam before installing flat casing that matches the home's window casing.

Doors like this aren't cheap, but they cost about the same as high-end entry doors from Europe. Each door required 100 hours of custom woodworking labor, 60 board feet (bd. ft.) of 4/4 cherry, 15 bd. ft. of 8/4 cherry, and 8 bd. ft. of 4/4 red oak. The doors have performed admirably during Vermont's frigid winter weather, keeping the homeowers comfortable and saving energy. But more than that, we all think the doors look great, and so does everyone else who visits the house.

Install a Sliding Barn Door

By Gary M. Katz

I've installed hundreds of interior pocket doors—everything from off-the-shelf hollow-core versions to custom hardwood doors 10 ft. tall—but they have always made me a little uneasy. My biggest problem is that the hardware is inaccessible for repairs. I don't like the thought of having to tear into walls to replace a worn roller or a broken track.

When I needed a space-saving door on the utility room in my new shop, I decided instead on a sliding barn-style door with an exposed track. Like pocket doors, sliding doors work great in tight locations. Unlike pocket doors, though, sliding doors have exposed hardware, so they're easy to fix when something breaks.

Barn-door hardware is available from several sources and in a variety of styles.

Picking a style and finish is only the first step in getting the right hardware. You also need to know the dimensions of the door, the thickness of the jamb, and the width and the thickness of the casing. You also need to know whether the door track should be drilled. You must decide all of these things before ordering hardware.

Mount the Track

When it comes time to hang a barn door, the most important factor is mounting the track in the right spot. I install the jambs first so that I can establish the location of the casing. The casing location determines where to mount the track.

Because sliding doors don't need a stop on the jambs, the jambs are made from primed 1x stock. It's important that the jamb legs be plumb and the head jamb level. This ensures that the casing also is plumb and level. If the casing isn't straight, the door edge won't line up with the casing when the door is closed, which will look terrible.

Once the jambs are installed, I lay out the side casing on the wall using a scrap of casing stock. I put another mark ½ in. beyond the casingthat corresponds to the length of the track. I also lay out the 5½-in.-tall head casing and place another mark ¼ in. above the casing that corresponds to the track bottom. The marks show where to put the track, but I still need to mark the track's mounting holes.

To make marking the holes easier and more accurate, I install a temporary ledger that lines up with the bottom of the track. After placing the track on top of the ledger and aligning the ends with the marks I made earlier, I mark the screw locations. I remove the track and drill pilot holes with a ⁵/₁₆-in. twist bit. I arrange the washers and standoffs as described in the instructions, and then fasten the track, starting with the center screw.

Barn-Door Basics

1. Mount the Track in One of Three Ways

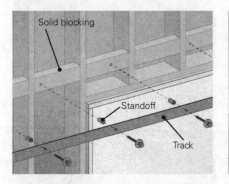

Solid blocking

Standoff

Track

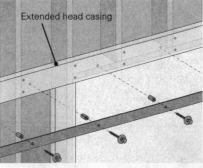

Extended head casing

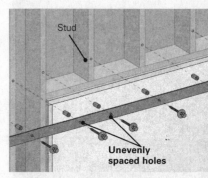

Stud

Unevenly spaced holes

A. Install solid 2x blocking behind the finished wall for mounting the track. For this method, order the track with the holes already drilled. This is the method the author used and ensures that the mounting screws are spaced evenly along the track.

B. Securely fasten a length of solid stock to the finished wall, and mount the track to the stock. The stock also acts as the head casing. For this method, you also should order the track with the holes drilled.

C. Mount the track directly to the wall studs. For this installation, you should order the track without the holes drilled. Instead, you'll need to locate the studs and then drill the track yourself to match the stud locations. It's unlikely that the holes will be spaced evenly.

Calculate the Correct Track Length

The length of the track varies with the style of hardware. With the author's hardware and door combination, it's twice the width of the opening, plus the width of one side casing, plus an extra ½ in. on each side. This extra ½ in. allows the door to be flush with the edge of the casing when closed and allows the hanger to be centered on the stile.

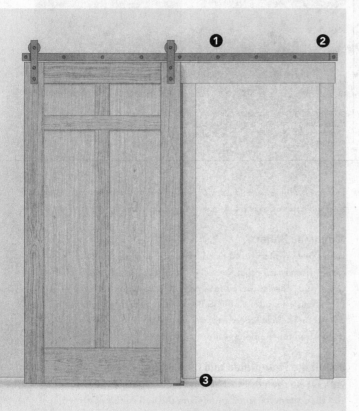

❶   ❷

❸

2. Match the Standoffs to the Casing

The standoffs included with the hardware package space the door away from the wall so that it can slide without hitting the casing. The standoff length is specified when you order the hardware. Here, the author chose 2-in.-long standoffs, a common length because it works well with

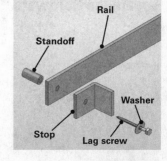

Standoff

Rail

Stop

Washer

Lag screw

a 1¾-in.-thick door and 5/4-in.-thick casing. Lag screws mount the track to the wall through the standoffs and are finished to match the track. The hardware manufacturer matches the screw length to the length of the standoffs, but thick wall coverings or unusually constructed walls may require longer screws.

3. Properly Position the Bottom Guide

The bottom guide is included with the hardware. When it's in the right spot, half of the guide's length is exposed when the door is fully open or fully closed. This prevents the door from swinging on the track and makes it easy to remove the door.

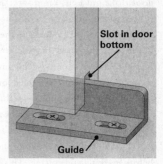

Slot in door bottom

Guide

Continued ➜

Install the Track with a Ledger

LOCATE THE TRACK. Once the jambs are installed plumb and level, use scrap stock for guidance to mark the locations of the head and side casings. In this case, the track must be at least ¼ in. above the top of the head casing.

MARK THE HOLES. A scrap-plywood ledger holds the track while the screw holes are transferred to the wall. The ledger is the width of the head casing plus ¼ in. The end is positioned so that it's ½ in. beyond the outside edge of the side casing, which accounts for the wheel stop.

FASTEN THE TRACK. After drilling the holes with a twist bit, fasten the track to the wall with the supplied hardware. Starting at the center, work toward the ends, where the L-shaped wheel stops are located.

Locate the Hardware

STAND UP THE DOOR. First, cut the door to length so that it's ¼ in. below the track and ½ in. above the finished floor. Next, shim it plumb, and place the rollers on the track. Center the mounting brackets in the door's stiles, and trace the screw holes for drilling.

Guide Bit for the Guide Groove

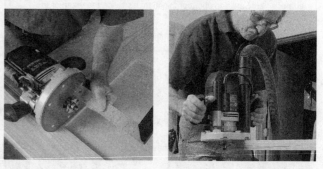

CUT THE SLOT. An L-shaped guide mounted to the floor prevents the door from swinging and hitting the wall or the casing as it's opened and closed. The guide aligns with a groove made with a slot cutter in the door bottom.

Cut the Door

Once the track is mounted on the wall, I turn my attention to the door. Like most custom doors, the door here was made a little tall so that it could be trimmed to size.

My first step is to stand up the door temporarily in the opening. For the bottom guide to work, the door needs to be ½ in. above the finished floor. I shim it by this amount, adding an additional thin shim if necessary to make the door plumb before marking the cut. It's better to cut the door twice than to make it too short.

The OSB subfloor in the photos is my workshop's finished floor, but if you haven't installed a finished floor under the door yet, you'll want to shim up the door the thickness of the finished floor before marking and cutting. This door is made of Douglas fir, which is beautiful but splintery, so I ease the edges with a sanding block.

Don't use a loose piece of sandpaper, or you may send a long splinter into the palm of your hand, a lesson I once learned the hard way.

Mount the Rollers

With the door plumb and lined up with the casing marks I made earlier, I make sure that the rollers' mounting brackets are parallel to the door edge and as close as possible to the center of the stiles. I then mark the pilot-hole locations with a pencil and return the door to my bench, where I mount the rollers and make a groove in the bottom for the floor guide.

Install the Floor Guide and the Casing

With the door on the track, I mark the location of the floor guide and then space the floor guide from the wall so that it's lined up

The Final Details

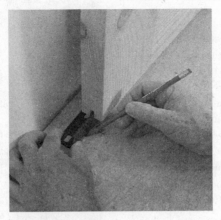

HANG THE DOOR. Aided by a helper, put the heavy door on the track. Unlike swinging doors, which are partially supported by their jambs, barn doors rely solely on their hardware and its connection to the framing. It's important to correct any weak framing before hanging heavy doors like this one.

MOUNT THE GUIDE. Space the bottom guide from the wall so that it aligns with the track above. One of its two mounting screws is accessible with the door fully open, and the other is accessible when the door is fully closed. This ensures that the door can be removed in the future.

FINISH UP WITH CASING. Barn-style doors are cased like conventional swinging doors. Secure the inside edge of the casing with 18-ga. brads, then fasten the outside edge with 15-ga. finish nails.

Tracks and hardware for all tastes

Sliding-door hardware has its origins in rustic architecture, but high-style, ultramodern hardware is also available. Hiding the track with a valance also can change the look or help a new sliding door to fit in with existing decor.

Hidden

Ultramodern

Unobtrusive

with the track above.

The guide is positioned so that one of its two screws is accessible when the door is fully open and the other is accessible when the door is fully closed. This allows the guide to be installed and removed with the door in place. It also makes it easier to remove the door for painting or for replacing worn hardware.

The final step is to install the casing. I first use an 18-ga. brad nailer to fasten the casings to the jambs. After I'm certain that the reveals look good and the joints are tight, I secure the casing to the jack studs and the header with 15-ga. 2½-in. nails spaced about every 16 in. I'm really pleased with how the door looks and how well it muffles the sound of my air compressor behind it.

Continued →

Hang a Split-Jamb Door

By Rick Arnold

Split-jamb doors are a lot like conventional prehung doors, but they have a two-piece jamb joined with a tongue and groove. The tongue-and-groove joint, which is hidden by the stop, allows both sides of the jamb to be cased at the millwork shop. Then the jamb can be separated when it's time to install the door.

Not only does the setup eliminate installing casing in the field, but it also gives you some wiggle room with regard to wall thickness. This quality makes split jambs great for old houses, which often have wavy plaster and odd-size studs. In addition, the millwork shop generally installs the casings and prepares the jambs for less than what I'd pay a competent finish carpenter to do the same work.

I've heard old-school carpenters deride split-jamb doors, claiming they can't be shimmed, but that's simply not the case. You just have to change your methods. I've never had a problem with any of the several hundred split-jamb doors I've installed over the years.

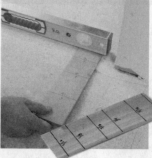
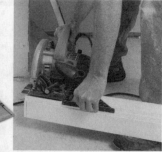

1. CHECK FOR LEVEL. The first step is to check the floor under the jambs for level. A 32-in. spirit level and a graduated shim make it easy to see how much the floor is off.

2. TRIM THE JAMBS. If the floor is out of level, cut one of the jambs a corresponding amount shorter than the other jamb. If a tile or hardwood floor will be installed later, raise the jambs with scraps to match the floor's final height.

3. TRY THE FIT. Confirm that the hinge-side jamb can be made plumb in the opening. Then remove the door, and pull out the duplex nail or hardware holding the door to the jambs. Replace it with a single finish nail.

4. CASING HOLDS THE DOOR PLUMB. Plumb the door with a level held along the casing leg, and drive 2½-in. finish nails through the casing into the jack studs and header.

5. FREE THE DOOR. Use a fine-tooth hacksaw blade held in a gloved hand to cut through the finish nail that holds the door closed. Go slowly so that you don't damage the jamb or stop.

6. SHIMS STEADY THE JAMB. Use 3-in.-wide shims (held vertically) to take up the space between the jamb and the rough opening. Tack the shims in place, but keep the nails away from the groove so that you can install the tongue side of the jamb later.

7. JOIN THE JAMB. Starting at the top, slip the remaining half of the split jamb onto the half already in place, and secure it by nailing through the stop and casing.

8. SCREW THROUGH THE HINGES. It's a good idea to swap one of the short screws in each hinge with one that goes into the framing. Plan for this; 2½-in. #9 wood screws in the correct finish are tough to find.

A Door Hanger's Tool Kit

The most important tools in the door hanger's kit are a pair of high-quality spirit levels to ensure a plumb door that doesn't open or close on its own.

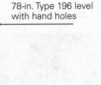

78-in. Type 196 level with hand holes

32-in. Type 196 level with hand holes

Stabila 37532
Two-level Jamber Set with hand holes

The 32-in. model is for head jambs; the 78-in. version is for side jambs. Buying the two levels together costs 20% less than buying them separately.

Hinge Adjustment for the Final Fit

By Tucker Windover

For finish carpenters, fine-tuning the fit of a new interior door offers plenty of bang for the buck. There's a lot of easy gratification for little effort. The final fit mostly involves door-hinge adjustment after the painters have finished.

First, I check that the door is swinging properly on its hinges. If the hinge leaf fastened to the door is not set fully in the mortise because of paint, plaster, tape, or misalignment, the hinges will bind. This might cause the door to creak or to spring back from a closed position. If the mortise in the jamb is set too close to the stop or if the leaf on the door is not set far enough across the width, the door will bind against the stop. If this is the case, you will probably see telltale signs of scraped paint on the door where it rubs.

When adjusting hinges, I often have to adjust the location of screw holes. Rather than struggle with a hole in the wrong spot, I simply tap in a plug and drill the hole where I want it.

After I get the door swinging properly, I adjust the hinges so that there is a consistent gap between the door and the jamb. When making corrections to the gap or any adjustments to the door, I make incremental changes. Often, going forward by small degrees is easier than going back by any amount.

Secure the Door to the Framing

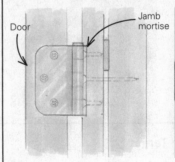

Door — Jamb mortise

Short screws installed at the factory secure the door to the jamb only. After the door is shimmed and nailed in place, a long screw can secure it to the framing.

SECURE THE DOOR WITH A LONG SCREW. Sometimes a door sags away from the hinge-side framing. To prevent this, I replace the short center screw of the top hinge with a 3-in. screw driven into the framing. Sinking this screw often changes the gap at the top and the opposite side of the door.

Continued ➔

A Proud Hinge Might Creak or Bind

Fine-tune the mortise for a good fit. A hinge leaf that stands proud of the jamb face can prevent a door from operating properly. Remove the screws to reveal the mortise. If the hinge leaf and the mortise were not aligned so that the hinge leaf fully seated in the mortise when the screws were driven, there will be a compression mark from the hinge. With a utility knife, carefully cut along this line to expand the mortise. Use a sharp chisel to remove the wood waste and to clear any paint, tape, or wood debris that might keep the hinge from seating fully in the mortise; then reattach the hinge.

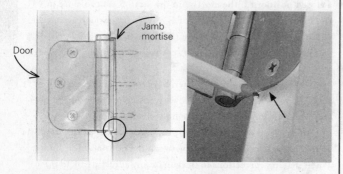

A hinge leaf not fully seated in the mortise will stand proud of the jamb. The individual leaf can be removed by backing out the screws and then removing the hinge pin.

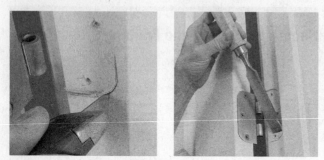

Adjust the Gap by Bending the Hinges

Open the hinge-side gap by spreading the hinges. I've seen shims used behind the hinge leaf to adjust the gap, but bending the hinge takes less time. I can widen the gap in small increments. Remember that when the gap is adjusted on one side, it affects the gap on the other side as well. (1) Place the butt end of a nailset between the hinge leaves up against the pin eyelet, or hinge knuckle. When the door is pulled toward the closed position, the nailset spreads the leaves and widens the gap. This technique puts a lot of force on the hinge, so go slowly to avoid damaging the hinge or bending it too far.

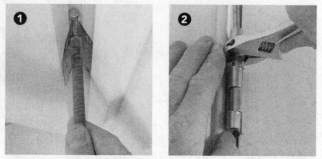

(2) Close the hinge-side gap by bending the knuckles. Set an open-ended adjustable wrench, also called a crescent wrench, just larger than the size of the hinge knuckle. Remove the hinge pin, and bend the door-side knuckles toward the door handle. This will close the gap. Go slowly. A difference of 1/16 in. is easy to notice.

Get the Screw Hole on Target

Centering a drill bit in a hinge hole without a self-centering bit is not impossible—but it takes a lot more time. Self-centering bits fit most hinge holes. The bit's shank is chucked in a drill, and the cutting end is encased in a sleeve with a beveled tip that centers it in the hinge hole. As the bit is pressed to the wood, the sleeve retracts, allowing the hole to be bored while keeping the bit centered. Self-centering bits come in sizes to fit cabinet and full-size door hinges. You can buy them at home centers or online.

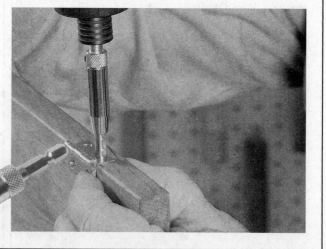

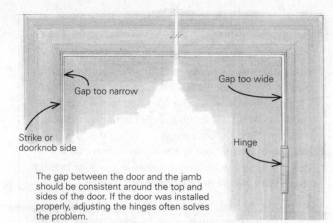

Gap too narrow

Gap too wide

Strike or doorknob side

Hinge

The gap between the door and the jamb should be consistent around the top and sides of the door. If the door was installed properly, adjusting the hinges often solves the problem.

A Binding Hinge Might Require Wood Plugs

A door that binds as it closes might be hitting the hinge-side stop. The mortise could be out of alignment, or more probably, the hinge was set slightly off.

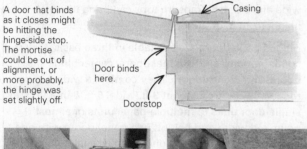

Casing

Door binds here.

Doorstop

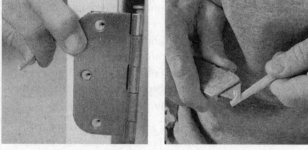

CORRECT OFFSET SCREW HOLES. Sometimes, the mortise is in the right place, but the hinge wasn't set properly at the factory. This can cause binding or gaps along the doorstop molding. To adjust the screw-hole locations, I whittle plugs from poplar. Poplar is a common hardwood for paint-grade trim material that holds the threads of a screw. Size the plug to fit snugly with a few hammer taps. Don't overdrive it and crack the door.

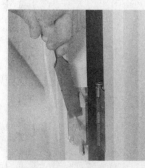

TRIM THE PLUGS FLUSH WITH A CHISEL. There is no need for glue. Friction holds the plugs in place when I drill new screw holes in the correct locations.

Pick the Perfect Patio Door

By Patrick McCombe

We ask a lot of patio doors. These huge panels of glass that provide wide-open views of the outdoors are expected to operate effortlessly while keeping us safe from drenching rains, high winds, pests, and intruders. We also expect them to keep our indoor-living spaces comfortable during the depths of winter and the dog days of summer. If that weren't enough, we want our patio doors to be attractive, complementing both the interior and exterior of our homes.

With myriad choices available, consumers buying patio doors face a challenge. The typical 6-ft.-wide patio door comes in dozens of styles and can cost anywhere from several hundred to several thousand dollars. But fear not. Here, I'll give you the tools that you need so that you can choose the best patio door for your situation.

Performance Ratings Are Easy to Come By

According to Rob Garofalo, patio-door product manager for Andersen, the best way to know you're getting a quality sliding patio door is to look for the performance-grade (PG) rating. This rating, developed jointly by the Window & Door Manufacturers Association and the American Architectural Manufacturers Association, replaces the former set of standards known as the design-pressure (DP) rating. Performance grade is a measure of a door's resistance to high winds and forced entry as well as its ability to keep out air and water during repeated cycles of positive and negative pressure. These cycles of pressurization and depressurization are common during strong storms and high winds. The scale ranges from PG 20 to PG 80. Garofalo suggests choosing a door with a PG rating of at least 40 in most of the country, with higher ratings for doors in coastal zones. The higher rating for coastal zones translates into a door that better resists wind and water during hurricanes and tropical storms.

You'll find PG ratings for all sliding doors, but unfortunately, PG ratings aren't yet standard for hinged patio doors, though many manufacturers still provide them for all or most of their hinged patio doors. If a door doesn't have a PG rating, you'll have to rely on the old design-pressure guidelines. A door with a DP rating of 40 is a good starting point for all but coastal zones. In either case, Christine Marvin of Marvin Windows urges door buyers to make an apples-to-apples comparison for a door's intended use. For example, doors with a "light-commercial" designation are held to a higher standard than those specified as "residential."

Of course, it's also a good idea to check a door's thermal performance. The easiest way is to look for an Energy Star logo, but a more thorough check is to identify the U-factor posted on the National Fenestration Rating Council (NFRC) label affixed to the glass. The lower the U-factor, the greater a window's resistance to heat flow and the better its insulating properties.

Continued ➜

Performance Must-Haves

As with most consumer goods, you get what you pay for in a patio door. Spend more, and quality, security, and efficiency increase. Here are some must-have performance levels and features for a decent patio door.

Acme Window and Door Company
Millennium 2000+
Vinyl-Clad Wood Frame
Double Glazing • Argon Fill • Low E
Product Type: **Inswing French**

ENERGY PERFORMANCE RATINGS	
U-Factor (U.S./I-P)	Solar Heat Gain Coefficient
0.35	**0.32**

ADDITIONAL PERFORMANCE RATINGS	
Visible Transmittance	Air Leakage (U.S./I-P)
0.51	**0.2**

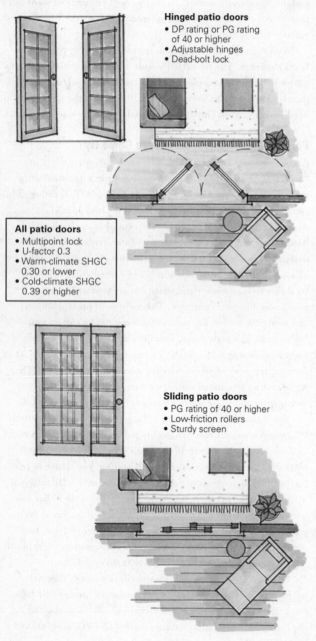

Hinged patio doors
• DP rating or PG rating of 40 or higher
• Adjustable hinges
• Dead-bolt lock

All patio doors
• Multipoint lock
• U-factor 0.3
• Warm-climate SHGC 0.30 or lower
• Cold-climate SHGC 0.39 or higher

Sliding patio doors
• PG rating of 40 or higher
• Low-friction rollers
• Sturdy screen

Swing vs. Slide

Sliding doors (sometimes described as gliding) have rollers that ride on tracks built into the door frame. The most common models have two panels, one of which is fixed. Either panel can be specified to operate at the time of ordering, although they're seldom switchable in the field. The big advantage of sliding doors is that they don't take up floor space when opened, which allows furniture to be placed closer to the door without interfering with the door's operation.

Unfortunately, sliding doors are the toughest to seal tightly, so inexpensive models typically have greater amounts of air leakage compared to similarly priced hinged doors. Sliding units are available in sizes from about 5 ft. wide and 6 ft. 8 in. tall to more than 16 ft. wide and 8 ft. tall. Transom tops can bring the total height to 10 ft. or more.

Hinged patio doors are available in three basic configurations: single-panel doors, center-hinge doors, and French doors. They come in a wide range of sizes, from about 3-ft.-wide, 6-ft.-8-in.-tall single-door units to multiple-panel units of almost unlimited width and height. Two-panel doors with one swinging panel are often described as center-hinge models. Center-hinge doors take up less floor space than doors with two operating panels, which are known as French doors. Center-hinge doors are easier to install and adjust than French doors, and they're generally more tolerant of rough openings that aren't quite plumb, level, and square.

By contrast, French doors are finicky to install and are less tolerant of imperfect openings. French doors also take up the most floor space. However, they're great at seamlessly connecting indoor and outdoor living spaces.

Patio-Door Materials

Patio doors are made of five basic materials: aluminum, fiberglass, steel, vinyl, and wood. All have strengths and weaknesses. Pricing assumes 6-ft.-wide by 6-ft. 8-in.-tall entry-level products with basic hardware and no extras. Larger sizes and options such as divided lites, factory-finishing, and upgraded hardware can add significantly to the cost.

ALUMINUM Aluminum can be uncomfortably cold during the winter and even frost over in cold climates. Aluminum's big advantages are strength and resistance to heat, even when the doors are painted a dark color. This makes aluminum doors popular where hot temperatures and dark exterior colors are the norm.

PROS Stands up to extreme heat even in dark colors, rot and insect resistant, inexpensive yet durable

CONS Unsuitable for cold climates, limited interior finishes, plain appearance

FIBERGLASS Not surprisingly, fiberglass has a rate of expansion that closely matches glass, so it's stable in all temperatures. It's also about three times stronger than vinyl and won't rot. Fiberglass doors are generally more expensive than aluminum, steel, and vinyl doors.

PROS Stable in all temperatures, times stronger than vinyl, rot and insect, resistant

CONS More expensive than steel, vinyl, or aluminum, some versions have fake-looking wood grain, often requires regular coats of paint or stain

STEEL Steel doors have cores of wood and insulating foam. This gives the thin steel skin strength and provides a means of attaching hinges and hardware. Steel doors rust without regular coats of paint. Steel doors are among the most affordable patio doors.

PROS Inexpensive, strong, temperature stable, rot and insect resistant

CONS poor corrosion resistance, easily dented, must be painted inside and out

VINYL The market for vinyl patio doors has grown steadily through the years, owing mostly to vinyl's affordability and minimal maintenance. Vinyl doors are generally sliders; the reinforcing steel needed for swinging doors makes them less affordable.

PROS Inexpensive, minimal maintenance, rot and insect resistant

CONS can soften in hot climates, few color options, hinged versions require costly reinforcement

WOOD Wood doors are appropriate for almost all residential styles. The big downside is having to protect the exterior from the effects of weather. Fortunately, most wood patio doors have vinyl, fiberglass, or aluminum skins (cladding) that protect the exterior.

PROS Most people find wood doors attractive, in infinite styles, Modern claddings mean less maintenance

CONS Most expensive, Unclad models require regular maintenance, Temperature and humidity can affect operation

Continued ➡

This information is also available in catalogs and on manufacturer websites.

Look for doors with a U-factor of 0.3 or lower, which is typical for a door with high-performance insulated glass. This glass is also better at blocking carpet- and furniture-fading UV-rays. The other valuable piece of information on the NFRC label is solar heat-gain coefficient (SHGC), which measures how much solar heat the glass admits. Cold-climate homes should have doors with an SHGC of 0.39 or higher. Warm-climate homes will be more comfortable with doors rated at 0.30 or lower, especially on unshaded western elevations.

When checking the SHGC and the U-factor, make sure the rating label features the "NFRC certified" stamp to ensure that the measurements given are for the whole door, including glazing, frame, and spacers, and not just the center of the glass. Center-of-glass measurements can make a door appear more efficient than it is.

Locks and Screens Matter, Too

Multipoint locks that activate additional latches in addition to the conventional latch at the handle are also an important feature on patio doors. These additional locking points boost security and weathertightness. If you're installing a sliding door, Todd Kippel of ThermaTru also suggests intermediate bolts that allow some ventilation by locking the door in a partially open position without providing enough room for entry.

Finally, it's a good idea to look at the quality of the screen doors. The best sliding screens have sturdy heavy-gauge frames that resist flexing and ball-bearing rollers that make sliding easy. Hinged screens, which are found on some hinged patio doors, should have sturdy frames and be easy to prop open so that you can move in and out of the house easily with food or furniture cushions.

Fit for a Passive House

Most patio doors perform much better than the doors of even 10 years ago, but for Passive Houses

and other homes where airtightness and weathertightness are taken to the highest level, only a few high-performance products from Europe, the United States, and Canada make the grade. These high-performance doors have triple glazing and precision hardware that can bring U-factors down to 0.15. They're made either from thermally broken wood frames or reinforced-vinyl or fiberglass frames. The downside to these good-looking precision products is price; they cost three or four times what a more conventional patio door would cost.

In-Swing or Out-Swing?

Hinged patio doors are available in in-swing and out-swing models. In-swing models dominate the market in Northern climates because snow and ice buildup can make a door difficult or impossible to open. In warmer parts of the country, both in-swing and out-swing doors are common. Out-swing doors perform especially well in coastal and other high-wind areas. As the wind blows harder against an out-swing door, more pressure is exerted on the bottom sweep and the weatherstripping, resulting in better resistance to wind and water.

The amount of space available also can influence the choice between an out-swing or an in-swing door. For tight indoor areas, an out-swing door makes more sense, because the door swing won't affect furniture placement inside the house. For tight outdoor areas, the opposite is true.

Door or Foldaway Wall?

The newest style of door includes multiple sliding or folding panels. These doors are especially popular in warm climates because they allow a seamless transition between indoor and outdoor living spaces. They operate with either folding or sliding hardware and can be used with openings of almost any width by increasing or decreasing the number of panels.

Seamless transition. When the weather is good, the four folding panels on this patio door from NanaWall can be pushed to the side, allowing the indoor and outdoor living spaces to flow together. For everyday use when the folding panels are closed, the single hinged patio door on the right provides access to the outdoors with minimal effort.

Prep Doors for Knobs and Dead Bolts

By Patrick McCombe

Boring and mortising a door for a knob or lock is not a hard job, but if you get the holes in the wrong spot, you're in for a tough fix. You might even have to buy a new door. Fortunately, it's easy to get the holes right if you pay attention to two critical dimensions and use the paper layout template that comes with the door.

You need a 2⅛-in. hole saw and a 1-in. spade bit for making the holes. A few dead bolts need a 1½-in. hole saw instead of a 2⅛-in. hole saw, though, so check the instructions to make sure you have the right one.

The first critical dimension you need to know is the door thickness. Exterior doors are generally 1¾ in. thick. Most interior doors are 1⅜ in. thick. When it's time to mark the door for boring, choose the mark on the template that corresponds to the door thickness. If the door is thinner than 1⅜ in. or thicker than 1¾ in., you'll likely need a special-order lock.

The second critical dimension is backset, which is the distance the center of the knob or dead bolt is from the edge of the door. Doors almost always have either a 2⅜-in. or 2¾-in. backset, and most modern locksets and dead bolts accommodate both. If you're

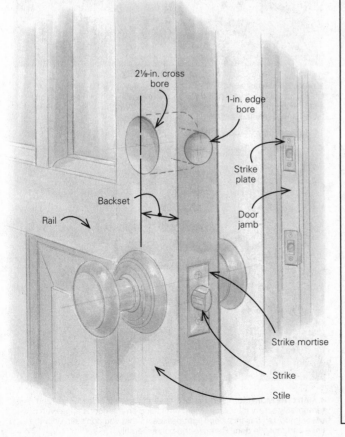

2⅛-in. cross bore

1-in. edge bore

Strike plate

Door jamb

Backset

Rail

Strike mortise

Strike

Stile

Tools for Preparing Doors

You can find cheaper hole saws than the ones shown below, but it's worth spending a few extra dollars for pro-quality saws with bimetal construction, which stay sharp longer than standard saws.

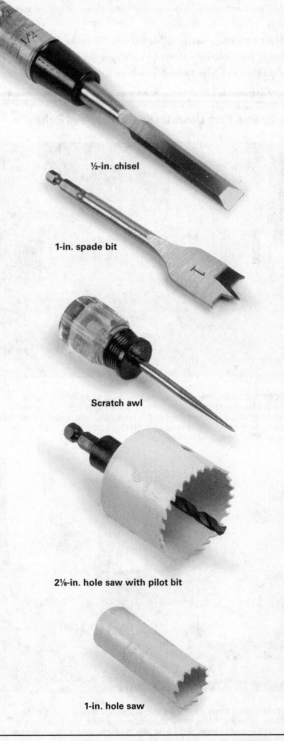

½-in. chisel

1-in. spade bit

Scratch awl

2⅛-in. hole saw with pilot bit

1-in. hole saw

Continued →

adding a dead bolt, match the backset of the existing doorknob; if you're starting with a new door, choose the backset based on the door. Generally, 2¾ in. is the preferred backset because it leaves more room for your knuckles when you're closing the door. However, narrow doors (less than 32 in.) and doors with narrow stiles, such as many full-glass doors, often look better with a 2⅜-in. backset because it brings the knob closer to the center of the stile.

Most doorknobs are installed between 32 in. and 36 in. above the floor; dead bolts are about 44 in. above the floor. However, you may have to adjust these dimensions slightly to match other doors or to avoid interfering with screen-door hardware.

Once you've drilled the door, mark the mortises with a sharp utility knife. I like to screw the strike and strike plate in place temporarily and then scribe around them. The knife groove makes it easier to locate the chisel accurately. Make sure your chisel is sharp, and work from the top and bottom toward the hole in the center to prevent slipping past the outline of the mortise. Finally, be sure to use the 3-in.-long screws that come with the dead bolts, because they provide much greater resistance to forceable entry than do shorter screws.

Step by Step Prep Doors for Knobs and Dead Bolts

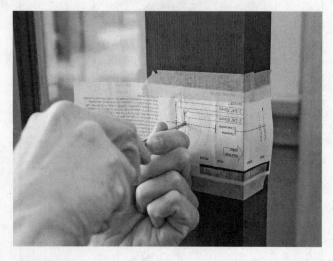

1. TAPE ON THE TEMPLATE. With the template level and attached to the door with painter's tape, mark the center of the cross bore with a nail or scratch awl, then mark the center of the edge-bore hole based on the door thickness. Make both marks deep enough to prevent the pilot bit on the hole saw from moving when you start the drill.

2. DRILL THE CROSS BORE. Using a 2⅛-in. hole saw or a 1½-in. hole saw (check the lock instructions), drill about 1 in. deep. Remove the hole saw, and use the pilot hole to register it for drilling from the other side. Keep the bit level, and maintain a firm grip on the drill.

3. DRILL THE EDGE BORE. Check the manufacturer's instructions for the edge-bore diameter. Most strike assemblies require a 1-in. hole. Use a spade bit for wood edges and a hole saw for metal edges. Keep the bit level and straight so that the bolt will operate smoothly.

4. MARK THE MORTISE. Insert the bolt assembly into the door edge, and temporarily screw it in place. Mark the shape on the door's edge with a utility knife. Do this in several light passes so that you don't slip with the knife and mar the door. Remove the bolt assembly.

5. CHISEL THE MORTISE. Use a sharp ½-in. chisel to cut the mortise for the bolt assembly. Work from the edges toward the hole to avoid slipping with the chisel and messing up the door's edge. Work incrementally, taking shallow passes and keeping the bottom of the mortise level. Deepen the mortise until the bolt fits flush with the edge of the door.

6. FASTEN THE BOLT. Using the screw holes made earlier, drive in the screws that secure the dead bolt to the door's edge. A conventional screwdriver is less likely to strip or damage the screw heads than a cordless drill or impact driver.

7. INSTALL THE LOCK ASSEMBLY. With the lock oriented correctly and right side up, align the parts to correspond with the proper backset (2⅜ in. or 2¾ in.), and drive in the long screws that attach the two halves of the assembly.

8. LOCATE THE STRIKE. Cover the end of the bolt with chalk powder. While holding the door shut, operate the lock to transfer the bolt location to the jamb. With the mark centered in the strike plate, trace the hole in the center of the strike.

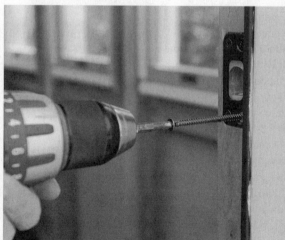

9. DRILL THE JAMB. Use a 1-in. spade bit to drill through the jamb for the lock bolt. Close the door, and check the lock operation. If the lock is tough to turn or won't engage fully, expand the hole with a small chisel or round file until the bolt engages easily.

10. INSTALL THE STRIKE. Screw the strike plate in place temporarily, and then use a utility knife to trace around the strike in several passes. Remove the strike, and mortise the recess with a ½-in. chisel. Use the provided 3-in. screws for the greatest resistance to break-in.

Continued ➜

Tubular Dead Bolts and Rim Locks

By Don Burgard

Doorknob assemblies for exterior doors include a lock that provides a minimal amount of protection against unauthorized entry. This lock will prevent a lazy thief from entering a home, but a more determined intruder will find that it's not much of a deterrent. As a result, add-on door locks are standard for homes in all types of neighborhoods. Although locks operated by a number pad are becoming more common, traditional keyed locks still dominate the market.

When shopping for a lock, be sure to check its ANSI rating. After undergoing operational and security tests, locks are graded 1 to 3, with 1 being the most secure. Most locks at home centers are graded 2 and 3, so if you want the best protection, you may need to look elsewhere.

Screws and Strikes

You can beef up the security of your grade-2 or grade-3 dead bolt with three simple enhancements to the strike:

- Attach the strike plate with 3-in. screws, which will secure it to the wall framing and not just the door jamb.
- Use a strike plate with four screw holes instead of two.
- Consider a strike plate with staggered screw holes, which help to prevent the jamb and the framing from splitting along the grain.

Tubular Dead Bolts

Unlike the common dead latch that is part of the knob assembly, a tubular dead bolt is not spring-loaded and is not beveled. For the door to open, the dead bolt must be fully retracted. If installed properly, a dead bolt also extends much farther beyond the strike plate than a dead latch; at least 1 in. is best. The farther the dead bolt extends into the doorframe, the harder it will be for someone to force the door open.

Single-Cylinder Dead Bolt

With a single-cylinder dead bolt, turning a key on the exterior side of the door moves a tubular bolt through the strike plate and into the doorframe. The same is accomplished on the interior side by a twist knob. If a window is close to the strike side of the door or if the door itself has a window, however, a thief can break the window, reach in, and twist the knob to unlock the door. If no windows are nearby, a single-cylinder dead bolt is the way to go.

Double-Cylinder Dead Bolt

If a window is present, you may want to consider a double-cylinder dead bolt, which is operated on both sides by keys. A thief who breaks the window can't reach in and twist a knob to unlock the door. Of course, if the home's occupant has left the key in the lock—not unusual, given the nuisance that losing the key would create—the thief can simply reach in and turn the key. Because of this, keep the key in the lock only when you're home. Even better is to hang it in a nearby location out of a thief's reach.

Double-cylinder dead bolts carry fire-safety risks. If during a fire the door is locked and the occupants can't find the key, they won't be able to exit the home through that door. For this reason, some fire codes prohibit the use of double-cylinder dead bolts.

Rim locks

Rim locks are surface-mounted to the inside of a door, with a cylinder that goes through the door and allows the lock to be operated by key from the outside. Unlike a tubular dead bolt, which requires drilling two holes and cutting out two mortises, a rim lock requires only one hole and perhaps a mortise.

1. Jimmyproof Dead Bolt

This type of lock is sometimes referred to generically as a Segal lock, after the company that introduced it. Designed to provide extra security for apartments in New York City, it's still the most common add-on lock found there, although it can be used on houses as well. The lock's position on the surface of the door gives it natural resistance to jimmying. A jimmyproof lock is operated by a key or knob that controls a two-part vertical bolt. The lock is engaged when the bolt descends or ascends into two rings on the strike. These locks can be installed with either a flat strike that is surface-mounted to the door casing or an angled strike mortised into the casing and the door jamb. Because it's secured on two sides, the angled strike provides greater holding power and greater resistance to excessive force used on the door itself. Jimmyproof dead bolts are available in both single-cylinder and double-cylinder models.

2. Slam Lock

The slam lock is essentially a jimmyproof lock that engages automatically when the door is shut. Rather than a vertical bolt, however, it has a spring-loaded crossbar that engages with three hooks on the strike plate. Turning the large knob to the unlocked position and pushing in the smaller knob disables the lock by keeping the crossbar in the open position.

3. Night Latch

The night latch has a spring-loaded beveled bolt that allows the lock to engage when the door is pushed shut. Many night latches have a button that essentially changes them into dead bolts. When this

button is pushed up or down, the night latch cannot be unlocked from the outside. The night latch has an angled strike that is secured on two sides and that requires a mortise in the jamb.

RIM DEAD BOLT the Outer Design of the Rim Dead Bolt Resembles That of the Night Latch, but the Locking Mechanism is Simpler: A Nonbeveled Dead Bolt That Locks or Unlocks Only with the Turn of a Knob or a Key.

Continued →

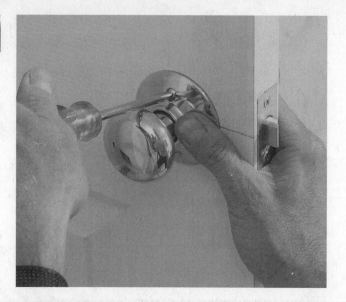

Installing a Lockset

By Tom O'Brien

Unlike old-fashioned and complicated mortise locks, most of the locksets you see these days are of the cylindrical variety and are fairly easy to install. Basically, installation requires a large hole drilled through the face of the door and a smaller hole drilled through the edge. After the holes are drilled, the most difficult part of the job is cutting the mortises for the strike and latch plates.

There are two keys to a successful installation: careful layout and sharp tools. In addition to a tape measure, a combination square, and a hammer, you'll need a scratch awl, a 2⅛-in. hole saw, a ¹⁵/₁₆-in. spade bit, and a 1-in. chisel. Assembling the lockset varies slightly from brand to brand, so it's important to read the manufacturer's instructions.

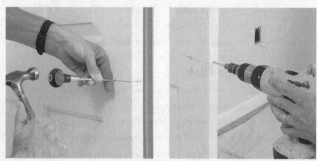

2. PILOT HOLES PAVE THE WAY FOR THE BIG BITS. To make sure the holes for the cylinders start in the right place and don't wander, use a scratch awl to punch the precise starting points. Then drill pilot holes with a ⅛-in. bit in the edge and in both faces of the door.

1. USE A COMBINATION SQUARE FOR LAYOUT. Most lockset packages include a paper template for locating the face and the edge bore. It's easier and more accurate to use a combination square, especially if you've got more than one lockset to install. Begin the job by wedging the door halfway open with a couple of shims under the bottom edge. Mark the face on both sides, 2⅜ in. from the leading edge of the door (2¾ in. for exterior doors) and typically 36 in. from the floor. The edge bore is marked at the center of the door, in line with the face marks.

3. DRILL THE FACE BORE FIRST. Holding the tool level and square to the door, drill halfway through one side with a 2⅛-in. hole saw. Then complete the bore from the other side of the door.

A Jig for Foolproof Hole Alignment

Carpenters who install door hardware for a living use commercial boring jigs that get the job done quickly and accurately. You can buy a light-duty version of the professional jig for a fraction of the cost. Made by Black & Decker (www.blackanddecker.com), this plastic jig clamps onto a door edge and aligns the face and edge holes automatically. Two hole saws (2⅛ in. and 1 in. dia.) and a common mandrel are included in the kit. The jig will handle both 2⅜-in. and 2¾-in. backsets.

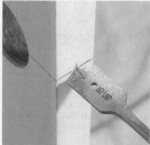

4. USE A NAIL TO MARK THE CENTER OF THE STRIKE-PLATE HOLE. Close the door and hold it tight to the stop, then push a 6d nail through the ⅛-in. pilot hole in the door edge until it pierces the door jamb; a pry bar provides leverage if necessary. Now drill holes for the latch and the strike using a ¹⁵⁄₁₆-in. spade bit. (A ⅞-in. bit is too small for most latch mechanisms, and the hole left by a 1-in. bit won't be covered completely by the latch plate.)

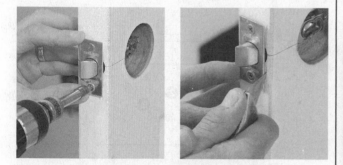

5. USE THE LATCH AS A TEMPLATE. After drilling the edge bore, insert the latch mechanism and secure it with the screws provided; then trace around the edges with a sharp utility knife. Be especially careful when cutting vertically along the grain because the knife may wander. Some carpenters prefer to use a scratch awl to cut along the grain.

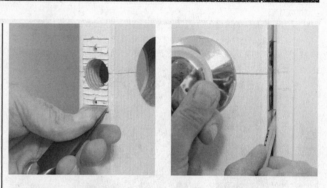

6. TAKE YOUR TIME WITH THE CHISEL. Hold a sharp chisel at about a 45° angle to the work, and score the face of the mortise by gently tapping the chisel with a hammer; cut across the grain in increments of ⅛ in. or so. Now carve away the waste, working the chisel toward the center. Check the fit of the latch plate; it should lie flush with the door surface. If you end up carving too deep, cut a piece of cardboard to shim the latch plate flush with the edge of the door. Align the strike with the latch. Close the door.

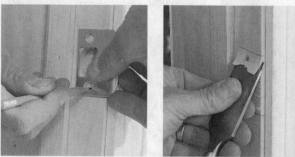

7. TRANSFER THE TOP AND BOTTOM EDGES OF THE LATCH PLATE TO THE DOOR JAMB. Now measure the space between the edge of the latch plate and the inside face of the door, and allow the same amount of space between the back of the strike plate and the doorstop. For a 1⅜-in. door (if the latch is centered properly), that space should be a heavy ⅛ in. The final task is to cut the strike mortise, following the same procedure used for the latch plate.

Continued ➡

Installing Replacement Windows

By Mike Guertin

Windows wear out before a house does. Sometimes the need for replacement windows is obvious, like when you encounter poorly functioning single-pane sashes with weights. But even windows with insulated glass become difficult to operate, suffer from damaged seals, or show signs of deterioration. The good news is that replacement windows do away with these problems, offering improved appearance, easier operation, and greater levels of energy efficiency. A whole-house window replacement can cut heating and cooling costs by as much as 25%.

Full-service replacement-window fabricators measure, make, and install new windows, On my first job, I asked a local company's sales rep to show me the measurement and installation process. I learned that replacement windows are easy to order and fast to install. I also discovered that I could save money by installing the windows myself.

Evaluate Existing Windows

The installation pictured here took place in a modest Cape Cod-style house that still had is original single-glazed, sash-weighted windows—a perfect candidate for replacement windows. I chose frame-and-sash replacement windows (also known as pocket windows) because the house's window jambs, sills, and trim were solid, and its siding was in good condition. Had the window frames been rotted or the siding in need of replacement, I would have had to install new-construction windows using the old rough openings. Also, the budget didn't allow for the extra labor to tackle full window replacement, which would have required the siding to be stripped back, and the interior and exterior trim to be removed and then reinstalled or replaced.

Finally, I didn't want to disturb the homeowners. Pocket windows are quick to install and create little mess inside or outside. On average, working alone, I can install one in less than 30 minutes. So I'd be in the house for only a day with no major mess to clean up.

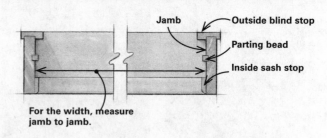

Jamb
Outside blind stop
Parting bead
Inside sash stop

For the width, measure jamb to jamb.

Measure Thrice to Avoid Ordering Twice

1. Use the shortest of three horizontal measurements.
2. Use the shortest of three vertical measurements.
3. Double-check for square by measuring the diagonal.

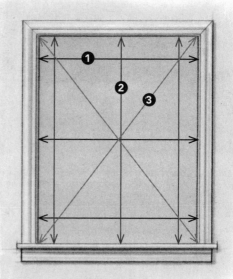

Remove the Old Window, and Prep the Opening

Once I've checked to make sure the windows I ordered fit in the opening, I lay down a drop cloth to catch paint chips, which could contain lead. Stripping out old window sashes is easy, but I still work carefully because the windows can be fragile and the glass can break easily. I'd rather spend extra time in preparation than on cleanup.

1. REMOVE SASH STOPS. Cut the paint at the jamb joint with a utility knife; then drive a stiff paint scraper into the joint to pry off the stops. Be careful not to damage anything because the sash stops will be reused.

2. CAREFULLY REMOVE THE SASHES. Swing the inside sash out of the window opening, and cut the counterweight cords to free the sash. Remove the small parting bead between the sashes, and take out the outer sash the same way.

3. REMOVE THE WEIGHTS. Open the counterweight doors to remove the weights and cords; then unscrew the pulleys and remove them. Some installation guides suggest hammering the old pulleys into the jamb, but I disagree. The pulley holes make good view spots when installing insulation.

4. INSULATE THE CAVITY. Use an old parting bead to slide strips of batt insulation into the cavity. Don't overstuff the cavity, or you'll reduce the insulation's R-value. Replace the counterweight doors, and scrape loose paint from the jamb and stops. Prime any bare wood on the jamb and sill to protect it from rot.

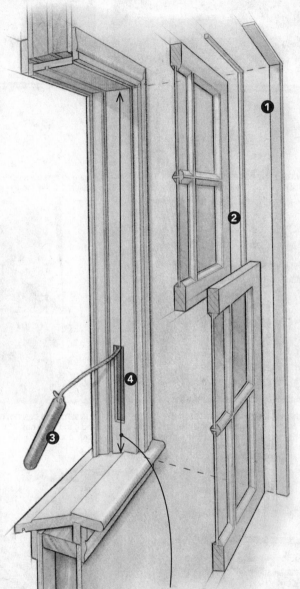

For the height, measure from where the sash rests on the sill up to the head or top jamb. Accurate measurements are critical.

Continued ➜

Install the New Window with Expanders, Shims, and Screws

Different manufacturers have different details for securing and weathersealing their windows. However, they all have a sill expander of some type at the top and bottom, and rely on screws to secure the frame to the jamb.

1. INSTALL THE BOTTOM SILL EXPANDER. I use a Speed Square to make a level reference line so that I can measure how much the sill slopes. I then can use a utility knife to cut the bottom sill expander to fit snugly against the sill. Tap the expander into the window frame with the butt of a hammer handle.

2. INSTALL THE HEAD EXPANDER. If the replacement window doesn't overlap the head stop, you need to add the head expander that fits over the top of the window and fill the airspace with low-expanding foam or fiberglass insulation.

3. INSERT AND CENTER THE WINDOW. Drive two mounting screws partway through the window frame and into the jambs to keep the window in place. Then use a small pry bar to get the frame centered, level, and plumb.

4. SECURE THE WINDOW. Insert shims between the window and the jamb as backing for mounting screws. Drive mounting screws in all the pilot holes. Sometimes these holes are concealed by sash stops or balance guards that can be slid out of the way or removed.

5. REPLACE THE SASH STOPS. The payoff for removing the old stops carefully is that they can be reused to finish the new window. Before installing the stops, I fill gaps between the window and the jamb with low-expanding foam, part of the weathersealing process.

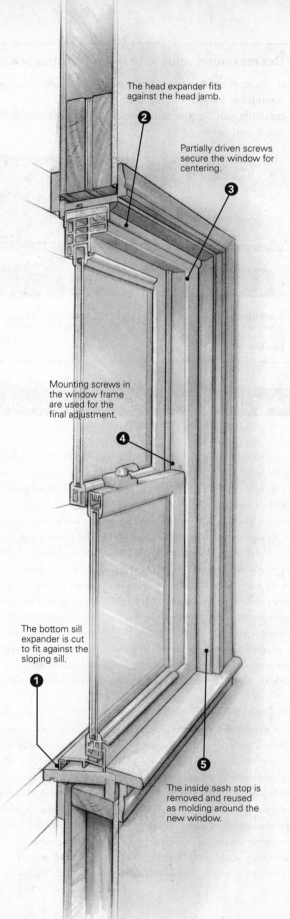

The head expander fits against the head jamb.

2

Partially driven screws secure the window for centering.

3

Mounting screws in the window frame are used for the final adjustment.

4

The bottom sill expander is cut to fit against the sloping sill.

1

5

The inside sash stop is removed and reused as molding around the new window.

Replacement windows Offer All the Features of New Construction

The same manufacturers that make windows for new construction also make replacement windows. In addition to the factors listed below, you'll need to consider cost and warranty details.

STYLE: Double-hung, single-hung, casement, awning, and other window styles are available.

GLASS: Choose between different types of insulated glass, including glass with heat-reflective coatings and gas-filled glass. You also can order windows with snap-in grilles or true divided lites.

MATERIAL: The type of material used in the window determines its price, its durability, and its appearance. Here's a quick tour:

VINYL
- Usually less expensive than other types
- Durable, low maintenance
- Limited color choice

WOOD
- Requires painting
- Compatible with historic houses

FIBERGLASS
- Stronger than vinyl and just as durable
- Available with wood interior surfaces
- Low maintenance
- Usually more expensive than other types

ALUMINUM-CLAD
- Durable exterior, wood interior
- Many colors available
- Aluminum can be painted

Choosing the Right Windows Is Challenging

In my area, I can order from more than a dozen replacement-window fabricators. Some manufacturers are national, some are regional, and a couple of the local fabricators have shops near where I work.

I advise shopping around, but be certain you're comparing equal products and services. Some companies' standard features are options that cost more from other fabricators. Frame-material thickness and extrusion designs can differ. Bargain windows could have lower-quality frames that require more time to shim and brace adequately for proper operation.

If I have a choice, I use high-quality vinyl windows made locally. Although they might not be a popular name brand my clients recognize, the warranty is good (20 years), and the price is reasonable. To reduce order errors, I purchase direct from the fabricator rather than through a dealer. A sales rep can help to

Continued ➜

measure orders and handle service issues. The windows cost a little more than those available through a national retailer, but there are few, if any, callbacks for operation, glass, or performance problems. If problems arise, I have someone local to call.

Accurate Measurements Are Critical

I always take measurements myself, and if the sales rep comes out to help, I check that person's work. Even though I do a little more work, I know that the information is right. The last thing I want is to show up for work on the morning of a whole-house window replacement and find out that someone else messed up the order.

The most important thing about measuring is checking multiple spots: top, bottom, middle, and diagonally for square. The new window has to be sized for the shortest measurement (drawing p. 426). I use a systematic approach with my own order sheet to note dimensions and window location. Writing down measurements on a block of wood just doesn't cut it. One wrong measurement, and you own a perfectly good window that doesn't fit.

Know How the Windows Are Sized

Replacement-window fabricators manufacture units on a ¼-in. basis, a ½-in. basis, or a combination of the two. This guideline forces you to order a unit smaller than anticipated when a dimension falls on a ⅛-in. increment, but undersizing a window is better than having it too tight. Window height is more forgiving than width due to the sill and head expanders, which is why many fabricators offer ¼-in. width sizing and only ½-in. height sizing. If I have to make a choice of leaving only ⅛ in. of wiggle room or having ⅝ in. to play with, I'll take the bigger measurement.

Some window fabricators take orders based on opening measurements, and they make the deductions to actual unit size from information you supply. I never order this way because it does not account for out-of-square conditions. Make your own deductions from the measured opening, and order the actual window size (sometimes called tip-to-tip size).

Guarantee a Smooth Installation

First, I keep my starting location flexible to accommodate the homeowner's schedule. Wherever I start, I move the furniture out of the way for clear access to the window, and I cover the floor with a drop cloth to collect paint chips and debris. I always bring a vacuum and a dust brush to clean out the windowsill and to clean up the floor when I'm done working.

Get maximum value with a good weatherseal

If I've spent the money, time, and effort to replace a window, I want to get the best performance I possibly can. Proper weathersealing calls for spray foam and caulk.

FOAM THE GAPS. Use low-expanding foam to fill gaps between the old jamb and the new window.

CAULK THE STOPS. Apply exterior caulk to the blind stop before installing the window; then caulk all the exterior trim joints.

New Life for Old Double-Hung Windows

By John Michael Davis

A client recently complained to me about how badly the old windows rattled in his historic home. He wanted to stop the noise as well as the air infiltration, but he didn't want me to replace the windows. Like me, my client understands the important role that original windows play in preserving an older home's historical integrity.

As a carpenter who specializes in restoration projects in New Orleans, I've come to appreciate not just the beauty of old windows but also their solid construction. All the sashes I see are made from locally milled cypress, a wood that has long been prized for its strength, its workability, and its rot-resistant qualities: ideal characteristics in this hot, wet climate. With the resources available today, boosting the efficiency of old sashes doesn't mean tearing them out or painting them shut. You can have smooth-working windows original to the house that don't rattle in the wind or make you dread next month's energy bill.

Old Sashes Work Better

Most people who want to address the issue of leaky windows tend to have a knee-jerk reaction: Either install storm units over the existing window opening, or remove the old sashes in favor of replacement windows (new units that insert in the old jambs). While storm windows can be installed to look unobtrusive, they are a pain to operate. To me, the much-more-expensive method of installing replacement-window units also has disadvantages. For starters, many of them don't come close to operating as effortlessly as old sashes hung with counterbalanced weights. Unlike the pulley-and-counterweight system, which has few

Simple Function, Easy to Disassemble

Traditional double-hung windows have a simple layout and basic operation. That's why many windows still work after more than 150 years of use. Each sash rides within a channel created by a stop and a parting bead. A sash cord or chain attached on each sideof the sash edge carries counterbalance weights. Toweatherize and update the window properly,it's necessary to remove the sashes fromthe window jamb. Here's how to do it.

Step One: Remove the Stops

Remove the interior stop first. Use a utility knife to break the seal between the stop and the casing. This piece keeps the lower sash in place and is generally nailed or screwed to the jamb and casing. It's necessary to remove the stop from only one side. Once removed, tip out the lower sash, and disengage the sash cord or chain.

To take out the upper sash, remove the parting bead, a thin strip of wood that sits in a groove between the upper and lower sash. If it's the

original bead, it will likely need to come out in pieces. A router equipped with a straight-cutting bit and an edge guide cleans up the parting-bead channel for a new parting bead. Skip this step if the upper sash will remain fixed.

Step Two: Remove the Weights

A pair of sash weights, sized to counterbalance the weight of the sash, allow the sash to be raised and lowered to any position. The weights are attached to the sash with sash cord or chain that rides over a pulley installed near the top of the side jamb.

Access to the weight is gained through a small access panel in each side jamb. This panel typically is held in

place with two screws. To make removing the panel easier, run a drywall screw in the middle of the panel to act as a handle before removing it.

Continued ➜

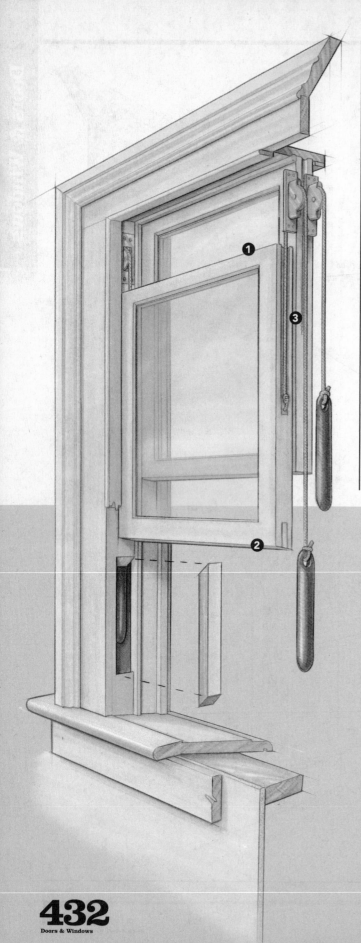

working parts, replacement windows contain many pieces that can break down over time, resulting in operation that deteriorates with age.

As an alternative course, I prefer to keep as many of the existing elements that make old houses unique and historical as possible, including the windows. Because windows have such a large impact on a house's appearance, updating them with new technology that doesn't detract from historical aesthetics is a far better (and more environmentally responsible) option.

My process involves removing the sashes from the opening, but it is far cheaper in the long run than the aforementioned alternatives. When upgrading windows, I usually repair damage to sashes, casings, jambs, and sills rather than replace them. Even highly durable cypress can fail in spots, rather than wholesale like lesser woods; repaired cypress will still be better than most any new wood everywhere else. I use two-part epoxy putties, adhesives, and special coatings to repair and protect these pieces.

The channel that the sashes move in should be tough but slippery. I coat the channel with DuPont Imron (www.dupont.com) two-part polyurethane over DuPont's Corlar epoxy enamel. These products are available only through industrial suppliers.

I don't use double-insulated glass for the new sashes I have made or update the glass of an original sash. If the sashes are single lite, the additional complication of modifying the sash to accommodate the thicker glass and the cost of ordering specially sized pieces (which can't be trimmed easily if they don't fit properly) might be justified in some harsh climates and with large budgets. To me, it seems a poor return on investment in this wet

Stop Air at These Three Places

Add leaf seals and a tube seal around the sash. The profiles shown below can be installed so that they are inconspicuous; they will maintain the window's original appearance.

1. Use at the meeting rails, where the top rail of the lower sash meets the bottom rail of the upper sash.
2. Use where the lower sash meets the sill. If the upper sash is not fixed, use where the upper sash meets the head jamb.
3. Use along both vertical edges of the sash, where the sash contacts the window jamb.

Mounting "arrow"

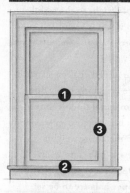

Seal Gaps Around the Sash to Stop Air Leaks

I use leaf seals and tube seals from Resource Conservation Technology (www.conservationtechnology.com) around all the working sashes. Slippery, flexible, and durable, leaf seals not only stop undesirable air movement, but they also help sashes to move more easily. The seals are installed in a groove cut in the sash. Because I bought in bulk, the price of materials to complete each window came to less than $10 for the seals I used. Once I was set up to work, I could fully gasket each window in about two hours. RCT offers variations of the seals mentioned below, so determine the needs for your project before ordering. If I'm permanently securing an upper sash, I run trim screws through the stiles, filling in gaps around the sash with backer rod as necessary, followed by paintable polyurethane caulk.

1. Where the two sashes meet

Cut a groove along the meeting rail of the lower sash using a slot-cutting bit in a router. Insert the WS87, an offset plastic leaf seal, into the groove to eliminate the gap between the meeting rails. If the leaf seal catches on the sash locks when the sash is raised, carve out a half-round piece of the seal for clearance. Available from Resource Conservation Technology, the 2mm by 8mm WS90 slot-cutting bit creates the exact groove required for this weatherseal.

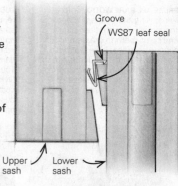

Groove
WS87 leaf seal
Upper sash
Lower sash

2. Where the sash meets the sill

After routing a groove along the bottom rail, tap WS10 tube seal into the groove with a hammer. Move across the sash only an inch or two at a time, and don't stretch the tube seal as you go. Be sure that the tube seal won't overcompress once the sash lock is engaged. To avoid over-compression, you might need to trim the bottom of the sash or run the seal in a dado cut in the rail. This approach is useful if the gap across the rail is not uniform. Refer to manufacturer's specifications for tolerances.

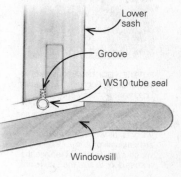

Lower sash
Groove
WS10 tube seal
Windowsill

3. On the outer edges of the sash stiles

For this project, I cut the mounting "arrow" off the seal and attached it to the sash with stainless-steel staples. Like all RCT's seals, the WS84, which I used here, is designed to sit in a groove. While this is usually a good approach, it did not work for this application. The wide rope channel left little "meat" along the stiles to run the groove, and the seal would have stood proud of the interior stop, which my client did not want.

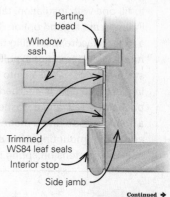

Parting bead
Window sash
Trimmed WS84 leaf seals
Interior stop
Side jamb

Continued ➤

Tune Up the Channels, Weights, Rope, and Pulleys

PRIME ALL BARE WOOD. Before reinstalling the sashes, I sand the jambs smooth, then prime and paint them to create a tough, slippery surface. I like DuPont's Corlar and Imron products, but they are available only through industrial suppliers. As an alternative, a high-gloss marine enamel works well.

LUBRICATE THE PULLEYS. Before reinstalling the ropes and weights, spray a lubricant into the housing onto the spindle/wheel center while you spin the wheel. Replace damaged pulleys with new ones. The one shown here from Van Dyke's Restorers (www.vandykes.com) includes nylon spindle bushings, which make for smooth operation.

PUT THE WEIGHTS BACK BEFORE THE SASHES. Because the weights I had weren't heavy enough, I added supplemental weights. The weights slip onto the sash cord and can be stacked on top of the main weights, as well as each other (www.architecturaliron.com). Once the weights are installed, I replace the access door to seal the side jamb.

A KNOT AND A FINISH NAIL DO THE TRICK. A knot at the end of the sash cord sits in a hole in the sash stile. For extra hold, I run a finish nail through the knot. I bend the remaining length of nail over the knot to push the knot into the channel so that it won't rub on the side jambs.

No weight pocket, no problem

If the weight pocket never existed or if you choose to fill one with insulation, tape balances made by Pullman are a good option. They operate much like a tape measure, providing the same counterbalance function as a traditional pulley, rope, and weight system. Once mortised into the side jamb and screwed in place, the tape is attached to the sash edge with a panhead screw and a washer. These tapes require only a shallow dado and a mounting pocket in the sash edges, but mounting them on your own can be tricky because the tension spring is incredibly strong.

climate. Such a lite would also add a lot of weight to the sash, perhaps making it harder to operate, and it would definitely send you out looking for much-heavier counterbalancing weights if you already had existing ones.

If sash weights are missing, there is an added challenge. With the retrofit project featured here, we were replacing badly done casement windows that had replaced the original double-hung sashes, and the weights were long gone. The homeowner weighed the lower sashes and bought approximate matching weights from local architectural salvage yards. New 1½-lb. and 2-lb. helper weights were ordered from Architectural Iron Co. (www.architecturaliron.com) to enable the proper balance to be set. I've heard of several methods for calculating sash weights, but a cast-iron slug half the weight of the sash on each side gets you close. From there, you can fine-tune the balance until the sash stays in position and also works with minimal effort.

The largest benefit of upgrading old windows comes from modern weatherseals. The system I use is from Resource Conservation Technology (www.conservationtechnology.com), which has seals for just about any situation. These seals stop air infiltration and also aid in operating the sashes because they reduce the friction caused by two painted surfaces rubbing against each other. Getting smooth plastic to slide on a painted surface is a huge improvement over having a painted surface slide on another painted surface. Painting the other wear surfaces with a high-gloss enamel is another big improvement.

Sash-Weight Cavities Can Be Insulated

During home restorations, it's sometimes necessary to remove the interior casing, which in turn fully exposes the window-weight cavity. If the rest of the house is to be insulated, as is usually the case, insulating the weight cavity is worth the effort.

In circumstances when a previously functioning upper sash is going to be permanently fixed, removing the outer set of weights frees space behind the exterior casing for rigid-foam insulation. I've heard of a technique in which the weight is placed inside a PVC pipe, with the pipe foamed into place. Whatever insulation method is used, it's important to maintain access to the weight through the jamb trap door and to be absolutely certain that the pocket can't move at any time in the future. I never permanently remove weights from a pocket, even if they are not being used. In the future, someone might want to restore a window's full function. Having the weights there to do it would be priceless.

With all this work and relatively inexpensive materials, you end up with windows looking the way they did 150 years ago. But more important, perhaps, is that they are as weathertight as anything being made today, and more durable. They can be operated easily with two fingers, and instead of looking gauche, with cheap and tricky details, the redone units have the look of quality. A lot of times, quality is defined most emphatically by what you don't see.

New Window in a Brick House

By Mike Sloggatt

In the 30-plus years that I've been a remodeling contractor, I've replaced hundreds of windows. The difficulties in window replacement vary by project, but one thing is certain: Replacements in brick-veneered homes are among the most challenging. Why? Masonry openings are difficult and expensive to change, and integrating a new window into a home's existing weather barrier is vastly more difficult when a layer of brick is in the way.

Further complicating matters, there are two ways to get a new window in an existing brick opening. The easier, less expensive option is a replacement window where only the sash and balance system are replaced. With a full-frame replacement, the entire window, including the frame, is replaced.

Given that a replacement window is cheaper and easier to install, why choose a full-frame replacement? If the frame is rotted or insect-damaged, a full frame is generally the better approach. Also, if there's evidence of water intrusion around the window opening, a full-frame replacement lets you find out what's going on and gives you access to fix it. The window in this house, which likely dates from the 1950s, was rotted badly enough that a full-frame replacement was the only sensible way to go.

Fortunately, most window manufacturers now make windows in custom sizes, and prices are affordable. You no longer have to alter masonry openings or pad the hole with trim to make a stock window fit. The only caveat is that you'll want to double- and triple-check all relevant measurements before ordering the unit, because getting the wrong size is an expensive mistake. Your window dealer or the manufacturer's website is a good place to look for guidance on proper measuring. In addition, custom window sizes may have longer lead times than stock sizes, so ask about delivery times when placing an order.

Here, I purposely shrunk the window so that it would fit

within the existing opening with the nail fin intact. The nail fin was covered with flat stock that matched the house's other existing windows. The result was a new energy-efficient window that matched the older units in the house well.

The first step in any window-replacement project is removing the old window. It's tempting to remove the old window as quickly as possible, but a go-slow approach means that you're less likely to damage plaster and finishes surrounding the window. On this house, the interior plaster was installed after the window and was keyed into the window frame. I couldn't have known this before I started removing the old window frame, and tearing the window apart would likely have resulted in significant plaster damage and a much bigger project, higher costs for the homeowner, and a headache for me.

Prep the Opening

PULL THE WINDOW. Start by removing the sash, the balance system, and the storm windows. Then cut the frame into pieces and gingerly pry them out. Here, the author is cutting nails that attach pieces of 1x wall sheathing to the window frame. This step prevents damaging the home's existing #30 felt weather barrier when these sheathing sections are removed.

THINK SURGICALLY. Use extra care when pulling the old window frame so that you don't damage existing plaster or drywall. On this house, the plaster is keyed into the window frame, so the author cuts the frame into sections and pulls out the sections one at a time.

EXPOSE THE WEATHER BARRIER. The most important part of replacing a window is integrating the new window with the existing felt or housewrap. Unfortunately, masonry openings often have chunks of mortar around the opening that must be removed before you can integrate the new flashing materials. Use an angle grinder and a chisel to remove the mortar without cutting or tearing the building paper.

ESTABLISH A ROUGH OPENING. A combination of 1x and 2x lumber is used to shrink the framing to match the window's specified rough opening. The smaller opening allows the window's nailing flange to fit inside the masonry. Leaving the nailing flange intact makes flashing the window easier and maintains the manufacturer's warranty.

Continued ➜

Flash the Rough Opening

Integrate New Wall Sheathing with Existing Building Paper

1. WRAP THE SHEATHING. Because there's no room behind the brick veneer to apply a weather barrier over the sheathing patches, the author covers the patches with a thin self-stick flashing tape before installing them.

2. SLIP IN THE SHEATHING. Made from ¾-in. stock, the sheathing patches around the new opening are coaxed behind the existing weather barrier with a 12-in. drywall knife. The knife helps to hold back the old felt while the patches are pushed in behind it.

3. LEAVE A FLAP AT THE TOP. The sheathing patch at the top of the opening has an extra flap of flashing tape. The release paper is left on the flap so that the window's top flange and head casing can be tucked under the flap, integrating them into the house's drainage plane.

Create a Site-Built Sill Pan

1. EXTEND THE WEATHER BARRIER. Aluminum flashing extends the weather-resistive barrier up to the new subsill. The flashing is lapped over the existing felt and is tacked in place with aluminum trim nails. The loose flap of flashing tape in the corners of the opening will eventually lap over a sill-pan flashing.

2. CREATE A BACK DAM. A back dam prevents infiltrated water from getting inside the house. A piece of vinyl wall edging (commonly used to protect wall-papered outside corners) makes a great low-profile back dam. It's temporarily held in place with flashing tape until it can be covered with the flexible sill-pan flashing.

3. SILL PAN STOPS WATER. After removing the release paper, the author carefully lays in a piece of DuPont FlexWrap as a sill-pan flashing. Where the sill meets the jack studs, he makes sure the flashing corners are pressed firmly to the opening so that they form a tight 90° corner. Other-wise, the window frame can cut through the pan flashing when the window is pushed into the opening.

4. ADD A STORM FLAP. To prevent wind-driven rain from getting under the window and behind the brick, it's a good idea to install a storm flap on top of the brick sill. This piece of foil-faced, self-adhesive flashing will be trimmed flush later. Although it's a good idea everywhere, this detail is especially important on second-story windows because the condition (or even the existence) of the weather-resistive barrier below the window can't be known.

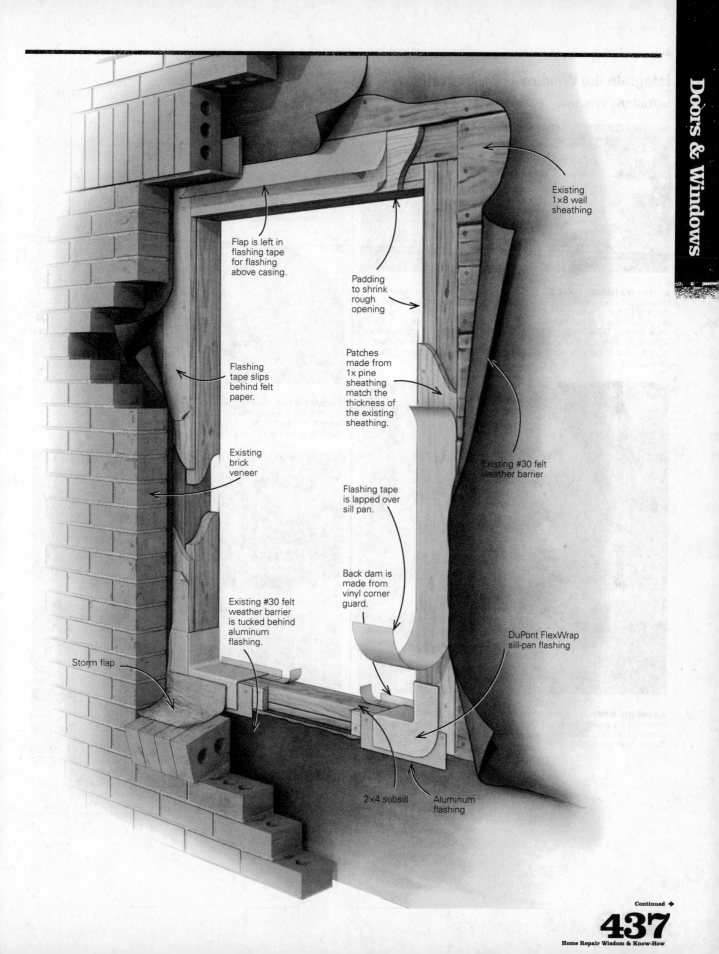

Existing
1×8 wall
sheathing

Flap is left in
flashing tape
for flashing
above casing.

Padding
to shrink
rough
opening

Patches
made from
1x pine
sheathing
match the
thickness of
the existing
sheathing.

Flashing
tape slips
behind felt
paper.

Existing #30 felt
weather barrier

Existing
brick
veneer

Flashing tape
is lapped over
sill pan.

Back dam is
made from
vinyl corner
guard.

Existing #30 felt
weather barrier
is tucked behind
aluminum
flashing.

DuPont FlexWrap
sill-pan flashing

Storm flap

2×4 subsill

Aluminum
flashing

Continued →

Integrate the Window with the Wall

Install the Window

1. CAULK THE NAILING FLANGE. The author puts a heavy bead of sealant on the window's side and top nailing flanges. The bottom is left uncaulked so that any infiltrated water can drain out. It's important that the flashing and the sealants are compatible because some solvent-based sealants attack some flashing tapes. With the frame resting on the rough sill and centered in the rough opening, tilt the window slowly into place. With the window centered in the opening, use two 1¼-in. pan-head screws to secure the nailing flange.

2. SHIM THE JAMBS. It's important to shim the frame straight before fully fastening the nailing flange on the exterior; otherwise, the window won't operate smoothly. Once the unit is shimmed, finish fastening the nailing flange—every hole for high-wind zones, every other hole elsewhere.

3. FOAM THE GAP. Minimally expanding window-and-door foam is used to seal the gap between the window frame and the rough opening. At the bottom, the author fills only an inch or so along the interior side of the opening. The single bead of foam stops air without trapping water.

4. FLASH THE FLANGE. Cover the side flanges and then the top flange with foil-faced flashing tape. The foil tape's adhesive is less tenacious, so it's easier to tuck the tape behind the brick. Tuck its top edge under the flap created with the first layer of flashing tape applied to the sheathing patches

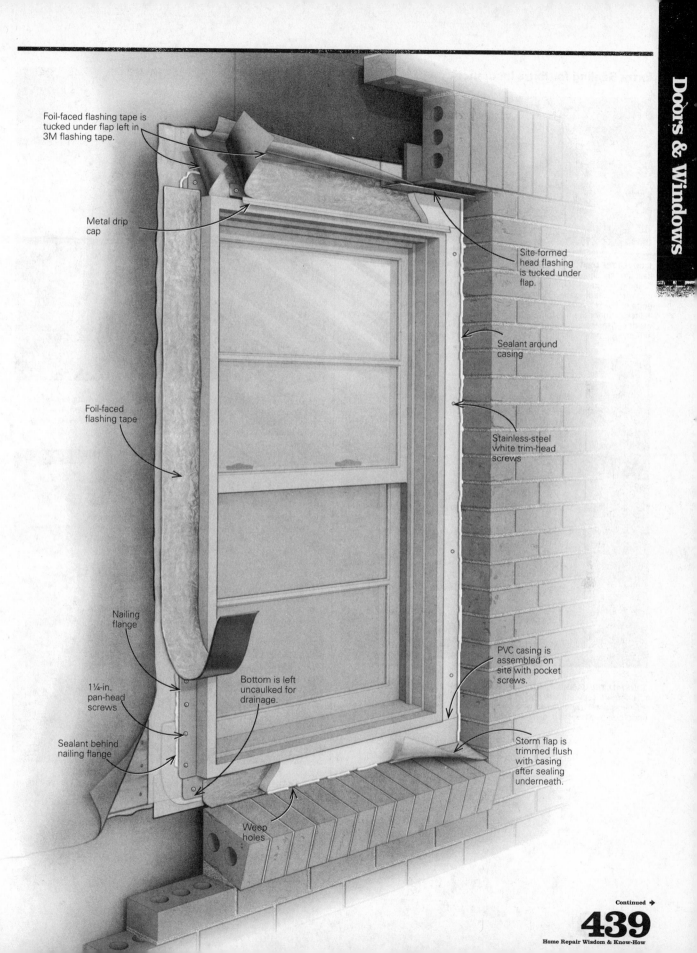

Foil-faced flashing tape is tucked under flap left in 3M flashing tape.

Metal drip cap

Foil-faced flashing tape

Nailing flange

1¼-in. pan-head screws

Sealant behind nailing flange

Bottom is left uncaulked for drainage.

Weep holes

Site-formed head flashing is tucked under flap.

Sealant around casing

Stainless-steel white trim-head screws

PVC casing is assembled on site with pocket screws.

Storm flap is trimmed flush with casing after sealing underneath.

Continued →

Extra Sealing for Extra Insurance

1. COVER THE DRIP CAP. A layer of foil flashing tape installed over the head flashing integrates the head flashing into the drainage plane. The top edge of the self-adhesive flashing is tucked under the flap left in the weather-barrier tape that covers the sheathing patch.

2. SLIP IN A HEAD FLASHING. An L-shaped flashing bent with a metal brake sheds water over the casing. Its vertical leg is tucked under the flap left in the weather-barrier tape that also shields the foil tape over the head flashing. Friction holds it while the casing is fit below.

3. INSTALL THE CASING. Made from cellular PVC, the site-assembled casing has corners secured with pocket screws. To make installation easier, the stainless-steel trim-head screws are started in the stock. The casing is ¼ in. undersize to allow for a ⅛-in. caulk joint around the perimeter.

4. SEAL AND TRIM THE STORM FLAP. Sealant under the storm flap keeps it in place and prevents wind-driven water from getting underneath. The flap is extra insurance against water infiltration and preserves the free-draining attributes of the other flashing materials.

5. CAULK THE TRIM. The final step is to caulk the casing to the window frame and the brick veneer with window-and-door sealant. The gap above the head casing and weep holes at the bottom remain uncaulked, allowing infiltrated water to drain out.

A Weatherproof Window Installation

By Brian Knight

As the building industry tightens up on air-sealing and improves energy efficiency, we need to be more aware of the risks associated with air and water intrusion. Materials that get wet won't dry out as quickly or easily as they used to do in leaky, poorly insulated houses, and many of the materials being used to build houses aren't as resistant to moisture as their predecessors. There's no doubt that with windows accounting for such a large part of the building budget, and being one of the most direct connections to the elements, their installation deserves extra attention.

Windows Are Complicated, and So Is Their Installation

Compared to solid areas of wall and roof, windows and their interface with the air barriers and water-resistive barriers (WRBs) of a house are complicated and vulnerable. Many builders and designers are confused about best practices, and inferior techniques are rampant. As windows, tapes, sealants, and WRBs evolve, so do the installation guidelines for these products. It's not uncommon for products that are typically used together to have conflicting installation instructions. When in doubt, I follow the window manufacturer's instructions as a bare minimum, and add improvements from there.

The best window installations include redundant layers of protection for keeping water out, incorporate measures for blocking the air movement that can draw that water in through weak spots, and provide an escape path for water that enters before it has a chance to cause damage.

Not all windows are created equal, of course, and it's tough to predict long-term performance. But I don't discriminate or try to predict. Every window I install—regardless of brand, material, or price—gets the same belt-and-suspenders treatment to ensure that air and water leaks aren't going to be an issue.

Aim for Waterproof, but Plan for Leaks

We should always assume that water will find its way into a window opening. Even if the installer does a perfect job with sealing and flashing, water can still leak through the window unit itself—especially as the materials, transitions, and sealants go through many cycles of expansion and contraction over time. Gravity, capillary action, blowing rain, and pressure differences can push and pull water into these weak points.

Water leaks from windows usually show up at the sill. Because this is the most vulnerable area of a window, it's also where the weatherproofing efforts begin.

As long as there is an air gap in place, a sloped and flashed rough sill is the best way to protect this vulnerable area. Creating a back dam along the rear edge of the sill flashing is one way to ensure that leaks under the window can't reach the interior of the opening, but I typically don't use back dams unless specifically

It Starts with the Sill

CREATE YOUR OWN SLOPED SILL. Remove stock from the rough sill to provide drainage in the case of leaks. Draw one line 3 in. from the outside face of the opening, and another about ¼ in. down from its outside edge. To create the slope, use an angle grinder equipped with a rough-grit flap disk.

WIDTH PLUS 12. Cut a piece of flashing tape 12 in. longer than the width of the opening, which allows 6 in. of tape to extend up each side.

KEEP THE TRANSITION TIGHT. Use a rafter square to press the tape tightly into the corners where the sill meets the sides of the rough opening, eliminating bubbles under the tape that are vulnerable to puncturing.

CONTINUOUS OUTSIDE CORNERS. You can buy flashing tapes made for curves, but they're expensive. Protecto Wrap tape is far more affordable and has enough flexibility to be stretched down onto the sheathing, where I tack it in place with button-cap nails.

Continued ➜

required by the window manufacturer. I've found that they can complicate rough-opening dimensions, interfere with shimming the window off of the sill pan, and make it difficult to air-seal the bottom of the window.

A piece of bevel siding laid across the rough sill of the opening is the traditional choice for creating a slope, but it requires planning to make sure there is adequate height in the rough opening to fit the siding and layers of flashing tape. Manufactured sill pans are another option and are certainly better than nothing, but I don't like them. The ones I've tried don't have the amount of slope I prefer; can make shimming, air-sealing, and trim installation more difficult; and often are two halves that need to be pieced together and are then never visible for inspection. I prefer to avoid questionable joints or seams in this vulnerable area.

My favorite method is to add the slope right to the rough-sill

framing. Sloping the sill after it has been framed eliminates any worry about reducing the height of the rough opening because you're actually enlarging it.

In addition to the sloped sill, the opening is protected with flashing tape, with the weakest interface being the spot where the sill meets the jack studs on each side. There are many ways of cutting flashing tape to fit this situation, but I prefer to stretch the sill flashing around the corner, eliminating the seam altogether.

If the window manufacturer allows it (some require continuous support at the sill), install the window atop spaced shims to increase the drainage and drying potential underneath the window unit and above the sloped, flashed sill.

The biggest obstacle in the drainage path is typically the window's bottom nailing fin. Do not caulk it, do not tape it, do not seal it in any way. Some window manufacturers call for a

Seal the Sides, but Let the Bottom Drain

SIDES ARE SIMPLE. Cover each side of the opening with a piece of flashing tape that bridges the gap between sheathing and framing and that extends down to and over the top of a horizontal piece of the same tape, reinforcing the seam where the sill flashing adheres to the wall. I like Zip System Tape or 3M All Weather Flashing Tape 8067.

CAULK THREE SIDES. Lay a bead of high-quality caulk along the sides and top of the opening, keeping it close enough to the edge so that the nailing fin will compress it. Never caulk across the bottom. If the corners of the nailing fin are designed to receive a piece of manufacturer-supplied adhesive flashing, skip the caulk in the top corners, as shown here.

BOTTOM FIRST. Rest the window on the edge of the sill, tip it upright, and slide it straight in against the caulked sheathing.

CAPS MAKE A GAP. To promote drainage, slide caps from button-cap nails under the bottom nailing fin, pressure-fitting one next to each nail. These caps are thick enough to create a gap but not so thick that they will complicate trim installation.

REINFORCE THE FIN. Zip System Tape is 3¾ in. wide, which is wide enough for it to be adhered to the sheathing, across the nailing fin, and onto the side of the window frame.

Easy Air-Sealing Opportunity

Regardless of window brand, material, or type, I eliminate the possibility of hidden air leaks through joints and seams in the window frame with vapor-permeable Pro Clima Uni-Tape before the window is installed.

Finish Strong on the Exterior

The exterior weatherization—the tape, the head flashing, the caulk, and their integration with the trim and the siding—is the last step in a well-detailed window installation. It's fairly common for people to unknowingly seal the crucial water exit points while missing some of the important leak-prone areas. Here are some general guidelines.

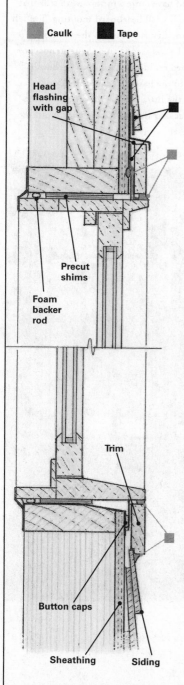

■ Caulk   ■ Tape

Head flashing with gap

Precut shims

Foam backer rod

Trim

Button caps

Sheathing   Siding

• Wherever there is flashing or a shingle-style transition in which one piece laps over another, such as clapboard over the head flashing, don't caulk. Any transition other than a lap, such as a butt joint where siding meets trim, should be caulked.

• Whatever the material, seal the top and bottom pieces of trim to the nailing fin or window frame to prevent water running behind it, even if the wall includes a vented or ventilated rain-screen assembly.

• Don't let installers place siding directly on top of the head flashing, and never add caulk in this location. Space the siding off the flashing to achieve a gap of ⅛ in. to ¼ in.; otherwise, paint can seal this water-drainage pathway.

Air-Seal from the Inside

A CONSERVATIVE BEAD OF FOAM. A thin bead of low-expansion spray foam offers limited air-sealing and insulation, but avoid filling the entire cavity, especially toward the bottom, to allow for drainage in the case of water entry.

A CAULK JOINT THAT WILL LAST. Foam backer rod cut and pressed in around the window jamb creates a flexible base for the bead of caulk that follows it. Use a wet finger to smooth the bead against the backer rod, creating the ideal hour-glass shape that allows the sealant to expand and contract without cracking or debonding.

TAPE IS THE INNERMOST AIR-SEAL. Applied so that it bridges the gap between rough frame and window jamb, flashing tape provides an easily inspectable air barrier that, like the backer rod and caulk, isn't affected by the shims along the four sides of the window.

dashed bead of caulk, but I believe this is just asking for trouble. It's also much easier to tell my crew "No caulk at the bottom" and get consistent results rather than "X lengths of Y diameter caulk with Z amount of space between them" and then hope for no problems. I like to go even one step beyond by providing a gap behind the nailing fin to promote further drainage.

Deal with Air from the Inside

In an ideal world, the window unit and any manufacturer-installed jamb extensions have airtight joints, but a builder's best method for assessing airtightness is the blower door, and that means the window is already installed. I'm sure that some manufacturers seal this connection, but it's safer not to assume.

Continued ➔

I eliminate the possibility of a leaky unit by applying tenacious acrylic-adhesive flashing tape over any seams and joints in the window frame before it's installed. It pays to seal the joints in the rough opening as well to eliminate short circuits or air leakage from surrounding stud cavities. Control the window unit, control the rough opening, and then you can confidently address the space that's left between the two.

Canned spray foam is probably the most common way of sealing between the window unit and the framing. My biggest gripe with this method is that it's difficult to inspect for quality without a blower-door test. On a house I tested recently, I was surprised to find air coming through the spray foam around windows and doors, most likely in the area of a shim, which I've found to be the most vulnerable leakage point.

There are many variables to consider if you're relying on spray foam as an air barrier in this location—the size, shape, and consistency of the bead; whether the can was shaken adequately; if the humidity is suitable; and the texture and temperature of the substrate—so I prefer to think of this spray foam only for insulating purposes. Backer rod and caulk followed by a layer of vapor-permeable flashing tape is what I use as my air-control layers.

I buy several packets of backer rod in diameters of $\frac{3}{8}$ in., $\frac{1}{2}$ in., $\frac{5}{8}$ in., and $\frac{3}{4}$ in. to accommodate the different-size gaps I typically encounter, and I always use a rod that is slightly fatter than the gap being filled. For gaps smaller than $\frac{3}{16}$ in., I skip the backer rod and simply caulk the gap. In all cases, I use a high-quality elastomeric or polyurethane sealant made for windows and doors, such as Sonneborne's NP1, Sika's Sikaflex, or Dap's 3.0. These sealants have better adhesion than typical silicone but still allow for plenty of expansion and contraction.

Flashing tape doesn't receive enough attention for use in this location. It's fast, durable, effective, and easy to inspect. Plus, it's the one air-sealing layer that's guaranteed to clear the shims installed around the window.

I prefer a tape that is vapor permeable—I use Pro Clima Uni-Tape—to eliminate it as a potential barrier should any moisture around the window need to dry toward the interior, but I would use something impermeable in a pinch. Tape is typically applied to the rough framing and the jamb-extension edge, but it's important to keep in mind the exposed reveals of the trim when placing the tape.

When followed by careful installation of the drywall, the exterior trim, and the head flashing (all of which are areas that should be handled with care to avoid damaging flashing tapes and air-sealing tapes), you've improved the performance of one of your building's weakest links.

Wainscot for a Window

By Gary Striegler

Window-trim details can have a huge effect on the overall look of a room. With the right combination of materials and molding proportions, window-trim details transform a drab space into an elegant one. Getting those details wrong, how-ever, really can disrupt the room's design.

Many of the houses I build have large windows with sills that are close to the floor. If I install a tall baseboard molding, I'm left with a strip of awkward-looking drywall beneath the window. To avoid that strip, I like to build a wainscot panel that extends from the windowsill to the baseboard molding. This detail grounds the window by connecting it to the baseboard and the floor. The window gains mass, and the little bump-out created by the wainscot has a big impact, breaking the wall plane with molding profiles that add visual interest.

Assemble Pieces on a Workbench

With the rails and stiles cut, I assemble the frame with pocket-hole joinery, then add the plywood. During assembly, I make sure that the good side of the rails, stiles, and plywood will face outward when the panel is attached to the wall. I find it easier to build the frame and apply the stool, apron, and inside-panel moldings on a workbench before installing it.

1. JOIN THE FRAME WITH POCKET SCREWS. I bore two pocket holes at each stile-to-rail joint, spacing the holes about 4 in. apart along the top rail where the stool will be attached later. Before attaching the plywood back, I smooth the frame with an orbital sander.

2. ADD THE INSIDE MOLDING AFTER THE PLYWOOD IS ATTACHED. I glue and staple ¼-in. plywood directly to the back of the frame, keeping it clear of the pocket holes on the top rail. On the front, I install the short pieces of panel molding first, then nail the longer pieces to fit so that I can spring them in slightly for a tighter joint.

TIP: Back-bevel the miters with a block plane or a utility knife for a tighter joint.

SCREW THE FRAME TO THE STOOL. I mill the stool from 1-in. poplar with a cove-and-bead bit, then attach it to the frame with pocket-hole screws. I use a combination square to set the frame back ¼ in. from the stool's edge, the thickness of the plywood attached to the back of the frame. Kreg's Right Angle Clamp has a foot on one end and a peg on the other to hold parts together until screws can be driven.

ADD THE APRON NOW TO SAVE YOUR KNEES. While the panel is upside down on the workbench, attach the apron molding and apron returns. Remember to run each return past the back of the frame ¼ in. so that it will meet the wall when it's installed.

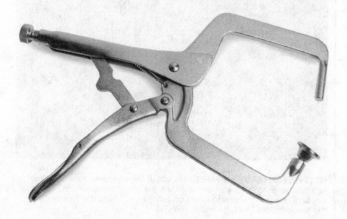

Continued →

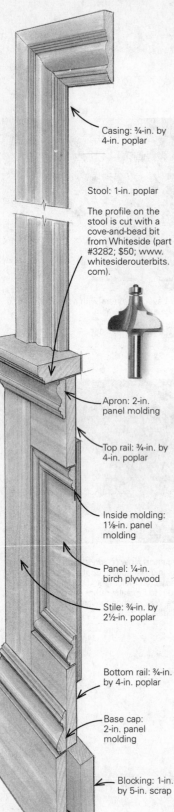

Casing: ¾-in. by 4-in. poplar

Stool: 1-in. poplar

The profile on the stool is cut with a cove-and-bead bit from Whiteside (part #3282; $50; www. whitesiderouterbits. com).

Apron: 2-in. panel molding

Top rail: ¾-in. by 4-in. poplar

Inside molding: 1⅛-in. panel molding

Panel: ¼-in. birch plywood

Stile: ¾-in. by 2½-in. poplar

Bottom rail: ¾-in. by 4-in. poplar

Base cap: 2-in. panel molding

Blocking: 1-in. by 5-in. scrap

Baseboard: ¾-in. by 5-in. poplar

Molding Profiles Dictate the Proportions

This wainscot detail works well when these profile sizes are used on a window from 18 in. to 30 in. off the floor with 6-in.- to 7-in.-tall baseboard. Use casing widths ranging from 3 in. to 4½ in. Working outside these dimensions can make the field of the panel either too small or too large, which creates awkward proportions. Before you cut, take the time to plan the size of the wainscot panel carefully, and make a cutlist for the rails and stiles. Because the area behind the panel is going to be hidden, I lay out the dimensions right on the wall, sometimes going as far as drawing everything to scale if I'm concerned about how the overall proportions will look. This takes some time, but it lets me work out problems before any wood has been cut.

Add the Final Moldings After the Panel Is on the Wall

Once the frame is built and the moldings are applied, I attach the unit below the window, keeping the top of the stool ¼ in. to 3⁄16 in. beneath the top of the jamb to create a reveal. Blocking and baseboard moldings are next; then I install the casing around the window to complete the job.

5A. LOCATE BOXES WITH CENTERLINES. Plumb a line down the wall at the window's center, and draw a line down the center of the back of the panel. Measure off these two lines and the top of the stool to pinpoint the cutout for an electrical box. An alternative approach is to have an electrician locate electrical boxes horizontally in the baseboard.

5B. LEVEL AND CLAMP THE PANEL IN PLACE. If the windows were installed properly, leveling the panel unit will keep the reveal between the stool and the jamb even. If the window isn't perfectly level, I hide the difference in the reveal before I nail the unit to the wall.

6. ADD BLOCKING AT STUD LOCATIONS TO SUPPORT THE BASEBOARD. Only a small part of the baseboard will overlap the bottom of the panel, so this backing provides nailing blocks for the baseboard.

7. NAIL THE BASE CAP TO THE PANEL AFTER THE BASEBOARD IS INSTALLED. I like to glue and nail the returns at the ends of the baseboard before attaching it to the wall. Once this is done and the base cap is on, I run a small cove strip to hide the ¼-in. gap left by the plywood panel. To eliminate this step, remove the drywall to allow the stiles to sit flush against the wall.

8. INSTALL THE HEAD CASING LAST. Nail the legs of the casing on first, keeping the same reveal between the casing and the jamb that was used between the stool and the jamb. Cut the head casing to fit, fine-tuning the angle as needed for a tight miter joint.

Installing High-Performance Windows

By Steve Baczek

The guiding principle of a Passive House is that its primary source of heat is the sun. Not only do you have to locate and size windows and doors to take advantage of that sunlight, but they have to be high-quality units capable of retaining that energy for times when the sun isn't shining. That's a tall order when you have 24 windows and three entry doors and your goal is a finished house with an air-leakage area that's roughly the size of an index card.

Most of the windows and doors that are built to handle these stringent criteria come from Europe. That's not because Americans can't build them; rather, it's because in Europe, there is a market that demands them.

For this job, we used Makrowin aluminum-clad, triple-glazed tilt-turn windows and matching full-lite doors with an overall thermal value of about R-7. Built in Slovakia, they are imported to the United States through a Massachussetts-based company called Yaro, which also provides the local product support necessary to bridge the gap between the builder and the distant European manufacturer.

In a typical American home, a window is fastened to the exterior sheathing through a nailing flange, and then the flange is sealed to the house's weather barrier with flashing tape. As is typical with European windows, the units used on this project had no nailing flange and were instead screwed through their jambs and air-sealed to the Zip System sheathing that was used to build the deep rough openings. The windows were then air-sealed inside and out with a combination of Siga Wigluv tape and expanding foam.

Custom Comes Standard

The beauty of these Makrowin windows, and many other European windows like them, is that they are customized. Windows that are built to suit are great from a design standpoint because I'm able to get what I need and want out of the windows without much restriction. For example, if we decide during the energy-modeling stage that we need to let in a little more sun to make the energy calculations work, we don't need to jump up to the next standard size; we can order the windows 1 in. wider or taller.

One thing to understand about high-performance windows and doors is that the frames are more costly than the insulated glazing units they hold. Therefore, larger windows are more cost-effective than smaller ones—not a bad bonus when windows make up 30% to 40% of the south wall of your house. Aside from function, these windows are just plain impressive in their fit, finish, and function. They close and latch with the heavy satisfaction of a bank vault and are perfectly balanced.

On-Site Torture Testing

Once all the windows were installed, I asked the builders to spray each one with a garden hose for about five minutes. I did this

Continued ➔

Anatomy of a Proper Installation

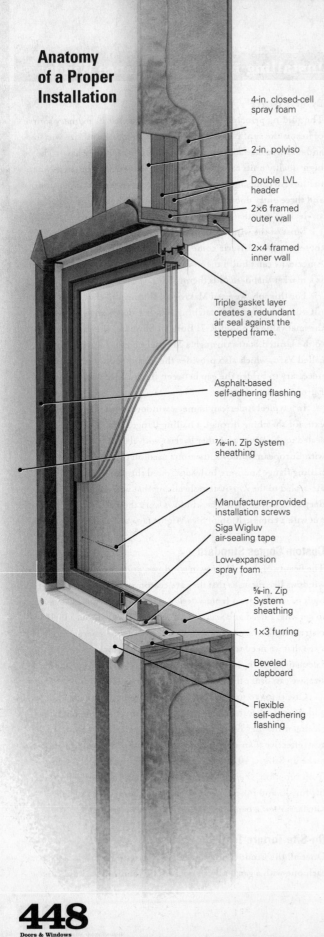

4-in. closed-cell spray foam

2-in. polyiso

Double LVL header

2×6 framed outer wall

2×4 framed inner wall

Triple gasket layer creates a redundant air seal against the stepped frame.

Asphalt-based self-adhering flashing

7/16-in. Zip System sheathing

Manufacturer-provided installation screws

Siga Wigluv air-sealing tape

Low-expansion spray foam

5/8-in. Zip System sheathing

1×3 furring

Beveled clapboard

Flexible self-adhering flashing

because I believe in testing success rather than just assuming it, but also because 15-in.-thick walls don't have the energy movement necessary to promote drying. In short, the stakes in this wall are high, and there's no room for error. If a window can withstand the spray from a hose, there's not likely to be a water issue from a rainstorm.

As it turns out, the spray test revealed minor leaks in two out of the 24 windows in this house, which we were able to address before moving forward.

Start Waterproof

CREATE A DRAINAGE PLANE. A sloped sill and back dam are built in place with a piece of beveled clapboard siding and a 1×4. Both pieces are then covered with Tyvek FlexWrap, which wraps over the outside edge of the opening. It is seated with a J-roller and tacked to the face of the Zip System sheathing with a pair of cap nails.

SEAL THE VERTICAL SEAMS. The sides of the rough opening, where the exterior sheathing meets the boxed window-frame assembly, are protected with lengths of Grace Vycor flashing, which lap over the sill flashing.

Installation Is Straightforward

IN AND UP. With 1/2-in. spacers setting a gap at the bottom and scrap 2xs tacked to the sides as temporary stops in the opening, the window frames (free of their heavy sashes) are tipped into place. The frames are square and robust, so after minimal shimming for level, the sides are fastened to the framing through predrilled holes with the included star-drive screws.

Tape and Foam Eliminate Air Leaks

FOAM AND SEAL FROM THE INSIDE. The installation screws are made to support the weight of the window, so the shims can be removed to allow the ½-in. space that remains around the wooden frame to be fully sealed with low-expansion spray foam. The final step is another round of Siga Wigluv tape to finish the redundantly air-sealed transition between the window and the framing.

TUCK THE TAPE ON THE OUTSIDE. To seal the window to the surrounding rough opening, the builders install Siga Wigluv tape from the sides of the rough opening to the wooden frame that extends around the perimeter on all four sides of the window.

Well-Proportioned Trim

By Bud Dietrich

Interior trim is such an important element of a room's design that it deserves more than just a few seconds' thought, yet that's often all it gets. In particular, there's often little thought given to one of trim's most important aspects: its size. Many builders and homeowners head to the local lumberyard or big-box store and buy what they find without thinking through whether it's the right size or if its proportions will enhance the room. Once it's installed, they see that rather than dressing up the room, the trim they've chosen leaves the room looking flat and dull.

Trim started out with the utilitarian purpose of covering the gaps between walls and floors and between walls and ceilings, as well as the gaps between dissimilar materials such as plaster walls and wood window frames. It quickly evolved into an important design element. Shaped and milled in many different manners and styles, trim has become a way to enrich our experience of a room. But this can happen only when trim is proportioned properly.

The good news is that getting trim proportions right doesn't take the keen eye of an experienced designer. All it takes is consideration and use of a few time-tested guidelines. The result is a room that provides a richer experience and is more comfortable to live in.

Continued →

Poorly Proportioned Trim

Sometimes referred to as "builder's standard," this trim package offers just the basics. With 3¼-in. base and 2¼-in. casing, this is the trim most readily found at big-box retailers. There is no crown molding, and window casing is typically installed in a picture-frame manner. Trim of this size is usually overwhelmed by the room's other architectural features and appears visually off. With no unifying elements, door and window openings appear as stand-alone features rather than parts of a whole, making the space appear flat and cartoonish.

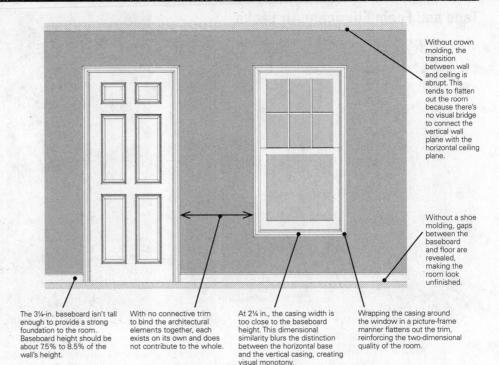

Without crown molding, the transition between wall and ceiling is abrupt. This tends to flatten out the room because there's no visual bridge to connect the vertical wall plane with the horizontal ceiling plane.

Without a shoe molding, gaps between the baseboard and floor are revealed, making the room look unfinished.

The 3¼-in. baseboard isn't tall enough to provide a strong foundation to the room. Baseboard height should be about 7.5% to 8.5% of the wall's height.

With no connective trim to bind the architectural elements together, each exists on its own and does not contribute to the whole.

At 2¼ in., the casing width is too close to the baseboard height. This dimensional similarity blurs the distinction between the horizontal base and the vertical casing, creating visual monotony.

Wrapping the casing around the window in a picture-frame manner flattens out the trim, reinforcing the two-dimensional quality of the room.

Properly Proportioned Trim

Simply increasing the size of the trim yields dramatic results. A 7½-in. base, 3¼-in. casing, and 3½-in. crown molding create a more interesting room, with the crown and shoe molding easing transitions from ceiling to wall and from wall to floor. Even with the window casing installed in a picture-frame manner, this larger, better-proportioned trim results in a more tailored look. This trim package costs more than the builder's standard, but it's readily available at most lumberyards and shouldn't break the bank.

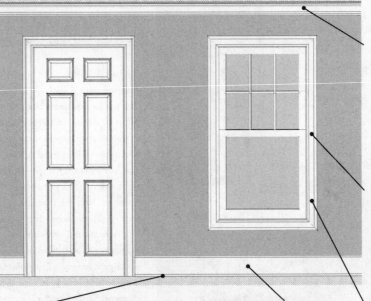

Crown provides a transition between wall and ceiling, connecting the two elements into a whole. Two rules of thumb can apply here: Use crown that's at least as tall as the casing is wide, or use crown that is about ½ in. tall for each foot of ceiling height. You'll have to gauge this with specific moldings, because each will project into the room differently.

The window casing is still installed in a picture-frame manner, but the larger dimension yields a more robust visual element.

The 3¼-in.-wide casing is about half the height of the baseboard, visually differentiating the two. This contrast emphasizes the casing's narrowness, and we tend to respond favorably to vertical elements that are not overly wide.

Shoe molding eases the transition between wall and floor and provides a tailored, finished look.

The 7½-in.-tall baseboard is about 8% of the height of an 8-ft.-high room. Like cuffed pant legs, this taller baseboard provides a strong base, anchoring the wall to the floor.

Beyond the Basic Trim Package

In this drawing, two strong horizontal trim elements—a picture rail and a chair rail—have been added to the room with well-proportioned base, casing, and crown. These horizontal elements unify all of the walls of the room, binding them together like the ribbon that wraps a gift. In addition, the window casing now includes a stool and an apron.

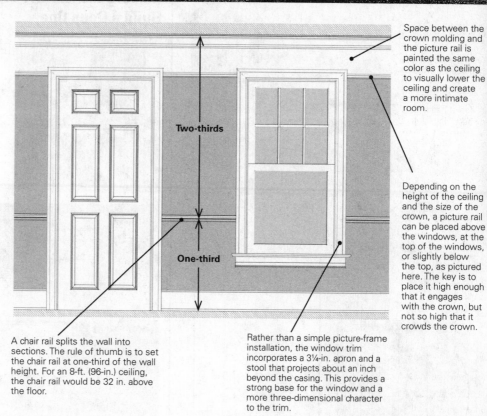

Two-thirds

One-third

Space between the crown molding and the picture rail is painted the same color as the ceiling to visually lower the ceiling and create a more intimate room.

Depending on the height of the ceiling and the size of the crown, a picture rail can be placed above the windows, at the top of the windows, or slightly below the top, as pictured here. The key is to place it high enough that it engages with the crown, but not so high that it crowds the crown.

A chair rail splits the wall into sections. The rule of thumb is to set the chair rail at one-third of the wall height. For an 8-ft. (96-in.) ceiling, the chair rail would be 32 in. above the floor.

Rather than a simple picture-frame installation, the window trim incorporates a 3¼-in. apron and a stool that projects about an inch beyond the casing. This provides a strong base for the window and a more three-dimensional character to the trim.

Trimming a Basement Window

By Chris Whalen

Finish carpentry is the art of making rough stuff look good. Even trimming a window can be a challenge because it's usually complicated by poorly aligned framing or uneven drywall. If things go well, you can tenderize the drywall with a hammer or shim the window into alignment. If not, the window jambs might need to be planed, the casing tweaked, or the miters back-beveled at odd angles. In the end, a bead of caulk is often needed to disguise the solutions.

Multiunit windows in thick walls, such as the basement windows featured here, are prone to even more problems. For starters, even if the windows were installed plumb, level, and square, they might not be parallel with the finished wall surface, meaning that the side jambs need to be tapered. Second, the individual units might not be installed in a straight line, meaning that the stool needs to be tapered. Third, access between the window and the interior-wall framing could be limited, which reduces options for attaching extension jambs.

First, Identify the Problems

The three window units here are in an 8-in.-thick concrete wall. A 2×4 wall covered with drywall sits inside. Before casing is applied to a window like this, the jambs and the stool need to be extended.

The first thing I do is determine how the window sits in relation to the drywall. With a multiunit window such as this one, I place a long straightedge along the top and bottom jambs to determine if the units are in the same plane and at the same elevation. In this case, the windows were at the same height, but the center unit was pushed out in relation to the flanking units. Next, I straddle the corners of each window unit with a short straightedge on the drywall and measure from the window jamb. This tells me how wide the extension jambs will be and if tapering is required. For reference, I write the measurement on the drywall along the edge of the opening where the trim will cover it later. If the variation is less than ⅛ in., there's no need to worry about tapering the extension jambs or stool. This discrepancy can be taken up by tipping the casing slightly. If the difference is greater than ⅛ in., the jambs need to be tapered.

Continued →

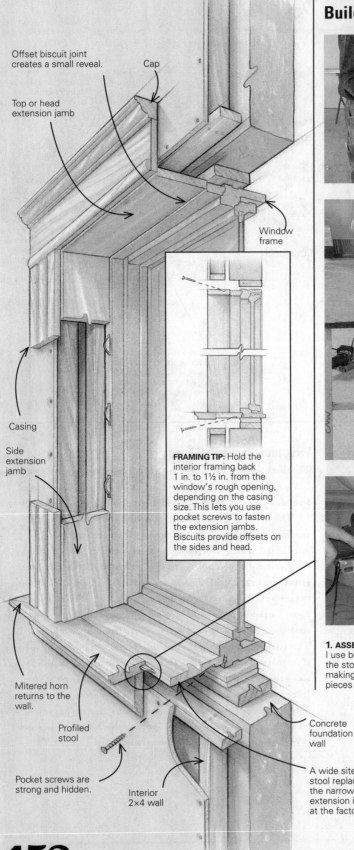

Offset biscuit joint creates a small reveal.

Cap

Top or head extension jamb

Window frame

Casing

Side extension jamb

FRAMING TIP: Hold the interior framing back 1 in. to 1½ in. from the window's rough opening, depending on the casing size. This lets you use pocket screws to fasten the extension jambs. Biscuits provide offsets on the sides and head.

Mitered horn returns to the wall.

Profiled stool

Pocket screws are strong and hidden.

Interior 2×4 wall

Concrete foundation wall

A wide site-made stool replaces the narrow stool extension installed at the factory.

Remove the Narrow Stool Extension, and Build a Deep One

The stool needs to be wide enough to get past the drywall while leaving room to scribe the final fit. To get the stool deep enough, glue and biscuit an extension to the profiled stool, keeping the two parts flush on top.

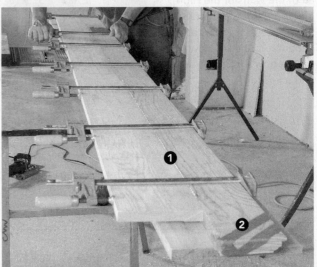

1. ASSEMBLE THE TWO-PIECE STOOL. I use biscuits and glue, then clamp the stool assembly overnight, making sure the tops of these two pieces are flush.

2. RETURN THE PROFILE TO THE WALL. I miter the returns at the end of the stool using two biscuits (stacked), glue, and blue painter's tape as a clamp.

Fit the Stool

With the deep stool assembled, scraped, puttied, and sanded, I turn to fitting. Ultimately, the stool needs to be tight to the window frame and drywall, and notched around the mullions. This begins with positioning the stool exactly parallel to the window and ends with a slight back bevel on the final cut. Rough- and final-scribing, cutting, and fine-tuning come between.

1. Rough-Scribe

MARK THE MULLIONS AND HORNS. The depth of the notch and the amount I cut off the horns is the distance between the window frame and the stool. I square the notch lines at this depth and scribe the horns accordingly.

2. Rough-Out

THE FIRST CUT IS THE DEEPEST. I use a jigsaw to cut the notches and horns, and a small circular saw to cut the length of the stool. The notches will be covered with trim later, so give yourself some wiggle room. The horns will be mostly covered, but not where they return to the wall.

3. Make the Final Fit

POSITION FOR FINAL SCRIBING. With the rough-cut stool back in place, I set my scribes to the widest gap. Next, I scribe the entire length of the stool, including the horns. This should make a perfect fit.

SOME CUTS MATTER MORE THAN OTHERS. The back edge of the stool is most important because it won't be covered by trim. To get a tight fit, I cut near the line with a saw, and then I ease the cut over to the line and back bevel with a block plane or sanding block.

4. Install with Pocket Screws

BORE MANY POCKET HOLES. I put a screw every 6 in. to 9 in. on window stools for a strong connection because people often sit or lean on them.

GIVE YOURSELF ROOM TO WORK. With space between the rough opening and the window frame, you can attach the stool extension with pocket screws.

Continued ➜

Fit the Top and Side Jambs with an Offset

For a great-looking joint that's fast to fit, I use a biscuit joiner with a clip-on offset plate. A ⅛-in. offset adds a shadowline to the profile and eliminates all the fussy fitting, sanding, and patching that a flush fit can require.

1. CLAMPS PROP THE TOP JAMB FOR SCRIBING. Just like the stool, the top extension jamb needs to be scribe-fit to all three window units. Don't get bogged down trying to get the exact length; it just needs to be long enough to land on the side jambs. What's important is that the top extension is parallel to the interior-wall surface when you scribe

2. SCRIBE THE BACK EDGE ALONG THE WINDOW FRAME, setting the scribes to the biggest distance that the front edge of the jamb sticks out past the drywall.

3. THIS FRAMING WASN'T HELD BACK ENOUGH FROM THE WINDOW, so I had to face-nail the head and side extensions into the framing rather than using pocket screws.

4. THE SIDE JAMBS NEED TO FIT TIGHTLY TOP TO BOTTOM AND ALSO ALONG THEIR WIDTH. If the framed wall isn't as plumb as the foundation wall (or as out of plumb), the board needs to be tapered. To get a tight fit top to bottom, I measure in two steps. First, I make a mark 20 in. up from the stool. Next, I measure down to the mark, and I add the two numbers together. This is more accurate (and faster) than bending my tape into a corner and guessing at the exact measurement.

⅛-in. offset

The Lamello Top 10 biscuit joiner has a clip-on offset plate.

Solutions Start with the Stool

Many windows have factory-applied 2-in. extension jambs that make the window suitable for a 2×6 wall. For basement walls, you need to extend the side and head jambs even more. I do this with a simple offset biscuit joint (more on that later). This offset joint looks good on the jambs, but it's impractical for a stool. That's why I carefully remove the factory-applied stool extension and replace it with a new full-depth stool.

The new stool needs to fit between the rough opening in the framed wall while extending past the side casings. The overall length of the stool is the sum of the distance between the side jambs, the width of the casings, the casing reveals (typically ¼ in.), and the amount of overhang beyond the casings. After cutting the stool to length, I miter the ends so that the profile returns to the wall. The extension is biscuited and glued to the back of the profiled stool. When this assembly is dry, I scrape excess glue, sand, fill gaps, and sand again, making it ready to install.

Set the new stool in the opening, and check its fit. The width will probably need adjustment. Because the three individual window units weren't perfectly in line on this project, I needed

to taper the stool in addition to notching around the mullions. I use a square and a scribe to measure and mark the notches and the ends of the stool extending past the window. After removing excess material with a jigsaw, I slide the stool into position again for final scribing and planing. Finally, I bore for pocket screws, clamp the stool into position, and screw it to the window frame. I use a lot of screws (every 6 in. to 9 in.) because someone is going to sit on this window stool sometime in the future, and I don't want it to break.

Install Jamb Extensions with an Offset Reveal

For the head and side jambs, I add a piece to the factory extensions using an offset reveal of about ⅛ in. The head jamb needs to be long enough to pass the side jambs, but it does not have to be fit to anything else. I cut it slightly longer than the overall length of the window. To scribe the head jamb, I set it in place with bar clamps and shims. Next, I measure at a few spots to determine what needs to be removed from the jamb stock, and I set the scribe and mark along the length of the jamb. I cut to the scribe line with a small circular saw, then use a power planer, a block plane, and a sanding block to adjust until the fit is

Complete the Assembly

The trim detail here was dictated by the trim in the existing house. I begin with the mullions, which need to fit tightly between the stool and the head extension. The side casings are cut ¼ in. long to establish the reveal for the head casing. The apron is installed last.

LONG HEAD CASINGS ARE A BIT TRICKY. I clamp the head casing in place and adjust the reveal to the head extension before nailing it off. I use a finish nailer with 2½-in. nails to attach the casing to the framing, and a brad nailer to fasten the casing to the extension jambs.

TIGHTEN THE STOOL. I use 2x blocks and shims to clean up the joints and make a solid stool. Last, I install the apron with mitered returns.

acceptable. As with the stool, the process takes a couple of fittings.

At this point, I use a biscuit joiner to create a consistent offset or reveal between the extension jamb I'm making and the one applied by the factory.

On the project here, because there wasn't as much clearance between the window frame and the rough framing on top of the window as there was on the stool, pocket screws wouldn't work. Instead, after applying glue and inserting the biscuits, I shimmed and nailed the head-jamb extension in place, making sure it was square to the side jambs.

The only difference in installing the side jambs is that the length needs to fit precisely between the new stool and head jamb. Rather than bending my tape measure into a corner, I measure in two steps: up from the stool 20 in., then down from the head to the 20-in. mark. I then add the two numbers together. I cut the jambs to length and then to width according to the numbers written previously on the drywall. Finally, I fit the pieces and then biscuit, shim, and nail them in place, making sure they are square and tight to both the head jamb and the stool.

The Rest Is Standard Procedure

The last few steps of the process aren't much different than regular window trimming: Apply the mullion trim, casings, cap, and apron. I start with the mullions and work my way out. Using the same two-step measuring technique as I did with the side jambs, I measure the mullions, then cut and nail them in place.

I cut side casings to length, making them ¼ in. longer than the distance between the stool and head jamb, thereby creating a reveal at the head. After nailing them in place, I measure, cut, shim, and install the head casing and cap. Before installing the apron beneath the stool, I permanently shim and block the stool so that it is level, straight, and solid. I then make an apron with mitered returns on the ends the same length as the head casing, and I nail on the apron so that its ends are in line with the outside edges of the side casings.

Whether you're trimming a basement window or one in a double-stud, adobe, straw-bale, insulated-concrete-form, or any other thick-wall structure, these techniques ensure a quality installation for an appealing assembly.

Continued →

Install a Bay Window

By Rick Arnold

I recently helped my mom and stepdad move into a small ranch house so that they'd be free of stairs and have an easier time getting around. The small house was in decent shape and livable, but the north-facing bedroom's lack of light made the space grim. With my stepdad's increasing mobility issues, it seemed likely that he'd be spending more and more time in there, so I decided to make the room more inviting by swapping the existing window for a projecting bay window.

Installing a bay window is one of the easiest ways to transform a room. By reaching beyond a home's wall, a bay window gathers light from three directions, creating an inviting, sun-collecting space that is perfect for displaying plants, cozying up with a good book, and brightening dark interior spaces.

Not surprisingly, installing a bay window is more involved than putting in a conventional window, so I'm covering the process in two parts. The first part deals with choosing a window and framing a good-looking roof to cover it—ahead of time. It may seem odd to frame the roof first, but it makes the whole project easier. The second part shows how to install the window and integrate it into the existing wall—make it weathertight and trim the exterior.

Part 1
Bay-Window Basics

The most common bay windows have outside corners that meet at a 45° angle, but other styles are available (see "Choosing aBay Window," p. 457). Fortunately, the installation methods for all types and sizes are similar. Bay windows are generally sold with head and seat boards that hold the window together and form its top and bottom. You also can get them without head and seat boards for installation in angled or curved walls. The 45° window that is featured here with head and seat boards is the most common type of window installed. I chose the narrowest window model that was available from this manufacturer so that the window wouldn't overwhelm the small bedroom.

Why Build the Roof First?

Through the years, I've learned that when a projecting window needs a roof, it's better to build the roof first. For starters, it's easier and safer to build the roof on the ground. In addition, having the roof framed yet removable makes it easier to cut back brick or siding for flashing and to integrate the window into the house. It also means that the house is vulnerable to bad weather for less time.

If you've ever seen a bay window that just doesn't look right, it might be because its roof has the wrong shape. The proper shape for a 45° window like the one featured here is based on a section of an octagonal roof with 22.5° hip rafters.

At this angle, the hip rafters bisect the window's front corners, giving the roof a pleasing shape. The pitch of the roof is also an important factor. When I'm installing the roof in a gable end, I like to use a steep pitch so that the roof has enough mass to balance the surrounding wall.

For this window's overhang, I added 4½ in. to the roof framing for a finished soffit made from a 1×5 board. A 5 -in. soffit works with most bay windows, but larger windows (8 ft. wide or more) may need wider soffits to match the overhang on the house's main roof better.

When deciding on a pitch and overhang for your window, be sure to consider architectural features such as other windows and house-roof overhangs that could interfere with the window's roof. Once you have a proposed design, make a sketch to see how it will look on the building. This roof's 12-in-12 pitch also complements the window's squarish shape.

Make a Template

I've seen these little roofs challenge even veteran framers, but my design method makes them easy to build. The first thing that I do is copy the shape of the window (in plan view) onto a piece of ¾-in. OSB. I use this OSB template to lay out and cut the 2×4s that form the roof's ceiling joists and subfascia. I call this assembly the base. Once I have the base, I rework the template into a nailer for attaching the rafters.

To make the template, I snap a line on the window's plywood headboard indicating the 4 in. that extends into the rough opening. Then I transfer the window's shape to the template. Using a scrap of stock, I add the overhang's width to the template and cut out the trapezoid-shaped OSB with a circular saw. Then I cut and assemble the ceiling joists and subfascia on top of the template.

I fasten the components with 2½-in. screws. I use screws because they allow me to hold the components with one hand while I fasten with the other. The screws hold better, too. This detail is important because the roof may be lifted onto the window and removed several times before it's put in place for the last time.

Make a Nailer for the Rafters

After the base is done, I rework the template into a nailer for the rafters. The rafters attach along the nailer's top edge; the whole assembly then is fastened to the house. If you're using the manufacturer's cable-suspension system to help carry the weight of the projecting window, the attachment bracket can be mounted on this OSB nailer, making the entire window installation easier.

You might assume the sides of the nailer are 45° like the sides of the base, but they're not. They're slightly less. In simple terms, it's because the roof is based on a segment of an octagon, not a box.

The right shape for the nailer is critical, and the math is somewhat complicated. I use a trick I learned years ago (see "Fashion a Rafter Nailer from the Template," p. 458).

Cut and Fit the Rafters

Before I take rafter measurements, I make sure that the rafter nailer is perpendicular to the base. If it isn't, I push or pull it

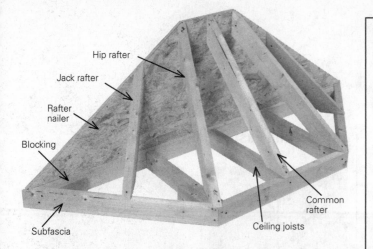

Hip rafter

Jack rafter

Rafter nailer

Blocking

Subfascia

Common rafter

Ceiling joists

Make a Template for the Roof Base

① Projection

①

4½ in.

Roof overhang

MEASURE THE WIDTH AND PROJECTION. Begin making a template for laying out the ceiling joist and subfascia by copying the shape of the window onto a sheet of ¾-in. OSB. (**1**) When making the template, don't include the 4 in. of plywood that extends into the rough opening.

ADD THE OVERHANG. Draw the window shape onto the OSB template, and add the 4½-in. roof overhang to the front and sides of the template.

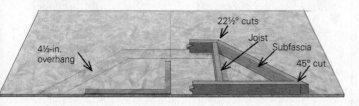

22½° cuts

Joist

Subfascia

45° cut

4½-in. overhang

Choosing a Bay Window

I once worked for a building-materials dealer that sold several brands of bay and bow windows. Clients were often surprised at the many choices available. For starters, bay windows can be built with casements or double-hung windows flanking the larger picture window. Most folks choose one or the other based on the other windows in their home, but that shouldn't be the only consideration. Casements, which open outward, can encroach on outdoor-living spaces, and double-hungs can be tough to open, especially when the bay is deep. You also can have a projecting window built from units that don't open at all.

Bay windows are commonly available with 30°, 45°, and 90° sides. While 45° models are the most common, 30° models stick out less from the building, making them a better option when the window has to open onto a cramped outdoor space. Bays with 90° sides have square instead of angled outside corners that better suit some home styles.

You also can get bow windows. These windows, which are usually made from a series of casement units, have a rounded shape. Most bay and bow windows have plywood head and seat boards that form the top and bottom, but they can be omitted when a window will be installed in a wall that matches the window's shape. The head and seat boards can be painted or stained by the window maker or finished on site. One big plus of both bay and bow windows is that they are an easy way to make a room slightly larger, often without encroaching on setbacks.

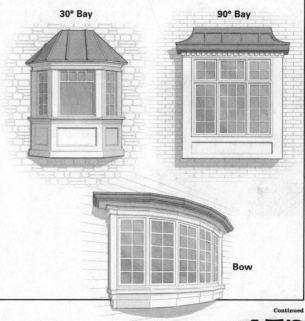

30° Bay

90° Bay

Bow

Continued ➡

Fashion a Rafter Nailer from the Template

Roof-base template

1. After cutting out and using the template to lay out and assemble the roof base, you can convert the template into a nailer for attaching the rafters.

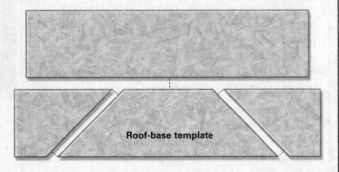

2. Hook a tape on the template corner to measure the angled side. Swing an arc the length of the angled side on the template.

3. Use a square to transfer the mark across the template.

4. Connect the outside corner to the new mark with a straightedge.

5. Repeat the process on the other side of the template, and cut out the shape. Trim ½ in. from the bottom edge of the nailer with a circular saw.

Without trimming, the nailer would project beyond the subfascia, preventing the sheathing and finished fascia from sitting flat. After trimming, the nailer should fit on the base so that the front side is flush with the subfascia.

Lay Out and Fasten the Common Rafter

MEASURE THE COMMON RAFTER. After using a framing square to ensure that the rafter nailer is perpendicular to the base (brace if necessary), measure from the top of the nailer (front side) to the outside edge of the subfascia. This will be the long side of the rafter. Cut 45° miters on both ends.

FASTEN WITH SCREWS. Drive 2½-in. drywall screws through the rafter end and into the roof base. At the top of the rafter, drive screws from the back side of the nailer into the rafter. Screws hold better than nails; this is important, because the roof will likely be moved several times before final installation on the window.

Lay Out and Fasten the Hip Rafters

MEASURE THE HIPS. The hip rafters run from the top corners of the rafter nailer to the outside corners of the top of the subfascia. Record the measurement, then subtract ⅜ in. to lower the rafter corners so that they are in plane with the subfascia.

MARK THE CUTS. Hip rafters on 45° bay-window roofs with a 12-in-12 pitch will have 43° cuts at the top and 47° cuts on the bottom. For pitches other than 12-in-12, use a construction calculator to figure the angles.

COMPOUND CUT ON THE TOP; MITER CUT ON THE BOTTOM. The bottoms of the hip rafters get a 47° miter without a bevel, but the tops need a 22.5° bevel in addition to a 43° miter. Tilt the saw to 22.5°, and follow the line made earlier.

CHECK THE FIT. Confirm that the first hip rafter fits correctly, then use it as a template to cut the other side. Arranged correctly, the bevels should form a point when the rafters are stacked. If not, the second bevel is sloping the wrong way.

THE PERFECT FIT. The rafters shouldn't protrude beyond the top of the rafter nailer or the subfascia. If the rafters are proud, the sheathing, which will be installed later, won't fit tight to the framing. If the rafters stick up slightly, trim their length from either end, using the same saw settings as the original cut.

Lay Out and Fasten the Jack Rafters

CUT AND FIT THE JACKS. Holding the tape perpendicular to the subfascia, measure to the front of the nailer and the top of the subfascia. The bottom cut has a 45° miter only. The top cut has a 45° miter and a 45° bevel. After checking the fit, use the rafter as a template for the other side by stacking the pair of rafters with one on top of the other as described on the facing page and above.

until it is; then I brace it in the proper position. The first rafter I cut is the common rafter. I measure from the outside edge of the nailer to the outside edge of the subfascia. Because the roof will have a 12-in-12 pitch, the common rafter will have a 45° cut on each end. After I screw the common rafter in place, I measure for the two adjacent hip rafters. They're longer than the common rafter, so they'll have slightly different angles. With a 12-in-12 roof, the hips will be 43° on the top and 47° on the bottom.

Getting the hips to fit correctly is important. I suggest being cautious when you cut; you can always trim them if they're too long. If the hips are too short, the sheathing won't fit correctly, so it's better to make a second cut than cut them too short the first time.

The hips bisect the 45° sides of the window, so the tops get a 22.5° bevel. After I check the fit, I use this first rafter as a template for the next rafter. I line it up and mark the bottom, then mark the bevel end. I keep it oriented the same way when I cut the rafter. Now I have a right and a left bevel.

The last pair of rafters go from the center of the angled subfascia to the center of the angled side on the rafter nailer. These are the jack rafters. They will have 45° angles on both ends and a 45° bevel at the top. Because the other side will be the same length, I use the first one as a template to mark the second.

Cut the Sheathing

With the rafters done, I cut the sheathing for the roof. I don't install it, however, because that would interfere with installing the stainless-steel cables that help to support the window. The second half of this two-part article will show how to install the cables.

To measure for the center piece, I first measure the fascia length. Then I measure the height. Finally, I measure the width at the top. To cut the center panel, I transfer the fascia measurement to the panel edge and mark its center. I use a framing square to ensure that the height measurement is perpendicular to the edge of the sheathing. Then I transfer the top measurement to the sheathing, centering it on the perpendicular line and using a square to form a right angle at the top.

To cut the side pieces of sheathing, I measure along the subfascia; then I measure the hip rafter and the length along the top of the nailer. I extend the tape to the imaginary point where the sheathing meets the building.

To lay out the triangular-shaped pieces of roof sheathing, I transfer the subfascia measurement to the edge of the panel. At opposite ends of the fascia measurement, I transfer the hip rafter and nailer measurements up. At the end of both measurements, I make a small arc by holding a pencil at the end of the tape. Where the two arcs intersect is the point at the top.

In part 2 of this article, I'll show you how to install the bay window, put on the roof, and integrate the whole window assembly into the wall.

Continued →

Lay Out and Cut the Sheathing

Center Sheathing

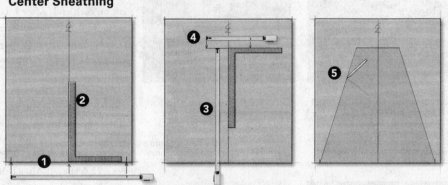

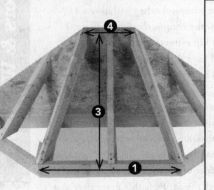

1. Transfer the fascia measurement to the panel edge, then find and mark the center of this measurement. **2.** Use a square to draw a perpendicular line from this mark. **3.** Measure the height, and transfer this measurement to the perpendicular line in the center. **4.** Measure the width at the top. Bisect this measurement on the vertical perpendicular line. **5.** Connect the ends of the lines. Cut out the shape with a circular saw, but don't attach the sheathing.

Side Sheathing

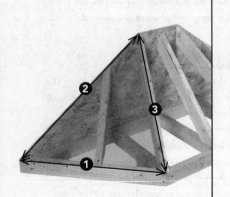

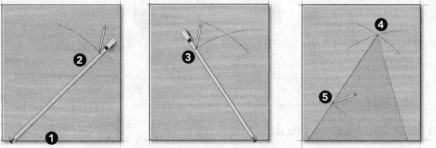

1. Measure the fascia edge, and transfer the measurement to the edge of the sheathing panel. **2.** Measure the side on the rafter nailer, and transfer this measurement to the sheathing by forming an arc at the end of the tape. **3.** Do the same for the hip rafter. **4.** The intersection of the two arcs is the point at the top. **5.** Connect this point to both ends of the fascia measurement, cut out the shape with a circular saw, and use the first piece as a template for the other side.

Part 2
Setting the Stage

I've learned that it's worth spending a little extra time to set up two levels of scaffolding to make the installation process easier. The first level is where you stand while working. The second, located above the first but just below the bottom of the rough opening, helps to support the heavy window while it's being installed.

Just about any type of scaffolding will do, but I use basic wooden A-frames (see "Simple Homemade Scaffolding," *Fine Homebuilding* #160) because their multiple rungs make it easy to get the window and the work platform at the correct heights.

Once the staging is set up, I pull off enough siding so that I can flash the opening and integrate the new window into the existing weather-resistive barrier. In this case, I removed the cedar-shingle siding about two courses (10 in.) higher than the top part of the bay window's roof, one or two shingles (depending on their width) on the sides, and one course at the bottom of the window opening. It's easier to do this work before the window is installed and restricts access to the siding around it.

I patched the missing and damaged sections of felt paper with new housewrap and covered the sides of the opening with flashing tape, which seals the vertical seams better. I also covered the rough sill with flexible flashing. Working from the bottom up ensures proper laps.

Bay windows are heavy, so before a second carpenter and I carry the window to the staging, I remove the operating sashes to make

Shim and Fasten

The window is moved into the rough opening from the outside. One carpenter moves inside to fasten the head board temporarily to keep the unit steady while it's shimmed and fastened. The other carpenter remains outside to check for plumb, adjusting the front of the window as necessary.

MAKE ANGLED SPACERS. A 2×4 with a 45° bevel fills the space between the bay window's angled casement windows and the rough opening. The pieces are best cut with a portable tablesaw.

FASTEN THE TOP AND BOTTOM. Secure the window's head and seat boards with 3-in. screws spaced every 6 in. or 8 in. Shims prevent the plywood boards from bowing as the screws are tightened.

FASTEN THE SIDES. With the angled spacers in place, secure the sides of the bay window with 3-in. screws driven through the jamb. The screws are spaced approximately 12 in. apart.

the window lighter and easier to handle. I also have some shims and plywood scraps handy so that we can use them to level the window on the staging once it's positioned in front of the opening.

We set the window on the lower level of staging and then climb up. We lift the window onto the upper level of staging and slide it into the rough opening. Using the plywood scraps on the stage, we level the window. While my co-worker steadies the window, I go inside to fasten it temporarily with a few screws. When the window is stable, we reinstall and lock the sashes to ensure that the window remains square while it's being fastened.

Fasten the Frame

When securing the window, it works best to have one carpenter hold a level on the exterior to check for plumb while the other shims the head and seat boards and checks for level on the inside. Once the window is plumb and level, it's secured by 3-in. #8 screws spaced from 6 in. to 8 in. apart, and run through the head and seat boards into the framing. As the screws are driven, we keep checking for plumb and level with 4-ft. levels.

With the top and bottom of the window secure, I fasten the sides. I first make angled spacers by cutting 45° bevels on a pair of 2×4s. These spacers prevent the window frame from distorting when I run screws through the bay window's angled side. I attach the spacers to the jack studs with 3-in. screws, and then I open the sashes and install 3-in. screws through the window frames and into the spacers. With the window securely fastened, I check the

Continued ➡

Install the Cable Supports

Once the assembled roof is screwed in place, stainless-steel cables are installed to keep the window from sagging over time. The tops of the two cables are attached under the roof, and the bottoms are attached to the seat board near the angled corners farthest from the building. The cable ends have threaded sections that allow the cables to be tensioned and adjusted later if needed.

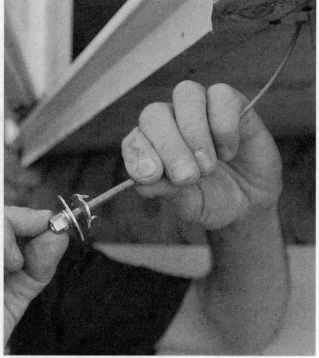

GO FISHING. Fish the cables that support the front of the window through the corners where the center picture window meets the flanking casements. Secure the cables at the top and the bottom, and then tension them.

MOUNT THE CLAMP. The manufacturer provides a paper template for correctly positioning the two-piece cable clamp that anchors the support cables. The clamp location varies depending on the type of bay window used and the blocking or studs behind it.

ASSEMBLE THE CABLE BOTTOM. The cable's threaded end allows tensioning and future adjustment should the house or window move. The end of the threaded section accepts a hex wrench, so the shaft doesn't turn when the hex nut is adjusted.

operating sashes to make sure that they open and close easily. I then go back outside to focus on drying in the installation. If the sashes are difficult to open, I check the gaps between the sash and the window frame to see if anything moved out of square while being fastened. I then shim and refasten until the sashes work correctly.

Insulate and Install the Roof

Projecting windows of all types can be cold and drafty, so before installing the roof I built previously, I add a 1-in.-thick layer of rigid insulation on the head board, 2-in.-thick rigid insulation beneath the seat board (covered with soffit material), and spray foam around the perimeter of the window to stop air leaks. The rigid insulation, which acts as an air barrier and thermal break, greatly improves the window's thermal performance.

It's now time to install the roof. The roof is centered on the window and is screwed to the framing with structural screws long enough to reach the framing under the wall sheathing. Connecting the roof's OSB back to the framing members—not

just the sheathing—is important; the roof's OSB back will later be the attachment point for stainless-steel cables that help to hold up the front of the window.

Install the Support Cables

When I started out as a carpenter 30 years ago, we supported bay windows with large brackets. The brackets take a surprisingly long time to build and install when the window is being put into an existing house. The siding must be cut away and additional blocking installed between the studs because the existing framing seldom corresponds with the bracket locations.

For all these reasons, I now use cable supports from the window manufacturer, which are faster and easier to install and can be adjusted later if the house settles or the window sags. When a client wants brackets under the window for aesthetics, I'll add them, but I still use the cables for proper window support.

The cables attach to the house with metal clamps mounted under the window's roof. The braided stainless-steel wires are

Install Flashing, Roofing, and Trim

With the roof sheathed and the overhang trimmed out, the asphalt roofing can go on. Step flashing is woven in between the roof shingles where the small hip roof meets the exterior wall. The flashing's vertical legs are taped to the wall and covered with housewrap. A small piece of trim over the roof shingles prevents the cedar-shingle siding from wicking water.

INSTALL THE TRIM. Size the overhang to complement the bay-window roof and to accept standard-width boards. The author chose PVC trim stock for this project because it needs minimal maintenance and can be left unpainted.

MAKE IT WATERTIGHT. A small piece of trim covered by an aluminum drip cap keeps the sidewall shingles' end grain off the wet roof shingles. Lap the housewrap over the drip cap's vertical leg before reinstalling the shingle siding.

A GOOD-LOOKING, WATERTIGHT WINDOW. The completed installation has redundant flashing and a good-looking roof that matches the scale and details on the rest of the house. The bedroom space inside is also brighter and more inviting than before.

fished through the window and connect to the seat board with nuts and a series of washers. The manufacturer provides plugs that allow access to the adjusting nut should the front of the window need to be raised or lowered later.

A pair of cables can safely support up to 1000 lb. If you have an especially large window or need greater capacity, consult the manufacturer for guidance. Sometimes additional cables or other means of support are required.

To begin the cable installation, I fish the cables through the hole locations specified by the window manufacturer and then attach hex nuts and washers to the threaded shaft on the bottom of each cable. The top of the cable is fastened to the metal clamps under the roof. After all the components are in place, I tension the cables by tightening the hex nuts on the bottom.

Roofing and Trim

With the window fully fastened in the opening, I place 6 in. of fiberglass insulation in the bottom of the roof before installing the roof sheathing (zipsystem.com). The sheathing has a waterproof surface and a companion tape to seal the seams. When used together, the sheathing and tape eliminate the need for shingle underlayment. I cover the roof with the same shingles used on the main roof.

Before attaching the exterior casing, I put another layer of flashing tape on the house and lap it onto the sides of the bay window to stop air and water. For trim, I use cellular PVC sheet stock on the bottom of the window and cellular PVC boards for the rest. After all the trim pieces are in place, I fill in the missing cedar shingles around the window and caulk any gaps in the trim for a finished look.

Despite installing a couple dozen or so bay windows during my career, I am always surprised at how long the process takes. Unlike a typical window replacement, bay windows have a roof to build; insulation, shingles, and flashing to install; support cables to connect; and additional exterior trim to attach. This particular installation took two skilled carpenters a full day to complete, although I think the improved living space makes the considerable effort worth it.

Continued ➔

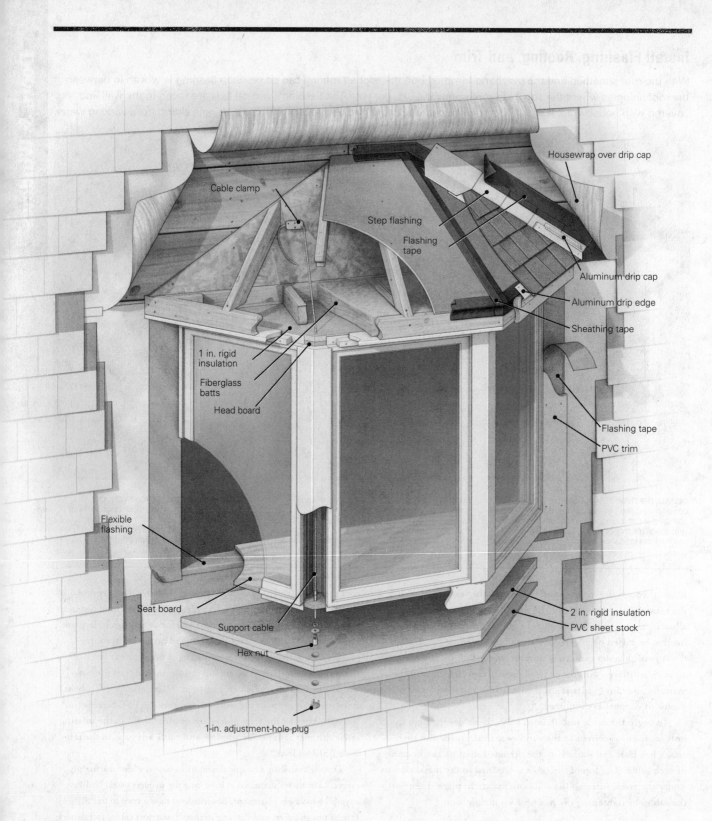

Cable clamp

Housewrap over drip cap

Step flashing

Flashing tape

Aluminum drip cap

Aluminum drip edge

Sheathing tape

1 in. rigid insulation

Fiberglass batts

Head board

Flashing tape

PVC trim

Flexible flashing

Seat board

2 in. rigid insulation

PVC sheet stock

Support cable

Hex nut

1-in. adjustment-hole plug

Contents

Heating & Cooling

Getting to Know Your Furnace

By Martin Holladay

Many different appliances can be used to heat a house, including boilers, water heaters, heat pumps, and woodstoves. According to the Department of Energy (DOE), however, most homes in the United States are heated by forced-air furnaces.

A forced-air furnace is connected to ducts that deliver heated air to registers throughout the house. Different types of furnaces are manufactured to burn a variety of fuels, including natural gas, propane, oil, and firewood. The most common furnace fuel in the United States is natural gas.

Even though the smallest available furnaces are often too big for a high-performance home (see "Heating Options for a Small Home," *Fine Homebuilding* #217), furnaces still have virtues that are hard to ignore. They are inexpensive, widely available, and easily serviced by local HVAC contractors. For many North American homes, they are a logical way to supply space heat.

A furnace is only as good as its installation, though, and research has shown that new furnaces and their distribution systems (ducts) often aren't sized correctly. According to a 2013 report prepared for the DOE, the problem is even more widespread when it comes to replacement furnaces. An oversize furnace often costs more than a right-size furnace, and improper duct installation results in reduced operating efficiency.

Efficiency Drives the Decision

When it comes to fuel efficiency, furnaces are grouped based on their annual fuel-utilization efficiency, or AFUE. These efficiency ratings are calculated using a laboratory method that tells you how much of the fuel going into the furnace is being converted to usable heat. AFUE is expressed as a percentage, and higher is better. Residential furnaces in the United States are divided into just two main categories: medium-efficiency furnaces (80% to 82% AFUE) and high-efficiency furnaces (90% to 97% AFUE). The reason that you can no longer buy a low-efficiency furnace is that the federal government now requires residential gas-fired furnaces to have a minimum efficiency of 80%.

The line between medium- and high-efficiency furnaces isn't arbitrary or driven by marketing campaigns; it's a function of the inner workings of those furnace types. Medium-efficiency furnaces are designed to keep flue gases hot enough to avoid condensation of flue-gas moisture, while high-efficiency furnaces deliberately encourage this condensation. Furnaces with an efficiency of at least 90%, sometimes known as condensing furnaces, draw so much heat out of the flue gases that the furnace exhaust can be vented through PVC pipe. PVC costs less than the stainless-steel pipe that would have to be used to vent hotter flue gases at risk of depositing corrosive condensate.

Continued ➔

Choose an Efficiency

Understanding Afue

The efficiency of a furnace is calculated using a laboratory procedure that measures an appliance's annual fuel-utilization efficiency, or AFUE. This calculation tells you what percentage of the energy in the fuel is being converted to heat, so higher is better.

What's Calculated
- Heat losses up the chimney
- Heat losses through the appliance jacket
- Heat losses due to on-and-off cycling

What's Not Calculated
- Electricity use (energy required to run fans and controls)
- Heat losses through ductwork connected to the furnace

Efficiency Categories

75%   80%   85%

Low: Less Than 75%

Although a low-efficiency furnace has traditionally been any model less than 75% efficient, the technology used in these older furnaces is now considered obsolete. The new minimum AFUE, mandated by the federal government, is 80%. Even though furnaces operating at low efficiency are no longer being manufactured, many are still in use throughout the country.

Medium 80% to 82%

Single- or two-stage (sometimes called "standard") furnaces can be equipped with either a single- or a variable-speed blower. They usually have a steel heat exchanger and rely on a natural draft to create a flow of exhaust gases up a chimney.

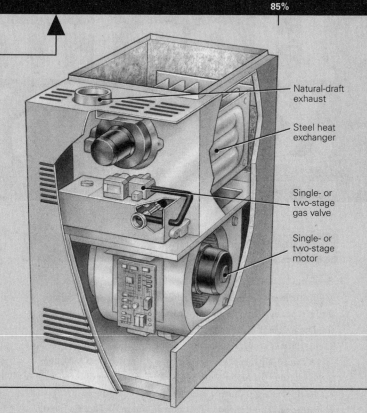

Natural-draft exhaust

Steel heat exchanger

Single- or two-stage gas valve

Single- or two-stage motor

Choose a Type

Single-stage These are the simplest furnaces because they only have one heat-output setting. If a furnace is rated with an output of 60,000 btu/hr, that is the furnace's output whenever it is running, regardless of exterior temperature or differences in temperature in different parts of the house.

Single-Stage, Two-Stage, and Modulating Furnaces

The simplest furnaces are single-stage models with single-speed blowers; they're either on or they're off. By contrast, two-stage furnaces can operate at two different output levels—either a high or a low Btu/hr setting depending on the demand. This is helpful because most of the time, a furnace only needs to operate at a low Btu/hr output to do its job. The higher output is needed only on the coldest days of the year.

Slightly more sophisticated than two-stage furnaces, modulating gas furnaces include an automatic fuel valve that varies the amount of fuel delivered to the burner. Many modulating furnaces also include a variable-speed blower motor—usually an electronically commutated motor (ECM)—that, like the automatic fuel valve, adjusts the airflow of the warmed air up and down in response to heating demand.

While it's fairly easy to design a gas valve that varies the amount of fuel delivered to the burner, it's harder to design such a valve for

What about 83% to 89%? From a technological standpoint, it's difficult to manufacture a furnace with an efficiency rating between 83% and 89%, so none are available in that range. A furnace with this rating would have sporadic condensation of flue gases, which would lead to corrosion problems. You either want dependable condensation (so that it can be dealt with and the thermal benefits of it can be harvested) or no condensation at all (to avoid the need for a condensate drain). Any condensation requires expensive features, including a method of collecting and disposing of the condensate; if the efficiency gains are small, the investment in these features isn't worth it. Also, very-high-efficiency furnaces with dependable levels of condensation lower the temperature of the flue gases to the point where PVC can be used as a flue; intermediate levels of condensation result in hotter flue gases, and hotter flue gases require a stainless-steel flue pipe, which costs more than PVC.

90%   95%

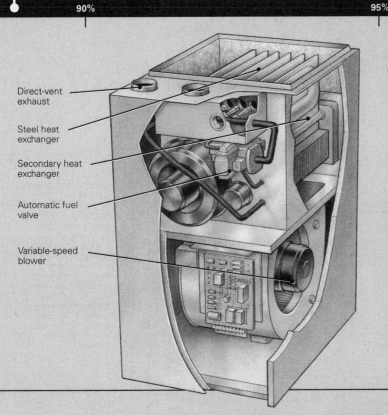

Direct-vent exhaust

Steel heat exchanger

Secondary heat exchanger

Automatic fuel valve

Variable-speed blower

High
90% to 98%

These furnaces can be either single-stage or two-stage models, but most have a variable-speed blower. Also, in addition to the standard steel-tube heat exchanger, high-efficiency furnaces have a secondary heat exchanger, which condenses the moisture in the escaping flue gases, turning it from vapor to liquid and squeezing out even more available heat in the process. These furnaces require a drain hookup to dispose of the condensate from this process. So much heat is drawn out of the flue gases that the exhaust can be vented safely through a PVC pipe going out the wall.

Two-stag A bit more sophisticated than single-stage models, these furnaces can operate at two different output levels. Most of the time, they operate at a lower btu/hr output—typically around 65% of full capacity. The higher output is needed only on the coldest days of the year.

Modulating These furnaces include an automatic fuel valve that varies the amount of fuel delivered to the burner. Since modulating furnaces can match the heating demand precisely, they provide heat more evenly than single-speed furnaces, which operate with a stop-and-go jerkiness.

delivering oil, so these furnaces are usually optimized for a single firing rate at a fixed Btu/hr output. That's why oil furnaces are usually single-stage furnaces.

Efficiency Leads to Direct Venting

Condensing furnaces are power-vented, so they include at least two fans: an air-handler fan that distributes warm air through the home's ductwork, and a power-vent fan to move exhaust gases through the flue pipe.

Most condensing furnaces are sealed-combustion furnaces, which means that the burners pull outside air into the combustion chamber through plastic ducts to feed the fire's needs. Sealed-combustion furnaces don't use any indoor air for combustion. The main advantage of a sealed-combustion furnace (compared to an old-fashioned atmospherically vented furnace) is that it is much less likely to suffer from backdrafting problems.

Continued ➜

Get Your Ducts Right

CHOOSE THE RIGHT DUCTS
Use rigid galvanized ducts wherever possible, and keep runs as short and straight as possible to enhance airflow. Flexible duct is hard to support and to keep straight, and its corrugations can cause turbulence that reduces airflow. Never use stud bays or other framing cavities as plenums to move supply air or return air. It's not only bad practice because it allows air to leak through miscellaneous gaps and cracks; it's also a code violation.

SEAL EVERYTHING
It's crucial to seal duct seams with mastic to prevent leakage, and you should apply foil tape or mastic to the plenum seams, too. If your furnace is located inside your home's conditioned space, these leaks may not matter very much, but if your furnace is located in a garage or vented attic, it can mean a substantial energy loss. Once sealed, the airtightness of the entire system should be evaluated with a Duct Blaster or similar duct-leakage tester.

PLAN FOR RETURN AIR
Return air has to have a path from every conditioned room back to the furnace's return plenum. You can ensure this either by including grilles in every room that are connected to the return-air duct system, or by installing jumper ducts or transfer grilles to connect rooms without a return to those with a return. Avoid a single, central return-air grille, which can cause bedrooms with closed doors to become pressurized, forcing conditioned air into walls and ceilings. Size return-air ducts to be as large as or larger than supply-air ducts. When in doubt, make them bigger.

RECONSIDER REGISTER PLACEMENT
Although traditionally located near exterior walls to counteract the chilling effect of windows, supply registers can be placed on interior walls if high-performance windows have been specified and the house is tight and well insulated. This method means shorter duct runs that operate more efficiently.

INCLUDE DAMPERS
Balancing dampers should be included on every branch duct running to a register to allow for airflow adjustments, a critical portion of the commissioning process.

A CENTRAL LOCATION IS BEST
To make sure that duct runs are as short as possible, locate the furnace in the center of your basement or in a mechanical room near the center of your house. Both the furnace and the ductwork should be located inside of the thermal envelope, not in an unconditioned attic or crawlspace.

Backdrafting occurs when a powerful exhaust fan—for example, a range-hood fan—depressurizes a house enough to draw combustion fumes down the chimney and back into the house. (For more information on this issue, see "How to Provide Makeup Air for Range Hoods," *Fine Homebuilding* #232.)

Sizing Matters

The most accurate method for determining the required size of a furnace is to do what's called a Manual J calculation. In its simplest form, a Manual J calculation takes into account the shape and orientation of a house, its insulation levels and airtightness, its square footage and surface area, and the various amounts of heat lost through all of the exterior surfaces. This information is then plugged into a Manual D calculation, which helps determine duct sizing.

Sounds easy, right? Well, it isn't. It can be difficult to find a residential HVAC contractor who is willing to perform Manual J, Manual D, or code-compliant alternative calculations, even though they're required by code. You should not assume that an HVAC contractor who agrees to do a "heat-loss calculation" will perform an actual Manual J calculation. (When in doubt, ask to see the paperwork.) Because heat loss and heat gain through building envelopes is governed by many factors, an accurate Manual J calculation requires many inputs, as well as dedicated computer software. Those who do perform the calculation need to be diligent and accurate about the details, because taking any guesses about building components and other fudge factors used to cover unknown defects in construction will push heat-loss estimates higher, leading to furnaces that are oversize.

You could argue that a pinpoint-accurate Manual J isn't necessary when furnace-size options aren't that numerous, but it's not uncommon for rule-of-thumb calculations to miss the mark by more than a little. Even if you aren't sold on the idea of conducting an accurate Manual J calculation to size a furnace, you should consider one for the room-by-room calculations it provides, which are necessary to perform a Manual D calculation. Failure to take Manual J seriously means that Manual D calculations suffer.

The Dos and Don'ts of Ductwork

During the 1950s and 1960s, fuel was so inexpensive that most heating contractors routinely installed ductwork without much attention to airtightness. In many areas of the country, contractors still install ductwork in vented crawlspaces or vented attics. These locations are outside of a home's conditioned envelope, and any air that escapes from leaky ductwork running through these areas is money wasted.

In the 1980s, energy-efficiency advocates responded to this issue with training programs to encourage HVAC installers to seal duct seams. After three decades of training, these programs are beginning to bear fruit in some areas of the United States. Unfortunately, the gospel of airtight ductwork hasn't reached every corner of the country, and many HVAC contractors are still installing ductwork the way their grandfathers did.

To make up for the fact that leaky duct systems waste large amounts of energy, many HVAC contractors install oversize furnaces with huge blowers. According to the DOE, 40% of contractors in one large-scale survey indicated that they purposely oversized equipment, citing reasons such as "To reduce callbacks," "To allow for future expansion," or "Customers demanded it."

Designing a duct system properly and installing it carefully costs more than doing sloppy work, but it provides two important benefits to homeowners: better comfort and lower energy bills.

A Low Thermostat Setting May Void Your Furnace Warranty

Energy columnists routinely advise owners of vacation homes to turn down their thermostats when the homes are unoccupied. As it turns out, homeowners following this advice not only are at risk of damaging their furnace; they are also at risk of voiding their furnace warranty.

If you read the fine print on the installation instructions for Carrier condensing furnaces, to take one example, you'll find this statement: "This furnace is designed for continuous return-air minimum temperature of 60°F ... or intermittent operation down to 55°F ... such as when used with a night setback thermometer [thermostat]. Failure to follow these return air limits may affect reliability of heat exchangers, motors and controls."

When I asked the Carrier Corp. whether setting one's thermostat to 50°F would void the warranty, the company had this response: "For optimal performance, Carrier Corp.'s 58MXB gas condensing furnace should be operated with return-air temperatures no lower than 60°F and no higher than 80°F. To support appropriate return-air temperatures, Carrier recommends that the 58MXB furnace be set within the range of 55°F to 80°F. Return-air guidelines and detailed operating instructions are included in the 58MXB owner's manual. Failure to operate the furnace according to the owner's manual could affect the furnace's reliability and void the factory warranty."

The bottom line: Condensing furnaces are more efficient than noncondensing furnaces, but their efficiency comes with the added risk that low return-air temperatures can contribute to the condensation of corrosive flue gases in the primary heat exchanger.

Continued →

Getting the Mechanicals Right

By Steve Baczek

Although many superinsulated houses are designed and built to be heated primarily by the energy from sunlight, there is almost always a secondary source of heating. The house shown here, which was covered in a recent series of five articles and videos, is no exception. It receives 50% of its total required heating from the sun—with another 25% from electronics, appliances, and occupants—but the remaining 25% must be handled by mechanicals. This heating requirement—about 6000 Btu—leads to some challenges.

The first is that such a small heating load makes it difficult to find right-size equipment. But even at twice the necessary output, the 12,000-Btu minisplit we ended up choosing is still more reasonable than the smallest furnace, which typically isn't designed to produce anything lower than 50,000 Btu.

The second problem is distribution of the conditioned air. Unlike a typical furnace and attendant ductwork, a ductless minisplit delivers the heating and cooling in bulk, and all in one location. Although the open floor plan of the house is designed to help distribution, there are still bedrooms and bathrooms that require some level of privacy and are therefore more difficult to keep comfortable. In other Passive House designs, I have solved this issue by spreading the work across multiple minisplits located in different areas of the house. In this home, we wanted to deliver the needed loads with a single minisplit, so we relied on the ERV (energy-recovery ventilator) to handle our distribution.

An essential element in this tight house, the ERV operates all day every day, taking stale air from the kitchen and the bathrooms and exchanging it with fresh outdoor air, which is then supplied to the bedrooms. The conditioned air from the minisplit is piggybacking on the circulation already provided by the ERV. This approach is working well, and the house stays at a comfortable 65°F to 70°F.

Wanting to have a backup plan—due to concerns that a single minisplit might have trouble keeping up with the summer dehumidification—we plumbed and powered a second minisplit rough-in should it be necessary to add a second unit.

We also outfitted the three bathrooms with small wall-mounted electric-resistance heaters. Although they were not necessary from a whole-house-heating standpoint, a bit of extra comfort is appreciated in bathrooms, especially on cold New England mornings.

ERV

Functioning as the lungs of the house, a Zehnder ComfoAir 350 brings fresh air through an intake in the lower gable on the left side of the house. Stale air discharges from a vent in the upper gable. The ERV operates continuously, pulling conditioned air from the kitchen and bathrooms, and transferring 75% of its energy to the incoming clean, fresh air that is then supplied to the bedrooms and the study.

Distribution Breakdown

The 10 corrugated ducts bringing stale air to the ERV must be balanced by the 10 ducts supplying clean air from the ERV. Each duct is designed to carry 12 cfm. Here's how the distribution works in this house.

Stale Air

FULL BATHS: 1 double-duct exhaust in each (24 cfm × 3 baths = 72 cfm)
HALF-BATH: 1 single-duct exhaust (12 cfm)
KITCHEN: 3 single-duct exhausts (12 cfm × 3 = 36 cfm)

10 DUCTS = 120 CFM

Clean Air

BEDROOMS: 2 single-duct supplies in each (24 cfm × 4 bedrooms = 96 cfm)
STUDY: 2 single-duct supplies (24 cfm)

10 DUCTS = 120 CFM

Clean air supplied to bedrooms and study

Stale air exhausted from bathrooms and kitchen

Solar Panels

Although solar panels were not allowed to be part of the Passive House calculations, the homeowner added a 8.75kw photovoltaic array, tipping the scale from Passive House to net-zero standards.

Ductless Minisplit

A 12,000-Btu Daiken Quaternity minisplit air-source heat pump has slightly more than twice this house's required heating load and also provides summer cooling. Although intentionally oversized to address the humid summers in this coastal location, this system contains technology that allows it to run at a high efficiency even at partial heating loads.

Geothermal Heat Exchanger

A Zehnder ComfoFond L connected to the ERV provides the initial tempering—either precooling or preheating—to the incoming fresh air. The heat exchanger kicks on only when necessary, circulating a mixture of water and glycol through a loop of PEX tubing that runs 7 ft. below grade, where the ground temperature is a constant 50°F to 55°F.

Water Heater

The 80-gal. A.O. Smith Voltex heat-pump water heater sources its heat from the surrounding air. Although it's equipped with a backup heating element, the homeowners have met their needs using only the heat-pump mode.

Supplemental Comfort

Each bathroom includes a TPI 3200 series fan-forced heater mounted on the wall opposite the toilet. Each 1500w heater is paired with an Aube TH115 thermostat and takes a few minutes to bring the bathrooms from 66°F to 74°F.

Continued ➜

471

Ground-Source Heat Pumps

By Justin Fink

Left to its natural devices, heat energy flows from areas of high temperature to areas of low temperature. A heat pump reverses this natural process, absorbing heat from a relatively cool environment and moving it to a warmer area.

A window air conditioner is a common example of a heat pump. The interior of a room is not cooled by pumping it full of cold air; rather, it's cooled by extracting heat from the room and dumping it outside. A heat pump can also be used to warm a room by reversing the process—that is, pulling heat energy from the exterior air and distributing it inside.

The flaw of air-source heat pumps (ASHPs), the most common type, is that their efficiency decreases with increased temperature extremes. The more frigid the air outside your house, for example, the harder the ASHP has to work to extract usable heat energy. That's why many homes are relying on ground-source heat pumps (GSHPs) for air-conditioning and heating at a higher level of efficiency.

Instead of air, a GSHP uses the relatively stable temperature of the earth as either a heat source or a heat sink depending on whether the system is in cooling or heating mode. Here's how it works.

Pump inside the house circulates water through high-density polyethylene tubing buried below grade.

Bentonite-based grout promotes thermal conductivity.

In heating mode, heat energy is extracted from the soil.

Heating and Cooling, Courtesy of the Earth

Although the temperature of the upper 6 ft. or so of soil varies based on the air temperature, if you dig to at least 20 ft., the ground temperature is roughly equal to the annual ambient temperature at that latitude. Depending on whether the house's heat-pump system is in cooling mode or heating mode, the soil is used either as a heat sink or a heat source.

The Refrigeration Cycle

Heat pumps rely on a closed loop of refrigerant, which is repeatedly condensed and evaporated in order to transfer heat energy from one place to another. The cycle works in both directions, allowing the same setup to be used for both cooling and heating, the latter of which is shown here.

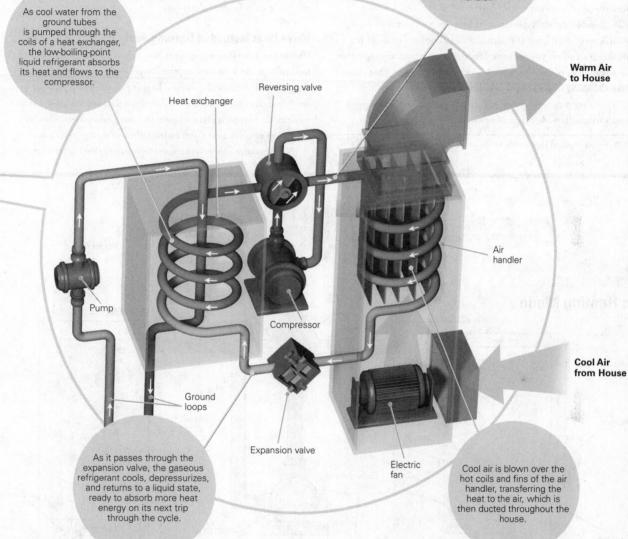

In the compressor, the heated refrigerant is condensed, creating a hotter, pressurized gas that is used to heat up coils and fins inside the home's air handler.

As cool water from the ground tubes is pumped through the coils of a heat exchanger, the low-boiling-point liquid refrigerant absorbs its heat and flows to the compressor.

Heat exchanger

Reversing valve

Warm Air to House

Pump

Air handler

Compressor

Cool Air from House

Ground loops

Expansion valve

Electric fan

As it passes through the expansion valve, the gaseous refrigerant cools, depressurizes, and returns to a liquid state, ready to absorb more heat energy on its next trip through the cycle.

Cool air is blown over the hot coils and fins of the air handler, transferring the heat to the air, which is then ducted throughout the house.

Loop Options Aplenty

The layout of the tubing in a ground-source heating system is somewhat customizable and can be changed to suit the site conditions, soil type, and desired heating and cooling load. The tubing may be placed in deep vertical wells from 100 ft. to 400 ft. below the surface, laid out in long horizontal trenches (either in straight runs or overlapping loops), or set below the surface of a body of water.

Continued ➡

Is a Heat Pump Right for You?

By Scott Gibson

High-efficiency gas-fired furnaces turn more than 95% of the fuel's energy potential into usable heat. Energy losses are low, and so are greenhouse-gas emissions. But what about a heating appliance capable of operating at efficiencies over 100%, producing multiple units of heat for every unit of energy it consumes? And what if it also is able to cool your house in summer and warm your water? High efficiency and versatility are two advantages of heat pumps. And at least on paper, that should make choosing one a slam dunk. Unfortunately, it's not that easy.

There are a variety of heat-pump types to choose from, with a proportionally wide range of prices. Here, I'll take a look at

NOTE: Prices cited in this article are from 2010.

both air-source (ASHPs) and ground-source, or geothermal, heat pumps (GSHPs) and some variations on both. Operating costs will vary depending on where you live, what type of heat pump you install, and your local electricity prices. Finally, there are significant caveats when comparing efficiency ratings between heat pumps and conventional heating and cooling equipment. If you're considering a heat pump, you'll have to wade deeply into these details before you can make an informed decision.

Move Heat Instead of Burning Fuel

Unlike most heating equipment that burns fuel to create warmth, heat pumps use a vapor-compression cycle to move heat from one place to another. In winter, heat is extracted from the air or the ground, concentrated, and distributed inside via air ducts or radiant-floor tubing. In summer, the same equipment runs in reverse to remove heat from indoor air and dump it outside.

Vapor compression is the same technology that makes a freezer

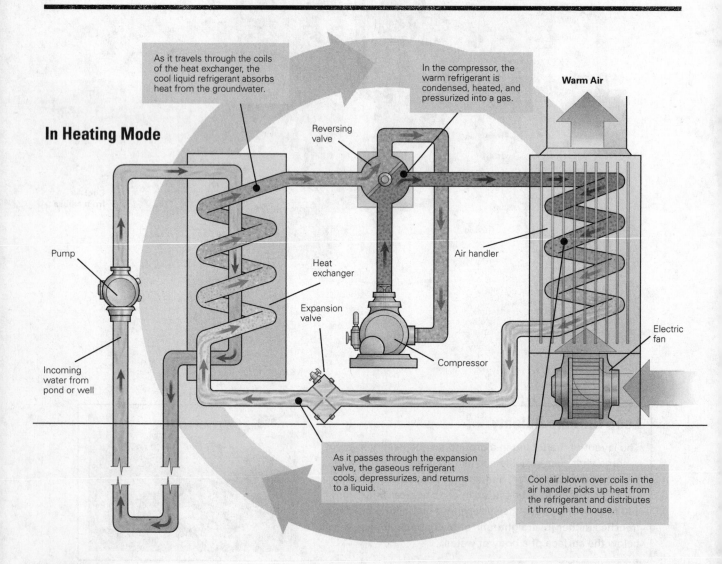

In Heating Mode

As it travels through the coils of the heat exchanger, the cool liquid refrigerant absorbs heat from the groundwater.

In the compressor, the warm refrigerant is condensed, heated, and pressurized into a gas.

Warm Air

Reversing valve

Pump

Heat exchanger

Expansion valve

Air handler

Compressor

Incoming water from pond or well

Electric fan

As it passes through the expansion valve, the gaseous refrigerant cools, depressurizes, and returns to a liquid.

Cool air blown over coils in the air handler picks up heat from the refrigerant and distributes it through the house.

or air conditioner work. With the help of a compressor and an evaporator, a refrigerant circulated through a closed loop absorbs and releases heat as it changes from a gas into a liquid and back again. Because the refrigerant has a low boiling point, it can extract heat even from air or water at or below freezing temperatures.

As the name suggests, ASHPs use outside air as the source of heat in winter and as the heat sink in summer. GSHPs use the earth for this exchange, either through tubing installed in wells or trenches or through a water source like a pond.

ASHPs are popular in the southeastern United States, where cooling is a bigger issue than heating and where winter temperatures are relatively mild. They cost less to install than ground-source heat pumps, but most don't operate as efficiently, especially in cold weather. When temperatures fall below 40°F, they may need a boost from either electric-resistance heaters or fuel-fired furnaces.

GSHPs can be designed either as "open loop" or "closed loop" systems. An open-loop system circulates water from a pond or well

How It Works

The technology behind a heat pump is the same technology used in refrigerators and air conditioners. A closed loop of refrigerant absorbs heat as a liquid and is compressed into a hot gas. When allowed to cool and return to a liquid, the refrigerant releases its heat. The open-loop ground-source heat pump shown in the drawings picks up or dumps heat into groundwater passing through the coils of a heat exchanger, depending on whether the heat pump is heating or cooling the house. An air-source heat pump uses outside air for this exchange. Because heat pumps can circulate the refrigerant in either direction, they can heat and cool your home.

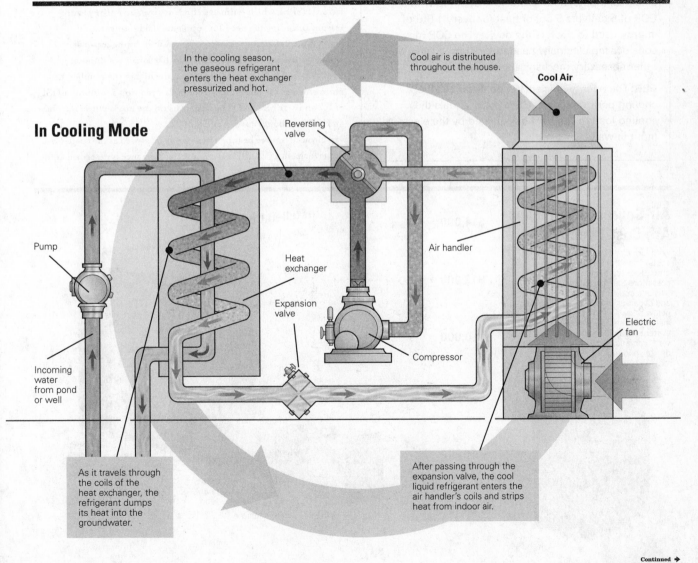

In Cooling Mode

In the cooling season, the gaseous refrigerant enters the heat exchanger pressurized and hot.

Cool air is distributed throughout the house.

Cool Air

Reversing valve

Pump

Heat exchanger

Expansion valve

Compressor

Air handler

Electric fan

Incoming water from pond or well

As it travels through the coils of the heat exchanger, the refrigerant dumps its heat into the groundwater.

After passing through the expansion valve, the cool liquid refrigerant enters the air handler's coils and strips heat from indoor air.

Continued →

Glossary

ASHP: Air-source heat pump

GSHP: Ground-source heat pump

HSPF: The heating seasonal performance factor is the heating-efficiency rating for ASHPs, which equals the total heat output, in Btu, divided by the electricity required to run the heat pump, in watt-hours.

SEER: The seasonal energy-efficiency ratio is the cooling-efficiency rating for ASHPs, which equals the total heat removed from the house, in Btu, divided by the power to run the device, in watt-hours.

COP: The coefficient of performance measures the heating efficiency of GSHPs. The COP equals heating output divided by some of the unit's electrical inputs, both in Btu. A heat pump with a COP of 5 delivers 5 Btu of heat for every 1 Btu of energy used to operate the device. The COP may not consider the electricity needed for pumps, fans, and other necessary mechanicals.

EER: The energy-efficiency ratio describes the cooling performance of GSHPs and equals the cooling load in Btu per hour divided by the electrical input in watts.

through the heat pump and returns it to the source. In a closed-loop system, water or an antifreeze solution circulates through tubing buried in the ground, picking up or dumping heat. There are also GSHPs that circulate refrigerant in buried copper tubing. No matter what the configuration, heat is transferred from the ground loop to a sealed refrigerant loop inside the heat pump. The site work required to install underground tubing makes ground-source heat pumps among the most expensive heating and cooling options, but they operate at very high efficiencies.

Efficiency Ratings Are Not Apples to Apples

If the basics of how heat pumps work are relatively simple, their efficiency ratings are anything but. ASHPs and GSHPs use different rating systems, and each is measured separately for heating and cooling efficiency. In addition, the efficiency ratings don't necessarily reflect how a heat pump will actually perform in a specific house at a particular location.

ASHP efficiency is gauged by the heating seasonal performance factor (HSPF), which estimates efficiency over an entire heating season, including the need for supplemental heating in cold temperatures. Cooling efficiency is measured by the seasonal energy-efficiency ratio (or SEER), just like an air conditioner.

For both HSPF and SEER ratings, the higher the number, the more efficient the heat pump. Federal law requires a minimum HSPF of 7.7 and a SEER of 13. The best units on the market these days have an HSPF of about 10 and a SEER of 22.

Ground-source heating efficiency is measured as the coefficient of performance (COP), and cooling performance is described as the

Air-Source Heat Pumps Are Cost-Effective

With higher efficiency comes higher costs. Even the least expensive ground-source heat pump is likely to cost more than either an air-source unit or a conventional gas-fired furnace and separate air conditioner. The chart below shows estimates for the total installed costs of a 3-ton (36,000 Btu) system. Keep in mind that costs can vary dramatically by contractor, system design, and region.

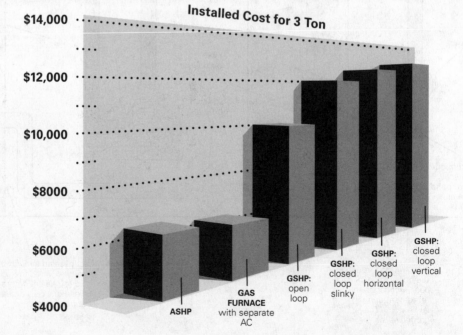

Installed Cost for 3 Ton

- ASHP
- GAS FURNACE with separate AC
- GSHP: open loop
- GSHP: closed loop slinky
- GSHP: closed loop horizontal
- GSHP: closed loop vertical

energy-efficiency ratio (EER). Based on the two different efficiency ratings of both ASHPs and GSHPs, the most important number will depend on how much of the year that you spend heating or cooling your home.

Unfortunately, these efficiency ratings are based on narrow test conditions, not actual site conditions. The rating systems for GSHPs, for example, do not consider the electricity needed for either the circulating pump to move fluid through tubing or for fans or pumps that distribute heat inside the house. Actual measured COPs (including pumping energy) for installed ground-source heat pumps typically fall between 70% and 74% of manufacturers' stated COPs. Other variables include temperature fluctuations in the earth around the tubing, and whether the system has been installed correctly.

Additionally, there's no simple way of comparing the rated efficiencies of GSHPs and ASHPs because they are, in effect, written in different languages.

The bottom line is that a heat pump may not perform as well as its efficiency rating would predict or, conversely, that it may do a little better than expected when site conditions are favorable. The best use of these performance numbers is for comparing similar heat pumps to one another.

Air-Source Heat Pumps Have Quirks

Most ASHPs are designed for forced-air heating and cooling

Desuper . . . What?

It won't likely be able to meet all your water-heating needs, but a desuperheater can be used to steal some of the heat produced by a heat pump and apply it to potable water. A desuperheater works only when the heat pump is running, and works best when used with ground-source heat pumps running in cooling mode.

---

systems, so the same ducts that distribute the heat also cool the house in the summer. They're often configured as split systems, meaning that there is one condensing coil inside and one outside, with a central air handler inside.

ASHPs produce warm air, not scorching heat. And that, says Harvey Sachs of the American Council for an Energy-Efficient Economy, can leave some homeowners feeling chilly. Airflow at 90°F warms the house, but not with the same punch as a woodstove, a hydronic radiator, or a gas furnace.

In winter, the outdoor condenser needs periodic defrosting. Most ASHPs send hot refrigerant down the line to take care of the problem, but while the condenser sheds its layer of frost, the air handler has to switch to a supplemental heat source. Other common problems include thermostats that force the heat pump to switch to supplemental heat, ducts that are poorly sealed or run through

---

Three Ways to Tap the Earth for Heat

A ground-source heat pump can tap into latent heat stored in the earth in several ways. Open-loop systems draw water from a well or nearby pond and pump the water back to its source. In closed-loop systems, plastic tubing containing antifreeze is submerged in a pond or lake, or is buried horizontally or vertically in the ground.

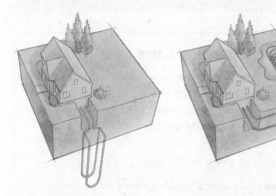

VERTICAL LOOP If you don't have a lot of property, you can drill a vertical-loop system. These closed-loop systems are often as deep as 400 ft. You can go vertical with an open-loop system by drilling two wells, one to draw ground-water, the other to return it.

POND LOOP Typically the most cost-effective and least disruptive installation is a pond loop. If you have a sufficiently deep pond, you can run either closed-loop horizontal pipes or an open-loop system that draws and returns pond water.

SLINKY LOOP It may be tough to beat the efficiency of geothermal heat pumps, but the installation is long, labor intensive, and disruptive to the property. The slinky coils shown here are part of a closed-loop, 8-ton retrofit.

Continued ➜

Getting Better: The Environmental Impact of Refrigerants

Refrigerators, freezers, air conditioners, and heat pumps rely on the ability of refrigerants to absorb and shed heat as they turn from liquid into gas and back again. Unfortunately, when they are released into the atmosphere, some refrigerants deplete the Earth's ozone layer.

Chlorofluorocarbons (CFCs) were proven to be the worst offenders, which led to the wider use of related compounds called hydrochlorofluorocarbons (HCFCs). R-22 is a common HCFC used in heat pumps. While much better for the environment, R-22 does not eliminate the ozone problem completely, and it is also scheduled for a phased withdrawal from the market.

Manufacturers are now turning to another refrigerant called R-410A. It contains no chlorine, so it will not damage atmospheric ozone, although it is considered a greater environmental threat than carbon dioxide. R-410A systems operate at higher pressures than those using R-22, so it's not simply a question of swapping one refrigerant for another. Some manufacturers, such as Water Furnace, switched to R-410A years ago, and all heat-pump makers were forced to do so as of January 2010.

---

unconditioned space, and systems charged with the wrong amount of refrigerant.

"I don't think we have any heating, ventilating, and air-conditioning technology out there that is more frequently screwed up by installers than heat pumps," Sachs says. "You need to have somebody who really understands heat pumps to get a satisfactory installation."

Ground-Source Heat Pumps Are Expensive to Install

Most GSHPs are connected to an air handler that distributes warm or cool air around the house. They can produce some of a home's hot water, and they also can be used for radiant-floor heating, although a duct system still is needed for air-conditioning in the summer. With water temperatures limited to about 130°F, GSHPs can't be used with most hydronic radiators, which require water that is at least 160°F.

There are lots of installation options for ground-source heat pumps. From a cost standpoint, the most attractive is an open-loop groundwater system, in which water is taken from and returned to a well or pond. According to a report by Kevin Rafferty, a consulting engineer and heat-pump specialist in Oregon, the ground loop alone costs between $600 per ton for a 5-ton system and $1000 per ton for a 3-ton system (a "ton" is 12,000 Btu per hour). A vertical, closed-loop system could cost nearly $1600 per ton because of the high cost of drilling. A horizontal closed-loop system comprised of straight tubing or coiled tubing, called a "slinky" ground loop, is somewhere in between. Current costs will vary from one system to another and between different parts of the country, but these numbers can still be useful for comparing the relative cost of one type of system to another.

Open-loop groundwater systems make the most sense in rural areas where a house will be served by its own well, providing the well produces enough water (2 gal. to 3 gal. per minute per ton). Even though a separate pump will be needed, this is commonly still the least expensive route.

Despite their higher cost, vertical closed-loop systems have one advantage over horizontal closed-loop systems: They don't need much property. Horizontal systems require long runs of trenches—

Estimate Operating Costs

If you can gather the local costs of fuel and the efficiency rating of the heating and cooling equipment you are considering, you can use these simple equations to compare estimated operating costs.

Fuel oil: (7.25 × $/gallon)/ Appliance efficiency

Propane: (11.1 × $/gallon)/ Appliance efficiency

Natural gas: (10 × $/therm)/ Appliance efficiency

Electric resistance: 293 × $/kwh

Air-source heat pump: (1000 × $/kwh)/ HSPF

Ground-source heat pump: (293 × $/kwh)/ COP

not an option for every suburban homeowner.

Overall, even the cheapest installation option for a ground-source system puts it at a higher cost than either an air-source heat pump or a gas furnace with a separate air-conditioning unit. Rafferty's estimated installed costs for a 3-ton system range from about $6000 for an ASHP to more than $12,000 for a closed-loop, vertical-well GSHP. But he warns that costs can be much higher.

Assumptions and Estimated Operating Costs

High efficiency doesn't automatically translate into low operating costs, which depend on the heating potential of each type of fuel and how much it costs locally. In comparing the cost of heating and cooling with either an ASHP or a GSHP and more conventional equipment, a useful common denominator is how much it costs to produce 1 million Btu of heat. These simple formulas estimate the operating costs, taking local energy prices into account (see "Estimate Operating Costs" p. 478).

To see how two different heat pumps would compare to the 85% efficient oil-fired boiler I have at my house, I plugged in local energy costs: 14¢ per kwh for electricity and $2.25 per gallon for #2 fuel oil. On the heat-pump side, I assumed the ASHP would have an HSPF of 8.5 and that the GSHP would have a COP of 3.5. The results showed that heating with fuel oil would cost $19.19 per million Btu, by far the most expensive option. An ASHP would do the same thing for $16.47, and the ground-source heat pump for $11.72.

Keep in mind that these numbers include assumptions about climate, installation, and system design that wouldn't necessarily hold true; nor do they factor in the up-front cost of the systems themselves. For that, I'd need more specialized advice from a manufacturer, HVAC contractor, or energy designer. But they are a place to start.

For More Info

- For guidance on installing a heat pump, visit the Web site of the Air Conditioning Contractors of America (www.acca.org).

- For efficiency ratings of various heat pumps, try the Air-Conditioning, Heating, and Refrigeration Institute's Web site (www.ahridirectory.org).

- Information on federal tax credits for installing air- and ground-source heat pumps is available here: www.energystar.gov.

- The Geothermal Heat Pump Consortium's Web site offers a wealth of information, including a directory of contractors and manufacturers (www.geo exchange.org).

When Ductless Minisplits Make Sense

By Scott Gibson

Widely used in other parts of the world, ductless-minisplit heat pumps (or minisplits) account for only about 5% of heating and cooling systems in the United States. Although minisplits are made by a number of companies, conventional air-source heat pumps are much more common. Despite that, minisplits are being promoted as a simple way to air-condition houses that lack central ductwork. That's true as far as it goes, but to a growing number of builders specializing in high-performance houses, that's just the beginning.

Like conventional air-source heat pumps, minisplits move heat from one place to another via refrigerant and insulated copper lines, using electricity for compressors and fans but not directly consuming any fuel to create heat for a building. In winter, a minisplit extracts heat from outdoor air and moves it inside. In summer, the process can be reversed so that the same equipment cools the house (sidebar p. 482).

Because they don't need ductwork, minisplits are easier and faster to install than conventional forced-air systems. They operate efficiently at much lower temperatures than standard air-source heat pumps, and they simplify zoned heating and cooling. In addition, they can sharply reduce distribution losses typical in ducted heating and cooling systems.

Minisplits can be used either in new construction or in retrofits. Best of all, in a tight, well-insulated house, a relatively modest minisplit can keep everyone comfortable at a much lower cost than a conventional HVAC system.

Refrigerant, Not Air, Moves Heat Through the System

Conventional air-source heat pumps and minisplits both generate heat or cooling in the same way. The big difference is in how it is distributed. With a conventional air-source heat pump, an outdoor condenser supplies refrigerant to a central indoor evaporator/air handler, which heats or cools air that is blown through duct-work to individual rooms (bottom drawing p. 480). With a ductless minisplit, one outdoor condenser supplies as many as eight individual indoor units (heads) with refrigerant through small-diameter supply lines. Each head contains a small evaporator and heats or cools by blowing air over the evaporator. When the system is being used for cooling, a drain carries condensation away from the head. Each indoor head can be controlled with its own thermostat, making it relatively simple to manage heating and cooling in different parts of the house (top drawing p. 480).

Advantages of Going Ductless

Eliminating ductwork simplifies installation, especially in a retrofit, where putting in ducts could be invasive and expensive. In a ductless system, refrigerant piping, control wires, and the

479

Home Repair Wisdom & Know-How

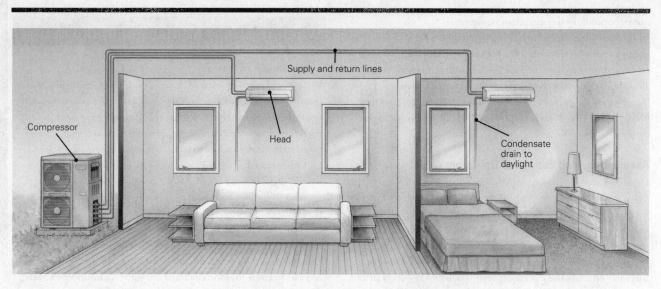

Minisplit Configuration

With surface-mount interior heat exchangers and no ducts, minisplits are relatively easy to retrofit in existing houses where there are no ducts. Each compressor can handle up to eight interior heat-exchanger heads, which makes zoning a simple matter. Well-insulated new homes often can be heated with a minisplit and a minimal number of heads, and efficient models can produce heat more cheaply than conventional fuel-burning systems.

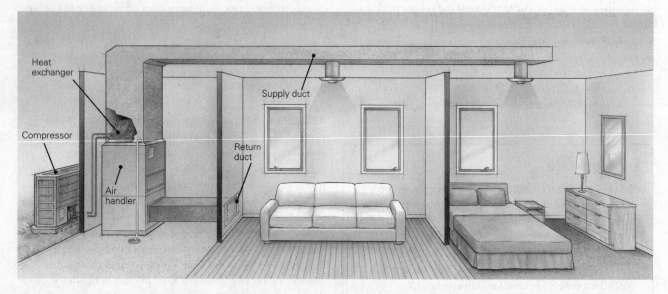

Conventional Heat-Pump Configuration

Conventional heat pumps send refrigerant to a heat exchanger in an air handler, heating or cooling air that is distributed to the house through ducts. Air handlers and ducts are often installed in unconditioned attics, making them highly vulnerable to heat loss. Even so, in conventionally insulated homes, ducted systems may be less costly to install than minisplits.

Supply lines

Drain line

Power

EASY TO FIT. The refrigerant lines, control wires, and condensate drain all fit in holes small enough to be drilled through a 2×4 wall plate.

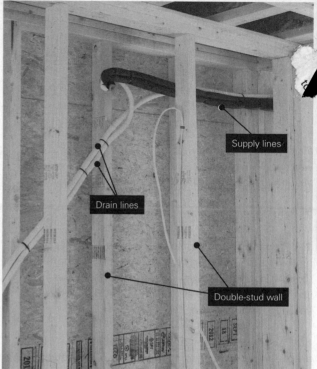

Supply lines

Drain lines

Double-stud wall

In homes with double-stud walls, you don't even have to drill the studs.

condensate drain fit together through holes small enough to be drilled in a 2×4 wall plate. A simple system that includes a single outdoor compressor and a few indoor heads can be installed quickly, with few of the construction headaches associated with conventional heating and cooling.

Ducts also are inherently wasteful, either because they're leaky or because they lose energy as they pass through unconditioned areas such as attics or crawlspaces. The U.S. Department of Energy estimates that as much as 30% of the heating or cooling energy in a conventional duct system is wasted.

Because the small-diameter refrigerant lines used in minisplit systems are insulated and don't have as much surface area as air ducts, they lose much less energy. Energy loss with minisplit refrigerant lines is as low as 1% to 5%, according to the National Association of Home Builders Research Center.

Minisplits Can Heat in Cold Temperatures

The inability of most conventional air-source heat pumps to operate efficiently in cold weather is one reason they are generally limited to moderate climates. As temperatures fall into the 40s, supplemental heating is usually needed to keep indoor-air temperatures comfortable. The supplement might take the form of electrical-resistance coils in the air handler, or a gas- or oil-fired furnace that kicks on when it's too cold for the heat pump to work.

Many minisplit models, however, continue to produce heat even when the outdoor temperature drops below zero. Mitsubishi says

its Hyper-Heat models work at 13 below zero, although at reduced efficiency (sidebar p. 484). Jim Godbot of Jim Godbot Plumbing and Heating in Biddeford, Maine, had one customer call him up on a windy, 20-below day to say how comfortable his minisplit-heated house was.

The Ductless Part Is Obvious, but What About Minisplit?

According to Fujitsu, split means that the system has indoor and outdoor components. Traditional residential and commercial central air-conditioning systems (which also are split) have capacities of 10 tons or more, which is the equivalent of 120,000 Btu per hour. Mini splits are simply smaller, with capacities of as little as 7000 Btu, Fujitsu says—hence, ductless minisplit. Mitsubishi Electric, however, doesn't like that term. "We prefer not to use the term minisplit, as it has been shown to cheapen the perceived value of our systems, instead favoring ductless systems or ductless split systems," the company said in a written statement. "We currently offer residential systems up to 4 tons [48,000 Btu] that can cover as many as eight rooms or zones from a single outdoor unit."

Continued →

How Heat Pumps Work

Heat pumps don't make heat; they move it. They can move it from outside to inside for winter heat, or from inside to outside for summer cooling. To understand how that happens, keep these four principles in mind.

1. Even when it's cold outside, there's some heat in the air. Think about it this way: 20°F might be cold, but it's warmer than minus 20°F. Until the temperature reaches absolute zero (minus 459.67°F), some heat is available.

2. Heat flows from warm to cold.

3. When the pressure of a gas increases, so does its temperature. This is why the lines to an air compressor's tank get hot. The inverse is also true: When pressure drops, so does temperature. This is why ice forms when you pop the top of a really cold beer.

4. When liquid changes to gas (boils or evaporates), it absorbs heat. When gas changes to liquid (condenses), it gives up heat.

Heat pumps are closed systems filled with refrigerant, a fluid with a boiling point that's typically around minus 40°F. In a heat pump, there is a low-pressure side where the refrigerant is cooler and a high-pressure side where the refrigerant is warmer. A compressor is used to pressurize the refrigerant, which raises its temperature. When pressurized refrigerant is allowed to expand, it cools down. The high- and low-pressure sides are joined with tubing (lines) and separated by an expansion valve that controls flow. The refrigerant runs through two separate heat exchangers: the evaporator and the condenser, which handle the low- and high-pressure sides respectively. Each heat exchanger can be either the evaporator or condenser depending on whether the system is in heating or cooling mode.

One heat exchanger is located outside, and the other is inside. (In a minisplit system, there is an interior heat exchanger at each head.)

In heating mode, the low-pressure side is outdoors. If the outside air is warmer than the low-pressure refrigerant vapor (which might be at minus 40°F), heat flows from the outside air to the refrigerant at the heat exchanger,

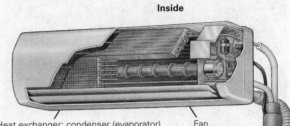

Inside

Heat exchanger: condenser (evaporator)   Fan

or evaporator. The heated refrigerant returns to the compressor, which pressurizes the vapor, warming it more. Now warmer than the air inside the house, the refrigerant flows to the indoor heat exchanger, or condenser. In the condenser, the refrigerant vapor condenses to a liquid, giving up the heat gained outside and warming the house. The cooled, now high-pressure liquid refrigerant passes through a thermal expansion valve. The valve meters the liquid refrigerant's flow, reducing its pressure on the outlet side, which causes the refrigerant to vaporize and cool inside the evaporator, where the cycle begins again. In the summer, a reversing valve inverts the process, condensers and evaporators swap roles, and heat moves from inside to out.

Condensate drain

Compressor

High-pressure liquid

Low-pressure vapor

Heat exchanger: evaporator (condenser)

Outside

Most systems use wall-mounted heads. Homeowners who object to that look can opt for flush-mount heads.

However, flush-mount heads may be harder to retrofit, and they gobble up precious insulation space in an exterior wall.

One potential disadvantage is that unlike most conventional air-source heat pumps, minisplits don't have any supplemental heating capacity. In superinsulated houses with low air leakage, this isn't a problem. In drafty, underinsulated houses in snow country, more powerful supplemental heat is needed. If the house is in an area where temperatures fall below the minisplit's capacity for extended periods, that secondary heat source would have to be able to handle the entire heating load.

Measuring Efficiency Can Be Tough

While minisplits can provide heat in very cold weather, efficiency drops as the outdoor temperature goes down. The National Renewable Energy Laboratory (NREL) says that measuring the efficiency of these systems, which it calls MSHPs (minisplit heat pumps), is challenging, in part because of their variable-speed components.

"Most public information on MSHP performance is provided by equipment manufacturers, and is typically limited to performance at a single operating speed for heating and cooling," says NREL's summary of a research paper on the topic.

NREL researchers developed testing strategies allowing them to measure the performance of two ductless-minisplit installations across a wide range of operating conditions.

"In the laboratory tests," the NREL report says, "researchers found that both MSHPs achieved manufacturer-reported performance at rating conditions. However, at other temperature

and humidity conditions, the heat pumps' capacity ranged from 40% above to 54% below the manufacturer-reported values. Knowing how performance varies is critical in order to reasonably estimate annual energy consumption of an MSHP and to compare MSHPs to other heating and cooling options. Minisplit heat-pump efficiency [measured as coefficient of performance, or COP] was seen to significantly exceed rated efficiency at low compressor speeds—a very important effect."

The tests suggest that variable-speed fans and compressors in ductless minisplits are more energy efficient than the simple on-off cycling of standard air-source heat pumps and are an important factor in minisplits' improved performance. According to NREL, "Two-stage forced-air systems must cycle on and off at loads below the low-stage cooling capacity. MSHPs can reduce the compressor speed to meet low cooling loads and have higher COPs under such conditions."

COP is an important measure of system efficiency, although not the only benchmark for heating and cooling equipment. It is the ratio of energy input to heating or cooling energy output. The higher the number, the more energy efficient the device. For example, if a minisplit consumed 1 unit of energy to put out 5 units of energy, the COP would be 5. NREL's tests found that COPs ranged from roughly 7 at an outdoor temperature of 55°F to a COP of 2 or less as outdoor temperatures fell to 5 below zero.

A useful guide to equipment efficiency is the directory of product performance available at the Air-Conditioning, Heating, and Refrigeration Institute's website (ahridirectory.org).

Continued ➔

Wall-Mounted Units Are Typical

Indoor units often are mounted on a wall close to the ceiling, and that makes them much more visible than other heat-distribution systems. For those who object to the looks, other options show only a flat grille when installed. However, cutting into the house to install them negates some of the low-installation-impact advantages that ductless minisplits advertise in the first place.

Another consideration is the exterior conduits that connect the compressor with interior air handlers. In new construction, supply lines can be buried inside walls, but the easiest way to install a system in an existing house is to run a line up the outside of the house, to bore a hole through the wall, and to attach wiring and refrigeration

lines to the indoor unit. Although manufacturers offer paintable covers that disguise the lines, they can't be hidden completely.

On the plus side, a compressor can be as much as 100 ft. away from an air handler, allowing it to be tucked on the back side of the house and mostly out of sight.

Do Minisplits Save Money? It Depends

Ductless minisplits can be a less expensive heating and cooling option than conventional HVAC equipment, especially in a high-performance house with reduced heating and cooling loads. A ductless system could be installed at a fraction of the cost of a ground-source heat pump, for example.

The National Association of Home Builders Research Center says the cost of installing a ductless minisplit has dropped as the technology has become more established. Of course, relative costs depend to a large degree on what you're comparing the minisplit to. Cost comparisons between ductless minisplits and other heating and cooling options are affected by the size and complexity of the installation, the heating and cooling loads, and whether the system is in new construction or a retrofit. With retrofits, the presence of existing ducts might make a traditional heat pump or air conditioner cheaper than a minisplit. Conversely, the cost of installing ducts in an existing house might make a minisplit system cheaper.

"The cost of ductless systems varies greatly depending on the application, size, zones covered, etc.," Mitsubishi Electric says. "While the units themselves are sometimes higher priced, the labor and installation component can be significantly less for ductless systems, and they will provide significant ongoing monthly savings."

Operating costs on the heating side can be a big advantage. In a blog post written for Green Building Advisor, engineer and energy consultant Marc Rosenbaum says that heating costs for his house on Martha's Vineyard in Massachusetts have run about $250 a year (figure from 2013)—one-quarter what it would have cost to heat with oil. Similarly, Jim Godbot says that he has installed several minisplit systems for air-conditioning in existing houses but found that the homeowners ended up using them for heat as well because they were cheaper to run than their existing gas- or oil-fired systems.

Rosenbaum also likes minisplits for three other reasons: variable-speed components that increase efficiency, the ease of zoning a house because each head's output is controlled with an individual thermostat, and the smaller drop-off in capacity at lower outdoor temperatures when compared to conventional air-source heat pumps.

He also adds a footnote to the cost discussion: The difference in cost between 2-ton and 4-ton minisplit systems is "significant," while the cost difference between an 80,000 Btu/hour furnace and a 120,000 Btu/hour furnace is not. That means money spent on insulation, good-quality windows, and air-sealing may leverage the use of a smaller, less expensive minisplit system.

Minisplits Are Plug and Play

Conventional ducted systems are prone to a variety of installation errors and oversights. As a result, forced-air systems often must be

---

Better Low-Temperature Performance

Why do most ductless minisplits operate so much more efficiently than standard air-source heat pumps at low temperatures? They use inverter technology. An inverter converts alternating current to direct current, allowing the use of variable-speed compressors and fans rather than standard heat-pump components that are either on or off. (Inverter technology is now finding its way into ducted systems.)

"By operating at higher rpm than traditional systems, our inverter-driven compressors ramp up quickly to provide instant warmth," Mitsubishi says. "Once the desired set point is reached, the system slows down to maintain the perfect temperature." A standard air-source heat pump, Mitsubishi adds, powers up more slowly, overshoots the desired temperature, and then shuts off. The building cools; then the cycle repeats, resulting in a broader temperature swing. In short, inverter technology allows the system to adjust its performance to match the demand for heating (or cooling) more closely. Additionally, variable-speed fans and compressors allow Mitsubishi's minisplits to operate at 100% capacity down to 5°F, while a standard heat pump operates at only 60% of capacity at 17°F.

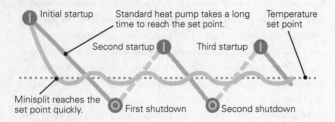

After it reaches the temperature set point, a standard air-source heat pump has to keep cycling on and off, which consumes lots of energy and results in large temperature swings.

A ductless minisplit runs continuously at variable speeds to maintain a consistent temperature, increasing comfort and decreasing energy use.

tested and adjusted, or "commissioned," after installation so that they perform as designed.

Rosenbaum says there's no need for that extra step with a ductless minisplit. "I can tell you what we haven't been doing: We haven't been commissioning our buildings with ductless minisplits," Rosenbaum writes. "If the building has a system with a lot of zones and a central controller, there may be some training from the rep, but no commissioning. These are self-contained products, so you are buying the control system with the unit. It's all packaged."

Ducting HRVs and ERVs

By Martin Holladay

Heat-recovery ventilators (HRVs) and energy-recovery ventilators (ERVs) are the most efficient devices for supplying fresh outdoor air to a house while simultaneously exhausting stale air from inside. To increase energy efficiency, both transfer some of the heat from the warmer airstream (the exhaust stream in winter, the supply stream in summer) to the cooler airstream. ERVs also transfer moisture from the more humid airstream (the exhaust stream in winter, the supply stream in summer) to the drier airstream.

Properly installed, either one does a good job. Of course, it's essential to follow the manufacturer's installation instructions, but these alone are not sufficient to ensure that your system will be energy efficient. Unfortunately, most manufacturers permit duct configurations that can lead to very high energy bills.

Fully Ducted Systems Are the Most Efficient

Of the three types of HRV/ERV installations—fully ducted systems, simplified systems, and exhaust-ducted systems—fully ducted systems are best. These systems usually pull stale air from bathrooms, laundry rooms, and kitchens. Fresh air is typically delivered to bedrooms and living rooms. With fully ducted systems, fresh air and stale air both are delivered exactly where the designer intended. These systems use less energy than systems connected to heating ductwork, and they are far easier to balance.

As with any system, duct runs should be as short and direct as possible, with a minimum of elbows or other fittings. Duct seams should be carefully sealed with mastic or HVAC tape.

Simplified Systems Are Expensive to Run

If a house already has ductwork for a heating or cooling system, it's possible to reduce HRV/ERV installation costs by installing a system without dedicated ductwork. The least expensive approach—often

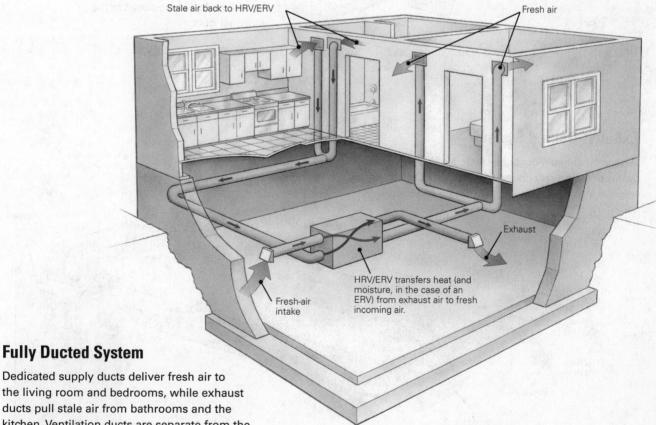

Stale air back to HRV/ERV

Fresh air

HRV/ERV transfers heat (and moisture, in the case of an ERV) from exhaust air to fresh incoming air.

Fresh-air intake

Exhaust

Fully Ducted System

Dedicated supply ducts deliver fresh air to the living room and bedrooms, while exhaust ducts pull stale air from bathrooms and the kitchen. Ventilation ducts are separate from the heating-and-cooling ducts.

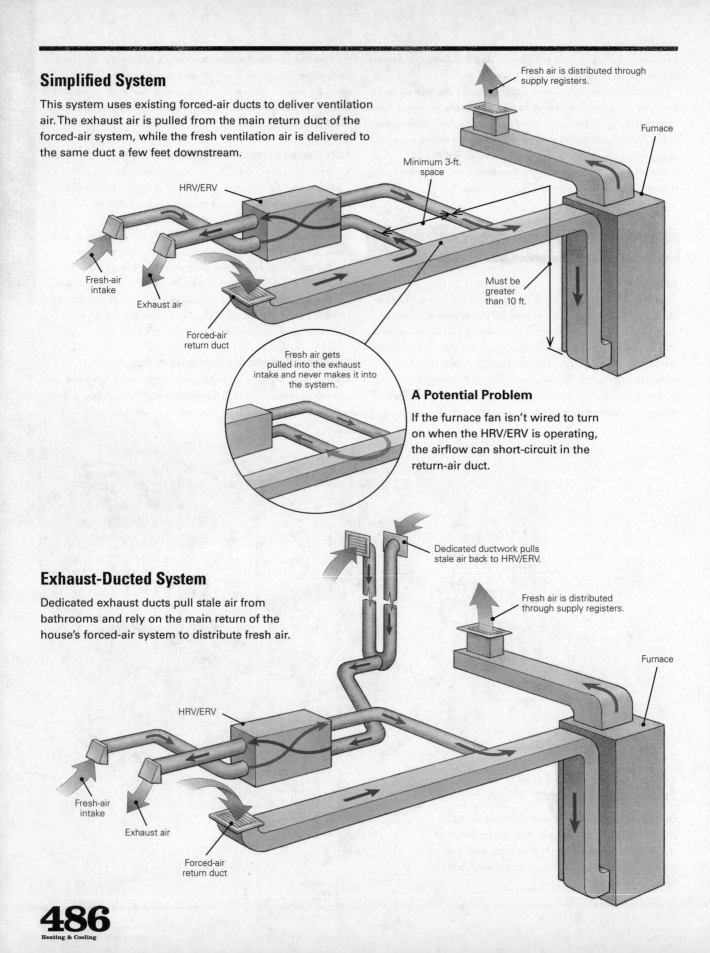

Simplified System

This system uses existing forced-air ducts to deliver ventilation air. The exhaust air is pulled from the main return duct of the forced-air system, while the fresh ventilation air is delivered to the same duct a few feet downstream.

Fresh air is distributed through supply registers.

Furnace

Minimum 3-ft. space

HRV/ERV

Must be greater than 10 ft.

Fresh-air intake

Exhaust air

Forced-air return duct

Fresh air gets pulled into the exhaust intake and never makes it into the system.

A Potential Problem

If the furnace fan isn't wired to turn on when the HRV/ERV is operating, the airflow can short-circuit in the return-air duct.

Dedicated ductwork pulls stale air back to HRV/ERV.

Exhaust-Ducted System

Dedicated exhaust ducts pull stale air from bathrooms and rely on the main return of the house's forced-air system to distribute fresh air.

Fresh air is distributed through supply registers.

Furnace

HRV/ERV

Fresh-air intake

Exhaust air

Forced-air return duct

called a simplified system—configures the HRV/ERV so that it pulls exhaust air from the main return duct of the forced-air system and dumps fresh air into the same duct a few feet downstream.

With this type of system, the point where the fresh-air duct joins with the return-air duct must be at least 10 ft. away from the furnace (measured along the return-air duct), and the exhaust-air connection must be at least 3 ft. upstream from the fresh-air connection.

A simplified system only works if there is an electrical interlock to turn on the furnace fan whenever the HRV/ERV is operating. If the ventilation fans operate without the furnace fan, fresh air is pulled backward toward the exhaust duct, which prevents any fresh air from entering the house.

The main problem with a simplified system is the huge energy penalty that comes from continuous operation of the furnace fan. Some furnace fans draw 800w, which can cost an arm and a leg if run continuously (in addition to the costs associated with the operation of the HRV/ERV). If the furnace has an energy-efficient blower with an electronically commutated motor (ECM), the energy penalty of continuous fan operation is reduced but not eliminated.

Exhaust-Ducted Systems Are Hybrids

An exhaust-ducted system straddles the fence between a fully ducted system and a simplified system. This installation has dedicated exhaust ductwork, but as with a simplified system, the HRV/ERV dumps the fresh air into the main return duct of the forced-air system.

With an exhaust-ducted system, an electrical interlock between the HRV/ERV fans and the furnace fan is an option. With an interlock, the system suffers from the same energy-penalty problem as a simplified system. If the fans aren't interlocked, the ventilation system uses less energy. When the furnace is operating, fresh ventilation air is distributed through the HVAC system's supply ducts. But when the HRV/ERV fans are operating and the furnace isn't, distribution gets quirky, and the fresh air enters the house through the HVAC system's return-air grilles. While this result is unconventional, the system still delivers fresh air throughout the house.

The exhaust- and supply-air flows of HRVs and ERVs need to be balanced after they are installed. This balancing process is known as commissioning. Exhaust-ducted systems without interlock wiring between the HRV/ERV and the furnace fan are particularly hard to balance because there are two different fan conditions: when the furnace fan is operating and when it isn't. Any attempt to balance the system with dampers will only be accurate in one of these two conditions, which is another reason why fully ducted systems make the most sense.

Upgrade to a Tankless Water Heater

By Brian Walo with Shannon Neff

As the lead electrician and plumber of a construction company, we install a number of tankless water heaters every year. We are firm believers in the energy savings of on-demand hot water, and it takes little convincing for our customers to agree to an upgrade. But it became harder for me to be in the field with Shannon installing these suitcase-size heaters while the 10-year-old tank-style heater in my garage worked hard to maintain 130°F water even when nobody was home to use it. I decided that it was time to practice what I preach, so I asked Shannon to help me install a Rinnai R75-LSi gas-fired tankless water heater (www.rinnai.us).

To get the most efficient operation, tankless heaters should be installed as close as possible to the fixtures that demand the most hot water, but this isn't always easy. Venting kits allow the units to be installed just about anywhere, but water, gas, and electricity must be routed to the desired location—easy in new construction, but a bit more work in a retrofit.

The best location often means compromising. For this installation, we were swapping out an electric heater located in my garage, and we decided to put the new water heater in the same location. I had to step down the 240v circuit to 120v, but the ¾-in.-dia. hot- and cold-water pipes were already in place, as was a discharge line for the pressure-relief valve and good access for the vent pipe. Also, because I wanted a gas-fired heater rather than one of the less efficient electric models, we needed to add a propane tank, and Shannon was able to install new gas lines easily through the wall to reach the tank outside the garage. The garage also was close to the kitchen and bath, which have the fixtures that use the most hot water.

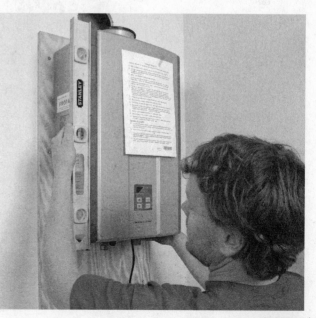

Continued →

Out with the Old

Tankless water heaters aren't much bigger than a carry-on suitcase, so they can be placed just about anywhere in a house. It's often cost-effective to use the same location as the heater you're replacing. The spot may seem remote, but most of the necessary plumbing and electrical should already be in place. The vent setup for most tank-style heaters, however, will have to be replaced with a concentric direct-vent pipe.

DRAIN IT, AND DRAG IT AWAY. After cutting the power at the electrical panel and shutting off the water flow to the old heater, attach a garden hose to the drain outlet, and empty the tank. While the tank drains, disconnect the electrical, and cut the hot and cold pipes so that the tank can be removed.

CAN'T FIND THE STUDS? If you can't find solid backing or if the installation requires a large hole to be cut into the wallboard, tie into the existing pipes in the wall cavity, then attach a piece of plywood to the finished side of the wall to cover the mess and to provide solid mounting for the heater.

CUT IT NOW; VENT IT LATER. If the heater will be installed in tight quarters, it's a good idea to cut the hole for the vent pipe before hanging the unit. Cutting the hole now allows for better access with the drywall saw and drill and prevents debris from falling into the heater's exhaust port.

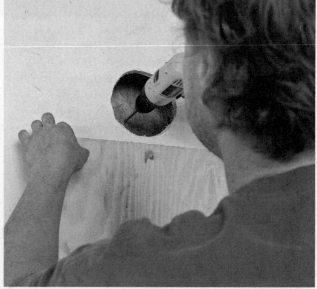

MARK THE CENTER. To make it easier to mark and cut the exterior opening later, drill through the wall sheathing at the centerpoint of the hole. Next, hang the heater from a single screw so that it can be pivoted to find plumb before sinking the rest of the screws.

Water In, Water Out

Tankless heaters need ¾-in.-dia. supply lines to feed the unit. If the water lines near the heater are only ½ in. dia., plan to install new plumbing from the nearest ¾-in. trunk line. The piping material you choose will be determined by local building codes and your personal preferences (see "Know Your Material Options," p. 492).

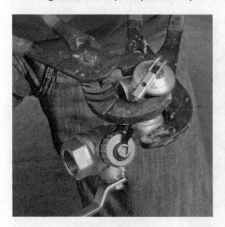

SOME (PRE)ASSEMBLY REQUIRED. Valve kits aren't complicated to install, but working in tight quarters can make some of the connections a hassle. To ensure that you have enough room to use two wrenches and lots of muscle, it's a good idea to attach the pressure-relief valve to the hot-water outlet before tying the whole thing into the couplers on the underside of the heater. Make sure to apply several wraps of Teflon tape followed by a coating of pipe dope to every joint.

SNIP AND CRIMP FOR A WATERTIGHT JOINT. With the hot and cold valves in place, thread a PEX coupling onto each valve. Cut the ¾-in. PEX tubing to length (making sure to subtract for the fittings), dry-fit all the pieces to check the fit, and fasten all the joints securely using a PEX crimper.

FLUSH THE SYSTEM. After the hot and cold connections have been made, it's a good idea to flush the lines to rid them of any harmful debris knocked loose during installation. Connect a garden hose to the cold-water cleanout first, opening the ball valve just enough to direct water into the hose but not into the heater. Next, move the hose to the hot-water cleanout, and open both the cold and hot valves to their full position.

Gas Work Demands Safety Measures

Installing gas lines isn't any more difficult than installing water lines. The stakes are a bit higher, though. It's common sense, but remember to extinguish any open flames and to refrain from smoking while working on or around gas lines. If your jurisdiction doesn't allow the unlicensed altering of gas lines or if you are at all uncomfortable with the procedure, call a licensed gas fitter/installer to handle this portion of the project.

A UNION FITTING FOR THE FUTURE. Best practices call for a ¾-in. union fitting to be installed where the gas lines enter the tankless heater. This allows the unit to be removed easily in the future if necessary. For this and all other threaded gas connections, apply a ring of pipe dope to the lead edge of all the male threads before making the connection.

DON'T DISREGARD THE DIRT LEG. Any loose debris trapped in a gas line can easily clog the small orifices in the guts of the water heater. A sediment trap, also known as a "dirt leg" or "dirt trap," is a must. Install a short leg of vertical pipe with a threaded cap just upstream of the unit to catch fragments and condensation and to provide a convenient cleanout in the event of a problem.

SOAPY-WATER LEAK DETECTION. After all the gas connections have been made, check the work for leaks. Do this by mixing up a spray bottle of soapy water, turning on the gas, and spraying the solution on each pipe connection. If you see any active bubbling, you've got a leaky joint to address.

Continued ➜

Compact Design and Clean Connections

Concentric vent pipe

Valve kits simplify the installation. It's possible to piece together the plumbing for a tankless water heater using fittings found in most hardware stores, but it's easier to buy a valve kit like the one shown below. The kit includes hot-water and cold-water shutoff valves with union fittings and cleanouts. Also, the code-required pressure-relief valve—which allows the heater to drain in case of an unexpected pressure buildup—threads right into the hot-water valve to save time.

Shutoffs are a must. Building codes require that a gas-shutoff valve be installed within 6 ft. of the heater. An old valve can be reused, but only if the new heater will use the same line as the old tank heater, and if the gas line is sized properly. If not, buy a new ball valve at any hardware store.

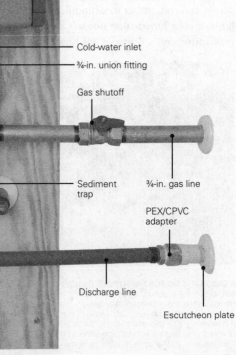

Hot-water outlet

Pressure-relief valve

Cleanout

Water shutoff

Cold-water inlet

¾-in. union fitting

Gas shutoff

Sediment trap

¾-in. gas line

PEX/CPVC adapter

Discharge line

Escutcheon plate

A single outlet provides a clean appearance, and the power cord should be coiled and stapled out of the way to prevent it from being accidentally unplugged from the wall.

Versatile Venting

Tankless heaters installed indoors can be vented up through a roof or out through an exterior wall, as shown here. The vent setup varies based on the installation location, so kits are sold separately (see "Know Your Material Options," p. 492). The required diameter and maximum length of the vent will be listed in the heater installation instructions, but keep the run as direct as possible. The more elbows required, the shorter the allowable length of the vent pipe.

SCRIBE A CIRCLE. Using the pilot hole from the interior as a centerpoint for a compass, draw a circle about ½ in. larger than the outside diameter of the pipe, and cut out the sheathing with a spiral-cutting saw or 5-in. hole saw.

SLOPE IT FOR DRAINAGE. To avoid the need for a condensation trap, horizontal vent piping can be pitched slightly toward the exterior (¼ in. per ft.). This allows any condensation from the exhaust gas to drip to the exterior. Use a torpedo level to check the pitch before fastening the pipe to the heater and to the wall.

BETTER LOOK, BETTER SEAL. After enlarging the hole in the first part of a vinyl mounting plate (see "Know Your Material Options," p. 492), peel back the siding and lap it under the housewrap or tar paper. Seal the area around the pipe with low-expansion foam, fill in the siding, and then slide the second part of the mounting plate into place, as shown above.

Minor Electrical Adaptations

Gas-fired tankless heaters consume little electricity, so adding a dedicated circuit isn't necessary. If you're replacing a tank-style heater and want to use the same wiring, though, you need to make some changes in the electrical panel. Before removing the panel cover, turn off the main breaker to de-energize everything below the switch. The cables and lugs above the main breaker will still be live, so work carefully.

BREAKER SWAP. Pull out the two-pole (240v) breaker that fed the old water heater, and remove the black and white wires. Attach the black wire to the new single-pole (120v) breaker and slide the assembly into the panel. The remaining white wire will be a neutral in the new setup; tie it to the neutral bus bar where the other white wires are connected.

COVER AND LABEL. With the new breaker in place, replace the panel cover, and snap in a plastic knockout to cover the remaining hole. Finish the job by relabeling the breaker on the door of the breaker panel.

Take the Temperature

Once all the water, gas, and vent connections are made and the unit is plugged in, use a digital thermometer to verify that the temperature on the heater's control panel matches the hot water at the faucet or other intended fixture. If the heater will be servicing the whole house, check several locations.

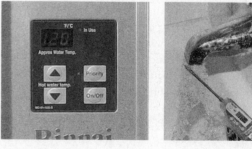

Continued ➜

Know Your Material Options

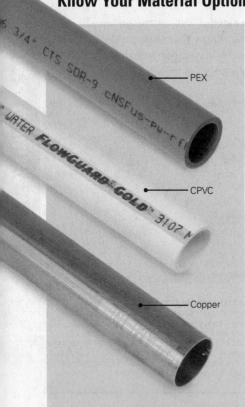

PEX

CPVC

Copper

Water Connections

Copper and CPVC pipes are common choices for the inlet and outlet water connections on a tankless water heater. Copper is durable but costs more and is more labor intensive to install. CPVC is less expensive and easier to install, but it isn't a great choice for a location where it might get knocked around. Although the easiest option is simply to tie into the existing plumbing using the same type of pipe, we prefer to use PEX tubing whenever possible. A wide selection of adapters makes PEX easy to attach to copper or CPVC, and the tubing can be snaked through joist and stud bays, making it a good choice if you need to tap into a trunk line buried in the wall, floor, or ceiling.

Gas Connections

Black steel piping is the traditional choice for routing natural gas or propane, though galvanized steel (used on this project) is also common in some areas. If it's allowed in your area, flexible corrugated stainless-steel tubing (CSST) is much faster and easier to route in remodeling projects, but it's more expensive. Hard pipe is also preferable in areas where the gas lines are likely to be banged up by boxes or grabbed by children playing hide-and-seek in the utility closet.

Black

Galvanized

Corrugated stainless-steel tubing (CSST)

Vent Connections

Some tankless heaters use separate intake and exhaust pipes, but according to Rinnai, a concentric pipe setup is not only simpler to install but is also safer. If the exhaust pipe in a two-pipe system were to leak, the harmful flue gases would be vented indoors. With a concentric-pipe setup, combustion air is drawn in through the outer pipe, and flue gases are expelled through the inner pipe, offering an additional layer of protection from potential exhaust leaks. Concentric "starter kits" typically include an appliance adapter, an exterior hood, and a 90° elbow with a couple of feet of pipe. Additional elbows and lengths of pipe are sold separately and can be added to the starter kit as needed.

Concentric pipe

Flange Upgrade

Some vent kits have a rubber flange that slides over the exterior vent pipe and gets caulked to the siding—not very reliable or attractive. Dress it up by enlarging the hole in a common two-piece vinyl-siding mounting plate.

Contents

Kitchens & Baths

Surgical Kitchen Remodel

By David Getts

The key to a successful small remodeling project is to make the new work match the existing details so that no one can tell that the space was ever modified. On this job, upgrading the double ovens in an existing kitchen meant that I had to create a little more room in a run of the 20-year-old cabinets for a new, larger oven cabinet, and then make everything look as though it had been built that way. The job was complicated because I had to modify the granite counter and base cabinet in place. It was more like kitchen surgery than remodeling.

My plan was to remove the ovens and the oven cabinet, as well as the upper cabinet to the right and the drawers below it, then to resize the upper cabinet and cut 3 in. from the counter and face frame below. If I worked carefully, the new oven cabinet would fit like a glove in the newly expanded space.

Ovens Out, Electrical In

First, I protected the area by taping down Ram Board on the floor, setting up Zip-Wall barriers in doorways, and taping 4-mil plastic over all the cabinets. I also checked the electrical requirements before the work began. Two new circuits were needed, and fortunately, there was a subpanel in the kitchen area

that I could easily tap into. This made it a one-day rough-in for the electrician. If we had needed to run the circuit from the main house panel, I would have had the electrician run it into the attic space above the kitchen before the demolition began to minimize any disruption to the homeowner.

Next, I removed the existing ovens and cut apart the cabinet to make them easier to pull out. After the electrician roughed in the new outlets, I patched and primed the drywall behind the cabinets.

Cutting a Granite Counter in Place

If the countertop had been short, I would have pulled it out and had it cut off site. Because the countertop extended around a corner, though, I thought that removing it was too risky. If the counter broke, it would be impossible to find a slab that matched.

I hired a granite fabricator, who arrived with an angle grinder fitted with a diamond blade. I thought he would use a saw and straight-edge guide, but he was more comfortable cutting the joint by hand. He drew his mark on a strip of painters' tape and carefully cut along the line. Another method would have been to use a small circular saw and an edge guide, but the final couple of inches would still have had to be cut with an angle grinder or a similar tool.

Reducing the Cabinets' Width

Of the two cabinets to be modified and reused, the upper was easier. I unscrewed it from the wall and took it back to my shop,

Continued →

Before

After

Remodeling by the Inch

The existing ovens were tired and ready to go. The problem was that they were an odd size, 27 in. wide, while most new ovens are 30 in. wide. Rather than struggle to find the same size, my client, Ginger, decided that she wanted the larger oven, which meant enlarging the space by 3 in. for the appliance cabinet. This cabinet occupied the center of one wall in her fairly small kitchen. To preserve working counter space, it made the most sense to expand the cabinet space in one direction toward the inside corner rather than toward the cooktop. The move in that direction also would help to minimize any visual impact of the remodel.

where I used a tablesaw, a small circular saw, and a straightedge to cut it down. Because the base cabinet was supporting the countertop, I left it in place and did the modification on site.

The most important aspect of field surgery is getting good, clean cuts so that the new work fits tight in the space. After applying painters' tape to minimize the tearout, I drew the layout in permanent marker.

I also consulted with the finisher before I started doing any modifications. On his advice, I avoided sanding, which meant that I had to be careful to align the new faces as flush as possible. Fortunately, all of the joints either were on the hinge side of the doors or were concealed behind the drawer faces, so any minor discrepancies were not noticeable.

Before any site work began, I built the oven cabinet so that it would be ready to install as soon as we needed it. One thing to keep in mind when building cabinetry for appliances is to follow the manufacturer's requirements, both for safety and for the warranty. The Miele appliances I installed here had specific venting requirements that led me to build the cabinet without a back and with open airflow throughout the height of the box.

After cutting down the upper cabinet, I attached a new side panel with biscuits and screws. I also reduced the width of the four drawers, making sure that the reassembled part of each drawer was on the side that was obscured when it was opened. The hardest, most labor-intensive part of the job was making the new oven-cabinet doors and a resized door for the adjacent cabinet. I built the cherry doors with a cope-and-stick frame and raised panel that had an uncommon radiused profile.

Reassembly on Site

Back from the shop, I prepped the flanking cabinets first. On the drawer bank, I added a new side. Above, I reinstalled the upper cabinet and cut slots in both upper and lower box edges for the biscuits that would attach the face-frame stiles. After rebuilding the oven-cabinet base, I pushed the big new cabinet into place, screwed it to the adjacent upper and base cabinets, and then biscuited the face-frame stiles into position.

After the drawer fronts and doors were installed, finisher Rick Fleming formulated a two-step stain process to match the existing finish. The first coat was a water-based aniline dye, followed by an oil stain and a clear topcoat, all of which he applied on site.

Cautious Demolition

REMOVE IN PIECES To avoid harming the neighboring cabinets, the author took apart the oven cabinet with reciprocating and circular saws.

THE EASY UPPER Because it didn't support the counter, the adjacent upper cabinet was simply unscrewed and brought back to the shop for resizing.

BACKSPLASH SURGERY A multitool was the first choice to remove backsplash tile in the footprint of the new cabinet. It was much easier to remove full courses of tile and then replace the missing partials after the new cabinet was installed.

NO MISTAKES HERE The counter was cut carefully with an angle grinder fitted with a diamond blade. The nozzle of the job-site vacuum was positioned at the blade to capture as much dust as possible. The crew also wore dust masks and protective eyewear.

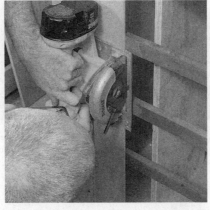

FOLLOW THE GUIDE To trim the lower cabinet's face frame, the author screwed a straightedge to the face-frame stile, then made the cuts with a small circular saw fitted with a 40-tooth carbide blade to minimize tearout. A multitool took care of the hard-to-get areas.

REPEAT AS NECESSARY After the face frame had been trimmed, the author used the same technique to trim the cabinet side and back.

Continued ➜

Back at the Shop

SLOWER FOR SAFETY'S SAKE Both the upper cabinet and drawers were cut down with the same techniques. After placing the drawer on its bottom and ripping it on a tablesaw, the author used a straightedge guide and a cordless circular saw to cut the narrower ends.

JOINERY OF CONVENIENCE Rather than try to reproduce the drawers' dovetail joinery, the author trimmed the drawer side and used tapered wooden dowels to join the butt joints.

HERE, THE INTERIOR MATTERS MOST The new oak plywood side joined to the newly resized upper cabinet had to be finished only on the inside; the exterior is concealed by the adjacent oven cabinet.

On-Site Installation

PREP THE OVEN BASE The new ovens needed a sturdy, level base, so the author reinforced the existing base with layers of plywood screwed and glued together and shimmed level.

ATTACH THE LOWER SIDE PANEL Because both faces of the new side would be concealed, the author mounted unfinished AC plywood to the cabinet with pocket screws.

BISCUITS INSTEAD OF NAILS The cleanest, fastest way to attach the new face-frame stile was to use biscuits and glue. The author cut slots in place, then transferred their positions to the stile.

WORKING SOLO EFFICIENTLY The rebuilt upper cabinet was installed with the aid of a cabinet jack, which held it in place until the mounting screws were driven.

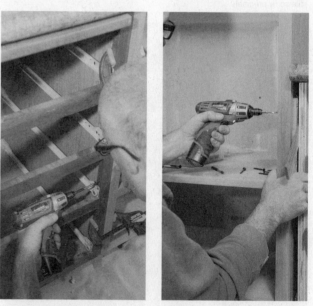

NOT MUCH WIGGLE ROOM With the oven cabinet in place, the author screwed it to the left-hand base cabinet. After adding plywood blocking, the oven cabinet was fastened to the right-hand base cabinet.

Continued ➜

THE EXACT WIDTH It was easier to fit the new right-hand stiles with the oven cabinet in place. The width of the stile was established by the distance between the oven cabinet and the drawer base rails. The author planed the stile to fit precisely.

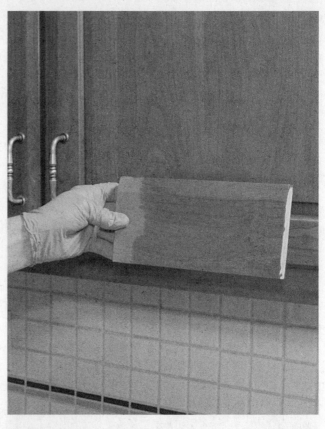

YOU HAVE TO BE THERE. Because a room's mix of natural and artificial light is unique, the finisher's best bet is to try various shades on site. Here, a water-based dye was followed by an oil-based stain and a clear coat of polyurethane.

MATCHING IS PARAMOUNT Like everything else on this job, the crown-molding profile was not stock, so the author had to re-create a section of the crown to blend in with the old.

Opening Up a Kitchen

By Reid Highley and Jim Compton

Hurried lifestyles have made it necessary for the functions of the kitchen and the main living areas of a house to overlap. In addition to cooking, kitchens have become places for dining, entertaining, working, paying bills, and studying. The ascendancy of the kitchen is a relatively recent development, however, and homes only a few decades old are likely to have cramped kitchens with little connection to the rest of the house.

Fortunately, many of these dated kitchens can be improved with relative ease. The kitchen pictured here is typical of what you might find in an original suburban home built in the 1970s. The sketches that follow illustrate three strategies for reconfiguring this kitchen to make it an open, multifunctional space. While your project won't have this exact layout, the three approaches illustrated here are easily modified, and they offer valuable insight into the potential that lies within remodels of various costs and levels of complexity.

Cost and Complexity: Low

The existing kitchen is kept intact, but a more open feel is achieved by removing the ceiling-hung cabinetry. This makes the room feel larger and facilitates interaction between the cook and those in the eating area. The storage capacity lost by eliminating the cabinets is offset with a built-in buffet that has a pass-through window to the dining room. The top of the buffet has glass doors on both sides to share light with the dining room. To unify the kitchen, new hardwood flooring is installed throughout the room. The existing cased opening is replaced by a 5-ft.-wide pair of glazed French doors to create a better connection to the living room.

Original plan

Dining

Living

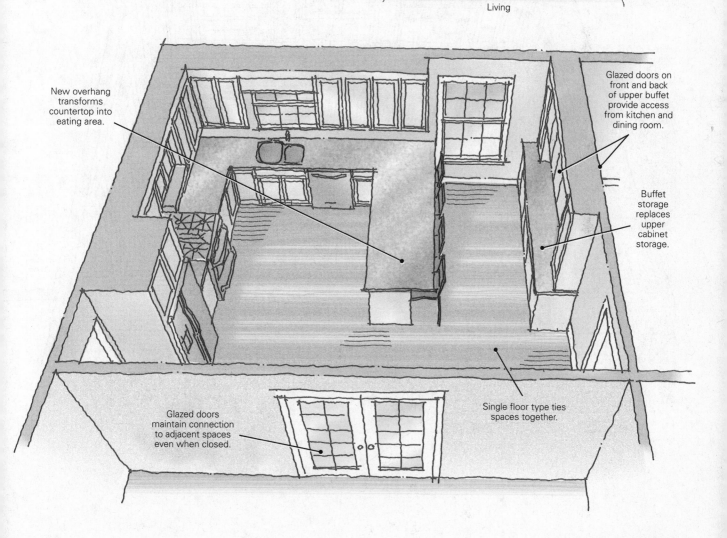

New overhang transforms countertop into eating area.

Glazed doors on front and back of upper buffet provide access from kitchen and dining room.

Buffet storage replaces upper cabinet storage.

Glazed doors maintain connection to adjacent spaces even when closed.

Single floor type ties spaces together.

Continued ➡

Cost and Complexity: Moderate

The breakfast area is annexed into the kitchen by removing the peninsula and ceiling cabinets. The cabinetry at the sink wall is extended, significantly increasing storage capacity. The range is moved to the middle of that wall, creating a long run of valuable counter space, and a large island provides eat-in functionality. To enhance the connection to the living room, a large opening that matches the width of the island is created. This opening is treated as a transition zone between the rooms and is enhanced with open shelving, which is handy for stashing cookbooks or displaying fine china. Though the flooring surface is hardwood in both the kitchen and the living room, a wide, flush wood threshold between the rooms provides a delineation of spaces. A wide opening with pocket doors is centered on the short side of the island to make an elegant connection to the formal dining room.

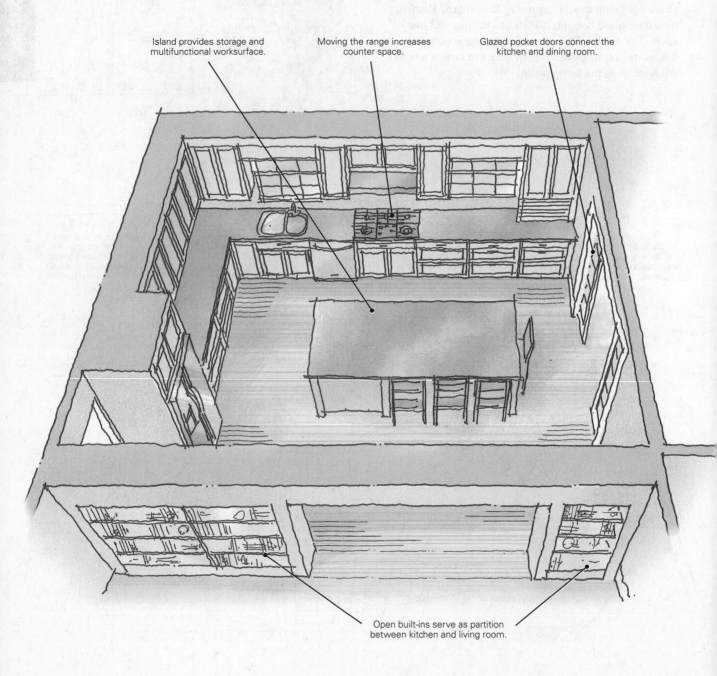

Island provides storage and multifunctional worksurface.

Moving the range increases counter space.

Glazed pocket doors connect the kitchen and dining room.

Open built-ins serve as partition between kitchen and living room.

Cost and Complexity: High

A flush header installed in the ceiling creates a continuous plane between the kitchen and the living room and allows removal of the wall that separates the spaces. This plan demands visual organization, so the cabinetry is laid out in an elongated U that wraps three sides of the room. The cabinetry cradles a large island with a sink at its center. The island acts as a visual marker of the transition from the living area to the kitchen. Large pendants suspended over the island will help to reinforce this transition. A cooktop with a decorative tile backsplash is aligned with the sink and becomes the kitchen's focal point. Tall cabinets for the wall ovens and the refrigerator bookend the cabinetry and countertops. New hardwood flooring helps tie the kitchen and the living room together.

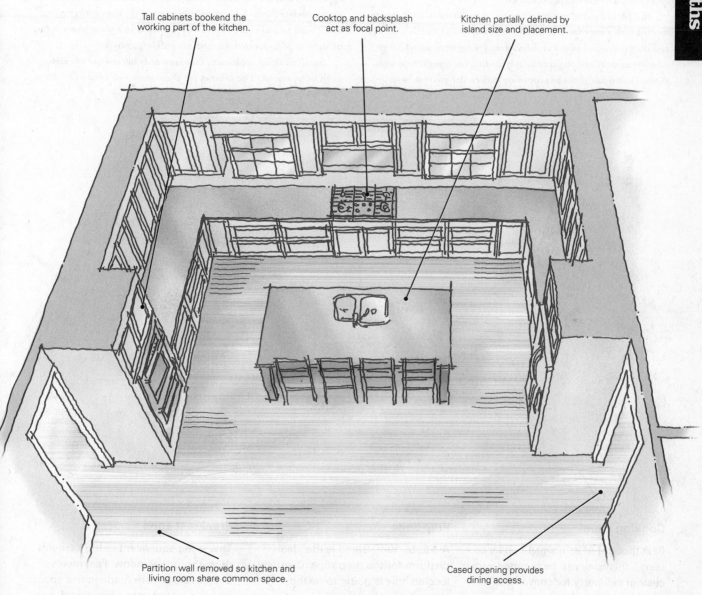

Tall cabinets bookend the working part of the kitchen.

Cooktop and backsplash act as focal point.

Kitchen partially defined by island size and placement.

Partition wall removed so kitchen and living room share common space.

Cased opening provides dining access.

Continued ➜

Zones for Small Appliances

By Bud Dietrich

At some point, most of us have been told that to design a kitchen well, we must get the work triangle correct. For me, however, the triangle concept—which is driven largely by the arrangement of the kitchen's major appliances—is a bit antiquated. Sure, it was appropriate for the days when kitchens had to satisfy only three jobs—storage, cooking, and cleanup—but those simple days and those simple kitchens are behind us.

In addition to the major appliances, many modern kitchens are stocked with a handful of small appliances that serve a variety of very specific purposes. Instead of shoehorning these items into kitchen cabinets as an afterthought or simply loading the countertops with them, I anticipate them by proposing kitchen designs that have established zones for small-appliance storage and room for their associated tasks. Here are three such zones to consider for your kitchen design.

The Cooking Zone

From the rice cooker to the waffle maker to the slow cooker, you should be able to access all of your small cooking appliances easily, use them as needed, clean them up, and store them with the least amount of effort possible. Because this category of appliances can be sizable in many homes, it's important to consider the appliances that are used most frequently and to design this zone to accommodate them. For example, if you use the slow cooker a lot, you'll want to make sure that this appliance is in a place where it can be slid out of its cabinet, turned on, and left to cook.

Small cooking appliances that have only occasional use also need to be stored. The cabinet for them does not need to be deep;

Cooking zone

Best thought of as a small-appliance corral, this zone can be outfitted with custom cabinetry for convenient access and storage of your most regularly used items.

Prep zone

A 4-ft. by 10-ft. island is the ideal platform for the prep zone. Centrally located, this is going to be the kitchen's workhorse in terms of meal prep and entertaining.

Breakfast zone

This is the equivalent of the kitchen's drive-through window. Fast meals and beverages are made in this space, which is intended to serve families on the go.

The Cooking Zone

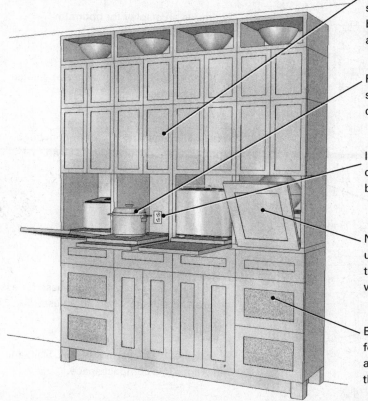

The cabinet space above the docking stations is deep enough for storing large bowls, platters, and infrequently used appliances.

Place the appliance on a slide-out surface so that lifting the top and stirring can be done easily.

Install an electrical outlet in each of these docking stations so that the appliance can be plugged in easily.

No matter the particular style of cabinetry, use doors on the docking stations so that the appliances can be kept out of sight when not in use.

Base cabinets can be outfitted with drawers for holding containers of flour, rice, beans, and other dry foodstuffs that are used in these types of appliances.

The Prep Zone

Food processors and mixers can be located on swinging shelves for easy access. Cabinets should have electrical outlets so that appliances can remain plugged in.

A small sink makes prep and cleanup easier and faster.

Refrigerator drawers in the prep zone provide ultimate convenience, particularly if the main refrigerator is more than a couple of steps away.

A trash and recycling cabinet is ideally suited to this zone because most waste is produced here.

Storage for cookbooks and a tablet keeps recipes close at hand.

Continued →

The Breakfast Zone

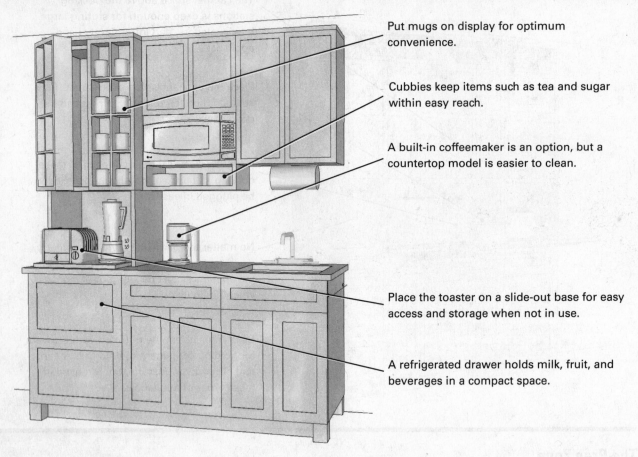

Put mugs on display for optimum convenience.

Cubbies keep items such as tea and sugar within easy reach.

A built-in coffeemaker is an option, but a countertop model is easier to clean.

Place the toaster on a slide-out base for easy access and storage when not in use.

A refrigerated drawer holds milk, fruit, and beverages in a compact space.

16 in. to 18 in. should be plenty. It doesn't have to be too large, either. A unit of about 6 lin. ft. should accommodate docking stations for three or four appliances.

The Prep Zone

From the food processor to the mixer, many of us slice, dice, mix, and blend routinely. You can stow all of these appliances in deep base cabinets and lug them out when you need them, or you can allow them and their snaking cords to clutter your countertops; you don't have to, though. Instead, integrate a prep zone close to the refrigerator and the cooking area.

Locating this zone at an island and between the refrigerator and prime cooking area is ideal. The chef then will be able to pivot between tasks and have everything within arm's reach. This means placing these small appliances in the base cabinets that make up the island. The island should be a good size if you wish to accommodate entertaining and food prep at the same time.

The Breakfast Zone

The days of the big breakfast are long gone. With everyone's hectic work and school schedules, it's a wonder we have time to make a morning meal at all. Dedicating an area to preparing grab-and-go cups of coffee, bowls of cereal, or toast can make a kitchen work more efficiently. A zone like this needs roughly 6 ft. of base cabinets and countertops, with corresponding upper cabinets. This run of cabinets will accommodate a 24-in.-wide undercounter refrigerator as well as a small sink. There should be a deep upper cabinet—say 16 in.—at one end of this area for housing the toaster and a blender or juicer.

This area can be tailored to serve as a beverage zone as well, enabling you to make smoothies in the morning and margaritas in the evening without disrupting the chef in the center of the kitchen.

Refinish Your Cabinets

By Philip Hansell

Refinishing kitchen cabinets is a difficult and labor-intensive painting project, but the payoff can be huge. For a fraction of the cost of new cabinets, refinishing can transform a well-worn kitchen into one that looks and feels new.

As with most painting projects, the secret to a high-quality finish on kitchen cabinets is proper preparation and the right tools and materials for the job. Here, I describe how my painting company goes about refinishing cabinets in a typical kitchen. The project shown is a high-end kitchen remodel in a handsome brick house in one of the nicest neighborhoods of Durham, N.C.

The kitchen design called for new tilework, lighting, and appliances. While the built-in appliances required new cabinets, the existing cabinets were in good shape, so the homeowners decided to save thousands of dollars by refinishing their existing kitchen cabinets.

Spraying Works Best

Unless the client's budget is supertight, we generally paint kitchen cabinets with an airless sprayer. Spraying costs more than brushing because of the additional masking and setup, but a high-quality sprayer in the hands of an experienced painter produces a flawless,

glass-smooth finish that's as good as or better than the factory finish on most mass-produced cabinets.

My company paints so many cabinets every year that we installed a spray booth in our shop. It's the same type of enclosure you'd find in an auto-body shop. Before we bought the booth, we made spray enclosures by hanging drop cloths or tarps from our shop ceiling. Tarp enclosures work fine, particularly if you'll be doing this only once, but the booth—with its bright lights and filtered air—provides a better finish in less time.

You can spray cabinets on site, too. In fact, we almost always spray cabinet boxes on the job because it's too time-consuming and expensive to remove them. Unfortunately, on most job sites it's tough to find a space large and clean enough to spray the many doors and drawers found in a typical high-end kitchen, which is why we do those in our shop.

Getting Started

The first step is protecting the countertops and floor with heavy kraft paper. If the kitchen has hardwood flooring that won't be refinished at the end of the project, we put down a thicker product called Floor-Shell (trimaco.com). We tape the paper or FloorShell around the perimeter and at seams to prevent the high-pressure sprayer from lifting it during spraying. We also cover appliances, light fixtures, backsplashes, and adjacent walls with ClingCover plastic drop cloths (trimaco.com) taped in place.

Continued ➜

Refrigerators need fresh air for operation, so we leave the plastic sheeting off the intake grilles until we're ready to spray. When it's time to spray, we turn off the refrigerator and cover the grille until we're done for the day. We always tell the homeowners about this ahead of time so that they can consume or move anything that's particularly perishable.

Remove Drawers and Doors

Once the space is protected, we remove the cabinet drawers and doors. Because cabinet doors have hinges adjusted for the individual cabinet box, we carefully label the doors, hinges, and cabinets so that everything can be returned to its original location when the job is done. This saves us from having to readjust the hinges. We do the labeling in an inconspicuous spot and cover the identifying marks with tape so that they won't be obscured with paint when the part or cabinet is sprayed.

We remove pulls and knobs before stacking the doors and drawers in our trucks. With the drawers and doors removed, we mask the drawer slides and accessory hardware, but we don't mask shelf standards because they look better when they're painted to match the cabinet color.

Surface Prep

After everything in the kitchen is masked, we fix any dents or scratches and sand the cabinet boxes with 320-grit paper. Afterward, we dust off the boxes with an old paintbrush and a shop vacuum equipped with a bristle-type nozzle. After vacuuming, we wipe everything down with a damp rag and then a tack cloth.

Previously stained cabinets are fully sanded with 150-grit paper and then wiped down with lacquer thinner before we spray on an oil-based primer such as Easy Sand from Sherwin-Williams.

Oil Works Best

We use oil products on most of our kitchen-cabinet jobs. Oil-based paint bonds and covers better than water-based products, and it sands more easily. In addition, oil paint and primer dry more slowly than latex, so any overspray has a chance to blend in with the coating that has been sprayed on top of it. Waiting too long to cover the overspray, though, will make the surface appear rough. To minimize the rough surface caused by overspray, we spray upper cabinets first and then the lower cabinets below, and we consistently work from one end of a cabinet run to the other.

The Right Gear

For finishing the cabinets, we use a Graco 395 or 695 sprayer with a 310 fine-finish tip, which has a 6-in. spray pattern. Thinning the paint or primer is not required unless the product is especially cold, which makes the solvents more viscous. It's better to let the paint or primer warm to room temperature, however, because thinned coatings don't cover surfaces as well.

We spray primer on the inside of the cabinet box first, and then we prime the exterior. When the cabinet backs are exposed, such

as on an island or a peninsula, we spray all the individual cabinet backs at the same time. Once the cabinets are fully primed and dry, we sand everything again with 320-grit paper before spraying on the topcoat.

The Right Paint

Our favorite paint for cabinets is ProClassic oil-based paint from Sherwin-Williams. We apply it in the same order as the primer. The secret for spraying is to apply the paint in multiple thin layers to prevent drips and sags, which have to be sanded out.

It's also important that the paint be fully atomized for even coverage. If you see that the spray pattern is formed by dots larger than $1/32$ in., or if there are discernible lines at the top and bottom of the spray pattern (called fingering), the paint is too thick, or you need more pressure.

Label Everything

To make reinstalling the doors and drawers easier with a minimum of hinge adjustments, the crew carefully labels and bundles the hinges and marks their locations. A piece of tape covers each mark so that it won't be painted over. The marks are located so that they'll be hidden when the kitchen is put back together.

DOORS. Cabinet doors are marked behind a cup hinge. The mark indicates which cabinet box the door came from.

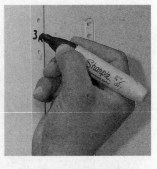

BOXES. Cabinet boxes are marked behind a hinge mount. The void in the finish will be hidden by the hinge.

HINGES. Individually labeled hinges are grouped by cabinet door and taped together. Bundles are labeled, too.

DRAWERS. Pullout shelves and drawers are labeled on the back side of the back panel to keep the marks hidden.

Sand and Clean

Once the floor is covered with kraft paper and adjacent surfaces and hardware are masked, any damage is filled with auto-body filler, sanded with 150-grit paper, and then spot-primed with sprayed oil primer. Finally, all previously painted surfaces are sanded with 320-grit paper.

SAND ALL SURFACES. Using 320-grit paper at the end creates a smooth surface for priming and painting. Changing sandpaper frequently yields quicker results.

CLEAN UP. Once everything is sanded, the kitchen is given a thorough cleaning, first with a shop vacuum and then with a damp rag. Just before spraying, cabinet surfaces are wiped with a tack cloth. All masking materials must be secured fully to prevent them from lifting during spraying.

Prime and Paint

Both old and new cabinet boxes are coated first with an oil-based primer. The author and his crew start with a bank of upper cabinets, then spray the lower cabinets below. They work in the same direction for both upper and lower cabinets. Painting and priming in this order ensures that any overspray is covered with wet finish before the overspray dries. Dried overspray leaves a rough surface.

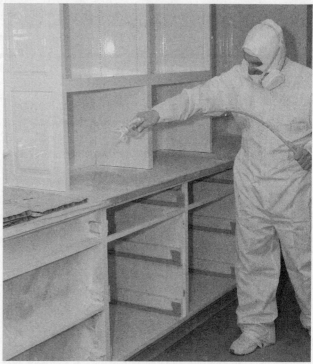

A COAT OF PRIMER. Both old and new cabinet boxes are sprayed with oil-based primer. The author prefers a Graco 395 or 695 sprayer with a 310 fine-finish tip, which has a 6-in. spray pattern. Insides are sprayed first, starting with the top, then the sides, bottom, and back. On the cabinet exterior, the crew starts with the sides and then sprays the front. When cabinet backs are exposed (on islands and peninsulas), all backs are sprayed at the same time by working from one end to the other, like a typewriter.

Continued ➔

Take Doors to the Spray Booth

Few residential construction sites have a space large and clean enough to prep and spray dozens of drawers and cabinet doors. The author takes these items to his spacious shop, where they can be prepped and then sprayed in his automotive-style spray booth.

PATCH, SAND, PRIME. Gouges are filled with body filler, sanded with 150-grit paper, and spot-primed. The whole surface is sanded with 320-grit paper before painting and priming.

FRONT, BACK, BACK, FRONT. Fronts are sprayed first, followed by two coats on the back. Finally, a second coat goes on the front, minimizing handling damage to the most visible side.

Finishing Touches

The last part of the job is to reinstall the door and drawer pulls. When the job calls for new hardware, the author fills the old holes, but it's the general contractor's job to drill new holes and install the new hardware. New drawer and door bumpers also are installed at this time: plastic bumpers for oil paint, felt bumpers for latex paint.

Don't use a spray tip that is overly worn, and don't spray at too high a pressure. Both of these situations result in excess overspray, which wastes paint and results in a smaller spray pattern prone to drips. It's also important to hold the spray nozzle parallel to the cabinet and to start moving before pulling the trigger.

When we're done spraying, we check our work with a bright light. We make any needed touch-ups and then let the paint dry for at least 48 hours.

Reassembly

Leaving the floor and countertop protection in place, we remove the masking inside the cabinet boxes and reinstall the doors and drawers. Then we remove the rest of the masking by working from the top down so that any falling paint flakes won't stick to the freshly painted surface.

The final step is to reinstall the pulls. We also install new bumpers on the drawers and doors at this time. I like clear plastic bumpers, which are durable and soften the impact of a slamming cabinet door. Because fresh latex paint sticks to plastic bumpers, we use felt bumpers with latex paint.

4 Quick Cabinet Upgrades

By Gary Striegler

Kitchen remodels are a priority for many of my clients, but some budgets won't allow me to gut the kitchen and install all new cabinets, fixtures, and appliances. So I've developed methods to give clients improved function and a style upgrade without breaking the bank. The concept is simple: Give the existing cabinets an overhaul. By adding new doors and drawers, upgrading storage, dressing things up with trim, and then applying a glazed paint job, I tie the new components in with the old ones for a seamless face-lift. Upgrading these cabinets took me six days and cost about $600 in materials. The backsplash cost about $225 and took another day to install. I hired out the granite countertop and the painting, which cost $1400 and $1000, respectively (figures from 2010).

There are a couple of prerequisites. First, the cabinet boxes need to be in sound condition. Adding new doors and drawers to poorly constructed boxes makes about as much sense as building a new house on a crumbling foundation. Second, the existing materials and style of construction are a big factor. The kitchen shown here had site-built face-frame cabinets made with a combination of solid wood and plywood, common in older houses. If the cabinets had been made from particleboard or didn't have face frames, the process would have been more complicated, and the return on investment less promising.

Improve storage and style for a fraction of the cost of new cabinets

Before

Continued ➔

1. Solid Doors Become Framed Panels

On this project, the existing cabinet doors were made from ¾-in. mahogany plywood. The plywood was in decent condition, so I wanted to find a way to reuse it. Most flat-panel cabinet doors tend to be made with ¼-in.- to ½-in.-thick plywood panels, which are lightweight and inexpensive but also feel cheap in terms of quality. I decided to use the old doors as panels, setting each in a new frame to create a more substantial cabinet door. If I hadn't been able to use the doors for the new panels, I would likely have chosen MDF, which is extremely stable and takes paint well.

For the door-frame stock, I chose poplar, a relatively inexpensive closed-grain hardwood that looks excellent in paint-grade cabinetry. Other hardwoods like maple and oak are good choices for stain-grade door frames as well. In terms of cost and durability, though, poplar can't be beat. The door construction is simple. It's crucial, however, that all of the wood be milled, that the rabbets be cut, and that beaded profiles be routed before the stock is cut to final size, or the cuts may not match up properly.

1. After the door-frame stock is cut to width and rabbeted to receive the panel, rout the other edge with a ⅜-in. beading bit.

2. A pair of pocket screws (Kreg micro jig) at each miter creates a tight joint. The holes then are plugged and sanded flush.

3. A hinge-boring jig makes quick work of preparing each door to receive the new concealed hinges.

4. Cut the old doors down to the appropriate size to become panels, and cut a matching rabbet around each so that it will sit about ¼ in. below the front face of the frame.

5. The panel molding, which also gets a shallow rabbet before assembly, is used to secure the panel in place and hide the joint.

2. New Drawers in an Hour

The existing drawers in this kitchen were made from 1x pine and assembled with glued rabbet joints reinforced with nails. Decades of use had loosened the drawer boxes and left the aluminum drawer slides sticky or falling apart.

This kitchen (and its budget) didn't warrant a high-end drawer with dovetail joints and hidden self-closing drawer slides. Instead, I built the drawers in this project from birch plywood. They are just as strong as the boxes found in high-end kitchen cabinets, and each takes me less than an hour to complete.

The construction of each drawer—butt joints, pocket screws, and a bottom panel captured in a dado—is simple. Installation is a bit more complicated, however, because site-built cabinets don't typically have back panels, so a plywood backer is needed for solid attachment of the drawer slides.

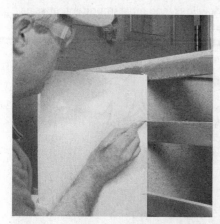

1. After cutting a backerboard equal to the interior width of each cabinet, use the face frame as a template to mark the drawer-slide mounts before nailing the panel into place at the back of each cabinet.

2. Attach the brackets and drawer slides to a plywood cleat, and install each preassembled unit as one piece.

3. Slide the drawer box into place, and use a straightedge to adjust the slides until the drawer box is flush with the face frame. Then drive the screws to secure the assembly.

4. Using a spacer jig to establish a consistent height above the cabinet doors, secure each drawer front from the inside of the drawer box with screws.

Doors and larger drawer fronts are routed with the bead profile before the stock is cut to length and assembled. Smaller drawer fronts can be made from solid poplar dressed up with a mitered bead detail installed separately using glue and pin nails.

Base cabinets with doors don't offer much accessibility. Either build a pullout shelf, or divide up the space with drawers by adding new rails with pocket screws.

Continued ➡

3. Fixed Shelves Become Adjustable

Site-built cabinets typically have shelves set into dadoes, so they can't be moved up or down to accommodate items of different sizes. I like to rip out these old fixed shelves and then install new painted side panels that cover the dadoes and allow for adjustable shelving.

1. You can make your own shelf-pin drilling template, but a self-centering bit and a compatible drilling guide make the job go much faster.

2. To remove the old shelves, drill a hole in the rear center of the board.

3. Cut up to the hole with a jigsaw so that the shelf can be removed in two pieces.

4. Insert the new side panel into place over the old inside of the cabinet, and secure it with finish nails.

4. Trim Takes It from Plain to Pretty

If I were building cabinets from scratch, I would install the boxes and add the molding on site. An old kitchen isn't much different because what you have is a bunch of plain boxes ready for molding.

Old-style cabinets were typically designed for utility, not so much for elegance. The addition of molding helps to balance the look of the new doors and drawer fronts, adds depth and shadowlines, and most important, gussies up the whole installation. For a job like this, I typically add band molding at the bottom, crown molding at the top, and picture-frame molding wherever end panels will show.

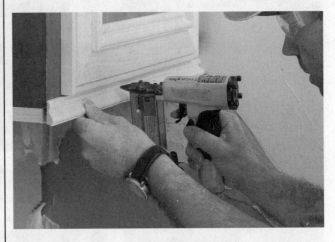

1. Depending on the space remaining below the cabinet doors, another nailer may be necessary to provide solid backing for the band molding. Some extra blocking may be necessary at the top, too. On this job, the author added a valance to provide solid nailing for part of the crown molding. If the cabinets don't extend to the ceiling, a nailer may be necessary at the top edge of the cabinet as well.

2. The best approach for end panels is to preassemble the picture-frame molding and install it as one piece. Use spacers to center the molding, and then attach it using nails that won't penetrate into the cabinet interior.

Get to Know Semicustom Cabinets

By Nena Donovan Levine

If your kitchen cabinets are decades old and you're homing in on a renovation, consider this advice: "Ya gotta know the territory." It's from The Music Man, a show as old as those very cabinets. Dispensed by a traveling salesman headed for River City, it's also a great mantra to use when surveying today's kitchen-cabinetry landscape.

In 2012, the cost of an average kitchen renovation was over $47,000, according to a National Kitchen and Bath Association member survey. Cabinetry consumes one-third or more of that amount. You can do the math, but it is safe to say this investment deserves careful consideration.

There are three broad categories of kitchen cabinets: Stock cabinets tend to be the most affordable but offer the least variety of style and finishes, are sometimes made from lower-quality materials, and may be constructed for a shorter useful life. Custom cabinets are at the other extreme in that they can be made of familiar or exotic materials to any size, style, and quality.

Semicustom cabinets fall between stock and custom cabinets and are arguably the best value. The Kitchen Cabinet Manufacturers Association defines semicustom as "built to order but within a defined set of construction parameters; available in standard widths but with more choices for depth and height modifications." According to one of the organization's recent member surveys, the semicustom category makes up 46% of the overall market.

MasterBrand Cabinets has lines in all three categories. Stephanie Pierce, manager of MasterBrand's design studio, says that unlike the company's stock line—which is limited to very specific dimensions, styles, and finishes—its semicustom lines, including Diamond and Decorá, offer designers and builders "flexibility within limitations." More specifically, these brands' offerings can be customized only to the degree of the shops' capabilities. At the custom end of the spectrum, Master Brand's Omega Cabinets will outsource any fabrication that its shop is not capable of.

Snapshot of a Giant Category

Semicustom cabinets are built upon receipt of an order, so lead time is longer than it would be for stock cabinets, which you can

SEMI-WHAT? Called semi-custom, the category of cabinetry that makes up the lion's share of the market is full of variety. These cabinets are chocolate-antiqued creme color. The island is burnished ebony stain. Details like the crown molding and island legs are often standard features of semicustom lines.

Continued →

Semicustom, Full of Options

Semicustom lines offer so many standard options that most of us don't need a custom shop to find what we're looking for.

FACE FRAMED, FRAMELESS, OR BOTH? You don't have to choose. These cabinets offer a clean, frameless look with face frames hidden behind the door and drawer fronts. Some installers prefer this arrangement for durability and ease of installation.

PULLOUT PANTRY IS NARROW ENOUGH. Standard cabinet widths start at 9 in. and can be specified in 3-in. increments (or smaller for an upcharge). This pullout spice rack from Merillat is a great use of narrow space next to the oven and cooktop.

HARDWARE MATTERS. Most manufacturers offer hardware options to enhance storage in their cabinets. Some can be outfitted with aftermarket hardware as well. These Diamond cabinets have elegant and useful storage that keeps cookware from getting lost deep inside the island.

sometimes get off the shelf at a home center. It's shorter than it would be for custom cabinets, however, although this varies based on the complexity of the cabinets and the builder's availability. Merillat's semicustom Classic line can ship in as little as five to 10 days. Canyon Creek's Katana line has a lead time as short as four weeks from order to delivery. Certain upgrades can push lead times out to six weeks or more.

Semicustom cabinets are offered in standard 3-in.-wide increments from 9 in. to 45 in. For an upcharge, you can modify this to ⅛ in. Such precise dimensions reduce the call for filler strips and minimize wasted space. Standard cabinet depths and heights also can be increased or decreased for an upcharge. So if using a standard 24-in.-deep base cabinet doesn't allow adequate clearance in a pantry or a passageway, you can reduce the box depth and still use the particular cabinets you were hoping for. Standard wall cabinets are 30 in. and 36 in. tall, but sometimes 33 in. or even 42 in. works better with a particular ceiling height. Again, with most semicustom lines, this level of customization is possible.

Semicustom cabinets are available with face-frame or frameless construction or both. The choice is mostly aesthetic: Face frames are more common on traditional-style cabinets, and frameless cabinets are more contemporary looking. But there are plenty of exceptions.

On face-frame cabinets, the doors can be inset or they can be overlaid to reveal more or less of the frames. The hinges attach to the face frames. Doors on frameless cabinets cover the cabinet box's finished front edge. Door hinges attach to the box sides. Frameless construction offers a more open interior and is typical of today's European cabinetry. In the United States, by contrast, face-frame construction outsells frameless, according to Danielle Mikesell, Merillat's director of marketing. Both traditional and frameless cabinets can be ordered with a panoply of door and drawer styles, wood species, finishes, crown-molding profiles, and box-construction options. Some manufacturers will even combine face-frame construction with a frameless aesthetic. When it comes to style and construction, most of what is commonly built by custom-cabinet shops can be found in semicustom cabinets.

Cabinet doors and shelves are typically ¾ in. thick. A loaded, ¾-in. shelf can span a 36-in.-wide cabinet, while thinner shelves may bow across that span. Full-depth shelves, adjustable in ½-in. increments, maximize storage. For organizing cabinet interiors, there are plenty of accessories, such as roll-out shelves and lazy susans. Companies such as Häfele, Knape & Vogt, and Rev-A-Shelf make bins, baskets, and recycling containers to complement semicustom lines.

Semicustom lines offer warranties that may equal the limited-lifetime warranty typical for custom cabinets. Canyon Creek, Merillat, and KraftMaid all offer such warranties on some lines that cover the product for as long as the purchaser owns it, with certain exclusions. Unfinished products are excluded, for example, as are normal wear and tear, instances of abuse, and improper installation. Merillat's Classic, also a semicustom line, has a 25-year warranty.

We Can't Tell You What It Will Cost

It would be great to read an article or visit a website and get a firm figure for what your cabinets might cost, but it's not that simple. Calculators, such as at finehomebuilding.com/cabinet-calculator, can give you a range, but the offerings of semicustom cabinetmakers are vast, and even some seemingly logical questions—such as whether face-frame or frameless cabinetry is more expensive—are not so easy to answer.

Let's explore that example: Frameless boxes ought to be ¾ in. thick to provide good purchase for door hardware, whereas a face-frame box can be ⅝ in., because door hardware is not attached to the box. So frameless cabinets, in general, must be more expensive. But without face frames, those European-styled cabinets don't use as much hardwood or require as much labor. So it seems that traditional cabinets must be more expensive. But filler strips can mar the clean lines of modern, frameless cabinets, so you'll want to specify custom box dimensions, increasing the cost. You still haven't specified a door and drawer style, a finish, or all the storage upgrades you want.

In short, distinguishing by frameless or traditional construction, dovetail or dowel joinery, or one particular feature or finish is not a meaningful way to compare prices. For every instance where one company's product costs more, there are others where you will find the opposite. Showrooms offering semicustom lines have a list of "retail" prices for every component in a cabinetry manufacturer's line. (Merillat's 2011 book for its Masterpiece line ran 664 pages.) What the showroom charges a customer, however, depends first on its discount calculation—a percentage assigned by the manufacturer—and then on how it adjusts that discount to cover its cost of business. The discount calculation varies based on the dollar volume of that cabinetry line sold by that showroom, among other factors.

The purchaser's price for a kitchen with dozens of components might include upcharges for customized dimensions, premium wood species, certain finishes and hardware, or glass doors (which require a finished cabinet interior). How badly a showroom wants the business can also affect price comparisons between showrooms. With so many factors influencing the final price, you'll have to talk to a designer or dealer to get a legitimate estimate.

Four Ways to Assess Quality

Experts agree on what distinguishes a quality semicustom cabinet: box construction, drawers, doors, and finish. In addition, hardware—drawer slides and door hinges—should be well-made and adjustable. Blum, Grass, and Häfele are examples of top-quality hardware brands.

Continued →

What's Not Semicustom

The distinction between stock, semicustom, and custom cabinets can be blurry. Some manufacturers offer lines in more than one category. Here's a look at the alternatives to semicustom.

Stock

Stock refers to cabinet inventory stocked—and sometimes stacked—at a manufacturer or retailer. Options for door style, wood species, finish, molding profile, and hardware are limited to what's there. Materials reflect a budget price point; for example, a stock cabinet door may be ½ in. thick, while a semicustom or custom door measures ¾ in. Cabinet-box size is limited to 3-in.-wide increments from 9 in. to 45 in. Depths for both wall and base cabinets are fixed, and warranties are the shortest on the market—often five years or less. Benefits of stock cabinetry include its entry-level price and fast (immediate or within a few days) delivery. Stock quality may suit a rental unit, starter house, or budget kitchen. Limited choices may inspire DIY creativity and yield excellent value.

Custom

Custom cabinets, originating in a small shop or a large manufacturing facility, are built to client specifications upon receipt of the order. They can incorporate curved doors, complex angles, odd box sizes, and unusual colors. If you want to hand-select or book-match exotic veneers, you can. Options for door style, wood species, finish, crown-molding profile, box selection, accessories, and hardware are enormous. Benefits of custom cabinetry include vast choice, tailored fit and finish, and individualized fabrication. Expect a premium price tag and longer remodel time, since custom lead times run eight weeks to several months. Large manufacturers offer generous (even lifetime) warranties for custom products. Small-shop warranties vary. Custom implies top quality, but it's not a given from every small cabinet shop.

Boxes

Today's semicustom cabinet boxes can be made from plywood, particleboard, or medium-density fiberboard (MDF). Even if different boxes meet the same testing requirements and have equal warranties, there are variations to note in the materials used.

To begin with, not all plywood is created equal. There are different grades, and the number of plies can vary. Assuming high-quality glue and fabrication methods are used—the more plies a panel has, the more stable the panel will be. Plywood is typically the most expensive option for cabinet boxes.

Another option, formaldehyde-free particleboard (sometimes called furniture board) is not the cheap, porous particleboard of the past. It is a dense and durable substrate for veneer and is often more affordable than plywood cabinet boxes. It can be sized and cut with great precision, as can MDF.

MDF is made from recycled wood fibers and resin. As the smoothest of the three box materials, it is an excellent substrate for both veneer and paint. MDF's downside is its heaviness.

Drawers

You're likely to find dovetailed and doweled drawer construction in most semicustom cabinet lines. Both are equally sturdy, though dovetails add character and a high-quality appearance. You won't likely find glued or stapled drawers in semicustom cabinets. If you do, consider upgrading. Dovetails and dowels not only look better, but they last longer.

For a durable drawer, the hardwood or MDF fronts should be applied to a four-sided drawer box, not used as the fourth box side. Drawer boxes typically have ½-in.- or ¾-in.-thick solid-wood sides, although Canyon Creek's semicustom lines feature a ½-in.-thick plywood drawer box. A drawer bottom of ³/₁₆-in.-thick plywood resists deflection even when fully loaded. Some semicustom European lines offer metal drawer boxes; a different look, it's perhaps the most durable option available.

When it comes to drawer hardware, full-extension slides separate semicustom cabinets from most stock offerings and provide full access to the contents of a drawer. Undermount slides support the drawer from the bottom; their concealment is aesthetically preferable to side-mounted slides, particularly with dovetailed drawers. A soft-close feature, available on many semicustom cabinets, means they'll close quietly and without slam damage. Avoid drawers that shake or rattle when you operate them, which is a sign of cheap drawer slides.

Doors

Doors don't express a cabinet's overall quality as reliably as the other three items. Even lesser-quality cabinets may have reasonably well-built doors. In any event, look for ¾-in.-thick doors made of hardwood, painted or veneered MDF, or veneered particleboard. Good particleboard is dense (Merillat Classic doors call for 48-lb. particleboard). All doors should have rubber bumpers to cushion their closing action and adjustable hinges from a reputable manufacturer.

Most doors consist of a four-piece frame plus a center panel. A center panel needs room to move in response to humidity, but that doesn't mean it should rattle around in the frame. A center panel may be hardwood or veneer, but its grain and color should closely match the frame. High-quality doors have a raised center panel set into the door frame facing either outward (a raised-panel door) or inward (a recessed flat-panel door). Raised panels—whether facing in or out—possess a thickness and solidity that distinguishes them from a ¼-in.-thick, flat center panel.

Continued →

Because they do not respond to changes in humidity, MDF doors in a raised-panel style are made of a single piece of material.

Door-edge, frame, and raised-panel profiles can be varied to individualize a semicustom door style, though not every style will be available for both framed and frameless cabinets. There are also laminate and thermofoil door options, but they are more commonly found in stock cabinetry.

Finish

Finish choices vary as much as door styles. Canyon Creek, for example, offers nearly 40 standard stain and paint colors on more than 10 wood species. Glazing, distressing, burnishing, and antiquing add subtle finish variations. Canyon Creek will also mix a finish color to match a paint-store chip.

Stain finishes comprise several steps, usually including stain application, heat curing, one or more sealer coats, and a topcoat. Cabinets are sanded by machine and by hand prior to staining, then sanded again between sealer coats. Companies typically cure stains, sealers, and topcoats with convection heat. The resulting baked-on finish is durable enough to support extended warranties. Bertch Cabinetry uses a blend of alkyd, amino, and vinyl resins in its sealers; the topcoats are alkyd and amino resins formulated into catalyzed conversion varnish. Sheen levels can be modulated from matte to glossy by varying the topcoat formulation, but all sheens should be equally durable.

"Painted" finishes are achieved using colored (opaque) catalyzed conversion varnishes. These dry harder than standard paint. Even when a semicustom manufacturer matches, say, a Benjamin Moore color, the resulting paint differs from what's available in retail because the cabinetry formulation must be sprayable and yield more sheen. The paint typically is applied as a primer coat topped with one or more additional coats, with sanding and heat-curing in between. Not all painted finishes receive a separately formulated topcoat as stain finishes do.

A painted finish must be applied to a smooth surface, so paint-grade maple is often used. Because this finish sits on the wood surface instead of moving into the wood like a stain, a painted finish can crack when the wood under it moves. Hairline cracks appear at door and face-frame joints, and are not considered defects. However, the finish should not peel or flake. Most manufacturers offer matching paint for touch-ups along with a cabinet order.

To assess a finish, you need to see actual product samples. The finish should be clear; a cloudy appearance is a sign of poor quality. It should be smooth and drip-free, without visible sanding marks. Molding and door edges should be crisp, with no finish buildup. Low- or no-VOC formulations are desirable.

Installing Semicustom Cabinets

By Isaak Mester

On the face of it, installing semicustom kitchen cabinets is pretty straightforward: Attach a run of boxes to the wall, make sure all the doors and drawers work, and don't scratch the paint. Unless kitchens are a regular part of your work week, however, you'll find that the installation can go sideways in a hurry if you don't pay attention to some key aspects of the job. In demonstrating the installation of this fairly typical kitchen, I illustrate the most important tricks of the trade that help to make this a professional-looking job.

First, Unpack Carefully

The designer and the client picked semicustom cabinets from Kraft-Maid for the kitchen. In price and quality, they usually represent a comfortable midpoint between small-shop custom cabinets and big-box-store economy cabinets. The carcases are made of plywood, and the face frames, doors, and drawers are hardwood. The quality of the finishes is excellent. The cabinets were configured with a mix of drawer and door bases, two lazy-susan corners, and some glass-door uppers. Cabinets like these are usually shipped to the job site. The first thing I do is check the shipping manifest against the items shipped, and note any damaged or missing boxes. The faster you start the return process, the faster you'll be able to finish the job.

When taking cabinets out of the boxes, use a knife only when necessary, and don't cut the box along the cabinet's face or you may scratch the finish. Inspect each cabinet to make sure there are no dings, and arrange the return of any damaged units.

Factory cabinets are manufactured in part with hot-melt glue, which tends to dry in heavy drips that can get in the way of an installation. Before installing a cabinet, scrape off any of these drips.

Start Off Organized

The best way to start an installation is to make sure that the space is clean and that your tools and materials are right where you need them. After unpacking the first run of cabinets, place them in the general vicinity of their future locations, leaving yourself enough space to work comfortably.

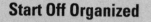

Trick of the trade
Painter's tape on one edge of a level protects the cabinet finish. When the tape gets dirty, though, it's not helping any longer. Change it often.

Trick of the trade
Before installing a cabinet, remove its drawers and doors, set them aside, and replace them when the cabinet is set.

Trick of the trade
You'll need more shims than you think. An empty bucket keeps them handy and portable.

Trick of the trade
When opening the cabinet boxes with a knife, steer clear of the face of the cabinet. Don't get excited and learn this simple tip the hard way.

Continued ➜

Measure and Mark for Level

A level run of cabinets starts from a reference point taken off the high spot on the floor or, when there are soffits, the low spot on the ceiling. It's especially important for the base cabinets to be level and flat so that they can adequately support long runs of countertop.

On this job, the kitchen's cathedral ceiling meant that there were no constraints to the upper cabinets, so we based our measurements on the floor. Using a 6-ft. level, I checked the floor along the base of the wall and found a high spot in the corner. Carried out on a level line, this would translate to a gap of more than an inch at the end of the cabinet run—too high to hide with a kick plate or shoe molding.

To avoid this gap, I moved my reference point to the end of the corner cabinet, where my original level line cleared the floor by about ½ in. I then marked a new reference point ¼ in. below the original line. From this new point, I measured up 34½ in. to establish the height of the base cabinets and drew a level line there. I then made another mark 19½ in. above that line to mark the bottom of the upper cabinets, drawing that line out level as well. When installing the cabinets, I scribed and cut the bases where the floor was higher than my reference mark, and shimmed the bases where the floor was lower.

Establish a Reference Line

Start a cabinet installation by finding the floor's high spot from which to create a level reference line on the wall to represent the cabinet tops.

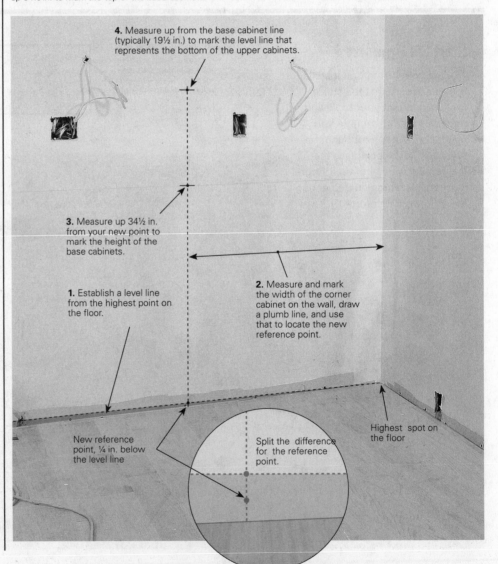

FIND THE HIGH SPOT. Use a 6-ft. level to find the highest point in the floor, which becomes the reference point to set the cabinets. Extend a level line outward to determine how much the adjacent cabinets will have to be shimmed. If the gap at the end of the run is too large to mask with trim, you'll need to adjust.

High spot

IF THE HIGH SPOT IS TOO HIGH, SPLIT THE DIFFERENCE. Mark a new reference point below the first line. Measure up 34½ in. to mark the top of the base cabinets.

4. Measure up from the base cabinet line (typically 19½ in.) to mark the level line that represents the bottom of the upper cabinets.

3. Measure up 34½ in. from your new point to mark the height of the base cabinets.

1. Establish a level line from the highest point on the floor.

2. Measure and mark the width of the corner cabinet on the wall, draw a plumb line, and use that to locate the new reference point.

New reference point, ¼ in. below the level line

Split the difference for the reference point.

Highest spot on the floor

Start in the Corner

Spend the time to get the first cabinet perfect, and it'll be much easier to install the rest.

Many installations start in the corner, so that cabinet must be plumb, level, and square. Here, I had to cut down the corner cabinet to compensate for a high spot in the kitchen's inside corner.

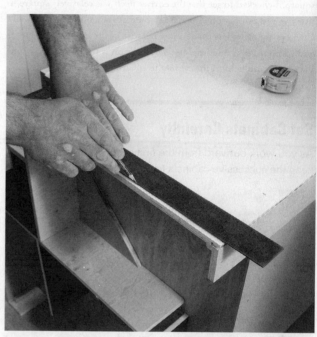

1. To make an accurate cut, I scribed the side panels.

2. Cut them down with a jigsaw.

3. Transferred those cuts to the interior base supports. A couple of strategically placed shims brought the cabinet into level compliance.

Continued ➔

Compensating for Corners

Once you've understood the state of the floor, you have to scope out the walls. It's a rare event when a kitchen's walls are plumb and square. I checked to see that the corner itself was relatively square so that the end cabinet on either side wouldn't flare out from the wall. Corners are often less than square because of the buildup of tape and compound. Sometimes the best solution is to cut or scrape out the compound behind the cabinet to square up the corner.

Set Cabinets Carefully

As you work outward from the first cabinet, it's important to keep the successive cabinets level and in line with the walls.

TRICKS OF THE TRADE When shimming the front of a cabinet, keep one finger on top of the face frame of the adjoining cabinet to avoid having to look to see when the two cabinets are even. Dedicated drill-drivers—one for drilling pilot holes and one for driving screws—save time.

TRICKS OF THE TRADE Use a small flat bar as a lever to gain more adjustment control when shimming a cabinet. A multitool does a clean and fast job of trimming shims without disturbing or splitting them.

I like to join the corner cabinet to the adjoining cabinets before attaching them to the wall so that I can carry the corner outward in two directions. If the corner isn't square, I can adjust the cabinet's angles so that there's an equal gap behind the end cabinets, which I usually conceal with a finished end panel. Here, because the line of cabinets was interrupted by appliances, I had the option of adjusting the position of the cabinets independently, but I always try to keep the counter overhang as consistent as possible.

There are times when joining your upper cabinets together on the ground will make the installation much easier and straighter. This is especially true with frameless cabinets, as there is absolutely no play in the installation. Some installers like to hang the upper cabinets first because they don't have to reach up and over the base cabinets. Many kitchen designs (like this one) are driven by appliance locations, though, so it's important to establish the base location first.

When it came to installing the upper cabinets, the first thing I did was to screw a length of scrap brick molding to the wall studs along the upper level line. This serves two purposes: First, it's a third hand to support the cabinets as they're installed; second, it makes a handy reference when locating screws inside the cabinet. If the area between the bases and the uppers isn't meant to be covered by a backsplash, it's easy enough to patch the screw holes in the walls.

Keep Plumbing and Electrical Neat

One of the details that adds to a good installation is careful integration of cable and pipes in the cabinets. I have encountered too many kitchens where the installers simply hacked out a square in the cabinet back for the water and waste lines, which is visible whenever the cabinet is open.

The first step I take to ensure this integration is to insist that the plumber leave everything stubbed out and capped. It makes it easier to do a careful layout, which in turn makes a neater installation.

Second, I find out what kind of undercabinet lighting is going to be installed later so that I can drill the holes in the proper locations of the cabinet. There's nothing worse than seeing the lights installed with 2 ft. of exposed wire running across the bottom of the cabinet to the hole that I drilled.

Scribing Shouldn't be Difficult

Once the cabinets are in, the next step is to scribe and attach the finished end panels. Base moldings, often part of the trim package in semicustom cabinets, cover any gaps between the panels and the floor, so the wall is the critical area to be scribed. After measuring the space, and determining the correct width or length of the panel, I shim or clamp the panel's tops equal to the top of the cabinet. Setting a compass to the distance of the largest portion of the gap between the wall and the panel, I scribe the wall's line onto the panel, check the measurement to make sure it's right, and cut away the waste. Full-length panels should be shimmed plumb before they're scribed.

Accurate Holes in the Sink Base are Important

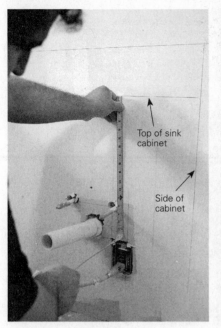

ESTABLISH THE REFERENCE. Find the centerline of the cabinet on the wall, then measure and mark the locations of the cabinet's side and top. Use only these two points to measure the plumbing and electrical locations.

TRANSFER TO THE CABINET. From the same two points, measure and mark the centers of the plumbing stubs and the outlet.

DRILLING FOR APPEARANCES. Drill ¼-in. pilot holes on the center marks from the cabinet back, then drill from the cabinet interior with a sharp hole saw, using its pilot bit as a guide, to minimize visible tearout.

Set Upper Cabinets with a Ledger

As with the lower cabinets, the upper-cabinet installation begins in the corner and works outward. Secondary support, such as a ledger or cabinet jack, helps to stabilize a cabinet's position while stud and wiring locations are marked and pilot holes drilled.

Screw a temporary ledger such as a scrap piece of brick molding to studs in the wall to help support the upper cabinets. When screwing a cabinet to the wall, transfer the locations of the ledger screws to the inside of the cabinet.

Use padded bar clamps to attach the next cabinet in line with the first, making sure to align the face frames. Always countersink a pilot hole for screws, and use decking or similar heavy-duty screws to attach cabinets to each other and washer-head screws to attach cabinets to the wall. Drywall screws are too brittle and shouldn't be used.

Move the wires to where they belong. Here, the undercabinet feeds should be above the cabinet bottom. On this job, a full backsplash will conceal the drywall repair.

Continued →

Be Precise with Crown and End Panels

THE EASIEST CROWN JOB. Because of the cathedral ceiling in this kitchen, the cabinet crown could be cut simply by registering its spring angles onto the miter saw's table and fence.

WORK CAREFULLY WITH PREFINISHED STOCK. To reduce visible nail holes, it's a good idea to use the smallest nail or brad possible when attaching crown or other exposed trim.

BACKING NOT INCLUDED. Finished trim panels on the back of peninsulas often require extra nailing support. Layout lines on the walls help to locate blocking in the right places.

KEEP FASTENERS CONCEALED. Meant to be covered by corner trim or base, the perimeters are good spots to attach the panels and still keep the appearance clean.

Tips for Installing Trim

The trim for semicustom cabinets is usually made from prefinished hardwood, and it's relatively expensive and difficult to replace once you've started. Make sure you have enough before you sign off on the delivery, although distributors often can send missing pieces within a few days. Because it's prefinished, the trim must be cut carefully to avoid tearout. Keep nail holes small so they can be concealed with a color-matched filler, and glue joints for extra holding power. When working with dark-stained crown, apply stain on the inside edges of miters so that any gaps won't show as prominently.

Installing Kitchen Cabinets Solo

By Mike Guertin

Installing kitchen cabinets is one of my favorite projects. Whether I'm working on a new home or on a remodeling project, cabinet installation signals that the end is in sight. And installing the right cabinets transforms an empty space into a functional, good-looking kitchen.

Even factory-made stock cabinets, though, can be fussy to install. Walls are rarely straight or floors flat. A two-person crew with basic tools requires at least a day to install an average-size

kitchen. But thanks to a few specialty tools and some techniques I've developed through many years spent working alone, I can do the same work by myself.

Good planning and joining cabinets together prior to installation are two important strategies. Tools like a laser level, face-frame clamps, and a cabinet lift save time while also improving the accuracy of my work. Throughout the process, I do everything possible not to damage the new cabinets.

Dings Don't Have to Happen

On most projects, a lot of work has gone into getting the kitchen ready for the cabinets. The cabinets are a finish item, and I take every precaution not to let them become damaged during installation, starting as soon as they are delivered. Even if the cabinets arrive on the job before I am ready for them, I unbox them immediately to make sure everything I ordered was delivered and to inspect them for damage. Before installing the cabinets, I number (on painter's tape) and remove the doors, shelves, and drawers to protect them from damage. Removing these parts also lightens the boxes and makes them easier to handle. I don't reinstall any parts until the rest of the kitchen is complete.

Put the Plans on the Floor

For me, part of planning a smooth installation is drawing the cabinet layout as well as important plumbing and electrical information on the floor and walls. I draw the layout on the floor early in the construction process to help other tradesmen and myself proceed. This system speeds the installation process and helps me to avoid mistakes.

On the floor, I mark three lines parallel with the walls: the face of the wall cabinets, the face of the base cabinets, and the face of the rough toe kick. Then I mark the location of the individual base cabinets, wall cabinets, and appliances. I write the cabinet size code in each box and label the appliances and their sizes.

With all this information written on the floor, I can determine if I need filler strips and identify any potential conflicts, like an off-center range outlet. The layout also shows the electrician and plumber where to locate rough-ins for appliances and fixtures. I also indicate on the floor and walls where pipe runs occur to avoid driving any cabinet-mounting screws into them.

Accurate Elevations Help You to Get the Right Heights

On the walls, I mark stud, blocking, and utility locations as well as the top of the base cabinets and the bottom of the upper cabinets. I factor in the thickness of the finished flooring before these elevations are marked.

Stock base cabinets are 34½ in. tall (1½-in.-thick countertops bring the finished elevation of the base cabinets up to 36 in.). If you install the base cabinets on the subfloor and then cover the floor with ¾-in.-thick hardwood flooring, the countertop height will be short. So when I mark the elevation of the top of the base

Continued ➜

Map and Mark

 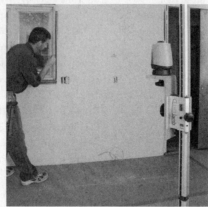 

1. START WITH AN ACCURATE MAP Lay out cabinet details on the floor. Here, I've taped resin paper over an old linoleum floor to show details more clearly. Mark the face of the wall cabinets, the face of the base cabinets, and the face of the rough toe kick. Also mark the locations of any individual cabinets and of the appliances.

2. MARK THE TOP OF THE BASE CABINETS AND THE BOTTOM OF THE UPPERS I use a laser level to mark the walls at the ends of each cabinet run. Then I snap chalklines to guide base- and upper-cabinet installation. Plan to shim the base cabinets off the subfloor the thickness of the finish flooring so that the 1½-in.-thick countertop will be 36 in. above the finish floor.

3. FIND THE STUDS A stud finder locates framing members quickly. I indicate the stud locations with a tick mark along the chalklines. The marks still will be visible when the cabinets are in place.

Install Blocking to Anchor Cabinets Solidly

You can fasten upper cabinets just to the studs, but horizontal blocking installed between the studs makes for a more secure installation. In new homes or gutted remodels, I install 2×4 or 2×6 blocks between studs. Make sure to locate blocking behind the cabinet's top mounting rail. When installing cabinets on existing walls (as shown here), I cut through the wallboard where the top mounting rail will land. I remove the wallboard and install 2×4 blocks with 3-in. screws. Then I cover the blocks with drywall and finish the seams with tape and compound.

cabinets, I add the height of the finished flooring. In this case, I added ⅞ in. for a tile floor.

I always measure the elevation from the lowest spot I can find on the subfloor and use a laser level to mark the elevations at the ends of cabinet runs. Then I snap a chalkline or connect the points with a long spirit level. I also find the elevation of the bottom of the upper cabinets and use a stud finder to locate and mark the studs along both elevation lines.

Join Wall Cabinets on the Floor

1. USE CLAMPS TO DRAW THE STILES TOGETHER I use three screws in stiles 24 in. or taller and two screws in those shorter. Drill a ⅛-in.-dia. pilot hole through both stiles and a shallow ³⁄₁₆-in. hole into only the first stile to counterbore each trim-head screw. If possible, I locate the screws so that they'll be hidden by door hinges.

2. ALIGN THE CABINETS WITH A STRAIGHTEDGE Before joining the back of the cabinets, I put a straightedge across the top to make sure the tops are level and the front is straight. Then I shim between the side panels at the rear of the cabinet, and drive screws to keep the ganged cabinets straight. The cabinets now can be installed as a single unit.

When I install the base cabinets, I set them on plywood strips to shim them to the proper height. In fact, I cut plywood strips that are both thicker and thinner than I need and use them to make up for low and high spots in the subfloor. I cut the strips to equal the distance from the rough-toe-kick line to the wall (around 22 in.). And I set a strip at each end of a run of base cabinets and everywhere two cabinets meet. Later, when the base cabinets are installed, I use cedar shims to level and make fine adjustments to raise the tops of the cabinets to the chalkline.

Upper or Base Cabinets First?

Professional kitchen installers debate whether the upper cabinets or the base cabinets should be mounted first. There's no right or wrong sequence, only preferences.

For many years, I installed the base cabinets first and laid boards over them to serve as a platform to rest the upper cabinets on during installation. But after damaging the face frames on a few base cabinets with my belt buckle and tools dangling from my belt, I changed to mounting upper cabinets first and haven't looked back.

Before I install the upper cabinets, I use a long spirit level, referencing the upper-cabinet positions marked on the floor, to draw plumb lines for the sides of the upper cabinets. This ensures that the upper cabinets will align with the base cabinets.

Don't Use Drywall Screws

Many cabinet companies now supply mounting screws, but years ago, we were left to our own devices. Like many installers, I made the mistake of hanging cabinets with drywall screws, which simply aren't strong enough to support loaded cabinets. These days, I use only special cabinet-mounting screws, preferably those with broad washer heads for full shoulder support (www.mcfeelys.com). To join stiles, I use trim-head screws. The smaller heads can be hidden easily by hinges, plugs, or wood putty.

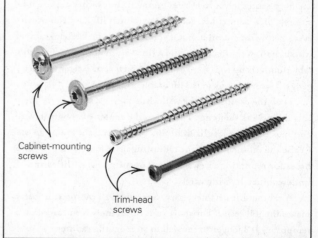

Cabinet-mounting screws

Trim-head screws

Continued →

Preassemble the Cabinets, and Forget About Wavy Walls

Walls are never flat. Even walls framed with engineered studs have bumps and dips at drywall seams. Sometimes cabinets aren't perfect, either. The side panels may be slightly out of square with the face frame, or a backing panel may not be flat across the rear. Imperfections in walls and cabinets make aligning the faces of cabinet runs difficult, particularly when cabinets are installed one at a time. I overcome these problems by ganging cabinets together before mounting them to the wall. This approach is faster and more precise than mounting cabinets individually.

Cabinets can be preassembled resting upright on the floor, on their backs, or elevated on a bench. I gang a run of cabinets together by screwing together the face-frame stiles and the rear of the cabinets. The trick is to clamp a straightedge along the top front of the cabinets while you screw them together. The front face and the top edge of the run need to be straight. Once the rear of the cabinets is joined, they will stay aligned.

I locate screws where they are least likely to be seen: behind the hinges or in the drawer spaces on base cabinets. If a screw is needed where it can't be hidden, I countersink trim-head screws and cover them with color-matched filler. Screws joining the rear of the cabinets can be driven through the cabinet side panels above the top panel, where they'll never be noticed. I use three screws to join stiles taller than 24 in. and two screws in anything shorter. Two screws are plenty to hold the cabinet rears together. Once screwed together, the individual boxes essentially become one long cabinet.

When I install the cabinet run as a unit, I still have to check the whole run for level using both a spirit level and the elevation lines. I make adjustments once for the whole run of cabinets instead of making many adjustments for each individual cabinet. I usually can move long runs of base cabinets into place by myself, but sometimes I need help with upper cabinets.

Wall Cabinets Get a Lift

Two people easily can lift a gang of three to six wall cabinets when the doors and shelves have been removed. But I work alone a lot, so I rely on a cabinet lift. For me, the cabinet lift has been worth every penny I spent on it, but if you're doing one kitchen-cabinet installation, you usually can find a lift at a rental center. The lift's table supports up to 6 ft. of ganged cabinets. For longer cabinet gangs, I screw a plank to the lift's table.

I roll the cabinets to the wall while they are still low on the lift, then crank them up. This keeps the center of gravity down and makes the lift less likely to tip. When I'm 3 in. from the wall, I raise the cabinets up to the mounting line; mark and drill pilot holes for mounting screws; and cut openings for utilities and undercabinet-lighting wires.

A cabinet lift isn't necessary to mount wall cabinets; it just makes the job easier. For short runs of cabinets, you can screw a temporary 1×3 ledger to the wall to support the cabinets. If you

Preinstalled Crown Molding

I think it's easier to apply crown molding to the cabinets with the preassembled unit on the floor. To do this, however, I first have to lift the cabinets into position and mark the bottom of the crown on each end of the bank of cabinets and at all cabinet joints. I then can lower the cabinets, screw blocking to the top rails, and install the crown by screwing through the blocking and into the crown from behind. With this technique, there are no nail holes that need to be filled with color-matched putty.

Preassembled Upper Cabinets Hang as One Unit

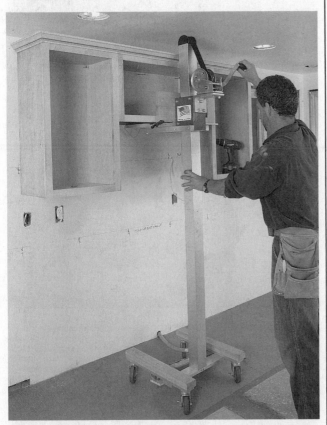

1. CRANK IT UP Cabinets make the lift top heavy, so I roll the lift close to the wall before cranking the ganged cabinets up and positioning them against their layout lines. Don't risk dropping the cabinets; clamp them to the lift's table until they are screwed to the wall.

2. DRILL HOLES FOR WIRING With the lift holding the cabinet close to the wall, I can drill holes to wire undercabinet lights exactly where they need to be.

3. DRIVE SCREWS INTO STUDS AND BLOCKING Cabinet-installation screws require pilot holes. I drive screws into the studs above the top panel of the cabinet, below the bottom panel, or through the back. When blocking is installed, I drill holes 2 in. from the side panels through the mounting rail and about 12 in. apart. With the unit secured to the wall with at least four screws, I remove the lift and drive the remaining screws.

Hanging Cabinets with a Ledger Instead of a Lift

If you don't have a cabinet lift, you can screw a temporary ledger board along the chalkline to support the back of a wall unit, and wedge a wood prop in place to support the front while you drive installation screws. But I prefer to have a helper, especially for longer runs of cabinets.

Continued →

Plywood Strips and Shims Set Base Cabinets to the Right Height

KEEP THE TOPS FLUSH AND THE FRONT STRAIGHT Join the base cabinets together with trim screws through the stiles. Shim between and screw together the panels in the back. Use a straightedge across the front of ganged base cabinets to keep the tops flush and the fronts straight. If the cabinets are imperfect, I sometimes have to plane the tops down to get surfaces flush.

USE A GAUGE STICK TO PAD OUT THE FLOOR Due to the fluctuations in the subfloor, the plywood strips won't all be the same thickness. I rip 2-in.-wide strips of ¼-in., ½-in., and ¾-in. plywood and use a 34¼-in. gauge stick (the height of the cabinets less the countertop) to determine which size strip to use. I place strips at each end of a run of cabinets and anywhere cabinets are joined.

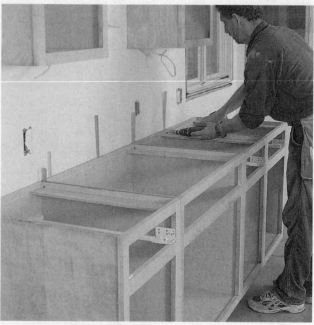

SET BASE CABINETS ON THE STRIPS, THEN SHIM After setting a gang of base cabinets into position on the plywood strips, I use shims to make sure they are sturdy and level.

SHIM FOR WAVY WALLS I drill pilot holes at each stud location, and drive screws to secure the cabinets. Shims fill the hollows between the mounting rails and walls.

Corner Details

BETTER SUPPORT FOR SINGLE CABINETS Cabinets less than 24 in. wide that stand alone or next to an appliance are prone to movement. I secure the bottom front on these cabinets by mounting a 2x block to the floor just inside the rough toe kick. I drop the cabinet over the blocking, and screw through the rough toe kick.

A FACE FRAME TAKES THE PLACE OF A CORNER CABINET Angled base cabinets for inside-corner sinks are expensive. Rather than buy an unnecessary box, I order an extra face-frame panel and a door from the cabinet company and use them to connect the base cabinets on both sides of the sink. The side panels of the adjoining cabinets and the painted drywall become the inside walls of the cabinet. I mount blocking to the sides of the adjacent cabinets and along the walls to support a plywood bottom panel with holes drilled for the plumbing. To support the countertop, I screw cleats to the walls. If the inside-corner cabinet will house a sink, I leave it open. If it is for storage, I make it a lazy susan.

use a ledger, drill pilot holes and twist screws into the holes at both ends of the cabinet run before lifting it to the wall. The ledger will help as you balance the cabinets with one hand and drive the screw with the other. Long gangs of cabinets can be lifted onto a ledger by two people. One person can hold the top against the wall while the other drives the screws.

I also preassemble the base cabinets. After shimming the ganged base cabinets to the appropriate elevation, I fasten them to the wall at each stud, using shims to fill any hollows.

Installing doors and drawers is the last thing I do on a project. I wait until the countertops are set, the plumbing is connected, everything is painted, and the flooring is installed. Waiting until the end of the project protects the cabinet doors and drawer fronts from collateral damage as the project is completed.

Breakfast-Booth Basics

By Roe A. Osborn

When I walk into a restaurant and I'm offered the choice of sitting at a table or a booth, I always choose the booth. Booths lend a feeling of informality to a meal, along with an element of fun. A booth can also seem like a private room for more-intimate dining.

A breakfast nook can create that same feeling at home. Nooks are typically carved from spaces too small for a conventional table and chairs. Just like in your favorite family-style eatery, a booth can add a note of fun and casual intimacy to a kitchen. On a bench, there's always room to squeeze in one more person.

Begin with the Bench Configuration

A breakfast nook can sit in a dedicated space such as a box bay or an angled bay, or you can put one in a corner with chairs that complement the built-in seating (drawings p. 532). If the nook breaks up a line of kitchen cabinets, the seats can extend to the front face of the cabinets so that the bump-out doesn't have to be as deep. Kneewalls can also define the nook.

As you determine which configuration works best in your kitchen, you also need to decide the length of the benches based on the number of diners to be accommodated. The book *Architectural Graphic Standards* (Wiley, 2004) suggests that benches 42 in. to 52 in. long are fine for two adults. A length of 48 in. uses materials most efficiently. Just remember that if a breakfast nook is built into a corner, the area where the two benches intersect should not be included when figuring the needed seating length. Two opposing 48-in.-long benches should be fine for two parents and three small kids.

Incidentally, an L-shaped booth with chairs along one side is especially well-suited to families with youngsters. Portland, Ore., architect Keyan Mizani says, "One bench side is great for keeping the kids in place, short of a force field. The parents get the chairs, making it easier for them to get to and from the table. Also, having more room on one side of the booth allows a high chair to be positioned at the end of the table with some extra legroom to get past."

Continued ➜

The Slant on Seats

Most folks agree that seat backs should be angled (about 3° to 5° off plumb) and that the seat level should be 18 in. off the floor, a height that includes cushions. While angling the seat back adds a modicum of comfort to a built-in bench, it also takes up more space. If space is at a premium, you might have to settle for straight backs.

I've never heard anyone complain about having too much storage in a kitchen, and if a breakfast nook is a solution to limited space, it makes a lot of sense to use the benches for storage. Drawers on the ends of the benches with full-extension slides are the best approach. Another way to take advantage of that space is with a hinged bench seat. Because the access is limited, though, hinged-lid storage should be a place for seldom-used items.

The Bottom Line on Cushions

I've sat on comfortable breakfast-booth benches both with and without cushions. Beyond padding for the posterior, cushions keep the hard edge of the bench from pressing into the backs of your legs. For optimum comfort, seat cushions should be at least 4 in. thick.

Keeping cushions clean can be a challenge. Salt Lake City architect Warren Lloyd sent his family's cushion-cover material to Americo (www.

Tips for Designing a Cozy, Comfortable Breakfast Booth

A nook built into a simple bump-out is probably the most common configuration. In this scenario, a table can be attached to the outer wall of the bump-out with a single support at the other end to maximize legroom. At 4 ft. deep, the booth seats two adults comfortably; any deeper could make serving meals difficult. A chair at the end provides additional seating, and a 6-in.-deep shelf at neck height allows you to tip your head back.

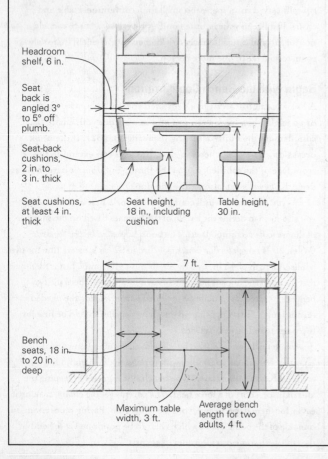

Headroom shelf, 6 in.

Seat back is angled 3° to 5° off plumb.

Seat-back cushions, 2 in. to 3 in. thick

Seat cushions, at least 4 in. thick

Seat height, 18 in., including cushion

Table height, 30 in.

7 ft.

Bench seats, 18 in. to 20 in. deep

Maximum table width, 3 ft.

Average bench length for two adults, 4 ft.

Same size booth, smaller bump-out

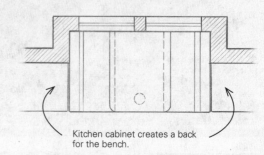

Kitchen cabinet creates a back for the bench.

In this scenario, the nook breaks up a run of kitchen cabinets. Extending the benches to the front of the cabinets translates into a much shallower bump-out, which might better fit a house's exterior design. The adjacent countertops also can act as staging areas for meals in the nook.

A kneewall replaces the bump-out

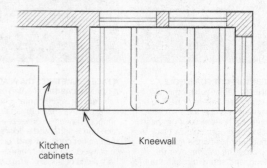

Kitchen cabinets

Kneewall

A kneewall makes it easy to build a nook with opposing benches without the expense of a bump-out. In this design, a kitchen corner creates one side of the nook, while a kneewall defines the opposite side. Kitchen cabinets end at the kneewall.

americo-inc.com) to be vinylized. Now the cushions in their breakfast nook are impervious to spills and stains.

Entering and exiting a booth usually requires sliding, and the right cover is critical. Smooth fabrics without a lot of nap are best; otherwise, you might drag the whole cushion with you when you slide. Seats without cushions should be sanded smooth and varnished to promote sliding and to discourage splinters. Less important are back cushions. They should not be as firm as seat cushions, and because they don't bear a diner's full weight, they don't need to be as thick; 2-in. to 3-in. foam is fine. If space is tight, forgoing back cushions can save a few inches of space per bench.

A Table for Legroom

A pedestal table with a center support that doesn't restrict legroom offers the easiest way of getting into and out of a booth. In a nook with a wall at one end, the table can be attached to the wall with minimal support at the other end.

Table height should be between 28 in. and 30 in., depending on your size. If you remember a booth that you've been comfortable in, I suggest measuring it and jotting down the dimensions of the table and benches. A table that's 30 in. to 36 in. wide has enough room for place settings with serving dishes in the middle, but it's not so wide as to diminish the intimacy of the nook. Because the table usually overhangs

Horseshoe booth maximizes seating

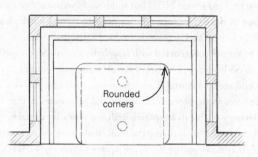

Rounded corners

To maximize built-in seating, a three-bench booth is the best way to go. The table in this arrangement has to be freestanding; rounded table corners make it easier to slide into and out of the "landlocked" bench. As in the corner plan, two adults might knock knees if they sit in adjacent corner seats.

Taking advantage of a kitchen corner

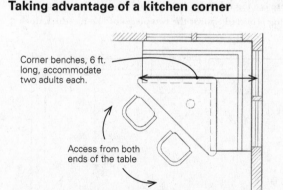

Corner benches, 6 ft. long, accommodate two adults each.

Access from both ends of the table

The table in this plan cannot be attached to the wall. Although the table can be square, a triangle is a viable option when space is at a premium. Chair seating is possible opposite the bench. Sitting in adjacent corner seats might be tricky as more than one person's legs try to occupy the same space.

A bench along one wall

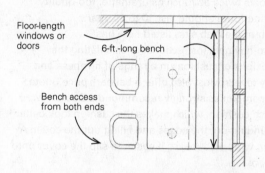

Floor-length windows or doors

6-ft.-long bench

Bench access from both ends

If the corner has full-length windows or doors, a built-in bench along one wall can be the answer. In this plan, the bench can be longer than in typical nooks, and the table can be attached to the adjacent wall or left freestanding to allow enough space at both ends for bench access.

Angled benches in a bay

Angled benches that follow the walls all but eliminate the cramped-corner effect. In this setting, a free-standing round or oval table works nicely, as does a table custom-built to fit the angles.

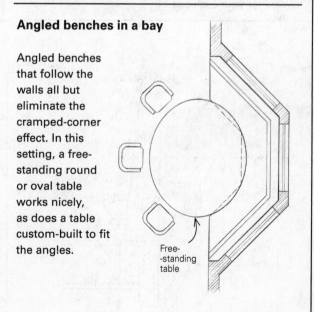

Free-standing table

the edge of the seats by 4 in. or 5 in., you'll have plenty of room to get into the nook but won't need to lean forward uncomfortably to reach your plate.

A freestanding pedestal table has its advantages. If you need a bit more room, the table can be moved slightly to let diners by.

Foam Facts

The type of foam you choose for breakfast-booth bench cushions can mean the difference between achy and comfy. The two most-common foam materials are latex and urethane. Both types of foam can be ordered in different levels of firmness (firm is better for seat cushions). Latex lasts twice as long and costs twice as much as urethane. Top-quality urethane foam should last 10 to 15 years.

Each of the Web sites listed here has easy-to-navigate instructions for calculating the dimensions of cushions in a range of firmness and quality levels. Most also offer a ballpark price quote. Most companies strongly recommend a Dacron wrap for each cushion, which makes the cushion look better by rounding out the edges and filling out the cover. A Dacron wrap also makes it easier to slip the cover onto the foam.

When calculating cushion size, foam companies suggest making the foam slightly longer (½ in.) and slightly thinner (½ in.) than the cover. The extra length of the foam plus the Dacron wrap fills out the cover nicely. If your plan includes back cushions, order them made of softer, thinner foam; a 2-in. thickness is typically fine. Many companies can also make custom covers for your cushions.

Build a Breakfast-Booth Bench

By John White

This bench is patterned after a Craftsman-inspired breakfast booth designed by architects Elliott Elliott Norelius of Blue Hill, Maine. Its comfortable proportions, straightforward lines, and readily available materials make it a great home-improvement project for beginners who want to learn about basic cabinetry, or for builders who want to expand their roster of built-ins.

The bench is composed of three boxes made of ¾-in. cabinet-grade plywood: the seat, the back, and the drawer. Once they are fitted together, the boxes can be trimmed with clear poplar or pine to create the legs, the drawer front, and the smaller details. The wainscoting on the seat back is formed MDF, but solid-wood wainscot can also be used. I gave all the edges of the trim a small bevel with a block plane, both to soften them and to provide for better paint adhesion.

The boxes are constructed with simple butt joints held together by 2-in. drywall screws. The boxes are plenty strong without the time and mess of gluing. For tight joints, drill countersunk clearance holes in the faces of the sheets and pilot holes in the edges. Having each bit in a separate drill can save a lot of time. To avoid trouble when applying the trim, make sure the plywood rectangles that make up the boxes are square so that the surfaces are flush where the pieces come together. As you cut the plywood into pieces, check them with a reliable carpenter's square, and also check that the opposite sides of each rectangle are identical in length.

Before placing the top panel on the base box, install the drawer-track hardware and test-fit the drawer. Next, attach the backrest, and set the assembly on sawhorses or on a worktable to do the trimwork. The bench is heavy enough now to require two people to move it.

There is a logical order to installing the molding. Almost everything is butted against the two pieces of 1⅛-in.-thick stock

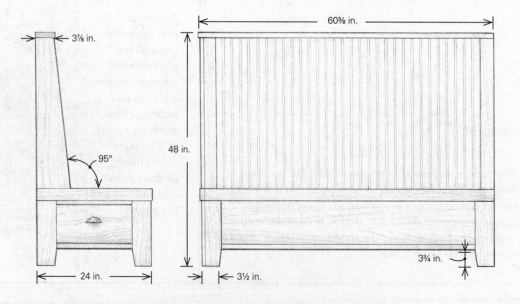

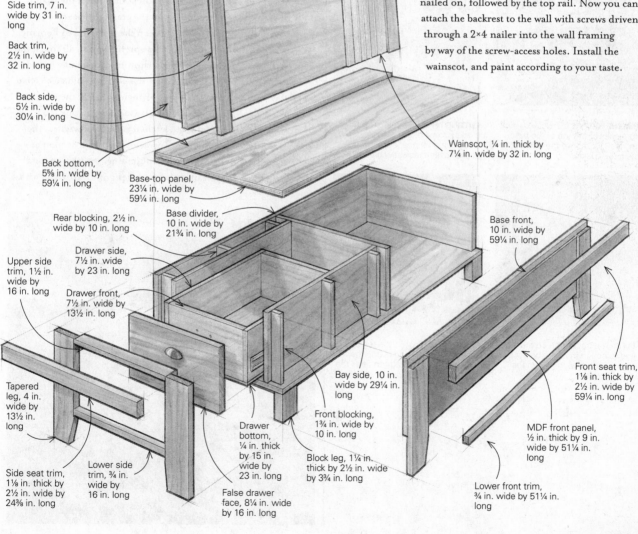

All material is ¾ in. thick unless otherwise indicated.

Cap, 1⅛ in. thick by 4¼ in. wide by 60⅜ in. long

Subtop, 2½ in. wide by 59¼ in. long

2×4 nailer, 57¾ in. long

Access hole, 2 in. dia.

Side trim, 7 in. wide by 31 in. long

Back trim, 2½ in. wide by 32 in. long

Back side, 5½ in. wide by 30¼ in. long

Back bottom, 5⅝ in. wide by 59¼ in. long

Rear blocking, 2½ in. wide by 10 in. long

Base divider, 10 in. wide by 21¾ in. long

Base-top panel, 23¼ in. wide by 59¼ in. long

Base front, 10 in. wide by 59¼ in. long

Upper side trim, 1½ in. wide by 16 in. long

Drawer side, 7½ in. wide by 23 in. long

Drawer front, 7½ in. wide by 13½ in. long

Tapered leg, 4 in. wide by 13½ in. long

Bay side, 10 in. wide by 29¼ in. long

Front blocking, 1¾ in. wide by 10 in. long

Front seat trim, 1⅛ in. thick by 2½ in. wide by 59¼ in. long

Side seat trim, 1⅛ in. thick by 2½ in. wide by 24⅜ in. long

Lower side trim, ¾ in. wide by 16 in. long

Drawer bottom, ¼ in. thick by 15 in. wide by 23 in. long

False drawer face, 8¼ in. wide by 16 in. long

Block leg, 1¼ in. thick by 2½ in. wide by 3¾ in. long

MDF front panel, ½ in. thick by 9 in. wide by 51¼ in. long

Lower front trim, ¾ in. wide by 51¼ in. long

Wainscot, ¼ in. thick by 7¼ in. wide by 32 in. long

(commonly called 5/4) that form the raised rim around the top of the base, so the rim pieces go on first. Like all the trim, they are nailed in place with finish nails.

Next, install the three visible legs with their tapered edges, along with the simple block leg in the back corner of the base. The three tapered legs all have blocks screwed to their back surfaces that serve to bear the weight of the bench. The blocks should be about 1/32 in. longer than the tapered legs so that all the weight rests on the blocks.

Once the legs are finished, install the smaller pieces of trim around the drawer opening and the front face of the base. The solid-wood false drawer face is cut to leave a bit of clearance on all four sides.

I use double-sided tape to temporarily attach the face to the drawer in the closed position. Once the face is positioned properly, I attach it permanently with screws driven from inside the drawer. A ½-in.-thick MDF panel completes the front of the base.

With the bottom half trimmed, the tapered trim on the end of the backrest can be cut and nailed on, followed by the top rail. Now you can attach the backrest to the wall with screws driven through a 2×4 nailer into the wall framing by way of the screw-access holes. Install the wainscot, and paint according to your taste.

Breakfast-Booth Bench

CUTTING PLYWOOD CAN BE UNWIELDY. Sometimes the best solution is to cut it with a circular saw guided by a fence.

INSTALL FULL-EXTENSION DRAWER SLIDES. Place the slides atop a spacer block during installation to ensure correct alignment.

TRIM THE TOP FIRST. The 1⅛-in.-thick rim pieces at the top of the base box rise ¾ in. above the plywood to retain the cushion.

CUTTING TAPERS. A pair of stop blocks screwed to a wooden sled position the tapered leg as it passes over a tablesaw blade.

ATTACH THE BACKREST. Screw the tapered box to the base box. Avoid screw points extending into the drawer section.

CLAMPS HELP. Test-fit the top and side trim pieces, and clamp them together to ensure a tight fit as the nails are driven home.

Build a Kitchen Island

By Rick Gedney

The function of a modern kitchen island can be traced to the familiar kitchen worktable that's been helping families to run the household and prepare meals for generations. An island's job is even tougher, though: A table from the 18th or 19th century didn't need to be a space for making pizza, checking email, or stir-frying. It also didn't have to integrate pipes, ducts, and wires.

I was recently called to a client's house for a full kitchen remodel. The young family wanted to renovate their existing, space-challenged galley kitchen, turning it into a wide-open room with an eat-at island. We looked at the available space and decided a single-level island with a farm sink made the most sense.

One often-overlooked item with island installations is how different floor coverings transition around the cabinets. On this project, we had to make an attractive transition between the wide pine floors in the adjacent living areas and the new kitchen's tile floor. We opted to make the transition at the end of the island and run the wide pine under the eating area. This seemed like the most logical spot to transition between the two types of flooring.

The installation of this island was pretty typical, although the open ceiling in the basement made running pipes and wires to the island a little easier. In this case, the plumber and electrician decided it would be best to do their rough-ins after the cabinets were installed, although such a process varies from one job to the next. When I'm designing a kitchen island, I always get the general contractor and the subcontractors involved as soon as we have preliminary drawings because plumbing, ventilation, and electrical requirements can make some designs unworkable with a typical budget.

Start with a Focal Point, then Follow the Plans

Light fixtures are typically centered over sinks and appliances, so this is a logical starting point for establishing the cabinet layout. From there, move left and right according to the plans, accounting for discrepancies in floor height as you move. With the cabinets aligned, screwed together, and at a consistent height, they can be fastened to the floor.

CENTER THE SINK. Using a pair of levels, transfer to the floor the location of the light fixture centered over the sink. This becomes the starting point for the layout.

WORK FROM THE END. With the position of the sink's overhead light as a starting point, use the kitchen designer's measured drawings to determine the end of the island. Measure from the wall cabinets to create a parallel line that the island will follow.

FIND MIDDLE GROUND. Many installers find the highest point of the floor to reference cabinet height, and then shim up the cabinets that sit on low spots. A better option is to find a cabinet at average height and then shim the low cabinets up and plane the high cabinets down. Shimming and planing should be minimal.

CHECK ACROSS THE GAP. Where there's a gap in the island's cabinet run for a dishwasher or other appliance, use a long level to ensure that both cabinets are at the same height. Check front and back to confirm that the cabinet tops are in the same plane. Also, make sure that the cabinets are spread the proper distance and that their sides are parallel.

Continued ➜

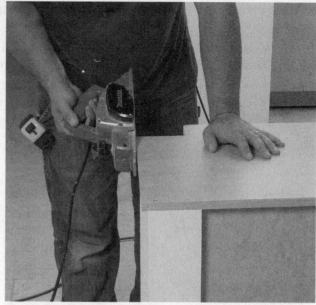

LOWER THE HIGH CABINETS. Using a level that spans from a high cabinet to one already at the correct height, center the bubble, and adjust your compass scribes so that they reflect the height difference. Use the same tool to mark the base of the cabinet for planing.

ADJUST THE HEIGHT. A few strokes with a power plane quickly remove enough stock to level the cabinet. This planer can remove about 1⁄32 in. with each pass while providing a smooth finish. Deeper passes leave a rough surface. Planing should be limited to a maximum of about 3⁄8 in.

CHECK ONE MORE TIME FOR INCONSISTENT HEIGHT. After the cabinet bottom is trimmed, put the cabinet in place, and check for level side to side and front to back. If necessary, make further adjustments with shims or planing until the cabinet is level in all directions.

FASTEN TO THE FLOOR. After two or three cabinets are screwed to each other, the cabinets are screwed to the floor. Drill pilot holes at an angle with a 7⁄32-in. twist bit, and then use 2½-in. square-drive screws to hold the cabinets to the floor.

Create a Seating Area

Rather than having extradeep or extrawide boxes, semicustom cabinets often have extended side panels for scribing to walls or other cabinets. These panels often work in conjunction with factory-finished plywood and solid hardwood to cover cabinet backs and empty cavities. The built-in eating area on this island is defined with a plywood panel that matches the cabinets. These additional parts are cut to size before they're fit and fastened.

TRIM FACTORY-FINISHED PANELS ON SITE. Using a track-guided saw, cut a plywood panel to form one side of the island's eating area. Cut it with a 45° bevel to correspond to a bevel on the cabinet's side panel.

GLUE MITERED JOINTS. The end and back panels meet with a mitered joint. A thick bead of wood glue prevents the mitered joint from opening with changes in humidity. While the glue dries, the joint is held together with 2-in.-wide masking tape.

BLOCKING REINFORCES THE PANEL. Use scraps of hardwood or plywood blocking to reinforce the eating area's plywood panels. Pocket screws are a strong, efficient way to make these connections. Previously installed cabinets make a great workbench for drilling pocket holes.

FASTEN THE BLOCKING. Using 1¼-in. coarse-thread pocket-hole screws, fasten blocking between the top of the plywood and the adjacent cabinet backs. The blocking prevents the plywood panel from warping.

Continued ➜

LOCATE THE LEGS. A pair of legs support the eating area's overhanging countertop. Use a pair of levels as straightedges to position the legs in plane with the cabinets.

CUT THEM TO LENGTH. Turn each leg upside down over where it will be installed so that it can be marked for trimming on a miter saw. **PRO TIP:** Cut the long part of the leg to keep the top consistent.

ANCHOR WITH HIDDEN FASTENER. Drive a 2½-in. drywall screw into the floor where the center of the leg will be installed. Cut off the head with lineman's pliers. This anchors the leg in place without visible fasteners.

ATTACH THE LEGS TO THE FLOOR. After drilling a hole in the center of the leg, fasten the leg to the 2½-in. drywall screw.

INSTALL AN APRON. Secured with pocket screws, a 2-in.-wide apron under the overhanging countertop supports the legs and provides a finished look. A 6-in. apron on the back of the island holds a receptacle.

ADD BRACING. Two-in.-wide stretchers attach the apron to the back of the cabinets, while angle braces keep the corners square. Both types of bracing are held in place with 1¼-in. coarse-thread pocket screws.

Finishing Touches

The finishing touches depend on the individual island, but most islands need drawer and cabinet pulls and some way to hide the obvious seams between cabinets. Appliances and fixtures may be installed now or after the top is in place, depending on the appliances. Once the cabinets are finished, it's time for the fabricator to measure for the countertop.

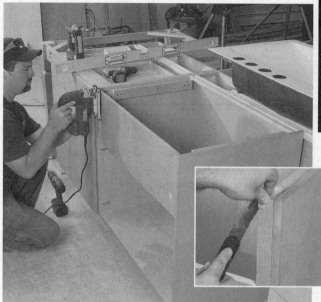

HIDE THE SEAMS AND SCREWS. The seam at the end of the island where the two cabinets meet is often hidden with a wine rack, bookshelves, or panels. This island has a pair of panels that mimic the cabinet doors. The seam between panels is offset from the cabinet seam, locking the cabinets together. Screws installed from the back side are hidden from view.

CUT THE FARM-SINK OPENING. Once the cleats that support the sink top are cut and secured to the sides of this cabinet, the installer cuts the blank panel at the front of the cabinet with a jigsaw and cleans it up with a rasp (photo inset above). When finished, the sink will be flush with the cabinet.

Time for Templating

With the cabinets in place, the eating area finished, and the farm sink installed, it's time for the stone fabricator to template the countertop. Decisions about thickness, the way the top overhangs the cabinets, and edge treatments should all be decided by this point.

Continued ➔

A Clever Kitchen Built-In

By Nancy R. Hiller

Modern kitchens are made for storage, but it never seems to be sufficient. Recently, my company built a cabinet to provide generous storage on a shallow section of wall in our clients' kitchen. It was space that normally would have gone to waste because it was too shallow for stock cabinets.

The inspiration for this custom-made cabinet came from a traditional piece of British furniture known as a Welsh dresser. In use since the 17th century, the dresser originally provided the main storage in a kitchen; built-in cabinets did not become the norm until the early-20th century. More commonly known in the United States by the less-elegant term hutch, the dresser typically has a shallow, open upper section that sits on a partially enclosed base. The dresser described here also exemplifies the sort of planning, production, and installation essential for genuinely custom built-in cabinets.

MORE PARTS MAKE CONSTRUCTION EFFICIENT. This type of modular cabinet construction allows a majority of the assembly work to be done in the shop. Consequently, I get more control over the processes and their costs.

Anatomy of a Built-In

Segmented construction let us assemble everything in the shop, break it down, and reassemble it in the kitchen. After the plywood boxes were screwed together in the shop, individual solid-wood face frames were glued to each box. The center cabinets had a complete face frame, while each side cabinet's frame, when joined to the center, would share the center's left or right stile.

At the client's house, we reassembled the base cabinets, shimmed them level, and screwed them to the framing. After scribing the counter to fit, we screwed it to the base cabinets. We installed the upper cabinets in the same way as the lower.

The partial face frame is attached to the outer cabinets prior to final assembly.

Countertop, ¾ in. thick by 13¾ in. wide

Undercounter Molding Detail

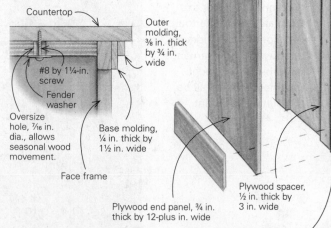

Countertop

Outer molding, ⅜ in. thick by ¾ in. wide

#8 by 1¼-in. screw

Fender washer

Oversize hole, ⁷⁄₁₆ in. dia., allows seasonal wood movement.

Base molding, ¼ in. thick by 1½ in. wide

Face frame

Plywood end panel, ¾ in. thick by 12-plus in. wide

Plywood spacer, ½ in. thick by 3 in. wide

Face-frame stile, ¾ in. thick by 2 in. wide

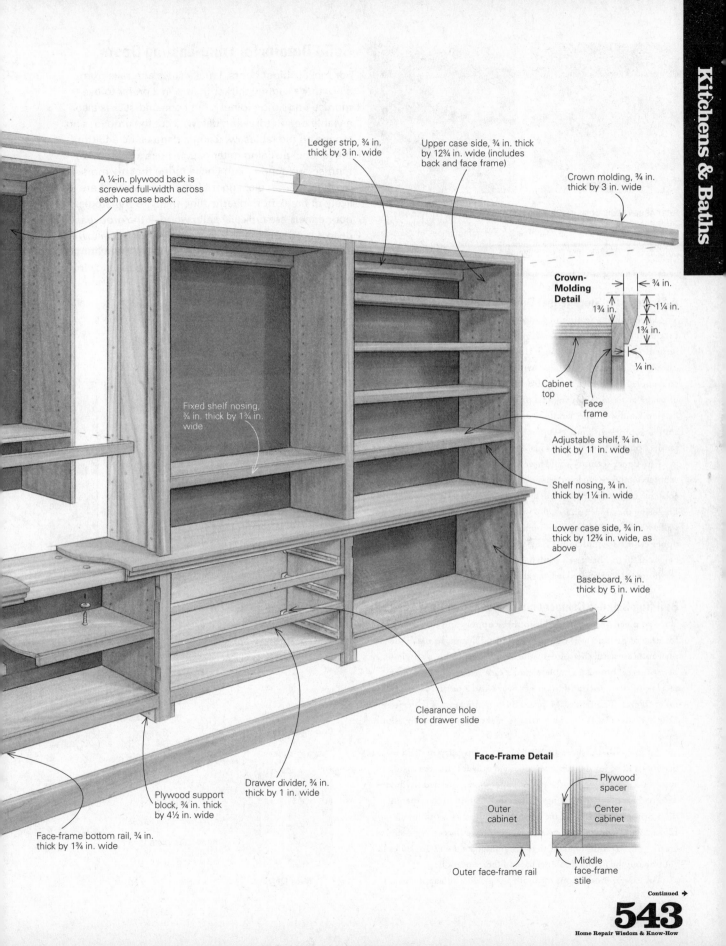

A ¼-in. plywood back is screwed full-width across each carcase back.

Ledger strip, ¾ in. thick by 3 in. wide

Upper case side, ¾ in. thick by 12¾ in. wide (includes back and face frame)

Crown molding, ¾ in. thick by 3 in. wide

Crown-Molding Detail

¾ in.

1¾ in.

1¼ in.

1¾ in.

¼ in.

Cabinet top

Face frame

Fixed shelf nosing, ¾ in. thick by 1¾ in. wide

Adjustable shelf, ¾ in. thick by 11 in. wide

Shelf nosing, ¾ in. thick by 1¼ in. wide

Lower case side, ¾ in. thick by 12¾ in. wide, as above

Baseboard, ¾ in. thick by 5 in. wide

Clearance hole for drawer slide

Face-Frame Detail

Plywood spacer

Outer cabinet

Center cabinet

Outer face-frame rail

Middle face-frame stile

Plywood support block, ¾ in. thick by 4½ in. wide

Drawer divider, ¾ in. thick by 1 in. wide

Face-frame bottom rail, ¾ in. thick by 1¾ in. wide

Continued →

FIRST ASSEMBLY IS DONE IN THE SHOP FOR A BETTER FINAL FIT. After Jerry Nees glued the center face frame to the center cabinet, he clamped the base cabinets together in the shop. The left and right portions of the face frame then can be scribed to fit and glued to their respective cabinets. The process is repeated for the upper cabinets.

A Strategy for Storage that Doesn't Waste Space

The kitchen had a section of unused wall about 11 ft. long, which I thought could be used for storage and display space without impeding traffic flow. Although 1 ft. of depth is shallow for a base cabinet, it is enough to hold a surprising variety of kitchen wares: cookbooks, decorative china, coffee mugs, small mixing bowls, jars of beans or pasta. Knowing that one of my clients had grown up in England and would be familiar with Welsh dressers, I suggested a similar cabinet with more-contemporary lines, customized for her family's budget and for the available space.

The upper sections would have open shelves, but the base cabinets would be enclosed with doors and drawers to keep their contents free of the dust and debris that collect at a kitchen's edges. Enclosing the lower sections also would give a nice visual weight to the wall without making it appear too heavy. The break between base and upper cabinets would be at 32 in., not the typical kitchen-counter height of 36 in., because I wanted this piece to look more like furniture than a regular kitchen cabinet.

Building Smaller Components Makes the Project Easier

The six-piece unit is divided into three uppers and three bases for ease of production, delivery, and installation. To make the six plywood cases and the solid-maple counter resemble a single piece of cabinetry, I used a complete maple face frame on the center section of the upper and lower casework and a partial face frame on each end. The end cases would butt tightly against the center unit and share its face-frame stiles to make the unit appear as one piece.

Although 10-in. slides are available for many purposes and would have been ideal for this job, they are rated only for drawers up to approximately 2 ft. wide. For smooth operation, I needed hardware designed for oversize openings. Given the location of the adjacent door casing, which limited the cabinet's depth to a maximum of 12¾ in., and a design that called for inset drawer faces, we needed to create ¼ in. of additional depth to accommodate the 12-in. slides by routing out the plywood cabinet back in those locations.

For ease of production, I typically use a full-width applied back

Solid Details for Long-Lasting Doors

For most cabinet doors, I make stiles and rails from stock that's slightly thicker than ¾ in. I prefer to use mortise-and-tenon joinery, but cope-and-stick is also a viable option (drawing below). I cut the grooves and tenons on the tablesaw, using a dado blade and (for the tenons) a sliding miter gauge. I use a 5/16-in.-wide mortise-and-tenon joint; I have found that my mortising machine's 5/16-in.-dia. auger bit and hollow chisel are less likely to break from overheating than are ¼-in. tools. My door panels are typically solid wood. If the groove is ½ in. deep, I make the panel ⅛ in. less all around to allow for some expansion. In summer, when the relative humidity is high here in Indiana, I make the panels extend closer to 7/16 in. into a ½-in.-deep groove.

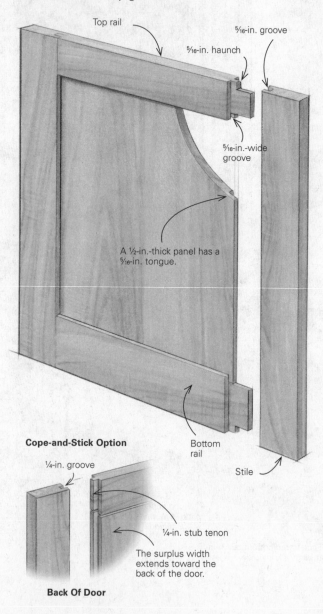

Top rail

5/16-in. groove

5/16-in. haunch

5/16-in.-wide groove

A ½-in.-thick panel has a 5/16-in. tongue.

Bottom rail

Stile

Cope-and-Stick Option

¼-in. groove

¼-in. stub tenon

The surplus width extends toward the back of the door.

Back Of Door

Drawer Construction and Installation: Hang the Box, then Attach the Face

I usually make drawers from ½-in. solid stock and dovetail the corners; it's a joinery option that my customers expect. (For less-expensive projects, I use biscuits or a rabbeted joint, as shown in the detail drawings at right.) I groove the inside faces of the front and sides to accept the drawer bottom (I use ⅜-in.- or ½-in.-thick plywood for the bottoms of extrawide drawers to prevent them from sagging). I also rip the back even with the top face of the drawer bottom so that I can slide in the bottom once the drawer sides are glued. Securing the bottom with small screws (but no glue) provides the option of a removable drawer bottom.

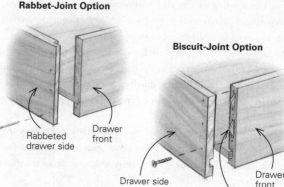

Rabbet-Joint Option

Rabbeted drawer side

Drawer front

Biscuit-Joint Option

Drawer side

Biscuits

Drawer front

Drawer front, back, and sides are made from ½-in.-thick solid maple.

These ⁷⁄₁₆-in.-dia. holes allow adjustment of the applied face. Drive these screws first to attach the face.

A ½-in.-thick drawer bottom slides in under the drawer back.

¾-in.-thick solid-maple applied face

The sides are dovetailed front and back.

½-in.-wide groove for bottom, located ½ in. from the bottom edge of the sides

Drill holes for setscrews that lock in the applied face.

on built-in cabinets rather than rabbeting the cabinet sides to accept the back. Scribed on site, a finished end covers the seam between the cabinet and the ¼-in. back. After cutting biscuit slots to join the case sides to the tops, I used cleats fastened with glue and brads or screws to support the case bottoms. The biscuit- and cleat-supported butt joints were reinforced with 1½-in. screws once the casework was put together.

As we assembled the cases, I checked for square and twist. I also cleaned off squeezed-out glue before it dried.

Solid-Wood Parts Need Special Consideration

Depending on the finish, I use either mortise-and-tenon joinery or pocket screws to assemble face frames before gluing them to carcases. Although pocket screws are quick and simple, I don't think the joint is as immobile as a glued mortise and tenon. While a hairline gap isn't as noticeable in natural wood, I've learned the

hard way not to use pocket screws for painted work that needs to look seamless. For this project, once the face frames were pocket-screwed, we glued and clamped them to the carcases.

The solid-maple counter was made by edge-joining two or three full-length boards. To increase the glue surface and to keep the boards even during clamping, I used biscuit joints about every 18 in. along the length. I determined the approximate location of the finished end so that I could avoid the nightmare of exposing a biscuit when I made the final cut. I sand and finish counters in the shop before I scribe and install them.

When I make cabinet doors, I keep the stock as thick as possible, at least ¾ in. and ideally ⅞ in. I flatten door stock on the jointer, then run it through the thickness planer to ensure that it is flat, square-edged, and uniform thickness. Using bar clamps rather than pipe clamps can help to keep doors flat. I lay the door directly on the clamp-bar surface so that I can detect any deflection, and clamp the

Continued →

door to the bar using smaller clamps if necessary. I check for square by comparing diagonal measurements and hold a straightedge across the top and bottom of the frame to ensure that the rail and stile joints are glued up flat, not bowed. I also check for twist, either by sighting across the bare surface of the door or with the aid of winding sticks. Finally, I check the back of the door to make sure the panel is centered in the frame, and I adjust it if necessary by applying pressure with a wide chisel.

When the doors are dry, I rough-fit them to the cabinet openings using a handplane or a tablesaw. Then I rout and chisel mortises for the butt hinges on the cabinets' face frames; the mortises in the doors will come later.

Next, I install the case backs and the solid ledgers. These hanging strips are screwed not just through the ¼-in. plywood cabinet backs, but directly through the top, the sides, or both. If the strips go only through the back and the back should somehow detach from the case, the entire assembly can fall forward, causing damage and possibly injury.

Installation Starts at the Highest Point of the Floor

Because this design called for an applied base molding, I could shim the casework up to level and count on the baseboard to hide the shims. I began from the high point on the floor and shimmed the cases up to level as necessary. The sections also were clamped together, so I could treat the three cabinets as a single unit if the wall behind them wasn't flat.

I use solid wood for counters because it generally holds up better than plywood and looks better with wear. When a solid counter is attached to a plywood case, the wood has to be able to move with changes in relative humidity. I set the counter in place and scribe as necessary, then attach it with screws in oversize holes that allow for wood movement.

As with the bases, I scribe the right face-frame stile to conform to irregularities in the wall, then screw together the upper units to form a single assembly before attaching it to the rear wall. No shimming is necessary because these upper cases are placed on a surface that should be level. I scribe the finished ends as needed and glue them in place. I also sand the face-frame edges flush if necessary.

Hang the Doors and Drawers After the Casework Is Locked In

After applying the baseboard and crown molding, we work on the doors. For inset applications, I like to plane doors and drawer faces to size after installing the casework. Although this technique is unconventional, I find it more efficient. Once in their final position, cabinets don't always sit quite the way they did in the ideal conditions of the shop, so postponing this final fitting until the installation is complete means the work is done only once.

After shimming the doors in place with the proper margins (about ³⁄₃₂ in. for stain grade, more for painted work), I mark the positions of the hinge mortises on the door stiles. Once marked, the door is clamped in a vise or on sawhorses, where I rout the mortises and mount the hinges. Once the door is rehung, I do a final fitting with a handplane.

Setting the drawers is the final stage. After finalizing the fit, I use a pair of screws and fender washers to hold the drawer face in position. Once I'm satisfied with the fit, I drive in four additional screws to lock the face to the drawer box.

Kitchens Illuminated

By Jeffrey R. Dross

We used to light kitchens with one fixture placed in the middle of the ceiling, an arrangement that rarely provided enough light in the right location and often made kitchens stark, gloomy places. Unfortunately, the trend today toward recessed-can lighting has not improved the situation. Often improperly placed and poorly chosen, recessed cans cast inopportune shadows and create undesirable washes of glare that make it almost impossible to see what you're cutting on the counter, even with the added benefit of undercounter lighting. The truth is that despite opulent fixtures, cans by the dozen, and undercabinet lights, many of the lighting layouts that I see today are ineffective because designers chose the wrong fixtures and didn't optimize their placement.

If, however, you follow a few simple steps that help you properly position those cans and choose the right lamps to put in them, your kitchens will suddenly seem bigger, look brilliant, and function beautifully.

Drawer Size and Weight Determine Drawer-Slide Hardware

A drawer that's 40 in. wide requires special slides to withstand the stresses placed on it when it's fully extended. However, the full-extension, heavy-duty 12-in. drawer slides from Accuride (model 3640; www.accuride.com) that  I chose turned out to be ¼ in. longer than the inside of the base cabinets. Fortunately, cutting a hole in the cabinet's back made just enough space.

To install the drawers, we hang the drawer box first and apply the face later. Typically, we hang the box with special low-profile screws that can be purchased with the drawer hardware. The box should be hung initially about ⅛ in. behind its final position. In this instance, we were working with ¾-in.-thick applied drawer faces, so the box was set back ⅞ in.

Light layering involves using several types of light in one room to serve different purposes. The basic layers are: **1** Ambient lighting **2** Task lighting **3** Accent or decorative lighting

The Foundation Layer

Good lighting consists of three basic layers: ambient (general) lighting, accent (decorative) lighting, and task (work) lighting. Strategically linking these layers creates a cohesive design that takes the place of that single light source of the past.

Like a basic coat of paint, ambient light serves as a backdrop for all other light. By itself, it may not be interesting, but it serves the total design and the visual comfort of the end user. In today's kitchens, ambient light is provided primarily by recessed cans. Unfortunately, it's in this initial ambient-lighting layer that most designers make their most egregious mistakes. Understanding how light is emitted from recessed fixtures is essential for positioning them correctly.

Beam Angle Is the Key to Spacing Cans

Unlike surface-mounted fixtures, which emit light in a 360° angle, light emitted from recessed fixtures forms a parabolic or cone-shaped beam. This is why they are also colloquially called downlights. Think of recessed cans as automobile headlights installed upside down on the ceiling.

The shape of the cone of light is determined by a reflector that focuses the light into a specific beam angle. This reflector may be

part of the fixture itself, or it may be built into the lamp (bulb). The "R" found in the popular bulb designations "R," "MR," and "PAR" indicates that these lamps have reflectors. In either case, whether built into the fixture or the bulb, you will find the beam angle specified by the manufacturer, generally on the box. This angle ranges from an extremely narrow 8° to a very wide 55°.

A narrow beam angle pushes all of the light into a slender cone, resulting in an intense quantity of light in a tiny space appropriate for illuminating a small worksurface, such as a cutting board or a sink. Wider beams take that same amount of light and disperse it over a broader area, which is generally more appropriate to ambient lighting. When using wide beam angles for ambient lighting, however, remember that the wider the beam, the lower the light intensity. To end up with an even distribution of the right amount of light, the quantity of fixtures and their beam angle must work in tandem so that beams overlap to cast even lighting, and that beams don't intersect upper cabinets to create shadows on worksurfaces.

When calculating ambient lighting for a kitchen, lighting designers take most of their lighting measurements at countertop level. It's the place where eyes generally focus when in the kitchen. The first rule of recessed-light placement is that cans must be positioned so that the beam angle will just miss the lower lip of

Continued ➡

Space Lights Using Beam Angle

Pay attention to the beam angle of overhead lights to eliminate glare and shadows in the kitchen. Wide-beam lights placed too close to cabinets create glare on the doors and shadows underneath. Improper placement of undercounter task lighting compounds this problem. Well-placed lighting positions the beam angle so that it misses the cabinet front, illuminating the countertop area and overlapping adjacent lights to produce solid overall illumination. Undercounter lights placed toward the front of the cabinets provide supplemental task lighting.

Poor Placement

Good Placement

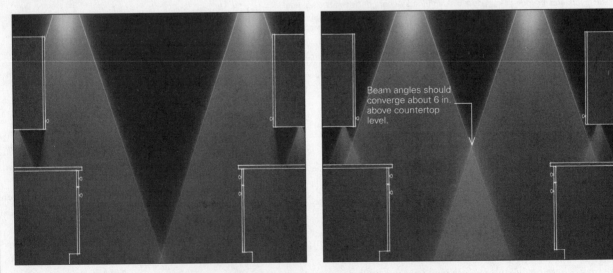

Beam angles should converge about 6 in. above countertop level.

Beam angle refers to the angle at which light radiates from a lamp. The narrower the beam, the more intense the light. Narrow beam angles often are used for highlighting objects; wider beam angles are used for general illumination.

the upper cabinets. If your light beam touches the front surface of the upper cabinets, it will cast an unfortunate shadow on the countertop worksurface below.

Plotting It on Paper

To position cans correctly, find the beam angle of your lights, which is listed on the fixture, the manufacturer's website, the packaging, or the lamp itself. On your kitchen section drawing (a side view of the kitchen showing cabinets), use a protractor to plot the beam angle you want to use (40° is a good place to start, although you may find you need to adjust this later). Plot the beam's path relative to your upper cabinets, placing the first row of cans so that the beam angle just misses the front edge of the upper cabinet. To pinpoint the perpendicular placement of the next can along this first row, use the protractor again, this time on an elevation drawing (front view of the cabinets). Find a point 6 in. above the worksurface, and intersect the first beam angle with the second. Working backward, place the second can where that beam angle hits the ceiling. Using the protractor and beam-angle method, place the remainder of the cans.

Following this simple method will help you to avoid the most basic and most frequent mistakes I see in kitchen lighting.

Calculating the Light Requirements

Once you've created a layout based on beam angle, you still have some work to do. The next step is determining how strong the lamps in your cans need to be to illuminate the space properly. The Illuminating Engineering Society (IES) recommends a minimum of 30 footcandles (fc) for general ambient lighting in a kitchen. This means you'll want an even distribution of 30 fc at countertop height.

This is an adequate amount of light for most kitchens. In some situations, however, more lighting might be needed. For example, if occupants are age 55 or older, the base recommendation from IES jumps to 40 fc. Someone with very poor vision may need much more. Young folks with excellent eyesight may get along with less, but stick to 30 fc as a starting point.

A footcandle is based on the output of one standard candle, burning 1 ft. away from the surface it illuminates. The other measure I use in lighting calculations is candlepower, which represents the traveling power of light emitted from a lamp.

These two measurements are the basis for the formulas I use to figure out how much light is needed at point A (the fixture) to see clearly at point B (countertop height).

Adjusting to the Situation

To complete our calculations, we have two more factors to take into account: room reflectance (how much of the lamp's light is absorbed or reflected) and ceiling height (the distance light has to travel to get to the countertop-height sweet spot).

A dark room absorbs light, requiring additional illumination. A kitchen finished with light colors requires less light. Because they become nonreflective black rectangles at night, windows increase

lighting needs. Countertop materials factor into reflectance as well: Black-granite countertops may be beautiful, but they do not reflect much light.

To deal with these variables, IES recommends adjustment factors that can be applied to the base recommendation (30 fc) to ensure proper illumination.

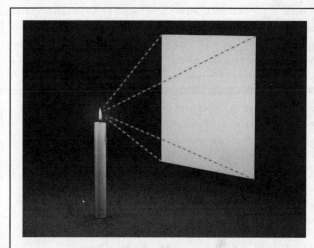

A FOOTCANDLE is a measurement of light intensity that represents the illumination of an average candle at a distance of 1 ft. from the surface being lit. Although largely abandoned abroad, footcandles (fc) are still used in the United States to express how much light is needed for a particular application, such as IES's recommended 30 fc for ambient lighting in an average kitchen.

CANDLEPOWER (CP) is a measure of light concentration in a light beam. The higher the candlepower, the more powerful the illumination is at that point. Also referred to as candela, mean candlepower, or center-beam candlepower (CBCP), this measurement is found on the same manufacturers' spec sheets where you'll find beam angle and other information.

A LUMEN represents how much light a lamp emits. Since the introduction of super-energy-efficient lighting, lumens have largely replaced watts as the go-to measurement for lamp intensity. As a result, it's the number you'll find on most lamp packaging (indoor lamps typically have light outputs ranging from 50 to 10,000 lumens). The number of lumens, however, does not take into account the intensity of the light at any one point in the beam. That is why professionals gauge the illumination power of focused lights (such as can lights) in candlepower rather than lumens.

Continued ➜

After these adjustments are made, one last formula is needed to determine the amount of light required from your fixtures. That's because a lamp placed 18 in. from a surface delivers a lot more light than the same lamp located 8 ft. away. To calculate how much candlepower a lamp must produce to get the required illumination where it's needed, lighting designers use the inverse-square law. According to this rule, the candlepower (cp) of your fixture should be equal to the distance from the light source to the countertop area squared (D^2) and then multiplied by the footcandles required. The equation is written $cp = D^2 \times fc$. The example at right demonstrates this formula for an 8-ft. ceiling.

Just a reminder: I've been measuring light needs at countertop height, but I'm focusing only on ambient light. For countertop tasks, you'll want to supplement this 30 fc of ambient light with another 40 fc or more of undercabinet lighting to reach the 70 fc recommended for worksurfaces.

Ceiling height makes a significant difference in the amount of illumination required to light a kitchen properly. If the ceiling height is just 2 ft. taller (10 ft.), you need almost twice as much illumination to deliver an adequate amount of light to that countertop sweet spot.

Now Find Your Lights . . . or Maybe Start Over

After you've established the location of your cans and calculated the beam angle and candlepower, you need to select the right lamps. Invariably, after looking through manufacturers' catalogs and websites, or receiving help from a lighting consultant, you'll seek out the product that emits the requisite candlepower combined with the beam angle you used in your lighting layout, only to discover that this lamp or integrated fixture does not exist.

So it's back to the drawing board for some recalculation. For example, if you planned the spacing based on a wide beam spread and the ceilings are very high, you may not find a lamp that can deliver the required amount of light. You may need to lay out the cans again and add more fixtures, using a tighter beam angle. Remember, fixtures that have a smaller beam angle deliver a larger concentration of light. Or you may opt to use fixtures that hang from the ceiling, effectively lowering the level of your light source.

You also may discover that you cannot place those cans in the ideal location because of a stray joist or other obstruction that sits in the middle of your perfect layout. I encountered this problem in my own kitchen. To provide the right amount of light on my counters, I sacrificed the amount of light at the center of the room. If a kitchen does not include an island, this is a good place for less light. I made the necessary adjustments in can placement to accommodate my joists, favoring worksurfaces and de-emphasizing perfect light in the center of the room. These kinds of adjustments are always a judgment call. Use logic and common sense, and you'll like the results.

Lighting by the Numbers

Getting ambient light right requires calculations based on real-world conditions. To demonstrate, let's look at the kitchen pictured on p. 547. This kitchen has an 8-ft. ceiling, and a floor and cabinets in midtone woods. The ceiling is white, and one wall is dark green. We'll assume the occupant is 58 years old. Here's how to calculate the ambient lighting needed for that room.

1. Plan for Cans

With a protractor, mark your chosen beam angle on a section drawing so that the beams from the first row of cans miss the cabinets and intersect just above countertop height. To place adjacent cans, repeat the process on an elevation or plan view, maintaining the same overlap.

2. Calculate Overall Ambient-Light Needs

Adjust ambient-light needs based on occupant age and room reflectance. IES adjustments are shown in charts 1 and 2, at right.

30 fc	Start with IES-recommended level of 30 fc.
30 fc x 1.33 = 39.9 fc	Multiply by age factor of 1.33 because the homeowner is 58 years old (see chart 1).
39.9 fc x 1 = 39.9 fc	Multiply by room reflectance factor of 1 because the wall, ceiling, and floor colors are of medium colorations (see charts 1 and 2).
39.9 fc x 1.33 = 53.07 fc	Multiply by countertop background factor of 1.33 because the countertops are dark (see chart 1).

Total footcandles required: 53.07. We can round to 53 before proceeding to the next step.

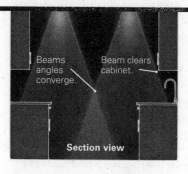

Beams angles converge.

Beam clears cabinet.

Section view

Plan view

Cans are spaced across the room by repeating the same beam angle with the appropriate overlap.

A section view (above) allows you to correctly position the cans relative to the cabinets. An elevation (frontal) view or a plan view (right) then can be used to space cans in each row for full illumination.

3. Calculate Required Candlepower

Based on the footcandle requirements established in step 2, we now factor in the ceiling height to arrive at the candlepower required for each fixture.

$$cp = D^2 \times fc$$
Start with the inverse-square law.

$$cp = 25 \times 53$$
The room has 8-ft. ceilings, so the worksurface is 5 ft. away; $5 \times 5 = 25$. We know the required fc is 53 from our calculations in step 2.

$$cp = 1325$$
Each recessed can must provide a candlepower of at least 1325 to illuminate the room adequately.

4. Find Fixtures

Match candlepower needs to a lamp or fixture with the right beam spread and candlepower. This information can be found on the manufacturers' spec sheets, websites, and catalogs. A little more candlepower is better than not enough.

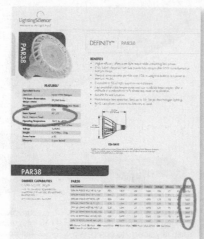

For more calculations, check out *Kitchen and Bath Lighting Made Easy* by Michael DeLuca (National Kitchen & Bath Association, 2001).

CHART 1

Adjustment factors for footcandle levels

Adjustment factor	0.66	1.0	1.33
Age	Under 40	40-55	Over 55
Average room reflectance (ceiling, walls, and floor)	Light (over 70%)	Medium (30%-70%)	Dark (under 30%)
Task background reflectance (countertop color)	Light (over 70%)	Medium (30%-70%)	Dark (under 30%)

CHART 2

Calculating room reflectance*

Wall or ceiling colors	Reflectance (%)
White, light cream	70-80
Light yellow	55-65
Light green, pink	45-50
Light blue, light gray	40-45
Beige, ocher, light brown, olive green	25-35
Orange, vermilion, medium gray	20-25
Dark colors (green, blue, red, gray)	10-15
Materials	**Reflectance (%)**
White plaster	80
White tile	65-75
Marble	30-70
Granite	20-25
Brick	10-20
Carbon/black	2-10
Mirror	95
Clear glass	6-8
Maple	60
Oak (light)	25-35
Oak (dark)	10-15
Mahogany	6-12
Walnut	5-10
Stainless	50-60
Aluminum	55-58

*If unknown, assume medium (30%-70%).

Continued ➡

Undercabinet Lighting

By Debra Judge Silber

There may be no place where advances in home lighting are more apparent than under kitchen cabinets. White-hot halogens and temperamental fluorescents are making way for a new crop of LEDs that are not just super-efficient—they're as aesthetically pleasing as the long-dominant incandescent. "Undercabinet lighting is one of the areas where LED is really ideal," says Joe Rey-Barreau, an architect and spokesman for the American Lighting Association who teaches at the University of Kentucky's College of Design. "There's nothing else I would even vaguely recommend." Improvements in color rendering, color temperature, and longevity are behind LEDs' seemingly universal acceptance by lighting designers. Their energy efficiency is remarkable, and they provide more lumens per watt than incandescent bulbs (or lamps, as they're called in the industry). Their life of 50,000 or more hours makes lamp replacement obsolete. Instead, in the case of many LED products, the presumption is that the fixture itself will be replaced after 15 to 20 years with a better and presumably less expensive version.

For all their benefits, high-quality LEDs remain expensive, in part due to the phosphor coatings used to enhance the quality of their light. Until that changes, alternatives such as xenon, halogen, and even fluorescent lamps will continue to be used in undercabinet fixtures.

This emphasis on the light source has overshadowed what used to be the decision in choosing undercabinet lighting: the fixture. Still, this choice remains important. Different types of fixtures not only install differently, but they cast light differently and create different architectural effects. This combination of light source and fixture has complicated the undercabinet-lighting decision.

Remember What It's There For

Make no mistake when specifying undercabinet fixtures: The primary reason to have light shining on your countertop is to aid in food preparation. In the practice known as light layering—that is, illuminating a space using different types of light with different functions—this is called task lighting. Because undercabinet lighting often plays a secondary role in accenting a backsplash or providing subtle illumination after hours (especially when dimmed), it's often regarded as accent lighting. This misconception can lead to choosing undercabinet lighting that does not provide enough illumination for countertop work.

With that understanding, the next step is to consider how the kitchen is used and who its occupants are. Jeffrey R. Dross, director for education and industry trends at Kichler Lighting, points out that older occupants want more illumination in the task area, as do avid cooks. "If you do a lot of home cooking, you're going to want more light than someone who uses the countertop to look at the Yellow Pages for carryout," he says.

Color Temperature Matters

Other factors to consider are the surfaces and style of the kitchen. The color temperature of the lamps you choose will determine whether your undercabinet lighting evokes a warm, traditional feel or a bright, modern one. Color temperature also impacts how food appears—worth remembering if you use your countertop for an impromptu buffet.

FLUORESCENT With modest improvement in color rendering, ⅝-in.-dia. T5 tubes remain an economical undercabinet option.

HALOGEN A reputation for burning hot and having a relatively short life compared to other lamps cost halogens their popularity.

XENON Low-voltage xenon lamps offer warm (not hot) operation, last about 10,000 hours, and provide adequate light at a moderate price.

LED Forget that blinding blue light. Today's long-lasting LEDs offer variable color temperatures and are vastly more efficient than incandescents.

Color Temperature

Whether your chicken soup appears golden yellow or simply pale may be a reflection of your cooking skills—or it may depend on the light source you're viewing it under. Old-school fluorescents—and more recently, inexpensive LEDs—had a reputation for casting an unflattering light on people and some foods because of their high (5000K) color temperature. This has all changed with the new generation of lamps, which offer a wide range of color temperatures. The difference can be seen in these apples photographed under LED lights of different color temperatures. While cool, crisp light enhances the green of the apple, warmer light brightens the wooden base.

Color temperature is measured in kelvins (K). Residential lamps typically have a color temperature that ranges from about 2700K (the light cast from an old-fashioned incandescent) to 5000K (the color of daylight). The higher the color temperature, the harsher and "colder" the light. In North America, where incandescent lighting has been the rule, designers tend to recommend warmer temperatures, edging a bit higher for contemporary kitchens. "The color of the light should match the color of the environment," says Dross, who recommends 2700K lamps for wood-tone kitchens and 3000K for white or steel kitchens.

One reason the new LEDs have taken undercabinet culture by storm is that manufacturers have discovered how to tame the cold, blue light of the LED with phosphor coatings that cast a warm, pleasant light. San Francisco-based lighting designer Randall Whitehead especially likes new LEDs that allow homeowners a range of temperatures. "This allows you to have a cooler color to show off your modern kitchen and a warmer color to show off your buffet," he says.

Color temperatures for halogens and xenons hover around 3000K. While large fluorescents are available in many color temperatures, Rey-Barreau points out that the smaller T5 tubes used in undercabinet fixtures haven't quite got the range. "For undercabinet lighting, it's hard to get fluorescent bulbs that have good color," he says.

In addition to temperature, you should look for a high color-rendering index (CRI) for your undercabinet lighting. CRI represents how well light interprets color and is rated on a sale of 0 to 100, with 100 being the best. Undercabinet lighting should have a minimum CRI of 85; for LEDs, Whitehead recommends 90. In general, the higher the CRI, the more expensive the lamp. If you can't find the CRI listed in the product literature of a lamp, don't buy it, Dross says.

The Right Light In The Right Place

The best task lighting puts light where you need it. Experts recommend placing undercabinet light sources toward the front of the cabinet, where they can illuminate the section of countertop where most prep work takes place. They shy away from direct-wire fixtures, which, because they tap directly into 120v stub-outs beneath the cabinets, are mounted against the backsplash. (Some manufacturers make up for this by aiming the lamps forward, a situation that can leave the backsplash in shadow.) Though wired to a direct current, many direct-wire products have a built-in transformer allowing the use of brighter, longer-life 12v or 24v halogen or xenon lamps. On the plus side, direct-wire fixtures are generally inexpensive, and their installation is familiar to most electricians.

The better choice, designers say, is modular low-voltage fixtures that can be mounted in a forward position and linked together to create a continuous line of light across the worksurface. Typically more expensive than direct-wire options, they also require more planning to determine what type of transformer will be used and where it will be mounted. One light per cabinet is typically recommended to ensure adequate illumination across the countertop.

An opaque lens guards against one of the major crimes of undercabinet lights, particularly LEDs: the annoying dots of light and multiple shadows produced by multiple light sources. "A lot of LED products have a clear or stippled lens," observes Whitehead. "On a shiny countertop, you'll see the individual diodes. You want to make sure it has a frosted lens to diffuse the light."

Puck or disk lighting is a mixed bag. Disks can create dramatic dots of light on a backsplash—but that's not ideal if the goal is useful task lighting. Halogen pucks in particular are notorious for damaging foodstuffs stored above them with their intense heat.

Continued →

New LED versions eliminate that concern, and some offer a much thinner profile, not to mention longer life and more efficient operation.

For all their hype, LED tapes present challenges in undercabinet applications because the light they provide is often not bright enough. Some manufacturers offer LED tapes in several intensities, including super-bright tapes that provide just enough power for adequate task lighting. Carefully chosen, these can work in applications where intensity is not a concern. Another option is to double up the tape for more light, but that means doubling the cost as well.

Trading Up Is Part of the Process

An important truth about LED tapes and most LED fixtures is that when the diodes die out, the entire unit, not the individual chips, will need to be replaced. This is a fundamental shift in lighting that few professionals and even fewer consumers have managed to get their heads around, says Rey-Barreau. Add to that the expense of LED lights and the rapid pace at which LED technology is progressing, and the potential for buyer's remorse becomes staggering.

Still, Rey-Barreau is upbeat. "The nice thing is that they have gotten to the point where the quality of the product and the efficacy is so good that even the thing you're stuck with is not bad," he says. "And 10 years from now, you'll replace it with a better product at a better price."

What's Going Under Cabinets Now

With improvements in both lamps and the fixtures that house them, there have never been more choices in undercabinet lighting. Here are some popular options.

Led Tape: Output Is Everything

LED tapes are all the rage, but most are better as accent lighting—under toe kicks or coves—than undercabinet task lights. Some manufacturers, however, have introduced high-output tapes that provide satisfactory undercabinet light. These include Maxim Lighting's Ultima Star 24v with an output of 254 lumens per ft., more than twice the 77-lumen output of its Basic tape. Both have a set color temperature of 3500K. The Color Flex tape ups the ante with a color temperature that adjusts from 2900K to 5000K. The key to getting a good LED tape is to test the product at a reputable lighting showroom that deals with established manufacturers. Complaints include adhesive failure and finicky connections, particularly among the many low-quality imports on the market.

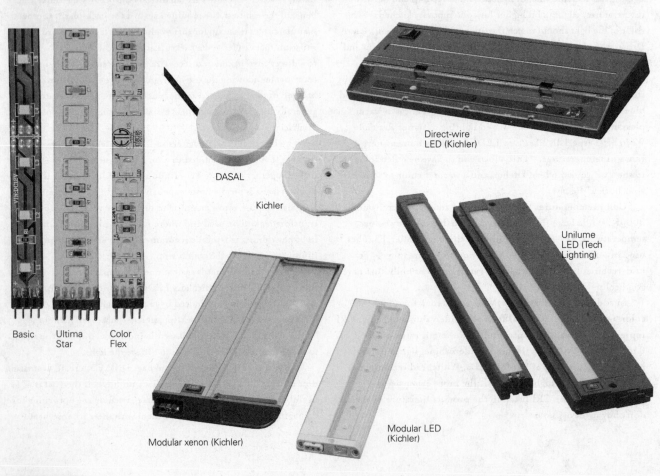

Basic
Ultima Star
Color Flex
DASAL
Kichler
Direct-wire LED (Kichler)
Unilume LED (Tech Lighting)
Modular xenon (Kichler)
Modular LED (Kichler)

Pucks: Improving a Spotty Reputation

Once-standard halogen and xenon puck lights are rapidly being pushed aside by LED versions, which not only are highly energy efficient but run much cooler. (Halogen pucks have been known to melt items stored in cabinets above them.) Some are so thin they're barely noticeable even under flat-bottomed European-style cabinets, such as Kichler's LED disk. DASAL Lighting's puck, challenges the warm cast of incandescents with a color temperature of 2700K. Regardless of lamping, pucks, disks, and buttons intended for undercabinet tasks should be weighed carefully with regard to beam spread and intensity to ensure sufficient illumination on the countertop. While some designers like the rhythmic pattern pucks produce under a cabinet, others dislike the spots of light or feel they interfere with functionality.

Low-Voltage Modular: Choose Your Location and Your Lamp

Low-voltage modular lighting is the undercabinet choice for many designers because fixtures can be mounted toward the front of the cabinets, where they deliver the most light. Modular LED units can be exceptionally slim but costly, which has allowed modulars outfitted with incandescent (typically xenon) lamps to remain popular. The 12v, 18w xenon lamps used in the Kichler model at right have a color temperature of 2700K and a CRI of 100, but their efficacy of 6 lumens per watt can't match the 41 lumens per watt of their LED counterpart.

Direct-Wire Led: Better Light in an Imperfect Place

Lighting designers typically caution against direct-wire undercabinet fixtures, because by necessity they're mounted against the backsplash—not near the cabinet front where their light is needed. But if the electrician has already stubbed out a line under each cabinet, or if you're hoping to upgrade the fluorescents you've had for years, direct-wire LED units may be the answer. A built-in driver steps down the current to power the LED chips.

Remote-Phosphor Lens Leds: Better Yet

If LEDs have one remaining drawback, it's this: It takes multiple LEDs to light a countertop, and those tiny multiple points of light create annoying multiple shadows on the workspace. That's been eliminated in LED fixtures where the yellow phosphor coating required to create white light from blue LEDs is applied to the lens rather than the individual chips. Commanding the category is Tech Lighting's Unilume line, which includes both modular and light-bar type fixtures.

Choose the Right Kitchen Sink

By Clair Urbain

Whether you're just fantasizing about your dream kitchen or are ready to roll up your sleeves to replace that chipped, stained, clumsy sink that's been there far too long, there are many options to consider when choosing this crucial kitchen fixture. What do you like and dislike about the sink you have? Is it too deep, too shallow, too big, or too small? What look are you trying to achieve, and what type of countertops do you have? You also need to consider how you use the sink, because an avid chef will have entirely different needs from a microwave master who serves quick-and-easy meals. To help navigate the countless options, break the decision into three areas: layout, material, and installation type.

NOTE: Prices cited in this article are from 2012.

Layout

Material

Installation Type

Continued ➡

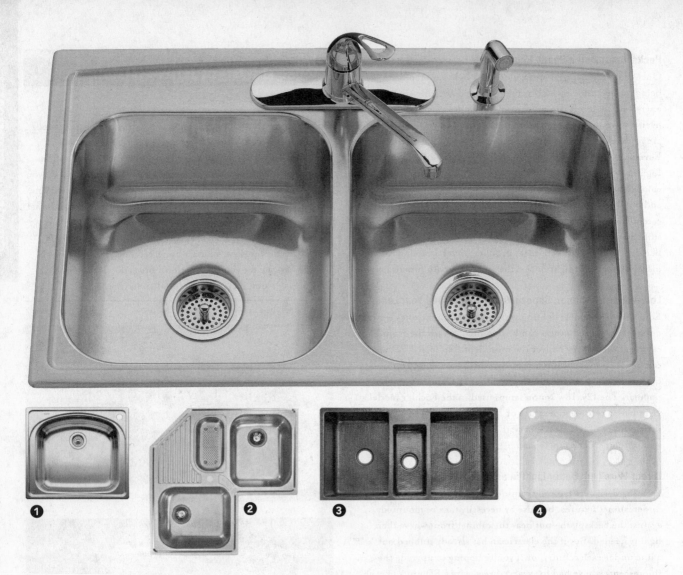

Choose a Layout

Sink manufacturers continue to develop the look and configuration of sinks so that they better match the needs of today's users. A wide variety of bowl configurations allows you to match sink type to the type of cooking, cleaning, and other chores you do. The type of faucet you choose and other accessories you may want to add, such as soap or hot-water dispensers, also affect your sink decision.

BOWL SHAPE AND ORIENTATION Bowls with straighter sides and tighter corner radii have more capacity. D-shaped bowls (1) with a curved back provide more room for maneuvering large pans but may require moving the faucet to the countertop behind the sink.

In corners or in tight locations, L-shaped sinks (2) or a sink placed on the diagonal may make better use of space.

NUMBER OF BOWLS Decide how many bowls you need based on the size of your kitchen and your typical activities in it. A large, single-bowl sink can be the best choice if you have a small kitchen or if you plan to wash most of your dishes in a dishwasher. Double bowls of equal size work well with multiple cooks in the kitchen, but if one cook focuses on prep work, a double-bowl design that includes a half-size or ¾-size bowl may be a better solution. Offset or shallow/deep double bowls and triple bowls (3) are becoming more common and may be better matches for your style of cooking and living. With a triple-bowl sink, one bowl can be used for dirty dishes, another can accept food scraps for the garbage disposal, and the third can be available for soaking or hand-washing. This luxury often means installing nonstandard cabinetry to accommodate a larger sink footprint.

BOWL DEPTH Because the standard sink-bowl depth is only about 8 in., dumping large pans or spraying down the sink can cause splashing. If you plan on washing large pans regularly, consider a sink with a 9-in.- or 10-in.-deep bowl. Some models have a lowered lip between the two bowls so that large pans can straddle both bowls comfortably and catch splashes during cleanup. Think about how bowl depth will be experienced by users of different heights. If the bowl is too deep, it may be hard for a shorter person to reach to the bottom and may make a taller person stoop too much.

CONSIDER ACCESSORIES First and foremost, make sure that the sink you choose can accommodate the faucet you want to mount to it. Does the sink have enough holes **(4)** for accessories, such as a sprayer and dispensers for soap and hot water? Do you need a dishwasher drain vent?

If you have your heart set on a certain sink but find that it has too many holes, you can attractively hide the holes you don't need with hole covers or extended baseplates.

Select the Sink Material

The decision process begins with a spectrum of materials ranging from steel to stone. With such a wide selection of mainstream and niche manufacturers, it's not hard to find examples of traditional or modern styling within each material category.

Composite

Composite sinks, best known by brand names such as Moenstone, Silgranit, Americast, and Swanstone, are made with a mixture of materials—usually quartz or granite—and a bonding agent. This combination produces a good-looking, resilient natural surface that can resist temperatures up to 500°F. Composite surfaces are also less vulnerable to dents and chips from dropped silverware or pans.

From a cost standpoint, composite sinks are an economical alternative to natural-stone sinks. They typically run between $200 and $700, but higher-end styles that incorporate drain boards cost nearly $1000. Expect to pay more for undermount sinks and multibowl models.

BOTTOM LINE Pros: Very durable; resistant to heat; can be a convincing alternative to granite and other natural stones. Cons: Moderately expensive.

Fireclay

Fireclay sinks are not only strong and beautiful, but they're also resistant to contamination and food-bacteria buildup. Unlike on enameled sinks, the glaze on fireclay is an inseparable part of the sink, rather than a coating. This means that fireclay generally can withstand much more abuse than porcelain-enameled cast iron. While strong, the fireclay surface can scratch, chip, and show burns. Also, fireclay sinks are comparatively brittle and may be incompatible with garbage disposals.

Fireclay can be cleaned with regular cleaners. Many fireclay sinks can even handle mildly abrasive cleaners, although nonabrasive varieties are recommended for everyday cleaning. Prices start at about $500, but can go as high as $2500 to $3000.

BOTTOM LINE Pros: Hygienic; strong; more durable than enameled sinks. Cons: More brittle and may not be compatible with garbage disposals.

Stainless Steel

Stainless steel is a popular material because it cleans easily, resists staining, withstands a wide range of temperatures, and is a fairly good value. It's also a natural complement to the stainless-steel appliances popular in today's kitchens.

Composite

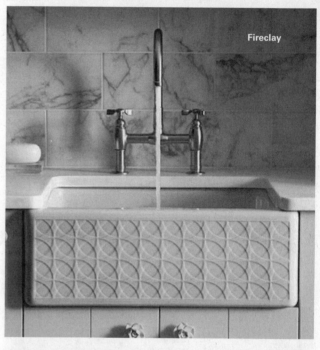

Fireclay

Stainless Steel

Continued ➜

Enameled

Glass

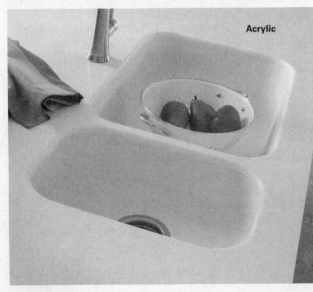

Acrylic

The thickness of stainless steel is measured by gauge—the higher the gauge number, the thinner the steel. Typically, commercial-grade sinks are made with 16-ga. steel, and the cheapest residential sinks are made with 23-ga. steel, which is noticeably thin, especially when saddled with a vibrating garbage disposal. Models with sound-absorbing undercoatings can muffle some of the noise from dish clatter and garbage-disposal use; this also helps to insulate the sink to reduce heat conduction from hot dishwater.

Because stainless steel is such a popular sink material, there is a wide variety of styles, and price closely follows steel gauge and complexity of bowl design. Typically, undermount stainless-steel sinks are slightly to substantially more expensive than drop-in models. Residential-grade, single-bowl kitchen sinks can be found for as little as $80; midgrade sinks cost from $100 to $400; high-end residential models are more than $500; and commercial-grade sinks can easily surpass $1000.

Most stainless-steel sinks have a brushed-satin finish, but higher-end and designer sinks may be highly polished. The satin finish does a better job of hiding minor scratches.

Stainless steel cleans up well with only soap and water and a quick towel dry, which helps the surface to form a strong, highly protective chrome-oxide film. Stubborn stains can be scoured lightly with a mild abrasive rubbed in the direction of the grain and then rinsed. Don't use steel wool on stainless-steel sinks because small particles can become embedded in the stainless steel and then rust.

Be sure to check that the model you choose is made from high-quality 304 stainless steel and that it meets ASME A112.19.3-2000 criteria for stainless-steel plumbing fixtures. Both pieces of information should be noted in the sink's specifications.

BOTTOM LINE Pros: Stain- and heat-resistant; easy to clean; a fairly good value; available in many shapes and sizes. Cons: Light-gauge models can be flimsy and noisy; highly polished sinks can show scratches.

Enameled

Enamel-on-cast-iron or enamel-on-steel sinks are available in a wide variety of colors and are easy to clean. They can take the shock of a hot pan or pot being placed in them, but their rigid enamel coating can chip and crack if heavy items are dropped on them. A crack in the enamel will expose the cast iron or steel to water and air, which encourages rusting.

Enamel sinks can be dulled by aggressive cleaning, which can lead to more dirt accumulation and staining. Enamel-on-steel sinks tend to be the least expensive sinks, with models beginning at $150. Enamel-on-cast-iron sinks start at about $200.

BOTTOM LINE Pros: Available in many colors; solid-feeling and heavy. Cons: Susceptible to chips and cracks; relatively heavy weight may complicate undermount installations.

Natural Stone

Exotic Metals

Glass

Although they constitute a small niche, glass kitchen sinks exist. One manufacturer is Jeannette Specialty Glass/JSG Oceana, a company that uses a special borosilicate glass commonly found in cooking and refrigeration applications and in pharmaceutical laboratories. The company claims that the glass has a low coefficient of expansion, can take repeated temperature shocks from boiling water, and is highly resistant to nonfluorinated chemicals, so its surface retains its clear and lustrous qualities over time and after repeated cleaning. Although it's scratch resistant and can stand up to bumps and drops from normal use, like porcelain, it can break from blows by heavy objects. JSG Oceana glass sinks are available in top-mount and undermount configurations, but they also can be free-formed for high-end kitchens. Standard bowl-type sinks cost around $400, and an undermount sink used in a double-sink configuration runs around $900 per sink. Custom sinks are priced based on specifications and desired look.

BOTTOM LINE Pros: Unique look; tolerant of high temperatures and temperature shocks. Cons: Can be severely damaged by hard impacts; limited number of manufacturers to choose from; may not be aesthetically compatible with all countertop options.

Acrylic

Acrylic sinks are light yet sturdy; come in a wide variety of colors, patterns, and shapes; and are less expensive than most other sinks. They are more vulnerable to scratches, however, and they have a low luster when compared with quartz or granite composites. Also, be careful where you put that hot pan; temperatures over 300°F can damage acrylic.

The material used in solid-surface counters, known under brand names such as Corian or Silestone, also can be molded into sinks. Because the material is the same all the way through

the sink profile, minor scratches can be buffed out. However, temperatures greater than 300°F may cause damage from melting.

Figure on paying $100 to $400 for simple to midrange sink designs and $500 or more for high-end models.

BOTTOM LINE Pros: Economical alternative to other sinks; lots of color options; solid composition means scratches can be buffed out. Cons: Sensitive to high temperatures; typically limited to undermount installations.

Natural Stone

Stone sinks can make bold design statements. They are hewn from solid rock such as granite, marble, quartz, limestone, sandstone, onyx, travertine, or soapstone. Semiprecious materials such as fossil wood also can be used.

Although several manufacturers and artisans sell standard styles of natural-stone sinks, the crystalline structure and veining of the material makes each sink unique. Few materials are more durable than rock, but because all rock formations are porous, these sinks must be sealed before use. Also, many types of stone have natural pocks and imperfections that must be filled with stone dust and epoxy, matching the natural stone as much as possible.

Typically, stone kitchen sinks cost between $500 and $1500, but prices can go much higher depending on the variety of stone and level of customization.

BOTTOM LINE Pros: Very durable; good sound-deadening properties. Cons: High price; may require sealing; heavy weight may complicate installation.

Exotic Metals

Stainless steel isn't the only type of metal sink. For a distinctive look, consider more exotic metals such as copper, brass, nickel, and even titanium.

Continued ➧

Copper has strong antibacterial and antiviral properties, even against E. coli, and because the surface oxidizes, slight scratches tend to "heal" themselves, although the patina can change.

High-quality brass or titanium sinks are actually a combination of stainless steel and either brass or titanium. A brass sink offers a warm, rich look, while titanium sinks come in three colors: anthracite, bronze, and gold. Beware of lower-quality brass sinks, which have coatings that can flake over time.

Depending on the material, exotic-metal sink prices range from slightly more than stainless steel for simple configurations of copper to thousands of dollars for high-end titanium or brass.

BOTTOM LINE Pros: Durable; hygienic; can offer a unique handmade look. Cons: Some metals can change slightly in appearance with age; cost can be high.

Choose an Installation Style

Typically, sinks are installed either by dropping them into the hole cut in the counter or by mounting them under the counter. Manufacturers typically have specific instructions that need to be followed to the letter, especially in undermount installations.

Drop-In

Drop-in sinks rest on top of the counter, making it more difficult to sweep crumbs and spills into the sink, but they are arguably the easiest to install. These sinks are fastened with either screw clamps that

integrate with a factory-attached track or, in the case of heavy sinks, a bead of sealant between the countertop and the edge of the sink. A word of caution for screw-clamp installations: Overtightening the fastener will strip it out of the base material, twist off the head, bend the screw, or even break the sink. If it's an in-place installation, be sure to have a good light source when working.

Undermount

Undermount, or rimless, sinks are gaining popularity, especially when used with granite, synthetic stone, or other materials that show the full-depth beauty of the countertop. However, they are more difficult to install and may require the use of special mounting brackets and tools (or, in the case of farmhouse sinks, often a solid platform). As a result, these sinks are often installed by the countertop fabricator. Don't use undermount sinks with laminate countertops because the slightest imperfection will expose the countertop's engineered-wood core to moisture, which can cause the wood to swell and the laminate to separate.

Epoxy

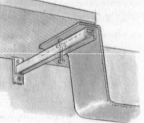

Brackets

Sealant-Secured

Inserts

Screw Clamps

Platform

Cut a Laminate Countertop for a Sink

By Andy Engel

When you're building or remodeling a kitchen, you can save time and money by using a ready-made laminate countertop. These tops, which generally have an integral backsplash and wraparound front edge, are durable and easy to find at home centers and lumberyards. Even if you have a laminate top custom-fabricated or you make it yourself, you can still use the sink-cutting methods described here.

Many sinks come with a layout template that makes marking the cut easy; you just trace the template with a pencil and cut out the hole with a jigsaw. If you don't have a template, trace around the sink rim with a pencil, and then adjust the line inward to get the proper fit. On dark tops like this one, I make the layout marks on light-colored masking tape so they're easier to see.

I cut most of the opening with a jigsaw equipped with a laminate-cutting blade. These blades cut on the downstroke to prevent chipping. If the countertop has an integral backsplash, there's usually not enough room for a jigsaw when making the rear cut (adjacent to the backsplash). I make this cut with an oscillating multitool.

After making the rear cut, I attach a cleat to the cutout with a single screw. The cleat supports the cutout in place to prevent the countertop from breaking as the cut is finished. I use one screw so I can rotate the cleat out of the blade's path while cutting.

To make less mess, you might be tempted to cut the top outdoors or in your shop and then move the prepared top to the sink base. I generally don't do this because with a large hole in the center, it's very easy to break the countertop while moving it.

Make the cut

To prevent damaging the laminate countertop, use a reverse-cutting jigsaw blade. These blades have teeth that cut on the downstroke instead of the upstroke. Go slowly, and apply steady downward pressure so that the saw doesn't bounce while cutting.

There's often not enough room to fit a jigsaw between the back of the sink and the backsplash. In these instances, use a fine-tooth blade in an oscillating multitool. Make the cut in several passes so you don't overheat the blade, which slows cutting and dulls the teeth.

Step-by-Step

1. CENTER THE SINK. Use a combination square lined up between the cabinet doors to establish the side-to-side location of the sink. Make sure the front cut won't hit the cabinet rail below.

2. TRACE THE LINE. Trace the template or the sink rim as the starting point for layout lines. A layer of tape helps you see the pencil lines.

3. MOVE THE LINE INWARD. Without a template, the layout line must be moved inward so it will be covered by the sink rim. The margins vary by sink, but the minimum is about ¼ in. Make a mark at both ends of all four sides.

4. CONNECT THE DOTS. Use a straightedge to connect the marks that correspond with the actual cutline. Connect the corners at an angle for an easier cut and better sink support.

5. DOUBLE-CHECK THE LAYOUT. Confirm that the cuts will be covered fully by the sink rim, then cross out the original lines to prevent cutting on the wrong line.

6. DRILL THE CORNERS. Drill the insides of every corner with a ⅜-in. spade bit. Make sure the holes are fully within the lines that mark the actual sink cutout.

Continued →

7. CUT THE BACK. Because of the backsplash, there's generally not enough room to cut the back side with a jigsaw. Instead, use a fine-tooth blade in an oscillating multitool.

8. ATTACH A CLEAT. To prevent the top from breaking as you finish the cut, secure a cleat to the top. A single screw in the center allows you to rotate the cleat out of the way while cutting.

9. FINISH UP WITH A JIGSAW. Use a jigsaw with a reverse-cutting blade to finish the sink cutout. Maintain downward pressure to keep the saw from bouncing as it cuts.

10. TEST THE FIT. After checking that the sink fits inside the cutout, clean all dust from the countertop, run a bead of silicone sealant around the rim, and install the clips that secure the sink.

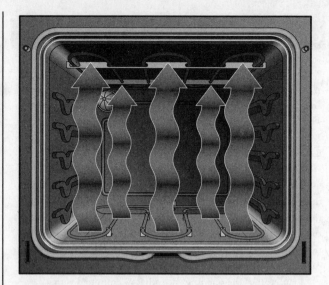

HOT AIR RISES. Set on "bake," a conventional oven produces heat from its bottom element. The top element is for broiling.

Electric Ovens

By Don Burgard

The growing popularity of outdoor kitchens and year-round grilling hasn't changed the fact that most cooking is still done inside. The typical kitchen has at least a conventional and a microwave oven; some kitchens have these plus a convection oven; and still others have ovens that combine conventional with convection cooking, or convection with microwave cooking. When outfitting a new or remodeled kitchen, it's important to think about how you cook, and then to consider which ovens you'll need. Here's a look at your options in electric ovens.

Conventional Ovens

In a conventional oven, food is cooked through radiation and conduction: A heating element on the bottom of the oven transfers thermal energy through the chamber via electromagnetic waves. This energy then heats the exposed parts of the food through radiation. It also warms the container holding the food, which then transfers heat to the unexposed parts of the food through conduction. As a result, the center is the last area to be cooked. This process is good if you like your food crispy on the outside and tender on the inside, but it also can result in food that looks done on the outside but isn't cooked all the way through.

The main drawback of this type of oven is that it does not create uniform heating conditions throughout the chamber. In a three-rack oven, items on the bottom rack cook most quickly because they are nearest the heating element, and items on the middle rack cook the slowest. Items on the top rack cook almost as quickly as those on the bottom rack because the hot air in the chamber rises to the top.

Convection Ovens

A convection oven has heating elements on the top and bottom, and a third element connected to a fan on the back wall of the chamber. This fan moves the air in the chamber, which cooks the food more evenly than in a conventional oven. This can be observed easily when baking three sheets of cookies. Unlike in a conventional oven, which requires rotating the cookie sheets through the racks for even baking, all three layers in a convection oven bake at the same rate.

Because moving air cooks more quickly than still air, the temperature in a convection oven doesn't have to be as high. A ballpark figure is to reduce the temperature by 25°F. The food will still cook faster, though; how much faster requires experimenting, but figure on somewhere between 10% and 25%. Manufacturer guidelines can help here, too.

If a convection oven cooks more evenly and more quickly than a conventional oven, why haven't convection ovens replaced conventional ovens? The food in a convection oven is cooked by circulating air, so anything that impedes the air from circulating freely—such as too many dishes or pans, dishes or pans with high sides, or covered dishes—reduces the oven's efficiency. If

A HOT-AIR JACUZZI. In a convection oven, heat is generated by elements at the top, bottom, and rear of the chamber. A fan circulates the hot air, keeping a constant temperature throughout.

thin-crust pizza is on the menu, therefore, a convection oven can have it ready sooner; if you're serving up a casserole, however, you're better off using a conventional oven.

Microwave Ovens

The microwave oven has come a long way since Raytheon introduced the Radarange, a 750-lb. appliance the size of a refrigerator that sold for $5000 in 1947. Its size, portability, and usefulness have made it a staple in North American kitchens, not to mention in employee lunchrooms and college dorm rooms. A microwave oven works by emitting electromagnetic waves at a certain frequency that penetrate food to a depth of up to 1½ in. These waves cause liquid-water molecules to become agitated and produce heat through friction. Areas deeper than 1½ in. are heated through conduction.

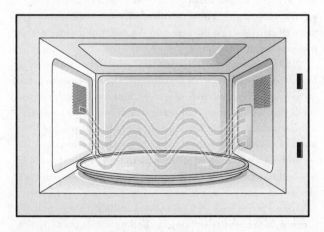

MAKE WAVES, NOT HEAT. Electromagnetic waves enter the chamber through the waveguide. A mica cover keeps food and liquid out of the waveguide while still allowing the waves to pass through.

It takes much longer to defrost food in a microwave oven than it does to cook it because ice molecules, unlike liquid-water molecules, can't rotate. Don't be tempted to speed things up by defrosting on anything other than the defrost setting, though. The moment liquid water is present in a certain area, the microwave will start cooking that area. You'll end up with food that's cooked in some areas but still frozen in others.

A microwave oven produces waves and not actual heat, which is why you can touch the inside of the chamber immediately after cooking and not burn your hand. Therefore, the microwave's settings control the percentage of the cooking time the unit is actually producing waves, not the temperature, as with a conventional or convection oven. For example, a 1000w microwave oven set at level 5 (or 50%) still produces 1000w of power, but it cycles on and off at equal intervals.

Cooktops from Simmer to Sear

By Sean Groom

Cooktops have never been as popular as ranges, which combine stove and oven, perhaps because a separate cooktop and wall oven costs at least twice as much as a decent-quality range. Installation is also more costly with two distinct appliances. A separate cooktop offers several advantages, however. Freed of the burners, the oven can be put at a more comfortable height, and the cooktop can be placed anywhere in the kitchen.

Installation heights can vary for comfort and can include space below for cabinets or for wheelchair access. Smooth-surface cooktops can integrate almost seamlessly into a countertop. Finally, having separate units allows you to pick cooktop features and oven features independently to match your needs exactly.

Choose the Fuel Type First

Today's market features three types of cooktop: gas burner, radiant electric, and induction. There are many reasons to choose one over another, but the detail that has the greatest impact on your cooking experience is heat response. You'll want to consider how finely you can tune the heat, how quickly the burners transfer heat to cookware, whether burners can cool rapidly and then return swiftly to high heat, and what the maximum and minimum heat-output settings are.

No rule of thumb will guide you to a particular type of cookware or pot size with burner or element output. Generally speaking, higher-Btu burners heat a pot quicker. As important as heat output, though, is the physical size of the heating elements. For example, a 19,000-Btu gas burner is great for bringing a 12-in.-dia., 16-qt. stockpot to boil, but if the largest pot you use is 7 in. or 8 in. dia., the flame pattern at the highest setting could be wider than the pot. Finally, look for burners or elements that accommodate specialty pots and pans you use frequently.

Continued ➜

Gas

Radiant

Induction

Gas: The Choice of Chefs

Gas is the serious cook's benchmark fuel for its nimble heating response. The flame on a gas cooktop seamlessly adjusts from steak-searing high to chocolate-melting low and back again. The open-grate system doesn't retain much heat, so the temperature transitions are nearly instantaneous.

Continuous grates let you slide cookware between burners; heavy cast iron provides even heating. Many grates are porcelain-coated, and some can be cleaned in the dishwasher, although most manufacturers suggest soaking and hand-scrubbing. Cleaning up spills with sealed burners on the full-size gas cooktops I researched means removing the grates and sponging out the depressed spill-collection areas.

Give serious thought to your ventilation choice if you are buying a gas-fueled cooktop (see "Breathe Easy With the Right Range Hood," at fine homebuilding.com) because in addition to cooking odors and moisture, you'll want to remove the carbon dioxide, soot, and PCBs generated by gas combustion. If efficiency is a concern, it's worth noting that only between 35% and 40% of the combusted fuel's energy potential is used for cooking. Unlike the gas stoves of the old days, all the models shown here have electronic ignition rather than a standing pilot light, which cuts down on fuel consumption and pollutants.

While 30-in. and 36-in. models are the most common, gas cooktops are available in sizes ranging from four-burner 24-in.-wide units to 60-in.-wide cooktops. The largest units use the extra real estate for additional burners and/or specialty surfaces such as wok burners, griddles, or grills. Basic models are among the most economical, starting at around $450, but prices can exceed $3000 (figures from 2012) for units with features that emulate the appearance or performance of restaurant-grade cooktops.

Radiant: Sleek and Easy to Clean

Electric elements used to mean unattractive, inexpensive, hard-to-clean coil burners. Although they're still used on entry-level ranges, they've largely been replaced with ceramic-glass-topped radiant elements. Electric cooktops are much more efficient than gas burners, and about 70% of the energy they consume is converted into cooking heat.

Radiant cooktops rely on a thin corrugated ribbon within an insulating "bowl" that directs heat upward. The element cycles on and off to maintain the desired temperature. Because glass is a poor heat conductor, the heat from the heating element warms the cookware without radiating far outward from the element. The roughly 30% heat loss comes from having to warm the glass before the pot.

Although a good electric cooktop can bring a pot of water to a boil faster than a gas cooktop, having the glass between the element and the pot makes for poor heat response. If you're warming a pot of milk on a gas cooktop and it's about to boil over, turning off the burner will stop the boiling almost instantly. On an electric cooktop, there's enough latent heat in the glass that milk will continue to boil.

Most radiant cooktops have at least one burner with a variable-size element that can operate at two or three different diameters. Look for a variety of element sizes that match an assortment of cookware sizes. Compared to the grate system on a gas cooktop, the smooth, sealed, glass cooking surface on an electric unit is minimalist and unobtrusive, and spills can be wiped away with a sponge—after the surface cools.

The surface does present a few potential problems, however. The glass can be scratched with abrasive cleaners, grains of sugar on the bottom of a pot, or even the rough surface of a cast-iron skillet. Blunt objects—a pepper mill, for instance—dropped from an overhead cabinet can crack the surface, and foods like sugar, sugar syrup, milk, and tomato sauce must be removed immediately. These items and some recalcitrant stains have to be scraped off with a razor blade held at 30° to the surface. (Cooktop manufacturers sell scrapers that make it easy to use a razor blade properly.)

Induction: Magnetism Gets Things Cooking

The coolest feature of an induction cooktop is that elements don't generate heat. In fact, these cooktops won't work unless an appropriate piece of cookware is on the glass surface (more on that in a moment). An alternating current of electricity energizes a coil of copper wire beneath each heating area on the cooktop, creating a magnetic field. When a pot or pan with iron content or magnetic stainless steel is placed above the coil, the magnet excites electrons in the pan, causing them to vibrate. The friction of this agitation heats the pan and its contents. Because the friction is in the pan, the cooktop doesn't heat up. Marketing campaigns for induction cooking show pans that have been cut in half, revealing things like ice melting in the pan but not on the exposed portion of the element. Although you can touch the cooking surface right next to a boiling pot, it's important to recognize that the glass beneath cookware warms from its contact with the hot pot in the same way that coffee warms a mug; therefore, touching it can still burn you.

Induction cooktops have even better heat response than gas, and control can be precise. There isn't any fiddling with a knob to adjust flame height. Push-button controls select the temperature, with up to 17 settings per element on the most flexible models.

Induction elements require cookware with ferrous content, so you may have to budget for new pots and pans in your kitchen renovation. Cookware manufacturers have begun adding an induction-compatible symbol to appropriate cookware. You can check your existing cookware or unlabeled new pots with a magnet. (It should stick.) To maximize efficiency, cookware bottoms should be flat. Cookware with an aluminum core is said to be best for taking advantage of induction's strengths.

Some people are put off by noises that can accompany the heating process. These can include a slight humming sound on high-heat settings or the sound of a fan in the cooktop cooling the electronics, but noises aren't that different from those made by a gas burner.

Next, Pick the Features

Once you've decided among gas, radiant, or induction, turn your attention to convenience features and appearance. The choices include timers and safety features. Some electric models even offer programs similar to those on a microwave.

Regardless of cooktop type, you should weigh two issues common to all cooktops. First, how easy is it to clean? Cleaning issues vary by cooking surface, so they're covered in the in-depth category discussions. Second, what type of controls and location do you prefer? Some cooktops mount controls vertically on the front. While this location frees space on the cooktop surface, it eats up more undercabinet space and positions knobs where they can be bumped while you work in the kitchen or where they can tempt children. Controls also can be mounted horizontally on one side of the burners or along the front edge. While twist knobs are de rigueur for gas burners, more expensive electric cooktops offer electronic touch controls that don't interrupt the smooth glass surface and typically have lockout features.

Bathroom Sinks: Seven Basic Styles

By Don Burgard

Kitchen sinks not only have to accommodate pots and pans but also have to withstand the beating that these items regularly inflict on sink basins (see "Choose the Right Kitchen Sink," p. 555). By contrast, bathroom sinks only have to be big enough to fit a pair of hands comfortably and durable enough to withstand hot tap water. Because of this limited purpose, manufacturers have been free to develop a dizzying array of designs, which can make choosing a bathroom sink as much an aesthetic decision as a practical one. Even so, most bathroom sinks come in a handful of basic styles, each of which has pros and cons.

Pedestal

Pedestal sinks look like birdbaths. They come in two parts, with a wall-mounted sink sitting atop a pedestal secured to the floor. The pedestal is open in the back to provide access for the drainpipe and supply lines.

PROS
- This can be a practical, attractive choice for a small space where there isn't room for cabinetry.
- If adequate storage exists elsewhere, a pedestal sink's unique design can enhance the look of a small or medium-size bathroom.

CONS
- The sink attaches to the wall, which means you'll have to install blocking behind the finished wall if it's not there already.
- Having no cabinet, shelves, or counter, a pedestal sink provides no storage space.

Continued →

Pedestal

Wall Mount

These sinks attach to the wall only and are open underneath. Some, called semipedestal sinks, come with shrouds that cover the plumbing all the way to the wall.

PROS
- Most units can fit into small or even tiny spaces.
- A wall-mount sink is the only type that doesn't take up any floor space.
- The open space underneath a wall-mount sink usually provides easy wheelchair access.

CONS
- As with a pedestal sink, you may need to install blocking in the wall.
- This sink provides no storage space.

Integral

An integral sink is of one piece with the surrounding counter and can be made from a wide variety of materials.

PROS
- Installation is simple: Sink and countertop are installed at the same time.
- One-piece construction means no crevices for capturing dirt, hair, or other debris.

CONS
- Replacing a sink means replacing a countertop as well, and vice versa.
- There's no opportunity for creatively matching a counter with a sink.

Drop In

Drop-in sinks, also called self-rimming sinks, fit inside a hole cut in the countertop. The rim rests on the edge of the hole and is secured to the countertop with a waterproof sealant such as silicone caulk. Fixtures are usually installed through the back of the rim, so these sinks can be purchased with the necessary holes already drilled.

PROS
- The cutout in the counter doesn't need to be finished; it can remain rough because it will be covered by the sink and won't be seen.
- The vanity cabinet hides the drainpipe and water supplies.

CONS
- The sink rim makes it impossible to wipe water from the counter into the sink.
- These sinks tend more toward the practical than the beautiful.

Undermount

Unlike a drop-in sink, an undermount sink is attached to the counter from below. This means that the counter edges must be finished rather than remaining rough cut. A support structure generally isn't necessary with cast-iron bathroom sinks, which are smaller and lighter than their kitchen counterparts.

Wall Mount

Integral

Drop In

Undermount

Vessel

PROS

- Has a sleeker appearance than drop-in sinks.
- With no rim in the way, you can wipe water from the counter directly into the sink.

CONS

- Unless you remove the vanity top, you can't install an undermount sink as a retrofit.
- An undermount installation leaves the edges of the cutout exposed, so undermount sinks can be used only with waterproof countertop materials such as granite, marble, or a solid-surface synthetic.

Vessel

Vessel sinks sit atop the vanity and are exposed on all sides. As a result, they often are as much pieces of sculpture as functional sinks. They come in the largest range of materials, including glass, marble, and cast bronze, as well as more common materials such as vitreous china and fireclay. Vessel sinks have no faucet holes, so fixtures need to be mounted on the wall or on the counter. They also don't have overflow holes, so if you have children and/or are absentminded, you'll probably want to install a grid drain rather than a stopper drain.

PROS

- No matter what they're made of, vessel sinks are visually striking.
- Because the hole cut in the countertop is very small, much more material remains, allowing the counter to complement the sink visually rather than just providing a place for it to rest.

CONS

- Although vessel sinks made from vitreous china can cost $200 or less, vessels made from other materials can cost thousands of dollars.

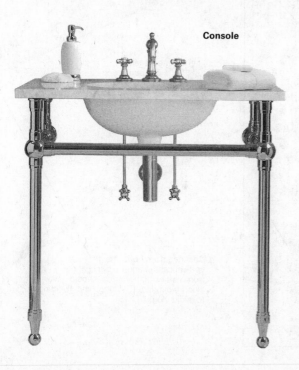

Console

- Because it sits atop the vanity rather than inside it, a vessel sink may need to be coupled with a vanity that is less than standard height.

Console

Console sinks share some characteristics with pedestal and wall-mount sinks. Like those styles, they don't sit atop cabinets, although some have drawers or a shelf for a limited amount of storage. Console sinks can either be freestanding, in which case they are supported by four legs, or mounted to the wall and supported by two or four legs. These legs can be anything from simple steel tubes to decorative posts made from the same material as the sink, such as vitreous china or fireclay.

PROS

- If the legs are far enough apart, a console sink can accommodate a person in a wheelchair.
- The extra width usually allows for some space on each side of the basin for toiletries.
- With some designs, towel bars can be added to the sides.

CONS

- Its extra width makes a console sink too big for a small bathroom.
- Plumbing is usually exposed, so PVC or ABS drainpipes are probably out of the question.
- For wall-mounted models, you may need to install blocking.

Drain-Waste-Vent Systems

By Justin Fink

Although hidden behind walls and in floors and ceilings, the pipes that make up a house's drain-waste-vent (DWV) system are the balance of the plumbing equation. They are the exit for the water provided through the supply lines, they carry waste from the toilet, and they connect to outside air for venting sewer gas and relieving pressure. These relatively large-diameter pipes rely solely on gravity, but they aren't easily routed through the structure of a house.

With three chapters in the IRC devoted to DWV systems, not to mention the tables and examples illustrated in the appendix, there is a lot to know about the layout and installation of such a system. Pipe sizes that vary based on usage; routes through framing bays that may already be packed with other mechanicals; pitch tolerances of plus or minus just ¼ in. per ft.; fittings with subtle differences in inlets, outlets, and applicability; and an array of minimums and maximums to consider when it comes to tying everything together are just a handful of the many situations, rules, and restrictions plumbers must understand.

The stakes are high, because an improper DWV setup can lead to slow drains, gurgling fixtures, sewer gas entering the living space, recurring clogs, and potentially hazardous overflows. When installed well, though, a DWV system will go unnoticed, with solids, liquids, and gases flowing smoothly. Here's how it works.

Continued ➔

Vent pipes should be pitched to drain accumulated moisture.

Every DWV system is required to have at least one 3-in. pipe venting outside.

For sinks of any kind, the most common branch fitting is the sanitary T. The vent attaches to the top inlet, and the trap arm attaches to the branch inlet.

To avoid bottlenecking and clogging, no component of the drain system can be larger in diameter than the downstream parts that are attached to it.

Toilets have their own traps built in.

Connections in a drain line should be made with a Y-fitting or TY-fitting, never a 90, to ensure a smooth and uninterrupted flow of waste.

Drain pipes should be sloped ¼ in. per ft. If they are not pitched enough, the flow will be inadequate. If they are pitched too steeply, the water will flow too quickly, leaving behind solid waste or debris.

Cleanouts (and 18 in. of open space for access) are required by code for clearing clogs.

Changes from horizontal to vertical can be abrupt, but changes from vertical to horizontal should have a combination of TY-fittings and 45-fittings to avoid clogs.

Getting the Trap Right

Good The trap is straight below and in line with the fixture drain, and the trap arm is sloped ¼ in. per ft. The trap arm falls no more than the diameter of the pipe it's plumbed with, allowing adequate room for air to flow in from the vent pipe as water drains.

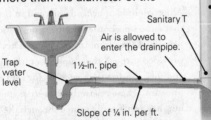

Stack vent

Sanitary T

Air is allowed to enter the drainpipe.

Trap water level

1½-in. pipe

Slope of ¼ in. per ft.

Bad If the trap arm is too long, pitched too steeply, or connected to the stack with the wrong fitting, the air intake will be below the level of the water flow and may start to siphon water out of the trap. Siphoning will continue until the water level in the trap drops enough to let air into the pipe, which then will leave it open for sewer gas to enter the room.

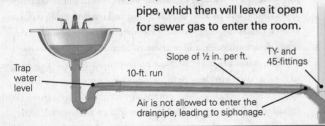

Stack vent

Trap water level

Slope of ½ in. per ft.

10-ft. run

TY- and 45-fittings

Air is not allowed to enter the drainpipe, leading to siphonage.

Evolution of the Modern Drain

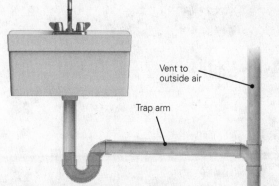

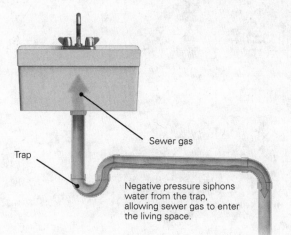

Sewer gas

Air and water mix, breaking the vacuum, but sewer gas is allowed to enter the living space.

Vent to outside air

Trap arm

Pressure is equalized by the vent, eliminating siphonage so that the water stays in the trap and blocks sewer gas.

UNPROTECTED If your sink, bathtub, and other fixtures were connected to drain lines that followed a straight, downward-sloping path to a main sewer outlet, water or waste would drain from each fixture with the help of gravity, air from the room would mix in and relieve the vacuum created by the draining water, and everything would flow without trouble. The problem with this setup is that air being allowed to flow into the drain system means that air also is allowed to flow out and into the room, bringing sewer gas with it.

TRAP AND VENT Nothing more than a connection to exterior air, a vent neutralizes air pressure within the drain lines. This neutral pressure can be achieved with lots of different configurations: an empty (dry) pipe that connects to the top of a trap arm like a snorkel, a waste (wet) pipe that is oversize in order to provide enough room for both water and airflow, and variations on these setups.

Sewer gas

Trap

Negative pressure siphons water from the trap, allowing sewer gas to enter the living space.

TRAP To prevent the entry of sewer gas, every fixture is required to have a U-shaped section of piping, known as a trap. Located downstream of the fixture (or in the case of a toilet, as part of the fixture itself), the trap holds water, blocking sewer gas from coming up through the fixture's drain. The problem with a trap is that as water flows through a drain line, it creates a vacuum behind it (negative pressure) and pushes air in front of it (positive pressure). The flow of this "water slug" can cause water to be sucked out of a trap that it's passing near, and it may also cause air to push through and gurgle in nearby traps downstream of its path. To relieve this pressure differential, code requires vents.

Miles of Tile

By Debra Judge Silber

The tile you choose not only has a substantial impact on the cost of a bathroom project, but it also affects how the new bath functions, ages, and impresses those who peek inside. If that's not daunting enough, consider the sheer volume of choices available inside the local tile showroom.

Designer-builder Patrick Sutton of Austin, Texas, suggests that clients avoid the tile store until they know what they're looking for. "I always tell people, 'I can't forbid you from going to a tile showroom, but I wish you wouldn't. Sit down first and make a list of what you're trying to do. Then go to the tile store.'" Lexington, Mass., architect Lynn Hopkins encourages clients to consider the style of the whole house before choosing one feature—which could be tile—to set the design tone for the bath. "Ask: What is this tile saying about the character of the room in which it wants to be? It gives you a context in which to make all those other decisions."

Aesthetics aside, there are other qualities you'll want to look for. One is strength, which will determine whether the tile is suitable for wall or floor applications (or both). Another is slip resistance. You can judge slip resistance based on the coefficient of friction (a COF of 0.5 or above is OK for floors), or you can do what many builders do: run your hand over the surface. A third feature to

Continued ➜

Porcelain

Natural Stone

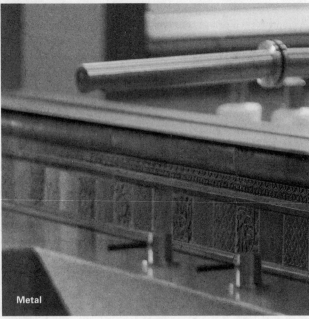

Metal

Glass

consider is shade variation, or the degree of difference in color and pattern from one tile to the next. Shade variation is designated by a V followed by a number from 1 to 4, with 1 having the least variation (minimal to no difference) and 4 having substantial, sometimes dramatic, variation in color or pattern between tiles.

Tile isn't forever, but try to choose one you can love for the long haul. "Find something you know you can be happy with for the next 10 to 20 years," advises Tom Meehan, a master tilesetter in Harwich, Mass. He adds that it's not just the tile, but also the complete design that matters. "When guests look in, you want them to say, 'What an incredible bathroom!' not 'What incredible tile!'"

Ceramic

Made of clay mixed with minerals and water, ceramic tile, like that used on the floor above, comes in a broad array of shapes, sizes, and colors. Initially fired to create bisque ware (unglazed ceramic), it can be fired a second time with a ceramic glaze to produce a surface that is stain and scratch resistant. The tile body itself is porous. Depending on its hardness rating, ceramic tile can be used on either walls or floors. For the most part, ceramic tile is easy to work with snap cutters and nippers, making it DIY-friendly. Although ceramic tile traditionally has been the most economical choice, the availability of porcelain tile in recent years has lessened ceramic's dominance in the market.

Porcelain

In the past decade, the price of porcelain tile has dropped; this and its many favorable attributes have led it to overtake ceramic in popularity. At the same time, new glazing techniques that closely mimic the look of natural stone have made it a durable, less expensive alternative to marble and limestone. "You get the look of old stone with zero maintenance," explains tilesetter Tom Meehan. Made of clay and finely ground sand, and fired once under high heat and pressure, porcelain is denser and stronger than typical ceramic tile. It is also less porous; with a water-absorption rate less than that of ceramic, porcelain tiles are often frostproof. Like ceramic tile, porcelain tile may be glazed or unglazed. Unglazed porcelain tile is sometimes called through-body, because the composition of the tile is uniform throughout. Much of the floor tile sold today is glazed porcelain, says Joshua Levinson, president of Artistic Tile, a distributor. "Porcelain production involves the use of fine-grained clays, which can be pressed more densely and fired at a higher temperature than traditional red-clay-body double-fire tile, making the product more resistant to wear," he says.

Natural Stone

Appearing in many forms in today's baths, natural stone shows up in formats that range from large slabs to tiny pebbles to uniform, cut tile. Add to that the many types of stone available—marble, granite, limestone, and slate among the most popular—and you have a wide variety of options. This

variety also presents considerable differences in qualities among stone types—such as stain resistance, durability, and porosity—so it's important to choose a type of stone that you can live with and that your tilesetter is confident installing. Limestone, for example, is popular, is fairly easy to work with, and comes in a variety of types; Jerusalem limestone is among the most dense and durable. Green marble, on the other hand, is more fussy: Contact with cement-based thinset will cause it to cup, requiring the use of resin-based thinsets.

Cutting stone tile requires the use of a wet saw, another reason why it's worth considering a professional installation. All stone tile should be sealed, but some tiles need more upkeep than others. Because much of the appeal of natural stone derives from surface variations from piece to piece, careful blending of shades—often by working from different boxes—is important for an attractive, "soft-slab" effect.

Metal

This material came on the scene with a splash some 10 to 15 years ago, and it remains popular primarily for accents. Not all metal-looking tiles are

---

Which Tile Where?

Shower walls

Tile on shower walls should extend at least 72 in. high for complete protection from water, although there's also the option of wrapping the ceiling for a complete enclosure. Large rectified tile allows for fewer and smaller grout joints, discouraging mold. Using the same tile in the shower as on the walls can help a small bath to appear larger. On the other hand, if the bathroom is large enough, a different tile can define the shower as its own space.

Shower floors

It's important that tile used on shower floors be slip resistant. Small tiles (1 in. to 3 in.) provide a secure grip and also accommodate the slope needed for drainage. Manufacturers typically match their larger-format floor tiles with smaller tiles specifically for shower floors. Stone pebbles are popular, but beware: Less expensive products can have irregular surfaces that are less than therapeutic.

Bathroom floors

Strength and slip resistance are key here. Tile manufacturers use coefficient of friction (COF) to rate slip resistance. A COF of 0.5 is acceptable; higher numbers offer more traction. Keep in mind that grout lines around smaller tiles improve traction. Floor tiles also need to be durable. The Porcelain Enamel Institute (PEI) rates tile durability on a scale of 0 to 5, with 5 being the toughest commercial-grade tiles. For residential floors, a PEI rating of 3 is fine.

Bathroom walls

You don't have to tile every wall in your bath, but it is a good idea to protect areas prone to splashes, including those behind the sink and toilet. Tile wainscot traditionally fulfilled this function, but it has started to fall out of favor. Wainscots typically range from 36 in. to 48 in., although taller, European-style wainscots of 54 in. are an option. How the wainscot meets the wall—with a decorative border, crown, or cap—can add to the bathroom's character.

Continued ➜

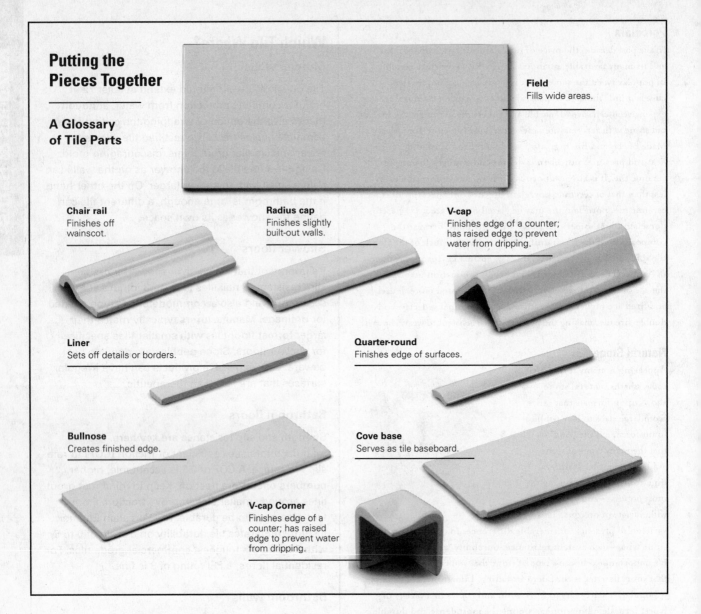

Putting the Pieces Together

A Glossary of Tile Parts

Field
Fills wide areas.

Chair rail
Finishes off wainscot.

Radius cap
Finishes slightly built-out walls.

V-cap
Finishes edge of a counter; has raised edge to prevent water from dripping.

Liner
Sets off details or borders.

Quarter-round
Finishes edge of surfaces.

Bullnose
Creates finished edge.

Cove base
Serves as tile baseboard.

V-cap Corner
Finishes edge of a counter; has raised edge to prevent water from dripping.

metal, however. Some are ceramic with a metal cap; still others are cast in resin and coated with a metallic finish. Stainless steel, nickel, and bronze are among the most popular. Generally, metal tiles install like ceramic tiles, although they are far more difficult to cut.

Glass

Often transparent and more brittle than ceramic or stone, glass tile requires careful installation, but the shimmer it adds to a bathroom can't be denied. Because glass is nonporous, sealing is not a concern, but glass can scratch and can be slippery, which is something to think about if you're considering a glass-tile floor. Available in luminous colors and often enhanced with texture or metal highlights, glass tile can be pricey—an argument for using it in small doses as a border accent, sink backsplash, or singular wall. Glass tiles are available with a percentage of recycled material.

"Glass is very big, and it's going to stay that way for a while," says Meehan. Its steady popularity has resulted in a large supply of glass tile of varying quality and individual characteristics that can complicate installation. This, Meehan says, makes it especially important to follow the installation instructions from the manufacturer of your particular tile. Artistic Tile's Levinson echoes that opinion, adding that anyone considering working with glass tile should consult the glass-tile selection and installation guide in the Tile Council of North America's Handbook for Ceramic, Glass, and Stone Tile Installation, available at tcnatile.com.

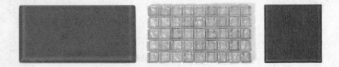

Sustainable Tile

Split-Face Tile

Trends in Bathroom Tile
Sustainable Tile

The availability of tile made from recycled materials keeps expanding, particularly in the area of glass tile, and manufacturers of all types are promoting their environmental friendliness. Ocean-side Glasstile takes environmental responsibility to the next level with its Blue brand tiles, which combine up to 82% postconsumer recycled content with a new melting technology that reduces energy use by 30%. Crossville Tile has developed a system of processing its own scrap tile back into powder, which then is used in manufacturing new tile. Many artisan tile makers practice good environmental stewardship as well, so it pays to seek them out. The Tile Council of North America's Green Squared Certification stamp identifies tiles that meet certain criteria in the use of sustainable materials and eco-friendly manufacturing and corporate practices. So far, several hundred tile lines from eight manufacturers have been certified (greensquaredcertified.com).

Mosaic Tile

It's hard to beat the variety available today in mosaic tile. Mosaics can come in many shapes and patterns—from Roman-style tesserae to sleek linear glass. Many combine several materials—including glass, natural stone, and metal—into one color-coordinated pattern. Several manu-facturers provide custom mosaics, with some offering online tools that allow you to create your own color blend or gradient in mosaic that the company then will produce for you. Tilesetter Tom Meehan acknowledges that mosaic tiles make a good DIY project, but he cautions that it's important to take your time.

Solid or opaque mosaics come mounted on a fiber mesh that makes installation easy; transparent glass mosaic tile comes face-mounted on paper.

Split-Face Tile

Tiles that pop from the wall literally add a new dimension to your bath design, but if you ask whether they're a good idea, get ready for a protracted conversation. The uneven surfaces referred to as split face that appeared a few years ago have found a limited audience. Installation challenges are one reason. "You can't grout the stuff, so you're relying on the backer to hold it in place," says designer-builder Patrick Sutton. Tilesetter Meehan is less harsh, but still cautious. "As a border or an accent, they're great," says Meehan, who nonetheless recommends grout release and professional installation.

Large-Format Tile

Defined as porcelain tiles with one edge measuring 15 in. or more and glass tiles with an edge measuring 3 in. or more, large tiles are, well, big. Popular sizes include 12-in. by 24-in. rectangles and 6-in. by 18-in. planks. They're not the right choice for every bathroom, though, particularly if you're going for an antique or vintage look. Also, the bigger the tile, the more stable the substrate needs to be to prevent cracking. Installation of large tiles can be tricky; particularly in the case of glass, large tile is best installed by a professional.

Continued ➡

Perfecting the Tiled Tub Surround

By Tom Meehan

Over my 35 years of installing tile, I've done well over a thousand tub surrounds. Take it from me: Tiling a tub surround might seem like the kind of remodeling project you can jump right into, but it's not. It takes quite a bit of planning and proper follow-through to get quality results; this is not a job I would recommend for a first-time installer. To this day, I still treat each new installation the same as the first. The key lies in knowing how the last tile will fit before the first tile touches the wall. This means knowing how well the tub was installed, where each course of tile will land, and how the cut tiles will lay out.

For this job, the customer asked for classic 3×5 white subway tile, which has never gone out of style in all the years I've been on the job. To give the tub surround a bit of a kick, I incorporated a band of mosaic tile into the layout and installed a marble corner shelf for shampoo bottles and a bar of soap. Neither of these little changes added much cost for materials or much time to the installation, but both help this space to stand apart from a typical tiled tub surround.

As is the case in any wet area, the tile substrate should be cement backerboard or another approved backer that will not deteriorate or harbor mold. In this case, because the tub surround met wall paneling on one side, I used standard ½-in.-thick Durock cementboard for most of the job, but installed ¼-in.-thick Hardie Backerboard, a fiber-cement product, on the wall that needed to be flush to the paneling.

Strategies for Success

I start all of my installations by making a story pole to help me in planning the horizontal and vertical layout. On the back wall of the tub, which is seen first and most frequently, I want the tiles laid out so that any necessary cuts land in the two corners and are of equal size. On the sidewalls, where symmetry is not as important, cuts can be hidden in the back corners.

If the tile will stop short of the ceiling, then you won't need to cut the top row. I usually run my tub surrounds right to the ceiling. I'd rather not end up with a small piece at the top, but I also want a full tile at the tub. Determining the size of each course can require a little compromise. If it looks as though the course of tile at the ceiling will be too narrow, I try reducing the size of the pieces on top of the tub. Also, if the tub is significantly out of level, a line of cut tile at the tub will make the problem less obvious. On the job shown here, the tub was out of level by about ¼ in. from end to end, which is a very common situation. I accounted for this by planning the bottom row so that full-height tile starts at the lowest point and is gradually adjusted and cut as needed to absorb the high spots.

Installing Tile Is the Fun Part

Once the layout has been determined, the hard part of the job is just about done. There will still be some tiles that need to be cut and some holes to be made for plumbing, but as long as you follow the plan and keep the tiles level, the next step will be the fast and gratifying part of the installation.

I always spread an ample amount of cement to get a full bond rather than skimping and leaving a few voids on the wall. When there's a good coating of thinset on the wall, I comb it with the teeth of the trowel in one direction. This makes a big difference in achieving a complete bond. Making sure that trowel lines all go in one direction reduces the possibility of voids in the thinset behind the tile. I also make sure to push each tile into the cement and give it a ¼-in. slide to achieve a good bond. Subway tiles often have self-spacing nibs to keep grout joints consistent. Regardless of the tile, though, you should always check with a level to ensure that the tiles are running at the same height and that joints are lining up at the corners.

I usually tile the lower half of all three walls of a tub surround before moving any higher. A pro can install about 25 sq. ft. of tile in 20 to 30 minutes. If you're a DIYer, plan on no more than half that square footage.

A Story Pole Eliminates Surprises

Unless you're really lucky, you'll have to cut some tiles to make the layout work. The key is planning where those cuts should land so that they are less noticeable. When properly laid out, cut tiles should be no less than half the size of a full tile. There are times, of course, when small pieces are unavoidable, but the problem can be minimized with a little effort and imagination.

A STICK TELLS THE STORY. Cut a piece of wood for the vertical layout and another for the horizontal layout, each a bit shorter than the distance between tub and ceiling or wall and wall. Place the tiles one at a time, including a space for grout between each if the tile isn't self-spacing, and mark the layout on the stick.

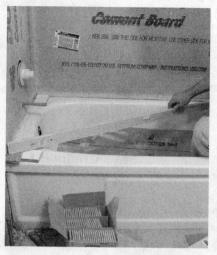

KNOW YOUR TUB INSTALLATION. It would be nice if every tub installation were dead level, but that's rarely the case. Before you can begin the tile layout, lay a level across the top of each side of the tub. The bottom row of tiles can be cut to follow the contour of the tub or to account for high spots, so the goal here is to find the low point, which becomes the starting point for the rest of the layout.

UP FROM THE BOTTOM. Set the end of the story pole on the tub's lowest spot, then draw a mark at least halfway up the wall that corresponds to the joints of your story-pole layout.

ESTABLISH A BENCHMARK. Transfer the halfway mark across all three walls of the tub surround, making sure it's level. This is your benchmark line.

PLAN FOR THE BAND. It's also a good idea to use the story pole to determine the position of the accent band and the way it will relate to shower hardware, and the position of niches or shelves in the tub surround.

FLIP IT FOR THE CEILING. Turned end for end and placed against the ceiling, the story pole indicates the amount that needs to be cut from the top row. Here, the cut will leave almost an entire tile, which is perfect.

Continued →

Installation Starts with the Bottom Half

With the layout established, the tiles go up quickly. Work the bottom half of the installation first, starting with the back wall and then tiling each of the sidewalls. Simple straights cuts can be made as you go, but tile as much as possible before slowing down to make the more complicated cuts, like those around plumbing fixtures.

AN EVEN SPREAD. Working from the benchmark line down, start with the lower part of the back wall, spreading the thinset cement with a ¼-in. square-notched trowel. Use a sag-resistant latex-modified thinset such as Laticrete 255 for tub surrounds because it reduces the chance that tiles will slide out of position before the cement sets up.

THE FIRST TILE ESTABLISHES THE PATTERN. On this job, the story pole confirmed that a full row of uncut tiles could fit along the back wall, so the first row begins with a full tile, followed by a half-tile below it to establish the running bond pattern. If a full row of uncut tile won't fit, it's better to start in the center of the wall and have the same cut on each end.

Basic Cuts

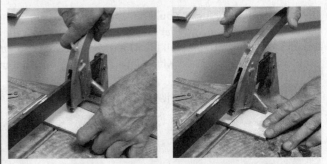

SCORE AND SNAP. For all straight cuts, a basic snap cutter works quickly and makes a clean cut. Score across the top of the tile, then give the handle a quick bump with the palm of your hand to break the tile at the score line. If the cuts are difficult, small, or notched, a tile saw is a better choice.

Irregular Cuts

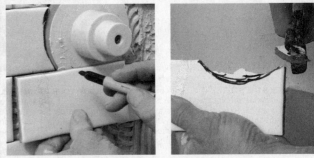

CURVES REQUIRE NIPPERS. After installing as many full tiles as possible around the showerhead and mixing valve, you can use a pair of nippers to fit in the remaining tiles. Holding the tile in place, use a permanent marker to outline the area that needs to be cut. Carefully nibble up to the marked line with a set of tile nippers. The cuts don't have to be pretty; just get close enough so that the tile easily fits the open spot in the layout. The gap will be covered by the fixture's trim plate.

Precision Cuts

KEEPING CUTS TO THE BOTTOM. Compensate for an out-of-level tub at the bottom row of tile. After using a straightedge to ensure that the highest completed row is straight, fill in the tiles at the tub. These cuts, which are often tapered and can vary from tile to tile, can be done on a snap cutter, but a wet saw is more accurate.

Kick Up the Character with Custom Features

I like to offer simple upgrades that make an impression but don't cost much or add much time to the job. I often include a built-in shampoo niche, which I've outlined in other articles (go to finehomebuilding.com/extras), but two of my other favorite upgrades are a corner shelf and a band of contrasting mosaic tile.

CORNER SHELF I typically make a corner shelf from a 12×12 stone tile. Here, I cut a piece of marble in half diagonally and then rounded over the edges with a rub brick. Installation is easy: Butter the back edge of the shelf with thinset and rest it atop a course of tiles. Trim the next course of wall tiles as needed. To keep water from pooling on the shelf, put a few temporary plastic wedge spacers under the shelf, all the way at the back of the corner, so that it sets up with a slight pitch.

ACCENT BAND As long as you're not using glass tile, which requires a slightly different approach (visit finehomebuilding.com/extras), you can install an accent band without changing your approach too much. Use a utility knife to cut sheets of mosaic tile into strips, set them into the thinset with firm pressure, and adjust individual tiles as needed to keep things even.

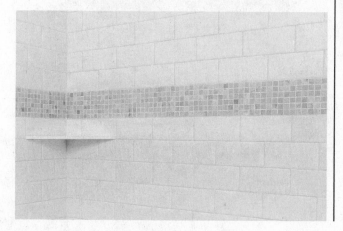

Grouting Can Make or Break the Job

As with laying out and setting the tiles, there's a right way and a wrong way to tackle a grout job. My father used to say, "A grout job can make a mediocre tile job look great or a great tile job look mediocre." Crisp, clean, and even grout lines are the goal, and there are a few key things to focus on.

PREGROUT CLEANUP. Before mixing up the grout, spend a few minutes looking over every joint in the tub surround. Even a day after it's been applied, the thinset is still fresh enough to be removed easily with a utility knife.

SPREAD AND SCRAPE. Use a margin trowel to load grout onto a rubber float, and then use the float to apply it to the wall. Spread the grout in broad, arcing strokes. Start with your arm extended, and pull the float toward your body. The first pass packs grout into the joints; the second pass scrapes away most of the excess.

PACK AND TOOL THE JOINTS. Once the grout has firmed up but before you wash down the tile, use the butt end of a Sharpie permanent marker as a grout stick to strike the grout joints. This packs in the grout tightly and makes the joint consistent.

WIPE AWAY THE HAZE. Once the tile has been washed down and all excess grout removed, let everything dry for about 15 minutes, or until a light haze develops on the surface of the tile. Then use a clean cloth or quality paper towel to wipe the haze off the surface of the tile, buffing it to a finished shine.

Continued →

Cutting the tiles is the hard part of the job. The cut pieces have to fit properly and the grout joints be spaced evenly so that everything blends together smoothly. Most ceramic, porcelain, and even some glass tiles can be cut with a snap cutter, which is a fast, portable, and nearly silent tool. Notches, curves, and other fairly simple nonlinear cuts can be handled with a pair of nippers. Almost all stone tiles, and even some handmade tiles, have to be cut with a wet saw, which is also indispensable for more complicated cuts or when working with fragile tiles.

Grouting for Consistency

If I'm using more than one package of grout, which in most surrounds will be a nonsanded grout, I mix everything together dry to ensure that the color is consistent. Then I mix the grout with clean water—that's a must. Generally, I spread the grout over the entire tub surround; by the time I finish spreading the last section, the first section is ready to clean. On hot days, grout will set up more quickly. In rainy weather or on humid days, the grout will take longer to firm up.

After spreading the grout, I wash the excess off the surface of the tile. It is important to wring out the sponge and not to use too much water. Also, when mixing the grout, I don't make it too watery. This weakens the strength of the grout in the long run. The next day, I wipe on a coat of sealer heavy enough to saturate the grout joints. I typically use a foam brush, but a rag also can work. I then wipe down the tiled area with a clean white cloth, leaving no sealer residue.

Tile Backerboard Options

By Martin Holladay

Forty years ago, ceramic floor and wall tiles were always set in a mortar bed. Then a few builders experimented with gluing wall tiles to water-resistant drywall (aka greenboard), a method that later was outlawed because it led to mushy drywall and moldy studs.

A better solution hit the market in the early 1970s when manufacturers introduced cement backerboard. These panels are impervious to water, so they proved to be an excellent substrate for tiled tub surrounds, shower walls, countertops, and floors.

Since then, several newer types of tile backerboard—made from materials including fiber cement, gypsum, and polystyrene—have been introduced. Most of them cost about the same (roughly $10 for a ½-in. by 3-ft. by 5-ft. sheet), except for polystyrene backerboard, which tends to be more expensive.

There is no consensus among tile contractors about which type of backerboard is best. Each material has its strengths; while one material might be more water resistant, a competing material might weigh less or be easier to cut. Adam Bey-Wagner, a tile contractor in New Fairfield, Conn., is a fan of Hardie-Backer. "HardieBacker is more fibrous than regular cementboards. There's not as much

aggregate. If you stand up a 3-ft. by 5-ft. piece of Durock or cement backerboard and shake it back and forth, it starts to lose its rigidity. HardieBacker stays stiff. It doesn't fall apart in water, and it's mold resistant."

Tom Meehan, a tile contractor in Harwich, Mass., has a different opinion. "My preferred backerboard, hands down, is Durock," he says. "It's lighter than other backer-boards, and it cuts beautifully. Durock is as close to Sheetrock as you are going to get. HardieBacker tends to break at the corners, and it's hard to get an even cut without the $180 shears. Plus, it can't be installed outdoors or in steam showers."

Jane Aeon, a tile contractor in Berkeley, Calif., agrees. "I like Durock," she says. "HardieBacker sucks up thinset, and the thinset sets up too quickly. When you are trying to adjust tiles, you have more time with Durock or WonderBoard."

As long as you choose a material recommended for the type of location where you intend to install it, any of the materials mentioned here should work well.

Cement

The first ½-in.-thick cement backerboard products on the market weighed between 3.75 lb. and 4 lb. per sq. ft. (WonderBoard still has a weight in that range.) Later, backerboards made with lightweight aggregate were introduced. These ½-in.-thick products weigh only 3 lb. per sq. ft.

Each brand of cement backerboard feels different. WonderBoard looks like the cement backerboard of the 1970s: very dense. Durock and Util-a-Crete have more air bubbles and a lighter aggregate than WonderBoard. As Jane Aeon says, "WonderBoard is more crunchy than Durock."

Different aggregates produce backerboards with different qualities. PermaBase, for example, includes small spheres of polystyrene that reduce the material's density. "Once I wanted to

Cement Backerboard

put in a soap dish the day after I had set some tiles," says Aeon. "When I took off the tiles, the PermaBase backerboard just disintegrated. Removing the tiles destroyed the backerboard. That wouldn't happen with any other type of backerboard."

Like concrete, cement backerboard is unaffected by water, so it can be installed indoors or outdoors, on floors, walls, ceilings, and countertops. While not susceptible to water damage, cement backerboard is not a moisture barrier, and it tends to wick water. In a wet environment (a shower, for example), it is important to install a waterproof membrane—either on top of the backerboard (when using a liquid-applied membrane) or behind the backerboard—to stop water from reaching the wall studs or subfloor.

Cement backerboard is available in a variety of thicknesses. Thin products (¼-in.- and ⅜-in.-thick panels) are reserved for use over plywood or OSB and for tiled countertops or floors. For walls, most installers choose ½-in. or ⅝-in. backerboard. While ½-in. backerboard is suitable for most jobs, ⅝-in. backerboard might be specified for heavy tile or to match the thickness of adjacent drywall. The most common panel size is 3 ft. by 5 ft., sized to make quick work of preparing standard tub surrounds.

Some types of cement backerboard are flexible enough to be installed on curved substrates. Be careful, though; bend them too far, and they will crack.

INSTALLATION: To cut cement backerboard, score it with a utility knife, and snap it like drywall. To cut holes for showerheads, toilet flanges, or other penetrations, carbide-tipped hole saws are an excellent choice. You can also score the circumference of the hole with a utility knife or by drilling a series of small holes, then knocking out the center with a hammer.

When installed on walls, cement backerboard requires a minimum stud spacing of 16 in. on center. It is fastened to studs with 1¼-in. backerboard screws or 1½-in. galvanized roofing nails spaced 8 in. on center (or 6 in. on center for ceilings). Backerboard screws are available from both U.S. Gypsum and Custom Building Products.

Most manufacturers require installers to leave a ⅛-in. gap between adjacent panels; the gap acts as a key for the thinset used to tape the seam. Seams should be taped with alkali-resistant fiberglass mesh tape. Don't use fiberglass drywall tape, which may not be able to resist the alkali corrosion associated with cement-based mortars.

When installed on a floor, cement backerboard must be set in a ¼-in.-thick support bed of thinset mortar. This leveling bed ensures that no voids under the backerboard can cause deflection.

When setting tile over cement backerboard, use either modified latex thinset or unmodified dry-set mortar.

STRENGTHS: Has unsurpassed water resistance.

DRAWBACKS: Weighs more than other types of backerboard. Because cement backerboard is brittle, some tile contractors don't like to use it on floors. According to Tom Meehan, "If you use cement backerboard on a floor, the tiles will have a tenacious bond, but if there is a little bit of give, you will get cracking of the tiles or grout."

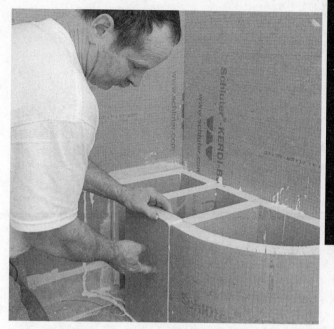

BEYOND BACKING. Polystyrene backerboards are lightweight, waterproof, and easy to cut. Schlüter's thicker panels can be used in place of framing for structural applications, such as a shower bench.

Polystyrene

Polystyrene backerboard consists of panels of either expanded (EPS) or extruded (XPS) polystyrene protected by facings made of fiberglass and polymer resin. Brands include FinPan ProPanel Lightweight Waterproof Backer Board, Schlüter Kerdi-Board, and Wedi Building Board. While the Wedi and Schlüter products have XPS cores, the FinPan product has a core of EPS.

Polystyrene backerboard is offered in a wide range of thicknesses and is suitable for use on walls, floors, ceilings, and countertops. Surprisingly stiff, it is strong enough to be used to build shower benches, curbs, or bathroom furniture, as long as panels of the material are used as "studs" for structural support where necessary.

Polystyrene Backerboard

INSTALLATION: Polystyrene backerboard can be cut with a utility knife. Most manufacturers advise using screws and washers to fasten the panels to walls or floors. For a waterproof installation, treat seams with sealant and waterproof sealing tapes.

Continued →

STRENGTHS: Weighs less than any other type of backerboard. It is waterproof and will not wick water, and once the seams are sealed, the panels provide a water barrier. Sheets are also available in more sizes and thicknesses than other backerboards.

DRAWBACKS: Polystyrene costs more than other types of backerboard. Schlüter's suggested retail price for a sheet measuring ½ in. by 48 in. by 64 in. is $78. That's $3.66 per sq. ft., compared to between 66¢ and 73¢ per sq. ft. for other backerboard options.

Fiber Cement

The same ingredients used to make cement backerboard are present in fiber-cement backerboard; the difference is that fiber cement also includes cellulose fiber.

The main brands of fiber-cement backerboard are HardieBacker and CertainTeed FiberCement BackerBoard. HardieBacker comes in two thicknesses: ¼ in. for floors or countertops and 0.42 in. for walls. At about ⁷/₁₆ in., 0.42-in.-thick HardieBacker is a little thinner than ½-in. cement backerboard, which is one reason why it is lighter (2.6 lb. per sq. ft.).

INSTALLATION: Fiber cement can be scored with a knife and snapped like drywall—although noncarbide utility-knife blades tend to dull quickly—or be cut using electric shears developed for cutting fiber-cement siding. Manufacturers recommend that fiber-cement not be cut with a power saw or grinder because such power tools create silica dust, a health hazard.

Fastening requirements for fiber-cement backerboard are the same as for cement backerboard: Use 1¼-in. backerboard screws or 1½-in. galvanized roofing nails spaced 8 in. on center. It is sometimes difficult to get screws to sit flush with the dense surface of fiber cement. If you're having this problem, use nails. Seams should be finished with thinset mortar and alkali-resistant fiberglass mesh tape.

Use only latex-modified thinset when installing tiles on fiber-cement backerboard.

STRENGTHS: Less brittle and weighs less than traditional cement backerboard. Because fiber-cement backerboard has a smoother surface than cement backerboard, it can be finished with paint or wallpaper. That makes it a good choice for finishing walls in damp areas like basements.

DRAWBACKS: Some traditionalists are reluctant to use products that contain cellulose in a wet environment. However, fiber-cement backerboard manufacturers warrant their products for use in showers and other wet areas.

Gypsum Core

While ordinary drywall has a paper facing, most brands of gypsum-core backerboard include a waterproof facing (usually a fiberglass mat). Brands include CertainTeed Diamondback Tile Backer, Temple-Inland GreenGlass, and Georgia-Pacific Dens-Shield.

Gypsum-core backerboard is available in the usual range of thicknesses: ¼ in., ½ in., and ⅝ in. The ½-in. product weighs 2 lb. per sq. ft., making it lighter than cement backerboard or fiber-cement backerboard. It can be used for walls, ceilings, and countertops, but it is not suitable for use on most floors or for any outdoor application.

Gypsum Core Backerboard

U.S. Gypsum's Fiberock is a gypsum-based backerboard that isn't really comparable to other gypsum-based products. Unlike Dens-Shield, Fiberock has no fiberglass-mat facing. According to the manufacturer, it is made of a "gypsum/cellulose-fiber combination" and is "water resistant to the core." The manufacturer warrants the use of Fiberock in wet areas like showers.

INSTALLATION: Gypsum-core backerboard can be scored and snapped like regular drywall. Fastening requirements are similar to those for other types of drywall: It can be fastened with 1¼-in. backerboard screws or 1½-in. galvanized roofing nails.

As with HardieBacker, latex-modified thinset should be used to set tile on gypsum-core backerboard.

STRENGTHS: Relatively light and easy to install; handles much like drywall.

DRAWBACKS: Best used in areas that are usually dry. It cannot be used outdoors, and most experts advise against its use in areas that experience daily wetting. Gypsum-core backerboard should never be used for a shower floor or shower curb, or in a sauna or steam room. Gypsum-core backerboard can't be used on floors with tiles that are smaller than 2 in. by 2 in.

Fiber Cement Backerboard

Install a Toilet

By Mike Lombardi

Ask a group of plumbers the proper way to install a toilet, and the conversation can get heated quickly. There are two major points of controversy: where to mount the flange and whether you should caulk the bottom of the toilet to the floor. When I install a toilet, I always make sure the closet flange is on top of the finished floor and anchored securely. This gives me the best chance for a sturdy, long-lasting, leak-free installation because the weight of the toilet and any occupant is transferred to the floor, not the connected piping.

Equally important, when the flange is on top of the finished floor, the outlet on the bottom of the toilet (the horn) is positioned so that it's below the top edge of the flange. This makes the wax seal last longer because the wax isn't being worn away by the constant flow of water. It also better protects the soft wax from the spiral-shaped hook at the end of toilet and drain snakes.

When connecting a toilet to the closet flange, I use plastic closet bolts made by Sioux Chief. The bolts have chunky shoulders that help to hold them upright so that they're ready to accept the toilet as it's lowered into place. The bolts won't rust and will break if overtightened, a safeguard against cracking the toilet's base.

Caulking the bottom of the toilet to the floor is required by the International Plumbing Code and the International Residential Code.

Step by Step

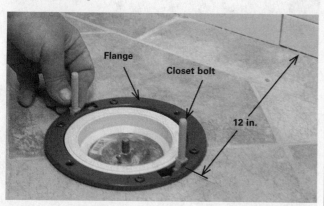

1. SECURE THE FLANGE. Dry-fit the flange so that when the closet bolts are at the end of the mounting slots, they will be 12 in. from the wall behind the toilet. When fitting is done, glue the parts together (see "Building Skills, *Fine Homebuilding* #229). Screw the flange to the subfloor with zinc-coated screws, and install the closet bolts.

Flange

Closet bolt

12 in.

2. DRY-FIT THE BOWL. To identify installation problems early, always do a dry-fit. Because this bowl isn't quite level and has a slight rock, the author uses rubber-gasket material as a shim. Once he's satisfied, he removes the bowl and trims the rubber to fit around the flange.

3. CAULK THE BOTTOM. With the bowl upside down, apply a bead of translucent adhesive caulk around the entire outside edge. This important sanitary measure is required by the IRC and the plumbing code.

4. INSTALL THE WAX RING. After removing the plug, place the ring in the flange. This ensures that the wax seal is centered over the toilet outlet. The author prefers the plastic-horned Hercules johni-ring.

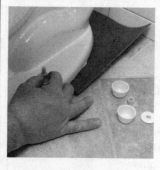

5. FASTEN THE BOWL. Carefully lower the bowl over the closet bolts. Lean on the bowl, compressing the wax seal until the bowl is in full contact with the floor. Then, with the cap bottoms in place, tighten the two bolts a little at a time.

6. TRIM THE SHIM. Holding a utility knife so that the blade angles in, trim the rubber gasket flush with the bottom of the toilet. Use a fresh blade, and make the cut in several passes so that the blade doesn't slip and scratch the floor.

Continued ➜

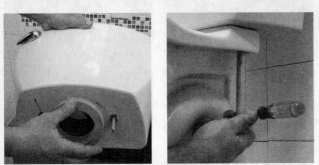

7. INSTALL THE TANK GASKET. In a conventional two-piece toilet, a soft rubber gasket seals the tank to the bowl. The brass bolts are tightened with a long socket provide by the toilet manufacturer. Go easy; overtightening can crack the tank.

8. CONNECT THE SUPPLY. The author likes to use braided supply lines with brass nuts at both ends. Choose one long enough to put a loop in the tubing. This puts less stress on the ends, which is where most leaks and breaks occur. Both ends have rubber washers, so the connections don't have to be tightened excessively.

9. CAULK AGAIN. Flush the toilet several times, inspecting the toilet and the basement for leaks. Once everything looks OK, apply another bead of caulk to seal the base to the floor, and smooth the joint with a moistened finger.

Problem-Solving Product: Best Bolts

Plastic closet bolts won't rust, and they'll break before they're tight enough to crack the toilet. Square shoulders keep the bolts upright in the flange.

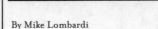

Trouble-Free Toilets

By Mike Lombardi

I've installed, removed, and replaced more toilets than I care to count. In some cases, a toilet has to be replaced because the necessary repairs to the inner workings of the tank aren't worth the effort when compared to the cost of upgrading to a new fixture. There's not much I can do to predict how long these internal components of a toilet will hold up, but I certainly can ensure that the plumber or homeowner who pulls the toilet isn't faced with additional repairs to the bathroom. I've pulled lots of toilets that have been in service for 50 years or more yet had no evidence of wax-ring failure, leakage, or rot. The difference isn't in the quality of the toilet, but in the quality of the installation.

In my experience, the three essential aspects of a long-lasting and trouble-free toilet installation are a stable floor frame, a closet flange that's installed at the right height, and a bead of sealant or grout around the base of the toilet where it meets the floor.

Closet flange

Hole centered on joist depth, with at least 2 in. above and below

Pipe slopes ¼ in. per ft.

3⅝-in. hole for 3-in. PVC pipe

Street 90 elbow slides directly into closet flange, allowing for a compact change in direction.

Reinforcement may be required on 2×8 and 2×10 joists and often can be achieved with gussets or additional framing.

Flange Over the Flooring

The underside of the closet flange should sit level and bear evenly on top of the finished floor. If new flooring has been added on top of the existing flooring, use spacer rings to extend the flange up. Although common, it's never OK to stack up wax rings to span the gap between a recessed closet flange and the horn of the toilet. A correctly installed wax ring is there to prevent sewer gas from entering the bathroom, not as a waterproof seal.

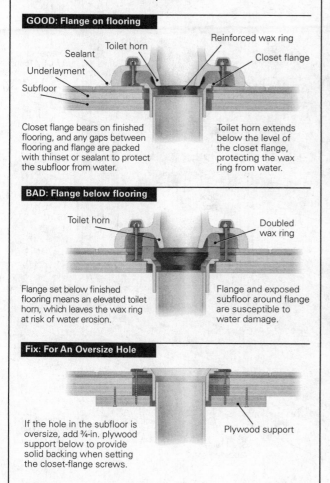

GOOD: Flange on flooring

Toilet horn · Reinforced wax ring · Sealant · Underlayment · Closet flange · Subfloor

Closet flange bears on finished flooring, and any gaps between flooring and flange are packed with thinset or sealant to protect the subfloor from water.

Toilet horn extends below the level of the closet flange, protecting the wax ring from water.

BAD: Flange below flooring

Toilet horn · Doubled wax ring

Flange set below finished flooring means an elevated toilet horn, which leaves the wax ring at risk of water erosion.

Flange and exposed subfloor around flange are susceptible to water damage.

Fix: For An Oversize Hole

Plywood support

If the hole in the subfloor is oversize, add ¾-in. plywood support below to provide solid backing when setting the closet-flange screws.

The Floor Frame Must Be Stable

From a framing perspective, there isn't anything special about the floor under a bathroom. If things go wrong, it's usually because somebody has reduced the strength of the floor by notching or drilling where they shouldn't, or because water damage has led to decay. Either of these problems will lead to movement in the floor, and that will affect the seal between the toilet and the closet flange.

Assess the condition of the floor by looking for loose tiles or feeling for sponginess. If there's access, always go below and look up for notched or drilled joists or for softness in the wood, which indicates rot. If the subflooring around the flange is rotten, it's best to cut out the old closet flange—either from below using a reciprocating saw, or from above with a specialty tool such as the Flange-off (keco.com) or the Ram Bit (pascospecialty.com)—and replace it along with the section of flooring.

If you have to drill holes in the floor joists to route the waste line, do so through their center, and be mindful of the structural restrictions. Although not permitted by a strict interpretation of the building code, drilling waste-line holes through 2×8 and 2×10 joists is often approved by building inspectors if you agree to reinforce the joists. Reinforcement options include doubled joists, plywood gussets, angle iron, headers for transferring the load, and a support wall.

Don't Skip the Sealant

Some plumbers argue that applying sealant where the toilet meets the floor will trap water and lead to rot if the wax ring ever fails. But sealant in this area is required by code, and for good reasons. The sealant prevents condensation on the outside of the bowl from wicking between the toilet and the floor, where it won't easily dry out. More importantly, it seals against soiled water following the same path if the toilet ever overflows. I always flush a newly installed toilet multiple times before sealing it to the floor with Phenoseal adhesive caulk.

Build Your Own Bathroom Vanity

By Justin Fink

The details of a bathroom make a statement, and a vanity is often a focal point that ties those details together. The simplicity and clean lines of Shaker-style furniture appeal to me because they aren't adorned with excessive trim, appliqués, or other embellishments, yet they are more inviting and comfortable than modern pieces in a starker style. In addition, I think the Shaker style can work as well in a suburban raised ranch as it does in a 200-year-old farmhouse.

To build this vanity, you don't need a cabinet shop, and you don't need weeks of build time. With some common power tools and a slight increase in cost, you can build a vanity that is stronger and far more stylish than a production model, and that requires only a couple of weekends to complete.

A Classic Look with a Lot Less Effort

When designing this Shaker-inspired piece, I started with the same height, depth, and compatibility with standard plumbing fixtures that would be present on a store-bought vanity. From there, I added some details that you won't easily find, such as mortised butt

NOTE: Prices cited in this article are from 2015.

Continued ➤

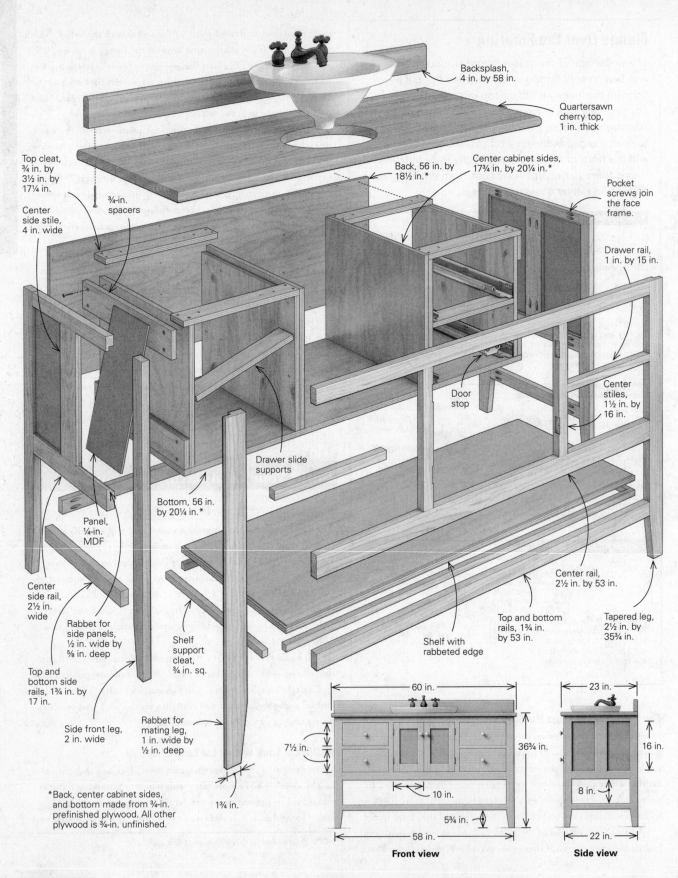

Backsplash, 4 in. by 58 in.

Quartersawn cherry top, 1 in. thick

Back, 56 in. by 18½ in.*

Center cabinet sides, 17¾ in. by 20¼ in.*

Pocket screws join the face frame.

Top cleat, ¾ in. by 3½ in. by 17¼ in.

¾-in. spacers

Center side stile, 4 in. wide

Drawer rail, 1 in. by 15 in.

Center stiles, 1½ in. by 16 in.

Door stop

Drawer slide supports

Bottom, 56 in. by 20¼ in.*

Panel, ¼-in. MDF

Center side rail, 2½ in. wide

Center rail, 2½ in. by 53 in.

Rabbet for side panels, ½ in. wide by ⅝ in. deep

Shelf support cleat, ¾ in. sq.

Top and bottom rails, 1¾ in. by 53 in.

Tapered leg, 2½ in. by 35¾ in.

Shelf with rabbeted edge

Top and bottom side rails, 1¾ in. by 17 in.

Side front leg, 2 in. wide

Rabbet for mating leg, 1 in. wide by ½ in. deep

1¾ in.

*Back, center cabinet sides, and bottom made from ¾-in. prefinished plywood. All other plywood is ¾-in. unfinished.

60 in.

23 in.

7½ in.

36¾ in.

16 in.

10 in.

8 in.

5¾ in.

58 in.

22 in.

Front view

Side view

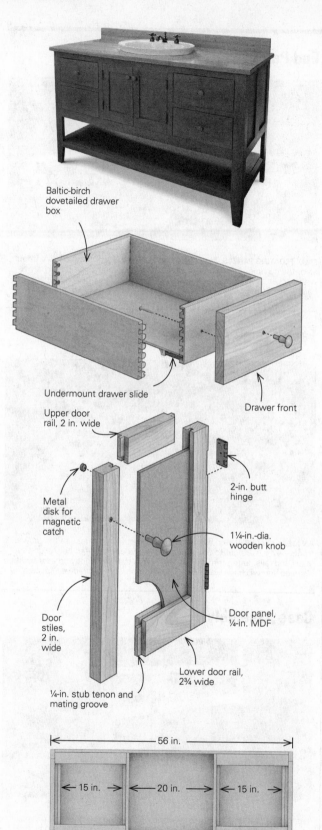

Baltic-birch
dovetailed drawer
box

Undermount drawer slide

Drawer front

Upper door
rail, 2 in. wide

2-in. butt
hinge

Metal
disk for
magnetic
catch

1¼-in.-dia.
wooden knob

Door
stiles,
2 in.
wide

Door panel,
¼-in. MDF

Lower door rail,
2¾ wide

¼-in. stub tenon and
mating groove

56 in.

15 in.   20 in.   15 in.

Plan view

hinges, full-extension ball-bearing undermount drawer slides, a solid-wood top, and a traditional milk-paint finish. Compared to the details on a production-line vanity, these small changes can make a big difference in the overall feel of the finished project, and they aren't that hard to execute. My goal in building this type of project is to respect the principles of traditional woodworking but challenge some of the techniques to make the building process a bit less fussy. Although the drawing may look intimidating, the necessary techniques for this build are basic, and I've included tips and tricks to increase your accuracy. The result is a vanity that looks and feels like a handcrafted piece of furniture, but one that goes together with more ease.

The most luxurious tools I used here were a track saw and a thickness planer, but even those are negotiable. If you don't have a track saw, then you can break down sheet goods with a circular saw and a homemade cutting guide. Also, even though you may be purchasing rough lumber that requires planing on its face and edges, most hardwood suppliers will do this work for a reasonable rate (my supplier charges 25¢ per bd. ft.) if you don't have a thickness planer.

Materials Chosen for Their Strengths

The build starts with the cabinet's plywood case, which is the foundation of the entire vanity—the part to which the rest of the components will be attached. The case consists of a continuous bottom piece, upright dividers to separate the center cabinet from the drawer sections that flank it, and a continuous back that locks everything into place. You'll need one sheet each of unfinished and prefinished ¾-in. plywood.

The unfinished plywood is used for the areas of the vanity that will either be painted or remain unseen. For water resistance and overall longevity of the undersink area, I prefer to use prefinished plywood. If you can't find a source for prefinished plywood, I recommend finishing both sides of a sheet of plywood with several coats of polyurethane and letting it cure before cutting the sheet into pieces. Otherwise, it can be a hassle to apply and sand clear coats of finish on the inside of an assembled box.

The joinery used in the plywood case won't be visible in the final piece; for that reason, you can use a finish nailer to tack most of the parts together. After assembling the face frame and attaching it to the boxes, lock the plywood together permanently with 2-in. screws.

Aside from the plywood used for the bottom shelf, all of the surfaces of the vanity that will be painted are built from 5/4 poplar (1-in. finished thickness) and ¼-in. MDF. Both of these are readily available, inexpensive, and stable, and they take paint well.

For the top of my vanity, I decided to use solid quartersawn cherry. Compared to more conventional flatsawn lumber, quartersawn boards have relatively straight-running grain, an inherently stable orientation that minimizes movement across the surface of the wood as its moisture content changes.

Continued ➜

Casework

MAKE SHEET GOODS MORE MANAGEABLE. A track saw is ideal for dividing sheets of plywood into smaller, rough-size pieces. A sheet of 1-in.-thick rigid foam is a perfect sacrificial base and support for cutoffs. Run the parts through a tablesaw for final sizing to ensure that matching parts are the same dimension.

FASTENED, BUT LEFT LOOSE. After screwing together the two pieces of plywood for each center divider and attaching the spacers to each end panel, tack the subassemblies to the cabinet bottom with 16-ga. nails. Nailed sparingly, the case parts are loose enough for adjustment once the face frame is attached.

Face Frame

ONE PART SIZES THE OTHERS. A sacrificial miter-saw fence and shopmade throat plate ensure cleaner cuts. They also make it easy to register the stock, so you only have to measure the first piece in each group of parts, which can then be laid atop the next piece for repeat cuts.

QUICK AND CLEAN TAPERS. The bottom of each leg stile receives a taper cut to give the finished vanity the look of a stand-alone piece of furniture. A plywood jig with an L-shaped fence allows the piece to be safely supported for a clean-cutting pass on the tablesaw.

End Panels

FAUX FLOATING PANELS. To achieve the look of true floating panels without all of the complex joinery, assemble each of the vanity side-panel frames with pocket screws, and then cut a ½-in.-wide by ⅝-in.-deep rabbet in the back side of the poplar stiles and rails to accept a ¼-in. MDF panel.

Face-Frame Assembly

AN IDEAL SPACER. When assembling the front face frame, use the drawer fronts—which are cut to the exact size of the opening—to help align the stiles and rails. Later, trim the drawer fronts to their slightly smaller finished size and you will have wasted no extra material on throw-away spacers.

Case Assembly

THE ORDER MATTERS. Because they are only tacked together, the plywood parts have room for adjustment, which allows you to bring the case and assembled frame into alignment. First, flush up and fasten the two long rails, then the two outermost stiles. Follow up with the inner stiles and then the drawer rails.

Pocket Holes Are Fast and Strong

The parts for the face frame, side-panel frames, legs, doors, and drawer fronts are all cut at the same time. All are crosscut to 1 in. longer than their final desired lengths, ripped ⅛ in. wider than their desired width, and then run through the thickness planer on all four sides to bring them to their final dimension before crosscutting them to their exact length.

Anywhere that I can, I use pocket-screw joinery as a fast and strong solution for hidden fastening. A pocket-hole jig is quick to set up, a cinch to use, and with hardly any moving parts, it just never seems to let me down. The only places on this project where I used a more traditional form of joinery were on the two doors.

Because the doors incorporate floating panels, the surrounding poplar pieces need to be grooved on a tablesaw to accept the ¼-in. MDF panels. But pocket screws won't work when driven through a groove-edge board, and even if they did work, the exposed grooves and pocket holes would be visible when the cabinet doors were open.

Making the Doors

ONE SETUP, TWO PASSES. Door stiles and rails receive ½-in.-deep grooves made by cutting to one side of a marked centerline, then flipping the piece to widen the ⅛-in. kerf into a ¼-in. groove. A featherboard ensures that parts stay firmly pressed against the fence.

NIBBLE THE TENONS. A stop block attached to the fence of a miter gauge registers each end of the door rails to create the shoulder cut of the ½-in.-long stub tenons, which are created by making a series of successive passes and testing the fit in the mating groove.

NOT LOOSE OR TIGHT, BUT SNUG. The panel and tenons should slide snugly into the grooves. If the tenons are too thin, glue shims to their cheeks. If they're too fat, hit them with a sanding block. After glue up, trim the door to final height.

Installing the Doors

MORTISES MADE EASY. After trimming the top and bottom of the doors, rout the hinge mortises on the doors and assembled face frame using a T-shaped plywood template and bearing-guided mortise bit.

ONE DOOR MARKS THE OTHER. With the first door sized, hung, and clamped in the closed position, temporarily hang the second door, and mark a line on the backside where the doors overlap.

DOUBLE-STICK SLED. The safest way to trim the second door, especially if the cut needs to be a slight taper, is to attach the door to a plywood sled with double-stick tape so it can be cut on the tablesaw.

Continued ➜

The Cabinet Top

TACKLE THE GLUING IN STAGES. Rather than trying to glue up a 23-in.-wide countertop all at once, glue up pairs of boards. This makes it easier to get parts clamped and misalignments corrected before the glue starts to set up. Join the pairs to make the whole top.

Decorative Edge Profile

CHAMFERS CREATE A RADIUS. To create a subtle radiused edge detail, use a 15° chamfer router bit to knock off the top and bottom edges of the counter. This leaves a narrow flat area that can be hand-sanded into a pleasing roundover profile.

Drawers

PERFECT DRAWER FACES. With the drawer boxes fixed to their slides and pushed into the cabinet, apply double-stick carpet tape to the back of the drawer face, and carefully press it into place. The tape is strong enough to allow the drawer to be opened so that the front can be fastened from the inside of the box with 1¼-in. pan-head screws.

Instead, cut stub tenons on the edges of the doors' top and bottom rails, allowing them to fit into the same groove that is already being cut to accept the MDF panel. All of this joinery can be cut on the tablesaw, provided you carefully set the fence and blade height for each step. After glue up and sanding, trim the doors to fit using a standard step-by-step door-fitting sequence (see "How to Install Inset Cabinet Doors," *Fine Homebuilding* #226).

Know When to Buy Rather Than Build

Drawer boxes aren't much harder to build than any other part of this vanity. But when I compare the convenience and low cost of ordering dovetailed drawer components with the steps and amount of time involved in making them myself, it's a simple decision. I buy my drawer components online from Barker Door, where the parts are cut to my specifications and arrive ready for glue up and finishing. For this project, the parts for all four drawers made of Baltic birch (a type of tightly veneered plywood) cost me $143, including shipping to my doorstep. Had I bought the plywood and built the boxes myself, I would have spent $116 for materials alone, and I consider my time worth more than the $27 savings.

For drawer slides, don't skimp. It's the one part of this cabinet that gets used daily, so it's the last place you want to save a buck. I use Blum undermount slides. They aren't cheap, but they install easily, ride smoothly, and have a soft-close mechanism.

Step Up to a Solid-Wood Top

For the top of my vanity, I bought rough-dimensioned 6/4 cherry boards and planed them to a 1-in. finished thickness. After gluing up and sanding the top, I cut the hole for the sink using a template and a jigsaw before applying the polyurethane finish. This sequence is important because it allows me to apply finish to the visible surface of the countertop and also to the edges of the sink cutout, which are likely to get wet at some point in the life of the vanity.

This vanity took about 30 hours to complete and cost me about $850 in materials—comparable in cash outlay to many commercially available vanities of this size and style. In fact, this vanity was less expensive than many similar models being sold online. Plus, I know mine is built solid in a classic style that I believe will remain timeless, and it has a handmade touch that you can't get from a factory-built vanity.

Contents

Flooring

Wood Flooring Problems and Solutions

By Charles Peterson

I love the look and durability of wood floors, and it's not just because I've been installing them since 1978. I'm impressed by a surface that receives such a tremendous amount of abuse yet—when installed properly—lasts as long as a house. Installing a wood floor requires a substantial investment in materials and labor. When problems arise or when a floor fails, it can be costly. Every year, an estimated $1 billion worth of hardwood-floor damage occurs across the country.

As a consultant and author for the National Wood Flooring Association (NWFA; www.woodfloors.org), I've made it my business to understand what causes all that damage. The good news is that if you take your time, use the appropriate tools and techniques, and understand wood acclimation, you can create a floor that lasts a lifetime.

1. Abnormal Gaps

Wood floors are prone to movement. Installed correctly, floorboards hold tight to one another during humid times of the year and might reveal gaps during drier times. Abnormal gaps are generally the result of flooring that's too wet when it is

NOT ALL GAPS ARE BAD, BUT THESE ARE. The gaps pictured here are too big and irregular. They take away from the overall look of the floor, which should be relatively uniform across its surface.

installed (sidebar p. 592), but they also can be the consequence of installing flooring in areas of excessive dryness. I've worked on floors that had abnormal gaps because floorboards were installed directly over heating ducts, in areas that received a lot of sunlight, and in homes heated with woodstoves, which creates a dry interior environment.

Gaps are an aesthetic issue and should be repaired when they disrupt the overall look of a floor, not when they measure a particular width. I repair abnormal gaps during the most humid

Continued ➔

time of year, when they are at their smallest. If I repair gaps when they are at their widest, I might not leave sufficient clearance between floorboards and create a floor that buckles when it expands.

Also, I never use wood filler to repair gaps. Instead, I make a patch by gluing slivers of wood to the edges of the floorboards. I'm careful to apply glue to only one side of the sliver so that I don't glue any boards together.

2. Cupping

When the bottom of a board is wetter than the top, its edges cup. Wide plank floors are more prone to cupping, but I've seen it happen to strip flooring as well.

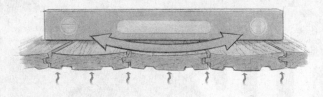

Most often, cupping happens when flooring is installed over a wet basement or crawlspace. A vapor retarder installed between the subfloor and the floorboards can help the condition by slowing moisture migration, but it shouldn't be relied on as a permanent solution to moisture problems. I use Aquabar "B" by Fortifiber (www.fortifiber.com) as a vapor retarder for strip flooring installed over conventionally framed floors. I use Bostik's MVP (www.bostik-us.com) trowel-applied membrane when I'm laying floors over slabs and radiant-heating systems and when I'm installing wide plank flooring.

Some cupped floors lie flat once moisture issues are corrected. Other floors might be deformed permanently. A floor that doesn't lie flat needs to be sanded, but only when the moisture content of the top and bottom of the boards is within 1%. I drive a moisture meter through the subfloor to check the bottoms of the boards. If you sand the peaked edges of a cupped floor too soon, you could have crowned boards when they're fully dry.

MOISTURE RESISTANT, NOT MOISTUREPROOF. Aquabar "B," which is composed of two layers of kraft paper laminated with asphalt, slows the movement of moisture through a subfloor, but it doesn't stop it. An elastomeric membrane has similar characteristics, but is best used in glue-down flooring applications.

3. Buckling

When wood flooring becomes too moist, it can expand to the point that it lifts off the subfloor, moves door frames, and pops trim from the wall. A floor can buckle because of a damp basement, because of a flood, or because the floor was installed when it was too dry. In any case, the cause of buckling is always moisture, and improper fastening can aggravate the condition. Nails could be the wrong size or could be spaced too far apart. On glue-down installations, using the wrong size trowel can lead to a poor bond between the floorboards and the subfloor.

I've been able to refasten some buckled floors, but others had to be removed. I reuse floorboards when possible, but if the tongues and grooves are torn apart or if the boards are cracked, I replace them. I don't repair buckled floors until the moisture issues in the home have been fixed and the moisture content of the floorboards and subfloor is at the appropriate level (sidebar p. 592).

BOARDS BUCKLE IF THEY CAN'T EXPAND. When floorboards aren't acclimated or are exposed to lots of moisture, they can crush together and lift off the subfloor.

4. Peeling Finish

Floor finishes peel because the floor was contaminated or improperly prepped when the finish was applied. Excessive sanding with high-grit paper can burnish wood and create a surface too smooth for the finish to adhere. Inadequate abrading or cleaning between finish coats, applying a top coat over a floor that is not dry, or working with incompatible finishes all can cause peeling. However, the most common cause of peeling that I see is stain residue that isn't cleaned from the floor prior to applying finish. To prevent a buildup of stain residue, I remove excess stain

A CONTAMINATED FLOOR WON'T HOLD FINISH. Dirt or chemicals on top of a floor or embedded in its finish can cause subsequent coats of finish to flake or peel off.

On floors that are not sanded finely enough, the finish settles in the bottom of the sanding grooves, but the tops of the grooves are covered with little finish. When the floor is exposed to foot traffic, the surface breaks down. I sand bare boards to 100 grit or 120 grit, depending on the finish I'm using. In other cases, I've seen layers of finish built up too quickly. When multiple coats of finish are applied without proper drying time, it can take six months for the finish to cure. By that time, the floor looks like it has aged 10 years.

Even when sanded and finished properly, wood requires regular maintenance. Grit left on wood floors acts like sandpaper when walked on, and unclipped pet nails or unprotected furniture feet can scratch a finish considerably. At times, I've been able to recoat a slightly worn floor without sanding off all the old finish. But when a floor has lots of wear and deep scratches, it's best to sand down the floor to bare wood and refinish it.

FINISHES ENHANCE THE BAD AS MUCH AS THE GOOD. Debris on the floor surface or in the finish, such as this hair, is magnified when the floor finish is dry.

no later than three minutes after it was applied and let the floor dry thoroughly before applying the finish. I don't apply multiple coats of stain or let stain sit in an attempt to darken wood.

The best way to fix a peeling floor is to sand it down to bare wood and restart the finishing process. Simply abrading the floor and applying a new top coat might not fix the problem. Without resanding, waxes, oils, and furniture polishes used to clean wood floors seep into the pores of the finish and can prevent the new finish from bonding successfully.

5. Excessive Wear

All wood floors eventually wear out, but when they're in rough shape only a couple of years after being finished, something went wrong. Likely, the floor wasn't sanded properly, the finish was built up too quickly, or the floor wasn't maintained correctly.

6. Debris in the Finish

Wet finish acts like a large piece of flypaper. Any dust or animal hair that finds its way into it will be magnified once the finish is dry. To prevent debris from ruining the finish, I clean all the room's surfaces prior to finishing the floor. I wipe down the walls and light fixtures. Then I vacuum the floor and go over it with a tack cloth. I never use tack cloths designed for use on cars, though. They can contain silicone, which compromises the finish. I also strain the finish and pour it into an applicator tray that I've lined with an inside-out garbage bag. Last, I remove any loose fibers from the applicator by washing and vacuuming it thoroughly.

If debris does find its way into the finish, I make repairs by sanding the floor as I would between coats of finish and apply a new top coat on the floor.

DON'T ALWAYS BLAME THE DOG FOR FAST-WEARING FLOORS. A worn floor lacks sheen and evenness in color. Poor finishing techniques can be the cause as much as family pets and household abuse.

Continued ➜

7. Sanding Blemishes

Worn abrasive screens or sanding pads used to sand between coats of finish can create unsightly scratches in the floor. Subsequent coats of finish magnify these imperfections. To remove the scratches, the finish needs to be sanded past the coat where the scratches were initially made. It's often difficult to tell which coat of finish the scratches were created in, so I tend to sand off all the finish and start again.

To prevent these scratches, I use 3M abrasive pads when sanding between each finish coat. I find that these pads leave smaller, more plentiful, but less noticeable scratches. They also create a scratch pattern that promotes a much better adhesion between coats of finish. I like to use 150-grit to 180-grit pads when sanding oil-based polyurethanes and 220 grit when sanding between coats of water-based finishes.

8. Stains

Stains built up on a floor finish can usually be removed with a wood-floor cleaner (www.minwax.com), but stains in the actual finish must be sanded out. The most difficult stains to deal with are those that penetrate into the wood fibers. Pets are the most frequent culprit in creating these types of stains, but water can be equally damaging.

PET-STAINED FLOORS CAN BE SAVED. This floor can be fixed by brushing two-part wood bleach over the surface. The floor is neutralized after a couple of hours, then sanded and refinished when it's dry.

Acclimate a Floor Correctly

Acclimating a floor is the process of adjusting the flooring's moisture content to correspond closely with the moisture content of the environment it's being installed in. Not all flooring needs to be acclimated, though.

From the Truck to the Subfloor

In remodels, flooring can be brought into the home as soon as there is space for it. In new construction, flooring should be brought into a home only after the HVAC system has been in operation for at least one week.

I remove strip flooring from its boxes and spread it over a clean, dry subfloor that has been covered with a vapor retarder. I stack wide plank flooring in a pile with shims between each board to increase air circulation. Then, I weight the top of the pile to keep the boards flat. Depending on how much moisture needs to be added or removed from the boards, I add a humidifier or dehumidifier to the room. I then take moisture readings periodically.

Install Flooring When It Has the Right Moisture Content

The interior temperature and relative humidity of a house determine the correct moisture content for a wood floor.

Relative humidity can be measured with a humidity gauge, which can be bought at hardware stores, and ideally should fall between 30% and 50%. In a home kept at 70°F with that humidity range, flooring should be installed when it has a moisture content of 7.7%. Homes don't always have ideal humidity levels or temperatures. It's best to determine the expected relative-humidity range and interior-temperature range and acclimate your flooring to fall in the middle of the spectrum (chart p. 593).

Environment and Floor Type Make Acclimation Tricky

Some homes have drastic swings in both temperature and relative humidity. Near the coast, for example, my house has a relative-humidity level of 30% and an average indoor temperature of 70°F in the winter. In the summer, when the doors and windows are open, the humidity level inside can spike to 78%. Engineered flooring or quartersawn flooring is the best choice for my home because they're less susceptible to movement. I still acclimated my floors to the midpoint of my moisture range at 70°F, so I don't have gaps in the winter or buckling in the summer. I install wide plank flooring when it has a slightly high moisture content. This provides extra room for floorboards to expand throughout the year.

I usually recommend replacing floorboards that have been deeply stained, especially by pet urine. But I have had success using two-part wood bleach (www.kleanstrip.com) to remove stains.

This treatment has some drawbacks, though. Bleach tends to break down wood fibers, which increases the wood's susceptibility to denting. Also, bleach isn't guaranteed to lift the stains from the wood, which means the floorboards might still need to be replaced. Finally, the entire floor should be bleached, not just one area. This results in a lot more work, but helps to create a floor that is consistent in color and sheen.

 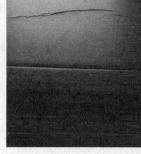

INSTALLATION ERRORS SHOW. The finish on the edge of this board was cracked by a flooring nailer that wasn't used correctly.

SMALL CRACKS CAN BE FILLED. A board with cracks in its face doesn't always need to be replaced. The board shown here may be repaired with a touch-up kit.

9. Fractures

I see more cracks in factory-finished floors than in any other type of flooring. The finish on these boards is easily damaged by flooring nailers. Most manufacturers, however, now make adapters for their nailers to prevent the nailers' force from concentrating on the surface of the floorboards. A board with a badly damaged edge should have been replaced when the damage occurred. If it wasn't, I take the time to replace it. (See "New Life for an Old Floor," online at finehomebuilding.com.)

Cracks also can form on the face of factory-finished and regular floorboards. This damage is generally attributed to checks in the wood. Some wood species are more prone to cracking than others. Cracking also can be caused by the manufacturer. If the wood is dried too quickly in the kiln, it can crack.

Factory-finished boards can be fixed with a manufacturer repair kit, which typically consists of wood filler, colored marker, and a bottle of finish. If I can't get a kit, I proceed the same way as I would with regular flooring. I replace the board, or I fill the crack with wood filler and apply a coat of finish over the entire floor so that colors, tones, and sheen match perfectly.

4 Steps to Properly Acclimated Boards

This chart, provided by the Forest Products Laboratory, indicates proper flooring moisture values with regard to relative humidity and interior temperature.

STEP 1: Determine the home's average interior temperature.

STEP 2: Determine the home's expected relative-humidity level in January, when levels are lowest.

STEP 3: Determine the home's expected relative-humidity level in June, when levels are highest.

Moisture content (%) at various relative-humidity values

°F	5%	10%	15%	20%	25%	30%	35%	40%	45%	50%	55%	60%	65%	70%	75%	80%	85%	90%	95%
30	1.4	2.0	3.7	4.6	5.5	6.3	7.1	7.9	8.7	9.5	10.4	11.3	12.4	13.5	14.9	16.5	18.5	21.0	24.3
40	1.4	2.6	3.7	4.6	5.5	6.3	7.1	7.9	8.7	9.5	10.4	11.3	12.3	13.5	14.9	16.5	18.5	21.0	24.3
50	1.4	2.6	3.6	4.6	5.5	6.3	7.1	7.9	8.7	9.5	10.3	11.2	12.3	13.4	14.8	16.4	18.4	20.9	24.3
60	1.3	2.5	3.6	4.6	5.4	6.2	7.0	7.8	8.6	9.4	10.2	11.1	12.1	13.3	14.6	16.2	18.2	20.7	24.1
70	1.3	2.5	3.5	4.5	5.4	6.2	6.9	7.7	8.5	9.2	10.1	11.0	12.0	13.1	14.4	16.0	17.9	20.5	23.9
80	1.3	2.4	3.5	4.4	5.3	6.1	6.8	7.6	8.3	9.1	9.9	10.8	11.7	12.9	14.2	15.7	17.7	20.2	23.6
90	1.2	2.3	3.4	4.3	5.1	5.9	6.7	7.4	8.1	8.9	9.7	10.5	11.5	12.6	13.9	15.4	17.3	19.8	23.3
100	1.2	2.3	3.3	4.2	5.0	5.8	6.5	7.2	7.9	8.7	9.5	10.3	11.2	12.3	13.6	15.1	17.0	19.5	22.9

Temperature

Step 4: Acclimate boards to moisture levels in the middle of these values.

Continued →

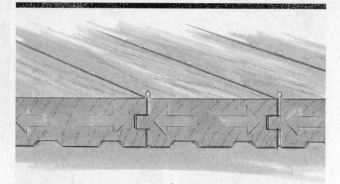

POLY BEADS ARE A SIGN THAT THE FLOOR IS MOVING. Polyurethane can be pushed from the cracks of a floor as it gains moisture and expands during the finishing process.

10. Poly Droplets

When small polyurethane droplets form along the edges of each floorboard, moisture is always to blame. The droplets are caused by polyurethane flowing into the gaps between floorboards while the floor is moving. The problem generally occurs when a floor is being finished during the change between dry and humid seasons. As the boards adjust to the climate, they expand, forcing any uncured polyurethane from the gap.

If caught in time, poly droplets can be removed with a razor blade, a rag, and floor cleaner. If a mess has already been made, either by walking on the droplets or by allowing them to cure, then each droplet needs to be cut off the floor by hand with a razor blade before the entire floor is abraded in preparation for a fresh top coat.

11. Irregular Floorboards

Dished-out deformities in floorboards are typically caused by poor sanding techniques or by heavy wear in spring wood. Spring wood, the part of the tree that grows quickly early in the season, has the least dense cell structure of any part of the tree. This wood

THE DISTORTION IS IN THE WOOD, NOT THE FINISH. Every floorboard contains both soft spring wood, which is the dark grain in each board, and dense late-season wood. The soft spring wood in this floor was dug out by improper sanding.

is softer and less durable than the slower late-season growth, where cells are stacked more densely. Spring wood is easily misshapen by heavy foot traffic, sliding furniture, pets, and other daily household abuse.

Poorly maintained drum sanders, low-quality abrasives, or incorrect sanding also can create irregular floorboards. Drum sanders with damaged sanding belts, damaged fan belts, or worn-out wheels can create chatter marks on a floor. Chatter marks appear uniformly across the grain of each board and result in a floor that looks wavy.

Fortunately, I've never seen irregular floorboards that couldn't be fixed. The floor needs to be flattened with a quality drum sander oriented at a slight angle to the boards; with a triplanetary sander, which has three orbiting heads; or with a buffer that has a hard-plate attachment. Of course, the floor will need to be refinished.

Wood Floors on a Concrete Slab

By Kevin Ward

Here in Texas, as in much of the South and West, houses are built on concrete slabs. For a flooring contractor like me, a slab can be a mixed blessing. Concrete is stable, doesn't bounce, and won't expand or contract seasonally like wood. However, it does limit the clients' choices for wood-flooring installations. Obviously, you can't use nails to attach the flooring. The advent of engineered flooring (hardwood veneer glued to a plywood substrate) made the choice of hardwood on a slab an easy one. Glued down with a urethane adhesive, engineered flooring doesn't move in service as much as solid wood, is easy to install with the right prep work, and looks great for years.

There are a few tricks to a successful installation, and in this case, preparation is more than half the job. Recently, my company was contracted to install more than 1000 sq. ft. of reclaimed-oak engineered flooring of random widths in a new house outside of Austin, and the job provided a good example of how we work.

Ensure the Substrate Is Flat and Dry

Before the job starts, I go to the site and check the slab's moisture content. There are a couple of different methods for doing this, but the easiest and most accurate is to use a moisture meter. The slab's moisture content should register about 4% or less. If you're working with a new slab, it's a good idea to allow it to cure for at least 90 days before checking its moisture content. If the slab is too wet, the flooring adhesive won't bond properly. Alternatively, you can use either a moisture-barrier membrane that's applied before the adhesive or a moisture-barrier/adhesive combination. (These alternatives are available from many manufacturers, but they cost twice as much as the simple adhesive process.) Even if I know the slab is dry, I always check and record the moisture reading in case something goes wrong later.

Next, I use razor scrapers to clean the accumulated paint, dirt, and gunk off the slab. Then I sweep and vacuum it clean so that nothing interferes when I check the slab's flatness.

I use a 10-ft.-long aluminum straightedge to find the high and low spots on the floor. Doorways, transitions, and floor outlets are the serial offenders here.

I grind down the high spots, checking with a straightedge as I go. I use a flooring buffer to scuff up the low areas. While I'm scuffing, one of my crew is mixing the self-leveling compound in a 5-gal. bucket. The compound's consistency must be liquid enough to seek its own level but stiff enough not to run across the floor.

After vacuuming and applying a polymer bonding agent to the low areas to be filled, I screed the leveling compound, trowel the edges into the slab surface, and let it dry overnight.

The next day, I use the buffer again to flatten any ridges in the compound. After a good vacuuming, I protect any finished surfaces close to the floor with painter's tape. At this stage, I also use an oscillating multitool and a scrap of flooring as a gauge to undercut door casings, cabinet stiles, and kicks so that the flooring has plenty of clearance.

Establish a Starter Row

The best way to start the installation is to create a starter row that's about 2 ft. wide and that runs across the entire room. I like to establish the starter row near the center of the room so that I can adjust in both directions. After measuring the space, I snap a chalkline along the long axis and check to see if it is parallel to each wall. A second line about 2 ft. from the first gives us the limits of the starter row.

Before spreading any glue, I start to fit the flooring to the doorways and bump-outs in the hall. It's important not to apply more glue than can be covered in about 40 minutes, the average working time for the urethane adhesive. Once the glue is applied, you only want to put the flooring down once. It's critical that the starter row remain straight, so I always check the distance to the chalkline after fitting a piece.

Even Out the Highs and Lows

A glue-down floor must be installed on a slab that has less than a 3/16-in. deviation in level over 10 ft. The slab must also be at the proper height so that the transitions are smooth between flooring and adjacent tiles, doorways, and stairs.

CHECK FOR FLATNESS. Examine the entire slab with a long straightedge (at least 10 ft. is preferable), and mark high and low areas with a pencil.

FLATTEN THE HIGH SPOTS. Use a rotary hammer or angle grinder to grind down high spots, periodically checking progress with a straightedge. Afterward, sweep and vacuum the area.

PRIME THE LOW SPOTS. Before the low areas can be filled, the slab surface must be abraded with a buffer and 36-grit sandpaper, then painted with an acrylic bonding agent.

MAKE IT FLOW. Mix the self-leveling compound, pour it onto a low area, and use a long straightedge as a screed to smooth its surface. Blend the edges into the slab with a trowel.

Continued →

Start the Layout in the Middle

To avoid accumulated errors, start the layout in the middle of the room and work toward the walls. Snap two lines about 2 ft. apart and parallel to both walls

DRY-FIT THE FIRST PIECES. Because the flooring must fit under the cut door jambs and around jogs in the walls, dry-fit those pieces, then check to make sure that they are parallel to the chalkline.

START SPREADING THE GLUE. After fitting and gluing the scribed areas in the hallway, use a ³⁄₁₆-in. V-notch trowel to spread the adhesive between the chalklines of the starter.

STAY BETWEEN THE LINES. Push the first course of flooring into the adhesive, and check to see that it's aligned with the chalkline. A couple of hammer taps help to set the pieces. As you fill in the rest of the starter, make sure the flooring isn't wandering over the line.

Work Toward the Walls

With the starter row established, continue the installation in one direction in increments approximately 2 ft. wide. Within a couple of courses' width of the wall, dry-fit the last course against the wall, then glue it down. Repeat the process on the opposite side of the room.

Trick of the Trade: Hide Cut Edges

Whenever I crosscut a piece of prefinished flooring, I knock off any fuzz from the cut end and then give it a quick swipe with the proper stain so the cut edge won't show.

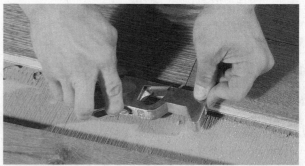

Tool of the Trade: Adjust Width with a Rabbet Plane

Occasionally, a board that's ¹⁄₁₆ in. or so wider than its nominal width gets installed. Rather than pull it out, it's sometimes easier to use a rabbet plane (I like the Stanley No. 92) to gradually reduce the excess width over the length of the piece.

Always Dry-Fit Tricky Areas

A glue-down floor must be installed on a slab that has less than a ³⁄₁₆-in. deviation in level over 10 ft. The slab must also be at the proper height so that the transitions are smooth between flooring and adjacent tiles, doorways, and stairs.

SWITCH PLACES. To scribe the last row of flooring, begin by aligning the piece to be scribed to the previous row.

SCRIBE THE LINE. Holding a short scrap of flooring (under 12 in.) of the previous row's width against the wall and on top of the piece to be scribed, trace its edge. Repeat along the wall until you've scribed the line along the entire piece.

RIP AND FIT. After ripping the piece at the pencil line, test the fit, then spread the glue and drop the piece in. The width of the tongue on the scrap piece creates the ³⁄₁₆-in. gap at the wall.

SQUEEZE IT IN. Use a flat bar to lever the last piece into place. A scrap of flooring used as a backer prevents the bar from damaging the drywall.

I spread this glue with a ³⁄₁₆-in. V-notch trowel within the chalked lines. (To set the starter on this job, I wanted at least 20 ft. of length.) I lay the flooring onto the glue, aligning it to the chalkline and staggering the joints at least 12 in. between courses. A few taps with a rubber mallet help to push each board into the glue. With three courses down, I stretch a piece of painter's tape across the row every couple of feet to help hold the boards together.

After checking to see that the starter row is on the line and parallel to the walls, I weigh it down with 5-gal. buckets filled with sand and let the adhesive cure overnight.

Switch to Production Mode

The next day, I measure out about 2 ft. from the starter courses, snap a chalkline, spread the glue, and lay down the flooring as before. I repeat this sequence to within two or three courses of the wall. Because the last course must be fit to the wall, I scribe, cut, and dry-fit the last course, then apply the adhesive, install the pieces, and bring in the sand buckets.

When the adhesive is dry and the floor is complete, I vacuum and sweep thoroughly until every speck of dirt is picked up. To protect the floor from the next wave of trades, I cover it with a tough, vapor-permeable covering such as Ram Board and tape all the seams. I also schedule a day to return and repair any scratches or blemishes, right before the clients are scheduled to move in.

Refinish Your Wood Floors

By Brent Kelosky

Although my company does all types of flooring installations, our bread and butter has always been refinishing worn hardwood. Our goal is to uncover the beauty under the decrepit surface of the floor, which involves no small amount of labor.

When we arrived on-site for the job shown here, the wall-to-wall carpeting had already been removed, revealing 750 sq. ft. of severely worn red-oak flooring that appeared original to this old Pennsylvania farmhouse. Although we got back down to bare wood quickly, that's just the beginning of a job like this.

The job took a two-person crew just under five days to complete. Refinishing a hardwood floor is an admittedly disruptive process, but you realize it's worth it when you first set eyes on the results.

The materials are straightforward—just a single coat of stain, a coat of sealer to lock in the stain, and two coats of polyurethane to provide the wear layer—but breathing new life into an old wood floor takes a lot of patience. It all starts with sanding.

Sanding Will Make or Break Your Job

Without question, the critical difference between a professional-looking finished floor and a poor attempt is how much care is taken during the sanding stage. Although you're only removing ¹⁄₁₆ in. or so of actual wood, the sanding process takes multiple days—that is, if it's done correctly.

In addition to some common hand and power tools, there are three specialized tools we use on our jobs: a belt floor sander, an orbital edger, and a buffer.

The bulk of the sanding work is handled by the large, very aggressive, 220v belt sander. Run back and forth through the room, working in the same direction as the floor's wood grain, the belt sander is used to take slow, overlapping passes.

Continued →

Although an upright orbital sander is the most common tool available at rental yards, we prefer to use a belt sander. (A drum sander is also an improvement over the orbital.) An orbital sander is a fairly gentle and forgiving tool, which may seem appealing if you're unsure of your abilities, but it also requires much more time to do the job. On badly damaged floors, you'll likely give up long before you get the blemishes sanded out.

A belt sander runs on wheels and uses a lever to lower the machine—which puts the sanding belt in contact with the floor surface—and then to lift it away. Because the machine is so aggressive, you can't allow it to sit in one spot for even a couple of seconds or you will end up with significant gouges. It should be lowered to the floor as it's being moved forward to start a pass, then lifted back off at the end of each pass.

A powerful handheld orbital sander called an edger is used to sand the perimeter of the room and any areas where the larger machine won't fit. The smallest details and corners are done by hand with a scraper and sandpaper. Later in the process, a buffing machine is outfitted for finer sanding, but first comes the rough cut.

Sand Incrementally and Patiently

Although it's not the coarsest option in our arsenal, 24 is typically the lowest grit we use for the rough cut. Such a coarse grit is only necessary when a floor has lots of built-up wax on the surface, and even then it's pretty inefficient for removing actual wood. In most cases, we start with 36-grit sandpaper, which removes the existing topcoats and stain, revealing fresh wood across most of the floor. From there, we sand the floor twice more with 50-grit and 80-grit paper, spending additional time on problem areas such as deep scratches or surface stains (see "Dealing with Damage," p. 599).

A crucial step that's often not considered by first-timers is blending together the sanding patterns from the belt sander and the edger. Because they have different weights, operate at different speeds, and are run in different directions, these two machines leave the sanded floor looking and feeling inconsistent, even when they're equipped with the same grit of sandpaper. The remedy for this problem is a random-orbit sander.

Even though we use 80-grit paper with the belt sander and the edger, experience has taught us that the random-orbit

Get Back to Bare Wood

The first pass with the belt sander and the edger, which we call the rough cut, typically relies on 36-grit paper to remove the existing finish and stain quickly, revealing fresh wood across most of the floor.

LARGE AREAS Heavy, powerful, and aggressive, a professional-grade belt sander (which can be rented)does the heaviest lifting in a floor-refinishing job. Slow, overlapping passes are made in the direction of the floor boards.

EDGES A powerful orbital sander known as an edger sands the flooring around the edges of each room and in any areas too small to be handled by the full-size belt sander.

CORNERS Scraping with a handheld draw scraper followed by some hand sanding quickly reveals bare wood in corners and around details where a sander won't fit.

STAYING SHARP Wherever the scraper goes, so does a metal file, which is used frequently to hone the scraper's cutting edge.

Dealing with Damage

We often see pet stains, traffic patterns, knife marks along the edges of the room left from the carpet installation, and missing wood or abandoned registers. Our first choice is always to sand out the damage if we can, but damage often extends beyond the missing, scratched, or dented wood.

Sanding can't fix everything, and often it's impossible to predict whether a damaged section can be sanded out until you try. For areas that can't be remedied with sanding, there are two options: acceptance or board replacement.

When sanding damaged areas, we take several passes with the belt sander at a slight angle to the wood

grain, alternating the angle of the machine between each series of passes. It sometimes helps to spray the surface of the damaged flooring with water—just enough to wet it evenly—between passes with the belt sander. The water raises the grain of the wood, lifting deeper stains to be within reach of the sander.

We typically don't bother filling large gaps with putty. Experience has taught us that the camouflage rarely lasts and that this repair isn't worth the effort. It's extremely difficult to fill an entire void, and seasonal movement combined with vibrations of walking usually open the gaps again. These imperfections are often best left as they are.

Sand with Patience

Although the sanding progress isn't as dramatic as during the rough cut, the incremental passes with belt sander, edger, buffer, and random-orbit sander are crucial and demand a slow, methodical system.

TRACK YOUR PROGRESS. To ensure that no spots are skipped, use a hard piece of rubber to mark across the grain of the floor before sanding. Rubber is more reliable than a marker, which can dry out quickly.

BACK IT UP ONE GRIT. Use a random-orbit sander to retouch the edges of the room. Although the rest of the floor is sanded to 80 grit, use 60-grit paper here to avoid a halo effect around the room's perimeter.

BUFF TO BLEND. The final sanding pass is done with a buffer that's equipped with a multidisk head and 80-grit paper. This setup blends the scratch patterns of the belt sander and the edger, ensuring a uniform look when stain is applied.

Continued ➜

Stain by Hand

When working in large, open areas, the fastest option is to apply the oil-based stain using a pad on the buffer machine. But for most jobs, the best way to apply stain is also the most labor-intensive: wiping it on by hand.

USE THE FLOOR AS THE SAMPLE BOARD. The most accurate way to decide between stain colors is to apply the stain options right to the floor after the first or second pass with the belt sander. They can then be sanded out with the next pass.

A TWO-PERSON STAINING TEAM. Working on padded hands and knees to prevent moisture spots that will keep the stain from penetrating evenly, the first person wipes the stain on using a folded cotton cloth while the second person follows behind, using another cloth to work the stain into the wood in a firm, circular rubbing motion.

sander should be equipped with 60-grit paper, which roughs up the perimeter of the room and any other areas where the two machines had overlapping passes. Although it seems counterintuitive, this ensures that the stain penetrates evenly. A final pass with the upright buffer machine is the last step in the sanding process before the floor undergoes a thorough vacuuming.

Staining Is Done By Hand

Although water-based stains are an option, I've found them to be inferior to oil-based products, especially in getting even stain color in large rooms. Along with the sealer and topcoats that come after it, we use stain from Bona Kemi. When using multiple cans of stain, we combine them in one bucket to ensure that the color is uniform. We apply the stain with a lint-free cloth, then wipe the excess before it dries in place.

It's critical to protect the unstained portions of the floor from moisture as you work. Water in the wood causes that part of the floor to absorb pigment differently, and even something as subtle as perspiration through the knees of your pants can leave discolored blotches in the finished floor. Always use disposable shoe covers when you're walking the floor; bare or socked feet are an absolute no. Kneepads are essential, as well as a rag under each hand. In hot weather, a cloth tied around the head will catch sweat dripping from your brow.

Sandpaper scratches that went unnoticed during the previous floor-prep phase often become obvious as they trap pigment during the stain application. These scratches can be sanded by hand with the same 80-grit paper used in the last pass of the sanders and then recoated right away with stain. There's no need to bother with the vacuum.

When the schedule allows, we like to let the stain dry overnight. If the sealer will be applied later the same day, we check for dryness by wiping a white cotton cloth across the stained surface. If no stain is transferred to the cloth, it's dry enough to move on to the seal coat, which is a waterborne product used to separate the stain from the topcoats that come next. Depending on the brand of polyurethane, the sealer may not be a strict prerequisite, but we use it to provide an extra layer of build above the stain, which enhances the visual depth of the topcoats. After the sealer dries, minor blemishes and nail holes can be filled with a putty that matches the stain color before the entire floor is abraded with the buffer. Then the floor gets another pass with the vacuum, followed by a pass with tack cloths to pick up any remaining dust.

Waterborne Polyurethane Is the Most Durable Choice

Although we use oil-based stain, we switch to a waterborne product for the polyurethane topcoats because the waterborne products have lower odor and faster dry times and are actually more durable than oil-based topcoats. For sheen, I encourage customers to opt for either satin or semigloss because wear

Topcoats Share the Same Technique

The topcoats on a floor—from the single coat of sealer through the two coats of water-based polyurethane—are applied using the same tools and techniques. Make sure to buff the floor after the seal coat, but you shouldn't need to sand between or after the coats of polyurethane.

1. EDGES COME FIRST. Working just ahead of the person applying finish with the T-bar, coat the perimeter of the room by pouring a thin line of finish directly onto the floor, then spreading it with a handheld applicator pad.

2. THE SNOWPLOW APPROACH. A T-bar applicator pushes the finish evenly across the floor. To prevent buildup at the edges of the room, apply each row by flowing it smoothly into the next using a continuous curving motion. Apply four to five overlapping rows at a time, which is about the limit of what can be reached easily without stepping in the wet finish.

3. RETOUCH THE CURVES. Remove the perimeter curve marks by feathering the finish from the edges of the room inward, wringing excess from the T-bar by pressing it firmly on the unfinished part of the floor.

4. SMOOTH THE SEAL COAT. Supplement a maroon (very fine grit) buffing pad with strips of 180-grit adhesive sandpaper to smooth out the dried coat of sealer, being careful not to walk on buffed surfaces.

5. PUSH-BROOM TACK CLOTH. After sanding the seal coat and vacuuming the floors, put on shoe covers and pick up the last bits of dust with a moistened towel wrapped around the head of a push broom. This ensures a clean surface for the first coat of polyurethane.

6. DON'T RUSH IT. We never apply more than two coats of finish in a single day. The most recent coat of finish always dries faster than what's under it and you don't want to risk trapping moisture.

patterns from pets and foot traffic are more obvious on floors with high-gloss finishes.

A small handheld foam pad is used to apply the polyurethane around the perimeter of the room, around details such as balusters and hearths, and in small areas. While the edges and details are still wet, a T-bar with a spongy applicator pad spreads finish across the rest of the floor in rows that follow the direction of the grain.

Optimum conditions for drying the topcoat are temperatures between 65°F and 80°F, with 40% to 60% relative humidity and some air movement to help wick away moisture, but not so much that it blows dust around.

The coat of sealer and the first coat of polyurethane are typically dry enough for a recoating in about four hours, but we never apply more than two coats of finish in a single day. My advice here is not to rush it, because the most recent coat of finish always dries faster than what's under it, and you don't want to risk trapping moisture, which leads to adhesion problems.

There should be no need for sanding between or after coats of polyurethane. After the last coat, the floor can be walked on gently in about four or five hours, but restrict normal foot traffic for 24 hours. Anything that might prevent drying, such as an area rug, shouldn't be replaced until after seven days to allow the finish to cure fully.

Continued →

Prefinished Wood Floors

By Charles Peterson

When working with prefinished flooring, it's important to keep in mind that the finish is permanent. While that may sound a bit obvious, many contractors who are used to installing unfinished wood flooring sometimes find it difficult to transition to prefinished products. They're used to working atop floorboards that will receive aggressive sanding before the job is done—a safety net of sorts. However, the margin for error when installing prefinished floorboards is small. The most minor mistake or oversight—a dropped hammer, a rock stuck in the sole of a boot, an exposed fitting on an air hose—can have costly consequences. From job-site setup to the layout to the actual installation, getting every detail right is imperative.

I recently installed solid, ¾-in.-thick, prefinished, quartersawn white oak of various widths in my house. The installation process is similar regardless of the type of prefinished flooring you choose. Many of the important lessons that you'll learn here can even be applied to the installation of prefinished engineered flooring.

Get a Superior Finish

Many builders are opting for prefinished wood floors for reasons of speed. Depending on the scope of the project, in as little as a single day you can install a beautiful new floor that the homeowners are able to use immediately without having to go through the inconvenience of a long and messy sanding and finishing process. Moreover, the finishes, which are applied in a factory, tend to be better from a consistency standpoint than anything applied on site.

Prefinished flooring is more sensitive to moisture changes due to its hard finish, which can be damaged if the floor is installed too dry. Acclimate the floor to the middle range of the expected interior moisture content of the house. (To calculate the ideal moisture content, see the chart on p. 593.)

As good as prefinished floors can be, read the fine print of the manufacturer warranties carefully before ordering. A 50-year warranty may include clauses that make it impossible to collect on a claim. For instance, some manufacturers allow 5% to 10% of the boards to have defects. They leave it up to you not to install them. Also, wear is not considered a defect, no matter how quickly it occurs. Warranties typically cover only flooring whose finish has been completely worn off to expose bare wood; they don't

The Subfloor Must Be Flat

The subfloor should be dead flat before a vapor retarder is installed. Raised plywood seams and other flaws can telegraph to the floor's surface. Adjust for flatness by sanding high spots or gluing down shims in low spots. The floor should be flat within ⅛ in. over 6 ft. Here, a layer of plywood was installed over the vapor retarder because the plank flooring will be glued down.

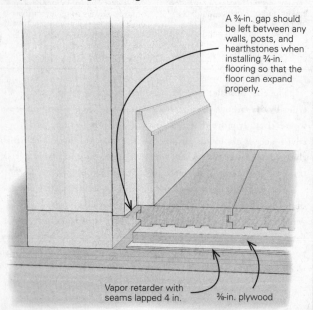

A ¾-in. gap should be left between any walls, posts, and hearthstones when installing ¾-in. flooring so that the floor can expand properly.

Vapor retarder with seams lapped 4 in.

⅜-in. plywood

The Layout Is Paramount

Figure out where to start the floor installation by finding the focal point of the room and working out from there. The focal point may be a window, a doorway, or in this case, a fireplace. Your eye is drawn to the focal point in the room, so you want maximum control over the length of boards in this area and the way they break. Notched, ripped, or tapered boards should be left for more inconspicuous areas.

RACK IT OUT. Lay out as much flooring as possible, but be sure to retain enough space for your flooring nailer. Racking gives you a preview of what the floor will look like. You'll notice boards with harsh, contrasting color tones or grain patterns right away, and you can refine how the boards break. Joints should be spaced at least three times the width of the flooring.

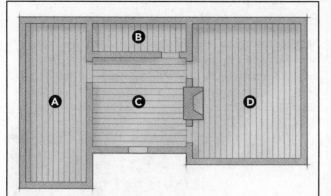

Directional differences
The direction in which the flooring runs has a profound impact on how a room looks and feels. Floorboards that run parallel to the longest wall in a room make the space feel longer and narrower (**A**), while boards running parallel to the shortest wall in a room make the space feel short and wide (**B**). Square rooms are simple because you can run the flooring in nearly any direction and it will look good (**C, D**).

cover the floor's cosmetic appearance. Maintenance is crucial. Variations in grain, color, or tone are also not considered defects, so carefully select the boards you will use in the racking process.

The Right Tools for a Flawless Floor

I recommend that you rethink every detail, from the type of boots you're going to wear—I wear nonmarring white-soled work boots—to the placement of your tools when not in use. I place all my tools on a work mat to prevent accidental scratches. While a refined method of work is important, you'll never achieve a quality installation if you don't have the right tools on hand, and there are only a few to consider.

Almost all manufacturers of flooring nailers use a poppet-type valve system. The harder you hit the gun, the more the valve opens, which lets more air in to drive the piston. It's difficult to control the penetration of the fastener this way, however, because if you don't hit the gun hard enough, you'll sink the fastener insufficiently. On the other hand, if you hit the gun too hard, the piston can come into contact with the wood and crack the tongue.

On this job, I used a Primatech P250 (www.primatech.ca). Primatech guns have a valve assembly that controls nailing impact independently from the mallet strike. Tap the striking surface, and the pneumatic reciprocal action of the valve drives the piston and fastener with a constant, regulated, and uniform push. I typically run this gun with my compressor set no higher than 90 psi. Excessive air pressure can create too much force on the edge of prefinished products, causing edge crushing, unsightly finish cracks, splinters, burnished areas, or broken tongues.

Manufacturers make adapters that fit on the base of flooring nailers to prevent damage to the board's edge. These essential adapters transfer the force of the gun to the flooring tongue

Cut the Flooring Cautiously

Cutting prefinished floorboards to length should not be met with trepidation. If done properly, the finished edges will retain their perfect sheen. As with any milling or cutting task, always be sure the blade or bit comes to a complete stop before moving the stock. Failing to do so is an easy way to chip finished edges.

TIP FROM A PRO: Crosscut blades with high tooth counts cut prefinished flooring best. Even so, a layer of painter's tape helps to reduce tearout.

CREATE A FACTORY END. With a slot-cutting bit in a router, restore the tongue or groove on the end of the board. To restore the factory bevel, make a few passes on the edge of the board with a palm sander.

FINISH CUT ENDS. After restoring the factory bevel, wipe a bit of polyurethane finish on the exposed edge. Mohawk clear-finish markers (www.mohawk-finishing.com) are available in different sheens and make this task a breeze.

BUTT JOINTS DON'T CUT IT. Restoring cut boards to their factory-milling tolerance not only makes each individual board look better, but it also locks the boards together at the same height so that the floor is even across its surface.

instead of the delicate surface edge. It's important to adjust an adapter for the thickness and contour of the flooring being installed. My gun is outfitted with a fully adjustable base, also made by Primatech, that has bearing-mounted rollers.

With fasteners, I always opt for cleats on prefinished flooring. Staples tend to fracture the flooring tongue and damage the board.

Other tools you'll want to have on site are a miter saw fitted with a sharp crosscut blade (the higher the tooth count, the better), a palm sander for beveling end cuts, and a router with male and female bits for milling the tongue and groove on cut boards. I like the carbide-tipped bits made by Amana Tool (www.amanatool.com) the best.

Finally, an 18-ga. finish nailer helps to fasten boards

Continued →

Hide Fasteners and Flaws

Nailing off the flooring is the easy part. After all, you already have your layout determined. Now it's simply a matter of pulling the pieces of the puzzle into alignment. Whether nailing with a finish nailer or a flooring nailer, be sure your compressor is set to the proper air pressure. Start with the air pressure at 70 psi to 75 psi, and adjust accordingly until the fasteners are set properly.

While you can get away with blind-nailing strip flooring, plank flooring needs extra hold-down power to keep it from moving radically. Before setting a board in place, apply a bead of urethane adhesive on the subfloor. Then nail the flooring every 6 in. to 8 in.

TIP FROM A PRO: Use a bash block made of scrap flooring to knock stubborn boards into place. The matching profile ensures that you won't damage the delicate edges of the floorboards.

TOP-NAIL, BUT SPARINGLY. Whether you're installing the first or last row of flooring, you'll need to top-nail the boards. Glue the board down before tacking it with an 18-ga. finish nailer.

Be Prepared to Navigate Transitions

Reducer strips and T-molding are often used to join one floor surface to another, usually at doorways. You won't be able to make these products on site, so be sure to order them along with the flooring if you don't opt for alternatives.

UNINTERRUPTED DOORWAYS. Instead of using a reducer or T-molding to join wood floors at doorways, you can simply use a piece of flooring. This doorway's casing needed a bit of trimming so that the piece within the door and the flooring butting up to the door would fit properly. Use a scrap of flooring as a guide and either a handsaw or a multitool to trim the casing and the doorstops to the right height.

CORK REPLACES REDUCERS AT THE HEARTH. It's important to install the flooring a full ¾ in. from any walls and hearthstones. Instead of covering this gap with reducer stock, you can fill it with cork. This cork was cut into rolls on the miter saw to match the thickness of the flooring and then fit snugly into the gap the floorboard was nailed off.

Cover Your Tracks

Whether spot-filling nail holes or covering up a mistake, these products can help touch up prefinished floors. **(A) PASTE FILLER**, tinted a variety of colors, can complement almost any wood species. **(B) WAX STICKS** can be melted by a butane torch to fill deep or shallow scratches. Waxes can be custom-blended to almost any flooring tone. **(C) WOOD-FINISHING PERMANENT MARKERS**, available in a range of colors from blond to black, help to hide shallow scratches in prefinished floors.

the flooring nailer can't reach, like the first and last row of floorboards parallel to walls, or boards held tight to a hearth.

Keep a Good Floor Looking Great

My greatest nightmare begins happily enough. I've just completed a prefinished floor with meticulous attention to detail, careful not to place a single scratch in a single board. Then the owners come home. They open the door, and in sprints the dog, digging in his nails as he fights for grip on the slick floor. Next come the kids from baseball practice, dropping bats, mitts, and dirt as they make their way to the kitchen in cleats, only to be followed by the parents, who grind that dirt into the floor with each step.

Wood floors and prefinishes are durable, but they still demand a little respect and proper maintenance. To help prevent damage, place mats and rugs in the areas that are used the most. Regularly sweep the floors with a soft-bristle broom or a vacuum with a soft-floor attachment, but never with a rug-beater attachment. Do not use wax or oil-based detergents or other household-cleaning agents on your floors; these products may dull or damage the finish. They also can leave a greasy film that makes floors impossible to recoat without sanding to bare wood. Most manufacturers make a no-wax wood-floor cleaner for their products.

If you have dogs or cats, make sure their claws are trimmed regularly because they can scratch the finish and even crush wood fibers. Also, all furniture should have a protective pad under each foot to prevent scratching or denting.

Even after all this care, there will come a time when the flooring needs to be refinished. Many of the new prefinishes have some form of mineral suspended in the finish. These minerals make the finish wear longer, but they are often the same aluminum-oxide minerals used in sanding abrasives. Abrading these finishes for a recoat can be a challenge. The buffer tends to leave scratch or swirl marks as some of the particles tear away from the finish and grind into the floor. For this reason, most prefinished-flooring manufacturers recommend chemical-bonding systems instead.

Chemical systems either etch the surface or prime it to create a surface for the new finish to bond to. Two such systems are Basic Coating's TyKote system (www.basiccoatings.com) and Bona's Prep system (www.bona.com).

Finally, extra floorboards should always be stowed in a safe place in case a board needs to be replaced. Matching the finish and sheen of a single board can be a nightmare if you don't have a stockpile of spares.

You Get What You Pay For

Not all prefinished flooring is created the same or costs the same. Basic prefinished flooring can range widely but is less expesnive than custom flooring, such as wide-plank hand-scraped, oiled products. Don't skimp on cost, though. Inferior products can be a pain to install. They also may wear faster than pricier products. Here are a few things you'll want to consider when shopping for your next floor.

1. Before you purchase flooring, put some of the floorboards together. Cheap flooring is hard to assemble, and you'll likely damage the boards. Also, their widths may be off by as much as ⅛ in.

2. Find out what the shortest, longest, and average-size boards will be. Many prefinished boards come in very short lengths that make your floor look like a butcher block. Quarter-Sawn Flooring (www.quarter-sawnflooring.com), the manufacturer I used on this project, produces boards with an average length of 5 ft., although some boards are as long as 12 ft.

3. Determine the manufacturer's overwood tolerance, which is the difference in height from one board to another when installed. I prefer overwood to be less than 0.012 in. Poor products will have tolerances of more than twice this amount and have large bevels on their edges to hide the difference.

4. Pay attention to the thickness of the finish, not the number of finish coats. Some flooring with 10 coats may have 0.0017 in. of finish, while other flooring with only three coats will have 0.0024 in. of finish.

5. Scratch the flooring in the showroom. Some finishes, but not all, leave behind noticeable white streaks when scratched. Scratching the floor before making a purchase gives you an idea of how it will look as it wears over time.

Beautiful Wood Scrap Floor

By Charles Peterson

You could say I have a passion for parquet floors. They are one of my specialties as a wood-flooring contractor, and I also teach courses in parquet-floor installation. As president of the International Parquetry Historical Society (www.parquetry.org), I've been able to walk on some of the most elaborate parquet floors in the world.

Parquet flooring is a mosaic of wood pieces usually arranged in repeating squares. The geometric variations within this square or rectangular format are just about limitless. Although you can purchase manufactured parquet squares, almost any parquet-floor pattern can be made from small pieces of scrap wood that otherwise might be thrown away. Because I am a flooring contractor, I have a readily available supply of flooring scraps, but any clear, kiln-dried lumber can be resawn to create an outstanding parquet pattern.

Continued →

Cut the Pieces, and Assemble the Squares

This work is a simple, repetitive production task that I can do in short sessions when I have extra time. The key is having a system and a dedicated work area so that I don't have to set up more than once.

RESAW TO THICKNESS. If I'm using ¾-in. scraps, I can resaw them to 5⁄16 in. thick and effectively double the amount of flooring I have. When resawing, make sure the scraps are long enough to handle safely on a tablesaw. Make the cut in two passes, cutting halfway through from each side. Always keep a push stick at hand.

USE A JIG TO MAKE ANGLED CUTS. Using the left side of the triangular fence on a crosscut sled, make the first 45° cut. Move the piece to the right side, and using the stop, make the second cut. As I go, I put the pieces in separate bins to keep them organized.

ROLL ON WALLPAPER GLUE. Water-soluble wallpaper glue is applied to a square of 40-lb. kraft paper that I cut to just less than the size of the parquet squares. I screw down 1×3 wood guide strips to form three sides of a square that is exactly the same size as the parquet pattern.

IT'S LIKE PUTTING TOGETHER A PUZZLE. First, place the biggest pieces on the outside; then work inward. The smallest pieces go in last. I always keep a finished parquet tile close by as a reference. By the time all the pieces are in, the glue should be dry.

Resaw the Lumber, and Make a Template

When you see the finished appearance of a parquet floor that has been cut, assembled, and installed one piece at a time, it's hard to believe how basic and efficient the process can be. But it is. Using a ripping blade on a tablesaw, I resaw scrap pieces of ¾-in.-thick strip flooring (walnut here) to create 5⁄16-in.-thick parquet stock. This material then can be ripped to finished width. At this point, I cull any pieces with knots, splits, or other imperfections. To make precise square or miter cuts in the parquet pieces, I use a crosscut sled on a tablesaw.

Any parquet-flooring project starts with the pattern. Once I've decided on a design and made a full-scale drawing, I cut all the pieces to fit in that drawing. These pieces then become templates to establish the stop settings on a crosscut sled and its miter-cutting jig.

When I have cut enough pieces to assemble a run of parquet squares, I jig up for that process as well. The 1×3s that I screw to a plywood worksurface form a perfect square, and they serve as guide strips. As shown in the photos at left, I glue the parquet pieces to a square piece of kraft paper, assembling from the outside in.

If I have a dedicated space to work, I can cut and assemble pieces as time allows. I once cut an entire floor during the halftimes of college-football games.

Find the Floor's Center, then the Starting Point

Once I've made all the parquet squares (plus a few extras) but before I glue down anything, I establish the layout. Keeping the parquet squares symmetrical with the walls is standard practice, but sometimes, the squares might need to line up with a focal point in the room, such as a stairway or a fireplace. Once I've found the exact center of the room, I dry-lay enough parquet

Cut Small Parts Precisely with a Crosscut Sled

One of the most useful accessories you can make for your tablesaw is a crosscut sled that rides on a pair of runners sized to fit the saw's miter-gauge grooves (see *Fine Homebuilding* #180). Front and back fences are fastened to the base at exactly 90° to the kerf made by the blade. For 90° cuts, place the workpiece against the back fence. For 45° cuts, I attach a right-triangle piece of plywood to the sled with a few drywall screws.

You need an adjustable stop on one side of the triangular fence for cutting identical parts. To make one, I cut a small kerf in the right-hand side of the fence and use five-minute epoxy to secure the blade of an inexpensive combination square. The square's adjustable head becomes a lockable stop.

Divide the Floor, and Lay the Parquet from the Center

Once you've found the starting point, bisect it with two perpendicular lines. Along these lines, screw down 8-in.-wide plywood strips to act as backerboards. Start from the center, spreading only as much glue as can be covered in five minutes.

SPREAD THE GLUE, AND INSTALL THE SQUARES PAPER SIDE UP. Use the notched trowel recommended by the manufacturer to spread adhesive evenly over the subfloor. Gently work the parquet squares back and forth to be sure that they adhere properly.

MOISTEN. After a few tiles are installed, wet the paper on the parquet squares sparingly with a sponge or spray bottle.

PEEL. After about 20 seconds, pull the paper off the parquet. Wipe up any excess moisture.

squares to go across the room in both directions. This test layout tells me what kind of a partial square I can expect to need at the intersections with walls.

Installed around the outside of a room, a border or an apron of strip flooring does a nice job of framing a parquet floor and serves as a transition from the decorative floor to the walls. Strip flooring also helps to de-emphasize walls that are not straight, to reduce the number of parquet squares that need to be made, and to help the transition into another room.

With parquet squares laid down along the layout lines, I can decide how wide I want to make the border, and then I can make any adjustments to the starting point.

Make Final Adjustments, and Fill the Gaps

For up to an hour after the squares have been set, they can be adjusted by hand. I do this as I work along, trying to get the floor as tight and as straight as possible. You can use a small hammer and a beater board to tighten the floor from the edges.

I don't walk on the floor for at least eight hours. When I can, I look carefully for gaps between pieces. These gaps can be filled with slivers of flooring material. Just glue the wood sliver in place, then shave off the excess with a razor blade.

Sanding is an essential step when installing a parquet floor, just as it is with other wood floors. But the different grain orientations in a parquet floor call for a special floor sander. I prefer to use a U-Sand machine (www.u-sand.com), which can be rented at many home centers. The machine is basically four large random-orbit sanders working in one device. These machines work well but are slow. To avoid scratches and to improve sanding effectiveness, be sure to remove dirt and debris, including loose sawdust.

Lay Down the Squares a Few at a Time

I like urethane adhesives for parquet flooring. Urethane is flexible enough to withstand the natural expansion and contraction of panels without losing its adhesive qualities.

No matter what glue is used, it always should be applied according to the manufacturer's instructions. I pay particular attention to open working time.

When I start gluing down the squares, I spread just enough glue that can be covered with parquet in about five minutes.

Continued →

Solid vs. Engineered Wood Flooring

By Bill Duckworth

If you want the warmth and beauty of real wood floors, choosing the species to install isn't your only decision. You first have to decide whether to put down solid-wood or engineered flooring. The latter is made of real wood veneers glued to either a plywood or a high-density fiberboard core.

Both solid-wood and engineered products can be first-rate floors. Here are some considerations to keep in mind.

Finished in Place or Prefinished?

Solid-wood flooring traditionally has come from the manufacturer in tongue-and-groove strips without a finish. Installers nail the strips in place, sand them flat, then apply a finish. The seams are tight and flush. Engineered-flooring manufacturers changed all that when they introduced prefinished flooring: no sanding, no malodorous finishes, and the floor can be used right away. Traditional manufacturers followed suit, and now they offer prefinished solid-wood flooring as well. The trade-off is that the edges have to be rounded or beveled slightly to mask minute differences in height between boards. The grooves can catch dirt, and the look may not be right for some tastes.

Look for thicker veneers, which allow more refinishing.

Costs

The cost of either type depends on thickness and species, though solid wood will be less expensive per sq. ft. than engineered flooring. But when you factor in the time and effort that sanding and finishing add to a solid-wood floor, the total costs for each type of flooring are comparable.

Stability

Solid-wood floors are famous for growing cracks between boards in winter and closing back up in summer. You can minimize this movement by using narrow strips of quartersawn lumber. The wider the boards, the more shrinking and swelling you can expect. Engineered lumber, on the other hand, is quite stable because of its plywood or fiberboard core. That makes it an excellent choice for areas that might be subject to high moisture, such as a finished floor in a basement over a concrete slab.

Engineered Wood Flooring

PROS

• More dimensionally stable, especially when wider planks are used.
• Prefinished flooring is ready to use as soon as it's installed; can be glued or used as a "floating floor" that lies atop the sub-floor without mechanical connection.
• More efficient use of materials; more environmentally friendly.
• Available in thinner thicknesses, so it can be applied over existing floors without raising thresholds.

CONS

• Because veneers are so thin, some engineered flooring can be sanded and refinished only once or twice, if that.
• Grooves can catch dirt.

Solid Wood Flooring

PROS

• Thicker stock can be resanded several times, down to just above the top of the tongue (about $5/16$ in. of material), allowing more refinishings over its life span.
• Inherent character and beauty in the grain patterns and color variety found in batches of wood milled from different trees.
• Slightly less expensive than the equivalent thickness of engineered flooring of the same species.

CONS

• Fewer sizes, species, and grades than engineered flooring.
• Must be nailed down, and typically sanded and finished in place.

Groove

No groove

Floor-Finish Applicators

By Charles Peterson

Applying finish to a wood floor is the final step in a long process. The application tools you use can either highlight your efforts or spoil them. Several types of floor-finish applicators are on the market, and each is used in a different manner. Whichever applicator you choose, select synthetic versions whenever possible. While 100% lambswool applicators work, they tend to shed. The resulting fibers might seem minute, but they're often magnified by the finish.

Wood Block

HOW IT'S USED: Either dip the block into a paint tray filled with finish and pull it across the floor, or pour the finish in a line and use the "snowplow" method. Always work with the grain, and start and stop at a wall. Never stop in the middle of a floor.

BEST APPLICATION: Residential floors.

NOTES: Bare wood can tear up lambswool wood-block applicators. Pros have a method to get the best finish. They use new applicators—which have been defuzzed with a vacuum cleaner—for the second coat of finish. Only after several uses are they suitable for applying finish coats. When finally overworn, they're used to apply first coats.

Wood block

T-Bar

HOW IT'S USED: Pour a line of finish along the length of the floor. Pull the T-bar applicator down the length of the room at an angle, "snowplowing" extra finish onto the area that will be coated next.

BEST APPLICATION: Large residential floors, commercial spaces, and basketball courts.

NOTES: T-bars come in different weights depending on the desired mil thickness of the finish. For example, a heavier bar creates a thinner finish.

T-Bar

Roller

HOW IT'S USED: Rolling a floor finish is similar to rolling paint on a wall. Take care not to overwork the finish, which can lead to unsightly air bubbles.

BEST APPLICATION: Works anywhere, but especially where wood grain goes in several directions, like on parquet floors. It's best to work with the grain as much as possible, but rolled finishes don't have to be applied in the direction of the grain.

NOTES: A yoke roller frame allows more-even pressure to be applied to the roller than a cage-style frame, resulting in a more-even finish.

Roller

Match the Applicator to the Finish

Choosing finishes and applicator materials that are incompatible can lead to ruined tools and floors. Follow the recommendations here to determine which finish works best with which type of applicator material.

100% lambswool
- Oil-modified urethane
- Lacquer sealer
- Moisture-cure polyurethane
- Shellac
- Varnish
- Stains
- Conversion varnish
- Varnish sealer
- Wax

100% lambswool

Synthetic lambswool
- Stains
- Varnish
- Water-based urethane
- Varnish sealer
- Wax

Synthetic lambswool

Synthetic pad/sleeve
- Stains
- Water-based urethane
- Bleach
- Conversion varnish

Synthetic pad/sleeve

Continued ➡

Replacing a Floorboard

By Andy Engel

Although the tongue-and-groove joints that unite the boards in a wood floor may seem to preclude replacing just one board, the process is pretty straightforward. Since the board to be replaced is toast anyway, removing it piecemeal makes that part of the process simple. Then it's a matter of removing the lip that forms the bottom of the replacement board's groove so it will fit over the tongue of the existing flooring. The new board is then fit in place and secured with glue. This type of repair is usually part of a floor-refinishing project because the new board has to be sanded even with the surrounding boards and finished to match.

You might think that finding a replacement board would simply entail visiting a lumberyard and buying one. It's rarely that simple, though. Even common ¾-in. by 2¼-in. red oak is sold in 20-sq.-ft. bundles for a few dollars per sq. ft. If your flooring is anything other than 2¼-in. red oak, you'll probably have to buy it from a specialty supplier or have a piece milled.

If you're lucky, though, you may have a solution at hand. The original builder may have left a few pieces of flooring up in the attic. It's worth a look, but if you aren't that lucky, don't give up. Odds are you can carefully remove a piece from inside a closet. Choose one from the edge so that you can get it out without having to split it in half, then replace it with whatever flooring you can scrounge or make.

Watch Where You Make That Cut

Careful installers pay attention to where they place the joints in a floor. A few things to avoid are butt joints closer than 6 in. to each other, evenly spaced joints that resemble stair steps, and patterns where three joints in consecutive rows resemble the letter H. When replacing a board, be careful to avoid creating one of these situations. A good rule of thumb is to not have any joints that are closer than the width of a floorboard over three neighboring courses.

Spacing flaws

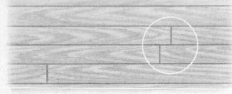

Closely spaced joints

Staircasing

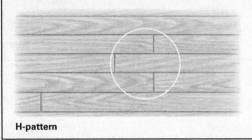

H-pattern

1. CUT LONG BOARDS. Remove a damaged short board entirely. With longer boards, it's less work just to remove 1 ft. or so of a bad section. Mark a square line across the board, and chisel a series of cuts about ¼ in. into the board.

2. CHOP OUT THE WASTE. Chiseling the damaged board toward the initial square cut, remove ¼ in. of wood at a time. Repeat these first two steps until you've cut all the way through the board. You also can make the cut with a multitool.

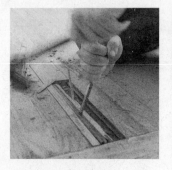

3. SPLIT THE BAD BOARD. Drive in the chisel parallel to the grain in several places. When the board splits, lever out the chunks with the chisel.

4. VACUUM OUT THE DEBRIS. If there's a layer of tar paper or rosin paper below the flooring, remove it to expose the subfloor before vacuuming up wood debris.

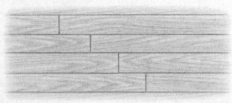

5. BREAK THE BOTTOM OF THE GROOVE. Lay the replacement board on a clean section of floor, and use a hammer to break the bottom lip that forms the groove.

6. REMOVE THE BOTTOM LIP. Clean up the broken edge with a knife or plane to ensure that the new board fits over the tongue of the abutting flooring.

7. CONSTRUCTION ADHESIVE SEALS THE DEAL. Put two beads of adhesive on the subfloor, and another along the tongue of the abutting board. Leave the other edge unglued to allow for seasonal movement.

8. SLIP IN THE REPLACEMENT BOARD. Engage the replacement board's tongue with the abutting groove, and push the groove edge down.

9. TAP IT HOME. Strike the replacement board with a heavy hammer, being sure that the hammer face hits squarely to minimize marring. If the board doesn't seat well, drive a couple of 6d finish nails into it to hold it down.

Flooring Options for the Kitchen

By Matthew Teague

As the most highly trafficked space in the house, a kitchen's floor has to withstand everything from spills to stilettos. The kitchen is the social heart of the home, playing host to dinner-party guests, friends, and family on a regular basis. The floor needs to look good, be comfortable to walk on, and wear well over time.

Sorting through the array of flooring materials can be a downright dizzying process, and finding the right balance between style and function is often the most difficult task. Each type of flooring has strengths and weaknesses, which greatly affect how it'll live in your kitchen. Whether you're looking for the charm of hand-scraped hardwood, the comfort of cork, the durability of concrete, or the "greenness" of palm, I'll pinpoint the benefits of each product, highlight its flaws, and attach a price tag to it. Before you dive in, remember: No single type of flooring material is best. The right kitchen-flooring choice is a reflection of your overall taste, the needs of your home, and your budget.

Wood Maintains a Tradition of Durability and Comfort

Aside from rock and dirt, wood floors probably have the longest history of any flooring type. While traditional, unfinished solid-plank flooring continues to be installed in kitchens across the country, there are two other wood-floor options available that just might outperform it. Engineered and prefinished wood flooring can be installed more quickly than unfinished solid-wood boards

MAKE NEW FLOORS OUT OF OLD TIMBERS. More and more companies, including Carlisle Wide Plank Floors (which made this walnut floor), use carefully managed old-growth trees, salvaged logs, and recycled beams to make new floorboards that offer rich character and antique charm.

Continued ➔

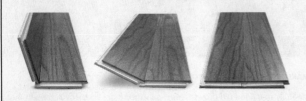

Solid-wood flooring

Engineered wood flooring

Similarities go only so deep

Solid-wood flooring's thickness allows it to be refinished time and again over its life span. Engineered flooring's thin top layer of wood is only 1/16 in. to 1/8 in. deep, making it difficult to refinish without causing damage to the veneer. Both types of flooring can be ordered prefinished, eliminating the on-site finishing process while providing a finish of higher quality in terms of durability.

CONS Can be expensive; susceptible to water damage; softer species dent easily; refinishing is an involved process; solid wood expands/contracts with humidity; prefinished floors offer limited stain options; limited refinishing options with engineered flooring.

Solid wood

Solid-oak floors have made up the bulk of the wood-flooring industry for years, but that doesn't mean that wood floors have limited style. Solid-wood flooring can be made out of everything from ash to zebrawood and milled to most any width you'd like. In the kitchen, hardwoods perform best. Although softwoods like pine look good and are readily available, they're not as tough as hardwood species and wear quickly under heavy use. Some hardwoods are harder than others, but all are rugged enough to handle everyday abuse in a kitchen. Solid hardwoods will last as long as your house, and they're also comfortable underfoot. Wood

without abandoning their look, comfort, or durability. A wood floor's longevity, however, is largely dependent on the way it is finished and maintained. For years, oil-based urethanes were the finish of choice, but modern water-based finishes are just as durable and can be applied faster and with less odor. Sweeping regularly helps to prevent dirt from wearing away the finish.

PROS Easy on your feet; warm underfoot; durable; wide range of species, stains, and prices; solid wood can be refinished multiple times; engineered wood installs quickly; pre-finished floors can be used immediately.

flexes just enough to ease the tension on your feet, legs, and back.

If your tastes lean toward traditional hardwood and you're in the market for an environmentally friendly floor, take a look at flooring made from recycled lumber or from the old-growth timbers now being hauled up from some lake bottoms.

Engineered wood

Engineered floorboards are more dimensionally stable than solid-wood flooring, meaning they're less likely to expand or contract due to humidity fluctuations. This stability makes them a great choice for flooring installed over a radiant-heating system. They're also just as comfortable as solid wood. The floorboards are made of multiple layers of wood stacked in a cross-grain pattern and glued up under pressure, much like plywood. The top layer features a veneer of the best-looking wood, while the layers underneath can be made of less expensive wood.

Engineered wood floors usually come prefinished. Manufacturers claim that their applied finishes are much more durable than any finish that can be applied on site. That said, kitchen activity can be ruthless, and even the most durable wood floors may need to be refinished at some point. Although some manufacturers boast that you can sand an engineered wood floor to refinish it, the top layer of wood is only 1/16 in. to 1/8 in. thick, making it difficult to sand without exposing the layers underneath.

Laminate Performs and Looks Better Than You Think

As much as some laminate flooring looks like solid wood, it is anything but. Laminate flooring is composed of four different layers of material and can be made to look like anything from marble to distressed oak. The top layer of a laminate board, called the wear layer, is usually a clear resin-based melamine that is incredibly durable and scratch resistant. Beneath the wear layer is a photo layer, which is a paper image of the specific material that you see on the face of the board. These layers are bound to a core made

Hardwood Flooring the Easy Way

Some engineered floors come prefinished and are installed simply by locking each board together with a specially designed tongue-and-groove joint.

Laminate Flooring

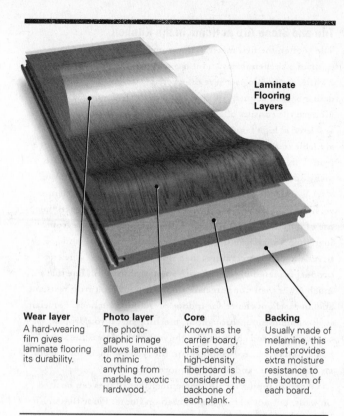

Laminate Flooring Layers

Wear layer
A hard-wearing film gives laminate flooring its durability.

Photo layer
The photographic image allows laminate to mimic anything from marble to exotic hardwood.

Core
Known as the carrier board, this piece of high-density fiberboard is considered the backbone of each plank.

Backing
Usually made of melamine, this sheet provides extra moisture resistance to the bottom of each board.

of high-density fiberboard (HDF) and a backing, usually made of melamine, that lends stability and moisture resistance. Because of the relatively inexpensive materials that go into laminate flooring, it is one of the most economical options available.

One of the major benefits of laminate flooring is the speed with which it can be installed. Laminate floors are floating, meaning they don't need to be fastened to a subfloor. While laminate floors of old had to be glued together, most new laminates snap together using an interlocking tongue-and-groove arrangement. This joint not only makes installation quick and easy, but it also pulls the boards tightly together, which helps to prevent liquids from penetrating the seams, a nice quality in a kitchen floor.

While the durability of laminate has always been high, the flooring tended to look fake. Newer laminate flooring is more convincing than ever. In addition to laminate's durability and low cost, the product offers plenty of deflection, making it comfortable underfoot. Caring for a laminate floor is easy and requires only occasional damp-mopping.

PROS Durable; easy on your feet; low maintenance; can be installed over old flooring; quiet; easy installation; low to moderate cost; scratch resistant; damaged planks can be replaced; built-in vapor barrier reduces moisture absorption.

CONS Cannot be refinished; some are expensive; limited style choices; not hypoallergenic; wet environments may cause fiberboard core to swell.

Linoleum Is Low Impact and Biodegradable

After falling out of vogue when vinyl became the kitchen floor of choice in the 1960s, linoleum has undergone a revival in recent years due to its standing as an environmentally friendly flooring option. Linoleum takes less energy to manufacture than most flooring, and it is made primarily from natural materials: linseed oil, wood flour, limestone, tree resins, and natural jute. Linoleum also can be installed using a solvent-free adhesive. When made of all-natural products, linoleum is 100% biodegradable and has no VOC emissions. Forbo, the company that introduced Marmoleum, even recycles all of its post-production waste.

Available in sheets and tiles of varying sizes and in more than 150 colors and patterns, Forbo's Marmoleum and Armstrong's Marmorette are highly versatile from a design standpoint. Linoleum also wears well and actually gets better with age: Exposure to air causes linoleum to harden, but it remains resilient, comfortable, and quiet underfoot. It's also hypoallergenic.

PROS Biodegradable; antistatic; resilient; comfortable underfoot; many colors available; hypoallergenic; homogeneous throughout; durable; easy installation.

CONS Difficult to repair; difficult to find installer; seams may be visible and intrusive.

Linoleum Flooring

Continued ➔

Vinyl
Flooring

Vinyl Is Low Maintenance

Vinyl has been vastly improved—in both design and quality—since its no-wax heyday in the 1960s. Sheet vinyl is available in widths ranging from 6 ft. to 12 ft., while vinyl tiles are usually sold in 12-in. squares. Vinyl even comes in plank form to mimic hardwood. Each type is available in an almost endless array of colors and designs.

Vinyl is generally composed of four layers. A clear wear coat, usually made of urethane, helps to prevent scratches and eases cleanup. A layer of clear vinyl provides durability. The printed layer, similar to laminate flooring, creates the look of the floor, while a backing of either felt or fiberglass adds rigidity. Vinyl with a felt backing must be glued to a subfloor. Fiberglass-backed floors are more comfortable and generally don't require any adhesive since they are far less likely to curl up at the edges.

Some manufacturers produce inlaid vinyl flooring in which granules of color are embedded to lend a richer appearance. Inlaid patterns wear better than vinyl with only a printed photographic image, but they typically cost a bit more. Many manufacturers also add texture to create a more realistic, 3-D effect that closely mimics the surfaces they intend to replicate.

PROS Resilient; durable; inexpensive; easy on your feet; quiet; low maintenance; water resistant; wide sheets hide seams in small rooms; easy to install; wide variety available; easy maintenance.

CONS Seams visible in wide rooms; seams susceptible to water damage; gloss finishes are slippery when wet; can fade or yellow; pattern can wear off; seams may lift.

Tile and Stone Are at Home in the Kitchen

Tile is often the first material that comes to mind when people think of a kitchen floor, and it has probably been that way for a while. Archaeologists have discovered thin slabs of fired clay dating back to about 4700 B.C. Today's tile isn't much different. Modern tile consists of clay and minerals that are shaped, pressed, and fired at high temperatures to create a hard surface. Tile is available in a variety of colors and shapes, and in sizes that range from 1-in. circles to 6-in. arabesques to 2-ft. squares. With so many options, the patterns possible with tile approach infinite.

Ceramic tiles are available in nonporcelain and porcelain versions. The current market, however, is seeing a surge in the use of porcelain in the kitchen. Porcelain tiles are made from ingredients similar to those found in fine dinnerware and are fired at higher temperatures than nonporcelain tiles. The end product is incredibly dense, with a water-absorption rate that's much lower than nonporcelain tile, which makes it frost resistant and an excellent choice for indoor or outdoor kitchens. Porcelain is also homogenous throughout, meaning that if you drop a cast-iron pan and chip the tile, the material below is the same color as the surface. Nonporcelain tiles achieve their color from an applied glaze, and damage is more noticeable.

When shopping for tile, remember that all tiles can be used on walls, but not all tiles can be used on floors. Floor tiles must be rated as such, and for durability, kitchen tiles must be at least a category III (out of a I to IV rating). What's a strength to some might be a weakness to others: Tile's density, hardness, and rigidity make it durable, but that also can translate into sore legs for cooks who stand in the kitchen for a long time.

Tile
Flooring

TRIED-AND-TRUE. Beyond its durability and ease of maintenance, tile offers the largest variety of colors, shapes, and sizes, which makes a one-of-a-kind kitchen much more attainable.

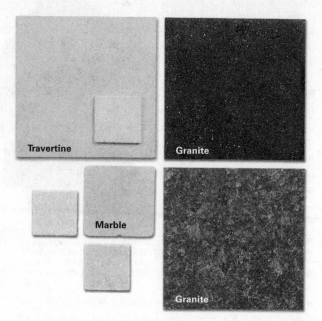

Travertine

Granite

Marble

Granite

Fringe Flooring

Concrete, brick, and stainless steel are less likely residential-flooring options, but they perform exceptionally well when placed in the kitchen, where durable, stylish materials are a must.

Concrete

Concrete can be stamped to simulate a tile, brick, or stone floor; finished in a variety of textures; and stained an almost endless spectrum of colors. Concrete can even be made into tiles.

Although concrete can be cold underfoot, it works well in conjunction with radiant-floor heat, it is easy to maintain, and it is arguably the most durable flooring material you can place in the kitchen. On the downside, concrete is extremely hard and does not deflect whatsoever when walked on or when a glass is dropped on it. It's also susceptible to staining if not sealed properly. Concrete is a low-cost product, but prices can soar when a professional finisher is called in to tackle the job.

Spills are inevitable in the kitchen, so look for tile that has good slip resistance. Unglazed tiles offer better traction than glazed tiles. However, unglazed tiles and grout lines must be sealed, and textured floors are more difficult to clean.

Stone flooring can bring the rustic feel of the outdoors into your kitchen, or it can be configured in sleek, uniform, tilelike orientations to create a more refined-looking floor. Uniform layouts demand precut stones, which increase costs substantially. For more money, stones can be cut into specific shapes to fit into the layout of your choosing.

Except for soapstone, all stone should be sealed to increase its stain resistance. To care for a stone floor, you'll need either a damp mop or a stone cleaner; consult your stone or floor specialist to determine the best cleaning practices for the type of stone you install. As with tile, the grout between stones must be sealed occasionally; the frequency varies from one type of grout to another.

One-of-a-kind designs are possible with stone floors. There are numerous types of stone to choose from: marble, granite, limestone, soapstone, travertine, and flagstone among them. An excellent conductor of heat, stone flooring works well with radiant-floor heating systems. Although some stone wears better than others, the average stone floor is incredibly durable. However, with this durability comes hardness, which can be unforgiving to your feet and to dropped dishware.

PROS Countless sizes, shapes, and colors; low maintenance; can be stain resistant; colors won't fade; works well with radiant-floor heat; can create very natural look (stone); inexpensive (some tile).

CONS Cold underfoot; susceptible to cracking or chipping; grout may stain or crack; grout requires maintenance; gloss finishes can be slippery when wet; hard on your feet; noisy; dropped items likely to break; must be sealed regularly (stone); can be very expensive.

Brick

Forgotten for many years and likely inspired by the urban-chic look of factories converted for loft living, the charm of brick flooring is once again popular. More often than not, today's clay-brick floors are composed of brick veneers ranging in thickness from ½ in. to ¹⁵/₁₆ in. New veneers offer a

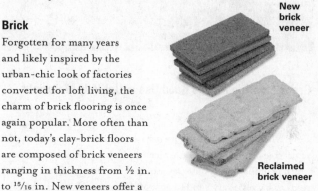

New brick veneer

Reclaimed brick veneer

smooth, consistent look, while veneers made from old reclaimed bricks tend to have a bit more character. Both types are installed just like unglazed ceramic tile. The slip resistance of brick and its durability make it a great choice for the kitchen. However, like natural stone, brick can be unforgiving on your feet, dishware, and wallet.

Stainless Steel

There's nothing subtle about a stainless-steel floor, but if it's a clean, modern look you're after, it might be the best option. These metal tiles, which come as large as 24 in. by 24 in., are screwed in place over a thin rubber underlayment. There is no need for adhesive, and the installation is quick and dust free. While smooth steel can be slippery when wet, metal flooring is often embossed to increase slip resistance and add style. Stainless steel may be durable, it's very expensive.

Continued ➡

Tile
Flooring

Green Flooring Makes Good Use of Unlikely Materials

Cork

Cork is harvested from live cork oak trees without cutting down the actual tree or corrupting the habitat in which it grows. The cork, which is similar to the outer layer of bark on a tree, regrows and is ready to harvest every 9 to 14 years. Multiple manufacturers now offer both unfinished and prefinished cork flooring in both tiles and glueless tongue-and-groove planks. Warm and comfortable to walk on, cork floors are also resilient. The flooring compresses underfoot, or under the impact of a dropped plate, and rebounds to its full volume. This resilience does have limits: If large appliances or furniture sits in the same spot for long lengths of time, the underlying cork can become permanently deformed.

Cork contains elements that repel bugs, mold, and mildew, so it's considered hypoallergenic. It also acts as an insulator to reduce noise transmission between rooms. You can buy cork floors that are natural in color or stained a variety of shades. You can even find cork floors with swirl patterns reminiscent of burlwood.

PROS Easy on your feet; warm; unique texture; environmentally friendly; fire-retardant; hypoallergenic.

CONS Edges of prefinished floors must be sealed; not the most durable flooring option.

Rubber

Designed to withstand the trials of commercial kitchens, machine shops, and automotive centers, rubber flooring has no trouble standing up to the rigors of a residential kitchen. Available in a variety of colors and patterns, rubber floors don't have to look as industrial as you might think. The various raised patterns on rubber floors are designed to improve traction, but they also lend a decorative, contemporary look to a kitchen. Rubber flooring is available in both sheets and tiles and is generally installed with a solvent-free adhesive. While a few rubber floors are marketed for residential use, you also might consider buying a commercial rubber floor through a flooring dealer.

Putting old tires to good use. This rubber flooring is vibrantly colored, comfortable, and durable, and is made of rubber that would otherwise be tossed in the trash.

If you're looking for the performance traits of rubber in an environmentally responsible product, look to the manufacturer Expanko and its residential product, Reztec. This flooring is made of a combination of postindustrial-waste rubber, virgin rubber, and recycled tires. Reztec is available in 48-in.-wide rolls and three different tile sizes.

PROS Comfortable underfoot; contemporary look; durable; easy maintenance; can be custom colored; resilient.

CONS Can be difficult to find; few experienced installers; expensive; some products can be damaged by spills.

Palm

Palm, a relative newcomer to the flooring market, is made from the hard, dark wood of plantation-grown coconut palm trees that no longer produce coconuts. After about 100 years, coconut palms grow so large that nutrients from the soil no longer reach the nuts, so the trees stop producing and have to be cut down. The lumber, which often went unused, is sliced, dried, and laminated together—much like plywood—using nontoxic adhesives.

Palm
Flooring

Sold in ⅝-in.-thick, 72-in.-long tongue-and-groove strips, palm flooring installs much like traditional hardwood flooring. The end product is about 25% harder than red oak, so it performs relatively well in the kitchen. Palm wears and reacts with water in very similar ways to traditional hardwood floors. The finishing and maintenance requirements are similar as well.

Palm flooring is available in both edge-grain or flat-grain orientations and can be purchased unfinished or prefinished with natural, walnut, or ebony stains.

PROS Warm and comfortable underfoot; durable; available prefinished; made of products that would otherwise go to waste.

CONS Limited color options; limited products on the market; prefinished planks leave seams unsealed.

Bamboo

As hard as maple and as durable as oak, bamboo is marketed as an environmentally friendly choice. Although the term sustainable has different meanings to different people, it's difficult to argue against the sustainability of bamboo. Tonkin and moso—the species of bamboo used to manufacture most flooring—grow to full height in about six months and naturally replenish themselves once harvested. A lot of manufacturers, however, allow bamboo to continue growing for four to six years. This late growth lends significant strength to the bamboo. Most of today's bamboo is harvested in Asia and South America, but a number of manufacturers are experimenting with bamboo stands in some Southern states.

There are four main styles of bamboo flooring on the market: flat grain, vertical grain, end grain, and strand woven. Each has a different price point, aesthetic, and level of durability. Flat-grain bamboo is considered the most economical because it's the least expensive type of bamboo flooring.

Bamboo is naturally pale yellow but is often put through a heating process, which caramelizes its natural sugars and gives it an amber tone. Bamboo flooring is available in

Which is the most durable? All bamboo is tough enough for the kitchen, but end-grain and strand-woven bamboo are the hardest.

a variety of other colors, too, in order to complement any design theme.

PROS Warm underfoot; durable; some give underfoot; available prefinished; available as an easy-to-install engineered product.

CONS Limited color options; limited products on the market; prefinished planks leave seams unsealed.

Flooring Options for the Bathroom

By Matthew Teague

Bathroom floors come with their own particular set of requirements. Like any floor, they should be chosen with style, durability, and comfort in mind. But a bathroom floor also must be able to handle moisture and humidity from daily use as well as any possible leaks that could occur in the future.

That said, not all bathrooms are created equal. While the family bath may have to endure splashing toddlers in the tub, you can use a master bath more responsibly, wiping up small spills as they occur. A guest bath or half-bath may be even less threatened by water. The less use your bathroom sees and the fewer fixtures it houses, the more options you have for bathroom flooring.

Choosing a bathroom floor that can handle the required amount of water is the first hurdle. You can expect a certain

Continued →

amount of water all the time—drips as you get out of the shower or puddles from the occasional overspray, for instance. Those minor mishaps are easily wiped up, but it's the months or years of that small bead of water dripping around a shower door or condensation running down the side of the toilet that is more likely to cause trouble. Also, because the bathroom has more plumbing than any other room in the house, it's the place most likely to spring a leak. Just hope it doesn't happen while you're on vacation.

In addition to the water you see, there's also the water you can't see: humidity, which affects some floors more than others. While a vent fan helps, you have to make sure that everyone turns it on. You also can wire it through a timer to run for a while after you leave the room.

Remember that all bathroom floors should be well-sealed and maintained, but that some require more work than others. Also, it's entirely possible that those splashing toddlers will turn into sloppy teenagers.

Despite Arguments, Wood Can Work
The arguments against solid- and engineered-wood floors in a bathroom are obvious: Wood not only absorbs water pretty easily, but it also swells in the process. The everyday humidity of a bathroom may test the limits of expansion joints where the floor meets the walls. In cases of prolonged leaks, it's almost a given that

any species of wood floor, and probably the subfloor, will have to be torn out.

Still, wood floors are beautiful and feel good underfoot, often providing a smooth transition from bedroom to bath. Although it is hard to find a designer who claims that putting wood flooring in the bathroom is a good idea, when pressed, almost all of them will admit to doing it regularly. It's really a case of risk assessment.

In a family bath that sees heavy use from kids, wood flooring just doesn't make sense. But in a master bath where the residents understand that standing water has to be wiped away, or don't mind the character and patina of water-stained floors, wood flooring will last as long as it will in any other room of the house.

Consider sectioning off the bathroom so that wetter areas are floored using a more moisture-friendly material. Architect David Edrington uses solid surfaces like stone or marble—often offcuts from countertops—to prevent condensation on the toilet from reaching wood floors. Because hardwoods exposed to humidity will expand and contract, high-quality vent fans are a must.

The maintenance for wood in the bathroom is the same as for any other room: Sweep and mop. But you should expect to refinish the floors at the first signs of a worn finish. Penetrating water not only expands the wood, but also bleeds down toward the subfloor. To assess the finish, perform the same water-droplet test used on tile.

The best chance at success is probably engineered-wood flooring. Not to be confused with laminates, engineered flooring is a layer of real wood backed by layers of plywood, which minimizes movement caused by humidity. Because it's less likely to cup or warp, there is less chance that gaps will open between planks, allowing water to penetrate. Factory finishes are often top quality, and they certainly ease installation, but to seal the joints between planks completely, opt for unfinished engineered hardwoods and lay on the finish yourself.

Think Twice Before Choosing Laminate Flooring
Because of their relatively low cost, laminates have become a popular choice in flooring. Most modern laminates—whether in planks or tiles—click together to form a floating floor with dry mechanical joints. While these joints are touted as being water-resistant, they aren't waterproof. Water may eventually reach the fiberboard core of the flooring, or the subfloor below. If you insist on laminate, opt for a style that installs with a one-piece continuous vapor barrier that covers the entire subfloor instead of having it attached to the bottoms of individual tiles or planks.

Tile Offers Sensible Style

Tile is likely the first option that comes to mind when you think of bathroom flooring, and for good reason—it's the most popular. Made of clay and other nonmetallic minerals shaped, pressed, and fired at high temperatures to create a hard surface, tile can handle water and comes in an almost endless variety of styles. You can choose from ceramic, porcelain, natural stone, or, in small doses, even glass. On the downside, tile is tough on your legs and back. In a room where you're often barefoot, it's also cold. It might feel nice on the Texas coast, but it is less than ideal for Maine winters. That said, adding radiant in-floor heat to a bathroom floor—tile or otherwise—is now easier than ever.

The important factors to consider when shopping for bathroom floor tile are water porosity and slip resistance.

SOME TILE IS ABSORBENT The higher the tile's porosity, the more water it will absorb. The determining factors are the body of the tile and, if any is used, the surface glaze. Porcelain, for instance, has a dense body and a durable glaze, so its absorption rate is about 0.5%. On the other hand, a Sausalito ceramic tile left unsealed can be up around 25%—basically a sponge. Your best bet for a bathroom floor is to use unglazed tiles with an absorption rate of no more than

0.5%, or glazed tiles with an absorption rate of 3% or less.

A higher porosity rate doesn't necessarily mean you can't use the tile, but it does mean that you'll have to seal it after installation and reapply the sealer every year or so to prevent standing water from reaching the vulnerable subfloor.

Every year or so, check the absorption of stone or porous tiles by placing a small amount of water on them. If the drops of water bead up and stand on top of the surface, it's sealed; if they absorb into the surface, it's time to reseal. The photo above illustrates the difference in absorption between a sealed and an unsealed terra-cotta tile.

SLIPPERY WHEN WET Slip resistance is rated with what's known as a coefficient of friction. Ideally, tile floors in showers should have a coefficient of "0.60 wet" or greater. It's not a bad idea to follow this same rule for the entire bathroom, which, at some point, is likely to be wet underfoot. These numbers, however, rule out heavily polished tiles or stones like granite, marble, or travertine, which have a much lower slip resistance. A lower rating doesn't mean that you can't use smooth tile, but if you push the limits,

Continued ➜

Where Tile Floors Go Bad

Want a long-lasting tile floor? Start with a proper installation.

REINFORCE THE SUBFLOOR Tubs, vanities, and toilets are heavy. Add tile, and it's often necessary to beef up the floor to prevent cracked tile or grout lines. Unless you're using an uncoupling membrane like Schluter-Ditra, which can be installed over ¾-in.-thick floor sheathing, use layers of plywood to create a subfloor thickness of 1⅛ in.

CHOOSE THE RIGHT CEMENT Never use mastic on the floor; tiles should always be placed in thinset cement. Choose a latex-modified thinset over a wood subfloor. Nonmodified thinset is a good choice for installing over concrete, but it will come loose from wood substrates.

DON'T OVERWATER THE GROUT Too much water added to the grout mix washes out the portland cement and weakens the grout. The same goes for washing off the grout after installation; keep the water to a minimum to keep the grout at its strongest.

WATCH FOR CRACKED CONCRETE Setting tile over concrete that already shows signs of cracking is a recipe for trouble. Use a crack-isolation membrane to separate the tile from failing concrete.

USE "SOFT" JOINTS WHERE NECESSARY Hard grout joints where the floor meets the tub or butts up to the tile baseboard will eventually expand and crack. Instead of grouting these edges, use a noncementitious caulk—sanded and nonsanded varieties are available depending on the type of grout—that matches the grout color.

it's a good idea to supplement the area with some type of rug or bath mat outside the shower and tub. Choosing a textured tile is a bit of a trade-off: More texture creates greater slip resistance and hides a little dirt, but it also makes the tile tougher to clean.

Remember that floor tiles can be used on walls, but not all wall tiles can be used on floors.

GROUT CHOICE MATTERS Modern tastes lean toward thin grout lines because no matter how nonporous the surface or how well you seal it, grout lines catch dirt. To reduce the dirty look as much as possible, choose a grout with a low absorption rate. The lower the absorption rate, the more resistant the grout is to staining and discoloration. Regular, nonmodified grouts run about 10%; modified grouts average about 5%; and epoxy grouts have an absorption rate of no more than 0.5%.

Most of the grouts on store shelves are latex- or polymer-modified; both are fine for most bathrooms. These products are just as easy to work with and offer the grout a little flexibility (about 1/64 in.) to combat cracking. Epoxy grouts have the reputation of being difficult to work with, but modern products are much easier to use than those of 10 or 15 years ago. Epoxy grout is dense and provides a tenacious bond. And while you can't leave coffee sitting on it for days, it's otherwise immune to staining, which is a welcome treat in the bathroom, where one of your major tasks is to wash away dirt.

The newest entrants to the market are glass grouts which use crushed glass (usually recycled) instead of sand. Glass grout is easy to work with and is less prone to shade differences because it has a lower absorption rate, somewhere between modified and epoxy grouts. And unlike the sand found in traditional sanded grouts, glass doesn't absorb water, which means that it cures to a more uniform color.

Resilient Floors Have Come a Long Way

Resilient floors, which compress a bit when walked on, are a good choice because they are quiet, feel good underfoot, and in many

more forgiving on your joints. Most cork flooring installs with click-together joints. Some claim that it forms a gasketlike seal, making it resistant to water infiltration, but a glue-down product is preferred in bathrooms. To help seal the joints between tiles and to increase water resistance, lay on a few extra coats of sealer after installation. You also can buy cork flooring in sheet form, which may be preferred in bathrooms.

Rubber

Rubber

For a more commercial look in the bathroom, consider a rubber floor. It's warmer than tile or even hardwood, and it feels good underfoot. Some consider it a green product: Expanko's Reztec is made of recycled rubber (often from old tires), and the company's XCR-4 is made of cork rubber. It comes in both sheets and tiles, though sheet rubber is less expensive and preferred in wet areas. While it can be laid loose, you're better off gluing it down with an adhesive that isn't water soluble. It's also a good idea to use a membrane or to paint on a waterproofing layer like Gacoflex before installing the floor. To minimize off-gassing and the resulting odor, Expanko recommends laying on a sealer coat before adding your finish coats.

Vinyl

Vinyl

Today's vinyl is made to mimic almost any flooring choice you can imagine, in both appearance and texture. The $1/16$-in. to $1/4$-in. flooring is composed of multiple layers: a wear layer, a decorative layer, a foam core, and a backing of either felt or fiberglass. Fiberglass backing is the best choice for bathrooms because felt backing doesn't react well to water. Fiberglass backing also has a layer of vinyl on the bottom, making the product itself completely waterproof.

Although it's available in tile up to 12 in. sq., 6- or 12-ft.-wide rolls are often a better choice for smaller bathrooms because they leave no unsightly, water-threatened seams. The material can be glued down, applied with a pressure-sensitive adhesive, or floated. For the ultimate peace of mind, opt for a glued-down floor. Leave a gap at the perimeter of the room, cover it with baseboard, and seal the joint with silicone. Where vinyl meets the tub, shower, or toilet, it's always best to run the flooring under the edges to eliminate that edge seam. If that's impractical, seal the joint with silicone. Maintenance of vinyl is minimal: Sweep and damp-mop, using manufacturer-recommended products.

cases are water resistant. Resilient floors are available in either sheets or tiles, but the fewer the seams, the better.

Linoleum

Linoleum was largely ignored from the 1960s to the 1990s, when vinyl dominated the resilient-flooring market. In the past 15 years, however, it has made a great comeback, due largely to its status as a green product. Modern linoleum, such as Forbo's Marmoleum or Armstrong's Marmorette, is made of all-natural products (linseed oil, wood flour, limestone, and tree resins pressed onto a natural jute backing), is biodegradable, and has few or no VOC emissions. It can be installed using a solvent-free adhesive and is naturally water resistant, antistatic, antimicrobial, and antiallergenic. Linoleum is homogenous throughout, which means the appearance suffers little with wear. It also ages well. Exposure to air hardens the linoleum, but it remains resilient.

Avoid seams by choosing sheet linoleum instead of tiles, and either run the material under the tub or seal joints with silicone to prevent water from working its way to the subfloor. Maintenance requires only sweeping and occasional damp-mopping using a pH-neutral cleaner. You also can reseal linoleum, and you should at least test the sealer every year. Linoleum pricing is comparable to wood or high-end vinyl.

Cork

Cork

Cork flooring can be classed as both an engineered product, because it consists of a sandwich of substrates, and a resilient floor, because it compresses and springs back, making it softer underfoot and

Continued ➜

Concrete Is a Durable, Stylish Choice

Concrete floors lend a modern, industrial look that is quickly catching on—and with good reason: They can be poured using local ingredients, making them a green choice. If you're already pouring a concrete slab, the expense of finishing and sealing is nominal. As far as handling the water present in a bathroom, well-sealed concrete shouldn't have any problem. On the downside, concrete almost always feels cold to the touch, so using heat mats or some kind of in-floor heat is a good idea.

While not a frequent choice, a concrete floor in the bathroom should, in many cases, be an obvious one. Concrete can be finished in a variety of ways using colors, stains, and aggregates of almost any kind. Concrete can be left rough or polished smooth, but before you buff it to a glasslike finish, remember that slip resistance is a major concern in the bathroom; a swept or textured finish might be better.

Maintenance for a concrete floor is minimal: Sweep and damp-mop as needed. But you should check the sealer on the floor every year or so. Again, use the water test: If a drop of water beads up, the floor is well-sealed; if it absorbs into the concrete, apply a fresh coat of sealer.

Easy Heat for a Bathroom Floor

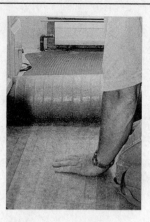

Warming the bathroom floor is much easier than it once was. There is a wide range of manufacturers offering electric, in-floor heating systems. These radiant systems feature electric coils woven through a section of matting. They are wired to a wall-mounted thermostat, or set on a timer to provide heat only when you need it. Although they won't provide enough heat to replace your main system, they'll keep your toes toasty. You can use them in conjunction with a wide range of flooring systems, including tile, stone, and engineered products.

These mats usually raise the floor level slightly, which means you'll have to use a floor-leveling compound to get over the wires. A few products can be set into the thinset during tile installation. You can buy prefab mats or have them custom-cut to cover the entire floor, which is more economical than you might imagine. These systems typically add only a few hundred dollars to the price of the floor.

Fix a Failing Bathroom Floor

By Mike Lombardi

In a perfect world, there would never be a battle between framing and plumbing. The reality, though, is that bathrooms are often small, and there frequently is precious little space to fit all the incoming and outgoing plumbing necessary for the tub, shower, vanity, toilet, and other fixtures. Without forethought in the design phase, upfront communication between subcontractors in the rough-in phase, and a willingness to do the job right in remodels, sacrifices are often made.

These problems usually are found in the floor system: Joists are notched carelessly, cut through, or drilled incorrectly, sometimes directly under a bathtub or toilet, where there is an added load on the framing. In the bathroom shown here, water leaking from the joint between the tile floor and the tub apron had rotted the floor sheathing, the original joist below, and a new joist that had been sistered in place to rescue the original. To make matters worse, the adjacent joist had been notched almost two-thirds of the way through to accommodate the tub's

Out with the Old, Prep for the New

1. OPEN THE FLOOR. Depending on the plans for the remodel, you can sometimes remove partition walls, which makes cutting the floor with a circular saw a quick task

2. Most of the time, the walls are staying in place, though, so use a reciprocating saw to cut the flooring flush to the plates.

3. POOR MAN'S PRY BAR. Used again\st the floor joists, a long 2x makes a great pry bar to help lift tongue-and-groove floor sheathing.

4. MAKE WAY FOR THE NEW WOOD. With the old subfloor removed, it's time to remove all nails from the tops of the joists and to remove or reroute any plumbing, electrical wiring, or ductwork that will interfere with the installation of the new subfloor and joists.

5. GET THE SAG OUT. It's not uncommon for an old floor joist, especially one that's been notched deeply, to have sagged over time. Before sistering a new joist to the old, string a line between the joists' two bearing points

6. Use a piece of framing lumber and a small sledgehammer to lever the joist up until the sag has been removed

waste line. These framing nightmares aren't uncommon, and though nobody likes to hear it, proper repair often means a full demolition of the bathroom.

The plans for this project included expanding the bathroom's footprint, so we had the luxury of removing the partition walls on both ends, which gave us lots of room to work. We had a full-height basement below the bathroom, which also made our work easier. Often, the ceiling below the bathroom has to be opened up or part of the rim joist removed so that new joists can be slid into place. The plans also called for a barrier-free shower, which meant lowering the floor so that the tilesetter could create a sloped mortar bed, a decision that has its own structural complications.

In the end, we elected to install doubled floor joists under the whole bathroom. Damaged joists were cut out and replaced with new lumber spanning from plate to carrying beam, and joists that were still in good condition were beefed up with new joists sistered alongside them. After notching the joists in place for the lowered floor, the whole assembly was tied together with ¾-in. subfloor sheathing.

Know the Signs of Trouble

The first signs of structural inadequacies in a bathroom floor usually show up in the form of cracked grout joints in floor or wall tile, or even cracks in the tiles themselves. Most fixtures in the bathroom are heavy, are used frequently, and can shed or leak enough water over time not only to wet the floor below, but also to wet it repeatedly so that it doesn't dry out. That's the perfect recipe for rot. These problems most often occur near the toilet, the bathtub, and the shower stall.

The toilet requires a large drainpipe connection (3 in. or 4 in. dia.), and in older homes, it was common for the plumber to notch the floor joists rather than to bore a clean hole through the framing to run the pipe. This notching can cause settling of the finished floor and can disturb the toilet flange's watertight connection. The damage in this case may be from a leak so small that it does not immediately show up, even when you're looking at the ceiling below the bathroom, but continuously wets the subfloor and framing to a point of decay and rot. Condensation also can contribute to floor and wall damage near the toilet. A

Continued ➜

Get a Good Fit without a Struggle

CUSTOM SIZING. If you're spanning between a mudsill and a carrying beam, you often can leave the joist long, sliding one end over the carrying beam while the opposite end is lifted into position.

If you're spanning between two walls or rim joists, the joists must be shorter to maneuver them into place.

The old joists may not be the same height as new lumber, but you can notch the bottom edge if needed

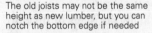

ROLL 'EM UPRIGHT. Slide one end of the joist over the top of the carrying beam so that the other end can be lifted and slid toward the rim joist. Start with the lower edge of the joist roughly in position, then roll the joist into place and persuade it into its final upright position with a small sledgehammer.

The joist may need to be raised slightly to ensure that it's carrying the load from the wall above. Use a pry bar to create space between the mudsill and joist, and then slide in opposing shims

toilet that is continuously running, especially during hot, humid conditions, will cause condensation to form on the tank, bowl, and cold-water supply piping. Although usually in small amounts, the constant drip of water causes damage to nearby subflooring, wooden trim, and eventually framing.

A bathtub uses a smaller drainpipe connection than a toilet, but the tub drain assembly (the trip waste and overflow) and the trap can interfere with the floor framing. A cast-iron tub is heavy. Add in 40 gal. to 80 gal. of water, and it's not hard to imagine the stresses being placed on the joists. The weakened floor can cause the tub to settle, which leads to cracked tile and fractured grout joints that allow water to wick into the subfloor below. I've also seen floors deflect enough that water from the showerhead has begun following the inclined tub rim into the grout joint fissure or onto the floor.

The Demo Phase Informs the Rebuild

When planning for a bathroom remodel, good preparation helps to prevent the possibility of future water damage. The demolition phase of the project usually reveals the areas that have been affected by moisture penetration and guides what needs to be corrected during the rebuild. Take pictures, make notes, and pay attention to details. Each job is different, but experience has taught me to focus on a few key areas.

First, know where your fixtures will go and how they will be installed. You may have to fur out walls, box out floor framing, adjust joist layouts, or even tweak the position of a fixture to avoid problems. Also, remember that solid, reinforced floor framing under the tub and toilet guarantees sturdy, level installations. It also pays to explore all fixture options. Often, you can find a tub or toilet with different rough-in requirements that may fit better with your floor framing.

Second, don't just seal around the fixtures after they're in place. Waterproofing should start with the subfloor and underlayment. Apply a good-quality silicone sealant where the tub apron meets the subfloor, where the tile backerboard meets the tub rim, and around all the shower faucet/fixture penetrations before, during, and after the tile is installed. The toilet flange should be sealed where it meets the finished floor, and the toilet bowl should be caulked or grouted to the floor. Toilet tanks can be purchased with an insulated liner that helps to prevent condensation from forming, an option that I always recommend when the bathroom has a history of water damage from condensation.

Prep for a Mortar Bed

The plans for this bathroom include a barrier-free shower, so the floor had to be lowered in preparation for a sloped mortar bed.

A plywood cleat screwed to the side of the joist serves as a guide for the circular saw.

At each end, an oscillating multitool or reciprocating saw finishes the cut.

A solid subfloor seals the deal. With the notches complete, the floor is tied together with ¾-in. tongue-and-groove subfloor sheathing laid in a bead of construction adhesive and fastened with screws or ring-shank nails.

A Helping Hand

Demolition should be an orderly operation, so rather than randomly cutting the joists and letting them fall, work carefully. Cut the damaged joists into 3-ft. to 4-ft. sections, making them easier to uninstall and carry out. To keep the unsupported ends of a damaged joist from falling as you make cuts, screw a scrap of wood to the top of the joist at a point just beyond where you will make the cut.

Invisible Repairs for a Hardwood Floor

By Scott Sidler

Other than refinishing hardwood floors, the most common repair my restoration company gets called to do is floorboard replacement. The typical reasons we replace boards are termite or water damage, pet stains that blacken the boards to a point sanding won't fix, and floor-plan changes that involve the removal of interior walls.

My goal is to find replacement boards that match the existing floor, and then integrate them for a natural appearance. It takes skill and patience, but the payoff is another 100 years or more of use without having to resort to an unfortunate solution: covering up the old floor with carpet, vinyl, or another layer of wood. The mark of success for a restoration carpenter is for nobody to realize you were ever there.

Identifying Wood and Its Installation

When I get called to look at a floor-repair job, the first thing I check is the species of the wood. The old homes I come across here in Florida usually have flooring of heart pine, red oak, or white oak; occasionally, they have Douglas fir. There are online guides to identifying wood grains, but this part of the job is hard to teach. Experience really is the best teacher.

I can usually identify the species by examining the grain of the planks, and I know some people who can determine the species by the smell of the sawdust or the weight of the boards. When in doubt, I remove a couple of boards and bring them to the salvage yard for help in finding a match.

The second thing I look for is whether the joints of the floorboards are randomly spaced, or set consistently at 16 in.

The key is finding boards that match and installing them with care.

Continued →

Patching Comes First

Many times the flooring repair is just the most visible part of a larger job that may involve rot repair or fixing other underlying damage to the subfloor and framing. On this job, we were called in to remove the return-air floor registers that fed the old, and now decommissioned, heating system. Before we could tackle the floorboard repair, we needed to install a framework in the hole and patch the subfloor.

STURDY SUPPORT. If the area to be patched is over a small opening, as it was here, you can frame it with 2×4s. Hold the 2×4s up tight to the underside of the existing subfloor, and take care to keep all of the pieces level and flush at the top as you fasten them with screws. With the framing in place, lay down a bead of subfloor adhesive.

SHIM IT FLUSH. Often the existing subfloor, usually ¾ in. thick, won't match the thickness of modern plywood, which is often slightly thinner than ¾ in. To make up for this discrepancy, glue and screw the new piece of plywood into place,

Before the adhesive sets up, back off the screws and add shims below. When the top edge is flush, drive the screws home.

Removing the First Board Is the Hardest

Tongue-and-groove flooring is fastened with nails driven through the tongue of each piece and down into the subfloor or framing below. The nails then are covered by the grooves of the next board that gets installed. To remove the boards, you have to gain access to the nails.

MARK A NEW LAYOUT. Use a marker to indicate which boards will be removed, and where any new butt joints will be added. Always carry the mark along the length of the board to avoid confusion when cutting, and stagger the joints by at least a foot or so.

DIVIDE THE BOARD. Using a circular saw set to the thickness of the flooring, make two parallel cuts along the length of each marked board, stopping shy of the end. If there are several boards in a row that will be removed, cut across their width to speed up the process.

PLUNGE TO FINISH THE CUT. The circular saw will leave a bit of uncut wood at the end of the board, which can be handled with an oscillating multitool. Plunge straight down until the blade hits the subfloor, being careful not to nick the adjoining board.

MAKE YOUR OWN JOINTS. When creating a new joint in the middle of an existing board, align a rafter square with the long side of the floorboard, and apply firm downward pressure to the square as you plunge the multitool along its edge.

CLEAR OUT THE WASTE. The center strip of the board can be lifted out by hand, which gives you access to the sides.

Use a cat's paw to pull these pieces toward the gap in the center, then lift them out.

Avoid Ripoffs

It's tempting to rip off the bottom half of the groove on every replacement board before dropping the board into place, but that's not as strong as having a full tongue-and-groove connection. To maximize the strength of the repair, I like to slide as many intact boards into place as possible. The fit has to be tight, so expect a lot of resistance. Once those boards are set and face-nailed sparingly, many of the remaining ones can be placed just as they would in a new installation. Drop in a new piece groove first, then toenail the tongue to the subfloor.

Face-nail the last board. For the final board, cut off the bottom half of the groove, and insert the board tongue first.

Carefully seat the groove side with a hammer and a piece of scrap wood. It should fit tightly but not feel forced into place. Face-nail the final board into place with 18-ga. nails—two at either end and one staggered every 12 in. along the length of the board—and be sure the nail heads are set below the surface to avoid problems when it's time to sand the floors.

TAKE OFF THE PRESSURE. To help a new board slide more easily into place, make sure the tongues and grooves of the existing and new boards are free of splinters or caked-on residue, and use a beater block to protect the end of the new board. A helper can drive a chisel into the subfloor and use it to leverage the nearby boards just enough to take the pressure off the board you're trying to slide in.

Wedge It

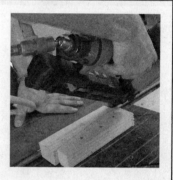

If you need to snug up the joint between a fastened and an unfastened floorboard, cut a pair of opposing wedges from a scrap of wood, fasten one half to the subfloor with screws, and hammer the other half into place to force the floorboards together. Nail the unfastened floorboard thoroughly before removing the wedges.

---

or 24 in. on center. Consistently spaced joints are usually an indication that there's no subfloor under the hardwood flooring. In my area of Florida, this is common to the oldest homes (1890s and earlier) and the homes in the low-end working-class neighborhoods built from the 1900s to the 1940s.

If there is a subfloor, I can use the replacement boards more efficiently, staggering the joints wherever I need. Without a subfloor, I have to use lengths in 16-in. or 24-in. increments and be careful not to fall through the floor while I'm working on large repairs. Also, in homes without subfloors, the planks run underneath the interior walls instead of butting against them, which means far more hassle when it comes to removing and replacing each piece.

Finding the Best Match

When it comes to finding replacement boards that will blend with the rest of the floor, there are a few options. In the case of this

project, we got lucky. The second floor of the house had been gutted by a previous owner, and the old flooring had been left behind, so we had a full stack of original floorboards to choose from. Without that, we would have had to start shopping around for a match.

Don't expect to get a good match just by driving to the local supplier to pick up some new wood of the same species. Wood looks different depending on where it was grown, when it was harvested, and how it was milled. For the best match, check an architectural salvage yard. First, though, arm yourself with as much information about the existing floorboards as possible.

Start by taking careful measurements of the existing boards. The width needs to be pretty accurate for a good fit and a satisfying match. In my area, I've seen heart-pine boards in 2¼-in., 2⅜-in., and 2½-in. widths. Why manufacturers decided to have such minimal differences is beyond me, but they do make a difference, so measure carefully. Fortunately, this is a pretty easy

Continued ➜

measurement to take right from the finished surface of the floor.

Accuracy is less crucial for the thickness of repair boards; as long as you're within 1/8 in. or so, the sanding should remedy any slight differences. That said, a replacement board that's too thick is better than one that's not thick enough.

To measure the thickness, you'll need to get creative. I typically look for a floor grate or a piece of baseboard I can remove in order to get an accurate measurement of the cross section of the flooring.

Pay attention to the position of the tongue of the board, too. The tongue is right in the middle of most floorboards, but with 7/8-in.- or 1-in.-thick boards, the tongue can be just below center. (This allows the boards to be sanded and refinished more times before replacement is necessary.) You need enough thickness above the tongue to match the rest of the floor, but the more crucial dimension is the distance between the tongue and the bottom of the board.

Finally, you need to find an appropriate grain and color match. For instance, if the floorboards in the house are quartersawn, then a replacement board with flatsawn grain will stick out like a sore thumb. The same holds true when comparing heartwood with sapwood. Some heart-pine floors have a lot of deep-red heartwood, while others are a bit more yellow.

Before you begin searching salvage yards for a match, find out the date that the house was built. If the homeowner isn't sure, check the property-appraiser's website, or visit the town hall. Ideally, the replacement boards will be from the same decade. If a decade match is not possible, at least look for similar grain patterns. Should you find nothing but replacement boards that are close but not quite perfect, there's still a back door. You can borrow flooring from a closet or pantry to do the more visible repair, and then put the new wood in these more remote locations where it will be less noticeable. It means more repair work, but the payoff is worth it.

Plan for a Full Refinish

A great repair job still can be hard to blend in with the surrounding boards. Even if the repair planks match the existing floor—as they did on this job—the new boards usually sit proud of the existing floor due to wear, as well as sanding and refinishing that may have been done over the years. Customers don't always like to hear it, but the best way to get a good match is to sand down and refinish the entire room, if not that whole level of the house.

If that's not in the budget, then you have to get creative with color-matching the stain and blending subtle differences with colored wood putty. You can draw in the grain on any puttied sections that aren't blending well enough. With the help of your thumb as a smudging tool, brown and black Sharpies can make almost any putty find the floor's true color.

Inlaying a Floor Medallion

By Charles Peterson

In the 20 or so years that I've been installing wood floors, I can't bear to throw out scraps, especially from the more beautiful, exotic wood species that I've been asked to use. Instead, I turn these scraps into the focal point of any hardwood floor. I recently dug into my scrap pile and used wenge, cherry, and maple to create a star medallion for an entry hall.

Assemble the Medallion

I always start with a full-scale drawing, labeling the wood species for each part. Most of the medallions that I make follow a pattern with a lot of similar shapes and sizes.

A Safe Rout

It's smart to mark the medallion's location before you begin to install the flooring. It's an easy way to avoid driving nails where they might make contact with the router bit.

The medallion pieces must be cut accurately. The fastest, safest, most accurate method for cutting is with a crosscut sled made to fit your tablesaw. These sleds are easy to make, extremely accurate, and more important, they help keep fingers safely away from the sawblade.

When all of the medallion pieces are cut, I assemble them into a single unit. If the medallion is made from ¼-in. stock, I glue together the pieces and apply clear packing tape over every seam. Thinner stock (such as the material that I used for this project) can be glued to)½-in. Baltic-birch plywood. Either way, the completed medallion then becomes a layout tool.

Install the Floor First

The easiest way to install a floor medallion is to rout out a hole in the flooring, then drop it in. If the medallion is for a new floor, I lay out its position on the subfloor before the flooring goes in. Because I install the flooring first and then cut out for the medallion, I make a bold reminder to the guy with the nailer (me) not to nail in the field of the medallion. As the boards go in, I also like to glue any butt joints that fall near the medallion. If the medallion is going into an existing floor, I position the medallion, then find all the nails in the field with a magnetic nail finder. If a nail falls in the way of my cut, I usually can move the layout slightly to avoid hitting it.

The Router Template Is Built in Place

When the floor is complete, I reposition the medallion on the floor. Because medallions are seldom perfectly symmetrical, I trace around the perimeter of the medallion and use index marks (on the floor and on the medallion) to make sure that I can reposition the medallion exactly.

Next, I cut blocks that fit tightly around the medallion for the

Assemble the Router Template Around the Medallion

The medallion is repositioned after the flooring is installed.

Template blocks are cut and numbered around the perimeter of the medallion.

Double-face tape holds the blocks in position, and each block is glued to its neighbor.

One block is left out so that the medallion can be removed easily.

router template. If I can get away with it, I tack the blocks directly to the floor. With this maple floor, nail holes would have been visible, so I attached the template blocks with double-face tape instead. For a smooth router cut, the blocks must remain stationary. So I also joined the template pieces to each other with glue. Because the template pieces fit tightly around the medallion, don't attach the last piece until you lift the medallion free.

Rout in Several Shallow Passes

To make sure of a tight fit for the medallion, I applied several layers of masking tape around the inside edge of the template. Then I drilled holes in the floor at several spots inside the template to help with starting the router.

I make the cuts with a pattern-cutting bit. This straight-fluted, carbide-tipped router bit has a top-mounted bearing that rides on the inside of the template. The first cut should be less than ¼ in. deep so that it just exposes the top of any nails I may have missed. If necessary, use a nail set to sink any nails safely out of the bit's path.

I make three or four passes to cut down to the subfloor, then remove the waste. A corner chisel squares off the rounded corners

Continued ➜

left by the router. Before testfitting the medallion, I make sure all the edges are clean and smooth, and that the hole is clear of debris.

I glue the medallion in place using urethane wood-flooring adhesive. As a last resort, I have used a plywood subfloor adhesive. Do not use a liquid-nail product; it is too rigid. I tap the medallion into place with a hammer and a wood block, and I weight it down until the glue is dry. A few passes with a floor sander level the medallion with the surrounding floor.

Template Blocks Guide the Medallion Cutout

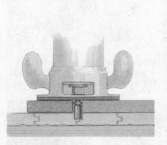

Template blocks installed with doubleface tape guide the router to cut the hole for the medallion. A straight-fluted bit with a top-mounted bearing does the cutting. Layers of masking tape smooth the inside of the template and decrease the size for a tighter fit.

Don't cut all at once. Several shallow passes with the router cut through the flooring safely and easily. Above, a crew member holds a vacuum to keep dust and mess to a minimum.

After the final cut, the waste is removed.

A corner chisel squares off rounded corners left by the router bit.

Glue and tap. Subfloor adhesive that stays flexible after it sets holds the medallion.

A wood block cushions the hammer as the medallion is tapped into place.

Linoleum vs. Vinyl

By Matt Higgins

Flooring options abound—even the options have options. But if you're looking for inexpensive flooring, especially in a potentially wet area such as a kitchen or bathroom, you're probably going to consider linoleum and vinyl. Although the terms are often used interchangeably, these materials are not the same. The mention of either sometimes conjures up images of second-rate products, but both have their place.

Linoleum and vinyl fall into the category of resilient flooring. According to Michele Zelman of Armstrong, which makes flooring products out of both materials, to call a flooring material resilient means that it can restore its shape. If a heavy object were to land on it, the material wouldn't necessarily be permanently dented. Linoleum is mostly, but not exclusively, limited to commercial applications. Vinyl is found in numerous residential and commercial applications. Both materials are available in sheets and in tiles.

Linoleum

First patented over 150 years ago, linoleum is an older product than most people realize, and like many innovations, it was discovered by accident. English inventor Frederick Walton observed how a solid but flexible film formed on top of linseed-oil-based paint. He experimented with this natural product and eventually found it to be a perfect floor and wall covering. Since linseed oil was the primary component, Walton called his new product linoleum.

DEEP COLOR. Because the color goes through to the backing, scratches don't readily show on linoleum.

Another important characteristic of linoleum that is largely unknown—but far more relevant to current home-building trends—is that it's all natural and biodegradable. In addition to linseed oil, linoleum includes pine rosin, limestone, cork flour, wood flour, jute as the backing, and coloring pigments. Its color goes through to the backing, so scratches don't readily show. Homeowners increasingly are selecting it as a green material that is relatively inexpensive.

Linoleum must be installed over a clean, smooth, and level surface, as imperfections in the floor can cause bumps. If the surface can't be smoothed, an underlayment may be needed. Linoleum is cut with a utility knife or a heavy-duty curved linoleum knife. Typically, it's secured with flooring adhesive, and depending on manufacturer specifications, a 100-lb. roller may be used to promote strong adhesion. Seams on some products can be heat welded. Rigid click-together tongue-and-groove tiles are also available that install over a thin foam underlayment without any adhesive or fasteners. These tiles typically are cut with a jigsaw.

Linoleum isn't as flexible as vinyl, and it is more difficult to cut. There are also fewer color options with linoleum, and the material isn't used nearly as widely as vinyl. New linoleum also has a temporary yellow cast called bloom that eventually disappears when exposed to light.

Linoleum requires only basic routine care such as sweeping and mopping with a product-specific pH-neutral cleaner, but the flooring must be polished with a sealer once or twice a year because the surface is porous.

Vinyl

Vinyl was also discovered accidently. Waldo Semon created it in the late 1920s while attempting to develop a glue for bonding rubber to metal. Today, vinyl is, of course, used in a huge variety of applications.

Even though they are often confused and can look similar once installed, vinyl and linoleum are significantly different in terms of composition. While linoleum is all natural, vinyl is a synthetic product made using a variety of toxic chemicals, primarily polyvinyl chloride (PVC) resin. Sheet vinyl flooring also contains

PRINTED SURFACE. Vinyl's surface is inexpensive to produce and allows for great variety, but scratches can show.

Linoleum Flooring

Vinyl Flooring

plasticizers for flexibility. Vinyl's large market share comes with a huge number of color and pattern options. Also, not all vinyl flooring is inexpensive. Luxury vinyl flooring (LVF, or LVT for tiles) is a higher-quality version of the product.

Like linoleum, vinyl flooring is available in sheets and tiles that get installed with flooring adhesive. A 100-lb. roller is often used, and the seams on some products can be heat welded. There is also a large selection of self-adhesive peel-and-stick tiles. Vinyl flooring is cut with a knife or shears, and since it generally is thinner and more flexible than linoleum, it's easier to cut.

Vinyl's color and patterns are printed, which allows for a tremendous variety and keeps costs low. It also means that deep scratches may show, since the color and patterns don't always go through to the backing.

Vinyl flooring requires no special care. In most cases, a mild cleaner is recommended by the manufacturer.

Cutting Ceramic Tile with a Tile Saw

By Andy Engel

If you're laying a significant amount of tile, a tile saw is an essential tool. Pros need their own, but if you lay tile only occasionally, you can find tile saws at rental yards. An alternative is to buy a tile score-and-snap cutter, which uses a carbide tooth to score the face of the tile. Once scored, tile is snapped along the line by pushing down on the handle. Scoring and snapping isn't as clean as cutting with a saw, though, and it doesn't allow you to make notching cuts as shown here.

All tile saws cut with a toothless, water-cooled diamond blade. While this blade is not as dangerous to flesh as a toothed blade, caution is still called for. With most tile saws, a sliding table is used to run the tile through the blade. Some saws, like the DeWalt shown here, also have a plunge function that allows the blade to be lowered into the tile. This makes cutouts easier, but it's not essential. To make the lesson more universal, we used the DeWalt saw as if it were a nonplunging tool.

Cutting Notches

1. LAYOUT HAS TO BE WATERPROOF. Use a permanent marker for your cutlines. Most cuts in tile don't need to be precise, so the wide line isn't a problem.

2. START CUTTING WITH THE GOOD SIDE UP. Align the mark with the blade, hold the tile tight to the fence, and push the tile and table into the blade. Finish the cut at the corner.

3. END THE SECOND CUT AT THE FIRST. Turn the tile, line up the second line, and make this cut just like the first one.

4. FINISH BY CUTTING FROM THE BACK. Flip the tile over, align the blade with the previous kerfs, and overcut the corners just enough to free the scrap. The thicker the tile, the longer the overcut needs to be.

Cutting U-Shapes

1. CUT FROM THE EDGE FIRST. Align the blade and make these cuts just as you would when notching a tile.

2. CUT THE TOP. If your saw doesn't plunge, align the blade to the cutline by eye and raise the tile to the blade. With the tile supported by the edge of the table, lift and tilt the tile into the blade.

3. FINISH BY BACK-CUTTING. As with a notch, back-cut the legs. To make the top cut, lift the tile into the blade.

Cutting Holes

1. CUT HOLES FROM THE BACK. Measure carefully, and lay out the cut on the back of the tile. Most holes are for tub or shower spouts and will be covered by an escutcheon, leaving room for error.

2. MAKE A SERIES OF CUTS. Slightly overcut the edges as with the top of a U-shaped cut, then cut a crosshatch pattern in the center.

3. TAP OUT THE HOLE. From the front, tap the hole location with the handle of a screwdriver or similar tool to clean out the waste. The shards are sharp, so be careful.

Diamonds Are a Saw's Best Friend

Used for cutting all types of tile including ceramic, porcelain, glass, and stone, tile saws rely on a blade whose rim is embedded with tiny diamonds. A constant water flow cools the blade and keeps the diamonds (which are just a form of carbon, like the charcoal in your grill) from burning up. Holes for plumbing can be cut with a tile saw, but a diamond hole saw can save time if you do a lot of tilework.

Continued ➡

Tile Floors: Layout Is Everything

By David Hart

Have you ever noticed the hallmarks of a bad tile layout? Slivers of tile at doorways or a line of tile that's not parallel to a long wall? I certainly have. A great tile installation doesn't start with the mortar, the wet saw, or even the grout. It starts with a proper layout. Not only will a well-planned tile floor or wall look better, but it also can save money by reducing waste.

I spend up to a day laying out a tile job before I do anything else. Essentially, I create a grid on the floor that tells me where the tiles will land. By determining a layout and shifting it as necessary, I can reduce cutting and eliminate the most difficult cuts, such as those around vents, outlets, and plumbing fixtures. Of course, I'll still have to cut around those obstacles, but with careful planning, I can make sure they don't fall inside a single tile, which can take far longer than making a couple of straight or U-shaped cuts in adjoining tiles. The whole idea is to streamline the process for the installer, which almost always yields a better tile job.

Establish a Reference

To create a layout grid, you need to know the size of the tiles. This determines the size of the grid squares. From there, you can establish horizontal and vertical reference lines, and superimpose the grid on the floor.

I start by laying a few tiles side by side along a straightedge, each separated by the width of the grout joint that I plan to use, and then measuring the length of the group plus a line of grout on one outside edge. I'm aiming for a unit of measure that's between 24 in. and 36 in., a distance I can comfortably reach on a typical floor installation.

Once I determine the unit measurement, I snap a reference chalkline parallel to the longest straight wall in the room. That reference line can be any distance from any wall, including a centerline between two main walls, or the reference line can be the cumulative measurement of tiles and grout joints from a single wall.

Next, I measure from that line to various stops, such as walls, entryways, and cabinet bases, to determine the cuts I'll have. I always plan for at least half a tile at the most obvious places—doorways and long, visible walls, for example. In some cases, it's impossible to have large pieces everywhere, so I place narrow pieces in closets, under cabinet toe kicks, or behind toilets.

If my first reference line doesn't give me a layout that works, I erase the line with a damp sponge, adjust the location, and snap a new one. Then I snap lines at the unit-measure increments parallel to my reference line. It's critical to make sure the measurements are precise; a ¼-in. or even ⅛-in. error can throw off the entire layout.

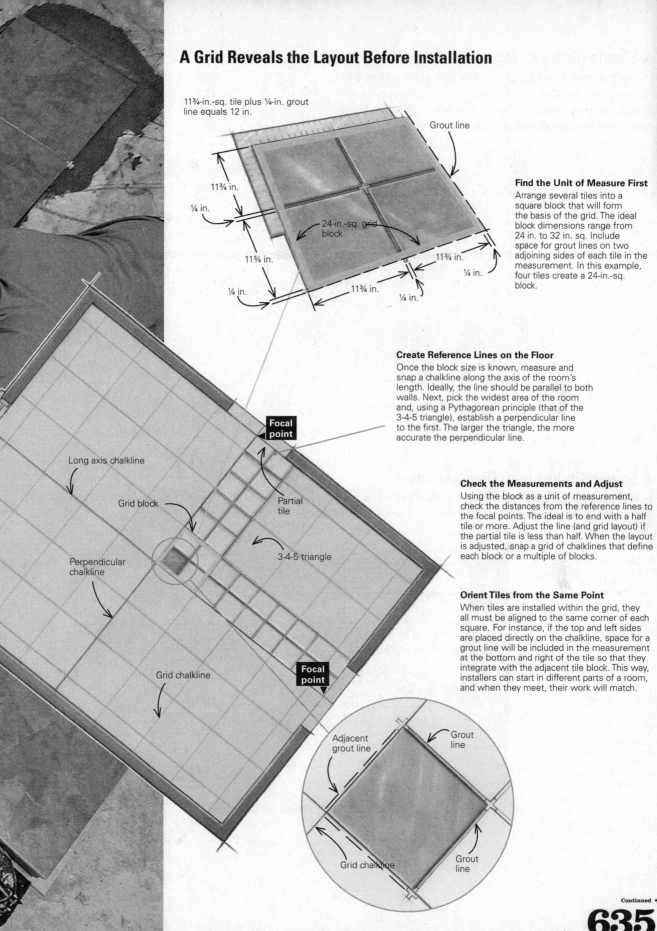

A Grid Reveals the Layout Before Installation

11¾-in.-sq. tile plus ¼-in. grout line equals 12 in.

Grout line

11¾ in.

¼ in.

24-in.-sq. grid block

11¾ in.

11¾ in.

11¾ in.

¼ in.

¼ in.

¼ in.

Find the Unit of Measure First

Arrange several tiles into a square block that will form the basis of the grid. The ideal block dimensions range from 24 in. to 32 in. sq. Include space for grout lines on two adjoining sides of each tile in the measurement. In this example, four tiles create a 24-in.-sq. block.

Create Reference Lines on the Floor

Once the block size is known, measure and snap a chalkline along the axis of the room's length. Ideally, the line should be parallel to both walls. Next, pick the widest area of the room and, using a Pythagorean principle (that of the 3-4-5 triangle), establish a perpendicular line to the first. The larger the triangle, the more accurate the perpendicular line.

Check the Measurements and Adjust

Using the block as a unit of measurement, check the distances from the reference lines to the focal points. The ideal is to end with a half tile or more. Adjust the line (and grid layout) if the partial tile is less than half. When the layout is adjusted, snap a grid of chalklines that define each block or a multiple of blocks.

Orient Tiles from the Same Point

When tiles are installed within the grid, they all must be aligned to the same corner of each square. For instance, if the top and left sides are placed directly on the chalkline, space for a grout line will be included in the measurement at the bottom and right of the tile so that they integrate with the adjacent tile block. This way, installers can start in different parts of a room, and when they meet, their work will match.

Long axis chalkline

Grid block

Perpendicular chalkline

Grid chalkline

Focal point

Partial tile

3-4-5 triangle

Focal point

Adjacent grout line

Grout line

Grid chalkline

Grout line

Continued ➔

A Simple Galley Kitchen

In this example, 12-in. tiles in a 24-in. grid are laid over a long narrow plan. The focal points are at the sink, the cabinet kick spaces, and the doorways. The potential complicating factor here is the hexagonal eating nook.

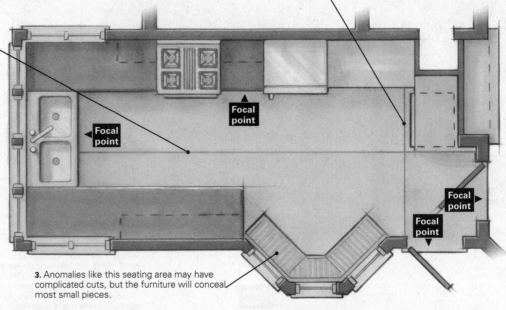

1. Start the first vertical line by measuring from the cabinet wall. The longest, straightest wall should always be the reference. Measure across to make sure the opposite wall is parallel to the line, and adjust if it isn't parallel.

2. Establish a perpendicular line at the widest point, then adjust for focal points.

Focal point

Focal point

Focal point

Focal point

3. Anomalies like this seating area may have complicated cuts, but the furniture will conceal most small pieces.

A Larger Kitchen with Obstructions

In kitchens, independent structures like islands can cause problems. Again, 12-in. tiles are used to form a 24-sq.-in. grid. The focal points are determined by sightlines from entrances and at the doorways themselves.

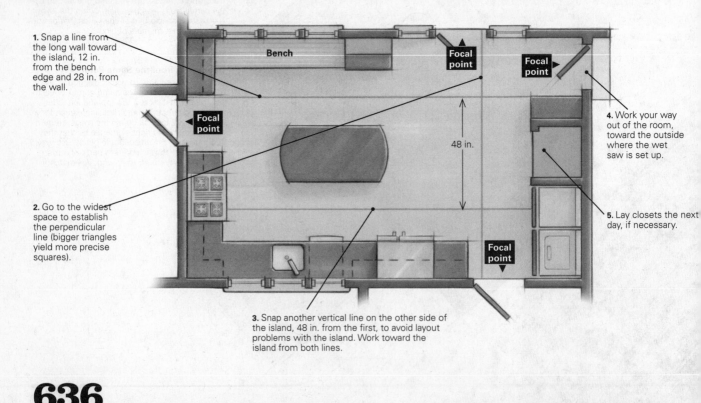

1. Snap a line from the long wall toward the island, 12 in. from the bench edge and 28 in. from the wall.

Bench

Focal point

Focal point

Focal point

48 in.

4. Work your way out of the room, toward the outside where the wet saw is set up.

2. Go to the widest space to establish the perpendicular line (bigger triangles yield more precise squares).

Focal point

5. Lay closets the next day, if necessary.

3. Snap another vertical line on the other side of the island, 48 in. from the first, to avoid layout problems with the island. Work toward the island from both lines.

Diagonal Layout in a Small Bath

In this example, 6-in.-sq. tiles are to be installed in a diagonal 18-in. grid. The focal points are at the sink and shower door. Smaller cut pieces of tile can be hidden behind the toilet.

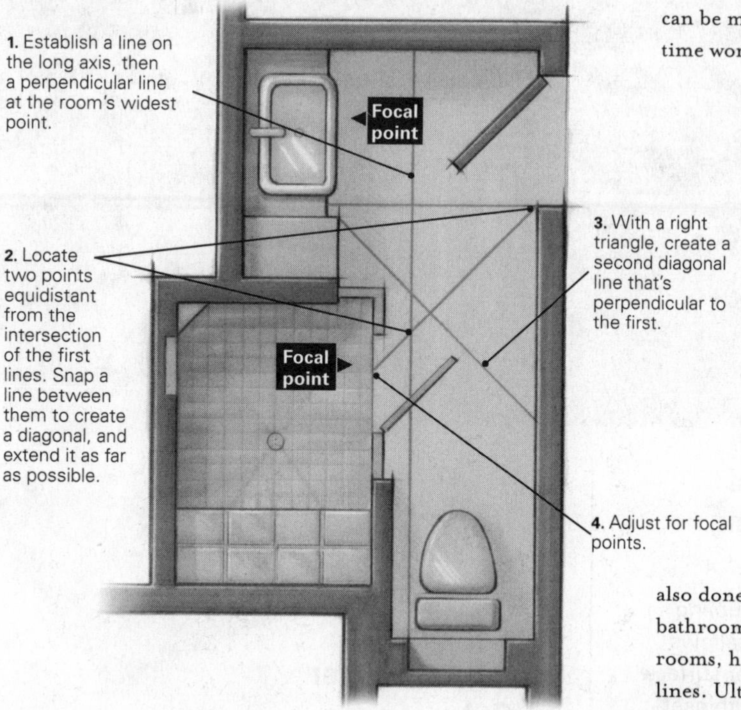

1. Establish a line on the long axis, then a perpendicular line at the room's widest point.
2. Locate two points equidistant from the intersection of the first lines. Snap a line between them to create a diagonal, and extend it as far as possible.
3. With a right triangle, create a second diagonal line that's perpendicular to the first.
4. Adjust for focal points.
Focal point
Focal point

Transfer the Grid to the Floor

Before I snap final lines, I review where the cuts will fall and then determine the best starting point. I choose an arbitrary point on my primary reference line and then measure in unit-measure increments to determine the locations of the cut tiles so that the largest pieces are in the most visible areas.

Once I determine my reference point on the vertical lines, I make a right triangle using the simple 3-4-5 rule governing right triangles. I use the longest combination of numbers, which will give me a longer perpendicular line. This serves as my primary horizontal line. I then snap lines at unit-measure increments, creating a grid of equal blocks on the entire floor. With that grid, I can start anywhere on the floor, as long as I remember that the tiles in each square must be started in the same corner. That allows me to fill in places that I might not be able to reach if I work in a continuous path—inside small closets, under appliances, and in tight corners.

Diagonal Grids Start the Same

Floors installed on a diagonal take a little more time to lay out, but the steps are basically the same. To start, I mark a centerline down the longest portion of the room and then snap a perpendicular line. Next, I measure an equal distance down one side of the horizontal line from the centerpoint and one side of the vertical line, and snap a chalkline through those marks. That gives me a diagonal reference line to determine cuts throughout the room. After I snap a series of lines, I can then go back and put down more lines to create a grid, following the same steps I use for tiles laid parallel to the room. Determining cuts on a diagonal can be much more time-consuming, and I often spend far more time working on the initial layout.

A Word About Choosing Tile

Many people say larger tiles make a smaller room look larger. I don't buy that theory, but then again, I'm just a tile installer. To me, a room doesn't look larger or smaller based on the size of the tile. I'm not a big fan of diagonal installations, either. The lines just get too overwhelming. Maybe that's just me, because plenty of people like a diagonal layout. The fact is, tile size, patterns, and layout are really a matter of personal taste. When dealing with a client, I do a dry run and lay a bunch of tiles on the floor both ways (straight and diagonal), then let the client decide between them.

My personal preference is for larger tiles. I think they look better, especially in larger rooms, but I've also done some installations with 18-in. by 18-in. tiles in smaller bathrooms and kitchens that looked great. Smaller tiles in big rooms, however, just look too busy; there are too many grout lines. Ultimately, what's really important is for the floor to look as though it has been there forever.

A New Way to Tile a Big Floor

By Tom Meehan

There are buildings in Europe with tile floors that are in perfect shape after more than 1000 years. However, on this side of the pond, tile floors routinely fail after less than 10 years. What did the Europeans of the first millennium know about tile that we have yet to learn?

New Material for an Old System

The answer is that Europeans developed what is known as an uncoupling system. The system began with a bottom layer of mortar covered by a thin layer of sand. The tile then was set into another layer of mortar on top of the sand. As the building settled and shifted over the years, the sand separated the tile from the floor below, allowing the tile to float on top, unaffected by the building's movement.

Without an uncoupling system, the tile floors of today move when the building moves. Results can include loose grout, loose tile, and in extreme cases, cracked tile as the floor surface under the tile moves and shifts, especially if the floor is big.

Continued →

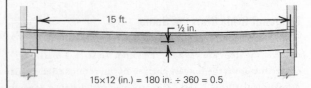

Both sides of an uncoupling membrane

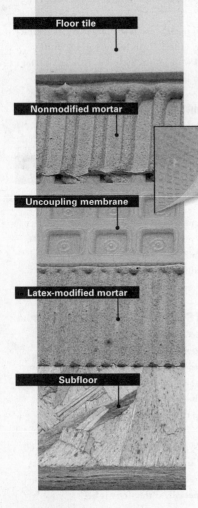

Floor tile

Nonmodified mortar

Uncoupling membrane

Latex-modified mortar

Subfloor

Ditra is an uncoupling membrane that allows the finished floor surface (tile, thinset, and grout) and the substrate (floor sheathing or a floor slab) to move independently of each other. A close look at Ditra reveals the way it works. A fabric backing on one side bonds to the floor, and a keyed plastic grid system on the other side bonds to the tile. When the floor moves, the fabric allows the plastic sheet above it to move without breaking the bond of the tile. Ditra cuts easily with scissors or a utility knife, and it can be pieced into smaller areas without losing effectiveness.

Is your floor strong enough for tile?

The Tile Council of America's (www.tileusa. com) standard formula for measuring maximum deflection under a tile floor is called L-360. Divide the total span of the floor joists by 360 for the maximum amount the floor can give in the middle under a live load of 40 lb./sq. ft., plus any long-term deflection due to the weight of the floor. For example, the maximum allowable deflection for a joist span of 15 ft. is ½ in. The L-360 standard applies to most ceramic, porcelain, and hard stone. But for certain soft-stone tile, such as limestone or light marble, the L-720 formula applies, cutting the maximum allowable deflection in half. Ways of reducing deflection include adding extra layers of plywood underlayment or installing additional support under the floor framing.

15 ft.

½ in.

15×12 (in.) = 180 in. ÷ 360 = 0.5

Spread Out the Membrane

TEST-FIT FIRST. Cut membrane to fit the floor with scissors or a utility knife. Cover the subfloor completely.

ONE COURSE AT A TIME. Spread only enough mortar for one course of membrane, then roll out the precut pieces.

MAKE A GOOD IMPRESSION. After the membrane is rolled out flat, a wooden float ensures a good bond with the mortar.

In the past, I've had pretty good luck by first making sure that the subfloor was thick enough, then applying felt paper, wire lath, and a layer of mortar before installing the tile. But that was a lot of extra work, extra materials, and extra thickness being added to the tile floor. Recently, I started using a product from the Schlüter Company (www.schluter.com; 800-472-4588), called Ditra, which applies ancient European concepts using some 21st-century materials.

Start with a Sound Floor

Adding a membrane under the tile may be a great way to lengthen the life of a tile installation, but the floor below has to be structurally sound. There are formulas for determining if a floor has too much deflection, but I've also learned to rely on feel. Too much give when I jump on the floor tells me that it probably needs strengthening.

Whenever possible, I check the framing below the floor to make sure the size and spacing of the joists are correct for the span of the floor. I've even been known to add extra support columns under bouncy floors.

The Membrane Goes Down Quickly

Before I begin installing tile, I roll out and cut pieces of membrane for the whole floor. It's OK to use small pieces in areas such as thresholds to make the installation easier. If I'm putting down a heat mat for a radiant floor, I install it before the membrane (*Fine Homebuilding* #159). The membrane helps to distribute heat from the mat, and it protects the mat if a tile ever needs to be replaced.

I snap chalklines for each course of tile before it's installed to help guide me so that I don't spread more thinset mortar than necessary. For an installation over a wood subfloor, I use a latex-modified thinset that bonds well to the fabric side of the membrane. I start

with a skim coat of thinset, pushing it into the pores of the wood with the straight edge of the trowel. Right away, I spread a second layer of mortar with a $^{3}/_{16}$-in. by $^{1}/_{4}$-in. V-notched trowel.

I keep the trowel lines going in one direction so that pockets or voids don't form, which could prevent the membrane from bonding properly. Then I roll the membrane into the fresh mortar and push it out flat. Once the membrane is in position, I use either a 75-lb. linoleum roller or a wooden float to press it into the mortar and establish the bond. Push out any excess thinset that may make the floor uneven.

Plan Tile Layout for Best Look and Least Waste

Once the first tile goes down, there's no turning back, so I take as much time as I need to get the layout right. This floor tile is 12×12 Turkish slate. It varies slightly in size and thickness, and has an uneven cleft face.

In this room, the focal point is the sliding door, so I began my layout there by measuring three courses from that wall and snapping a chalkline across the room. Next, I dry-fit a row of tiles in front of the door to see what cuts I'd end up with beside the slider and at the two sidewalls. I found that centering the tile on the middle of the door left 11-in. pieces on both sides of the room for minimal waste. Before lifting the tiles in front of the door, I marked the center tile's edge.

Once I have the line across the room and the line for the center course of tile, I project a perpendicular line down the middle of the room with a straightedge and a 3-4-5 A-Square (C.H. Hanson Tool Co.; www.asquaretools.com; 800-827-3398). Measuring off the sidewalls, I extend the centerline to the other end of the room and snap a chalkline. I confirm that the line is perpendicular to the first line between the sidewalls, and when I'm satisfied, I trace over the chalkline with a waterproof marker.

As a final check, I lay out one course of tile along both

Continued ➔

Tiling Starts with Careful Layout

Dry-fitting a couple of tile courses enables you to determine the best layout and mark up the floor with layout lines.

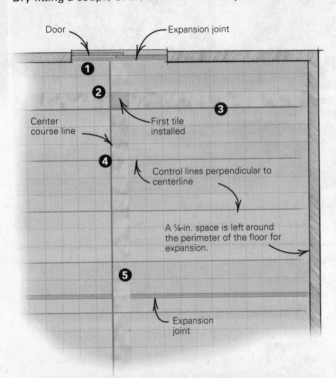

Door

Expansion joint

① ② ③

Center course line

First tile installed

④

Control lines perpendicular to centerline

A ¼-in. space is left around the perimeter of the floor for expansion.

⑤

Expansion joint

1. After tiles are dry-fit in front of the door, measuring the width of the room determines whether the layout should be centered on a tile or on a grout joint for the best use of materials.

2. Mark the edge of the center tile course.

3. Measure three tile courses off the wall, and snap a chalkline across the room.

4. After marking the edge of the center tile, use a large folding square and a straightedge to extend the layout into the room. Measurements to the wall guide the center course line to the other end of the room. Straightedges confirm that the layout lines are perpendicular to each other.

5. A dry course of tile on top of the membrane confirms the side-to-side layout, and another course along the center course line sets the installation spacing every three courses.

perpendicular lines without mortar. As I pick up the tile, I mark every three courses and snap parallel chalklines at each mark to keep the courses running straight and true.

Tile Locks into Membrane

I install the tiles over the Ditra using a dry-set thinset mortar instead of latex-modified thinset. Dry-set, or nonmodified, mortar is easier to work with, is easier to clean up, and is about one-third the price of good latex-modified thinset mortar.

Because the slate is uneven and has voids in its surface, I spread the thinset with a coarse ⅜-in. square-notched trowel. Before I comb it with the notched side of the trowel, I push the thinset with the straight edge of the trowel to key it into the recessed dovetailed edges of each square in the membrane. Then I go back over the thinset with the notched side of the trowel, again keeping the lines moving in just one direction.

The first tile determines the position of every tile in the floor, so I set it at the point where the two layout lines intersect. As I work down the floor, I apply thinset to an area in which I can set tile within about 15 minutes, usually about 30 sq. ft. at a time. For each set of courses, I install the first tile at the intersection of the layout lines. As each tile goes in, I apply a little downward pressure and slide the tile into place, which helps to lock the tile into the layer of thinset.

Because these tiles vary in thickness, I butter the backs of thinner tiles with a little thinset to bring them to the height of the other tiles. If a tile is extremely irregular in either shape or thickness, I put it aside for cuts or to be used in a closet.

Each piece of stone tile varies in shade and color. To keep color variations consistent across the floor, I work with tile from several boxes at a time. If a color is too extreme, I set it aside.

Expansion Joints Give Tile Extra Breathing Room

In large floors, expansion joints should be installed every 20 ft. to 24 ft. Without expansion joints, there's an increased risk of cracks as the tile expands and contracts due to temperature changes.

The expansion joints I use (also made by the Schlüter Company) are available L-shaped for along walls, or T-shaped for between tile courses. A section of L-shaped expansion joint was needed in front of the sliding doors, where it also helps to prevent the tile and grout from cracking as the door is opened and closed repeatedly.

Because this room is just over 24 ft. long, I put a T-shaped expansion joint between two courses roughly in the middle of the room. Once I determine where the joint will be, I press it into the thinset, measuring to keep the joint at the right distance from the previous course. I trowel a little thinset over the flange before setting the tile.

I like to lay tile before baseboard goes in, so I leave a ¼-in. expansion gap along the walls for seasonal tile movement. The baseboard will hide the gap when it's installed. If the base is in before I tile, I can put L-shaped expansion joints around the perimeter of the floor.

Continued ➜

Setting Tile

Expansion joints, recommended every 20 ft. to 24 ft. or wherever tile butts against a wall surface, such as in front of a sliding door, allow the tile to expand and contract with changes in temperature.

L-shaped expansion joint

T-shaped expansion joint

1. An L-shaped joint goes against the door. After caulking the edge of the joint with silicone, press it into the mortar and against the door.

2. The first tile set at the intersection of the layout lines establishes the position of every tile in the room.

3. .01 T-shaped expansion joint goes between tile courses. First, position the joint, then apply a thin layer of mortar over the flanges to keep the joint in place while you set the tile.

Grouting

1. Applying the first coat of sealer with a rag keeps it from going into open grout joints.

2. The author pushes a large volume of grout to make sure it is packed deep into all the joints.

3. To bridge the uneven edges between the stone tiles, a gloved palm shapes the grout into a bevel.

4. The second coat of sealer seals the grout and adds extra protection to the stone tile.

Seal Tile Before You Grout

After all the tile is in, but before it's grouted, I give the floor a thorough cleaning. I not only wash the surface of the tile, but I also remove any thinset that is too high in the joints between the tiles. The thinset should be at least 1/8 in. below the surface of the tile.

After the tile is clean, I wipe the first of two coats of sealer onto the tile with a rag to avoid getting sealer into joints. I prefer Miracle Sealants Porous Plus (800-350-1901; www.miraclesealants.com). Because slate is porous and has an irregular surface, the sealer makes cleaning off grout easier.

To spread the grout and push it deep into the joints, I begin with the grout trowel at a 30° angle. Next, I scrape the residue off the tiles with the trowel at a 60° angle. Finally, I remove excess grout by dragging the trowel across the tiles and joints at a 45° angle to avoid pulling the grout out of the joints. Because of the uneven edges of the slate tile, I use the palm of my hand to bevel the grout between tiles as I spread it.

After the grout has set up, I wipe down the tile with terrycloth to remove grout crumbs. Then I clean the tile with cool, clean water and a sponge. Cleaning requires extra diligence to remove all the grout from the uneven surface of the slate. Finally, after I've finished cleaning the floor, I let it sit for 24 to 48 hours, then apply a second coat of sealer with a sponge. On a large floor, I usually use a pump sprayer on the final coat.

High-Traffic Tile Floor

By Tom Meehan

There aren't many rooms in a house that get more foot traffic than a foyer. On this particular job, the foyer has two interior doorways, a front door, and a stairway. Add in a family of four and a pair of very active dogs, and this floor will see some abuse. I always try to provide a tile job that will stand the test of time, but when I'm told by a customer that durability is the biggest priority, I pull out all the stops.

This is an old house, and even though the plank subfloor was topped with ½-in. plywood, I decided to top off the subfloor with an uncoupling membrane to provide additional crack resistance. The handmade, Arts and Crafts–style 8×8 tiles chosen by the customer have a naturally imperfect look, so I wasn't worried about them showing signs of wear and tear. Modern stain-resistant grouts do a pretty good job of living up to their name, but when it comes to resisting muddy shoes and dirty dog paws, nothing is as stain resistant and rock solid as epoxy grout.

Prevent Cracks with a Membrane

Too many tile floors are doomed from the start because of poorly prepped subfloors. Antifracture membranes, sometimes called crack-isolation membranes or uncoupling membranes, are sheet coverings that are applied on top of the subfloor or slab before the tile is installed. The main purpose of these membranes is to prevent any expansion, contraction, or flexing in the structure from leading to failed grout joints or loose and cracked tiles.

START WITH A DRY FIT. The orientation and size of each piece of Ditra mat don't matter. Just cut them to fit with a knife or scissors, tracing the location of each piece onto the subfloor with a permanent marker.

BURNISH, THEN COMB. Working in the sections marked out in the previous step, spread thinset and burnish it into the wood with the straight edge of a ¼-in. square-notch trowel to ensure a good bond. Comb out the cement with the notched side of the trowel until it's an even thickness, with ridges eventually going in the same direction.

POSITION WITH CARE. Don't make contact with the thinset until the Ditra is properly positioned. Hold the piece above where it will be installed, then align one end and work your way toward the other end, making sure to stay on layout.

BOND IT WITH PRESSURE. To ensure a flat surface and a good bond with the thinset below, use a wooden mason's float to push out any bubbles. Start near the center of each piece, and work toward the edges. Use your body weight to lean into the float.

Get Rid of Bounce

Jump up and down in the middle of the floor to see if it will flex; then, if possible, look at the floor framing from the basement. Bottom line: If the floor isn't structurally sound, do not install tile on it, no matter what anyone says.

Continued ➜

Plan Around Focal Points

One of the easiest ways to spot an amateur tile job is to look at the layout. Beginners tend to start with a full tile on one side of the room and cut the last row to fit, no matter how awkward the resulting sliver of tile. If done well, you should never even notice the layout; it should just "go away." To achieve that, plan the layout around focal points while also hiding cuts and out-of-square walls as much as possible. Each space is different, and some are trickier than others. Here's how this room played out.

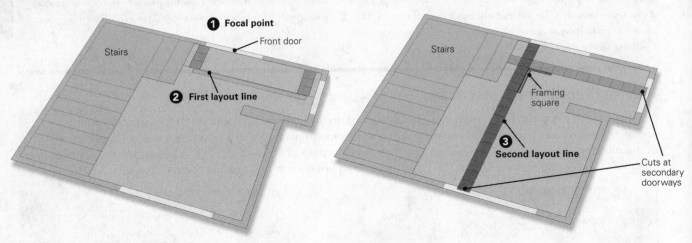

1. START WITH A FOCAL POINT. The focal point is where your eye goes first and most often. I like to start with full tiles where they will be most visible, but only if this leaves a decent remainder at the opposite wall. If the remainder is less than half of a tile, it often looks better to split the difference.

2. SET THE FIRST LAYOUT LINE. In this room, the focal point is the large front door, so I measured the length of three tiles out from the front wall of the foyer, then set a long straightedge to establish the first leg of my intended layout.

3. ESTABLISH A PERPENDICULAR LINE. With the first leg of the layout in place, I needed to project an accurate line perpendicular to this leg so that I could be sure my tiles wouldn't wander and leave me with an out-of-square floor. To find this line, I used a long straightedge in combination with a framing square.

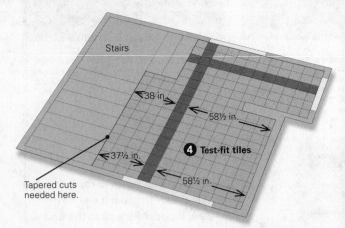

4. TEST-FIT TILES. With my two layout lines established, I worked out from those lines to see where I would need to cut around obstacles and how I would deal with any out-of-square walls. Everything looked like it would work out well, so I drew those two layout lines directly on the floor with a permanent marker. At that point, I was ready to start laying tile.

Install Tile to Stay Stuck

You've taken the time to fully prepare the subfloor, so don't get lazy with the thinset. There are different kinds of adhesives for different applications; for this project, unmodified thinset is ideal for bonding to the Ditra mat. It should be mixed so that it's firm enough to hold a paddle mixer upright for a few seconds. You also need to match the type of trowel to the tile being installed. The slightly irregular 8×8 tiles installed on this job called for a ¼-in. by ¼-in. notched trowel, which helped fill in any voids in the back of the tile for a better bond.

1. SET THE FIRST TILE. After burnishing and combing the thinset as you did under the Ditra mat, set the first tile, pushing it firmly into the cement with a ¼-in. sliding motion to ensure that it bonds well.

2. MIND THE LAYOUT. Work in sections, spreading thinset in patches only as big as you can reach across while in a kneeling position. Stop the spread just shy of the marked lines so that you don't cover them and lose track of the layout.

3. CHECK THE BOND. The best way to be sure that the tile has bonded well to the floor is to set one piece of tile and then pry it up to look at the backside. There should be even coverage of thinset across the back of the tile. Any missing spots mean that you're either not using enough thinset or spreading the thinset with the wrong trowel.

4. MARK CUTS DIRECTLY ON THE TILE. There's no need for a tape measure when determining tile cuts. Just hold the piece above where it will be set, and mark one edge with a permanent marker.

5. USE A TILE SAW FOR CUTS. A score-and-snap cutter is great for straight cuts in ceramic tile; for anything more than that, you want a decent tile saw. If you do only a few tile jobs a year, it's better to spend $40 to $60 to rent a good saw than $100 to buy a piece of junk.

6. MIND THE GAP. The author aims for tiles to leave no more than a ¼-in. gap where they meet the wall. Any more than that, and you'll be wasting grout where it's not needed and taking a risk that the baseboard molding will not conceal the gap.

Not Just Any Thinset Will Do.

The thinset you use has to be compatible with the substrate you're applying it to. The basic rules of thumb are to use latex-modified thinset with plywood or HardieBacker, and unmodified thinset with concrete or with cement backerboard.

Continued ➡

Work Your Way Out of the Room

With the layout locked in, the rest of the job is just a matter of keeping an eye on the grout joints and filling in tiles as you work your way toward an interior exit from the room. Every room is different, but you always want the last tiles you set to be the ones closest to a doorway or other exit.

KEEP MATERIALS CLOSE AT HAND. To avoid a lot of up and down, keep a stack of tiles, a bucket of thinset, and a sponge nearby.

CLEAN AND SEAL AS YOU GO. You won't be able to walk across the tile until the thinset has set up, so now is your chance to keep the surface neat. After laying tile in each section, wipe the surface with a tile sponge and as little water as possible, then apply a coat of sealer. The sealer is especially important when grouting stone tile or tile with a flat finish.

USE YOUR EYE, NOT TILE SPACERS. Some tile installers use temporary spacers to ensure a consistent layout, but with handmade tiles like these, the variations in size and squareness of each piece make the spacers useless. Lay a small section, then adjust the tiles until the joints look even. When you get to doorways, use a level or a piece of wood as a guide to ensure a straight edge.

Finish Strong with Epoxy Grout

The grouting process for epoxy is basically the same as with conventional grout—pack the joints firmly, but leave as little excess as possible—only the stakes are a bit higher. You need to work quickly and clean off excess grout thoroughly before it sets up, being mindful that setup time can vary based on temperature. Once the grout sets up, it sets up for good.

CLEAR THE WAY FOR GROUT. The next day, after the thinset has hardened, use a utility knife to loosen any chunks of cement from between tiles, and then vacuum the whole floor.

KNOW THE ABCS OF MIXING. Combine part A and part B, the pouches of liquid epoxy, in a clean bucket. Mix the two liquids together with a margin trowel, and then add part C, the carton of colored filler.

TAKE THE RIGHT ANGLES OF ATTACK. Spread the grout, and push it into the tile joints using a premium quality rubber float held at a 30° angle to the floor. After switching the float angle to 60°, scrape off the excess, being careful not to dig into the side of the joints.

CLEAN AND SHINE. The grout kit includes two packets of powder that are added to water to create a cleaning solution. About 15 to 20 minutes after the grout has been applied, use the first solution and a thoroughly wrung-out sponge to clean off the remaining residue. Follow up with the second cleaning solution, and finish by buffing away any haze with a lint-free cloth.

Don't Grout More Than You Can Clean.

I find Laticrete's portioned kits of Spectralock epoxy to be the most user-friendly. Don't try to mix several batches at once, though, or you'll risk the first parts setting up before you've had a chance to wipe them clean. Instead, mix, spread, and clean one batch at a time.

A Fearless Approach to Epoxy Grout

By Tom Meehan

For the past 25 years, tilesetters have been relying on epoxy grout as their ace in the hole for grouting stain-prone areas such as countertops, showers, and high-traffic bathroom floors. The early forms of epoxy grout quickly earned the material a reputation for being difficult and messy. I can attest to that fact, too. Epoxy grout used to be tricky to mix and difficult to spread, and the smell always left me feeling sick by day's end. Unless the mixture was perfect, the temperature was fixed, and the moon was in alignment with Saturn and Pluto, the goopy grout would sag in wall joints and settle below the edges of floor tiles. The cleanup, which was unforgiving in every sense of the word, often concluded with my work clothes being tossed in the garbage. If you can approach the material with an open mind, though, I think you will find that today's epoxy-grout products have changed for the better.

Several manufacturers make epoxy grout, and although their products differ slightly, all have significantly simplified the installation process. The Laticrete product I use is sold in kits, which include individually measured components that ensure the right mix every time. A pair of gloves in each bucket guards against the temptation to work unprotected, packaged additives make cleanup easier, and a fresh sponge means less chance of leaving yellow bits of debris in cured joints. If you throw in your own grout float and heed the advice offered here, a smooth installation is in the bag.

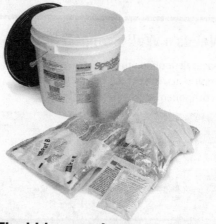

The kit's a good start

The kit shown includes most of the materials you need for a smooth installation. Part C, which adds color, is sold separately. If you choose another brand, make sure to have these essentials.

BUCKET If the epoxy-grout kit doesn't come in a bucket, you will need one. Be sure to wash out remaining grout before using the bucket for cleanup.

FLOAT Some manufacturers offer special epoxy-grout floats, which are made from a harder rubber. I've found that a premium-quality traditional float (a new one, preferably) is a fine substitute.

GLOVES Epoxy chemicals aren't just messy. They also can irritate your skin. Kits include thin latex gloves, but I prefer slightly thicker grouting gloves.

MIXING TOOLS I use a margin trowel for mixing small batches of grout, but if the job requires a large portion, I use a drill-powered paddle mixer. Clean tools right after mixing.

RAGS Avoid materials such as terrycloth towels that could leave fuzz in the grout joints; a clean cotton cloth is the best bet.

SPONGE Don't risk being left with yellow sponge crumbs in cured grout joints. Use a new sponge for every installation.

Continued ➜

Epoxy Grout Needs a Well-Prepped Surface

Now that the necessary supplies are close at hand, there are a few housekeeping items to check off the list before mixing the epoxy components.

CLEAN THE JOINTS. Use a utility knife or the edge of a margin trowel to remove any hardened chunks of thinset from the tile. Nothing in the joints should be within ⅛ in. of the tile surface.

VACUUM THE JOINT. This step is often skipped, but it's a must. Any dust or small specks of debris left on the floor will appear in the grout joints. The tacky epoxy makes debris difficult to remove before it hardens.

SEAL THE TILE. This is especially important when grouting natural stone (two coats if the stone is extremely porous), but is also a good idea for porcelain and ceramic tile with a flat finish. Allow the sealer to dry for at least a couple of hours.

PROTECT THE AREA. Don't risk getting this stuff on your bathroom vanity, baseboard trim, door threshold, carpet, or hardwood flooring. Anything that's near the tile but is not supposed to be grouted should be masked off with painter's tape.

Once You're Mixing, the Clock Is Ticking

Expect to have about 80 minutes of working time, but don't try to beat the clock by making only partial batches of grout. If the A:B:C ratio isn't exact, the product won't perform as expected.

Part A

Part B

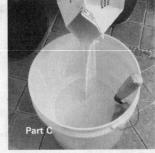

Part C

MIXING MADE EASY. Combine Part A and Part B in a clean (preferably new) bucket, mixing with a margin trowel and rolling each bag like a tube of toothpaste to squeeze out as much liquid as possible. After stirring, add Part C, the cement-based colorant. Blend all three components until the mixture has a consistency similar to sticky cake batter.

Spread Quickly, and Clean Completely

The grouting process for epoxy is basically the same as with conventional grout—pack the joints firmly, but leave as little excess as possible—only the stakes are a bit higher. Work quickly and thoroughly; recklessness will leave you with a mess.

SCOOP, SPREAD, AND SCRAPE. Use the margin trowel to scoop a small pile of grout onto the floor, and begin spreading it across the tile, holding the float at a 30° angle to the floor. Once the grout is pushed firmly into the joints, scrape off the excess, holding the float at a 60° angle to the floor. Be careful not to dig into the side of the joints, or you'll remove the grout.

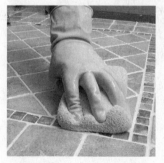

DON'T WAIT TOO LONG TO WASH. The floor should be ready to wash after about 15 to 20 minutes; much longer than that, and the epoxy begins to harden. Make sure to wring out the sponge thoroughly before scrubbing. Too much water dilutes the epoxy, making it weak and discolored.

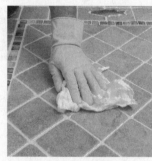

BUFF AWAY THE HAZE. After both washes have been completed, use a cotton rag to wipe off the remaining haze. Avoid pushing down too hard with the rag; buff the surface firmly, as if you were waxing a car. Don't stop wiping the surface until every bit of sticky residue is removed. If you are working your way out of the room, make sure to watch out for footprints left on the tile surface.

Replacing a Broken Tile

By Jane Aeon

It was bound to happen. The new floors have been finished for less than a week, and someone already has dropped a hammer on the kitchen's tile floor. Unless the tile guy is still on the job, you're either going to wait a long time or fix it yourself.

Luckily, it's a fairly easy fix, as long as you use the right technique. Although you can use a hammer and an old chisel to break out the damaged tile, this technique can be risky. Within grout joints tighter than 3/16 in., hammer blows can chip or crack adjacent tiles. Hammering also can pulverize the substrate beneath the damaged tile.

Occasionally, I use a hole saw to cut out the center portion of a cracked tile. This technique is good for removing soft-bodied tile. It's usually a slow process, but I'm left with a hole in the tile that makes it easy to pry with the tip of a chisel or a screwdriver.

My preferred technique, however, is to use an angle grinder outfitted with a 4-in. diamond blade and a shop vacuum. This technique is good for thick, softbodied tiles such as saltillo, but it works on others as well. The tile must be larger than 4 in., or there won't be room for a 4-in. grinder blade.

Basically, the trick is first to isolate the tile from neighboring tiles by removing the surrounding grout line, then carefully break the tile into pieces and remove it. Using a grinder can be messy unless you keep a vacuum nozzle trained on the dust stream. I mask off any surrounding cabinet faces or furniture, and also protect neighboring tiles with sheet metal or plywood in case I overcut. I mask off myself as well, donning safety glasses, a dust mask, and hearing protection.

I start by making diagonal cuts, then make separate cuts that run parallel to the edges.

The parallel cuts along the tile edges make it possible to position a chisel from the edge of a tile facing in so that the neighboring tile is not damaged. This technique is good for removing tiles with tight joints, like marble. There's also a cordless 3⅛-in. saw made by Makita with a slightly smaller diamond blade that comes in handy; I also use a Dremel tool fitted with a small #7134 diamond-point bit in the corners where the grinder can't reach.

Once the tile is removed, I scrape out any remaining thinset and vacuum the substrate. With fresh thinset and a new tile, the job is finished, except for the grouting work.

Continued ➜

Replacing a Broken Tile

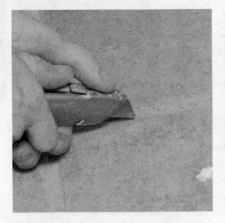

1. ISOLATE THE VICTIM. To keep the neighboring tiles intact, the first step is to score the grout lines with a utility knife. A few light passes do the trick.

2. PROTECTION IS PREVENTION. Before cutting, it's a good idea to mask off any nearby cabinets or furniture with plastic and tape. On the floor, angle brackets taped to the surrounding tiles protect them from inadvertent slips of the grinder's blade.

3. DIAGONAL CUTS OPEN UP THE TILE. With both hands firmly holding the grinder, the author carefully plunges the blade into the tile's center and cuts diagonally, then along the tile's sides. A helper holds the vacuum hose to catch the dusty exhaust.

4. A JUNKY TOOL STILL HAS ITS USES. Using a hammer and an old chisel or putty knife, the author works from the outside toward the tile's center, carefully prying out the pieces.

5. MAKE A CLEAR SPACE. After the tile is removed, all old thinset and grout are scraped from the substrate, which then is vacuumed clean.

6, BACK TO SQUARE ONE, AGAIN. After making sure the replacement tile fits, the author mixes a small batch of thinset, trowels it into the space.

7. SET THE TILE. After the thinset dries, the tile can be grouted.

Decorative Concrete Floors

By Shellie Rigsby

When I started my business, decorative concrete floors were still a new trend. I'll never forget walking onto my first paying job carrying my tools tucked into a yellow mop bucket. A plumber sat in the garage fitting pipe and abruptly asked, "Are you the cleaning lady?" Rather than explain that I was there to stain the concrete floors, I replied, "I am today."

The truth is that cleaning the concrete is one of the most important and time-consuming aspects of staining a concrete floor, but the old plumber still made me wonder if I was crazy for deciding to get into this business. That was almost a decade ago, and today, business is better than ever. As word spreads about the benefits of concrete floors, their popularity grows.

You can color concrete in a few different ways. Manufacturers tint ready-mixed concrete with integral pigments before it is poured, and still-wet concrete floors can be colored with powdered color hardeners. I prefer to use acid-based stains on cured concrete instead.

Staining concrete is inexpensive, and the results are a natural-looking stonelike floor. Acid-based stains create rich, variegated colors, and the effects can range from simple and understated to elaborate and artistic. Thanks to concrete floors' increasing popularity, the tools and materials you need to stain them are readily available.

Living with Concrete Floors

Although I've seen people cringe at their mention, stained-concrete floors feel surprisingly nice underfoot. The silky satin or gloss finish applied to the stained concrete has a smooth, supple glide. Homeowners in warmer climates benefit from the passive-cooling properties of concrete floors, and homeowners in colder climates appreciate their warmth when paired with a radiant-heat system.

Most of the cost of staining a concrete floor is labor, which makes this a particularly inexpensive do-it-yourself project, though you will have to rent a rotary floor machine for a couple of days and buy a good-quality garden sprayer. If you hire a professional, the cost of stained concrete is similar to installed carpet or inexpensive ceramic tile.

Continued ➜

First, the Floor Gets a Good Cleaning

To create color, acid-based stains penetrate the concrete and react with the lime. Any contaminants, like PVC glue or paint that dripped onto the floor, prevent the stain from penetrating and show in the finished floor. For this reason, the first and most important step is a thorough cleaning.

1. Although it may seem easier to hang the paper from the top down, apply tape to the lower edge of the wall first. Then use small pieces of tape every few feet along the top of the paper to hold it up.

2. Mix 1 tablespoon TSP with 1 gallon warm water, and wet the floor with the solution.

3. Use a rotary floor machine with a stiff abrasive pad to clean the floor.

TROUBLESHOOTING Wet concrete will show more contaminants. Hand-scrape anything stuck to the floor that the machine couldn't remove.

4. Vacuum the dirty solution from the floor, and neutralize the concrete with clean water. Vacuum again, and let the floor dry.

As long as they are protected by a coat of good-quality wax or sealer, stained-concrete floors are easy to maintain. Depending on the amount of traffic, rewaxing or resealing may need to be done only every two or three years. Sweeping and an occasional damp-mopping will keep the floor clean, and unlike carpet, concrete doesn't harbor allergens.

However, staining concrete is an unpredictable process. Because it involves a chemical reaction, guaranteeing the color or pattern is impossible. Some find the variation appealing; for others, it is a drawback. Another disadvantage is that like stone floors, concrete does not absorb sound. Most homeowners use rugs and furniture to balance noise in rooms with concrete floors.

Can I Stain an Old Concrete Floor?

Acid-based stains will work on any concrete that contains lime. Although the results are more predictable with new concrete, old concrete can be stained, too. If the concrete is cracked or looks worn, these imperfections likely will show through the finish. Slight or hairline cracks are common and often resemble veins in stone. I prefer to leave these cracks to add to the character of the finished floor. If the cracks bother you, consider another flooring option because chances are that even if you fix the cracks now, new cracks eventually will appear.

A Good Scrubbing Allows the Stain to Penetrate

If I'm staining the floors in a new house, I like to do the job as soon as the house is weatherproof but before the electrical rough in is done or the drywall is hung. This way, I don't have to worry too much about damaging adjacent surfaces with cleaning products or overspray. I still mask and paper all surfaces adjacent to concrete floors, including walls, built-ins, and other flooring.

Thoroughly cleaning the concrete is one of the most important parts of this process. Drips of adhesive, drywall compound, paint, or plain old dirt will prevent stain from penetrating the concrete and reacting with the lime. The results show up in the floor as uncolored spots.

Acid-Based Stains Change the Color of the Concrete, Permanently

Unlike paint, acid-based stains do not create a film on concrete. And although they do penetrate like a wood stain, the color actually comes from a chemical reaction that takes place between the acid and the lime in the concrete. Acid-based stains are made from a mild hydrochloric-acid base and trace minerals (metal ions or metallic salts). These stains are limited to organic colors because they are produced from minerals such as copper, magnesium, phosphorous, and iron. When applied to concrete, acid-based stains permanently change its color. Therefore, the color doesn't chip, peel, or fade but wears as the concrete does.

I start by wetting the floor with a solution of trisodium phosphate (TSP) and warm water. A concentration of about 1 tablespoon TSP to 1 gallon water works well. Then I scrub the floor with a stiff-bristle pad on a rotary floor machine. I use a wet/dry vacuum to suck up the dirty water.

After the initial cleaning, I neutralize the concrete by mopping the floor with water. (Some stain manufacturers recommend neutralizing with a solution of water and baking soda.) As I mop, I look for irregularities. If you see areas that do not darken from the water or that show a noticeable pattern, check to make sure the concrete is clean.

You can use a razor scraper to remove stubborn contaminants. It doesn't happen often, but I also have resorted to using paint stripper and other solvent-based products like lacquer thinner to clean spots off concrete. No matter what, though, do not acid-wash the concrete; it can inhibit the staining process. If you use a solvent-based cleaner at this point, you'll need to neutralize the floor again, vacuum the water, and let the floor dry.

Most Floors Take Two Coats of Stain

Staining is easier than cleaning. I mix stain and water in a garden sprayer using the manufacturer's instructions and adjust the spray pattern for a light mist. This is a good time to check the color before you stain the entire floor. You often can do this in a different room where the concrete is going to be covered by carpet, tile, wood flooring, built-ins, or appliances. If not, closets are good test areas.

Spray the stain quickly in a random manner. Do not spray in a consistent pattern, because it will show in the final color and texture. First, I apply a light coat, just enough to wet the entire floor without applying so much stain that it runs or puddles, which also will show. The color appears slowly but should reach its peak two hours to four hours after application, depending on the room temperature, the mix of the concrete, and the amount of stain applied to the floor.

A second coat is not always necessary but can increase depth of color or can even the color if there is a lot of variation. This time, be sure to cover areas that are too light or that didn't get enough stain with the first coat.

As the stain reacts, it produces a chalky, oily residue. Once the stain is dry (never walk on wet stain), you should remove the residue with a scrub brush or a stiff-bristle push broom and plenty of water. As you pour water onto the floor, scrub vigorously, then vacuum the residue before it settles back into the concrete. You may need to do this more than once to remove all the residue. Allow the floor to dry overnight before sealing or waxing.

Mimic the Look of Stone with Grout Lines

To make a stained-concrete floor look more like stone or tile, you can cut shallow grooves to resemble grouted joints. The most common scoring pattern is 36-in. squares laid diagonally across a room. Because most saws cannot cut all the way up to a wall, I usually cut a border around the room where the pattern ends.

The easiest way to score a concrete floor is with a circular saw and a masonry blade set to as shallow a cut as possible (⅛ in. to 1⁄16 in.). I snap chalklines to show the pattern on the floor and use a straightedge to guide the saw.

Scoring is a dusty process. Score the concrete before cleaning the floor, and always wear a good respirator.

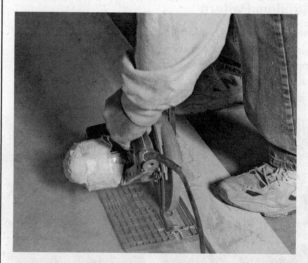

Continued ➜

A Wear Layer Is Protective and Sometimes Decorative

Concrete is porous, so you have to protect the floor from wear and discoloration. There are a few options for protecting concrete that can be used alone or in combination. Paste wax can be used alone; sealers need a finish coat, typically a floor-wax product.

On this job, I used an oil-based sealer to darken, or saturate, the color along the border. I carefully applied the sealer with a roller only around the edges of the room. Then I applied about ¼ cup of paste wax at a time and spread it with a stiff natural-bristle brush on the rotary floor machine. Each application of wax covers about 6 sq. ft. After waxing the entire floor, I switched to a soft white pad and polished the floor to a glossy sheen.

I let the wax sit for 24 hours before walking on the floor. In heavy-traffic areas, the floor may need rewaxing in a year or two. In low-traffic areas, it will last even longer.

Mist the Stain over the Floor in a Random Pattern

Acid-based stains are easy to apply with a clean plastic garden sprayer. Test the sprayer and the color in an inconspicuous spot before starting. Be cautious; the stain can be harmful to bare skin. Wear gloves, a respirator, long sleeves, and safety glasses when staining.

1. Mix the stain and water in the sprayer according to the manufacturer's instructions.

2. Mist the floor with stain in a random pattern. After the first coat has dried and color appears, apply a light second coat.

TROUBLESHOOTING If the color doesn't appear evenly, brush stain into the light areas on the second coat. Follow the brushing with one last mist of stain.

3. After the stain has reached the desired color, remove the residue with a stiff-bristle brush and plenty of water. Vacuum the water and residue from the floor.

Sealer vs. Wax

All concrete floors need a protective finish. You can use a water- or oil-based sealer, a stand-alone paste wax, or both. Consult the stain manufacturer for sealer or wax product recommendations. Here are some pros and cons for each.

Sealers

- Produce a high-gloss sheen.
- Have a good nonslip rating.
- Are chemical resistant.
- Are easy to apply with a roller or a sprayer.
- Can be used indoors or outdoors.
- Can be used to add color to the floor or to deepen stain colors.
- Should be waxed or will need regular reapplication.
- Can scratch.

Paste Wax

- Can produce a satin or high-gloss finish.
- Penetrates into the surface and is scratch resistant.
- Is long lasting.
- Can be used to add color to the floor.
- Requires minimal maintenance.
- Can be used only indoors.
- Is not chemical resistant.
- Is labor-intensive to apply.

Protect and Polish the Stained Floor

Although the color is now permanent, the concrete still needs to be protected. Here, a sealer is used to darken the color around the border, and the entire floor is waxed for a protective wear layer.

1. Sealers can be used to protect an entire floor. Here, though, an oil-based sealer is rolled on only around the border for a decorative effect.

2. After the sealer has dried, apply a stand-alone paste wax with a rotary floor machine and a stiff natural-bristle brush. Finish by polishing the floor with a soft white polishing pad.

Contents

Painting

10 Tips to Paint Like a Pro

By Philip Hansell

As a professional painter with nearly 20 years of experience, I've developed a thriving business. Getting there hasn't been easy, though, and I've made my share of mistakes. However, I've used these mistakes to improve my technique and to seek out high-quality, problem-solving products that I now rely on for almost every job. Here, I'll share some of my favorite products and some tips for getting the best possible exterior paint job.

The 2200-sq.-ft. house featured here was in rough shape when we started, and it demonstrated that it's best not to neglect exterior painting for too long. Regular maintenance could have prevented much of the prep work and saved thousands of dollars when it came time to repaint. Because of the home's condition, we had between four and eight painters on the job for nearly two months, which pushed the clients' bill to more than $30,000. The price included removing the existing vinyl shutters; pressure-washing the entire house; scraping, priming, and painting all the trim and overhangs; stripping much of the siding down to bare wood; and painting the porches, siding, and window sashes. Finally, we painted and hung new, historically accurate wooden shutters.

In April 2008, the EPA released new rules for painting and remodeling houses that have lead-based paint. If you're a contractor and you're caught ignoring the EPA's RRP (renovation, repair, and painting) rule, you're risking your livelihood. One Connecticut-based company was recently fined more than $30,000 for violations. Homeowners doing their own work are exempt, but that doesn't mean they should disregard the requirements. If you're a homeowner planning to repaint your own house, I suggest reading up or taking a class on handling lead-based paint.

Tip 1: Scrape and Sand Before Washing

When there is a lot of scraping and sanding to do, as there was on the house featured here, we like to do it before the house is washed. Many painters make the mistake of washing first and then doing a lot of heavy sanding afterward. The dust left behind makes it hard for the paint to bond. After the scraping and sanding are done and the house has been washed, check all scraped areas to make sure the washing didn't loosen any more paint.

Tip 2: Stick to Low Pressure When Washing

We add about a tablespoon of dish soap to our mix of TSP (trisodium phosphate) and bleach. Dish soap creates suds that help the solution to cling to the siding and trim instead of running off the house. Then we rinse the house with a pressure washer on a low setting. Never use high pressure, which can force water into the wood and damage siding and windows.

Continued →

Windows get extra attention. With the glazing putty replaced and the window scraped and primed, the author's crew fills screw holes left by the old shutters with auto-body filler. The patches are then sanded with 150-grit paper and primed.

Tip 3: Cover Plants, Cars, and Exterior Light Fixtures

We use lightweight canvas drop cloths to cover plants. They don't break branches, and they let the plants breathe. Plastic covers can heat up like a greenhouse and kill plants. We cover lights, windows, and doors with Cling Cover plastic. Unlike with traditional poly sheeting, tape sticks well to the slightly textured surface. This material comes in 9-ft. by 400-ft. rolls. Automobile covers are one of those inexpensive touches that show our clients we do quality work and care about their possessions.

Tip 4: Consider Special Primers Instead of Whole-House Paint Removal

If we are working on a house that has old oil-based paint that is peeling and cracking badly and complete removal is not an option, we like to use XIM Peel Bond primer. It's a high-build, clear acrylic primer that can be applied up to 30 mils thick. It's great at leveling cracked surfaces, and it costs two-thirds less than stripping down to bare wood. We used this product on the porch ceilings and on the second story of the house shown here as a way to make the project more affordable. We stripped the lower part of the house down to bare wood so that it would have a flawless finish at eye level.

Tip 5: The Right Tool Makes All the Difference

With the EPA's new RRP rule for dealing with lead-based paint in effect, we had to rethink how to prepare surfaces that test positive for lead. When we were introduced to the Festool sander/vacuum

Sometimes You Have to Start from Scratch

On old houses, paint can be in such rough shape that complete removal is the only way to go. We like a stripping product called Peel Away, which has the consistency of joint compound **(1)**. We apply it with a mud knife in a ¼-in.-to ⅝-in.-thick coat **(2)**, then cover it with the waxy paper included with the product **(3)**. We leave it covered for 12 to 72 hours, checking it about three times a day until we see that it has worked its way through all the layers of paint. After scraping off the softened paint onto 6-mil plastic with a putty or taping knife **(4)**, we apply with pump sprayers the neutralizer that comes with the product **(5)**. We work it in with stiff nylon brushes, let the wood dry for a couple of days, then neutralize and scrub again. The final step is a scrub and rinse with clear water. After the wood is dry, we check the pH with a test strip. If the pH is too high, we go through the neutralization process again. Once neutralization is complete, it's important to check the wood's moisture content before priming. Anything below 15% is acceptable. Peel Away is labor intensive, but when done correctly, it gives great results. On this house, we used it on the siding up to the bottom of the second-story windows.

combo by a local cabinet builder, I was really impressed, but I was hesitant to buy one because of the price (more than $1000). The tool works so effectively, though, that after we bit the bullet on the first one, we ordered two more soon after. Now we use all three every day on lead jobs. The vac's EPA-approved HEPA filter captures 99.97% of particles down to 0.3 microns. We love that these vacuums protect our employees from lead exposure and reduce our cleanup time. In fact, we like them so much that we plan to buy six more this year.

Tip 6: Pick the Right Primer

With so many primers out there, it's easy to get confused about which one to use. We almost always use a slow-drying oil-based primer for exterior wood. Because it dries slowly, it has time to penetrate the wood and provides the best base for all types of paint. Many people think that if they are going to use latex paint, then they must use latex primer, which is incorrect. As long as the primer has time to dry, it's perfectly fine to topcoat with latex paint. For fiberglass and PVC trim that needs to be painted, we've had good success with an adhesion primer. One often-overlooked step is to wipe these materials with denatured alcohol to remove any manufacturing oils before priming. When priming new wood, watch out for mill glaze. I've heard carpenters and painters say they don't believe in mill glaze, but if the wood appears shiny or

especially smooth or if it's been in the sun for a few weeks, sand it lightly before priming. For more on primers, see "What's the Difference: Primers" online at finehomebuiling.com.

Tip 7: Allow Extra Time for Painting Windows

When painting old windows, it's best to remove loose glazing putty and peeling paint and then reglaze where needed. It's OK to leave portions of old glazing putty if they're well adhered. Once the glazing putty is dry (we like to wait two to three weeks), we mask the perimeter of the window with 1½-in.-wide blue tape, which protects the glass from scratches and speeds up priming and painting. After masking, we sand all the wood and old glazing, then wash the window with a solution of TSP, bleach, and detergent. We let it sit for 10 to 15 minutes, then rinse the window with clear water. After the window is dry, we prime the sash and glazing putty with a slow-drying oil-based primer. Once the primer is dry, we sand the wood lightly, caulk where needed, and apply the first coat of paint. Then we pull off the tape and clean the glass with spray-on glass cleaner and paper towels. For the final coat, we lap the paint ¹/₁₆ in. onto the glass. This prevents water from getting behind the glazing putty, which is what causes the putty to fail. Before the paint dries, we open and close the window a few times to prevent it from becoming sealed shut with paint.

Continued ➡

Tip 8: Wrap Up Painting by Early Afternoon in the Fall and Spring

Surfactant leaching is something that most people haven't heard about but have probably seen. It occurs when ingredients in the paint leach to the surface as a result of moisture. It's common in the fall and spring with their warm days and cool nights. At night, condensation forms on the paint film; then the water breaks down the water-soluble components in the paint and brings them to the surface. When the water evaporates, it leaves behind a waxy-looking area that usually wears off on its own, but it's hard to convince a customer of this. To prevent surfactant leaching, we stop painting around 1 p.m. in the spring and fall. We do surface prep in the early morning, paint from late morning to shortly after lunch, and then resume prep work until the end of the day. This process takes longer, but it avoids problems.

Tip 9: There's a Quick Fix for Sticky Doors and Windows

Have you ever tried to open a cabinet door that feels like it is glued shut? This condition is known as blocking, and it is common on places where cured latex paint tries to stick to itself, such as on wood windows, painted doors without weatherstripping, and garage doors. Most exterior paints are not resistant to blocking, so we apply a thin coat of clear Briwax to window sashes, garage-door panels, and places where doors meet door stops.

Tip 10: Don't Forget Home Maintenance

Most people think that if they clean their gutters twice a year, they've maintained their home. We recommend that our customers hire us to wash their homes every other year and to have us check the caulking and touch up the paint where needed. We have customers who have 11-year-old paint jobs that look nearly new. The cost for this service can add years to a paint job and costs the fraction of a new one. I've seen something simple like cracked caulking between trim and a windowsill ruin many window frames. These costly repairs could have been avoided with a tube of caulk and a few minutes of work.

DIY One Side at a Time

If you are a homeowner trying to tackle a large exterior paint job yourself, my first advice is to set plenty of short-term goals. If you set out to paint the exterior of your house without a plan, you're going to run out of steam or end up hating painting. I recommend working on one side of the house at a time, preferably starting on the least visible elevation. This will give you time to develop your technique and to perfect your painting skills. If you're like me, there are probably a few projects around the house that you haven't finished, so you don't want to add exterior painting to the list.

With such a long-term project, you're likely to get rained out on occasion. I suggest keeping some work in reserve, such as prepping and painting shutters and sashes, that you can do in the garage or basement on rainy days. Make sure to protect yourself and your family from lead paint by avoiding any dry-sanding or scraping and by keeping a neat work area free of paint chips.

How to Tackle a DIY Whole-House Paint Job

1. Remove all shutters and storm windows or screens.
2. Remove all loose window glazing.
3. Glaze the windows where needed.
4. Scrape and sand the overhangs.
5. Wash and prime the overhangs.
6. Scrape and sand the siding.
7. Wash and prime the siding.
8. Scrape and sand the windows, doors, and trim.
9. Wash and prime the windows, doors, and trim.
10. Scrape and sand the shutters.
11. Wash the shutters.
12. Wash, prime, and paint the shutters.
13. Caulk.
14. Paint the overhangs.
15. Paint the siding.
16. Paint the windows, doors, and trim.
17. Clean the windows.
18. Hang the storm windows or screens.
19. Hang the shutters.

NOTE: If you are going to try Peel Away, do a test spot first, because sometimes it works in hours and sometimes it takes days. Don't apply more than you can remove in one day. Letting the wood sit bare for a couple of months isn't a problem unless you live in an area with a lot of rainfall. If the wood is going to be bare for weeks or months, tack up some 6-mil plastic to protect it. When we need to protect bare siding from rain, we wrap the plastic around a 2×4 and screw it to the house. We keep the plastic rolled up as much as possible so that the wood under it can dry, and we let it down only when there is a good chance of rain.

Paint in the Right Order

Sometimes it's hard to know where to start on an exterior paint job. Below are outlines that show how we paint homes in good condition and homes that have been neglected.

Home with Minor Peeling

1. Remove the shutters and screens.
2. Wash the exterior, shutters, and screens.
3. Scrape all loose paint and glazing putty.
4. Replace any rotten wood.
5. Sand all scraped areas.
6. Spot-prime all bare wood.
7. Apply caulk and glazing putty where needed.
8. Brush all overhangs and high trim.
9. Paint all siding.
10. Paint the windows, doors, and trim.
11. Paint the porch floors.
12. Hang the shutters and screens.

Home with Major Peeling

1. Remove the shutters and screens.
2. Scrape all loose paint and glazing putty.
3. Sand where needed.
4. Wash the exterior, shutters, and screens.
5. Check the scraped areas, and sand where needed.
6. Replace any rotten wood.
7. Prime all wood.
8. Apply caulk and glazing putty where needed.
9. Paint all shutters.
10. Brush all overhangs and high trim.
11. Paint all siding.
12. Paint the windows, doors, and trim.
13. Paint the porch floors.
14. Hang the shutters and screens.

Sashes must look good inside and out. The last step in painting windows is to scrape excess paint from the glass and to give it a thorough cleaning. If the window sticks because of the recent paint job, the sides of the frame are given a coat of paste wax.

Continued →

All About Brushes

By Cody Hall and Don Burgard

Bristle Shape

Paintbrush tips can be angled or flat. A flat-tipped brush is good for flat surfaces with no obstructions, such as horizontal siding. Although many pros use angled brushes for painting flat surfaces, they are more often used for cutting in and for covering areas, such as window muntins, that require precision. The best brushes have tapered filaments of various lengths that hold paint throughout the brush and release it smoothly. Look at the brush from the side. If it comes to a point at the end, it is tapered. If the thickness is the same from base to tip, it is not tapered and will not apply paint evenly and cleanly. Quality brushes also have flagged, or split, ends, which create more surface area for holding paint and leave fewer brush marks.

Ferrule

The ferrule is the metal band that protects the base of a paintbrush. Ferrules on most professional-grade brushes are made from stainless steel, nickel-plated steel, or copper-plated steel. Cheap brushes often have ferrules made of tin-plated and brass-plated steel, which are not as corrosion resistant. The rust that develops after repeated cleanings could end up staining the paint. If you need to cover a large area by brush, you may want to consider a brush with a semioval ferrule. Its larger bristle capacity makes it able to hold more paint. Regardless of the metal it's made of, a ferrule should hold the shape of the bristles.

Handle

The handles on most professional-grade brushes are made from unfinished wood, although handles made of finished wood, plastic, and other materials are available. Unfinished wood absorbs perspiration, which means the brush won't slip out of your hand. You also should consider shape: rattail, beaver tail, fluted, flowing, Shasta, block, round. The choice comes down to three related factors: comfort, balance, and size. Comfort is in the hand of the painter. Someone with a small hand might prefer a thin, light brush, while someone with a large hand might choose a wide, heavy brush. Manufacturers match handles to brushes in part to provide balance between the handles and the bristles. Better balance means more control. At times, however, size may outweigh balance. A brush with an extrashort handle, for example, may not feel balanced, but it might be just the right tool to reach a narrow corner.

Why Pay More for Paint?

By Scott Gibson

At one end of Lowe's 60-ft.-long paint aisle is a shelf stocked with Valspar Duramax exterior latex paint, $33.98 a gallon. Nearby is Olympic Premium exterior latex paint, $22.98 a gallon (figures from 2008). Is the Valspar 33% better than the Olympic? And other than price, how would a buyer know?

"Good paint and cheap paint look the same when you open the can," says Bob Welch, technical director for the Master Painters Institute. Where they differ is in the binders, pigments, and additives the manufacturer has used to make them. How long paint lasts, how easy it is to apply, and how well it hides surface imperfections all depend on its ingredients.

Even if the ingredients are listed on the label (often they're not) or on the material safety data sheet, buyers likely won't understand what they are or what they do. Still, there are ways to narrow the field. Understanding how the basic components of paint work together is a good place to start.

Latex Has Won the Paint Wars

Increasingly, house paint means latex paint. Water, rather than oils or alkyds, makes up the carrier, a liquid that disperses other ingredients into a uniform paint film. One reason for the shift toward latex paint is tougher government regulations on the amount of volatile organic compounds (VOCs) allowed in paint. Another is that latex paints perform well, especially outside, and now rival the workability of oil-based paint.

Manufacturers haven't abandoned oil paints, but that's not where their money is going. "They are not investing research-and-development dollars into alkyd technology," says Steven Revnew, marketing director at Sherwin-Williams. "It's all going into waterborne technology."

Professional painters have made the switch, too, although some prefer oil-based paints for high-wear surfaces like handrails or kitchen cabinets because they think the paint film is harder and more durable. Tim Leahy, a painter in Newport, R.I., loves the "beautiful, hard, glossy oil shine" and the way oil-based paint behaves in spray equipment. Leahy also likes exterior oil-based primer because it soaks deep into raw wood.

Leahy isn't alone, but latex paint is getting undeniably better as oil-based paint becomes harder to find. "The reasons for using oil are shrinking as each year goes by," Richmond, Va., painter Brian Doherty says, somewhat wistfully.

Binders Add Durability, Flexibility, and Sheen

Of the main ingredients in paint, the binder (also called the resin or polymer) is among the most expensive. Binders are the glue that holds the paint film together, and they are the key to durability, resistance to UV-light, color retention, flexibility, and a variety of other performance attributes that are particularly important in exterior paints. The most common binders used in latex paints are acrylic and vinyl acrylic, though styrene resins are sometimes used.

All-acrylic paints are typically more durable and more expensive than paints made with vinyl-acrylic binders. This distinction should be clearly marked on the label. Revnew calls vinyl-acrylic the "entry point" for exterior coatings. Using vinyl-acrylic instead of all-acrylic binders reduces costs, but it also lowers the paint's ability to expand and contract and to protect against damage from UV-light.

The supremacy of 100% acrylic resin is not absolute, though. Welch prefers to think of it as an indicator of quality, not a guarantee. Manufacturers can make proprietary resin blends that are just as good. Unfortunately, you might not know it from reading the label.

Resins also help to give paint its hardness and sheen. In paint-industry lingo, flat paints have a high pigment-volume concentration, or a high ratio of pigments to binders. Gloss and semigloss paints have a lower pigment-volume concentration. Because binders often cost more than pigments, glossier paints are generally more expensive.

Pigments Help Paint to Cover Effectively

Pigments give paint its color and what the paint industry calls hide, the paint's ability to cover a surface with a minimum number of coats. Prime pigments include red and yellow iron oxide, phalocyanine green or blue, and titanium dioxide. Titanium dioxide is white in color but is used in both light and dark paints. It is an important pigment because it is particularly effective at giving paint better covering qualities than low-cost bulk pigments, called extenders.

Getting the right proportion of titanium dioxide in a paint formulation is tricky. "The challenge is that more isn't always better," says Revnew. "It's really the whole pigment package. There is a certain level of titanium dioxide where you optimize hide, and adding any more is not going to make a difference."

Extenders, such as calcium carbonate, talc, silica, and clay, could cost less than prime pigments, but Welch says it would be a mistake to think their only role is to make paint less expensive to manufacture. "The proper combination of prime and extender pigments will give better performance than using only prime pigments and add properties not obtainable with prime pigments alone," Welch says.

Taken together, pigments and resins make up most of paint's solids, the materials that form the film when the carrier has evaporated. One old chestnut in the paint industry is that higher solids content predicts a better-performing paint. Is at least this much true?

"It can be," says Jim Stange, senior brand manager at ICI Paints, which manufactures several brands. "It's one of the things that indicate quality. Paint solids are one thing, but thickness (viscosity) and ease of application also are important."

Continued →

Inside the House

Most rooms require at least three different types of paint, one for the ceiling, one for the walls, and one for the trim. Color is an important factor, but so is sheen. Kitchens and baths have requirements all their own.

Walls

If durability and scrubbability are priorities, choose a higher sheen. Higher sheens typically mean better wear resistance and washability, but they also show surface imperfections. Flat paints, on the other hand, hide imperfections on older walls but could develop shiny burnish marks if scrubbed. At the high end of the cost range, manufacturers are introducing lower-sheen paints with good burnish and stain resistance. Higher prices also mean better coverage and ease of application, and less splatter.

Trim

Interior trim and built-ins are two of the last strongholds for alkyd paint. Many pros love the way oil paint levels out into a glass-smooth finish before curing, and the hard paint film holdv to wear. High-end, semigloss latex paints and enamels are starting to rival this performance, and regulations limiting volatile organic compounds will speed the trend.

Ceiling

Durability is not a common issue on the ceiling, so flat paints that mask surface flaws and touch up easily are preferable. Top-quality ceiling paints are more uniform in sheen and cover in fewer coats with less roller splatter. Ceiling paints that change color as they dry (from pink to white, for example) make it easy to get even coverage on a shadowy overhead surface.

Kitchens & Baths

Kitchen and bath paints are no gimmick. In these hardworking, wet rooms, durability, scrubbability, and mildew resistance are extra important. These paints have excellent wear resistance and stain-release characteristics so that surfaces can be washed without damaging the film. They're also formulated with mildewcides that block the growth of mold and mildew. Satin sheen is a good choice for the walls. Use semigloss trim paint for cabinetry, and consider using a ceiling paint with a mildewcide.

Additives Improve Workability and Performance

Additives are the last principal ingredient of paint, and they can affect everything from workability and mildew resistance to leveling, stability, and splatter control. Although additives are not high-volume ingredients, they make a big difference in performance.

Mildew resistance is especially important for exterior and kitchen and bathroom paints, and it should be clear from the label whether a particular type of paint contains a mildewcide, according to Debbie Zimmer of the Paint Quality Institute. Mildewcides are expensive to manufacture and handle, Zimmer says, so leaving this ingredient out is an easy way to save money. Really cheap exterior paint might not have one at all.

In general, consumers have no real way of knowing what additives a manufacturer has used. It's a fair bet that a com- pany's top-of-the-line exterior paint will have more additives than its economy-grade interior paint. According to Welch, when buying paint, it is important to be specific about where it will be used. For example, additives that allow exterior paint to shrink and expand with changes in moisture and temperature and that protect the color from fading aren't often important for interior paint. Paint for high-moisture areas such as bathrooms could have different additive packages than paint that won't be subjected to high humidity.

Professional painters use several aftermarket additives to increase paint's workability and performance. A favorite is Floetrol (or Penetrol for alkyd paints), a conditioner made by Flood (www.flood.com) that is used to improve flow and leveling, minimize brush and roller marks, and make it easier to use paint in spray equipment.

Don DeMair, a New Jersey pro, keeps Floetrol on hand and says it can make a big difference in extremely dry conditions when paint would set up too quickly. If he uses an additive, however, DeMair says he's careful to mix it into all the paint he's using so that sheen and color are the same from one can of paint to the next.

Packaged mildewcide can be added as further protection against mold and mildew growth. Top-quality paints might already contain this type of protection, and a mildewcide doesn't guarantee that mildew won't appear on a painted surface under the right conditions.

"I'm more of a fan of doing an extreme wash preparation before I paint," says Rhode Island pro Tim Leahy. He uses a commercial cleaner like Jomax (www.zinsser.com) and believes that starting with a clean, mildew-free surface is probably the best insurance.

Virginia painter Brian Doherty, however, uses a mildewcide if he thinks it will help. "If I can see that mildew is a recurring problem, I will go ahead and use a mildewcide no matter how good the paint itself is, just as a backup," he says.

Although additives can be helpful, the paint industry doesn't

Warranties

Written warranties are an indication of the manufacturer's confidence in the paint's durability, and therefore are a good measure of overall quality. Warranties range from a year or two all the way up to a "lifetime," typically meaning for as long as the paint buyer owns the house.

Duration, a top exterior paint from Sherwin-Williams, for example, is warranted not to blister or peel for as long as the purchaser owns the home. If the paint film does fail, the company says it will provide enough paint to fix the problem or will refund the original purchase price.

The catch, of course, is that you'll have to provide proof of purchase if you want to file a claim. And manufacturers don't pay for the labor required to prep the surface and apply a new coat of paint. Also, the deal is off if the surface has been improperly prepped or if the paint has been applied incorrectly.

Lifetime warranties from other manufacturers are similar for the best (and most expensive) paints in their lines. The warranties are generally not transferable to a new owner.

Whatever the fine print says, longer warranties are typically a sign of better-quality paint.

universally recommend them. Zimmer says that additives have the potential to hamper paint performance, especially when used in excess. "While you may be able to apply the paint better and have it open longer, down the road that paint may not perform as well as you expected," she says.

The best advice is probably to use additives judiciously, and never in higher concentrations than recommended by the manufacturer. As Zimmer puts it, if it's 100°F outside and the paint dries on the brush before you can apply it, maybe it's not the best day to be painting.

Everyone Agrees That You Get What You Pay For

While consumers have little way of knowing exactly what's in a can of paint, both the paint industry and paint professionals say price is a good indicator of quality. "The do-it-yourselfer can most often identify the top-of-the-line paint by a top-of-the-line price." says Zimmer. "Purchase your favorite manufacturer's paint, but always ask for the highest price point because in a can of paint, you will absolutely get what you pay for."

Pros agree. "It definitely matters," says Leahy. "Quality is there with the higher-priced paints. You get what you pay for. If you go to a big-box store and buy cheap paint and apply it, you're going

Continued →

Outside the House

The preparations that go into exterior painting are grueling tasks. Don't let your hard work go to waste by choosing inadequate paint. When in doubt, stick with mildew-resistant, 100% acrylic paint.

Siding
Choose all-acrylic water-based formulations over those made with vinyl-acrylic or styrene binders, but keep in mind that some manufacturers use proprietary ingredients that might not be listed on the label. Higher prices buy better grades of binders and additives that offer higher mildew and UV-resistance, better color retention, and more film flexibility to reduce cracking and peeling. Expect to pay $20 to $55 per gallon.

Trim
As is the case with siding paint, all-acrylic latex trim paint lasts longer than other blends and endures seasonal wood movement. For decorative purposes, trim paints often have slightly more gloss than siding paint. But more gloss also translates to higher durability. Expect to pay $20 to $55 per gallon.

Floors
Few surfaces take as much abuse as a floor. More expensive paints that are labeled specifically for porches and floors have all the characteristics of other exterior paints plus increased abrasion resistance and better adhesion. Expect to pay $25 to $50 per gallon..

to be repainting your house in 500 days."

In the end, buyers will do well by sticking with a brand they've come to trust, or by relying on recommendations from a professional. Whether it's Benjamin Moore, Sherwin-Williams, Pittsburgh, or Farrow & Ball, you can be sure that it won't be their cheap stuff.

One other thing: Even the most expensive paint will fail if you don't prepare the surface properly. "If you do proper prep and the surface is ready to go, sometimes that cheaper paint might do OK," says Leahy. "But if you do a lousy prep job, it's going to fail."

Painting the Way to Better Air Quality

What's coming out of paint is just as important these days as what's going into it. Government regulations and a push for healthy indoor-air quality are driving down the levels of volatile organic compounds (VOCs) allowed in paint.

VOCs, the solvents that waft into the air as paint dries, are a contributor to smog. Rules in effect nationally allow 380 grams of VOCs per liter (g/l) in nonflat paints and 250 g/l in flat paints. (Specialty paints have higher limits.)

In two regions of the country, however, the regulations are less forgiving. The Ozone Transport Commission, which writes model regulations for 11 states in the Mid-Atlantic and Northeast, limits VOCs in nonflat paints to 150 g/l and flat paints to 100 g/l. Rules in the South Coast Air Quality Management District, covering parts of the Los Angeles area of California, are even tougher. The national rules are due to stiffen in 2009.

Manufacturers are already producing low- and no-VOC paints, but there's a catch: Government VOC rules apply to the tint base, not to the colorant added at the paint store. Further, national rules cover only VOCs that contribute to smog while exempting potentially harmful chemicals such as acetone and limonene, a powerful citrus solvent.

Both latex and alkyd paints have traditionally been tinted with universal colorants, and their contribution to the total VOC content of paint can be "significant," says Carl Minchew, director of product development at Benjamin Moore. How much, exactly, depends on the color and the volume of tint added at the store, but Minchew says it's possible that a colorant could push paint over the allowed threshold for VOCs even though the tint base itself falls within the guidelines.

Benjamin Moore and ICI are among manufacturers that have developed new types of colorants that do not add VOCs to paint. Benjamin Moore's is called Gennex, which goes into its Aura line of latex paints. ICI's no-VOC colorant can be found in its Freshaire paints. A number of smaller companies also have developed no-VOC and low-VOC paints.

At least three organizations set green standards for paint— Green Seal, Greenguard, and the Master Painters Institute (MPI)—and they list certified products on their Web sites.

Green Seal's certification requirements (called GS-11 standards) cover several performance standards as well as limit VOC content and ban some chemicals altogether (www. greenseal.org). Green Seal's revised rules released earlier this year cap VOCs at 100 g/l for nonflat and 50 g/l for flat paints. By 2010, GS-11 standards also will cover colorants added at the point of sale.

Greenguard takes a different approach, measuring chemical emissions from applied paint rather than setting limits on what's in the can. As a result, its standards already measure the effect of colorants (www .greenguard.org).

MPI, which also writes performance standards for paint for the U.S. and Canadian governments, maintains a list of approved green products at its Web site (www.paintinfo.com).

Air-emission standards are becoming increasingly important for builders trying to meet green-building requirements, such as those of the LEED for Homes program, a set of criteria that covers a long list of construction and performance issues. When it comes to paint, LEED for Homes uses Green Seal's GS-11 rules.

There's No Escaping the Scraping

By Hugh Schreiber

When it comes to exteriors, the word painting can be misleading because it refers only to the last step of an important process. Although this deception can come in handy when luring your friends into servitude (hint: the shrewd recruiter never says, "Want to help me scrape my house this weekend?"), it leaves a lot to interpretation where prep work is concerned.

If exterior paint has a job, it is to protect a house from the damaging effects of sun, wind, and rain, and look good doing it. If you fail to provide paint with good working conditions, like any employee, it will become flaky and quit. Properly applied paint can last for years, but don't expect it to seal cracks, stop peeling layers beneath it, or stick to damaged wood.

A lot has to happen before a house is ready for paint, and one of the biggest challenges is making sure that the work all gets done efficiently and in the right order. The sequence is always the same: clean, scrape, sand, repair, prime, and caulk.

I try to work in one direction around the house, but logistics and weather conditions sometimes dictate where and when I decide to do certain things. This can get confusing. For me, the best way to keep track of progress and to make sure nothing is missed is to make a simple line drawing of the exterior, then divide the house into manageable numbered sections. This map becomes the daily to-do list that helps me to assign tasks and to keep on schedule.

Use a Pressure Washer, But Let the Soap Do the Work

The first thing on the to-do list is to wash the entire house to remove dirt, mold, mildew, and other contaminants that can interfere with paint adhesion. A pressure washer can scour walls clean and even strip peeling paint, but I don't use it this way. At close range, a pressure washer can damage the house and drive water deep into the walls. Because trapped moisture is a leading cause of paint failure, I use the pressure washer only to apply soap and to rinse.

The hard work is actually done by the detergent, which is a blend of warm water, bleach, and trisodium phosphate (TSP), a strong cleanser that is available in powder form at any paint or hardware store. Ready-made house-washing products that don't contain bleach or phosphates are easy to find at any paint store, but I like the TSP-and-bleach combination because it kills mildew and cuts through contaminants to leave a dull, etched surface that is ready for repainting.

I mix the detergent with 1 cup of bleach and 1 cup of TSP for each gallon of water. You also can add a couple of tablespoons of powdered laundry or dish soap to help with rinsing. In the siphon mode on my pressure washer, water combines with detergent at a 4-to-1 ratio, so I make the mix four or five times stronger.

At this concentration, the TSP is a powerful deglosser, great for prep but bad for the finish on your car and sensitive body parts.

I protect plants, trees, and shrubs with drop cloths; saturate the ground with water; and wear goggles, gloves, and a raincoat when washing. I'm very cautious if I have to use a ladder. The detergent makes things slippery, and the gun can have a powerful kick.

I wet each part of the house before applying the detergent. Although I mostly work from the ground, I keep the spray at the lowest possible angle and pressure to avoid driving water under the siding while still reaching the highest parts of the house. I don't spray directly at the edges of windows and doors; I hand-scrub these and other dirty areas if necessary.

The detergent needs time to work, so I move ahead in 10-minute intervals before going back to rinse from the top down. In hot weather, it may be necessary to resoap after five minutes to keep the detergent from drying on the surface. I check the results by running my palm over the dry surface. If the house feels slippery or leaves residue on my hand, it needs to be washed and rinsed again.

Scraping Paint Is No Fun, But It Must Be Done

Peeling paint can be caused by a number of conditions, including wood movement, moisture problems, and the buildup of excess

Continued ➔

Follow the Rules of Lead-Paint Safety

If your house was built before 1978, there is a 75% chance that it contains lead paint. Undisturbed lead paint is harmless, but dust or paint chips created during paint prep or other remodeling projects pose health hazards, especially to young children. The EPA recommends professional testing, which can cost a few hundred dollars. If that money is not in your budget, you can purchase a home testing kit at a hardware store (www.leadinspector.com; 800-268-5323). And the National Lead Information Center (800-424-5323) has a list of accredited testing labs where you can send paint samples for testing. The center's pamphlet Lead Paint Safety: A Field Guide for Painting, Home Maintenance and Renovation Work is available for free online (www.hud.gov/offices/lead/training). For more information on lead-paint safety, log on to www.nsc.org, the National Safety Council's Web site, or www.epa.gov/lead to find local abatement firms.

paint in low spots and corners. While washing a house, I look for peeling paint, which presents one of the most daunting prep tasks: scraping.

There are many different methods for paint removal, from chemical strippers to power tools. If I'm sure that a house contains lead paint (sidebar opposite; and "Lead-Paint Safety," *Fine Homebuilding* #150), I use only hand scrapers and remove as little paint as possible.

Hand-scraping is arguably the worst job in all the trades, but a few tips can make it a little less painful. First, always work with a sharp scraper blade. A good two-handed carbide-blade scraper is a must-have for any paint-scraping enthusiast. Because there's actually no such thing as a paint-scraping enthusiast, most people end up using the more-common, less-expensive mild steel-blade scrapers. Steel replacement blades are inexpensive, but they dull so quickly that I often resharpen them on the job with a belt sander. With practice, you can tell when a scraper becomes too dull just by listening. A properly sharpened blade makes a distinct hissing sound as it cuts. Sharp scrapers also leave a feathered edge where successive layers of paint can be seen receding from the bare wood.

A typical scraper has a long handle and a large, flat knob behind the blade. I've seen people use this knob to push and pull the blade vigorously over the surface as if they were scratching an itch. Like a lawn-mower blade, however, a scraper is designed to work in one direction only. Two-handed scrapers must be pulled toward the body. Pushing dulls the blade, gouges the wood, and wears you out.

After scraping, the remaining paint should be able to pass the "fingernail test": Its edge can't be lifted with your fingernail. Once an area is scraped successfully, it's time to sand.

Sanding Smooths the Surface

The main objective in the sanding process is to smooth the transitions from painted wood to bare wood. This allows for an even film thickness when primer and paint are applied.

I use 80-grit sandpaper and an orbital sander to soften the sharp transition scraping leaves between paint and bare wood.

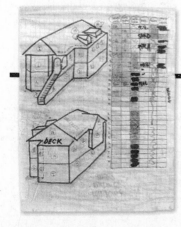

Dirty Areas May Need to Be Scrubbed by Hand

Use a pressure washer to scrub a house, and you're asking for trouble. Instead, use it to apply detergent with light pressure, and rinse the house after the detergent has had 10 minutes to work. If the house is still dirty, consider hand-scrubbing.

Homemade House-Wash Solution

This solution will cut through dirt, mold, and mildew. When applying this solution with a pressure washer, make sure to adjust the concentration for the machine's water-to-detergent ratio.

- 1 cup of TSP
- 1 cup of bleach
- 1 gallon of water

Use a scrub brush around windows and doors and on excessively dirty areas, but unlike this guy, wear gloves when you do. Scouring with a pressure washer can damage siding and force water into walls.

Stand back and rinse. Keep the pressure and the spray angle as low as possible while rinsing the house with clean water. Check the dried surface for cleanliness and soap residue before moving on with the prep.

A Simple Drawing Organizes a Big Job and Becomes a Useful To-Do List

Preparing a house for paint is a big job with many different phases that must be done in order: wash, scrape, sand, repair, prime, and caulk. Sometimes, when tall ladders and staging are involved, it makes more sense to complete all the tasks in one area before moving on. A line drawing of the house helps to break the work into manageable sections and becomes a checklist as the job proceeds.

Continued ➡

Removing Peeling Paint Is a Two-Part Process

Most houses require scraping to remove loose paint. Unless recently primed or washed with TSP, surfaces should be sanded lightly to create a tooth for better adhesion. Edges where existing paint meets bare wood may need more extensive sanding to create a smooth, finished look.

Scrape Away the Loose Stuff With a Two-Handed Scraper.
Apply pressure to the blade with one hand and pull the scraper toward your body with the other hand.

Feather the Edges With an Orbital Sander.
Smooth the transition from painted to bare wood with 80-grit sandpaper. Use 100-grit sandpaper to promote adhesion on questionable surfaces.

Old houses usually have been painted many colors. When properly scraped and sanded, the edges of a scraped area will show a narrow rainbow of color. This sanding helps to hide an uneven surface. Whether it's new or recently scraped, I sand all bare wood to remove mill glaze (burnishing left by sawblades at the mill and pressure from the scraper blades) and the gray layer that develops on the surface.

Sanding harsh transitions is necessary, but it takes a lot more work to render a perfectly smooth surface where the siding has been peeling. To stay within a budget and limit the amount of lead paint disturbed, I often reserve the highest cosmetic standards for the money shots: the front of the house and the other highly visible areas.

This isn't cheating or poor craftsmanship. It's just being practical. As a recovering perfectionist, I've come to realize that the success of a big painting job is measured not only by the results but also by the way limitations are managed. If the exterior of the house has been neglected severely, cosmetic sanding is one area where I can make concessions to the budget without sacrificing the longevity of the paint job.

Repairs Are Part of Painting

By this point, I've seen every inch of the house, and I'm aware of all the damage. Paint will cover it up, but not for long. And I don't like to work backward.

The first repairs I make are to window sashes because new glazing can take up to two weeks to cure (see "Restoring Window Sashes," *Fine Homebuilding* #161). Next, I move on to repairing and replacing damaged trim and siding. Before priming, new wood should be seasoned until its moisture content is less than 18%. If you think wood might be too wet to be primed, you can check it with an inexpensive moisture meter. It's also a good idea to avoid flat-sawn lumber and sapwood for repair work because primer has a hard time bonding to dense grain and bleeding resin. Both sides of the wood should be primed before installation.

If a damaged board is easy to replace, I replace it. It sometimes even makes sense to flip over a cosmetically damaged board and fill the nail holes. If the damage is minimal or is part of a complicated system like a windowsill, a repair might be in order. For a tough, permanent repair that cures evenly and quickly, I use Bondo. You don't need to waste your money on a high-priced epoxy. Used correctly, Bondo will outlast us all. Paint stores also carry two-part hole fillers that work fine.

The fact is that wood repairs don't fail because of the product but because of wood movement. To keep filler from being rejected, you have to immobilize the surrounding wood by saturating the area with a resin-based treatment like Minwax Wood Hardener.

New work doesn't need repairing, but it might have nail holes to be filled. I fill nail holes with nonshrinking vinyl exterior spackle available at any paint store. If a lot of holes need to be filled, I use a wide taping blade to speed along this job and try to

Four Ways to Get the Paint Off a House

Hand Scrapers

The $30 or so you spend on a carbide-blade paint scraper is money well spent if you're painting a house that requires selective paint removal. The sharp blades cut loose paint away from the surface with ease and disturb the least amount of firmly bonded paint (a plus if lead paint is a concern). Hand-scraping paint is hard work and usually requires follow-up sanding, but it is the most common and least expensive method unless the entire house needs stripping. Mild steel-blade scrapers cost less and dull much more quickly.

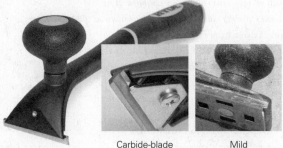

Carbide-blade scraper

Mild steel-blade scraper

Power Scrapers

Power scrapers like the Paint Shaver (www.paintshaver.com) are hundreds of dollars, but they make quick work of removing large areas of paint from flat surfaces like clapboards and shakes. A vacuum hose connected to a shop vacuum collects the paint, keeping the mess and the user's exposure to lead minimal. Nail heads hidden just under the paint are one of the weaknesses of mechanical scrapers. Corners are another.

Paint Shaver

Chemical Strippers

Ideal for removing paint from intricate details and tight spaces, most chemical strippers are brushed onto the surface and take a few hours to work. When the paint blisters or appears to be degenerating, it can be scraped gently from the surface without damaging the wood or creating a cloud of dust or pile of chips. Although this process might seem ideal for lead-paint removal, the best strippers can be bad for your health as well. Chemical strippers should be used with extreme caution.

Stronger chemical stripper

Safe chemical stripper

Heat

Electric heat guns, heat plates, and even infrared heat (www.silentpaintremover.com) are effective for loosening paint without risk of surface damage. Like chemical strippers, heat does the work and requires only a gentle scraping to remove the paint. Unfortunately, heating a surface to remove paint is a slow process and can be dangerous. The heat can create hazardous lead fumes and fire. Torches and other open flames never should be used to remove paint.

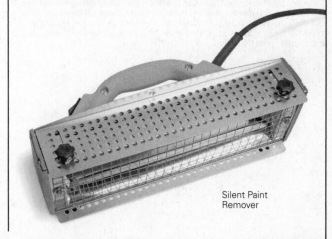

Silent Paint Remover

Continued ➔

Primer Seals the Surface and Highlights the Last of the Prep

When changing colors or painting a long-neglected house, everything should be primed. If the house is in good shape and the color change is minimal, spot-priming bare wood and repairs still is required. White primer highlights gaps that need caulk and rough surfaces that need more cosmetic sanding. Primer should be painted within two weeks, or it will need a light sanding.

If You Spray, You Have to Back-Brush.
Sprayers are a great way to apply primer to a surface, but the primer still needs to be worked into the porous wood and smoothed out when it builds up in corners and low spots. Spray only small areas at one time and go back, or have someone follow you to smooth the paint with a brush.

Caulk to Seal and Beautify.
Caulk can be used to seal gaps and prevent water from getting behind trim and siding, and it can be used to create a smooth transition between walls and trim, allowing you to cut a clean line. However, certain gaps, such as those between clapboards, are essential for allowing moisture to escape and should never be sealed.

leave just a small amount of spackle proud of the surface. Before priming, I go over the new work with a quick pass from an orbital sander.

Priming Is Almost the Last Step

Although each step is critical to the process, priming always seems most important because it locks in the progress and ends the bulk of the prep work. Primer's main purpose is to seal, unify, and bond with the various substrates so that the finish coats adhere evenly; it also highlights gaps that need caulk and areas that need further repairs.

Although I typically apply Benjamin Moore exterior latex paint as a topcoat, I spot-prime bare wood and repaired areas with a Benjamin Moore alkyd primer formulated to be compatible with both water- and oil-based finishes. The primer penetrates bare and painted wood and various fillers for an even, firmly bonded undercoat. Oil primer also helps to blend the transitions from bare to painted wood, and it even can be sanded. Freshly applied water-based primers tend to gum up when sanded.

Adhesion test. Let paint on a primed area dry overnight; then attach a piece of tape to it. Remove the tape a few minutes later. If paint sticks to the tape, the surface should be sanded lightly and rinsed.

Depending on the situation, I use rollers or a sprayer to apply primer quickly (for tips, visit www .finehomebuilding.com). Either way, the primer has to be back-brushed to even it out, to work it into porous areas, and to keep it from building up in the corners. Primer should be painted within two weeks, or it will need a light sanding to remove oxidation. To test preprimed material or surfaces primed weeks earlier, perform an adhesion test.

The last official step is caulking. The primary purpose of caulking is to seal gaps that would allow water to penetrate the house. I also use caulk selectively to smooth joints between siding and trim so that a straighter line can be cut between finish colors.

Some gaps should never be sealed. As a rule, I never caulk the bottom edge of a window casing or the horizontal spaces between clapboards. Some people insist on caulking these gaps for a clean look, but this is a mistake; they're critical to a house's ability to release moisture.

Ideally, the builder will leave behind only small gaps to be filled with caulk. When this fails, I stuff deep crevices with foam backer rod. Without it, the caulk would go in too thick and never cure fully.

A Long-Lasting Repair Ensures a Long-Lasting Paint Job

Wood fillers fail when the wood moves. To create a patch that will last as long as the paint job, clean and prepare the damaged area with wood hardener, and repair the damage with a two-part filler like Bondo.

REMOVE ROT, AND PIERCE THE WOOD AROUND THE DAMAGE. Clean the damaged wood and remove all rot. Then use an awl or other pointy tool to make small punctures all around the general area to ensure that the wood hardener penetrates.

SOAK THE WOOD WITH HARDENER. A baby-bottle nipple fit onto a bottle of Minwax Wood Hardener makes it easy to apply. Soak the entire area. When the wood appears dry, it is stable and ready for repair.

MAKE THE REPAIR. Mix just enough two-part filler to repair the wood. Then apply and smooth the patch with a wide putty knife.

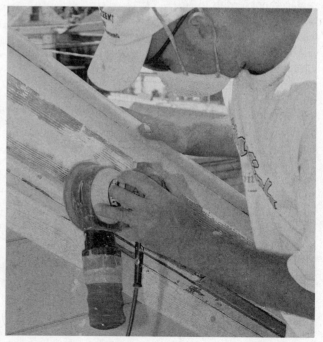

SAND THE REPAIR SMOOTH. Two-part fillers dry quickly and usually can be sanded within 30 minutes of application.

Continued ➤

Spray or Brush

By Scott Gibson

A good painter knows that prep work is everything. Once that's done, though, there are two choices for applying paint or stain: with a brush or roller, or with a spray gun. You'll find professional painters on both sides of the fence. Some stick with painting by hand, either because that's how they learned the trade or because their customers prefer it. Many others use spray equipment, either by itself or, more frequently, in tandem with brush and roller.

There's no question that spraying an exterior finish is much faster than brushing or rolling alone. But before pulling the trigger, spray painters have to make sure all surfaces are protected against overspray, the inevitable drift of atomized paint particles that bounce off the surface or are carried away by wind. This takes time, so the question becomes: Does the time saved by spraying the finish outweigh the effort of getting ready to spray?

The answer depends as much on the person who is holding the brush or sprayer as it does on the type of finish, the type of trim and siding, the time available, and the weather conditions.

The Case for Spraying

Although many painters combine spraying with brush and roller work, there are circumstances where a sprayer alone is the best approach. Rhode Island painter Tim Leahy found one such opportunity in the restoration of a period brick home in Newport, R.I., where carpenters had installed a wide band of complex trim at the top of the second story. The house had already been staged, allowing painters to move quickly. Although masking off the wall below the trim took an hour, it took one painter just 30 minutes to spray a 60-ft. section of soffit, a job that would have taken two painters with brushes half a day to complete.

Easy access and calm winds helped to guarantee a high-quality spray finish in a very short time. A smooth substrate also helped: The trim was sprayed with primer before it left the shop. After installation, nail holes were puttied, the surface was resanded, gaps were caulked, and the trim was primed again.

Spray or Brush? It All Depends on . . .

. . . What's in the Can

Why I Spray

People see the airless sprayer as a replacement for the brush and roller. It's not. I wouldn't use a sprayer without having a brush or a roller on hand to help spread the paint evenly without over-applying. That said, an airless sprayer is the fastest and most consistent way to get a lot of paint onto the building. It's like carrying 5 gal. of paint in your hand.

Paint	**SPRAY:** All exterior finishes can be sprayed, given the right spray-gun tip and paint viscosity. Thick finishes may need thinning to atomize properly. **BRUSH:** Many paints can be applied right out of the can, although thinning can help thick paints to level out in hot or very dry conditions. Choose a good-quality brush that matches the finish: synthetic bristles for acrylics, natural bristles for oil-based paints.
Stain	**SPRAY:** On bare wood, back-brush the surface after spraying to ensure even film and penetration. **BRUSH:** Because stains are usually thinner than paints, watch for drips along edges. Keep a wet edge to avoid lap marks in the finish surface. If you have to stop midjob, look for a natural break, and cut to that point so that lap marks won't show later.
Primer	**SPRAY:** Back-brush or back-roll for good penetration and even distribution on the surface. Thinning can help primer to penetrate the surface, but don't exceed the manufacturer's recommendations. **BRUSH:** Thinning may help penetration.
Oil	**SPRAY:** Overspray is more of a threat to distant objects because oil takes longer to dry. Oil paint's slower drying time allows it to flow out smoothly after spray application to a nearly flawless finish. Equipment must be cleaned with solvents that contain volatile organic compounds. Brush: Application is slower, but brushing fills minute gaps and seams effectively, and using a brush gives you more control than using spray equipment. Some brush marks will be evident.
Latex	**SPRAY:** Water-based finishes dry quickly. Atomized paint dries quickly and will fall as dust sooner, reducing chances of damage due to overspray. Paint sprayed in direct sunlight on a hot day may not have a chance to flow to a smooth surface before it dries. Additives such as Floetrol help. Brush: The finish may dry too quickly in direct sunlight. An additive such as Floetrol can help paint to level before it dries.

That's the key to a good spray-only finish. Aluminum siding, metal meter boxes, and smooth metal fencing—the smoother the surface, the better it responds to a spray gun alone. In the hands of a skilled painter, a spray gun leaves a blemish-free finish without roller or brush marks.

When It's Best to Break Out the Brushes

Nonetheless, it takes time to set up a sprayer, to mask off areas to be protected, and to clean the equipment at the end of the day. When that outweighs the speed advantage of spraying, out comes the brush or roller.

Stan Hallett found that to be the case as his crew repainted a sprawling condominium last summer in a Portland, Maine, suburb. Although a sprayer made sense on the sidewalls, it was easier to paint the simple trim by hand because nothing had to be masked. As one painter applied solid stain to clapboard and shingle walls with a gun and brush, a second followed with just a brush for the trim.

Hallett and Leahy both weigh the circumstances carefully before they make their choice. "Why would we go through all the hassle of spraying when we can just fly right along with a brush?" Leahy asks. "We make our decision based on complexity and how much time we can save. If you have a big soffit with corbels and brackets and decorative trim, it'll take two guys all day to paint with a brush, and you can spray it in an hour. If you have a simple trim detail that two guys can knock out in a half-hour by brush, then you lose the reason to spray."

Sticking with a brush or roller also makes sense when there isn't much paint to apply. "It always comes down to the volume of paint," says Berkeley, Calif., contractor Hugh Schreiber. "If you're doing less than a gallon of paint, I would say it's not worth cleaning the sprayer."

Working around lots of obstructions is another reason to stick with a brush, Schreiber adds. In an area with lots of windows, doors, and fixtures, it may not be worth the effort to mask everything.

Other painters apply finish exclusively by hand because that's what their customers expect. Brian Doherty, a Richmond, Va., area painter, never uses spray equipment even though he's well aware of its speed advantages. Why? First, because that's

. . . What's Being Painted

		Why I Brush
Wood shingle	**SPRAY:** A spray gun spreads finish effectively into cracks between shingles, but make sure to back-brush on at least the first coat to ensure even penetration into pores of wood. **BRUSH:** Provides more control when working near plants, trim, and other surfaces that could be damaged by overspray, but is much slower. Watch for drips along the bottoms of shingles.	My customers really don't want to know anything about sprayers because they think it's going to get all through their ventilation system. I learned how to paint by hand, and my customers are willing to pay me to do that. But if I was starting out in painting, if I was trying to start up a business, I would be seriously looking into how to operate a sprayer.
Clapboard (wood or fiber cement)	**SPRAY:** Application is fast, but back-brush on the first coat. Sand the surface of wood clapboards first to eliminate slick surface called "mill glaze" that can hamper the penetration of finish. Fiber cement usually comes preprimed. **BRUSH:** Application is slower but offers more control in tight spots. Be wary of mill glaze.	
Brick	**SPRAY:** Application is fast as long as masking windows and trim isn't overly complicated. Brick must breathe, so use an acrylic finish. Back-roll after spray application. Use an alkali-resistant primer. **BRUSH:** Provides more control, but application is slower. For small areas, brush application may be faster than spraying when masking is considered.	
Concrete	**SPRAY:** Large areas with minimal masking can be finished quickly. Back-roll at least on the first coat. **BRUSH:** Rolling is much faster than brushing, although not as fast as spraying. For small areas where masking is required for spray equipment, rolling may be the best option.	
Vinyl siding	**SPRAY:** Vinyl's smooth surface may mean no back-brushing is required. Make sure surface chalk and mildew are removed. **BRUSH:** Brushing is faster when the surface to be finished is relatively small or required masking is extensive. The finish surface probably won't be as smooth.	
Intricate trim	**SPRAY:** Much faster than brushing detailed profiles, especially when trim can be painted before windows or siding is installed and masking is held to a minimum. Count on back-brushing at least the first coat unless the prepped surface is very smooth. **BRUSH:** Although slower than spraying, brushing offers more control. No masking is necessary, so it may even be faster when trim is not extensive or especially complicated.	

Continued ➔

how he learned the trade. And second, his traditionally minded customers don't want spray equipment in or around their homes for fear of damage from overspray.

Combining Spray and Stroke

Spraying gets a lot of finish on the surface quickly and evenly, and a brush or roller works the finish into the surface for good penetration, better coverage, and ultimately, better durability. Combining the two—called back-brushing or back-rolling—offers all the advantages of both.

"Spraying by itself would be wonderful if it worked well because it's very quick," says Hallett. "But it doesn't do a good job. That paint is going to be gone in 10 years. We spray only as a means of getting the paint onto the surface."

Hallett's technique is common. After masking off nearby surfaces, a painter sprays a section of wall, then works the same area with a brush or roller to even the coat and push paint into the surface. The paint film is more uniform, and the pressure from the gun forces paint into all the depressions that a brush or roller by itself might not reach. Surfaces with uneven texture, such as

Spray or Brush? It All Depends on . . .

. . . Who's Doing the Painting, and With What

Experience of crew	**SPRAY:** Advertisements featuring inexperienced homeowners applying flawless finishes are unrealistic. No one learns how to spray overnight, so expect some missteps in the beginning, such as overspray, finishes that go on too thick or too thin, and improperly thinned paints. Choosing the right tip and gun pressure and knowing when to thin and how to cope with weather variables take years of practice. **BRUSH:** Much easier to learn, but experience is still valuable, especially when it comes to painting complex trim, window muntins, door panels, and similar elements. Knowing when and how to thin paint or use additives takes experience.
Size of crew	**SPRAY:** One person with a spray gun and two others to handle masking, small areas of trim, and other details are enough to paint a small house in three to five days, depending on the complexity of the job. **BRUSH:** To paint the same house by hand would take the same crew five to six days, all things being otherwise equal.
Equipment	**SPRAY:** A homeowner-grade airless sprayer is fine for simple jobs under good conditions, but it won't atomize the finish as effectively, is noisier, and doesn't offer the same range of adjustments as professional-quality equipment. A pro-level kit can easily top $2000. **BRUSH:** Much less expensive to get started. Whether you brush or spray, you'll still need ladders, drop cloths, and possibly staging.

. . . Time Factors

Preparation	**SPRAY:** Same as for brush painting; the additional task of masking windows, doors, and roofing on a 2500-sq.-ft., two-story house might add half a day for a professional crew. **BRUSH:** Basic surface prep, but no masking.
Application	**SPRAY:** Huge time advantage for complex trim and large expanses of wall. Depending on site conditions and the surfaces being painted, application could be 10 times as fast. **BRUSH:** Application much slower.
Dry time/ recoating	**SPRAY:** No significant difference, although sprayed finishes may dry marginally faster because the paint film is thinner. **BRUSH:** A heavy coat will take longer to dry than a thin coat applied by a spray gun.
Cleanup	**SPRAY:** 15 minutes or so to clean lines and gun tips in solvent (water or paint thinner), plus time to clean any brushes and rollers that are used and to remove and dispose of masking materials. **BRUSH:** Somewhat faster.

. . . Conditions

Wind	**SPRAY:** A very light breeze in an area where overspray isn't an issue is OK. As soon as the wind starts to affect the spray pattern, work should stop. Atomized paint carried off by the wind means more wasted materials and increases the risk of damage to plants, cars, and other parts of the building. **BRUSH:** Wind has much less of an effect, although it can cause finishes to dry too quickly, especially in direct sunlight.
Heat	**SPRAY:** Surfaces that dry too quickly may not level properly. Avoid spraying in direct sunlight, especially as the mercury climbs. **BRUSH:** Brushing in direct sunlight also can mean an uneven surface. An additive can help by increasing the drying time.
Cold	**SPRAY:** Follow manufacturer's recommendations on minimum temperature, and make sure the surface will stay at the temperature while the paint dries, not just at the time of application. **BRUSH:** Same considerations as for spraying.
Humidity	**SPRAY:** Very high humidity can trap moisture in the paint film, causing it to blister. **BRUSH:** Same considerations as for spraying.

rough-sawn clapboards, shingles, and split-face masonry block, are especially well suited to this approach.

Manuel Fernandes, chief inspector for the Master Painters and Decorators Association, says new work always should be back-rolled or back-brushed on the first coat. "If you spray it only, the paint just sits on top of the substrate," he says. "You're not forcing the paint into the pores of the wood."

But back-rolling or back-brushing on subsequent coats is a judgment call. Rough-textured surfaces may benefit from a second round of back-rolling or back-brushing, but a sprayed second or third coat on a smoother substrate may not need any further attention. That's where experience counts.

Choose Spray Equipment

An airless sprayer is the most common choice for painting professionals. As the name suggests, an airless system does not use an air compressor as a means of atomizing the finish. Instead, a powerful pump forces the paint through a tip at very high pressure (3000 psi or more), causing it to break into tiny droplets.

According to Jeff LaSorella, owner of Finishing Consultants in Seattle, airless sprayers get a higher percentage of paint on the surface than either conventional high-pressure guns or high-volume low-pressure (HVLP) equipment. This "transfer rate" is 70% with an airless sprayer, versus as little as 35% with a high-pressure gun powered by an air compressor and 65% for an HVLP sprayer.

Less common but even more efficient are Airmix or air-assisted sprayers, according to LaSorella. Airmix, a proprietary technology owned by a company called Kremlin, uses a pump to develop hydraulic pressure at the tip while slight air pressure helps to disperse paint particles in a fan-shaped pattern. LaSorella says transfer rates of 90% are possible. Air-assisted airless spraying uses similar technology to achieve a transfer rate of 75%.

Although airless sprayers are highly efficient, they carry risks. Extremely high fluid pressure can cause injury if the tip comes into direct contact with skin. Never remove the gun's guard.

Airless sprayers start at a couple hundred dollars at big-box stores, but expect to pay more for professional-quality equipment with higher pressure at the tip for better atomization, longer hoses, and greater durability. Air-assisted equipment is even pricier. For example, while Graco's model 390 professional airless sprayer is available for $700*, the price rises to $1650 for the air-assisted airless model. The smallest Airmix Kremlin, a top pro brand, starts at around $2500 for the pump and gun. Professional-quality equipment may be rented from a local big-box store or rental center. For about $80 a day, The Home Depot rents an Airlessco airless sprayer that retails for more than $1500. If you rent, make sure you get the right tip size for the finish you're using, and check that filters and hoses are clean before you leave the store.

*Note: All prices cited are from 2010.

Paint-Spraying Pointers

Manuel Fernandes, chief inspector for the Master Painters and Decorators Association and a professional painter for 34 years, offers these suggestions for anyone using spray equipment:

• Always work in the shade. Paint sprayed on a substrate in direct sunlight dries too quickly and doesn't adhere well.

• Be wary of wind. When wind is affecting the spray pattern or when spray drift is obvious, stop spraying.

• Always back-roll or back-brush after applying a first coat of paint or stain by sprayer.

• Most finishes can be reduced for better atomization and a smoother finish by following directions on the can for thinning.

• Never paint (by brush or spray) when the humidity is greater than 85%.

• Multiple thin coats are better than one thick coat.

• Let paint cure thoroughly between coats.

Don't Be Afraid to Spray

By Philip Hansell

During the more than 20 years I've been a painter, I've used an airless sprayer to apply thousands of gallons of paints and coatings of all types. Compared to brushing and rolling, spraying saves time on both interior and exterior projects, lays down a perfect coat of paint, and has helped my company build a reputation for high-quality work.

For a novice, using an airless sprayer conjures thoughts of a huge mess, unreasonably long cleanup, and a poor finish, but using a sprayer efficiently and with minimal mess is not that hard. It just takes somebody more experienced to walk you through the process of how to set up, operate, and maintain an airless sprayer

Continued ➜

Motor

Manifold Filter

Pressure control

Bypass/prime valve

Pump/fluid section

Bypass hose

power to spray through the largest tips. Heavy exterior latex, which requires a 0.019 tip, and high-build primers (0.027 tip) pose the greatest difficulty (see "Choosing Tips," p. 677). These paints have a high percentage of solids, which makes them more viscous and more difficult to spray than oil paints and varnishes. Most residential water-based paints require at least 2000 psi and a 0.019 or smaller tip. To know the exact tip size and spraying pressure for a specific product, go to the paint manufacturer's website and look for the product data sheet. There you'll find the recommended tip size and spraying pressure, as well as special handling or safety precautions. If you're renting a sprayer, it probably makes sense to buy your own tip, because you can't tell the condition of a tip just by looking at it: There's more than one style of tip and tip guard, so be sure everything fits the gun that comes with the sprayer before leaving the store.

Airless sprayers can be rated by how many gallons of paint they can spray weekly. It's an easy way to match the pump and motor to the size of the jobs you'll be doing. For remodelers and hardcore DIYers, a small sprayer like the Graco 390 or 395, which are rated for 25 to 30 gal. of paint a week, would be a good fit. If you spray between 30 to 50 gal. a week, you'll want a midrange sprayer like Graco's 695 or 795. If you're painting over 50 gal. a week, you'll need a model like Graco's 1095 or larger.

The gallons per minute (GPM) rating is another useful way to compare sprayers. For example, Graco's 390, which is their smallest contractor sprayer, has a GPM rating of 0.47, a maximum psi of 3300, and a maximum tip size of 0.021. For comparison, a Graco 1095 (the largest sprayer we regularly use) has a GPM rating of 1.2, a maximum psi of 3300, and a maximum tip size of 0.035. Even though the 1095 and the 390 have an equal psi rating, the smaller 390 can only sustain a consistent finish at that pressure for a short amount of time. How long depends on the paint being applied and the tip size.

to produce a smooth finish. With these lessons in mind, there is no reason to keep from spraying on your next painting project.

Picking the Right Type

Although my crew and I also have HVLP (high-volume, low-pressure) and air-assisted sprayers, we mostly use airless sprayers because of their speed, the wide range of coatings they can apply, and their reliability. Airless sprayers pressurize the paint with a pump that forces it through the hose until it's atomized by the spray tip as it exits the gun. Although I've tried all the pro-quality airless spray rigs, I've had the best luck with Graco sprayers. They're widely available in my area, too, so it's easy to get tips and repair parts.

For a professional painter like me, spending several hundred to several thousand dollars on a sprayer is an easy business decision, but for GCs, remodelers, and DIYers, spending that much money on a tool for occasional use might not make sense (see "Cost and Quality," p. 680). But you can rent sprayers such as the Graco 695 at home centers, paint stores, and rental yards. A sprayer like that can spray almost any residential coating short of foundation tar, high-build drywall primers, and concrete-block fillers.

Whether buying or renting, you need to match the sprayer to the coating you'll be applying. Smaller sprayers don't have enough

Picking the Right Model

If you're considering a purchase and will be moving the sprayer by yourself, get a small model. Two people are needed to get a medium or larger sprayer into a vehicle. If you're considering a particular model, find out if there's a local supplier for spray tips and filters. The best spray guns cost a little more, but their consistent paint delivery makes it easier to get a smooth finish.

If you are regularly spraying trim or built-ins (which commonly have a glossy finish), then you'll want a sprayer with a computer-controlled pressure regulator. Without computer control, the pressure is regulated by a mechanical pressure switch. With a mechanical switch, the spray pulses as the pressure switch cycles the pump on and off. Sometimes described as deadband, this pulsating affects spray uniformity and may be visible in the finish, depending on the paint's sheen. The higher the level of gloss, the more it will be obvious.

I have found that a Graco 695 Ultra Max II is the right sprayer for most jobs we do. We usually buy the upgraded pro-contractor models, which have computerized controls, a sturdy cart, and a nice hose reel. We also have a couple of 1095s for spraying thick paints that require a large tip, and we use some 395s for residential repaints and small jobs. One of our favorite features of Graco sprayers is the easy-to-remove fluid section on the pump. If there's a problem, it can be swapped without tools, so we keep backup fluid sections in our vans to minimize downtime. Another nice feature of this sprayer is the "WatchDog" pump-protection system, which turns off the pump when the paint runs out or if there's a leak in the hose.

Getting Ready to Spray

Before any spraying begins, I cover the floor with a heavy butyl-backed drop cloth for extra floor protection around the sprayer. I put on a cartridge respirator and a Tyvek suit, and I cover my head with a spray sock. I put a little Vaseline on my eyelashes, which makes it easy to wipe off any overspray. While I unravel the hose, I inspect it carefully for scuffs, kinks, bubbles, cuts, or pinches. This is important because a damaged hose not only makes a mess, but it can seriously injure someone if it breaks. When paint is injected under the skin, the resulting injury is very serious, even if it only looks like a scratch. If you or someone in the vicinity gets hit with a sprayer's high-pressure stream, go to the ER immediately and tell the staff you have a "fluid-injection injury." Bring a paint-can label or the material safety data sheet to help the medical staff administer the right treatment.

When spraying ceilings or walls, keep the gun 12 in. to 15 in. away from the surface, and overlap the spray pattern by 50%. The product data sheet will tell you how thick the coating should be

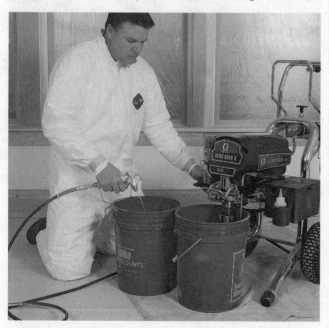

FLUSH WITH SOLVENT. Fill the pump with a solvent compatible with the coating you're spraying. Spray it through the line at low pressure until it's running clear and smells clean (without traces of the previous coating or nonwater-based solvent).

Choosing Tips

Spray tips are the key to airless spraying. They are sized by a three-digit code that indicates spray pattern and orifice size. Doubling the first digit tells you the width of the spray pattern, while the second and third digits are the size of the orifice in thousands of an inch. For example, a 311 tip has a 6-in. spray pattern and an orifice that's 0.011 in. dia. Small orifices atomize the coating into smaller droplets for a fine finish, but small tips build the coating thickness slower and clog more easily than larger tips.

Many tips can be turned backward for clearing clogs. I consider these so-called reversible tips a must. After turning the tip so the arrow on the tip handle is facing the gun, spray into a waste container until the tip is cleared, and then return the tip to the spray position. You can find the proper tip size for a specific coating by referring to the product data sheets, which you'll find on the coating manufacturer's website.

When the spray pattern has diminished to 75% of its original size, it's time to replace the spray tip, because at this point you're spraying more paint over a smaller area. With latex coatings, this could be necessary every 30 to 50 gal. If you continue to use the tip, more and more paint will be applied to a smaller and smaller area, yielding an inconsistent finish. To minimize tip wear, filter your paint through a mesh strainer bag before spraying, spray at the lowest pressure that still produces a full pattern, and clean the tips and all the filters after every use.

Match the Tip Size to the Finish

Lacquer, clear coat.009 - .011
Shellac.009 - .013
Stain.011 - .013
Water-borne lacquer.012 - .014
Acrylic latex (interior).013 - .015
Polyurethane.013 - .015
Solid stain.013 - .015
Interior latex.013 - .017
Exterior latex.015 - .019
Latex primer.015 - .017
Oil primer.017 - .019
Heavy latex.021 - .025
High-build drywall primer.025 - .039

Continued ➔

when wet. You can check the wet thickness with simple tool called a wet-film thickness gauge, which you can find at most paint stores. Work from the top down and from the back of the room toward the exit. If you are spraying a small area such as a closet, begin with the corners and then fill in the bare areas.

Once you go through the setup and cleanup process two or three times, spraying becomes second nature, and you'll be amazed at how fast and easy it is to get a great finish.

Get Spraying

Start each job by completely unrolling the hose and checking it for nicks, cuts, and abrasions. Also, make sure the power cord isn't damaged and that it's fully grounded to prevent severe shocks from static electricity. Don't use the sprayer if any parts are broken or missing. Confirm that the pressure-control switch is turned all the way down and the power switch is off before plugging in the machine.

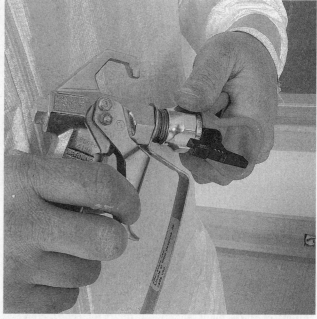

3. INSTALL THE TIP. Install the tip into the tip guard so that the arrow is pointing away from the gun. Screw the tip assembly onto the gun, and align the guard to choose a vertical or horizontal spray pattern. Make the connection hand tight.

1. PRIME THE PUMP. Place the suction tube into the paint, and put the bypass hose into an empty can or bucket. Turn the bypass valve to the prime setting, and turn the pressure-control switch all the way down. Turn on the sprayer and slowly increase the pressure, but no more than halfway. When a steady stream of paint comes out of the bypass hose, turn the pressure back down to zero. Turn the bypass valve to the spray setting. The pump is now primed.

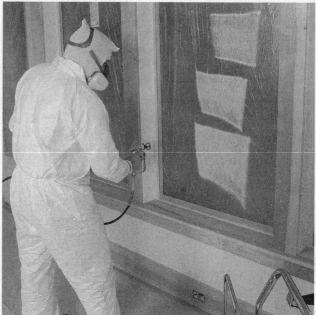

2. FILL THE HOSE. The gun should not have the tip guard and spray tip installed yet. Unlock and pull the trigger while aiming the gun into an empty can. Slowly turn up the pressure. When a steady stream of paint starts coming out of the gun, switch the flow into the fresh-paint container for several seconds to clear air from the hose. Turn the pressure all the way down again, and lock the trigger on the spray gun.

4. ADJUST THE PRESSURE. Use the lowest pressure that fully atomizes the paint. Make a test spray on the masking materials, and gradually increase the pressure until there are no small lines, called "fingers," at the top and bottom of the spray pattern. If you see fingers, increase the pressure until the spray pattern shows full and even coverage across its width.

Clean Up

Sprayers save time and money, but improper cleanup and storage can negate any savings through downtime and repairs. Fully flush the coating from the pump, the hose, and the gun after every use. Filters must be fully cleaned during wash up and replaced if they're damaged or are more than 20% clogged. The tip and guard should also be fully cleaned before breaks and at day's end. Always lock the trigger when you're not spraying.

3. FLUSH WITH SOLVENT. Turn the bypass valve to the spray position, and turn up the pressure while pulling the trigger. Aim the flow into the paint can. Once the paint is emptied from the hose and solvent starts coming out of the nozzle, move the stream to a waste bucket. Continue running solvent through the system until it's nearly clear.

1. RELIEVE THE PRESSURE. Without touching the bypass valve, turn the pressure all the way down. Remove the tip and guard, and place them in a container of appropriate solvent. Slowly pull the trigger to release the pressure.

2. PUMP OUT THE PAINT. Place the suction tube into a clean bucket of solvent, and turn the bypass valve to the bypass setting. Slowly turn up the pressure to flush the pump with solvent. Paint will come out of the bypass tube, which can be put back in the can. Once solvent starts coming out, collect it in a waste container.

4. CLEAN THE FILTERS. Remove the inlet strainer, manifold filter, and gun filter, and shake them in a bucket of solvent to clean them. Reassemble the sprayer without the filters, and run solvent through the sprayer and bypass hose until it's nearly clear. You can reuse the solvent later.

Continued ➜

Cost and Quality

Internet retailers and home centers have an assortment of airless sprayers in stock with prices that range widely. Even the most expensive consumer model costs about half what my cheapest pro sprayer costs. So are these inexpensive sprayers worth considering for folks who are painting only a few times a year? In many cases, the more expensive airless sprayers available at home centers can do a good job for oil-based and light latex coatings. The most expensive models, such as the Graco ProX9 below, may be able to spray exterior latex, but less expensive models will struggle to spray latex paint without thinning because they have smaller pumps and motors. If you're considering one of these sprayers, research what tip sizes you'll need for the coatings you intend to spray, and see if the tool you're considering is up to the job. Consumer sprayers have lower-quality components compared to pro models, so they may not hold up if they're used beyond their capabilities. Also, they're loud.

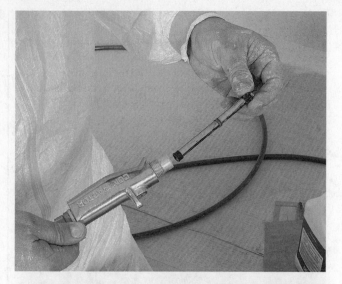

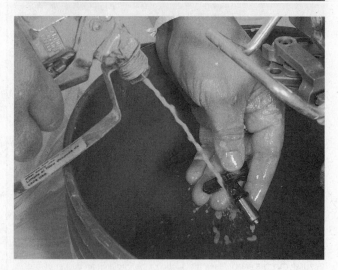

Clean the tip and the guard. Shake the tip and the guard in the pail of solvent to clean them. You can use a toothbrush to remove stubborn residue. Don't leave water in the sprayer in freezing temperatures and never for more than a day or two. Instead, fill the pump with RV antifreeze prior to storage to prevent corrosion and freezing.

Drop Cloths

Plastic, Canvas, or Alternative Products

When painting, the most important and effective measure of protection from splatters and spills is a drop cloth. The two most common types of drop cloths are plastic and canvas. However, other products like rosin paper, cardboard, and natural and synthetic recycled fibers are available. While each type serves the same essential purpose, each functions differently.

Plastic Is Cheap

Plastic drop cloths are useful, but serve a more limited purpose. They are lightweight, disposable, and inexpensive.

PROS: Lightweight, so they can be hung and draped easily. Impermeable.

CONS: Dangerously slippery on hardwood and carpeted floors. Easily ripped or torn. Must be taped to be kept in place.

BEST USE: Plastic can be hung with painter's tape, making it the best drop cloth for covering upper cabinets, light fixtures, and tall furniture.

Canvas Is the Standard

Next to a paintbrush, the most universal item in any painter's possession is the canvas drop cloth. A heavy-duty 12-oz. drop cloth is best because paint is less likely to seep through it.

PROS: Durable, long lasting, and reusable. Rubber-backed versions are impermeable.

CONS: Can be slippery on hardwood floors. Won't lie dead flat, which can create a tripping hazard.

BEST USE: General flooring coverage, tool and material staging, countertop and furniture coverage, exterior applications (like deck or walkway protection).

Alternative Products Vary in Effectiveness

While some people use rosin paper and cardboard as drop-cloth material, I don't. They just don't offer the performance and ease of "installation" of other products. However, a fibrous drop cloth, like Clean & Safe (www .dropcloth.com), is a good option in some situations.

PROS: Lies flat, skid resistant, impermeable, reusable, easier to detail around transitions and stairs than other drop cloths.

CONS: Difficult to drape or hang. Distribution is limited, and online orders offer only larger quantities.

BEST USE: As floor protection over hardwood and carpet. Performs particularly well on stairs because it's less likely to bunch up.

Continued ➜

Prep Before You Paint

By Jim Lacey

For a lot of people, painting is dreadful. They complain that it's messy and fussy, and that they don't always get the results they hoped for. The truth is that most people end up with less-than-desirable results because they ignore the importance of proper preparation.

In the 20 years that I've been painting houses, I've learned how to size up quickly the results of poor prep work. The signs include paint peeling in sheets off doors and trim, mildew seeping through layers of paint, and bleeding spots on walls and ceilings—paint failures that easily could have been avoided.

At each job, I follow a basic routine that ensures a long-lasting, attractive paint job. I start by removing items from the room. Large items, such as couches, can be moved to the center of the space and covered with drop cloths. With a fresh canvas, I can begin the real prep work.

Step 1
Drop the entire room. After the furniture is covered or removed, cover the floor with heavy-duty canvas drop cloths. Use 9-ft. by 12-ft. drop cloths near walls, 4-ft. by 5-ft. cloths under tools and paint, and a 12-ft. by 15-ft. cloth to cover a large area of flooring or furniture. Don't skimp on the drop cloths. Cheap products can allow paint to seep through, and plastic drop cloths can be slippery, especially on hardwood floors.

Step 2
Organize and stage essential tools. Keep all commonly used tools close at hand. This helps the work to go smoothly. Place these tools on their own drop cloth in an easily accessible but out-of-the-way area. Large items, such as step ladders and vacuums, also should be kept close by.

Step 3
Light the space. Set up halogen lamps on a stand, and clamp circular incandescent lamps wherever possible. Set the lights in a position that eliminates shadows and works best with the natural light coming into the room. Adjust the lights as conditions change.

Step 4
Remove wall and ceiling obstructions. Don't try to paint around easily removable elements such as window treatments, sconces, outlet covers, switch covers, thermostats, and recessed-light trim rings. Large fixtures, such as chandeliers, can be covered with plastic instead of being removed. The escutcheons can be unscrewed and lowered.

Step 5
Wash down everything. One-quarter cup of trisodium phosphate (TSP) per 2 gallons of water will remove dirt, smudges, smoke residue, and most surface grime. Pay particular attention to high-touch areas such as door jambs and areas around light switches. Bleach and TSP work best on mildew stains. Use a light hand when washing; you don't want to soak the wall. Also, wear heavy-duty rubber gloves. Allow the walls and ceiling to dry completely before moving on.

Tackle the Bulk of the Surface Prep in the Final Five Steps

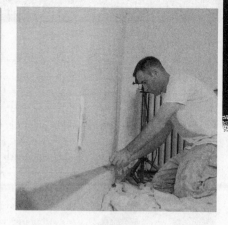

Step 6

Assess the existing paint. Glossy finishes need to be sanded with 120-grit sandpaper, while moderate-gloss paint can be sanded with 120- to 150-grit sandpaper. Very hard surfaces may need to be prepped with a palm sander, but most often, you can get away with using a sanding sponge or sandpaper. Remove dust from the wall with a brush and a tack cloth.

Step 7

Repair any damage, and fill any gaps. Joint compound is ideal for repairing cracks, holes, or dents in both drywall and plaster walls. (Visit finehomebuilding.com for more on wall repair.) Use a high-quality wood filler for repairs on wood trim and doors. Sand the repairs, and remove dust from the wall with a tack cloth, a brush, and a vacuum. Any gaps that have developed between the trim and the wall or ceiling should be caulked. Acrylic caulk performs well in most applications. However, in damp areas such as bathrooms or kitchens, consider a vinyl adhesive-based caulk, such as Phenoseal (www. phenoseal .com), for greater longevity.

Step 8

Mask conservatively. Mask only those horizontal areas that are most vulnerable to paint splatter, like the tops of chair rails and the tops of baseboards if they're not going to be repainted. If baseboards are going to be repainted, mask the area where the wood flooring meets the baseboard.

Step 9

Always prime walls, but not ceilings. Roll primer on walls to give paint a flat, uniform base to adhere to. Ceilings don't always have to be primed because they're often in good shape and are typically painted with flat paint. Recoating flat paint is less demanding than recoating glossy paint. You should, however, spot-prime areas with repairs, such as places that had water leaks or drywall cracks. Tinting the primer to the finish color helps to improve coverage and gives a better sense of how the room will look when it's done—much better than small paint swatches, which can bleed through subsequent coats of paint and ruin the final finish. Universal acrylic primers perform better than ever and have little odor.

Step 10

Give the wall a final sanding and cleaning. Sand all wall and ceiling surfaces with a medium-grit sanding sponge, and inspect the surface for any irregularities, such as hardened paint or primer drips. This is an ideal time to make any final touch-ups or repairs prior to painting. If you make a repair, remove the dust, and be sure to spot-prime the area before starting to paint.

Must-Have Materials

- Step ladder
- Canvas drop cloths
- 5-in-1 tool
- Multibit screwdriver
- 2½-in. angled brush
- Acrylic caulk
- Cut bucket
- Extension cords
- Taping knives
- Paint trays
- Roller handle
- Tinted primer
- ⅜-in. roller sleeves
- Roller extension pole
- Bleach or TSP
- Rubber gloves
- Sponges
- Joint compound
- Tack cloths
- Sandpaper and sponges
- Rags
- Shop vacuum
- Auxiliary lighting

Continued →

Painting Trim the Right Way

By Tim Leahy

Most people who are new to painting see the job in terms of applying the finish coat, but that's just the icing on the cake. The real work that makes or breaks a paint job is how you prepare the surface. If you're painting interior trim and you don't do a good job of sanding, cleaning, and priming, the final coats of paint won't look pristine. At the very worst, a poor prep job can make the finish coats fail. I work in high-end restoration, where the end result is paramount. Over the years, I have developed the following procedures for a great paint job.

An aftermarket HEPA filter (inset) improves the performance of a typical job-site vac.

Step 1: Clear the Air

Whether it's your spouse, the construction manager, the homeowner, or any combination of the three, everyone needs to know when the painting stage of a job is set to begin. Other trades need to be out of the area, and the air needs to be right, especially for the last finish coats. The inside temperature should be between 55°F and 80°F, and the humidity level should be less than 50%. Humidity between 50% and 80% is less than ideal. When the humidity shoots over 85%, the paint won't dry properly, which may cause blushing, sags, wrinkling, or film failure.

Air quality is very important, especially during the finish-coat stage, so we try to eliminate all airborne dust by using fans fitted with filters to draw in clean air and exhaust dusty air from the work area.

Step 2: Clean and Protect the Room

A dirty floor and fresh paint don't mix. The dirt gets airborne when kicked or when cords, hoses, or ladders are moved. Once everyone has left the area, the first thing we do is vacuum. Sawdust, dirt, and other debris on the floors and walls need to be cleaned off with a powerful vacuum that has nonmarring attachments. Vacuums equipped with high-efficiency particulate absorption (HEPA) filters are the best, although they can be expensive.

Any hardware should be removed or protected. We remove hardware, tag it with tape, label it with a marker, and place it into plastic bags or clean cups. If there is a lot of hardware, I use a camera or a sketch pad to document the layout before taking everything apart.

If the area has finished floors, we use one of three levels of protection. If we happen to be priming in a room where the flooring hasn't been finished, we tape down rosin paper, which helps keep the dust and dirt to a minimum. If the finish is in place, then we switch to a thicker, more protective paper product such as Ram Board, and sometimes even add a plastic layer to block moisture. The ultimate protection is paper first, followed by a layer of plastic and a layer of luan plywood.

FIRST THINGS FIRST. Before starting the prep, thoroughly vacuum the floor and all horizontal edges to eliminate dirt and dust.

COVER THE FLOOR. It's a good idea to cover the floor with builder's paper to contain any embedded dirt. The author uses this quick method of footwork to apply tape to the paper.

Step 3: Fill the Holes

On many of our jobs, paint-grade trim comes to the site already primed. Once it has been installed (and if not primed, see step 5), the next step is to fill the fastener holes. For typical finish-nail holes, I use lightweight spackle. I like UGL brand, which dries quickly and expands out of the hole when dry, which makes it easy to sand flush with the surface. For large screw holes, I use a two-part wood filler. Lots of folks use auto-body filler, but I use a two-part filler from Minwax that is made for wood.

For dents and shallow imperfections, I use Elmer's interior Wood Filler. This product has better adhesion than spackle, so it works on fine dents and scratches. It tends to shrink, though, so I have to compensate with a slight overfill or a second application.

FILL NAIL HOLES. Use a lightweight filler such as UGL spackling to fill small holes. Press the filler into the holes, and allow it to expand to prevent shrinkage.

LEVEL DENTS. Use a medium-body product such as Elmer's Wood Filler to fill any shallow depressions in the trim. Overfill slightly so that sanding will create a flush surface.

THINK BODY SHOP. For wide holes deeper than ¼ in., use a two-part acrylic product that is similar to auto-body fillers, such as Minwax's Wood Filler.

Step 4: Sand Surfaces and Soften Edges

When the fillers have dried, it's time to sand everything smooth. This prep stage creates a uniform profile over the trim surface. Hand-sanding and checking your work by feel is critical; your fingertips can detect imperfections that your eyes would miss. I always use a disposable mask with a N100 rating when sanding.

I begin with 180-grit sandpaper to smooth the entire surface and to level all fills. Since fillers are often softer than the wood around them, I make sure to keep the paper flat so as not to dig out any filler. Working from the bottom up means not sanding over dust from above. I feel every inch as I go to ensure the surface is buttery smooth. At this point, it's OK to burn through the primer on some edges and profiles and to remove heavier raised grain. The primer used in the factory is typically applied heavily, which results in a poor texture that has to be sanded down quite a bit to create a truly flat surface.

Sharp edges are easily worn and chipped, so it's best to soften them with 150-grit paper. Remember, it's all about the feel. After everything has been sanded, I use a vacuum to thoroughly clean the surfaces, and then a raking light to inspect for defects. It's better to fill a spot now than it is to interrupt your workflow in the middle of painting to spackle a divot.

PROPER TECHNIQUE. It's easier to control the work if you sand by hand. Fold the sheet into thirds, and hold it between your pinky and ring finger to keep it from sliding around.

DON'T FORGET THE EDGES. Make all surfaces consistent by sanding the edges of trim pieces and the adjoining wall areas.

SHINE A LIGHT. When a section is complete, use a strong light to make sure that all the imperfections are filled.

CLEAN UP. After sanding, be sure to vacuum the dust from the trim and the surrounding surfaces. Use soft attachments that won't ding the trim surfaces.

Continued →

THIN IS BETTER. Many modern oil primers must be diluted with turpentine or paint thinner (about 1 part thinner to 10 parts paint) so that they soak into the wood.

START FROM THE EDGE. To avoid buildup, brush first from the edges of the trim, making sure to hit the seam between the trim and the wall.

GET RID OF THE EXCESS. It's difficult to brush away more paint than the brush can hold, so use a rag to wipe off the flats before proceeding.

CREATE A GOOD FOUNDATION. Working in one direction, brush out the face of the trim in even, straight strokes, being sure to avoid laps and drips.

Step 5: Apply the Primer

We always make sure the trim has a total of two coats of primer. If you begin with unprimed trim, apply an oil-based primer to the entire surface. I like to use Zinsser's Cover-Stain Primer because it seals off the grain and tannins better than water-based products, it sands smooth, and it can be topcoated with oil or latex. I have used water-based primers, but they tend to raise the grain, which means I have to prime and sand two or three times until the grain texture is tamed.

The second coat builds the surface, giving it an even color and texture that's a good substrate for any type of finish paint. Be sure to brush the primer onto the adjacent walls to create a better seal for the caulk. This foundation coat has to have straight brush strokes, minimal build, and no fat edges or overlaps. Brushing needs to be done in proper sequence: first the edges, then the flats.

Step 6: Sand Both Primer Coats

I lightly sand the trim after both the first and the second coat of primer to remove dust nibs or unwanted texture. I also wipe down the adjacent walls and vacuum to remove dust before caulking.

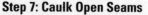

It makes a difference. After each coat of primer has dried, I use 320- or 400-grit sandpaper or an extra-fine nylon abrasive pad to prepare the surface.

Step 7: Caulk Open Seams

For the last step before the finish paint, I fill all cracks and seams with a high-quality acrylic adhesive caulk. The main trick with caulk is to make sure that a good bead of it gets forced behind the surface of the crack. Joinery with gaps of less than $1/16$ in. don't need to be filled as deeply, but anything larger should be filled behind the crack, not just on top of it. If the bead is too thin, the caulk will crack at the slightest movement of the underlying material. Once I've applied the bead, I use my finger to push the bead into the crack and smooth it out at the same time. I don't use rags, as they tend to wipe away too much caulk. Larger fills are prone to shrink and may need a second application.

Step 8: Apply the Topcoat

Vacuum as needed, then ensure that the air is as free of dust as possible and within the manufacturer's recommended temperature and humidity levels. Add heat to the room if it's too cold; if it's too hot and there's no air-conditioning, work at night. Allow for extra drying time if the humidity is high.

EPA regulations have adversely affected the performance of oil-based finish paints, especially in terms of their tendency to yellow over time. Fortunately, manufacturers have improved the performance of acrylic paints so that they level better and work easier than before. On this job, I used Benjamin Moore's Advance, which is a water-based paint with a small alkyd component to help it work and be tough like oil. Slight thinning according to the label directions is OK, but you shouldn't need any additives such as flowing agents.

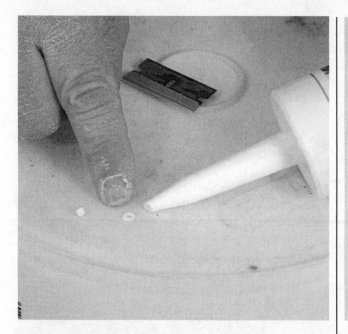

CONTROL THE OUTPUT. When you're about to use a new tube of caulk, cut off the tip at an angle so that the caulk can be easily directed into cracks without too much waste.

MIND YOUR STROKES. When applying primer or finish coats, keep the brush strokes definitive along transitions such as miters and other joints.

PULL, DON'T PUSH. With the angled tube facing the crack, pull the tube along the seam as you squeeze out a consistent amount of caulk.

DIGITAL WORKFLOW. Use a fingertip to smooth out the bead of caulk and to push it into the seam. Use a rag only to wipe off your finger, not the seam.

SCUFF AND BUFF. After the first finish coat has dried overnight, rub all areas lightly with an extrafine nylon pad or 400-grit sandpaper to smooth any imperfections and to dull the surface for the final coat. After vacuuming, wipe everything down with a tack cloth.

APPLY THE SECOND TOPCOAT. The final coat of paint should provide a perfect sheen and an extra layer of protection. After it has dried, check for missed spots and then clean the area, remove any masking, and reinstall the hardware.

Paintbrushes

For even brushwork, you need a decent brush. A high-quality China-bristle brush works best for oil-based paint, while a good nylon brush works well with water-based finishes. Look for evenly cut, feathered ends on the bristles, which help to smooth out the paint. Purdy and Wooster are reputable brands.

Continued →

Cutting in Trim and Corners

By Jim Lacey

One of the benchmarks of a good paint job is crisp, straight transitions of color where trim meets a wall or a wall meets a ceiling. I've found that cutting in these areas is as much about having the right tools as it is about having the right technique. It all starts with the right brush.

My favorite is a Corona 2½-in. Excalibur angled sash brush. First, it works well with both oil- and water-based finishes. It's also good for a wide variety of painting tasks besides cutting in, and its Chinex bristles are long-lasting and easy to clean.

Most painters, pros and do-it-yourselfers alike, hate cleaning brushes; even some pros wrap their brushes in plastic wrap or aluminum foil for later use. Unless I'm in an extreme rush, though, I don't do it. Clean bristles produce a much better finish, and it really doesn't take long to clean a high-quality paintbrush.

Having a clean brush is so important that I wash my brushes both at lunchtime and at the end of the day. In hot or dry conditions, I may wash my brush three or four times a day. The problem with storing brushes in plastic wrap, foil, or even zip-top bags is that the paint near the top of the bristles dries in a few hours and becomes difficult to remove completely. Before long, the bristles don't hold as much paint or flex as they should, which contributes to a rough finish and ragged lines where you're cutting in.

Besides the brush, you need a paint pail. I like metal pails because they don't flex unnervingly like plastic pails; however, the seams in metal pails make them more difficult to clean. If you find this a problem, look for a paint store that sells liners for metal pails. I use them whenever I'm changing colors several times a day.

I fill the pail about one-quarter full so that there's plenty of room to tap off excess paint on the side. Generally, I find high-quality, well-mixed paint (I like Benjamin Moore) to be fine right out of the can, but in extremely hot or dry conditions, a paint additive such as Floetrol or Penetrol (www.flood.com) can reduce brush marks and even the transitions between brushed and rolled areas. Follow the additive directions carefully to avoid problems.

1. WET THE BRISTLES. Before painting, wet the bristles in the appropriate solvent (check the can), and then squeeze out the excess. This makes cleanup easier and prevents paint from creeping up the bristles.

2. GET A GRIP. Hold the pail with four fingers on the bottom and your thumb wrapped around the handle. Keep only an inch or two of paint in the pail to keep your brush and workspace clean and to minimize spills.

3. TAKE A DIP. Dunk the brush into the pail so that paint covers about one-third of the bristles. You can adjust the paint depth by tipping the pail slightly to the side.

5. APPLY THE PAINT. Starting from ½ in. to ¼ in. away from the trim or ceiling, use a single stroke to apply the paint. Looking slightly ahead of the bristles, pull the brush toward you; keep dragging until the paint stops covering.

4. ONE TAP. Tap one side of the brush against the side of the pail, and then gently drag the bristle tips over the rim. While painting, keep the pail in your left (or nondominant) hand for maximum productivity.

6. WORK IT OUT. With the brush rotated 90°, take a second pass with the bristles just touching the trim or corner. The paint should level out, leaving a smooth line free of ridges. Take a third pass only when necessary.

A Kit for Cutting In

Cutting in nice, straight lines starts with the right brush and a high-quality paint pail. A good choice is an angled sash brush with Chinex bristles. This bristle works well with both oil and latex paint. Pails come in several sizes. Choose one that's comfortable to hold and has enough room for tapping excess paint off the brush.

Leaktite 5-Quart Steel Paint Pail

Leaktite 5-Quart Paint Pail Liner

Corona Excalibur 2½-in. Angled Sash Brus

Continued ➡

By Philip Hansell

The paint protecting your doors and windows has a tough and important job to do. It must endure hostile weather, punishing wear, and up-close scrutiny every day. Paint made for doors and windows used to be judged by how much lead it contained—the more lead, the better. These coatings worked great. The heavy metal helped the paint to stick and to move seasonally. As is well-known now, however, lead is toxic and is especially dangerous to kids. For this reason, lead has been banned from household paint since 1978.

Old doors and windows generally have high concentrations of lead paint, so it's important to protect yourself and any children who live in the house by working lead safe. This means containing and collecting dust and chips and minimizing airborne particles. Wear a good particle mask when scraping and sanding, and use a HEPA vacuum. Thoroughly clean up the work area every day, and change your clothes before playing with the kids. (See "The Best Practices for Lead-Safe Remodeling" online at finehomebuilding. com for more information on working lead-safe.

Key Preparations

As with all painting projects, proper preparation is key for painting doors and windows. Before starting, my painters and I wash the glass with glass cleaner and paper towels. We then mask the hardware and the perimeter of the glass panes.

Once the door is cleaned and masked, we fill any damaged areas with two-part auto-body filler and sand the dry filler with 180-grit paper. For the initial sanding on the rest of the door, we use 220-grit paper on the interior and 180-grit on the exterior. For the second sanding (between the first and second coats), we use 320-grit paper for interior work and 220-grit for exterior work. A rougher grit on the outside gives the surface a little more "tooth" for better paint adhesion.

The weatherstripping on modern doors is generally easy to remove for painting. The vinyl-covered foam, sometimes identified as "Q-Lon" after one brand, is removed by starting at one end and gently pulling it out of the kerf that holds it. Removing the strip eliminates a lot of tedious masking. I replace it when the door is fully dry—24 hours for latex and about four days for oil. It easily pushes back into the slot it came out of.

I recommend leaving hardware in place. Disassembly and keeping track of the many small parts is an unnecessary and sometimes expensive hassle. Asking a client to forego doorknobs and locks for two or three days is an even bigger problem.

Choosing Paint

My favorite paint for interior work is Sherwin-Williams Pro Classic. I like both latex- and oil-based versions. Most clients choose satin or semigloss, which are easy to keep clean but don't

All Painting Starts with Prep

The prep work is the same for both windows and doors. The surrounding area is protected with disposable drop cloths, and the glass is cleaned and masked to prevent scratches. Any scratches or damage are repaired and spot-primed with oil primer. New doors and windows get a full coat of oil primer before painting. Tinted primer helps dark-colored topcoats to cover the surface fully.

Mask Glass and Hardware
Clean the glass, then mask the glass perimeter and any nearby hardware with painter's tape. High-quality tapes may seem expensive, but they are less likely to leave a sticky residue.

Scrape Loose Paint
Using a paint scraper or a painter's tool, scrape any loose paint. Sand out any scratches that don't reach the underlying surface.

Fill Deep Scratches
Two-part auto-body filler is great for repairing dog scratches and other deep imperfections. Apply it with a putty knife.

Sand Repairs
Once it's dry (in about 15 min.), sand the filler with 180-grit paper. Repairing significant damage may take more than one application.

produce an overly shiny finish.

For new exterior work, I prefer slow-dry oil primers because they penetrate and stick well and they prevent brown stains caused by wood tannins. Slow-dry primers must dry for four days or more before a topcoat is applied. Otherwise, the evaporating solvents in the primer can cause blistering and poor adhesion of the topcoat.

For a topcoat on both new and old work, I use acrylic latex paint, such as Sherwin-Williams Duration or Sherwin-Williams Emerald. Acrylic latex paints have greater elasticity and are more

Painting Doors:

Start Outside

Painting an entry door requires leaving it open for several hours. You'll need to manage small children and pets accordingly. If the sun is directly on the door, open it fully so that it's shaded by the home's interior. Keeping the door cool prevents lap marks and deep brush marks. (In the photos on the at right, the panes of glass are completely taped over. I would not do this ordinarily, but the photographer was unable to get good pictures with the western sun streaming through the glass.)

Clean Up as You Go
Wipe off excess paint and drips right away. Remove masking materials when the paint is dry to the touch. Reinstall weatherstripping when the paint is fully dry (one day for latex; four days for oil).

Apply the First Coat
Starting at the top of the door, paint all of the rails and muntins, and then paint the stiles one at a time.

Spot-Prime as Needed
Once any damage is repaired, lightly sand the rest of the door surface with 180-grit (exterior) or 220-grit (interior) paper. Cover repairs with stain-blocking oil-based primer.

Remove Weatherstripping
Most exterior doors have kerf-in weatherstripping that's removed by gently pulling on it. Removing it eliminates a lot of tedious masking.

Finish Inside

Work from the Top Down
After an initial sanding with 220-grit paper and a wipe down with a tack cloth, paint the top rail and any muntin bars. Because this door was painted previously and was free of damage, priming was unnecessary. New doors and repaired areas should be primed before painting, however.

Apply the First Coat
Starting at the top of the door, paint all of the rails and muntins, and then paint the stiles one at a time.

Panels First, Stiles Last
Paint stiles one at a time. Brush away any drips where panels meet stiles and rails as soon as possible. Look for and correct drips near locks and hardware.

Sand, Tack, and Recoat
Sand the door with 320-grit paper, and wipe the surface clean with a tack cloth. Turn the cloth often to pick up the maximum amount of dust. Apply the second coat in the same order as the first. The inside of the door isn't exposed to weather, so you can leave the tape on the glass for both coats.

Continued ➜

vapor permeable than oil paints, which makes them better at dealing with seasonal moisture and wood movement.

The Right Equipment

For exterior painting on doors and windows, I like a 2½-in. angled-sash brush. My favorite is a Corona with Chinex bristles. It works well with both latex- and oil-based paint and cleans up easily, even on hot, sunny days.

For painting the interior of doors and windows, I like an "all-paints" 2½-in. nylon-bristle brush from Corona or Purdy. Indoors, where brushes don't get baked by the sun, I prefer nylon bristles because they shed less than other bristle types.

When I'm painting large areas such as stiles, rails, and panels, I dip one-third of the bristle length into the paint and then slap both sides of the brush on the inside of the paint pot. For smaller, more precise locations such as muntin bars, I dip the brush, slap the sides of the pot, and scrape both sides of the brush along the rim. This removes excess paint from the sides of the brush, helping to prevent drips at corners.

The Right Order

It's best to work from the inside out to prevent messing up work you've already completed. When painting the interior side of double-hung windows, I start with the upper sash; when working on the exterior side, I start with the lower sash. On doors, I start with the muntin bars and panels. Rails come next, and then the stiles. The edge of the door with hinges gets painted the exterior color. The latch edge is painted to match the door's interior side.

Finish the Upper Sash
Paint the top rail and then the stiles. A final pass with a dry (undipped) brush yields straight and uniform brush marks. Push up the painted sash with a painter's tool.

Paint the Bottom Sash
Working from the top down, paint the lower sash. Once you're done, brush out any drips where vertical and horizontal parts meet.

Paint the Trim
Start with the head casing, and then paint the sides. Finish by coating the stool and the apron. As you finish each part, make a final pass with a dry brush.

Lower the Upper Sash
Begin by painting the muntin bars on the top sash, then lower the sash to coat the bottom rail and the lowest part of the stiles.

Raise the Upper Sash
Raise the upper sash and lower the bottom sash to expose the stiles and the top rail of the upper sash. Leave the sash partly open to paint the top rail.

Strain Your Paint
Old paint should be strained before use. Squeezing the paint through the strainer with a gloved hand saves time. Afterward, pull the glove off inside-out to prevent a mess.

The Right Gear for the Job

The tool kit below is all you need for painting doors and windows. You can find everything here at paint stores that cater to professionals.

¾-in. high-quality masking tape

Two-part auto-body filler

1½-in. putty knife

2½-in. angled-sash nylon-bristle brush

2½-in. angled-sash Chinex-bristle brush

180-, 220-, and 320-grit sandpaper

5-in-1 painter's tool

Tack cloth

Elastic-top strainer

2½-gal. paint pot

Disposable latex gloves

Continued ➡

Brush-Painting a Steel Door

By Andy Engel

While steel entry doors are durable, reasonably priced, and energy efficient, their details don't match the visual warmth of a well-built wood door. Still, a good paint job can go a long way to making a steel door look as welcoming as a wood one.

The key to a good-looking paint job on any door is the direction of the brushmarks. On a wood door, the grain dictates the direction that you paint. With a steel door, think how the grain would run if the door were wood, and paint accordingly.

Paint in moderate conditions. If you work in the direct sun or in very hot temperatures, the paint can dry too quickly, making it hard to clean up errant brushstrokes or blend more paint onto freshly painted areas. Although many paints can be used in temperatures as low as 35°F, working in the cold makes paint harder to spread. And if the temperatures drop below the minimum, the paint won't cure properly.

Buy a quality acrylic paint and follow the directions. Acrylic paint holds up well and is easy to clean from brushes with water. The door shown here is a fire door for separating a garage from living space, so I didn't prime over the factory primer. Had this been an exterior door, I would have primed it using the same sequence as in the photos.

Although you can paint doors while they're hanging in their frames, I prefer to work with them lying flat. Drips and sags in the paint are less likely, and there's no chance you'll spill paint on the foyer floor.

3. PAINT THE PANEL MOLDING FIRST. Here, the brushmarks should go in the long direction of each edge.

4. BRUSH THE PANEL ENDS. Use careful, short brushstrokes running in the same direction as the length of the panels, never across their width.

5. COVER THE PANEL CENTERS. Make broad brushstrokes along the length of the panels, brushing toward the previously painted ends.

6. PAINT THE CENTER STILES. Brush up and down. Painting onto the abutting rails is necessary and OK.

1. CLEAN THE DOOR. Use window cleaner to remove dirt and oil from the door. The cleaning agents are meant to evaporate and to leave glass free of streaks, so they don't leave residue that could interfere with paint adhesion.

2. ROUGH UP THE SURFACE. Use your fingers to guide a synthetic steel-wool pad into all the nooks and crannies. Use a microfiber tack cloth to pick up the dust.

7. DO NOT LET THE OVERLAPS DRY. Right after brushing onto the rails from the center stiles, brush this paint out across the width of the door, keeping a straight brush line at the "joint" between the center stile and rail.

8. PAINT THE RAILS. Brush in the long direction, and lap onto the edge stiles. As in the previous step, brush out the overlaps in the direction of the stiles' "grain" before the paint begins to set up.

9. PAINT THE OUTER STILES. Paint in long, sweeping brushstrokes, and include the door's edges. At the holes for the knob and deadbolt, keep the brushmarks straight, passing directly over the holes rather than dragging the brush around them. You might get drips into the holes, but that's OK.

Plastic Makes Painting Easier

Synthetic steel wool doesn't fill my fingers with sharp metal fibers the way actual steel wool can. The grit of 3M's synthetic steel wool is indicated by its color. The maroon pads are fine enough that they aren't likely to abrade through the factory primer and damage the door's galvanization. (Any scratches that penetrate the zinc coating on the steel skin can rust.)

Angled sash brushes get in the corners better than square brushes. For acrylic paints, synthetic bristles are best, and I've found that Purdy brushes work well and last for years. I like a 3-in. brush because it's big enough to speed up the job but small enough to be maneuverable. Finally, a 1-qt. plastic container (you can use a clean takeout-soup container) is easier to work from than a 1-qt. paint can. The 3-in. brush fits more easily into the plastic container's larger opening.

Painting Walls with Glazes

By Patricia McTague Pontolilo

Every time I pick up a new decorative painting product at the paint store, I am discouraged by the lack of instructions. The directions tend to be oversimplified and fail to mention the many little tricks that make a decorative-painting project successful. Glazing kits are a perfect example.

A glaze is a semitransparent layer of paint applied over a complementary solid color, or base coat. You've probably heard of ragging, bagging, or sponging. These glazing techniques are named for the tools used to create the texture. For centuries, artisans have used glazes to add texture and depth to art, furniture, and walls. Glazes are a great alternative to solid colors and wallpaper, and are an excellent way to hide flaws in imperfect walls.

Mixing the glaze is the easy part. You don't need a kit, just a few basic ingredients, the right color combination, and good technique. As a decorative painter, I've learned a lot about using glazes, but one thing I can't stress enough is that practice makes perfect.

Start with a Sample Board

I do sample boards for every job. Sample boards give me a chance to try different color combinations and textures, and to establish the right glaze formula. Most important, though, sample boards are a great way to practice technique and to see how colors interact.

I use 2-ft. by 2-ft. pieces of tempered hardboard for my samples, but you can use a scrap piece of drywall or any other smooth surface as a sample board. Remember, bigger is better. When you put the sample in the room, a larger board gives a better reading of what the color and texture will look like on the walls.

Priming the boards before you start is a good idea. This way, the boards won't swell and the paint will adhere well so that you can use one board for multiple samples. The first sample is rarely a screaming success. On this job, the homeowner liked my first sample but asked that I make it "just a little bit darker" when I did the walls. Even though it was a simple adjustment, I did one last sample to make sure the glaze was right.

Match the Colors to the Room

You'll need two paint colors: a base-coat color and a glaze color. You can start by choosing one overall color as a starting point for the glaze. I usually use the furniture, the art, or a fabric in the room for inspiration. Matching paint to objects is always easier than matching objects to paint. Here, I based the color combination on an existing Asian carpet.

I use paint chips to decide on the first color, then choose a second color either a little lighter or a little darker than the first choice, but in a similar hue. I've had the best results using different values of the same color paint. In this case, I used two shades of orange.

When I make my samples, I usually do two versions, reversing

Continued ➡

START WITH PAINT AND GLAZING LIQUID. Most paint stores have graduated buckets ideal for measuring glazes. Mix 1 part paint with 2 parts glazing liquid in a bucket, and stir them well. Then test the glaze on a sample board (inset photo). The glaze should spread a little more easily and thinly than paint. Add thinner as needed to help the paint flow across the surface. For coverage, refer to the glaze label.

BASE-COAT WITH THE RIGHT PAINT. Base-coating the walls for a glaze is just like painting a wall normally. Cut in the ceiling and trim, and roll out the walls. Use a midrange sheen like satin or pearl, and expect to use two coats to cover primed walls.

the base-coat and glaze colors. Most of the time, I find that darker glazes over lighter base coats work best. The lighter base coat gives the impression of light coming through, and the glaze creates texture and depth. Of course, decorative painting is as much an art as it is a science, so don't be afraid to experiment with color or texture.

Texture and Technique Take Practice

There are positive and negative glazes. A positive glaze is applied and textured in one step. Sponging a glaze onto the wall is positive glazing. Negative glazes are applied and textured in separate steps. Applying the glaze with a brush, roller, or pad and then creating texture by dabbing a sponge against the wall is negative glazing. The texture here is created by removing glaze from the surface.

I do almost all negative glazing, but I use a variety of tools to create different textures. This glaze, textured with cheesecloth, softens the appearance of the walls and produces an organic, atmospheric feeling. Alternatively, a strié—streaky vertical lines—is created with a dry, stiff-bristle brush and can be more formal and pronounced.

Use your sample boards to find and refine a texture that is right for your project. There are a number of tools—from expensive horsehair stippling brushes to plastic shopping bags—that can be used to texture a glaze.

Open Time Matters

In some states, oil-based paints (or alkyds) are no longer available because they don't meet VOC standards. For now, they are still available in Connecticut, where I do most of my work. Although I use water-based paints wherever I can, including base coats, I mix my glazes with oil-based paint and glazing liquid. Because I work alone, I appreciate the longer open time of oil-based paint. Open time is the amount of time I can work the glaze before it starts to set up. Weather also can affect open time. The best time to glaze is on a cool, damp day.

Glazes have three ingredients: paint, glazing liquid, and paint thinner. The paint adds color, the glazing liquid extends the paint's open time, and the paint thinner thins the glaze. I was taught to start with 1 part paint, 1 part glazing liquid, and 1 part paint thinner. That formula is easy to remember, but I often found that I had too much paint and thinner in the mix. Now I start with 1 part paint, 2 parts glazing liquid, and no thinner. This way I can adjust the glaze without making an excessive amount.

When I make my first samples, I mix a small amount, about ½ quart, of glaze. If I want more color saturation or a denser texture, I add a little paint at a time until I'm happy with the sample. The glaze should spread across the sample board (and later, the walls) more easily and thinly than paint. If it is too thick, I add small amounts of paint thinner until it flows easily across the surface. Be careful, though. If you thin the glaze too much, the paint thinner decreases the open time, and although the glaze might look good on a horizontal board, it might not hold a texture and could run down the walls.

GLAZING CAN BE MESSY. Cover the floors with drop cloths, and tape the trim and ceiling.

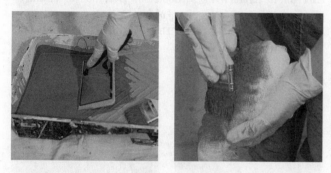

WET YOUR TOOLS. If you start with a dry pad and texturing tool, the glaze will change as you work and the tools become saturated with paint. Here, the author is using a ball of cheesecloth for texture. To keep the glaze consistent, she works some of the glaze into the pad and cheesecloth before starting.

Keeping Up With Fast-Drying Latex Glazes

Although I prefer to mix glazes with oil-based paints, I have done plenty of glazing with latex products as well. Here is a list of things I do to extend open time and work more efficiently when glazing with latex.

Add paint conditioner to the glaze. I mix latex glazes the same way I mix oil glazes: 1 part latex paint, 2 parts water-based glazing liquid, and a little water (instead of paint thinner) to thin the glaze. But I also add a fourth ingredient. To increase open time and emulate the smoothing properties of oil-based paint, I use a small amount of a latex glaze extender (www.benjaminmoore.com) or a paint conditioner, such as Floetrol (www.flood.com).

Wet the walls. To increase open time and to prevent dragging, I wet the walls before applying the latex glaze. In a small bucket, I mix warm water and a drop of dish soap to keep the water from evaporating. Just before I'm ready to apply the glaze to an area, I dip a rag or sponge into the water and wipe down the wall only enough to dampen it, but not so much that the water drips.

Work with a partner. One of the keys to any successful glaze is working quickly. When I glaze with latex, I like to work with a partner. One person applies the glaze, and the other textures. Working with a partner is efficient, and the applicator should have plenty of time to step back from the wall and inspect the glaze in progress.

Seal the finished walls. Latex glazes are not as durable as oils. After the glaze has cured for 24 hours, I seal it with a low-luster water-based polyurethane. I use a brush or pad to apply the clear coat, but not a roller. You won't see them until the wall dries, but roller marks will be visible in the clear coat.

When the glaze dries, it will acquire the sheen of the paint that you used. I prefer a low-luster look, so I use only matte, flat, or eggshell paints for my glazes.

Prep and Base Coat First

The prep work for glazing is the same as for any other interior painting. Fill any holes, caulk the trim, sand damaged paint, and prime the walls if they are old or in bad condition.

Base-coating is also straightforward: Cut in the ceiling and trim, and roll out the walls the way you would any painting project. Be sure to use paint with the right sheen. I use two coats of Benjamin Moore's latex pearl finish for most of my base coats. It has midrange sheen, between eggshell and semigloss, which is ideal for glazing. Glazes dry too quickly on flat sheens, and they don't adhere well to glossier surfaces. I always let the final base coat set up for 24 hours before glazing.

I glaze one wall at a time, so I tape the adjacent unglazed walls to keep them clean. Wall edges are one of the most commonly flawed areas because people worry about getting glaze on adjacent surfaces. Even if I don't tape all the surrounding areas, I don't sacrifice the quality of the glaze to avoid making a mess. Instead, I'm always prepared to clean or touch up the adjacent unglazed wall, ceiling, or trim later.

Continued ➡

Glaze One Wall at a Time

Once you start glazing, you'll need to move quickly to get the job done before the glaze begins to set up. Start in a corner and stop at the end of each wall. This way, when you're done with the wall, you'll be able to go back and fix any flaws while the glaze is still open.

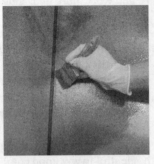

1. BEGIN WITH A TRIANGLE IN A CORNER. Apply the glaze with a pad, starting in an upper corner. Stay about 1 in. from the trim, ceiling, and adjacent wall.

2. WORK THE EDGES WITH A BRUSH. Before texturing the glaze, work it up to the edges with a small disposable brush. Don't brush the glaze; push it with the tips of the bristles to create texture.

3. GLAZE IN A DIAGONAL PATTERN. As you work across the wall, apply and texture the glaze in 12-in. to 18-in. diagonal bands. Work first from the top down, then from the bottom up.

Pay Attention to the Edges

If you did a sample on a horizontal surface, expect gravity to change things a little on vertical walls. Start in an inconspicuous location, and keep your eyes peeled for runs or drips.

I glaze 12 in. to 18 in. at a time, diagonally from left to right. I work quickly from top to bottom first, then bottom to top. This motion not only is efficient, but it also helps to prevent lap marks, those dark spots where glaze overlaps. Lap marks are tough to avoid completely; applying the glaze diagonally makes them less noticeable.

When I apply a glaze, I like to stay about 1 in. from the edges of the walls. Often, the texturing tool I'm using is too big to get into the corners and just makes a mess of the adjacent surface. I use a small disposable brush to work the glaze into the edges instead.

I also don't texture all the way to the edge of the glaze I've applied. This is called the wet edge, and I leave the glaze heavy and untextured until my next pass. Keeping a wet edge allows me to work back into the previously textured area.

Once the wall is completed, I step back and take a look. With an oil-based glaze, I still may be able to touch up the texture or fix a run. Be careful fixing a troublesome area, though. Messing around with paint that is starting to set up can cause obvious flaws. And don't be too critical. The glaze will become more subtle as it dries.

4. KEEP A WET EDGE. Don't texture all the way to the edge of the most recently applied glaze. Leave it wet and heavy to keep it from setting up. On the next pass, work the newly applied glaze into the wet edge.

5. MARRY TWO GLAZED WALLS CAREFULLY. When you reach the end of a wall and meet a recently glazed wall, it is important to get all the way into the corner without getting any glaze on the adjacent surface. Use the disposable brush again to push the glaze carefully into the corner.

Colors and Textures Customize Any Room

One of the benefits of glazing is that you can produce a one-of-a-kind look at a low cost. Two variables, color and texture, can be used to create a custom finish. Varying shades of the same color tend to work well together, but color combinations are limited only by your imagination. You even can use stain instead of paint for a dark glaze. For a subtle texture, try dabbing a stippling brush, a ball of cheesecloth, or a sponge over the glaze. More dramatic textures can be created with rags and plastic bags. Stiff brushes, combs, and other homemade tools can be used to create linear textures. And remember, glazes are not reserved for walls. They also can be used on cabinetry and trim.

ONE-OF-A-KIND WALLS. Glazing is a great, inexpensive route to a custom look. From a subtle, rustic texture with analogous colors to a bold strié, glazes open a lot of possibilities for your walls.

Paint Failure

By Tim Leahy

We've all seen it. A drive through almost any neighborhood in the nation reveals homes whose paint is perfect and pristine next to others whose paint is bubbled, peeling, or actually flaking off. Paint failure not only looks bad, but it invites water and weather inside the building envelope where it can cause serious damage.

In the coastal New England communities where I work, a good exterior paint job should last about three years. In a less harsh environment, a paint job on exterior wood should last five years or more. When premature paint failure occurs, it leaves homeowners, contractors, and paint suppliers with the same question: Why?

Although there are some telltale signs that point to a specific cause for a paint job gone bad, many of the factors leading to premature paint failure are related to conditions during application, making assessment after the fact difficult. It is far easier to identify conditions that can lead to failure and eliminate them at the time of application—before they result in separation of the paint from the surface it was designed to protect and beautify.

Poor Surface Prep

The bond between paint and wood is a mechanical one, so sanding the surface is critical for strong adhesion. New clapboards, in particular, have a dense, shiny "mill glaze" that, unless removed, interferes with the ability of the primer or stain to penetrate the wood. When repainting previously coated surfaces, it is important to ensure that the old paint is adhering well and that the surface is abraded so the new coat grabs tight.

Continued ➜

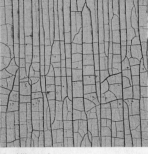

❶ Alligatoring

❷ Chalking

❸ Blistering

❹ Cracking/flaking

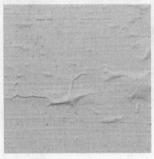

❺ Peeling

❻ Mildew

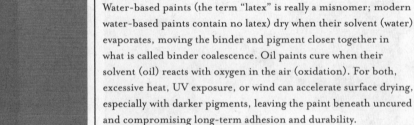

❼ Gloss retention

❽ Incompatiblity

❾ Wrinkling

❿ Fading

Sun and Wind

Water-based paints (the term "latex" is really a misnomer; modern water-based paints contain no latex) dry when their solvent (water) evaporates, moving the binder and pigment closer together in what is called binder coalescence. Oil paints cure when their solvent (oil) reacts with oxygen in the air (oxidation). For both, excessive heat, UV exposure, or wind can accelerate surface drying, especially with darker pigments, leaving the paint beneath uncured and compromising long-term adhesion and durability.

❸ ❹ ❺ ❼ ❾

Contaminants

Where there is dust, mildew, or salt glaze, paint will adhere to that and not the surface. These can be removed with specialized house washes such as Jomax.

❸ ❹ ❺ ❻

Surface Moisture

Paint applied too soon after power washing or rain, or when condensation is present (a risk when the temperature is within 5°F of the dewpoint), exposes the new film to excess moisture and weakens it in ways that might not show up until later. This affects both oil-based and water-based products. When a moisture meter reads above 15%, it's best before painting to allow the surface to dry or to correct the condition causing the moisture.

❸ ❺ ❾

No Primer

Primer seals in tannins, fills pores, and binds wood fibers to create a nonabsorptive, sandable surface to which topcoats readily adhere; it also protects end grain from damaging moisture. Without primer, paint can absorb into the wood, which will make it dry too fast, compromising film integrity.

❸ ❹ ❺ ❻ ❾

Cold

If applied at too low a temperature (below 50°F, generally), the binder in water-based paint is unable to fully coalesce with the pigment into a durable film. Cold retards the curing of oil paints as well but results more often in surface imperfections than film failure.

❸ ❹ ❺ ❼

High Humidity

Relative humidity slows the drying of water-based paint and affects the curing of oil-based paint, compromising film formation.

③ ⑤ ⑥ ⑨

Poor Quality

Water-based paints that contain 100% acrylic binders provide superior flexibility and durability. Paints that contain blends of acrylic and other resins may not perform as well.

① ② ③ ④ ⑤ ⑥ ⑦ ⑧ ⑨ ⑩

Incompatible Coats

Modern formulations have negated many rules of thumb regarding the application of oil paint over water-based paint or vice versa. Without those guidelines, it is critical to adhere to manufacturers' instructions for compatibility with other paints or primers. Recoating old oil paint with modern acrylic paint, however, often leads to failure as the new flexible coating bonds to the old brittle paint, yanking it off the surface.

① ④ ⑤ ⑧

The Wrong Product

Exterior and interior paints and primers are engineered for specific surfaces and conditions. Exterior paints are formulated to stand up against UV radiation, temperature swings, and surface movement. Interior paints are formulated for easy leveling and durability against cleaning. Primers are formulated to create an optimal surface for paint. Choosing the right product yields the best results.

① ② ③ ④ ⑤ ⑥ ⑦ ⑧ ⑨ ⑩

Consistency

Overthinning weakens the molecular structure of all paints, resulting in a weaker surface (think of a latex glove being stretched too thin). Modern paints rarely need thinning, but if a paint is too thick, it will dry on the surface but not underneath, causing failure due to improper curing.

② ④ ⑦ ⑩

Continued ➔

Cleaning Paintbrushes and Roller Covers

By Jim Lacey

As a professional painter, I have one rule for purchasing paintbrushes and roller covers: Buy the best ones available. These high-quality tools are the first step to ensuring a professional finish. However, higher-quality tools come with a higher price tag and should be considered an investment. To get the best and longest performance from brushes and roller covers, you have to clean them properly after each use. The process is not difficult or time-consuming, and with proper and regular cleanings, you can expect to get close to a lifetime of service from a paintbrush, and two or three uses out of each roller cover.

Cleaning brushes and roller covers in a sink is a lot easier than cleaning them in a bucket, but both options work. Keep in mind that while the cleaning process is the same no matter the type of finish you've been applying—primer, paint, or stain—you have to substitute paint thinner for water when cleaning oil-based products from your tools. Paint thinner shouldn't be dumped down the drain. Dispose of it properly, or store it for future use.

Also, I recommend cleaning brushes more than once a day. This may seem excessive, but depending on several factors, including humidity, the type of work you're doing, and the type of paint you're using, it's often necessary. This practice keeps brush bristles fresh and ultimately makes your work easier and more pleasant.

Rinse, Brush, Rinse

1. WASH OUT THE LIQUID PAINT. Half-fill a clean bucket with warm water or paint thinner (for rinsing oil-based paints), or use a sink if one is available. Dip the brush into the water, and flare its bristles against the bottom of the bucket or sink. Dab the brush several times to allow the water or thinner to penetrate the bristles.

2. BRUSH OUT ANY DRY PAINT. After a rinse, brush the bristles with a steel brush, moving from the handle toward the tip of the bristles. This helps to loosen any dry paint that has hardened in the brush, especially just below the ferrule. Rinse the brush again. Repeat this process until the water or thinner coming out of the brush runs clear.

3. TAP AND STOW. Once clean, extract as much water or thinner as you can from the bristles, either by spinning the brush between your hands or by tapping the brush on the toe of your shoe. Give the bristles a final brushing with a steel brush or a brush comb to restore their shape, and return the brush to its wrapper or case.

The 5-In-1 Tool Shines When Cleaning Roller Covers

1. REMOVE EXCESS PAINT. With a 5-in-1 tool, scrape any excess paint out of the roller into a paint can.

2. WASH THE ROLLER. Work the roller under warm water—either in a sink or in a bucket—with the 5-in-1 tool until the water runs clear. If the roller was used on oil-based products, simply discard it. It's not cost-effective to clean this tool with paint thinner.

3. SPIN TO DRY. Return the roller to the roller handle, and spin it until most of the water has been removed. Place the roller cover in its plastic wrapper, and store it flat.

Choose the Best Product

Not all paintbrushes and roller covers are created equal. The best last a long time if you treat them well. Most painters that I've talked to use brushes made by Purdy (www.purdycorp.com) or Corona (www.coronabrushes.com). According to these painters, these two manufacturers make some of the best paintbrushes available. The type of bristle you choose depends on the finish. Universal bristles, such as Chinex, can be used with both water-based and oil-based finishes. However, some manufacturers suggest dedicating one brush to oil-based finishes and another to water-based finishes. Nylon, polyester, or nylon-polyester blended bristles should be used only with water-based products; China-bristle brushes should be reserved for oil-based finishes.

When choosing a roller cover, buy the most expensive product your budget will allow because price is often indicative of quality. You'll still get only two or three uses from each roller, but quality rollers are far less likely to shed fibers during painting. The fibers on a good roller cover are usually made of nylon, polyester, or a similar synthetic blend. The core should be made of rigid plastic, not soft cardboard. A roller cover with a ⅜-in. nap is a good option for most painting tasks.

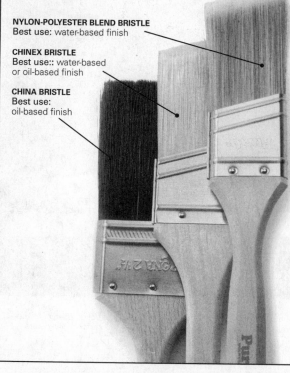

NYLON-POLYESTER BLEND BRISTLE
Best use: water-based finish

CHINEX BRISTLE
Best use:: water-based or oil-based finish

CHINA BRISTLE
Best use: oil-based finish

Finishing Secrets for Furniture-Grade Trim

By Tim Leahy

As far as work in the trades is concerned, I'm a lucky guy. For the past 12 years, I've spent my days as a finish foreman with a company that remodels and restores historic mansions and builds new homes in Newport, R.I. Our carpenters install custom-milled trim, cabinetry, doors, and windows. Then my crew and I go in and finish them. Given all that—and the ocean views—it's a sweet deal.

There's no doubt that the craftsmanship that precedes us sets the stage for us to do our best work. But delivering flawless finishes is no easy task. Staining and clear-coating the mahogany mantelpiece featured here—and the paneled library that it's in—took three of us two weeks to complete. Yes, we were methodical and took great care when applying the stain and the final clear coats. But nothing got more of our attention than the prep we did before popping the lid off the first can of stain.

Sand Every Inch

On one of our recent jobs, someone accidentally dripped water on an oak floor that my crew and I had just prepared for stain. Unfortunately, that someone never told us what had happened. When we applied the stain, there—in deep, dark splotches—was the evidence. The water had raised the grain, creating an uneven surface. Unlike a layer of paint, which hides the wood, stain highlights it. Unfortunately, stain also highlights watermarks, fingerprints, dried glue, and swirl marks left by power sanders. To get consistent results with stain, you can't just sand the blemishes; you need to sand the entire project evenly.

Sanding everything evens the porosity of the wood. Let me explain: When wood is run through a planer or shaper, its outer fibers are compressed, which leaves it with a glazed or glossy appearance. If stain is applied directly over those compressed fibers, it doesn't penetrate the wood the way it's meant to. Sanding opens the fibers evenly, allowing stain to soak into the wood.

The amount of sanding you should do depends on the quality of the wood. If you are staining molding or cabinetry made at a high-quality woodshop or in your own shop, chances are you'll need to sand the surface only lightly. Wood from big-box stores and moldings or cabinetry that has been exposed to temperature and humidity changes will likely need more work. In either case, using the proper grit sequence is important.

Because of the high quality of wood we work with, we typically use a two- or three-step sanding sequence. We thoroughly inspect all the wood first for the problem areas mentioned above, as well as for planer snipe. We do this by holding a light at a 45° angle close to the wood so that the light rakes across the surface. Don't use halogen work lights; they create too much glare. An aluminum clip-on work light with a 150w bulb works best.

We remove the illuminated trouble spots by sanding along the

Continued ➜

Step 1: Sand

After protecting the surrounding area with rosin paper and masking tape, spot-sand blemishes with 120-grit sandpaper. Then sand all the woodwork in two passes, first with 120-grit sandpaper, then 150 grit. This grit sequence is good for hardwoods, like the mahogany shown here. On softer woods, start with 150 grit or 180 grit, and proceed up to 220.

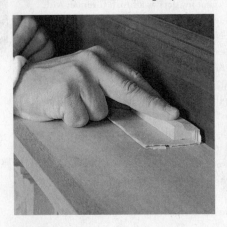

HIT THE IMPERFECTIONS FIRST. The area around an errant nail becomes a lump in the surface. To flatten it, use 120-grit sandpaper wrapped around a flat, square-edged block. Once all imperfections are sanded, begin sanding the entire surface.

EASE SHARP EDGES, BUT DON'T ALTER THE PROFILE. Sharp joints and edges splinter easily and don't take finish well. Use gentle pressure, and sand in the direction of the grain. Sandpaper wrapped around a wooden dowel works well on crown, especially in the cove portion of the profile.

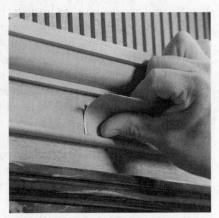

SAND EVERY INCH, NO MATTER HOW SMOOTH IT LOOKS. Planer and profile-cutting knives compress the top layer of wood fibers so much that stain can't penetrate the surface the way that it's designed to. That's why it's necessary to sand everything before applying stain.

One section at a time. Sand each shape or plane separately so that you don't sand one spot more than another or in the wrong direction relative to the grain. Be sure to get into grooves and crevices, and around corners. Keep the area well-lit and vacuumed so that you can see the surface. Make sure everything feels smooth before proceeding to Step 2.

grain with 120-grit sandpaper. We also lightly sand sharp corners and edges at this point because they splinter easily and don't take finish well.

Once the imperfections are removed, we sand the entire surface with 120-grit paper. Then we sand with 150-grit paper, still working with the grain. We maintain even pressure as we sand, making sure that we don't bear down with our fingertips. Doing so could leave sanding marks and stripes.

You can use a random-orbit sander on flat stock and cabinets, and sanding sponges are great for molding profiles. Just make sure to use high-quality sponges from 3M or Norton; their sanding surface is consistent, the granules don't flake off, and they have a stiff sponge material, which gives them crisp edges. Cheap sponges fall apart easily and often lack crisp edges.

Once everything has been sanded, we vacuum and clear sawdust from nooks and crannies with an air hose. We check the surface one more time with our bare hands to make sure it's smooth. Then we lay tarps around the area and bring out the staining supplies.

Premixed Stain Isn't for Every Wood

I've seen plenty of beautiful woodwork virtually destroyed by stain because it was applied to wood that's difficult to finish. Pine, cherry, maple, and birch can absorb stain unevenly, often resulting in a blotchy look. To prevent blotching, use a wood conditioner prior to staining these woods. Woods like oak, mahogany, walnut, chestnut, ash, and hickory are easier to stain. Their porosity is more consistent, so they take stain more evenly.

Off-the-shelf oil-based wiping stains such as Minwax (www.minwax.com) are easy to use. They are premixed, so they are ready to use straight from the can. They also dry slowly, so they can be pushed around the surface easily to avoid lap marks. Dye stains, on the other hand, require mixing and dry much more quickly, so they are more difficult to use. Dye stain can be the best option for blotch-prone woods, however.

Using premixed stain, as we did on this project, is a two-step process: applying the stain, then wiping it off. We apply stain from the bottom up so that an errant drip doesn't hit bare wood. It's possible to apply it with a rag, but a tapered top-quality

Step 2: Stain

Staining wood is a two-step process. First, brush on the stain; then wipe it down with a clean rag. Let the stain sit for several minutes to achieve its full color potential. Additional coats yield a darker color but can muddy the grain. Let the stain dry fully before proceeding to Step 3.

CUT IN WITH A BRUSH. Working in small sections, apply the stain liberally, and let it sit for several minutes before wiping it off. Apply stain in a neat, orderly process. Excess stain can drip, run, and puddle, which can leak or leach out from behind moldings afterward.

WIPE WITH A CLEAN RAG. As you're working across the surface, keep the soaking time consistent for all sections, and pay attention to the edges, profiles, and corners. Replace the cloth when it gets loaded with stain.

AFTER WIPING, USE A CLEAN BRUSH TO GET INTO CREVICES. Inexpensive brushes are great for removing excess stain from tight spots. Have a dry cloth handy to keep bristles dry.

The Secret to Dealing with Blemishes: Wet Sanding with Stain

When water or glue stains appear after stain is applied, sand the spot with 180- or 220-grit wet/dry sandpaper and stain. Apply stain to the wood and also to the paper; then sand the area in the direction of the grain. Wipe and repeat to remove the spot. Use longer strokes to feather out the area if needed. After the wet sanding, the glue spots are erased. This process also works wonders on scratches.

Find the blemish

Sand with stain

Wipe and repeat

Continued →

paintbrush with natural bristles is the best choice. These brushes offer better control over the stain, which is crucial when working around molding profiles. To prevent lap marks, we cut in every surface as if we were painting trim. To remove any excess stain, a rag is the tool of choice, though brushes are helpful in tight spots.

To heighten the level of finish on open-grain woods like oak, hickory, and mahog-any, we often apply a grain filler like Behlen's Pore-O-Pac (www.behlen.co.uk) once we're done staining. Grain filler produces a smooth surface and is often used on fine furniture and musical instruments. Whether we end the coloring process with stain or grain filler, we wait at least 18 to 24 hours before applying the finish coats.

Topcoats Serve Many Purposes

Topcoats protect. They also affect the overall feel and final look of the wood. Products like teak oil, furniture oil, or Danish oil create a natural look. They highlight the grain, but because they soak into the wood, natural finishes don't leave a durable film that protects the surface. Use them for projects that won't be exposed to much sunlight or wear and tear. Oil finishes are typically brushed on, then wiped off with a rag, so they're easy to work with.

Film-forming finishes create a hard, durable surface and a lens that allows light to accent color and grain. The most commonly used film-forming finishes include varnish, shellac, polyurethane, and lacquer, which I'm applying here. Two-part conversion finishes are available, but they're difficult to apply and typically are used on production cabinetry and furniture.

Each of the film finishes I mentioned is available in waterborne and solvent-based formulations. To protect wood from alcohol, water, and ultraviolet (UV) light, we typically use varnish or a conversion finish with UV-blockers. For a durable finish that comes close to an antiqued look, choose lacquer or shellac. And, as you guessed, the most commonly used hand-applied finish is polyurethane. It doesn't spray well, so we don't use it often. We like to use lacquer because it is easy to spray and dries quickly.

We prefer to spray clear coats because spraying produces the smoothest finish. Spraying also allows us to apply thin layers so that it's easy to fix problems that present themselves after the first coat. We can sand down the initial thin layer to fix a stain blemish that we missed, and we can blend the clear finish around that area when we're done. Despite the great working conditions and projects, there always seems to be something that needs a little extra attention.

Step 3: Fill the Grain

Add a grain filler to accent the grain and to smooth the surface of open-grain woods such as mahogany. Filler also can be used on bare wood if no stain is to be applied. If you don't want to use grain filler, skip this step and proceed to Step 4.

Mix the grain filler with the stain to add color to the grain. Follow the label directions for the proper filler-to-stain ratio and consistency. Here, I accented the grain by using a darker stain. It's also possible to use a lighter stain for a different effect.

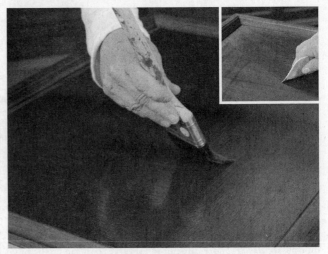

Apply along the grain, then perpendicular to it. Use a brush, and work in both directions to force the material into the wood pores. Wait for the sheen to dull; then use a rubber squeegee or plastic spreader to remove the excess. Work across the wood at a 45° angle to the grain.

Finish the removal with a clean rag. First, work across the grain, then with the grain. I like to fold the rag flat and wipe off the residue as if waxing a car. Overrubbing with the grain can remove too much filler. Letting the residue dry for too long makes it difficult to remove.

Don't forget profile transitions. Filler left on edges or in grooves results in a sloppy look when the piece is finished. A dull putty knife or pointed stick works well to clean these areas.

Step 4: Topcoat

Apply three to four coats of clear finish to protect the wood and to enhance its tones. Fill the nail holes after the first coat. If you fill them before the wood is sealed, the filler will penetrate the pores around the holes, creating a smudged look. Sand between each coat with fine sandpaper, and rub down the surface with a tack cloth between coats.

A properly applied spray finish gives a furniturelike quality to this library. The first coat of precatalyzed lacquer makes the wood come to life. When spraying lacquer or any other finish, maintain a wet edge at all times. Safe working conditions require good ventilation, a respirator, and a Tyvek suit.

Brushed-on polyurethane is a great choice, too. Always use a high-quality brush. Also, thin the first coat with mineral spirits or naphtha for a base layer void of brush marks. Then follow with two coats straight from the can. Make sure the area and the air are clean so that dust doesn't settle on the surface as the polyurethane dries.

LAST-MINUTE TOUCH-UP. I like to fill imperfections and nail holes after the first topcoat so that the putty matches the wood tone exactly. Force the material into the hole; then wipe it clean. You might need to mix two or three colors to match various tones in the piece.

Scuff each coat for the smoothest result. Use 400- or 600-grit sandpaper, 0000 steel wool, or fine Scotch-Brite pads to remove dust nibs and to prepare the surface for subsequent topcoats. Be careful not to sand through the clear coat and remove stain around profile edges.

Continued ➜

Restore a Wood Entry Door

By Sean Clarke

Several years ago, I wandered into a small East Coast shipyard. In the center of a quaint workshop was a shipwright kneeling alongside a wooden skiff. I watched as he applied epoxy by brush to the boat's exterior. At that moment, I realized that if a finish could stand up to brutal ocean conditions and nearly relentless sun exposure for a season, then surely this same finish could get a wood entry door through a couple of years of use.

Wood entry doors can be strikingly beautiful. Unfortunately, because they are exposed to weather and heavy use, they often show their age prematurely.

With a little research and lots of samples, I adopted an epoxy-based finishing system that changed the way I finish wood doors. I have completed dozens of doors with this approach, and I have to admit that my initial assumption about longevity was wrong. You can expect this finish to last from five to 10 years, depending on its exposure.

Here, I'll show you how to prep a wood door properly whether it has been painted or varnished, how to make minor repairs, how to apply an epoxy sealer, and finally, how to build up a varnish finish that yields a durable, clear shine.

Remove Existing Finish

Whether it's paint or varnish, removing the existing finish on a door is accomplished with the same techniques.

With the door placed level in its jig (sidebar p. 709), I apply a semipaste methylene-chloride-based stripper to the face of the door with an old paintbrush. Because methylene chloride is an aggressive chemical, be sure to wear nitrile gloves and to work in a well-ventilated area.

I find that stripping one-half of the face of the door at a time is best. If you're stripping only one side of the door, mask the back surface and any edges you don't want stripped. If you intend to finish both sides of the door, you can simply flip the door in its jig after the front face is complete.

It doesn't take long for the stripper to soften an existing finish. However, if I am stripping several layers of paint, I may

need to leave the stripper on for 30 minutes to an hour to cut through all the layers. The bulk of the paint or varnish can be removed with a taping knife or a paint scraper.

I switch to a Scotch-Brite pad and nylon brush to remove any residual finish left in crevices and molding profiles. Don't use steel wool or wire brushes for this process. Fragments from the metal can break off, become lodged in the wood fibers, and cause mineral spotting, which reveals itself in the form of tiny black spots that appear after the finish coat has been applied. The spotting typically is caused by a reaction between the mineral in the steel and the tannin in the wood, and is most commonly a problem with species like cherry, walnut, or white oak.

After all the finish and stripper are removed, I wash the door with acetone and a clean Scotch-Brite pad. I follow the wash with a clean cotton rag before the acetone evaporates. The acetone removes the wax residue left behind by the stripper. Many paste strippers contain wax to make the stripper easier to apply and to slow its drying time. If left on the door's surface, the wax residue would compromise the ability of the stain and sealer to penetrate the door as well as the ability of the varnish to bond to the door. The acetone also helps to remove any remaining finish from the pores in the wood.

Make Surface Repairs

Damage to the door should be remedied before any sanding takes place. Typical damage includes lifting or loose veneer and chips in the wood surface. For loose or lifting veneer, I clean the surfaces between the veneer and the substrate with 150-grit sandpaper folded in half. I push the sandpaper between the two surfaces and gently sand back and forth, removing any old glue or loose debris. I apply yellow wood glue to the back side of the veneer and the face of the substrate, and clamp down the veneer until the glue dries.

For chipped areas or in places where the veneer is in bad shape and has to be removed, I either fill the void with a two-part wood epoxy and then sand it flush, or I insert a new piece of veneer, depending on the size of the void or its location. When I clean around the edges of the missing piece of veneer, I try to follow grain lines to minimize the appearance of the fix.

Sand the Door Evenly

After repairs are done, I sand all the door's surfaces and moldings with 150-grit sandpaper. On doors without raised panels or molding details, I use an orbital dual-action palm sander. Otherwise, I sand by hand with a sanding block and a loose sheet of sandpaper.

I start by sanding the raised panels and their molding profiles or the rails and stiles that divide the panels. I always save the rails and stiles around the exterior of the door for last. This prevents unsightly sanding marks on the surface of the door.

I don't sand the door beyond 150-grit sandpaper because finer grits polish the wood, which makes it less receptive to the stain and sealer coats.

Prep for Stain

Removing the door's existing finish and repairing surface damage, which typically includes lifted or chipped veneer, should be done before all surfaces are sanded.

1. STRIP THE FINISH. Apply a chemical stripper with an old paintbrush. When the finish has softened, remove it with a scraper or taping knife. After stripping all the finish, wash the door with acetone to remove any residual finish and stripping residue.

2. FIX DAMAGED VENEER. Use a utility blade and chisel to clean up the edges of missing or damaged veneer. Follow grain lines to minimize the appearance of the fix. Glue and clamp a patch in place, and remove the waste with a sharp block plane.

3. SAND ALL SURFACES. Sand the door's middle rails and stiles or raised panels first, then the perimeter rails and stiles with 150-grit sand-paper. Use a sanding block on flat surfaces and loose sheets of sandpaper on molding profiles.

Continued ➨

Add Color

Use oil-based stains to achieve the desired color tone on the door. To avoid unsightly lap marks, start by staining raised panels first. Then stain the rails and stiles that divide the panels before staining the peri-meter rails and stiles. Let the stain dry for 12 hours before moving on to sealing.

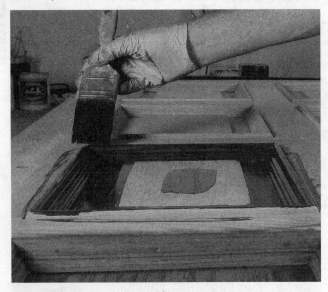

1. STAIN THE PANELS. Apply the stain to the raised panels and molding profiles with a quality brush. Quickly wipe up the excess stain, in the direction of the wood grain, with a cotton rag.

2. STAIN THE REST OF THE DOOR. Apply an even coat of stain to the stiles and rails and the door edges, working on one part at a time before wiping up the excess with a cotton rag. Always stain with the grain, never across it.

Apply the Sealer

Clear penetrating epoxy sealer protects the door from moisture, which causes rot as well as wood contraction and expansion.

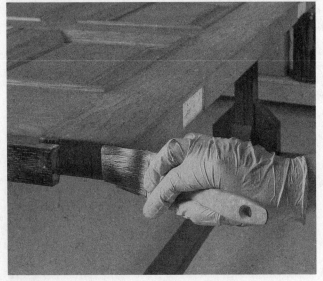

1. COAT THE END GRAIN. Apply the sealer to the end grain on the top and bottom edges of the door first. End grain wicks up the sealer as it is applied. Keep applying sealer to these areas until the door no longer accepts more, which is evident when the finish remains glossy.

2. COAT THE REST OF THE DOOR. Apply a single coat of sealer to all the faces of the door, including the raised panels and the door edges. Don't forget to apply sealer to the lockset and hinge mortises. Reapply sealer to any areas that seem to be drying too quickly. Let the sealer dry for no more than eight to 12 hours before applying the varnish.

Oil-Based Stains Are Better Than Water-Based

I make my own oil stain from dry pigment, a varnish binder, and a mineral-spirit reducer. The oil stain I make is purely pigment-based, and pigment-based stains don't fade as fast as dye-based stains when exposed to direct UV light. However, many over-the-counter oil stains can be used. Stains from Minwax and General Finishes, for example, are readily available and come in a variety of colors.

Don't use water-based stains for entry doors. They introduce water to the door surface. At this point in the process, the door's moisture content should be kept as low as possible.

Using a 2-in. flat China-bristle brush, I apply the stain to panels or middle stiles and rails first, then to perimeter stiles and rails to prevent unsightly lap marks. I also stain the top, side, and bottom edges of the door. After the entire door has been stained, I let it sit for a minimum of 12 hours, which helps to ensure that all the stain, including the stain that found its way under the raised panel moldings, is dry.

If any part of the door appears lighter than the rest, I simply sand that part with 220-grit sandpaper, remove the dust, and reapply a coat of stain to the area.

Sealer Protects the Door

Sealing the door against moisture is one of the most critical steps in ensuring a long-lasting finish. The Smith's sealer that I use does an excellent job at treating dry rot, which is common on many of my restorations, but it also provides good moisture protection and serves as a good base for the varnish coats.

I let the sealer dry for eight to 12 hours, depending on the temperature in my workspace, before adding the first coat of varnish. Applying varnish to the sealer coat before it's fully cured allows the varnish to bond chemically to the sealer.

A High-Gloss Finish Is the Most Durable

I use Epifanes marine spar varnish to build up topcoats because of its flexibility, leveling properties, and high UV-resistance and sheen-retention ratings.

The longevity of this finish hinges largely on its gloss level. A high-gloss finish reflects more UV light than a matte finish. Satin and matte finishes have added solids to dull their appearance; these solids absorb light and decrease the longevity of the finishes. A semigloss finish is acceptable, but that's the lowest sheen I use. I guarantee this finish for three years. I once had a client specify a satin finish for his doors. I documented the work for liability purposes, and sure enough, the finish didn't last three years.

To get the longest-lasting finish possible, I apply eight to 12 coats of varnish to my doors. For all but the last coat, I use Epifanes Wood Finish Gloss Varnish that has been thinned with Epifanes Brush Thinner. Each coat dries for 24 to 48 hours before receiving another coat of varnish.

Before I apply the last coat of finish, I release the floating raised panels from the door framework. When too much varnish builds up in this area—more than 6 mils, say—it can buckle and crack. Once all the panels have been released, I sand the door again with 220-grit sandpaper and clean up the dust.

I apply a final coat of Epifanes High Gloss Clear Varnish, which has great UV stability. After 24 hours, all the hardware can be reinstalled, and the door can be removed from the jig.

Once the door is free of the jig, I fill the screw holes in each end of the door with a two-part epoxy resin. I then sand these epoxy plugs flush and apply a single coat of varnish over the entire edge of the door. After the varnish cures for 12 hours, the door is ready to be hung back in its frame.

A Jig Makes the Work Easier

You can lay the door on sawhorses or a worktable to apply the finish, but building a jig takes little time, materials, or money, and has several advantages:

• Finishing both sides of the door at the same time is possible only when it's placed in a jig.
• The door can be rotated in the jig to ensure that varnish coats spread evenly over the face of the door.
• The jig and the door can be moved easily.
• All the door's edges are easily accessible when in the jig.
• The door can be stored on edge to prevent it from bowing.
• The door can be stored face down in the jig to eliminate debris buildup on the uncured face.

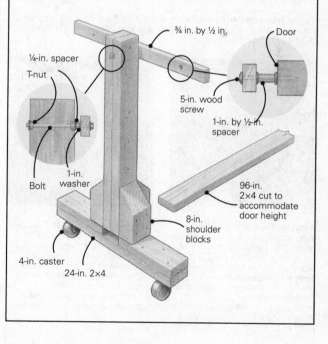

Continued →

Build the Finish

Reduce the varnish approximately 20% with a manufacturer-recommended brush thinner, or use mineral spirits or naphtha. This will allow the varnish to flow more easily. For the best results, apply the varnish with a 2-in. stiff China-bristle varnish brush. This varnish has an open time of approximately 10 to 15 minutes.

1. APPLY THE VARNISH. Working in the direction of the wood grain, apply a coat of varnish to all panels, rails, stiles, and door edges. Let the finish set up for five to 10 minutes.

2. ROTATE THE DOOR. Flip the door in its jig, catching any runs with the brush. Place the door face down for 10 to 15 minutes, then flip the door face up for 10 to 15 minutes. Repeat this rotation three or four times. Let the door dry face down for 24 hours before applying another coat of varnish. Repeat steps 1 and 2 until you've applied eight to 12 coats.

3. PREP FOR A FINAL COAT. Release the raised panels by scoring the finish along the molding edge with a utility knife before sanding all surfaces with 220-grit sandpaper. Buff with a clean Scotch-Brite pad, and remove any dust before brushing on a final coat of high-gloss varnish.

Use Dyes to Transform Poplar into Cherry

By Peter Gedrys

When we updated the kitchen in our 1920s home, we decided the cabinets should be made of cherry. However, I wanted everything else to be visually in tune with the new cabinets, and an adjacent door happened to be made of clear-finished poplar (a common choice back then). My solution was to turn the poplar into cherry. Historically, furniture makers also used stained or dyed poplar as an inexpensive alternative to the more desirable cherry. Using a sample cabinet door, I'll show how I transformed the color. You can use the same techniques to change the color of almost any species of wood.

Although close scrutiny will always reveal the poplar's grain pattern to be different, matching the color fools the eye into believing it is seeing cherry. The easiest way to begin the finish is with a dye; unlike pigmented stains, dyes are transparent and won't muddy the surface of the wood. I prefer to make dyes from water-soluble powders. If the color is too weak at first, I can easily add more powder to intensify the color. Water-based dyes are also extremely economical. You can make a gallon of color for as little as about $20, and it goes a long way.

The only problem with a water-based dye is that it will raise the wood's grain, so before applying the dye, I sand, lightly dampen the surface, let it dry for 10 minutes, and then give it a final sanding. Another option is to dye the wood, wait until it's dry, then seal the surface with a thin wash of shellac. The raised fibers will be locked in the sealer and can be easily sanded smooth without affecting the color.

Make Color Samples First

The biggest mistake many people make is trying to get the right color in one shot. I make a color sample in four steps. First, I pick the general color range (yellow brown, red brown, deep brown, etc.), and then dye a sample piece of the same species. I put the sample next to the color I want to match. If my sample looks light or washed out, I add more powder to the dye mix and adjust the warmth or coolness as required. Next, I adjust the color depth by making sure the value (light or dark) matches. Finally, I apply a coat of the clear finish I plan to use, which enlivens the color.

For these samples, I used two colors, both from W.D. Lockwood (www.wdlockwood.com): golden amber maple and antique cherry. A small scale is handy for weighing exact amounts of powder, but for this project, I measured by volume. I mixed about 2 oz. of powder into 16 oz. of water. As I mixed the dye, I put some on a white paper plate to see through the color. If it looked weak, I added more until it looked correct.

Apply a Base Layer of Color

Mix dye powder into hot distilled water, and let it cool. Check the strength of the dye on white paper, and adjust accordingly. Just to be safe, strain any undissolved dye particles with a fine paint filter. Flood the surface with dye, starting with the panel and progressing to the frame. Allow it to sit, and wipe off any excess.

Add More Dye until the Color Is Right

After the first layer of color is dry, a second dye can be applied to modify the color further. When that's dry, brush the surface with a thin wash coat of shellac. The color can be tweaked further with a layer of stain before the final top coat is applied.

CATCH DRIPS BEFORE THEY START. When finishing paneled doors, it's a good idea to blow a little compressed air around the hips of the panel to force out the dye that has migrated behind the rails and stiles. Otherwise, pooled dye will dry and create a halo along the hip.

MOVE THE PROCESS ALONG. Because the dye doesn't have a flammable base, you can use a heat gun or hair dryer to speed up the drying time between coats.

TOP COAT READY. When the color closely resembles cherry, the clear finish can be applied, which adds the final depth to the color.

Continued →

Deck Stain

By Matthew Teague

Deck stain keeps new wood looking good and helps to refurbish old, weathered boards. Stain shouldn't be confused with deck sealer, though. Terminology differs slightly among manufacturers, but sealers generally impart little or no color to wood. They simply seal it against air and moisture. Stains, which perform better than sealers, use pigments that add color to wood. Although the intended purpose of applying a deck stain may be only to return a deck to its natural tone, it's actually the pigment that helps to protect wood from weathering caused by exposure to UV-light from the sun.

Most stains are engineered to color and protect wood in a single coat and are available in oil-based, water-based, and water-based epoxy-fortified mixtures.

More Pigment Offers Better Protection

Although you might want your deck to have a clear finish—especially if you've spent top dollar for mahogany—a pigment-free finish is seldom a good choice because it offers little to no protection against UV-rays.

All three types of deck stain come in four versions:

transparent, semitransparent, semisolid, and solid. Transparent stains appear clear to the eye, but they actually contain pigment. The best stains contain pigments called transoxides (look for them on the label) that provide UV-protection without adding color, much like a sunscreen.

Semitransparent stains add slightly more pigment but still allow some wood grain to show, while semisolid stains conceal much of the wood's natural character. With the highest percentage of pigment, solid stains offer the best protection but have an appearance just short of paint.

Water-Based Stains Are More Durable Than You Think

Most water-based stains don't penetrate wood well, but some manufacturers, such as Defy (www.saversystems.com), Penofin (www.penofin.com), and Benjamin Moore (www.benjaminmoore.com), are using additives to help their stains penetrate better, preventing the cracking and peeling common with older versions. Most water-based stains actually last longer than oil-based stains. While water-based stain can typically last two to three years and is more environmentally friendly (it's solvent-free), its refinishing process can be more work. Unlike oil-based stain, it's often necessary to remove the old water-based stain entirely before a fresh coat is applied, which usually requires a combination of sanding, stripping, and scraping.

Oil-Based Stains Are Easier to Maintain

Manufacturers traditionally use linseed, tung, and soy oils in their oil-based finishes. This mixture allows the stain to penetrate deep into the wood, but not all oils perform the same. Critics say that linseed oil is a fantastic source of food for mold, so a mold-resistant chemical has to be added to stains containing linseed oil. Applying an oil-based stain is much easier than a water-based product, but oil-based stains require more frequent maintenance. However, refinishing oil-based stain, which should take place every one to two years, is much less involved. The wood simply needs to be cleaned of dirt, grime, and mildew, then recoated. There's no need to recoat the entire deck if you don't have to; just touch up the areas that need it. Oil-based stain's major shortcoming is that it typically has a high VOC content and is more difficult to clean up.

Epoxy-Fortified: The Next Generation of Stain

Among the latest deck finishes to hit the market are water-based epoxy-fortified stains, such as the stain manufactured by Defy. A small amount of epoxy is combined in a synthetic resin to improve the stain's wear, durability, and color retention. Formulated to develop a deep sheen reminiscent of old-style oil-based finishes, these stains contain chemical additives to help break surface tension and allow the finish to penetrate the wood. Epoxy-fortified stain still forms a film finish, though, so the refinishing process is the same as with other water-based stains, which means a lot of scraping and sanding. The good news is that epoxy-fortified stain is supposed to create a much more durable deck, so you won't have to refinish it as often. Manufacturers of these stains say that their products last from three to five years before needing to be refinished.

A Classic Finish for a New Wood Floor

By Jim Leahy

One way to create a wood floor that looks old is to install flooring made from reclaimed or salvaged lumber. But if the high price, long lead time, and limited availability of antique flooring put you off, there's another option that my company likes a lot. By using a combination of stains, glazes, and clear topcoats, it's possible to give a newly laid wood floor a convincing antique appearance. You can effect this transformation using standard finishes and equipment available from any paint supplier or home center.

The technique discussed here was done on quartersawn white oak and works best on open-pore woods like oak, hickory, and ash. Starting with a level sanded surface is important, as is making sure you have all the resources necessary to tackle a floor-finishing project—including extra help. Because some finishes (shellac, for instance) dry quickly, it's wise to have more than one person applying them.

Step 1: Water Opens the Pores

Wetting bare wood with water sounds like a bad thing to do, but it can be beneficial to the overall look of the floor's finish. When wet, the wood's pores open, allowing the color to penetrate for a richer, deeper tone. Use a 50/50 mix of denatured alcohol and distilled water, though water alone works, too. The alcohol quickens the drying time, but be sure the room is ventilated sufficiently. Don't use tap water, because it contains minerals that adversely affect the coloring process.

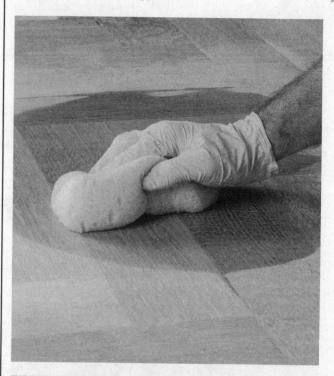

THE FLOOR SHOULD BE WET BUT NOT SOAKED. Application goes quickly with a sponge or mop. Allow the floor to dry for two to four hours, then lightly sand off the raised fibers by hand using 180-grit sandpaper. Vacuum the floor before continuing to the next step.

Continued ➜

Step 2: Oil-Based Stain Sets the Tone

One coat provides a base color that will be refined or toned by the glaze coat that follows. I use oil-based stains for the base because I like the richness they provide. Latex stains are fine, but the tones aren't nearly as rich. Although dyes can be used, they are tough to apply uniformly to large unfinished surfaces. To arrive at the custom color for this project, I mixed a gallon of Minwax's Colonial Maple with a gallon of Golden Pecan stain.

APPLY THE STAIN LIBERALLY. With the walls protected by resin paper and tape, use a brush to cut in around the edges and a lamb's-wool applicator to spread stain over larger areas of the floor. Spread the stain uniformly; don't let pools develop.

DON'T LET THE STAIN SIT. After a minute or two, wipe stained areas with soft cloths (100% cotton cloths work best). The longer the stain sits, the darker the color gets, which lessens the contrast with the glaze coat. Give the stain a final wipe in the direction of the grain.

Step 3: Sanding Sealer Locks in the Color

Use dewaxed shellac sanding sealer, which can be topcoated with almost any finish; traditional shellac contains a wax that can keep some topcoats from adhering. The sealer locks in the base color and enhances the grain definition in the wood, but straight from the can, it is too thick for this process. A sealer coat that's too thick won't allow the glaze coat to penetrate sufficiently.

I use a 1-lb. cut, or thinned mix, of the dewaxed shellac. I thin the shellac with denatured alcohol, following the directions on the can.

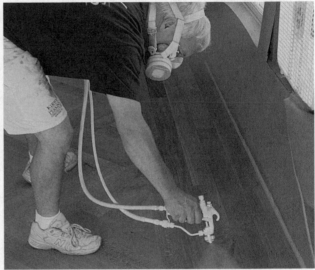

APPLY A THIN, EVEN COAT. You can apply the shellac with a brush or synthetic pad, but I prefer to spray it on because spraying is faster than other methods. Whatever technique you use, don't apply a thick coat. The sealer dries fast, so work quickly and maintain a wet edge. Depending on humidity level and temperature, the floor will be ready to sand in two to three hours.

SORRY, BUT HAND-SANDING WORKS BEST. The purpose here is to scuff-sand the sealer to a dull finish. I do this by hand because I am less likely to penetrate either of the preceding layers. Although 220-grit sandpaper does the job, fine sanding sponges work better because they don't clog as easily. Vacuum the floor completely after sanding.

Step 4: A Glaze Coat Pops the Wood's Figure

A coat of colored glaze highlights the grain and pore structure of the wood. The effect can be mild, extreme, or anywhere in between. For this step, I mixed a quart of Aged Oak with a quart of Walnut gel stain (quart is the largest size available). Gel stains are easy to use and dry overnight. The color of the gel stain directly affects the overall outcome and look of the finish. A glaze much darker than the base color creates a more dramatic effect than a similar color. The overall process is similar to applying the base coat, except that the gel should be applied only with a brush.

FORCE THE COLOR INTO THE PORES. Using a 4-in. natural-bristle brush, apply the gel stain liberally. Spread only as much as you can reach from one spot without moving your position. Then use two cotton cloths to wipe up the stain: one for the initial wipe and a second, cleaner cloth for the final wipe. Let the glaze coat dry for 12 to 14 hours before applying the final polyurethane coats.

Step 5: Clear Polyurethane Protects the Finish

I prefer to use oil-based polyurethane as a topcoat for floors because of its proven durability. A minimum of three coats provides years of trouble-free service. Here, I used two coats of clear gloss to start because I like the clarity it provides. I followed with one coat of satin for a hand-rubbed look.

After the first coat dries, lightly scuff the floor with a fine sanding sponge, which removes bits of dust or small imperfections from previous layers. Vacuum and wipe the floor with a tack cloth. Repeat the process for the second coat; then apply the satin.

Touch Up the Border with Gel Stain

The mahogany border here is a nice accent, but it had some lighter boards that looked awkward next to darker ones. I used a gel stain that closely matched the darker boards to stain the lighter boards. Gel stains are easy to control, almost like paint. Lightly feather the color back into the darker boards with a brush. Test small areas first to see how the stain matches.

Continued →

Work Safely

Safety precautions are crucial when using all finishing products, especially oil-based finishes. Read all the instructions on the cans of finish you use. Make sure the room has good ventilation; if good ventilation isn't possible, wear a chemical respirator equipped with filter cartridges rated for use with organics, vapors, and solvents (OVS). Minimize skin contact by wearing protective gloves, and remember that oil-soaked rags and sawdust pose a serious fire hazard. Place these materials in an airtight, water-filled container, and dispose of them in accordance with local fire regulations.

Tips for a Smooth Finish

A tack cloth removes fine particles that vacuuming tends to leave behind. The tack cloth can leave a sticky or oily residue, however, which can affect water-based finishes. If applying water-based finishes, be sure to use tack cloths that are made for use with water-based products.

Use preshrunk T-shirt-grade cotton rags. Run them through a laundry cycle before use to remove all loose fibers.

Slowly hand-stir the polyurethane. If you stir it fast by hand or with a mixer, air bubbles will form and make their way onto the floor's surface. Popped air bubbles create an orange-peel effect—which is exactly what you don't want.

To remove any loose fibers, run the pad of a lamb's-wool applicator through a laundry cycle before using it to apply polyurethane. If you don't have time to throw it in the washer and dryer, vacuum the applicator.

Contents

Insulation & Weatherproofing

Control Layers

By Allison Bailes III, Ph.D.

Air Barriers, Vapor Barriers, Water-Resistive Barriers, and Insulation

The purpose of a building enclosure is to control the transmission of air, water (liquid and vapor), and heat. We use different materials in houses to achieve the various levels of control we need, and what any one house needs depends on the climate and on what its occupants do when they're inside.

These materials often are described as control layers. A properly enclosed house has a water-vapor control layer, a liquid-water control layer, an air control layer, and a thermal (heat) control layer. Calling them all control layers reminds us that they have a similar task, but they are more commonly known by other names: The water-vapor control layer is also called a vapor retarder or vapor barrier, the liquid-water control layer is also called the drainage plane or the water-resistive barrier (WRB), the air control layer is also called an air barrier, and the thermal control layer is also called insulation. I encounter lots of confusion around the differences among these control layers. While the details of how each one works in relation to the others in any particular house can get complex, the basic distinctions are simple.

Do I Need a Vapor Barrier?

The biggest point of confusion seems to be about what a vapor barrier is. Most often, people say they need a vapor barrier when they really mean they need a WRB. Housewrap is great for controlling liquid water, but most of the ones used are not vapor barriers, nor do they need to be. For example, DuPont's Tyvek HomeWrap has a vapor permeance of 58 perms, putting it way into the vapor-permeable range. (A material is considered vapor permeable if it has a value greater than 10 perms.) It's generally more important for building assemblies to be able to dry out than it is to prevent water vapor from moving into them.

A vapor barrier, also known as a Class I vapor retarder, is a material such as polyethylene or metal. When you put one in an assembly, it lets almost no water vapor diffuse through. About the only places you need to use a full-blown vapor barrier are under a slab or when you encapsulate a crawlspace.

Housewrap is the most common material used as a WRB. It keeps water that gets behind the siding from damaging the sheathing. If the sheathing does get wet, housewrap's high vapor permeance allows it to dry. Housewrap is rarely installed well enough to be a good air barrier, but that's OK because in most homes it's stapled to a material that, when properly taped, is: plywood or OSB.

Continued →

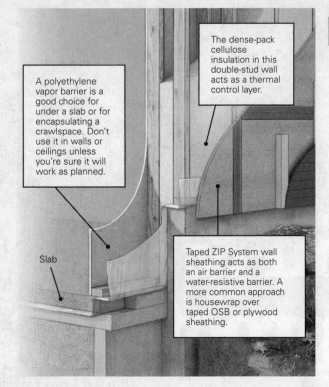

A polyethylene vapor barrier is a good choice for under a slab or for encapsulating a crawlspace. Don't use it in walls or ceilings unless you're sure it will work as planned.

The dense-pack cellulose insulation in this double-stud wall acts as a thermal control layer.

Slab

Taped ZIP System wall sheathing acts as both an air barrier and a water-resistive barrier. A more common approach is housewrap over taped OSB or plywood sheathing.

What Does Insulation Do?

I also frequently encounter confusion about what insulation controls. Insulation is available in both air-permeable (fiberglass and cellulose) and air-impermeable (spray foam and rigid foam) forms. Putting in more fiberglass or cellulose insulation won't give you the airtightness you need in a house. Those fluffy insulation materials are thermal control layers but not air control layers. Spray foam and rigid foam of the proper thickness are both.

Open-cell spray foam can control heat and air, but not water vapor or liquid water. Closed-cell foam can control heat, air, water vapor, and liquid water. Rigid-foam insulation, depending on type and facings, also can control all four.

When you're looking at plans or actual building assemblies, go through the materials layer by layer and identify the functions of each. Is the material controlling heat, air, liquid water, or water vapor? Is it controlling more than one? Even if it's there for structural reasons, you need to know how it might affect the flow of heat, air, and moisture. OSB and plywood sheathing, for example, are vapor semi-permeable and can reduce an assembly's ability to dry.

Detailing Walls with Rigid Foam

By Steve DeMetrick

Wall construction has changed dramatically since I started in the trades 20 years ago. The 2×4 walls insulated with R-13 fiberglass batts that everyone built back then don't come close to complying with today's energy code in climate zone 5, where I live. And even with today's stricter codes, building just to code is like settling for a D in school. A house that only meets the minimum standard is the worst that can legally be built.

On this house, the combination of 2-in. foil-faced polyisocyanurate exterior foam and 6 in. of fiber insulation create a high-performance wall that exceeds the IRC requirements. But even meeting the minimum wall R-values required by the new energy code can be hard to achieve with cavity insulation alone. In climate zone 5, walls are required to be at least R-20, and standard batts yield R-19. In cold climates, exterior insulation in addition to the cavity insulation is becoming a de facto code requirement. But there are pitfalls, including moisture condensation, detailing challenges around windows and other penetrations, and the lack of a solid base for attaching the siding. Here's how I navigate them.

Walls That Make Sense

As a consultant on this build, I worked with carpenter Andrew Gallant of Gallant Builders on the wall details. Our combination

Thermal Bridges

Small paths that bypass the foam sheathing could have a big impact on the wall's performance. At the windows, a layer of 1-in. foam topped with 5/4 pine nailers provides both insulation and attachment.

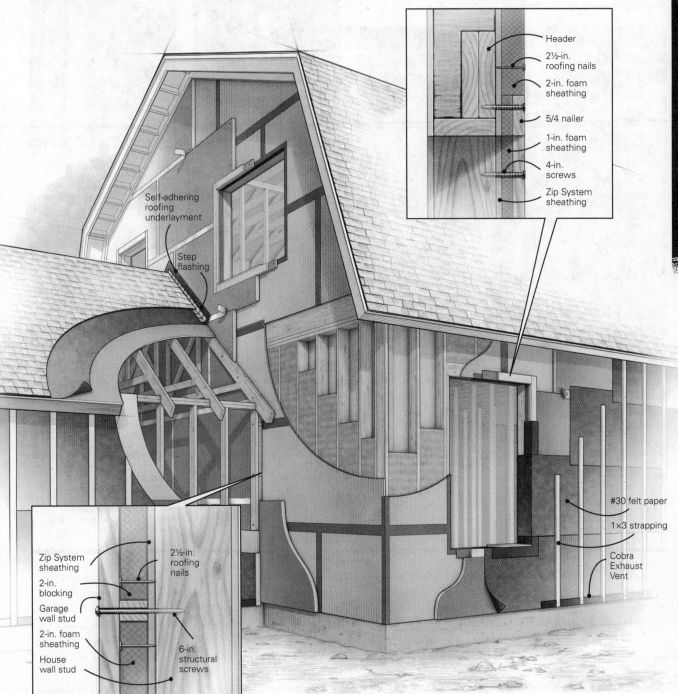

Header

2½-in. roofing nails

2-in. foam sheathing

5/4 nailer

1-in. foam sheathing

4-in. screws

Zip System sheathing

Self-adhering roofing underlayment

Step flashing

Zip System sheathing

2-in. blocking

Garage wall stud

2-in. foam sheathing

House wall stud

2½-in. roofing nails

6-in. structural screws

#30 felt paper

1×3 strapping

Cobra Exhaust Vent

To minimize thermal bridging, blocking and foam separate the unheated garage's framing from the house.

Detailing Rough Openings

Sheathing with foam is mostly dirt simple, with windows and doors being the trouble spots. The main things to keep in mind are providing solid nailing while avoiding creating a thermal bridge, and providing adequate flashing to keep out water.

INSTALL NAILERS. Screw rough-pine 5/4×3 nailers over the 1-in. foam to build the assembly out to the plane of the main 2-in. foam insulation.

BUTT THE WALL FOAM TO THE BUILD-OUT. Installation of the rest of the insulation is simply a matter of cutting to fit and fastening with 2½-in. roofing nails.

CREATE A THERMAL BREAK. Nail foam strips 1 in. thick and 3½ in. wide around the opening.

ADD A SOLID SILL. To create a base for windows and doors, fasten a piece of ¾-in. sheathing to the bottom of the rough openings.

PROCEED NORMALLY. With solid nailing established, installing windows or doors and integrating them with the WRB and the flashings is the same as on any other job.

---

of foil-faced foam and Zip System sheathing has created walls that are essentially impervious to moisture on the outside, meaning that they can only dry inward. To allow this, the wall cavities will be insulated later with unfaced fiberglass or mineral-wool batts, and the interior finish will be gypsum board, plaster, and vapor-permeable latex paint, all of which allow free movement of water vapor.

Because moisture generally moves from warm locations to cool ones, in this predominantly heating climate, the vapor drive is outward for most of the year. That makes controlling interior moisture a critical component of the house's system. Otherwise, water could condense on the back of the sheathing,

causing rot. Accordingly, interior moisture will be managed by a combination of timed bath fans, kitchen exhaust fans, and an energy-recovery ventilator (ERV). Not too many years ago, the standard approach would have been to use an interior Class I vapor retarder such as polyethylene sheeting. Today we know that having vapor-impermeable surfaces on both sides of a wall traps any moisture that does sneak in, often leading to rot.

In addition to keeping out exterior moisture and air, being able to dry, and reducing thermal conductivity, walls also should be simple to build. A goal in all of my projects is to detail walls so that carpenters can build with familiar materials and tools. The walls shown here are a good example of that approach. The

Insulation Ratio Determines Vapor-Retarder Type

When designing a wall, think about the risk of condensation within the wall cavity. The inside of the sheathing must be kept warmer than the dew point so that moisture doesn't condense there, so the ratio of exterior insulation R-value to cavity insulation R-value is critical. Either the exterior insulation needs to be sufficient to keep the sheathing above the dew point, or the cavity insulation needs to leak enough heat to achieve the same end. Colder climates require higher ratios and/or less permeable vapor retarders. To find the insulation ratio of a wall, divide the exterior R-value by the cavity R-value. In the chart at left, use the insulation ratio and the climate zone to determine whether a vapor retarder is needed, and if so, what class to use (e.g., Class II: kraft facing; Class III: latex paint).

Climate zone	Class II interior vapor retarder	Class III interior vapor retarder
1 to 3	No limit	
4	0.2	
5	0.2	0.35
6	0.25	0.5
7	0.35	0.7

studs are 2×6s on 16-in. centers. The Zip System sheathing, with its seams carefully taped, doubles as the air barrier. Although the sheathing could also function as the house's water-resistive barrier (WRB), it was easier to detail the wall so that the WRB is just behind the siding.

Continuous foam significantly reduces thermal bridging through the studs and wall plates, increasing the total R-value of the wall. The assembly needs to be thought through before framing begins. The first step is to indicate on the plans exactly where the foam-insulation plane is located and then identify any places where there are connections that might break the continuity of the foam.

Installing the Foam

The 4×8 sheets of 2-in. polyisocyanurate are fastened to the wall sheathing with 2½-in. roofing nails. Only a few nails per sheet are needed because 1×3 strapping applied later provides the real holding power. There are many ways to cut the foam. My tool kit includes a Festool track saw, a Japanese pull saw, and a Tajima retractable knife whose long blade is handy for making quick cuts when I'm not standing at the cut table. The foam seams are taped with 3-in. foil-faced tape.

Windows and doors are the biggest stumbling block with

There's More Than One Way to Skin a House

Of the four common types of insulating sheathing, the foil-faced polyisocyanurate used here offers the highest R-value per inch (R-6.5). In addition, it's readily available and practically vapor impermeable (it's a Class I vapor retarder). Extruded polystyrene (XPS) is also readily available, is slightly vapor permeable (Class II), and offers an R-value of R-5 per in. Expanded polystyrene (EPS) may be a little harder to find, has an R-value of around R-4 per in., and is several times more vapor permeable than XPS (although it still falls within the Class II range). Finally, there is mineral-wool board, a denser material than mineral-wool batts. Mineral wool is open to vapor transmission and has an R-value of about R-4 per in.

Foil-faced polyisocyanurate R-6.5 per inch

Extruded polystyrene R-5 per inch

exterior foam. You need solid material at the surface to attach to. Building out to the plane of the foam with solid blocking would create a thermal bridge around every opening. Instead, Gallant nailed 3½-in.-wide rips of 1-in. foam around the windows, followed by 5/4×4 rough pine screwed to the framing through the foam, creating a thermally broken attachment point for the windows and doors. The 2-in. foam butts to this assembly. To create a solid base for supporting the windows and doors, Gallant screwed ¾-in. sheathing to the bottoms of the rough openings, which were built ¾ in. taller to accommodate the thickened sill. With this treatment, the window and door openings can be flashed just as on a typical wall.

Expanded polystyrene R-4 per inch

Felt Paper Keeps Out the Rain

The most critical element of any wall assembly is the WRB and its flashings. On this project, the taped Zip System sheathing and the taped foam act as redundant WRBs, but the primary WRB is #30 felt paper and self-adhering flashings that go over the foam. From remodeling century-old oceanfront homes that stayed dry, I know that properly lapped and flashed felt paper works over the long term. I'm not so sure about WRBs that rely on the adhesion of tape to keep out water.

Mineral wool R-4 per inch

The felt paper is attached with 2½-in. roofing nails and is lapped shingle-style over all of the window and door flashing, as well as over the

Continued →

roof step flashing. To avoid having to hand-drive pounds and pounds of roofing nails to hold the felt paper if the wind kicked up, Gallant worked in small sections, installing the felt paper and following up immediately with strapping.

With very tight houses, it's important to seal the small holes made for items such as wires and pipes. On a Passive House I built, a first-floor window leaked significantly during a rainstorm through a 1-in.-long tear in the flashing tape. In a typical house, that wouldn't result in a pronounced leak, but this house was extremely airtight. The problem was located in the second-floor wall, where two 6-in. holes for the ERV intake and exhaust hadn't yet been connected. The wind depressurized the house through these holes. Because the house had so few leaks, enough negative pressure was created to suck water in.

With that in mind, wires for outside lights were taped to the sheathing prior to the installation of the foam. Once taped, wires were routed down the face of the wall a few inches and to the fixture or outlet to prevent water from following the wire into the wall. Larger holes for pipes or ventilation fans were first air-sealed at the sheathing with EPDM gaskets (foursevenfive.com) and then flashed to the foam with 3M's All Weather Flashing Tape.

The final step before installing the siding was to attach the 1×3 vertical strapping over the foam to provide nailing for the siding and trim. The strapping is fastened through the foam and the sheathing to the studs with 5-in. screws. The ¾-in. space formed by the strapping creates a generous drainage gap for water that gets behind the siding. The airspace also will ventilate the siding so it can dry evenly, resulting in a more durable installation and paint job. I know of similar houses that have gone 15 years without repainting. To keep vermin out of the space while allowing airflow, Gallant nailed Cobra Exhaust Vent between the strapping at the bottom of the wall.

New Insulation for Old Walls

By Justin Fink

When it comes to insulating floors, walls, and ceilings, nothing compares to the blank canvas of a newly framed house. The house is wide open, so contractors can add any type of insulation they want to achieve the best possible thermal performance. Those guys have it easy.

What about us remodelers, though? The people living in houses built with minimal insulation, or none at all? The ones who don't have the luxury of gutting their walls? The ones who work on or live in houses that hemorrhage heat in the winter and bake like an oven during the summer? What can we do to improve the thermal performance of these homes? A lot, actually.

Techniques and materials for retrofitting insulation in old walls have improved over the years. Many times, insulation can be added from the interior or exterior of the house without gutting the walls. Even so, I'm not going to sugarcoat this: Adding new insulation to closed walls is a hassle.

Pick the Low-Hanging Fruit First

If you are thinking about adding insulation to your walls, chances are that you have already tackled the other major weak spots in the house. If you haven't, you should, and your efforts should begin in the attic, where the most heat loss typically occurs (see "Attic Insulation Upgrade," *Fine Homebuilding* # 200 and online at finehomebuilding.com). If, however, after air-sealing and insulating the attic and plugging some other common energy trouble spots (see "Home Remedies for Energy Nosebleeds," *Fine Homebuilding* #190 and online at Fine Homebuilding.com) your house still feels drafty and your energy bills are still too high, it's

Balsam Wool   Urea-Formaldehyde Foam   Vermiculite

time to consider the walls.

There's a lot to consider when it comes to adding new insulation to old walls. The first step is to find out what type of insulation, if any, is in the walls. Once that is determined, you can assess the thermal performance of the walls and make a more informed decision about the potential benefits of an upgrade. You might find that the existing insulation is astonishingly inferior and that a small outlay of cash would mean a significant decrease in your energy bills. Then again, you could be surprised to find that a high-dollar retrofit will offer only a minuscule return on investment.

What's in My Walls?

The first step to narrowing your upgrade options is to learn the type and amount of insulation, if any, in your walls. Houses built before 1930 often were left uninsulated, so you will find either empty stud bays or insulation that was added later. Houses built in the '40s, '50s, and beyond were typically insulated, but often with thin batts that didn't fill the wall cavity.

The possibilities shown here represent the most common types of early insulation, but it's not a comprehensive list. Many of the earliest forms of insulation were driven by the local industry. If the town was home to sawmills, the surrounding houses could be insulated with sawdust. If the town was an agricultural hub, rice hulls were fairly common. What you find in your walls is limited only by the whim of the builder and the previous homeowners.

Balsam Wool (1940s)

WHAT IS IT? Wool is a bit misleading because this insulation is essentially chopped balsam wood fibers.

POSITIVE ID Although some installations may have been loose fill,

How to Find Out

Electrical outlets: You often can get a peek at what's in walls by removing electrical-outlet coverplates and shining a flashlight into the space where the drywall or plaster meets the electrical box.

Look up or down: Drilling a hole up into the wall cavity from the basement, or down through the top plate from the attic may be helpful. A piece of wire bent into a hook is a helpful probing tool here.

Cut a small hole: This last resort should be done in a location that will go unnoticed once patched up. Cut a neat hole with a drywall saw—a small square or rectangle will be easiest to replace—and keep the piece to use later as a patch.

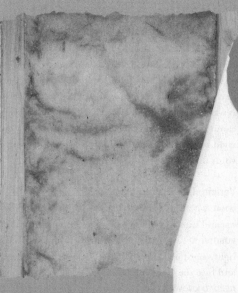

Fiberglass

Rock Wool

Cotton Batts

Continued ➜

this tan/brown insulation was most often packaged and installed in black-paper-faced batts. The tan fibers look similar to sawdust.

NEED TO KNOW Balsam wool is not a health hazard, but take care when investigating this insulation; a dust mask is a good idea. Because the paper batts are likely to be brittle to the touch, disturbing them too much may leave holes that will decrease thermal performance.

UPGRADE OUTLOOK This insulation was typically fastened to wall studs, similar to fiberglass batts. Balsam wool should still yield an R-value of between R-2 and R-3 per in. if installed correctly, but the batts are likely only a couple of inches thick. Consider filling the remaining empty space in the stud cavities with blown cellulose or fiberglass. Some manufacturers of pour foam also recommend their product for this type of installation.

Urea-Formaldehyde Foam (1950 To 1982 — Mostly in the Late 1970s)

What is it? Also known as UFFI, this once-popular retrofit option is a mixture of urea, formaldehyde, and a foaming agent that were combined on site and sprayed into wall cavities.

POSITIVE ID Lightweight with brownish-gold coloring, this foam is fragile and likely to crumble if touched (hence the smooth chunks shown here).

NEED TO KNOW Because this open-cell foam was banned in 1982 and most of the off-gassing happened in the hours and days following installation, chances of elevated levels of formaldehyde are slim.

UPGRADE OUTLOOK Although it's rated at R-4.5, UFFI rarely performs at this level. This foam is well known for its high rate of shrinkage and tendency to deteriorate if in contact with water, and it also crumbles if disturbed during remodeling. The result is walls that likely have large voids, but this insulation isn't a good candidate for discreet removal. The best option here is to add rigid foam to the exterior to help to make up for the large air voids that are likely hidden in the wall.

Vermiculite (1925 To 1950)

WHAT IS IT? This naturally occurring mineral was heated to make it expand into a lightweight, fire-retardant, insulating material.

POSITIVE ID Brownish-pink or brownish-silver in color, these lightweight pellets were typically poured into closed wall cavities and into the voids in masonry blocks.

NEED TO KNOW Seventy to eighty percent of vermiculite came from

a mine in Libby, Mont., that was later found to contain asbestos. The mine has been closed since 1990, but the EPA suggests treating previously installed vermiculite as if it is contaminated. If undisturbed, it's not a health risk, but if you want to upgrade to a different type of insulation, call an asbestos-removal professional.

UPGRADE OUTLOOK Vermiculite doesn't typically settle and should still offer its original R-value of between R-2 and R-2.5 per in. This low thermal performance makes it an attractive candidate for upgrade, especially because it's a cinch to remove; cut a hole and it pours right out. But the potential for asbestos contamination makes the prepwork and personal protection more of a hassle, and the job more costly as a result. If cavities are not filled to the top, consider topping them off; fiberglass, cellulose, or pour foam will work if there is access from the attic.

Fiberglass (late 1930s to Present)

WHAT IS IT? This man-made product consists of fine strands of glass grouped together in a thick blanket.

POSITIVE ID Most often yellow, though pink, white, blue, and green are possibilities. Older products were typically paper-faced batts.

NEED TO KNOW Official health information on fiberglass is ambiguous; the argument over whether it's a carcinogen continues. Even if it's not a cancer-causing material, it will make you itchy and irritate your lungs if disturbed. Be on the safe side if you plan to remove this insulation; wear gloves, long sleeves, goggles, and a respirator.

UPGRADE OUTLOOK Fiberglass has a decent thermal performance between R-3 and R-4.5, but early products were typically only about 2 in. thick. Consider filling the remaining empty space in the stud cavities with blown cellulose or blown fiberglass. Some manufacturers of pour foam also recommend their product for this type of installation.

Rock Wool (mostly in the 1950s)

WHAT IS IT? Rock wool is a specific type of mineral wool, a by-product of the ore-smelting process.

POSITIVE ID This fluffy, cottonlike material was typically installed as loose fill or batts. It usually started out white or gray, but even the white version will likely be blackened or brown from decades of filtering dirt out of air flowing through the cavity.

NEED TO KNOW Research indicates that this is a safe material. It's still in use today, and it's gaining popularity among green builders.

UPGRADE OUTLOOK Rock wool is fairly dense, so it's less likely than other materials to have settled over time. If installed correctly, it should still yield a value of R-3 to R-4 per in., about the same as blown fiberglass or cellulose insulation. If anything, consider adding housewrap or a thin layer of rigid foam to the outside of the wall to air-seal the structure. If more insulation is desired, go with rigid foam.

Cotton Batts (1935 To 1950)

WHAT IS IT? A naturally grown material, cotton batts are treated to be flame resistant.

POSITIVE ID This white insulation is dense, but still fluffy. It's not as refined as cotton balls; instead, it's likely to have more of a pilly, fuzzy appearance. Although several companies manufactured cotton batts, one of the most popular seems to have been Lockport Cotton Batting. Look for a product name (Lo-K) and company logo on the batts' paper facing.

NEED TO KNOW Cotton is all natural and is perfectly safe to touch, but don't remove the batts or otherwise disturb the insulation without wearing at least a nuisance dust mask or respirator to protect your lungs. Also, cotton by nature is absorbent, so if it gets wet, it will take time to dry out.

UPGRADE OUTLOOK The growing popularity of green-building materials has brought renewed interest in cotton batts. Although these modern versions of cotton batting, often referred to as "blue-jean insulation," have an R-value of R-3.5 to R-4 per in., there is some controversy over the R-value of the old versions. Some sources claim the old products perform similarly to the modern versions, and others estimate the R-value to be as low as R-0.5 per in. Considering the density of the old cotton batts, such a low R-value seems unlikely.

Upgrade Options: Foam

Rigid Foam Always Works

It doesn't matter how the walls were built, what type of insulation they have now, or how many obstructions are hidden in the wall cavities: Rigid-foam panels installed over the exterior side of the walls are always an option. However, installation is not as easy as cutting the lightweight panels with a utility knife and nailing them to the framing, though that's part of it.

Rigid foam must be applied directly to the framing or sheathing, or on top of the existing siding, and then covered with new siding. In either case, you are faced with a full re-siding job and maybe a siding tearoff as well. Also, depending on the added thickness of the panels, windows and doors might need to be furred out, and roof rakes and eaves extended. As long as the installation is detailed carefully ("Save Energy With Rigid-Foam Insulation," *Fine Homebuilding* #181), though, the result is wall cavities that stay warm

Rigid Foam

Continued →

and dry, allowing your existing insulation to perform at its best.

Panels are available in 2-ft. by 8-ft. or 4-ft. by 8-ft. sheets, and typically range from ½ in. to 2 in. in thickness. The vapor permeability of the foam is determined by the type of foam and the presence of a facing. Panels faced with foil or plastic are class-I vapor retarders (commonly referred to as vapor barriers) and should not be used if the house already has poly sheeting or an equivalent vapor retarder under the drywall. Unfaced or fiberglass-faced panels will allow water vapor to pass and won't be problematic in combination with a class-I retarder.

Expanded polystyrene (EPS) These white, closed-cell panels are made from the same polystyrene beads used in disposable coffee cups. EPS is the least expensive option and has the lowest R-value of the group (about R-4 per in.). Some EPS is unfaced, which makes it more fragile to handle but also allows the passage of water vapor. Unfaced EPS should be installed in combination with #15 felt paper or housewrap.

Extruded polystyrene (XPS) XPS falls in the middle of the three types of rigid-foam insulation in terms of cost and performance. Easy to spot by its blue, pink, or green color, XPS is slightly more expensive than EPS and also offers better performance (about R-5 per in.). Panels are commonly unfaced, and though water-vapor transmission slows on thicker panels, all XPS panels greater than 1 in. thick are considered class-II vapor retarders, which allow water vapor to pass.

Polyisocyanurate (polyiso) This is the most expensive type of rigid foam, but also the best insulator (about R-6.5). Polyiso is a popular choice for retrofit applications because it packs more insulation into a thin package—less hassle for detailing windows and doors. All polyiso boards are faced, most with foil, which retards the flow of water vapor.

Pour Foam Is the Most Thorough

This water- or HFC- (hydrofluorocarbon) blown mixture is injected into the wall cavity from either the interior or the exterior through two or more ¾-in.- to 1-in.-dia. holes. The foam flows to the bottom of the stud cavity, where it slowly expands upward, surrounding even the most complicated plumbing and electrical obstructions, and filling every gap to create an airtight wall assembly.

Pour foam follows the path of least resistance as it expands, so the bottoms of stud cavities (in the basement or crawlspace) need to be sealed in balloon-framed houses. Old houses with siding installed directly over the studs will likely have foam squeeze-out between siding courses, which must be removed with a paint scraper once cured.

Blowouts or distortions in drywall, plaster, or siding are also possible, although this is typically not a concern if the foam is installed by trained professionals. Still, this is the reason why most pour-foam companies don't sell directly to the public, instead relying on a network of trained installers. Tiger Foam, on the other hand, sells disposable do-it-yourself kits to homeowners.

Although there are videos on the Internet showing pour foam being injected into wall cavities that have fiberglass insulation—compressing the batts against the wallboard or sheathing—most manufacturers do not recommend this practice. The pour foam could bond to individual strands of fiberglass and tear it apart as it expands, creating voids. Tiger Foam is the exception, but the company recommends the use of a long fill tube to control the injection.

Installation from the exterior requires removal of some

Pour Foam

clapboards or shingles. Installation from the inside is easier, but requires more prep work (moving furniture, wall art, drapes, etc.). Homeowners can expect a slight odor after installation and for the day following; proper ventilation is a must.

For a professional installation, prices range depending on job specifics and foam choice. The prices for Tiger Foam do-it-yourself kits depend on the quantity you buy. Open-cell foams—which are more permeable to water-vapor transmission—are about R-4 per in.; closed-cell, around R-6 per in.

Upgrade Options: Blown-In

The Most Common Approach

This method begins with compressed packs of dry cellulose or fiberglass, which are dumped into the hopper of a blowing machine, where they are agitated and loosened. A 1-in.- to 2-in.-dia. hose runs from the blowing machine through a hole in the interior or exterior side of the wall and is lowered to the bottom of the stud cavity. The installation process usually involves either one hole at the top of each cavity and a long fill tube that is withdrawn as the insulation fills the space, or a "double-blow" method, where two holes are used—one about 4 ft. from the floor and a second near the top of the wall.

Both cellulose and fiberglass do a good job of surrounding typical plumbing and electrical utilities routed through the wall, but the finished density of the insulation is crucial. Cellulose that's installed too loosely will settle and create voids in the wall, and fiberglass that's packed too densely will not offer the performance you paid for.

Cellulose

Cellulose

This insulation is made from 80% post-consumer recycled newspaper and is treated with nontoxic borates to resist fire and mold. It's a good choice because of its balance between cost, thermal performance, and environmentally friendly characteristics. Also, unlike fiberglass insulation, cellulose doesn't rely only on its ability to trap air to stop heat flow. Cellulose can be packed tightly into a wall cavity to resist airflow—a practice called "dense-packing"—yielding an R-value of R-3 to R-4 per in.

Although blowing loose-fill cellulose into attics is a pretty straightforward process (and is touted as a good do-it-yourself project), dense-packing is more complicated. As the material is blown into the cavity, the blowing machine bogs down, letting the installer know to pull back the hose a bit. This process repeats until the wall is packed full of cellulose. Although it is possible to pack cellulose too densely, the more common problem is not packing it densely enough. Most blowing machines that are available as rentals are designed for blowing loose cellulose in an open attic. These machines aren't powerful enough to pack cellulose into a wall cavity, and unpacked cellulose can settle and leave voids. The Cellulose Insulation Manufacturers Association (www.cellulose.org) recommends that dense-pack cellulose be installed only by trained professionals with more powerful blowing machines.

Finally, if soaked with water, cellulose is likely to settle, leaving voids. Then again, if there's liquid water in the wall cavity, voids in the insulation will be the least of your worries, and the least of your expenses.

Fiberglass

This loose-fill insulation is made from molten glass that is spun into loose fibers. The material is available in two forms, either as a by-product of manufacturing traditional fiberglass batts and rolls, or from "prime" fibers produced especially for blowing applications. In either case, the material is noncombustible, will not absorb water, and is inorganic, so it will not support the growth of mold.

Fiberglass resists heat flow by trapping pockets of air between fibers, so the insulation must be left fluffy to take advantage of the air-trapping nature of the material. The R-value (typically between R-2.5 and R-4) is dependent not only on the thickness

Continued ➜

Fiberglass

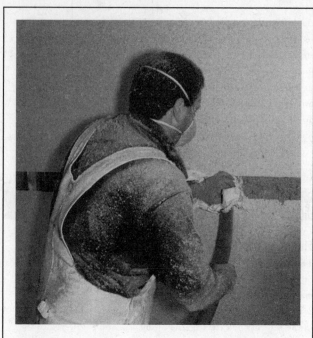

of the wall cavity but also on the density at which the insulation is installed. For information on ensuring that the fiberglass is installed to provide the stated R-value, visit the North American Insulation Manufacturer's Association (www.naima.org) for a free overview.

Because fiberglass doesn't need to be blown to such high densities, it's a more user-friendly installation for nonprofessionals. On the other hand, loose fiberglass is not as readily available as cellulose, which is often a stock item at home-improvement centers. Finally, fiberglass advocates contend that their product won't absorb water, and cellulose will—though fiberglass will still sag if it becomes wet.

Out with the Old

If your walls are filled with old insulation and your remodeling plans don't involve gutting the house, then you can either add rigid insulation to the exterior of the house (p. 727), or in some cases, surgically remove the old insulation.

Vermiculite can be removed by drilling a hole through the wall at the bottom of the stud cavity and letting gravity empty the stud bays. In balloon-framed houses, which have wall studs that run continuously from the foundation to the roofline, blocking in the basement can be removed to access the stud cavities above.

Batts or dense fibrous insulations can be removed by cutting a "bellyband" in which a narrow strip of wall is removed about 4 ft. from the floor (this can be done from the exterior as well). With this strip of wall open, the batts can be pulled out—a homemade hook helps—and new insulation can be blown or poured into the cavities through the same openings (photo left) before being patched.

Making Fiberglass Work

By Lee Kurtas

When building science and home efficiency really took off in the mid-1990s, insulation contractors started hearing regularly about how the type of insulation used affects a building's energy efficiency. Blower-door testing and thermal imaging of existing homes proved that fiberglass—as it's typically installed—didn't

Air-Seal Before Insulating

Before the insulation is installed, all gaps in the sheathing (or other air barrier) must be sealed with spray foam, caulk, or durable air-sealing tape. The same is true with mechanical penetrations.

FILL WITH FOAM Before insulating, an air-sealing crew seals all holes with canned spray foam. They also seal any gaps between the sheathing and the framing. After this work is checked by a foreman for completeness, the batts can be installed.

SEAL WITH SPRAY CAULK The air-sealing crew offers spray-applied caulk for air-sealing as an upgrade. The caulk shown here, from Knauf, stays flexible to better accommodate seasonal movement. Owens-Corning offers a similar product.

perform as well as other types of insulation, especially spray foam. As a result, builders and architects doing projects with energy-performance benchmarks started specifying spray foam as a way to ensure better airtightness and thermal resistance.

These builders and architects liked spray foam because it seals around penetrations such as pipes, ducts, and wires, and because it fills odd-shaped cavities quickly and easily. But spray foam does have a significant downside: cost. Insulating a typical new home with spray foam in my area costs two to three times what it costs to use fiberglass. Because of its low cost, fiberglass insulation is easily the most popular building insulation here in Houston and in the rest of the country. For example, fiberglass makes up 85% of my company's insulation business, while spray foam represents only 10%. The rest is cellulose.

Provided it is installed according to the highest standards, fiberglass performs very well. My company has developed a cost-effective and quality approach you can adapt to meet the same standards.

Installed Right, Fiberglass Works

For fiberglass to be effective, its installation must involve three factors. First, the building must have a durable and continuous air barrier such as taped sheathing. Second, any gaps and mechanical penetrations must be fully air-sealed with durable tape or sealant.

Fit, Fill, Fluff

Properly installing batt insulation starts with a piece of insulation that fills the cavity and is in full contact with the framing and the sheathing or other air barrier behind the insulation.

FIT THE BATT With the batt tight to the top plate, an installer cuts the batts to length and width in place using a batt knife. When the cavity is longer than the batt, a piece is added to the bottom.

FILL THE CAVITY Once the batt is sized, it's inserted carefully into the cavity. The installer uses his batt knife to push the sides, top, and bottom flush to the sheathing. If you're careful, you can do this without compressing the batt.

FLUFF THE EDGES Once the batt is in place, any compressed areas are fluffed out with the batt knife. For out-of-reach sections, a long pole with a spike in the end places and fluffs the insulation.

A BETTER BATT KNIFE. The author's installers lengthen their square-point knives with PVC pipe. The duct-taped end makes it easier to grab from a tool belt.

Continued ➡

Making the Grade

Inspectors from Residential Energy Services Network (RESNET) give batt-insulation installations a rating of Grade I, II, or III. The grades describe the quality of the installation and the completeness of the air barrier. Grades I and II assume a durable and continuous air barrier. Installations without an adequate air barrier are automatically downgraded to Grade III or "uninsulated."

Grade I
This is the best possible job, one in which the batts fill each cavity without voids or compression. The batts are cut to fit tightly around penetrations. The insulation is in full contact with framing and sheathing. Occasional very small gaps are allowed.

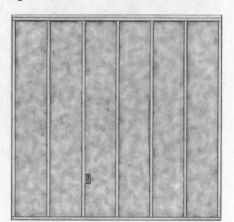

Grade II
Moderate to frequent defects such as gaps and compressed edges are present in this installation. The compressed areas (up to 30% compression) can be no more than 10% of the insulated surface area. Insulation can't be missing from more than 2% of the surface area.

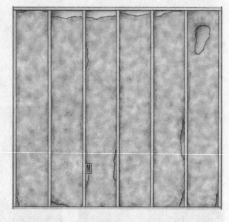

Grade III
In this installation, more than 2% but less than 5% of the total surface area is compressed or missing. This rating also includes insulation that isn't in substantial contact with the sheathing or that lacks sheathing or another air barrier. Insulation that's installed worse than Grade III is described as uninsulated.

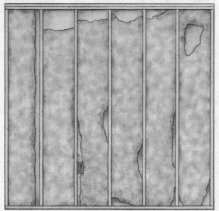

Finally, the batts must be fit and placed with care and minimal compression.

When these three factors are present, fiberglass performs as well as other insulation types. And that's not just my opinion. Summarizing their recent findings in a multiyear head-to-head test of six insulation types, researchers at Building Science Corporation (BSC) said, "When walls are constructed with the same R-value in the stud space, and are air-sealed both inside and outside, they exhibit essentially the same thermal performance regardless of the type of insulation material used."

The important caveat in that quote—"and are air-sealed both inside and outside"—refers to the air barrier that separates interior and exterior air. Creating a good air barrier and detailing penetrations properly are essential to getting the maximum energy performance from fiberglass batts.

What Is an Air Barrier?

It can be helpful to think of a home's air barrier as an air-filled balloon. The balloon's skin, which represents the air barrier, separates inside air from outside air. For the balloon to hold air, the skin must be sturdy enough and continuous enough to resist the air pressure inside the balloon. It's an apt analogy, because a balloon, like a home's air barrier, is not perfectly airtight. Even the most stringent building-performance programs allow some air leakage. The goal is to make the air barrier as complete and free of leaks as possible.

On most homes, the air barrier is the exterior sheathing. In Texas, we see both foam and OSB sheathing. In places where

Work with a Net

On garage walls and other places where there will be drywall on both sides, the crew staples 24-in.-wide fiber mesh to the stud faces. This holds the insulation in place until the drywall is installed.

Slow Down for Obstacles

Blocking, odd-size cavities, and penetrations make installing insulation much harder than it would be without them. Getting to Grade I requires careful fitting and piecing in these problem areas.

PIECE AND FIT BEHIND PIPES Raters always look around large waste lines because insulating behind them is slow and tedious. Small scraps should be tucked behind the pipe with a batt knife.

FILL AROUND REFRIGERATION LINES When possible, installers split the insulation so that the pipe is between layers. This is easier with small-diameter tubing. The larger, insulated tubing often requires piecing around the pipe.

SPLIT AROUND WIRES Cables are generally run in the center of the wall, so installers split the batt in half and pull the rear section behind the cable. The front half is laid on top.

USE SCRAPS WHEN NECESSARY Switch boxes and other spots with multiple pipes or wires generally have to be pieced together with scraps. Raters pay special attention to these areas, so it's important to fill every void.

Continued ➜

there is no sheathing, such as attic kneewalls, builders use an inexpensive fiberboard material on the back of the studs. Called Thermo-ply, this material stops air movement in these locations. Builders also use it behind fiberglass tubs and showers.

Get Better or Lose Business

About the same time we started hearing about air barriers and blower doors in the mid-1990s, a visionary group of Houston energy raters and production builders realized that boosting a home's energy efficiency produces a higher quality, more comfortable home. This led to greater homeowner satisfaction and ultimately increased sales.

One strategy for improving efficiency was to install fiberglass insulation with greater care. As insulation contractors, we now had to pass third-party insulation inspections conducted by certified energy raters every time we finished insulating a new home.

At first, we didn't have trouble meeting the requirements, but as home-performance programs such as Energy Star got traction in the new-home market, the focus on the building envelope became more important. As a result, the scrutiny with which the raters evaluated fiberglass installations increased greatly. We started getting failed-inspection calls almost overnight.

Working with the raters, we retrained our installers so that we could meet the new Residential Energy Services Network (RESNET) Grade I standards. Fast forward 20 years: Most of the mid-range and high-end new homes in our market are now insulated to Grade I.

Even though getting to Grade I is hard to achieve, it's worth the extra effort. The builders we work with build very efficient homes. They have optimally sized heating-and-cooling systems that require a good thermal envelope for peak efficiency.

Proper insulation and air-sealing also make a home that's more durable. In our humid climate, poorly insulated areas can become condensing surfaces that lead to rot and mold. Insulating to Grade I also pays lifelong dividends to the homeowner in the form of greater comfort and lower utility bills.

Achieving Grade I

Most of the builders in our market build a limited number of designs in their large developments, so we get a chance to insulate a given design many times. When the rater identifies a consistent air-barrier or insulation problem, the rater, the builder, and I meet to come up with a way to achieve Grade I. Sometimes we have to get the framer or mechanical contractor involved. Sometimes the framer can modify problem spots to make insulating easier. Similarly, the plumber or HVAC tech might be able to run pipes and ducts in different spots.

These efforts are necessary because failed insulation inspections mean returning to completed jobs to fix things, which in turn creates scheduling problems for us, the builder, and other tradespeople.

Installing fiberglass to the highest standards costs more than

---

Five Facts About Fiberglass

1. FIBERGLASS IS THE MOST POPULAR BUILDING INSULATION IN THE COUNTRY. The manufacturing process for fiberglass looks a lot like how cotton candy is made at a summer fair. Molten glass is fed into a spinning drum with small holes. The liquid glass, which can be up to 50% recycled content, is forced out of the drum into long fibers. The loose fibers are then bound together into large billets with an acrylic adhesive. The billets are cut into various sizes and packaged for transport and sale.

2. FIBERGLASS INSULATION STARTS OUT WHITE. Some insulation is brown because the corn-based binder holding the white fibers together is brown. In the past, manufacturers used formaldahyde-based binders, but the modern adhesives are said to be more environmentally friendly and less irritating. Even the pink insulation starts out white and is made pink with red dye.

3. FIBERGLASS CAN BE MANUFACTURED WITH OR WITHOUT A KRAFT-PAPER FACING. The facing is a vapor retarder meant to slow moisture accumulation resulting from water vapor diffusing through the drywall. In cold climates, the vapor retarder faces the living space, opposite the sheathing. In hot climates, it faces the exterior, against the sheathing. However, building scientists now generally advise using unfaced insulation in all but the very coldest climates because vapor retarders can hamper seasonal drying.

4. DIFFERENT PARTS OF THE COUNTRY HAVE DIFFERENT INSULATION REQUIREMENTS FOR WALLS, FLOORS, AND CEILINGS. The specific requirements can be found in table N1102.1.1 of the International Residential Code (IRC). Some manufacturers label their products "for walls" or "for floors and ceilings," indicating where they should be used. This can be helpful for less-savvy consumers, but to satisfy code, you must insulate to the R-values specified by the IRC. You can't assume that the product bearing a label for a particular application will meet code requirements.

5. FIBERGLASS CAN IRRITATE THE LUNGS AND SKIN. When installing fiberglass, wear a N95 particle respirator to prevent inhaling glass fibers, and wear long pants, a long-sleeve shirt, gloves, and a hat to prevent skin irritation.

doing a poor job because it takes longer and you have to pay someone who's more skilled to do the work. Before the 1990s, an experienced installer could handle 5000 sq. ft. of batts per day. Under Grade I requirements, installing 3000 sq. ft.—a 40% drop—is difficult.

To deal with the slower pace, we had to raise our prices somewhat, but we couldn't raise them by 40%. To compensate, we only keep the best installers (and we pay them above the average). With their help, we've developed systems that make a Grade I job go as efficiently as possible.

A Day in Our Life

At least a day or two before we begin a job, our three-person air-sealing crew fills gaps between the framing and sheathing with canned spray foam. They seal around penetrations, doors and windows, and anywhere else the air barrier is compromised.

When the three people on the insulation crew get to the job, they distribute the material throughout the house. Through experience, they know how much insulation will be required in which places.

One crew member starts with the upper parts of the wall on the top floor. He makes sure each batt is tight to the top plate and works his way down the stud cavity carefully, making sure not to compress the edges. He also installs any ceiling insulation he can reach as he moves along in a rolling scaffold. He carries both types of insulation on the scaffold with him.

Every installer carries a long-bladed batt knife that he routinely resharpens on a concrete slab. The installers use this knife to cut the batts in place. They also use the knife's blunt tip to fluff up any insulation compressed during fitting. The insulation should be touching the back side of the drywall once it's installed.

When the installer on the scaffold has a sufficient head start, another installer does the lower parts of the wall. He begins by finishing the batt started by the guy on the scaffold. If the batt isn't long enough, he cuts a piece for the bottom and carefully fits that, too. The third installer works on the rest of the ceiling and on any other high areas. Sometimes he wears stilts to reach the ceiling.

All the installers are trained to split the insulation around small-diameter pipes and wires. The batt is pulled apart near the middle, then one-half is slipped behind the pipe or wire and the other half placed on top.

When splitting is impossible, the installers place scraps around the obstruction, being careful to fill every part of the cavity. Electrical boxes get special scrutiny from raters, so the installers either insulate behind them with canned spray foam or fit small pieces of fiberglass behind them. At the end of the job, they gather the scraps and the packaging for disposal.

This Isn't Going Away

Installing fiberglass to Grade I might seem like a lot of work compared to how most fiberglass is installed, but judging from the continued focus on insulation in each IRC update, I don't think Grade I requirements are going away.

In addition, insulation is one of the few aspects of a house that are nearly impossible to upgrade once the drywall is up. This makes it even more important to get it right the first time.

Continued →

Insulating Unvented Roof Assemblies

By Martin Holladay

If you plan to insulate a sloped roof, you need to decide if you want a vented or an unvented assembly. An unvented assembly can perform well, but it's important to get the details right to avoid sheathing rot. Air-permeable insulation such as fiberglass batts, dense-packed cellulose, or blown-in fiberglass can't be used alone for an unvented assembly, since these types of insulation can allow moist indoor air to reach the cold roof sheathing, leading to condensation or moisture accumulation in the sheathing. Unvented roof assemblies should be insulated either with air-impermeable insulation (rigid foam or spray polyurethane foam) or with a combination of foam and air-permeable insulation. If you don't want to use SIPs or nailbase, there are four basic approaches.

Four options for building an unvented roof assembly

1. Rigid foam above roof sheathing

You can install all of the insulation above the roof sheathing, but the foam has to be thick enough to meet minimum code requirements for ceiling R-value. The rigid foam will be fairly thick (see "How much insulation?" below right).

2. Rigid foam on roof sheathing with air-permeable insulation between the rafters

Rigid foam also can be installed above the roof sheathing in tandem with air-permeable insulation between the rafters. In this case, the rigid foam can be thinner than when it's used alone. Code specifies the minimum R-value of the rigid-foam layer.

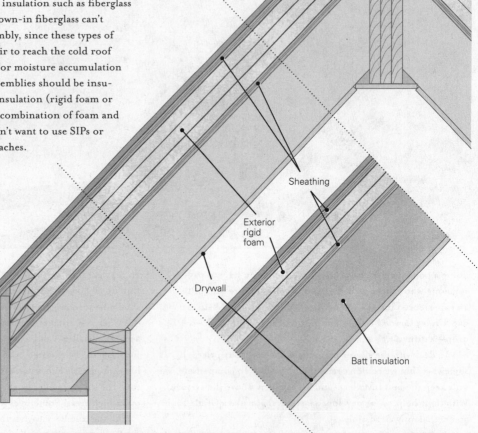

Sheathing

Exterior rigid foam

Drywall

Batt insulation

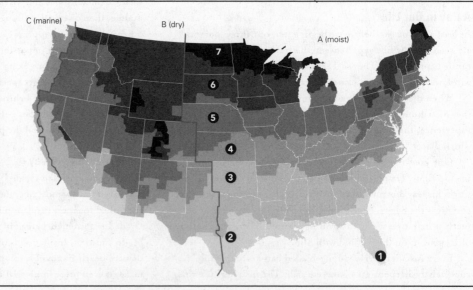

3. Spray polyurethane foam

Since it's air impermeable, spray polyurethane foam can be installed alone on the underside of roof sheathing. The foam must be thick enough to meet minimum code requirements. The main drawback is high cost. Other concerns: Closed-cell spray foam uses blowing agents with a high global-warming potential, and open-cell spray foam needs a carefully detailed vapor barrier to prevent moisture accumulation in the sheathing.

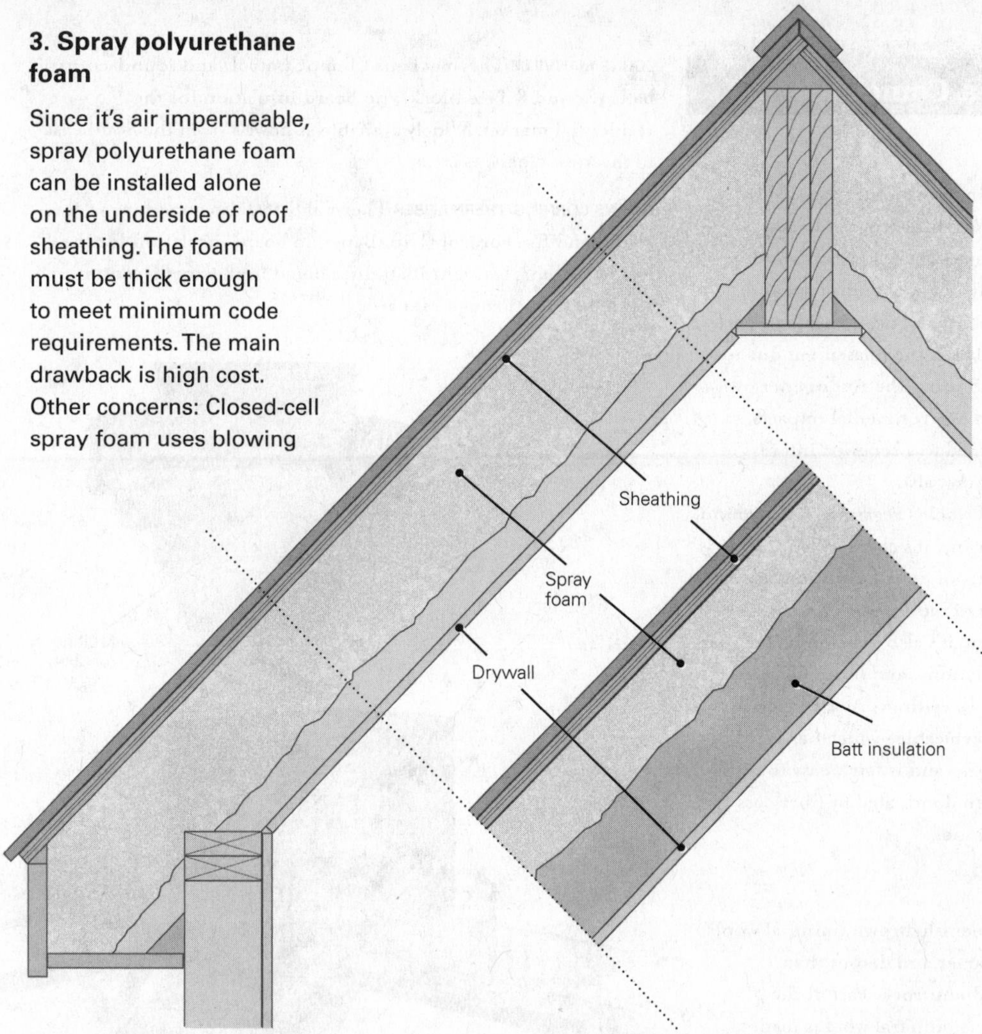

4. Spray foam with air-permeable insulation

A layer of spray polyurethane foam can be installed against the underside of the roof sheathing, with the rest of the rafter cavity filled with air-permeable insulation. You must meet the same minimum code requirements for the spray-foam layer and the total assembly as for the rigid-foam-plus-air-permeable-insulation approach.

Sheathing

Spray foam

Drywall

Batt insulation

How Much Insulation?

Most building codes include a table showing minimum R-value requirements by climate zone. Insulation, whether a single type or combination, must at least meet these requirements. When combining foam and air-permeable insulations, code requires the foam layer to meet specific minimum R-value requirements, which vary by zone. This chart is based on table R806.5 of the 2012 IRC.

Climate zone	Air-impermeable insulation	Minimum total R-value
1, 2, 3	R-5	R-30
4a, 4b	R-15	R-38
4c	R-10	R-38
5	R-20	R-38
6	R-25	R-49
7	R-30	R-49
8	R-35	R-49

Mineral Wool Makes a Comeback

By Mike Maines

Mineral-wool insulation has been in use since the late 1800s, so it's nothing new. But as the market shifted in the 1960s to less-expensive and better-promoted fiberglass insulation, the mineral-wool industry shifted its focus to industrial and manufacturing applications, where mineral wool became a perfect replacement for the asbestos materials being phased out due to health concerns. Yet over the last 25 years, the cost of energy, the public's awareness of health and environmental impacts, and building-science research have led to a renewed interest in mineral wool for the residential market also.

It's not hard to see why mineral wool is regaining lost ground. It's got an R-value of 3.8 to 4.3 per in., it's chemically inert, it contains almost no VOCs, it's fireproof, it absorbs sound, and its embodied energy is lower than that of most petroleum-derived foams. Sold most commonly as batts, it's also available as boards and as loose fibers for blown installations, and it can be used in all the critical locations: walls, floors, ceilings, roofs, exteriors, and even below grade. It is vapor permeable—which has its disadvantages as well as its advantages—and is fairly easy to install well. In a category that has long been dominated by fiberglass batts, mineral wool is worth a fresh look.

Yes, It's Made of Rocks

Ranging from tannish-yellow to greenish-brown, mineral wool has a matted-wool texture that's coarser and denser than fiberglass, thanks to its main ingredient: rock. Part of the fibrous insulation family of products, mineral wool is made by spinning molten basalt and/or blast-furnace slag (a by-product of the processing of iron ore and other minerals) to form short, multidirectional fibers.

Supply and Demand

Although more available than ever before, mineral wool still competes for shelf space. Batts are typically 60% to 70% more expensive than fiberglass, and boards are at least 80% more expensive than rigid-foam boards.

JOHNS MANVILLE Thermal batts (TempControl) and sound-control batts (Sound & Fire Block); no board insulation for the residential market. Widely available at Lowe's from the Southeast to the West Coast.

OWENS CORNING/THERMAFIBER Thermal batts, also good for sound and fire control (UltraBatt); no board insulation for the residential market. UltraBatt distributed in the north-central United States through Menards.

Centrifuge

Melting furnace

Raw fibers

Pleating/press machine

Curing oven

Cutters

The Options Look Familiar

Batts
Mineral-wool batts come in widths and thicknesses typical for residential construction, but only in 48-in. (or sometimes 47-in.) lengths, and never in rolls. Batts are formed slightly wider than typical 16-in. or 24-in. framing cavities to create a tight friction fit, and they don't move or change significantly over time or with changes in temperature. Mineral wool is dense, ranging from 2 lb. to 4 lb. per cu. ft. versus 0.4 lb. to 1.4 lb. per cu. ft. for fiberglass.

Boards
Mineral-wool boards are almost as stiff as rigid foam and are always about 48 in. long, between 16 in. and 96 in. wide, and between 1 in. to 3 in. thick. Denser than mineral-wool batts as well as rigid-foam boards, which have a density of between 0.75 lb. and 3 lb. per cu. ft., these boards range from 4.4 lb. to 8 lb. per cu. ft. (and up to 15 lb. per cu. ft. for commercial grades). They can be used both for interior and exterior applications.

Blown
Mineral wool is available for blown installations either by itself as loose fill (generally for attics), or mixed with a binder and sprayed into framing cavities or onto foam as a fire retardant.

ROXUL Thermal batts (ComfortBatt) and sound-control batts (Safe'n'Sound) in widths designed for 16-in. and 24-in. framing cavities; board insulation (ComfortBoard IS insulating sheathing) in 1¼-in., 1½-in., 2-in., and 3-in. thicknesses, and in 24-in., 36-in., and 48-in. widths (also available is the 1-in.-thick ComfortBoard FS firestop product, sold in 16-in. and 24-in. widths) Batts commonly available nationwide; board insulation typically special ordered and only in large quantities, but internet retailer Small Planet Workshop stocks smaller quantities

AMERROCK Loose mineral wool for blown installation (Rockwool Premium Plus) and FireStopTB sprayed thermal barrier; no boards or batts. Available nationwide through insulation distributors, or direct from the manufacturer

More Points of Comparison

HEALTH CONCERNS Although mineral wool is chemically inert and contains essentially no VOCs (the products with formaldehyde binders are cured before leaving the factory), respirators and other personal protective equipment are still recommended during installation, as with installations of other types of fibrous insulation. Some people find the fibers itchier than fiberglass, but others consider them less so. According to manufacturers, the fibers settle out of the air quickly due to their relatively heavy weight, so the itch factor may depend on the individual and whether the itch is from contact or airborne fibers. MSDS documents list mineral wool as "not classifiable as carcinogenic to humans." Although products with a mineral-oil additive may

Continued ➡

create some smoke in the presence of fire, there is no danger of the thick, toxic smoke that accompanies burning foam.

MOLD As do the manufacturers of many building products, mineral-wool producers exercise care with the phrasing "does not support mold growth." In other words, the insulation itself does not provide a food source for mold or other fungal growth, but if temperature and humidity levels are high enough, mold could still appear in framing cavities. In fact, one of mineral wool's other markets is as a growing medium for plants.

ENVIRONMENTAL IMPACT Considered green for its typically high recycled content (although some brands use all virgin material), fire resistance, low formaldehyde content, high thermal resistance, and vapor-permeable composition, mineral wool compares favorably to most other insulation products in terms of environmental impact. According to a Building Green report, mineral wool's lifetime global-warming potential is lower than that of most foam products and about the same as fiberglass. The only insulation material that scored significantly better than mineral wool was cellulose.

LIQUID WATER Thanks both to a light-bodied oil added during the manufacturing process and to the nonporous nature of its fibers, mineral-wool insulation is highly resistant to water absorption. Mineral-wool fibers are stocky, allowing liquid water to drain without harm, even in batt products.

PESTS Other than its density, there is nothing in mineral wool to deter rodents or insects, and birds have been known to nest in exposed exterior mineral wool. As with most types of insulation, care should be taken in other ways to keep pests out.

How Mineral Wool Stacks Up to Other Types of Insulation

Although it's not easy to do a direct comparison, mineral wool proves to be a strong contender in many areas.

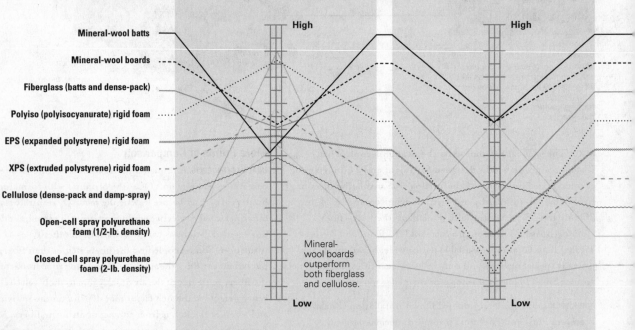

Thermal R-value
With R-values from 3.8 to 4.3 per in., mineral wool outperforms the thermal resistance of conventional fiberglass and cellulose, and it lands in the middle of the pack compared to the aged R-values of foam insulation. With a very low coefficient of thermal expansion—just 4% to 8% that of rigid foam—shrinkage in cold weather is also a nonissue.

Water-vapor permeability
In all its forms, mineral wool is very vapor permeable (30 to 40 perms). By code, this requires that vapor retarders be used on interiors in colder climates, but it also means that building assemblies can dry.

Type of Insulation

- Mineral-wool batts
- Mineral-wool boards
- Fiberglass (batts and dense-pack)
- Polyiso (polyisocyanurate) rigid foam
- EPS (expanded polystyrene) rigid foam
- XPS (extruded polystyrene) rigid foam
- Cellulose (dense-pack and damp-spray)
- Open-cell spray polyurethane foam (1/2-lb. density)
- Closed-cell spray polyurethane foam (2-lb. density)

High — Low

Mineral-wool boards outperform both fiberglass and cellulose.

At Home in Most Applications

Manufacturers and insulation contractors cite sound attenuation and fire safety as the two major reasons for using mineral wool, but the product has plenty of thermal advantages as well. Here's what you need to know about installing it in various applications.

CAVITY INSULATION Mineral-wool batts can be installed in framing cavities, but expect them to be heavier than fiberglass and less likely to compress. Manufacturers recommend cutting them with a serrated bread knife because they are not as easy to cut with a utility knife as fiberglass batts.

BASEMENTS AND FOUNDATIONS When insulating first-floor joists, or the ceiling of a crawlspace or basement, keep the batts tight to the floor sheathing, and add a vapor retarder. Because of the risks involved, avoid using mineral wool or any permeable insulation on the interior face of a basement wall.

A study by the Danish Technological Institute found that mineral wool installed below grade remained effective and unaltered by compression over 30 to 35 years. Damp proof or waterproof the exterior face of the concrete before installing the mineral wool, backfill with well-draining soil and filter fabric, and extend the insulation to the top of the foundation wall. Cover it with cementboard, stucco, or another material.

Roxul's ComfortBoard IS is approved for use below slabs at non-load-bearing locations, but it is not approved for use under frost-protected shallow foundations.

EXTERIOR INSULATION According to Building Science Corporation, the water-resistive barrier (WRB) should go on the face of the sheathing when installing exterior mineral-wool board insulation. You also can use a sheathing with an integral WRB, such as

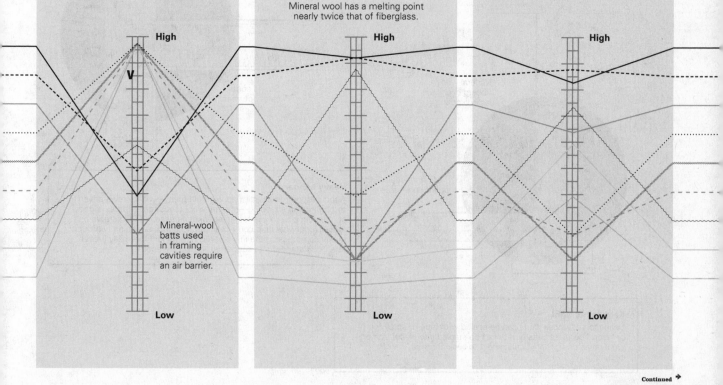

Airflow resistance
Although dense enough that wind washing (diminished insulating value due to movement of air) is not a big concern for board products or in attics, mineral wool is still air permeable, and even when it's tightly fit, there still may be some gaps in the installation. For this reason, batts in framing cavities should be combined with some form of air barrier.

Mineral-wool batts used in framing cavities require an air barrier.

Fire control
Naturally fire resistant and noncombustible without relying on chemical additives, mineral wool has a melting point of over 2000°F and is code approved for use as both draft stopping and as fire blocking. Its flame-spread and smoke-development ratings are low to zero, depending on the specific product.

Mineral wool has a melting point nearly twice that of fiberglass.

Sound control
The physical characteristics of mineral wool make it excellent at absorbing sound. "Sound batts," made somewhat denser and in different sizes than batts intended solely for thermal use, can be installed in interior framing cavities to minimize sound transfer. Manufacturers note that mineral wool is only one part of a sound-attenuation strategy, though; for the best performance, refer to assemblies rated for sound-transmission class (STC).

High

Low

Continued →

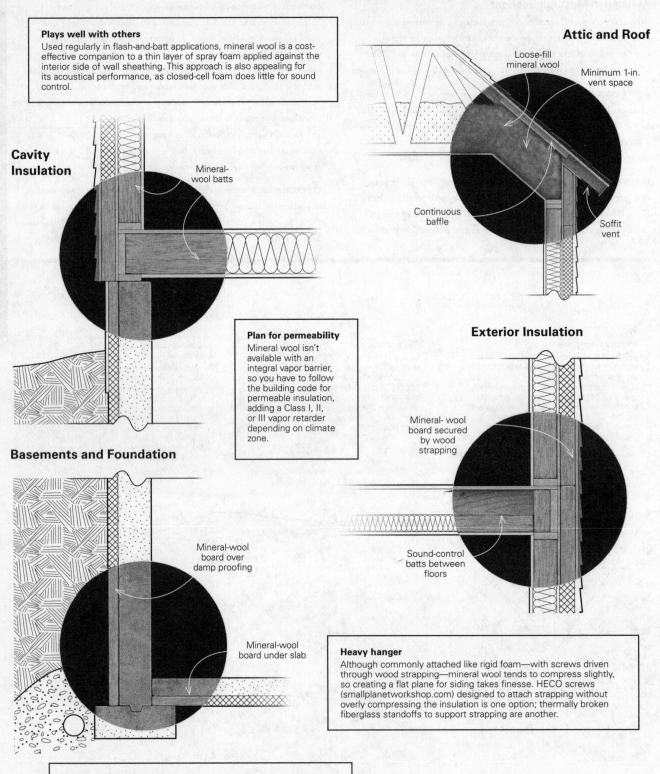

Plays well with others
Used regularly in flash-and-batt applications, mineral wool is a cost-effective companion to a thin layer of spray foam applied against the interior side of wall sheathing. This approach is also appealing for its acoustical performance, as closed-cell foam does little for sound control.

Attic and Roof

Loose-fill mineral wool

Minimum 1-in. vent space

Continuous baffle

Soffit vent

Cavity Insulation

Mineral-wool batts

Plan for permeability
Mineral wool isn't available with an integral vapor barrier, so you have to follow the building code for permeable insulation, adding a Class I, II, or III vapor retarder depending on climate zone.

Exterior Insulation

Mineral- wool board secured by wood strapping

Sound-control batts between floors

Basements and Foundation

Mineral-wool board over damp proofing

Mineral-wool board under slab

Heavy hanger
Although commonly attached like rigid foam—with screws driven through wood strapping—mineral wool tends to compress slightly, so creating a flat plane for siding takes finesse. HECO screws (smallplanetworkshop.com) designed to attach strapping without overly compressing the insulation is one option; thermally broken fiberglass standoffs to support strapping are another.

Keep joints tight
Unlike foam (whose joints can be sealed with tape or spray foam) or faced fiberglass batts (which can be stapled into place), mineral wool relies on tight physical contact to avoid thermal "short circuits."

Huber's Zip System product. The WRB or sheathing layer is also a good location for the air barrier in all climates as long as the framing cavities allow drying toward the inside (i.e., no closed-cell foam). It is also a good location for the vapor retarder, when required, as long as the proportion of exterior insulation to interior insulation keeps the vapor retarder above the dew point. Keep in mind that because of its lower R-value per inch, a thicker layer of mineral-wool board insulation is required to reach the same R-value as foam.

ATTIC AND ROOF On attic floors (above a vapor retarder in colder climates), install batts between joist bays, then place a second layer perpendicular to the first. Combining a layer of 5½-in. batts (R-23) and a layer of 7¼-in. batts (R-30), with all seams offset, creates an attic with a nominal R-value of 53, which exceeds the R-49 minimum-required value for cold zones in the United States (zones 6, 7, and 8 in IRC 2009, plus zone 5 and marine zone 4 in IRC 2012). Alternatively, use the loose-blown product.

For a vented roof with a sloped ceiling below, such as a typical vaulted or cathedral ceiling, simply allow for at least a 1-in. gap between the top of the insulation and the underside of the roof sheathing. Best practice is to air-seal this gap by using continuous baffles.

Unvented roofs are more challenging. The use of permeable insulation such as mineral wool is allowed as long as an impermeable insulation (foam) to prevent condensation is installed either directly above or directly below the roof sheathing. Generally, a greater proportion of impermeable insulation is required the farther north you are.

Stop Drafts with a Drop-Down Door Seal

By Jay B. Lane

As a custom-door and window installer, I always include weathersealing as part of the job. This final step not only improves comfort and energy performance, but it also shields the home's interior from wind-driven water, insects, and street noise.

While the weathersealing around the sides and at the top of a door is straightforward, I find that sealing an exterior door at the threshold can be tricky. In most cases, I use an interlocking threshold with a water pan underneath and a rubber silicone bead kerfed into the bottom of the door. However, this approach still leaves a visible metal threshold.

For a seamless transition between interior and exterior spaces, I use an auto-drop threshold seal. It's an adjustable device with a neoprene seal that retracts when the door is opened to allow for a hidden weatherseal. When the door closes, the door jamb depresses a pin on the hinge side of the door. This action engages a leaf spring inside the mechanism, allowing the neoprene seal to drop into place. I use a Pemko automatic door bottom (www.pemko.com) because of its reasonable price and solid assembly.

1. TRIM THE DOOR BOTTOM. For the weatherseal to operate correctly, the bottom of the door must be no more than ½ in. above the top of the threshold. After marking this dimension on both the hinge and latch sides of the door bottom (inset photo), I trim the door using a circular saw and a straightedge guide. For a review of different guides, check *Fine Homebuilding* #182, or online at finehomebuilding.com.

2. CUT THE GROOVE WITH MULTIPLE ROUTER PASSES. The Pemko mechanism requires a groove 9/16 in. wide and 1 9/16 in. deep. After fitting a ½-in.-dia. bit (www.freud.com) in my router, I attach and adjust a fence to center the groove in the door's bottom edge. Then I rout the groove in multiple passes, increasing the cutting depth ¼ in. to 3/8 in. each time. I widen the groove to 9/16 in. by adjusting the router fence on the final pass.

3. CUT THE SEAL AND HOUSING IN ONE STEP. After I've checked the mechanism's fit in the groove and scribed it to match the width of the door, I move the scribe line clear of the door's edge and cut the entire mechanism to length with an abrasive grinding blade (a fine-toothed hacksaw will work as well). Note: The neoprene bumper can move laterally inside the housing, so before you cut, make sure its opposite end is flush with the end of the housing.

Continued ➡

4. SECURE WITH SCREWS GLUED IN PLACE. After sealing the inside of the groove and the door bottom with polyurethane sealant, I position the mechanism, drill pilot holes, and attach it with screws. I squeeze a small amount of wood glue into each hole before securing each fastener. I secure the bumper by crimping the aluminum bar at one end.

A hidden auto-drop seal won't work for every door configuration. The stiff aluminum bar crimped to the neoprene bumper needs a fairly flat surface to seal against. Large gouges or dips and undulations in the floor or threshold below the door cause a gap in the seal. Also, the bottom of the door must be within ½ in. of the threshold. If the door needs to pass over a thick rug, the threshold can be built up to allow the bottom of the door to be higher. This seal is not recommended for high-exposure areas, but for a clean, seamless look, nothing works as well.

Dial in the Drop

When the door closes, a spring-loaded pin compresses against the hinge-side door jamb to drop the seal. Depressing the pin releases tension on the spring and allows the seal to drop into place. Turning the pin with a screwdriver adjusts the seal up or down. A screw driven flush to the door jamb contacts the pin and prevents it from creating a depression in the wooden jamb. When the door opens (photo below), the seal retracts.

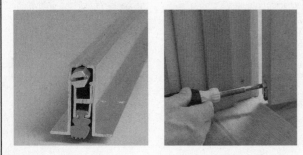

Gutters

By Don Burgard

Gutters are kind of like baseboard heaters. They serve a useful function but can present a design challenge for homeowners who don't like the way they look. By building deep overhangs and observing proper drainage practices around a house's foundation, it's possible in many areas to make do without gutters. In fact, three of the six winners of Fine Homebuilding's 2012 Houses awards—homes in Northern California, Massachusetts, and North Carolina—have no gutters.

Still, most houses in most climates have gutters, and the choice of materials is wide enough so that gutters don't have to intrude on a house's aesthetics. In some cases, gutters can even enhance a house's appearance. Gutters made from the materials featured here are available in the two most common profiles: half-round and ogee, or K-style. To determine what kind of gutters work best on a particular house, it's important to know the differences between the materials.

Vinyl

Vinyl gutters are the easiest to install, so they are popular with DIYers. Only a few basic tools are required, and parts fit together without sealants. Joints in gutters from some manufacturers are sealed with neoprene gaskets, while in others, pieces are joined permanently with PVC cement. Of all the gutter materials, vinyl expands and contracts the most. To account for this movement, the inside of the downspout connector is marked with various temperatures. When installing gutters, you cut the piece that ends at the downspout connector to a length that corresponds to the current temperature. Vinyl gutters are attached to the fascia with either one-piece or two-piece hidden brackets.

Vinyl gutters are widely available in white and brown, although some manufacturers offer gray and various shades of brown. They are easy to clean and never need to be painted, although they can be.

Over time, vinyl gutters can become brittle, particularly in cold climates. In areas prone to snow or ice storms or even heavy rainfall, vinyl gutters will likely not hold up as well as metal gutters, in part because their brackets typically are attached with screws much shorter than those used to attach metal gutters. These screws often aren't long enough to reach the rafters or trusses behind the fascia. Vinyl gutters also are unlikely to support the weight of a person on a ladder.

but expansion joints in long runs can prevent wrinkling or seam failure.

Aluminum gutters should not be used where the roof is covered with algae-resistant shingles, whose granules are covered in a thin coating of copper. In areas with little rainfall or in coastal areas with frequent salt fog, runoff from the shingles can remain in the gutters and lead to galvanic corrosion.

Copper

Copper gutters have practical advantages: They are naturally rust resistant, they experience minimal expansion and contraction, and they last a century or more under normal conditions. It's their distinctive appearance, however, that is the primary reason why some homeowners are willing to spend a lot of extra money to have them on their house. Individual pieces of copper gutter are soldered together and also may be pop-riveted prior to soldering. Copper gutters are held in place with strap hangers, hidden brackets, or exterior brackets; decorative exterior brackets add to the cost. Over time, copper develops a greenish patina that many people find attractive. Those who wish to maintain the shiny appearance of their gutters must treat them periodically with a sealant to prevent the copper from oxidizing.

Aluminum

Aluminum is the most common material used for gutters, and for good reason: It is widely available, lightweight, rustproof, durable, and relatively inexpensive. It is made from stock ranging in thickness from 0.018 in. to 0.032 in., with the thickest stock providing the greatest resistance to damage from snow, ice, falling tree branches, and ladders. The aluminum gutters sold in most home centers are painted white or brown, but they can be found elsewhere in other colors; of course, they can be repainted in any color. Traditional aluminum gutters carried by home centers come in 10-ft. sections that can be joined by slip-joint connectors and sealant.

Aluminum gutters can be installed in several ways, including strap hangers that attach to the roof sheathing, hidden brackets, exterior brackets, or 7-in. screws or spikes with ferrules. Aluminum expands and contracts with temperature changes,

Continued →

Steel

The strongest residential gutters are made of steel. Stainless-steel gutters are expensive and rare. Steel gutters most often are made from galvanized steel or painted steel, and as with copper, individual pieces are soldered together and also may be pop-riveted. These gutters are held in place by strap hangers, hidden brackets, or exterior brackets. They are better than aluminum and vinyl at resisting damage from hail, ice, snow, and falling branches, and they also provide more support for ladders. Of the gutter materials profiled here, steel expands and contracts the least; still, in areas with big temperature variations, long runs of steel gutters may need expansion joints. Whether made from galvanized or painted material, steel gutters eventually rust. If you're looking for the strength of steel but want a higher degree of corrosion resistance, consider Galvalume gutters, which are made from steel and are coated with an aluminum-zinc layer.

Seamless Gutters

Aluminum, steel, and copper gutters can be fabricated on site by running metal coil through an extruder that spits out gutters in seamless lengths much longer than the 10-ft. sections available in home centers. Fewer seams, of course, mean fewer places where leaks can develop. Seamless-gutter companies can handle the entire job, or they can leave custom-cut lengths at the site if you want to do the installation yourself.

Fixing Common Gutter Blunders

By Brent Briggs

As a home-improvement contractor for the past 30 years, I've seen an inordinate amount of damage to homes that can be attributed to rain-gutter problems. From stains on the siding, to major foundation problems, to flooded basements and interior mold, poorly installed rain gutters always cause a host of problems. Here are fixes for the most common ones I encounter. Many of these problems can be corrected easily, except for poor roof design, which is often based more on looks than practicality and is very difficult to change after the roof has been built. Even then, installing a larger gutter or increasing the number of downspouts can make a difference. Here, I explain how to get gutters right the first time, including how to size them correctly based on roof size and climate.

Nine Ways to Do Gutters Right

Fixing the gutter blunders exemplified on the house shown here requires a three-pronged approach. The first is good design: Avoid details that concentrate flows, and size gutters for the climate and roof size. The second is proper construction: Pitch gutters to drain, and install them with an eye to avoiding restrictions that cause clogs and overflows. The third is the right materials: Use durable sealants, fasteners that stay tight, and quality guards that keep out leaves and debris.

1. Exclude Leaves Trim overhanging trees, and use gutter guards. Plygem's guards also stiffen gutters, so they're less likely to bend if a ladder is leaned on them.

2. Lead Water Away Buried pipes lead water to daylight or to a dry well at least 10 ft. from the house.

3. Install More Downspouts If gutters are longer than 30 ft., pitch them from the middle toward a downspout on each end. The second downspout doubles the capacity of that gutter.

4. Pitch Gutters Properly To keep water moving, pitch gutters at least 1 in. over their length. A greater pitch is better but may not look as good.

5. Use the Right Sealant To avoid slow drips at joints, use elastomeric sealant such as quad or geocel that resists UV rays and stays flexible for the long term.

6. Extend Corners To hide downspouts on the side of a house, extend the gutter 3 in. beyond the eave.

7. Design Wisely The best roofs don't concentrate flow, and their upper gutters drain through downspouts leading to lower gutters and downspouts.

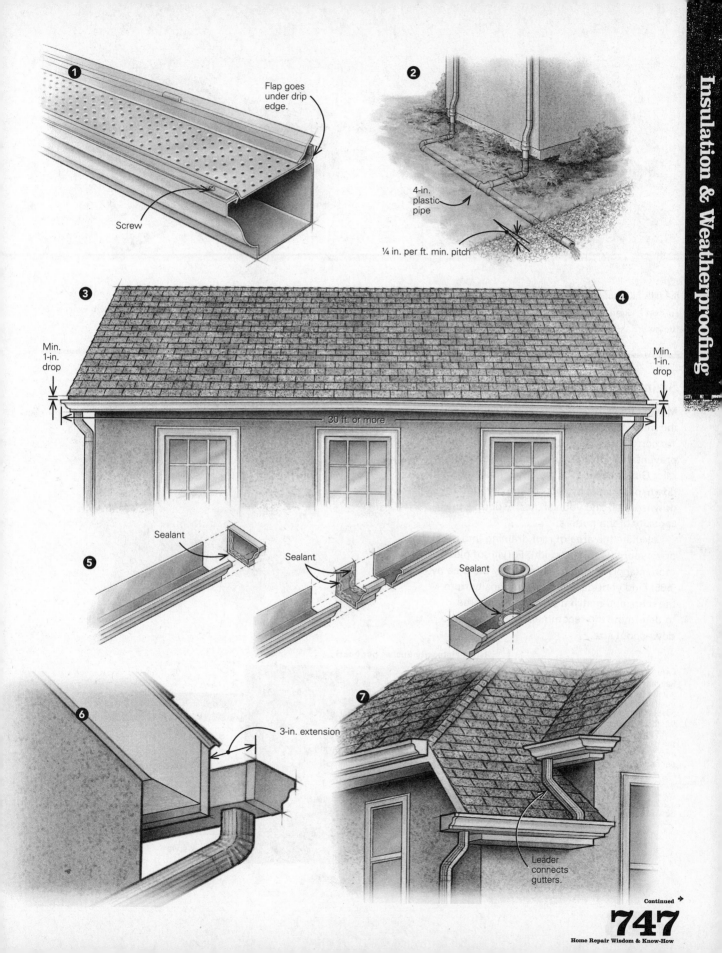

1 Flap goes under drip edge.

Screw

2 4-in. plastic pipe

¼ in. per ft. min. pitch

3 Min. 1-in. drop

4 Min. 1-in. drop

30 ft. or more

5 Sealant · Sealant · Sealant

6 3-in. extension

7 Leader connects gutters.

Continued ➔

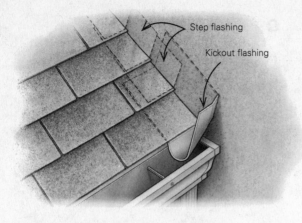

Step flashing

Kickout flashing

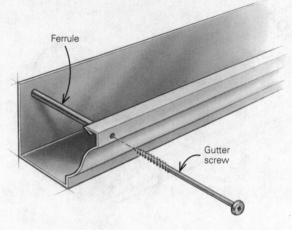

Ferrule

Gutter screw

8. Install Kickout Flashing Integrated with the step flashing by the roofer, kickout flashing diverts water away from the wall and into the gutter.

9. Use Gutter Screws Unlike spikes, which back out and allow gutters to sag and overflow, screws hold tight. Space them every 2 ft.

Sizing Gutters and Downspouts

Most builders default to 5-in. K-style gutters, the most commonly available size and style. Yet correctly sizing gutters is simple and can prevent them from being overwhelmed with rain. Gutter capacity is directly related to downspout capacity: Double the number of downspouts, and you can nearly double the capacity of the gutters.

Calculate the area of roof draining into each downspout (length × width). For a roof pitched more steeply than 5-in-12, multiply the area by 0.85. Find your design rainfall intensity from the map, and match it with your roof area to determine the recommended gutter and downspout size.

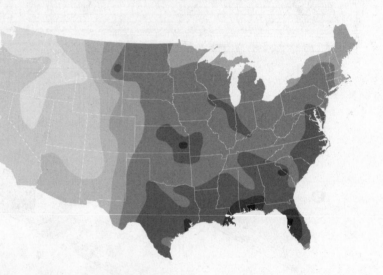

Example

Say that the roof area to be drained measures 21 ft. by 40 ft. (840 sq. ft.), that the pitch is 4-in-12, and that the local rainfall intensity is 5 in. per hour. That requires at least a 5-in. K-style gutter with at least a 2-in. by 3-in. downspout.

Rainfall intensity (inches per hour)

3	4	5	6	7	8	9	10	Gutter size and type	Downspout size
			Roof area (square feet)						
775	581	465	387	332	291	258	232	5 in. half-round	3 in. dia.
1272	954	763	636	545	477	424	382	6 in. half-round	3 in. or 4 in. dia.
763	572	458	382	327	286	254	229	4 in. K-style	2 in. by 3 in.
1399	1050	840	700	600	525	466	420	5 in. K-style	2 in. by 3 in. or 3 in. by 4 in.
2279	1709	1367	1139	977	854	760	684	6 in. K-style	3 in. by 4 in.

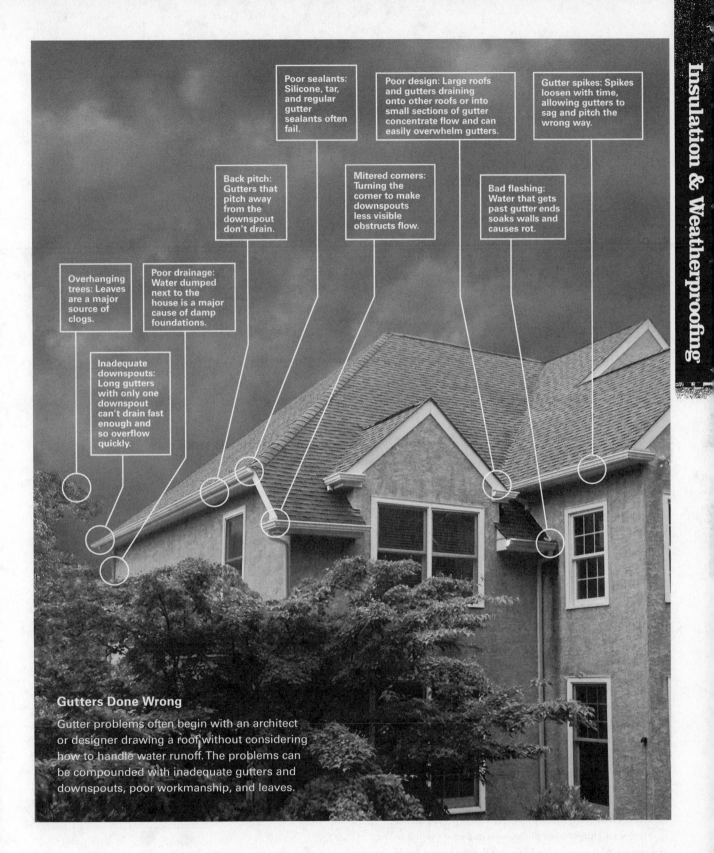

Poor sealants: Silicone, tar, and regular gutter sealants often fail.

Poor design: Large roofs and gutters draining onto other roofs or into small sections of gutter concentrate flow and can easily overwhelm gutters.

Gutter spikes: Spikes loosen with time, allowing gutters to sag and pitch the wrong way.

Back pitch: Gutters that pitch away from the downspout don't drain.

Mitered corners: Turning the corner to make downspouts less visible obstructs flow.

Bad flashing: Water that gets past gutter ends soaks walls and causes rot.

Overhanging trees: Leaves are a major source of clogs.

Poor drainage: Water dumped next to the house is a major cause of damp foundations.

Inadequate downspouts: Long gutters with only one downspout can't drain fast enough and so overflow quickly.

Gutters Done Wrong

Gutter problems often begin with an architect or designer drawing a roof without considering how to handle water runoff. The problems can be compounded with inadequate gutters and downspouts, poor workmanship, and leaves.

Designing for Durability

By Jay Crandell and Jamie Lyons

Have you Googled "housing durability" lately? Probably not. But you might be surprised that one of the most popular downloads on the U.S. Department of Housing and Urban Development's (HUD) website is a guide we were commissioned to write called Durability by Design. It's a collection of best design practices for housing durability from the ridge vent to the footings, and it covers moisture, UV radiation, corrosion, mechanicals, insects, and other topics. According to Dana Bres of HUD, who was instrumental in creating both the original guide and its recent update, one reason it's been so popular is that "the practices which make for good durability are often the same ones that make houses more sustainable and efficient. In searching for those details, builders and designers find us."

It struck us that the original 2002 publication is kind of like a time capsule that shows the building methods and materials commonly used in that era. "Era" makes it sound long ago, but homes really do work a lot differently today than they did a decade ago, and this affects durability. We've seen these changes along the way through our work in building consulting, training, research, inspections, and forensics, but updating this 12-year-old durability guide really put the changes into focus for us.

Here we highlight some of the most important topics in the new version of the guide. We hope you'll give the new guide a read and find it as interesting as we did in producing it.

Control Water with Overhangs

Rainwater control has always topped the list of durability-fostering details. The improved insulation and air-sealing of today's exterior walls means that they have a greater sensitivity to moisture. Keeping rain from hitting walls, which is the job of roof overhangs, is more important than ever. In the revised guide, we place the important factors for rainwater management into a clear decision-making framework that includes recommendations for roof-overhang width based on risk of decay—which differs by region—as a way to reduce the risk of water intrusion in walls.

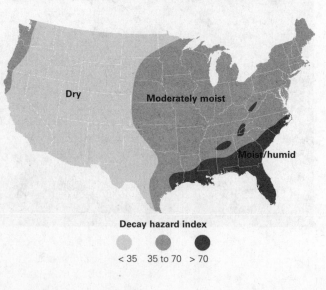

Decay hazard index

< 35   35 to 70   > 70

Roof Overhangs by Region

The overhang a house should have is based on the local decay hazard index. In places where the index is less than 35, overhangs aren't that important, but they matter a lot in many other regions.

Design Walls Based on Local Rainfall

Although a wall's durability and performance depend on far more than its exterior cladding, the design and installation of that cladding and its underlayment are critical factors in protecting a building from rainwater and moisture accumulation. The revised guide lays out a three-step procedure for selecting a durable and climate-appropriate method of constructing exterior walls to ensure performance in specific climates.

Step 1: Assess the Site's Climate

Begin by categorizing the climate based on the potential for wetting of walls, especially wetting from wind-driven rain. These classifications are a bit subjective, as there aren't clearly defined criteria in the United States for assessing the effects of wind-driven rain. As a proxy, we use a wind-driven-rain map in the revised guide to help classify the severity of the climate.

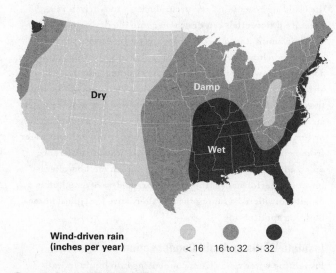

Wind-driven rain (inches per year)   < 16   16 to 32   > 32

Step 2: Assess Building Exposure

The terrain surrounding a building affects its exposure to wind-driven rain, as does the ratio of roof overhang to the height of the wall below. Increased shielding of the site against wind tends to reduce the effects of rain. Similarly, wide roof overhangs relative to wall height effectively reduce the exposure.

Reference the table at right to determine a building's exposure level based on the climate, the roof-overhang ratio, and the wind. The exposure level provides a basis for selecting an appropriate exterior-wall assembly. We can drill down further by applying the exposure levels in the table to specific walls of a house or even elements such as glazing. By understanding the exposure at this simplified level, a builder or designer can make decisions about flashing details or consider the benefits of using wider overhangs.

Building Exposure Levels

Wind exposure	Overhang ratio*	Site climate		
		Wet	Damp	Dry
Little or no wind protection from surrounding buildings and/or natural obstructions	0	High	High	Moderate
	0.1	High	Moderate	Low
	0.2	Moderate	Low	Low
	0.3	Moderate	Low	Negligible
	0.4	Low	Low	Negligible
	≥ 0.5	Low	Negligible	Negligible
Wind protection from surrounding buildings and/or natural obstructions	0	High	High	Moderate
	0.1	High	Moderate	Low
	0.2	Moderate	Low	Negligible
	0.3	Low	Negligible	Negligible
	0.4	Low	Negligible	Negligible
	≥ 0.5	Negligible	Negligible	Negligible

*Find the overhang ratio by dividing the roof overhang by the wall height.

Step 3: Select a Wall Assembly

Based on the building exposure level determined in step 2, use the table at right to select an appropriate exterior-wall assembly. With a reasonable level of installation quality and maintenance, a wall rated "good" has a low risk of failure during its likely service life. A "fair" wall may require more careful attention to detailing, installation quality, and maintenance, and it has a tolerable risk of failure during the likely service life. "Not recommended" means that the wall shouldn't be used on a wood-framed house in that climate.

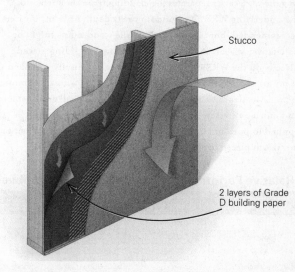

Stucco

2 layers of Grade D building paper

Concealed Barrier

The concealed-barrier method relies on porous cladding material adhered to or placed directly on an internal water barrier or drainage plane. A common example is conventional stucco applied over two layers of Grade D building paper. This method relies primarily on deflection of rainwater, but it also has some

Continued →

ability to absorb and retain moisture, which can dry out later. These walls allow water to seep out through weeps at the bottom, but there is no open pathway to allow water to drain freely. Also, moisture stored in the cladding from a recent rain can be driven into the wall by the sun as vapor, especially when the wall uses a vapor-permeable water-resistive barrier (WRB) material such as building paper and many housewraps. Synthetic stone is another example of a concealed-barrier cladding.

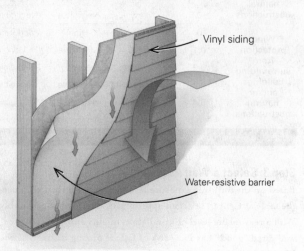

Vinyl siding

Water-resistive barrier

Drained Cavity

Drained cavities increase the life of exterior finishes on wood surfaces by promoting drying. The method relies on deflection, drainage, and drying to protect the wall from moisture damage. In general, a cavity separates the cladding from the surface of the underlying WRB. A minimum cavity depth of ⅜ in. is often recommended, but this may vary. While wood siding might be nailed over spacers to create such cavities, vinyl siding placed directly on the WRB creates a cavity whose continuity is broken at points of contact, and masonry veneer is laid with a minimum 1-in. cavity depth to allow space for drainage as well as placement and mortar excesses. The drained-cavity approach also can be applied to portland-cement stucco with use of a drainage mat or metal lath placed over spacers to create the cavity.

Relative Performance Of Exterior-Wall Assemblies

Exposure level	Concealed barrier	Drained cavity	Basic rain screen
High	Not recommended	Fair	Good
Moderate	Fair	Good	Good
Low	Good	Good	Good
Negligible	Good	Good	Good

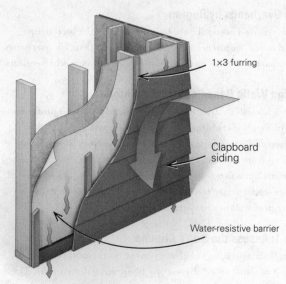

1×3 furring

Clapboard siding

Water-resistive barrier

Basic Rain Screen

A rain screen is similar to the drained-cavity method, but it has added features to reduce air-pressure differentials across the cladding system that can occur during wind-driven rain. Pressure differentials can draw water into the drainage cavity. At a minimum, this approach uses a rigid air barrier such as sheathing behind the cladding that is able to resist wind pressures. This reduces wind pressure across the cladding (which is not airtight) and is less likely to result in water being sucked behind the cladding. Also, the cavity between the cladding and the water/ air barrier must be compartmentalized by use of airtight blocking or furring at corners of the building. This feature prevents water from being sucked into the cavity due to a pressure difference on an adjacent wall. Although the rain-screen method offers improved performance, the simpler drained-cavity method is usually considered a more practical alternative for typical home-building applications.

Insulate Walls to Avoid Condensation

Preventing water vapor from condensing into liquid in walls is incredibly important for durability. Recently added to the International Energy Conservation Code (IECC), continuous rigid exterior insulation combined with traditional batt or blown cavity insulation is detailed as an option for many climate zones. This change can affect how moisture in walls behaves in ways that the code did not seem to anticipate. We can prevent condensation in walls by keeping the interior of their sheathing from falling below the dew-point temperature. In the prescriptive wall assemblies, the continuous exterior insulation must hold enough heat in, or the cavity insulation must let enough heat through, to keep the sheathing interiors warmer than the dew point. Durability requires a climate-specific look at the ratio between the R-values of the exterior insulation and the cavity insulation, as well as the permeance of the vapor retarder.

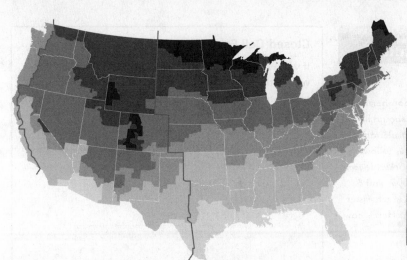

Minimum Insulation Ratios for U.S. Climate Zones

Climate zone	Class II interior vapor retarder	Class III interior vapor retarder
1 to 3	No limit	
4	0.2	
5	0.2	0.35
6	0.25	0.5
7	0.35	0.7

Match the Insulation to the Vapor Retarder

The insulation ratio is the R-value of the exterior insulation divided by that of the cavity insulation. For example, R-5 (1 in. rigid foam) ÷ R-20 (6 in. fiber insulation) = 0.25. Used with low-perm exterior foam insulation, Class I vapor retarders such as plastic can trap moisture. Class II (kraft-paper-faced batts) or Class III vapor retarders (many paints) allow drying to the inside. Using the map and the chart above, match the type of vapor retarder to the insulation ratio and the climate zone to avoid condensation.

Think Beyond the Building Code

Both the walls below meet code, but one might have condensation in a cold climate. One option in the 2012 IECC for all climate zones is an R-20+5 wall. However, its insulation ratio of 0.25 can cause condensation in zones 5 and up if used with a Class III vapor retarder. The IECC considers an R-13+10 2×4 wall to be thermally equivalent to an R-20+5 wall. With an insulation ratio of 0.77, this wall should perform well up to zone 7 with a Class II or Class III vapor retarder.

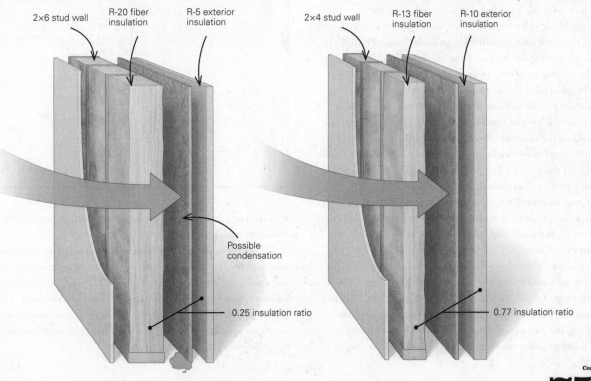

2×6 stud wall
R-20 fiber insulation
R-5 exterior insulation
Possible condensation
0.25 insulation ratio

2×4 stud wall
R-13 fiber insulation
R-10 exterior insulation
0.77 insulation ratio

Continued →

Adding Insulation to Basement Walls

By Martin Holladay

If you live in South Carolina, Alabama, Oklahoma, Southern California, or anywhere colder, your basement walls should be insulated. In climate zones 3 and higher, basement insulation is required by the 2012 International Residential Code as follows: R-5 in climate zone 3, R-10 in climate zone 4 (except marine zone 4), and R-15 in marine zone 4 and climate zones 5, 6, 7, and 8.

If your home lacks basement-wall insulation, it's much easier to install interior insulation than exterior insulation. Here's how to do it correctly.

Make Sure Your Basement Is Dry

Before installing any interior-wall insulation, verify that your basement doesn't have a water-entry problem. Diagnosing and fixing water-entry problems in existing basements is too big a topic to be discussed here (but see "Build a Risk-Free Finished Basement," *Fine Homebuilding* #248). Suffice it to say that if your basement walls get wet every spring or every time you get a heavy rain, the walls should not be insulated until the water-entry problem is solved.

Use Foam Insulation

The best way to insulate the interior side of a basement wall is with foam insulation that is adhered to or sprayed directly on the concrete. Any of the following insulation materials are acceptable for this purpose: closed-cell spray polyurethane foam or either XPS, EPS, or polyisocyanurate rigid foam.

Rigid foam can be adhered to a poured-concrete or concrete-block wall with foam-compatible adhesive or with special plastic fasteners such as Hilti IDPs or Rodenhouse Plasti-Grip PMFs. To prevent interior air from reaching the cold concrete, seal the perimeter of each piece of rigid foam with adhesive, caulk, high-quality flashing tape, or canned spray foam.

Building codes require most types of foam insulation to be protected by a layer of gypsum drywall. Many builders put up a 2×4 wall on the interior side of the foam insulation; the studs provide a convenient wiring chase and make drywall installation simple. (If you frame a 2×4 wall, don't forget to install fire blocking at the top of the wall.)

If your basement has stone-and-mortar walls, you can't insulate them with rigid foam. The only type of insulation that makes sense for stone-and-mortar walls is closed-cell spray polyurethane foam.

If you plan to insulate your basement walls with spray foam, the best approach is to frame your 2×4 walls before the foam is sprayed, leaving a gap of 1½ in. to 2 in. between the back of the studs and the concrete wall. The gap will be filled later with spray foam.

If you live in an area where termites are a problem, your local building code may require that you leave a 3-in.-high

Closed-Cell Foam

If you want to insulate the interior of your basement wall with spray foam, specify closed-cell spray foam, not open-cell foam. Closed-cell foam does a better job of stopping the diffusion of moisture from the damp concrete to the interior. Frame the 2×4 wall before the spray foam is installed, with a gap of about 2 in. between the 2×4s and the concrete.

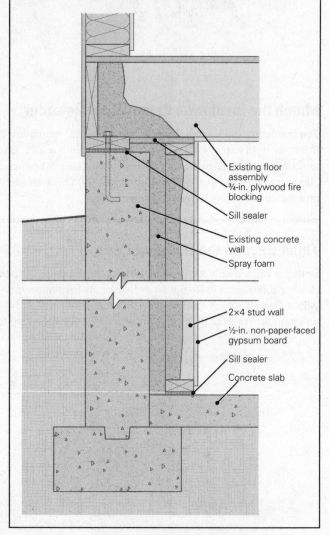

Existing floor assembly

¾-in. plywood fire blocking

Sill sealer

Existing concrete wall

Spray foam

2×4 stud wall

½-in. non-paper-faced gypsum board

Sill sealer

Concrete slab

termite-inspection strip of bare concrete near the top of your basement wall.

While reduced costs might tempt you to use fibrous insulation such as fiberglass batts, mineral-wool batts, or cellulose, these materials are air permeable and should never be installed against a below-grade concrete wall. When this type of insulation is installed in contact with concrete, moisture in the interior air can condense against the cold concrete surface, potentially leading to mold and rot.

Rigid Foam

A 2-in. layer of XPS foam (R-10) is adequate in most of climate zone 4. However, if you live in marine zone 4 or in zones 5, 6, 7, or 8, you need at least 3 in. of XPS or 4 in. of EPS to meet the minimum code requirement of R-15. Furring strips should be fastened to the concrete wall through the rigid foam.

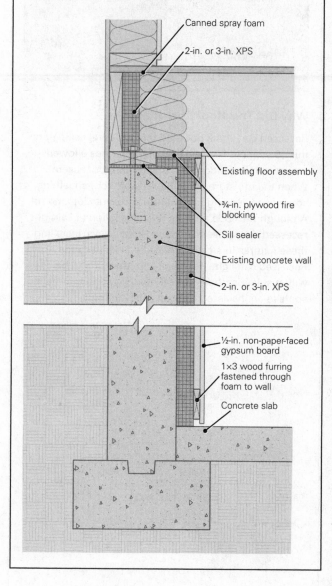

Canned spray foam

2-in. or 3-in. XPS

Existing floor assembly

¾-in. plywood fire blocking

Sill sealer

Existing concrete wall

2-in. or 3-in. XPS

½-in. non-paper-faced gypsum board

1×3 wood furring fastened through foam to wall

Concrete slab

Don't Worry About Inward Drying

Some people mistakenly believe that a damp concrete wall should be able to dry toward the interior—in other words, that any insulation on the interior of a basement wall should be vapor permeable. In fact, you don't want to encourage any moisture to enter your home by this route. Don't worry about your concrete wall; it can stay damp for a century without suffering any problems or deterioration.

Avoid Polyethylene Vapor Barriers

Basement wall systems should never include polyethylene. You don't need any poly between the concrete and the foam insulation, nor do you want poly between gypsum drywall and the insulation. If your wall assembly includes studs or furring strips, polyethylene can trap moisture, leading to mold or rot.

Basement Insulation Is Cost-Effective

If you live in climate zone 3 or anywhere colder, installing basement-wall insulation will almost always save you money through lower energy bills. It will also provide an important side benefit: Insulated walls are less susceptible to condensation and mold. This means that insulated basements stay drier and smell better than uninsulated basements.

Insulating a Cathedral Ceiling

By Martin Holladay

Because older cathedral ceilings are usually insulated with thin fiberglass batts, they are often thermal disasters. These ceilings usually leak air, leak heat, create monumental ice dams, and permit condensation and rot. Roofers sometimes try to solve these problems by improving ventilation openings at the soffits and ridge, but these "improvements" often make every symptom worse.

Fortunately, there are better ways to build cathedral ceilings. Whether they are vented or unvented, such ceilings can perform well, as long as they are properly detailed.

Although many builders still follow the time-tested technique of installing vent channels directly under roof sheathing, a vented cathedral ceiling makes sense only if the geometry of your roof is simple. You need a straight shot from the soffits to the ridge. That's easy on a gable roof without any hips, valleys, dormers, or skylights, but if the geometry of your roof is complicated, it's impossible to ensure adequate airflow through all of the rafter bays. Until recently, building codes required that insulated sloped roofs be ventilated. For complex roof designs, the International Residential Code (IRC) now allows unvented cathedral ceilings.

Vented Cathedral Ceilings Can Be Difficult to Insulate Well

Ventilation channels maintain an air gap between the insulation and the roof sheathing. The component that creates the gap is called a variety of things, including a ventilation baffle, a

Continued ➜

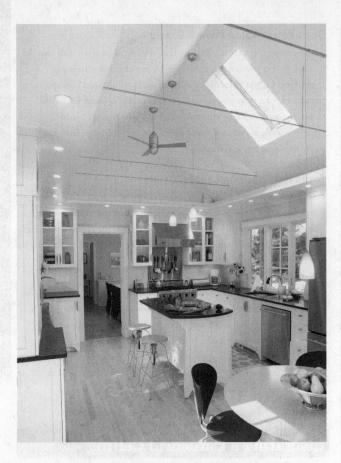

Why Did This Roof Rot? Air Leaks

Recessed can lights doomed the cathedral ceiling on this 10-year-old house. Leaky light fixtures allowed moisture-laden indoor air to enter the roof assembly. When the moisture encountered cold roof sheathing, it condensed, leading to moisture accumulation and rot. Although the code permits the installation of "airtight" recessed can lights in insulated rafter bays, installing these fixtures in a cathedral ceiling is a bad idea. Recessed can lights take up room that should be filled with insulation; they give off heat, creating thermal hot spots in an insulated roof; and they leak air.

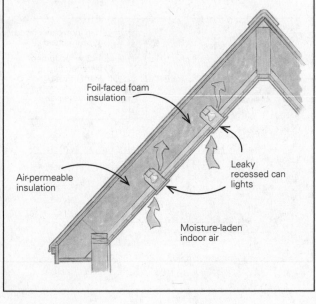

ventilation chute, a ventilation channel, or a product such as Proper-Vent.

The first vent baffles to hit the market—the classic Proper-Vents of the 1970s and '80s—were flimsy items made of thin polystyrene. These baffles don't work well. Being thin and flexible, they can't resist the pressures from dense-packed cellulose; they don't ventilate the entire width of the rafter bay; and as usually installed, they allow air to leak out the top of the insulated assembly.

Eventually, manufacturers began offering stiffer alternatives that were able to resist the pressures of dense-packed insulation. Many of these products are no longer available. At one time or another, it was possible to buy baffles that were made of cardboard, vinyl, and compressed cellulose fibers. These days, the best available vent baffle is probably the AccuVent baffle, which is made from stiff vinyl.

Some builders make their own site-built baffles. According to the IRC, "A minimum of a 1-inch space shall be provided between the insulation and the roof sheathing and at the location of the vent." Such a vent space can be created by tacking 1-in. by 1-in. "sticks" in the upper corners of each rafter bay, followed by stiff cardboard, thin plywood, OSB, fiberboard sheathing, or panels of rigid-foam insulation. Many experts advise that 2-in.-deep vent cavities are even better (see "A Crash Course in Roof Venting," at finehomebuilding.com).

Eight Ways to Get to R-45 or Better

Because rafter cavities are generally shallow, it is hard to meet minimum energy-code requirements when insulating cathedral ceilings. There are at least a few ways to compensate for this: furring down the rafter, adding rigid foam to the top or bottom of the roof, and using high-performance insulation. Depending on your climate zone and which version of the code your building department uses, this may or may not be enough.

If you plan to replace your roofing, adding exterior rigid foam is a no-brainer

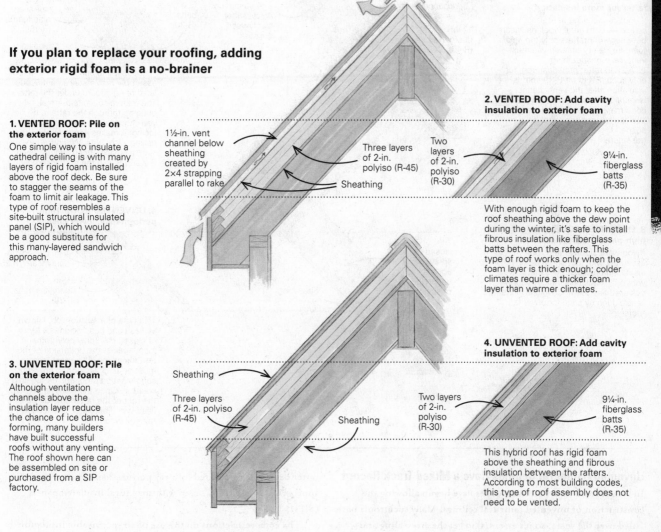

1. VENTED ROOF: Pile on the exterior foam

One simple way to insulate a cathedral ceiling is with many layers of rigid foam installed above the roof deck. Be sure to stagger the seams of the foam to limit air leakage. This type of roof resembles a site-built structural insulated panel (SIP), which would be a good substitute for this many-layered sandwich approach.

1½-in. vent channel below sheathing created by 2×4 strapping parallel to rake

Sheathing

Three layers of 2-in. polyiso (R-45)

2. VENTED ROOF: Add cavity insulation to exterior foam

Two layers of 2-in. polyiso (R-30)

9¼-in. fiberglass batts (R-35)

With enough rigid foam to keep the roof sheathing above the dew point during the winter, it's safe to install fibrous insulation like fiberglass batts between the rafters. This type of roof works only when the foam layer is thick enough; colder climates require a thicker foam layer than warmer climates.

3. UNVENTED ROOF: Pile on the exterior foam

Although ventilation channels above the insulation layer reduce the chance of ice dams forming, many builders have built successful roofs without any venting. The roof shown here can be assembled on site or purchased from a SIP factory.

Sheathing

Three layers of 2-in. polyiso (R-45)

Sheathing

4. UNVENTED ROOF: Add cavity insulation to exterior foam

Two layers of 2-in. polyiso (R-30)

9¼-in. fiberglass batts (R-35)

This hybrid roof has rigid foam above the sheathing and fibrous insulation between the rafters. According to most building codes, this type of roof assembly does not need to be vented.

When installing any type of vent baffle, it's important to pay attention to air-sealing, especially if you plan to install fibrous insulation in the rafter bays. Seal the edges of each panel with caulk, and tape the seams between panels with a high-quality tape.

Some builders locate their vent channels above the roof sheathing instead of below it. You can create 1½-in.-high vent channels above the sheathing with 2×4s installed on the flat; locate these 2×4s above the rafters, 16 in. or 24 in. on center. Although this approach is less fussy than installing vent baffles under the sheathing, it usually costs more, because most types of roofing require a second layer of

plywood or OSB on top of the vent channels.

In some cases, these vent channels are installed above rigid foam. It's also possible to purchase nail base (a type of structural insulated panel with OSB on one side instead of two) that includes integrated vent channels between the OSB and the rigid foam; one brand is Cool-Vent from Hunter Panels.

If you choose a vented roof assembly, include soffit vents and ridge vents. (To calculate how much soffit and ridge venting you need, see "A Crash Course in Roof Venting.")

Continued →

If you do not plan to replace your roofing, either make the rafters deeper or improve the insulation

1. VENTED ROOF: Fur down the rafter for more insulation

If you are installing fiberglass, cellulose, or mineral-wool insulation between your rafters only (no rigid foam inside or outside), you must vent the roof sheathing.

A 2×10 rafter provides room for only about 8¼ in. of R-30 fibrous insulation after the vent channel is installed. This is less than the code minimum in most climates. You can deepen the rafter bays by suspending 2×4s with plywood gussets.

3. UNVENTED ROOF: Use high-performance insulation

If you want an unvented roof assembly with just one type of insulation between the rafters, your only insulation choice is spray polyurethane foam. Cellulose alone is forbidden by code for unvented roofs.

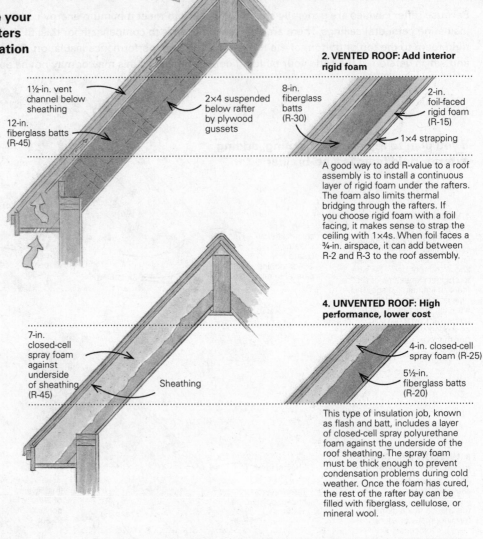

1½-in. vent channel below sheathing

12-in. fiberglass batts (R-45)

2×4 suspended below rafter by plywood gussets

8-in. fiberglass batts (R-30)

2-in. foil-faced rigid foam (R-15)

1×4 strapping

2. VENTED ROOF: Add interior rigid foam

A good way to add R-value to a roof assembly is to install a continuous layer of rigid foam under the rafters. The foam also limits thermal bridging through the rafters. If you choose rigid foam with a foil facing, it makes sense to strap the ceiling with 1×4s. When foil faces a ¾-in. airspace, it can add between R-2 and R-3 to the roof assembly.

7-in. closed-cell spray foam against underside of sheathing (R-45)

Sheathing

4. UNVENTED ROOF: High performance, lower cost

4-in. closed-cell spray foam (R-25)

5½-in. fiberglass batts (R-20)

This type of insulation job, known as flash and batt, includes a layer of closed-cell spray polyurethane foam against the underside of the roof sheathing. The spray foam must be thick enough to prevent condensation problems during cold weather. Once the foam has cured, the rest of the rafter bay can be filled with fiberglass, cellulose, or mineral wool.

Unvented Cathedral Ceilings Have a Mixed Track Record

In recent years, most building codes have begun allowing the construction of unvented cathedral ceilings. Many such roofs have failed over the years, so it's essential to get the air-sealing and insulation details right.

First, you can't use air-permeable insulation (for example, fiberglass batts, mineral-wool batts, dense-packed cellulose, or blown-in fiberglass) to insulate an unvented cathedral ceiling unless the roof assembly also includes a layer of air-impermeable insulation (either spray polyurethane foam or rigid-foam panels) directly above or directly below the roof sheathing. If you go this route, make sure that the foam layer is thick enough to avoid condensation problems. For information on how thick the exterior foam should be, see section R806.4 of the 2009 IRC.

If you want to use just one type of insulation in unvented

rafter bays, you are limited to spray polyurethane foam. Another approach is to build your roof with structural insulated panels (SIPs).

The code restrictions on the use of air-permeable insulation between rafters were developed to prevent the roof sheathing from rotting. When fiberglass batts are installed in unvented rafter bays, the batts often allow moist indoor air to reach the cold roof sheathing. When the moist air hits the cold sheathing, that leads to condensation or moisture accumulation in the sheathing, followed eventually by rot. By preventing air movement, spray-foam insulation almost eliminates this problem.

Insulating Rim Joists

By Martin Holladay

In older homes, rim joists (also called band joists) are often uninsulated, even though the only materials that likely separate them from outdoor air are sheathing and siding. Rim joists are above grade, so it makes sense to insulate the joists to the same level as above-grade walls. At the rim-joist area, many building components come together—the foundation wall, the mudsill, the rim joist, the subfloor—so it's also important to seal all cracks against air leakage.

The time-honored practice of insulating rim joists with fiberglass batts is no longer recommended. Because fiberglass batts are air permeable, they do nothing to prevent warm, humid interior air from contacting the rim joists. During the winter, when the rim joists are cold, condensation can cause mold and then rot.

To prevent these problems, only air-impermeable insulation—either rigid foam or spray polyurethane foam—should be used to insulate the interior of a rim joist. Two-story homes usually have another ring of rim joists above the first-floor ceiling. If you need to insulate these rim joists, it's best to hire a cellulose-insulation contractor.

Rigid Foam Is Affordable

If you're ready to insulate the rim joists in your basement or crawlspace, you have to decide between rigid foam and spray foam. Using rigid foam keeps the material costs low, but it also requires more labor than using spray foam. Rigid foam also has a few other downsides: Compared to spray foam, it's harder to install in awkward areas (for example, in a tight space where a rim joist is close to another parallel joist). Rigid foam is also fussy to install if the rim joists are the site of lots of wiring and pipe penetrations.

Any of the three common types of rigid foam—polyisocyanurate, expanded polystyrene (EPS), or extruded polystyrene (XPS)—can be installed against a rim joist. Polyisocyanurate is considered the most environmentally friendly of the three foam types; it has an R-value of between R-6 and R-6.5 per in. In colder climate zones, it's a good idea to install at least 3 in. to 4 in. of rigid foam, either in a single layer or in multiple layers. (For a less pricey approach, you can install 2 in. of rigid foam and a layer of fiberglass insulation.) In warmer climates, 2 in. of foam may be enough.

To ensure that humid indoor air won't reach the cold rim joist, the crack at the perimeter of each piece of foam (and at any penetrations) should be sealed with caulk or canned spray foam. If you use canned spray foam, you may want to buy a few lengths of flexible vinyl tubing with a slightly larger diameter than the plastic nozzle that comes with the can. This will make it easier to reach awkward corners. Discard the vinyl tubing when it gets clogged.

Seal Rigid Foam in Place

Fiberglass batts should never be installed near a rim joist unless the rim joist is first insulated with at least 2 in. of rigid foam or spray foam. The edges of each piece of rigid foam should be carefully sealed with caulk or canned spray foam. If you're using canned spray foam, you'll find that wide cracks are easier to seal than narrow ones, so it's a good idea to cut the rectangles a little small.

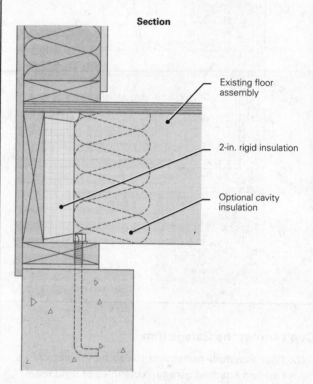

Section

Existing floor assembly

2-in. rigid insulation

Optional cavity insulation

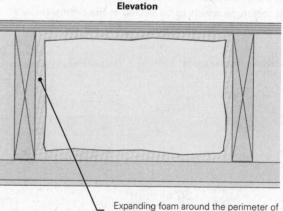

Elevation

Expanding foam around the perimeter of loosely fit rigid insulation

Hit Everything with Spray Foam

To create an effective air barrier, spray foam should extend from the top of the concrete all the way to the subfloor. For good thermal performance, the foam should cover all of the exposed concrete at the top of the wall.

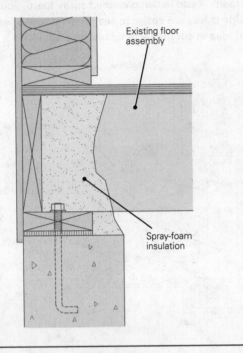

Existing floor assembly

Spray-foam insulation

Don't Forget the Garage Rim

If the floor assembly penetrates the air barrier between a house and an attached garage, rectangles of rigid foam should be installed between each joist to prevent air leaks. Each rectangle needs to be sealed at the perimeter with caulk or canned spray foam.

Conditioned interior space   **Unconditioned garage space**

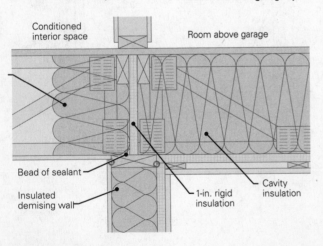

Conditioned interior space

Room above garage

Bead of sealant

Insulated demising wall

1-in. rigid insulation

Cavity insulation

Spray Foam Insulates and Seals

One advantage of using spray foam to insulate rim joists—an approach sometimes called the critical-seal method—is that a single product performs two tasks: sealing air leaks and insulating. In mild climate zones, either open-cell spray foam or closed-cell spray foam will work; however, in climate zone 6 and colder zones, it's safer to use closed-cell spray foam.

Unless you hire a spray foam contractor for the job, you'll probably be buying a two-component spray-foam kit. These kits are available at most lumberyards. If you want to install 3 in. of foam in an area that measures 1 ft. high by 130 ft. long, you'll need about 400 bd. ft. of spray foam. Once cured, this type of spray foam has an R-value of about R-6.5 per inch. (Most two-component spray-foam kits use closed-cell foam.)

If your basement is cool, store a spray-foam kit in a warm location for 24 hours before you begin. Be careful; uncured spray foam is messy. If you get uncured spray foam on your skin, you won't be able to wash it off. If you get it on objects in the basement, the foam may be impossible to remove. Before spraying, clear movable objects from the work area, and use a tarp to protect things that can't be moved. Wear a respirator, rubber gloves, goggles, a cheap hat, and either a Tyvek suit or old clothes.

What the Code Says

Most building codes require rigid foam to be protected with a layer of 1/2-in. drywall as a thermal barrier. The drywall can be screwed to the rim joist through the foam.

Dow Thermax polyisocyanurate, one type of rigid foam, has a facing that has passed fire-safety tests. That means that most building inspectors don't require Thermax to be protected with a drywall layer, making it a good choice for this application.

Spray-foam requirements differ from those for rigid foam. As long as your cured spray foam is no thicker than 3 1/4 in., the International Residential Code (IRC) allows spray foam at the rim-joist area to be left exposed, without any protective drywall. The relevant provisions can be found in section R314.5.11 of the 2006 IRC and in section R316.5.11 of the 2009 IRC.

More Options for New Homes

If you're building a new house, you can insulate the rim joists using one of the methods suggested for older homes. It often makes more sense, however, to insulate rim joists on the exterior rather than the interior. This can be done by recessing the rim joist 2 in. from the outer edge of the mudsill to provide room for 2 in. of rigid foam.

It's also possible to install a layer of rigid foam on the exterior side of your OSB or plywood wall sheathing; if you go this route, the rigid foam will cover the rim joists as well as the walls.

A third option is to buy engineered rim joists with integral foam insulation. These joists are available from Emercor (Claresholm, Alta.), which manufactures the E-Rim, and from Structural Wood Corp. (St. Paul, Minn.), which manufactures the Insul-Rim Plus.

Insulating Attic Stairs

by Martin Holladay

Builders of energy-efficient homes often make attic access deliberately inconvenient—for example, by providing a small exterior door in the gable wall of the attic (accessible only with an extension ladder) rather than an interior attic hatch or stairs. That's because both fixed and pull-down attic stairs present air-sealing and insulation challenges. It's important to acknowledge the conflict between convenient attic access and energy efficiency. Although most homeowners want convenient access to their attic, it's actually a bad idea to use an unconditioned attic for storage. If you have no other option, plan for storage by relocating insulation from the attic floor to the roof assembly, creating a conditioned attic.

Retrofit Options

Most pull-down attic stairs are leaky and poorly insulated. You can remove the stairs and replace them with a smaller hatch. The hatch should be insulated with at least 6 in. of rigid foam, should have weatherstripping, and should be equipped with two latches that draw the hatch tightly closed.

Note that code requirements for hatches have recently been tightened. According to the 2009 IECC and IRC, "Access doors from conditioned spaces to unconditioned spaces ... shall be weatherstripped and insulated to a level equivalent to ... surrounding surfaces." If you live in a climate zone where R-38 attic insulation is required, your access hatch also should be insulated to R-38.

If you insist on keeping your pull-down stairs, you'll need to purchase or make an insulated lid to cover the top of the stairs. Several manufacturers sell such lids; the best available product at this time appears to be the R-39 Energy Guardian Pull-Down Ladder Kit (photo above).

If you choose to build your own insulated lid, you'll need to make a strong, airtight box out of thick rigid foam. The lid needs to be heavy enough to compress the weatherstripping at its base.

If your house has fixed stairs leading from a conditioned room to an unconditioned attic, you need to investigate whether the builder provided adequate insulation and air-barrier details. Your first question should be "Where is the air barrier?"

The usual location of the air barrier is at the base of the stairs. In this case, you'll need to make sure that the door is insulated and weatherstripped. If you don't want to buy an exterior door, you can attach a layer of rigid foam to the back of your existing door, and you can reduce air leaks by installing weatherstripping.

The two triangular walls on either side of the stairway need to be insulated. The underside of the attic stairs—the sloped ceiling created by the bottom of the stair stringers—also needs to be insulated and air-sealed. This can be tricky; treads and risers usually leak air, and there isn't much room above the sloped drywall to accommodate insulation. One approach is to remove the plaster or drywall under the stairs and to spray polyurethane foam against the treads and risers from below. Or, if the headroom is generous, it may be possible to install one or two layers of rigid foam in this location, followed by a new layer of drywall.

Some attic stairways lead to a small room that encloses the top of the stairway. In this case, there should be a door at the top of the stairs. This type of stairway is part of the conditioned space, and it is easier to insulate than one with the air barrier at the base of the stairs. First, make sure that the door is insulated and weatherstripped. Then check the walls and ceiling of the attic room to ensure they are well insulated. If necessary, install an attic-side air barrier (for example, sheets of foil-faced polyisocyanurate) at these locations to prevent air leaks and to improve the R-value of the insulated assemblies.

Continued ➜

Better bought than built. A tight cap for pull-down attic stairs is hard to build. The weatherstripping details can be tough to execute, and the necessary weight of the hatch can be difficult to achieve. The Energy Guardian, shown here, is available from ESS Energy Products (essnrg.com). The company also makes kits for kneewall access, walk-up stairways, and more.

New Construction Details

If you are building a new house with stairs that lead from conditioned space to unconditioned space, you have a couple of options.

In most homes, the drywall is part of the air barrier. To maintain continuity of the air barrier above and below the stair stringers, it's best to install some type of sheet good behind the stair stringers—usually a sloping band of ½-in. plywood—with an exposed lip above and below the stringers, in order to provide a surface to tape the drywall to. Another approach is to install a sloped 2×4 as blocking between the stringers and the studs; once the drywall is hung, the gap between the drywall and the 2×4 can be sealed with canned spray foam.

It's best to insulate the walls on either side of the stairway before the stair stringers are installed. If the treads and risers separate conditioned space from unconditioned space, the underside of the stairs will need to be insulated—either with spray polyurethane foam or with a thick layer of rigid foam. In either case, pay attention to air-barrier continuity and thermal-barrier continuity at the edges of the sloped assembly.

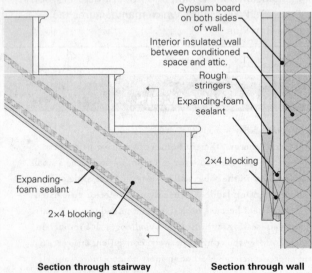

Section through stairway **Section through wall**

Gypsum board on both sides of wall.

Interior insulated wall between conditioned space and attic.

Rough stringers

Expanding-foam sealant

2×4 blocking

Expanding-foam sealant

2×4 blocking

Seal the Gap Behind the Stringers

If there is a door at the bottom of your attic stairs that separates conditioned space from unconditioned space, then the stair assembly and adjacent walls need to be insulated and air-sealed. Because drywall typically is installed after the stairs are framed, you need to find a way to create a continuous air barrier up the walls. One way is to install 2×4 blocking behind the stringers. Once the drywall is installed, you can fill the gap with spray foam. The stairs themselves also need to be insulated, and the bottom of the stringers should be air-sealed with airtight drywall.

Requirements for Energy Star Homes

Builders of Energy Star homes need to comply with the Thermal Bypass Checklist, a document that specifies air-sealing and insulation requirements for attic stairs. The EPA's Thermal Bypass Checklist Guide includes these directions:

Staircases adjoining exterior walls, garages, or attics need complete air barriers throughout the framed assembly ... A common area missing an air barrier at staircase walls occurs at small areas under enclosed landings or bottom stairs. Once framed, staircases can be difficult to complete with insulation and air barriers so it is important to coordinate details with the framing subcontractor ...

• Structural sheathing can be used to extend above and below stringers to allow for taping with joint compound.

• Air barrier shall be fully aligned with insulation and any gaps are fully sealed with caulk or foam ...

• Similar to attic hatches, attic drop-down stairs represent very large thermal holes to the attic when not fully insulated and sealed ... When insulating attic drop-down stairs, the insulation should not be installed between the steps ... because it blocks the stairs themselves and is typically compressed in place, undermining its effective R-value ...

• Attic drop-down stair shall be fully gasketed for a snug fit. However, gaps in weatherstripping to accommodate hinge hardware shall be acceptable ...

• Factory made attic drop-down stair assemblies that are fully gasketed and include a rigid insulation panel much like an exterior insulated door are a great simple solution.

Are Drainable Housewraps Enough?

By Justin Fink

In an ideal world, the exterior cladding on a house would be smooth, continuous, nonabsorbent, and completely waterproof, protecting the moisture-sensitive structure beneath. But we aren't building submarines—we're building houses. Clapboards, sidewall shingles, and other cladding options all are leaky.

But leaky cladding is OK. Building scientist John Straube, who has long studied the effects of moisture in walls, wrote in 2010 that we must "accept that some water will penetrate the outer surface and remove this water by designing an assembly that provides drainage."

Although most housewraps are able to protect sheathing from occasional wind-driven rain, they don't provide a purposeful route for water that gets behind the siding to drain away or dry out. For that, you need a physical gap between the back of the cladding and the sheathing it's attached to. That's where a new breed of drainable housewraps comes into play.

Essentially, housewraps that have been wrinkled, dressed with bumps, or otherwise designed to maintain a gap provide a small space for water to drain away before it has a chance to cause problems such as peeling paint or rotten sheathing. Unlike when incorporating furring strips or another form of vented drainage, these drainable wraps require none of the additional detailing or rethinking of transitions between windows, trim, and siding, which means they are more likely to get used by builders who aren't willing to change their building details. But the real question is whether a drainable wrap is just a premium version of standard smooth housewrap, or whether it is a comparable substitute for a true ventilated rain-screen system.

Lessons Learned from Stucco

Drainable housewraps may seem like a new idea, but they actually were borne from the hard-earned lessons of past failures. The problems builders have encountered with stucco are an excellent example.

Stucco is a so-called reservoir cladding, which means that it can absorb and hold water. Warmth from the sun pushes moisture from the surface of the stucco farther into the wall, where it can sit against the sheathing and lead to rot. Decades ago, builders installed a single layer of asphalt-impregnated building paper over the wall sheathing to protect it against this moisture. Scientists realized later that the reason why this single layer worked so well is that as the stucco dried, it debonded from the building paper and left small gaps, which allowed water to drain away. Over time, however, the manufacturing methods for building paper changed, and a single layer of the newer paper maintained its bond with the stucco rather than debonding like the old stuff; as a result, the drainage space wasn't created. Around the same time, builders started switching from plywood sheathing to OSB sheathing, which is more moisture sensitive (see "Taking Care of Mold," p. 893). You can guess how the story ended: Lots of builders were forced to deal with catastrophic cases of rotten sheathing.

To solve the problem, builders started applying two layers of building paper instead of just one. The outermost layer bonded with the stucco and was meant to be sacrificial, while the inner layer was undisturbed and able to protect the sheathing. Best of all, a small gap between the two layers provided drainage.

Nowadays, a double layer of building paper (or a membrane with performance equivalent to two layers of building paper) is required by building codes for stucco and manufactured-stone installations.

Continued ➜

Are You Sure You Know What a Rain Screen Is?

In the building industry, the loose usage of terminology can lead to confusion. For years, people have been using the term rain screen to describe a variety of different wall assemblies.

By definition, a rain screen is just one component of what's known as a drained wall system. There are several variations of this system, but it usually includes four components.

1. A rain screen (i.e., the clapboards, brick, or other cladding) acts as the first layer of deflection for sun, water, and dirt.

2. A drainage plane is the waterproofing layer in the assembly and is protected by the rain screen. This plane is typically in the form of housewrap or felt paper, but it also can be taped foam sheathing or water-resistant sheathing such as Zip System, among other things.

3. A drainage gap is a space between the back of the rain screen and the drainage plane.

4. Drainage openings at the bottom of the wall cavity provide an outlet for any liquid water that is driven into the wall or that accumulates between the back of the rain screen and the face of the drainage plane.

The catch is that a wall with these four components is technically a vented assembly, because the drainage openings allow water to flow out and air to flow in. But in order to be a ventilated assembly (what most of us are likely thinking of when we say a house has a rain screen), it must also include openings at the top of the drainage gap. Working in conjunction with the drainage openings at the bottom of the assembly, the wall now has continuous airflow.

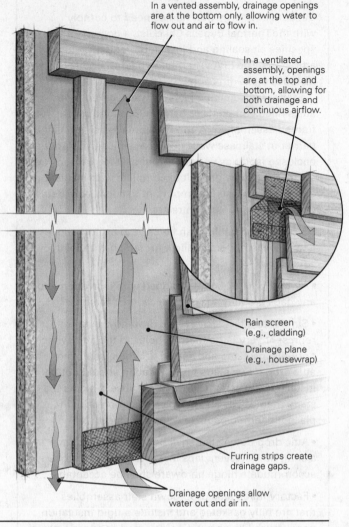

In a vented assembly, drainage openings are at the bottom only, allowing water to flow out and air to flow in.

In a ventilated assembly, openings are at the top and bottom, allowing for both drainage and continuous airflow.

Rain screen (e.g., cladding)

Drainage plane (e.g., housewrap)

Furring strips create drainage gaps.

Drainage openings allow water out and air in.

A Small Gap Is Enough

The benefits of drainage extend beyond masonry. In a 2004 paper, Straube declared drainage behind the siding of a house to be "the first and fastest means of removing water that penetrates [cladding]."

Straube's research—which has since been supported by others and carried like a trophy by manufacturers of drainable housewraps—proves that even an extremely small gap (1 mm, or about 1/32 in.) drains water from behind cladding faster than rainwater can penetrate, even under extreme weather conditions. (Not coincidentally, all of the drainable housewraps I looked at for this article provide a gap of between 1 mm and 1.5 mm.)

Benjamin Obdyke's website states that the company's HydroGap drainable wrap "drains moisture from wall assemblies at least two times faster than the leading drainable housewrap and removes 100 times more bulk water than standard housewrap." Tamlyn claims on its website that its TamlynWrap produces the "drying capability of a ⅜-in. rainscreen without the cost

by creating a needed cavity." But the picture being painted by drainable-housewrap marketing—a stream of water running harmlessly behind the cladding thanks to the gap provided by the membrane—isn't the best representation of the problems most builders are faced with.

That's not to say that the drainable housewraps won't provide this level of drainage, just that this much water getting behind cladding isn't common. A more likely problem is water penetrating a wall in less obvious ways that are just as damaging and that may not be solved with drainage alone (see "Why all the wet walls?" above).

Big Enough for Drainage, But Is Drainage Enough?

Although a small gap can make a big difference in allowing liquid water to pass, the increased levels of wall insulation and the moisture-sensitive building components used in today's houses call for more purposeful airflow than can be provided by

Why All the Wet Walls?

Builders have been dealing with water for as long as they've been building walls. So why are we talking much more these days about the need for drainage and airflow behind siding? Some of the biggest changes affecting wall durability in recent years have been the introduction of housewrap, the shift from plywood sheathing to OSB, and the increase in levels of insulation, much of it highly vapor retardant. But these changes in building materials aren't the reason for this new focus on drainage and airflow; they're just more-sensitive indicators of the same moisture problems we've been seeing (and getting away with) for years.

Moisture can affect walls through precipitation, capillarity, diffusion/air movement, stored moisture, and groundwater.

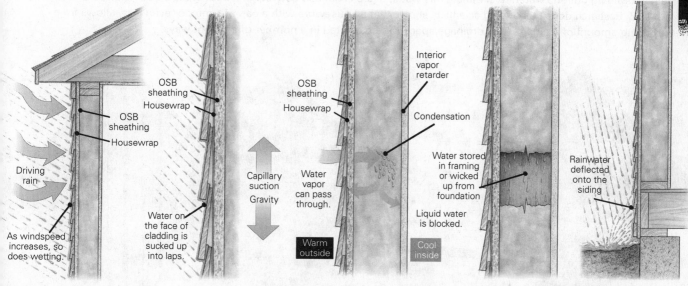

Precipitation

Although it is possible for water to be sucked behind the cladding due to wind-related pressure differences, this is rarely the smoking gun when it comes to leakage. The chances of leakage do increase when it's windy, particularly at butt joints and penetrations, but that's because the walls are faced with driving rain (the minimum threshold depends on the overhang and topography), and the amount of water on the wall increases in proportion to the wind speed.

Capillarity

Although capillary suction is more commonly associated with water moving through porous materials—a concrete wall, for instance—it can also be a problem with nonporous materials. When two pieces of siding are lapped tightly, the narrow gap between them can itself become a capillary pore, defying gravity by sucking moisture that has clung to the face of the siding upward and suspending it in the lap joints.

Diffusion/air movement

Housewrap is designed to block liquid water while still allowing the passage of water vapor. But if that water vapor condenses in the wall cavity, it will be unable to pass through the housewrap to dry to the outside, and drying toward the interior is often limited by an interior vapor retarder (e.g., poly sheeting behind the drywall) or high levels of insulation that limit the amount of available heat energy.

Stored moisture

Whether it comes directly from the building materials we use—green framing lumber and concrete that isn't fully cured are two common examples—or from building components being exposed to the elements during construction, stored moisture can take a year or more to dry fully.

Groundwater

The mechanisms at work here aren't wholly different from those of driving rain: gravity and capillarity. In this case, however, gravity takes the form of rain splashing off the ground and onto the siding, and capillarity may come from high concentrations of moisture at ground level (for example, if there are lush garden beds at the base of the wall).

Continued ➡

a drainable wrap. Liquid water may be able to drain, but liquid water isn't the only worry.

According to Straube's 2004 paper, "A significant amount of water deposited by condensation or rain penetration will remain in an enclosure, absorbed by the materials and adhered to the surfaces." It's this absorbed moisture that's most problematic, because it will not easily dry without the help of air movement, which is not a benefit of a drainable housewrap. So if a 1.5-mm gap provided by a drainable housewrap isn't enough, what is?

Engineer Joe Lstiburek, principal at Building Science Corporation, wrote in a 2010 article that a ⅜-in. ventilation gap is "a pretty safe dimension with stucco, manufactured stone veneers, wood claddings or other claddings like fiber-cement that lie flat against the housewrap and OSB." (Vinyl and aluminum siding have plenty of air gaps behind them and so don't require any additional airspace.)

Lstiburek called this ⅜-in. gap "very, very conservative" and said that it can be much smaller, depending on the severity of the climate and other variables that scientists haven't accurately measured yet. Lstiburek recommends playing it safe: "With a ⅜-inch gap I have never, ever, anywhere known of anyone to have a problem."

This approach is helpful in every climate, but it's particularly important in rainy climates; in fact, a ⅜-in. gap is a building-code requirement in coastal British Columbia and Oregon.

One situation where drainable housewraps are finding their niche is in wall assemblies that include rigid-foam insulation installed on the outside face of OSB sheathing and either vapor-impermeable insulation or a vapor barrier that prevents drying to the inside, all of which are being used more frequently

1 mm Goes a Long Way Toward Drainage

Although water-resistive barriers (WRBs) are able to protect sheathing from incidental water intrusion, they need extra help at draining built-up water. To eliminate this water, a gap is needed between the back of the cladding and the face of the WRB. Research done by building scientists shows that a housewrap with a gap of 1 mm, or even less, allows for a surprising amount of drainage. This drainage space can be created in a number of different ways.

Bumpy

Benjamin Obdyke's HydroGap (shown) and Tamlyn's TamlynWrap are two examples of how a drainage space can be achieved by simply adding dabs of soft rubber or plastic to the face of a woven housewrap.

Crinkled

Tyvek's StuccoWrap and DrainWrap (shown) are among the first products in this category of housewrap. Resembling housewrap that's been scrunched into an accordion pattern, they have minimal drainage channels that must run vertically to be effective.

Stamped

Similar to the surface of a basketball, the texture of wraps such as Barricade Building Products' WeatherTrek (shown) is nondirectional, as on bumpy housewraps, to ensure drainage regardless of the wrap's orientation in relation to the siding.

Channeled

Although the space created by the exaggerated weave of Kingspan's GreenGuard Raindrop 3D (shown) and similar wraps isn't especially deep, it's good enough. As with crinkled wraps, the channels must run vertically to be effective.

these days. Lstiburek says that in these cases it's possible to get a sufficient amount of outward drying by providing a small gap between the OSB sheathing and the rigid foam so that water can diffuse. A drainable housewrap not only is helpful in this regard, but it's actually the best solution. A gap larger than 1 mm or so means a reduction in the insulating effectiveness of the exterior rigid foam. According to Lstiburek, with drainable housewrap you lose next to nothing in terms of thermal performance compared to the increased durability and diminished risk of the wall assembly.

A Judgment Call

It seems that the proper role of drainable housewraps is still somewhat unclear. On the one hand, they provide a space behind siding for drainage, which is one of the best safety mechanisms that can be incorporated into a house. And when it comes to making sure that exterior foam plays nicely with OSB sheathing, they are a true silver bullet, balancing effective moisture redistribution with a very small reduction in thermal performance.

The research findings are pretty well understood and agreed upon when it comes to airflow: A physical gap behind siding is a good thing (although there is a sliding scale), and planned ventilation is even better. In his 2010 article, Lstiburek wrote that providing ventilation is "simple, elegant, and unbelievably effective in helping out drying."

On the other hand, drainable housewraps have limitations compared to an assembly with a more substantial gap. A drainable housewrap will not provide purposeful airflow—certainly not enough to compete with the performance of a ventilated rain-screen wall.

It may be helpful to think of drainable housewraps as falling somewhere in the "better" zone, trailed by a "good" traditional housewrap installation, but not as beneficial as the "best" option: a true ventilated rain-screen assembly.

Creating a Sealed Crawlspace

By Martin Holladay

If you live in the eastern half of the United States and want a damp, moldy crawlspace, just make sure that it is vented to the exterior. Within a few short years, the fiberglass batts installed in the crawlspace ceiling will become so damp that they'll hang down like stalactites. You'll end up with a classic moldy crawlspace—one that represents a significant source of moisture for the house above.

During the summer months, warm outdoor air holds more moisture than cooler crawlspace air. When that humid outdoor air enters the crawlspace vents, it hits cool surfaces—concrete, water pipes, and air-conditioning ducts—and condensation forms and begins to drip. One remedy that is sometimes attempted is to add a fan to the space, but that just increases the occurrence of condensation. The more you ventilate, the wetter the crawlspace

Unvented Crawlspace

Code requires the walls of an unvented crawlspace to be insulated. In most cases, there is then no need to install any insulation between the floor joists above the crawlspace. Some code authorities require rigid foam to be protected by a layer of ½-in. drywall, but an exception is often made for Thermax, a brand of polyisocyanurate that has passed fire-safety tests.

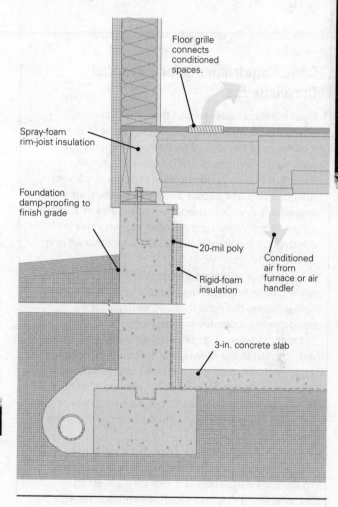

Floor grille connects conditioned spaces.

Spray-foam rim-joist insulation

Foundation damp-proofing to finish grade

20-mil poly

Rigid-foam insulation

Conditioned air from furnace or air handler

3-in. concrete slab

gets. Crawlspace vents also can cause problems during the winter by introducing frigid outdoor air into the space, which can cause pipes to freeze.

Properly designed unvented (sealed) crawlspaces stay drier than vented crawlspaces, the pipes within them are protected from wintertime freeze/thaw cycles, and they require less insulation than vented crawlspaces (since the area of the perimeter walls is less than the area of the crawlspace ceiling). They also bring any ducts running through the crawlspace into the conditioned envelope of the house—an improvement that usually results in

Continued →

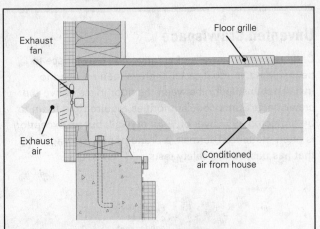

Exhaust fan

Floor grille

Exhaust air

Conditioned air from house

Code Requirements for Unvented Crawlspaces

Most building codes permit the construction of unvented crawlspaces. In recent versions of the International Residential Code, requirements for unvented crawlspaces can be found in section R408.3. If an unvented crawlspace has a dirt floor, the code requires exposed earth to be covered with a continuous vapor retarder with taped seams: "The edges of the vapor retarder shall extend at least 6 inches up the stem wall and shall be attached and sealed to the stem wall."

In addition to the requirement of a duct or floor grille connecting the crawlspace to the conditioned space above, the code lists two options for conditioning unvented crawlspaces.

Option 1 (above): Install a continuously operating exhaust fan in the crawlspace that blows through a hole in the rim joist or an exterior wall. Make sure that the fan isn't too powerful (1 cfm for each 50 sq. ft. of crawlspace floor area), because the makeup air entering the crawlspace is conditioned air from the house.

Option 2 (right): Install a forced-air register to deliver supply air from the furnace or air handler to the crawlspace (again, 1 cfm for each 50 sq. ft.). Assuming the house has air-conditioning, this introduction of cool, dry air during the summer keeps the crawlspace dry.

energy savings.

New-construction crawlspaces may require temporary dehumidification to remove construction moisture. Once the home is dried in, it's a good idea to install a dehumidifier in the crawlspace and run it for three or four months until the interior relative humidity stabilizes. Also, remember that any combustion appliance (for example, a water heater or furnace) in an unvented crawlspace should be a sealed-combustion unit.

Detailing an Unvented Crawlspace

If you want to build an unvented crawlspace, follow these recommendations.

· To help keep the crawlspace dry, make sure the exterior grade slopes away from the foundation.

· Remove all rocks and debris from the crawlspace floor, and rake the dirt smooth. In new construction, it's best for the crawlspace floor to be higher than the exterior grade.

· If the crawlspace is subject to water entry, slope the floor to a sump equipped with a drain or a sump pump.

· Install a durable vapor barrier—for example, a 20-mil pool liner or Tu-Tuf poly—over the floor. Extend it up the crawlspace walls, leaving 3 in. uncovered at the top to create a termite-inspection strip.

· Attach the top of the vapor barrier to the wall with horizontal battens secured with masonry fasteners.

· Seal the seams of the vapor barrier with a compatible tape or mastic. Many builders use duct mastic embedded in fiberglass-mesh tape.

· Install a 2-in.- or 3-in.-thick concrete slab to protect the vapor barrier, or install a sacrificial layer of 6-mil poly on top of the permanent vapor barrier to protect it from damage during installation of mechanicals and insulation.

· If testing shows high radon levels, install a passive radon-collection system below the crawlspace floor.

· Insulate the interior of the walls and rim joists with rigid foam or spray polyurethane foam. Many builders use Thermax, a polyisocyanurate foam that in most jurisdictions does not require a thermal barrier or ignition barrier. (Alternatively, you can insulate the exterior of the walls.) If your crawlspace has stone-and-mortar walls, you must use closed-cell spray polyurethane foam. Install at least as much insulation as required by the 2012 IRC for basement walls: R-5 for climate zone 3, R-10 for climate zone 4 (except marine zone 4), and R-15 for marine zone 4 and climate zones 5, 6, 7, and 8.

· Install an exhaust fan or a forced-air register as required by code (see "Code Requirements for Unvented Crawlspaces," left). Be sure that the fan does not exceed airflow requirements for the size of the crawlspace, since exhaust fans always carry an energy penalty.

Breaking the Thermal Bridge

By Stephen Bonfiglioli

You might say I've always been ahead of the curve as far as building performance goes. When I started building in 1977, my houses had 2×6 walls and R-19 insulation, while code-built homes had 2×4 walls with R-11 insulation. Other builders, subs, and suppliers said I was crazy for installing more insulation than the building code required, but I've always thought that building energy-efficient homes made perfect sense. In my quest for efficiency and comfort, I tried just about every high-performance wall assembly there was, all of which seemed overly complex and expensive. Then one day 12 years ago, I asked myself, "What if I fur out the interior wall with strips of rigid foam and strapping?"

I reasoned that the foam strips would address thermal bridging, add thickness to the wall to accommodate high-density fiberglass batts, and cost less than alternative methods. I have been building my walls this way ever since.

Foam Selection

I assemble lengths of 1-in.-thick high-density expanded polystyrene (EPS) foam and 1×3 strapping picked up from my local lumberyard. While the strapping is readily available, the high-density foam isn't always a stock item, so I buy my foam from Insultech in Bridgewater, Mass. (insultech-eps .com). This foam resists compression more than regular EPS, and it comes in convenient 1½-in. by 4-ft. pieces. Alternatively, I could cut full sheets of rigid foam into 1½-in.-wide strips on a tablesaw.

While it may appear to make sense to use extruded polystyrene (XPS) or polyisocyanurate insulating strips, both of which have higher R-values, R-value matters very little in this application. EPS is the least expensive type of rigid foam, and with an R-value of R-4 per in., it creates enough of a thermal break to sufficiently slow heat transfer through the framing.

Speed and Strength

Once we have a new house dried in or a remodel gutted, we can add the foam strips to an entire 3000-sq.-ft. house in a day or less, saving us considerable time and money when compared to more-complicated wall assemblies. Also, because the foam strips are covered with 1×3s, drywall and trim can be installed with conventional fasteners instead of using long nails or screws to find the framing behind the foam. The 1×3s also allow the homeowners to hang pictures and shelves more easily later on.

Don't Forget the Air Barrier

Air-sealing is paramount when using fiberglass batts (see "Making Fiberglass Work," *Fine Homebuilding* #246), so we fill any holes or gaps with spray foam before installing the high-density R-30 batts. We're careful to fill the stud cavities completely with minimal compression.

Our locality requires vapor retarders on the interior-facing side of exterior walls, so we use MemBrain vapor retarder (certainteed.com) in combination with air-sealing tape and acoustical sealant to create a complete air barrier that prevents warm interior air from condensing in the wall cavities during the winter. MemBrain is a so-called smart vapor retarder with a

Two Kinds of Foam-Backed Furring

The foam strips are assembled by arranging 1×3 strapping on sawhorses and then fastening the foam strips to the strapping with a roofing nailer and 1¼-in. roofing nails.

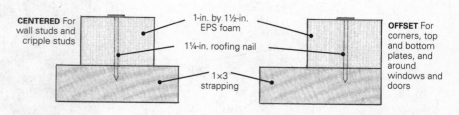

CENTERED For wall studs and cripple studs

1-in. by 1½-in. EPS foam

1¼-in. roofing nail

1×3 strapping

OFFSET For corners, top and bottom plates, and around windows and doors

Continued ➡

Installation Details

Attach offset foam furring strips first to the top and bottom plates with cement-coated 3½-in. ring-shank nails. Then, working from one end of the wall to the other, nail the foam-backed strips into corners, onto studs, and around doors and windows. Space the nails about every 12 in. to 16 in.

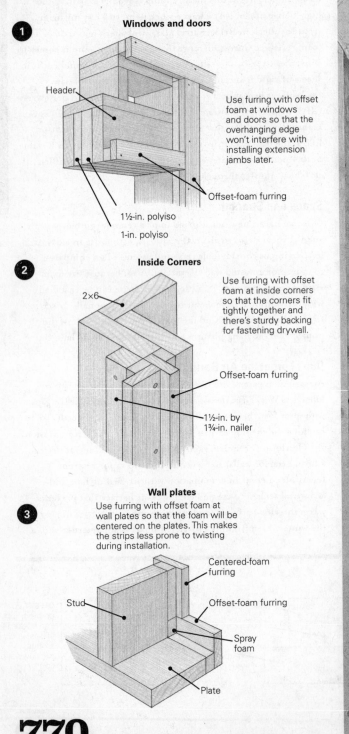

① Windows and doors

Header

1½-in. polyiso

1-in. polyiso

Offset-foam furring

Use furring with offset foam at windows and doors so that the overhanging edge won't interfere with installing extension jambs later.

② Inside Corners

2×6

Use furring with offset foam at inside corners so that the corners fit tightly together and there's sturdy backing for fastening drywall.

Offset-foam furring

1½-in. by 1¾-in. nailer

③ Wall plates

Use furring with offset foam at wall plates so that the foam will be centered on the plates. This makes the strips less prone to twisting during installation.

Centered-foam furring

Stud

Offset-foam furring

Spray foam

Plate

What About Electrical Boxes?

Adding foam-backed furring strips—and building an airtight assembly—hamper the typical electrical-box installation. We modify our installation method with plywood blocking and Lessco airtight and vapor-tight enclosures.

Start with a plywood scrap. A piece of ¾-in. plywood is nailed to the side of the stud to provide a solid installation point for the nail on electrical boxes.

Install the enclosure and box. The green enclosure, which helps air-seal the electrical box, is nailed to the furring; then the electrical box is nailed to the plywood scrap. The last step is sealing the cables with foam.

permeability that increases as humidity rises to promote drying. To ensure drying to the exterior, we complete the assembly with plywood, carefully detailed housewrap, and wood siding.

Cost Comparison

My wall is much less expensive than alternatives such as SIPs or exterior foam. Labor and materials—including the foam strips, strapping for attaching trim and drywall, and batts of high-density R-30 fiberglass insulation—cost $1.50 per sq. ft. of living space (figure cited from 2015). For comparison, installing 1½-in. or 2-in. rigid insulation over plywood or OSB sheathing and adding blocking or furring for windows, siding, and trim costs more than $3 per sq. ft. of living space.

Insulating a Low-Slope Shed Roof

By Martin Holladay

Low-slope shed roofs that range in pitch from nearly flat to 4-over-12 are common in the Southwest and in dense urban neighborhoods of the Northeast. These roofs are either framed with deep trusses or framed with rafters that are separate from the ceiling joists. Because of their limited space between the sheathing and the ceiling joists, these roofs are often difficult to insulate properly.

Although some builders insulate a low-slope roof with the same techniques used for a house with a big attic, they should be

Continued →

Insulating a Vented Low-Slope Roof

A vented roof needs intake vents at the attic perimeter and cupolas at the center of the roof to maintain airflow between the sheathing and the top of the insulation. The ceiling must be airtight to prevent condensation on the underside of the sheathing.

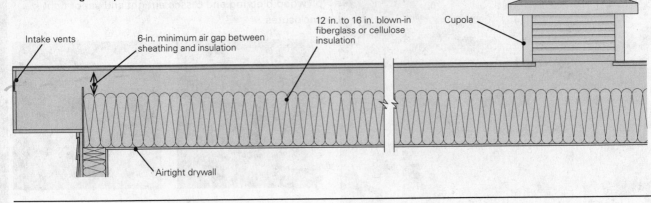

Intake vents

6-in. minimum air gap between sheathing and insulation

12 in. to 16 in. blown-in fiberglass or cellulose insulation

Cupola

Airtight drywall

Five Ways to Insulate an Unvented Low-Slope Roof

Of the various methods to insulate a shallow roof, applying insulation to the exterior is easier than working in a space with limited access. Whatever method is used, the amounts of insulation must achieve R-values mandated by local codes.

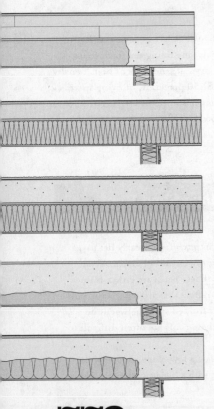

1. Exterior rigid foam

Install a thick layer of rigid-foam insulation (usually 6 in. thick or more) above the roof sheathing.

2. Exterior rigid foam plus interior insulation

Install a more moderate layer of rigid-foam insulation (2 in. to 4 in. thick) above the roof sheathing, supplemented by a layer of air-permeable insulation (such as blown-in fiberglass or cellulose) below and in direct contact with the roof sheathing.

3. Exterior closed-cell foam

Spray a layer of closed-cell polyurethane foam on top of the roof sheathing, supplemented by a layer of air-permeable insulation below and in direct contact with the roof sheathing.

4. Interior closed-cell foam

Spray a thick layer of closed-cell polyurethane foam on the underside of the roof sheathing.

5. Interior closed-cell foam and blown-in fiberglass or cellulose

Spray a more moderate thickness of closed-cell polyurethane foam on the underside of the roof sheathing, supplemented by a layer of air-permeable insulation below and in direct contact with the underside of the cured spray foam.

using a different approach. If the roof is vented, the ceiling must be air-sealed to prevent moisture-laden air from reaching the attic. If the roof is unvented, there are several ways to efficiently insulate the space either from the exterior, from the interior, or from a combination of both.

If there is at least 18 in. (or in a cold climate, at least 24 in.) of room between the top-floor ceiling and the roof sheathing, these cramped attics can be vented and insulated with fluffy insulation such as fiberglass or cellulose. However, the system only works if the builder includes a generously sized cupola in the center of the roof. Ventilation air doesn't move from the "eaves" to the "ridge" in the same way it does in a steeply sloped roof. Turbine (whirlybird) vents or ridge vents are not recommended for low-slope roofs because they don't provide enough airflow.

If you want to vent a low-slope roof, here's what you need to do:

• Specify roof trusses or conventional framing deep enough for 12 in. to 16 in. of insulation, plus room for an air gap of at least 6 in. between the top of the insulation and the roof sheathing.

• Provide soffit, fascia, or wall-mounted vents at the perimeter of the shallow attic that will allow exterior air to connect with the air gap between the top of the insulation and the underside of the roof sheathing.

• Near the center of the roof, provide one or more vented cupolas, each measuring at least 2 ft. by 2 ft. by 2 ft., with rectangular vents on all four sides of each cupola. Most building codes require a minimum of 1 sq. ft. of net free vent area (NFVA) for every 300 sq. ft. of attic floor area. Locate between 50% and 60% of the NFVA at the perimeter of the building, and 40% to 50% of the NFVA at the cupolas near the center of the roof.

• Before installing the insulation, make the ceiling as airtight as you can.

One Pro's Method for Insulating a Cramped Attic

What if you need to insulate an existing unvented low-slope roof, say 3 ft. high at the high side, with very limited attic access? You could rip out the ceiling or tear off the roof, but there is a third method.

Bill Hulstrunk is the technical manager at National Fiber, a manufacturer of cellulose insulation. "Our installers crawl in and do as much air-sealing as possible on the side with good access," Hulstrunk explains. "There is a point where the attic gets too confined and you can't do any air-sealing. So they'll dense-pack the side of the attic with limited access, and then they'll blow in loose-fill cellulose on the side of the attic where there was enough access for air-sealing work. It is always a good idea to have vents on the high-side walls, above the top of the insulation, to provide some connection between the air above the loose-fill insulation and the outside. If they've done a good job with the air-sealing, they've reduced the amount of moisture that will get up there. But in case there is some moisture that gets through, it's good to have some way to allow the moisture to make its way to the exterior."

Because codes don't permit air-permeable insulation to be installed in contact with the roof sheathing unless the sheathing is covered with a layer of rigid or closed-cell spray foam, not all code authorities accept Hulstrunk's retrofit insulation method, so check with your local code inspector before attempting this technique.

Unvented Roofs Are Easier

In many ways, it's easier to build an unvented low-slope roof, and there are several ways to do it.

If you install a combination of closed-cell foam and vapor-permeable insulation, you need to be sure the foam is thick enough to keep the roof sheathing (or the lower surface of the foam insulation) above the dew point during the winter. (Don't use open-cell foam; it's vapor permeable.) The International Residential Code specifies the following minimum R-values for the foam layer of these hybrid insulation sandwiches: R-5 in zones 1-3, R-10 in zone 4C, R-15 in zones 4A and 4B, R-20 in zone 5, R-25 in zone 6, R-30 in zone 7, and R-35 in zone 8.

While vented roof assemblies are designed to dry to the exterior, unvented roof assemblies are designed to dry to the interior. That's why an unvented roof assembly should never include interior polyethylene. If a building inspector insists that you install some type of interior vapor retarder, you can always install a "smart" vapor retarder such as CertainTeed's MemBrain to satisfy your inspector.

Attic-Ventilation Strategies

By Martin Holladay

Except in some specific cases, building codes and shingle warranties require new roofs to be vented. If you're building a house with an unconditioned vented attic, the necessary attic-ventilation details are fairly straightforward, especially if the house has a gable roof. They include soffit vents (and usually a ridge vent) along with ventilation baffles that provide open pathways for air to travel from the soffit vents along the underside of the roof sheathing to the ridge.

Although the essential components for attic ventilation are straightforward, mistakes are common. Believe it or not, sometimes it's as simple as the fact that the roofers forgot to cut back the roof sheathing at the ridge before they installed the ridge vent. Here are some key points to remember.

Provide Enough Clearance Between Top Plates and Roof Sheathing

If you plan to install 14 in. of insulation on your attic floor, then you should have at least 16 in. of clearance between the top plate of your perimeter walls and the underside of your roof sheathing. To make sure that your clearance is adequate, order raised-heel trusses. For a stick-framed roof, set your rafters on a raised 2x plate installed on top of your attic floor joists.

Don't Use Flimsy or Undersize Ventilation Baffles

Some energy experts believe that the code-minimum ventilation-gap height (1 in.) is inadequate. Even if you're willing to accept a 1-in. airspace, many commercial ventilation baffles are so flimsy that they easily collapse when insulation is blown or tucked into place, which can leave an airspace that measures ½ in. or less. Joseph Lstiburek, a principal at Building Science Corporation, recommends that ventilation channels be at least 2 in. deep, an approach that requires site-built baffles made from thin plywood, stiff cardboard, or rigid foam attached to 2-in. spacers installed in the corners of the rafter bays.

Protect Against Wind Washing

To prevent cold wind from blowing through the blown-in or batt insulation and degrading its performance—a phenomenon called wind washing—you need to install a solid block of rigid foam above the top plate of the wall in each rafter bay. The foam should be cut to conform to the shape of the opening, and all four edges of the rigid foam should be sealed with canned spray foam.

You Can Still Vent Roofs That Don't Have Ridges

On a hip roof, the ridge is short or absent. There are two ways to vent an attic under a hip roof: You can install mushroom vents in the field of the roof, or you can use the code formula that allows roofs with adequate soffit venting to omit ridge vents.

Continued →

4 Steps to Calculate Vent Area

If an attic measures 900 sq. ft., code requires that there be a minimum of 3 sq. ft. of ventilation area (1 sq. ft. for every 300 sq. ft. of attic-floor area), with between 40% (1.2 sq. ft.) and 50% (1.5 sq. ft.) of ventilation area at the ridge and the remainder at the soffits. If there is no ridge vent, this same attic would require 6 sq. ft. of ventilation area at the soffits. Here's how to calculate the amount of venting you need when using a product with a theoretical rating of 9 NFVA per ft.

1. Find total ventilation area.

900 sq. ft. ÷ 300 sq. ft. = 3 sq. ft. of ventilation area

2. Convert sq. ft. to sq. in.

3 sq. ft. × 144 in. per sq. ft. = 432 sq. in.

3. Assign the areas of soffit and ridge.

60% of 432 = 259 sq. in. (soffit)
40% of 432 = 173 sq. in. (ridge)

4. Divide the areas by the NFVA of the vent—in this case, 9—and assign venting.

Soffit vents
260 ÷ 9 = 28.8 lin. ft.
(14.4 ft. per side)

Ridge vent
173 ÷ 9 = 19.2 lin. ft.

Many hard-to-vent roofs, including roofs without soffits and shed roofs that die into a higher wall, can be vented with specialty products from manufacturers such as DCI Products and Cor-A-Vent. These slim-profile structures are typically integrated into the shingle field at mid-roof or higher.

Follow Code Requirements for Sizing Vents to Achieve Adequate Flow

To meet code, check the formula for calculating the necessary size of soffit and ridge vents for a particular roof, which can be found in section R806.2 of the 2012 International Residential Code (IRC).

If the ventilation openings are split between the soffits and the ridge, the formula requires

1 sq. ft. of ventilation area for every 300 sq. ft. of attic-floor area; between 40% and 50% of the ventilation area should be at or near the ridge. Manufacturers of soffit and ridge vents specify the net free vent area (NFVA) of their products, which typically is expressed in square inches per lineal foot. You'll need the NFVA information to accurately calculate the amount of product necessary to ventilate the roof properly (see "4 Steps to Calculate Vent Area," left).

If a roof has only soffit vents and no ridge vents, the code requires 1 sq. ft. of ventilation area for every 150 sq. ft. of attic floor area.

If you need to install ventilation baffles to maintain an open path for air to travel from the soffit vents to the attic, the baffles must comply with section R806.3 of the 2012 IRC, which requires that "a minimum of a 1-in. space shall be provided between the insulation and the roof sheathing and at the location of the vent."

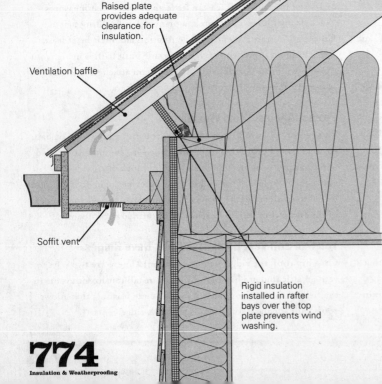

1-in. minimum space between roof sheathing and baffle

Ridge vent

Rafter

Raised plate provides adequate clearance for insulation.

Ventilation baffle

Soffit vent

Rigid insulation installed in rafter bays over the top plate prevents wind washing.

Build a Risk-Free Finished Basement

By Steve Baczek

Finishing a basement can create extra living space with far less cost and complexity than an addition that expands the home's footprint. Perhaps for that reason alone, finishing a basement is a popular project for many homeowners. But a well-designed basement remodel is much more than an assembly of studs and drywall thrown up over a foundation wall, then trimmed and painted. Understanding and managing the risk of moisture and bulk water are imperative to developing a successful basement design, as is getting the insulation and air-sealing details right.

By assessing your site and basement accurately, and detailing your foundation floor and walls appropriately, not only can you improve the comfort, health, and efficiency of your home, but you can tackle the fit and finish of your basement with complete confidence in its durability and longevity.

Economics of Performance

As with all construction projects, risk and performance in a basement remodel exist on a sliding rule of cost. Minimizing risk, providing durability, and ensuring proper performance come with a price. But when is good enough really good enough? It is easy to think of a basement as "cheap" space, but if the remodel is not well planned, it could easily be an inexpensive project that leads to expensive problems down the road. Improper water management can lead to health and durability risks; improper thermal management can lead to comfort risks. When it comes to considering the budget for a basement remodel, it's helpful to follow the general guideline that as cost decreases, risk increases. The challenge is to find a suitable balance between cost and risk.

Rating the Conditions

Because of the below-grade location of most basements, the existence of water is generally the measuring stick of risk. I typically rate existing foundations as having low, moderate, or high levels of risk. To me, low-risk foundations are not challenged at all by water infiltration. They are most often located in a high, well-drained area, and they have no evidence of water problems from the walls or the slab. Remodels should still be detailed carefully, though, since dramatic weather-related water events could occur at any time. I have also seen basements compromised because site conditions changed naturally, or more frequently, because neighboring properties were developed.

A basement with a moderate risk level has seasonal challenges. In colder climates, water from the spring thaw can saturate the ground. In warmer climates, water might become a problem during the rainy season. Regardless of the source, a moderate-risk scenario has water issues for up to half of the year. If you've lived in the house for a period of time, you certainly know if and when water issues are a problem. If you're working on a home without

Code Considerations

Many code requirements for basements apply directly to occupant health and safety. Here are a few worth investigating before moving forward in any basement design.

• Ceiling height or beam height is always a challenge in basements, especially in older homes. According to IRC R304.3, minimum ceiling height of a habitable space is 7 ft.

• Egress demands increase dramatically when the basement remodel includes adding bedrooms. Refer to IRC 310.1.

• Proper alarms for smoke, fire, and carbon monoxide should be installed and maintained in accordance with IRC R314 and R315.

• Sealed-combustion mechanical equipment that separates the combustion air within the device from the basement air is required in some jurisdictions and is a good idea in all of them.

• Natural ventilation is a calculated requirement in many jurisdictions. Start by researching section R303 in the IRC.

• Radon testing and mitigation are required in some jurisdictions. Radon can become a problem as a basement gets tighter.

Continued ➜

Roof overhangs and eaves not only aid in preserving your above-grade walls by preventing water infiltration, but they also prevent water from flowing directly along the exterior of the foundation wall, where it can enter the basement. While other solutions may also be warranted, adding overhangs to a house without them should be considered whenever roof work takes place.

Curtain drains installed above the house can effectively channel runoff away from the foundation to a lower portion of the site. Drains should terminate at daylight.

Regrading the site directly around your home to slope away from the foundation prevents the pooling of runoff and can help direct water around your home to a lower portion of the site where it's no longer a threat to the basement.

Basement-window sills should be at least 4 in. above grade. This can be accomplished with a window well of stone, metal, or timber. The base of the window well should have a minimum of 12 in. of stone or drainable fill.

A Dry Basement Starts With Site Management

Before beginning any basement remodeling work, make the effort to minimize the amount of water challenging the foundation walls. By keeping storm water, snowmelt, and runoff away from your home, you decrease the risk level of the basement renovation, which can help reduce the cost and complexity of the remodeling work. Here are the primary things to keep in mind as you create a strategy for keeping water away from the foundation.

historical context, look for evidence of bulk water in the basement in the form of staining on the slab and/or mineral streaks along the foundation walls. Your new neighbors might also be able to provide some insight into existing conditions, but keep in mind that every property is unique. Just because your neighbor's basement is dry doesn't mean yours is.

A high-risk basement faces water infiltration for more than six months of the year. Water might even be a daily challenge. High-risk basement remodels can be managed effectively, but demand a system of water management that requires a perpetual solution.

Site and Foundation Assessment

The initial steps in designing any finished basement are straightforward. First, if any water exists on the site, try to minimize the amount of water near the foundation as much as you can prior to beginning your work. The less water you have to deal with, the smaller the problem will be, and therefore, the smaller and less expensive the management system needs to be.

Once the site is analyzed and a plan for correction or improvement is developed, the foundation itself needs to be assessed. Different foundation types perform differently and can demand different approaches to management. Stone, brick, concrete block, and concrete all have specific characteristics that challenge a finished basement. Stone, brick, and concrete-block foundation walls are all mortared systems. The amount of mortar and the manner in which it was laid (neat and full vs. sloppy and spare) help determine the ability for water to penetrate the foundation wall. Because of their continuous casting, concrete walls offer a more formidable defense to the infiltration of

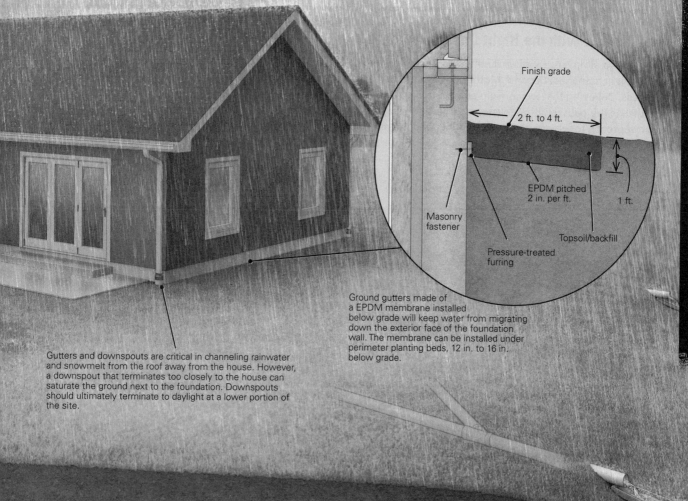

Finish grade

2 ft. to 4 ft.

EPDM pitched
2 in. per ft.

1 ft.

Masonry
fastener

Pressure-treated
furring

Topsoil/backfill

Gutters and downspouts are critical in channeling rainwater and snowmelt from the roof away from the house. However, a downspout that terminates too closely to the house can saturate the ground next to the foundation. Downspouts should ultimately terminate to daylight at a lower portion of the site.

Ground gutters made of a EPDM membrane installed below grade will keep water from migrating down the exterior face of the foundation wall. The membrane can be installed under perimeter planting beds, 12 in. to 16 in. below grade.

groundwater. Make no mistake, though—if water exists, it will get in eventually.

Managing Moisture

Moisture in its vapor form is usually not a cause for concern in a basement. It only becomes a problem when it is given the opportunity to cool and compress to its saturation limit and condense on cool surfaces. For this reason, controlling surface temperatures in the basement is critical. For example, I recommend thermally breaking the framed walls from the concrete slab with a piece of rigid insulation under the bottom plate. This prevents vapor from permeating through the slab and condensing on the cool wood framing, where it could conceivably cause rot and mold growth.

Some builders try to control vapor by applying vapor barriers between the slab and finish flooring or between the foundation walls and the finished space. In some cases, this approach might be successful, but I tend to stay away from barrier systems in favor of management systems. I typically allow the vapor to migrate into the basement and then manage the level of moisture in the basement air with my mechanicals. A heat-pump water heater, for instance, provides partial dehumidification of the air as it heats the domestic water supply. This appliance, though, needs its own drain line for condensate.

When it comes to managing bulk water infiltrating the basement, the strategy is straightforward. The objective is to manage, collect, and discard water from the basement. Depending on the level of risk and the amount of water infiltration, an

Continued →

Balance Risk with the Right Design

There are two simple rules when it comes to designing a finished basement. First, water is never stopped, halted, or detained; it is managed. Second, Mother Nature and Father Physics are formidable opponents, with a very long history of success. Believing that we can win against their natural forces is simply a fantasy. Water management that aligns with their rules is the path to ultimate success. The following examples illustrate adherence to these rules and insight into the proper approach to waterproofing, insulating, and finishing foundations that vary in risk level.

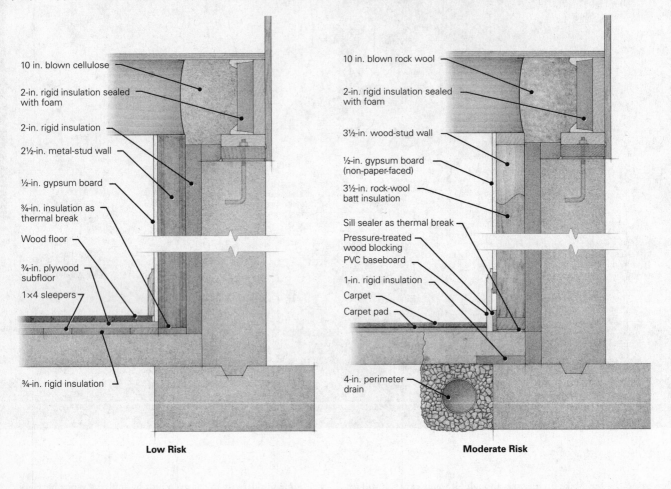

Low Risk

- 10 in. blown cellulose
- 2-in. rigid insulation sealed with foam
- 2-in. rigid insulation
- 2½-in. metal-stud wall
- ½-in. gypsum board
- ¾-in. insulation as thermal break
- Wood floor
- ¾-in. plywood subfloor
- 1×4 sleepers
- ¾-in. rigid insulation

Moderate Risk

- 10 in. blown rock wool
- 2-in. rigid insulation sealed with foam
- 3½-in. wood-stud wall
- ½-in. gypsum board (non-paper-faced)
- 3½-in. rock-wool batt insulation
- Sill sealer as thermal break
- Pressure-treated wood blocking
- PVC baseboard
- 1-in. rigid insulation
- Carpet
- Carpet pad
- 4-in. perimeter drain

appropriate drainage plane must be employed to manage this water. With a moderate level of risk where water moves through the wall by capillarity or saturation, the drainage plane could be as simple as a layer of rigid insulation applied to the foundation wall and its seams taped. At a higher level of risk, where bulk water comes through the wall, a drainage curtain or drainage mat would be needed. A drainage curtain needs to be linked physically to a subslab perimeter-drain system in cases where a footing drain isn't already in place. This is the "collect" part of the strategy. After the infiltrated water is collected, it is directed to a sump pump for discharge. If the exterior grade allows, however, the perimeter drain can be directed to daylight at some point on the

property. By virtue of its subslab position, the perimeter drain handles any groundwater challenging the slab from below.

Insulation and Air-Sealing

In most unfinished basements, moisture issues cause few problems because a leaky above-grade envelope allows the moisture to dry. In many homes, though, attempts have been made to separate the basement from the conditioned living space above with batt insulation installed in the first-floor joist bays. These attempts usually fail, since air movement between the floors goes unchecked. In addition, as the lowest point in the house, the basement is subject to the highest negative pressure

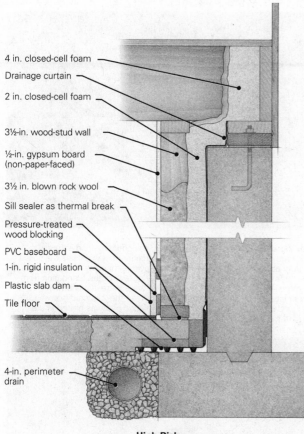

4 in. closed-cell foam

Drainage curtain

2 in. closed-cell foam

3½-in. wood-stud wall

½-in. gypsum board
(non-paper-faced)

3½ in. blown rock wool

Sill sealer as thermal break

Pressure-treated
wood blocking

PVC baseboard

1-in. rigid insulation

Plastic slab dam

Tile floor

4-in. perimeter
drain

High Risk

half of my basement-wall R-value. At a minimum, these numbers usually work out to an R-10 slab and an R-20 foundation.

Rigid insulation, spray foam, blown insulation, and batt insulation all have their place in certain basements. I typically consider batt or blown insulation to be an additional level of insulation rather than my primary insulating method. I refrain from putting any of them directly against the foundation wall for a couple of reasons. First, they allow air movement between the foundation and the wall assembly, making it more difficult to control the surface temperature of the framing and drywall. Second, water permeating the foundation can easily move through the insulation and damage the framing and drywall.

I like to control the surface temperature of the foundation wall with rigid foam or spray foam. After one of them has been installed, I determine the risk of adding batt or blown insulation. I tend to avoid batt or blown insulation in high-risk basements, and I use it sparingly or as bulk-fill insulation in lower-risk basements.

In terms of air leakage, the concrete walls and slab do a fine job of providing air-barrier continuity along their surfaces. With a stone, brick, or concrete-block foundation, the air barrier becomes more of a challenge. In these cases, I tend to use a drainage curtain, rigid insulation with sealed joints, or spray foam as the primary air barrier linking the slab to the mudsill.

Fit and Finish

When it comes to finish materials in the basement, I have heard hundreds of opinions on which ones to use, where to use them, and why. I rely on my initial risk assessment to guide me in material selection with my clients, but I try to accommodate their wishes. In most cases, the installation methods of the selected materials are of prime importance, not the materials themselves. For example, if drywall is to be used in a moderate- or high-risk basement, then I will install a tall (8-in. or 10-in.) synthetic baseboard and hold the bottom edge of the drywall just under the top of the baseboard, which I will fasten to blocking. If the basement incurs a flood, the drywall is likely not to be part of the resulting problem. If a client desires carpet in a low-risk basement, I probably won't have a problem with installing it wall-to-wall. In basements of moderate and high risk, a better option is either an engineered-wood floor or a tile floor with large area rugs. Area rugs are easy to remove, clean, and reuse if they are part of a flood.

In summary, my approach is pretty simple: As risk increases, materials used in a finish basement should be less permanent or more resistant to moisture and water.

(air infiltration) due to the stack effect. Whether the basement is insulated or not, the mechanical system located there is unavoidably tasked with conditioning the basement. In many cases, adding a proper thermal barrier in the basement allows the mechanical system to work less and still be able to provide the required heating or cooling of the insulated basement.

When it comes to insulating the basement, there are code-minimum R-values that vary based on where the home is located. My approach is to provide an R-value that is proportional to my thermal goals above grade. I typically strive for a basement-wall R-value that is at least half of my above-grade wall-insulation value. My target slab R-value is typically at least

Continued →

Manage Risk and Reap the Rewards

Risk is related directly to the threat of water and moisture in the basement. The more water challenging the foundation, the higher the risk level. Because no two basements are alike, each one demands its own method for keeping the space below grade dry and healthy. While finish and furniture selection can be inspired by other projects, it's important to design your finished basement around your specific needs and challenges. The approach to low-, moderate-, and high-risk projects outlined here is not theoretical. It can be trusted in practice. Below are three of the author's designs, built by Two Storey Building of Bolton, Mass., that afforded his clients the additional living space they dreamed of while also offering them peace of mind.

LOW This basement was a 1757-sq.-ft. remodel for clients looking for a family room, a fitness area, and a recreation area. The design is enhanced by a full-height walkout, which allows lots of daylight to enter the family room. This low-risk basement had an existing perimeter drain that emptied to daylight, but there was no evidence or history of water intrusion. The foundation wall was insulated with 2 in. of closed-cell foam, while the wood-framed walkout was insulated to R-19 with cellulose.

HIGH This design called for a media area, a kitchenette, and a fitness area with a full bath. The remodel was considered high risk, as the space endured occasional water intrusion. To provide proper water management, a drainage curtain was placed on the interior face of the foundation from the mudsill to a new perimeter drain. The walls were insulated with 2 in. of closed-cell spray foam placed between the 2×4 stud wall and the foundation wall. An additional R-15 unfaced batt was placed in the wood-framed stud cavity.

MODERATE This 1616-sq.-ft. basement remodel added a media room, a bar and recreation area, a fitness room with a flat-screen TV, and a large pantry at the bottom of the basement stairs for storing bulk items. The homeowners were looking for a casual environment for entertaining and a place for their three children to be with their friends. The basement was at a moderate risk level and required a new perimeter-drain system. In this remodel, the foundation walls were insulated with 2 in. of polyisocyanurate. A 2×4 stud wall was then framed over the rigid foam and filled with R-15 unfaced batts. Finishes in this space are casual and comfortable, and they are easily replaced if needed.

Air-Seal Windows and Doors

By Mike Sloggatt

To the uninitiated, it might appear that once a new door or window is in the rough opening and the exterior is flashed, the installation is done and it's time to install the trim or move on to something else. Stopping the installation there, however, leaves out a very important step: air-sealing the interior. Air leaks around doors and windows not only significantly increase energy losses and make a house less comfortable, but the resulting cold spots inside the wall also can create condensing surfaces that wet insulation and damage framing and finishes.

Modern spray foam makes air-sealing around windows and doors fast and easy. The secret is to use a low-pressure, low-expansion, closed-cell foam designed for windows and doors, and to apply it with a pro-style foam gun.

Don't use expanding foams (often marketed as crack-and-gap fillers), which can exert enough pressure to distort frames and hinder door and window operation. Also, before air-sealing, make sure that the door or window works perfectly, because the foam makes later adjustments extremely difficult.

Polyurethane foam sticks tenaciously to just about anything it touches, so keep it away from finished surfaces and home furnishings. Also, wipe away messes on hard surfaces as soon as they occur.

You can clean up uncured foam on soft materials with acetone or aerosol cleaners made by foam manufacturers, but when the foam is sitting on the surface, it's generally easier and less damaging to let it dry and then to cut, pick, or scrape it off.

> Consider extension tips. Some guns accept small-diameter metal extension tips that make it easier to slip the nozzle into the space between the jamb and the rough opening. Other guns have a barbed tip that accepts flexible plastic nozzles. Both styles work well.

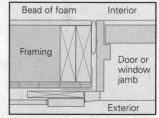

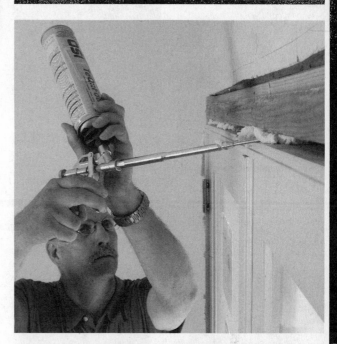

1. Start at the top.
With the foam-gun nozzle inserted between the door or window frame and the rough opening, close the gap with a single bead of foam. Leave the rest of the space between the frame and the rough framing open so that infiltrated water can drain. Start as far away as you can reach, and work toward yourself.

Bead of foam | Interior
Framing
Door or window jamb
Exterior

2. Seal the sides.
Once the top is done, seal the sides by working from the top down and using the edge of the jamb to guide the nozzle for a neater job. To make cleanup easier, periodically wipe the gun's nozzle of accumulated foam with a rag or paper towel before it dries.

3. Seal manufactured sill pans with caulk.
The tiny gap between window and door frames and manufactured sill pans is better sealed with window-and-door caulk rather than foam (see the sidebar in "Energy Smart Details," *Fine Homebuilding* #212). Seal only the top edge of the pan's back dam so that water can drain from beneath. A strip of painter's tape ensures a tidy job.

Continued →

4. Seal site-built sill pans with foam.

For site-built sill pans made from flexible flashing, use a single bead of foam at the rear of the pan to keep out air and water. The single bead allows water to drain while stopping air movement.

5. Trim the foam.

Once the foam has had a chance to set up thoroughly, usually after about an hour, trim the foam flush with the opening using a reciprocating-saw blade or a keyhole saw. The author likes this razor-sharp contractor's saw from Tajima (www.tajimatool.com).

6. Cover the shims.

If you haven't already trimmed the shims used to level the unit, cut them off so that they're flush or below the framing. Cover the ends of the shims with foam, and fill any remaining gaps in the foam previously installed.

7. Keep a can of foam on the gun.

Polyurethane foam cures with exposure to humidity, so make sure the gun is airtight by keeping a can of foam on it at all times, even if the can is empty. If you won't be using the gun for several weeks, replace the can of foam with a can of cleaner. Run the cleaner through the gun until the spray is clear.

Go with a Pro

A pro-style foam gun is vastly superior to the plastic straw that comes with the cans of foam sold at home centers. The tool features a small nozzle that can fit in tight spots and an adjustable trigger for improved control. The cans of foam it accepts are also a better value than straw-dispensed cans, yielding more foam at a lower cost with almost no waste.

Pro-style foam gun

Foam cleaner

Gun-dispensed foam

Cooking spray
A light coat of cooking spray on the gun's nozzle prevents dispensed foam from sticking to the gun, resulting in a neater job and easier cleanup.

Seeing storm damage firsthand.
Following an outbreak of deadly tornadoes in the spring of 2011, the author surveyed hundreds of storm-damaged homes in a multistate investigation. His research revealed that many of the most-badly damaged homes could have fared much better had their builders adopted a few simple and inexpensive wind-resistant framing methods.

Wind-Resistant Framing Techniques

By Bryan Readling

You've seen photos and videos of massive tornadoes ripping through towns and wiping neighborhoods off the map. Given the destruction, you might guess that any house close to an advancing tornado is doomed. The reality, though, is that weaker twisters—those rated EF-0, EF-1, and EF-2 by the National Weather Service—make up 95% of all tornadoes. A carefully constructed house often can survive a hit from one of these smaller, more common storms.

As an engineer for APA-The Engineered Wood Association, I spend a lot of my time studying wind damage to houses and figuring out ways to boost a house's resistance to hurricanes, tornadoes, and windstorms. My work includes plenty of travel, because tornadoes and hurricanes affect most of the country and high-wind events happen everywhere.

My latest field-research project was in April 2011, when two storms two weeks apart spawned tornadoes in seven Southern states. The second storm caused the single largest tornado outbreak in recorded history. In our subsequent investigation of wind-damaged houses 10 years old and newer, my colleagues and I discovered that most of the structural failures were caused by a lack of continuity in the load path that connects a house's structural elements from the foundation to the roof.

Roof Failures

The most common and often most devastating load-path failures occurred when rafters and trusses were pulled from exterior walls. Many of the most severely damaged houses had roof framing attached to the walls with toenails, an inherently weak connection because it relies on the nails' withdrawal capacity. Modern building codes allow toenailed rafters in most nonhurricane areas, but many engineers don't believe toenails have the strength to meet some International Residential Code requirements.

Roof failures were not limited to houses with toenailed trusses and rafters. Failures also occurred when metal hurricane ties were nailed on the interior of the top plate instead of the exterior. Exterior-mounted metal connectors hold better because they line up with the wall sheathing's load path.

Wall Failures

Another common observation, especially in the hardest-hit areas, was houses blown off their foundations. Most had their walls attached to the foundation with hand-driven, cut masonry nails and, in a few locations, pneumatic framing nails. Obviously, anchor bolts are a better choice, especially when the bolts have large square washers to prevent them from pulling through the plate.

A gable end is often poorly connected to the rest of the building. We saw many houses where the triangle-shaped gable end had blown in, often leading to greater damage from wind and water. The gable end is especially vulnerable to failure because its walls are often not backed with drywall. Walls backed with drywall in living space generally hold up better because the drywall provides additional resistance to wind and debris. Failures like this were even more common when the gables were covered with foam sheathing and vinyl siding because both materials are vulnerable to wind pressure and flying debris.

Poorly Fastened Sheathing

When the houses we studied were at least partially intact, the loss of wood wall and roof sheathing often could be attributed to improper attachment. Nails used as prescribed in the building codes provided good performance, while staples performed poorly because they offer less pullout resistance than nails and must be used in greater quantity. Poorly attached roof sheathing at the last rafter or gable-end truss was identified as a weak link in roof construction.

We also saw many cases where breaches in the exterior walls due to wind pressure or flying debris caused pressurization of the building, sometimes resulting in homes that blew apart completely. Field and wind-tunnel research has revealed that wind and flying-debris damage to doors, windows, and nonstructural claddings like brick and vinyl siding often lead to more catastrophic structural failures. Large openings such as garage doors are especially vulnerable to impact and wind-pressure damage.

A Small Price to Pay

Most of these above-code improvements are easy to implement and surprisingly affordable. In researching the 2013 Georgia Disaster Resilient Building Code, the Georgia Department of Community Affairs determined that the added cost of implementing the APA's recommendations is about $595. This estimate, which includes materials and labor, is based on a 2100-sq.-ft. slab-on-grade ranch house with a 10-in-12 roof pitch and three gables.

Beyond Code for High-Wind Resistance

The framing details shown here are not complicated or expensive to execute when they are incorporated into the plans for a new house. In addition to these measures, there are other ways to protect houses in hurricane- and tornado-prone areas.

First, protect large openings. Picture windows, sliding-glass doors, garage doors, and other large openings are vulnerable to damage in high-wind events. Breaches can lead to pressurization of the building interior and increased loads on the structure. Consider installing windows, doors, and garage doors rated for high winds and impact damage.

While a stronger, more wind-resistant structure is certainly safer for occupants, think about adding a safe room in a basement or central space.

Finally, consider using hip roofs, which are more aerodynamic and provide better support to the tops of exterior walls than gable roofs.

Tie down rafters
Secure rafters and trusses with metal connectors. The roof-to-wall connection is subject to both uplift and shear. Inexpensive framing connectors make this important connection simple. Place connectors on the outside of the wall, where they'll do the most good.

Use enough nails
Nail wall sheathing with 8d common (0.131 in. by 2½ in.) nails 4 in. on center at ends and edges and 6 in. on center in the intermediate framing. This installation will greatly increase wind and racking resistance compared to code-minimum requirements.

Lap the sill
Extend wood structural-panel sheathing to the sill plate. The connection of the wall sheathing to a properly anchored sill plate is an important part of the load path. Available at many pro-oriented lumberyards, 9-ft.-long and 10-ft.-long OSB simplifies this connection.

Bolt sill plates
Anchor sill plates with ½-in. anchor bolts equipped with 0.229-in.-thick, 3-in. by 3-in. square plate washers. Space the bolts from 32 in. to 48 in. on center. The IRC requires a minimum spacing of 6 ft. for houses subjected to wind speeds up to 110 mph, but tighter spacing greatly improves wall performance.

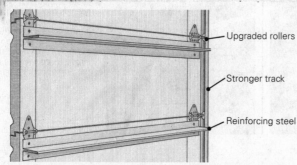

Ring-shank nails on roof

Nail roof sheathing with 8d ring-shank or deformed-shank (0.131 in. by 2½ in.) nails at 4 in. on center along eaves and panel ends and 6 in. on center at intermediate framing.

Sheathe gables

Sheathe gable ends with plywood or OSB. Foam sheathing works better when used with drywall inside the house. The easiest way to avoid interior gypsum at the gable end is to use wood sheathing on the exterior.

Tie gables to walls

Tie gable-end walls back to the structure. Gable ends should be tied to the wall framing below with metal straps and by lapping the gable sheathing onto the wall below.

Connect levels

Break upper-story and lower-story sheathing at the band joist or engineered rim to provide lateral and uplift load continuity. Continuous sheathing also provides an additional layer of protection if siding or brick veneer is lost during storms.

Protect openings

Strengthened with steel struts and upgraded hardware, garage doors should be rated for the maximum wind speeds specified in the IRC's building-planning section. Dealers and manufacturers can offer guidance on choosing a garage door appropriate for local conditions.

Upgraded rollers

Stronger track

Reinforcing steel

Investigating Real-World Storm Damage

The author's recommendations for improving a house's resistance to high winds are based on the structural failures he saw after surveying storm damage for APA-The Engineered Wood Association in the wake of two devastating Southern storms in 2011.

Missing anchor bolts
Far from the foundation. This house, which was attached to its masonry foundation with cut nails, was pushed 6 ft. off its foundation by tornado-driven wind. Similar failures occurred with houses that were nailed to slab foundations.

Missing connectors
Blown-away roof. Unless it's adequately secured, roof framing can be pulled from the walls that it's attached to during high winds. Toenailed roof framing ripped from walls was the most commonly observed serious building failure in the author's poststorm research.

Unbacked foam sheathing
The weak little triangle. Foam sheathing performs better when the interior is covered with drywall. Gable ends without drywall, like the gables on these neighboring homes, should be sheathed with structural panels.

Connectors on the wrong side
Fastened, but not well enough. This house's roof framing was attached to the walls' top plate with metal hurricane ties. Unfortunately, the ties were fastened on the inside of the top plate, where they aren't as strong as connectors aligned with the wall sheathing on the exterior.

Ice Dams

By Martin Holladay

What do northerners from North Dakota to Maine call the period between Valentine's Day and Easter? Ice-dam season, of course. During snowy winters, many northern homes are plagued by ice dams, which form when escaping heat warms the roof sheathing and melts the under-side of the snow layer on the roof. As the melted water refreezes at the eave, the resulting dam interferes with drainage. Water can then back up, get under the roofing, and lead to interior damage. Although the impulse of many homeowners is to respond to a water leak by calling a roofer, leaks from ice dams are just a symptom of a larger problem that usually stems from air leaks or insulation defects. Sealing the roof eaves with flashing membranes adds extra insurance against ice dams. In a few rare cases, increasing the amount of roof ventilation may help. However, air-sealing the connection between the living space and the roof or attic and then improving insulation is usually the best way to solve the problem. The best course of action is to ignore the contractors who talk about roof repair and ventilation improvements and instead find a home-performance contractor who knows how to identify air leaks using such tools as a blower door, an infrared camera, or a fog machine. But before you call anybody, it helps to have a good understanding of what causes an ice dam to form. Here's how it works.

How Ice Dams Form

1. Warm interior air entering an attic (or roof assembly in a cathedral ceiling) raises the temperature of the roof sheathing, causing the under-side of the snow to melt.

2. Water trickles down the roof until it reaches the eave—which is significantly colder than the rest of the roof—where it refreezes.

3. This recurring process causes the ice at the eaves to get thicker and thicker, forming an ice dam.

4. Eventually, water from melting snow backs up behind the ice dam. If the water reservoir is large enough, it can seep up under the roof shingles, leak through the roof sheathing, and cause damage.

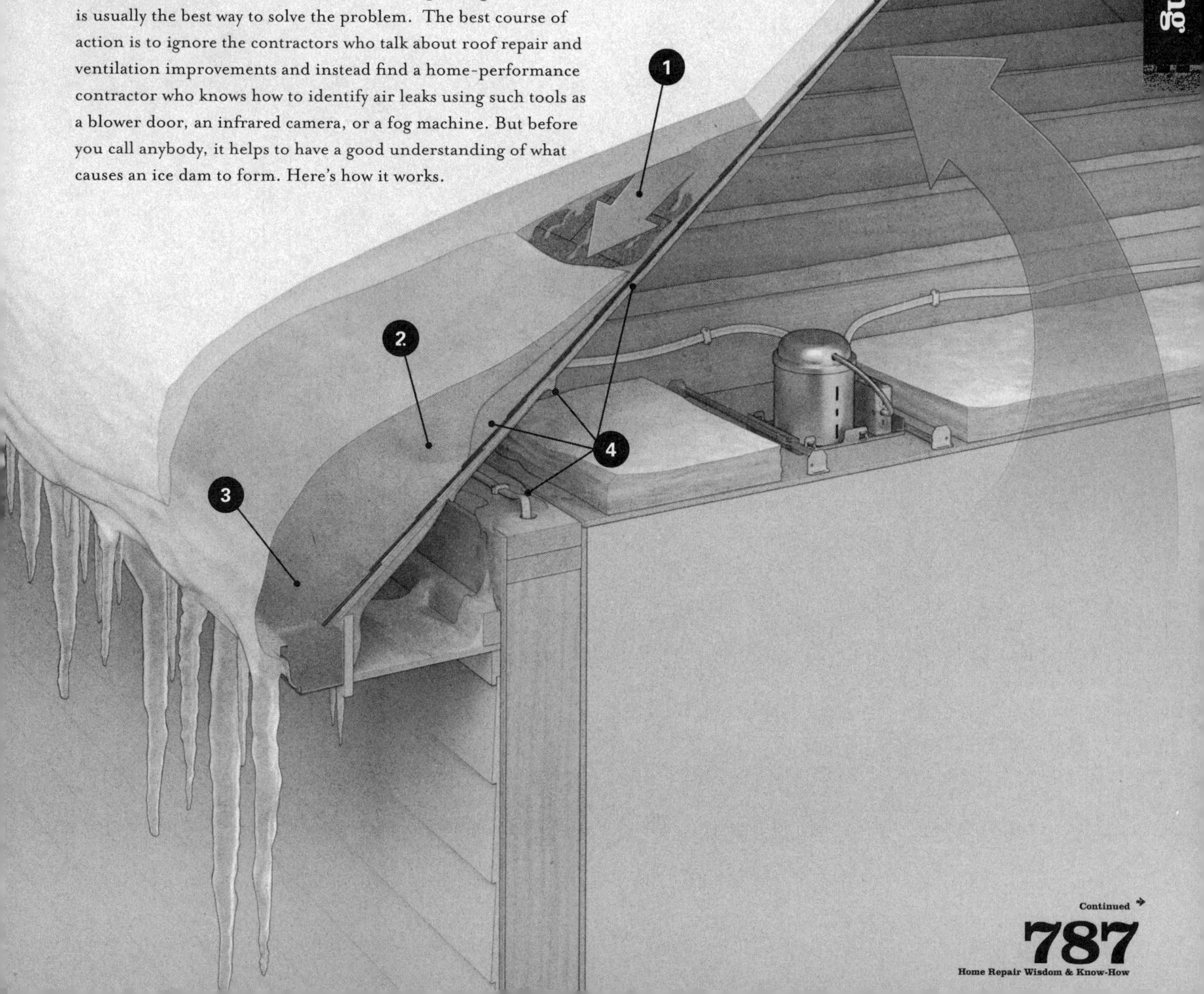

Continued →

How to Fix Them

Ice dams are not a roofing problem; they're an air-sealing problem. There are four possible ways to prevent ice dams, and they are best taken in order of priority. Step 3 shouldn't be attempted until steps 1 and 2 have been addressed, and in many cases, not every step is necessary. 1. Seal air leaks. Canned spray foam, rigid air barriers, and/or sealants are your tools, and any gap, crack, or joint is your target. Seal gaps around recessed can lights, ceiling-mounted electrical boxes and duct boots, bath exhaust fans, plumbing vent pipes, seams between partition top plates and partition drywall, and holes drilled through top plates.

1. SEAL AIR LEAKS. Canned spray foam, rigid air barriers, and/or sealants are your tools, and any gap, crack, or joint is your target. Seal gaps around recessed can lights, ceiling-mounted electrical boxes and duct boots, bath exhaust fans, plumbing vent pipes, seams between partition top plates and partition drywall, and holes drilled through top plates.

2. ADD MORE INSULATION. Cellulose or fiberglass can be blown atop an existing layer of undersize or poorly installed fiberglass batts. If there isn't adequate room under the rafters to reach full insulation depth, it may make sense to spray the underside of the roof with closed-cell polyurethane insulation. Insulated sloped-roof assemblies (cathedral ceilings) are best addressed by installing one or more layers of rigid foam above the roof sheathing, followed by an additional layer of OSB or plywood sheathing and new roofing.

3. IMPROVE VENTILATION. In the past, many building inspectors falsely concluded that the only way to stop ice dams was by improving ventilation, which they believed kept sheathing cold enough to prevent snow from melting. The truth is that increasing ventilation can help, but only after you've air-sealed and insulated; otherwise, the increased ventilation will actually increase air leakage through the ceiling, bringing more heat than ever against the roof sheathing.

4. INSTALL A WATERPROOFING membrane. Although not a solution, self-adhering membrane on the eaves of the roof (a code requirement) is cheap insurance against ice dams that form due to unusual weather conditions.

Install a self-adhering membrane extending at least 2 ft. from the exterior wall.

Baffles, preferably made from rigid foam, create an air gap (1 in. to 2 in. deep) between the roof sheathing and the insulation below.

Add an insulation dam at the perimeter of the attic to contain the insulation and to separate it from the flow of exterior air.

Code Minimums

Requirements for roof or ceiling insulation vary by climate zone and are not as lenient as they were in decades past. Here are the current building-code minimums:

- R-30 in climate zones 1, 2, and 3 (8½ in. of insulation)
- R-38 in climate zones 4 and 5 (10½ in. of insulation)
- R-49 in climate zones 6, 7, and 8 (14 in. of insulation)

Contents

Porches, Patios & Decks

Add a Screened Porch

By Paul DeGroot

When the weather's right, there's no better place than a porch to enjoy a meal, to watch the kids play, or to entertain friends. But to keep mosquitoes and flies from ruining the fun, you need screened-in walls. Like a giant screened door, a screened porch opens your home to fresh air. Done right, a screened porch has plenty of daylight, pleasant views, and good ventilation.

Make It Easy for People to Gather

Social rooms—kitchens, family rooms, and dining areas, for example—facing the backyard are an ideal location for screened porches. Although a porch with two screened sides provides some cross ventilation, three screened sides work much better. Accordingly, try to avoid placing the porch at the inside corner of an L-shaped floor plan. Not only does an inside corner limit airflow, but it also can make hassles with a tricky roof merger.

Also, avoid overlapping the porch with a bathroom window, and don't overlap a bedroom window or bedroom door unless the porch is relatively private with limited access.

You want to tie the porch to the landscape, inviting people to use both the porch and the backyard. You can create more-inviting stairs by breaking tall stair flights into shorter sections with terraces or landings and by dressing up these intermediate levels with barbecue grills, sunny seating, and potted plants.

The Size Should Be Just Right

The porch should be sized in proportion both to the adjoining room(s) and to the overall scale of the house. A tiny porch off the grand family room of a large home looks and feels incongruous. Likewise, an oversize porch linked to a small bungalow kitchen seems out of character architecturally. Respect the scale of the house by using existing eave lines and roof shapes; this helps to keep the porch from overwhelming the house.

The furniture and activities you're planning for the porch also are constrained by its size. Seating four comfortably for dinner requires a 48-in.-sq. or 48-in.-dia. round table, while lunch for six requires a 60-in.-dia. round table or a 60-in. by 30-in. rectangular table.

You can push back and get up from a table with as little as 24 in. between the table and a wall or other furniture, but 36 in. or more

Continued ➜

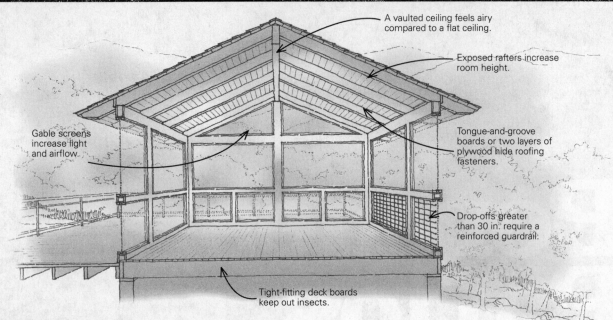

A vaulted ceiling feels airy compared to a flat ceiling.

Exposed rafters increase room height.

Gable screens increase light and airflow.

Tongue-and-groove boards or two layers of plywood hide roofing fasteners.

Drop-offs greater than 30 in. require a reinforced guardrail.

Tight-fitting deck boards keep out insects.

Maximize Screened Area

Exposing the rafters and the underside of the roof deck lends a casual, sometimes rustic, feeling to the space. It also increases the height of the room. Splurge on tongue-and-groove wood decking, or use two layers of plywood thick enough to hide staples and nails. Put the attractive face downward.

Elevated porches require a code-approved barrier for the bottom 3 ft. of wall. Design the barrier into the wall/screen assembly so that it doesn't look like an afterthought. A reinforced guardrail also protects the screening, something you might want to include regardless of drop-off height if you have kids or pets.

Make It Bright and Airy

Screened porches create nice, sheltered outdoor space, but they reduce the amount of light in adjoining rooms. Low ceilings block more light than vaulted ceilings. In northern climates, you may notice lost solar gain in winter as well. Add skylights if you can't vault the ceiling, and especially if it's lower than the ceiling of the adjoining room. Skylights boost the amount of daylight to the screened porch and bounce more light into the house. Lighter paint colors, wood tones, and light-colored floors also help to reflect additional light indoors.

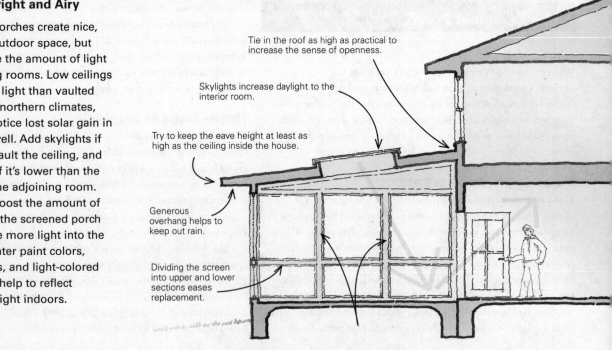

Tie in the roof as high as practical to increase the sense of openness.

Skylights increase daylight to the interior room.

Try to keep the eave height at least as high as the ceiling inside the house.

Generous overhang helps to keep out rain.

Dividing the screen into upper and lower sections eases replacement.

Design for Flow

Add windows and doors where you can to increase the glass area, visually expanding the interior space. They also allow for good airflow and, placed properly, provide convenient traffic flow.

Traffic patterns are critical when planning door locations and furniture layout. Create a direct route between the kitchen and the outdoor eating area so that people aren't forced to walk through the cook's work area. Also, avoid traffic patterns through a living-room conversation group or in front of the TV. On the porch, the house door and the screened door should isolate the traffic zone to one side or a corner, maximizing floor area for furniture and keeping the porch size in check.

The screened-porch door should open onto a comfortably sized landing area. You don't want to be teetering on the top step as you open and close the door.

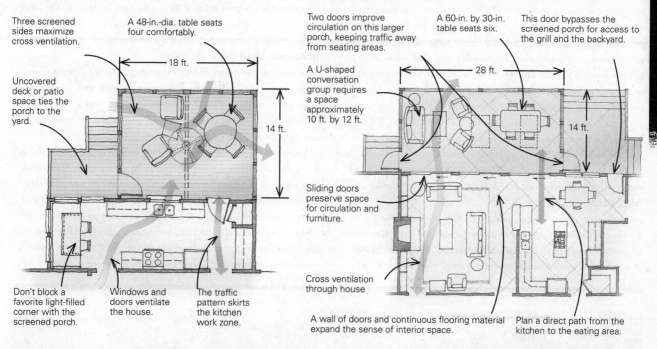

Three screened sides maximize cross ventilation.

A 48-in.-dia. table seats four comfortably.

Uncovered deck or patio space ties the porch to the yard.

18 ft.

14 ft.

Don't block a favorite light-filled corner with the screened porch.

Windows and doors ventilate the house.

The traffic pattern skirts the kitchen work zone.

Two doors improve circulation on this larger porch, keeping traffic away from seating areas.

A 60-in. by 30-in. table seats six.

This door bypasses the screened porch for access to the grill and the backyard.

A U-shaped conversation group requires a space approximately 10 ft. by 12 ft.

28 ft.

14 ft.

Sliding doors preserve space for circulation and furniture.

Cross ventilation through house

A wall of doors and continuous flooring material expand the sense of interior space.

Plan a direct path from the kitchen to the eating area.

is easier on your back and keeps chairs from banging the walls. Add at least another 24 in. if the "scoot-back" zone is also a walking zone. (You can get by with less additional space if the walking zone is seldom used.) Plan for serving and storage, too. You might want to keep seat cushions, candles, and other items below a serving counter. Built in or not, storage and serving stations need floor space.

Add Headroom for Comfort

Screened porches reduce the amount of daylight entering adjacent rooms, so the brighter and loftier you can make the porch, the better. In general, the farther the porch extends away from the house, the higher the ceiling should be. While a flat 8-ft.-high ceiling for a porch only 8 ft. deep might be OK, that same ceiling for a 14-ft.-deep porch will seem low.

If the adjoining rooms have 9-ft. ceilings, then shoot for at least a flat 9-ft. ceiling for the porch, or vault the ceiling for extra airiness. As a rule, don't increase the ceiling height by setting the porch floor below that of the interior rooms. A continuous floor plane beyond the threshold creates nice visual continuity. Also, interrupting that plane with

a code-required landing and steps chews up floor space, limits mobility, and invites accidents. If you can't get a tall ceiling, you can use several strategies to boost daylight in the screened porch (drawings p. 790).

Block the Bugs and Protect the View

When you choose screening, you need to balance your desire for transparency with your need for durability. Standard fiberglass screen is low cost, easy to install, and flexible enough to stay taut when stretched without denting or creasing. Aluminum screening costs a bit more but visually is more transparent. However, it is prone to oxidation and dents easily—pets and kids can make aluminum screening look bad in a hurry.

Traditionally, screen mounting is done by stretching and stapling rolled screening over openings framed in the wall and then hiding the staples with battens. However, getting screens tight can be challenging. I let a window-screen company make custom panels to fit framed wall openings. Sandwiching thin aluminum frames between a fixed stop on the outside and a removable one inside makes for a finished look that is easily replaceable if damaged.

Continued ➜

The Precut Porch

By Michael Patterson

Make it look like the pretty picture. That's our job as carpenters—
to bring someone's ideas to life in three dimensions. Sometimes,
though, the carpenter and the customer have different visions, and
details get lost in the translation. Avoiding that issue is one reason
we have drawings.

There's another reason as well. Good drawings help me to
complete the work quickly. A recent project where I built a portico on
top of an existing concrete-and-brick stoop provides a good example
of how drawings speed my work. Efficiency starts with thinking the
details through beforehand. That sounds pretty obvious, if only
because every job needs a materials list, a plan for how to proceed,
and a time estimate. But in cases such as this small portico, I expand
the concept. In the past, I would have estimated the rough dimensions
of the parts and pieces to order the material. Once on site, I'd have
figured out the exact dimensions of the framing, cutting the pieces to
size just before installing them. Next, I'd have measured the installed
framing to determine the sizes of the trim pieces, spending a lot of
time running up and down a ladder. Complicating matters would be
doing all that outside.

A few years ago, I started tackling smaller projects by first
developing a detailed drawing and a cutlist with the exact dimensions
of nearly every piece in the project. From that detailed list, I cut
as much of the project as possible in my shop, right down to the
trim. I usually still have to cut a piece or two on-site when existing
conditions vary enough to make precutting dicey. Even on those
pieces, though, I still do as much dimensioning or shaping as
possible in the shop.

The advantages are obvious. The cutting is done with shop
tools, which tend to be more accurate than job-site tools. Much of
the work is done out of the elements, and because the on-site time
is minimized, there is less disruption to the client's life. My shop is
at my home, so I have no commute, which is nothing to sneeze at
in the traffic-clogged Washington, D.C., area. I also find that I can
complete the job more quickly, in part because my trips up the ladder
are only to install the components, not to measure for them.

Measure, Then Draw in Detail

This portico was designed by Amy Stacy, an architect with whom
I work regularly. Her drawings were accurate enough for me to
estimate from, but to build a computer model and a cutlist with
dimensions that were guaranteed to fit, I needed to quantify the
site conditions exactly.

Conditions I check include not only dimensions but such things
as whether the existing construction is plumb and level. A house wall
that leans out far enough could, if not accounted for, leave the new
column bases overhanging the edge of the stoop. I did find that this
stoop wasn't level, so the posts had to be trimmed on-site. Since the
new portico roof had to tuck just beneath and run parallel to the rake
board on the existing roof, I verified that the roof pitch was drawn
correctly on the plans. I also checked to see if the concrete stoop was

The Job
It was clear that the existing facade, while nice enough, would benefit both
visually and functionally from an entry portico.

Sketchup as a Tool
A computer model of the architect's plan was superimposed over a photo
to show the homeowner what the final portico would look like.

centered on the door, or if it was offset. This would affect where the columns could be located.

One aspect I didn't check came back to bite me. I assumed that the house's brick walls were structural, a common detail in this neighborhood that would mean I could cut pockets into the brick and support the insides of the roof beams on the house wall. However, they turned out to be brick veneer, which by code can't be used structurally to support a load. This meant that I had to add structural posts down the face of the wall. Because of how these posts ended up having to be spaced, I had to move a light, which led me to add the paneling around the door. This is a good reminder to make no assumptions and to check everything carefully.

You can draw the parts of the structure underlying that pretty picture a number of different ways. In the past, I often drew things out full scale on a piece of plywood using a construction calculator and a framing square. Then I discovered a free drawing program called SketchUp. While it is not as powerful as a traditional CAD program or design-specific software programs such as Chief Architect or Revit Architecture, it lets me draw on the computer like I had so often drawn on plywood.

To develop the cutlist for this portico, I began by looking at the finished dimensions on the architect's plans. Then thinking from the outside in, I built a model of the portico in SketchUp with exact board-by-board dimensions. First came the trim, whose outside dimensions sprang from the architect's plans, and then the framing members, whose size was determined by the trim's dimensions. Math doesn't lie. Assuming you have accurate measurements, if it

fits together on-screen, it will fit on-site. The computer model's dimensions became my cutlist.

Working things out on-screen allowed me to explore the easiest way to build certain details. For example, it became obvious that the barrel-vaulted ceiling would be easier to build if I assembled its arched ribs and straight rafters into trusses in my shop, to be set as units on-site. Another example was a fiber-cement panel on the inside gable face that had to meet the curve of the barrel vault. I wondered how I'd make that curved cut, but when doing the SketchUp drawing, I realized that instead of the difficult task of cutting the fiber-cement panel to fit the ceiling boards, I could frame the roof so that the panel dropped in from above. Then I could butt the ceiling boards to the panel—a simpler, faster, and cleaner approach. Small details like that add up to a real time savings and a better-executed project.

Make the Parts Like the Drawing

I did everything I could in the shop, including rabbeting the back of the fascia for the soffit panels, cutting the angled gable boards, and assembling the rake returns, box beams, and roof trusses. Of course, there's a limit to the size of such assemblies. They have to be small and light enough to be placed easily.

An advantage to working in the shop is that it keeps the material dry. Using dry stock is particularly important when cutting a project ahead of time, as any dimensional changes can throw the fit off. Expecting the wood to expand a little bit once it's exposed to moisture, I take the layout lines when cutting the framing. On the

Precut and Assembled
Most components were cut, and some were assembled, in the author's shop. Site time was reduced, benefiting both carpenter and client.

The Perfect Fit
The completed portico deviates from the computer model only in the railing and the door treatment, the result of decisions made later in the process.

Continued →

"Build" It on the Computer First

Drawing building components in SketchUp helps you to understand how to build the real version, but expect a learning curve (online tutorials help). Approach it like you're building something. To model a roof, draw the components—rafters, ridge, soffit, and fascia—individually, and then assemble them. This helps with dimensioning the parts and understanding how the real project will come together.

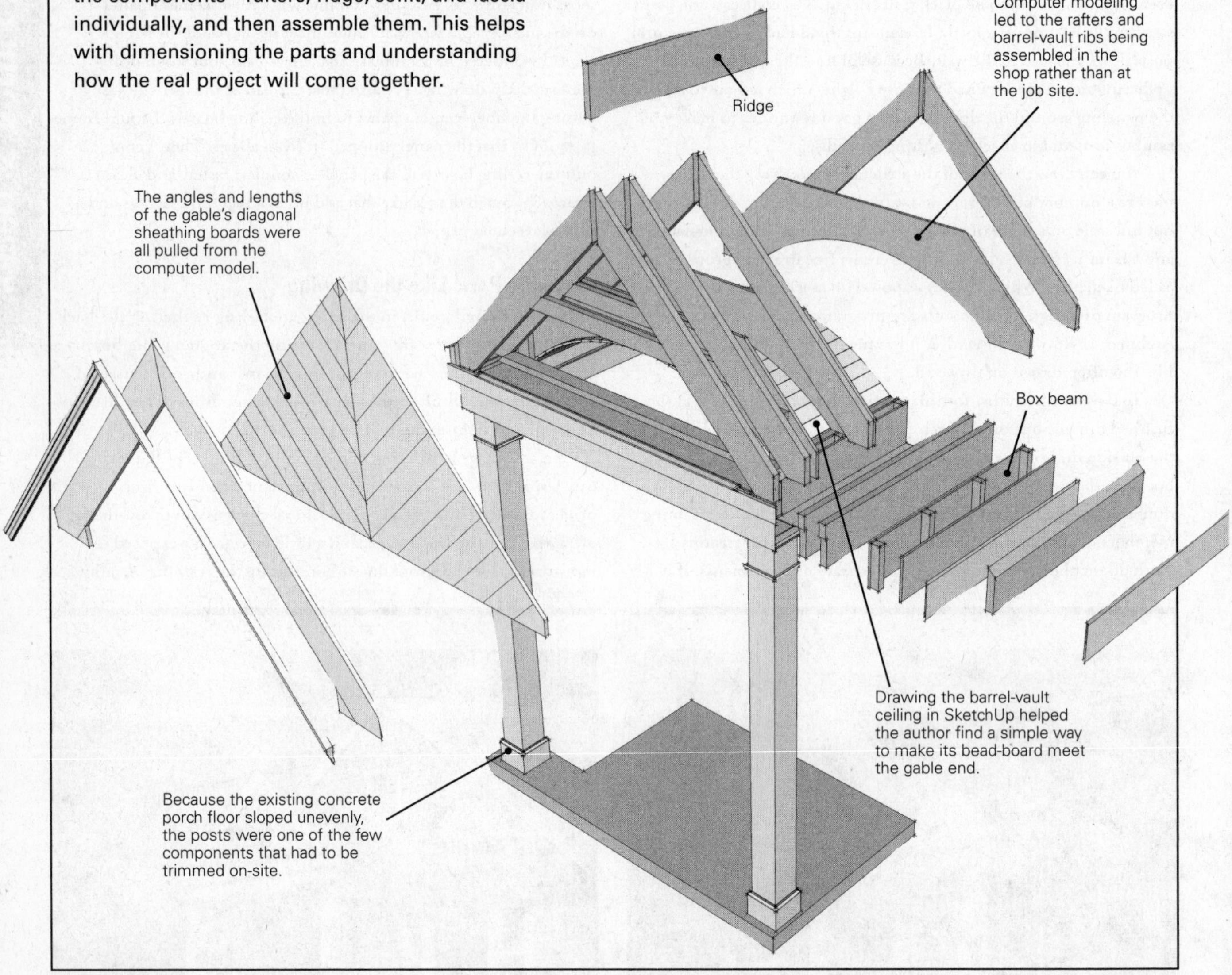

The angles and lengths of the gable's diagonal sheathing boards were all pulled from the computer model.

Ridge

Computer modeling led to the rafters and barrel-vault ribs being assembled in the shop rather than at the job site.

Box beam

Drawing the barrel-vault ceiling in SketchUp helped the author find a simple way to make its bead-board meet the gable end.

Because the existing concrete porch floor sloped unevenly, the posts were one of the few components that had to be trimmed on-site.

trim, I cut right to the lines, so it's a little bigger than the framing it will cover. I'd rather have to take a little off a piece of trim than have it be too short.

Once I was on-site for this project, the only measuring and cutting I had to do was on the two outer support posts. The post locations were not level with each other, and it was easier to account for this variance on-site. Because everything else was cut, with some of it built into assemblies in the shop, I just had to install it. I had printouts of my drawings and cutlist, so it was easy to check and cross-check as I went along, making sure that the components went together as planned.

I spent about two hours drawing the portico in SketchUp and making the cutlist. Shop work, delivery, and installation took an additional 59 hours, for a total of 61 hours. If I'd built the portico entirely on-site, I estimate that the job would have taken around 75 hours. The savings of 14 hours is not too shabby, and it doesn't include time saved by avoiding rain delays. Plus, some of that time was spent in a comfortable shop rather than out in the cold scratching my head.

1. Build in the shop

Pocket screws from the back create a hidden connection between the rake boards and the cornice returns. It's a sturdy joint that looks good and can survive transportation to the site.

2. Load on the truck

All the components of the portico fit in one truckload for delivery to the site. Sitting on top are the roof trusses.

3. Assemble at the job site

After the posts were trimmed, erected, and braced, the lightweight box beams were lifted easily into place. Layered on top of the framing, the precut trim was nailed into place quickly and easily.

Continued ➜

Perfect Screened Porch

By Scott Gibson

Replacing a dilapidated deck on the back of our house with a new screened porch was the best renovation money I have ever spent. The outdoor space has the feel of a room, and we use it for everything from drinking coffee and reading the paper in the morning to eating supper at night. Best of all, it's free of bugs.

That, of course, is the whole point, no matter what the porch's style or size. Without this refuge, enjoying the great outdoors in summer means fighting a losing battle with creatures that bite, sting, and just plain annoy.

With increased exposure to the weather, larger-than-average wall openings, and less structural bracing than other rooms in the house, screened porches pose special construction and detailing challenges.

NOTE: Prices cited in this article are from 2005.

Whether the porch is designed for a shingle-style cottage on Martha's Vineyard or a contemporary lakeside house in Michigan, decisions must be made about designing the floor system, framing the walls to accommodate the screen openings, and attaching the screening. Builders and architects have approached these challenges in many ways. The best screened porches, however, are easy to maintain, are bright and airy, and exhibit inspiring craftsmanship.

Frame the Floor for Maintenance

Most screened porches are built over wood framing and flooring, but Virginia builder Scott McBride, like others, also has built them on masonry surfaces over a concrete base. The advantage, he says, is that a stone, brick, or concrete surface is highly resistant to wear, won't decay, and is cool underfoot.

Screened porches built over wood framing raise at least one prickly maintenance problem. If porch walls are built on top of the flooring or the decking, it is difficult to replace flooring down the road when the weather takes its toll. The trick is to isolate the

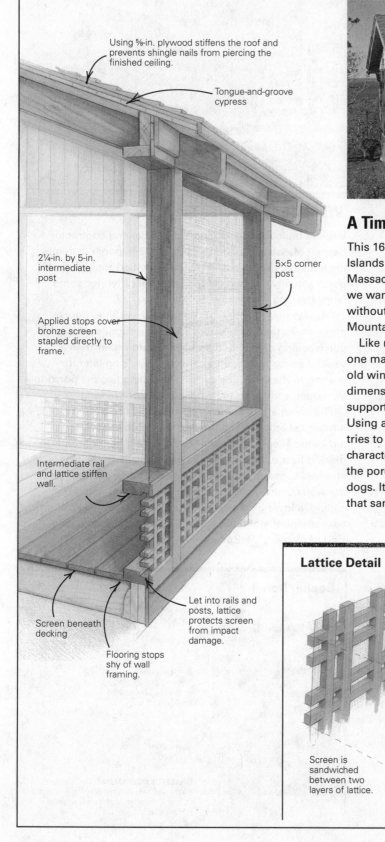

Using ⅝-in. plywood stiffens the roof and prevents shingle nails from piercing the finished ceiling.

Tongue-and-groove cypress

2¼-in. by 5-in. intermediate post

5×5 corner post

Applied stops cover bronze screen stapled directly to frame.

Intermediate rail and lattice stiffen wall.

Screen beneath decking

Flooring stops shy of wall framing.

Let into rails and posts, lattice protects screen from impact damage.

A Timber-Frame Porch

This 16-ft.-square porch overlooks the Elizabeth Islands off the western shore of Martha's Vineyard in Massachusetts. "It's a house with a wonderful view, and we wanted the porch to take advantage of that view without obstructing it," says John Abrams, whose South Mountain Company built both house and porch.

Like many of the porches South Mountain builds, this one makes ample use of salvaged lumber. Staves from old wine or beer vats are 2⅜ in. thick, a nearly ideal dimension for posts. They provide plenty of structural support without obscuring too much of the view. Using a formula developed over the years, Abrams tries to keep spacing between posts 28 in. to 32 in. A characteristic detail is the latticework at the bottom of the porch wall, which protects the screen from kids and dogs. It's made from two layers of ½-in.-thick cypress that sandwich bronze screen.

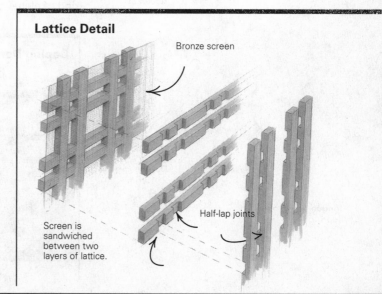

Lattice Detail

Bronze screen

Half-lap joints

Screen is sandwiched between two layers of lattice.

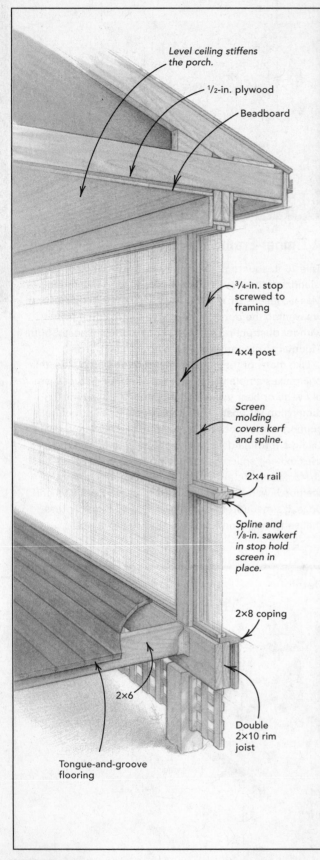

Level ceiling stiffens the porch.

½-in. plywood

Beadboard

¾-in. stop screwed to framing

4×4 post

Screen molding covers kerf and spline.

2×4 rail

Spline and ⅛-in. sawkerf in stop hold screen in place.

2×8 coping

2×6

Double 2×10 rim joist

Tongue-and-groove flooring

Walls That Preserve the View

Virginia builder Scott McBride joined general contractor George Massie to build this 16-ft. by 18-ft. porch. It meets the house at the eave of a low-pitched shed roof, so the porch actually has two gable ends. That called for some fancy framing.

Worried that this tenuous connection with the house might make the porch wobbly, McBride suggested a solid porch ceiling of plywood and beadboard rather than a vaulted space with open framing. "There's no lateral bracing in the walls," he says. "The ceiling ties the porch to the house and keeps the whole thing from racking."

The porch also includes a piece of 2×8 pressure-treated lumber set atop the rim joist to support the posts. The technique keeps the structure's weight off the floorboards, making future flooring repairs less difficult. Screen is attached to stops grooved to accept a spline. At floor level, the stop covers the gap between the flooring and the coping, allowing screen to be run to the floor. "There's no base member along the bottom, so it's transparent, and kind of elegant," McBride says.

Coping Detail

2×8 coping

Skirtboard

Gap between flooring and coping is covered by screen molding.

Vertical 1×2 blocking for circulation

GRACEFUL MINIMALISM. The slender posts and rails are made of ipé, a richly colored, durable, and tough tropical hardwood.

wall framing from the flooring material. Some common methods are adding an extra joist a few inches from the wall's bottom plate to support the ends of the flooring, connecting the posts directly to the floor framing and fitting the floor pieces around the posts, or using a 2×8 coping to support the wall, as McBride does.

Level Floors Are Fine on a Porch

The roof usually shelters screened porches from the worst of the weather, especially if the overhang is greater than 12 in. The insect screen also keeps at least some water from blowing inside. Still, moisture is bound to get in. Water won't pool on porches with gapped decking, of course, but what about porches that have tongue-and-groove flooring?

Some years back, McBride designed a screened porch for his own house with a floor that sloped like a shallow hip roof. The idea was that the flooring would shed water in three directions.

Screens for Every Budget and Need

Screen is available in a variety of materials, but aluminum and fiberglass are by far the most common. Specialty screening includes extra-heavy pet-resistant screen; screen that blocks as much as 90% of solar-heat gain; and noncorroding bronze, monel (an alloy of nickel and copper), or stainless steel for coastal installations.

Standard door and window screen has a mesh size of 18×16, indicating that there are 18 strands per inch in one direction and 16 in the other. This screen can be used on a porch, but a mesh size of 18×14 uses a slightly larger-diameter wire, is stronger, and spans larger openings. If your area is plagued by tiny biting insects (sometimes called "no-see-ums" by their victims), 20×20 mesh may be a better choice.

Fiberglass

Standard fiberglass insect screen is made from vinyl-coated fiberglass threads in charcoal and silver gray. It won't crease like aluminum screening, but it's more opaque. It's also more flexible and, therefore, easier to install in an aluminum frame with a spline or in one of the proprietary screen-framing systems.

Some sun-control and pet screening is made from vinyl-coated polyester, which is stronger and heavier than fiberglass.

Standard fiberglass screen comes in widths up to 84 in. and costs about 17¢ per sq. ft. Pet screening is about 60¢ per sq. ft., and Phifer's Super Solar screen (www.phifer.com), in charcoal and silver gray, costs $1.53 per sq. ft.

Standard fiberglass

Sun control

Pet screening

Metal

Available in bright, charcoal, and black finishes, aluminum screening is the least visible to the eye. Aluminum, however, dents and creases fairly easily, and it can oxidize in coastal areas. It's available in widths up to 72 in. and costs about 26¢ per sq. ft.

Probably the most common of the high-performance alloy screens, bronze won't readily oxidize in salty air along the coast. It turns from a bright, coppery color to a dark brown, or even green, with age. It's available in widths up to 60 in. and costs about $1.10 per sq. ft.

Stainless steel and monel stand up extremely well to salty air, but their durability comes at a cost—anywhere from $2.25 to $5 per sq. ft., depending on weave and quantity.

Aluminum

Bronze

Stainless
steel

Continued ➡

BRINGING THE INSIDE OUT. The large screened openings on this elevated porch make the most of the view, while the wide frieze and wood-strip ceiling continue design elements from inside of the house.

A Porch With Removable Floor Sections

Dominic Mercandante designed this 12-ft. by 16-ft. porch overlooking the water near Schoodic Point, Maine, as part of the house's living and dining areas. The porch, where the owners enjoy many of their summer meals, is actually a roof deck over a basement space. Removable cedar floor sections, called duckboards, conceal an EPDM membrane that keeps water out of the basement. The waterproof subfloor is sloped to channel the water through scuppers below the screen.

Elevated and freestanding on three sides, the porch enjoys steady breezes throughout the day. Simple butterfly clasps hold the removable aluminum-framed screen panels in place. The screen panels can be replaced with glass panels to extend use of the porch into chilly weather or to keep out wind-driven rain and snow during the off-season.

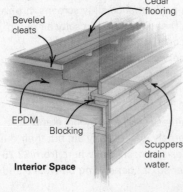

Cedar flooring

Beveled cleats

EPDM

Blocking

Interior Space

Scuppers drain water.

"I don't know that I would go to that trouble again," McBride says now, "because the water that blows inside the porch is pretty much held there by surface tension. I don't think water starts to run until you get a serious amount of pitch." Most of the water that blows inside sits on the floor until it evaporates.

So build the floor flat, McBride suggests, even if you're using tongue-and-groove flooring, and don't worry too much about adding weep holes at the bottom of the wall to allow water to drain. Unless you plan to hose down the porch regularly, it would be rare that enough water could collect behind the bottom plate to make weep holes useful.

One final consideration for an open-decking floor is whether insect screen should be stapled to the tops of the joists before decking is laid. Most builders I spoke with recommend the practice, but I skipped the screen there because I thought it would create a great repository for dirt and dog hair. We haven't had any problems with insects finding their way up through the floor, perhaps because the porch deck is about 3 ft. above well-drained soil that is almost pure sand.

See-Through Walls Need Careful Framing

Screened porches have less structure than conventional walls framed 16 in. or 24 in. on center. Because the whole point is leaving big spaces to admit light and air, framing members tend to be farther apart, spans are longer, and wall sheathing is frequently missing altogether. Planning the size of screened openings is a question of aesthetics as well as structure. The framing typically is on display, and it determines the view.

John Abrams, whose South Mountain Company on Martha's Vineyard builds a lot of screened porches, looks for a rhythm and symmetry in the spacing of the vertical posts that form openings for screen. He spaces posts equally along the walls, directly under roof rafters, and keeps openings to no more than 32 in. That's a convenient width for the bronze screen he uses.

For those buying material at the lumberyard, Abrams recommends ordering 3×6 lumber; the proportions are more pleasing than conventional 2x and 4x stock.

With larger wall openings, the double 2×4 top plate of a conventionally framed wall has to be replaced by something heavier, either a solid beam or one made from built-up 2xs. The 5-in.-square beams Abrams uses are strong enough for openings of 4 ft. McBride's rule of thumb is to use a double 2×6 for openings 4 ft. wide and a double 2×8 for openings 5 ft. wide.

Abrams lets the posts into the beam at the top of the wall for an attractive and simple connection.

Most of the builders I spoke with, though, simply toenail the parts in place. This approach works fine if posts are made from 2x material that will be wrapped with 1x lumber because nail or screw heads will be hidden. If framing members are left exposed, you can conceal screw heads by using a pocket-hole jig and capping the holes with tapered wood plugs.

Posts made from heavier timbers—4×4s and up—can be notched to accept a double 2x beam, one on each side of the post.

If notches are made deep enough to seat the 2x fully, what's left is a ½-in.-thick tenon between the 2xs. The connection can be screwed, nailed, or through-bolted. This arrangement leaves the outside of the 2x in the same plane as the outside face of the posts, simplifying trim and screen installation.

Intermediate Rails or Kneewalls Can Stiffen the Structure

Another decision with both structural and aesthetic consequences is whether to add an intermediate rail or even a full kneewall between posts. Intermediate rails or kneewalls offer additional bracing and can help to keep children and pets from pushing through screened openings. Rails and kneewalls also serve as a convenient shelf for a glass of iced tea.

Porches with freestanding walls on three sides gain some stiffness from an intermediate rail set in the lower third of the wall. Although the work takes some additional time, cutting a groove in the posts to accept the rails is a neat, attractive way to make the connection. If the framing will be hidden, just butt the rails to the posts and toenail from the bottom side with screws or nails.

A solid kneewall 24 in. to 30 in. high is even better insurance against racking. Typically, the outside of the kneewall is sheathed in plywood to add stiffness and is covered with siding to match the house.

South Mountain Company has developed its own system for adding lateral bracing and protecting the screen from damage. Screening is sandwiched between two ½-in.-thick lattice panels. The panels are made by cutting a series of half-lap joints in intersecting pieces. When the screen is installed and the 1-in.-thick panel is assembled, it can be screwed into a rabbet cut into porch posts below the intermediate rail. This custom-built detail protects the screen from both sides and gives the porch a distinctive appearance.

Some designers, however, want a cleaner look and choose to run screen the full distance between top and bottom plates. In this case, the porch framing may have more flex than you'd like. McBride suggests beefing up the roof by using plywood sheathing as a ceiling, which will increase the walls' racking resistance. Similarly, metal strapping nailed to rafters across the porch in an "X" pattern helps to brace and stiffen the framing.

Screening Should Be Easy to Replace

The final step of building any screened porch is installing the screen itself. There are two key considerations: One is getting the screen taut so that it doesn't look like a bedsheet billowing in the wind. The other is anticipating how sections of screen can be replaced when they become damaged, a virtual certainty over time.

The simplest method of installing screen is to stretch it over the openings by hand, staple it directly to the outside of the framing, and then cover the staples with trim. This method has the advantage of low cost, but it's difficult to get the screen tight. In addition, the fragile screen molding often breaks when damaged screen is replaced. If you decide to staple the screen,

Skylights Make the Porch Brighter

John Scholz and Meg Barclay renovated his mother's old shingle-style house to add a porch for refuge from Maine's notorious mosquitoes and for views of the water.

Homeowners often hesitate to add an enclosed porch that might block light to existing rooms. On this project, the architects knew that a solid roof would limit sunlight to the adjoining kitchen. "It's rather dark on the first floor," Barclay says, "and we really wanted to be sure that the kitchen received as much natural light as possible, hence the skylights." Four skylights in a ceiling recess 11 ft. long make the kitchen as well as the porch brighter.

The 9-ft.-wide by 21-ft.-long porch, sized for meals as well as siestas, is designed to match an open porch elsewhere on the house. Its broad screened openings are anchored by a lower railing, and the dark-green accent paint highlights the traditional post-and-railing porch construction. The mahogany screen panels are held in place with simple butterfly clasps and can be removed easily for the winter season. "Part of the reason we made these removable screens is that there's nothing more irritating than trying to repair a torn screen in place. It's so nice to be able to pop it out and take off the molding and staple in a new screen," Barclay says.

SCREENS SHOULD BE EASY TO FIX. The screen panels are simple mahogany frames held in place with butterfly clasps. The frames are nearly impervious to rot and remove quickly for repair or cleaning.

Continued →

heavier, more durable molding installed with trim-head screws will save time when screen must be replaced.

McBride borrows his approach from manufactured screen panels. He cuts a ⅛-in.-wide sawkerf in the edges of ¾-in. trim boards and fastens them to the inside of framed openings. Screen is rolled into the kerf with a screen-spline tool, then capped with a flexible vinyl spline. A separate piece of trim covers the kerf and spline.

It's possible to skip this detail work altogether and buy aluminum screen panels or proprietary screening systems that simplify installation and repair (sidebar p. 803).

Although there are dozens of ways to handle the details of a screened porch successfully, what counts in the end is the space itself. These spaces meld inside and outside, expanding a floor plan in delightful ways.

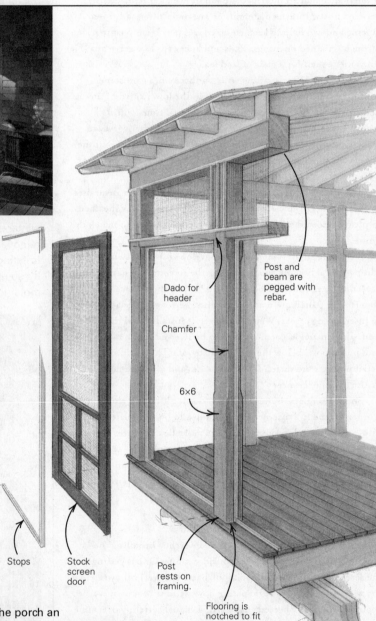

Screen Panels from Stock Doors

Cambridge, Mass., architect John Cole designed this southeast-facing screened porch for a shingle-style house to let the owners reap the maximum possible reward from their lakeside setting.

The 3-ft. spacing of the posts was a time-saving decision by Cole. "The screened panels are actually off-the-shelf screened doors—a trick I've used often that makes life a lot easier for everybody," he says. The panels are screwed to stops at the tops and bottoms of the openings. Spaces above the panels also are covered by screen.

The 12-ft. by 15-ft. structure is reached through an informal dining room, encouraging the homeowners to use it for eating as well as sitting. The screened porch can seat up to a half-dozen people comfortably.

The 10-ft. height of the walls helps to give the porch an airy, open feeling. "Maine, to me, is being outside," Cole says. "It's nice when you can have exposure on three sides so that you really feel as if you're outdoors, but you're protected from the sun and the bugs."

The walls are framed with 6×6 hemlock posts let into the beam at the top of the wall and pinned from above with lengths of rebar. Similarly, the hemlock headers above the screen panels are let into the posts.

Stops

Stock screen door

Post and beam are pegged with rebar.

Dado for header

Chamfer

6×6

Post rests on framing.

Flooring is notched to fit around post.

Save Time with Screening Systems

If you're looking for something beyond the stretch-and-staple approach of installing screen, there are several alternatives.

Custom Panels

Buying premade panels of wood or aluminum, which are installed against stops applied to framed openings, is faster than installing screen yourself, and the panels can be removed and rescreened individually if they become damaged. Storm panels can be substituted for screen to extend the use of a porch into cooler weather. Connecticut Screen Works Inc. (www.connscreen.com) is one such supplier. It has made panels as large as 9 ft. by 18 ft., but the company recommends that buyers limit the maximum size to 48 in. wide by 80 in. tall. Prices for a basic panel with aluminum screen start between $50 and $75 per running foot, which includes a screen door and mounting hardware for the panels.

Proprietary Track Systems

At least two companies manufacture track that is attached to the framing and holds the screen tightly in place. Both types work best with fiberglass screen, although you can use aluminum screen. These systems make screen repair a snap.

Screen Tight
www.screentight.com
A plastic extrusion is attached to the framed openings, and the screen is held in place with a spline and capped with a separate extrusion. If you get the hang of using the spline tool, replacing damaged screen is relatively simple. An 8-ft.-long section of track and cap is about $7.50.

ScreenEze
www.screeneze.com
The screen is tightened as a piece of vinyl trim is snapped over an aluminum extrusion mounted to the framing. No splines are used. To replace a piece of torn screen, pull off the trim, cut a new piece of screen, and reinstall the trim. The track and cap retail for about $2 per ft.

The best screened porches are easy to maintain, are bright and airy, and exhibit inspiring craftsmanship.

Continued →

A Porch with a Rooftop Deck

By Michael Maines

Covered porches are great places to enjoy the outdoors while being protected from the weather. The views, however, are often better from the porch roof. If built properly, the porch structure is substantial enough to support outdoor living space above, so why not take advantage of it and build a rooftop deck?

Starting on p. 869, Emanuel Silva shows how to build such a structure. Here, I show how to get the design right. To illustrate the rules of thumb I follow, I've designed a porch and deck for a one-and-a-half-story farmhouse, a home that's popular in many parts of the country. As with any other project, the ideal situation doesn't always exist, so I offer some alternatives where appropriate.

1. Layout

Long, shallow porches typically look best. A depth of 8 ft. is a comfortable target. However, porches deeper than 8 ft. should be given boxy, roomlike dimensions instead—10×14 or 12×16, for example.

2. Columns: Size and Shape

Don't be afraid to use generously sized columns, but keep in mind that square columns appear wider than round columns because of their diagonal cross section. Round or turned columns usually look best with a gentle curve that narrows at the top, referred to as an entasis. Square columns can be straight, have entases, or be tapered.

3. Columns: Spacing

Place columns so that they create an opening that relates to the shape of the house. For example, a tall, narrow house looks best with closely spaced columns that create vertically oriented rectangular openings. Try to keep the columns evenly spaced and with an odd number of openings. Align these openings with windows and doors when possible.

4. Beams

The beams, more correctly called lintels, should match the width of the top of round columns. If square columns are used, the beam can overhang the columns slightly; in this case, the beam should extend beyond the columns ¾ in. on each side. In general, the face of the beam should be about one-and-a-half times as tall as the beam is wide.

5. Gutters

The roof can drain into conventionally installed gutters or concealed gutters built into the roof, or the runoff can be allowed to spill out freely and be picked up (or not) by ground gutters. In warm climates, internal drains may work, but they're not recommended in cold climates, where they may clog with ice.

6. Posts

Railing posts should be one-half to two-thirds the width of the columns. Posts should align with the columns below and have similar or less-elaborate trim. Match square columns with square posts. If the columns are round, the posts can be round or square.

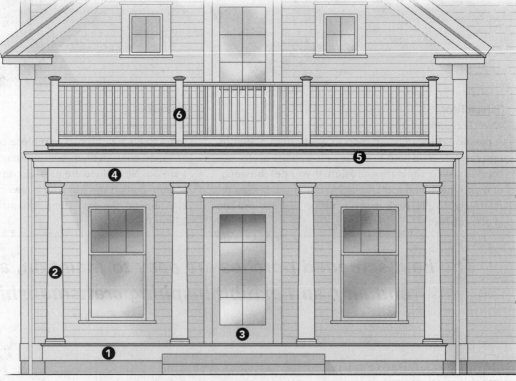

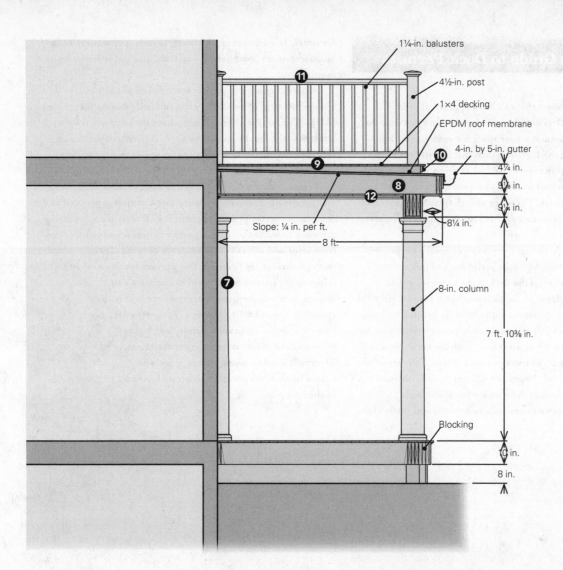

Labels in diagram:
- 1¼-in. balusters
- 4½-in. post
- 1×4 decking
- EPDM roof membrane
- 4-in. by 5-in. gutter
- 4¼ in.
- 9⅛ in.
- 9⅛ in.
- 8¼ in.
- Slope: ¼ in. per ft.
- 8 ft.
- 8-in. column
- 7 ft. 10⅜ in.
- Blocking
- 10 in.
- 8 in.

7. Pilasters

The beams supporting the roof and the deck above can be supported visually by pilasters where they meet the house, or by freestanding columns placed a few inches away from the siding. Pilasters are more classically correct.

8. Roof

The roof should be sloped at least ¼ in. per ft. It's common to put a deck above a low-pitched shed roof. However, if the roof is deeper than 4 ft., it typically looks better to create a shallow hipped roof so that the eaves on all three sides are a consistent dimension.

9. Decking

The deck boards should be attached to pressure-treated 2x sleepers, tapered to offset the roof pitch so that the deck surface is level. If the deck boards are installed as removable panels, cleaning the surface under them is much easier.

10. Trim

A fascia board can hide the sleepers, but a ½-in. drainage gap must be maintained between the fascia and the porch roof. The outside face of the fascia should be in line with the outside face of the beam below.

11. Railings

If the porch below has railings, match them or use a scaled-down version of them above. If the porch has no railings, the deck railings should be as visually light as possible. Where the railing meets the house, there should be a wall at least as tall as the railing. The railing can terminate directly into the wall, but it looks best when it ends at a postlike pilaster or a post held 2 in. to 3 in. from the siding.

12. Ceiling

Ideally, the porch ceiling is in the same plane as the porch-roof soffit. The depth of the porch-roof overhang should match the overhang on the house or be reduced by one-third.

Continued ➡

Homeowner's Guide to Deck Permits

By Glenn Mathewson

Building a deck is a project that's within the grasp of most experienced DIYers. Decks can be enticing, because not only do you end up with a pleasant outdoor space for your family, but decks also offer one of the highest returns on investment of any remodeling project. In many ways, a deck is pretty simple. Home centers sell all the materials necessary and are quick to offer encouragement and advice. There are well-defined members and hardware to connect them, and detailed instructions are widely available.

Simple as they seem, though, decks can conceal a surprising number of safety hazards. An improperly attached ledger—the structural member that joins the deck to the house—can fail, causing the deck to collapse when it's loaded with people. An improperly flashed ledger can cause the framing behind it to rot. (Flashing is the system of sheet metal and adhesive membrane that directs water away from the house.) Even with the code-required fastening, the ledger can fail and the deck collapse if the structure it's attached to isn't sound. Improper railings present obvious hazards. As a consequence of these and other risks, most jurisdictions in the United States require permits and inspections for decks. In addition to a building permit, permits for zoning, historic-district compliance, wetlands, and so forth may be required.

A permit generates project records and allows code requirements to be verified by the authority-having jurisdiction (AHJ). The AHJ is often the city where the property is located, but it may also be the county or state. Building departments are often located at the city hall or in some other prominent government location.

Permits allow an unbiased group of professional inspectors and plan reviewers to help ensure that a project is planned and completed correctly—a real benefit for DIYers. If you're hiring someone to build the deck, a permit fosters accountability in a contractor and offers you some peace of mind. Permits ensure that contractors are licensed. But permits cost money, and while skipping the permit might yield momentary cost savings, it is usually just a matter of time before that approach comes back to bite you. Property sales, tragic accidents, insurance claims, and future projects draw these skeletons from the closet. The result is often more money, time, and heartache than if a permit had been obtained in the first place.

When Is a Permit Needed?

A building permit is local-government permission for a construction project on a property. In most urban locations, the government has authority over many more construction projects than you may think. A few less obvious examples can be window-, water-heater, and furnace replacements. Generally, however, anything that is "finish work" does not require a permit. Wall and floor coverings, trim molding, and interior doors come to mind. In some regions, replacing only deck boards is considered finish work, and a permit is not required. When in doubt, ask your building department.

Building permits must be applied for, reviewed, and picked up before any construction work that requires a permit begins. There is no consistency across the various jurisdictions in the United States for when decks require permits. All editions of the International Residential Code (IRC), the most widely adopted model code in the country, have language that exempts decks of certain heights and sizes, among other specifics, from requiring a permit:

2012 IRC, R105.2 Work exempt from permit, Building, #10

Decks not exceeding 200 sq. ft. in area, that are not more than 30 in. above grade at any point, are not attached to a dwelling, and do not serve the exit door required by Section R311.4.

However, local jurisdictions frequently amend the IRC prior to adopting it, so this exception may not apply where you live. Provisions that affect when permitting and inspection are required have political and economic aspects that must be evaluated for each jurisdiction; as a result, they are rarely uniform. For example, two neighboring suburbs in the Denver metro area, whose distinction can only be seen from the change

in logo on the street signs, are on opposite extremes. One doesn't require permits for any deck less than 30 in. above the ground, while the other requires permits for all decks. This is nothing unusual. When planning a deck, always find out for certain if a permit is required.

It's understandable to want to get started building a deck right away, and waiting for a permit can seem like a unnecessary delay. However, when a permit is required, even demolishing an existing deck or digging holes for footings can be considered "work without a permit," something that often comes with a fine. Quite often, curious neighbors seeing or hearing any such work call the AHJ, prompting an inspector's uninvited visit. That said, some jurisdictions allow demolition to proceed and footing holes to be dug once the permit application is in. Ask your inspector; the worst answer you'll get is no.

Even purchasing construction materials before obtaining a permit is a bad idea. If the plan reviewer calls for changes in your construction plans, then having purchased the wrong material may cost you a restocking fee and second delivery charge. Decks are regulated with unbelievable variety across the country, so what was right on target at your last house may be prohibited at your new one. In the worst examples, you may even find the project you planned and purchased materials for is not allowed at all, or it must be built in a manner that costs more than you budgeted. The permit process can take anywhere from a few minutes to a few weeks, depending on your jurisdiction and whether any issues arise. A stack of pressure-treated 2×10s might become a twisted and bowed mess if it sits in your driveway through a long permit delay. All of these are good reasons to avoid purchasing any material until you know exactly what will be required and have clear permission to move forward.

Who Is Responsible for Getting the Permit?

The expectation of nearly all building authorities is that the person acting as the contractor is responsible for obtaining the permit. If you're the homeowner and are doing all the work, you're the contractor. If you do no physical work but design, organize, and contract all the various pieces of the job yourself, you are still acting as the contractor, even if you are not a tradesperson.

Some homeowners have no involvement other than cutting the check. In most cases such as this, the person hired to build the deck should be responsible for permitting. If a contractor asks that the homeowner get the permit, it's often because the contractor isn't licensed. While some jurisdictions don't require contractor licensing, in others the licensing system can be a political mess. If it's regulated at the state level, then a contractor's license should be valid anywhere within that state. But licensing is often done at the municipal level, and a contractor may build a deck perfectly legally on one side of a street but not on the other, because that's a different municipality and requires a separate application and fee for yet another license.

If you as the homeowner obtain the permit on behalf of a contractor, beware of a few potential problems. Primarily, you might become responsible for any failure of the contractor's work to meet code. If the contractor isn't willing to pull a permit, it should raise questions about that person's professional standing. Does he or she have liability and workers' comp insurance, for example? Also, in many jurisdictions, unlicensed contractors cannot file liens or sue for nonpayment.

There is little consistency in this process other than the fact that, in most places, homeowners who occupy their residential property may obtain permits without being licensed contractors. The necessity of occupancy is to avoid having professional property flippers sidestep licensing requirements. Often the term homeowner permit is used, but that's a bit misleading. Generally, it is simply the qualifications necessary to pull a permit that are softened for homeowners. Once the permit is issued, the expectations regarding code compliance, inspections, and procedures are the same.

How Do You Get a Permit?

The permit process always begins with an application, and in some locales this may be the full extent of it. However, it will probably take a bit more effort. The application is likely generic for many types of work, and it's intended to convey the details about the property, owner, and contractor. A "work description" or "project scope" field is likely but is nothing more than a written description: "Construction of a 250-sq.-ft. composite deck with stairs" would be an example of a basic project description. The information on this application allows the person who accepts the application to enter it into the plan-review process. In some areas, the plan review is conducted by the same person who accepts the application; in others, it is passed to a plan reviewer or is placed

If you as the homeowner obtain the permit on behalf of a contractor, beware of a few potential problems. Primarily, you might become responsible for any failure of the contractor's work to meet code.

Which Code?

That may seem like an odd question. The International Residential Code (IRC) applies almost everywhere, so there's no choice, right? Well, there may be. The American Wood Council, which produces the document that the IRC is largely based upon—the National Design Specification (NDS) for Wood Construction—also produces an alternative building code for decks called the Prescriptive Residential Wood Deck Construction Guide and referred to commonly as the DCA 6. It's updated periodically, and the most recent version is the DCA 6-12. It can be downloaded for free at awc.org, and many jurisdictions accept it as an alternative to the IRC.

Why bother? The IRC is a performance-based code, that is, it specifies the minimum standards a structure must adhere to. It doesn't tell you how you must achieve those standards, though, leaving design professionals a lot of leeway but also leaving DIYers with the task of figuring out how to transform code requirements into construction plans.

The DCA 6, on the other hand, is a prescriptive code. It tells you how to build the deck and provides lots of construction details. Design professionals may find that restrictive, but those details can be very useful to a builder or DIYer.

The Permit Process

First, you have to go down the hall to the third office on the left...

I need a building permit for a deck. What? I have to go where first?

ZONING: You have to show that the deck fits within the property setbacks and that it's a permitted use in that zone. You may need a professionally drawn plan of the property to ensure that's so.

PLANNING: In some communities, the deck may have to meet appearance requirements. In towns with historic zones, you may have to show that a modern structure such as a deck won't be visible from the street.

HEALTH: In areas that rely on septic systems, you may have to show that the deck won't be over the septic tank or leach fields. You may need to have those systems located, if not shown on existing property plan.

FLOOD ZONES: If the project is near water, you may need a professional to prove that it won't impact flooding or affect the ecology of wetlands.

TAXES: You may need confirmation that property taxes are current.

OK, I have all the other approvals. Once the plan reviewer examines my proposal, I'll be able to get a building permit.

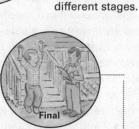

I got a call that my permit is ready. The fee is $299. I'll need to call for inspections at different stages.

Footings

OK, so my holes are deep and wide enough.

Framing

The framing looks good, and the ledger flashing, ledger bolts, and joists appear as on the plans.

Mechanical

I've got my GFCI outlet and the gas line for the grill.

Final

The stairs and railings meet code. I'm done!

Continued ➡

Inspections are intended to verify that the work is being done in the location, at the size, and with the materials that were approved. Inspections also visually verify that work is being performed in general accordance with the building code.

Land-use Permits Make Sure Your Project Plays Nice With the Neighbors

Even for a deck, the building permit is often the last in a string of permits for which you need to apply and pay. In fact, getting the building permit can be the easiest and fastest step in the process. Here's a list of common prerequisites.

Zoning: An area's zoning laws determine whether the proposed construction is a permitted use in that area and if the planned project is within the property's building envelope. Most jurisdictions have setbacks, that is, areas within a specific distance from the property lines where building is not allowed. Setbacks vary between jurisdictions; even within the same jurisdiction, front, side, and rear setbacks usually differ. They may also depend on the neighborhood or whether a street or public property is adjacent.

You'll need to show that what you propose to build does not intrude on the setback limits, which may require a plot plan of the property that shows the relationship of the new deck to the property lines. Plot plans are usually created by surveyors, and you may have a copy in the title work for your mortgage on which you can draw the proposed deck. There may also be such a plan filed with your property records at the town hall that you can copy. When a deck is proposed well away from the setback limit, a hand-drawn plot plan may be acceptable. On the other hand, construction near the setback line may require a new survey and a professional rendering.

Planning: Housing in planned urban areas and historic districts is often regulated strictly for a consistent community appearance. Homeowners associations may have similar requirements. Style, colors, and materials may be regulated; for example, a new deck may require brick columns or a specific type of guardrail. In historic districts, you may not even be allowed to build something as modern looking as a deck if it will be visible from a public way.

Flood zones and wetlands: If your proposed deck is near water, in a flood zone, or over specific drainage channels within your property, you may have to show that it won't affect drainage. In dense housing developments, regulations require each property to work with the overall storm-drainage plan of the entire community. Any construction that could potentially disrupt this may require a review by municipal civil-engineering professionals. Also, some jurisdictions regulate any construction near wetlands to preserve the ecological and hydrological benefits they offer. These circumstances may require you to hire an engineer to provide a plan that meets regulations. This can add months to the permit process.

Taxes: Many jurisdictions will not issue a permit for new construction if property taxes are in arrears.

Health department: In areas where septic systems are used, you may have to show that your new deck isn't going to be built above the tank or in the reserve area, a spot kept open for a new leach field should the existing one fail. This usually requires a survey of your property, but that information also may be on an existing plot plan.

Call Before You Dig

IT'S THE LAW: Before you begin digging holes, you have to call to have any underground utilities located. The nationwide number is 811. Call it, and you'll be put in touch with your locating service. Someone will show up within two to three days to mark the approximate location of gas, power, and communication lines so that you can avoid them. There's no charge, unless you hit an electric line with a shovel. Then there's a really big charge.

in a queue for a later plan review.

Depending on the project, supporting "construction documents" must also be submitted. For a deck, that often includes a plot plan of the site as well as plan and section views of the deck that show the structural elements such as the footings, beam, joists, railing design, and ledger-attachment details. In many cases, the plans for a deck can be simple, hand-drawn renderings.

Additionally, if any electrical work or gas lines are planned, separate permits are required. Some jurisdictions that allow homeowners to obtain building permits may require licensed contractors to perform electrical or gas work. Usually, when a licensed contractor is required, that person is responsibile for obtaining the permit. In that instance, the homeowner can usually drop off the permit application that the contractor has filled out and signed.

There is almost always a fee associated with any permit, and it is based on a percentage of the construction cost. However, for small jobs, a minimum fee may apply. That's why permit applications ask for the cost of the job. These fees help to offset the cost of inspectors and the supporting bureaucracy.

Getting Inspections

After a permit is obtained and the work begins, the next step is inspection. Inspections are intended to verify that the work is being done in the location, at the size, and with the materials that were approved. Inspections also visually verify that work is being performed in general accordance with the building code. It is important to understand that inspection is not intended to guarantee code compliance. Compliance is always the responsibility of the person building the project. An inspector only performs periodic inspections and can only verify what is observed. Inspections are snapshots of the process. Permitting and inspection should not be construed as quality control for a contractor's work.

For a deck, the common inspections include the footing holes before concrete is poured, a rough inspection of the framing before any portions are covered up, and a final inspection to verify such things as railing height and whether stair dimensions are within the code. In some areas and for certain designs, the framing inspection can be performed at the same time as the final. However, fixing any code-related errors to the structure is often much more costly in time and materials after the job is

complete, so I encourage getting a separate framing inspection. Any electrical work, such as adding a receptacle on the deck, requires rough and final electrical inspections as well. Extending a gas pipe out to a grill or fire pit on the deck? That requires a plumbing inspection.

Although working through the bureaucracy may feel like a burden, building codes, permits, and inspections are a necessary part of urban civilization, even for work on our own homes. If you step back, history shows that construction standards are important. They have grown as a result of building failures and the injuries and lost lives resulting from those failures.

We've come to expect a certain level of safety from our houses and buildings, and government oversight of construction makes those societal expectations possible. Beyond the added safety they provide—admittedly, often with added expense—permits help with keeping property taxes properly apportioned and land records up to date. Ultimately, permitting is just a wise investment. A house is a major investment, and selling your home with good permit records is like selling a car with comprehensive maintenance records. It validates the value below the shiny wax, or in the case of decks, below the ipé decking.

Tips

Work as positively with your building authority as possible. Those folks are not the enemy that they are often made out to be.

Ask questions when you do not understand, but do not expect building inspectors to be your personal code teachers or project designers. Their job is generally to review and approve. You will often get more service from them, but consider it a bonus.

Take the time to prepare good, detailed plans. Do not be afraid or upset about plan changes (redlines). They are far easier to introduce on paper than at the job site. Prefer the eraser over the sledgehammer, and treat your plan reviewer as your ally.

When potential contractors refer to code requirements that differ between bids or that drastically affect the cost or intent of the design, check with the building authority directly. Decks are often regulated inconsistently, so assumptions can be incorrect.

Continued →

Designing a Small but Elegant Deck

By Clemens Jellema

Last year, I was asked to design a deck for Fine Homebuilding's Project House. They were looking for a simple yet elegant design that would not be too complicated to build. It would be close to grade, accessed through a pair of French doors connected to a family room, and measure roughly 15 ft. by 12 ft. The deck would feature some built-in benches and planters, and provide a connection to the backyard.

Before I start on any design work, I always check first to see if there are any limitations. These can include slopes, setbacks, easements, and local codes or homeowners-association rules. In this project, the biggest challenge was to create a usable entertaining space while allowing access from both sides of the deck. Typically, stairs create a traffic path where furniture can't be placed, therefore limiting a deck's usable space.

The initial size limitation for this deck project also meant we only had room for a seating area. To make room for a dining set as well, I expanded the project area to include a secondary lower-level deck or a patio at ground level. In designing this deck, I used RealTime Landscaping Architect software (ideaspectrum.com). It is fun to work with and easy to learn, and it can create pretty much anything I can think of. It's also capable of importing models from SketchUp and produces realistic designs. The illustrations here use that software.

As I would with any client, I worked through several designs before arriving at one that satisfied us all. The process offers an instructive glimpse into developing a design for the perfect deck, no matter what the size.

Option 1

In the initial drawing, the focus was on getting the overall design right, with a good traffic flow. Two stairs—one alongside the French doors and the other wrapping the opposing corner—provide two ways for moving to or from the yard. I chose a corner stair because it provides a nice wide entrance to the deck from the patio and a strong connection between the two spaces. This deck is less than 2 ft. off the ground, so rather than a railing, I suggested enclosing the other outside corner with bench seating, using a rosewood-colored variation of the decking to add interest to the tops of the benches and to the stair treads. Because of the deck's small size, I suggested locating a dining area off to the side, on a patio that could be built in a second phase. Skirting added around the deck gives the space a more finished look when viewed from the yard.

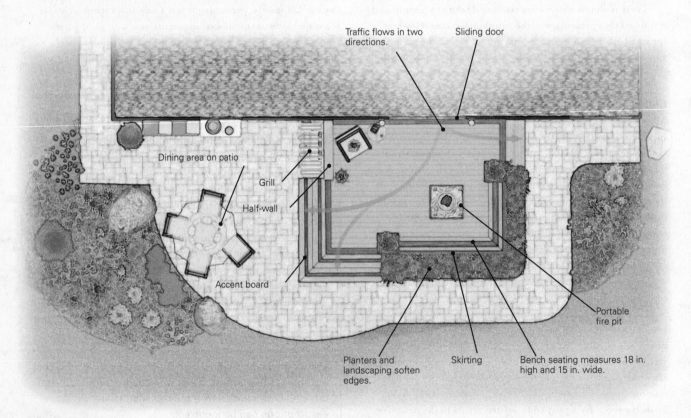

Traffic flows in two directions.

Sliding door

Dining area on patio

Grill

Half-wall

Accent board

Portable fire pit

Planters and landscaping soften edges.

Skirting

Bench seating measures 18 in. high and 15 in. wide.

Option 2

Although the plan had been to keep the deck simple, I also suggested this version, with a nearly grade-level platform that would accommodate the dining set. To be comfortable, a dining set needs 4 ft. of clearance all around (2 ft. for chairs and 2 ft. of open space). For example, a 4-ft.-dia. table requires a 12-ft.-wide space. A small platform extension supports the grill and keeps it out of the way. When I place a dining area on a low deck like this, I normally add 2×4s of the decking material around the perimeter to prevent chairs from sliding off the edge. Steps built into the inside corner formed by the two levels allow direct access from the patio. If budget were a concern, this project could be done in stages.

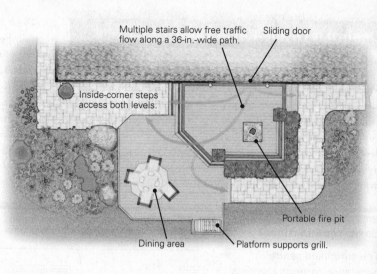

Multiple stairs allow free traffic flow along a 36-in.-wide path.

Sliding door

Inside-corner steps access both levels.

Portable fire pit

Dining area

Platform supports grill.

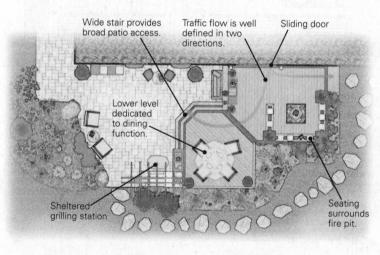

Wide stair provides broad patio access.

Traffic flow is well defined in two directions.

Sliding door

Lower level dedicated to dining function.

Sheltered grilling station

Seating surrounds fire pit.

Option 3

The lower deck in this version is closer in height to the main deck and functions entirely as a dining area. To do this, I eliminated the small step on its right side and moved the grill to the patio. This creates a confined place where people can entertain out of the circulation paths. I also moved the steps to the patio so they wrap around one side of the lower deck. This provides a path from the table to the grill, which now is sheltered with a pergola. The deck is shifted to the right in this expanded design, creating a slightly wider patio and allowing me to wrap the built-in benches around the fire pit without interrupting circulation. This is a more elaborate design than the others, and it can handle more guests. If budget would allow it, this would be my favorite.

The Choice

In the end, we returned to the concept of a simple deck. We kept the positioning we had in option 1 to maximize the patio, but traded the paver path for stepping stones. To make framing easier, we chose to run the decking parallel to the house, as in options 1 and 2. I should also mention here that the corner stair treads, at roughly 14½ in. wide, are suitable for seating and potted plants. This type of "stadium stair" is fine if the deck is not higher than 30 in. To dress up the deck a bit, I added a white fascia and stair risers, something that will look particularly nice with the eventual addition of white window and door trim on the house.

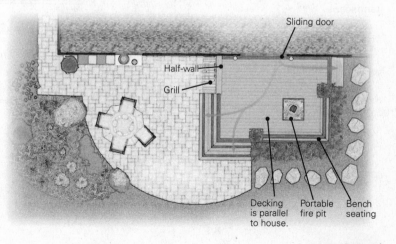

Sliding door

Half-wall

Grill

Decking is parallel to house.

Portable fire pit

Bench seating

Continued →

Design a Grade-Level Deck

By James Moffatt

Starting on p. 835 carpenter Chris Ahrens shows how to navigate the construction sequence of a grade-level deck. Before you can begin to consider its ledger attachment or its beam construction, however, the deck needs to be properly designed. Grade-level decks are popular among my clients for several reasons. Most significantly, these low decks create a closely connected outdoor living experience that they find appealing.

To get the most out of your deck, you need to consider carefully how it will be used. Tailoring the deck's design to its intended functions will yield the most pleasing results. Most every deck should have spaces for cooking, dining, and entertaining, with comfortable circulation paths between.

As with any project, enhancing any of these elements can drive up deck size, construction costs, and complexity. To illustrate how the design of a deck can be altered to accommodate various budgets while retaining the qualities of a good outdoor living space, I offer here three versions of a modern deck for a family that spends a lot of time entertaining and relaxing outdoors.

Basic Yet Functional

The simplified central circulation through this deck creates two distinct areas of use: one for relaxing and the other for dining. Each space is intended to feel intimate and unencumbered by traffic. The sitting area is anchored by built-in seating that doubles as storage for cushions.

The dining area easily accommodates eight and could expand for larger parties. Grilling is located right outside the door to allow short trips to and from the kitchen.

The landscape along the edge of the deck provides a sense of levitating above the vegetation, with a small opening for access to the yard. Perennial fern or inkberry would work well in this landscape.

Features

• Built-in bench with storage
• Built-in or freestanding grill
• Dining for eight
• Two access points to grade
• Size: 315 sq. ft.

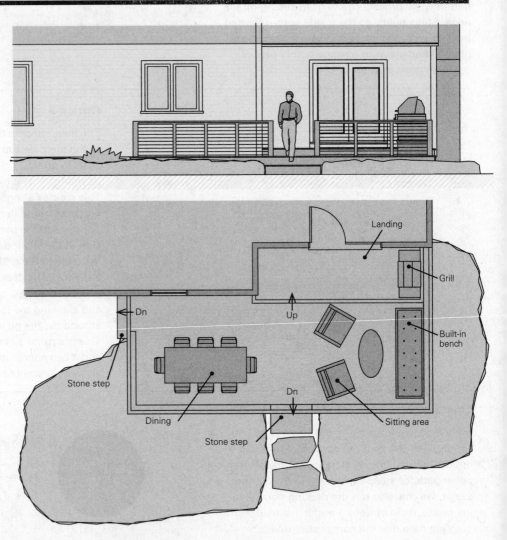

Modest and Modern

This deck design breaks from the orthogonal lines of the house to create a sculptural and dynamic form. The angles of the deck extend into the landscape in the form of a low stone wall.

With the help of some low plantings, the wall directs people through an intimate garden space. To add to the sculptural theme, and to help distinguish the sitting area, a metal fireplace is positioned at the apex of the angle. The box near the entry to the house provides dry and convenient storage for firewood.

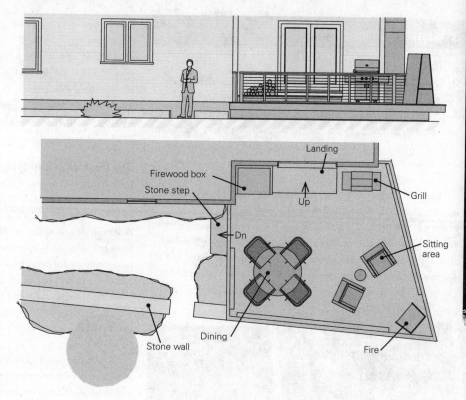

Features

- Metal fireplace
- Firewood storage
- Freestanding grill
- Dining for four
- One access point to grade
- Size: 322 sq. ft.

Large and Inviting

This deck design begins with a stone-wall foundation. The wall helps organize the main sitting area by supporting its dramatic focal point, a fire element that appears to grow out of stones and through the decking.

The main deck, which is in front of the home's sole back door, is designed as the key entertaining space. Its slight elevation offers the homeowners and their guests a broader view of the large backyard.

The dining area is now dropped one step from the main deck. Free of railings, it allows an intimate experience that is tied more closely to the landscape.

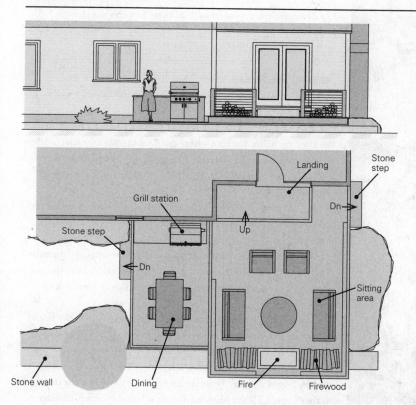

Features

- Fire pit as focal point
- Firewood storage
- Built-in grilling station
- Dining for six
- Two access points to grade
- Size: 447 sq. ft.

Continued ➔

A Grade-A Deck

By Scott Grice

My clients were frustrated with their house, a 1960s-style ranch that had just been renovated. After this long process was over, they quickly realized two things: First, having the kids play outside meant that a little bit of yard rode in on their feet every time they entered the house (this is Portland, Ore.); and second, the two doors opening to the backyard weren't leading to a welcoming destination.

Even when the renovation got under way, there had been talk of a deck in the backyard, but those discussions were sidelined in the push to get back into the house. Now the homeowners knew they needed to structure the yard both to mitigate the dirt entering the house and to create an inviting outdoor space.

Because I had done the renovation, I had a good sense of both the house and their needs.

Dirt mitigation is easy enough, but "inviting" provided more of a challenge.

I ended up building a long wraparound deck positioned to catch the most sun on this forested site. The largest section adjoins the public part of the house, with a smaller platform off the master bedroom. The two sections are connected by a narrower strip of decking that runs along the side of the bedroom wing.

One Deck with Multiple Details

Linking the two sections gave me the opportunity to build in a few features that would make this simple, on-grade deck stand out. To start, I wanted a picture-frame border. Picture-framing is a clean way of hiding the visible ends of the deck boards by running a long deck board perpendicular to those ends, giving them something to die into. Because the deck turns a corner and wraps partway around the house, I faced having a field of deck boards running at right angles to each other. This would be a perfect spot to run a herringbone weave; 45° miters only open over time, and having a stark junction of perpendicular boards interrupts the flow of a deck.

The homeowners also requested an opening with removable panels in the deck to accommodate a small tree. Because this tree was to be installed after I completed the project, I had to frame the opening in a way that would support removable deck panels that went around the tree and also would allow the landscapers to remove enough of the deck frame so that they could plant the tree.

Although the appeal of each of these features is primarily visual, modifying the framing is the first step in constructing each of them and what I'll focus on here.

Framing the Border

Although most of the joist system was straightforward, I made slight modifications for the picture-frame border. When creating this type of border, I find it's a good idea to leave a drainage gap in the framing below the line where the deck boards meet the border so that water won't pool there. The framing also has to provide enough support to the border, which cantilevers off the edge of the deck by 1¼ in.

My answer was a triple 2×8 joist with ¾-in. shims (angled on top so that water will shed off them) placed between the second and third 2×8s.

The double joist sits under the border. The single joist catches the end of the deck boards dying into the border, and the spacers allow water to drain. I left the rim board of this tripler long so that I could through-screw it into the end beam.

Installing the frame boards requires marking where the board will sit on the structure, snapping that line, and face-screwing the piece to the line. Hidden fasteners can't be used here because the boards sit over a 4×8 beam. Because I didn't want the screws visible, I used a ¼-in. Forstner bit to recess the screw 5/16 in. so that I could fill the hole later with an ipé plug. After making the hole for the future plug, I drilled pilot holes and then used stainless-steel trim-head screws to fasten the board in place.

Because frame boards overhang the deck's skirtboard, the board can move a bit to remain parallel to the house or to true up a corner. With the frame boards in place, the field boards could be cut and installed. Before I did that, though, I put a 1/8-in. roundover bit in my router and used it on the cut ends of the deck boards to give them a more finished look.

Solutions for Tight Spots:

The Lowdown on Working on Grade

The house sits low to the ground. I had about 14 in. from the ground to the kitchen door's threshold and 12 in. at the family-room door. That left enough room to bring the top of the deck in just under the house's cedar skirtboard. I planned to have a ledger to pick up the deck's load at the house and to run beams to carry the leading edge of the deck.

I cut spacers from 3/4-in. pressure-treated plywood to allow drainage between the ledger and the foundation. Before installing the ledger boards, I cut them to length, tacked them in place with regular concrete screws, and temporarily placed the 4×8 beams that would carry the other end of the deck. I strung lines around the deck's perimeter and marked the footings.

Once the footing holes were dug, I cut the beams to length. I then temporarily placed the first beam and determined the joist layout. Because the deck sat so low to the ground, I took down the ledger and attached all the hangers for the joists with the ledger boards and beams on sawhorses. With the hardware installed, I bolted the ledger boards to the foundation with 5/8-in. by 6-in. Simpson Titen HD concrete lag bolts (photo below), then set the beams.

With the deck so close to the ground, the beams sat right in the post bases. I put the bases on the beam first and then, using a stringline, a laser level, and some stakes, set the beams for final placement. With the beams in place, I filled the footings. While the concrete cured, I measured and cut the joists, returning the next day to install them.

HELD FAST. The ledger boards are bolted to the foundation. Spacers allow drainage and prevent rot.

Continued ➜

When Hardwood Meets Hidden Fasteners

For this deck, I used Deckmaster hidden fasteners. I've tried several hidden-fastener systems, but none has performed as well as Deckmaster. Ipé is a strong wood, and if it decides to move—which some ipé deck boards do—I have found that screws are the only things that hold fast.

Ipé is beautiful wood, but it is rarely straight and is difficult to make straight. Before installation, I take some scrap ipé and cut a bunch of shims the thickness of the gaps between the deck boards. I cut a lot and all at the same time for consistency. With my bag of shims and sized deck boards, I begin installation. As indicated in the photo at right, I use pipe clamps to get the board where I want it; then I use two drills, one to make a pilot hole, the other to install the screws. Here's more on the challenges of working with ipé and hidden-fastener systems.

MOUNTING THE HARDWARE IS THE EASY PART. Deckmaster brackets mount on alternate sides of the joist. Having the ends overlap slightly ensures that a bracket is always available.

PIPE-CLAMP PERSUASION. Deck boards are rarely perfectly straight, and ipé is no different. The difference is how much force you need to straighten them. Use bar clamps. They can span almost any distance, allow a great deal of precision, and by reversing the heads can be made to push instead of pull. Use scraps for spacers to maintain a uniform gap.

IPÉ NEEDS PILOT HOLES. Use a drill bit slightly smaller than the diameter of the screw. Use a stop collar to prevent drilling all the way through the deck board. Many drills now come equipped with headlights, which are helpful for this type of work.

BAD FOR THE BACK. Be forewarned: While this system is easy to install on the joists, installing the screws through the brackets and into the bottom of the boards when the only access is from above will have deleterious effects on knees and backs.

Crafting a Herringbone Corner

Because the deck turns a corner and wraps partway around the house, I would have a field of deck boards running at right angles to each other—a perfect spot for a herringbone weave. This, too, required a minor alteration to the framing: To support the corner, I had to run a double joist at a 45° angle into that corner (top photo, below). This allowed me to keep my regular joist layout and to catch the ends of the boards where they meet together in the weave. The double joist consists of two 2×8s with ¾-in. spacers sandwiched between.

With the boundaries of the herringbone set, I measured all the boards in the corner, and cut and detailed the ends. I then used spacers to lay them all in place to see if any adjustments were necessary to make the deck boards parallel to the house.

Everything was square in this case, but had the corner been slightly off, I've found that playing with the reveal between the boards will erase most discrepancies. Once I knew that the layout worked, I started with the longest board and worked my way to the corner.

TURNING A CORNER. The finished weave lets the deck turn the inside corner without interrupting the flow.

Tie one header into the ledger

Double the side and header joists

Set removable supports

Planning for a Built-In Plant

Frame the Opening

My approach to building the removable panels to accommodate the small tree my clients wanted to plant in the corner of their deck was basically the same as my approach to the picture-frame border. Like the border, the deck boards would die into the frame of the panels.

I used the normal joist layout to determine one side of the box. From there, I laid out the dimensions of the box on the surrounding joists and built the frame of the box.

The side and header joists have to carry extra weight, so they are doubled.

I also extended the ledger board to the header to help tie everything together. I built triplers to support the panels and to allow for drainage. In this case, I left the framing loose in the hangers so that the landscapers could remove the framing when it came time to plant the tree. After the tree was planted, I used additional joists for center support.

I ran the deck boards around the box so that I could be certain that the layout of the boards in the panels matched the layout of the surrounding deck and so that I would have only full boards in the panels, not ripped pieces.

Shop-Built Panels Are Detailed and Fitted on Site

I built the removable panels in my shop. The two panels were actually built as one unit and then cut down the middle to form the two units. This helps to ensure that everything is aligned.

I started by using a compass to mark the hole for the tree. Then I cut the two side rails and clamped them in position on my workbench. Next, I measured and cut the infill pieces.

Using spacers and clamps, I laid out the whole thing face

Planning for a built-in plant

Use spacers to lay out panels

Continued →

down. Once it was laid out, I marked where I wanted to cut the dadoes for the ⅜-in. by ¾-in. ipé stretchers that hold the panels together.

With everything marked, I cut the grooves and dadoes on a tablesaw, put the whole puzzle together again, then glued and screwed the stretchers in place. After the glue dried, I cut the panel in two and used a jigsaw to trim the middle stretcher flush with the panel's edge. Later, on the deck, I used a router with a roundover bit to put the finishing touches on the tree hole.

The finished panels have framing support on all sides except where they meet in the middle. Where the two panels meet, I screwed a 1×2 on the bottom side of one panel to support the other panel.

Attach center supports

Glue stretchers in place

Trim middle stretchers

Finish edges of panels

An Elegant Border for Your Deck

By John Michael Davis

There are a lot of parts in a deck, but in the end, it's the decking that everyone notices. One thing I've learned building decks in New Orleans's brutal climate is that of all a deck's parts, the decking also takes the most serious beating.

My default method for fastening deck boards is to use stainless-steel screws run in such dead-straight lines that they become part of the design. On this project, however, the homeowners wanted ipé decking, so I decided to upgrade to a hidden fastening system to showcase the wood. I speculated that the time and material expense for using hidden fasteners would not be much costlier or labor intensive than screws.

At the time, everything I knew about hidden fasteners came from a *Fine Homebuilding* article ("Deck-Fastener Options," online at finehomebuilding.com). I remember being impressed by the EB-TY system (www.ebty.com), even in a field of other innovative products, so I decided to give it a try on this project.

EB-TY fasteners come in different sizes for various thicknesses and types of decking. Here, I used the EBE004, which has a built-in spacer of $^3/_{32}$ in. and is specified for the 5/4-in. ipé I was installing. I made some jigs and took a production-minded approach to installation that kept labor time similar to screwing down the boards. The EB-TY system cost about twice what screws would have, but to me, it's a good value. There are no fasteners visible, so the deck looks clean and elegant. Also, the top surface remains unbroken, which makes for a more durable board.

Use Butt Joints Outside

During the design, I decided to wrap the rim joists with a 1×10 pressure-treated clear-and-better southern-yellow-pine fascia board. Given the anatomy of this deck, I knew that some lags, screws, and nails would be visible in various places around the rim joist. Because I would need to use stainless-steel fasteners and take extra time installing them so that they looked like part of the design, a fascia board that hides the fasteners seemed like a logical option. This tack turned out to be of dubious economic value when compared with the price of stainless-steel fasteners, but it does dress things up.

I also decided to create a border with three courses of deck boards. Framing the perimeter with a border isn't a new concept, but corners are typically done with mitered joints. In my experience, mitered joints in exterior applications don't fare well. Wood moves across the grain, so miters are prone to opening. I was wary of this fact even with ipé, which doesn't move much, and especially with the southern-yellow-pine 1x fascia.

With wood movement in mind, I stuck to square cuts and butt joints for the decking and the fascia. I ran the border around a field of deck boards and, instead of miters, made a herringbone design in the corners. The fascia boards die into corner blocks,

which I incorporated into the design (drawing on p. 822).

Clean, Shape, and Seal Every Board

Although the ipé showed up on the job site in good condition, I took the time to clean and dress up the boards. After choosing the best side, I sanded it lightly with 80-grit paper on a random-orbit sander to remove surface flaws. Next, I put a ¼-in. radius on the two top edges with a roundover bit and router. Later, when the boards were cut to length, I rounded over the ends, too.

Once the boards were prepped, I cleaned them with naphtha, then laid them out across the joists, where I applied a coat of Flood's CWF-UV Clear Wood Finish (www.flood.com) to the tops. This brought out the wood's true glow. Once the deck was complete, I applied a second coat for further protection.

The dense ipé soaked up the sealer in varying amounts, which left some boards darker than others. I sorted the boards into a pleasing arrangement, taking into account grain pattern and direction, and placed the most beautiful boards where they would be most visible. Then I numbered each for sequence on the bottom and drew an arrow for direction.

Start with the Border

This deck is fairly large, about 17 ft. wide by 15 ft. deep, and is broken up into three sections. I treated each section separately, starting with the first course of border boards, then the second, then the third. Once the border was established for each section, I filled in the field boards, working from one side of the deck to the other.

The key when laying the border was to establish a square corner. If I had been using screws and plugs to start the border, this process would have been tedious. But I used biscuits, so I was able to rely on the groove they run in. The groove parallels the

Continued ➔

edge of the deck board and locks into the fascia, which is attached directly to the square framing.

The perimeter also had to be established first to determine the length of the field boards, so I completed a corner with all three courses. This corner became a reference point for determining the length of the field boards. I cut them all to the same length so that each would hang over the rear rim joist equally.

Lay the Field Production Style

Installing the corner boards took some time. I glued and clamped the outer boards, then cut the EB-TY slots in place with a router. Then I dry-fit the next two courses, marked the joist layout directly on them, and cut the slots. This was the best way to make sure I got the herringbone corner joints exactly where I wanted them. There were more than 1000 slots to cut in the field boards, though, which could have been a daunting task. So I built a site-made slot-cutting jig with the materials I had on hand.

The two boards that were to be laid last became the base for the jig. A stop block screwed into one end aligned each board to layout lines marked on the jig's base. Then I placed the first board upside down on top of the fixture boards and locked it in place with cleats. Now it was merely a matter of placing each board in the fixture in the correct direction and sighting the layout lines with the biscuit joiner, which made a tedious task fast, accurate, and easy.

Finally, I found out quickly that it was easier and faster to do everything I could while the boards were in the fixture. Therefore, once the slots were cut, I installed the EB-TYs and drilled pilot holes for the screws. Drilling pilot holes is mandatory with ipé and a good idea with pine. The self-drilling screw tips might let you slide when using pine, but the screw would probably run with the grain in some spots, causing splits.

The Border Starts with Two Boards in One Square Corner

Three courses of deck boards weave together in the corners to form the herringbone pattern. Boards are held in place by EB-TY fasteners, which fit into slots and attach to the joists. Blocking beneath the joints supports the pattern and fasteners. The perimeter boards get two grooves (inset below). The inner groove receives biscuits that run along the fascia and help to start things off square. The outer groove acts as a drip edge to keep water out of the biscuited joint. Fascia boards terminate into corner blocks in lieu of miter joints.

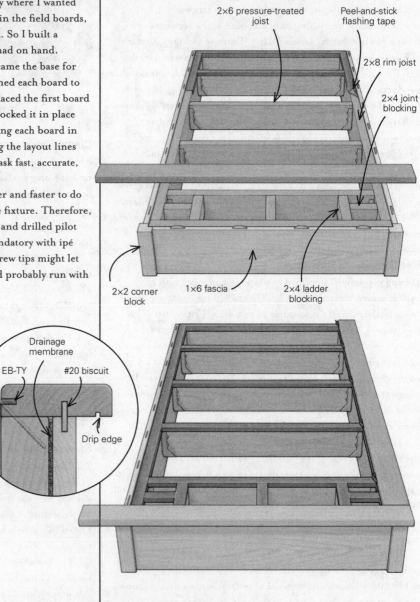

2×6 pressure-treated joist

Peel-and-stick flashing tape

2×8 rim joist

2×4 joint blocking

2×2 corner block

1×6 fascia

2×4 ladder blocking

Drainage membrane

EB-TY

#20 biscuit

Drip edge

Biscuits replace screws. Instead of using screws and plugs through the face of the perimeter boards, the author chose to biscuit them to the fascia. Run the starter board long; it will be cut after the field is laid. Dry-fit the starter board with the biscuits in place. After applying glue to the biscuit slots, the biscuits, and the groove, reapply the board and clamp it in place.

Slot the first board in place. After gluing and clamping the first board, determine where the second board will intersect and where the third board will end. Cut the slots using a router outfitted with a slot-cutting bit. Bending over the board to make a cut like this is dangerous, so use caution. Using a biscuit joiner before the board is installed is another option.

Finish the Corner, and Fill the Field

Move from the corner out. Once the first herringbone corner is complete, install the field. Cut the field boards the same size, and use a biscuit joiner to slot both edges of the board at each joist location. Each board interlocks with the previous one. Move in this fashion until there are only three boards left to install.

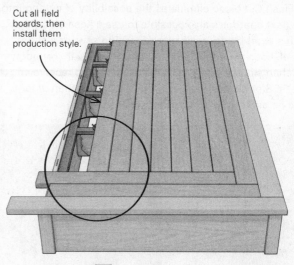

Cut all field boards; then install them production style.

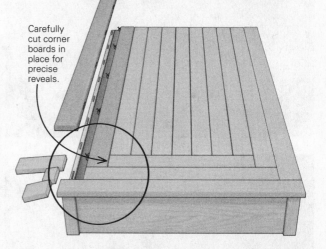

Carefully cut corner boards in place for precise reveals.

Continued ➡

Cut, Slot, and Weave to Finish

Cut the front boards in place. Before installing the last two boards, cut the innermost border board in line with the edge of the last field board. Start the cut with a circular saw, ideally a 4½-in. trim saw. Trim saws are easier to control and create a thinner kerf. Fein's Multi-Master (photo right) is the best tool for finishing the cut because its Flush Cut blade eliminates the possibility of cutting into the next board. It's also possible to use a jigsaw outfitted with a short blade, a Japanese finishing saw, or a sharp chisel. Ease the edge of the cut end with a ¼-in. roundover bit, then slot the end and its mating board to receive an EB-TY. Slot only one edge on the last board; then glue, biscuit, and clamp it in place.

Fastener Feedback

An EB-TY, which looks like a plastic biscuit with legs, slips into a slot cut in the edge of the board directly over each joist. The legs, or splines, hold the fastener off the joist and create a ³⁄₃₂-in. gap between deck boards (other sizes are available for 2x decking). A stainless-steel trim-head screw goes through the EB-TY and deck board at a 45° angle into the joist.

• While I erred on the side of "dead-on" when aligning the slot center with the joist center, I learned quickly that there is about ⅜ in. of wiggle room from side to side.

• The EB-TY itself has about the same amount of built-in "slop" in the slot as a wooden biscuit, which gives you a slight amount of additional play. I figure that just sighting the jig's layout lines with the joiner, rather than marking the board for every slot, produced around a plus or minus tolerance of ⅛ in., which is fine if everything else is also that close.

• Once fastened, the EB-TYs were pleasantly forgiving when accepting the next board's slot. It is possible to torque the outer flange over by cinching down too much on the screw. But I quickly got a feel for just right by putting a finger under the flange as I drove in the screw. There was also a slight click when the screwhead seated into the EB-TY's hole.

• Once I figured out the jig arrangement for cutting slots, the process went quickly, considering the huge amount of repetitive motion. I appreciated that the gap spacing is automatically built into the system, which helped both in consistency and in labor time savings.

• The ³⁄₃₂-in. gap between boards is too narrow to be practical; it won't let plant debris fall through. But much of this deck is covered, so the gap seemed acceptable.

Top 10 Deck-Building Mistakes

By Glenn Mathewsons

The process of building decks is not nearly the same today as it was a decade or more ago. While the outdoor environment and the endless design possibilities have remained constant, emerging technologies and new products and materials require a stronger sense of industry codes and best practices for you to be able to build a deck properly.

As a deck builder, inspector, and plans analyst, I have seen a lot of inferior deck-building practices from professionals and do-it-yourselfers. I've also seen an abundance of bad information that perpetuates problematic designs and poor construction practices. A badly built deck is more prone to failure than a correctly built one, and it's dangerous for those who use it.

Here, I highlight the most common errors I see in deck building and offer solutions to help ensure that your next deck is safe and that it lasts.

The post in the middle of this flight of stairs interrupts the top of the railing, which was designed to serve as the handrail. A new continuous handrail, albeit an unsightly one, had to be added.

1. Failing to Install a Continuous Handrail on Stairs

THE ERROR: For construction or aesthetic purposes, builders regularly install handrails interrupted with newel posts. It's also common to see a guardrail used as a handrail.

THE SOLUTION: Code provision R311.7.8.2 requires that a continuous handrail be installed on any set of stairs that has four or more steps. A continuous guardrail free of midspan posts extending through the top can be used as a handrail, but only if it meets specific geometric requirements. To be considered a handrail, the guardrail must be graspable by those walking up and down the stairs.

If a post interrupts a guardrail, a true handrail must be added to the guardrail running along the stairs.

Always follow manufacturer guidelines for appropriate fastener types and sizes, and use stainless-steel or galvanized fasteners if you are using pressured-treated lumber.

2. Using the Wrong Fasteners and Installing Them Incorrectly

THE ERROR: Incorrect fasteners in hangers are a notorious mistake. For example, deck screws are not a proper way to attach joist hang-ers, and using 1¼-in.-long 10d nails where 3½-in. 16d nails are required is a sure sign that manufacturer instructions were not followed.

Fasteners that don't have the correct corrosion-resistance rating will fail quickly when installed in treated lumber. Also, using only one-half of a two-part post-to-beam connector and installing undersize bolts in 6×6 post bases are common installation errors.

THE SOLUTION: For hardware to work as the manufacturer claims it will and the way the inspector expects it to, follow the manufacturer's installation instructions. Proprietary hardware is not specified in the code; therefore, it is considered an alternative. Alternatives are approved via testing or engineering, and that information must be provided to the building official. The only way to be sure hardware will perform as expected is if it is installed as it was tested or designed. Beyond code compliance, valid product warranties depend on proper installation.

Bolting beams to posts as shown here can result in failure. The bolt may not shear, but the wood can shred. Use a galvanized-steel post cap, and keep the beam firmly seated atop its support post.

3. Bolting Beams to the Sides of Posts

THE ERROR: A tragedy brought to us from the aisles of big-box stores, directions to deck builders to bolt deck beams to the sides

Continued →

of support posts. The average backyard deck has relatively few posts. Fewer posts result in greater loads at beam connections. It would take a huge load to shear a ½-in.-dia. machine bolt, but long before that occurs, the wood around the bolt would be crushed and distorted, resulting in a failed connection.

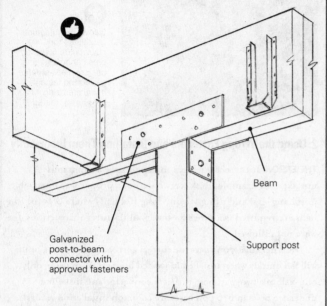

Galvanized post-to-beam connector with approved fasteners

Beam

Support post

THE SOLUTION: A beam should be bolted to the side of a post only for low-level decks that have short-spanning joists and beams and many support posts. Of course, that means lots and lots of foundation piers, which are not the best choice in a region with a significant frost depth. With all the hardware available to handle various direct-bearing applications of different-size beams and posts, there is little reason not to place deck posts directly beneath beams.

To meet the span tolerance of this diagonally installed composite decking properly, additional joists and hangers had to be added to the existing deck framing.

4. Overspanning Composite Decking

THE ERROR: The maximum span of wood-and-plastic composite decking generally depends on the type of plastic used in the product. It's important to follow the span limits of a specific product as outlined in the manufacturer's installation instructions, which some builders fail to review. Overspanning composite decking is most commonly a problem when deck boards are run diagonally over joists or when they're used as stair treads.

THE SOLUTION: Floor joists for a deck are typically installed at 16 in. on center, which won't properly support some composite-decking products when installed on an angle. In new construction, be sure floor joists are installed at the correct spacing. In existing decks, adding more floor joists is the only remedy. Similarly, additional stair stringers might have to be added to stairs where composite decking is used for the treads. Stair treads must be able to resist a concentrated load of 300 lb. over an area of 4 sq. in. This requirement puts a lot of pressure on the actual tread material to support concentrated loads. Some composite products are limited to an 8-in. maximum span when used as stair treads, which require the support of four stringers in a 36-in.-wide stairway.

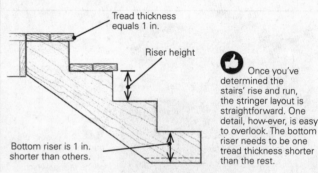

Tread thickness equals 1 in.

Riser height

Bottom riser is 1 in. shorter than others.

Once you've determined the stairs' rise and run, the stringer layout is straightforward. One detail, how-ever, is easy to overlook. The bottom riser needs to be one tread thickness shorter than the rest.

5. Building Stairs with Incorrect Riser Heights

THE ERROR: Often, the bottom step on a set of deck stairs is roughly 1 in. taller than the rest. Code allows a maximum variation of only ⅜ in. between riser heights. This guideline often confuses inexperienced carpenters, who insist that they cut every notch in the stringer the same.

THE SOLUTION: Every notch cut into a stringer has an identical riser height except for the bottom one. The steps notched out of the stringer in the middle of the flight have treads placed above and below each step, effectively adding the same tread thickness to each riser height so that they remain constant. The bottom step doesn't have a tread below it, though, so you must subtract the thickness of the tread from the height of the bottom riser, which is the bottom of the stringer.

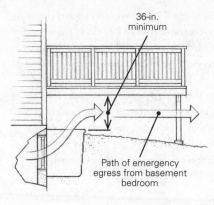

36-in. minimum

Path of emergency egress from basement bedroom

👍 Some clearances around a deck are code-required, like providing a minimum 36-in.-tall escape path from a basement egress window, while others are simply practical, like ensuring access to hose bibs. Each clearance should be considered with equal diligence.

6. Ignoring Clearances and Inhibiting Access

THE ERROR: Although well constructed, some decks create code violations and safety hazards just by how they interact with the house. For example, some stairs on multilevel decks end up near windows that the builder has not replaced with tempered-glass units. Other decks are built too close to the house's main electrical service panel or the service conductors overhead—which need to be at least 10 ft. above a deck or 3 ft. to the side of a deck, according to code (E3604.2.2).

THE SOLUTION: No matter what features exist on the exterior of a home—windows, air-conditioning compressors, low-hanging soffits, exterior lights, outdoor receptacle outlets, dryer vents—identify the required clearances before starting a deck design. While some features will influence the shape and location of the deck, other features may require only that appropriate access be integrated into the design of the deck.

👍 If sistering deck joists to floor joists isn't an option, adding a beam, posts, and footings can help to relieve some of the stress placed on the fasteners connecting the ledger to the end grain of the cantilevered floor joists.

7. Attaching Deck Ledgers Poorly

THE ERROR: The majority of deck plans end with a straight, continuous line at the ledger, rather than details as to what the ledger is connecting to. Unfortunately, the way a ledger attaches to a house is one of the most critical elements in deck construction, and many builders get it wrong. For example, they bolt ledgers straight

to brick, stucco, or EIFS cladding. These practices violate the code.

One of the more egregious ledger mistakes is connecting the ledger to a rim joist nailed to the end grain of cantilevered floor joists—those that support a kitchen bump-out, for example.

The solution: Detailing a ledger properly depends on the building type, the cladding material, and the site conditions. Of all the parts of a deck, the ledger can rarely be treated the same from job to job. Long before construction begins, considerations must be made as to, for example, whether stucco needs to be cut back with new weep screed installed or whether a few courses of lap siding need to be removed to bolt and flash the new ledger properly.

A ledger connection to a cantilevered floor requires specific considerations. Instead of attaching a ledger to the ends of the cantilevered floor joists, it's often stronger to sister the deck joists to the existing floor joists.

When set above an area's frost line, footings can heave (top photo). Piers set below the frost line with bell-shaped bases (bottom photo) stay in place and distribute the deck's weight. Even where the ground doesn't freeze, footings must be set 12 in. into undisturbed soil and not directly on grade (middle photo).

8. Setting Piers in Disturbed Soil

THE ERROR: When it comes to digging footings for their deck piers, some builders are lazy. Usually, a deck's foundation piers are not set below the region's frost line. To avoid deck-ledger failures, freestanding decks are becoming popular, but the piers nearest the home's foundation are often set atop backfill.

In areas where the frost depth is not an issue and precast foundation blocks are commonplace, they're often set on top of the exposed grade.

THE SOLUTION: Just about every deck is built on an isolated-pier foundation system. Foundation systems are required to extend

Continued ➔

a minimum of 12 in. into undisturbed soil (R403.1.4). In cold climates, where the earth is subject to freezing, a pier foundation must extend to a depth below that which is likely to freeze—anywhere from 36 in. to 48 in. This prevents the soil below the pier from freezing and heaving the pier upward.

To install deck piers properly, the piers must bear on undisturbed soil and be set below the frost line in cold-climate regions. However, if the piers are in a backfill region, as is the case with piers nearest the house on a freestanding deck, the footing depth may have to be as deep as 10 ft. to reach undisturbed soil and to comply with code.

Precast foundation blocks must be set at least 12 in. into the ground. However, even in the middle of a lot, the topsoil is tilled roughly 6 in. prior to seeding, so it's likely that the footing needs to be at least 18 in. deep to comply with code. Assume that all deck piers and foundation blocks require some digging.

Don't use nails or screws to fasten railing posts to deck framing, as shown above. Use bolts. More specifically, use blocking and bolts, as shown below, to create a stronger railing than one with posts connected to rim joists that are nailed only to the end grain of the joists.

9. Incorrectly Attaching Guardrail Posts

THE ERROR: Insufficiently connecting a guardrail post to a deck is among the most dangerous deck-building errors. Fastening guardrails to deck rim joists or floor joists with wood screws is not acceptable. While some builders get the guardrail-to-rim-joist connection correct, they don't always ensure that the rim joist is attached to the deck framing properly.

THE SOLUTION: The code (table R301.5) requires a guardrail to be capable of resisting a concentrated load of 200 lb. in any direction along its top. Depending on the design of the guard assembly, a stout guardrail-post-to-deck connection can be accomplished with blocking and through-bolts or with horizontally oriented hold-down hardware. In some rail designs, most of the load resistance is handled by the post connection to the deck. In those instances, the post should be attached to the joists, not the rim, because the rim is not usually fastened to the joists in a manner capable of transferring the load. Rims are typically nailed into the end grain of the joist, the weakest possible connection for withdrawal resistance.

The design methods for guardrail assemblies are as vast as the imagination, and homeowners admire that creative expression. However, serious consideration must be made as to how the guardrail is ultimately assembled.

The strength of a guardrail assembly is provided by a lot more than just the post-to-deck connection. The concentrated load must be resisted at any point along the top of the rail. With a common 5-ft. to 6-ft. distance between the posts, the load must transfer through the connection of the horizontal rails to the post. When a continuous top cap runs across the posts, it acts like a horizontal beam to help distribute the load over a larger area. When a post is run long, through the top of the guardrail, there is a considerable reduction in strength.

10. Making Beam Splices in the Wrong Places

THE ERROR: When a long built-up beam spans multiple posts, many builders run one ply long and extend it beyond the support posts. Many builders believe this practice is good because splices of opposing beam plies are greatly separated as opposed to being only inches apart on top of a post. Unfortunately in these cases, an engineer's evaluation or a rebuild of the beam is required.

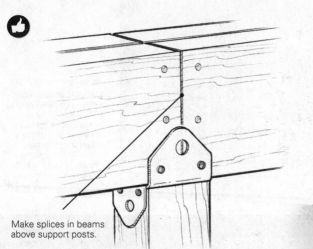

Make splices in beams above support posts.

Beams suffer the greatest amount of deflection at the center of their post-to-post span. Therefore, strong beams are spliced atop posts. If you can't stagger splices over different posts, then placing them over a single post is permissible.

THE SOLUTION: Beams are under two stresses, bending and shear. Shear forces act perpendicular to the length of the beam and are greatest near the bearing ends.

Bending changes the beam's shape, a force called deflection, and is greatest in the center of the beam span. The code lists maximum allowable limits for deflection. In deck beams, the deflection limit is typically reached long before shear limits are a consideration. Any reduction in bending resistance also increases deflection potential and ultimately ends in code noncompliance.

Beam splices that miss the bearing point by a small amount don't greatly affect bending or deflection, and the shear strength of one fewer ply is likely still sufficient. In these cases, the cost of an engineer's review might just get you the OK to build. If a design calls for a splice in the center of a span, it will be smarter and cheaper to build the beam so that splices land atop posts.

A Solid Deck Begins with Concrete Piers

By Rick Arnold

Dig a hole and fill it with concrete. How hard can that be? I've seen old decks built on top of little more than a shovelful of concrete, cinder blocks up on end, and even 8-in. by 12-in. patio blocks. I've also seen old decks—not to mention a couple of new ones—sink and pull away from a house, heave up with the same results, and even both sink and heave from one end to the other.

An insufficient design or a bad installation of this simple foundation system can have disastrous consequences in terms of safety, aesthetics, and a builder's reputation. That's why I approach piers with the same care as I do a house or addition foundation.

Soil conditions and load requirements determine pier size and spacing

Piers Transfer the Deck's Weight to the Soil

To do so effectively, they need to be sized and spaced according to the deck's design load and the soil's bearing capacity. In cold climates, piers always should sit below the frost line to prevent frost heaves. Check your local code for pier-depth requirements.

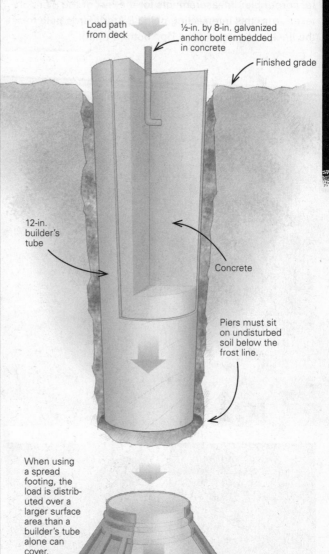

Load path from deck

½-in. by 8-in. galvanized anchor bolt embedded in concrete

Finished grade

12-in. builder's tube

Concrete

Piers must sit on undisturbed soil below the frost line.

When using a spread footing, the load is distributed over a larger surface area than a builder's tube alone can cover.

24-in.-wide spread footing

Continued ➔

Use Two Lines for a Dead-On Layout

With the ledger location transferred to grade level, I can measure out from the house foundation and run a stringline to represent the centerpoint of the piers. A single line parallel to the house intersecting a line perpendicular to the house locates the center of the far-corner pier. Measurements for the rest of the piers are taken from this intersecting point. Batterboards help to set the lines accurately ("Tool Tip," bottom right).

1. PLUMB DOWN FROM A HIGH LEDGER. With a Stabila plate level (www.stabila.com), I carry one end of the ledger down to the grade. I drive a stake into the ground here to anchor a line that will run perpendicular to the house.

2. THE PIER CENTERLINE RUNS PARALLEL TO THE HOUSE. The batterboards I use make it easy to adjust the string until it's exactly the right distance from the house foundation. I set the batterboards a couple of feet beyond the corner-pier locations so that the boards won't be disturbed when holes are dug.

3. A² + B² = C². Pulled diagonally from the foundation, my tape forms the hypotenuse of a right triangle. A helper shifts the line that extends from the house to intersect with the right measurement, identifying the center of the far-corner pier.

3. $A^2 + B^2 = C^2$. Pulled diagonally from the foundation, my tape forms the hypotenuse of a right triangle. A helper shifts the line that extends from the house to intersect with the right measurement, identifying the center of the far-corner pier.

4. MARK PIERS WITH PAINT. Measure the remaining piers from the far-corner pier. A dot marks the centerpoint, and a rough circle highlights where to dig. Pull the stringlines and prepare to dig, but keep the batterboards in place.

5. THE BEST HOLES HAVE NO ROCKS. But just in case you encounter a few, make sure to have a long digging bar in addition to a post-hole digger. Take care not to disturb the batterboards or their settings because you'll have to reattach the strings later. Dig down deep enough so that the bottom of the pier rests on undisturbed soil below the frost line.

Tool Tip

Rousseau makes a reusable batterboard system that is easy to install with foundation spikes, and allows for horizontal, vertical, rough, and precision adjustments of the string with a couple of thumbscrews. www.rousseauco.com

Because piers perform the same job for the deck that the foundation does for the house, it's critical to size and space them properly.

I begin by figuring out how many piers I'm going to need. This decision depends mostly on deck design. For this project, I was building a simple 12-ft. by 16-ft. rectangular deck with a double rim joist to act as a beam that could span about 8 ft., with posts running down from the beam to the piers. In this type of application, I start with two piers on the corners and divide the 16-ft. double rim joist until I get a figure of 6 ft. or less. Here, I found that dividing the rim joist into three sections gave me a span of roughly 5 ft. 4 in., which came out to four piers. Even though my double rim joist could span 8 ft., I chose to use a 5-ft. 4-in. pier spacing to minimize the pier diameter.

After calculating the number of piers I need, I determine the size they need to be. The size of builder's tube dictates the size of the bottom of the pier, which is the area that will be in contact with soil at the bottom of the excavation. To figure this out, I calculate the maximum weight each pier must be designed to bear (by code). For the deck in this article, I figured a 1600-lb. load on each of the two inside piers (sidebar left). Then I compared that to the bearing capacity of the soil at the bottom of the hole. I was building on hard-packed gravel, which easily has a bearing capacity of more than 3000 lb. per sq. ft. (psf).

The bearing capacity of a 10-in.-dia. tube in 3000 psf soil is 1650 psf (0.55×3000). The design load of each inside pier is 1600 lb., so a 10-in. tube will work. However, by jumping up to a 12-in. tube, the bearing capacity becomes 2370 psf (0.79×3000), which can carry the 1600-lb. load more easily. For just a bit more concrete, I ensure the pier is well designed. I typically ignore the pier weight because there is enough fat in these calculations to justify this simplification.

The two outside-corner piers are required to bear only half the weight, but to simplify the work process, I use the same-size tubes for all four of the piers.

The depth you set the piers at depends a lot on the region of the country you're working in. In climates where frost is an issue, the minimum depth is established by code. For this project, the bottoms of the piers have to be 36 in. below finished grade.

Wherever you live, it is important to dig past soil that contains organic matter (topsoil) and any uncompacted fill. Organic matter decomposes over time and settles; loose fill also settles over time. In most cases, the depth of undisturbed soil is not known until the excavation is well under way.

Begin Layout with Deck Dimensions

Once I know the size and the number of piers I'm going to use, the next step is to lay them out on site. If the deck details aren't drawn on the plans, I sketch the outside deck framing to determine exactly where the center of the supporting posts are in relation to the outside dimensions of the deck. Then I use those locations to form a layout rectangle. I use batterboards and string

How Many and What Size?

Three things affect the number and the size of piers you use: the way you frame the deck, the weight the deck is designed for, and the load-bearing capacity of the soil. For the deck I'm building, I chose to support the double rim joist with piers instead of a cantilevered approach that uses piers beneath a beam. I use the International Residential Code's design load for decks, which is 50 lb. per sq. ft. (psf) (40 psf live load, 10 psf dead load). Different soils have different bearing capacities (measured in psf); consult table 401.4.1 of the IRC for the bearing capacities of different soil types.

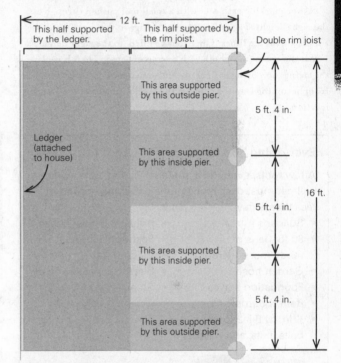

Step 1. Space Piers Evenly Beneath the Double Rim Joist
Because I'm using a double rim joist to support the floor joists, I support this 16-ft. deck with four piers.

Step 2. Distribute the Deck's Weight onto the Piers
A 12-ft. by 16-ft. deck is 192 sq. ft. Multiply by 50 psf to determine the design load, 9600 lb. Half of that weight (4800) is carried by the ledger; the other half is carried by the piers. Because the corner piers carry only half the weight that the inside piers carry, dividing 4800 lb. by three tells me the two inside piers must each bear 1600 lb.

Step 3. Transfer the Weight to the Soil
For this project, I was working in hard-packed gravel, which I estimate to have a bearing capacity of 3000 psf. Using the table below, I multiply the square-foot equivalent of each tube by 3000 psf to find one that will work in this soil. A 10-in. tube will bear 1650 psf, which is close, but I chose to bump up to 12-in. piers for peace of mind. To keep things simple, I made the corner piers the same size.

Continued ➔

to locate the exact center of the post, which is also the location for the anchor bolts that hold the post hardware in place.

Once the post locations are identified and marked with surveyor's paint, I remove the strings and dig the pier holes. When the holes are deep enough, I rough-cut the builder's tubes, drop them in, and replace the stringlines. I keep the tubes centered on the strings while they are backfilled, and I double-check the measurements with a tape measure.

Rather than try to cut tubes to exact height, I leave them long and pour concrete to the desired height inside the tube. In most cases, I like the pour to come a couple of inches above the finished grade. If the piers are on a pitched elevation, the tops of the piers won't be level with each other. On this job, the finished grade was level, so I used a long level to carry the elevation across the piers.

After marking each pier with a small nail pushed through at the right height, I again remove the strings so that I can pour the concrete into the tubes. Once they're filled to the right height, I float the concrete smooth with a scrap of wood. Then I replace the string, and using a slight up-and-down motion to prevent air from becoming trapped, I insert the anchor bolts in their proper locations.

Everything You Need

A few tools, even fewer materials, and a little sweat will get most deck foundations out of the ground in less than a day.

- Builder's tubes
- 80-lb. bags of ready-mix concrete
- Garden hose
- Foundation spikes
- Batterboards
- ½-in. by 8-in. anchor bolts, nuts, and washers
- Adjustable post bases
- Post-hole digger
- Digging bar
- Electric concrete mixer
- Stabila plate level

Fine-Tune the Layout Before and After the Pour

Once the holes are dug, put the stringlines back on the batterboards. When setting each builder's tube, use the lines and a tape measure to center them according to layout, adjusting the hole locations as needed. Take the time to check the tube locations often as you backfill to keep them on layout. After all the fill is in place and the final layout check is made, fill the tubes with concrete, and insert the anchor bolts.

1. BACKFILL WITH MEASURING TAPE AND SHOVEL. I cut the builder's tubes so that they stick out a few inches above grade when placed in the hole. To make sure a tube is placed precisely, I hold it on its layout while a helper backfills. Pack the soil around the tube every so often as you go.

2. DOUBLE-CHECK THE CORNERS. I spend a little extra time checking the location of the final corner pier to make sure that it's in the right spot, because I won't get a chance to move it once the concrete is poured. Use a nail to mark the finished height of the piers, keeping it a couple of inches above the finished grade. If you need to have piers all at the same height, use a long level or a transit to locate their finished height.

3. A SHOVEL MAKES UP FOR BAD AIM. Fill the tubes with concrete until it reaches the nail. The concrete should be just slightly on the wet side, about the consistency of thick oatmeal. As the concrete is poured into the tube, a helper uses a shovel to agitate the mix every 8 in. to 10 in. to work out air pockets.

4. PLACE ANCHOR BOLTS ACCURATELY. Once all the piers are poured, I go back and insert anchor bolts in the center of the piers. I measure from the line running perpendicular to the house to set anchor bolts accurately. Be sure to leave the threads high enough so that a post base, washer, and nut can be added later.

5. ADJUSTABLE POST BASES ALLOW FOR FINAL TWEAKS. After the concrete is cured completely, I attach adjustable post bases. I like to use Simpson ABA-style bases because they allow me to fine-tune the post location after the post is attached.

How Much Concrete Do I Need?

To pour the piers for an average-size deck, I use 80-lb. bags of concrete and an electric mixer.

For major pours, I have a concrete truck deliver a 2500-lb. mix. Either way, the basic formulas below will help you to estimate the number of bags or cubic yards of concrete required based on pier size and depth.

Example
Size of tubes: 8 in.
Number of tubes: 8
Average depth per tube: 4 ft.
0.53 (8×4) = 17 bags

Mix Concrete by the Bag

By Scott Grice

Some people might assume that mixing concrete is an obvious task: Buy a bag of premix, dump it in a wheelbarrow with some water, and mix it up. Sounds simple, right?

As a fence and deck contractor, I have learned otherwise. I often have to mix five to ten bags in an afternoon, then have to push around wheelbarrow loads of wet concrete. This chore was a strong motivator for me to come up with an efficient, reliable mixing system.

The first step to smarter concrete-mixing is to use my truck's tailgate as a platform for emptying the concrete premix into the wheelbarrow. This setup limits the number of times I have to move the bags of concrete and keeps them at a comfortable working height. Second, I put the water in the wheelbarrow before the concrete. This step helps to keep down the dust and prevents dry pockets in the mix. Third, I use a stiff rake to mix the concrete. A rake mixes more efficiently and is easier to work with than a hoe or a shovel. Finally, to keep from straining the operator (me), I mix only one 90-lb. bag at a time. I don't think mixing two bags at once is any faster, and I know it tires me out sooner.

After I've finished, I pour any excess concrete into a compact lump to be removed once it hardens. Then I wash out the wheelbarrow so that it's ready to work another day.

Tip: Use a piece of dry wood as a depth gauge. The water level shows clearly.

1. PUT IN THE WATER FIRST. For this size of wheelbarrow (sidebar, p. 834), add water to a depth of about 1 in. Too little water is better than too much because you always can add more later.

Add the concrete. Place the unopened bag in the water. Then use a utility knife to open the bag with a single cut along the end. Grab the bottom of the bag and tip it up so that the concrete slides out rather than pours out. This technique minimizes dust.

Continued →

5. ADD WATER IN SMALL AMOUNTS. Too much will weaken the concrete, so add a little water at a time, then mix. Aim for the texture of dry cottage cheese.

6. THE FINAL TEST. I'm done when all the concrete is wet and I've scraped the rake along the bottom and sides to remove any dry pockets. The mix passes my personal slump test when it's all wet but still firm enough for the rake's furrows to hold their shape.

3. Move the mix to where it's needed. To maneuver through tight areas without hanging up the rake, put the working end of the rake in the wheelbarrow with the handle pointing ahead.

Make a Lagoon in the Island of Concrete

4. STAND IN FRONT TO MIX. Pull the concrete to the front, and water will flow in behind it. Because I'm standing at the front of the wheelbarrow, I now can work the concrete without having the wheelbarrow move as I push back and forth. Let the water flow in after each push-and-pull stroke. Keep mixing until most of the water is absorbed.

Sturdy, Stable, and Sized Right

When it comes to wheelbarrows, bigger is not always better. A medium-size 6-cu.-ft. tray is large enough to hold as much wet concrete or rock as I can move comfortably but is not so big that it's unwieldy. I prefer a tray made of heavy-gauge steel that, unlike plastic, is not affected by UV-rays and won't crack if the temperature dips into single digits. Nice extras on any wheelbarrow are solid hardwood handles for easy gripping and anti-tilt-back supports on the feet to reduce the chance that I'll end up with a load of concrete exactly where I don't want it. All this adds up to a wheelbarrow that can take the abuse of a full-time professional. For more information, visit www .jacksonprofessional.com.

Framing a Grade-Level Deck

By Chris Ahrens

The traditional raised deck frame is a beautiful balance of structural function and adjustability. A ledger attaches through the wall sheathing and into the floor frame of the house, joists extend out from the ledger across the top of a built-up beam, and weight is transferred down support posts to footings below. The height of the deck is usually driven by the elevation of the house's floor framing, and then a set of stairs runs from the deck to the ground.

It's an easy template for any intermediate builder because it includes lots of flexibility when it comes to footing heights, post lengths, and beam leveling. It also offers plenty of underdeck access for grading and moisture management. Many builders assume that constructing a grade-level deck means shifting to a different technique—ditching the ledger and going to a freestanding structure, or swapping a carrying beam for a flush beam—but in fact, all of the traditional methods can still be used. You don't need to make drastic changes to the way the deck is assembled; you just need to modify how you tackle three of the structural components: the ledger, piers, and beam.

Working within a foot or so of ground level means that you have less room for adjustment. On the deck shown here, for instance, there wasn't enough space for posts, so the beam sits right on the footings. This single change meant that footings had to be poured level to each other and that their height couldn't be figured accurately until the ledger was set on the wall.

The Challenges Begin with the Ledger

A typical ledger-supported deck is fastened to the house at the rim joist. But to set the deck close to grade, the ledger might need to

be attached to the foundation. This involves both challenges and advantages.

To start with, fastener options will change. On solid-concrete foundations like this one, you can attach the ledger with wedge bolts or with standard bolts set in epoxy or acrylic adhesive. Gone are the days of using lag shields for ledger attachments; they aren't up to snuff for structural deck connections. You can't use wedge bolts if you're attaching to a hollow-block foundation, but adhesive anchors will do the job as long as you set them in mesh screening or tubes, which gives the adhesive solid purchase inside the hollow block.

Continued ➜

Attaching the ledger to the foundation may also mean spanning cast-in-place windows (see "Q&A," *Fine Homebuilding* #248). On this job, we had two. Your building official has the final word on this subject, as there are no deck-specific requirements in the codes. From a structural standpoint, though, this is not a major departure from standard floor framing. Building codes for floor framing allow the use of a single structural header when spanning a space of 4 ft. or less, provided the header is the same size or larger than the joists attaching to it.

Another challenge that you might encounter is how to deal with a foundation that has dips and humps on its face. Attaching a ledger to the rim joist generally goes easily because it would have been in the best interest of the framer to set that rim straight when building the first floor. By contrast, the dips and humps left in a foundation wall by its form boards aren't crucial to anybody but the deck builders trying to put a ledger onto that wall, so the concrete might be pretty out of whack.

Don't fuss with trying to get the ledger straight, though; just secure it tightly to the wall, and adjust things at the outer edge of the deck frame by letting joists run long, snapping a chalkline, and cutting the joists to an even length.

If all of this sounds like a hassle that you don't need, consider one major benefit: There's often no need to peel back siding or worry about ledger flashing—that is, unless you pulled off an old deck and had to patch in siding, as we did on this job. It's still a good idea to run flashing up under the bottom course of siding if the ledger will be set tight to the siding, but there's no need for that if the ledger is lower on the foundation wall. The only concern here is water getting behind the ledger and not being able to dry out easily. This problem is prevented by applying a bead of sealant at the joint between ledger and foundation.

The last piece of advice I have on this topic is to think ahead about how to handle the logistics of holding, aligning, tacking, and permanently fastening the ledger. Wet pressure-treated lumber is heavy, but it seems to get even heavier when you're in a crouched position trying to hold a long ledger to a snapped chalkline while freeing up one hand to fasten the board to the wall. Whenever possible, I use powder-actuated nails to tack temporary support blocks to the foundation to ease my back, free up my hands, and let me focus on positioning the ledger just right.

If you prefer, you can also tack the blocks to the wall framing above and then lift the ledger up tight to the blocks before pinning it to the foundation. This method is helpful if your deck will have a landing between the main part of the frame and the door to the house, which is the situation we had on part of this deck. In this case, we established our final height and then cut blocks from the framing lumber that would be used later for the landing, creating a sort of real-life story pole.

Whatever you do, take your time at the ledger. Installed carefully, it will make the footings, the beam, and the rest of your deck frame easier to build.

The Ledger Sets the Elevation

The ledger is not only the structural connection between the deck and the house; it's also what establishes the overall height and levelness of the entire deck frame. On this project, the 2×10 joists of the main deck frame sit just about even with the top of the foundation, and a landing framed with 2×8s sits atop the main frame, serving as a transition point between the lowered deck and the patio door.

1. Any level line will do. You don't have to bother adjusting the height of a laser to project a ledger guideline at just the right elevation. Instead, project a level line somewhere near where the ledger will attach, and then snap a line to be used as an offset benchmark for the rest of the elevations.

2. Gauge blocks guide the ledger. After determining where the ledger will attach in relation to the benchmark line, mark the offset on both ends of a pair of 2×8 cutoffs—the material that will be used to frame the landing. Align the marks on the blocks to the benchmark line, and screw them to the wall.

3. Two nails let you focus on the drilling. Lift the ledger so that it's tight against the bottom edge of the gauge blocks, and then shoot a powder-actuated nail into each end of the ledger to tack it in place. Drill a hole and set a bolt on each end of the ledger before drilling all of the other bolt holes.

4. Nuts before hammers. Use the predrilled ledger as a template for boring the holes in the concrete. But before whacking the wedge anchors into place, put a washer and a nut onto each bolt. A hammer can damage a bolt's leading threads and make it impossible to get the nut started if it's not already in place. Give the nut enough spins to ensure that it won't be hit by the hammer.

Ledger Fastening by the Code

5½-in. min. for 2×8
6½-in. min. for 2×10
7½-in. min. for 2×12

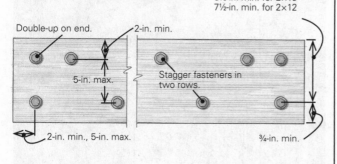

Double-up on end.

2-in. min.

5-in. max.

Stagger fasteners in two rows.

2-in. min., 5-in. max.

¾-in. min.

Dealing with a Dropped Deck

Attaching a deck ledger to concrete rather than the house's framing can mean dealing with some new challenges. The most common ones I've found are jogs in the foundation that aren't square, concrete walls that aren't straight, and basement windows that are in the ledger's path.

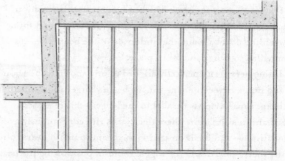

Out-Of-Square Corners
If the deck will wrap around corners or jogs in the foundation, check the foundation corners for square before setting the ledger. If you simply follow the jogs of the foundation, you could end up with an out-of-square frame.

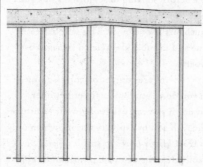

Wavy Walls
Always knock off excess concrete left by the form ties to help ensure that the ledger lies flat against the wall. Even then, the ledger might not be perfectly flat. If you try to set joists cut to size, the opposite ends won't line up. Instead, let the joists run long over the beam. Before attaching the rim, snap a straight cutline, and trim the joists evenly.

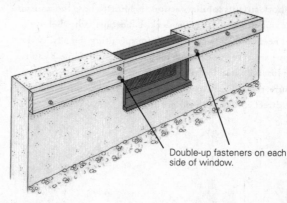

Double-up fasteners on each side of window.

Basement Windows
As long as the building official approves your plan, you can span the ledger right over small basement windows. In these cases, double-up the ledger fasteners on each side of the opening, holding them back from the window frames by about 3 in.

Continued ➡

Piers Are Hard to Get Perfect

When digging 42-in.-deep holes 7 ft. apart in rocky soil, then placing footing tubes in a straight line and filling them with concrete to the same finished height, there are any number of ways for mistakes to creep in. It's important to aim for perfection, but it's crucial to understand how to deal with problems.

If piers aren't poured level to one another, the only option is to find the highest pier and then shim under the beam on the lower ones to meet the same finished height. In this situation, I still anchor the post bases to the concrete, but then I add shims between the post base and the underside of the beam after it's been nailed together and set in place.

If the piers aren't perfectly aligned to one another, then you have to find a new centerline for the beam. Forget about whether the beam runs perfectly parallel to the ledger—this really isn't important in a situation where deck joists run continuously over a beam anyway—and focus on setting the beam so that it bears fully on the piers. This desire for wiggle room in positioning the beam is why I use 12-in.-dia. footing tubes, even if I can get away with smaller ones, and why I opt for bolt-down post bases rather than the anchors that are cast in place.

The last thing to check before starting to set joists is that your site is graded and detailed to deal with moisture. A deck set low to the ground won't have much airflow below it. This will increase the risk of rot in the frame and of moisture-related issues above it, such as cupped deck boards.

The basics of moisture control are simple: Start by sloping the ground for drainage; you don't want water to settle under your deck. After that, put down several inches of gravel. Moisture wicks up to the surface through soil by capillary action, which only works when water can go from larger pores to smaller ones. Such a path is found easily in soil. Gravel creates a layer of larger pores that short-circuits capillary action, helping to keep the moisture in the soil and away from the deck. Landscape fabric below the gravel keeps dirt out and weeds from sprouting. Finally, never let any part of the deck frame touch the ground. Unless you're using lumber rated for ground contact—a rating that common pressure-treated lumber does not carry—the wood is not meant to be in direct contact with the ground.

Calculate Pier Heights

The height of concrete piers isn't crucial on a raised deck, because leveling the beam is a matter of adjusting the length of each post running between pier and beam. But for a grade-level deck, where the beam is set right on post bases anchored to the top of the concrete piers, there is far less room for error.

USE THE TOP TO FIND THE BOTTOM. Align a laser to the top edge of the fastened ledger, and then use a story pole to measure down the footing tubes to determine the finished height of each concrete pier.

NAILS MARK THE POUR. Rather than cutting the tubes at the finished height before pouring concrete, poke nails through the cardboard to serve as height indicators.

Build the Beam in Place

It may be only inches from the ground, but the carrying beam in a grade-level deck does the same job as a structural beam 10 ft. overhead. It should be built strong, set level, and protected against rot.

ALIGN AND FASTEN. One person holds the two halves of the beam so that the tops are in alignment before the second person nails them together. Building codes recommend the use of 10d threaded nails set in two staggered rows, with 16 in. between nails. The author nails more liberally.

PROTECT THE SEAM. The joint between pieces of lumber in a built-up beam is a notorious trap for water and debris, and will eventually lead to damage, even with pressure-treated lumber. A strip of self-adhered flashing is a cheap weapon in the fight against the elements.

Straight Trumps Parallel

It's not crucial for the beam to be exactly parallel to the ledger and the deck rim; it just has to be straight and to land fully on the piers. With the ideal beam centerline (red) marked on the two end piers, stretch a chalkline across the row of footings to visualize the centerline of the other post bases. Before snapping the chalkline, adjust the two ends of the line either in or out to be sure that each post base will bear fully on its pier.

Don't Forget the Shims and Spacers

Post bases are designed to be used with 4×4 or 6×6 posts, so two- and three-ply built-up beams require wood or plywood spacers installed on one side at each pier.

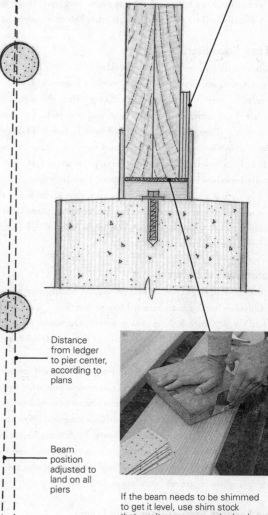

Distance from ledger to pier center, according to plans

Beam position adjusted to land on all piers

If the beam needs to be shimmed to get it level, use shim stock that won't compress under load and won't deteriorate from rot or rust. Galvanized metal tie plates (sometimes called strap ties) are a good option and can be bent in half for extra thickness.

Continued →

Better Ways to Frame a Deck

By John Spier

The wood frame of a deck leads a hard life. Without the protection of roof or walls, a deck frame is completely exposed to the weather. Though subjected to heavy loads, a wood deck is supported by just a few posts or piers instead of a solid foundation. And it's a rare homeowner who gives a second thought to maintaining a deck once it has been built. In spite of all this, a deck is expected to be safe and attractive, and to last as long as the house that it's hanging from.

These goals aren't unreasonable if you pay attention to the details and materials that I'll explain in this article. Although the deck featured here is framed against a new addition, these details work equally well when a new deck is added to an existing house.

Off to a Good Start

I've been building houses on Block Island, R.I., for almost 20 years, and unless otherwise requested, I frame decks with pressure-treated lumber, which stands up well to the rigors of weather. I use straight material free of major defects. For fasteners, I prefer hot-dipped galvanized nails driven by hand. The deck ledgers attach with galvanized bolts and lags. I use gun-driven nails only to tack framing in place until permanent fasteners are installed, such as when nailing the spacers to the ledger.

Laying out and installing piers is an article all by itself, so I'll start with the assumption that the piers are in place (and in the right place) with metal post bases installed. A quick check confirms these facts before I start.

Waterproof, then Frame

Before the ledger goes on, I waterproof the house sheathing with an adhesive-backed membrane. I like to use Grace Ice & Water Shield (W.R. Grace & Co.; www.graceconstruction.com). The membrane goes on well above the top of the deck ledger and runs 6 in. or so past the end.

Above the deck, the housewrap has to overlap the membrane and flashing, but below the ledger, the membrane must overlap the housewrap. If the housewrap hasn't been installed (as in this case), I score the membrane's peel-off backing and leave about 3 in. along the bottom of the membrane so that the housewrap can be tucked under at a later date. A combination of careful detailing and high-quality flashing materials completes the waterproofing measures (drawing p. 842).

Two Ledgers Protect House and Frame

The actual deck framing starts with a ledger securely fastened to the house. For decks less than 8 ft. wide, a single ledger may suffice, but for most decks, I prefer a double ledger that's fastened to the house with through-bolts and lag screws. The two-ledger system lets me attach the deck board nearest the house without perforating the flashing.

I establish a level line for the ledger based on the floor inside the house. Installing the deck 3 in. to 4 in. below the floor level keeps water and debris away from the door threshold and makes a comfortable step into the house. Holding a level in the window openings near each end of the deck, I measure down, make marks on the membrane, and then snap a chalkline for the top of the primary ledger. A few nails hold this ledger in place until the bolts and the lags can be installed.

Pressure-treated plywood spacers separate the two ledgers. I make the spacers about 3 in. wide and ½ in. shorter than the width of the ledger (9-in. spacers for 9½-in.-wide 2×10 ledgers). The top of each spacer is pointed to shed water. I install the spacers 32 in. o.c. Because the spacer layout is also the layout for the bolts and lags, I plan for the spacers to fall between the deck joists and between the floor joists in the house. I tack the spacers to the first ledger with a couple of nails in opposite corners where I won't drill into them later.

The secondary ledger is laid out for both the bolts and the deck joists. Before the ledger goes up, I counterbore each through-bolt and lag location so that the washer and bolt stay below the surface of the ledger and away from any water running off the deck. The secondary ledger then nails to the first at every spacer, with just enough strategically placed nails to hold it in place until the bolts can be installed. At this point, I drill and insert one bolt in every other layout location to keep the ledgers

Waterproof First

Adhesive-backed membrane applied to the wall sheathing protects the house by isolating the deck ledger. The membrane backing is scored carefully; a narrow strip left in place allows the housewrap to tuck underneath the membrane later (top photo).

The floor of the house determines the level of the deck, so one person measures down to the floor on the inside while another measures to the top of the framing (bottom photo). A snapped line guides ledger placement.

in place while the rest of the framing process continues.

6×6 Posts and a Double Rim Joist Add Strength

Once the ledgers are installed, I turn to the posts that support the opposite side of the deck. The posts fit into metal post bases bolted to the piers. On occasion, I've used custom-fabricated stainless-steel bases, but I usually use Simpson Strong Tie ABU66 (www.strongtie.com). The post bases provide a secure connection, so the piers hold the deck down as well as up.

A common choice for deck posts is 4×4 stock, but I prefer 6×6s, which can be notched to hold a double rim joist and still stay strong enough to support the deck railing. To get the length of the first post, I level over from the top of the ledger and measure down to the post base.

After squaring the bottom of the post, I transfer the measurement to locate the notch. Corner posts are notched on two adjacent sides, while the notch runs along only one side of intermediate posts. I first cut the top and bottom of each notch at the proper depth. Then I plunge-cut the edges of the notch. A rap with a framing hammer knocks out the waste, and I clean up the corners with a sharp chisel.

While the posts are resting on sawhorses, I cut the tops, using the railing, trim, and framing details to establish the length. Because 6×6 posts tend to look massive, I often soften the edges with routed chamfers.

Inner rim joists are installed first. Before setting the first post in place, I cut the inner rim joist for that end of the deck. The rim joist attaches to the double ledger at the house and slips into the notch on the corner post. After starting a few nails to hold the rim joist in place, I adjust the post base until the post is plumb in both directions. When I'm satisfied, I drive the nails home. Then I square the rim joist to the ledger using a large measured triangle, such as a 6-8-10, and brace it in position.

With the first post braced plumb and square, I move to the post on the opposite corner of the deck. I connect the first corner post to the opposite corner post with a long 2×10 for the inner rim joist. This rim joist holds the post plumb in one direction, while a regular joist keeps it plumb in the other direction.

This is a good place to explain that this deck wraps around the addition with 45° corners, so instead of framing for a 90° corner with a single post, I used two posts to form the 45° angle. I modified the notches for these posts to hold the 45° rim joist.

For the intermediate post between the corner posts, I simply measure down from the rim joist to the post base for the height of the notch. If the distance between posts cannot be spanned with a single length of framing, I stretch a taut string between the posts and measure down. As each intermediate post slips into place, I install a regular joist nearby to hold the rim joist straight and the post plumb.

Continued ➔

Install a Two-Layer Ledger

A double ledger allows for a strong frame and an impenetrable flashing system that protects the house (drawing below). Nails hold the first ledger in place until the bolts and lags are installed later. The plywood spacers come next, made with pointed tips to shed water (1).

Before the secondary ledger is installed, counterbore holes for two bolts and a lag screw are drilled at each spacer location (2). With the secondary ledger held in place by nails, one person bores through the framing members, and bolts attach the ledger assembly to the house (3).

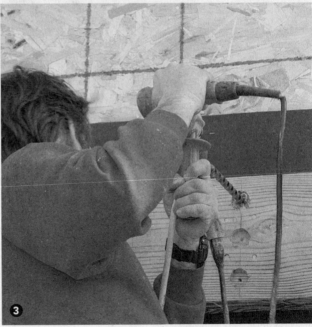

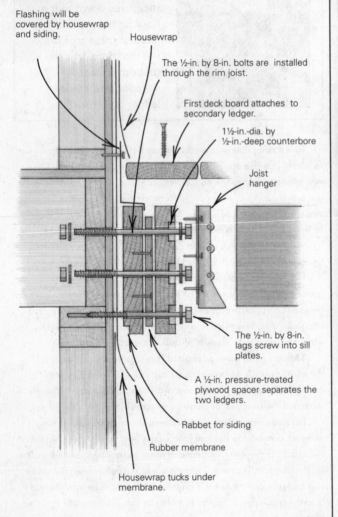

Flashing will be covered by housewrap and siding.

Housewrap

The ½-in. by 8-in. bolts are installed through the rim joist.

First deck board attaches to secondary ledger.

1½-in.-dia. by ½-in.-deep counterbore

Joist hanger

The ½-in. by 8-in. lags screw into sill plates.

A ½-in. pressure-treated plywood spacer separates the two ledgers.

Rabbet for siding

Rubber membrane

Housewrap tucks under membrane.

Prep the Posts

Leveling over from the ledger determines the length of the posts (1). Instead of rolling each post to square the bottom, line up the framing square underneath the post and draw the line with the pencil out of sight (2). Cut the top and bottom of the notch first, then plunge-cut along the edges (3). A routed chamfer softens the edges of the 6×6 posts (4).

LONGER LEVEL. I use this handy level in all phases of house framing. For deck framing, the level extends up to 13 ft., making it useful for plumbing tall posts or for leveling over from a ledger to a pier. Extendable Level by Plumb-It (www.plumb-it.com).

BIGGER SAW. My brother-in-law is a timber framer who works on our crew frequently. His big circular saw cuts to a 3¾-in. depth, which lets me work on 6×6 posts without having to dig out my handsaw. Milwaukee 10¼-in. circular saw (Part No. 6460; www.milwaukeetools.com).

Joists Are Nailed Twice

If the outside walls of the house are relatively straight and the corner posts are the same distance from the house, I cut all the deck joists to the same length. I reject stock that's excessively crowned or bowed. I mark crowns on all the joists and set them where they can be accessed easily.

Joists have to be installed with proper hangers, and in an ideal world, you would set the hangers first, drop in the joists, and nail them off. But even the best grades of framing material vary too much in width for this approach. So I nail the joists in place first and then install the hangers. Following those steps keeps the tops of the joists aligned properly with the tops of the ledger and rim joists. With just the inner rim joist in place, I can drive nails directly into the joists to secure them. A toenail on each side holds each joist in place at the ledger end.

Once the joists are in place, I check the posts with a level, casting an eye along the perimeter to make sure everything is straight. Then one crew member tacks the hangers in place with the integral tabs on them; another follows with a pneumatic positive-placement nailer. We finish installing the ledger by drilling and driving through-bolts and lags. If the deck is large, I break out an automotive pneumatic nut driver, which makes quick work of the bolts and lags.

The last step is installing the outer rim joist. For the strongest assembly, I offset any butt joints from the joints in the inner rim joist. On this deck, the outer rim joist was also the finished surface, so I chose the nicest-looking stock and mitered the corners for a more finished look.

Although the frame is now ready for the decking, I often cover the joists with plywood while the project is under way. As with the finished floors inside, I try to install the decking after the heaviest work has been done to keep it looking nice.

Continued ➡

Square the Corners

Notches in the 6×6 posts keep the double rim joists flush with the outside of the posts (drawing below). The first rim joist connects the corner post to the ledger and holds the post plumb (1). After the joist is checked for level (2), it is held square while a diagonal brace is nailed into place. Another rim joist helps to establish the opposite corner (3), which is checked for square with a diagonal measurement and secured temporarily with a 2×4 brace (4).

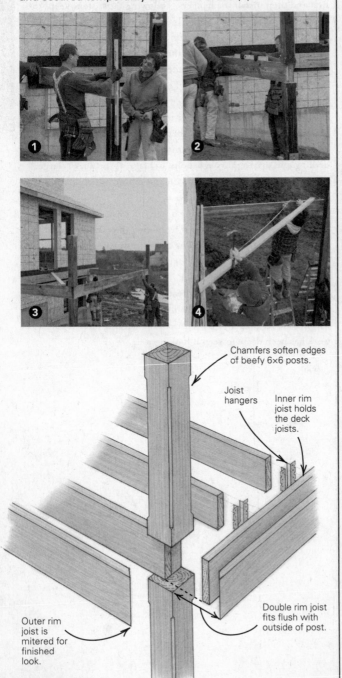

Chamfers soften edges of beefy 6×6 posts.

Joist hangers

Inner rim joist holds the deck joists.

Double rim joist fits flush with outside of post.

Outer rim joist is mitered for finished look.

Finish the Frame

With the inner rim joist set around the perimeter, the tops of the deck joists align with the rim, and nails through the rim hold them in place until the hangers can be installed (1). The ledger end of each joist is toenailed. For this deck, the outer rim joist is the finished face, so the best-looking stock is used. Mitered corners create a more finished look (2).

ACCURATE NAILER. The most tedious part of deck building is putting in joist hang-ers. On the first job, the Paslode nailer paid for itself in time saved. Boredom relief was a bonus. Paslode Positive Placement Framing Nailer.

FASTER WRENCH. Whenever I have a lot of lags to drive, my impact wrench comes to the rescue of my bruised knuckles. Porter-Cable ½-in. pneumatic impact wrench (Part No. PT502; www.porter-cable.com).

Framing a Deck with Steel

By Robert Shaw

My company focuses on building high-quality decks. Over the years, one of our biggest issues had been the quality of the pressure-treated lumber available for framing. The joists weren't uniform in depth, and always twisted and warped as they dried.

When I heard about light-gauge steel deck framing in 2006, I was impressed by its apparent advantages: It's light, straight, and uniform in size. Still, the available information was limited, and I spent a few more years sorting through wet, heavy, pressure-treated framing lumber, culling out bad boards, crowning joists, sorting joists by variation in depth, planing the joists after installation, and trying my best to build a perfectly flat frame, only to come back the next day to more warped joists.

In 2009, I decided to give steel framing a shot. I faced three main hurdles, however: dealing with building departments that were used to wood framing, finding a supplier, and learning how to work with steel. Once I overcame these hurdles, steel's advantages made it a no-brainer for me, even though it costs more per piece than lumber. Despite steel's higher cost per piece, on a high-quality project with synthetic or hardwood decking and a manufactured rail system, the framing is a relatively small part of the whole cost.

Although it's lighter than wood, steel offers greater spans in smaller profiles than wood, allowing for more-flexible designs and fewer footings, which can compensate for some of steel's higher cost. Steel is rotproof (although it can corrode), noncombustible, termite proof, and free of chemicals. It can be ordered in custom lengths to minimize field cuts, and any scrap is easily recycled.

First Hurdle: The Building Department

Even though the International Residential Code (IRC) devotes page after page to steel framing, it's much more common in commercial buildings than in houses. Most building departments aren't used to the idea of a steel-framed deck and so may be somewhat resistant. Despite the depth of coverage the IRC gives to light-gauge steel framing, most of it is specific to house walls, floors, and roofs, not to decks.

I've found that talking face to face with inspectors helps the process along best. Bring along some information (including this article) so that you can show them what you're talking about. Still, the line you'll probably hear is "I can approve this only with an engineer's design stamp."

If this happens, find an engineer who specializes in light commercial construction, because he or she most likely will be familiar with the use of light-gauge steel. Once again, have some information to present. If you demonstrate a thorough

Continued ➝

understanding of steel framing and present high-quality, detailed drawings, an engineer might be willing simply to review and stamp your plans for a small fee. The big details on the plans won't be much different from those you'd see for a wood deck; there are still posts, beams, and joists. The main differences are in the details for fastening and blocking.

Second Hurdle: Finding a Supplier

Your local lumberyard or home center probably won't have a clue about light-gauge steel. The place to buy light-gauge steel is usually a drywall-supply house that also deals in steel studs. Knowing this, I contacted drywall-supply houses and asked about material for decks. I got confused salespeople on the phone and funny looks at the store.

I changed my approach. Rather than explaining that I was building a deck and asking if they could supply the framing, I simply started using nomenclature from the engineer's plans. Once I learned how to speak the language, buying steel became a lot simpler.

Steel joists are technically referred to as studs. Studs fit inside tracks, which are supplied just slightly wider than the studs to ensure a proper fit. (Because of how I use these studs, I refer to them here as joists; when ordering, though, I call them studs to avoid confusing the supplier.) Like framing lumber, steel framing is sold in certain depths, but it's also sold in a variety of

flange widths, which is sort of like being able to buy 3x and 4x lumber as well as 2x lumber. Steel also comes in various gauges, or thicknesses. (For more information, go to the Steel Stud Manufacturer's Association website: ssma.com.)

Steel used outside must be galvanized. Many galvanization levels are available; G60, G90, and G135 are typical. The number indicates the ounces of zinc applied per square foot of material. For example, G60 has 0.6 oz. of zinc per sq. ft. (0.3 oz. on each side), while G135 has 1.35 oz. per sq. ft. This is the same system used for framing hardware intended for wood decks, which comes with a G185 coating. Before 2004, when the standard wood preservative was CCA, G60 and G90 coatings were commonly used on hardware. The G185 standard is a response to the greater corrosiveness of the chemicals that replaced CCA. Because it doesn't contact treated lumber, steel framing doesn't require the same galvanization level as hardware. Where I build, G90 is sufficient. If you live in a wetter environment or near a road that's treated with deicing salt, consider thicker galvanization. If you live on the seacoast, steel framing may not be acceptable at all.

Steel studs typically come with holes already punched for wiring and plumbing. Order yours without them. They're unsightly, unnecessary on a deck, and could line up with a spot where a screw is required.

Joists + Tracks = Beams

Light-gauge steel is identified in dimensions like this: 800S200-54. That piece is an 8-in. stud (or joist) with a 2-in. flange made from 54-mil-thick (or 16-ga.) material. A piece identified as 800T200-54 is the same, except it's a track. The edges of a track's flange are straight, not curled like a stud's. Tracks are sized so that studs fit between their flanges.

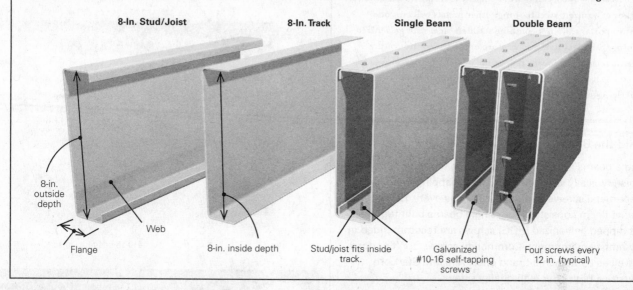

8-In. Stud/Joist

8-In. Track

Single Beam

Double Beam

8-in. outside depth

Web

Flange

8-in. inside depth

Stud/joist fits inside track.

Galvanized #10-16 self-tapping screws

Four screws every 12 in. (typical)

Begin with the Ledger

The ledger on a steel-framed deck is a piece of track that's bolted or screwed to the house. Lay out the ledger so that the bolts don't interfere with joist connections. Unlike with a wood ledger, holes have to be drilled in steel even for structural screws. Drill ⅛-in. starter holes on layout, then switch to a step drill and enlarge the holes to fit the fasteners. After all the holes have been drilled, spray the exposed steel with Rustoleum cold galvanizing compound.

DRILL HOLES IN THE LEDGER. Lay out the holes for the mounting screws so they don't interfere with the joist layout. Start the holes with a ⅛-in. twist bit, and finish with a step drill marked at the desired hole diameter.

JUST LIKE CUTTING WOOD. Cut steel with a circular saw. The author likes Freud's Diablo steel blades. The hot metal chips produced call for full-face protection.

SCREW IT UP. Just like a wood deck ledger, steel ledgers must be properly bolted to the house framing and installed level.

DON'T CREATE OPPORTUNITIES FOR RUST. Coat all cuts and holes with cold galvanizing spray.

GRINDER FOR THE NOTCHES. An inexpensive abrasive cutoff wheel in a die grinder makes short work of little cuts.

Continued ➔

Third Hurdle: Putting It Together

There's a lot about framing a steel deck that's no different from framing a wood deck. The footings are the same, although there may be fewer of them. Ledger flashing is the same, with one caveat: If your flashing will contact the framing, use either vinyl or galvanized-steel flashing; other metals will corrode. Most important, do not combine stainless steel with galvanized framing. Stainless steel and zinc are on opposite ends of the galvanic scale. This means that in the presence of moisture, the zinc galvanization will rapidly oxidize and will expose the underlying steel, which then will rust.

Build the Beam

Single beams are built up by screwing together a track and a joist, typically with ¾-in. #10-16 self-tapping galvanized sheet-metal screws through the flanges every 12 in. A double beam consists of two single beams built together. Hot-dipped galvanized (HDG) screws are recommended in any moist environment. Commodity screws don't perform as well as some name-brand ones. Hilti and Starborn Industries both offer high-quality screws.

BUILD BEAMS STRAIGHT. Sight the length of a track to be sure it's supported flat and straight before joining it with a joist into a beam.

Building Beams from Tracks and Joists

Beams are made by combining tracks and joists. A single beam consists of one joist nested inside one track and typically fastened with one screw through the flanges every 12 in. A double beam is made by screwing two joists together back to back, then adding a track on each side.

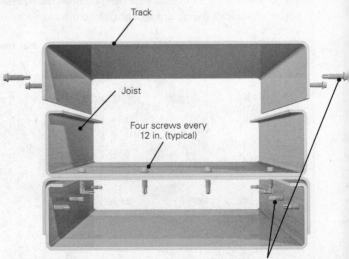

Track

Joist

Four screws every 12 in. (typical)

#10-16 self-tapping screws

A JOIST AND A TRACK MAKE A BEAM. Join the two nested members with self-tapping sheet-metal screws through their flanges.

WOOD POSTS ARE EASIER. In most cases, it's faster to notch and bolt a wood post to a steel beam than it is to assemble a steel post from tracks and joists.

Install Joists and Blocking

Without help, steel joists aren't as laterally stable as wood joists. So that they don't tip under load, steel joists require blocking (joist stock) where they bear on a beam. Depending on the span, additional blocking may be required at the center of the deck. You usually only need to block every other bay because each piece of blocking stabilizes the two adjacent joists. Alternating the joists so that flat faces flat simplifies blocking. Where the blocking is over a beam, add two screws through the flange of the block into the beam below. Joists attach to the ledger with standard Simpson Strong-Tie or USP Structural Connectors framing-angle hardware. Steel joists are dead straight, so there's no need to crown them before installation. Fastening joists to a beam takes one screw through the flange and into the beam below. The rim is a piece of track that fits right over the ends of the joists and is then screwed through its top and bottom flanges.

ALTERNATE SIDES. Face each pair of joists away from each other so that the flat sides face every other bay. This is to simplify blocking installation.

BLOCK EVERY OTHER BAY. Each block stabilizes two joists.

STANDARD FRAMING ANGLES JOIN JOIST TO LEDGER. Fasten the framing angle to both members with self-tapping sheet-metal screws.

SCREW JOISTS TO BEAM. Connect a joist to a beam with a screw between the flanges.

BLOCK BETWEEN THE JOISTS. Self-tapping screws fasten framing angles to blocking and to the joists. Two additional screws secure the blocking to the beam.

SCREW RIM TO JOISTS. Sight along the rim as you screw it to the joists to keep the edge of the deck straight.

Continued ➔

Custom Details Make a Better Deck

By Michael Ayers

Decks often are referred to as outdoor rooms, and this added living space can receive as much furnishing attention as any room in the house. These outdoor rooms are subject to outdoor weather, though, which affects durability and usability. Most home-owners accept the fact that they won't be able to use an outdoor room in December, but they expect to be able to use the deck full time in August. Even in cold climates like Montana's, the August sun gets hot. Shady seating can be provided with store-bought chairs, benches, and umbrellas, but a more elegant option is to build in the seating and the shading. A pergola is an attractive way to create shade, and as long as you're building one, why not add some benches to sit on underneath?

Freestanding Decks Don't Cause Rot

One of the most difficult aspects of decks is how to attach them to a house without allowing water to infiltrate house framing. When my crew and I dug in to the house featured here, we found considerable rot in the rim joist and sill plate where moisture had been wicking in through an old porch for years. Rather than devising a complicated strategy for attaching and flashing the new deck ledger through the stucco siding, my crew and I thought, "Why not make the deck freestanding?"

By simply adding a couple of beams and their associated posts and piers, we could eliminate the need for flashing a ledger altogether. This design had the added benefit of eliminating joist hangers because the deck joists sit atop site-built beams bolted through 6×6 posts. And because we had called in an excavator to dig the holes for the piers (the frost line in Montana is about 3½ ft. below the surface), adding a few more holes didn't add much cost.

Posts Must Be Aligned Perfectly

Taking time to ensure a good layout is the key to making the job easier as you move from framing the deck to building the pergola and the benches. Some deck posts in this design run continuously through the deck and support the bench and the pergola above, one runs through the deck to support the bench framing, and the others support only floor framing.

Because of this design, the posts must be placed thoughtfully, and they must be aligned perfectly. Thoughtful post placement means that they won't interfere with windows, doors, or travel paths. Equally important, they need to be spaced to adequately support the floor beams. Post placement starts with excavation, but you have opportunities to refine their position: when setting the concrete tubes in the holes and with adjustable post bases.

Beams Are Built in Place

In Montana's high mountain desert, using pressure-treated

lumber for durable decks is unnecessary except in ground-contact situations. If the deck is close to the ground, we use pressure-treated lumber for the floor framing, but not for the visible wood. On this deck, the posts, the benches, and the pergola are fir. The framing is pressure-treated, and the decking is composite (www.trex.com). The post bases elevate the posts enough to keep moisture from wicking into them.

Because the posts are finish work, they need to look good, and it's much easier to cut, sand, and detail them while they're on sawhorses. To calculate post length, I use a rotary laser to shoot grade on the bases. I establish the high point as the benchmark, then figure out how much I need to add to each post to keep the tops level. It's not imperative that the tops be perfectly level because they'll be integrated into a pergola frame, but they should be within ¼ in.

The more important aspect of shooting grade is beam placement. For a grade-level deck such as this one, the elevations can be tricky. The decking should be about 1 in. below the door threshold, and the beams should be above the ground. To squeeze a beam and floor joists into the space between threshold and ground, we used 2×10s for the beam and 2×8s for the floor joists. Along with 1-in. decking, this puts the beam 1 in. to 2 in. above the ground. Post placement and joist spacing need to be part of the equation when choosing lumber dimensions, so consult

The Design Revolves Around a Post

Anchored to concrete piers, the tallest posts extend through the deck, bench, and pergola; beams are bolted to the posts to support deck joists, bench framing, and pergola rafters. This freestanding design eliminates the need for a ledger. Because the posts are central to the design, alignment and plumb installation are critical.

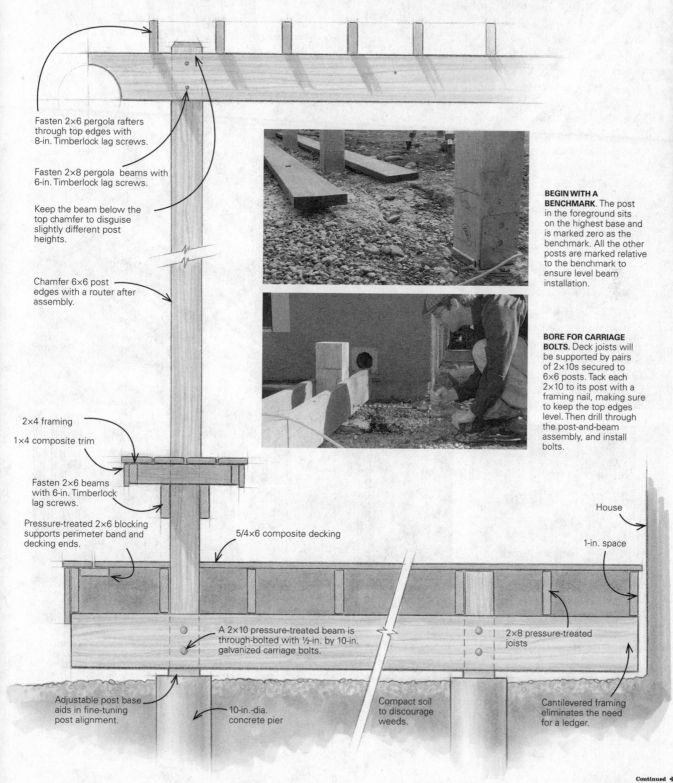

Fasten 2×6 pergola rafters through top edges with 8-in. Timberlock lag screws.

Fasten 2×8 pergola beams with 6-in. Timberlock lag screws.

Keep the beam below the top chamfer to disguise slightly different post heights.

Chamfer 6×6 post edges with a router after assembly.

2×4 framing

1×4 composite trim

Fasten 2×6 beams with 6-in. Timberlock lag screws.

Pressure-treated 2×6 blocking supports perimeter band and decking ends.

5/4×6 composite decking

A 2×10 pressure-treated beam is through-bolted with ½-in. by 10-in. galvanized carriage bolts.

Adjustable post base aids in fine-tuning post alignment.

10-in.-dia. concrete pier

Compact soil to discourage weeds.

House

1-in. space

2×8 pressure-treated joists

Cantilevered framing eliminates the need for a ledger.

BEGIN WITH A BENCHMARK. The post in the foreground sits on the highest base and is marked zero as the benchmark. All the other posts are marked relative to the benchmark to ensure level beam installation.

BORE FOR CARRIAGE BOLTS. Deck joists will be supported by pairs of 2×10s secured to 6×6 posts. Tack each 2×10 to its post with a framing nail, making sure to keep the top edges level. Then drill through the post-and-beam assembly, and install bolts.

Continued ➜

Frame the Floor and Then Slide It Over to the House

FACE-NAILING IS FASTER THAN JOIST HANGERS.
Because the rim joist isn't attached to the house, I eliminated the need for 20 joist hangers, which saved a lot of time. I frame the floor far enough away from the house to provide nail-gun clearance. Then, with some assistance, I slide the deck into place.

TOENAIL JOISTS TO BEAMS. Straight joists mean straight lines of screws in the decking. After toenailing the joists on the layout, I add blocks around the posts to catch the ends of decking boards.

CUT THE JOISTS WITH DECK BOARDS IN MIND.
I let the outboard ends of the joists run long. Then I calculate the depth the deck needs to be to finish with a full-width deck board. This saves time and improves the deck's finished appearance. After snapping a line to establish uniform joist length, I square it with a Speed Square and cut the joists in place.

applicable span tables.

With a felt-tip pen, I mark the highest post zero; this is the benchmark. The other bases are marked with the fraction of an inch that they differ from the benchmark (+⅛, +¼). When nailing the posts into the bases, it's the last chance to align them accurately. It's also a good idea to plumb them at this point; temporary braces can help to hold them in place.

To find the top of the beam, hook a tape measure to the bottom of the post, and add the fraction written on the post to the beam height (9¼ in. in this case). I tack the beams to the posts with a framing nail, making sure the two-piece beams are level to each other. Then I drill through each post and beam with a ⅝-in.-dia. auger bit. Carriage bolts tie everything together. It's a good idea to double-check that the posts are plumb and spaced properly before you really tighten the carriage bolts and move on to floor framing.

Spread the joists on layout atop the beams, and attach the rim closest to the house first. With that end of the floor framed, I slide the frame in place, leaving it about 1 in. from the house, and toenail the joists to the beams.

Next, I cut the joists to length, but not just any length. Instead, I calculate the number of deck boards needed to cover the distance, including trim board, gaps, and overhang. This way, I won't have to rip the last deck board where it meets the house. It takes about the same amount of time to calculate this number as it does to rip the final board, and it looks a lot better. After cutting the joists, I attach the opposing rim and any blocking needed to support the deck boards around the posts and along their ends where they butt into the perimeter band.

Space the Decking Consistently

With the deck framed, I square up the outside corner, apply a fascia board to the deck's rim, and lay deck boards along the perimeter, mitering the corners. I overhang this "picture frame" past the trim by about 1 in.

Because the joists' lengths were calculated precisely to accommodate a particular number of deck boards, it's important to gap the deck boards consistently as I work back toward the house. As with other composite-decking materials, Trex requires specific spacing between boards and at butt joints because the material shrinks and swells with temperature variations. The gap size depends on the temperature during installation; the specs are printed on the end tags. I cut a few shims on a tablesaw to keep the gaps consistent.

To space the ends of the decking consistently away from the house, I use a scrap of ½-in. oriented strand board (OSB) as a spacer. I also check the decking as I proceed toward the house: Staying parallel to the house is important. After notching around the posts, I snap a chalkline as a guide, and when I get about halfway across the deck, I start measuring from the house to the deck boards.

This also confirms that I can finish with a full-width deck

Use Spacers to Keep the Expansion Gaps Consistent

ENDS AND EDGES NEED GAPS. Composite decking shrinks and swells with temperature variation, so gapping butt joints is necessary. I also cut spacers a little wider and narrower than the specified gaps to keep the decking parallel to the house.

TIP: Speedy screwing template. If you don't want to place screws by eye, mark your Speed Square with a felt-tip pen; slide the square along or mark the boards individually.

board. If the numbers are a little off here, I can make a correction using a larger or smaller spacer at one end or the other. Then I can phase in the correction over many boards so that it won't be as visible.

Frame the Benches and Pergola

The beams carrying the pergola are 2×8s lag-screwed to the posts with Timberlock screws (www.mcfeelys.com); the pergola rafters are 2×6s. Both framing members have decorative cuts on their

Continued ➜

Detail the Ends of the Pergola Beams and Rafters

Multiple cuts warrant a template. I detailed the ends of the beams and rafters with a simple radius cut. Because the beams are wider than the rafters, they need a slightly different radius to maintain the same proportions. Scraps of OSB make good templates. (1) Trace the outline, and rough-cut it with a jigsaw. (2) Cut a line with a razor knife to avoid tearout caused by a pattern-cutting router bit (3). The finished cut needs to be shaped with a round-over bit, then cleaned up with a sander.

ends. Square or angular cuts can be made with a circular saw or a sliding compound-miter saw. Rounded or notched details can be cut with a jigsaw and a router. When cutting 2x stock with a jigsaw, the final cut probably won't be square. I either need to clean it up with a belt sander or make a router template of ½-in. OSB. The template guides a pattern-cutting bit. At the end overhanging the house roof, I cut an angle to match the slope of the roof, leaving at least an inch of clearance off the roof shingles.

The benches are framed the same way as the deck, only on a smaller scale: a frame atop a beam bolted to posts. In this case, the beams are 2×6s attached to the posts with small lag screws. The 2×4 bench frame is built on top of the beam. The width of the frame again is set by the number of full-width deck boards that will be placed on top, which eliminates the need to rip any deck boards to fit. I wrap the bench frame with 1×4 finish trim, and then I run the decking on the benches. As with the deck boards, I picture-frame the benches, screwing the outer frame in place first, then decking the interior. This gives a finished look to the ends of the benches, capping the end cuts.

The pergola rafters are set north and south, which casts a wide afternoon shadow over the deck on hot summer days but allows sunlight into the house during cold winter months. If more shade is needed, a perpendicular layer of 1×2 material can be added to the top of the rafters.

With a couple of light fixtures mounted in the corners and a gas grill outside the kitchen door, the built-in pergola and the benches give a cozy feel to this inviting 300-sq.-ft. outdoor room.

The Benches Are Like Long, Skinny Mini-Decks

Deck boards dictate the bench width. The 2×4 bench framing should be sized to accommodate full-width deck boards, an overhang, and a 1×4 trim board. The bench's perimeter, like the deck's, is picture-framed.

Deck Refinishing

By Jim Grant

Keeping decks looking good in a sunbaked climate can be a challenge, but it provides me plenty of work as a professional deck refinisher. In San Diego, where I live and work, outdoor living space is important, and my clients expect a deck to look as good as the interior of a house. Maintaining a deck can be a huge challenge. Poorly handled cleaning or refinishing usually results in a deck that has to be redone.

I was recently called to look at a hardwood deck in Solana Beach, Calif. This deck, which was about three years old, needed a good cleaning and refinishing. In addition, black streaks emerged from every fastener on the stairs, the privacy fence, and the glass-paneled walls that protect deck occupants from coastal winds.

The stains resulted from the nails' rusting. Apparently, the builder had used galvanized nails to fasten everything but the decking. I see this black staining regularly despite the sound advice of distributors who suggest stainless-steel fasteners for tropical hardwoods. Fortunately, the deck surface was unaffected because the decking was attached with blind fasteners (ebty.com).

Begin with a Thorough Cleaning

This project was typical of the deck-refinishing work my crew undertakes. First, we clean the wood with a concentrated detergent. Then we follow up with a wood brightener. After each step, we power wash using a wide-angle (40°) nozzle.

A pressure washer in the hands of a novice can destroy landscaping, force water into a house, and ruin a wood deck. We've handled many projects where homeowners or contractors have damaged the deck surface with a power washer. Fixing the resultant gouges requires extensive sanding and sometimes new decking. Before I let new employees touch someone's deck with a pressure washer, I teach them how to feather the stream of water onto the surface when starting out and how to let the cleaning chemicals do the majority of the work. We always use a wide-angle nozzle on decking, even if it takes a little longer to get the surface clean.

On this deck, once the wood was cleaned and brightened, we turned to the rusting fasteners. To prevent water from getting into the nail holes and causing a recurrence of staining, we filled the holes with a wax-based exterior filler. We heated the filler slightly with a tea-light candle and carefully pushed it into the 400-plus holes. Minor sanding with a medium-grit sanding sponge removed the excess filler. We used a light touch, because excessive sanding can result in a noticeable change in the wood texture that shows up later when the deck is finished.

Apply the Finish

With the surface clean and free of rust stains, it was time to apply the coating. Choosing a coating can be confusing to homeowners and contractors alike, and mistakes in application can result in serious problems, including peeling from improper adhesion, blotchiness from improper surface prep, or the use of too much finish. Usually, the coating has to be chemically removed and the deck recoated.

I've done my own testing on 50 products over the past 23 years and continue to test finishes. For this deck, I used an oil-based stain for hardwood decking from Superdeck (superdeck. com). This coating enhances the natural look of the wood with penetrating oils that protect the surface and prevent mildew and water damage. The high density of hardwood decking makes using the proper application method important. We use several different types of applicator pads and make long strokes to avoid leaving lap marks and applying too much coating. After the coating has fully penetrated (usually in 10 to 15 minutes), we use a lint-free cloth to remove the excess material.

For tight corners and other hard-to-reach areas, we use a natural-bristle brush and then wipe away the excess coating with a lint-free cloth. We also watch the amount of absorption, because the density of individual boards can vary. As a result, some boards need more finish than others.

Start with a Good Cleaning

SPRAY ON THE CLEANER. Starting with vertical surfaces and working from the top down, apply deck cleaner. Allow it to work for 10 to 15 minutes.

SCRUB THE SURFACE. Moving in the direction of the wood grain, use a stiff-bristle brush on a telescopic pole to clean the wooden surfaces. Horizontal boards are usually the dirtiest. Use smaller handheld brushes for hard-to-reach areas.

POWER RINSE. Starting with the vertical surfaces and working from the top down, rinse the deck clean with a pressure washer equipped with a wide-angle (40°) nozzle. Nozzles with a tighter spray pattern can strip out soft areas, leaving gouges.

Continued →

Use Brightener to Make Old Wood Look New

BRIGHTEN THE CLEAN WOOD. After allowing the wood to dry, apply an oxalic-acid-based wood brightener to all surfaces. Mix 1 gal. of the brightener with about 3 gal. of water. The author uses a homemade spray rig to apply it (sidebar below). Allow the brightener to work for about 15 minutes, then scrub the wood with a stiff brush and rinse it with a pressure washer.

SCRUB AGAIN. Once the wood brightener has worked for about 15 minutes, scrub the surfaces with stiff-bristle brushes. A long handle provides additional leverage.

RINSE CLEAN. A gas-powered pressure washer equipped with a wide-angle (40°) nozzle rinses and cleans the surface without damage. The pressure washer doesn't apply the two cleaning chemicals; it sprays only water.

Spray It on, Work It in, Wipe It Off

ONE BOARD AT A TIME. To prevent lap marks, coat the deck boards with finish individually. After covering each board, stop spraying, and wipe away excess coating as necessary.

SPRAY, THEN SMOOTH. A painter's pad on a long pole helps to smooth the layer of finish applied with the sprayer. The pad works the finish into the grain and evens the application so that it's absorbed uniformly.

WIPE OFF THE EXCESS. Once the finish has had a chance to be absorbed fully by the decking (10 min.), remove the excess with a rag (small areas) or a rag-covered scrub brush (large areas).

A Better Sprayer

Frustrated with constant pumping and all-too-frequent refills when using a garden sprayer, the tool commonly used to apply cleaner and wood brightener, the author devised his own spray rig. At its heart is a small AC-powered transfer pump. The inlet has a short hose that's dunked into a bucket of cleaning solution. The outlet side has a Tee Jet spray wand (sprayingequipmentsupply.com). To make transport easier, the rig is contained in a plastic toolbox that holds the pump, cord, and inlet hose.

Tips for a Better Finish

MIX THOROUGHLY. Stir the individual cans of finish so that any settled pigments are mixed with the solvent. Mix together all the cans for a uniform color.

START AT THE TOP. The author applies the finish with a Wagner 1075 airless sprayer, but you also can use a 7-in. painting pad. Cover with canvas drop cloths any surfaces and vegetation that could be damaged from overspray.

BRUSH TIGHT SPOTS. Use a brush to cover stairs and other areas too awkward to spray. Allow the coating to penetrate for a few minutes, then wipe away the excess with a clean lint-free cloth.

USE A SMALL PAD FOR SMALL SPACES. A disposable, handheld painting pad is good for applying finish to areas too small to spray and too big to brush.

A Fix for Rusty Fasteners

Despite recommendations to use stainless-steel fasteners for hardwood decks, we often see decks built with galvanized fasteners. Unfortunately, it doesn't take long for the nails to rust, leaving black streaks that can make an otherwise beautiful deck look really bad.

In most cases, the cleaner and brightener remove the marks, but in some badly stained areas, only a sander can remove them. This is a last resort, however, because it means sanding the whole board or having a board with an inconsistent appearance between sanded and unsanded areas.

Once the black marks are gone, we fill the holes with a color-matched, wax-based wood filler. It's important to pick the right color, or the filled holes will be as obvious as the black stains.

SAND AWAY MARKS. In spots with the worst black staining, the cleaner and wood brightener are not fully effective at removing discoloration. In these spots, the only solution is to use a random-orbit sander equipped with 120-grit paper over the board.

FILL AND SMOOTH. Once a matching color has been found, the wax filler (fastcap.com) is applied with a plastic spatula included with the kit. The same tool scrapes away the excess.

Continued ➜

Deck Railings Grow Up

By Scott Gibson

Trex started a stampede of new building materials in the 1990s with the introduction of an alternative decking made from wood flour and recycled plastic. Many other manufacturers since have introduced their own composites, and low-maintenance decking options have grown to include a variety of plastics and metal. Yet the development of matching railings lagged behind. Now that's changing, too.

Wood still accounts for as much as 80% of all residential deck railings. But a number of other choices offer the same advantages that are behind the steady rise of composite decking: resistance to insects and decay, weather hardiness, and very little maintenance.

Of these low-maintenance options, wood/plastic composite railings make up a fast-growing category, but there's also aluminum-reinforced vinyl, stainless-steel cable, cellular polyvinyl chloride (PVC), molded polyurethane, and powder-coated metal. Even on the low end, wood alternatives are more expensive. PVC railings are often the most affordable, and they can be three or four times as expensive as a pressure-treated rail. At the other end of the scale, molded urethane can top $150 per running ft. for the heaviest, most elaborate styles.

Newer rail systems, however, are often easier and faster to install. At their most basic, lumberlike composite railings assemble the same way as wood. But producers have devised special clips, brackets, and templates to speed up the job. Some rail comes packaged in 6-ft. or 8-ft. ready-to-assemble kits that manufacturers say can be installed in minutes per foot.

"The more consumers are getting educated to new railings ... the more they want them," says Steve Scholl, a busy deck builder in the Detroit metro area. None of this will ever satisfy anyone who wants real wood, but to a generation with an increasing aversion to maintenance, it's very appealing.

Cable Rail: Less Is More

Cable rail is made from the same kind of wire and hardware used for sailboat rigging, and it won't block a million-dollar view.

Stainless-steel cable is typically ⅛ in. dia. for residential railings and heavier for commercial applications. The most common (and one of the strongest) is 1×19, made up of 19 individual strands of wire.

Cable railing is moderately expensive, starting at $65 to $75 per running ft. for an all-metal horizontal installation but about half of that cost when cable and fittings are combined with wood posts and top rails. Both surface-mounted and through-post cable terminations (below) are available; turnbuckles allow the cable to be tightened as needed. Keeping railing turns to a minimum will reduce hardware and installation costs.

NOTE: Prices cited in this article are from 2006.

PROS

· Unobtrusive. Won't block scenic views.

· Flexible. Can be built with a variety of wood or metal post and rail components as well as tensioning hardware.

· Cables can run horizontally or vertically.

· Glass panels can be used in some aluminum-rail systems.

CONS

· More expensive than some other options.

· Horizontal railings barred in some areas because they pose a "climbing hazard."

· Not compatible with all architectural styles.

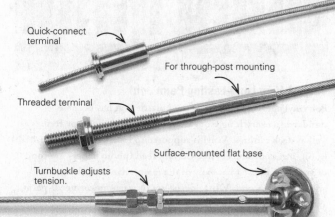

Quick-connect terminal

Threaded terminal

For through-post mounting

Surface-mounted flat base

Turnbuckle adjusts tension.

❶ STRONG AND TRANSPARENT. Custom steel posts and stainless-steel cable open the views to this lakeside deck. The posts were fabricated and designed by Keuka Studios in Honeoye Falls, N.Y. Cable assembly by Feeney.

❷ CABLE RAIL CAN BE SURFACE-MOUNTED. If you use wood, corner posts have to be sturdy. Producers usually recommend a 4×4 at minimum because the 11 cables typical for a 36-in.-high rail exert a great deal of lateral force. Railing by Atlantis.

❸ THERE'S AN UPCHARGE FOR A DIFFERENT LOOK. Vertical installations require beefy top and bottom rails as well as more cable terminations and labor. Railing by Atlantis.

Metal: Old-World Look with a Friendly Price

There is no mistaking powder-coated aluminum and steel railings for something else. These railings are not trying to look like any material other than metal.

Given the strength of metal parts, baluster and post styles tend to be thinner and less massive than other alternatives. Metal also is a versatile material that can be fabricated into many styles, from plain to ornately detailed filigree, as in the example from Anderson Welding (photo above right).

Producers point to speedy installation as another advantage. Rail sections arrive already assembled so that the installer only

has to mount the posts, cut rails to length, and attach them. Post-to-post spans of 10 ft. are possible without any intermediate supports.

Aluminum, iron, and steel railings may look the same, but it might be best to stay away from ferrous metals in saltwater areas. Although powder-coating offers good protection from the elements, even a pinhole can allow moisture below the paint film, where it will cause rust.

Basic aluminum railings are typically more expensive than vinyl but not as costly as many composites. Expect to pay about $35 to $40 per running ft.

PROS

· Quick installation.

· High strength and long unsupported spans.

· Material highly adaptable to custom shapes.

· Very low maintenance.

CONS

· Appearance may not be appropriate with some architectural styles.

· Railings made from ferrous metals can rust if finish is damaged.

DON'T LET THE CORROSION START. When bolting metal posts to the deck, use nylon washers to prevent cracking the powder coating on the mounting flange. Railing above by L&L Railings.

Continued ➡

Posts Are Still Wood

Many railing systems come with a post sleeve that fits over the 4×4, as in this Alcoa railing; the railings are attached through the sleeve into the post. Vinyl sleeves tend to be thinner-walled than composite sleeves.

Hidden Mechanicals

Rail/post connections typically are made with the help of metal brackets that are screwed through the post sleeve into the wood beneath; some models' brackets are hidden by a trim cover, as in this Genova railing.

Vinyl: A Very Long-Lasting Paint Job

Polyvinyl chloride is a widely used plastic that has become standard in everything from siding to window and door frames as well as deck railings. Vinyl is supposed to look like freshly painted wood, but as producers like CertainTeed (photo above) are fond of saying, it doesn't have any of the maintenance problems that go along with wood. Vinyl doesn't rot or warp, never needs paint, and is unaffected by insects.

Now in very wide use even on upscale houses, vinyl has done a lot to shed its image as a cheap building material. Alcoa, for example, guarantees its vinyl railing for as long as you own the house. Yet some home-owners complain that vinyl railings can be squeaky when flexed.

Vinyl railing tends to be one of the least-expensive wood alternatives and should be available for about $20 to $25 per running ft.

PROS

- Durable; very low maintenance.
- Longer unsupported rail spans than wood-plastic composites.
- Has the appearance of painted wood.
- Railing comes in kits that can be assembled quickly.

CONS

- It's still plastic, which won't appeal to all homeowners.
- Limited color selection.
- Some consider the manufacturing process environmentally hazardous.

Metal Bones.
Vinyl-rail sections typically are reinforced with aluminum or steel for added stiffness, like the Royal Crown Ltd. railing to the right. The result is a span of up to 10 ft.—and that's without any support blocks beneath the lower rail.

PROS

· Appears more wood- like than other low-maintenance options, so railings blend nicely with wood-composite decking.
· Feels more like wood than plastic railings.
· Wider color selection than vinyl.
· Unlike wood, won't split, crack, or warp.
· Trex railings can be ordered in curved sections.

CONS

· Relatively expensive.
· Because wood composites contain organic material, they can support the growth of mold.
· With the exception of the PVC-coated variety, dark colors can fade in sunlight. Effect varies by brand.
· Requires support blocks under bottom rail to prevent sagging.

Composites: A New Life for Wood Chips and Plastic Bags

Composites are a recycling success story, keeping millions of pounds of plastics per year out of landfills. Although they still make up a small slice of the deck and railing business, composite producers are elbowing their way into the market in increasing numbers.

Composites are fairly flexible—polyethylene products like Trex more so than polypropylene composites—so bottom rails must be supported by squash blocks as frequently as every 18 in. so that they don't droop.

A newer type of composite (photo right) is capped with a layer of PVC in a process that is called co-extrusion. This process gives the railing the look of a painted finish that, like solid-PVC railings, is nonporous and is not as susceptible to fading.

Composites are available as dimensional lumber that can be used to make railings conventionally or as kits that are designed to go together more quickly. Costs start at about $45 per running ft.

When it comes to assembly, site-built rails offer more options. Composite railings like the Alcoa Oasis shown above are made from solid, lumberlike stock (1) and are built the same way as wood railings. Railing kits such as Trex's co-extruded Artisan are made of preregistered and precut parts (2). They may be faster to assemble, but their design isn't as flexible in terms of baluster spacing, railing height, and other design options.

Continued ➡

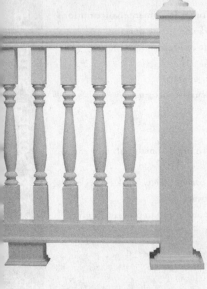

The Other Plastics: Variations on a Theme

Pricey Elegance

Molded-urethane railings are made by Fypon, which produces a line of well-known trim under the same trade name; it is the most expensive railing option I found. Prices go above $150 per running ft. for large-scale railings and oversize balusters with the proportions of carved stone. But the look is unlike just about anything else (photo left). Styles can be very ornate, better-suited to period homes than the more limited offerings in vinyl or wood composite. Rail widths range from 5 in. to 12 in.

Urethane railing components, which are reinforced with PVC pipe (photo right), are available in straight and curved sections. Newel posts also are reinforced with PVC pipe. Railings can span up to 12 ft. between posts (10 ft. for the 5-in. system) with squash blocks required below the bottom rail every 4 ft. to 5 ft. Fypon arrives primed and can be painted. It won't absorb water, crack, or rot.

As Strong as Aluminum

Fiberglass railings made by Armor-Rail (photo right) are similar in composition to a fiberglass ladder and, the manufacturer says, have about the same strength as aluminum. They are made with "pultruded" fiberglass, a process in which continuous glass strands are pulled through a die.

Posts are hollow in section with walls about ¼ in. thick. They can be installed over a 4×4 or mounted over a proprietary support (photo left) that's bolted to the deck framing.

Rail sections come completely assembled. The maximum distance between posts is 12 ft., with one squash block below the bottom rail. There are several rail and baluster styles and four colors to choose from. These railings cost more than vinyl but not as much as some composites.

Foam and Wood

Cellular PVC is a type of plastic foam that is molded into different profiles for railing parts. It's made by several companies and typically is reinforced with another material to meet code requirements for strength. Novaline's Wood Collection railings use a composite higher than most in wood-fiber content plus cellular PVC. Novaline's hollow posts can be installed on 4×4s or over their steel-tube stanchion (photo right). The railing is in about the same price range as wood composites.

Ideas for Custom Railings

By Debra Judge Silber

While there's no shortage of off-the-shelf railing systems from decking manufacturers, there still can be advantages to building your own system. Cost is one. Craft is another. Still another is the ability to deliver a unique outdoor feature that fits a client's desires—and a deck's design—perfectly. "It's a lot more fun to play with different ideas and to create something that's more than the sum of its parts," says North Carolina builder Michael Chandler, who incorporated agricultural panels and coil stock in the railing shown on p. 858. "There's an alchemy in taking something very prosaic, like galvanized flashing and goat wire, and turning it into something that's high value and more attractive than premade cast-aluminum stuff."

Maryland deck builder Clemens Jellema used two types of manufactured balusters in the railing he designed for a home near the Chesapeake Bay (photo below), but he supported them in a cedar framework detailed with ipé plugs and a rope-wound top rail. In Jellema's case, with the high labor costs associated with a metropolitan area, it pays to incorporate some ready-made components.

Nautical Details

Maryland deck builder Clemens Jellema produced this design for a client who wanted a rail with nautical features that wouldn't obscure his view of the nearby woods and river. Jellema achieved the shipshape appearance with a top rail of 1-in. copper pipe wrapped with marine-grade roping. To preserve the view, he chose tempered-glass balusters from Deckorators. For the stair rails and deck sections facing the yard, he used the company's stainless aluminum balusters and connectors. In those sections, a single cedar 2×4 was used for each top and bottom rail.

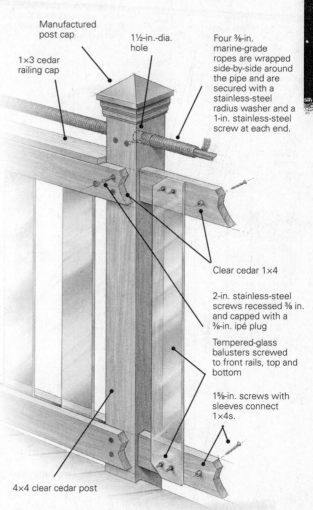

Manufactured post cap

1×3 cedar railing cap

1½-in.-dia. hole

Four ⅜-in. marine-grade ropes are wrapped side-by-side around the pipe and are secured with a stainless-steel radius washer and a 1-in. stainless-steel screw at each end.

Clear cedar 1×4

2-in. stainless-steel screws recessed ⅜ in. and capped with a ⅜-in. ipé plug

Tempered-glass balusters screwed to front rails, top and bottom

1⅝-in. screws with sleeves connect 1×4s.

4×4 clear cedar post

Continued ➔

Wire Panels for a Wide-Open View

When budget concerns arose, North Carolina builder Michael Chandler corralled the cost of this 600-sq.-ft. deck project by using agricultural wire—goat panels—for the guardrails rather than the custom metalwork initially planned. The panels are made of $7/32$-in.-dia. wire in a 4-in. grid pattern that's stiff enough to stand in for traditional balusters. The ends of each panel are inserted in holes drilled into the posts or, along the bottom, in a 1-in.-dia. rigid-steel conduit that serves as the bottom rail. Rope lights tucked under the top rails provide illumination.

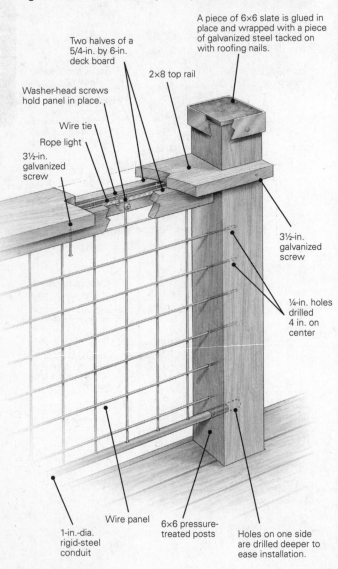

Two halves of a 5/4-in. by 6-in. deck board

A piece of 6×6 slate is glued in place and wrapped with a piece of galvanized steel tacked on with roofing nails.

2×8 top rail

Washer-head screws hold panel in place.

Wire tie

Rope light

3½-in. galvanized screw

3½-in. galvanized screw

¼-in. holes drilled 4 in. on center

Wire panel

1-in.-dia. rigid-steel conduit

6×6 pressure-treated posts

Holes on one side are drilled deeper to ease installation.

Durable Deck Stairs

By Scott Grice

Deck stairs for a small yard had better be beautiful to look at because there's no way to hide them. Although this might sound like a risky situation, it is also an opportunity. Deck stairs done well can add a sense of balance and unity to a small yard and can become a feature to be celebrated rather than a utilitarian eyesore.

I recently took on a job where I had just such an opportunity. The homeowner's backyard was small, and the landscaping had been mostly destroyed during a remodeling project that was nearing completion. The homeowner had a fresh slate for landscaping, and the deck stairs that I built would be the first feature there. I knew that in the future, the stairs would be a prominent part of a fastidiously landscaped backyard haven.

The Finished Look Affects the Framing

For both durability and aesthetics, ipé was the decking choice. Ipé is highly resistant to rot, it is incredibly dense, and when sealed with tung oil, it develops a dark-brown patina over time. Also, ipé is heavy and hard to cut, and it has been known to pull itself loose from framing because of the extreme force it exerts with seasonal move- ment. The ipé risers for these stairs are made from ¾-in.-thick decking, but the treads are 2×12s. I frame stairs as strong as possible, but because this deck called for ipé, the framing was particularly important.

I did a few things to ensure the framing was strong enough. First,

choose boards with a slight crown (I orient the crown up to help fight gravity), but without cups, twists, bows, or checks. Also, I buy lumber that is long enough to catch the framing square when I'm laying out the cuts for the top and bottom connections.

I use stair gauges on a framing square to lay out stringers. To increase accuracy, I use a Speed Square to mark the transition from one step to the next. When I draw and number the steps, I leave a little room at the top and bottom of the board. At the top step, I draw the way the stringer will attach to the deck. Once that is done, I make adjustments for tread thickness. If I had cut these stringers and installed them without accounting for tread thickness, the first step up from the concrete would have been taller than the other steps.

Accounting for tread thickness is easy. From the height of the first riser, I subtract the thickness of the tread. I mark a new cutline on the stringer and label it. Typically, I account for the thickness of the decking at the top of the stairs by including it in the overall height calculation. But just to make sure, I draw and label the decking on the stringer along with all the other framing elements that affect stringer framing or stair height.

Before I start cutting, I double-check measurements and layout marks for accuracy. I use a circular saw to make cuts. At inside corners, however, I finish the cuts with a handsaw instead of overcutting and weakening the stringer. After the first stringer is cut, I use it as a template by clamping it to an uncut stringer board and tracing the outline. After I've cut all the stringers and fastened the strongbacks, I coat all the fresh-cut surfaces with wood preservative.

Finishing Details Affect the Experience

You don't typically hear someone say, "I had a great experience with my deck stairs today," but any casual observation of a backyard party assures us that deck stairs are used for more than simply climbing up and down. People set plates on them. They sit and lounge on them. They stop to talk midspan. During quieter times, deck stairs collect flowerpots and garden art and even substitute as a potting bench. Consequently, I like to make the deck stairs as inviting as possible.

Wide is better than narrow. I like the stairs to be at least 3½ ft. wide at the inside of the newel posts, and wider if possible. I make the treads at least 11 in. from front to back to allow enough room for people and pots. I chamfer all sharp edges and sand rough spots. Finally, I hide all the fasteners by screwing from underneath or countersinking the screws and plugging the holes. As I mentioned, hiding the fasteners improves the look of the stairs and reduces the chance of water damage, but it also makes the stairs nicer to the touch and eliminates the fastener location as a source of slivers.

Obviously, all deck stairs should conform to local code requirements. I installed the cable-rail system according to the manufacturer's specifications. I beveled the top of the handrail to shed water and to make it more comfortable to grab. In some code jurisdictions, I also would have to install an additional handrail that is easier to hold.

I minimized the distance the stringers had to span by eliminating one step. This increased the stair rise to 8 in., which is tall but still within acceptable range. To ensure the stringers wouldn't flex under load, I used pressure-treated 2×12s (the largest dimension available at the lumberyard). Also, I nailed 2×4 strongbacks to both sides of the middle stringer and to the inside of each outside stringer. Strongbacks dramatically increase the rigidity of stringers, so I never build exterior stairs without them.

The transitions at the top and bottom of the stairs also affected the framing. At the top, the last riser needed to continue seamlessly as the deck's fascia. The fascia was spaced off a 4×8 supporting beam by the thickness of the newel posts, which complicated the stringer attachment. I solved the problem by using the stringer strongbacks and the top newel posts to help support the stairs.

The bottom transition incorporated an existing concrete slab to support and secure the stairs. To ensure solid newel posts and to protect the entire stair assembly from racking or twisting, I beefed up the landing step. With extra blocking and all-thread rods, I created a rigid box at the bottom of the stairs that includes the newel posts. I bolted this assembly to the concrete slab.

Meticulous Stringer Assembly Pays Off

Beefy stringers don't do much good if they are not cut or crowned properly. Stringers are the backbone of the staircase, and I've found that less-than-perfect stringers compound problems down the road. Perfect stringers begin at the lumberyard. Pressure-treated lumber is not high quality in the first place, so I take the time to select stringer boards that are free of big knots. I

Continued →

Stronger Stairs, Top to Bottom

At the top of the stairs, newel posts are incorporated into the framing to create a seamless transition from stairs to deck. At the bottom of the stairs, a rigid box is incorporated into the landing step using epoxy, ½-in.-dia. bolts, and ¼-in.-dia. all-thread. This ensures sturdy newel posts and a solid connection to the concrete slab. The stringers that connect the deck and the slab are strengthened with 2×4 strongbacks.

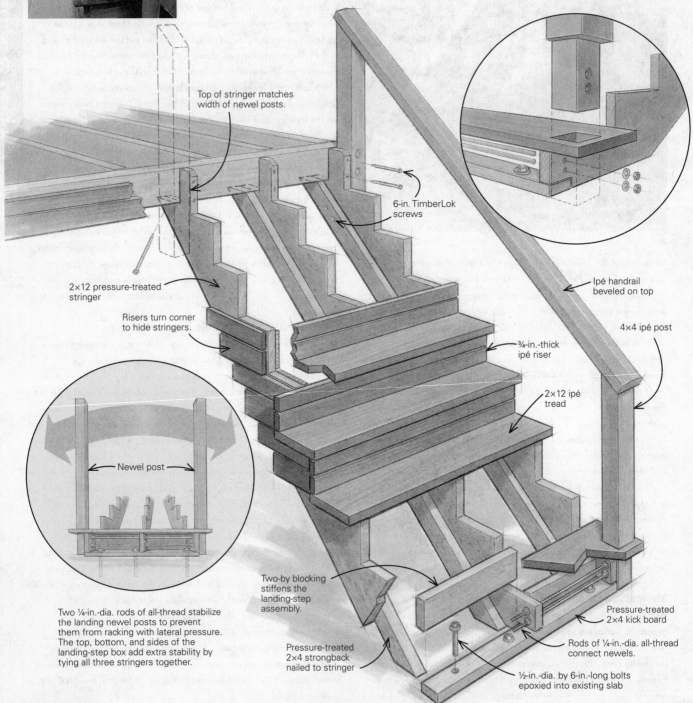

Top of stringer matches width of newel posts.

6-in. TimberLok screws

2×12 pressure-treated stringer

Risers turn corner to hide stringers.

Newel post

Ipé handrail beveled on top

4×4 ipé post

¾-in.-thick ipé riser

2×12 ipé tread

Two-by blocking stiffens the landing-step assembly.

Two ¼-in.-dia. rods of all-thread stabilize the landing newel posts to prevent them from racking with lateral pressure. The top, bottom, and sides of the landing-step box add extra stability by tying all three stringers together.

Pressure-treated 2×4 strongback nailed to stringer

Pressure-treated 2×4 kick board

Rods of ¼-in.-dia. all-thread connect newels.

½-in.-dia. by 6-in.-long bolts epoxied into existing slab

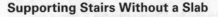
Be Organized and Accurate When Making Stringers

The first step in constructing deck stairs is to figure out where and how the stringers will connect the deck to the ground. Once I establish the exact number and size of treads and risers, I draw all the elements on the stringer before I begin cutting. I take the time to be as accurate as possible and double-check my measurements. Also, even for a small set of stairs, I ensure that the stringers are strong enough to carry the load and are protected against rot.

TAKE TIME TO BE ACCURATE. When laying out the stair's rise and run on a pressure-treated stringer, I use a Speed Square placed against the stair gauges to mark the exact location of the next rise. When marking the next rise and run, I align the framing square to that line. This reduces the margin of error introduced when marking each step.

USE THE STRINGER AS A STORY POLE. Before making any cuts, I draw all the cutlines as well as any other important elements, such as the height of the decking, the thickness of the treads, and the top of the concrete.

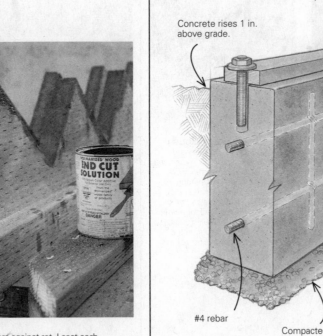

MAKE STRINGERS THAT LAST. To protect stringers against rot, I coat each cut surface with wood preservative. To prevent a stress failure, I attach one strongback (a 2×4 cleat nailed flush to the back edge of the stringer) to each side of the center stringer and one strongback to the inside of each outside stringer.

Supporting Stairs Without a Slab

When I don't have the luxury of an existing slab, I build a big footing and hide it under the stair framing. A stair footing is simply a block of reinforced concrete that carries the weight of the stairs and prevents the bottom of the stairs from kicking out. I usually make the footing big enough to support the stair framing fully but small enough to be hidden when the stairs are finished. The back side of the footing is under the stairs, so I run it thicker than necessary to give myself a little wiggle room.

With the footing laid out, I excavate to below frost level, compact 2 in. of gravel at the bottom, and build a form. I keep the top of the form no more than 1 in. above grade, but high enough to keep the bottom of the stringers out of the dirt, if possible. The form is typically small enough that I can mix the concrete I need by hand. Depending on the depth of the form, I add one or two pieces of rebar across the width to reinforce the concrete. Once the concrete has cured and the stair stringers are connected to the kick board, I drill holes with a rotary hammer and use epoxy to secure ½-in.-dia. by 6-in.-long bolts through the kick board and into the footing.

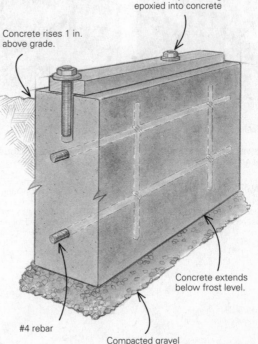

½-in.-dia. by 6-in.-long bolts epoxied into concrete

Concrete rises 1 in. above grade.

Concrete extends below frost level.

#4 rebar

Compacted gravel

Continued ➡

Use Newel Posts to Strengthen Stringer Connections

Top and bottom stringer connections are potential weak points for any set of stairs. At the top, a combination of TimberLok screws secures the stairs to the deck. At the bottom, I created a box assembly with enough rigidity to anchor the landing newel posts firmly. I secured this box assembly to the existing slab to prevent the stair stringers from moving away from the deck over time.

TIMBERLOK SCREWS SECURE THE TOP. I secure the top of the stringer to the deck's beam by driving 6-in. screws through the vertical face; however, this mainly prevents lateral movement. To carry the load, I drive fasteners up through the strongbacks into the deck beam. Additionally, the newel posts (installed later) at each side of the top of the stairs help to carry the load by being fastened to both the beam and the stringers.

THE NEWEL POST SLIPS THROUGH THE TREAD. I cut down the bottom of the newel post to allow it to pass through a hole in the tread. Because the tread helps to stabilize the newel post, I keep the tolerances between the hole and the post as tight as possible.

CONNECT THE NEWELS THROUGH THE BASE. I pass ¼-in. all-thread through holes I've drilled in the base of the newels and matching holes drilled in the ends of the stringers. Countersunk into 1-in. holes, nuts tightened over washers secure the newels and can be used for plumb adjustment. To increase adjustability, I place washers and nuts on the all-thread rods at both sides of the center stringer.

Add Durability by Adding Detail

A little attention to detail will raise the craftsmanship of stairs from pure utility to an ornamental feature in the yard. The easiest way I've found to improve the look of deck stairs is to hide the fasteners and framing lumber. This not only creates a better look but also can help the stairs to last longer.

SCREW THE TREADS FROM UNDERNEATH. I use the Deck Master hidden-fastener system (www.grabberman.com) because I found the galvanized J-channel system is strong enough for ipé, a dense wood that exerts a lot of force with seasonal movement. Also, securing the treads from below does not create a place for water to penetrate the framing and potentially cause rot.

HIDE THE STRINGERS. I continue the riser detail around to the sides of the stringers, spacing the boards ⅛ in. to allow for water drainage (inset photo). The gaps also add to the visual interest of the stairs.

STREAMLINE THE POST CONNECTION. The top riser is continuous with the deck's fascia for a clean transition. The outside course of decking is full width and is notched around each newel post.

Decking Over a Roof

By Emanuel A. Silva

There are tons of reasons to build a deck over a roof, from creating a romantic outdoor breakfast nook off a second-floor master bedroom to providing a second-floor porch on a city house. No matter the reason, the keys to a long-lasting deck above a living space are the same: a reliable roof membrane and details that minimize any damage to the roof from the deck loads. I like rubber roofing for this, combined with a floating deck floor. The rubber roofing I've been using for 15 years—a glue-down, 60-mil EPDM membrane from International Diamond Systems—offers several advantages. It's reliable, it's fairly easy to work with, and it requires no special tools. That said, a lot of people subcontract the roofing work and build the deck themselves. Either way, the roofing has to be right.

Framing the Roof

Whenever I install decking over a roof, I make sure the framing is structurally sound and properly pitched to drain water. The project illustrated here was a complete teardown and rebuild, so I framed the roof with 2×8s spaced on 16-in. centers, supported by a beam and a ledger as on most decks. Because these 2×8s were also the framing for the ceiling below, and because I wanted to keep all the cuts square, I framed the roof level. To pitch the upper surface ¼ in. per ft. for drainage, I ripped 2×4s on a taper and screwed them to the tops of the joists.

It might seem like it would have been easier to start with 2×12s and rip them to a taper. The trouble with that approach is that the allowable span of a joist or rafter depends on both its species and its grade. The grade depends largely on how close knots and other defects are to the edge of the board. In ripping a board, a knot that had existed harmlessly in the center is now close to the ripped edge, compromising the board's strength. For that reason, code does not allow the use of ripped lumber for structural purposes.

Continuous notched 4×6 posts support the framing and also serve as rail posts. The roof sheathing is ¾-in. CDX plywood, glued and screwed to the framing.

To create a smooth surface and to protect the bottom of the rubber roofing from any fasteners or rough edges on the plywood, I installed ½-in. fiber roof underlayment as a final substrate. Each board is secured with 16 1⅝-in. screws and 3-in.-dia. sheet-metal washers.

Where the roof ties into the house, I removed the siding about 2 ft. up the wall and about 1 ft. out on each side. This enabled me to fully adhere the roofing membrane about 2 ft. up the sheathing and then counterflash with a self-adhering butyl membrane. I pulled back the existing building paper after stripping the siding, installed the butyl membrane, and lapped the building paper back over it. This procedure makes for a watertight connection on ordinary rainy days, but it also protects against wind-driven rain or deep snow sitting on the deck up against the house.

Continued →

Epdm Membrane

Tapered Sleeper

½-In. Fiber Roof Underlayment

¾-In. Plywood Sheathing

Epdm Membrane

Peel-And-Stick Epdm Tape

Drip Edge

Glue Down the Epdm Roofing

EPDM roofing is available in a variety of widths and in lengths up to 100 ft. Here, I needed enough rubber to overhang about 1 ft. on each end, and it had to be wide enough to run about 2 ft. up the house wall and to overhang the edge of the deck by at least 2 in. Because I was using up leftovers from another job, I did this roof with two pieces of rubber, which I joined in the middle with Rubberall Splicing Adhesive. In most cases, though, I'd simply buy membrane big enough to cover the roof in one piece. After sweeping the underlayment clean and making sure there were no protruding fasteners, my helper and I laid the rubber down on the underlayment and fitted it to the house and against the posts. I made cutouts for the posts, then split the rubber beyond the cutouts so it could be placed around each post.

Next, we rolled back the rubber about halfway toward the posts. Working about 2 ft. at a time, we wiped the membrane with Rubberall's membrane cleaner and then spread its bonding adhesive on both the underlayment and the membrane using a paint roller. It's a contact adhesive, so once the glue was set enough that my finger barely stuck to it, we slowly rolled the membrane over the glued area, making sure not to make any air bubbles, and smoothed it with a J-roller.

Fiber Underlayment Protects Roofing

Nails can back out of plywood or OSB over time. A layer of fiberboard prevents them from penetrating the roofing.

DON'T OVERLAP THE SEAMS. Offsetting the joints in the fiberboard from those in the sheathing makes a smooth surface.

USE THE BIG WASHERS. Screws and 3-in.-dia. sheet-metal washers mean that only 16 1⅝-in. fasteners are needed per sheet. The washers are sold by roofing-supply houses.

Running the Rubber

Installing large sheets of rubber is easier than it looks, although it's a big help to have a second pair of hands on the job.

DRY-FIT FIRST. Roll out the rubber sheet so that it's square to the roof, then use scissors to make the cuts needed around penetrations such as posts. Before gluing the rubber, be sure to clean it with a manufacturer-recommended solvent.

ROLL THE RUBBER MEMBRANE HALFWAY BACK. Working in approximately 2-ft. swaths, spread the adhesive on both the rubber and the substrate.

MAKE IT PERMANENT. Once the glue is barely tacky, unroll the rubber over the glued area, and smooth it out with a J-roller.

UP THE WALL. Adhering the rubber about 2 ft. up the adjacent wall is part of creating a watertight system.

We continued toward the house in 2-ft. sections and finished by gluing the rubber about 2 ft. up the wall. We then turned around and glued the rubber around the posts and over the PVC fascia. The glue extends about 2 in. down the fascia. We let the excess rubber hang for the time being.

To protect the outer edge from damage, we installed a 3-in. aluminum drip cap all around the perimeter, fastening it every foot with 2-in. hot-dipped galvanized roofing nails. I trimmed the rubber with a knife so that it would be even with the bottom of the drip edge. To waterproof the inside edge of the drip cap and to protect the nail penetrations, I covered the joint with uncured-EPDM peel-and-stick tape. Starting with the bottom edge of the roof and finishing up with the sides yields a shingle effect that will prevent water from entering.

Integrating the posts into the roofing is the hardest part of this job; getting roofing to seal around the corners of the posts is both vital and challenging. I could have bought premade corners for the posts, but they're expensive. Instead, I made corners from membrane scraps, overlapping them and gluing them in place with splice adhesive. I counterflashed with a butyl membrane to about 3 ft. up the post, and eventually wrapped the posts with PVC trim.

Let the Sleepers Lie

The next step was to lay out the sleepers 16 in. on center, on top of the joists below. To prevent the sleepers from wearing through the EPDM roof, I laid additional 4-in.-wide strips of rubber membrane below the sleepers' locations.

I wanted the tops of the sleepers to be level, so I ripped pressure-treated 2×6s in half so that their bottoms tapered to match the roof pitch. At their thinnest part, the sleepers are 1½ in. deep, so the 2-in. decking fasteners won't stick through. Cutting pressure-treated lumber exposes the untreated core, so I applied Wolman CopperCoat wood preservative to all the cut sides and ends to help prevent rot.

Any penetrations in the roof membrane made by fasteners are potential leaks, so the sleepers just rest in place. The post wraps help prevent the decking from uplifting.

So that the finish would have time to dry, I had coated all six sides of the mahogany deck boards with Penofin a week earlier and had stacked them with sticks between the layers. As I worked, I recoated all the cut edges. To secure the decking, I used 3M 5200 Marine Adhesive Sealant, a tough, waterproof urethane normally used as boat glue. I followed the adhesive with stainless-steel finish nails. The nails' main function is to clamp the boards while the glue cures, which is what provides the real strength. I finished up by applying another coat of Penofin to the boards. This helps to hide and seal all the small nail holes and gives the boards one more layer of protection.

With the decking down, the rest of the job was the same as any other porch. I wrapped the posts with a ¾-in. PVC trim board and added railings, then replaced the siding and called in the painter.

Continued ➔

Detailing the Roof Edge

Use permanent trim around a permanent roof. PVC won't rot, it takes paint well, and you can glue rubber roofing to it.

GLUE THE ROOFING TO THE FASCIA. Spread the adhesive on the rubber roofing and about 2 in. onto the board below.

DRIP EDGE PROTECTS THE CORNER. Nail a 3-in. aluminum drip edge over the corner of the roof. Guide a knife along it to trim the excess rubber.

SEAL THE DRIP EDGE. Use uncured EPDM tape to cover the nails and seal the drip edge to the roof. Uncured EPDM must be protected from UV rays, which the decking will do once installed.

Flash the Posts

Any penetration in the EPDM membrane is a potential leak, so the posts on this roof required special attention. They were wrapped with rubber and then flashed to the roof with scraps of rubber and splicing adhesive. The challenging areas to flash are the post corners.

WRAP THE POST FIRST. Wrapping the post with membrane provides a reliable base for gluing additional rubber for flashing.

PAINT ON THE GLUE. Spread splice adhesive on the roof and on the post wrap.

START AT THE BOTTOM. Split a scrap of rubber so it can go around the corner while lying flat on the roof. Stretch the rubber a little so the apex of the split is placed above the roof plane.

OVERLAP THE FIRST LAYER. Split a second scrap of rubber like the first. Install it to wrap the corner and splay onto the roof. The apex of its split must be on the roof so that the two apexes don't align and create a potential leak.

COUNTERFLASH. Once the post is fully flashed to the roof, counterflash with layers of bituminous membrane going up the post about 3 ft.

Finally, It's Time to Deck

Installing the decking is straightforward. Tapered sleepers ripped from 2x material ensure a level walking surface. Glue and nails secure the decking.

PLACE THE SLEEPERS. Strips of 4-in.-wide EPDM provide a layer of protection between the sleepers and the roof. The sleepers aren't fastened in place, and the floor floats.

GLUE DOES THE WORK. The decking nails are mainly there to clamp the boards until the urethane sealant sets up.

NAIL DOWN THE DECKING. Short, 2-in. stainless-steel finish nails fasten the mahogany decking to the sleepers. PVC trim will hide the gap between the decking and the post and help to hold the decking down.

JUST DETAILS LEFT TO GO. A second coat of Penofin (the boards were all coated and dried before installation), rails, trim, siding, and paint are all that's left.

Simple Shade Structure

By Robert Shaw

As a contractor who lives at the foot of the Rockies, I spend my days outside building decks and shade structures to help my customers enjoy our great climate. In spring, summer, and fall, the weather and the views call us to be outdoors. Even when it's hot, our low humidity makes being outside a good proposition—if you can find some shade.

This home has a great view of the Front Range, but along with that view comes the western sun. Until it would lower behind a stand of cottonwoods, the mid-afternoon sun used to beat down on the deck and the kitchen just inside, making the spaces too hot to use. When the owners hired me to build a new deck, adding shade was a key part of the project.

Whenever I design a pergola, a lot of factors come into consideration. The more shade desired, for example, the more purlins (the uppermost members) are needed. I don't have a strict formula for determining their size and spacing, but this deck's 2×4 purlins are spaced on 12-in. centers, which is a typical layout I use. If there's any doubt, I place the purlins without fastening them and see how my customer likes the layout.

By spacing the purlins this close together, snow and wind loads become a concern. This is Colorado, and we get a lot of snow, plus the winds coming down from the Rockies can be fierce. Because of these concerns, my engineer designed the pergola for the same loads as a roof. Made from rough-sawn western red-cedar timbers, this pergola fit together attractively in a simple, budget-friendly design that blocks a considerable portion of the sun, making the deck and the kitchen more comfortable by lowering the afternoon temperature in each space.

Continued ➜

Run the Posts from the Ground to the Sky

Having been built at the same time, both the deck and the pergola are supported by three posts that run from the ground to the pergola's outer beam. Post bases connect the posts to the footings, resisting both lateral loads and wind uplift. Notches in the posts support the deck beam and the pergola beam.

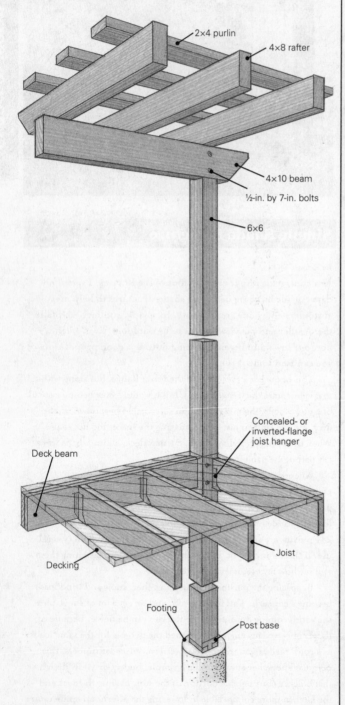

- 2×4 purlin
- 4×8 rafter
- 4×10 beam
- ½-in. by 7-in. bolts
- 6×6
- Concealed- or inverted-flange joist hanger
- Deck beam
- Joist
- Decking
- Footing
- Post base

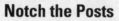

Notch the Posts

A trio of cedar 6×6 posts supports the deck, the railing, and the pergola. The posts require careful notching where they will support the deck framing and the 4×10 pergola beam. If the pergola were being added to an existing deck, the floor joists would have been doubled or tripled below the post locations, and a manufactured post base would secure the post to the framing. The posts were finished with deck stain before installation.

LAY OUT THE NOTCHES. The outline of the beams is marked on the posts a consistent distance above the decking. The top of this beam is 8 ft. above the deck.

A BIG SAW HELPS. The 10-in. blade on a Big Foot circular saw cuts most of the way through the 6×6 in one pass. A 7¼-in. saw also can do the job, but it leaves material in the center to be cut by other means.

FINISH WITH A JIGSAW. Not even the 10-in. saw cuts all the way through. A jigsaw with a coarse-tooth 5-in.-long blade completes the cut.

SEAL THE NOTCHES. Even in Colorado's dry climate, it's a good idea to seal end grain and cut areas where water might be trapped and cause rot.

Cut and Install the Beam

Two 4×10s meet over the center post, forming a beam that runs the width of the pergola. The ends of the beam cantilever 1 ft. beyond the outer posts for looks. All the prep work of cutting, beveling, laying out the rafter locations, and staining is done on the ground. The bolt holes were drilled after the beam was placed.

FIND THE CROWN. Lumber is rarely straight, and beams should be installed with any curve facing up. Finding the curve, or crown, that determines the top requires sighting along the beam.

BEVEL THE BEAM. One pass with a 10-in. circular saw cuts a decorative 45° angle on the bottom of the 4×10. A 7¼-in. saw would take two passes, and you'd have to clean up the cut with a belt sander.

POSITIONING A 4×10 OVERHEAD TAKES HELP. For support, the joint in the beam has to land on the center post.

BOLTS LOCK THE JOINT. A pair of ½-in. by 7-in. hot-dipped galvanized bolts with nuts and washers tie the beam to the post. An impact driver makes quick work of tightening the nuts. After installation, the exposed metal is painted black to match the rest of the hardware.

Install the Ledger and the Rafters

As with a deck, the inside of the pergola is supported by a ledger attached to the house. Because of Colorado's dry climate and the generous overhang directly above the ledger, no flashing was required. In most cases, though, pergola ledgers require flashing that's similar to deck-ledger flashing. As with the beam, the 4×8 rafters were cut to length, beveled, laid out, and stained on the ground. Installed on 24-in. centers, they overhang the beam by 24 in.

SCREW THE LEDGER TO THE HOUSE. A pair of 5-in. LedgerLok structural screws driven into each stud secures the rough-sawn 2×8 ledger to the house. LedgerLoks don't require pilot holes, as lags do.

NAIL THE RAFTER TO THE LEDGER. Black-painted Simpson L70 angles connect the rafter and ledger. After installation, dings in the paint are touched up using an artist's brush.

RAISE THE RAFTERS IN STAGES. The outer end of each rafter is placed on the beam, then the inner end is lifted into place.

SCREW THE RAFTERS DOWN. Each rafter is held in place by two 10-in. TimberLok screws driven with an impact driver from above.

Continued ➜

Finishing Touches

The final bit of carpentry was the installation of the 2×4 rough-sawn purlins atop the rafters. The purlins cantilever 12 in. beyond the last rafter. For more shade, they are spaced 12 in. on center.

BEVEL THE PURLINS. Because of their smaller size, it's faster and easier to use a miter saw to bevel the ends of the purlins that will extend past the last rafters.

SHORT PIECES ARE FINE. To make the best use of the available lumber lengths, short lengths were pieced into the center bay. A pair of 3-in. deck screws holds each of the purlins to each rafter.

A Concrete-Paver Patio

By Dick Henry

On those first warm days of spring, a patio tucked into a sunny corner of the backyard begs you to spend time outside. Throughout summer and into fall, that versatile outdoor room can be a solitary retreat or a place to entertain guests. Regardless of the season, a flat and firm patio made from simple materials adds value to your home.

Traditionally, patios have been made of brick, flagstone, or poured concrete, but I prefer installing concrete pavers. Pavers are widely available, and you can buy them in different shapes and colors. The cost of a patio made with concrete pavers is roughly twice that of poured concrete and comparable to clay-brick pavers. Site conditions and labor costs vary widely. I like the durability of concrete pavers, and their consistent size makes for ease of installation.

When you're installing a paver patio or walk, it's what you do before the pavers go down that makes all the difference. If you plan carefully (see "Before You Begin," below) and prepare a good base, you'll set the stage for a patio that looks great and will stay that way for a long time.

Before You Begin

- Use spray paint to outline the patio on the ground.
- Before excavating, call a local utility or service to locate under-ground hazards.
- Cover or protect sensitive plants.
- Find a flat, convenient location to unload pavers, stone, sand, etc.
- Do you need to remove soil? If so, decide where it will go.
- Patios change the way water drains around your house. Determine what drainage alterations will be necessary to move water away from the house.
- Plan outdoor-lighting and power locations, and install underground lines as necessary.

Stringlines Guide the Excavation

To end up with a flat patio that drained water away from the house, I created a virtual patio of string as a reference during construction. I chose 7 in. below the back-porch floor, the height of an average step, as the patio's high point. I tied a string to the first grade pin at this height, and to guard against losing the mark, I wrapped duct tape at the same height. At the patio's far end, I drove another grade pin and stretched a string between the two pins. Measuring down from the string tells whether the soil below is too high, too low, or just right.

Staking Out the Patio

I used a 4-ft. level to adjust the string to a slope of about ⅛ in. per ft. Once established, I transferred this elevation across to the curved side.

High point is 7 in. below back-porch floor.

Patio drains this way with a slope of ⅛ in. per ft.

String represents finished patio elevation.

¾-in.-dia. by 30-in.-long steel grade pin

1
2
3
4

Extend the stone base 10 in. to 12 in. beyond the patio. This allows for minor adjustments in the size of the patio and provides stability at the edge.

Anatomy of the Patio

1. Concrete pavers
2. 1-in. coarse-sand setting bed
3. 6-in. to 7-in. compacted-stone base
4. Existing soils, high in clay

The Stone Base Is Critical

For a lasting job, nothing is more important than getting the stone base firm and flat. I excavate the site 9 in. to 10 in. below the finished grade to make room for the stone base. Slope the excavation to promote drainage, following the stringlines. A Bobcat makes quick work of moving stone; a plate compactor packs and flattens the base.

I HIT A SOFT SPOT After excavating to the desired depth, I still have unstable soil to take care of. I install geotextile fabric over this area. The geotextile helps to spread the weight of the ensuing stone base, creating a stable surface.

SPREAD THE STONE IN THIN LAYERS. The ABC stone we used for the base includes all gradations of stone from dust to 1½-in.-dia. gravel. This mix can be packed flat and dense without losing its drainage properties. Apply the base in several 2-in. to 3-in. layers, wetting it down to aid compaction. Repeat the layering process until the base is 3 in. from the finished elevation.

Continued →

Use Coarse Sand for Bedding the Pavers

A maximum of 1 in. of clean, coarse sand is installed on top of the stone base. Initially, I bring in a little more sand than I need. After running the plate compactor, I'll end up close to my target elevation, but I don't worry about perfection at this stage. Perfection comes with the final screeding.

FINE-TUNE THE SETTING-BED LAYER. After spreading and compacting the coarse sand over the base, I extend stringlines from the grade pins to identify the finished height of the patio. Then we use a paver and a 4-ft. level (or other straightedge) to fine-tune the setting bed. The final smoothing fluffs the sand a little after compaction so that the pavers bed nicely in the sand.

Circular Pattern Starts with a Kit

We chose a circular pattern for this patio because it complements the curve in the retaining wall. These pavers came from Belgard (Oldcastle Architectural Product Group; www.belgard.biz), so we bought their starter kit for circular pavers. The kit includes a couple of sizes of wedge-shaped pieces, which can be used in various combinations to create the first dozen or so rings. After that, the square and rectangular pavers continue the pattern. Like most paver manufacturers, Belgard provides a good installation guide for anyone unfamiliar with the process.

1. Start in the Center

WHERE'S THE CENTER? Matching the paver pattern to the retaining wall would have placed the pattern's center too close to the house, so we started closer to the center of the patio. When installing pavers in running rows, we're careful not to line up the joints.

2. Make Straight Cuts in Place

STRAIGHT RUNS ARE EASY. Snap a chalkline, then use a cutoff saw with a diamond blade to make a quick scoring cut along the top of the paver. Make a final pass, cutting through the pavers and slightly into the sand.

3. Make Straight Cuts in Place

MARK CURVES with ¾-in. braided rope, which bends and holds a curve. When the curve is formed, mark it with a pencil, and score it lightly with the saw to make a smooth curve. Take each piece out and complete the cut.

4. Anchor Pavers Around the Edges

ON THIS JOB, WE USED A MASONRY BORDER (from Belgard) with plastic inserts that poke into the pavers and then are spiked into the ground. My favorite edge restraints are the 8-ft. polyethylene strips, which can form curves if you snip the intermediate tabs.

5. Lock the Pavers Into Place

SWEEP SAND INTO THE CRACKS. We spread clean, coarse sand over the patio and sweep it into the cracks. Then we vibrate the pavers with a compactor to lock the pavers into place. We repeat the process at least one more time: spread, sweep, and vibrate.

Continued →

Laying Concrete Pavers

By Joseph Cracco

My company, Modern Yankee Builders, specializes in remodeling. We end up doing all sorts of work, from framing to high-quality trim. Sometimes we even get to spend nice days outdoors, working on landscaping projects. This particular job was typical for us. It included a small kitchen addition and replacement of the old asphalt driveway with a new one made of concrete pavers. (A backyard patio or a sidewalk would use the same techniques.)

Concrete pavers offer a bunch of advantages for driveways and patios: A wide variety of styles and colors is available, uniform sizing eases installation, and aside from the excavation (which we subcontract), the few special tools needed are readily rented.

Designing for the Site

Because the number of paver styles available is vast, visiting supply yards to review the possibilities and obtain samples is a good idea. A decent supply yard should be able to help with design and with determining how many of each size of paver are needed. A word of caution: Some pavers can be ordered only by the full pallet. So if I require a third of a pallet of, say, small squares to three pallets of rectangles, I'm out of luck. If my supplier quoted a price based on a per-paver basis, I may find out that what I thought was a $150 purchase now costs $450 because of that two-thirds of a pallet of small squares I don't want. I need to find a place for those extra small squares or to change my pattern.

Where I work, patios usually don't require a building permit; for driveways, however, some towns require the local public-works department to do an existing-conditions survey (sometimes they just snap a photo) prior to issuing a certificate allowing the work to proceed. When the new driveway is complete, someone returns to verify that you didn't alter the size or location of the driveway's intersection with the street. Other jurisdictions are much more restrictive, particularly for the first 20 ft. or so where a driveway meets the street. I always check local requirements before commencing work, and I start with a site survey if I'm going to be anywhere near the property lines.

Planning the excavation and fill depth was critical for making sure that the new driveway matched the height of the neighbor's driveway. To have a clean edge to butt our pavers against, we needed to cut a straight line through the neighbor's asphalt driveway and along the edge of the street. Two things were critical in cutting the asphalt. First, the cuts needed to penetrate the existing pavement completely or the excavator would hook the uncut asphalt and rip up big sections beyond the cut. Even after patching, this never looks right. Second, the cuts needed to be dead straight as well as perpendicular to each other or the job would look bad, forcing us to waste time trimming the full pavers to fit.

We could have made the cuts ourselves, but when we added up the time to rent the saw, cut 60 ft. of asphalt, and return the saw,

Pavers Need Layers

The showy part of the driveway is the pavers on top, but what's below matters just as much. Choose the right materials, and compact them correctly for a flat, durable installation.

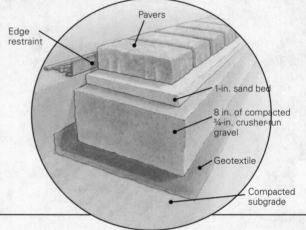

Edge restraint
Pavers
1-in. sand bed
8 in. of compacted ¾-in. crusher-run gravel
Geotextile
Compacted subgrade

Get the Base Right

A GOOD EXCAVATOR IS CRUCIAL. When digging down to the required depth of the base stone, be sure that the subgrade is flat so that the succeeding layers are of a consistent depth.

GEOTEXTILE SEPARATES THE LAYERS. The main purpose of geotextile is to prevent the crusher run from mixing into the subgrade over time and losing its bearing capability.

SPREAD THE CRUSHER RUN. A mix of stone from ¾ in. to dust, the crusher run helps to spread the loads from the pavers above to the subgrade below.

TAMP TO PREVENT SETTLING. Place the crusher run in two 4-in.-deep lifts. Compact the first lift, then place and compact the second.

Make a Flat Sand Bed

DETERMINE THE ELEVATION. A piece of conduit resting atop a few pavers determines the height of the sand bed. The partially buried pieces of conduit are used as screed guides. Set them ½ in. high to allow for compaction.

START IN A SQUARE CORNER. This helps create two straight edges to work from, easing the balance of the installation. The mitered corner blocks are a simple custom touch.

LAY THE PAVERS. Place the pavers carefully so that they maintain proper contact with each other. Standing on boards spreads out your weight and prevents the set pavers from tipping.

SCREED THE SAND FLAT. A level or other straightedge rides on the conduit guides (later removed) to screed the sand.

INSTALL EDGING. Spike plastic edge restraints to the ground as the job progresses.

A CIRCULAR SAW WITH A DIAMOND BLADE CUTS PAVERS EASILY. A light water mist cools the blade, extending its life and preventing it from warping due to heat, and it keeps the silica-laden dust down. Make sure to be plugged into a GFCI-protected outlet.

and then factored in the rental rate, the cost to hire a specialized contractor to cut a dead-straight line was only a little more.

Base Prep Is Key

No matter the kind of paver project, success depends on installing the base correctly. Pavers require a sand setting bed atop a base of crushed stone for drainage and support, as well as underlying subsoil that can handle the loads. Each paver manufacturer has specific requirements, but the ones here are fairly typical.

Elevation restrictions on all sides controlled the depth of our excavation. The driveway had to end up flush with or just a bit higher than the road and the neighbor's driveway. The edge near the front of the house needed to meet the front walk. The back had to rise slightly to eliminate what would have been a difference in height between the driveway and the client's planting bed. Ultimately, the adjacent asphalt driveway and the road were the critical control points. For the height to work out, the final elevation of the 1-in.-deep sand bed directly below the pavers would need to be 3 in. lower than the neighbor's driveway and the street. On other jobs, we might be looking for a crown to drain water off each side, or maybe a dead-flat, pitched base to send water in one direction. Over a 10-ft. span, the base has to be graded to within ¼ in. of flat. (Flat doesn't mean level, just planar.) The goal is to make adjustments by adding or subtracting from the crushed-stone base so that the sand setting bed ends up a uniform depth.

On any paver job, the excavation and the base materials that follow have to extend at least 8 in. beyond the edge of the pavers so that the edge of the base doesn't crumble under load. In this case, that didn't apply to the side that abutted the neighbor's drive because there was an existing compacted base there. Fortunately, the subsoil was suitable. If the soil had had significant amounts of clay or organic matter (both of which can hold a great deal of water, causing frost heave in cold climates), we would have had to excavate to good soil and to use more crushed-stone fill, driving up the cost of the project.

After Don Lemonde, our excavation contractor, removed the old asphalt driveway and hauled it to a recycling facility, he dug out all the soil down to a little more than 12 in. below what would be the final elevation of the pavers. After grading the subsoil to eliminate pockets, which retain water, Don compacted the excavation with a 4000-lb. walk-behind vibrating compactor, running over it twice in perpendicular directions. Compactor weight refers to the force the compactor exerts as it vibrates, not the machine's actual weight. These walk-behind machines weigh a little more than 200 lb. and are readily rented.

Fill the Excavation Back Up

The next step was to install a layer of geotextile, a synthetic fabric that increases the stability of the soil and the aggregate base. Geotextiles keep fine soil particles from migrating into the aggregate, which helps to maintain its drainage capacity. This becomes even more important when the base assembly is below a permeable pavement.

Continued →

Compact and Fill

Before Compaction

After Compaction

POUND 'EM DOWN. With a layer of plywood as protection, use a plate compactor to set the pavers firmly in the sand bed.

FILL THE JOINTS. Sweep a graded material such as fine stone dust over the pavers until the joints are full.

FILL THE JOINTS AGAIN. Sweep in more joint filler after compaction to bring it up to the level of the pavers.

FINALLY FILLED. When done, the filler should end just below the level of the pavers.

Above the geotextile, Unilock, the paver manufacturer, required 8 in. of compacted ¾-in. crusher-run gravel, a blend of crushed stone ranging in size from ¾ in. down to dust. Manufacturers specify how big a lift (or layer) of gravel can be installed at one time, based on the size of the compactor. A 4000-lb. vibrating compactor allows for 4-in. lifts.

After Don finished, we had the pavers delivered. The pattern called for three different paver sizes, plus another for a border. We had the pallets placed as close as possible to the work area to save time and labor. We try to stage the correct quantity of each size paver so that the first ones to be used are close at hand and the others become more accessible as the work progresses. With the limited space here, we ended up locating a third of the pallets on the front lawn and the remaining pallets at the back of the property.

Create a Sand Setting Bed

The crusher run was to be topped with ¾ in. to 1 in. of coarse, angular sand (concrete sand, as opposed to mortar sand or play sand) in which to bed the pavers. Before my helper Kevin and I tackled that step, however, we verified Don's grade. He had it perfect, but if he'd been off, we'd have adjusted it by adding or subtracting crusher run with shovels and rakes, then compacting again.

To make the setting bed a uniform depth, we set 1-in.-dia. EMT-conduit guides at the correct height, filled around them with sand, and used a straightedge to screed off the excess. There are a number of methods for setting the exact level of the screed guides. A simple way is to set a string ½ in. higher than where you want the tops of the pavers to end up. The extra ½ in. allows for the pavers to be compacted into the sand bed. Set the screed guides on the subbase, and place pavers on each end. Adjust the guides up or down by adding or removing material below them until the pavers are even with the strings. If the base is right, little adjustment should be needed. In this case, because the neighbors' asphalt controlled our elevation, we simply set a ½-in. spacer on their driveway and used a 10-ft. piece of conduit in place of the strings.

A large magnesium screed typically used for concrete flatwork is ideal for flattening the sand, but a straight 2×4 or even a level also will work. Keeping some sand in front of the screed as you go will help to fill low spots, but letting too much build up can bow the screed and throw off the grade. Once the sand bed is flat, we gently pull out the guides and sprinkle sand into the depressions. I'm looking for a variation in the sand bed of no more than ⅛ in. in 10 ft. More than this means that you'll end up with dips that hold puddles. Over time, these areas will sink even more because the water will wash the fines out of the soil below the low spot in a vicious cycle. We build the sand setting bed in 10-ft. sections, the length of the screed guides, laying pavers over each section before building the next. You could do the entire sand bed at once, but if you end up not laying pavers over an area, odds are that you'll come back to find that kids, dogs, or cats have destroyed your work. Once the sand is down and screeded, don't walk on it, or you'll create divots.

Don't Play Around With Sand

For bedding, we use concrete sand (also known as coarse sand or sharp sand). Unlike play sand, whose grains are smooth and round, concrete sand is angular. Its flat sides engage each other, creating a solid bed. In comparison, play sand's grains move around like ball bearings. If you drove over pavers set in play sand, they would rotate, digging in on one side and lifting on the other as the play sand moved. Concrete sand's stability minimizes this motion. Ultimately, this means that the pavers will remain flat much longer.

A Case for Permeable Pavers

Unlike traditional concrete-slab or asphalt driveways, paver driveways can be permeable, as the one is in the project shown here. This means that rather than increasing runoff, rainwater can soak through these pavers into the ground.

Storm-water runoff is an environmental problem. When water can't soak into the ground where it falls, the runoff can cause damaging erosion and carry sediments and pollutants into waterways. Humans exacerbate this problem by constructing buildings and paving over the ground. When water can soak into the ground directly, pollutants such as motor oil are retained at the point of origin, where they can be digested by naturally occurring microorganisms. Densely populated municipalities usually limit the percentage of a lot that can be covered with impermeable structures, such as roofs or traditional pavement. This means, for example, that you might not be able to build as large an addition as you'd like. Here, because we replaced an impermeable concrete driveway with permeable pavers, the percentage of impermeable coverage on the lot shrank, even though we had just built an addition. It's not just the pavers that must be permeable, but the filler as well. On this job, we filled the joints with Aqua Rock, a granite product made specifically for permeable-paver joints. It fulfills the requirements for lateral-load transfer as well as the appropriate flow of water.

Setting the Pavers

If you don't count how your back feels by the end of the day, setting pavers is the easy part. We usually start at a corner, guided by an existing fixture such as a foundation wall, or in this case, the neighbor's driveway and the street, and then fill in the field using a picture of the pattern as our guide. Without such an edge, we'd create a square starting corner by installing heavy plastic angles called edge restraints atop the base, fastening them with long galvanized spikes per the paver-manufacturer's requirements.

It's important to keep the pattern running straight and true. On this project, we had a 67-ft.-long straight line for one edge and only a 9-ft.-wide driveway, so we didn't need additional benchmarks. In other situations, we set up a centerline to guide the layout. To establish a centerline, you can set a stringline, which often gets in the way, or you can snap a chalkline on the sand setting bed, which is my preferred method.

It's important to set pavers flat, making sure not to dig a corner into the sand bed. When the pavers are compacted, the disturbed sand may even out, but I don't leave this to chance. It's easy to hold the paver about 1 in. above the setting bed, move it in contact with one or, preferably, two sides of the adjacent pavers, then slide it straight down onto the sand.

The pavers used here are made with ribs that bear on neighboring pavers to maintain a consistent gap. Without this contact, the entire assembly would be compromised. Each paver's ability to withstand vertical loads depends on its resisting lateral loads while pushing straight down on the underlying base. If a paver can rock under load, it will eventually fail. (Imagine a tire rolling over a single paver; first one edge and then the other would be pushed into the sand.) Each paver's ability to withstand lateral loads depends on its distributing the load to the pavers around it. If you have 8 ft. of pavers but 8 ft. 1 in. of space to fill, don't gap each of the pavers a little bit to take up the extra space. You must either cut fillers or move the edge in 1 in.

Similarly, before the pavers are compacted into the sand bed, they are susceptible to rolling if you step on the edge instead of the middle. I lay walk boards on the pavers I've just set, and move them as the setting progresses. Not only can I walk across the planks and not worry about rolling the pavers, but the planks also act as a great place to stage the next row without the risk of chipping the set pavers.

We picked from several pallets at once to ensure an even distribution of any color variation. Once we distributed the pavers, Kevin and I laid them as a team. Each paver went from the pile to Kevin's hands to mine, and then to the sand bed without having to be put down and picked back up again.

On the house side, we placed edge restraints as we installed the pavers. Long galvanized spikes secure the edging to the base.

Cutting Pavers

Edges often mean cutting pavers. I use a wet saw to minimize dust, which is laden with silica and is a real health hazard. On a project with a lot of cuts, I set up my tile saw on a stand. We set all of the full pavers, then my helper marks the cuts and brings them to me at the saw. While I'm cutting the paver he just marked, he takes the paver I just cut, places it where it belongs, then marks the next paver to be cut.

For efficiency, I plan the job to make as few cuts as possible. There were only eight on this entire driveway. When there are

Continued →

Design Possibilities

There are several concrete-paver manufacturers, each with its own product line. Offerings vary by region as well, so you'll have to shop around.

Brussels Block

Belpasso

Camelot

Courtstone

few cuts to make, I don't drag out the tile saw. Instead, I use an old circular saw with a diamond blade. The pavers on this job had distressed edges, so I roughed up the cut edges with a hammer. The final step in setting the pavers was to backfill against the edge restraints with soil.

Finishing Up

With all the pavers laid, we were ready to compact them into the base and to fill the joints. It's important to compact as soon as possible after setting is complete. Wait too long, and rain or traffic can tilt pavers out of alignment. If heavy rain hits before we can compact, we wait a day for the sand to dry out a little. We closely inspect the pavers before compacting, replacing any damaged ones. Once compacted, heaven and earth need to be moved to get a paver back out.

Pavers should be isolated from the compactor to prevent damage to their surface. Special "paver saver" pads can do this, but our rental yard doesn't have them. Instead, we used scrap sheets of ¼-in. lauan plywood.

Compacting is done in two steps. The first compaction drives the pavers down into the sand and levels each paver to the adjacent ones. This operation also drives some of the sand up between the pavers. After running the compactor in two passes over an area determined by how much plywood we had, I moved up the driveway while Kevin started filling the joints with graded joint material. Using a stiff-bristle broom on the area I had just compacted, he swept off the excess so that it wouldn't be ground into the paver surface with the second compaction.

When I reached the driveway's end, I doubled back to begin compacting the areas Kevin had filled. This second compaction vibrated the joint filler and settled it well below the surface of the pavers. Kevin then swept in more filler to top off the joints.

Contents

Healthy Home

Radon-Mitigation Systems

By Martin Holladay

Radon is a naturally occurring and potentially dangerous radioactive gas that is present in nearly all soils. People who live for many years in a house with elevated levels of radon gas have a higher-than-average chance of developing lung cancer. About one in 15 homes has a high-enough level of radon to be of concern.

Radon enters a house via the stack effect, which often causes soil gases to be drawn into houses through cracks in the foundation. High radon levels are possible in new houses as well as old houses, and in tightly sealed houses as well as leaky ones.

It's possible to have a high indoor radon level in any state in the country, so the only reliable way to determine the radon level in your home is to test the indoor air. If testing reveals radon at levels above 4 picocuries per liter—the standard "action level"—you should arrange for a contractor to install a radon-mitigation system in your house.

A variety of do-it-yourself radon test kits are available. These kits must be left in your home for a period of days or weeks, after which you mail them to a lab for analysis. If the results of a short-term test (one that takes less than 90 days) show radon levels near or above 4 picocuries per liter, it's best to follow up with a long-term test, which will be more accurate than a short-term test. There is no need to test the air in an unfinished basement; instead, test air on the first floor.

Start Passive

A passive radon-mitigation system allows soil gases to flow from the soil beneath the slab through the vent pipe to the outdoors. The driving force is the stack effect. In most houses, a passive system is adequate to keep radon levels safe. New houses should include these essential system components:

- A layer of clean ¾-in. crushed stone under any basement slab or a slab on grade
- At least one horizontal length of 4-in. perforated PVC pipe in this layer of stone, with one end connected to an elbow or a T that's connected on the other end to a nonperforated 4-in. PVC riser (a vertical pipe that penetrates the home's roof)
- A layer of 6-mil polyethylene above the stone layer
- Caulk or a permanent seal for cracks and seams in the slab and for all penetrations through the slab and the slab perimeter
- An airtight sump lid (if the basement has a sump)
- An electrical power supply in the attic near the vertical vent pipe in case an exhaust fan is needed in the future.

The vent pipe should terminate 12 in. above the roof. Exposed sections of the pipe should be labeled "radon vent system."

If testing shows that radon levels are still high in a house with passive radon mitigation in place, then an exhaust fan can be installed. This turns the passive system into an active system. Radon exhaust fans should not be located within a home's conditioned

Continued ➜

New Homes

Start with a Passive System

All new homes should include a passive radon-mitigation system that vents radon gas from the soil below the slab through the roof. Once the home is finished, you can test radon levels in the house. If levels are too high, it is simple to add a fan to make the system active and to lower radon levels in the house further.

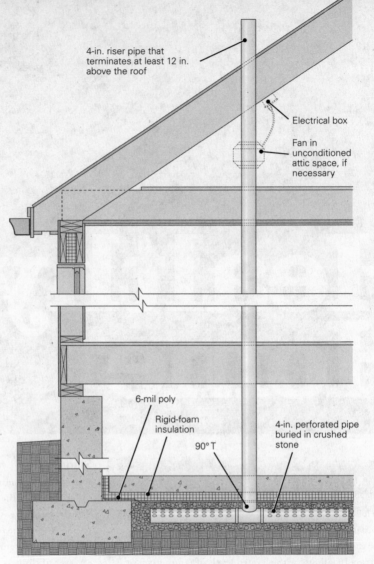

4-in. riser pipe that terminates at least 12 in. above the roof

Electrical box

Fan in unconditioned attic space, if necessary

6-mil poly

Rigid-foam insulation

90° T

4-in. perforated pipe buried in crushed stone

Retrofit

Dig a Hole Beneath the Slab

In existing homes, you need to create a void beneath the slab, which can be left empty or filled with crushed stone and a perforated pipe. Seal the pipe to the slab well, make sure the slab and basement walls are airtight, and always use a fan.

Slab patch

3-in. or 4-in. riser pipe sealed to the slab with hydraulic cement

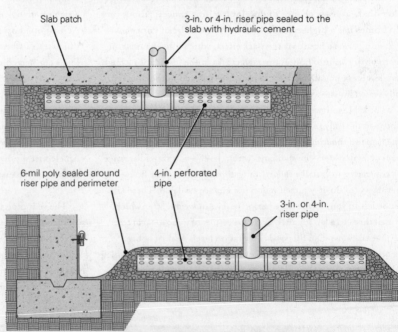

Retrofit

Dirt Floors

In existing homes with dirt basement or crawlspace floors, lay the perforated pipe on the floor. Cover the pipe and the entire floor with a well-sealed layer of polyethylene. Make sure to seal the riser pipe to the poly.

6-mil poly sealed around riser pipe and perimeter

4-in. perforated pipe

3-in. or 4-in. riser pipe

envelope; all pressurized lengths of pipe need to be outside the conditioned space. They are usually in the attic.

Radon exhaust fans usually draw between 20w and 100w and are rated at 60 cfm to 200 cfm. The fans need to operate continuously. Low-flow fans work well for homes with a porous layer of crushed stone under the slab; high-flow fans are required when the soil under the slab is dense and damp.

The main drawback to an active radon-mitigation system is the cost of the electricity required to run the fan. At 12.5¢ per kwh, a radon fan costs $22 to $110 per year to operate (figures from 2014).

Retrofits Are Active

Older houses usually lack a layer of crushed stone under the slab, so passive radon-mitigation systems rarely work. Installing an active subslab depressurization system usually costs between $1000 and $2000 (figures from 2014).

Radon contractors begin a retrofit by drilling a 4-in.-dia. hole in the slab. Unless the contractor discovers a layer of crushed stone under the slab, it's necessary to remove enough soil to make a void equal in volume to a small wastebasket. Then a 3-in. or 4-in. riser pipe is installed; the pipe originates just below the bottom of the concrete slab. Alternatively, the contractor may break up enough of the slab to add a perforated pipe in a layer of crushed stone, as shown in the center drawing.

In either case, the gap between the pipe and the slab needs to be sealed. The contractor will also seal all visible cracks in the slab. If the basement walls are made of concrete blocks, it may be necessary to seal them, too. The rest of the system resembles the system described for new construction.

In basements or crawlspaces with a dirt floor, a length of horizontal perforated pipe is installed on the floor. Polyethylene sheeting is placed above the pipe. One end of the perforated pipe is connected to a riser that penetrates the polyethylene through a carefully sealed hole. The rest of the system is similar to systems installed in homes with concrete slabs.

Balanced Ventilation

By Sean Groom

Houses need fresh air. Without ventilation, the quality of indoor air can rapidly become worse than that of the outside air; that holds true even in urban areas. Common contaminants include gases, odors, and moisture, and these can stem from utility rooms, garages, basements, bathrooms, and kitchens.

Until recently, fresh air entered a typical house through various openings, whether intentional (a fan or open window) or unintentional (holes and leaks around windows, rim joists, door jambs, and sheathing penetrations). Over the last few decades, however, houses have become tighter, and the unintentional flow of air through the building envelope has been reduced.

Once a house reaches about five air changes per hour (ACH), it's important to start thinking about using mechanical ventilation to ensure indoor-air quality.

In regions with moderate to significant heating and/or cooling loads, HRVs and ERVs are the most efficient means of mechanical ventilation. Depending on the efficiency of the heat exchanger, it can transfer anywhere from 50% to 91% of the conditioned air's heat and energy to the supply air.

Homeowner satisfaction with a recovery ventilator will depend on the answers to three questions: Does it keep the air temperature comfortable? Is it cheap to operate? Is it excessively noisy?

Does It Keep the Air Temperature Comfortable?

Comfort speaks to a unit's thermal efficiency. Thermal efficiency is the recovery ventilator's ability to transfer the temperature of the outgoing air to the incoming air. When a unit transfers a high percentage of the heat or cold to the incoming air, the fresh air can be diffused directly into the living space without creating cold drafts in the winter and warm eddies of air in the summer.

How Much Ventilation Is Enough?

ERVs and HRVs must be able to run at two ventilation rates: the background ventilation rate required to ensure the right number of air changes per hour for the house, and a second, higher rate when the bathrooms and kitchen need a boost. The boost rate is typically 50% higher than the background rate. The background ventilation rate is determined by the home's exhaust requirement. Depending on whom you ask, this can be determined by the number of bathrooms, the number of occupants, the infiltration rate of the house, and the size of the house—either in isolation or in combination. Recovery-ventilator manufacturers offer guidance for sizing a unit, but the ultimate arbiter is your local building code. Many codes have adopted the American Society of Heating, Refrigeration, and Air Conditioning Engineers' standard, referred to as ASHRAE 62.2. This standard requires 7.5 cfm per person (calculated by number of bedrooms, with the master bedroom counting twice) plus 3 cfm per 100 sq. ft. Prior to the 2013 revision, this calculation used only 1 cfm per 100 sq. ft., and the increased ventilation rate has met with strong resistance from building scientists and ventilation engineers who argue that for new, tight houses, the new standard imposes a stiff energy penalty by overventilating. At least one competing standard has emerged from Building Science Corporation, but it's too early to know what standard the building codes will adopt.

Continued →

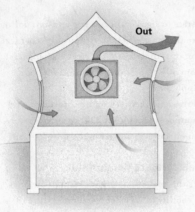

Bad

Exhaust-only ventilation uses a relatively low-volume bathroom fan run either continuously or at intervals on a timer to expel stale air from the home. Although excellent for their intended use, bath fans aren't ideal as a whole-house ventilation solution. Drawing air through the fan creates a slight negative pressure in the house and pulls outside air through leaks in the envelope. There is no control over the source of incoming air. It could as easily come from the garage, basement, or utility room as around the jambs of a second-floor window.

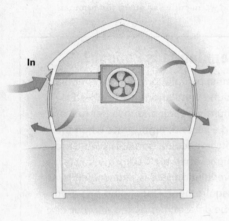

Better

Supply-only ventilation is the inverse of the exhaust scenario: A fan pulls fresh air into the house; under pressure, air finds its way out of the house through cracks. This is an improvement over the exhaust-only system because pressurizing the house makes the fan less likely to pull air from the garage and because incoming air can be filtered. Depending on the system, though, it can be inefficient to use the furnace fan to distribute air.

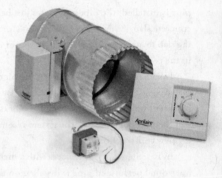

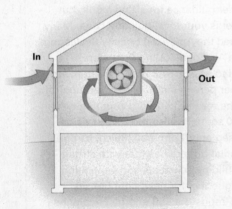

Best

Balanced ventilation makes the most sense if you intend to control the source of your fresh air. By relying on separate intake and exhaust fans working as a system, the amount of air that you expel from the house is matched by the amount of fresh air supplied by the ventilation equipment. This avoids depressurizing or pressurizing the house; the source of incoming air is planned and controlled, and it's filtered. The fans are small and cheap to operate. Best of all, balanced systems are available with heat exchangers to recover the heating or cooling energy in the outgoing air.

Balanced Ventilation Should Be Recovery Ventilation

There are three types of balanced mechanical ventilation. Each relies on one or more fans to bring fresh air into the house and to exhaust stale air out of the house. These are called balanced systems because the volume of air moved in each direction should be the same. Because differences in duct lengths and the number of elbows affect airflow, these systems need to be tested and tuned to achieve balance. This process, called commissioning, should be part of any installation.

AIR EXCHANGER By pulling outdoor air into the house at the same rate it expels indoor air, an air exchanger provides balanced ventilation at a relatively low rate, say 60 cfm. Your fresh air won't be quite as fresh as with a recovery ventilator, your stale air won't be completely removed, and the mixing of airstreams is an inefficient way of conditioning supply air. The appliance itself, however, is far less expensive than an HRV or ERV.

Filter

Fresh air from outside

Exhaust to outside

Improved air to indoors

Fan

Stale air from inside

Filters

Fresh air from outside

Stale air from inside

Exhaust to outside

Fan

Heat exchanger

Fan

Fresh air to inside

Condensate drain

HRV A heat-recovery ventilator is perfectly suited for a heating climate. The idea behind it is simple: Outgoing stale air and incoming fresh air pass through a heat exchanger so that the warm air gives up its heat to the cool airstream. In winter, the outgoing warm air heats the incoming cold air; in summer, the incoming warm air gives up its heat to the outgoing cold air. The two airstreams are kept separate to prevent contaminants in the outgoing air from tainting the incoming fresh air. Efficiency is a function of how long the air spends in the heat exchanger. There are two heat-exchanger designs: crossflow and counterflow. The greater surface area of counterflow designs makes them more efficient, and there are three design types within this category: vertical flat panel, horizontal flat panel, and cellular. Vertical-flat-panel models are the least efficient (50% to 70%), followed by horizontal-flat-panel models (70% to 80%) and cellular heat exchangers (more than 80%).

ERV An ERV is ideally suited for a cooling climate. Although it's commonly referred to as an energy-recovery ventilator, ERV actually stands for enthalpy-recovery ventilator. Put simply, an ERV is a moisture- and heat-recovery ventilator. The only difference between an HRV and ERV is a vapor-permeable membrane between the exhaust and intake sides of the heat-exchange chamber. Instead of the aluminum or polypropylene that you'd find in an HRV, the material between the outgoing and incoming chambers in an ERV is a fabric akin to Gore-Tex. Vapor can pass through the material, but air, gases, odors, and bulk water cannot. Because ERV cores don't have as much surface area as HRVs, they are not as efficient at heat removal. The typical efficiency penalty is about 10%.

Fresh air from outside

Filters

Stale air from inside

Exhaust to outside

Fan

Heat exchanger

Fan

Fresh air to inside

Continued ➜

To compare the effects of efficiency on indoor-air temperature, let's say the indoor temperature is 70°F and the outdoor temperature is 30°F. The makeup air an HRV that's 75% efficient distributes through the house is 60°F—a far cry from the 30°F air pulled in by an air exchanger, but cool enough to be uncomfortable in a 70°F environment. A 90%-efficient HRV will raise the temperature of the makeup air to a more comfortable 66°F.

The Home Ventilation Institute (HVI), an independent agency, tests and reports the performance of HRVs and ERVs. You can compare the thermal efficiency of different units on its website (hvi.org), including both sensible recovery efficiency and apparent sensible effectiveness (see sidebar below). It's worth checking this database instead of relying on a manufacturer's advertising.

Is It Cheap to Operate?

A recovery ventilator should be airtight and well insulated, and it should have an ultra-efficient motor. The degree to which it diverges from this ideal determines overall efficiency and operating cost.

Recovery ventilators run continuously, so motor efficiency is critical. The most efficient machines use electronically commutated motors (ECMs). The best measure of overall efficiency is expressed as cfm/w, or how many watts it takes to exchange a cubic foot of air per minute. Plenty of recovery ventilators have a cfm/w ratio under 1.0, but aim for a value of 1.5 or better.

Is It Excessively Noisy?

A well-insulated house reduces sound transmission from the outside; as a side effect, noises from mechanical systems inside the house become much more noticeable. It's important to install the recovery ventilator in a utility room away from the bedrooms.

Unfortunately, no independent organization tests these ventilation products for operating noise. The two recovery-ventilator brands I know that publicize noise levels are Lunos and Zehnder. Ratings are in decibels and not sones, which is the measure used for bath fans. Zehnder is the only system I'm aware of that incorporates a duct silencer.

In talking with architects and building scientists who have specified equipment for projects, I've heard a few brands consistently mentioned as quiet: Fantech, Venmar, and Zehnder. One feature consumers can look for are ECMs; in addition to being efficient, they are quieter than alternating-current (AC) motors.

Do You Want an ERV or HRV?

One thing that often confounds people looking at recovery ventilators for the first time is whether they should choose an HRV or an ERV. The essential difference between the two is that an ERV transfers moisture, as well as heat, between the two airstreams. If you live in a region with a very consistent climate, then the answer is simple: Choose an HRV for cold climates and an ERV for hot, humid climates.

The problem is that a lot of North America falls into the mixed-climate category. To choose between an ERV and HRV in

One Machine but Two Efficiency Scores

Recovery ventilators report thermal efficiency in two categories: sensible recovery efficiency (SRE) and apparent sensible effectiveness (ASE). SRE is the true measure of the heat exchanger's efficiency; it measures only the amount of heat transferred across the plates of the heat exchanger, not including any outside variables. ASE includes heat from sources other than the exchanger itself. Waste heat generated from the unit's motors, air leakage between the exhaust- and fresh-air streams, and heat from other appliances in the room can skew the apparent efficiency of the ventilator by more than 10%.

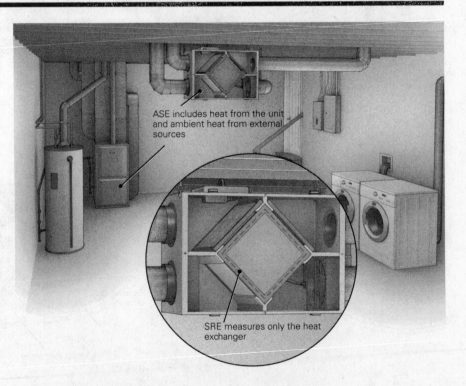

ASE includes heat from the unit and ambient heat from external sources

SRE measures only the heat exchanger

Stale air is stripped of its heat and then exhausted outside.

Stale air is picked up from the bathrooms and the kitchen.

Fresh air enters the house.

Conditioned fresh air is supplied to bedrooms.

Forget HVAC. You Want HAV & V

To get the most out of a ventilation system, decouple it from the heating and cooling systems. The potential problem with connecting your recovery ventilator to a forced-air heating and cooling system is that the furnace becomes the distribution fan for ventilation. A furnace fan is larger and less efficient than a recovery ventilator. Without a FanCycler or similar device, this overventilates the home and does so at a higher price.

The other problem with using HVAC ducts for ventilation is that it short-circuits the air-exchange process. Properly installed ventilation creates airflow through the house by establishing a cascade of air from supply vents to exhaust vents (drawing left). Supply diffusers are placed in bedrooms or walk-in closets, while exhaust vents are placed in the bathrooms and the kitchen. The idea is that fresh air is delivered to the sleeping areas, drawn through the hallways into the common living spaces, and then vented out of the house from the bathrooms and the kitchen. This cascade design flushes stale air out of the house at relatively low cfm, reducing both energy use and noise. Adding air-supply diffusers in general living areas or having vents and supplies in the same room will short-circuit air movement, causing fresh air to flow directly from supply to exhaust. Bath vents should have boost switches, which increase the fan rate when moisture accumulates, either by humidistat control or a manually activated timer switch.

In the kitchen, a recovery ventilator intake cannot take the place of a range hood. Separate ventilation is needed for airborne oils. To keep ventilation rates balanced, system designers often recommend an induction cooktop because there's no combustion. A recirculating hood can then be used to trap oil and to push air back into the kitchen so the ERV or HRV can exhaust it.

Continued →

a mixed climate, you've got to look at the length of the cooling season, the amount of outdoor humidity, and the conditions inside the house.

First, consider that the flow of moisture in an ERV is from the warm, moist airstream to the cold, dry airstream. This means that in the summer, humidity is transferred to the colder stream, which is exhausting outside the house. In the winter, though, the colder stream is incoming, so the ERV is raising humidity levels in the house. That's why home size and the number of occupants can make an ERV the wrong choice in some situations.

In a small, sufficiently air-sealed house with many occupants, the relative humidity in winter may be fairly high, and capturing and returning humidity to the house with an ERV could raise relative humidity to unhealthy levels. On the other hand, a larger house with few occupants could be made more comfortable by returning the relatively low moisture content to the house with an ERV. In these cases, an ERV might raise relative humidity 8% to 10% above the 35% to 45% relative humidity you'd get with an HRV.

In regions where the cooling season is dominant and there's outdoor humidity, an ERV is the clear choice. When an ERV reduces the humidity of the incoming air, it's making you more comfortable; it's also easing the burden on your air-conditioning system by reducing the amount of moisture it has to remove from the air.

In colder regions, an HRV makes the most sense. There might be a slight comfort bump from an ERV's raising of the relative humidity in winter, but it would be outweighed by the greater thermal efficiency of an HRV.

Lead-Safe Remodeling

By Justin Fink

Lead safety has been a hot topic since the Environmental Protection Agency (EPA) issued its new Renovation, Repair, and Painting (RRP) Rule. Professional contractors working on pre-1978 houses are now required by law to take extensive job-site precautions to protect themselves and a house's inhabitants from the potential effects of lead dust.

Homeowners working on their own property are exempt from the new rules, but that isn't an excuse to ignore the health dangers of lead dust. Although children under the age of 6 are most at risk of lead-related developmental and behavioral problems, lead poisoning is a concern for everyone.

While this article is not meant to be a manual for the RRP regulations, the information found here will be no surprise to contractors who have already taken the EPA training for lead testing, site and personal protection, and proper disposal of hazardous waste. However, the tools and general approach to dealing with lead safely are universally applicable.

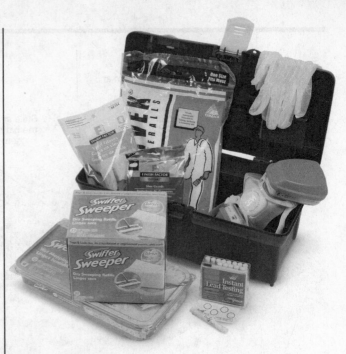

Triple-Test It

Before going to the trouble of setting up drop cloths and donning full coveralls, verify that lead is present in the work area. Unless you're planning on dealing with lead only on a one-time basis, it makes sense to create a dedicated supply kit. Along with lead-test swabs, you should have wet- and dry-cleaning cloths, disposable gloves and booties, and a respirator. Rather than relying on test results from just one area of the work zone, test in three different spots. On the project featured here, the door casing, window casing, and clapboard siding all were tested.

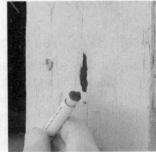

GO BEYOND THE SURFACE. Lead may be lurking under more recent coats of paint, so use a sharp knife to remove a V-shaped chunk of wood, and then test that freshly cut area. To help keep track of the test locations, use Post-it notes that are labeled to correspond with the individual test swabs.

NOT ALL TEST KITS ARE CREATED EQUAL. Several lead-testing swab kits are on the market, but LeadCheck is the only one that has met the EPA's stringent qualifications for false positives and false negatives. Although the goal is simply to determine if lead is present, these swabs also indicate, roughly, the concentration level. A swab that barely changes color indicates only a minor amount of lead, whereas bright red—as was found on this project—indicates a high level.

Follow the 10-Ft./20-Ft. Guideline

If the test indicates that lead-based paint is present in the work area or will be disturbed in the process of working, the next step is to create a two-stage containment area. The outer area—a radius of 20 ft. from the work being done—alerts passersby to the presence of lead paint. It also prevents kids, pets, or other tradespeople from entering the work area. The inner area—a radius of 10 ft. from any part of the building where lead will be disturbed—is where the dust, paint chips, and building debris will be collected.

1. BLACK PLASTIC IS THE BEST CHOICE The first step is to protect the ground beneath the work area. Use 6-mil black plastic because it's durable and because dust and debris show up clearly when it is time to clean up later. Secure the plastic to the house with nails or staples, and then seal it with 2-in.-wide painter's tape.

2. WATCH OUT FOR WIND. Even a gentle breeze can cause the plastic ground covering to lift or dust to blow around. Use framing lumber to create a dam, and lay scraps of wood over the plastic to keep it flat. If stronger winds are likely to be an issue, plastic wall barriers are a good idea.

3. SEAL ANY OPENINGS. Make sure all windows and doors in and around the work area are sealed so that lead dust doesn't get into the house, and so that no one enters the work area in the middle of the job.

Keep Dust to a Minimum

The goal is to keep lead under control, so the EPA frowns on a few tools and tasks that generate fumes or large amounts of dust. Avoid devices such as heat guns that operate at greater than 1100°F, or tools that grind, scrape, or sand and are not attached to a HEPA-filtered vacuum system.

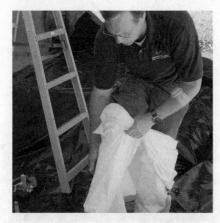

PROTECT YOURSELF FROM HEAD TO TOE. Personal safety is obviously a concern, so a respirator and gloves are musts in the inner containment zone. You also have to make sure that lead dust doesn't hitch a ride on your clothes or shoes when you leave, so wear your disposable coveralls and booties.

MIST AND SCORE BEFORE REMOVAL. Before removing any lead-painted materials, mist the surface with water to help keep down the dust. Then cut along any joints before removing material. This way, the worst you're going to do is fracture the wood, not shatter it and create a lot of dust.

GET THE RIGHT RESPIRATOR. Disposable respirators are acceptable when working around lead, but they must bear the N100 or P100 classification. If you are likely to be working around lead dust for an extended amount of time or on multiple occasions, a reusable respirator like the one shown here may be a better option.

Continued →

Don't Cut Corners on Cleaning

After remodeling work is complete, cleanup begins. Disposal is just as important as the prep work and execution of the remodeling. Every piece of debris removed from the containment area must be bagged or wrapped to ensure that lead dust won't be released during transportation to the landfill. Tools and protective gear that will be reused have to be cleaned thoroughly, too.

1. BAG WHAT YOU CAN, AND WRAP THE REST
Any item containing lead dust should be double-bagged while it's still within the defined containment area. If it's too big to fit in a bag, it should be wrapped in plastic and then vacuumed before removal. With all scraps and tools removed, it's time to deconstruct the work area.

2. VAC IT UP, WET IT DOWN. First, use a vacuum to collect light debris (flip the vac nozzle on edge, as shown here, so that it won't get hung up by its own suction), then wet down the plastic to keep dust from becoming airborne. A HEPA vacuum filter is a must, but it won't do much good in a bargain-bin vacuum. For the best protection, the filter should be used in a vacuum designed so that all the air drawn into the machine passes through the HEPA filter—with no leakage or "blow-by"—before being expelled.

3. FOLD THE PLASTIC IN ON ITSELF. Start folding up the plastic at the edges, working your way toward the center. Then remove your protective gear, and do a quick pass over yourself with the vacuum while standing in the plastic. Discard your coveralls with the plastic.

Interior Work Is a Bit Different

Most of the testing, prep, work, and cleanup rules that are best practice for exterior work also apply to interior work, but there are a few changes and additional steps.

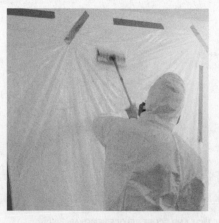

SHRINK THE CONTAINMENT ZONE. The 10-ft. containment zone used outdoors shrinks down to a single zone of only 6 ft. for indoor work. Fitting your tools and waste in this small area can be tough. If you can, find a helper so that you can hand off contained waste.

CLEAN VERTICAL SURFACES, TOO. Interior walls should be covered in plastic. This way, the surface can be wiped, vacuumed, and thrown out at the cleanup stage, eliminating the chance of lead dust remaining on the wall.

MAKE A FINAL PASS. After vacuuming off your coveralls and disposing of the plastic, do one more pass with the vacuum. Finish up with a wet-cleaning cloth, which should be used to wipe no more than 40 sq. ft. before being replaced with a fresh one.

Taking Care of Mold

By Joseph Lstiburek

Mold isn't a bad thing. Without it, we wouldn't have beer, blue cheese, or penicillin. When mold starts attacking the inside of your house, however, it is a bad thing. Even before the memorable onslaught of hurricanes in 2004 and 2005, we'd seen a lot more moldy buildings. Mold claims in Texas alone increased by five times a few years ago and cost homeowners' insurers more than $1 billion in 2001. Why?

Mold is a water problem. Excluding the flooding in the Gulf states, though, there suddenly isn't more water, so why is there more mold? The problem is that the water we've always had is hanging around in a new generation of building materials that can't tolerate water as well as yesterday's building materials could. Today's building materials are also more palatable to mold because they're more refined.

Many of the wood products that make our lives convenient during the construction process can make our lives inconvenient later on. These deficiencies don't show up, though, until something bad happens. It can be a single event like a hurricane, or an ongoing event like a roof valley that lets water into the house every time it rains.

While "toxic mold" makes headlines, news stories tend to offer more hype than hope. It's really not difficult to avoid mold problems if you understand how mold works. Getting rid of mold isn't so difficult, either.

Today's houses make it easier for mold to find the food and water it needs to thrive. The cure is a quick cleanup and smarter choices in materials.

Can Moldy Framing Lumber Cause Rot?

Mold can grow on framing lumber as soon as it leaves the sawmill. You've probably seen the telltale black stains on bundles of 2x material at the lumberyard. But mold growth on studs is mostly a surface phenomenon; if it bothers you, you can wash off the spore-producing fruiting bodies of mold and sapstain fungi with soap, water, and an abrasive pad. Decay, or rot, is caused by different fungi, ones that can attack the cell walls of wood and eventually cause structural failure.

Because of the extractives in heartwood, both mold and decay fungi prefer sapwood. Framing and sheathing are made from tree species with lots of sapwood (southern yellow pine, Douglas fir, aspen, spruce); as a result, today's houses have more potential mold and decay food than earlier houses built with lumber such as chestnut, oak, hickory, and other hardwoods as well as lumber cut predominantly from the heartwood of softwood species.

Wet framing lumber can support the growth of mold and decay fungi, but by itself, moldy lumber can't cause rot. It takes a decay fungus to do that. Because the growth rate of decay fungi is relatively slow

Heartwood   Sapwood

LIKE MOLD, THIS BLUE-STAIN FUNGUS CAN'T PENETRATE HEARTWOOD. As a tree ages, sapwood is converted to heartwood and often gains decay resistance.

compared with mold, you are more likely to see mold growth. As long as wetted lumber isn't wet too long and the dried lumber stays dry, you won't see decay fungi.

Continued ➜

Today's Wood Products Are Easy for Mold to Eat

Refining wood makes the mold nutrients more accessible to mold. As we go through this refining process, we also switch to tree species that are high in sapwood content and make them more susceptible to mold.

Solid Lumber
Even young, violent mold with a bad attitude can't get the sugar from old-growth timber-frame structures. That's because most of the lumber is heartwood cut from species like Douglas fir, white pine, and white oak. Mold can live on a sapwood surface, but it doesn't like the heartwood that's common in old buildings.

Sheathing
Rather than cutting the tree into ¾-in.-thick boards for sheathing, we now peel the tree and smash the layers together under heat and pressure. This heat and pressure caramelizes the wood sugars into mold candy, or plywood. We also flake the mold candy and put the flakes in a vat to make oriented strand board. OSB is the Spam of mold food. Because we peel and flake the tree, we can use smaller trees that are faster-growing and contain mostly sapwood. If you're mold with the choice between 2×4s and OSB, which are you going to choose? OSB, every time.

Particleboard and MDF
We take those candy fibers, and we grind them down to make sawdust. Then we add nitrogen to make particleboard (the nitrogen is like Cajun seasoning for fungi). We make furniture, cabinets, flooring, and underlayment from this. If you're mold with the choice between OSB and MDF, which are you going to choose? MDF, every time.

Paper-Faced Drywall
Finally, we grind the sawdust and reconstitute it to make nature's most perfect mold food: paper. Old mold with no teeth can eat paper. We glue the paper on both sides of drywall and wrap the insides of buildings with it. On commercial buildings, we wrap the outside, too. Even the dumbest of the three little pigs didn't build his house with paper. Sometimes we color it green to fool the mold and put it in the shower. We glue tile to the paper, and we hose it down with hot water twice a day. Unless you're mold, repeat after me: paper, water, bad.

Mold Likes Sugar, and Trees Are Made with Sugar

To engineers like me, trees are just big batteries. Let me explain: A tree stores the energy it converts from the sun (through photosynthesis) in the form of glucose, which is a hunk of sugar. When we burn the tree, we convert the energy in glucose into heat.

Mold prefers the sugar found in dead plants, which is in the form of cellulose. Unfortunately, we build houses out of dead plants and dead-plant by-products. That's OK as long as we don't make it easy for mold to get to the cellulose. Unfortunately, as wood is refined from a log to the paper facing on drywall, the cellulose is chopped, baked, ground, and seasoned to become easier for mold to eat.

Mold Likes Water, and Houses Leak

Living inside of mold food isn't too much of a problem as long as we make it hard for mold to eat the food. We do this by avoiding moisture problems. When houses get wet at a rate that exceeds their ability to dry out, moisture accumulates. When the rate of accumulation exceeds the storage capacity, we have a moisture problem. The house can't dry out. The amount of water coming in isn't the problem; it's the balance of how much water is coming in compared with how much is going out.

Unfortunately, both the storage capacity and the drying potential of houses have decreased over the past 100 years. You can store a lot of water in lath and plaster, but you can't store much in drywall. The drying potential has shrunk because of thermal insulation and the lower permeability of roof and wall materials (plastic vapor barriers).

Ductwork: The Mold Superhighway

We've made building materials into better mold food as we move down the processing stream from tree to paper, we've reduced the drying capacity of houses by adding insulation and vapor barriers, and we've reduced the storage capacity of houses by using newer materials that can't store much water (if any at all).

The last big change in our buildings is that they now are hollow. Walls, floors, and ceilings are hollow cavities. These hollow cavities with insulation in them can't control airflow or moisture. We're inadvertently building complex three-dimensional airflow networks.

The classic example is a commercial building where the dropped ceiling acts as the return plenum. The dropped-ceiling return plenum is connected to the exterior walls, and the interior walls are connected, too. We've got a three-dimensional airflow network where every interior partition wall is connected to the exterior walls by the floor and the ceiling assembly, so everything is connected to everything else. That network is the contaminant interstate. It transports mold from wet walls to the breathing zone of the space via the building's mechanical system.

Residentially, we do the same thing with forced-air heating and cooling when HVAC contractors bang a few pieces of sheet metal on the underside of a floor joist or a stud cavity and call it an air return. Basically, they're drawing air through wall and floor cavities. And the floor and the partition walls are connected to the cavities of the exterior envelope with holes cut for plumbing and electrical. We're connecting the envelope to the breathing zone via

Mold Thrives on the Moisture in Today's Houses

Mold can't survive and reproduce without water, so the ability of particular building materials to wick away, absorb, and store water (their buffer capacity) is related directly to whether mold can thrive in your house. Materials with higher buffer capacities produce fewer puddles, making it harder for mold to set up shop.

Let's Compare the Buffer Capacity of Three 2000-Sq.-Ft. Houses

Most wood-frame houses average 5% moisture content (MC). When solid lumber reaches MC of around 16%, mold is active. If the MC is under 15%, mold is dormant. Mold becomes a problem only when we push the MC from 5% to above 15%. The difference between 5% and 15% is 10%, so the typical moisture-storage capacity of a wood-frame house is around 10% by weight. In other words, the house can store 10% of its weight in moisture before mold can break out of dormancy and reproduce.

In a typical 2000-sq.-ft. house, the wood weighs 5000 lb. The buffer capacity is 10% of that, or 500 lb. So the house can hold 500 lb. of water before mold can cause a problem. A gallon of water weighs 8 lb. (which is a lousy number to divide by, so for simplicity, let's call it 10 lb.); 500 lb. divided by 10 lb. equals 50 gallons. This house can have 50 gallons of leaky plumbing, bad flashing, and poor drainage, and mold won't be a problem.

Swap steel studs and gypsum sheathing for plywood and 2×4s. Steel studs can hold 0% of their weight in moisture. Gypsum sheathing can hold about 0.7% of its weight in moisture (0.7 is a lousy number to divide by, so for simplicity, let's call it 1%). The gypsum sheathing in the house weighs 3000 lb. The buffer capacity (1% of 3000) is 30 lb., or about 3 gallons of water.

In a 100-year-old masonry house with plaster walls and a rock foundation, the buffer capacity works out to be about 500 gallons.

500 gal.

50 gal.

3 gal.

Can Mold Make Me Sick?

Most molds reproduce by making spores, which are small enough to mix and move freely with air. When spores become airborne, you can be exposed three ways: You can inhale spores into your lungs, you can absorb them through your skin, or you can ingest them.

Mold's musty odor is caused by volatile organic compounds (VOCs) that can create reactions including eye irritation, runny nose, cough, wheezing, laryngitis, headaches, and nausea. Some types of molds also produce mycotoxins that can be irritating to breathe, touch, and ingest. Remediation workers handling mold-contaminated materials without skin protection have developed skin lesions, skin dryness, and rashes. Similarly, ingesting food contaminated with mycotoxins can cause digestive problems such as diarrhea.

In most cases, the symptoms disappear when exposure to mold is curtailed or eliminated. That's why it's important to dispose of moldy materials, stop mold growth, and wear protective gear when doing mold cleanup. (See "How Do I Clean Up Mold?" on p. 899.)

After a flood or sewer backup, more than mold can make you sick. You also could be exposed to bacteria and human pathogens, which can cause sickness or death if you're not properly prepared to handle them.

Continued ➜

Win the War on Mold by Choosing Materials Wisely

Combined with good details such as flashing and a sloping grade away from the house, materials can have a big effect on a house's mold tolerance. Smart decisions can be made everywhere between basement and roof sheathing.

DRIVEWAYS Make porous driveways with pavers or bricks set in gravel. This type of driveway reduces runoff, which can cause problems for you and your neighbors.

FOAM SHEATHING Use foam sheathing to insulate inside basements and crawl-spaces because it doesn't absorb water. Using foam outside wall sheathing eliminates the condensing surface on the plywood's inside face.

FRAMING For hurricane- and flood-prone areas, use framing lumber treated with antimicrobial coatings.

EXTERIOR WALLS AdvanTech (www.huberwood.com) and plywood are the best sheathing choices; regular OSB is second best. The worst choice is paper-faced drywall.

HOUSEWRAPS Nonperforated housewraps, asphalt-saturated kraft paper, or asphalt-impregnated felt repel water and let vapor escape.

SIDING DRAINAGE Plastic mat material or wrinkled housewrap allows water to drain out.

SIDING Aluminum, vinyl, and fiber-cement siding are more water-tolerant than wood. If you use wood siding, it needs a drainage plane, and all the ends must be sealed with primer.

SPRAY FOAMS Spray-foam insulations are breathable and water-tolerant.

LOOSE-FILL INSULATION Borate-treated cellulose has big buffer capacity.

TILE BACKERBOARD Use cementboard or a fiberglass-faced drywall for tile backing in a shower or other wet area.

ROOF SHEATHING Use sheathing with sprayed-on membrane and tape that actually sticks. Or use AdvanTech or plywood covered entirely with a self-stick membrane. Stickiness is key; the membrane shouldn't blow off during construction or in hurricanes.

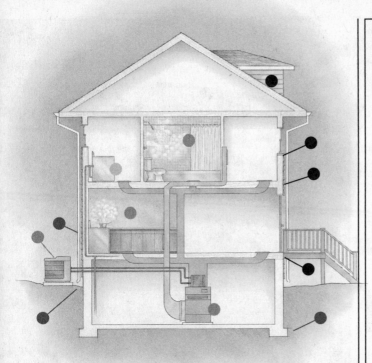

Water Can Attack a House from Many Directions

Some common water problems are easy to fix after construction, but many are complicated and expensive to repair retroactively; they're best addressed in the design stage before construction begins. Four major water sources attack your house.

● Plumbing

Supply or waste pipes in exterior walls, where they don't belong.

Clothes washers or water heaters on an upstairs floor, where they don't belong.

● Rain

Poorly detailed valleys, chimneys, and roof-to-wall interfaces

Poorly flashed windows and doors

No drainage plane on outside of wall

Poor deck-to-wall flashing

● Surface and Ground Water

Ground sloped toward the house

Gutter downspouts not directed away from the house

Bad footing-drain detail

● Interior Moisture

Vapor barrier and vinyl wall coverings

No exhaust fan in kitchen and bathrooms

Poor interior ventilation

Oversize air-conditioning unit

How Do I Clean Up Mold?

Consider the size of the mold problem when deciding who should do the cleanup. You can tackle most small jobs (less than 10 sq. ft.) yourself. Big jobs require a professional.

Small mold problems usually result from small water problems. If you don't fix the water problem, the mold will grow again. And don't put off the cleanup; do it within 48 hours. The longer you let it go, the more mold you'll have.

If the source of the water was clean, such as that from a pipe leak or from rain, mold can be cleaned by scrubbing hard surfaces with detergent and water. You don't need bleach. Then dry everything thoroughly. Throw away most soft or porous items if they get moldy because they are difficult or impossible to clean. For mold caused by contaminated water (sewage), consider using a cleaner/sanitizer, which is widely available in grocery stores and hardware stores.

It's also important to avoid exposing yourself to mold while cleaning it up because mold produces both allergens and irritants. Wear an N-95 respirator, goggles (without ventilation holes), and water-resistant gloves. You can get this protective gear at most hardware stores.

—Laura Kolb works with the U.S. Environmental Protection Agency's Indoor Environments Division (www.epa.gov/mold).

the mechanical system. To me, that's the greatest danger and the greatest tragedy of the buildings that we're constructing today. The principle is the same for residential and commercial, whether we're in Alaska or in Florida. This inadvertent linkage of the occupants to the envelope via the mechanical system is something that nobody expected or predicted. When we add this piece to the three others that I've described, it answers the question, "Mold, why now?"

View mold as the canary for all other contaminants. If they're carried by air, decay fungi and other pollutants are likely to be trans-ported along this three-dimensional airflow network into the breathing zone of building occupants.

The Fix: Smart Design and Remediation

We build houses of materials with little buffer capacity and with thousands of pounds of water in cast concrete. We fill them with insulation, we wrap them with vapor barriers on the inside and on the outside, we heat them and cool them without any understanding of the physics, and we look around and wonder why they're turning into mush and falling down. But there's no mystery here.

Continued ➜

The solution starts with selecting materials systems differently. We can choose smart materials and simple systems or simple materials and elegant systems. When you have a water problem, fix the problem quickly and dry it out, or replace the damaged materials. Don't wait for the lawsuits to establish who's at fault. Fix the problem quickly, and it won't be worth quibbling over who pays for it. The cost will be minimal.

And please, don't blame mold and indoor-air quality problems on energy conservation. Yes, if houses were leaky, we wouldn't have these problems, but the answer isn't to take out the insulation and make the house leaky. The answer is to understand what went wrong, get past this issue, and build even higher-performing buildings. As a society, we can't afford to build disposable structures. People aren't disposable, and buildings shouldn't be disposable, either.

16 Ways to Improve the Air You Breathe

By Jamie Lyons

From the spotless houses of the Cleavers and the Bradys to the showcases featured in contemporary advertising, we've been taught that a good house is a clean house. So we sweep, spray, and scrub with an ever-increasing arsenal of tools and cleansers. But what about the part of a house that we don't see yet breathe into our lungs thousands of times every day? Indoor air is a fundamental part of how our houses affect us, but it's often overlooked and misunderstood.

Americans spend up to 90% of their time indoors. According to the Environmental Protection Agency (EPA), indoor air can actually be more polluted than outdoor air. The consequence of spending so much time indoors and breathing polluted air can be seen in the increase of asthma and chronic respiratory disease among Americans.

What makes indoor-air quality (IAQ) most difficult to understand is that it can't be easily or accurately tested. There's a vast world of contaminants to test for, and for most of them, there aren't clear exposure limits to compare against. Plus, testing is just a snapshot of a home's conditions. Because many factors can affect IAQ, testing is not a realistic option in most cases. Instead, looking at the sources of pollutants and the way they enter the living space is the best way to determine if your house is as healthful as it can be.

Both Tight Houses and Leaky Houses Have Issues

We didn't hear much about IAQ 30 years ago. Building science was still in its infancy, and our houses were different.

In the name of energy efficiency, modern houses are wrapped, caulked, and spray-foamed until air leakage through the building shell is reduced to a mere whisper of outside air. This has eliminated the natural air infiltration that once served as an IAQ

Cooking generates strong odors, smoke, grease, and humidity. These contaminants should be exhausted directly outdoors (not recirculated) with a range hood.

Band-Aid by diluting pollutants and, occasionally, helping to dry out moisture.

Before you call a tight house an unhealthful house, though, remember that the air infiltrating a leaky house can cause just as many problems as it fixes. For example, hot, humid outside air that finds its way inside simply adds moisture to your house. Incoming outside air can introduce pollutants such as car exhaust. Although tight houses can prevent pollutants from escaping, they also decrease the amount of contaminants that are entering the living space and allow indoor conditions to be better managed.

Three Threats Revealed

While a number of pollutants can create poor IAQ, there are three common sources: poor construction, faulty or improperly designed mechanical systems, and human activity.

Poorly designed and poorly executed construction details can allow moisture to enter a house. Bulk-water leakage leads to IAQ problems such as mold growth. High levels of water vapor, which is measured as relative humidity (RH), can result from water leakage or a host of other problems. High RH can have just as serious an impact on IAQ as bulk-water leakage. RH levels greater than 70% spur mold growth, and a 50% RH level allows dust mites to thrive. (Dust mites foster asthma.) A variety of factors influence indoor-moisture levels. For example, incorrectly flashed windows, unsealed rim joists, and cracked foundations all can contribute to excess moisture in a house.

Monitoring your house's RH is easily accomplished with an inexpensive battery-powered digital hygrometer, and could tip you off to much larger moisture problems. While different people will be comfortable at different indoor RH levels, certain limits can be established to help maintain healthful IAQ. To help control dust mites and mold growth, keep indoor RH at a level below 50%.

When you're analyzing mechanical systems, the goal is relatively simple. They should operate as they were designed. When these systems fail, problems arise. Return-air ducts in a forced-air system can be particularly troublesome. The ducts are under negative pressure, so they pull air from wherever it's available. Ideally, they draw air only from the living space, but leaky ducts can draw air from crawlspaces, attics, and basements where dust, pollen, mold spores, moisture, and even radon can be lurking.

Other mechanical-system failures can have a more dire affect. A combustion appliance that's not working correctly can emit carbon monoxide into a house, and a radon-mitigation system that's not performing can allow the cancer-causing gas to seep into living spaces.

Not all contaminants are nature's fault (like radon) or the result of poor construction. The truth is that homeowners introduce many contaminants. These pollutants include the formaldehyde found in cabinets and plywood, and the volatile organic compounds (VOCs) found in carpets, adhesives, and paints. Homeowners also introduce contaminants like cooking by-products and more subtle offenders such as the products used to clean the house. Product and material substitution works in some instances. Look for sources at LEED for Homes (www.

Mold

Dust Mites

usgbc.org) and GreenGuard (www.greenguard.org). However, installing a ventilation system is the best way to rid a home of contaminants.

Clean Air in, Bad Air Out

The solution to existing IAQ problems in a house is proper ventilation. This is true of old houses and new houses. There are two types of ventilation to consider: whole-house ventilation and spot ventilation.

Spot ventilation—also referred to as local exhaust ventilation—includes range hoods and bathroom exhaust fans.

Knowing whether you need spot ventilation can be pretty obvious. Lingering odors, condensation, and mildew are all easy signs to recognize.

Whole-house ventilation systems supply fresh outdoor air, exhaust stale indoor air, or do both to help manage IAQ. Whole-house ventilation provides a steady, predictable amount of indoor-outdoor air exchange. Not all systems perform well in every climate, so it is wise to do some research before installing a ventilation system in your house.

Exhaust-based whole-house systems use one or more bath exhaust fans to pull stale air out of a house. The fresh air from the outdoors makes its way into the home through cracks and openings in the building's shell. Alternatively, passive vents or dampers can be built in to provide a specific entry point for fresh air. These systems are the easiest to install in an existing house, and they don't rely on central ductwork.

If central ductwork is accessible, supply systems and balanced whole-house systems are options. A supply system draws outside air into the central blower and distributes it through the house. Because the house is pressurized, it forces stale air and its contaminants out of the house through cracks and gaps. These systems rely on a much bigger blower to introduce fresh air, so they're best used in combination with high-efficiency models.

Balanced systems draw fresh air into a house and exhaust stale air at the same rate. Balanced systems usually use a heat-recovery ventilator or an energy-recovery ventilator to improve the efficiency of the system.

While ventilation technology has improved over the years and has helped to improve the air quality in our houses, keep in mind that it doesn't negate the importance of preventing IAQ problems at their source. Ventilation doesn't trump proper design and construction.

Human Activities

Discovering the causes of poor indoor-air quality is the first step in creating a healthful home.

1. Cooking generates strong odors, smoke, grease, and humidity. These contaminants should be exhausted directly outdoors (not recirculated) with a range hood. For best performance, match the hood's flow rate with the range's heating capacity (about 1 cfm

Continued ➜

per 100 Btu). The fan's noise rating should be 1.5 sones or less at low speed.

2. Cabinets and pressed-wood products are often made with adhesives containing formaldehyde, which is emitted into the home. Whole-house ventilation can remedy existing sources of formaldehyde, but it's best to select materials free of the compound or that meet standards for low emissions.

3. Carpets harbor dust mites, and new carpeting can emit VOCs into a home. Dust mites can be controlled by maintaining RH below 50%. When installing new carpeting, select products with low VOC emissions, and ventilate the area for 48 to 72 hours following its installation.

4. Many household-cleaning products emit harmful VOCs when they're used and stored. When choosing cleaning products, select items that are listed as solvent-free. If using a product made of harmful chemicals, provide ample ventilation with your house's mechanical systems and open windows.

5. Showers add humidity to indoor spaces. Control this moisture load with exhaust fans ducted to the outdoors. These fans should move air at a rate no less than 50 cfm. (Fans often deliver less flow than their nominal rating.) Increase airflow with short, direct duct runs, and look for fans with 6-in. ports

that can accommodate 6-in. ductwork. These fans should be quiet—2 sones or less.

6. Garages often are home to toxic chemicals, car exhaust, and VOCs that can migrate into a house. Isolate the garage from the house with self-closing and weatherstripped entry doors and tightly air-sealed ducts (if routed through the garage, which they shouldn't be) and through-wall penetrations. It's also wise to consider using exhaust ventilation to the outdoors.

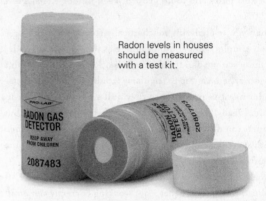

Radon levels in houses should be measured with a test kit.

Clothes dryers generate large amounts of humidity.

Backdrafting from combustion appliances can introduce deadly carbon monoxide.

Unvented gas fireplaces can transfer combustion by-products into the house.

Equip the central blower with a (MERV) 8 filter.

Mechanical Systems

Poor mechanical systems and faulty appliances can increase indoor-pollution levels. The resulting IAQ issues range from mold exposure to death by carbon-monoxide poisoning.

7. Clothes dryers generate large amounts of humidity and also draw about 150 cfm of air from the surrounding space when they're operating. Vent dryer exhaust directly to the outdoors with approved ducting. If natural-draft combustion appliances are nearby, make sure the dryer isn't causing backdraft issues.

8. Leaky return ducts in crawlspaces or basements can draw contaminants into a house. Seal joints with duct mastic, and design floor plans to keep ducts out of unconditioned spaces.

9. Radon, a naturally occurring radioactive gas found in soil, needs to be kept from indoor spaces. Radon levels in houses should be measured with a test kit. If levels are too high, install an active mitigation system, which uses a fan and vent piping to exhaust radon from under the slab to the exterior of the house, usually through roof vents.

10. Backdrafting from combustion appliances can introduce deadly carbon monoxide. Backdrafting occurs when the negative pressure around a combustion appliance, such as a water heater, pulls combustion gases back down a flue instead of letting them flow to the outdoors. Backdrafting can be caused by exhaust devices (fans, dryers), fireplaces, leaky return ducts, and the stack effect. Select sealed-combustion or power-vented combustion equipment (water heaters, furnaces, boilers) to ensure that combustion gases are exhausted properly. In any house, ensure that all mechanical equipment is vented properly, and install carbon-monoxide alarms close to the appliance and sleeping areas.

11. Unvented or "vent-free" combustion appliances, such as gas fireplaces, can transfer combustion by-products into the house

Install pan flashing, integrate the housewrap with the unit, and seal the flanges with flashing tape.

A cracked slab can allow radon and moisture into the house.

Continued ➔

Seal gaps in the exterior envelope with caulk or spray foam.

Install gutters and downspouts properly.

appliances, install a carbon-monoxide alarm near sleeping areas and close to the combustion appliance.

12. Prevent contaminants from circulating through the house by equipping the central blower with a minimum efficiency reporting value (MERV) 8 filter. Be sure filters on air handlers (like HRVs) are cleaned regularly. When designing an HVAC system, account for the increased static pressure of the filter. A more powerful central blower might be needed to achieve proper airflow.

Construction

When a home is built or remodeled without attention to construction details, then the home as a system can fail. Below are some of the most problematic areas of a house. By addressing them properly, you can manage your home's IAQ more easily.

13. Poorly flashed windows, doors, and other through-wall penetrations can allow moisture to enter the living space. Install pan flashing, integrate the housewrap with the unit, and seal the flanges with flashing tape. Spray foam between the jamb and the rough opening to help keep moist air out of the house.

14. Gaps in construction allow dust, humidity, and other pollutants to enter. Seal gaps in the exterior envelope with caulk or spray foam. Pay particular attention to attics and rim joists, which are prone to leakage. A blower-door test helps to reveal the areas that you've missed and that need attention.

15. Basements with moisture problems increase humidity levels and promote mold growth. Keep a foundation dry by properly grading the exterior soil, by installing gutters and downspouts properly, and by waterproofing foundation walls correctly. If bulk-water infiltration is an issue, make sure you've got a working sump pump, and add a dehumidifier if necessary to keep relative humidity below 50%.

16. A cracked slab can allow radon and moisture into the house. Cracks and openings in the slab, such as those around drainpipes, should be sealed to keep moisture and radon at bay.

Index

Continued →

Continued ➤

Continued →